HANDBOOK OF LATIN AMERICAN STUDIES: No. 57

A Selective and Annotated Guide to Recent Publications in Anthropology, Economics, Geography, Government and Politics, International Relations, and Sociology

VOLUME 58 WILL BE DEVOTED TO THE HUMANITIES: ART, HISTORY, LITERATURE, MUSIC, PHILOSOPHY, AND ELECTRONIC RESOURCES

EDITORIAL NOTE: Comments concerning the *Handbook of Latin American Studies* should be sent directly to the Editor, *Handbook of Latin American Studies*, Hispanic Division, 101 Independence Avenue SE, Library of Congress, Washington, D.C. 20540.

HANDBOOK OF LATIN AMERICAN STUDIES: NO. 57

SOCIAL SCIENCES

Prepared by a Number of Scholars
for the Hispanic Division of The Library of Congress

LAWRENCE BOUDON, *Editor*
KATHERINE D. McCANN, *Assistant Editor,*
Acting Editor for Volume 57

2000

UNIVERSITY OF TEXAS PRESS   *Austin*

International Standard Book Number 0-292-75243-1
International Standard Serial Number 0072-9833
Library of Congress Catalog Card Number 36-32633

Requests for permission to reproduce material
from this work should be sent to
Permissions, University of Texas Press,
Box 7819, Austin, Texas 78713-7819.

First Edition, 2000

The paper used in this publication meets the minimum requirements of American
National Standard for Information Sciences—Permanence of Paper for Printed
Library Materials, ANSI Z39.48-1984. ⊗

CONTRIBUTING EDITORS

SOCIAL SCIENCES

Juan M. del Aguila, *Emory University,* GOVERNMENT AND POLITICS
Benigno E. Aguirre-López, *Texas A&M University,* SOCIOLOGY
Amalia M. Alberti, *Independent Consultant, San Salvador,* SOCIOLOGY
G. Pope Atkins, *University of Texas at Austin,* INTERNATIONAL RELATIONS
Melissa H. Birch, *University of Kansas,* ECONOMICS
Jacqueline Braveboy-Wagner, *The City College-CUNY,* INTERNATIONAL RELATIONS
Roderic A. Camp, *Claremont-McKenna College,* GOVERNMENT AND POLITICS
William L. Canak, *Middle Tennessee State University,* SOCIOLOGY
Gustavo Enrique Cañonero, *Independent Consultant,* ECONOMICS
César N. Caviedes, *University of Florida,* GEOGRAPHY
Marc Chernick, *Georgetown University,* GOVERNMENT AND POLITICS
Jeffrey Cohen, *Pennsylvania State University,* ANTHROPOLOGY
Harold Colson, *University of California, San Diego,* ELECTRONIC RESOURCES
Lambros Comitas, *Columbia University,* ANTHROPOLOGY
William Van Davidson, *Louisiana State University,* GEOGRAPHY
David Dent, *Towson University,* GOVERNMENT AND POLITICS
Gary S. Elbow, *Texas Tech University,* GEOGRAPHY
Damián J. Fernández, *Florida International University,* INTERNATIONAL RELATIONS
Michael Fleet, *Marquette University,* GOVERNMENT AND POLITICS
James W. Foley, *University of Miami,* ECONOMICS
Jeffrey Franks, *International Monetary Fund,* ECONOMICS
Daniel W. Gade, *University of Vermont,* GEOGRAPHY
Eduardo A. Gamarra, *Florida International University,* GOVERNMENT AND POLITICS
José Zebedeo García, *New Mexico State University,* GOVERNMENT AND POLITICS
Ivelaw L. Griffith, *Florida International University,* GOVERNMENT AND POLITICS
Kevin Healy, *Inter-American Foundation,* SOCIOLOGY
Darrin Helsel, *University of Maryland,* SOCIOLOGY
John Henderson, *Cornell University,* ANTHROPOLOGY
Silvia María Hirsch, *Trenton State College,* ANTHROPOLOGY
William Keegan, *Florida Museum of Natural History,* ANTHROPOLOGY
Roberto Patricio Korzeniewicz, *University of Maryland,* SOCIOLOGY
Susana Lastarria-Cornhiel, *University of Wisconsin-Madison,* SOCIOLOGY
Paul Lewis, *Tulane University,* GOVERNMENT AND POLITICS
Robert E. Looney, *Naval Postgraduate School,* ECONOMICS
Peggy Lovell, *University of Pittsburgh,* SOCIOLOGY
Markos J. Mamalakis, *University of Wisconsin-Milwaukee,* ECONOMICS
Tom L. Martinson, *Auburn University,* GEOGRAPHY
Nohra Rey de Marulanda, *Inter-American Development Bank,* ECONOMICS
Betty J. Meggers, *Smithsonian Institution,* ANTHROPOLOGY

Keith D. Muller, *Kent State University*, GEOGRAPHY
Deborah Nichols, *Dartmouth College*, ANTHROPOLOGY
Robert Palacios, *The World Bank*, ECONOMICS
David Scott Palmer, *Boston University*, GOVERNMENT AND POLITICS
Ransford W. Palmer, *Howard University*, ECONOMICS
Jorge Pérez-López, *US Department of Labor*, ECONOMICS
Timothy J. Power, *Florida International University*, GOVERNMENT AND POLITICS
Catalina Rabinovich, *Independent Consultant, Chevy Chase, Maryland*,
   ECONOMICS
Martín Rama, *The World Bank*, ECONOMICS
Joanne Rappaport, *Georgetown University*, ANTHROPOLOGY
Dereka Rushbrook, *Independent Consultant*, ECONOMICS
René Salgado, *Independent Consultant*, GOVERNMENT AND POLITICS
David W. Schodt, *St. Olaf's College*, ECONOMICS
Russell E. Smith, *Washburn University*, ECONOMICS
Paul Sondrol, *University of Colorado, Colorado Springs*, GOVERNMENT AND POLITICS
Dale Story, *University of Texas at Arlington*, INTERNATIONAL RELATIONS
Scott D. Tollefson, *Kansas State University*, INTERNATIONAL RELATIONS
Antonio Ugalde, *University of Texas at Austin*, SOCIOLOGY
Aldo C. Vacs, *Skidmore College*, INTERNATIONAL RELATIONS
Timothy Wickham-Crowley, *Georgetown University*, SOCIOLOGY
Robin M. Wright, *Universidade Estadual de Campinas (Brazil)*, ANTHROPOLOGY
Clarence Zuvekas, Jr., *Consulting Economist, Annandale, Virginia*, ECONOMICS

HUMANITIES

Edna Acosta-Belén, *State University of New York-Albany*, LITERATURE
Maureen Ahern, *The Ohio State University*, TRANSLATIONS
Severino João Albuquerque, *University of Wisconsin-Madison*, LITERATURE
Félix Angel, *Inter-American Development Bank*, ART
Uva de Aragón, *Florida International University*, LITERATURE
Barbara von Barghahn, *George Washington University*, ART
María Luisa Bastos, *Lehman College-CUNY*, LITERATURE
Alvaro Félix Bolaños, *University of Florida*, LITERATURE
Dain Borges, *University of California-San Diego*, HISTORY
John Britton, *Frances Marion University*, HISTORY
Francisco Cabanillas, *Bowling Green State University*, LITERATURE
Sara Castro-Klarén, *The Johns Hopkins University*, LITERATURE
Don M. Coerver, *Texas Christian University*, HISTORY
Edith B. Couturier, *National Endowment for the Humanities*, HISTORY
Edward Cox, *Rice University*, HISTORY
Joseph T. Criscenti, *Professor Emeritus, Boston College*, HISTORY
César Ferreira, *University of Oklahoma*, LITERATURE
Francisco J. Fonseca, *Princeton University*, ELECTRONIC RESOURCES
José Manuel García García, *New Mexico State University*, LITERATURE
Magdalena García Pinto, *University of Missouri, Columbia*, LITERATURE
John D. Garrigus, *Jacksonville University*, HISTORY
Miguel Gomes, *University of Connecticut*, LITERATURE

Lance R. Grahn, *Marquette University*, HISTORY
María Cristina Guiñazú, *Lehman College-CUNY*, LITERATURE
Michael T. Hamerly, *Independent Consultant, Seattle, Washington*, HISTORY
Robert Haskett, *University of Oregon*, HISTORY
José M. Hernández, *Professor Emeritus, Georgetown University*, HISTORY
Rosemarijn Hoefte, *Royal Institute of Linguistics and Anthropology, The Netherlands*, HISTORY
Joel Horowitz, *Saint Bonaventure University*, HISTORY
Regina Igel, *University of Maryland*, LITERATURE
Nils P. Jacobsen, *University of Illinois*, HISTORY
Peter T. Johnson, *Princeton University*, ELECTRONIC RESOURCES
Erick Langer, *Carnegie Mellon University*, HISTORY
Pedro Lastra, *State University of New York at Stony Brook*, LITERATURE
Asunción Lavrin, *Arizona State University at Tempe*, HISTORY
Peter Linder, *New Mexico Highlands University*, HISTORY
Maria Angélica Guimarães Lopes, *University of South Carolina*, LITERATURE
Carol Maier, *Kent State University*, TRANSLATIONS
Teresita Martínez-Vergne, *Macalester College*, HISTORY
David McCreery, *Georgia State University*, HISTORY
Joan Meznar, *Westmont College*, HISTORY
Molly Molloy, *New Mexico State University*, INTERNET RESOURCES
Elizabeth Monasterios, *State University of New York-Stony Brook*, LITERATURE
Naomi Hoki Moniz, *Georgetown University*, LITERATURE
José M. Neistein, *Brazilian-American Cultural Institute, Washington*, ART
José Miguel Oviedo, *University of Pennsylvania*, LITERATURE
Suzanne B. Pasztor, *University of the Pacific*, HISTORY
Daphne Patai, *University of Massachusetts-Amherst*, TRANSLATIONS
Anne Pérotin-Dumon, *Pontificia Universidad Católica de Chile*, HISTORY
Charles Perrone, *University of Florida*, LITERATURE
René Pricto, *Southern Methodist University*, LITERATURE
José Promis, *University of Arizona*, LITERATURE
Inés Quintero, *Universidad Central de Venezuela*, HISTORY
Susan E. Ramírez, *DePaul University*, HISTORY
Jane M. Rausch, *University of Massachusetts-Amherst*, HISTORY
Oscar Rivera-Rodas, *University of Tennessee, Knoxville*, LITERATURE
Humberto Rodríguez-Camilloni, *Virginia Polytechnic Institute*, ART
Mario A. Rojas, *Catholic University of America*, LITERATURE
Kathleen Ross, *New York University*, TRANSLATIONS
William F. Sater, *California State University, Long Beach*, HISTORY
Jacobo Sefamí, *University of California-Irvine*, LITERATURE
Susan M. Socolow, *Emory University*, HISTORY
Robert Stevenson, *University of California, Los Angeles*, MUSIC
Barbara A. Tenenbaum, *Hispanic Division, The Library of Congress*, HISTORY
Juan Carlos Torchia Estrada, *Consultant, Hispanic Division, The Library of Congress*, PHILOSOPHY
Lilián Uribe, *Central Connecticut State University*, LITERATURE
Stephen Webre, *Louisiana Tech University*, HISTORY
Raymond L. Williams, *University of California, Riverside*, LITERATURE
Stephanie Wood, *University of Oregon*, HISTORY

Foreign Corresponding Editors

Teodoro Hampe-Martínez, *Universidad Pontificia Católica de Lima*, COLONIAL HISTORY MATERIALS IN GERMAN AND FRENCH LANGUAGES
Kotaro Horisaka, *Sophia University, Tokyo, Japan*, JAPANESE LANGUAGE
Mao Xianglin, *Chinese Academy of Social Sciences*, CHINESE LANGUAGE
Magnus Mörner, *Stockholm University, Sweden*, SCANDINAVIAN LANGUAGES
Inge Schjellerup, *Nationalmuseet, Denmark*, DANISH LANGUAGE

Special Contributing Editors

Christel Krause Converse, *Independent Consultant, College Park, Maryland*, GERMAN LANGUAGE
Barbara Dash, *Bowdoin College*, RUSSIAN LANGUAGE
Georgette M. Dorn, *Library of Congress*, GERMAN AND HUNGARIAN LANGUAGES
Zbigniew Kantorosinski, *Library of Congress*, POLISH LANGUAGE
Dolores Moyano Martin, *Independent Scholar, Library of Congress*, SPECIAL PUBLICATIONS
Vincent C. Peloso, *Howard University*, ITALIAN LANGUAGE
Juan Manuel Pérez, *Library of Congress*, GALICIAN LANGUAGE
Iêda Siqueira Wiarda, *Library of Congress*, SPECIAL MATERIAL IN PORTUGUESE LANGUAGE

CONTENTS

ECONOMICS

INTERNATIONAL RELATIONS

INDEX

EDITOR'S NOTE

I. GENERAL AND REGIONAL TRENDS

As the Cold War came to an end more than ten years ago, a number of scholars predicted that new issues and themes would compete with more traditional concerns in the field of Latin American studies, particularly in areas concerning US foreign policy and security interests. Indeed, as the literature reviewed in this volume demonstrates, the often stifling constraints of the Cold War have given way to what one political scientist described as "a vibrant eclecticism in the research agenda" (Dent and Sondrol, p. 399). In the section on Government and Politics, for instance, established themes such as democratization and social movements continue to receive substantial attention, but are now joined by a growing body of work examining institutional design and reform, the impact of drug trafficking, neoliberalism and its consequences, and the rise of indigenous movements. Moreover, there was no underlying theme in the section, as there has been in the past.

Perhaps no discipline was more influenced by the Cold War than International Relations, which since 1989 has been forced to re-evaluate, though not discard, the dominant paradigms on which it was based: realism and Marxism. As one specialist noted, "identifying the current era as 'post-Cold War' reflects an understanding that previously utilized analytic and policy constructs are no longer valid" (Atkins, p. 547). And while security issues continue to attract substantial scholarly attention, another political scientist points out that, "issues once deemed low politics, such as the drug trade, immigration, and the environment, are now of high import" (Fernandez, p. 577).

Some topics that appeared prior to 1989 have continued to be relevant into the mid-1990s, while other topics have evolved. The attention devoted to democratic transitions in the 1980s, for example, has segued into research on democratic consolidation. Sociology, on the other hand, has demonstrated remarkable thematic continuity, even though in some countries the focus of the scholarship has shifted. In Chile, which experimented with neoliberal economics before any of its neighbors, sociologists no longer focus on the social impact of structural adjustments as they continue to do in Argentina and Mexico, *inter alia*. According to one sociologist: "Instead, most works have turned their attention toward examining changing social conditions among more specific sectors of the population" (Korzeniewicz, p. 712). Similarly, in Central America, the end of the Cold War coincided with the end of the civil wars that had wracked the region in the 1980s. "The decline of organized, civil war/revolutionary violence by the mid-1990s has unsurprisingly turned some scholars away from analyses of violence and toward examinations of 'returns to normalcy'," wrote another sociologist (Wickham-Crowley, p. 646).

While the field of Economics was not as directly affected by the end of the Cold War, the literature reviewed this biennium nevertheless "reveals a striking shift in focus," according to one economist (Foley, p. 171). The scholarship has moved away from the debt crisis, agrarian reform, and radical solutions to Latin

America's problems, toward the impact of structural adjustment and neoliberal reforms on income distribution, regional integration and trade, labor markets, and privatization, among other themes. In economic terms, a perhaps more significant event for Latin America was the 1989 implementation of the Brady Plan. Despite this official end to the debt crisis, however, most Latin American countries still struggle with tremendous foreign debt obligations. Nevertheless, the end of the Cold War that same year did impact Economics, as a discipline, to the extent that it narrowed the debate. As one economist notes, "the relative lack of radical tracts is perhaps best explained by the fall of communism in Eastern Europe and the ascendency of free-market policies in both developed and underdeveloped areas of the world" (Foley, p. 171). Consequently, most scholars stopped looking for alternatives to neoliberalism and began analyzing its impact, particularly on poverty and income inequalities. In addition, the advent of the Southern Cone Common Market (Mercosur) and the North American Free Trade Agreement (NAFTA) has attracted substantial scholarly attention, even in areas not directly involved in the trading blocs, such as Central America.

The fields of Anthropology and Geography were largely unaffected by the end of the Cold War, although each experienced certain changes to their research agendas in the mid-1990s. While the dominant anthropological themes have for the most part continued, an important new trend in Andean research is, according to one anthropologist, "the growing scholarly voice of native Andean peoples" (Rappaport, p. 138). In Geography, the environment remains the dominant issue overall this biennium, but the 1992 celebration of Columbus' voyage to the Americas continued to prompt the publication of geographical works related to that event.

Turning to some of the outstanding individual contributions and thematic undercurrents within each field, certain topics transcended the often nebulous boundaries between disciplines, underscoring the fact that the social sciences, in general, and Latin American studies, specifically, are becoming increasingly interdisciplinary. Without exhausting the list of possibilities, broad subject areas such as democratic transitions and consolidation, the implementation and impact of neoliberalism, drug trafficking, indigenous movements, gender studies, and regional integration are characteristic of interdisciplinary themes.

One excellent example of a work that transcends the traditional lines of its field is Tulchin's edited volume *The consolidation of democracy in Latin America* (item **2938**), which features essays on the political, economic and international aspects of the democratization process. An outstanding work on Mexico (item **3017**), focusing primarily on technocratic leadership within the country, addresses the interrelationship between economic and political reforms. In the mid-1990s, Mexico was in the midst of its democratic transition and considerable attention has since been paid to the political and social impact of economic reforms begun there in the 1980s (items **3039**, **3084**, and **3099**).

Whereas Mexico was arguably democratizing in the mid-1990s, the democratic political systems in other countries—particularly Colombia and Venezuela—were under siege. Meanwhile, in Cuba, modest economic reforms were not accompanied by a comparable political opening. In all three cases, interdisciplinary approaches have helped scholars to better understand the processes of democratic transitions and consolidation.

While Colombia continues to be understudied by US scholars, their Colombian counterparts have, to some extent, taken up the slack. As that country sank deeper into a seemingly endless cycle of violence, scholars in Colombia have begun using an interdisciplinary approach to studying the problem known as *violentología*. Combining political science, sociology, economics and international relations, *violentólogos* are seeking to understand why Colombia has been thus far incapable of ending the oldest internal armed conflict in the Americas which, in recent years, has claimed the lives of at least 35,000 people. One outstanding work that examines drug trafficking is *Drogas ilícitas en Colombia: su impacto económico, político y social*, sponsored by the United Nations Development Program (item **3378**). Other notable studies of violence include articles by Pecaut (item **3397**), Granada and Rojas (item **3389**), and an excellent rural study directed by Jesus Antonio Bejarano, who was killed on the grounds of the National University in September 1999. Indeed, the escalating violence in Colombia has, as one sociologist noted, threatened to curtail the valuable research that might eventually help resolve the seemingly intractable internal conflict. "Many [sociologists] are taking low profiles and others have emigrated" (Canak, p. 685). In December 1999, well-known Colombian sociologist and *violentólogo* Eduardo Pizarro was seriously wounded by a would-be assassin and has since left the country.

At the time that volume 57 of *HLAS* was being published, Venezuela was undergoing the most radical changes of any country in the Western Hemisphere. The literature reviewed herein reflects upon the upheaval of the mid-1990s that one political scientist said was "marked by a changing political mood and increasing economic challenges" (Salgado, p. 467). The actions taken in that era contributed directly to the December 1998 election of populist "outsider" Hugo Chávez and, almost exactly one year later, to the approval by popular referendum of a new political constitution hailed by its promoters as democratic and attacked by its detractors as authoritarian. Readers interested in the events leading up to this critical juncture will benefit from works by Giordani on the Movimiento al Socialismo political party (item **3458**) as well as from Yepes Salas' treatment of the Causa R political party and its rise from relative obscurity (item **3484**). Two other notable edited volumes are those by Blanco on current sociopolitical issues (item **3483**), and Serbín *et al.* on the political and economic crisis (item **3481**).

In Cuba, the demise of the Soviet Union has forced the Castro regime to introduce limited economic reforms while, at the same time, attempting to keep a lid on political dissent. The scholarship reviewed in *HLAS* 57 reflects this development, with numerous works devoted to the economic reforms of 1993–94 (items **1917**, **1930**, and **1934**), together with the reforms thereafter aimed specifically at the external sector (items **1934**, **1938**, and **1940**). While the literature on Cuban foreign policy has been somewhat slow to react to the new post-Cold War reality, new studies on the Bay of Pigs (item **4242**) and the Cuban Missile Crisis (item **4229**) are worth noting. In addition, Caunedo's article "La siempre fiel isla de Cuba: la realidad del cambio" (item **3331**) reflects the unresolved tension between the economic and political realms.

With the debt crisis on the back burner, many Latin American countries sought to expand their international trade by signing bilateral or multilateral agreements with partners within and outside the hemisphere. A bilateral trade accord between Brazil and Argentina blossomed in 1990 into the Southern Cone Common Market (Mercosur) while, to the north, Mexico joined with Canada and the United States in creating the North American Free Trade Agreement (NAFTA), which went into effect January 1, 1994. It is not surprising that a substantial amount of research has been devoted to these two agreements and their impact on politics, society, the international arena, and even on indigenous groups.

Within the field of International Relations, the authors writing on regional integration recognize the limitations of the current agreements but, as of the mid-1990s, maintained a relatively optimistic view of Mercosur. Notable works on that trading bloc include those by Hirst (item **4324**), Manzetti (item **4327**), Peña (item **4330**), and Yore and Palau (item **4318**). Volumes edited by Karlsson and Malaki (item **1352**), Echerri-Carrol (item **1406**), and Nishijima and Smith (item **1287**), analyze Mercosur, NAFTA, and the proposed Western Hemisphere Free Trade Area (WHFTA) from an economic perspective.

With regard to NAFTA, Weintraub's two works (items **4133** and **4134**) discuss the implications for US-Mexican relations, while the Economist Intelligence Unit's comprehensive examination (item **1622**) attempts to forecast the impact of the agreement on Mexico's major economic sectors. Also noteworthy are a pair of studies, each of which analyzes and discusses the effects of NAFTA on Central American exports and trade (items **1731** and **1740**). More focused works examine the impact of Mercosur on Brazil's relations with its neighbors (items **2331** and **2374**), on regional disparities within Brazil (item **2381**), and on specific economic sectors in that country (items **1421**, **2338**, and **2353**).

On a related topic—neoliberalism—particular attention is being paid to the detrimental impact of neoliberal economic reform and privatization on income distribution and poverty, as well as their possibly negative affect on democracy. At the regional level, works by Morely (item **1402**) and volumes edited by Bulmer-Thomas (item **1408**), Lustig (item **1288**), Sautter (item **1349**), and Psacharopoulos (item **1424**) are of particular interest, as is an interdisciplinary volume edited by Smith, Acuña and Gamarra (item **1373**). At the national level, two studies tackle the political impact of economic reforms in Bolivia (items **2196** and **2201**), one looks at the Argentine labor market (item **2272**), while two other works focus on income distribution inequalities in Brazil (items **2373** and **2330**). In Uruguay, several articles (items **3830**, **3835**, **3840**, **3842**, and **3847**) address the transformation of the political party system from one of Latin America's most institutionalized two-party arrangements into a decidedly four-party system, due to what one political scientist argues is "the challenge of neoliberalism" (Lewis, p. 506).

Studies of the relatively recent rise of indigenous movements draw upon different disciplines, including Political Science, Sociology and Anthropology. Whereas in the past, Latin American indigenous groups by and large sought to isolate themselves from the often repressive and hostile Hispanic nation-states in which they lived, political and social changes have not only made it possible for them to organize, but have given them a stake in the political and economic arenas. In Ecuador, indigenous movements have arisen in response to threats to their homelands posed by environmental degradation and multinational firms engaged in extractive activities, together with a growing desire to establish and protect indigenous rights (items **3429**, **3439**, and **3440**). Moreover, sociologists are studying the impact of education on indigenous groups (item **5032**), the successful Protestant conversion movement (item **5028**), and indigenous elements in mestizo ethnic identity (item **5023**).

The appearance on January 1, 1994, of the *Ejército Zapatista de Liberación Nacional (EZLN)* guerrilla group sparked interdisciplinary research into the movement's historical antecedents (items **695** and **761**). In *From Olmecs to Zapatistas: a once and future history of souls*, (item **729**), Gossen argues that the Zapatista rebellion has as much to do with the construction of a pan-Mayan movement as it does with the stated demand for agrarian reform. Similarly, anthropologists are examining indigenous resistance movements to see how studying past experiences can be useful in building and maintaining current and future indigenous movements in the Amazon region (items **926** and **946**).

Studies of indigenous cultural issues also are increasing in number and quality. One anthropologist singled out four works for their outstanding contribution to ethnology in this biennium. Poole's study of Andean photography (item **1046**), Romero's collection of essays on Andean music and dance (item **1209**), Arnold's analysis of Andean ethnography and family relations (item **1042**) and Larson and Harris' collection of Andean market studies (item **1040**) all represent refreshing and innovative avenues of research. In addition, there is a growing body of ethnological literature produced by indigenous peoples, themselves, covering topics such as traditional medicine (items **1201** and **1087**), popular religion (item **1169**), and technical themes (item **1191**).

In the field of Archaeology, recent research is casting new light on several long-held assumptions, such as the belief that the Olmec were the "mother culture" of Mesoamerican civilization. Ongoing investigations on the Pacific and Gulf Coasts of Chiapas have revealed that sedentary villages were present there as early as 1550 BC (items **33** and **113**), while ranked societies may have developed earlier there than in the Olmec heartland. In a similar vein, archaeologists are uncovering "abundant evidence for pre-Clovis presence in southern South America" (Meggers, p. 52), adding to the controversy over the antiquity of human arrival in the Americas (items **417, 426, 427, 481, 515, and 517**). Moreover, a growing debate over the existence of precolumbian settlements in the Amazon is fueled, on one side, by scholars who rely on European descriptions of advanced cultures (items **403, 409, 410, 491, and 597**) and, on the other, by those who insist that any such settlements were either impermanent or more recent (items **595, 596, and 600**).

One of the fastest growing areas of research in Latin America is women's studies. Due to the universal nature of the field, these works embrace every discipline in the social sciences, including international relations, where feminist theory has begun to challenge the traditional paradigms. Its scope notwithstanding, the bulk of gender studies can be found in the sociology section. Among the more compelling scholarship concerning women in the mid-1990s are Bolivian works on discrimination toward migrant women in La Paz (item **5084**), grassroots development (item **5094**), and women's experience as political party leaders (item **5098**). Two innovative Paraguayan studies analyze the impact of educational reform on university women (item **5100**) and female reproductive behavior (item **5103**). In Brazil, *Estudios Feministas* is an excellent journal for research on gender. Other works examine the country's feminist movement and the political history of women (items **5300** and **5297**). Also noteworthy are two Peruvian volumes edited by Portocarrero (item **4542**) and Ruiz-Bravo (item **5052**) and Massolo's outstanding investigation of women and Mexican social movements in the 1970s (item **4617**). Finally, Eber's study of Mayan women and alcohol bridges the gap between sociology and ethnology (item **718**).

In addition to ongoing research on the environment, geographers are turning their attention to the impressive growth of urban centers in Latin America. General works include those by Villa Soto (item **2451**) and Martín, Asunción and Múscar Benasayag (item **2429**), while among the more focused publications are two books on Puebla, Mexico, by Cabrera Becerra (item **2528**) and Melé (item **2562**), two studies of Guatemala City by Gellert (item **2502**) and Pérez Sáinz (item **2507**), and works from Chile and Argentina by Gross (item **2809**), Larraín (item **2819**) and Randle (item **2765**).

One interesting and expanding area of research in the English Caribbean is the study of Rastafarianism, both from an anthropological and a sociological perspective. An entire volume of a three-volume conference proceedings, *Rastafari and other African-Caribbean worldviews* (item **819**), is dedicated to the movement. The volume argues, among other things, that the signature dreadlocks worn by men are not only a symbol of separation from the world, but also of male dominance. A separate work by Lake describes the subordinate role played by Rastafarian women, despite the rhetoric of liberation (item **857**). Within sociology, Lewis examines the experience of Rastafarians in the United States (item **4858**), Herrera describes the evolution of the movement since its inception in the 1950s (item **4846**), while two additional studies address its internationalization (items **4922** and **4836**).

Finally, it is important to mention a number of groundbreaking works and new research areas that do not fit neatly into the preceding thematic discussion. With regard to new research areas, it is heartening to see that scholars are beginning to study the increasingly active role that Canada is playing in inter-American affairs. Prior to the 1980s, Canada's presence in Latin America was minimal but, in part due to the negotiations that eventually led to NAFTA, Ottawa began to see itself as part of the Western Hemisphere and, in 1990, Canada became a full member of the Organization of American States. One noteworthy piece of scholarship is Rochlin's historical analysis of the evolution of Canadian foreign policy toward Latin America (item **4043**).

In terms of individual works that are worthy of praise, a volume that stands out is Tomassini's edited work on democracy, public policy and State-civil society relations in Chile (item **3652**). Significant works on the Chilean economy include those by former Foreign Minister Juan Gabriel Valdes on the impact of the Chicago School during the Pinochet era (item **2137**), by Hojman on Chilean political economy in the 1990s (item **2100**), two studies of the Aylwin era (items **2092** and **2121**) and a comprehensive study of the social security system (item **2111**). Extrapolating from Barrington Moore's seminal work, Paige traces the paths to democracy in El Salvador, Nicaragua and Costa Rica in his long-awaited study on coffee and power (item **4733**).

Lawrence Boudon, *Editor*

II. CLOSING DATE

The closing date for works annotated in this volume was mid-1997. Publications received and cataloged at the Library of Congress after that date will be annotated in the next social sciences volume, *HLAS 59*.

III. ELECTRONIC ACCESS TO THE *HANDBOOK*

Web Site

The *Handbook*'s web site, *HLAS Online*, continues to offer, free of charge, all bibliographic records corresponding to *HLAS* volumes 1–60. Records that did not appear in a print volume are not annotated, and some records may be in a preliminary editorial stage. The web site also includes a list of *HLAS* Subject Headings, a list of journal titles and the corresponding journal abbreviations found in *HLAS* records, searchable tables of contents for volumes 51–56 (http://lcweb2.loc.gov/hlas/contents.html), and introductory essays for early volumes of *HLAS*. The web address for *HLAS Online* is http://lcweb2.loc.gov/hlas/.

Online Public Access Catalog
HLAS records from volumes 50–60 may also be searched through the Library of Congress online catalog. Some searches at this site may be limited by language, publication date, and format. The address for the catalog web site is http://www.loc.gov/catalog/.

CD-ROM
Volumes 1–55 (1935–1996) of the *Handbook* are also available on the *Handbook of Latin American Studies: CD-ROM: HLAS/CD (v.2.0)*. This retrospective version is produced by the Fundación Histórica TAVERA (Madrid, Spain) and distributed for them by DIGIBIS. For ordering information, contact DIGIBIS:

DIGIBIS: Publicaciones Digitales
Duque de Medinaceli, 12–1 Dcha.
28014 Madrid SPAIN
phone: (91) 420-10-74 OR (91) 429-80-03
fax: (91) 429-80-71
http://www.digibis.com/(home page)

IV. CHANGES FROM PREVIOUS SOCIAL SCIENCES VOLUME

Changes in Coverage
There is no Electronic Resources chapter in this volume. The chapter will reappear in subsequent volumes.

Anthropology
Deborah L. Nichols of Dartmouth College collaborated with John Henderson on the preparation of the Mesoamerican chapter. Jeffrey H. Cohen, Pennsylvania State University, annotated materials on Middle America, while Robin M. Wright of the Universidade Estadual de Campinas (Brazil) and Silvia María Hirsch of Trenton State College reviewed materials on Brazil.

Economics
Dereka Rushbrook, Independent Consultant, collaborated with Clarence Zuvekas, Jr. on Central America. Martín Rama of the World Bank contributed the annotations on Paraguay and Uruguay, and Gustavo Enrique Canoñero, Independent Consultant, reviewed materials on Argentina.

Geography
William Van Davidson, Louisiana State University, annotated all general materials.

Government and Politics
Paul C. Sondrol, University of Colorado, Colorado Springs, collaborated with David Dent, annotating all general materials. Publications on the Caribbean and The Guianas were canvassed by Ivelaw L. Griffith of Florida International University.

Sociology
Patricia L. Richards assisted Antonio Ugalde with his review of general materials. Timothy P. Wickham-Crowley, Georgetown University, prepared the chapter on Mexico. William L. Canak, Middle Tennessee State University, assumed full responsibility for the chapter on Colombia and Venezuela. Materials on Peru were reviewed by Susana Lastarria-Cornhiel of the University of Wisconsin-Madison. Roberto Patri-

cio Korzeniewicz, University of Maryland, assumed responsibility for annotating materials on Argentina, Chile, and Uruguay.

Subject Index

The *Handbook* uses Library of Congress Subject Headings (LCSH) when they are consistent with usage among Latin Americanists. Differences in practice, however, make adaptation of LCSH headings necessary: 1) the *Handbook* index uses only two levels, while LC headings usually contain more; and 2) *Handbook* practice is to prefer a subject-place pattern, while LC generally uses a place-subject pattern. Automation of the *Handbook* has required that the subject index be compiled with two audiences in mind: users of the print edition and users of the online database. It has also demanded that index terms, once established, remain as stable as possible. A list of subject headings used in indexing *HLAS 50* onward is available on the *HLAS Online* web site (http://lcweb2.loc.gov/hlas/subjects.html). Since the *Handbook* is arranged by discipline, readers are encouraged to consult the table of contents for broad areas of coverage.

Advisory Board

Cole Blasier, former chair of the Advisory Board and former chief of the Hispanic Division will step down from his position on the board. The *Handbook* has greatly benefitted from his farsighted counsel; his presence on the board will be missed.

We are pleased, however, to announce that Dolores Moyano Martin, former *HLAS* Editor, and David Scott Palmer of Boston University will be joining the Advisory Board.

V. ACKNOWLEDGMENTS

The past biennium saw several *HLAS* staffing changes, most significantly, the retirement of *HLAS* Editor, Dolores Moyano Martin. It was also a period of important technical changes, primarily the LC's conversion from a mainframe computer system to an integrated client-server system, implementation of a new web interface, and development of new searching tools. As a result, this will be the last volume to use the production system developed for *HLAS* in 1989. While this period of transition was not without its frustrations, these temporary setbacks were far outweighed by the encouragement offered to the *Handbook* staff from various sources. It is no exaggeration to say that the publication of volume 57 would have been impossible without the help, advice, and hard work of an exemplary group of Library of Congress staff members and the professionalism and patience of the *HLAS* Contributing Editors.

Faced with limited time and staff, we appealed to the Contributing Editors to complete their end-of-cycle proofreading in record time. During the end-of-semester rush, they swiftly responded to our request with characteristic diligence and attention to detail.

Among Library of Congress staff, we are particularly grateful to the *Handbook* Transition Team led by Kathryn Mendenhall, Product Development Supervisor of Cataloging Distribution Services, who calmly steered the *Handbook* through the conversion to the new computer system, keeping us on track at all times. The core members of the team, Jim Agenbroad, Mary Bader, Ardie Bausenbach, Mary Ann Ferrarese, and Andy Lisowski demonstrated unhesitating willingness to answer questions, solve problems, and even check on progress from home. Their guidance, along with their unwavering patience and sense of humor, helped *HLAS* staff through many late nights and weekends and ultimately enabled us to meet our production deadlines. We also extend our wholehearted thanks to several other staff members for contributing their time and energy when both were extremely scarce resources at the LC. Sally Arason, Randy Barry, Dave Reser, and Ann Della Porta were instrumental in ensuring the transition of the *HLAS* bibliographic records from a MUMS to a MARC environment.

Each year the *Handbook* benefits from the assistance of a diverse group of temporary helpers, interns, and volunteers who share an appreciation for Latin America. Pablo Tagre, the Hispanic Division/Esteban Torres intern, worked through piles of editing and error reports with an impressive combination of speed and concentration. Claudia Cuevas and Nora Luaces, both Lampadia Fellows, offered guidance with the nuances of the Spanish language, while work-study Damarys Raquel Martínez assisted with mailings, photocopying, and record inputting, all with unflagging enthusiasm. Many thanks to Eddie Mazurek for his sympathetic technical advice and constant optimism. In addition, we are grateful to our Library of Congress managers Winston Tabb and Carolyn T. Brown and to Hispanic Division Chief Georgette Dorn for their continuing suppport of the *Handbook* and its staff.

Finally, we cannot fail to recognize the members of the Seminar on the Acquisition of Latin American Library Materials (SALALM) for their generous support of the *Handbook*. SALALM's membership is dedicated to the collection, dissemination, and preservation of research materials and works related to Latin America. Their generosity has enabled us to continue to work on a new print production system, while maintaining free online access to *HLAS* bibliographic records. The organization's commitment to research and publication in Latin American studies provides a welcome example of professional cooperation and the continuing belief in the value of scholarship and learning.

Katherine D. McCann, *Acting Editor for Volume 57*
Tracy North, *Assistant to the Editor*

ANTHROPOLOGY

GENERAL

1   Alcina Franch, José. Arqueólogos o anticuarios: historia antigua de la arqueología en la América española. Barcelona, Spain: Serbal, 1995. 212 p.: bibl., ill. (Libros del buen andar; 39)

Important social history of archaeology in Mesoamerica, the Andes, and the Antilles covers period 1492–1830 and focuses on personnel, motivations, ideologies, and political implications.

2   Alcina Franch, José. Cooperación política en Mesoamérica y los Andes en época precolombiana. (*Rev. Indias*, 55:204, mayo/agosto 1995, p. 279–300, table)

Argues that political confederations developed in Mesoamerica and the Central Andes for mutual economic advantage and that they represent an alternative stage in the evolution of States. [B. Meggers]

3   Benson, Elizabeth P. Birds and beasts of ancient Latin America. Foreword by Susan Milbrath. Gainesville: Univ. Press of Florida, 1997. 162 p.: bibl., ill. (some col.), index, map.

Categorization of animals by domesticated, hunted, anomalous, birds, amphibians and reptiles, fish, crustaceans, and mollusks reveals common themes among depictions from Mexico, Belize, Guatemala, Costa Rica, Panama, Colombia, Ecuador, and Peru.

4   Bremer, Thomas. The constitution of alterity: Fernando Ortiz and the beginnings of Latin American ethnography out of the spirit of Italian criminology. (*in* Society of Caribbean Research. International Conference, *1st, Berlin, 1988*. Alternative cultures in the Caribbean. Frankfurt: Vervuert Verlag, 1993, p. 119–129)

Reviews lifework of Cuban anthropologist Fernando Ortiz, the most important figure in the creation of Latin American anthropology and ethnography. Examines influences of Lombroso and the Italian school of criminology on Ortiz. Includes comments on Ortiz's ethnographic approach and the international ramifications of his work. [B. Aguirre-López]

5   De Suiza a Sudamérica: etnologías de Alfred Métraux. Recopilación de Claude Auroi y Alain Monnier. Geneva: Museo de Etnografía de Ginebra, 1998. 101 p.: bibl., ill., plates.

Excellent tribute to Swiss scholar Alfred Métraux (1902–63), the greatest pioneer of South American ethnology, author of multi-volume classic *Handbook of South American Indians*, and one of the first *HLAS* contributors. Compiled by Geneva's Ethnographic Museum, volume includes eight fine articles on his life and work (some by his former students); several of his drawings; many of his splendid photos of South American Indians dating from the 1920s–30s; a biographical chronology; and a comprehensive bibliography. Highly recommended. [D. Martin]

6   Díaz Polanco, Héctor. Indigenous peoples in Latin America: the quest for self-determination. Translated by Lucia Rayas. Boulder, Colo.: Westview Press, 1997. 1 v: bibl., index. (Latin American perspectives series; 8)

An important book first for its critical history of *indigenista* policies in Latin America and the limits these policies placed on social autonomy; and second for its examination of the development of indigenous autonomy, particularly in Nicaragua. Argues that autonomy is no panacea; rather, it is one possibility given current social, economic, and political processes. [J. Cohen]

7   The emergence of pottery: technology and innovation in ancient societies. Edited by William K. Barnett and John W. Hoopes. Washington: Smithsonian Institution

Press, 1995. 285 p.: bibl., ill., index, maps. (Smithsonian series in archaeological inquiry)

Includes chapters by A.C. Roosevelt on Amazonia; A. Oyuela-Caycedo on San Jacinto I, Colombia; C. Rodríguez on north coastal Colombia; J.E. Damp and L.P. Vargas on Valdivia, Ecuador; R. Cooke on Monagrillo, Panama; J.W. Hoopes on the Central American isthmus; B. Arroyo on El Salvador; and J.E. Clark and D. Gosser on Mesoamerica.

8 Fernández, Fiz Antonio. Antropología cultural, medicina indígena de América y arte rupestre argentino. v. 1–3. Buenos Aires: Editorial Galerna, 1992. 3 v.: bibl., ill.

Vols. 1 (Origins, North and Mesoamerica) and 2 (Circum-Caribbean, South America) summarize ethnohistorical, ethnographic, and archaeological information on illnesses, symptoms, treatments, fractures, practitioners, and other aspects of indigenous medicine. Vol. 3 provides 300 illustrations of Argentine rock art. Absence of bibliographic sources subsequent to 1976 limits utility to an introductory level. [B. Meggers]

Five hundred years after Columbus: proceedings. See *HLAS 56:437.*

9 Galindo Trejo, Jesús. Arqueoastronomía en la América antigua. Madrid: Editorial Equipo Sirius, 1994. 263 p.: bibl., ill. (some col.). (Col. La ciencia y la tecnología en la historia)

An astrophysicist draws on codices, stelae, ethnohistorical sources, and architectural alignments to summarize astronomical knowledge among preshistoric populations of Mesoamerica and the Andean area.

10 History of Latin American archaeology. Edited by Augusto Oyuela-Caycedo. Aldershot, England: Avebury, 1994. 212 p.: bibl., index.

Most of the 12 chapters focus on countries outside of the Intermediate Area. Nevertheless, entire volume is of value to scholars working throughout the Caribbean area. Oyuela-Caycedo's introduction sets the tone by pointing out that the conventional history of archaeology in the region is unfortunately biased by US perceptions and the English language. Fitzgerald reviews recent developments in Panama; Hastorf discusses changing approaches to maize research throughout the region; and Roe uses regional examples to examine the relationship between ethnology and archaeology. [W. Keegan]

11 Lagarde, Marcela. Los cautiverios de las mujeres: madresposas, monjas, putas, presas y locas. 2a ed. México: Univ. Nacional Autónoma de México, 1993. 878 p.: bibl. (Col. Posgrado; 8)

Mexican anthropologist, one of the few theorists of radical feminism in the region, offers detailed examination of a "feminist anthropology of women" (p. 831). Discusses status of women in patriarchal societies and identifies motherhood, sexuality, and religion as key components of female oppression. Main contribution of this work is its focus on five "models" that typify female oppression: mother-wives, nuns, prostitutes, women prisoners, and demented women. Lagarde's thesis quickly became popular throughout Latin America. [A. Lavrin]

12 MacNeish, Richard S. The beginnings of agriculture in the New World. (*Rev. Arqueol. Am.,* 6, 1992, p. 7–34)

Author summarizes his "Trilinear Theory" and applies it to highland Mexico and the Andes, lowland Mesoamerica and the Andes, and the Colorado Plateau and Eastern Woodlands of North America. Dating of early plant domesticates from Mexico is currently under reevaluation, which may have implications for this model. [D. Nichols]

13 Martín Barbero, Jesús. Communication, culture and hegemony: from the media to mediations. Translated by Elizabeth Fox and Robert A. White. Introduction by Philip Schlesinger. London; Newbury Park, Calif.: SAGE Publications, 1993. 272 p.: bibl., index. (Communication and human values)

Important contribution to Latin American cultural studies focuses on popular culture within a general theory of hegemony. Also relates how mass media define national identities. [J. Rappaport]

14 Patterson, Thomas C. Social archaeology in Latin America: an appreciation. (*Am. Antiq.,* 59:3, July 1994, p. 531–537)

A leading Marxist archaeologist briefly reviews influence and development of Marxist thought on Latin American archaeology. Considers writings of Mexican archaeologists, including M. Gándara. [D. Nichols]

15 Piperno, Dolores R. and **Gayle J. Fritz.** On the emergence of agriculture in the New World. (*Curr. Anthropol.,* 35:5, Dec. 1994, p. 637–643)

Piperno comments on Fritz's revised chronology (see *HLAS 55:109*) for the origins of agriculture in the Americas and argues that chronology revision for Mesoamerica is premature and that microfossil evidence from Central America should be considered. Fritz in her reply agrees with importance of Central American research, but sees need for further chronological analysis. [D. Nichols]

16 Schwartz, Marion. A history of dogs in the early Americas. Selected drawings by Susan Hochgraf. New Haven, Conn.: Yale Univ. Press, 1997. 233 p., 4 p. of plates: bibl., ill. (some col.), index, maps.

Using archaeological (skeletal remains, depictions), historical, ethnographic, mythological, and linguistic evidence, work surveys various roles of domesticated dogs throughout the Americas.

17 Sorenson, John L. and **Martin H. Raish.** Pre-Columbian contact with the Americas across the oceans: an annotated bibliography. 2nd. ed. rev. Provo, Utah: Research Press, 1996. 2 v: index.

Deletion of 1,250 of the 5,613 references in the 1990 edition, substitution of 600+ new titles and 900 new abstracts, and a more detailed index enhance the utility of this indispensible resource. Annotations emphasize content rather than criticism, and are especially valuable for early titles in obscure sources. Sorenson's formidable accomplishment and perceptive introduction bring objectivity to the most controversial topic in New World archaeology.

Sušnik, Branislava. Interpretación etnocultural de la complejidad sudamericana antigua. v. 1, Formación y dispersión étnica. See item **404.**

18 Textile traditions of Mesoamerica and the Andes: an anthology. Edited by Margot Blum Schevil, Janet Catherine Berlo, and Edward Bridgman Dwyer. Austin: Univ. of Texas Press, 1996. 503 p.: bibl., ill., index, maps.

Chapters provide detailed information on manufacturing (spinning, weaving, dyeing, decorating); communicative significance (ethnicity, identity, tradition, rank, geographic origin); and marketing and commercialization among contemporary groups of indigenous descent.

ARCHAEOLOGY
Mesoamerica

JOHN HENDERSON, *Professor of Anthropology, Cornell University*
DEBORAH L. NICHOLS, *Professor of Anthropology, Dartmouth College*

ALTHOUGH SCHOLARS HAVE increasingly taken a more interpretive, comparative, and theoretical approach to Maya archaeology, a substantial amount of the literature is still highly descriptive. Most of these descriptive publications consist of field investigation summaries (settlement pattern studies, excavation projects) or technical analyses (sourcing studies, especially of obsidian).

The fundamental theoretical perspectives that shape the work of Maya scholars can be classified into two groups (item **99**). One set represents the continuing impact of processual archaeology, is empirically oriented, and tends to emphasize ecology, subsistence, population, and economy. The second is a more humanistic, non-scientific perspective. It emphasizes cultural realms, such as religion, a less constrained style of interpretation, and, while it has much in common with some varieties of "post-processual" archaeology, it also represents a continuity of art historical and culture historical approaches that have consistently been strong components of Maya studies.

Core-periphery perspectives continue to provide the most common explicit theoretical models for processually-oriented Maya archaeology (item **128**). World systems theory, originally developed by the historian Immanuel Wallerstein, remains the most persistent version of these models. However, critiques of its applicability to prehistoric societies have sharply limited its popularity within the archaeological field.

The most prominent dimension of the growing emphasis on an interpretational approach is the array of studies based on decipherment of Maya hieroglyphic writing and on related insights based on iconographic analysis (items **301, 311,** and **130**). The popularity of these approaches among Maya scholars, and their appeal to the general public, has increased steadily over the past two decades, and the trend shows no sign of abating. Some of these studies focus on specific aspects of ancient Maya religion, mythology, and symbolism (items **281, 29, 161, 298, 195, 303, 306, 318,** and **319**); others, assuming similarity among all Maya societies, attempt a more global, synthetic interpretation of the ancient Maya (item **68**).

Interpretive approaches also include attempts to understand the principles and institutions that underlay the political and economic organization of ancient Maya societies. Some of these studies on the emergence and nature of ancient states are informed by comparative theoretical perspectives (items **44** and **102**). Others, more focused on reconstructing the political landscape of the ancient Maya world, draw heavily on advances in decipherment and on iconographic analysis and tend to be highly interpretive, even speculative (items **101, 88,** and **323**). Explorations of economic organization, by contrast, tend to hold back from interpretation, emphasizing a grounding in empirical data (items **248, 271,** and **280**). These economically oriented studies, along with investigations of the environment, ecology, and subsistence (items **196, 241, 242, 256, 122,** and **272**), represent the processual thread within Maya archaeology.

Documenting and understanding the history, formation, and development of precolumbian civilizations and their antecedents dominates archaeological research in Mexico. Although scholars have, in recent years, conducted relatively less field research aimed at uncovering the origins of maize cultivation in Highland Mexico, the estimated timing of this agricultural development has stirred a considerable amount of controversy (item **15**). Reanalysis of early maize from the Tehuacan Valley, using the accelerator mass spectrometric (AMS) method of radiocarbon dating, has yielded more recent dates, suggesting that the critical time-frame for maize domestication was 3500–2500 BC, and not 5000–3500 BC as has been generally accepted. The debate surrounding early American agricultural chronology is likely to continue as additional studies, now underway, uncover new clues. This issue highlights not only the value of reanalyzing material collections, but also the need for new field research in the highlands on the Archaic and early formative periods.

The Pacific and Gulf Coasts of Chiapas, once backwaters of contemporary archaeology, have become the focus of a series of on-going investigations concerning the origins of sedentary villages and early complex societies (items **113** and **33**). Sedentary villages were present here by 1550 BC, and ranked societies developed as early, if not earlier, than in the more famous Gulf Coast Olmec heartland; the notion of the Olmec as Mesoamerican civilization's "mother culture"—an artifact of the history of archaeological investigations—is simply no longer tenable. At the same time, the regional approach taken by the San Lorenzo Tenochtitlan Archaeology Project, combined with excavations of residential areas and hinterland centers, is providing much needed details of Olmec chronology and their social, political, and economic organization.

Theories recently advanced to account for these and later developments encapsulate broader disciplinary trends that emphasize human agency, political economy, history, and ideology—approaches that are becoming the "normal science" of archaeology (see Cowgill in item **34**). Marcus and Flannery, in their book, *Zapotec civilization* (item **100**), argue that action theory provides a way to incorporate humans as actors of social change within a scientific and comparative explanatory framework, and thus serves as a counter-balance perspective to structural and syncretic models.

Ideology figures prominently in Hosler's *The sounds and colors of power* (item **85**), in which she argues that metallurgy was adopted in west Mexico from northern South America through coastal trade networks, not principally for utilitarian purposes, but because sensory properties and relative scarcity linked metals to sacred precepts and the hierarchy of human social relations. Hosler's work suggests a number of avenues for future research in west Mexico.

Current research on the origins and evolution of Mexica (Aztec) society has complemented the ethnohistorical shift away from the standard Spanish chroniclers to local sources by focusing on the culture's political economy. The picture now emerging from the combined and sometimes, as in the case of *Aztec imperial strategies* (item **32**), collaborative research of archaeologists and ethnohistorians of the Mexica is not that of a monolithic centralized State, but of a State that employed various imperial strategies to control and manipulate networks of social, political, and economic relationships among diverse city-states and factions.

The number of recent general, regional, and topical syntheses—including the three-volume *Historia antigua de México*, written by leading archaeologists but accessible to non-specialists—suggests that archaeologists are making greater efforts to present their findings to a broader audience. Also notable is the number of collaborative symposia, conferences, and publications involving Mexican and North American archaeologists. The Univ. of Pittsburgh's Latin American Archaeology Publications now distributes books published in Mexico by INAH and UNAM's Instituto de Investigaciones Antropologicas, making salvage and research archaeology results more accessible in North America.

Nichols' contribution to this chapter was written while she was on sabbatical leave from Dartmouth College. She gratefully acknowledges the expert assistance of Patricia Carter and the staff of the Inter-Library Loan Office (Baker Library, Dartmouth), Dr. Ridie Ghezzi (Baker Library, Dartmouth), and Dr. Gregory Finnegan (Tozzer Library, Harvard). The authors are grateful for the help and support of Amy Puryear and others on the staff of *HLAS*.

GENERAL

Alcina Franch, José. Arqueólogos o anticuarios: historia antigua de la arqueología en la América española. See item **1**.

19   The ancient mind: elements of cognitive archaeology. Edited by Colin Renfrew and Ezra B.W. Zubrow. Cambridge, England; New York: Cambridge Univ. Press, 1994. 209 p.: bibl., ill., index, maps. (New directions in archaeology)

Collection of articles seeks to define a scientific approach to prehistoric cognition. In an important paper, Marcus and Flannery look at the evolution of Zapotec religion and ritual and the transformation of Monte Albán and the Zapotec state. [DN]

20   Andrews, Anthony P. First cities. Montreal: St. Remy Press; Washington: Smithsonian Books, 1995. 176 p.: bibl., col. ill., index, col. maps. (Exploring the ancient world)

This introductory-level book of the "Exploring the Ancient World" series deals with urbanism in six parts of the world. One chapter overviews Mesoamerica and discusses Olmec centers, Monte Albán, and Teotihuacán. Reflecting the author's interests, ancient Maya cities are discussed in a separate chapter. Color photographs and drawings. [DN]

21 Antología de Cacaxtla. v. 1–2. Recopilación de Angel García Cook y Beatriz Leonor Merino Carrión. Coordinación de Lorena Mirambell S. México: Instituto Nacional de Antropología e Historia, 1995. 2 v.: bibl., ill. (Antologías. Serie Arqueología)

Useful collection of 36 previously published articles dealing with the Epi-Teotihuacán center and surrounding parts of Tlaxcala. Vol. 1 contains an introduction by the editors, an excerpt from Diego Muñoz Camargo's *Historia de Tlaxcala*, early papers by Pedro Armillas and Wiberto Jiménez Moreno, along with more recent articles that are continued in vol. 2. [DN]

22 Antropología mesoamericana: homenaje a Alfonso Villa Rojas. Recopilación de Víctor Manuel Esponda Jimeno, Sophia Pincemín Deliberos y Mauricio Rosas Kifuri. Tuxtla Gutiérrez, Mexico: Gobierno del Estado de Chiapas, Consejo Estatal de Fomento a la Investigación y Difusión de la Cultura, DIF-Chiapas/Instituto Chiapaneco de Cultura, 1992. 545 p.: bibl., ill., map. (Serie Nuestros pueblos; 10)

Appropriately, most of the contributions to this *festschrift* in honor of one of Mexico's foremost ethnographers are biographical or focus on ethnographic topics. A few, however, deal with archaeological and ethnohistorical subjects: excavations at Ocozocuautla, Chiapas; precolumbian Maya sacbes and hydraulic works; precolumbian Maya scribes; Yucatán at the time of the Spanish invasion; Mesoamerican and Asian calendars; and astronomical alignments at Monte Albán. [JSH]

23 Archaeological views from the countryside: village communities in early complex societies. Edited by Glenn M. Schwartz and Steven E. Falconer. Washington: Smithsonian Institution Press, 1994. 230 p.: bibl., ill., index, maps.

Important collection of articles on rural settlements of ancient Mesoamerican and Near Eastern civilizations. Documentation of heterogeneity in rural settlements is a central theme. Articles on Mesoamerica deal with the Maya site of Colha, Belize. and chert

production; Matacapán, Veracruz, and the organization of craft production; Aztec period settlements in Morelos; and households and settlement patterns in the Copán Valley. [DN]

24 Arnold, Philip J. An overview of southern Veracruz archaeology. (*Anc. Mesoam.*, 5 : 1, Spring 1994, p. 215–221)

Paper provides a concise summary of current research trends. Early and middle formative Olmec societies continue to be an important area of research; other recent work has focused on classic and postclassic periods at Matacapan (Tuxtla mountains) and La Mixtequilla (southern Veracruz), political economy, specialization, and exchange. [DN]

25 Arqueología del occidente y norte de México. Edición de Eduardo Williams y Phil C. Weigand. Zamora, Mexico: Colegio de Michoacán, 1995. 224 p.: bibl., ill., maps. (Col. Memorias)

Diverse topics are covered in this collection: recent work on the Tarascan state, groundstone from Carapan, Michoacán, "conch" shell artifacts, turquoise mining, ceramic and lithic artifacts from the borders of Hidalgo and Querétaro, ceramics from the Sierra Tarahumara, and investigations of the Boca de Potrerillos project in Nuevo León. [DN]

26 Arqueología Mexicana. Vol. 3, No. 15, 1995. México: Editorial Raíces.

Focuses on the Mexica (Aztecs) of Mexico. Short articles draw on ethnohistory and recent archaeological investigations of the Templo Mayor and Tlatelolco to discuss religion and human sacrifice, art and politics, architecture, the history of the Triple Alliance and the organization of Nahua society. Also includes article on the quetzal bird, whose feathers were highly valued by prehispanic societies. Color photographs.

27 Arqueología Mexicana. Vol. 3, No. 16, 1995. México: Editorial Raíces.

Issue devoted to mural painting with an overview of prehispanic development and technology. Other articles cover Teotihuacán and central Mexico, Monte Albán, El Tajín, Bonampak, and the postclassic Maya. Discussion of monastic mural painting and the later 20th-century muralist movement notes change and continuity in Mexican muralism. [DN]

28 **La arqueología mexicana en el umbral del siglo XXI: proyectos especiales de arqueología.** México: Consejo Nacional para la Cultura y las Artes; Instituto Nacional de Antropología e Historia; Museo Nacional de Antropología, 1994. 47 p.: ill. (some col.).

Catalog of exhibition presenting results of 14 archaeological excavation and restoration projects from 1992–94. Brief descriptions of each project by its director. Color photographs of the sites, reconstructed buildings, and key artifacts. Projects focus on rock art in Baja California; Paquimé in Chihuahua; Bega de la Peña in central Veracruz; Monte Albán in Oaxaca; Teotihuacán, Xochicalco, Xochitécatl, and Cantona in central Mexico; and Palenque, Toniná, Dzibilchaltún, Chichén Itzá, Calakmul, Dzibanché in the Maya world. [JSH]

29 **Bassie-Sweet, Karen.** At the edge of the world: caves and late classic Maya world view. Norman: Univ. of Oklahoma Press, 1996. 263 p.: bibl., ill., index, map.

Reconstruction of classic period Maya beliefs about the structure of the universe based on imagery and hieroglyphic texts from lowland cities. Focuses on cosmological meanings of caves in defining the Maya world and connections with supernatural realms, especially the underworld. [JSH]

30 **Baudot, Georges.** Utopia and history in Mexico: the first chroniclers of Mexican civilization, 1520–1569. Translated by Bernard R. Ortiz de Montellano and Thelma Ortiz de Montellano. Niwot: Univ. Press of Colorado, 1995. 585 p.: bibl., ill., index, map. (Mesoamerican worlds: from the Olmecs to the Danzantes)

Important historical analysis of 16th-century accounts concerning indigenous people. Examines context in which chronicles—considered among the earliest ethnographies—were written (and censured and ignored), and Franciscan beliefs about the Indians' future within the millennial kingdom. First English translation. [DN]

31 **Beltrán, Ulises et al.** El Michoacán antiguo: estado y sociedad tarascos en la época prehispánica. Coordinación de Brigitte B. de Lameiras. Fotografía de Ricardo Sánchez González. Paleografía de J. Benedict Warren, Alberto Carrillo Cázares y Silvia Méndez Hernández. Zamora, Mexico: Colegio de Michoacán; Gobierno del Estado de Michoacán, 1994. 463 p.: bibl., ill. (some col.), index, maps (some col.).

Interdisciplinary volume provides current syntheses of ethnohistory, archaeology, linguistics, and ethnography by leading scholars. Transcription and index of document "El Proceso contra Pedro de Arellano, su valor histórico," originally recorded in 1532. Illustrated with striking color photographs and line drawings; printed on glossy paper. Oversize format. [DN]

32 **Berdan, Frances et al.** Aztec imperial strategies. Washington: Dumbarton Oaks Research Library and Collection, 1996. 400 p.: appendices, bibl., ill., index, maps.

Based on a ten-week working seminar in 1986, offers new interpretations of the extent, organization, and imperial strategies of the Aztec empire. Analyzes data from the major chroniclers and from individual towns and places throughout the empire. Information obtained from early colonial Spanish administrative documents and archaeology is presented in appendices. [DN]

33 **Blake, Michael et al.** Radiocarbon chronology for the Late Archaic and Formative periods on the Pacific coast of southeastern Mesoamerica. (*Anc. Mesoam.,* 6:2, Fall 1995, p. 161–183)

Detailed analysis of recent dates is used to propose a refined archaeological chronology between 4000–650 BC (late Archaic to middle formative periods). Analysis dates initial appearance of sedentary villages to ca. 1550 BC and the development of early rank societies to 1400–1250 BC. [DN]

34 **Blanton, Richard E. et al.** A dual-processual theory for the evolution of Mesoamerican civilization. (*Curr. Anthropol.,* 37:1, Feb. 1996, p. 1–14, map, tables)

In a special section, "Agency, Ideology, and Power in Archaeological Theory," authors propose an influential agency-based theory of political economy and the development of complex societies. Teotihuacán and lowland Maya civilizations are used to distinguish different strategies of political power. Commentaries by other scholars included. [DN]

35 **Bones of the Maya: studies of ancient skeletons.** Edited by Stephen L. Whittington and David M. Reed. Washington:

Smithsonian Institution Press, 1997. 301 p.: bibl., ill., index, maps.

Collection defines current state of Mayan skeletal studies. Coverage spans the formative through colonial periods, with a geographic focus on the Maya lowlands of northern Guatemala, Belize, and western Honduras. Includes osteological, dental, bone chemistry, and DNA analyses. Diet and health status of Maya populations is a major theme, especially in relation to social status, gender, and the historical problem of the "collapse." [JSH]

36   Boone, Elizabeth Hill. The Aztec world. Montreal: St. Remy Press; Washington: Smithsonian Books, 1994. 160 p.: bibl., col. ill., index, col. maps. (Exploring the ancient world)

Well-illustrated overview of the Aztec empire and society's development drawn from ethnohistoric sources and excavations at major imperial centers. Basic introduction for nonspecialists. [DN]

37   Brambila Paz, Rosa. Bibliografía de arquitectura de Teotihuacán. México: Univ. Nacional Autónoma de México, Facultad de Arquitectura, 1994. 1 v.: bibl.

Issue devoted to a bibliography of Teotihuacán architecture. Includes published and unpublished scholarly works and sources for general audiences. Over 1,000 entries from 1865–1992. [DN]

38   Caciques and their people: a volume in honor of Ronald Spores. Edited by Joyce Marcus and Judith Francis Zeitlin. Ann Arbor: Museum of Anthropology, Univ. of Michigan, 1994. 311 p.: bibl., ill., maps. (Anthropological papers/Museum of Anthropology, Univ. of Michigan; 89)

Articles review Spores' contributions to Mixtec archaeology, ethnohistory, and ethnology. Other topics include archaeological theory, the colonial period, Xaltocán, Cholula, codex-style vessel from Nochixtlan, Codex Selden, irrigation in Mixtec *cacicazgos* and Cuicatlan, Mixtec *cacicazgos* organization, Spanish conquest of Oaxaca, Zapotec inauguration, and Tehuantepec barrio organization. [DN]

39   Carpio Rezzio, Edgar H. La práctica arqueológica en Guatemala, 1954–1970: un análisis crítico. (*Estudios/Guatemala*, 1, 1994, p. 33–60, bibl.)

Assessment of Guatemalan archaeology within a national political context during the 1950s-60s. Emphasis on development of a distinctively Guatemalan approach to archaeology, and especially on the relationship between the agendas of foreign, mainly North American, archaeologists and those of Guatemalan archaeologists. [JSH]

40   Castañeda, Quetzil E. La economía *escritural* y la invención de las culturas mayas en el *museo* de Chichén Itza. (*Rev. Esp. Antropol. Am.*, 25, 1995, p. 181–203, bibl.)

Consideration of the processes by which various interest groups—academics, spiritualists, tourists, providers of tourist services, etc.—use remains of the past to create and manipulate images of the ancient Maya. Focuses on case study of the events which surround the equinox sunset shadow patterns on the stair of the Castillo at Chichén Itzá. [JSH]

41   The ceramic legacy of Anna O. Shepard. Edited by Ronald L. Bishop and Frederick W. Lange. Niwot: Univ. Press of Colorado, 1991. 484 p.: bibl., ill., index.

Revised papers from a 1988 conference on the history of ceramic technology in archaeology. Part I examines Shepard's research, covering her contributions to Mesoamerican archaeology. Part II deals with current issues, including a discussion of Mesoamerican Plumbate Ware. Part III concludes with an assessment. In addition to valuable historical analysis, important theoretical and methodological issues are addressed.

42   Cerámica de Cultura Maya. Nos. 17/ 18, 1996. Philadelphia: Temple Univ., Dept. of Anthropology.

Last two numbers of journal devoted to Mesoamerican (especially Maya) ceramics and methods of ceramic analysis. These issues contain retrospective essays on the history of ceramic analysis in the Maya world; listing of major repositories of ceramic collections; comprehensive author, title, and subject indices to the journal; and extensive indices of taxonomic categories. [JSH]

43   Chance, John K. The barrios of colonial Tecali: patronage, kinship, and territorial relations in a central Mexican community. (*Ethnology/Pittsburgh*, 35:2, Spring 1996, p. 107–139, bibl., tables)

Through an analysis of documentary

sources, argues that prehispanic Tecali, Puebla, was organized by noble houses (*teccalli*). Although this system of personal loyalties was replaced during the colonial period by a territorial model consisting of barrios, indigenous people manipulated these colonial divisions and adapted them to non-Spanish institutions. For ethnologist's comment, see item **711.** [DN]

44   Chase, Arlen F. *et al.* The Maya state: centralized or segmentary? (*Curr. Anthropol.*, 37:5, Dec. 1996, p. 795–830)

Forum on models for ancient Maya political organization. Drawn from research at Caracol in Belize, the case is made by A. Chase and D. Chase for centralized precolumbian Maya States; Cook and Fox, referring to ethnohistorical and ethnographic data on the Quiché and the Yucatec, argue that they were segmentary. [JSH]

45   Chase, Arlen F. and Diane Z. Chase. A mighty Maya nation. (*Archaeology/New York*, 49:5, Sept./Oct. 1996, p. 66–72)

Popular overview of recent excavations at the Maya city of Caracol in western Belize. Emphasizes population size, and the scale and influence of its State during the classic period. [JSH]

46   Chase, Diane Z. and Arlen F. Chase. Maya multiples: individuals, entries, and tombs in Structure A34 of Caracol, Belize. (*Lat. Am. Antiq.*, 7:1, 1996, p. 61–79)

Tombs in one structure of Caracol's Central Acropolis suggest that multiple burials and reuse of old tombs were relatively common at this classic-period city. [JSH]

Chepstow-Lustry, A.J. *et. al.* 4000 years of human impact and vegetation change in the central Peruvian Andes—with events parallelling the Maya record? See item **616.**

47   Chipping away on earth: studies in prehispanic and colonial Mexico in honor of Arthur J.O. Anderson and Charles E. Dibble. Edited by Eloise Quiñones Keber with the assistance of Susan Schroeder and Frederic Hicks. Lancaster, Calif.: Labyrinthos, 1994. 266 p.: bibl., ill.

Collection of papers deals primarily with documentary 16th-century studies. Topics include: the production of the Florentine Codex, Sahagún's ethnography, Nahua, Mixtec, and Yucatec Maya documents, Nahua society before and after the Spanish Conquest, and the history and archaeology of Texcoco and the Alcolhua domain. For ethnohistorian's comment see *HLAS 56:416.* [DN]

48   Cobos, Rafael. Síntesis de la arqueología de El Salvador, 1850–1991. San Salvador: Dirección General de Publicaciones e Impresos, Consejo Nacional para la Cultura y Arte, Dirección General del Patrimonio Cultural, 1994. 104 p.: bibl., ill. (Col. Antropologá e historia; 21. Arqueología)

Covers the history of archaeological work and the cultural history of preclassic, classic, and postclassic periods. [DN]

49   Congreso Internacional de Mayistas, 1st, San Cristóbal de Las Casas, Mexico, 1989. Memorias. v. 2., Mesas redondas, arqueología, epigrafía. México: Univ. Nacional Autónoma de México, 1992–1994. 1 v. bibl., ill., maps.

Proceedings from a 1989 international conference on the Maya held in San Cristóbal de las Casas (Mexico). Vol. 2 includes general sections on archaeology (20 papers), epigraphy (4 papers), recent fieldwork in Guatemala (3 papers), economic development of the classic Maya (5 papers), and Oxkintok (7 papers).

50   Congreso Internacional de Mayistas, 2nd, San Cristóbal de Las Casas, Mexico, 1995. Memorias. México: Univ. Nacional Autónoma de México, Instituto de Investigaciones Filológicas, Centro de Estudios Mayas, 1995. 750 p.: bibl., ill.

Proceedings of a 1995 international conference on the Maya held in San Cristobal de las Casas (Mexico). Papers focus on lowland Maya archaeology, especially of the Yucatan peninsula. Featured essays focus on bird symbolism; images of the Maya as represented in archaeological and ethnographic literature; similarities between Quiche myths in the Popol Vuh and those of central Mexico; architecture of ancient Becan (Campeche); and oral literature of modern Santa Catarina Palopo in the Guatemalan highlands. Eighteen additional papers on the archaeology of the Yucatan, ten on sites in Tabasco, Chiapas, Belize, and Peten (Guatemala), six on linguistic themes (including one on epigraphy), and two on biological anthropology. [JSH]

51   Cortés de Brasdefer, Fernando. Los mascarones de Chakanbakan. (*Mexicon/Berlin*, 16:2, 1994, p. 32–34)

Describes the large stucco masks that flank the stairway of a classic period pyramid at a Maya city in southern Quintana Roo. Reports on recent damage to the masks by looters. [JSH]

52 Culture and contact: Charles C. Di Peso's Gran Chichimeca. Edited by Anne I. Woosley and John C. Ravesloot. Albuquerque: Univ. of New Mexico Press, 1993. 326 p., 8 p. of plates: bibl., ill. (some col.), index, maps (some col.). (Amerind Foundation New World Studies series; 2)

In addition to biographical contributions, this *festschrift* includes papers focusing on the North American Southwest and northern and western Mexico. Topical focus on patterns and mechanisms of interaction among these regions. [JSH]

53 Curtis, Jason H.; David A. Hodell; and Mark Brenner. Climate variability on the Yucatán peninsula, Mexico, during the past 3500 years, and implications for Maya cultural evolution. (*Quat. Res./New York,* 46:1, July 1996, p. 37–47)

Reconstructs climatic change based on changes in sediment and oxygen isotopes in a core from Lake Punta Laguna of the Yucatán. Results indicate relatively wet conditions from before 1000 BC until about AD 200; drier conditions until approximately AD 1100, followed by a return to a wetter regime. Frequent droughts between 850 and 1050 may have contributed to the process of cultural transformation that signaled the decline of many city-states of the southern Maya lowlands. [JSH]

54 De Montmollin, Olivier. Patrones fronterizos de los reinos mayas de clásico en los altos tributarios del río Grijalva. (*Arqueología/México,* 7, 1992, p. 57–67)

Article summarizes a recent settlement pattern study of the Upper Grijalva tributaries, and proposes that in late/terminal classic period this southwestern periphery of the Maya lowlands contained a network of small polities. Discussed, with greater detail, in a recent book by same author (see item **55**). [DN]

55 De Montmollin, Olivier. Settlement and politics in three classic Maya polities. Madison, Wis.: Prehistory Press, 1995. 386 p.: bibl., maps. (Monographs in world archaeology, 1055–2316; 24)

Settlement pattern data from the Greater Rosario Valley, Chiapas—the southwest periphery of lowland Maya civilization—are analyzed with an emphasis on the late/terminal classic period. A variety of settlement/political models, from the household to regional levels, are considered; favors a segmentary-state system of political organization. See also item **54**. [DN]

56 Demant, Alain *et al.* El proyecto Michoacán, 1983–1987: medio ambiente e introducción a los trabajos arqueológicos. Coordinación de Dominique Michelet. México: Centre d'études mexicaines et centraméricaines, 1992. 197 p.: bibl., ill., maps. (Col. Etudes mésoaméricaines. II, 0378–5726; 12. Cuadernos de estudios michoacanos; 4)

Focus on prehispanic settlement and environment of north-central Michoacán. Inventory of 367 sites/loci and a summary of radiocarbon dates. Most of the volume is devoted to the region's geomorphology, including Lake Zacapú; and to discussion of human-induced environmental changes, the subject of recent controversy. [DN]

57 Drennan, Robert D. What can be learned by estimating human energy costs? (*Anc. Mesoam.,* 5:1, Spring 1994, p. 209–212)

Commentary on the energetics of long distance transportation of goods in prehispanic Mesoamerica. Discusses common misunderstandings and argues that because of transporatation costs, long distance movement of staple foods was not profitable in energetic terms. [DN]

58 Eighth Palenque round table, 1993. San Francisco, Calif.: Pre-Columbian Art Research Institute, 1994. 498 p.: ill. (The Palenque round table series; 10)

Proceedings of an international conference on the Maya held at the ancient Maya city of Palenque. Like earlier Palenque meetings, the 1993 conference emphasized the iconography and epigraphy of the classic Maya lowlands, with a few contributions on Olmec art and other kinds of archaeological data. [JSH]

59 Fähmel Beyer, Bernd Walter Federico. La arquitectura de Monte Albán. México: Univ. Nacional Autónoma de México, Instituto de Investigaciones Antropológicas, 1991. 201 p.: bibl., map.

Architectural analysis of Monte Albán's (Mexico) central plaza. Especially useful line drawings and photographs. [DN]

60   Fähmel Beyer, Bernd Walter Federico. En el cruce de caminos: bases de la relación entre Monte Albán y Teotihuacán. México: Univ. Nacional Autónoma de México, Instituto de Investigaciones Antropológicas, 1995. 32 p.: bibl., ill.

Draws on recent architectural studies with an emphasis on ritual and astronomy, to analyze and discuss relations between Monte Albán and Teotihuacán. [DN]

61   Faugère-Kalfon, Briggitte. Algunos aspectos del Clásico en el centro-norte de Michoacán. (*Arqueología/México*, 7, 1992, p. 39–50)

Based on work conducted between 1983–87 by the Centro de Estudios Mexicanos y Centroamericanos, article reviews archaeology of north-central Michoacán's classic period. [DN]

62   Fedick, Scott L. Indigenous agriculture in the Americas. (*J. Archaeol. Res.*, 3:4, 1995, p. 257–303, bibl.)

Review of studies published between 1987–94. Discusses transition from foraging to agriculture, plant domestication and dispersion. Includes regional overviews of prehistoric agricultural systems and examines process of agricultural change, suitability of tropics for foraging economies, and the application of precolumbian agricultural practices in contemporary experimental settings. Includes bibliography. [DN]

63   Finsten, Laura et al. Circular architecture and symbolic boundaries in the Mixtec Sierra, Oaxaca. (*Anc. Mesoam.*, 7:1, Spring 1996, p. 19–35)

Systematic survey of the Peñoles area between the Valleys of Oaxaca and Nochixtlan identified a series of enigmatic circular stone foundations, which are interpreted as remains of *temazcales* or sweatbaths. Based on their distribution, these structures may be symbolic boundary markers of postclassic Mixtec kingdoms. [DN]

64   Finsten, Laura. Jalieza, Oaxaca: activity specialization at a hilltop center. Nashville, Tenn.: Vanderbilt Univ. Press, 1995. 98 p.

Monograph discusses results of intensive surface collections that represent the first systematic investigation of a secondary hilltop center from the classic period, and presents evidence for ceramic, obsidian, and local chipped stone production in classic and early postclassic periods. [DN]

65   Flannery, Kent V. Ignacio Bernal, 1910–1992. (*Am. Antiq.*, 59:1, January 1994, p. 72–76)

Obituary of this important figure in Mexican archaeology includes a personal and intellectual biographical overview. Annotated bibliography covers 20 of Bernal's most notable publications, which total 267. [DN]

66   Foro de Arqueología de Chiapas, 2nd, Chiapas, Mexico, 1991. Segundo y Tercer Foro de Arqueología de Chiapas. Tuxtla Gutiérrez, Mexico: Gobierno del Estado de Chiapas, Consejo Estatal de Fomento a la Investigación y Difusión de la Cultura, Instituto Chiapaneco de Cultura, 1993. 247 p.: bibl., ill., maps. (Serie Memorias)

Important papers from conferences on archaeology of Chiapas pertaining to the preclassic and protoclassic periods. Topics include Olmec sociopolitical organization, writing, San Lorenzo Tenochtitlán, preclassic and protoclassic Chiapas, Kaminaljuyú, Izapa, Los Cerritos, and preclassic Campeche.

67   Foro de Arqueología de Chiapas, 4th, Comitán de Domínguez, Mexico, 1993. Cuarto Foro de Arqueología de Chiapas. Tuxtla Gutiérrez, Mexico: Gobierno del Estado de Chiapas, Consejo Estatal de Fomento a la Investigación y Difusión de la Cultura, Instituto Chiapaneco de Cultura, 1994. 211 p.: bibl., ill., maps. (Serie Memorias)

Collection of conference papers on diverse Maya archaeological topics: linguistics, ritual, relations between Tikal and Dos Pilas, Palenque, Bonampak, eastern Chiapas, Tenan Puente, and classic period settlement in the upper Rio Grijalva. Two papers discuss ethnohistory, the Maya (Chol and Zoque), and the colonial period. [DN]

68   Freidel, David A.; Linda Schele; and **Joy Parker.** Maya cosmos. (*Camb. Archaeol. J.*, 5:1, 1995, p. 115–137)

Authors provide introductory remarks about *Maya Cosmos*, their highly interpretive, anecdotal treatment of Maya religion and mythology which assumes a great deal of continuity through time and space. Commentaries focus on the "personal," nonscientific approach (Sanders), theoretical considerations in the use of iconographic data (Graham), problems associated with decontextualized data (Tedlock), the postulated shamanic character of Maya kings (Webster), and structural similarities between Maya and South American astronomical beliefs (Rose). [JSH]

Garavaglia, Juan Carlos. Human beings and the environment in America: on "determinism" and "possibilism." See *HLAS 56:865.*

69   Garza, Mercedes de la. Aves sagradas de los Mayas. México: Univ. Nacional Autónoma de México, Centro de Estudios Mayas del Instituto de Investigaciones Filológicas, Facultad de Filosofía y Letras 1995. 138 p.: bibl., ill.
      Examination of birds within Maya thought and imagery (including hieroglyphs that are pictographic representations of birds). Emphasizes birds' symbolic role, especially in connection with supernatural beings. [JSH]

70   Good, Catherine. Salt production and commerce in Guerrero, Mexico: an ethnographic contribution to historical reconstruction. (*Anc. Mesoam.*, 6:1, Spring 1995, p. 1–13, bibl., maps, photos)
      Discusses an ethnographic study of contemporary salt production along the Costa Chica of Guerrero and reconstructs itinerant Nahua salt trade in the Balsas Valley during early-mid 20th century. Briefly examines recent economic change. Relevant to studies of prehispanic salt production, contemporary economics, and use of oral history. [DN]

71   The Gran Chichimeca: essays on the archaeology and ethnohistory of northern Mesoamerica. Edited by Jonathan E. Reyman. Aldershot, Great Britain; Brookfield, Vt.: Avebury, 1995. 352 p.: bibl., ill., index, maps. (Worldwide archaeology series; 12)
      Core of this collection, in honor of Charles C. DiPeso, includes an especially important paper on Casas Grandes and its redating. Discusses archaeology of northern Mexico. Mesoamerica-Southwest interaction is a major theme. Concludes with section on North American Southwest. [DN]

72   Grube, Nikolai. The emergence of lowland Maya civilization: the transition from the Preclassic to the Early Classic. Möckmühl, Germany: Verlag Anton Saur-

wein, 1995. 201 p.: bibl., ill, index. (Acta Mesoamericana; 8)
      Collection of papers assesses the processes by which Mayan populations developed complex societies during the centuries just before and after the beginning of the Christian Era. Includes site-focused essays on Tikal, Río Azul, Cuello, and the Guatemalan Pacific coast. Topical papers on the environment and subsistence, monumental architecture, burials and caches, iconography, and writing. [JSH]

73   Guevara Sánchez, Arturo. Arquitectura prehispánica del estado de Chihuahua. (*Cuad. Arquit. Mesoam.*, 28, 1995, p. 43–48)
      Briefly discusses importance of small settlements and semi-subterranean houses in the region. [DN]

74   Guevara Sánchez, Arturo. El sitio arqueológico de la Ferrería, Durango: trabajos de 1993. Durango, Mexico: Instituto Nacional de Antropología e Historia; Secretaría de Educación, Cultura y Deporte, 1994. 135 p.: bibl., ill., maps. (Col. Durango)
      Brief description of major structures, associated artifacts, and consolidation program. [DN]

75   Guillén, Ann Cyphers. Chalcatzingo, Morelos: estudio de cerámica y sociedad. México: Univ. Nacional Autónoma de México, Instituto de Investigaciones Antropológicas, 1992. 364 p.: bibl., ill., maps.
      Primarily a description of ceramics from 1970s investigations of this important formative period site. Includes line drawings and frequency distributions. [DN]

76   Gyarmati, János. Investigaciones arqueológicas en el Valle del Río Necaxa, Veracruz, Mexico. (*Mexicon/Berlin*, 17:4, 1995, p. 67–70)
      Short article reports on an archaeological settlement survey that located 51 sites; all sites with diagnostic ceramics date to the postclassic period. [DN]

77   Hassig, Ross. Mexico and the Spanish conquest. London; New York: Longman, 1994. 215 p.: bibl., index, maps. (Modern wars in perspective)
      Offers a new interpretation of the conquest by considering perspective of indigenous peoples. Argues that indigenous rulers who allied with Cortés to pursue their own goals were a significant factor, even though

their intentions and understandings differed from those of the Spanish. [DN]

78 Hatch, Marion Popenoe. Kaminaljuyú/ San Jorge: evidencia arqueológica de la acitvdad económica en el Valle de Guatemala, 300 aC a 300 dC. Guatemala: Univ. del Valle de Guatemala, 1997. 266 p.: ill. (some col.).

Summary of recent excavations at an ancient highland Maya community buried beneath modern Guatemala City. Emphasizes new evidence of canals, reservoirs, and other extensive water control systems. [JSH]

79 Healan, Dan M. Identifying lithic reduction loci with size-graded macrodebitage: a multivariate approach. (*Am. Antiq.*, 60:4, October 1995, p. 689–699)

Demonstrates new method of identifying archaeological locations where stone was reduced or worked, based on size sorting of macrodebitage. Applies this method to obsidian concentrations from the Toltec capital city of Tula, Hidalgo. The confirmed presence of an obsidian workshop within a residential complex suggests a family mode of production. [DN]

80 Henderson, John S. The world of the ancient Maya. 2nd ed. Ithaca, N.Y.: Cornell Univ. Press, 1997. 345 p.: bibl., ill. (some col.), index, maps.

General overview of the ancient Maya begins with summary discussions of the history of Maya studies, the environment and geography of the Maya world, and the European invasion. Text is devoted primarily to a synthesis of the history of Maya cultural traditions based primarily on archaeological data and complemented by epigraphic and ethnohistorical information. [JSH]

81 Hirth, Kenneth G. Urbanism, militarism, and architectural design: an analysis of epiclassis sociopolitical structure at Xochicalco. (*Anc. Mesoam.*, 6:2, Fall 1995, p. 237–250)

Article examines sociopolitical implications of defensive architecture at this key Epiclassic center and surrounding fortified precincts in Morelos. Architectural patterns suggest that the city was divided into wards similar to Aztec *calpulli*, that the military had a segmentary organization, and that Xochicalco headed a regional confederacy. [DN]

82 Historia antigua de México. v. 1, El México antiguo, sus áreas culturales, los orígenes y el horizonte preclásico. Coordinación de Linda Manzanilla y Leonardo López Luján. México: Consejo Nacional para la Cultura y las Artes; Univ. Nacional Autónoma de México; M.A. Porrúa, 1994. 1 v.: ill., maps.

Articles in the Pt. 1 provide background information on biological anthropology, cultural history, and the northern and southern boundaries of Mesoamerica. Pt. 2 concerns the earliest—Paleoindian and Archaic—occupations and the formative period in the Basin of Mexico, the Gulf Coast, and Oaxaca. [DN]

83 Historia antigua de México. v. 2, El horizonte clásico. Coordinación de Linda Manzanilla y Leonardo López Luján. México: Consejo Nacional para la Cultura y las Artes; Univ. Nacional Autónoma de México; M.A. Porrúa, 1995. 1 v.: ill., maps.

Collection contains new overviews of the classic period in Mesoamerica's major regions: the Gulf Coast, Oaxaca, lowland Maya, central highlands, and west, northwest, and northeast Mexico. Concluding chapter examines the Epiclassic period in the Valley of Morelos at Xochicalco. [DN]

84 Historia general de Centroamérica. v. 1., Historia antigua. Edición de Robert M. Carmack. Coordinación general de Edelberto Torres-Rivas. Madrid: Comunidades Europeas; Sociedad Estatal Quinto Centenario; FLACSO, 1993. 1 v.: bibl., ill., index, maps.

Introductory chapter sets out the ecological, geographical, and historical context. Following chapters explore prehistory of the northern (Maya) zone, the central sector, and southern Central America. Concluding chapter indicates general patterns of Central American societal organization and contrasts these to changes that occurred at the time of the Spanish invation. For historian's comment on all six volumes see *HLAS 56:1633*. For ethnohistorian's comment on vol. 1, see *HLAS 56:468*. [JSH]

85 Hosler, Dorothy. The sounds and colors of power: the sacred metallurgical technology of ancient West Mexico. Cambridge, Mass.: MIT Press, 1994. 320 p.: bibl., ill., index, maps.

This major study suggests that prehispanic metallurgy was adopted in western

Mexico ca. AD 600 from northern South America. Presents technical analyses and a comprehensive theory for development of Mesoamerican metallurgy. Argues that metals were a ritual and elite material that expressed sacredness and social relations. [DN]

86   Iwaniszewski, Stanislaw. Archaeology and archaeoastronomy of Mount Tlaloc, Mexico: a reconsideration. (*Lat. Am. Antiq.*, 5:2, 1994, p. 158–176)
    New interpretation of the archaeoastronomy of the Aztec ritual sanctuary atop Mount Tlaloc in the Valley of Mexico suggests it was part of a sacred geography based on calendric-astronomical alignments with important mountains and ceremonial centers in the valleys of Puebla and Mexico. [DN]

Jones, Grant D. The Canek manuscript in ethnohistorical perspective. See *HLAS 56:473.*

87   Jones, Lindsay. Conquests of the imagination: Maya-Mexican polarity and the story of Chichén Itzá. (*Am. Anthropol.*, 99:2, June 1997, p. 275–290)
    Analysis of archaeological interpretations of a Maya city in Yucatán. Argues that former orthodox interpretation of archaeology and history of Chichén Itzá—in which an older Yucatec community was conquered by western Mesoamerican foreigners—reflects European ambivalence toward Native Americans and a resulting tendency to conceptualize them in terms of simplistic oppositions, in this case the peaceful Maya versus the warlike invaders from the west. [JSH]

88   Jones, Lindsay. Twin city tales: a hermeneutical reassessment of Tula and Chichén Itzá. Photographs by Lawrence G. Desmond. Niwot, Colo.: Univ. Press of Colorado, 1995. 494 p.: bibl., ill., index. (Mesoamerican worlds)
    Comparative study of ritual architecture of Toltec Tula (Hidalgo) and Chichén Itza of the northern Maya lowlands(Yucatán). Offers new interpretations of architectural symbolism and its relationship to forms of power and rulership that explain formal architectural similarities between these postclassic cities. [DN]

89   Joyce, Rosemary A. *et al.* Engendering Tomb 7. (*Curr. Anthropol.*, 35:3, June 1994, p. 284–287)

Commentaries on the McCaffertys' work (see *HLAS 55:323*) engendered reinterpretation of Tomb 7 and Skeleton A at Monte Albán, Oaxaca. Most opinions are favorable and accept the reinterpretation of the skeleton and associated artifacts. Others dispute important points, including the interpretation of weaving implements and the extent of Caso's androcentrisim. Reanalysis of the skeletal remains is needed. [DN]

90   Kellog, Susan. The woman's room: some aspects of gender relations in Tenochtitlán in the Late Prehispanic period. (*Ethnohistory/Society*, 42:4, Fall 1995, p. 563–576)
    New interpretation of gender relations in Mexica (Aztec) society emphasizes the importance of class and argues that gender relations were conceived of as both parallel—with male and female spheres where men and women held positions of authority—and hierarchical. [DN]

91   Langenscheidt, Adolphus. Historia mínima de la minería en la Sierra Gorda. Windsor, Canada: Rolston-Bain, 1988. 164 p.: bibl., ill.
    Overview of mining history from precolumbian times through 20th century in the Sierra Gorda mountain range that runs through Querétaro, San Luis Potosí, Hidalgo, and Guanajuato. Photographs of rarely preserved precolumbian mining tools of wood, bone, and fiber. [DN]

92   Lathrop, Jacqueline Phillips. Ancient Mexico: cultural traditions in the land of the feathered serpent. 4th ed. Dubuque, Iowa: Kendall/Hunt Pub. Co., 1991. 199 p.: bibl., ill.
    Updated and expanded version of introductory text that devotes a chapter to each major time period: Paleo-Indian/Archaic, preclassic,classic, and postclassic. The Spanish conquest is discussed in the conclusion. Most useful for students and those unfamiliar with Mesoamerican archaeology. [DN]

93   Leal Rodas, Marco Antonio. Ríos y arqueología de Petén. (*Estudios/Guatemala*, 2, dic. 1993, p. 7–38, bibl., maps, photos)
    Summary of the physiography of Guatemala's Petén dept. and adjacent regions. Emphasizes relationships between waterways and the distribution of ancient Maya communities. [JSH]

94 **The legacy of Mesoamerica: history and culture of a Native American civilization.** Edited by Robert M. Carmack, Janine Gasco, and Gary H. Gossen. Upper Saddle River, N.J.: Prentice Hall, 1996. 511 p.: bibl., ill., index. (Exploring cultures)

Comprehensive overview of Mesoamerican cultural traditions. Introductory chapter sketches the Mesoamerican physical setting and the field of Mesoamerican studies. Six chapters of volume's first section present the history of Mesoamerican peoples from prehispanic times to the present. The bulk of the text is devoted to topical essays on key issues in Mesoamerican studies: religion, gender, politics and economics, language, and native literature. [JSH]

Lian, Yunshan. Shei Xian Daoda Meichou [Who first arrived in America?] See *HLAS 56:736.*

95 **Lima Soto, Ricardo E.** Aproximación a la cosmovisión maya. Guatemala: Univ. Rafael Landívar, Instituto de Investigaciones Económicas y Sociales, 1995. 198 p.: bibl., ill. (Serie Socio-cultural)

Introductory essay by the editor suggests a basic configuration of beliefs about nature, time, the supernatural, ritual, and values, based mostly on the Quiché of the Guatemalan highlands (as they are today and as they are reflected in the Popol Vuh, their mythic history), with some discussion of precolumbian beliefs, especially in relation to the calendar. Five essays by other scholars assess various aspects of Guatemalan indigenous groups, especially in relation to the heavily European-derived national culture. [JSH]

96 **López Luján, Leonardo.** The offerings of the Templo Mayor of Tenochtitlan. Translated by Bernard R. Ortiz de Montellano and Thelma Ortiz de Montellano. Niwot: Univ. Press of Colorado, 1994. 542 p.: bibl., ill., index.

This important book presents detailed descriptions, analyses, and interpretations of offerings recovered during the last 50 years from excavations of the Aztec Great Temple in Mexico City. Argues that the offerings formed part of a cosmovision and are more varied in content, and presumably meaning, than previously thought. [DN]

97 **Lucet, Geneviéve** and **Claudia Lupone.** A computerized register of pre-Hispanic architecture. (*CAA/Oxford,* 1995, p. 145–148)

Briefly discusses application of computer-assisted three dimensional (CAD) models to architecture from the important Cacaxtla site. [DN]

98 **Lupone, Claudia** and **Geneviéve Lucet.** A methodology for recording pre-Hispanic mural paintings. (*CAA/Oxford,* 1995, p. 245–248)

Briefly describes the application of computer drawing (CAD) of scanned images of murals from the important Maya site of Cacaxtla, where CAD facilitated analysis of mural imagery and the study of damage and restorations. [DN]

99 **Marcus, Joyce.** Where is lowland Maya archaeology headed? (*J. Archaeol. Res.,* 3:1, 1995, p. 3–53)

Assessment of trends reflected in the recent history of Maya archaeology. Focuses on the relative strength of settlement pattern studies, comparative perspectives on the State, and other processual approaches on the one hand, and epigraphic, iconographic, and other less structured interpretive frameworks on the other. [JSH]

100 **Marcus, Joyce** and **Kent V. Flannery.** Zapotec civilization: how urban society evolved in Mexico's Oaxaca Valley. New York: Thames and Hudson, 1996. 255 p.: bibl., ill., index. (New aspects of antiquity)

Important new synthesis of the Paleo-indian through classic periods. Develops an action theory framework to explain formation of the first Zapotec State and the founding and growth of Monte Albán. Written in an accessible style and exceptionally well illustrated with drawings and photographs (some color) on glossy paper. [DN]

101 **Martin, Simon** and **Nikolai Grube.** Maya superstates. (*Archaeology/New York,* 48:6, Nov./Dec. 1995, p. 41–46, ill., maps, photos)

Interpretation of the political landscape in the southern Maya lowlands during the late classic period, based mostly on new interpretations of hieroglyphic texts. Emphasizes role of Calakmul in southern Campeche, the largest known classic Maya city. By the late seventh century, Calakmul was also the dominant city in the Maya lowlands, with a vast sphere of allies and subordinate States. [JSH]

102   McAnany, Patricia Ann. Living with the ancestors: kinship and kingship in ancient Maya society. Austin: Univ. of Texas Press, 1995. 229 p.: bibl., ill., index, maps.

Argues that ancestor veneration is a fundamental feature of the Maya cultural tradition at all socioeconomic levels. Uses ethnographic, ethnohistorical, and archaeological information to explore relationships among ancestors, lineages, and land tenure on the one hand, and systems of social inequality and political power on the other. [JSH]

103   McCafferty, Geoffrey G. Reinterpreting the Great Pyramid of Cholula, Mexico. (*Anc. Mesoam.*, 7:1, Spring 1996, p. 1–17)

Reevaluates the Pyramid's construction history based on recent excavations. Suggests that the Pyramid was not abandoned at the end of the classic but continued to be occupied throughout the early postclassic, which has important implications for regional cultural history. Also considers religious meanings and ethnic associations. [DN]

104   McCafferty, Sharisse D. and Geoffrey G. McCafferty. The conquered women of Cacaxtla: gender identity or gender ideology. (*Anc. Mesoam.*, 5:1, Spring 1994, p. 159–172)

Article proposes a provocative reinterpretation of the "Battle Mural" at this important early postclassic site in Tlaxcala, Mexico. Argues, based on costume details, that the two central bird-warriors are female, not male as usually assumed, and that these captives were not sacrificed but saved for royal marriages. [DN]

105   Mexico. Secretaría de Gobernación, Consejo Nacional de Población. El poblamiento de México: una visión histórico-demográfica. v. 1, El México prehispánico. México: Secretaría de Gobernación, Consejo Nacional de Población, 1993. 1 v.: bibl., col. ill.

Overview of prehispanic historical demography written by leading scholars for non-specialist readers. Covers general topics—initial populating of the Americas, agricultural origins, urbanism, and population movements. Also discusses major ethnic groups and regions: the Mexica, Maya, Mixtec

and Zapotec, Tarascan, and northern Mexico. Glossy paper with excellent drawings and color photographs. [DN]

106   Mixteca-Puebla: discoveries and research in Mesoamerican art and archaeology. Edited by Henry B. Nicholson and Eloise Quiñones Keber. Culver City, Calif.: Labyrinthos, 1994. 263 p.: bibl., ill.

Collection of papers from a 1991 symposium focuses on Mixteca-Puebla concept and associated stylistic/iconographic tradition of the postclassic period. Includes papers on history of the concept and discussions of particular regions/subregions: Tlaxcala, Puebla, Cholula, Mixteca, Oaxaca, central Mexico, Tehuacán, and Nicoya. Illustrations include color plates. [DN]

107   Monte Albán: estudios recientes. Coordinación de Marcus Winter. Oaxaca, Mexico: Proyecto Especial Monte Alban, 1994. 134 p.: ill., maps. (Contribución; 2)

First published results of the 1992–94 Mexican government-sponsored archaeological investigations. Includes discussions of the new topographic map of Monte Albán, architectural patterns, Teotihuacán-style ceramics, Zapotec writing, astronomy and calendars, and chronology. New radiocarbon dates are presented. [DN]

108   Montúfar, Aurora. Estudios palinoecológicos en Baja California Sur y su posible relación con los grupos cazadores-recolectores de la región. México: Instituto Nacional de Antropología e Historia, 1994. 68 p.: bibl., ill., maps. (Col. científica; 277)

Results of an ethnobotanical study of three sites: La Laguna in the Cabo region, the Rancho de San Joaquín, and El Parral *arroyo* in San Ignacio. Background data on soils, climate, and geology are included. [DN]

109   Morelos G., Noel. Proceso de producción de espacios y estructuras en Teotihuacán: Conjunto Plaza Oeste y Complejo Calle de los Muertos. Mexico: Instituto Nacional de Antropología e Historia, 1993. 285 p.: bibl., ill. (Col. científica; 274)

Discusses urban form and evolution of Teotihuacán in four parts: 1) analyzes architecture of the West Plaza Group and the Street of the Dead Complex; 2) synthesizes ecology, population, and urbanization; 3) presents a model of the evolution of Teotihuacán; and 4) presents plans and diagrams. [DN]

110 Mountjoy, Joseph B. Propuestas para el futuro de la arqueología en el occidente de México. (*Estud. Hombre*, 1, nov. 1994, p. 205–210, bibl.)

Outlines an expanded conservation program for archaeological sites, calling for a systematic *municipio* by *municipio* identification and evaluation of sites. Also recommends the development of formal cooperative agreements between the Instituto Nacional de Antropología e Historia, universities, scientific organizations, and state and municipal governments. [DN]

111 Nelson, Ben A. Complexity, hierarchy, and scale: a controlled comparison between Chaco Canyon, New Mexico, and La Quemada, Zacatecas. (*Am. Antiq.*, 60:4, October 1995, p. 597–618)

These sites were once thought to have been linked by turquoise trade, but recent chronological analysis has shown they were not contemporaneous. This comparative study argues that although La Quemada was more hierarchically organized, it was not a Toltec outpost nor did it influence the development of the Chacoan system. [DN]

112 Ohnersorgen, Michael and **Mark D. Varien.** Formal architecture and settlement organization in ancient west Mexico. (*Anc. Mesoam.*, 7:1, Spring 1996, p. 103–120)

Weigand's unpublished settlement pattern data from the Teuchitlán region are analyzed using a gravity model that he interprets as a four-tiered regional settlement hierarchy, with settlement concentrated in six habitation zones. The statistical analysis suggests refinements and alternative models of settlement organization that require further study. [DN]

113 Los olmecas en Mesoamérica. Coordinación de John E. Clark. Fotografías de Rafael Doniz. México: Citibank, 1994. 298 p.: bibl., col. ill.

Important collection of articles summarizing current research on the preclassic Gulf Coast Olmec and inter-regional relations. Topics covered include chronology and antecedents, San Lorenzo Tenochtitlan, El Manatí, La Venta, economics, monumental art, sociopolitical organization, cosmology, and relations with Chiapas, Oaxaca, Guerrero, Chalcatzingo, and the altiplano. Printed on glossy paper with color photographs; oversize format. [DN]

114 Patterson, Thomas C. Conceptual differences between Mexican and Peruvian archaeology. (*Am. Anthropol.*, 98:3, Sept. 1996, p. 499–505)

Draws on Marxist theory to argue that power relations and nation-State hegemony in the late-19th and 20th centuries underlie Mexican archaeologists' emphasis on "civilization" as an organizational framework, while Peruvian archaeologists emphasized "culture." [DN]

115 Paz, Josef. The vicissitude of the alter ego animal in Mesoamerica: an ethnohistorical reconstruction of tonalism. (*Anthropos/Switzerland*, 90:4/6, 1995, p. 445–465, bibl.)

This historical reconstruction of the alter ego concept and tonalism and nagualism in Mesoamerica relates the origins of the alter-ego concept to beliefs in a guardian spirit, identification with animals, and pre-destination (the calendar) during the formative period. [DN]

116 Pohl, Mary D. *et al.* Early agriculture in the Maya lowlands. (*Lat. Am. Antiq.*, 7:4, 1996, p. 355–372)

Recent evidence from investigations in wetland regions of northern Belize suggests that domesticated maize and manioc were grown there by about 3500 BC. Rapid deforestation which began about 2500 BC may represent the spread of agricultural economies. Argues that wetfield farming involving canal construction began about 1000 BC as a response to rising groundwater levels and that these facilities were abandoned because they were submerged after about 400 BC. Suggests that evidence of wetfield systems proposed for later periods and other parts of the Maya lowlands should be reevaluated. Also reviews new evidence and interpretations on the emergence of agriculture in southwestern Mexico and central Panama (where forest clearance is claimed to have begun by 10,000 BC and maize cultivation is posited before 4000 BC). [DN]

117 Ramos de la Vega, Jorge and **Amalia Ramírez Garayzar.** Sitios arqueológicos del municipio de León. 2a. ed. León, Mexico: Univ. Iberoamericana, Plantel León, 1993. 65 p.: bibl., ill., maps. (Entorno; 3)

Catalog of sites in northeastern Guanajuato includes brief descriptions, maps, and a bibliography. [DN]

118 Rivera Dorado, Miguel and **Ascensión Amador Naranjo.** Más opiniones sobre el dios Chak. (*Rev. Esp. Antropol. Am.*, 24, 1994, p. 24–46, bibl., ill.)

Dense discussion of the nature of the deity Chak, based heavily on archaeological and iconographic analysis of terminal classic representations from the Maya lowlands. The last pages of the article consider related 20th-century Maya beliefs. [R. Haskett]

119 Robles García, Nelly M. Las canteras de Mitla, Oaxaca: tecnología para la arquitectura monumental. Nashville, Tenn.: Vanderbilt Univ., 1994. 71 p.: bibl., ill. (Vanderbilt Univ. publications in anthropology; 47)

Description of prehispanic quarry sites in the vicinity of Mitla where construction stone was cut and prepared. Includes discussion of technology and petrographic analysis. See also item **120.** [DN]

120 Robles García, Nelly M. La extracción y talla de cantera en Mitla, Oaxaca: tecnología para la arquitectura monumental. (*Arqueología/México*, 7, 1992, p. 85–112)

Summary of prehispanic quarries where construction stone was extracted. Discusses lithic technology. See also item **119.** [DN]

121 Rousseau, Xavier. Arqueología y utopía en el Occidente de México. (*Estud. Hombre*, 1, nov. 1994, p. 193–204)

Discusses efforts of the Laboratorio de Antropología at the Univ. de Guadalajara to develop an integrated program of anthropology dedicated to the study of past and present societies and cultures of western Mexico. Also considers why the archaeology of this region has received less attention than other areas. [DN]

122 Sabloff, Jeremy A. Drought and decline. (*Nature/London*, 375:6530, June 1, 1995, p. 357)

Suggests that a period of drought that began about AD 800 may have exacerbated a variety of other stresses and thereby contributed to the decline of many city-states in the southern Maya lowlands during the 9th century. [DN]

123 Santley, Robert S. The economy of ancient Matacapán. (*Anc. Mesoam.*, 5:1, Spring 1994, p. 243–266)

Reviews recent research at this regional center in the Tuxtla Mountains, Veracruz, that apparently had a Teotihuacán enclave during the classic period. Presents regional settlement pattern data to argue that Matacapán—a center for ceramic production and distribution—dominated a dendritically organized political economy. Alternative models are also possible. See also item **124.** [DN]

124 Santley, Robert S. and **Philip J. Arnold.** Prehispanic settlement patterns in the Tuxtla Mountains, southern Veracruz. (*J. Field Archaeol.*, 23:2, 1996, p. 225–249)

A recent systematic regional survey, which recorded sites ranging from the early formative through the late postclassic, indicates development of a major settlement hierarchy during the classic period when Matacapán became a large regional center. Comparisons are made with regional settlement patterns in other Gulf Coast regions. See also item **123.** [DN]

125 Saphieha, Nicolas and **Anglea M.H. Schuster.** El Tajín: abode of the dead. (*Archaeology/New York*, 47:6, Nov./Dec. 1994, p. 43–47)

Brief photographic essay of the late classic center of El Tajín, Veracruz. [DN]

126 Sarmiento Fradera, Griselda. Las primeras sociedades jerárquicas. México: Instituto Nacional de Antropología e Historia, 1992. 135 p.: bibl. (Col. Científica. Serie Arqueología; 246)

Develops a model for the formation of hierarchical societies that incorporates Marxist theory and considers processes and relations of production. Discusses archaeological correlates, including activity area concept—which has been criticized—and formation processes. Briefly reviews the formative period of the Gulf Coast, Oaxaca, and Basin of Mexico, but emphasis is conceptual. [DN]

127 Saunders, Nicholas J. Predators of culture: jaguar symbolism and Mesoamerican elites. (*World Archaeol.*, 26:1, June 1994, p. 104–117)

Challenges previous interpretation that prehispanic jaguar symbolism represents worship of jaguar deities. Argues that symbolism is instead associated with high sociopolitical status and warfare. [DN]

128 Schortman, Edward M. and **Patricia A. Urban.** Living on the edge: core/periphery relations in ancient southeastern Mesoamerica. (*Curr. Anthropol.*, 35:4, Aug./Oct. 1994, p. 401–430, bibl., maps, table)

Assesses the utility of "core/periphery" concepts for understanding southeastern Mesoamerica. Emphasizes the varied nature of sociopolitical relationships in the region. Draws on authors' investigations in the Naco Valley of western Honduras for illustrative data. Includes commentaries by other scholars and the authors' response. [JSH]

129 Séjourné, Laurette. Arqueología e historia del Valle de México. v. 1–2. México: Siglo Veintiuno Editores, 1990–1991. 2 v.: bibl., ill. (some col.). (Antropología)

Republication of two-volume work dealing with ethnohistoric data on several cities of the Valley of Mexico. Vol. 1 covers the history of archaeological work at Culhuacan and Aztec ceramics. Vol. 2 covers ethnohistory of the Chalco-Xochimilco region and formative, classic and postclassic ceramics. Especially useful are the illustrations of pottery and figurines. See also *HLAS 33:757* and *HLAS 49:440* [DN]

130 Seventh Palenque round table, 1989. Edited by Merle Greene Robertson and Virginia M. Fields. San Francisco, Calif.: Pre-Columbian Art Research Institute, 1994. 294 p.: ill. (Palenque round table series; 9)

Proceedings of the seventh in a series of international conferences on the Maya held at the ancient Maya city of Palenque. Like the earlier conferences, iconography and epigraphy of the classic Maya lowlands were emphasized. Includes few contributions on other themes, mainly Maya architecture and Olmec art. [JSH]

131 Sharer, Robert J. The ancient Maya. 5th ed. Stanford, Calif.: Stanford Univ. Press, 1994. 924 p.: bibl., ill., index.

Comprehensive synthesis of ancient Maya scholarship. Extensive summary of the archaeology of the Maya world provides the historical context for a detailed topical synthesis of chronological and geographic variability within the Maya cultural tradition. [JSH]

132 Sharer, Robert J. Daily life in Maya civilization. Westport, Conn.: Greenwood Press, 1996. 249 p.: bibl., ill., index, map. (The Greenwood Press "Daily life through history" series, 1080–4749)

Popular overview of Maya civilization. Begins with basic observations about archaeology and the Maya, then presents a synthesis of Maya history to provide the context for a topically organized characterization of the Maya cultural tradition. Essentially a streamlined version of Sharer's *The ancient Maya* (see item **131**), though less detailed and less extensively illustrated. [JSH]

133 Simposio de Investigaciones Arqueológicas en Guatemala, 7th, *Museo Nacional de Arqueología y Etnología, 1993.* Actas. Recopilación de Juan Pedro Laporte y Héctor L. Escobedo. Guatemala: Ministerio de Cultura y Deportes; Instituto de Antropología e Historia; Asociación Tikal, 1994. 778 p.: bibl., ill., maps.

Proceedings of the annual conference on archaeology sponsored by the Guatemalan Instituto de Antropología e Historia in 1993. Includes descriptions of work in the highlands and Pacific coast region (10 papers), the Petexbatun area (7), Nakbé (7), Oxkintok (5), and other lowland regions (13), as well as four papers on epigraphy and iconography, three dealing with biological anthropology, and two on ethnohistory and colonial archaeology. [JSH]

134 Simposio de Investigaciones Arqueológicas en Guatemala, 8th, *Guatemala, 1994.* Actas. v. 1–2. Recopilación de Juan Pedro Laporte y Héctor L. Escobedo. Guatemala: Museo Nacional de Arqueología y Etnología, 1995. 2 v. (849 p.): bibl., ill., maps.

Proceedings of the 1994 annual conference on archaeology sponsored by the Guatemalan Instituto de Antropología e Historia. Includes descriptions of work in the highlands and Pacific coast region (12), and the lowlands (18), along with five contributions on epigraphy and iconography, five concerning the Maya "collapse," six on osteology and mortuary patterns, two dealing with palaeontological and faunal remains, and four on ethnohistory and colonial archaeology. [JSH]

135 Simposio de Investigacions Arqueológicas en Guatemala, 9th, *Museo Nacional de Arqueología y Etnología, Guatemala, 1995.* Actas. v. 1–2. Recopilación de Juan Pedro Laporte y Héctor L. Escobedo. Guatemala: Ministerio de Cultura y Deportes; Instituto de Antropología e Historia; Asociación Tikal, 1996. 2 v. (759 p.): bibl., ill., maps.

Proceedings of the 1995 annual conference on archaeology sponsored by the Guatemalan Instituto de Antropología e Historia. Includes descriptions of investigations in the Maya lowlands (Petén—18, Campeche—2, Belize—3); in the Guatemala highlands, especially at Kaminaljuyú (11); and the Pacific coast and piedmont of Mexico, Guatemala and El Salvador (6); along with six essays on colonial archaeology in Guatemala and Mexico. [JSH]

136 Simposium sobre Arqueología en el Estado de Hidalgo: Trabajos Recientes, Mexico City, 1989. Actas. Coordinación de Enrique Fernández Dávila. México: Instituto Nacional de Antropología e Historia, 1994. 156 p.: bibl., ill., maps. (Col. científica; 282. Serie Arqueología)

This collection of important recent work by Mexican archaeologists contains several papers on the obsidian industry at Tula and the Sierra de las Navajas. Other topics covered include Tula and the Mexica (Aztec), mortuary practices at Tula, excavation of a well-preserved Zapotec tomb at Tepeji del Rio, and multidisciplinary research in the Mezquital Valley. [DN]

137 Smith, Michael E. and T. Jeffrey Price. Aztec-period agricultural terraces in Morelos, Mexico: evidence for household-level agricultural intensification. (*J. Field Archaeol.*, 21:2, 1995, p. 169–179)

Discusses an archaeological study of terraces/check dams at Capilco and Cuexcomate in Morelos. These and other data from nearby excavated houses suggest late postclassic agricultural intensification was a response to household demographic change. [DN]

138 Smith, Michael E. et al. The size of the Aztec city of Yautepec: urban survey in central Mexico. (*Anc. Mesoam.*, 5:1, Spring 1994, p. 1–11)

Archaeological survey and surface collections trace the size and extent of Yautepec, Morelos. Yautepec's size, in area and estimated population, is compared with other Aztec cities in Morelos and the Basin of Mexico. Concludes that politico-administrative

activities were the most important urban functions of Aztec cities. [DN]

139 Stark, Barbara and L. Antonio Curet. The development of the Classic-Period Mixtequilla in south-central Veracruz, Mexico. (*Anc. Mesoam.*, 5:1, Spring 1994, p. 267–287)

Based on systematic survey and surface collections, the authors discuss ceramic and settlement patterns during the preclassic and classic periods. Current evidence does not support a direct Teotihuacán presence; stylistic influences may reflect emulation rather than commercial trade, although the possibility of indirect Teotihuacán administration remains open. [DN]

140 Steadman, Sharon R. Recent research in the archaeology of architecture: beyond the foundations. (*J. Archaeol. Res.*, 4:1, 1996, p. 51–93, bibl.)

Overview focuses on recent trends in architectural archaeology research, with an emphasis on domestic architecture. Focuses on Mesoamerica, where much basic research on household archaeology has been conducted. Discusses recent work on communicative aspects of architecture. Bibliography of recent literature. [DN]

141 Thompson, John Eric Sidney, Sir. Maya archaelogist. Foreword by Norman Hammond. Norman: Univ. of Oklahoma Press, 1994. 301 p.: ill., index, maps.

Autobiographical account of the early days of modern Maya archaeology by the most influential Mayanist of the middle decades of the 20th century. A foreword by Norman Hammond highlights Thompson's immense contribution to Maya studies, but also points out that changes in the field since publication of the original edition in 1963 (see *HLAS 27:254*) have resulted in the rejection of some of Thompson's ideas. This thoroughly readable account of Thompson's work during the 1920s–30s provides a fascinating glimpse of a critical formative period in Maya archaeology. [JSH]

142 Transformaciones mayores en el Occidente de México. Coordinación de Ricardo Avila Palafox. Guadalajara, Mexico: Univ. de Guadalajara, 1994. 305 p.: bibl., ill. (Col. Fundamentos)

Collection covers wide range of topics on western Mexico, including archaeology, ecology, Teuchitlán architecture, the colonial hacienda, prehispanic bronze metallurgy, linguistics, archaeology of the Cuenca de Sayula, the work of Isabel Kelly, and ceramic ecology. [DN]

143   Valadez Moreno, Moisés. Antecedentes y avances de los estudios arqueológicos en el noreste de México. Monterrey, Mexico: Archivo General del Estado, 1995. 39 p.: bibl. (Serie Orgullosamente bárbaros; 2)
        Brief overview of archaeology in Tamaulipas, Coahuila, and Nuevo León accompanied by bibliography. [DN]

144   Valdez, Francisco *et al.* The Sayula Basin: lifeways and salt flats of central Jalisco. (*Anc. Mesoam.*, 7:1, Spring 1996, p. 171–186)
        A systematic survey has identified approximately 100 sites within the 800 sq. km. study area, including agricultural hamlets and villages and salt-making stations. Excavations provided additional details concerning the technology and changes in the organization of salt production from classic period industry workshops to postclassic household-based workshops. [DN]

145   Voorhies, Barbara and Douglas Kennett. Buried sites on the Soconusco Coastal Plain, Chiapas, Mexico. (*J. Field Archaeol.*, 22:1, 1995, p. 65–79)
        Survey of all river cuts between the towns of Pijijiapan and Mazatán addressed problem of buried late Archaic and early formative sites. Survey found more buried early and middle formative sites in inland settings than recorded by Voorhies' earlier survey. [DN]

146   Weeks, John M. Maya civilization. New York: Garland Pub., 1993. 435 p.: ill., indexes. (Garland reference library of the humanities; 1796. Research guides to ancient civilizations; 1)
        Research guide on the Maya includes summary of Maya cultural history, capsule descriptions of North American museums and research institutions that have been involved in Maya studies, and an extensive annotated bibliography. The guide to the literature strongly emphasizes English-language sources. Listings are organized topically and indexed by author, place name, and subject. A site-by-site listing of publications will be particularly useful for students. [JSH]

147   Weigand, Phil C. The architecture of the Teuchitlán tradition of the *occidente* of Mesoamerica. (*Anc. Mesoam.*, 7:1, Spring 1996, p. 91–101)
        Analyzes the distinctive tradition of monumental circular architecture with a focus on the classic period. Argues that the size of, and labor invested in, these structures reflects a regional political hierarchy, and that the formal characteristics of these structures relate to cosmology and religious rituals. [DN]

148   Wilkerson, S. Jeffrey. The garden city of El Pital. (*Res. Explor.*, 10:1, 1994, p. 57–71)
        Intriguing claims are made about this site: it was the largest and most complex Gulf Coast center during the early classic period; it was associated with massive drained field systems; and El Pital, not El Tajín, was the source of Gulf Coast pottery at Teotihuacán. Claims remain unsubstantiated. [DN]

149   Women in archaeology. Edited by Cheryl Claassen. Philadelphia: Univ. of Pennsylvania Press, 1994. 262 p.: bibl., ill., index.
        Pt. 1 of this collection presents a history of women in Americanist archaeology, including a biography of Dorothy Hughes Popenoe who conducted early stratigraphic excavations in Honduras. Pt. 2 focuses on the current status of North American women in Mesoamerican archaeology and problems of gender bias. Valuable discussion of issues, but non-US archaeologists are not covered. [DN]

150   Zeitlin, Robert N. Accounting for the prehistoric long-distance movement of goods with a measure of style. (*World Archaeol.*, 26:2, Oct. 1994, p. 208–234)
        A preliminary study of inter-regional interaction applies coefficients of ceramic similarity to formative pottery from the southern Isthmus of Tehuantepec and the northern Isthmus Coast; Chiapas Central Depression; Valley of Oaxaca; and Soconusco. Despite sampling limitations, author finds strong correlations with patterns of obsidian procurement. [DN]

Zhou, Shixiu and Corcino Medeiros dos Santos. O descobrimento da América pelos chineses. See *HLAS 56:789*.

FIELDWORK AND ARTIFACTS

151 A propósito del Formativo. Coordinación de María Teresa Castillo Mangas. Tecamachalco, Mexico: Subdirección de Salvamento Arqueológico; México: Instituto Nacional de Antropología e Historia, 1993. 136 p.: bibl., ill., maps.

Collection of short articles presents results of small salvage archaeology projects at important formative period sites in the state of México: Azcapotzalco, Cuicuilco, Ecatepec, Tlapacoya, Xico, and Zacatenco. Projects in Guanajuato, Guerrero, and the Gulf of Mexico are also briefly reported. [DN]

152 Abrams, Elliot Marc and **Ann Corinne Freter.** A late classic lime-plaster kiln from the Maya centre of Copán, Honduras. (*Antiquity/Cambridge*, 70:268, June 1996, p. 422–428)

Reports the only known classic Maya lime-burning installation at Copán in western Honduras. The kiln for making plaster used to coat masonry architecture is associated with an ordinary residence, suggesting that plaster-making was not a high-status occupation. [JSH]

153 Alvarez Aguilar, Luis Fernando and **Ricardo Armijo Torres.** Excavación y consolidación de la Estructura 3 de Calakmul, Campeche. (*Información/Campeche*, 14, 1994, p. 42–55, bibl., ill.)

Summary of excavation and architectural consolidation of a classic period residential palace in southern Campeche. The building, atop a 15 meter platform, consists of 12 rooms arrayed around three sides of a patio. Associated lithic debris and artifacts indicate that one of the rooms served as a flint workshop. [DN]

154 Amaroli, Paul. A newly discovered potbelly sculpture from El Salvador and a reinterpretation of the genre. (*Mexicon/Berlin*, 19:3, 1997, p. 51–53)

Reports the discovery at Teopán in western El Salvador of a late formative potbelly sculpture representing a female. Argues that the potbelly figure genre depicts a pregnant female, perhaps an earth-fertility goddess giving birth. [JSH]

155 Andrews, Anthony P. and **Roberta Corletta.** A brief history of underwater archaeology in the Maya area. (*Anc. Mesoam.*, 6:2, Fall 1995, p. 101–117)

Assesses the state of underwater archaeology in the Maya world. Includes a history of underwater investigations and a review of recent projects focusing on precolumbian remains in freshwater lakes and cenotes and historic wrecks offshore. [JSH]

156 Aoyama, Kazuo. Microwear analysis in the southeast Maya lowlands: two case studies at Copán, Honduras. (*Lat. Am. Antiq.*, 6:2, 1995, p. 129–144)

Report analyzes indications of wear on two sets of chipped stone tools associated with public buildings in the Acropolis area of the classic period Maya city. Experimental replication of wear marks on similar stone tools suggests activity such as shell jewelry manufacturing in the vicinity of Str. 16, and more intense usage, such as food preparation, in the vicinity of Str. 22A, the hypothetical council house. [JSH]

157 Arnauld, Charlotte *et al.* Arqueología de las lomas en la cuenca lacustre de Zacapu, Michoacán, México. México: Centre d'études mexicaines et centraméricaines, 1993. 230 p.: bibl., ill. (Col. Etudes mésoaméricaines, 0378-5726; II-13. Cuadernos de estudios michoacanos; 5)

Report of a 1983–86 investigation by a team of French archaeologists describes results of survey, surface collections, and test excavations, along with larger scale excavations of a stratified mortuary site dating ca. 100 BC–AD 500. Well illustrated. [DN]

158 Aronson, Meredith. Technological change: ceramic mortuary technology in the valley of Atemajac from the late formative to the classic periods. (*Anc. Mesoam.*, 7:1, Spring 1996, p. 163–169)

Compares late formative/early classic and classic period mortuary ceramics from the site of Tabachines to ceramics from the core of the Teuchitlán tradition. Speculates that abrupt changes during the classic period in mortuary practices at Tabachines more closely parallel influences from Teotihucán than Teuchitlán. [DN]

159 *Arqueología Mexicana.* Vol. 3, No. 17, 1996. México: Insituto Nacional de Antropología e Historia, Editorial Raices.

Prehispanic clothing and textiles of Mexico are the focus of this issue that begins with an overview of clothing types, followed by regional (Oaxaca, Veracruz, Huasteca, and Maya) and topical (weaving, dying, and military regalia) articles. Contemporary textile production is also discussed. Useful introduction to subject. Color illustrations. [DN]

160 Arroyo, Barbara. Early ceramics from El Salvador: the El Carmen site. (*in* The emergence of pottery: technology and innovation in ancient societies. Edited by William K. Barnett and John W. Hoopes. Washington: Smithsonian Institution Press, 1995, p. 199–208)

Describes early formative Bostan phase pottery from a coastal village site of western El Salvador. The pottery, which shows strong similarities to contemporary ceramics of Pacific coastal villages in Guatemala and Mexico, is the earliest so far discovered in El Salvador. [JSH]

161 Baudez, Claude. Arquitectura y escenografía en Palenque: un ritual de entronización. (*Res/Harvard*, 30, 1996, p. 172–179)

Analysis of the sculptural and architectural iconography of the enthronement of classic period Maya kings. Focuses on Palenque as a case study. [JSH]

162 Beach, Timothy and **Nicholas P. Dunning.** An ancient Maya reservoir and dam at Tamarindito, El Petén, Guatemala. (*Lat. Am. Antiq.*, 8:1, 1997, p. 20–29)

Describes an ancient Maya dam which closed off the outlet of a natural depression in an area of elite houses at the Maya city of Tamarindito in the Petexbatun region of the southern Maya lowlands. Probably built in the late classic period (AD 600–800), the 60-meter-long construction created a small reservoir that could have provided a defensible domestic water supply (Tamarindito was involved in conflict during the classic period) and irrigation for nearby fields. [JSH]

163 Becquelin, Pierre *et al.* Proyecto arqueológico *Xcalumkin, en su trayectoria cronológica:* segunda temporada. (*Mexicon/Berlin*, 16:5, 1994, p. 93–99)

Preliminary summary of investigations aimed at locating and characterizing residential remains at a Maya city in Campeche, and at clarifying the development of the Puuc architectural style. [JSH]

164 Beekman, Christopher S. Political boundaries and political structures: the limits of the Teuchitlán tradition. (*Anc. Mesoam.*, 7:1, Spring 1996, p. 135–147)

Based on systematic testing and mapping, analyzes defensive features in the La Venta corridor that links the Teuchitlán and Atemajac Valleys. Argues that these features were part of a strategy to monitor the boundaries of a centralized polity in the Teuchitlán Valley; the applicability of Southhall's models appears premature. [DN]

165 Benavides, Antonio. Edzná, Campeche, México: temporada de campo 1993. (*Mexicon/Berlin*, 17:1, 1995, p. 7–10)

Reports on excavation and restoration efforts at the Templo del Norte in the Gran Acropolis and on investigation of adjacent buildings. The building sequence runs from early in the first millennium (late formative/early classic) to the 14th century (early postclassic). Architecture reflects the Petén and Chenes-Río Bec styles, along with a local terminal classic-early postclassic hybrid that may reflect the arrival of Chontal groups. [JSH]

166 Benavides, Antonio. Okolhuitz, Campeche, 1995 field season. (*Mexicon/Berlin*, 19:2, 1997, p. 33–35)

Reports on preliminary mapping and repair of buildings at a Maya town near Xpujil, Campeche. The architectural style involves a blend of Petén and Río Bec elements, and suggests a date near the transition from early to late classic. [JSH]

167 Beutelspacher, Ludwig. Exploraciones arqueológicas en Itzantún, Chiapas. México: Instituto Nacional de Antropología e Historia, 1993. 79 p.: bibl., ill. (Col. Científica; 270. Serie Arqueología)

Monograph on a salvage project in a 250 sq. km area of northeastern Chiapas to be impacted by the Itzantún dam. Systematic survey recorded 15 sites, ranging from the middle formative to late classic. Sites and associated ceramics are described. [DN]

168 Bey, George; Craig A. Hanson; and **William M. Ringle.** Classic to Postclassic at Ek Balam, Yucatán. (*Lat. Am. Antiq.*, 8:3, 1997, p. 237–254)

Reports excavation of a building spanning the late to terminal classic period (Pure Florescent) at a Maya city in northern Yucatán. One building, a C-shaped structure of the type usually identified with the postclassic period, is associated with classic-period Cehpech pottery. Suggests that the building had an administrative function and may relate to attempts to maintain order in the face of widespread terminal classic political disruption. [JSH]

169 Boxt, Matthew A. Interesting litter: notes on unexpected historical finds at Sarteneja, an ancient Maya site in northern Belize. (*J. Caribb. Hist.*, 27:2, 1993, p. 160–175, ill., maps)

Describes a newly discovered historic sugar mill in northern Belize. Uses archaeological finds along with historical sources to provide an overview of the local sugar industry during late-19th and early-20th centuries. [JSH]

170 Brady, James E. *et al.* Preclassic cave utilization near Cobanerita, San Benito, Petén. (*Mexicon/Berlin*, 19:5, Sept. 1997, p. 91–96)

Describes a series of caves near Lake Petén Itzá, modified with artificial clay floors and interior walls. One has hieroglyphic texts painted in multiple colors. Associated pottery is almost exclusively middle and late formative, consistent with evidence of early cave utilization at Naj Tunich, Dos Pilas, and elsewhere; as in other caves, carbonized maize may reflect ancient ritual activity. See also item **171**. [JSH]

171 Brady, James E. Settlement configuration and cosmology: the role of caves at Dos Pilas. (*Am. Anthropol.*, 99:3, 1997, p. 602–618)

Uses ethnography to develop a model of modern Maya sacred geography in which caves were an important factor in determining settlement location and layout. Applies the model to the classic period city of Dos Pilas, where building location is closely correlated with the locations of caves. See also item **170**. [JSH]

172 Braniff C., Beatriz. La frontera protohistórica Pima-Ópata en Sonora, México: proposiciones arqueológicas preliminares. v. 2–3. México: Instituto Nacional de Antropología e Historia, 1992. 2 v.: bibl., ill., maps. (Col. científica; 241–242. Serie Arqueología)

Vol. 2 presents descriptions and analysis of artifacts from excavations at the site of Ojo de Agua, occupied ca. AD 1200–1640. Vol. 3 describes archaeological sites of the Curcurpe area, including artifacts from El

Ranchito, and surveys of the Ríos San Miguel, Dolores, Sarachic, Remedios, Cocóspera, Bacanuchi, and San Pedro. Other articles discuss the ethnobotany of Río San Miguel, ceramics in the Wasley collection (Arizona State Museum), and classification of historic period artifacts from Sonora. For the anthropologist's comment on vol. 1 see *HLAS 55:214.* [DN]

173 Braswell, Geoffrey E. El intercambio comerical entre los pueblos prehispánicos de Mesoamérica y la Gran Nicoya. (*Rev. Univ. Val. Guatem.*, 7, 1997, p. 17–29)

Summary of evidence of commercial exchange (mainly obsidian from the Maya highlands) linking precolumbian Costa Rica with eastern Mesoamerica. [JSH]

174 Brüggemann, Jürgen K. *et al.* Zempoala: el estudio de una ciudad prehispánica. México: Instituto Nacional de Antropología e Historia, 1991. 400 p., 6 folded leaves of plates: bibl., ill., maps, plans (Col. científica; 232. Serie Arqueología)

Recent investigations of the postclassic center of Zempoala, Veracruz are discussed, including results of surface collection and mapping, seriation, excavations and reconstruction, and artifact catalogs. [DN]

175 Cabrera García, María Teresa. La muerte en el occidente del México prehispánico. México: Univ. Nacional del Autónoma de México, Instituto de Investigaciones Antropológicas, 1995. 190 p.: bibl., ill., photos.

Study of prehispanic mortuary patterns in west Mexico using previously published data. Most useful is the summary of data from a large sample of sites. Illustrated with photographs and line drawings. [DN]

176 Cacaxtla: proyecto de investigación y conservación. Tlaxcala, Mexico: Consejo Nacional para la Cultura y las Artes, Instituto Nacional de Antropologia e Historia, Centro Regional Tlaxcala: Gobierno del Estado de Tlaxcala, Consejo Estatal de Cultura Tlaxcala, 1990. 98 p.: bibl., ill. (some col.), plans.

Collection of miscellaneous papers on the central Mexican palace complex which contains elaborate mural painting in a Maya style. Includes general contributions on the site, its chronology, and the identity of its inhabitants; discussions of mortuary practices, offerings, and other finds; analyses of the murals' style and iconography; and examinations of the conservation of the buildings and their decoration. [JSH]

177   Caran, S. Christopher *et al.* A Late paleo-indian/early archaic water well in Mexico: possible oldest water-management feature in the New World. (*Geoarchaeology/ New York*, 11:1, 1996, p. 1–35)

Detailed presentation of geomorphologic and archaeological data on a large hand-dug water well in the Tehuacán Valley, Puebla, whose radiocarbon date ranges from 9863 to 5950 BC. Implications for hunter-gatherer mobility and the origins of agriculture are discussed. The well's connection to contemporary archaeological settlements has yet to be established. [DN]

178   Carpenter, J.P. Huatabampo y Aztatlán: el montículo funerario de "El Ombligo" y las fronteras culturales en el norte de Sinaloa, México. (*in* Simposio de Historia y Antropología de Sonora, *19th, Hermosillo, México, 1994.* Memorias. Hermosillo, Mexico: Instituto de Investigaciones Históricas de la Univ. de Sonora, v. 2, p. 93–115, bibl., maps, tables)

Analyzes artifacts from the funerary mound of "El Ombligo" at the site of Guasave, Sinaloa, originally excavated by Gordon Eckholm between 1937–40. Views Huatabampo culture as intermediate between western Mexico and southwest US. [DN]

179   Carrasco Vargas, Ramón. Chicanná, Campeche, un sitio de la frontera sur: estudio arquitectónico. México: Univ. Nacional Autónoma de México, Instituto de Investigaciones Filológicas, Centro de Estudios Mayas, 1994. 157 p.: bibl., ill., plans.

Analyzes architecture of an eastern Campeche Maya city. Investigations revealed a long occupation which peaked during the classic period when its architecture reflected the Río Bec style of southern Yucatán. Volume focuses on four well-preserved buildings consolidated during the 1980s, including data on architectural development derived from the excavations. [JSH]

180   Carrasco Vargas, Ramón and **Marc Wolf.** Nadzca'an: una antigua ciudad en el suroeste de Campeche, México. (*Mexicon/Berlin*, 18:4, 1996, p. 70–74)

Reports the mapping of a newly-discovered Maya city located 40 kilometers west

of Becán-Xpuhil-Chicanná. Presents a brief description of the site layout and architectural styles (a blend of Petén and Chenes-Río Bec). Twenty stelae have been found thus far, six with traces of carving; the best-preserved has a text with a terminal classic date. [JSH]

181   Castillo V., Donaldo Arnulfo *et al.* Estilo Maya en Abaj Takalik durante los períodos preclásico tardío-clásico temprano (300 A.C. al 500 D.C.). (*Estudios/Guatemala*, 2, 1994, p. 7–23, bibl., ill., maps, photos)

Preliminary summary of investigation of a terraced platform and associated sculpted monuments in the south-central sector of this southwestern Guatemalan site. Emphasizes the appearance, in the late formative period, of Maya features in the architecture, sculpture, and hieroglyphic texts. These changes suggest the arrival of a foreign Maya group who subdued, and took the place of, the local rulers. [JSH]

182   Clutton-Brock, Juliet and **Norman Hammond.** Hot dogs: comestible canids in preclassic Maya culture at Cuello, Belize. (*J. Archaeol. Sci.*, 21, 1994, p. 819–826)

Analysis of dog remains from early deposits at the Maya village in northern Belize suggests these animals were raised for consumption. Dogs apparently represented a significant (but not dominant) portion of the Cuello villagers' meat supply. [JSH]

183   Coyoc Ramírez, Mario Alberto. Entierros explorados en la zona arqueológica de Calakmul, Campeche. (*Información/Campeche*, 14, 1994, p. 85–105, bibl., ill.)

Preliminary summary of five burials found during the 1984–85 excavations at a Maya city in southern Campeche. Includes brief descriptions of the burials' context, associated offerings, and basic observations on skeletal characteristics. Bones were generally in poor condition, in part because most of the burials were secondary or were disturbed during the remodeling of buildings in which they were interred. [DN]

184   Cruz Antillón, Rafael. Análisis arqueológico del yacimiento de obsidiana de Sierra de Las Navajas, Hidalgo. México: Instituto Nacional de Antropología e Historia, 1994. 121 p.: bibl., ill. (Col. Científica; 281. Serie Arqueología)

Results of recent mapping of an obsidian source area called Cerro Cruz del Milagro, a portion of the Sierra de Las Navajas (Pachuca). Artifacts and archaeological features such as mines are described. Monograph also contains a valuable oversized plane map, b/w photographs, and line drawings. [DN]

185   Cyphers, Ann Guillén. Olmec sculptures. (*Res. Explor.*, 10:3, 1994, p. 294–305)

Well-illustrated article on four recently discovered "Azuzul" sculptures at Loma del Zapote, a secondary early preclassic center of southern Veracruz. Excavations indicate the deliberate arrangement of two human sculptures (ritually mutilated to remove insignia) and two feline sculptures (made from recycled monuments), suggesting ritual placement. [DN]

186   Danforth, Marie Elaine; Keith P. Jacobi; and Mark Nathan Cohen. Gender and health among the colonial Maya of Tipu, Belize. (*Anc. Mesoam.*, 8:1, Spring 1997, p. 13–22, ill., map, tables)

Summarizes the analysis of numerous skeletal remains from the western Belizean city of Tipu, a center which maintained its prominence for two centuries after the Spanish invasion. Skeletal features indicate the population enjoyed relatively good health before and after the invasion, with only minor growth disturbances. This is consistent with other archaeological and ethnohistorical indications of successful indigenous accomodation to the presence of Europeans; in contrast with the situation in other regions, contact with Europeans apparently was not a biological disaster at Tipu. [JSH]

187   Day, Jane Stevenson; Kristi Butterwick; and Robert B. Pickering. Archaeological interpretations of west Mexican ceramic art from the late Preclassic period: three figurine projects. (*Anc. Mesoam.*, 7:1, Spring 1996, p. 149–171)

Three in-progress analyses of figurines from shaft tomb—ball-game figures, architectural models, and dog figurines. Of limited interest until studies are completed. [DN]

188   De Montmollin, Olivier. A regional study of Classic Maya ballcourts from the upper Grijalva basin, Chiapas, Mexico. (*Anc. Mesoam.*, 8:1, 1997, p. 23–41)

Analysis of late to terminal classic period Maya ballcourts of eastern Chiapas in relation to regional settlement and political

systems. Distribution of ballcourts matches that of civic centers, reflecting the important ritual and political functions of the ballgame in that region; the unusual number of ballcourts may likewise relate to particularly intense political competition. [JSH]

189   Demarest, Arthur A. *et al.* The Vanderbilt pretexbatum regional archaeological project, 1989–1994. (*Anc. Mesoam.*, 8:2, Fall 1997, p. 207–364)

Preliminary summary of results from long-term, multi-disciplinary investigations of the prehistory of Guatemala's southwestern Petén region. Focuses on the Maya "collapse." Includes papers on paleoecology, settlement systems, warfare and defensive architecture, skeletal analyses, production and exchange of pottery, and several individual ancient cities (Dos Pilas, Aguateca, Tamarindito, and Arroyo de Piedra). [JSH]

190   Domínguez Carrasco, María del Rosario. Calakmul, Campeche, análisis de la cerámica. Campeche, Mexico: Univ. Autónoma de Campeche, 1994. 357 p.: bibl., ill., index. (Col. Arqueología; 4)

Analysis of ceramics from a large Maya city of southern Yucatán. Presents classification and description of middle formative through terminal classic pottery, using a type-variety analytical framework. [JSH]

191   Domínguez Carrasco, María del Rosario and Miriam Judith Gallegos Gómora. Informe de trabajo del Proyecto Calakmul, 1984, Estructura 7. (*Información/Campeche*, 14, 1994, p. 56–83, bibl., ill., maps)

Preliminary summary of excavation efforts on a classic period temple at a southern Campeche Maya city. The building stands upon a tall platform on one side of the central plaza. A vaulted tomb chamber within contains remains of an individual whose bones were disarticulated and burned before being interred with rich offerings of ceramics, jade, shell, stone tools, and perishable material. [JSH]

192   Domínguez Carrasco, María del Rosario. Tipología cerámica de Calakmul, Campeche, México. (*Mexicon/Berlin*, 16:3, 1994, p. 51–53)

Listing of middle formative, late formative, early classic, late classic, and terminal classic period ceramic wares and types for a Maya city in southern Campeche. [JSH]

193 Dunning, Nicholas P. and **George F. Andrews.** Ancient Maya architecture and urbanism at Siho and the western Puuc region. (*Mexicon/Berlin*, 16:3, 1994, p. 53–61)

Describes architecture of a classic period Maya city in Campeche and compares it with Edzná, Oxkintok, and other neighboring cities. Interprets Siho as within Oxkintok's political sphere, and relates it to the Puuc region and to the western coast. [JSH]

194 Estrada Belli, Francisco *et al.* Patrones de asentamiento y uso de la tierra desde el Preclásico al Postclásico en la costa del Pacífico de Guatemala: la arqueología de Santa Rosa, 1995. (*Mexicon/Berlin*, 18:6, 1996, p. 110–115)

Survey of southeastern Guatemala's coastal zone summarizing an occupation sequence from the early formative to conquest periods. Distribution of sites in relation to environmental zones suggests changing patterns of land use. Proposes preliminary interpretations of ceramics as indicators of long-distance interaction and patterns of regional ceramic manufacture and consumption. [JSH]

195 Fash, William L. and **Barbara Fash.** Building a world-view: visual communication in Classic Maya architecture. (*Res/Harvard*, 30, 1996, p. 127–146)

Discussion of visual messages in public architecture of classic period Maya cities. Draws heavily on the architectural sculpture of Copán in western Honduras for illustrative material. [JSH]

196 Fedick, Scott L. Land evaluation and ancient Maya land use in the upper Belize River area, Belize, Central America. (*Lat. Am. Antiq.*, 6:1, 1995, p. 16–34)

Summarizes the distribution of precolumbian settlements in the upper Belize River drainage and relates them to soil characteristics. Argues that settlement location can be understood in terms of the agricultural potential of surrounding land. [JSH]

197 Fedick, Scott L. Predicting the past and preserving it for the future: modeling and management of ancient Maya residential sites. (*in* Belize: selected proceedings from the second interdisciplinary conference. Lanham, Md.: Univ. Press of America, 1996, p. 1–22, bibl., maps, tables)

Reviews potential of new sources of data on soil, land use, and agricultural potential—especially digital maps—for locating and analyzing archaeological sites, as well as for identifying areas in which sites are likely to be threatened by modern agriculture. Draws on data from investigations in the Belize River Valley. [JSH]

198 Feinman, Gary M. and **Linda M. Nicholas.** Household craft specialization and shell ornmanet manufacture in Ejutla, Mexico. (*Expedition/Philadelphia*, 37:2, 1995, p. 14–25)

Non-technical but useful article discusses recent excavations of a classic period household workshop that manufactured shell plagues, disks, beads, pendants, and bracelets. Describes techniques of shell working. The household made other crafts, including ceramic production, lapidary working, and possibly spinning. [DN]

199 Flannery, Kent V. and **Joyce Marcus.** On the perils of "politically correct" archaeology. (*Curr. Anthropol.*, 35:4, Aug./Oct. 1994, p. 441–445)

This commentary critiques McCafferty and McCafferty's reinterpretation of Skeleton A in Tomb 7 at Monte Albán, Oaxaca (see *HLAS 55:323*). Disputed points include: characterization of Alfonso Caso's initial interpretation as androcentric, centrality of Skeleton A in tomb, and identification of weaving tools. Includes reply by McCafferty and McCafferty. Reanalysis of Skeleton A is essential. [DN]

200 Folan, William J. *et al.* Calakmul: new data from an ancient Maya capital in Campeche, Mexico. (*Lat. Am. Antiq.*, 6:4, 1995, p. 310–334)

Summary of recent mapping, excavation, and architectural clearing and consolidation at a Maya city of southern Campeche. Emphasizes the emergence of Calakmul as a prominent center during the late formative period, and its architectural scale and political reach at its developmental peak during the late classic period. [JSH]

201 Folan, William J. and **Abel Morales López.** Calakmul, Campeche, México: la Estructura II-H, sus entierros y otras funciones ceremoniales y habitacionales. (*Rev. Esp. Antropol. Am.*, 26, 1996, p. 9–28, bibl., facsims., maps)

Describes one of the major structures

on the main plaza of a southern Campeche Maya city and its associated elite burials. Constructed during the late formative, the platform and its superstructure were remodeled several times during the classic period. The late classic building served elite residential and ceremonial functions. It was the site of the burial (or reburial) of two individuals who were accompanied by costly offerings of painted ceramics, jade, and other exotic materials. [JSH]

202   Folan, William J.; Joyce Marcus; and W. Frank Miller. Verification of a Maya settlement model through remote sensing. (*Camb. Archaeol. J.*, 5:2, 1995, p. 277–283)

Presents new data on the settlement pattern of communities in the region surrounding the ancient Maya city of Calakmul in southern Campeche, Mexico. Elevated roads, or *sacbeob*, connected the city with smaller dependent towns and with more distant, presumably independent, cities such as El Mirador. Authors argue that the roads confirm Marcus's hypothesis, presented in the 1970s, that the distribution of smaller communities around Calakmul corresponds to a Central Place lattice and an implied administrative hierarchy. [JSH]

203   Ford, Anabel et al. Obsidian procurement and distribution in the Tikal-Yaxha intersite area of the Maya lowlands. (*Anc. Mesoam.*, 8:1, Spring 1997, p. 101–110)

Summarizes analysis of obsidian from formative to terminal classic period refuse heaps associated with 12 residential units between the northern Guatemalan Maya cities of Tikal and Yaxhá. Most of the formative obsidian originated from the San Martín Jilotepeque source; during the classic period it came from El Chayal (some was imported from the Pachuca source in central Mexico during the early classic); Ixtepeque obsidian appeared only during the terminal classic. [JSH]

204   Fowler, William Roy. Caluco, historia y arqueología de un pueblo pipil en el siglo XVI. San Salvador: Proyecto Venga y Busque con Nosotros, Patronato Pro-Patrimonio Cultural; Fundación Interamericana, 1995. 152 p.: bibl., ill.

This study of Caluco, one of the principal early colonial towns of western El Salvador, represents one facet of a larger investi-

gation of the Izalco region, home to Pipil speakers who were major cacao producers just before and after the Spanish invasion. Emphasizes description of the 16th-century church of San Pedro y San Pablo, one of the best surviving examples of early colonial architecture in Central America, based on excavation and a survey of the standing architecture. Includes a historical overview of the early colonial town drawn from documentary sources. [JSH]

205   Fox, John Gerard. Playing with power: ballcourts and political ritual in Southern Mesoamerica. (*Curr. Anthropol.*, 37:3, June 1996, p. 483–509, bibl., ill., graphs, tables)

Analyzes archaeological evidence of the construction, dedication, and use of ballcourts. Emphasizes data from west-central Honduran field investigations in which the author participated. These data, along with ethnohistorical and ethnographic accounts, suggest that ballcourts were scenes of competitive sponsorship of feasting as well as of the game itself. Also imply that sponsors employed these rituals in order to establish and maintain power, and to resolve political conflict. [JSH]

206   Franco Velázquez, Francisca; Rubén Cabrera; and Luis Torres Montes. Los artefactos metálicos de Tzintzuntzan, Michoacán: su deterioro y tratamiento. (*Arqueología/México*, 7, 1992, p. 51–56)

Article describes gold, silver, and copper artifacts (e.g., needles, clasps, bells, nails, awls). Corrosion was chemically analyzed to assess conservation procedures. [DN]

207   Freter, AnnCorinne. The Classic Maya collapse at Copán, Honduras: an analysis of Maya rural settlement patterns. (*in* Archaeological views from the countryside: village communities in early complex societies. Edited by Glenn M. Schwartz and Steven E. Falconer. Washington: Smithsonian Institution Press, 1994, p. 160–176)

Analyzes trends in demography and settlement patterns within the Copán region of northwestern Honduras at the time of the so-called classic Maya "collapse" after AD 800. Argues that complex socioeconomic processes occurring during the period had varying effects on different segments of the Copán population, especially outside of the city's core. Suggests that strain on environmental resources produced by growing populations was a key factor in the failure of the Copán State. [JSH]

208 **García Targa, Juan.** Arqueología colonial en el área maya: aspectos generales y modelos de estudio. (*Rev. Esp. Antropol. Am.,* 25, 1995, p. 41–69, bibl., ill., maps)

Reviews recent archaeological investigations of the early colonial period in the Maya lowlands. Discussion focuses on the different ways in which Maya societies responded to the 16th-century European invasion, particularly in terms of the varying intensity of European pressure. [JSH]

209 **García Targa, Juan.** Unidades habitacionales en el área maya. (*Bol. Am.,* 33 : 42/43, 1992/93, p. 231–254, bibl., ill.)

Residential archaeological studies and their place within the history of Maya archaeology is briefly discussed. Reviews recent field projects in the Maya world which focus on household archaeology. [JSH]

210 **Gillespie, Susan D.** Llano de Jícaro: an Olmec monument workshop. (*Anc. Mesoam.,* 5 : 1, Spring 1994, p. 231–242)

Discusses archaeological survey and excavation findings at a quarry where monuments were carved from basalt boulders into preforms. Investigations found preforms, a tabletop altar, stone tools for carving, debitage, and a habitation area where stonecarvers probably resided. [DN]

211 **Gómez Serafín, Susana *et al.*** Enterramientos humanos de la época prehispánica en Tula, Hidalgo. México: Instituto Nacional de Antropología e Historia, 1994. 156 p.: bibl., ill. (some folded). (Col. científica; 276)

Results of mortuary and osteological analyses of burials found during salvage excavations of 1980–81 within the Tula archaeological zone. From the area now covered by the museum, 123 burials were recovered dating from the Corral through Late Tollan phases. [DN]

212 **Gonlin, Nancy.** Rural household diversity in Late Classic Copán, Honduras. (*in* Archaeological views from the countryside: village communities in early complex societies. Edited by Glenn M. Schwartz and Steven E. Falconer. Washington: Smithsonian Institution Press, 1994, p. 177–197)

Describes archaeological evidence for rural settlement in the Copán valley of northwestern Honduras. Analyzes the relationships between rural and urban social segments. Demonstrates considerable variability in prosperity within the rural sector. [JSH]

213 **González Crespo, Noberto *et al.*** Archaeological investigations at Xochicalco, Morelos, 1984–1986. (*Anc. Mesoam.,* 6 : 2, Fall 1995, p. 223–236)

Article describes excavation of public architecture conducted by the Instituto Nacional de Antropología e Historia during the 1980s. Results include a ditch and defensive terrace complex, residential complexes, and drainage system, and platform mounds used for administrative and military purposes. [DN]

214 **Graham, Elizabeth A.** The highlands of the lowlands: environment and archaeology in the Stann Creek District, Belize, Central America. Madison, Wis.: Prehistory Press, 1994. 392 p.: bibl., ill., maps. (Monographs in world archaeology, 1055–2316; 19)

Technical report on a survey and excavation program in east-central Belize, including the coast and inland regions that rise toward the Maya Mountains. Focus is on natural environments and the ancient Mayas' adaptation to them. Includes descriptions and analyses of pottery, chipped and ground stone, and animal bone. [JSH]

215 **Grove, David C.** La Isla, Veracruz, 1991. (*Anc. Mesoam.,* 5 : 1, Spring 1994, p. 223–230)

The 1991 archaeological investigations at this site near the Olmec center of Laguna de los Cerros identified formative, classic, and postclassic period components and discovered fragments of carved Olmec monuments. Argues that Olmec centers in different resource zones engaged in complementary exchanges under the control of an hereditary elite. [DN]

216 **Guderjan, Thomas H.** Maya settlement and trade on Ambergris Caye, Belize. (*Anc. Mesoam.,* 6 : 2, Fall 1995, p. 147–159)

Reports of a survey and excavation program on an island off the Belizean coast. Synthesizes results with information from other excavations. Classic period communities were oriented toward maritime trade networks. After AD 1000 coastal trading sites were abandoned except for Marco González, and settlement patterns shifted to focus on the interior and farming. [JSH]

217 Hall, Barbara Ann. Formation processes of large earthen residential mounds in La Mixtequilla, Veracruz, Mexico. (*Lat. Am. Antiq.*, 5:1, 1994, p. 31–50)

Concludes that a gradual accumulation of structures and artifacts contributed more to the size of a classic period earthen mound than deliberately deposited fill and considers implications for using mound dimensions to infer social organization. [DN]

218 Hammond, Norman and **Theya Molleson.** Huguenot weavers and Maya kings: anthropological assessment versus documentary record of age at death. (*Mexicon/Berlin*, 16:4, 1994, p. 75–77)

Discusses the apparent age estimate discrepancies for King Pacal of Palenque. One method analyzed skeletal remains; the other, hieroglyphic texts. Data from historic burials in London suggest skeletal indicators of age are very imprecise. [JSH]

219 Hammond, Norman; Amanda Clarke; and **Sara Donaghy.** The long goodbye: Middle Preclassic Maya archaeology at Cuello, Belize. (*Lat. Am. Antiq.*, 6:2, 1995, p. 120–128)

Discusses evidence of building construction, mortuary ritual, and subsistence from the middle preclassic period (ca. 900–400 BC). Revisionist interpretations of the village of Cuello in northern Belize are based on new radiocarbon dates and a new synthesis of the stratigraphic sequence. [JSH]

220 Hammond, Norman et al. Survey and excavation at La Milpa, Belize, 1996. (*Mexicon/Berlin*, 18:5, 1996, p. 86–91)

Report on 4th season of investigations at a Maya city in northern Belize. Investigations outside the site's core confirm that most remains are of short-term late to terminal classic occupations, suggesting rapid population growth. Excavations within the site core elucidate the long construction history which begins during the late formative period and continues through the terminal classic. Stelae were erected during the early classic and terminal classic, with a hiatus at least in the 7th century, which coincides with the conflict between Tikal and Calakmul. [JSH]

221 Haviland, William A. and **Anita de Laguna Haviland.** Glimpses of the supernatural: altered states of consciousness and the graffiti of Tikal. (*Lat. Am. Antiq.*, 6:4, 1995, p. 295–309)

Analysis of prehispanic graffiti at the lowland Guatemalan Maya city of Tikal. Concludes that most depictions were not random scrawls produced by visitors to abandoned buildings after Tikal's collapse, but rather representations of visions experienced during trance states. [JSH]

222 Haviland, William A. The rise and fall of sexual inequality: death and gender at Tikal, Guatemala. (*Anc. Mesoam.*, 8:1, Spring 1997, p. 1–12, ill., map, table)

Analysis of differential burial treatment of males and females at a Maya city in northern Guatemala. Preferential treatment for males (tomb location and construction, quantity and quality of grave goods) correlates with centralized political organization which began shortly after the rise of the dynastic State and declined during the terminal classic when central political authority was also being transformed. [JSH]

223 Healy, Paul et al. Pacbitun, Belize and ancient Maya use of slate. (*Antiquity/Cambridge*, 69:263, June 1995, p. 337–348, bibl., maps, photos, tables)

Concentration of slate artifacts and manufacturing refuse suggests that mirror backs, figurines, maces and other slate artifacts were manufactured at Pacbitun in western Belize and probably traded to other lowland Maya communities. Slate slabs were also used locally to roof elite tombs. Slate is available at several localities within the vicinity of Pacbitun and analyses designed to characterize the different source areas are in progress. [JSH]

224 Hester, Thomas R. and **Harry J. Shafer.** The ancient Maya craft community at Colha, Belize, and its external relationships. (*in* Archaeological views from the countryside: village communities in early complex societies. Edited by Glenn M. Schwartz and Steven E. Falconer. Washington: Smithsonian Institution Press, 1994, p. 48–63, bibl., ill., map)

Summary description of chert tool production at Colha. Analyzes distribution to communities beyond the immediate hinterland of Colha. See also item **225.** For ethnohistorian's comment see *HLAS 56:462.* [JSH]

225   Hester, Thomas R. et al. The Colha preceramic project: preliminary results from the 1993–1995 field seasons. (*Mexicon/Berlin*, 18:3, 1996, p. 45–50)

Excavation reports from the Colha and Kelly sites on the edges of the chert-bearing zone of northern Belize indicate that extensive lithic quarrying had begun by at least 3000 BC when forest clearance and farming was established in the region. Identifies several precolumbian chert tool production locales. See also item **224.** [JSH]

226   Hill, Robert M. Eastern Chajoma (Cakchiquel) political geography: ethnohistorical and archaeological contributions to the study of a late postclassic highland Maya polity. (*Anc. Mesoam.*, 7:1, Spring 1996, p. 63–87, bibl., map, photos, tables)

Identifies the territory of the Chajoma (Akajal or Akal in documents produced by their neighbors) in the central highlands of Guatemala and characterizes the late postclassic Chajoma polity with its capital at Mixco Viejo. [JSH]

227   Hirth, Kenneth G. The investigation of obsidian craft production at Xochicalco, Morelos. (*Anc. Mesoam.*, 6:2, Fall 1995, p. 251–258)

Concludes from test excavations of surface concentrations of obsidian debitage that most are workshop locales, except in areas altered by downslope erosion. Most workshops are located in or adjacent to households. Interestingly, the location of two workshops in nonresidential contexts suggests different modes of production existed during the epiclassic period. [DN]

228   Hodell, David; Jason H. Curtis; and Mark Brenner. Possible role of climate in the collapse of Classic Maya civilization. (*Nature/London*, 375:6530, June 1, 1995, p. 391–394)

Summary of data on oxygen isotopes and sediments in a core from Lake Chichancanab of central Yucatán indicates a period of unusually dry conditions between AD 800 and 1000 when a process of cultural transformation was bringing an end to many city-states of the southern Maya lowlands. [JSH]

229   Hohmann, Hasso. Form and function of four lost structures on the Acropolis of Copán. (*Arch. Völkerkd.*, 49, 1995, p. 187–194, bibl., ill., maps)

Analyzes four classic period buildings on the Acropolis at a Maya city of western Honduras that were destroyed during a 1934 earthquake. Uses records from a Harvard expedition of the 1890s, along with the few surviving traces of the structures and sculptural decoration fallen from them to reconstruct their form. Suggests that associated imagery may link two of them with the Bat House and House of Knives which appear in the Popol Vuh, the conquest-period Quiché epic. Interprets another structure as a steambath with holding cells for sacrificial victims. [JSH]

230   Inomata, Takeshi and Kazuo Aoyama. Central-place analyses in the La Entrada region, Honduras: implications for understanding the Classic Maya political and economic systems. (*Lat. Am. Antiq.*, 7:4, 1996, p. 291–312)

Analysis of late classic Maya settlement systems in two adjacent valleys of northwestern Honduras. Argues that differential distribution of obsidian from two different regional sources confirms the usefulness of central place theory in analyzing local economic and political spheres. [JSH]

231   Jacob, John S. Ancient Maya wetland agricultural fields in Cobweb Swamp, Belize: construction, chronology, and function. (*J. Field Archaeol.*, 22:2, 1995, p. 175–190)

Identifies channels at the Maya town of Colha as relics of an ancient irrigation system designed to control water levels and to allow for farming along the swamp margins. Their construction began by at least the late classic period and perhaps as early as the preclassic period. The field was buried during the terminal classic period by eroded material from adjacent upland areas. [JSH]

232   Jacob, John S. and C.T. Hallmark. Holocene stratigraphy of Cobweb Swamp, a Maya wetland in northern Belize. (*Geol. Soc. Am. Bull.*, 108:7, 1996, p. 883–891)

Report on reconstruction of the landscape history of a depression adjacent to Colha, a center of chert tool production in northern Belize. Deforestation and erosion beginning as early as 1400 BC reflects the activities of Maya farmers; these processes reached their peak intensity about AD 1000 when many Maya city-states were collapsing. [JSH]

233 **Joyce, Arthur A.** *et al.* Exchange implications of obsidian source analysis from lower Río Verde valley. (*Lat. Am. Antiq.*, 6:1, 1995, p. 3–15)

Neutron activation analysis of obsidian artifacts from four formative and classic period sites indicates that most of the obsidian came from sources in the Basin of Mexico and Michoacán. Discusses implications for interregional exchange patterns and changes to them over time. [DN]

234 **Joyce, Arthur A.** Late Formative community organization and social complexity on the Oaxaca coast. (*J. Field Archaeol.*, 21:2, 1995, p. 147–168)

Results of excavations at the important late formative site of Cerro de la Cruz support the view that the site formed part of a coastal chiefdom, although status differences are not as pronounced as in other contemporary ranked societies on the coast. [DN]

235 **Kaplan, Jonathan.** The Incienso throne and other thrones from Kaminaljuyu, Guatemala: Late Preclassic examples of a Mesoamerican thorne tradition. (*Anc. Mesoam.*, 6:2, Fall 1995, p. 185–196)

Describes a class of four-legged benches from early late preclassic (ca. 400–200 BC) Kaminaljuyu of highland Guatemala that possibly functioned as thrones, or formal seats for high-ranking political figures. Several examples bear relief carvings, often depicting richly dressed lords, and have been misidentified as "table altars" or stelae, including the well known Stela 10. [JSH]

236 **King, Eleanor** and **Daniel Potter.** Small sites in prehistoric Maya socioeconomic organization: a perspective from Colha, Belize. (*in* Archaeological views from the countryside: village communities in early complex societies. Edited by Glenn M. Schwartz and Steven E. Falconer. Washington: Smithsonian Institution Press, 1994, p. 64–90, bibl., ill., maps)

Summarizes evidence for specialized lithic tool production at the small community of Colha. Argues that specialization, differentiation, and other aspects of economic complexity must be examined independently of site size hierarchies. For ethnohistorian's comment see *HLAS 56:478.* [JSH]

237 **Köhler, Ulrich.** Rectangular mushroom stones from Oaxaca, Mexico. (*Mexicon/Berlin*, 17:4, 1995, p. 70–73)

Based on the rectangular-shaped caps of four "mushroom stone" artifacts displayed in the Museo Frissell de Arte Zapoteca (Mitla), author rejects earlier interpretations linking similar artifacts with hallucinogenic mushrooms. Proposes to redefine this class of objects in descriptive terms and suggests that mushroom stones may be potter's molds. [DN]

238 **Laporte, Juan Pedro** and **Vilma Fialko.** Un reencuentro con Mundo Perdido, Tikal, Guatemala. (*Anc. Mesoam.*, 6:1, Spring 1995, p. 41–94)

Summary of excavations in the Mundo Perdido sector of central Tikal. Emphasis is on the developmental history of the major public building complexes, beginning in the late formative period. During the classic period, Mundo Perdido architecture strongly reflected Teotihuacán styles. [JSH]

239 **Laporte, Juan Pedro; Paulino I. Morales;** and **W. Mariana Valdizán.** San Luis Pueblito: un sitio mayor al oeste de Dolores, Petén. (*Mexicon/Berlin*, 19:3, 1997, p. 47–51)

Reports on recent investigations at a late classic Maya city in southeastern Petén with substantial public architecture, including a central plaza with pain stelae and altars, an acropolis complex, a ballcourt, and causeways. Survey of the surrounding region has revealed smaller communities in the center's hinterland. [JSH]

240 **Laporte, Juan Pedro.** Los sitios arqueológicos del Valle de Dolores en las montañas mayas de Guatemala. (*Mesoamérica/Antigua*, 13:24, dic. 1992, p. 413–439, chart, maps)

Preliminary summary of archaeological investigations in the Valle de Dolores region in Guatemala's northwestern sector of the Maya Mountains, a major lowland Maya communication route. Descriptions of geographic and ecological settings, site layouts, and architectural features of sites ranging from the late formative to late postclassic periods. [JSH]

241 **Lentz, David L.** *et al.* Foodstuffs, forests, fields, and shelter: a paleoethnobotanical analysis of vessel contents from the Cerén site, El Salvador. (*Lat. Am. Antiq.*, 7:3, 1996, p. 247–262)

Describes carbonized plant remains preserved from rapid burial in volcanic ash from an eruption that occured in approximately AD 600. Cultivated plant species include maize, beans, squash, chile peppers, cacao, and cotton, as well as wild species of fruits, fiber, and wood. [JSH]

242 Lentz, David L.; Carlos R. Ramírez; and Bronson W. Griscom. Formative-period subsistence and forest-product extraction at the Yarumela site, Honduras. (*Anc. Mesoam.*, 8:1, Spring 1997, p. 63–74)

Analysis of excavated botanical remains from an early village site in Honduras provides evidence for cultigens and the exploitation of wild plants, including local plant products and those procured from longer distances. Specific plants documented include several species of wood, maize, squash, and cashew (probably introduced as a domesticate from South America). [JSH]

243 MacKinnon, J. Jefferson. Stone weights from an ancient Maya fishing net used on the Sermis River, Belize. (*Mexicon/Berlin*, 18:1, 1996, p. 14–17)

Reports the discovery, on an ancient river course, of a cluster of notched stones that probably formed part of a net left on the riverbank. [JSH]

244 Magaloni Kerpel, Diana Isabel. Metodología para el análisis de la técnica pictórica mural prehispánica: el Templo Rojo de Cacaxtla. México: Instituto Nacional de Antropología e Historia, 1994. 86 p.: bibl., ill. (some col.). (Col. Científica; 280. Serie Arqueología)

The methodology developed for analyzing the Cacaxtla murals begins with *in situ* observations followed by optical and electron microscopic examination and gas chromatography of small samples. The objective is to better understand the technical aspects of ancient murals in order to develop more effective preservation methods. [DN]

245 Martínez López, Cira and Marcus Winter. Figurillas y silbatos de cerámica de Monte Albán. Oaxaca, Mexico: Proyecto Especial Monte Albán 1992–1994, Centro INAH-Oaxaca, 1994. 148 p.: bibl., ill., photos. (Contribution . . . del Proyecto Especial Monte Albán 1992–1994; 5)

Catalog and description of figurines, whistles, and molds recovered during investigations conducted between 1992–94. Illustrated with line drawings and photographs. [DN]

246 Masson, Marilyn A. Cultural transformation at the Maya Postclassic community of Laguna de On, Belize. (*Lat. Am. Antiq.*, 8:4, 1997, p. 293–316)

Comparison of late classic and early postclassic Maya settlements at Laguna de On in northern Belize suggests a strong continuity, especially in domestic contexts, and no indication of population displacement after the collapse of political hierarchies during the terminal classic period. New patterns of settlement, architecture, and craft production are best understood as transformations of earlier institutions. [JSH]

247 Maya maritime trade, settlement, and populations on Ambergris Caye, Belize. Edited by Thomas H. Guderjan and James F. Garber. San Antonio, Texas: Maya Research Program; Lancaster, Calif.: Labyrinthos, 1995. 210 p.: ill.

Papers describe ancient Maya settlement patterns on Ambergis Caye, Belize. Interpretation emphasizes the participation of these settlements in maritime trade networks extending north along the coast of Yucatán and south to the Gulf of Honduras. [JSH]

248 McKillop, Heather. Ancient Maya trading ports and the integration of long-distance and regional economies: Wild Cane Cay in south-coastal Belize. (*Anc. Mesoam.*, 7:1, Spring 1996, p. 49–62)

Report on an investigation of ancient Maya sea trade in southern Belize. Identifies the offshore island of Wild Cane Cay as a trading port during the classic and postclassic periods. Its role in the distribution of salt from coastal production sites and of obsidian and other exotic goods from distant sources made it the focus of coastal-inland economic relationships, especially during the late classic peak of inland occupation. [JSH]

249 McKillop, Heather. Traders of the Maya coast: five field seasons in the swamps of south coastal Belize, 1988–1993. (*Mexicon/Berlin*, 16:6, 1994, p. 114–119)

Preliminary summary of the results of five years of regional survey and test excavation along the coast of southern Belize and on the offshore islands. The investigations focused on the nature of ancient Maya sea trade. [JSH]

250 McKillop, Heather. Underwater archaeology, salt production, and coastal Maya trade at Stingray Lagoon, Belize. (*Lat. Am. Antiq.*, 6:3, 1995, p. 214–228)

Describes remains of a submerged Maya site off the coast of Belize that indicate inhabitants extracted salt from sea water. This local salt production was presumably related to the region's involvement in maritime exchange networks that connected communities along the Yucatán coast. [JSH]

251 Medrano E., Angélica María and María Honoria de Jesús Hurtado. Análisis de restos arqueológicos de Las Ventanas. (*Estud. Jalisc.*, 23, feb. 1996, p. 5–20, ill., map)

Brief report describes artifacts found at the site in 1989. [DN]

252 Miller, Mary E. Imaging Maya art. (*Archaeology/New York*, 50:3, 1997, p. 34–40)

Non-technical summary of recent comprehensive photographic recording and digital enhancement of the famous classic period murals at Bonampak. [JSH]

253 Mock, Shirley B. Monkey business at Northern River Lagoon: a coastal-inland interaction sphere in northern Belize. (*Anc. Mesoam.*, 8:2, Fall 1997, p. 165–183)

Summary of investigations at a coastal salt-producing site in northern Belize. During the late and terminal classic periods, Northern River Lagoon exchanged salt (and salted products) for chert produced at Colha. Argues that the shared iconography on painted plates may reflect the emergence of specialized elite identities. [JSH]

254 Ojeda M., Heber. Reconocimiento arqueológico en el sureste de Campeche, México: informe preliminar. (*Mexicon/Berlin*, 19:1, 1997, p. 5–12)

Report on the first phase of a survey project in southeast Campeche. Descriptions of several previously unreported formative and classic period sites. Two newly discovered sites have monumental architecture and sculpture, and probably functioned as regional political centers. Settlement patterns and architectural styles suggest ties with Petén and northern Belize. [JSH]

255 Olay Barrientos, María de los Angeles. El Sumidero, Mexico: un sitio del Clásico Tardío. Tuxtla Gutiérrez, Mexico: Gobierno del Estado de Chiapas, Consejo Estatal de Fomento a la Investigación y Difusión de la Cultura DIF-CHAPAS, Instituto Chiapaneco de Cultura, 1993. 259 p., 12 folded leaves of plates: ill., maps. (Serie Antropología)

Describes a clearing and excavation program at a modest town on the banks of the Río Grijalva in Chiapas. Excavations in the central zone of public architecture indicate that El Sumidero flourished during the late classic period (ca. AD 600–1000). Therefore, it was not, as has sometimes been suggested, the capital of the Chiapanecs, who dominated the region at the time of the Spanish invasion. Includes analysis of architecture, pottery, chipped and ground stone, and other artifacts. [JSH]

256 Paine, Richard R. and AnnCorinne Freter. Environmental degradation and the Classic Maya collapse at Copán, Honduras (A.D. 600–1250): evidence from studies of household survival. (*Anc. Mesoam.*, 7:1, Spring 1996, p. 37–47)

The terminal classic transition that resulted in the abandonment of the Copán valley began during the 9th century and lasted some 300 years. Analysis of the relationship between the abandonment date of residential groups derived from obsidian hydration and their ecological settings indicate that houses in ecologically vulnerable locations were abandoned earlier, probably as a consequence of environmental degradation (especially soil erosion in the uplands) resulting from agricultural intensification caused by the need to feed a growing population. [JSH]

257 Paine, Richard R.; AnnCorinne Freter; and David L. Webster. A mathematical projection of population growth in the Copán valley, Honduras, A.D. 400–800. (*Lat. Am. Antiq.*, 7:1, 1996, p. 51–60)

Backward projection of growth rates based on late classic data suggests that Copán's early classic population was somewhat larger than other estimates suggest, but was still well under 10,000. [JSH]

258 Peraza Lope, Carlos. Unidades cerámicas de San Gervasio, Cozumel, Quintana Roo, México. (*Mexicon/Berlin*, 18:4, 1996, p. 67–70)

Listing of classic and postclassic period ceramic complexes, groups, and types from an ancient Maya town on the island of Cozumel off the east coast of Yucatán. [JSH]

259 Pincemín Deliberos, Sophia. Amate-nango del Valle, Chiapas: supervivencia de la alfarería prehispánica. (*Anu. Inst. Chiapaneco Cult.*, 1993, p. 196–202, bibl.)

Brief overview of modern ceramic production in this Tzeltal Maya community of highland Chiapas, Mexico, which has been occupied since the preclassic period. This first stage in a long-term project examines continuities between prehispanic and modern ceramic production. [DN]

260 Pincemín Deliberos, Sophia. Entierro en el palacio: la tumba de la estructura III, Calakmul, Campeche. Campeche, Mexico: Univ. Autónoma de Campeche, Directorio de Servicios Educativos de Apoyo, 1994. 218 p.: bibl., ill. (some col.). (Col. Arqueología; 5)

Detailed description and analysis of an early classic period tomb beneath the floor of a palace at a Maya city in southern Campeche. The tomb's occupant, a noble (possibly royal) male, was buried with costly offerings: elaborately painted pottery vessels, jade mosaic masks and jewelry, stingray spines, pearls, shells and shell ornaments, and perishable objects. [JSH]

261 Pincemín Deliberos, Sophia. Remontando el río: reconocimiento arqueológico del río Candelaria, Campeche. Campeche, Mexico: Univ. Autónoma de Campeche, 1993. 297 p.: bibl., ill., cartes, tables. (Arqueología; 2)

Report on archaeological survey project in the Candelaria drainage of southwestern Yucatán. Provides descriptions and plans of sites and discusses their dating (based on ceramic collections), site typology, settlement patterns, communication routes, and canal systems. Incorporates a more detailed account of El Tigre, the largest site in the region, which reached its peak during the late postclassic period. Focuses on its relationship to ethnohistorical accounts of Acalan, a State that dominated the region at the time of the Spanish conquest. [JSH]

262 Ramos de la Vega, Jorge and **M. Lorenza López Mestas Camberos.** Datos preliminares sobre el descubrimiento de una tumba de tiro en el sitio de Huitzilapa, Jalisco. (*Anc. Mesoam.*, 7:1, Spring 1996, p. 121–134)

Reports on salvage excavations at this late formative/early classic center of the first

unlooted, major shaft tomb associated with architecture of the Teuchitlán tradition. Calibrated radiocarbon dates of associated materials cluster within the first century BC. [DN]

263 Rattray, Evelyn Childs. The Oaxaca barrio at Teotihuacán. Puebla, Mexico: Instituto de Estudios Avanzados, Univ. de las Americas, 1993. 90 p.: bibl., ill., maps. (Monografías mesoamericanas; 1)

Discusses excavations in the Oaxaca Barrio in Teotihuacán, Mexico, conducted by the Univ. de las Américas and the Teotihuacán Mapping Project during the 1960s. Provides detailed descriptions and analyses of architecture, ceramics—including neutron activation—chronology, and mortuary patterns. Significant contribution to studies of ethnic groups and Oaxaca-Teotihuacán relations. [DN]

264 Reyes-Valerio, Constantino. De Bonampak al Templo Mayor: el azul maya en Mesoamérica. México: Siglo Veintiuno Editores; Agro Asemex, 1993. 157 p.: bibl., col. ill. (Col. América nuestra; 40. América antigua)

Study of "Maya blue" an intense sky-blue pigment used to decorate precolumbian pottery (especially but not exclusively Maya polychromes) and for precolumbian and early colonial period murals. Concludes that the pigment was produced by combining mineral pigments with indigo. Includes many color illustrations of ceramic vessels, figurines, and murals with Maya blue paint. See also item **293.** [JSH]

265 Reyna Robles, Rosa Ma. La cultura mezcala: su caracterización preliminar a través del análisis cerámico en la Organera-Xochipala, Guerrero. (*Arqueología/México*, 7, 1992, p. 9–27)

Ceramics from the site are described and compared, most are late classic and/or epiclassic, although some postclassic, Aztec II, and Aztec III types are also present. [DN]

266 Rivera Dorado, Miguel. Arquitectura, gobernantes y cosmología: anotaciones sobre ideología maya en los cuadernos de Oxkintok. (*Rev. Esp. Antropol. Am.*, 25, 1995, p. 23–40, bibl., map)

Analyzes the architecture and urban layout of a Maya city in western Yucatán in terms of cosmological symbolism and political functions. [JSH]

267   **Rivera Dorado, Miguel.** Sobre la crono-
      logía de Oxkintok. (*Rev. Esp. Antropol.
Am.*, 26, 1996, p. 57–75, bibl., table)
      In the absence of reliable suites of radio-
carbon dates, chronological perspectives on
this Maya city in western Yucatán have been
characterized by discrepancies stemming
from reliance on different classes of archaeological data (ceramics, architecture, iconography, etc.). This synthesis proposes general
cultural phases defined in terms of all available data sets. [JSH]

268   **Rivera Estrada, Araceli.** Panorama
      general de la arqueología en el sur de
Nuevo León: Cueva de la Zona de Derrum-
bes. Monterrey, Mexico: Archivo General del
Estado, 1995. 25 p.: bibl. (Serie Orgullosamente bárbaros; 4)
      Brief report on six burials excavated
at cave site (NL92) in the Río Santa Rosa Valley. [DN]

269   **Robles García, Nelly M.** Las unidades
      domésticas del preclásico superior en
la Mixteca Alta. Oxford, England: B.A.R.,
1988. 166 p.: bibl., ill., maps, plans. (BAR
international series; 407)
      Descriptive monograph on results of
excavations at San Juan Yucita Nochixtlán,
Oaxaca, that focused on late formative residential areas. [DN]

270   **Rodríguez M., María del Carmen** and
      Ponciano Ortiz Ceballos. El Manatí:
un espacio sagrado olmeca. Xalapa, Mexico:
Univ. Veracruzana, Dirección Editorial, 1994.
60 p.: bibl., ill. (some col.).
      Brief, popular description of a site on
the Río Coatzacoalcos in Veracruz where
ritual offerings were continuously buried for
several centuries during the early formative
period. The most spectacular finds—a series
of unique wooden sculptures preserved as a
result of water-logging—are in the Olmec
style and date to the period around 1200 BC
when San Lorenzo was the region's dominant
Olmec center. Other offerings include bits of
rubber balls, fragments of stone mortars and
grain-grinding slabs, axes, greenstone beads,
and pottery vessels. Fire-cracked rock suggests that burning, perhaps food preparation,
formed part of the ceremonies, which to judge
by pottery remains, may have begun as early
as 1500 or 1600 BC, in pre-Olmec times. [JSH]

271   **Santone, Lenore.** Transport costs, con-
      sumer demand, and patterns of intrare-
gional exchange: a perspective on commodity
production and distribution from northern
Belize. (*Lat. Am. Antiq.*, 8:1, 1997, p. 71–88)
      Analysis of the distribution of chipped
stone tools made at Colha in northern Belize
during the late preclassic (400 BC-AD 250)
and late classic (AD 600–800) periods suggests that increasing reliance on water transport correlated with a growing number of
communities in the region around Colha that
used stone tools manufactured there. [JSH]

272   **Scarborough, Vernon L. *et al.*** Water
      and land at the ancient Maya commu-
nity of La Milpa. (*Lat. Am. Antiq.*, 6:2, 1995,
p. 98–119)
      Describes a system of water channels
and reservoirs at a Maya city in northwestern
Belize. Includes comments on the role of
water storage, water management, and erosion control in the economic systems of the
lowland Maya. [JSH]

273   **Schieber de Lavarreda, Christa.** A
      Middle Preclassic clay ball court at
Abaj Takalik, Guatemala. (*Mexicon/Berlin*,
16:4, 1994, p. 77–84)
      Reports the discovery of a ball court
at an early center in the piedmont of Pacific
Guatemala and compares the structure with
the few known contemporaries. [JSH]

274   **Schlegel, Suzanne.** Figuras de estuco en
      un chultú en Xkipché. (*Mexicon/Ber-
lin*, 19:6, 1997, p. 117–119)
      Describes six stucco figures of animals
modeled on the walls of a cistern found at a
Maya site in the Yucatán. Figures include
frogs, turtles, and a monkey with a pronounced phallus. Comparable figures have
been found at chultunes in the Puuc region.
Imagery may reflect water symbolism. [JSH]

275   **Schmidt Schoenberg, Paul.** Arqueolo-
      gía de Xochipala, Guerrero. Apéndices
por Luis Barba Pingarrón y Magalí Civera Ce-
recedo. México: Univ. Nacional Autónoma de
México, Instituto de Investigaciones Antropológicas, 1990. 301 p.: appendices, bibl., ill.,
maps.
      Monograph on recent investigations
of an 80 square km area of the Río Mezcala
Basin surrounding Xochipala describes the results of stratigraphic test excavations of sites

found through informants and road and trail surveys. Primary objective was to better understand the cultural history of prehispanic occupations in this poorly known region. [DN]

276 **Sierra Sosa, Thelma Noemí.** Contribución al estudio de los asentamientos de San Gervasio, isla de Cozumel. México: Instituto Nacional de Antropología e Historia, 1994. 156 p.: bibl., ill., maps. (Col. científica; 279. Serie Arqueología)

Study of settlement patterns surrounding the Maya community of San Gervasio on the island of Cozumel off the coast of Yucatán. Description and classification of structures and a reconstruction of the ancient settlement systems of San Gervasio from the classic period (beginning about AD 200) through the 17th century. [JSH]

277 **Siffre, Michel.** Découvertes dans les grottes mayas. Paris: Arthaud, 1993. 187 p.: col. ill., maps.

Popular account of recent discoveries of ancient Maya cave paintings and carvings. See also item **281**. [JSH]

278 **Simmons, Scott E.** Maya resistance, Maya resolve: the tools of autonomy from Tipu, Belize. (*Anc. Mesoam.*, 6:2, Fall 1995, p. 135–146)

Description and analysis of stone tools from Tupu, the principal town in the Maya polity of Dzuluinicab in western Belize during the invasion period. Suggests that stylistic variability in arrow points may reflect ethnic differences among regions. [JSH]

279 **Smyth, Michael P. et al.** The origin of Puuc Slate Ware: new data from Sayil, Yucatán, Mexico. (*Anc. Mesoam.*, 6:2, Fall 1995, p. 119–134)

Investigates the production of terminal classic (AD 800–1000) Puuc pottery. Recent investigations at Sayil have revealed evidence that Puuc Slate Ware, widely distributed in northern Yucatán, was produced locally on a large scale. This pottery is chemically similar to Sayil area clays, while other Puuc wares show closer relationships to Loltun area clays. [JSH]

280 **Spence, Michael W.** Commodity or gift: Teotihuacán obsidian in the Maya world. (*Lat. Am. Antiq.*, 7:1, 1996, p. 21–39)

Green obsidian from Pachuca sources of Central Mexico is found in relatively small quantities in eastern Mesoamerica, and often in ritual contexts. Spence suggests that green obsidian in Maya communities is better interpreted as a symbolic marker of a Teotihuacán connection than as an indication that obsidian was a major exchange item. [JSH]

281 **Stone, Andrea Joyce.** Images from the underworld: Naj Tunich and the tradition of Maya cave painting. Austin: Univ. of Texas Press, 1995. 294 p., 8 p. of plates: bibl., ill. (some col.), index, maps.

Describes the cave site of Naj Tunich in the southeastern Petén region of Guatemala. Includes an analysis of the cave painting style and iconography and (with Barbara MacLeod) of the hieroglyphic texts that accompany some of them. A survey of cave paintings from other parts of the Maya world and elsewhere in Mesoamerica provides a broad comparative context. See also item **277**. [JSH]

282 **Taschek, Jennifer T.** The artifacts of Dzibilchaltun, Yucatán, Mexico: shell, polished stone, bone, wood, and ceramics. New Orleans, La.: Middle American Research Institute, Tulane Univ., 1994. 318 p.: bibl., ill., index, maps. (Publication; 50)

Description and classification of a variety of artifact types: shell, bone, pottery, wood, jadeite, and other fine stone jewelry; copper bells; ceramic figurines, stamps, and musical instruments; bone and antler tools; basketry. Emphasizes excavation contexts and associations and their interpretive implications. Includes a phase-by-phase chronological summary. [JSH]

283 **The Teotihuacán valley project final report.** v. 3, The Teotihuacán period occupation of the valley; pt. 1, the excavations. Edited by William T. Sanders. University Park: Pennsylvania State Univ., Matson Museum of Anthropology, 1994. 1 v.: ill., maps. (Occasional paper in anthropology; 19)

Results of important excavations of rural classic period sites in the Teotihuacán valley, Mexico undertaken during the 1960s. Includes illustrations and a spatial analysis of artifacts with maps from residential compounds at one site (TC-8). [DN]

284 The Teotihuacán valley project final report. v. 3, The Teotihuacán period occupation of the valley; pt. 2, Artifact analyses. Edited by William T. Sanders. University Park: Penn. State Univ., Matson Museum of Anthropology, 1995. 1 v. (Occasional paper in anthropology; 20)

Analyzes artifacts excavated at rural classic period sites during the 1960s. Descriptions, frequency distributions, and illustrations of pottery, figurines, and obsidian are included. Obsidian analysis suggests that most of the blade-core material came to rural sites from quarries and not from the urban workshops at Teotihuacán. [DN]

285 The Teotihuacán valley project final report. v. 3, The Teotihuacán period occupation of the valley; pt. 3, The surface survey. Edited by William T. Sanders. University Park: Pennsylvania State Univ., Matson Museum of Anthropology, 1995. 1 v.: ill., maps. (Occasional paper in anthropology; 21)

This volume reports on the recently revisted Teotihuacán (classic) period sites first recorded during the 1960s. Data on each site are presented in narrative and tabular form accompanied by maps and photographs. Reevaluation of the data has prompted revised interpretations of Teotihuacán's impact on rural settlements and population. [DN]

Textile traditions of Mesoamerica and the Andes: an anthology. See item **18**.

286 Torres Soria, Pablo. La ficoflora de la zona arqueológica de Palenque, Chiapas. México: Instituto Nacional de Antropología e Historia, 1993. 117 p.: bibl., ill. (Col. Científica; 271. Serie Conservación y restauración)

Study of lichens and other plants that grow on buildings, stone sculpture, and modeled stucco of the classic period Maya city of Palenque in Chiapas. Focuses on the destructive effects of these plants on the ancient momuments, and on methods to control and eliminate them. [JSH]

287 Tourtellot, Gair; John R. Rose; and Norman Hammond. Maya settlement survey at La Milpa, Belize, 1994. (*Mexicon/Berlin*, 18:1, 1996, p. 8–11)

Reports on mapping in and around the center of a Maya city in northern Belize. Traces of formative and early classic period occupation found only around the main plaza, suggesting that the community was highly concentrated early in its history. La Milpa reaches its peak in terms of settlement size in the late and terminal classic, when terraces suggest intensified agriculture. [JSH]

288 Tourtellot, Gair et al. More light on La Milpa: Maya settlement archaeology in northwestern Belize. (*Mexicon/Berlin*, 16:6, 1994, p. 119–124)

Report of mapping and excavation of central zone of a Maya city in northern Belize in 1993. Public construction began in the late formative period and the city reached its peak in the late to terminal classic; during the postclassic, some older monuments were reset and venerated. Settlement survey located two chert quarries. Occupation density varies within the city. Names of two late classic period rulers have been identified within hieroglyphic texts. [JSH]

289 30 años de arqueología en Nicaragua. Recopilación de Jorge Eduardo Arellano. Managua: Museo Nacional de Nicaragua, Instituto Nicaragüense de Cultura, 1993. 150 p.: bibl., ill.

This collection of articles ranges from site reports to brief summaries of various aspects of archaeology in Nicaragua over the last three decades. Useful bibliography. [DN]

290 Valetín Maldonado, Norma. Análisis del material arqueozoológico procedente de San Luis La Loma, Guerrero, México. (*Arqueología/México*, 7, 1992, p. 29–38)

Article describes faunal remains—anthropoids, mollusks, and vertebrates—from salvage excavations in the town's modern market place. [DN]

291 Varela Torrecilla, Carmen. La secuencia histórica de Oxhintok: problemas cronológicos y metodológicos desde el punto de vista de la cerámica. (*Rev. Esp. Antropol. Am.*, 26, 1996, p. 29–55, bibl., graphs, map, tables)

General discussion of factors that support limited use of ceramic analysis for the development of a chronological sequence for a Maya city in western Yucatán. Focuses on the inadequate attention paid to variability in functional contexts and scanty comparative data. Detailed discussion of periods in which the correlation of ceramics with architecture, epigraphy, and other data types is particularly problematic (early-middle classic, late-terminal classic, and postclassic). [JSH]

292   The view from Yalahau: 1993 archaeological investigations in northern Quintana Roo, Mexico. Edited by Scott L. Fedick and Karl A. Taube. Riverside: Latin American Studies Program, Univ. of California, 1995. 159 p.: bibl., ill., maps. (Field report series; 2)

Eleven papers present the preliminary findings of a project designed to explore ancient Maya subsistence, settlement patterns, and political organization in northeastern Yucatán. Investigations focused on settlement survey and documentation of monumental architecture, especially at the large center of Naranjal. Results suggest that occupation was most intense during the terminal formative and early classic periods, with a decline during the late and terminal classic and renewed activity in the late postclassic. [JSH]

293   Yacamán, José M. *et al.* Maya blue paint: an ancient nanostructured metal. (*Science/Washington,* 273, 1996, p. 223–225)

Maya blue, a precolumbian pigment widely used in mural painting, and for decoration of pottery and other objects, is famous for the quality of its color and for its resistance to degradation. Its chemical composition, however, has remained elusive. Electron microscopy and complementary analyses attribute the distinctive color to a combination of palygorskite clay, the plant dye indigo, and metal impurities present in the form of nanoparticles. See also item **264.** [JSH]

294   Yadeun Angulo, Juan. Toniná: el laberinto del inframundo. Fotografía de José Ignacio González Manterola y Pablo Oseguera Iturbide. Presentación de José Patrocinio González B. Garrido. México: Gobierno del Estado de Chiapas, 1992. 127 p.: bibl., ill. (some col.). (Chiapas eterno)

Popular account of recent archaeological discoveries at the classic period Maya city of Toniná in Chiapas. Highly interpretive analysis of monumental architecture, modeled stucco, and relief carving in relation to royal political organization and religious thought. See also item **295.** [JSH]

295   Yadeun Angulo, Juan. Toniná. Investigación, textos y dibujos de Juan Yadeun. Fotografías de Rafael Doniz. México: El Equilibrista, 1992. 158 p.: bibl., col. ill.

Popular summary of recent archaeological investigations at the classic period Maya city of Toniná in Chiapas. Extensively illustrated with high-quality color photographs of its architecture and sculpture. See also item **294.** [JSH]

296   Zapata Castorena, Alicia and **Lynda Mary Florey-Folan.** Investigaciones arqueológicas en la Estructura 1 de Calakmul, Campeche. (*Información/Campeche,* 14, 1994, p. 27–41, bibl., ill., maps)

Preliminary summary of excavation and consolidation of a classic period temple at a Maya city in southern Campeche. The building, atop a tall terraced platform, reaches a height of some 50m, and is one of the largest in the city. An earlier construction stage indicates that building was begun during the late formative or at the very beginning of the classic period. [JSH]

NATIVE SOURCES AND EPIGRAPHY

297   Alcina Franch, José. Cielo e inframundo en la cosmovisión mexica: análisis iconográfico. (*Anu. Estud. Am.,* 50:2, 1993, p. 13–44, ill., photos, tables)

Offers an iconographic analysis of sculptural, ceramic, and pictorial representations of the Mexica (Aztec) cosmovision and the tripartite division of sky, earth, and underworld. [DN]

298   Bricker, Harvey M. and **Victoria R. Bricker.** Astronomical references in the throne inscription of the palace of the governor at Uxmal. (*Camb. Archaeol. J.,* 6:2, 1996, p. 191–229)

Identifies references to zodiacal constellations in a hieroglyphic inscription above the central doorway of a terminal classic building at an ancient Maya city in northern Yucatán. Convincingly relates the astronomical references in the text to the building's orientation and sculptural ornamentation, which have long been interpreted as reflecting a connection with Venus. [JSH]

299   Bricker, Harvey M.; Victoria R. Bricker; and **Bettina Wulfing.** Determining the historicity of three astronomical almanacs in the Madrid Codex. (*Archaeoastronomy/England,* 22, 1997, p. S17-S36)

Analysis of three calendrical texts in

one of the four surviving Maya books. Argues that the three almanacs form a related set that correlates equinoxes, solstices, and eclipses with positions in the Maya calendar. Attempts to show that these almanacs refer to events in the early-10th century AD, close to the date expressed in a structurally parallel table of the Dresden Codex. See also item **300.** [JSH]

300 Bricker, Harvey M. and **Victoria R. Bricker.** More on the Mars table in the Dresden Codex. (*Lat. Am. Antiq.*, 8:4, 1997, p. 384–397)

Analysis of a calendrical table in one of the four surviving Maya books. Argues that the table is not just a weather and agricultural almanac, but is concerned with the movements of the planet Mars and that it, like several other tables in the Maya codices, was used to correlate calendrical and astronomical cycles. See also item **299.** [JSH]

301 Bricker, Victoria R. Advances in Maya epigraphy. (*Annu. Rev. Anthropol.*, 24, 1995, p. 215–235)

An excellent compact summary of current understandings of the nature of Maya hieroglyphic writing, grammatical aspects of the script, and kinds of information recorded in surviving texts. [JSH]

302 Byland, Bruce E. and **John M.D. Pohl.** In the realm of 8 Deer: the archaeology of the Mixtec codices. Norman: Univ. of Oklahoma Press, 1994. 312 p.: bibl., ill. (some col.), index, maps.

A multi-disciplinary approach reinterprets the Mixtec codices and argues that they present a Mixtec history of the political fragmentation that occurred in Oaxaca following Monte Albán's decline. Through archaeological survey and informant interviews, authors correlate specific postclassic archaeological sites with the codices. Additional research needed to substantiate correlations. For ethnohistorian's comment see *HLAS 56:405.* [DN]

303 Grube, Nikolai and **Linda Schele.** Kuy, the owl of omen and war. (*Mexicon/Berlin*, 16:1, 1994, p. 10–16)

Analysis of classic period Maya imagery and texts involving owls. Demonstrates a close association between owls and warfare. [JSH]

304 Grube, Nikolai and **Linda Schele.** New observations on the Loltun relief. (*Mexicon/Berlin*, 18:1, 1996, p. 11–14)

Interpretation of relief carving outside a cave in northern Yucatán as the earliest evidence for royal iconography in the region. Relief resembles early images of rulers at Nakbé and Uaxactún. Suggests that the hieroglyphic text includes an abbreviated Maya date that would correspond to approximately AD 100. [JSH]

305 Houston, Stephen D. Literacy among the precolumbian Maya: a comparative perspective. (*in* Writing without words: alternative literacies in Mesoamerica and the Andes. Edited by Elizabeth Hill Boone and Walter D. Mignolo. Durham, N.C.: Duke Univ. Press, 1994, p. 27–49)

Considers literacy of ancient Maya society in the context of writings on literacy in Old World societies. Emphasizes the problematic aspects of determining the functions of ancient writing and of characterizing the various contexts in which it was used. Argues persuasively that it is essential to distinguish the ability to read from the ability to write and to consider the likelihood that the level of mastery of each varied by social and occupational group. [JSH]

306 Houston, Stephen D. and **David Stuart.** Of gods, glyphs and kings: divinity and rulership among the Classic Maya. (*Antiquity/Cambridge*, 70:268, June 1996, p. 289–312)

Explores the classic period lowland Maya concept of relationships between deities and kings based on decipherment of hieroglyphic texts. Rulers laid claim to divinity through titles that involve the epithet "holy" or "sacred". [JSH]

307 Houston, Stephen D. The shifting now: aspect, deixis, and narrative in Classic Maya texts. (*Am. Anthropol.*, 99:25, June 1997, p. 291–305)

Discourse analysis, particularly tense and aspect, of classic period lowland Maya hieroglyphic texts. Concludes that the precolumbian written texts show the same patterns found in modern oral discourse, suggesting that some hieroglyphic texts were performed. [JSH]

308 Houston, Stephen D. Symbolic sweatbaths of the Maya: architectural meaning in the Cross Group at Palenque, Mexico. (*Lat. Am. Antiq.*, 7:2, 1996, p. 132–151)

Texts in the shrines in the late classic period temples of the Cross Group at Palenque appear to refer to them as sweatbaths, although there is no evidence that they had the normal architectural features of such buildings. Houston interprets the shrines as symbolic sweatbaths, which were ritually important in ancient Mesoamerica, especially in connection with healing, purification, and childbirth. [JSH]

309 Love, Bruce. A Dresden Codex Mars table? (*Lat. Am. Antiq.*, 6:4, 1995, p. 350–361)

Reexamines evidence that a calendar table in the Dresden Codex—one of four surviving prehispanic Maya books—records the movements of Mars. Concludes that the table is an agricultural alamanac. [JSH]

310 Macri, Martha J. The five-door temples at Piedras Negras and Palenque. (*Mexicon/Berlin*, 16:5, 1994, p. 100–102)

Maintains, on the basis of architectural similarites and textual references, that Structure O13 at the classic Maya city of Piedras Negras was built as a deliberate copy of Palenque's Temple of the Inscriptions. [JSH]

311 Macri, Martha J. Maya and other Mesoamerican scripts. (*in* The world's writing systems. Edited by Peter T. Daniels and William Bright. New York: Oxford Univ. Press, 1996, p. 172–182)

Brief summary of present understanding of precolumbian writing systems in Mesoamerica, emphasizing the Maya script. [JSH]

312 Nahm, Werner. Hieroglyphic Stairway 1 at Yaxchilán. (*Mexicon/Berlin*, 19:4, 1997, p. 65–69)

Analysis of a long, poorly preserved hieroglyphic text carved on a stairway at a classic Maya city on the Río Usumacinta. The text, commissioned by King Yaxun Balam IV ("Bird Jaguar") begins with a list of predecessors since the founding of the dynasty, from whom he claimed descent, and ends with a list of his military conquests. Text appears to have been carved over an earlier version. [JSH]

313 Nahm, Werner. Maya warfare and the Venus year. (*Mexicon/Berlin*, 16:1, 1994, p. 6–10)

Presents additional evidence that, during the classic period, the Maya scheduled warfare in relation to the cycle of visibility of Venus. [JSH]

314 Navarrete, Carlos; Thomas A. Lee, Jr.; and Carlos Silva Rhoads. Un catálogo de frontera: esculturas, petroglifos y pinturas de la región media del Grijalva, Chiapas. México: Univ. Nacional Autónoma de México, Instituto de Investigaciones Filológicas, Centro de Estudios Mayas, 1993. 137 p.: bibl., ill., map.

A descriptive catalog of prehispanic sculptures, petroglyphs, and paintings from the middle region of the Grijalva or Mezcalapa river—Chicoasán, Malpaso region, Colonia López Mateos, Peñitas region, and Las Palmas plantation. Includes drawings and photographs. [DN]

315 Palka, Joel. Sociopolitical implications of a new emblem glyph and place name in classic Maya inscriptions. (*Lat. Am. Antiq.*, 7:3, 1996, p. 211–227)

Tentatively identifies a new emblem glyph that may refer to a town in the upper Usumacinta region. Speculates about political relationships among towns whose texts refer to it. [JSH]

316 Pohl, John M.D. The politics of symbolism in the Mixtec codices. Nashville, Tenn.: Vanderbilt Univ., 1994. 169 p.: bibl., ill., maps. (Vanderbilt Univ. publications in anthropology; 46)

Offers a new interpretation of these codices from Oaxaca based on evaluation of costume and dress as symbols of sociopolitical relations. Argues that the codices present a Mixtec history of royal genealogical descent and alliances during the postclassic period. [DN]

317 Ringle, William M. and **Thomas C. Smith-Stark.** A concordance to the inscriptions of Palenque, Chiapas, Mexico. New Orleans: Middle American Research Institute, Tulane Univ., 1996. 371 p.: bibl., cd-rom, ill. (Publication/Middle American Research Institute; 62)

The concordance for all known hieroglyphic texts from the late classic lowland Maya city of Palenque employs a very useful revision and extension of the standard Thompson system for transcribing Maya glyphs. A transcription of the texts includes brief commentaries indicating generally accepted interpretations (and sometimes corresponding Mayan readings) for many of the more straightforward glyphs. Includes a revised glyph catalog with a full listing of changes to Thompson's system and discussion of the rationale for them. [JSH]

318 Schlak, Arthur. Venus, Mercury, and the sun: GI, GII, and GIII of the Palenque Triad. (*Res/Harvard*, 30, 1996, p. 180–202)

Attempts to demonstrate that the "Palenque Triad," deities in imagery and texts at Palenque (and some other classic period Maya cities), represents the sun, Venus, and Mercury. This interpretation is based on the iconography of these figures and their association with celestial events involving those astronomical bodies. [JSH]

The sky in Mayan literature. See *HLAS 56: 525.*

319 Stuart, David. Kings of stone: a consideration of stelae in ancient Maya ritual and representation. (*Res/Harvard*, 30, 1996, p. 148–171)

Argues that stelae were not just vehicles for texts and imagery designed for the glorification of rulers, but were themselves the focus of ritual activity. Summarizes new decipherments of classic period Maya texts indicating that ceremonies revolved around stela placement and dedication. [JSH]

320 Toorians, Lauran. Codex Zouche-Nuttall: some observations concerning its history. (*Mexicon/Berlin*, 17:4, 1995, p. 73–75)

Briefly critiques the explanations for the pre-1854 history of the Codex. Ends with suggestions for future research. [DN]

321 Urcid, Javier *et al.* Escritura zapoteca prehispánica: nuevas aportaciones. Coordinación de Marcus Winter. Oaxaca, Mexico: INAH, 1994. 105 p.: bibl., ill. (Contribución no. 4 del Proyecto Especial Monte Albán 1992–1994)

Description and analysis of inscriptions carved on stone monuments discovered during excavations at Monte Albán between 1992–94. Includes articles discussing the sociopolitical context of Zapotec writing. [DN]

322 Urcid, Javier. A peculiar stone with Zapotec hieroglyphic inscriptions. (*Mexicon/Berlin*, 17:5, 1995, p. 87–92)

Analysis of epigraphy on a carved stone monolith in Museo Regional, Oaxaca, suggests that monolith originally may have been part of some type of commemorative structure related to a prominent person (5 Jaguar) named on the stone. [DN]

323 Valdés, Juan Antonio and **Federico Fahsen.** The reigning dynasty of Uaxactún during the Early Classic: the rulers and the ruled. (*Anc. Mesoam.*, 6:2, Fall 1995, p. 197–219)

Traces the history of monumental public architecture with political and religious functions (palaces, temples, building complexes aligned with astronomical phenomena) at a lowland Maya city during the late preclassic and early classic periods (ca. 300 BC–AD 600). Combines data from hieroglyphic inscriptions, architecture, and burials to propose a sequence of rulers for the period from AD 250–550. [JSH]

324 Wagner, Elisabeth. The dates of the High Priest Grave (*Osario*) inscription, Chichén Itzá, Yucatán. (*Mexicon/Berlin*, 17:1, 1995, p. 10–13)

Analysis of an inscription at Chichén Itzá, in northern Yucatán, dated by Eric Thompson to AD 998, much later than other dates at the city. Since the associated imagery shows a Toltec-style figure, Wagner argues that the date should be changed to a century earlier, within the range of other dates. Therefore, the Maya and foreign "Mexican" features at Chichén Itzá are contemporary. [JSH]

325 Wanyerka, Phil. The carved monuments of Uxbenka, Toledo District, Belize. (*Mexicon/Berlin*, 18:2, 1996, p. 29–36)

Describes the nine carved stelae from a Maya town in southern Belize. Three early classic period monuments have features that suggest connections to Tikal (for example, a possible reference to the Tikal lord "Jaguar Paw"). Uxbenka may have been part of the communication route linking Tikal with Copán and other cities in the southeast. [JSH]

326 **Writing without words: alternative literacies in Mesoamerica and the Andes.** Edited by Elizabeth Hill Boone and Walter D. Mignolo. Durham, N.C.: Duke Univ. Press, 1994. 322 p.: bibl., ill., index.

This interdisciplinary collection of articles focuses on pictorial and iconic systems of the Maya, Mixtec, Aztec, and Inca, and the social contexts of writing during the colonial period, to challenge western conceptualizations of art, writing and literacy. The final papers offer stimulating discussions of interactions between European and indigenous writing systems. For ethnohistorian's comment see *HLAS 56:551.* [DN]

Caribbean Area

WILLIAM KEEGAN, *Curator of Caribbean Archaeology and Assistant Director of Research and Collections, Florida Museum of Natural History, University of Florida, Gainesville*

LOWER CENTRAL AMERICA

IN THE LAST REVIEW I noted the lengths to which archaeologists in Lower Central America had gone to distinguish their region as more than the periphery of the Maya and Inca worlds. Recent reviews and edited volumes suggest that this is indeed the trend. Instead of being treated as the handmaidens to their better-known neighbors to the north and south, their work appears in volumes on equal footing (items **332** and **327**). Moreover, Drennan's review of the Intermediate Area expands the purview from Lower Central America to include Northwestern South America as part of the same cultural region (item **329**). Research in this region reflects a growing interest in two themes that incorporate all of the Americas: the evolution of social complexity, and the study of evidence for the earliest arrival of humans and the origins of pottery making.

CARIBBEAN ISLANDS

A new generation of archaeologists continues to spread across the islands, producing a wealth of materials. Two of the main themes of research, Lithic and Archaic Ages (1994) and the European Contact Period (1996), were the subjects of recent review articles (items **379** and **356**). Although a regional review of Ceramic age cultural development has not been attempted, reports of long-term research (items **364** and **351**) and summaries for specific islands are welcome additions to the literature (items **340, 339,** and **350**). In addition, the proceedings of the XV International Congress for Caribbean Archaeology were published on schedule (item **352**).

RECENT DOCTORAL DISSERTATIONS

Clement, Christopher. Landscapes and plantations of Tobago: a regional perspective. University of Florida, 1990.

Fung, Christopher David. Domestic labor, gender, and social power: household archaeology in terminal classical Yoro, Honduras. Harvard University, 1995.

Hofman, Corinne L. In search of the native population of precolumbian Saba (400–1450 AD)—Part one: pottery styles and their interpretations. Leiden University, 1993.

Hoogland, Menno L.P. In search of the native population of precolumbian Saba (400–1450 AD)—Part two: settlements in their natural and social environment. Leiden University, 1995.

Howson, Jean. Colonial goods in the plantation village: consumption and the internal economy in Montserrat from slavery to freedom. New York University, 1995.

Leshikar, Margaret E. The 1794 wreck of the Ten Sail, Cayman Islands, British West Indies: a historical study and archaeological survey. Texas A&M, 1993.

Rostain, Stéphen. L'occupation Amérindienne ancienne du littoral de Guayane. University of Paris I—Pantheon/Sorbonne, 1994.

Santone, Lenore M. Demand structure, transport cost, and patterns of intraregional exchange: aspects of the prehistoric lithic economy of Northern Belize. University of Texas-Austin, 1994.

Simmons, Scott E. The households of Ceren: form and function in middle classic period. El Salvador, 1996.

Smith, C. Wayne. Analysis of the weight assemblage of Port Royal, Jamaica. Texas A&M, 1995.

Walker, Jeffrey B. Stone collars, elbow stones and three pointers, and the nature of Taino ritual and myth. Washington State University, 1993.

LOWER CENTRAL AMERICA

327 Archaeology in the lowland American tropics: current analytical methods and applications. Edited by Peter W. Stahl. Cambridge; New York: Cambridge Univ. Press, 1995. 328 p.: bibl., ill., index, maps.

Collection of 11 papers about analytical methods and their recent applications. Methods include survey techniques, community organization, landscapes, environmental stress, paleoethnobotany, plant microfossils, zooarchaeology, human osteology, stable isotope analysis, pottery analysis, and historical evidence. Regional coverage includes Puerto Rico, Panama, Ecuador, Colombia, Bolivia, and Peru.

328 Archaeology, vulcanism, and remote sensing in the Arenal region, Costa Rica. Edited by Payson D. Sheets and Brian Ross McKee. Austin: Univ. of Texas Press, 1994. 358 p.: bibl., ill., index, maps.

This book contains 17 chapters by 13 authors; 10 are single-authored and the others by various combinations of multiple authors. The work is meticulous ranging from regional to site descriptions, and covering remote sensing applications, chipped stone, ground stone, jewelry, phytoliths, pollen, and macrobotanicals. An excellent account of the archaeology in this region beginning with Paleoindian occupations. Provides a complementary data set to those collected under similar circumstances in El Salvador and Panama.

329 Drennan, Robert D. Betwixt and between in the Intermediate Area. (*J. Archaeol. Res.*, 4:2, 1996, p. 95–132, bibl., map)

A comprehensive review of recent archaeological research (mostly post-1987) in the Intermediate Area. Drennan defines the Intermediate Area's northern boundary in central Honduras, with the southern boundary including Ecuador, Colombia, and western Venezuela. Covers "early inhabitants," "hunters, gatherers, and cultivators," "early pottery," and "complex social patterns." Extremely important overview that includes a bibliography of more than 250 recent publications.

330 Fonseca Zamora, Oscar. La conformación de los espacios históricos: el caso de América Central y noroccidente colombiano. Recopilación de Marcio Veloz Maggiolo y Angel Caba Fuentes. (*in* Seminario de Arqueología del Caribe, *1st, Altos de Chavón, Dominican Republic, 1995.* Memorias. Altos de Chavón, Dominican Republic: Museo Arqueológico Regional, 1996, p. 100–121, bibl.)

Interpreta cultural development in the Chibchoide historical area, extending from Colombia to Honduras, in terms of social archaeological categories. [B. Meggers]

331 Helms, Mary W. Chiefdoms, rivalries, control, and external contacts in lower Central America. (*in* Factional competition and political development in the New World. New York: Cambridge Univ. Press, 1994, p. 55–60)

Helms briefly describes the two-tier chiefdoms of Panama, in an effort to detect whether factions played an important role in their political development. She concludes that there is presently no evidence for or against the operation of factions, and notes her preference for a personalistic, rather than factional, interpretation of intended goals.

Jopling, Carol F. Indios y negros en Panamá en los siglos XVI y XVII: selecciones de los documentos del Archivo General de Indias. See *HLAS 56:1656.*

332 Precolumbian jade: new geological and cultural interpretations. Edited by Frederick W. Lange. Salt Lake City: Univ. of Utah Press, 1993. 378 p.: bibl., ill. (some col.), index.

Monumental work that includes detailed studies of jade from across Central and South America is divided into three parts. Pt. 1 includes eight chapters on geology and minerology; Pt. 2, eight chapters on cultural contexts; and Pt. 3, six chapters on artifacts. Of special note is that the Motagua Valley of Guatemala remains the only known source of jadeite for the entire region. Invaluable compendium for archaeologists working in the region who have recovered jade from their sites. For Mesoamerican archaeologist's comment see *HLAS 55:145.*

Redmond, Elsa M. and **Charles S. Spencer.** The cacicazgo: an indigenous design. See item **365.**

333 Shelton, Catherine N. A recent perspective from Chiriquí, Panama. (*Vínculos/San José,* 20:1/2, 1995, p. 79–101, bibl., ill., maps, tables)

A report on sites discovered during surveys along the Río Chiriquí Viejo and at San Vicente. Results indicate that the relationship between La Concepción phase and Late Bugaba phase ceramics may be more continuous than previously recognized.

CARIBBEAN ISLANDS

Alcina Franch, José. Arqueólogos o anticuarios: historia antigua de la arqueología en la América española. See item **1.**

334 Allaire, Louis. Visions of cannibals: distant islands and distant lands. (*in* The Lesser Antilles in the age of European expansion. Gainesville: Univ. Press of Florida, 1996, p. 33–49, bibl.)

What is the derivation of the name *Carib,* and what is its meaning? Allaire addresses this question beginning with the first use of the term in Columbus' *diario.* Throughout this discussion, Allaire assumes that the Tainos of the Greater Antilles were familiar with the Island Carib of the Windward Islands, and that the names Columbus recorded reflect that knowledge. Keegan offers a contrasting view in his essay from the same edited volume (item **354**).

335 Archaeological investigations on St. Martin, 1993: the sites of Norman Estate, Hope Estate, Anse des Peres. Edited by Corinne Lisette Hofman and Menno L.P. Hoogland. Basse-Terre, Guadeloupe: Direction Régionale des Affaires Culturelles de Guadeloupe, Service Régional de l'Archéologie, 1995. 1 v.: bibl., ill.

In 18 chapters, various researchers describe the results of their studies from three sites on St. Martin. Artifacts studied include lithics, stone tools, mollusk shell, pottery, and the faunal, botanical, and human remains. An important contribution to understanding cultural development on the small islands of the northern Lesser Antilles.

336 The archaeology of Aruba: the Tanki Flip site. Edited by Aad H. Versteeg and Stéphen Rostain. Oranjestad, Aruba: Archaeological Museum Aruba; Amsterdam: Foundation for Scientific Research in the Caribbean, 1997. 519 p.: bibl., ill., maps. (Publications of the Foundation for Scientific Research in the Caribbean Region, 1381–2491; 141. Publications of the Archaeological Museum Aruba; 8)

Vast archaeological report on the Tanki Flip site which includes more than 10 precolumbian houses, a palisade, pottery kilns, and tens of thousands of finds and artifacts. Uses recurrent shell form approach to study certain artifact categories. Presents anthropological data from the opposing mainland to provide a context for the Tanki Flip site. [R. Höefte]

337 Arrazcaeta, Roger and **Robin García.** Guara: una región pictográfica de Cuba. (*Rev. Arqueol./Madrid,* 15:160, agosto

1994, p. 22–31, bibl., ill., maps, photos)

Pictographs from three caves near Havana share a common style. Unique in the region. Focuses on hunting scenes and quadrupeds.

338   Berman, Mary Jane and **Perry L. Gnivecki.** The colonization of the Bahama archipelago: a reappraisal. (*World Archaeol.*, 26:3, Aug. 1995, p. 421–441, bibl., ill.)

Authors contend that Cuba is the source for the first ceramic-age colonists in the Bahama archipelago based on a comparison of artifacts from the Three-Dog site, San Salvador, Bahamas, with artifacts from Arroyo del Palo, Cuba. They also cite recent paleoenvironmental data arguing that the southern Bahamas were too arid to have been settled before AD 950.

339   Between St. Eustatius and The Guianas: contributions to Caribbean archaeology. Edited by Aad H. Versteeg. St. Eustatius, Netherlands Antilles: St. Eustatius Historical Foundation, 1994. 300 p.: bibl., ill., map, photos. (Publications/St. Eustatius Historical Foundation; 3)

Three of the four papers in this collection concern St. Eustatius. Versteeg describes the history of archaeological research on Statia, beginning with the diary of J.P.B. de Josselin de Jong and concluding with the Leiden Univ. Expedition in 1985. Kooijmans picks up where Versteeg leaves off, presenting "Old World" perspective of the work at the Golden Rock site by archaeologists from Leiden Univ. over the past 10 years. Finally, Delvoye reports on the coastal and underwater ecology of Corre Corre Bay. In the fourth paper, Rostain describes the prehistoric archaeology and the cultural historic sequence along the coast of French Guiana. The collection is valuable because it provides a historical context to the work conducted by Leiden researchers and offers an English overview of Rostain's work, especially published in French.

340   Boomert, Arie. The prehistoric sites of Tobago: a catalogue and evaluation. Alkmaar, The Netherlands: Arie Boomert, 1996. 133 p.: ill. tables.

The first detailed inventory of the prehistoric archaeological sites and structures from Tobago discusses 82 prehistoric sites encompassing 103 separate occupations ranging from Archaic through the post-contact (and post-Suazoid?) Culloden complex (Koriaban

subseries). An invaluable compendium of data for the southern Lesser Antilles.

341   Coppa, A. et al. Dental anthropology and paleodemography of the precolumbian populations of Hispaniola from the third millenium BC to the Spanish contact. (*Hum. Ecol.*, 10:2, April/June 1995, p. 153–167, bibl., ill., tables)

Study of dental characteristics in preceramic and Taino groups showed a reduction in the incidence of enamel hypoplasia which they interpret as evidence for a slight improvement of life conditions among the latter. Dental nonmetric traits show a strong homogeneity within the Taino samples, while the preceramic group shows more marked differences when compared to others. These traits suggest that preceramic and Taino groups come from different demes.

342   Curet, L. Antonio. Estructuras domésticas y cambio cultural en la prehistoria de Puerto Rico. (*Rev. Cent. Estud. Av.*, 14, 1992, p. 59–75, bibl., ill.)

An excellent discussion of ethnohistoric descriptions of Taino houses and an overview of house structures identified during archaeological investigations in Puerto Rico.

343   Curet, L. Antonio. Ideology, chiefly power, and material culture: an example from the Greater Antilles. (*Lat. Am. Antiq.*, 7:2, 1996, p. 114–131, bibl., ill.)

Reviews archaeological evidence for cultural change in eastern Puerto Rico. Suggests that these changes are related to the development of social complexity as elite groups exert increasing control over the use of symbolism represented in the artifacts.

344   Dacal Moure, Ramón and **Manuel Rivero de la Calle.** Art and archaeology of pre-Columbian Cuba. Translated by Daniel H. Sandweiss. Edited by Daniel H. Sandweiss and David R. Watters. Foreword by Thor Heyerdahl. Photographs by Kristine Edle Olsen. Pittsburgh, Pa.: Univ. of Pittsburgh Press, 1996. 158 p.: bibl., ill. (some col.), maps. (Pitt Latin American series)

First overview of Cuban archaeology published in English in 50 years. Highly illustrated volume (102 b/w and 16 color plates) provides some of the first images of important artifacts and classes of artifacts. Excellent introduction to recent investigations in Cuba.

345 Davis, Dave D. Revolutionary archaeology in Cuba. (*J. Archaeol. Method Theory,* 3:3, Sept. 1996, p. 159–188, bibl.)

In contrast to Dacal Moure and Rivero de la Calle's insider perspective on Cuban archaeology (item **344**), Davis examines the context in which Cuban archaeology has been conducted since 1959. Davis discusses how archaeological practices in Cuba reflect the aims of the revolutionary government, the influence of Soviet archaeology, the legacy of prerevolutionary approaches in North American archaeology, and the Cuban sense of *patria.*

346 DeFrance, Susan D.; William F. Keegan; and Lee A. Newsom. The archaeobotanical, bone isotope, and zooarchaeological records from Caribbean sites in comparative perspective. (*in* Case studies in environmental archaeology. New York: Plenum Press, 1996, p. 289–304, bibl., ill., tables)

These specialists discuss the contradictory diet reconstructions that emerge from their different data sets. Although they do not reconcile these differences, they offer suggestions for resolving them.

347 Delpuech, André. Archéologie amérindienne en Guadeloupe: recherches récentes et perspetives. (*Bull. soc. hist. Guadeloupe,* 109, 1996, p. 21–38)

French archaeologist conducting excavations in the islands of Guadeloupe and nearby Marie-Galante, the Saints, and Désirade describes findings and offers first assessment of the archaeological program undertaken in 1992. Analyzes challenges unique to the region—variations in sea-level related to frequent hurricanes and volcano eruptions—and shows that Guadeloupe's position halfway down the arc of the Lesser Antilles makes it a prime site to study Carib cultures. [APD]

348 Delpuech, André. Habitats amérindiens dans l'archipel guadeloupéen. (*in* Comité des travaux historiques et scientifiques (CTHS) *120th, Aix-en-Provence, France, Oct. 23–26, 1995.* L'homme préhistorique et la mer, p. 307–381)

Analyzes the results of excavations conducted since 1993 by a Franco-Dutch team in four major sites among the 120 then identified in Guadeloupe. Draws some important preliminary conclusions about Carib settlements from 1500 BC: a marked tendency for settlements to be on the coast due to their increasing reliance on sea-products, the different characteristics of defensive and religious sites, and the crucial need to document more sites dating from the time of the European encounter. [APD]

349 Dubelaar, C.N. The petroglyphs of the Lesser Antilles, the Virgin Islands and Trinidad. Amsterdam: Natuurwetenschappelijke Studiekring voor het Caraïbisch Gebied, 1995. 498 p.: bibl., ill., maps, photos. (Uitgaven/Natuurwetenschappelijke Studiekring voor het Caraïbisch Gebied; 135 = Publications/Foundation for Scientific Research in the Caribbean Region; 135)

The most comprehensive overview of petroglyphs in the region. Discussions of their distributions, as well as similarities and differences, are accompanied by detailed measurements and drawings. Volume includes 689 figures, most of which are b/w photographs.

350 Haviser, Jay B. In search of St. Martin's ancient peoples: prehistoric archaeology. French translation by Daniella Jeffry. Philipsburg, St. Martin: House of Nehesi, 1995. 58 p.: bibl., ill., maps.

A general introduction to the prehistory of St. Martin.

351 Hoogland, Menno L.P. and Corinne Lisette Hofman. Kelbey's Ridge 2: a 14th-century Taino settlement on Saba, Netherlands Antilles. (*Analecta Praehist. Leiden.,* 26, 1993, p. 164–181, bibl., ill., maps)

The discovery and excavation of a Taino outpost on the tiny island of Saba is one of the most significant archaeological finds in recent years because it extends the influence of the Classic Tainos of the Greater Antilles well south into the Lesser Antilles.

352 International Congress for Caribbean Archaeology, 15th, San Juan, 1993. Actas. Recopilación de Ricardo E. Alegría y Miguel Rodríguez López. San Juan: Centro de Estudios Avanzados de Puerto Rico y el Caribe, 1995. 671 p.: ill., maps.

This up-to-date overview of recent investigations in the West Indies includes 53 papers by the leading practitioners in the field. Topics include: method and theory (3); historical archaeology (4); prehistoric technologies (5); interaction, adaptation, and migration (11); preceramic age (2); ceramic age (9); physical anthropology (2); underwater (1); and rock art (6).

353 Keegan, William F. Bahamiam archaeology: life in the Bahamas and Turks and Caicos before Columbus. Nassau: Media Publishing, 1997. 100 p.: bibl., ill., index, maps, tables.

First book-length treatment of Bahamian archaeology designed for use by students and the general public. Includes a description of all aspects of Lucayan material culture and lifeways, as well as notes on archaeological method and theory.

354 Keegan, William F. Columbus was a cannibal: myth and the first encounters. (*in* The Lesser Antilles in the age of European expansion. Gainesville: Univ. Press of Florida, 1996, p. 18–32, bibl., map)

In an attempt to clarify the derivation of the name *Carib* and its meaning, Keegan addresses the use of associated terms in Columbus' *diario*. In contrast to Allaire's essay in the same edited volume (item **334**), Keegan argues that the Tainos did not tell the Spanish about the people they knew to be living in the Windward Islands (today called Island Caribs). Instead the Tainos were using names derived from mythological categories which were more appropriate to these strange beings from across the sea.

355 Keegan, William F. Modeling dispersal in the prehistoric West Indies. (*World Archaeol.*, 26:3, Aug. 1995, p. 400–420, bibl., ill., maps)

Keegan presents new information about the colonization of the West Indies in a theoretical framework that can be applied to all episodes of population expansion by humans. He argues that most of the southern Lesser Antilles were bypassed during the initial ceramic-age expansion from South America to the central Caribbean, and that the islands were settled by multiple migrations of related ethnic groups from South America and within the Antilles. He also describes the 1,000-year pause in population expansion and discusses the second wave of expansion that commenced around AD 500.

356 Keegan, William F. West Indian archaeology 2: after Columbus. (*J. Archaeol. Res.*, 4:4, 1996, p. 265–294, bibl., ill., map)

Second in series of review articles on West Indian archaeology. Focus is on Spanish colonial archaeology, shipwreck archaeology, and native societies at the time of European contact. Bibliography contains references to more than 250 recent works on West Indian archaeology, most published after 1989.

357 Kerchache, Jacques. L'art des sculpteurs taïnos: chefs-d'oeuvre des Grandes Antilles précolombiennes; exposition, Paris, Musée du Petit Palais, 24 février–29 mai 1994. Direction de Jacques Kerchache. Organisation des Musées de la Ville de Paris. Paris: Paris-musées, 1994. 269 p.

Oversized catalog illustrating Taino sculptures from the Greater Antilles displayed in Paris exhibition from Feb. 24–May 29, 1994. The 143 color prints are accompanied by 10 brief articles about Taino life and the objects themselves. An incomparable collection of Taino art.

358 Kiple, Kenneth F. and **Kriemhild C. Ornelas.** After the encounter: disease and demographics in the Lesser Antilles. (*in* The Lesser Antilles in the age of European expansion. Gainesville: Univ. Press of Florida, 1996, p. 50–67, bibl., tables)

Possible known disease vectors present during the early centuries of European contact are discussed. Special attention is directed toward the Island Caribs and subsequent populations in the Lesser Antilles.

359 Pendergast, David M. The Los Buchillones site, north coastal Cuba. (*NewsWARP/Thorverton*, 19, 1996, p. 3–6)

Very brief account of the Royal Ontario Museum's efforts at this submerged site. In addition to well-preserved ceramic, shell, and lithic artifacts, the anaerobic environment has yielded a substantial quantity of wooden artifacts including ceremonial stools and elaborate figurines.

360 Peterson, James B. Archaeology of Trants, Monserrat, part 3: chronological and settlement data. (*Ann. Carnegie Mus.*, 63:4, 1996, p. 323–361, bibl., ill.)

Third in a series on the archaeology of Trants. Chronological and settlement data used to help establish the size and configuration of the site as well as its antiquity and duration. For a review of part 1 see item **377** and for a review of part 2 see item **366.**

361 Petitjean Roget, Henry. Éléments pur une étude comparèe des mythologies taïnos et Caraïbes insulaires (Kalinas) des Antilles. (*Espace Caraïbe*, 2, 1994, p. 91–107)

Comparison of myths among the Tainos and Island Caribs. Contact between the two is evident since the Tainos had to obtain their most valuable artifact, a gold-copper alloy called Guanin, from South America. The Island Caribs served as intermediaries in the exchange. The myths also contain similar elements, such as the rainbow as the supernatural source of maladies. Yet each has a distinctive view of gender in the supernatural realm: the Tainos placed emphasis on feminine beings, while the Island Caribs emphasized masculine beings.

362 Petitjean Roget, Henry. Les pierres à trois pointes des Antilles: essai d'interprétation. (*Espace Caraïbe*, 1, 1993, p. 7–26, bibl.)

Elements of Taino mythology as recorded by Ramón Pané are reviewed and used to develop a diadic model of Taino myth, which in turn identifies three-pointed stones from the Lesser Antilles as reflecting these divisions. The author argues that three-pointers cannot be associated with a single Zcmí, but instead reflect a chain of the meanings related to childbirth and fertility. He also cites evidence that these stones were attached to sticks.

363 Pons Alegría, Mela. El diseño pintado de la cerámica saladoide de Puerto Rico. San Juan: Col. de Estudios Puertorriqueños, 1993. 154 p.: bibl., ill. (some col.). (Col. de estudios puertorriqueños)

Following a brief introduction to Saladoid ceramics, the author provides 100 pages of line drawings depicting linear, geometric, abstract, figurative, and polychrome designs. Three colors are used in illustrations with multiple original colors. A very useful compendium of Saladoid designs from Puerto Rico.

364 Puerto Real: the archaeology of a sixteenth-century Spanish town in Hispaniola. Edited by Kathleen A. Deagan. Gainesville: Univ. Press of Florida, 1995. 559 p.: bibl., ill., index, maps. (The Ripley P. Bullen series. Columbus quincentenary series)

Long-awaited monograph concerning archaeological investigations conducted between 1975–83 at this 16th-century Spanish town near Cap Haïtien, Haiti. The results are detailed in 13 chapters by the researchers who were responsible for particular studies. Topics include the contexts and discovery of the site, community organization and the public sector, Spanish households, economy, transculturation, and the site's abandonment and aftermath. Deagan's introduction and epilogue place these investigations in the broader context of historical archaeology.

365 Redmond, Elsa M. and **Charles S. Spencer.** The cacicazgo: an indigenous design. (*in* Caciques and their people: a volume in honor of Ronald Spores. Ann Arbor: Univ. of Michigan, 1994, p. 189–225)

Detailed accounts of the Taino cacicazgos of Hispaniola, as described by the Spanish, and of the cacicazgos in the Cuicatlán, southern highlands of Mexico, are used to illustrate the florescence and emergence of this indigenous American form of political organization.

366 Reitz, Elizabeth J. Archaeology of Trants, Montserrat, part 2: vertebrate fauna. (*Ann. Carnegie Mus.*, 63:4, 1994, p. 297–317)

The second of a series describes the analysis of vertebrate remains on the Trants site. Both fishes and terrestrial animals were consumed. Humans also introduced terrestrial animals, and drove some indigenous species to extinction. The results show that people living on each island knew well how to make use of local animals and were not simply transient South Americans unfamiliar with the resources offered by Caribbean Islands. For a review of part 1 see item **377** and of part 3 see item **360.**

367 Robiou Lamarche, Sebastián. Encuentro con la mitología taína. San Juan: Editorial Punto y Coma, 1992. 82 p.: bibl., ill.

Generously-illustrated book reexamines Ramón Pané's account of Taino mythology. Includes a glossary of Taino mythology and a new version of Taino cosmology.

368 Rodríguez, Miguel A. Diversidad cultural en la tardía prehistoria del este de Puerto Rico. (*Rev. Cent. Estud. Av.*, 15, 1992, p. 58–74, bibl., ill.)

Prepared for an SAA symposium focusing on the late prehistory of the northeastern Caribbean. Rodríguez describes cultural development in eastern Puerto Rico beginning with the terminal Saladoid. Conclusions are based on the results of his pioneering survey of the Río Loiza drainage.

369 **Roe, Peter G.** Style, society, myth, and structure. (*in* Style, society, and person. New York: Plenum Press, 1995, p. 27–76, bibl., ill.)

An important paper on how cultural factors constrain aesthetic and technical styles. Roe explores the hierarchical nature of style, and applies his model to the evolution of stylistic traditions in lithics and ceramics from Puerto Rico. This case illustrates the ideational factors that articulate style with self and society on the mythic and structural levels.

370 **Saunders, Nicholas J.** and **Dorrick Gray.** Zemís, trees, and symbolic landscapes: three Taíno carvings from Jamaica. (*Antiquity/Cambridge*, 70:270, Dec. 1996, p. 801–812, bibl., ill.)

The reporting of three wooden statues from Jamaica provide the foreground for this discussion of Zemís and the Taino spirit world. The authors' maintain a traditional view of Taino spirituality. Important discussion of wooden objects. Casts Taino mythology in the language of today.

371 **Siegel, Peter E.** Ideology and culture change in prehistoric Puerto Rico: a view from the community. (*J. Field Archaeol.*, 23:3, 1996, p. 313–333)

This paper explores linkages between the archaeological record at the community level and ideology to discuss culture change in the West Indies. Working from the premise that settlements are physical models for the cosmos, Siegel considers the structure of social behavior, relations of power, and activity organization by examining how participants interact with and interpret cosmology.

372 **Siegel, Peter E.** An interview with Irving Rouse. (*Curr. Anthropol.*, 37:4, Aug./Oct. 1996, p. 671–689)

Interesting retrospective on the doyen of Caribbean archaeology. Irving Rouse's view of West Indian archaeology for most of the past 58 years is presented in a nutshell.

373 **Stokes, Anne V.** and **William F. Keegan.** A reconnaissance for prehistoric archaeological sites on Grand Cayman. (*Caribb. J. Sci.*, 32:4, 1996, p. 425–430, bibl., maps)

An archaeological survey of Grand Cayman concludes that the island was uninhabited prior to the arrival of Europeans in the 16th century.

374 **Ulloa Hung, Jorge** and **Juan M. Reyes.** Vínculos prehistóricos entre Cuba y Haití. (*Del Caribe*, 23, 1994, p. 104–109, facsims., tables)

Comparison of prehistoric ceramic styles in Cuba and Haiti. Authors detect an interchange of style between Meillac and Carrier before these were exported to Cuba. Critical of Rouse's unilear scheme of cultural development, and suggests instead that cultural diversity existed in Cuba before Columbus.

375 **Van Gijn, A.L.** Flint exploitation on Long Island, Antigua, West-Indies. (*Analecta Praehist. Leiden.*, 26, 1993, p. 183–197, bibl., ill.)

Report on a survey of Long Island, an islet off the coast of Antigua, which was a major source of flint for the Lesser Antilles. The survey uncovered various raw material sources. Test excavations at Flinty Bay site show a standardized reduction sequence whose aim was to produce high quality cores that could be transported easily.

Veloz Maggiolo, Marcio and **Elpidio Ortega.** La fundación de la villa de Santo Domingo: un estudio arqueo-histórico. See *HLAS 56:1900.*

376 **Veloz Maggiolo, Marcio.** La isla de Santo Domingo antes de Colón. Santo Domingo: Banco Central de la República Dominicana, 1993. 211 p.: bibl., ill., maps.

While other accounts of the precolumbian populations of Hispaniola rely primarily on the writings of European invaders, this book uses archaeological investigations conducted over the past 20 years as its basis. An indispensible work by one of the most highly regarded archaeologists in the West Indies.

377 **Watters, David R.** Archaeology of Trants, Montserrat, part 1: field methods and artifact density distributions. (*Ann. Carnegie Mus.*, 63:4, 1994, p. 265–295)

First in a series of articles on the Trants site. Watters compares and evaluates the different research strategies used during fieldwork in 1978–79 and 1990. Radiocarbon dates indicate that the site was first occupied around 500 BC, making it one of the oldest sites in the West Indies, while terminal dates point to its abandonment around AD 330. The "collection corridor" strategy employed in 1990 revealed an oval-shaped core area of the site. For a review of part 2 see item **366** and of part 3 see item **360**.

378 **Watters, David R.** and **Richard Scag-lion.** Beads and pendants from Trants, Monserrat: implications from the prehistoric lapidary industry of the Caribbean. (*Ann. Carnegie Mus.*, 63:4, 1994, p. 215–237)

Analysis of a collection of lithic beads and pendants from Montserrat suggests that the Trants site may have been a lithic bead manufacturing center specializing in carnelian beads. This Saladoid age site has yielded one of the largest collections of small lithic jewelry recovered in the West Indies. It has important implications for the study or regional exchange patterns and ethnic identities.

379 **Watters, David R.** Mortuary patterns at the Harney site slave cemetery, Montserrat, in Caribbean perspective. (*Hist. Archaeol.*, 28:3, 1994, p. 56–73)

Mortuary patterns at the 18th-century Harney site slave cemetery include demographic, burial, and artifact information. This study informs broader perspectives on the mortuary patterns of enslaved populations within the Caribbean region.

380 **Weeks, John M.; Peter J. Ferbel;** and **Virginia Ramírez Zabala.** Rock art at Corral de los Indios de Chacuey, Dominican

Republic. (*Lat. Am. Indian Lit. J.*, 12:1, 1996, p. 88–97)

Drawings of petroglyphs from a gallery along the banks of the Río de Chacuey, near Dajabón in western Dominican Republic, are illustrated, although no scales are provided. Possible meanings of the petroglyphs are discussed in the context of Taino shamanism.

Whitehead, Neil L. The Mazaruni dragon: golden metals and elite exchanges in the Caribbean, Orinoco, and Amazon. See item **410**.

381 **Wing, Elizabeth S.** and **Stephen R. Wing.** Prehistoric ceramic age adaptation to varying diversity of animal resources along the West Indian archipelago. (*J. Ethnobiol.*, 15:1, 1995, p. 119–148)

Island biogeographic principles are applied to the analysis of archaeological faunas from Caribbean Ceramic age sites. Authors showed decreased diversity in faunal assemblages with distance from the mainland and a positive correlation between diversity and island size. They also comment on new species introduced by human colonists.

382 **Wolves from the sea: readings in the anthropology of the native Caribbean.** Edited by Neil L. Whitehead. Leiden: KITLV Press, 1995. 176 p.: bibl., index. (Caribbean series, 0921–9781; 14)

Collection of seven papers mostly new, refreshing perspectives on the Island Caribs of the Windward Islands. Drawn from ethnohistory, archaeology, linguistics, ethnology, critical theory, and cross-cultural comparisons, the papers reinvent the Island Carib, whose culture had become stultified as the war-like "cannibal" opponents of the "peaceful Arawaks." For ethnologist's comment see *HLAS 55:846.*

South America

BETTY J. MEGGERS, *Research Associate, Department of Anthropology, Smithsonian Institution*

TWO MAJOR CONTROVERSIES have pushed South American archaeology into the headlines during this biennium: 1) the antiquity of human arrival and 2) the existence of precolumbian civilizations in Amazonia.

The earliest accepted North American date ca. 12,000 BP has been challenged as incompatible with associations between lithic complexes and extinct fauna in South America. The "Clovis barrier" was breeched as a consequence of extensive documentation in the final report on Monte Verde, Chile (item **500**) and inspection of the site by skeptical US specialists (items **492** and **514**). However, two other candidates for pre-Clovis antiquity remain contested. A conference attended by European, US, and Latin American experts to evaluate evidence for a 50,000 BP occupation at Pedra Furada in Northeastern Brazil led the US delegation to reject human presence prior to ca. 10,000 BP (item **472**). Although this assessment has been challenged by the excavation team (item **472**), it is compatible with the date from a nearby site (item **477**). Claims for the antiquity of Pedra Pintada, a rock shelter in central Amazonia (item **597**) have provoked multiple rebuttals by US specialists, who challenge the dates, associations, stratigraphy, and inferred tropical forest context (Tankersley 1996, Science 1996, 1997).

Concurrently, South American archaeologists have strengthened the case for human presence contemporary with or earlier than Clovis. Well-documented sequences have been described from Santana de Riacho, Minas Gerais (item **481**) and Serranopolis II, Goiás in Brazil, at Quero (item **517**) and Taguatagua (item **515**) in Chile, and at sites in several parts of Argentina (items **417, 426,** and **427**) and interpretations of ethnicity, subsistence preference, and adaptation to diverse habitats based on archaeological evidence have been supplemented by experimental replication of lithic technologies (items **512** and **400**). A symposium in Bogotá with participants from Ecuador, Colombia, Venezuela, and Panamá (item **384**) and a study of the cranial morphology of early skeletal remains (item **401**) provide a continental perspective. The abundant evidence for pre-Clovis presence in southern South America raises the question: where are the antecedent North American sites?

The controversy over the existence of precolumbian states and civilizations in Amazonia is increasingly acrimonious. Proponents reject archaeological evidence and environmental constraints in favor of early European descriptions of dense populations, hierarchical societies, and advanced technology (items **403, 597, 410, 491,** and **409**); opponents report only impermanent settlements with relatively recent dates and no evidence of metallurgy, social complexity or other advanced features (items **595, 596,** and **600**). Although Denevan (item **461**) has reduced his previous estimates of floodplain productivity, he maintains large permanent settlements were sustainable. In Colombia, by contrast, impressive highland and north coastal remains are attributed to autonomous chiefdoms linked by exchange of elite items, rather than centralized states (items **533, 553, 392, 398,** and **536**).

In spite of increased length, this section does not adequately reflect expansion of archaeological research by South Americans. In the case of Argentina, for example, annotation of contributions in conference proceedings would double the number of titles (item **388**) and many articles on local topics have been omitted for lack of space. Other multi-authored volumes attest to increasing collaboration among neighboring countries: Argentina/Chile (item **406, 422, 506,** and **396**), Colombia/Ecuador (items **574** and **547**), Colombia/Ecuador/Peru (item **407**), Peru/Argentina (item **389**). Conferences with international participation focus on faunal exploitation, mortuary practices (item **408**), and environmental adaptations (item **384**). Tabulations of authors by country of origin shows that nationals still far surpass foreigners in Argentina, Brazil, Chile, and Colombia. The biggest change is Peru, where entries have declined from a third to a quarter of the total and national authorship has increased to about 40 percent.

GENERAL

383 Adamska, Anna and **Adam Michczyński.** Towards radiocarbon chronology of the Inca State. (*Andes/Warsaw*, 1, 1996, p. 35–58, bibl., tables)

Calibrated C14 dates from Inca architecture and artifacts from Peru, Chile, Argentina, and Ecuador. Evaluations use various statistical procedures and agree with the historical chronology.

384 Ambito y ocupaciones tempranas de la América tropical. Edición de Inés Cavelier y Santiago Mora Camargo. Bogotá: Fundación Erigaie; Instituto Colombiano de Antropología, 1995. 154 p.: bibl., ill.,index.

Nine articles discuss lithic industries and C14 dates from Sabana de Bogotá, Popayán, Calima, upper Magdalena, and middle Caquetá valleys in Colombia; upper middle Orinoco, Venezuela; Panama; and Ecuador.

385 Andean art at Dumbarton Oaks. Edited by Elizabeth Hill Boone. Washington: Dumbarton Oaks Research Library and Collection, 1996. 2 v.: bibl., ill. (some col.), maps. (Pre-Columbian art at Dumbarton Oaks; 1)

The first of four catalogs documenting each piece in the Bliss Collection, work includes topical essays on the collector's perspective (E.H. Boone), the Andean world and technology of metal and cloth (H. Lechtman), textile structure amd meaning (W.J. Conklin), and Peruvian textile art (A.P. Rowe). Object descriptions grouped by cultural affiliation include technological data, iconography, cultural significance, and reference to similar objects elsewhere.

386 Archaeology and environment in Latin America. Edited by Omar R. Ortíz-Troncoso and Thomas van der Hammen. Amsterdam: Instituut voor Pre- en Protohistorische Archeologie Albert Egges van Giffen, Univ. van Amsterdam, 1992. 305 p.: bibl., ill., maps.

Sixteen articles examine various aspects of cultural/environmental interactions ranging from Paleo-Indian to historic periods in Panama, Colombia, Venezuela, Brazil, Uruguay, and Patagonia.

387 Arqueología Contemporánea. No. 4, 1993. Explotación de recursos faunísticos en sistemas adaptativos americanos. Recopilación de José Luis Lanata. Buenos Aires: Programa de Estudios Prehistóricos.

Articles discuss catfish productivity in Panama, camelid resources in the Puna, extinct fauna in southern Chile, archeofaunal preservation in northwest Argentina and Patagonia, and ethnographic perspectives from Venezuela and Tierra del Fuego.

388 El arte rupestre en la arqueología contemporánea. Editado por María Mercedes Podestá, María Isabel Hernández Llosas y Susana F. Renard de Coquet. Buenos Aires: M.M. Podestá, 1991. 150 p.: bibl., ill.

Seventeen articles examine aspects of theory, methodology, documentation, style, conservation, and interpretation of rock art, including appropriate computer databases.

389 Congreso Peruano del Hombre y la Cultura Andina, 11th, Huánuco, Peru, 1995. Actas y trabajos científicos. v. 1. Recopilación de Hernán Amat Olazábal y Luis Guzmán Palomino. Huánuco, Peru: Univ. Nacional Hermilio Valdizán de Huanuco; La Plata, Argentina: Univ. Nacional de La Plata; Lima: Centro de Estudios Histórico-Militares del Perú, 1997. 1 v.: bibl., ill. (some col.), maps.

Cardich traces Andean cultural development prior to 4500 BP; 15 Peruvian and Argentine archaeologists discuss aspects of the Andean formative, the Inca State, and Argentine archaeology and ethnohistory.

Davies, Nigel. The Incas. See item **621.**

390 DeBoer, Warren R.; Keith Kintigh; and **Arthur G. Rostoker.** Ceramic seriation and site reoccupation in lowland South America. (*Lat. Am. Antiq.*, 7:3, 1996, p. 263–278, bibl., ill., tables)

Quantitative differences in vessel inventory among contemporary households in a modern Sipibo settlement refute the validity of seriation for differentiating discontinuous occupation from long-term occupation of prehistoric habitation sites.

391 Diálogo Andino. No. 14/15, 1995/96. Prehistoria del norte de Chile y del Desierto de Atacama: simposio homenaje a Percy Dauelsberg Hahmann. Arica, Chile: Univ. de Tarapacá.

Contains six articles on Dauelsberg's life and work, and chapters on Inca roads, reticulate irrigation, a formative settlement in the Atacama Desert, intercultural relations in the Azapa Valley, interpretation of Chinchorro mummies by early Spanish chroniclers, correlation between coca chewing and tooth loss, and Late-Period relations between north Chile and the Titicaca Basin.

392 Gassón, Rafael A. La evolución del intercambio a larga distancia en el noro-oriente de Suramérica: bienes de intercambio y poder político en una perspectiva diacrónica. (*in* Chieftains, power & trade: regional interaction in the intermediate area of the Americas = Caciques, intercambio y poder: interacción regional en el área intermedia de las Américas. Bogotá: Depto. de Antropología, Univ. de los Andes, 1996, p. 133–154)

Comparison of prehistoric, contact, and colonial periods indicates a change from low-intensity, long-distance exchange in luxury goods among autonomous groups to aggressive and competitive commerical distribution with loss of local independence.

393 Guliaev, Valeriĭ Ivanovich. Viajes precolombinos a las Américas: mitos y realidades. Traducción de Iván Cevallos Calderón. Quito: Abya-Yala, 1992. 314 p.: bibl., ill. (Col. Tierra incógnita; 2)

Asserts establishment position that if transoceanic contacts occurred, they had no significant impact.

394 Hoopes, John W. Ford revisited: a critical review of the chronology and relationships of the earliest ceramic complexes in the New World, 6000–1500 B.C. (*J. World Prehist.*, 8, 1994, p. 1–49, bibl., maps)

A comparison of ceramic chronologies in lowland Brazil, northern Colombia, coastal Ecuador, coastal Peru, central Panama, southern Mesoamerica, and southeastern and central US indicates that initial complexes were distinct and implies at least eight independent inventions of pottery in the Americas, a conclusion jeopardized by uncritical acceptance of C14 dates.

395 Ibarra Grasso, Dick Edgar. Sudamérica indígena. Buenos Aires: Tipográfica Editora Argentina, 1994. 715 p.: bibl., ill. (some col.), maps.

Distinguishing discovery (appropriating something existing in nature) from invention (no natural antecedents) reveals that Old World specialists generally accept single origins of inventions, whereas New World specialists propose multiple independent origins

of many traits. This review of New World cultural history indicates it was part of a single global process. This liberally illustrated publication is the most comprehensive treatment of a controversial topic.

396 Jornadas de Arqueología e Interdisciplinas, *Buenos Aires, 1993*. Actas. Buenos Aires: Consejo Nacional de Investigaciones Científicas y Tecnicas, Programa de Estudios Prehistoricos, 1994. 236 p.: bibl., ill.

Chapters discuss potentials and problems of applying evidence from paleopalinology, geoarchaeology, biological anthropology, C14 dating, paleomagnetism, paleontology, ethnography, and sea-level change to interpreting cultural remains.

397 *Journal of the Steward Anthropological Society*. Nos. 1/2, 1995. Current research in Andean antiquity. Edited by Ari Zighelboim and Carol Barnes. Urbana, Ill.: Steward Anthropological Society.

Articles discuss revision of formative chronologies in south coastal Peru and southeastern Titicaca Basin, Casma Valley settlement pattern, social implications of spatial analysis, and specialized ceramic production in Tiwanaku.

398 Langebaek, Carl Henrik. Patterns of human mobility and elite finances in 16th-century northern Colombia and western Venezuela. (*in* Chieftains, power & trade: regional interaction in the intermediate area of the Americas = Caciques, intercambio y poder: interacción regional en el área intermedia de las Américas. Bogotá: Depto. de Antropología, Univ. de los Andes, 1996, p. 155–174, maps)

Differences in development of chiefdoms and States reflect relative success in replacing local control over staples and raw materials with centralized control over production and circulation, which in turn reflects differences in local access to varied microenvironments.

399 Meggers, Betty J. Possible impact of the mega-Niño events on precolumbian populations in the Caribbean area. (*in* Seminario de Arqueología del Caribe, *1st, Altos de Chavón, Dominican Republic, 1995*. Ponencias. Altos de Chavón, Dominican Republic: Museo Arqueológico Regional Altos de Chavón; Organization of American States, 1996, p. 156–176, bibl., ill.)

Revision of seriated ceramic sequences from coastal Colombia (lower San Jorge, Carrizal) and Venezuela (Agüerito, Macapaima, Barrancas, El Cuartel) reveals discontinuities that correlate with mega-Niño events ca. 1500, 1000, and 700 BP, implying disruption of local populations.

400 Nami, Hugo Gabriel. New assessments of early human occupations in the Southern Cone. (*in* Prehistoric mongoloid dispersals. Oxford, England; New York: Oxford Univ. Press, 1996, p. 254–269, bibl., map, tables)

Archaeological evidence from a dozen localities documents environmental diversity, varying adaptive strategies, and sophisticated flint-knapping techniques during the Pleistocene-Holocene transition.

401 Neves, Walter *et al.* O povoamento da América à luz da morfologia craniana. (*Rev. USP*, 34, 1997, p. 96–105, maps, table)

Multivariate analyses on skeletal remains from 30 sites in Brazil, Chile, and Colombia suggest two peoplings: one premongoloid ca. 12,000 BP, and another mongoloid ca. 9,000–8,000 BP.

402 Redmond, Elsa M. Tribal and chiefly warfare in South America. Ann Arbor: Museum of Anthropology, Univ. of Michigan, 1994. 148 p.: bibl., ill., maps. (Memoirs of the Museum of Anthropology, Univ. of Michigan; 28. Studies in Latin American ethnohistory and archaeology; 5)

Preparations, organization, weapons, strategies, rituals, and mortuary treatments associated with warfare among contemporary Jivaro and Yanomamo, and among contact-period Colombian and Panamanian chiefdoms, provide criteria for differentiating tribal and chiefdom levels; these are evaluated using archaeological data from various regions and periods.

403 Roosevelt, Anna C. The rise and fall of the Amazonian chiefdoms. (*Homme/Paris*, 33:126/128, avril/déc. 1993, p. 255–283, bibl., ill.)

Summarizes previous arguments for powerful and populous chiefdoms throughout Amazonia prior to European contact, invalidating existence of environmental constraints on intensive exploitation.

Shimada, Izumi. Pre-hispanic metallurgy and mining in the Andes: recent advances and future tasks. See item **665.**

404 Sušnik, Branislava. Interpretación etnocultural de la complejidad sudamericana antigua. v. 1, Formación y dispersión étnica. Asunción: Museo Etnográfico Andrés Barbero, 1994- . 1 v.: bibl., ill., maps.

Three maps show the centers of origin and directions of dispersal of initial hunter-gatherers, ceramic traditions, and major linguistic/ethnic groups. Text summarizes diagnostic settlement, social and economic features, and forms of interaction. An original and important contribution combining archaeological and ethnographical data.

405 Sušnik, Branislava. Interpretación etnocultural de la complejidad sudamericana antigua. v. 2, El hombre, persona y agente ergológico. Asunción: Museo Etnográfico Andrés Barbero, 1994- . 1 v.: bibl., ill., maps.

Detailed information on body ornament (tattoos, deformation, hair style, dress, paint), types of shelter, pottery, basketry, and weaving makes this work an important reference. Descriptions and illustrations of houses are particularly useful for archaeological interpretation.

406 Taller de costa a selva: producción e intercambio entre los pueblos agroalfareros de los Andes centro-sur. Edición de María Ester Albeck. Tilcara, Argentina: Instituto Interdisciplinario Tilcara, Facultad de Filosofía y Letras, UBA, 1994. 403 p.: bibl., ill., maps, tables

Seventeen chapters by Argentine and Chilean archaeologists discuss relationships between complementarity, production, and trade, and differences in environment and cultural complexity.

407 Tecnología y organización de la producción cerámica prehispánica en los andes. Recopilación de Izumi Shimada. Lima: Pontificia Univ. Católica del Perú, Fondo Editorial, 1994. 517 p.: bibl., ill., maps.

Seventeen chapters discuss aspects of technology, composition, production, and use of pottery in Peruvian, Ecuadorian and Colombian cultures ranging from Formative to Inca periods. A detailed description of pottery making in a traditional north coastal Peruvian community provides leads for archaeological inference.

408 Tombs for the living: Andean mortuary practices; a symposium at Dumbarton Oaks, 12th and 13th October, 1991. Edited by Tom D. Dillehay. Washington: Dumbarton Oaks Research Library and Collection, 1994. 425 p.: bibl., ill., index, maps.

Ancient Peruvian practices are summarized by J.H. Rowe; Chinchorro mummies by M.S. Rivera; San Agustín, Colombia, by R.D. Drennan; Moche by C.B. Donnan; Nasca by P.H. Carmichael; south coastal Peru by J.E. Buikstra; human sacrifice and trophy heads by J.W. Verano. Observations on rituals among contemporary Bolivians (J.W. Bastien) and Araucanians (T.D. Dillehay), and in colonial documents (F. Solomon), provide comparative data.

409 Whitehead, Neil L. Amazonian archaeology; searching for paradise?: a review of recent literature and fieldwork. (*J. Archaeol. Res.*, 4:4, 1996, p. 241–264, bibl.)

Claims recent archaeological evidence refutes ecological, geological, and climatological evidence for limitations to sustainable intensive exploitation by dense, sedentary populations.

410 Whitehead, Neil L. The Mazaruni dragon: golden metals and elite exchanges in the Caribbean, Orinoco, and Amazon. (*in* Chieftains, power & trade: regional interaction in the intermediate area of the Americas = Caciques, intercambio y poder: interacción regional en el área intermedia de las Américas. Bogotá: Depto. de Antropología, Univ. de los Andes, 1996, p. 107–132)

Argues that retrieval of a gold object of Tairona style from the Mazaruni river substantiates historical accounts of gold production in the central Guianas and diffusion from there to coastal Colombia.

ARGENTINA

411 Aschero, Carlos A.; Cristina Bellelli; and Rafael A. Goñi. Avances en las investigaciones arqueológicas del Parque Nacional Perito Moreno, Provincia de Santa Cruz, Patagonia Argentina. (*Cuad. Antropol. Pensam. Latinoam.*, 14, 1992/93, p. 143–170, bibl., ill., maps, tables)

Archaeological remains from sites occupied between 6800 and 2800 BP are interpreted in the context of environmental differ-

ences and climatic changes to reconstruct subsistence strategies and settlement behavior.

412 Austral, Antonio G. and Ana María Rocchietti. El Ojito: un área de domesticidad indígena en el sur de Córdoba. (*Rev. Univ. Nac. Río Cuarto*, 13:2, 1993, p. 205–223, bibl., graphs, ill., maps, tables)

Excavations in a rock shelter in Piedra de Aguila produced charred Rhea shell, llama bones, lithics, and pottery. A C14 date of 1900 BP suggests an earlier adoption of pottery than previously documented.

413 Bellelli, Cristina and Hugo Gabriel Nami. Hojas, experimentos y análisis de desechos de talla: implicaciones arqueológicas para la Patagonia Centro-Septentrional. (*Cuad. Antropol. Pensam. Latinoam.*, 15, 1994, 199–223, bibl., graphs, ill.)

Experimental replication of stages and techniques of blade manufacture indicates that all stages are present in archaeological refuse in Campo Moncado, Río Chubut, occupied 5000–3000 BP.

414 Bengtsson, Lisbet. Architectural remains as archaeology: ideas and attempts in a Sub-Andean context. Göteborg, Sweden: Univ. of Gothenburg, Dept. of Archaeology, 1992. 148 p.: bibl.., ill. (GOTARC, 0282–94798. Serie C, Arkeologiska skrifter; 9)

Detailed examination of three sites of the Santa María culture gives no indication of existence of a central plan. Evidence of intra- or inter-site hierarchy or of specialized function is also lacking. Architectural features imply a long-lived local tradition.

415 Boschín, María Teresa. Arte rupestre patagónico: problemas no resueltos y propuestas para su discusión. (*Anu. IEHS*, 9, 1994, p. 323–354, bibl.)

Coexistence of numerous rock art styles and varieties implies production by specialists who maintained the symbolic codes and techniques of execution.

416 Boschín, María Teresa. Historia de las investigaciones arqueológicas en Pampa y Patagonia. (*Runa/Buenos Aires*, 20, 1991/92, p. 111–144, bibl.)

Changes in theoretical perspective identify periods, each illustrated by representative publications. Diagnostic features are summarized, critiqued, and evaluated in the context of prevailing sociopolitical attitudes.

417 Cardich, Augusto; Paunero, Rafael; and Alicia Castro. Analísis de los conjuntos líticos de la cueva 2 de Los Toldos—Santa Cruz, Argentina. (*An. Inst. Patagon./Hum.*, 22, 1993/94, p. 149–173, bibl., graphs, ill., maps, tables)

Microwear analysis of lithics associated with the Toldense and Casapedrense industries identifies technological, stylistic, and functional differences.

418 Contribución a la arqueología del Río Pinturas, Provincia de Santa Cruz. Dirección de la publicación de Carlos J. Gradin y Ana M. Aguerre. Concepción del Uruguay, Argentina: Búsqueda de AYLLU, 1994. 375 p.: bibl., ill., maps. (Col. Estudios arqueológicos; 987560081X.)

Details on sediments, palynology, lithics, fauna, and human remains from Alero Cárdenas, Alero Charcamata, and Enterratorio Puesto El Rodeo. Thirty-six C14 dates extend from 4910 ± 70 to 430 ± 50 BP.

419 Earle, Timothy. Wealth finance in the Inca Empire: evidence from the Calchaqui Valley, Argentina. (*Am. Antiq.*, 59:3, July 1994, p. 443–460, bibl., ill., tables)

High frequency of metallurgical, marine shell, and mica manufacturing debris in elite-sector households at three sites implies craft production for export and use in the imperial economy.

420 Escola, Patricia et al. Prospecciones arqueológicas en las quebradas de la margen occidental del Salar de Antofalla, Catamarca, Puna Meridional Argentina: resultados preliminares. (*Cuad. Antropol. Pensam. Latinoam.*, 14, 1992/93, p. 171–189, bibl., maps)

Survey in four quebradas documented occupations during the regional formative by agro-pastoralists and periodic herders, and an important obsidian source. Ceramics are related to the Tebenquiche, Ciénaga, and Aguada traditions.

Fernández, Fiz Antonio. Antropología cultural, medicina indígena de América y arte rupestre argentino. v. 1–3. See item **8.**

421 Gambier, Mariano. Prehistoria de San Juan. San Juan, Argentina: Editorial Fundación Univ. Nacional de San Juan, 1993. 109 p.: bibl., ill., maps.

Synthesizes 25 years of investigation to reconstruct prehistoric adaptation after ca. 8000 BP. Cultural innovations are traced to northern influences and are documented with maps, dwelling reconstructions, characteristic artifacts, and photographs of well-preserved human remains.

422 Jornadas de Arqueología de la Patagonia, 2nd, Puerto Madryn, Argentina, 1993. Ponencias. Puerto Madryn, Argentina: Centro Nacional Patagónico, CONICET, 1993. 1 v.: bibl., ill., maps, tables.

Forty-five articles discuss Pleistocene and Holocene occupations, rock art, arqueofauna, lithic technology, and biological anthropology.

423 Kirbus, Federico B. Arqueología argentina. Buenos Aires: El Ateneo, 1994. 127 p.: bibl., ill. (some col.). (Serie Historia y geografía)

History of archaeological investigations in northwest Argentina and guide to notable sites is directed toward a nonprofessional audience.

424 Legoupil, Dominique. El archipiélago del Cabo de Hornos y la costa sur de la Isla Navarino: poblamiento y modelos económicos. (*An. Inst. Patagon./Hum.*, 22, 1993/94, p. 101–121, bibl., graphs, maps, photos, tables)

Detailed analysis of faunal remains reveals significant differences in subsistence emphasis, with marine mammals and birds dominating in the archipelago assemblages and mollusks in the coastal site.

425 Manzo, Alberto and María Gabriela Raviña. Augustukuy: rito de la multiplicación de los rebaños; ceremonias rurales y su articulación con el registro arqueológico. (*Publicaciones/Córdoba*, 48, 1997, p. 1–53, bibl., ill.)

Traces of semicarbonized *Erythroxylum coca* in cavities of camelid images suggest precolumbian antecedents of contemporary rites.

Massone Mezzano, Mauricio; Donald Jackson; and Alfredo Prieto. Perspectiva arqueológica de los selk'nam. See item **510.**

426 Mazzanti, Diana L. and Carlos A. Quintana. Asociación cultural con fauna extinguida en el sitio arqueológico Cueva Tixi, provincia de Buenos Aires, Argentina. (*Rev. Esp. Antropol. Am.*, 27, 1997, p. 11–21, bibl., ill.)

Eutatus seguini and *Canis avus* were identified in the initial occupation, with C14 dates of 10,375 ± 90 and 10,045 ± 95 BP.

427 Mazzanti, Diana L. Excavaciones arqueológicas en el sitio Cueva Tixi, Buenos Aires, Argentina. (*Lat. Am. Antiq.*, 8:1, 1997, p. 55–62, bibl., ill., map)

Abundant lithics and faunal remains define at least four occupations reflecting variable use beginning ca. 10,375 BP.

428 Mazzanti, Diana L. El período tardío en la arqueología bonaerense. (*in* Huellas en la tierra: indios, agricultores y haciendados en la pampa bonaerense. Recopilación de Raúl Mandrini y Andrea Reguera. Tandil, Argentina: Univ. Nacional del Centro, IEHS, 1993, p. 31–44, graph, map, tables)

Compares location, cultural remains, rock types, and fauna from 10 sites.

Ocampo E., Carlos and **Pilar Rivas H.** Caracterización arqueológica preliminar del suroeste de la Tierra del Fuego. See item **518.**

429 Pelissero, Norberto A. El sitio arqueológico de Keta-Kara en el sistema cultural de la Ceja de Puna, Departamento de Tilcara, Provincia de Jujuy. Buenos Aires: Centro Argentino de Etnología Americana, 1995. 170 p.: ill. (Col. Mankacén)

A detailed local ceramic chronology permits reconstructing growth and decline of a settlement occupied AD 1000 to Inca expansion. Considers demographic history, environmental potential, and impact of external populations.

430 Pérez Gollán, José Antonio. Los sueños del jaguar: viaje a la región de la sabiduría y de los señores iluminados. (*in* Los sueños del jaguar: imágenes de la puna y la selva argentina. Santiago: Museo Chileno de Arte Precolombino, 1994, p. 14–61, ill., map)

Synthesis of cultural development during the Integration Period, ca. 150 BC–AD 750, is beautifully illustrated in color.

431 *Prehistoria: Revista del Programa de Estudios Prehistóricos.* No. 2, 1996. Salvataje arqueológico e investigaciones prehistóricas en el área de influencia de la represa hidroeléctrica Piedra del Aguila, provincias del Neuquen y Río Negro. Buenos Aires:

Consejo Nacional de Investigaciones Científicas y Técnicas.

General description of salvage operations includes specialist reports on stratigraphy, plant and animal remains, palynology, and artifact typology of two rockshelters: Piedra del Aguila II and Cueva Epullán Grande. Chronological chart summarizes changes in artifacts, fauna, and environment since 10,000 BP.

432 Quiroga, Adán. Calchaquí. Comentarios de actualización por Rodolfo A. Raffino. Buenos Aires: Tipográfica Editora Argentina, 1992. 475 p.: bibl. ,ill.

Contains the principal contributions of a remarkably versatile late-19th-century scholar to local history, rock art, and folklore.

433 *Revista del Museo de Historia Natural de San Rafael.* Vol. 27, Nos. 1/2/3/4, 1995. Arqueología del noreste argentino.

Eleven articles summarize recent investigations, historical archaeology, and use of space in prehistoric and historic Guaraní settlements.

434 Rodríguez, Jorge Amilcar. Introducción a la prehistoria de la cuenca del Plata oriental. (*Sarance/Otavalo*, 24, 1997, p. 71–97, bibl., ill., maps)

Synthesis of cultural development between the Río Uruguay and the coast from Paleo-Indian to European contact periods emphasizes adaptation to changing environments.

Schávelzon, Daniel. Arqueología histórica de Buenos Aires. v. 1, La cultura material porteña de los siglos XVIII y XIX. See *HLAS 56:3122.*

435 Sempé, María Carlota and **María Amanda Caggiano.** Las culturas agroalfareras del Alto Uruguay, Misiones, Argentina. (*Rev. Mus. Arqueol. Etnol.*, 5, 1995, p. 27–38, bibl., ill., map, tables)

Provides detailed tabulation of pottery types by level from excavations at two habitation sites of the Tupiguarani Tradition; a single C14 date of AD 1030.

436 Stern, Charles R. *et al.* Obsidiana negra de los sitios arqueológicos en la precordillera andina de Patagonia central. (*An. Inst. Patagon./Hum.*, 23, 1995, p. 111–118, bibl., map, tables)

Similarity of trace elements, strontium isotopic composition, and age indicates black ryolite obsidian in three areas is from the same unidentified source.

437 Yacobaccio, Hugo D. Etnoarqueología de pastores surandinos: una herramienta para conocer el registro arqueológico. (*in* Jornadas de Arqueología e Interdisciplinas, *Buenos Aires, 1993*. Actas. Buenos Aires: Consejo Nacional de Investigaciones Científicas y Técnicas, Programa de Estudios Prehistóricas, 1994, p. 203–236, bibl., graphs, map, tables)

Data on composition of herds, butchering, processing, and disposal collected during the annual round of a contemporary group from a permanent base to two temporary camps in the *puna* of Jujuy are used to evaluate inferences from 100 collections of bones from all three locations. Results provide important insights into bias of the archaeological record.

BOLIVIA

438 Albarracín-Jordán, Juan. Tiwanaku, arqueología regional y dinámica segmentaria. La Paz: Plural Editores, 1996. 393 p.: bibl., ill. (some col.).

Based on evidence obtained at 17 preceramic, 20 early Tiwanaku, 3 classic Tiwanaku, 1 late Tiwanaku, and 4 Inca sites, argues that interpretations of State formation have been distorted by European perspective. Archaeological, historical, and ethnographic evidence support a segmentary State model rather than a centralized bureaucracy.

439 Alconini Mujica, Sonia. Algunas reflexiones sobre la formación de la arqueología en Bolivia. (*Etnología/La Paz*, 15:19, 1991, p. 57–68)

Character and degree of support for archeology reflect changing perceptions of its political relevance.

440 Alconini Mujica, Sonia. Rito, símbolo e historia en la pirámide de Akapana, Tiwanaku: un análisis de cerámica ceremonial prehispánica. La Paz: Editorial Acción, 1995. 238 p.: bibl., ill.

Uses a new ceramic chronology based on vessel form and function to define four periods from AD 400–1150, permitting reconstruction of the rise and abandonment of the pyramid and its symbolic and social significance.

441 Barba, Josep; Efraín Barbery; and Jordi Juan. Lago Pajaral: nuevos petroglifos en el oriente boliviano. (*Rev. Arqueol./Madrid*, 15:162, oct. 1994, p. 24–29, bibl., maps, photos)

Concentric rings and anthropomorphic faces occur on boulders subject to inundation in Santa Cruz Province.

442 Bermann, Marc. Lukurmata: household archaeology in prehispanic Bolivia. Princeton, N.J.: Princeton Univ. Press, 1994. 307 p.: bibl., ill., index, maps.

Comparison of "capital-centric" and local household perspectives using a 1,500-year-long chronology of pottery, artifacts, and architecture at Lukurmata identifies Tiwanaku as a State rather than a trade or religious network. The greatest changes occurred in shape, size, layout, and diversity of household buildings; domestic pottery remained relatively stable.

443 Escalante Moscoso, Javier F. Arquitectura prehispánica en los Andes bolivianos. La Paz: CIMA, 1993. 507 p.: bibl., ill.

Wankarani, Chiripa, Tiwanaku, Mollo, Señoríos Aymaras, and Inca architecture are liberally illustrated with plans, elevations, structural details, measurements, reconstructions, and photographs. Specifications of materials, standards of measurement, and other details make this a valuable reference.

444 Estudios arqueológicos del período formativo en el sur-este de Cochabamba, 1988–1989. Cochabamba, Bolivia: Univ. Mayor de San Simón, Instituto Antropológico y Museo, 1995. 180 p.: bibl., ill., maps. (Cuadernos de investigación. Serie Arqueología; 8)

A relative ceramic chronology derived from stratigraphic excavations at four sites defines three periods in a continuing tradition extending from 3395 to 2065 BP (11 C14 dates), after which the region suffered a population decline.

445 Ponce Sanginés, Carlos. Arqueología política y el estado precolombiano de Tiwanaku. (*Pumapunku/La Paz*, 4:8, enero 1995, p. 15–87, bibl., facsims., map, photos)

Reviews alternative theories on the identity of Tiwanaku, concluding that it was a State and that its capital was an urban center.

446 **Ponce Sanginés, Carlos.** Tiwanaku, 200 años de investigaciones arqueológicas. La Paz: Producciones CIMA, 1995. 448 p.: bibl., ill., index, photos.

Historical overview by a leading participant includes photographs of all significant investigators and descriptions of selected fieldwork.

447 **Stanish, Charles et al.** Archaeological survey in the southwestern Lake Titicaca Basin. (*Diálogo Andin.*, 1995/96, p. 97–143, bibl., ill., maps)

Provides typologies of sites, ceramics, and tombs, and their spatial and temporal distributions, based on nearly 500 single and multi-component sites in a 360 sq. km. area.

448 **Stanish, Charles.** The hydraulic hypothesis revisited: Lake Titicaca Basin raised fields in theoretical perspective. (*Lat. Am. Antiq.*, 5, 1994, p. 312–332, bibl., maps, tables)

Data support a causal link between increasing agricultural productivity and political complexity, but indicate that managerial control by an elite was not a significant factor.

449 **Tiwanaku and its hinterland: archaeology and paleoecology of an Andean civilization.** v. 1, Agroecology. Edited by Alan L. Kolata. Washington: Smithsonian Institution Press, 1996- . 1 v: bibl., ill., index, maps. (Smithsonian series in archaeological inquiry)

Discusses physical environment, paleoecology, raised fields, groundwater control, nutrient fluxes, long-term sustainability, experimental rehabilitation, and impact of climate fluctuations on the decline of the Tiwanaku State.

450 **Walter, Heinz** and **Hermann Trimborn.** Investigaciones de arqueólogos alemanes en Bolivia. Buenos Aires: Centro Argentino de Etnología Americana, 1994. 136 p.: bibl., ill. (Col. Mankacén)

Translations of articles originally published in German in 1966 and 1967 on excavations of Huancarani Mound in La Paz Department and on Samaipata, the "sculptured mountain" near Santa Cruz.

BRAZIL

451 **Afonso, Marisa C.** and **Paulo A.D. de Blasis.** Aspectos da formação de um grande sambaqui: alguns indicadores em Es-

pinheiros II, Joinville. (*Rev. Mus. Arqueol. Etnol.*, 4, 1994, p. 21–30, bibl., graphs, map, photos)

Salvage excavations provide C14 dates of 2970 ± 60, 1270 ± 120, and 1160 ± 45 BP.

452 **Aguilar, Alice.** Bibliografia sobre registros rupestres no nordeste do Brasil. (*Clio Arqueol./Recife*, 11, 1996, p. 187–200)

Useful compilation of publications to 1994.

453 **Albuquerque, Paulo Tadeu de Souza.** Projeto arqueológico "O Homem das Dunas," RN. (*Clio Arqueol./Recife*, 1 : 10, 1994, p. 175–188, bibl., map, photos)

Dunes throughout coastal Rio Grande do Norte produced lithics of the Itaparica Tradition; pottery of the Tupiguarani Tradition and a local tradition was also encountered.

454 **Alves, Marcia Angelina.** As estruturas arqueológicas do Alto Paranaíba e Triângulo Mineiro—Minas Gerais. (*Rev. Mus. Arqueol. Etnol.*, 2, 1992, p. 27–47, bibl., graphs, maps, photos)

Provides maps of patches of dark soil at six sites, but no information on associated lithics or ceramics.

455 **Arqueología nos empreendimentos hidrelétricos da ELETRONORTE: resultados preliminares = Archeology in the hydroelectric projects of ELETRONORTE: preliminary results.** Brasília: Centrais Elétricas do Norte do Brasil, 1992. 93 p.: bibl., ill. (some col.).

Site locations, settlement patterns, pottery types, lithics, seriated sequences, and C14 dates document prehistoric occupation on the lower Jamarí, Rondônia (Usina Hidrelétrica Samuel); the lower Uatumã, Amazônas (Usina Hidrelétrica Balbina); and the lower Tocantins, Pará (Usina Hidrelétrica Tucuruí). Evidence in all three regions supports adoption by 2000 BP of settlement behavior characteristic of contemporary indigenous groups.

456 ***Arquivos do Museu de História Natural.*** Vol. 15/16, 1994/1995. Bibliografia da arqueologia brasileira. Belo Horizonte, Brazil: Museu de História Natural, Univ. Federal de Minas Gerais.

Academic publications, unpublished manuscripts, and abstracts on archaeology and related topics are arranged alphabetically by author.

457 **Barbosa, Márcia; Maria Dulce Gaspar;** and **Débora Rocha Barbosa.** A organização espacial das estruturas habitacionais e distribuição dos artefatos no sítio Ilha da Boa Visa I, Cabo Frio—R.J. (*Rev. Mus. Arqueol. Etnol.*, 4, 1994, p. 31–38, bibl., graph, tables)

Spatial differences in domestic activities are inferred from frequencies of stone, shell, and bone artifacts in the habitation zone and surrounding area of a shell midden.

458 **Barreto, Maura Vianna.** História da pesquisa arqueológica no Museu Paraense Emílio Goeldi. (*Bol. Mus. Para. Goeldi*, 8:2, 1992, p. 203–294, bibl., ill., map)

Synthesis of archaeological investigations conducted by staff since Museum's inception is especially useful for descriptions of unpublished fieldwork in eastern Amazonia during the past decade.

459 **Beber, Marcus Vinicius.** Arte rupestre do nordeste do Mato Grosso do Sul. São Leopoldo, Brazil: Instituto Anchietano de Pesquisas/UNISINOS, 1995. 157 p.: bibl., ill., map, tables.

Superpositions in four rock shelters indicate three styles: the earliest with red and yellow geometric motifs, the second with monochrome geometric motifs, and the most recent with biomorphic figures.

460 **Dantas, José de Azevedo.** Indícios de uma civilização antiquíssima. Text and preface by Gabriela Martin. João Pessoa, Brazil: Fundação Casa de José Américo; Instituto Histórico e Geográfico Paraibano, 1994. 200 p.: ill.

Publication of manuscript and 156 plates with rock art from Rio Grande do Norte, dated 1926, from the library of the Instituto Histórico e Geográfico Paraibano.

461 **Denevan, William M.** A bluff model of riverine settlement in prehistoric Amazonia. (*Ann. Assoc. Am. Geogr.*, 86:4, Dec. 1996, p. 654–681, bibl., maps, tables)

Retreats from previous estimates of large floodplain settlements, but argues that high density could be sustained on bluffs by combining floodplain and terra firme resources.

462 **Dias, Ondemar F.** Considerações a respeito dos modelos de difusão da cerâmica Tupi-Guarani no Brasil. (*Rev. Arqueol./São Paulo*, 8:2, 1994/95, p. 113–132, bibl., tables)

Defends western derivation based on priority of southern C14 and TL dates and on dissimilarity of coastal and Amazonian painted decoration.

463 **Dias, Ondemar F.** As origens da horticultura no Brasil. (*Rev. Arqueol. Am.*, 7, 1993, p. 7–52, bibl.)

Reviews direct and indirect evidence in preceramic sites for incipient cultivation, including environmental context, climatic changes, plant remains, settlement pattern, tool wear, and dental attrition.

464 **Galindo, Marcos.** Dois sítios da Tradição Nordeste em Pernambuco. (*Clio Arqueol./Recife*, 1:10, 1994, p. 125–134, bibl., facsims., maps)

First documentation of rock art of the Northeast Tradition in Pernambuco.

465 **Girelli, Maribel.** Pesquisas arqueológicas no Pantanal do Mato Grosso do Sul. (*Estud. Leopold.*, 32:147, maio/junho 1996, p. 91–107, ill., map, photos)

Describes petroglyphs extending across four large, horizontal granite outcrops, consisting principally of circles and small pits without systematic arrangement.

466 **Guidon, Niède et al.** Nature and age of the deposits in Pedra Furada, Brazil: reply to Meltzer, Adovasio, and Dillehay. (*Antiquity/Cambridge*, 70:268, June 1996, p. 408–421, bibl., ill.)

Authors argue that comments by Meltzer et al. (see item **472**) are based on "partial and incorrect knowledge."

467 **Kern, Arno Alvarez.** Antecedentes indígenas. Porto Alegre, Brazil: Editora da Univ. Federal do Rio Grande do Sul, 1994. 139 p.: bibl., ill., maps. (Síntese rio-grandense; 16–17)

Presents authoritative overview of prehistory of Rio Grande do Sul in the context of environmental change, population movements, and cultural diffusion.

468 **Kern, Dirse C. et al.** O potencial espeleoarqueológico da região de São Geraldo do Araguaia-PA. (*Bol. Mus. Para. Goeldi*, 8:2, 1992, p. 157–183, bibl., ill.)

Survey in the Andorinhas hill region recorded 14 rock shelters with preceramic occupation, several Tupiguarani Tradition sites, and two rock art locations, one extending across a horizontal surface 50m x 250m.

469 Machado, Lilia Cheuiche and **Lina Maria Kneip.** Padrões dentários, dieta e subsistência das populações dos sambaquis de Saquarema, RJ. (*Rev. Arqueol. /São Paulo,* 8:1, 1994, p. 45–57, bibl.)

Comparison of trauma on teeth from three shell middens revealed a 50 percent higher frequency of the severe abrasion to be associated with emphasis on molluscs over fish.

470 Martin, Gabriela. Os rituais funerários na pré-história do Nordeste. (*Clio Arqueol./Recife,* 1:10, 1994, p. 29–46, bibl., ill., map)

Describes burials from four locations, including Pedra do Alexandre with three skeletons dating prior to 8000 BP.

471 Meggers, Betty J. Amazonia: man and culture in a counterfeit paradise. Rev. ed. Washington: Smithsonian Institution Press, 1996. 214 p.: bibl., ill., index, maps.

Epilogue reviews recent archaeological evidence for the precolumbian antiquity of social and settlement behavior of indigenous Amazonian groups. For annotations of first edition of this work see *HLAS 35:1293* and *7107.*

Meggers, Betty J. Amazonia on the eve of European contact: ethnohistorical, ecological, and anthropological perspectives. See item **595.**

472 Meltzer, David J.; James M. Adovasio; and **Tom D. Dillehay.** On a Pleistocene human occupation at Pedra Furada, Brazil. (*Antiquity/Cambridge,* 68:261, Dec. 1994, p. 695–714, bibl., ill.)

Authors reject human occupation prior to ca. 10,000 BP, based on extensive experience in Paleo-Indian excavations and inspection of the site, artifacts, and environment. See also item **466.**

473 Milder, Saul Eduardo Seiguer. Uma breve análise da fase arqueológica Ibicuí. (*Rev. CEPA,* 19:22, março 1995, p. 41–63, bibl., ill., map)

Disputes association between lithics and Pleistocene fauna based on reevaluation of the stratigraphic evidence.

474 Noelli, Francisco Silva. Os Jê do Brasil meridional e a antigüidade da agricultura: elementos da lingüística, arqueologia e

etnografia. (*Estud. Ibero-Am. /Porto Alegre,* 22:1, junho 1996, p. 13–25, bibl.)

Ethnobotanic and linguistic evidence supplements archaeological data for establishing antiquity of agriculture and the latter's role in promoting defense of territorial boundaries.

475 Noelli, Francisco Silva. Por uma revisão das hipóteses sobre os centros de origem e rotas de expansão pré-históricas dos Tupi. (*Estud. Ibero-Am. /Porto Alegre,* 20:1, julho 1994, p. 107–135, bibl.)

Reviews disagreements among linguists, ethnologists, historians, and archeologists concerning origin and dispersal of speakers of Tupi languages.

476 Ott, Carlos. As culturas pré-históricas da Bahia. v. 1–2. Salvador, Brazil?: Editora Bigraf, 1993- . 2 v.: bibl., ill., maps.

Polemic and idiosyncratic review of the history of archaeology in Bahia rejects archaeological interpretations by Valentin Calderón de la Vara and linguistic reconstructions by Aryon Dall'Igna Rodrigues.

477 Parenti, Fabio. Estratigrafia do Caldeirão do Rodriguez, São Raimundo Nonato, Piauí. (*Clio Arqueol./Recife,* 11, 1996, p. 119–135, bibl., ill.)

Recent excavations affirm occupation 10,000–6000 BP related to production of rock art.

478 Pesquisas. No. 52, 1996. Arqueologia nos cerrados do Brasil central: sudoeste da Bahia e leste de Goiás; o Projeto Serra Geral. São Leopoldo, Brazil: Instituto Anchietano de Pesquisas.

Survey along the Rio Corrente and two tributaries sampled *cerrado* and *caatinga* environments. Preceramic sites predominate, represented by open camps in the *cerrado* and rock shelters in the *caatinga.* Late ceramic occupations affiliate with the Una Phase; intrusion by the Tupiguarani Tradition, Painted Subtradition is rare.

479 Pesquisas. No. 53, 1996. Escavações arqueológicas do Pe. João Alfredo Rohr, S.J. São Leopoldo, Brazil: Instituto Anchietano de Pesquisas.

Detailed descriptions of sites, faunal remains, burials, and artifacts from two preceramic and one ceramic (Itararé Tradition) sites excavated by Rohr on the Santa Catarina coast. Preceramic dates extend from 4515 to 3815 BP.

480 Programa de salvamento arqueológico da UHE Nova Ponte: atividades desenvolvidas pelo Centro de Estudos e Pesquisas Arqueológicas-CEPA, Universidade Federal do Paraná; relatório final. Belo Horizonte, Brazil: Leme Engenharia, 1995. 345 p.: bibl., ill., maps.

Survey on the lower Rio Quebra Azul, western Minas Gerais, documented two preceramic and three ceramic traditions. Aratu/Sapucaí Tradition sites predominate; Tupiguarani and Neobrasilian presence is slight.

481 Prous, André; Marcos Eugênio Brito; and Márcio Alonso. As ocupações ceramistas no Vale do Rio Peruaçu, MG. *(Rev. Mus. Arqueol. Etnol.,* 4, 1994, p. 71–94, bibl., ill., map, photos)

Differences in lithics, ceramics, shell, bone, and plant remains from rock shelters and surface sites identify the Una and Tupiguarani Traditions and a possible early historic occupation during the past two millennia.

482 Prous, André; Emílio Fogaça; and Márcio Alonso. As últimas indústrias líticas do Vale do Peruaçu, MG-Brasil. *(Rev. Arqueol./São Paulo,* 8:2, 1994/95, p. 49–64, bibl., ill.)

The lithic industry associated with ceramics is dominated by tools made from thick cortical flakes.

483 Registros rupestres: formas de levantamento e conservação; novas metodologias de pesquisa. *(Rev. Arqueol./São Paulo,* 8:1, 1994, p. 283–364, bibl., ill.)

Six articles discuss classification and significance of rock art from various parts of northeastern Brazil.

484 Reunião Científica da Sociedade de Arqueologia Brasileira, 7th, João Pessoa, Brazil, 1993. Actas. João Pessoa, Brazil: UFPB/Editora Universitária, 1993? 205 p.

Abstracts of papers on the archaeology of coastal Brazil and Uruguay, with emphasis on northeastern Brazil.

485 Reunião Científica da Sociedade de Arqueologia Brasileira, 8th, Porto Alegre, Brazil, 1995. Anais. v. 1–2. Organização de Arno Alvarez Kern. Porto Alegre, Brazil:

EDIPUCRS, 1996. 2 v.: bibl., ill., maps. (Col. Arqueologia; 1)

Symposia discuss history of Brazilian archeology, historical archeology, rock art, coastal sites, hunter-gatherers, agriculturalists, and human skeletal remains.

486 Ribeiro, Pedro Augusto Mentz. Arqueologia do vale do Rio Pardo, Rio Grande do Sul, Brasil. *(Biblos/Rio de Janeiro,* 7, 1995, p. 9–87, tables)

Authoritative overview of environment, settlement, subsistence, chronology, and other features of the major lithic and ceramic traditions, and their interactions from 10,000 BP to European contact, is followed by a detailed list of wild subsistence resources, a glossary, and a bibliography of 442 titles.

487 Ribeiro, Pedro Augusto Mentz. Levantamentos arqueológicos no médio e alto Jacuí, Brasil. *(Biblos/Rio de Janeiro,* 8, 1996, p. 9–42, bibl., ill., photos)

Preliminary descriptions of ceramics and lithics from 47 habitation sites of the Guaratã Phase, Tupiguarani Tradition, Corrugated Subtradition.

488 Schaan, Denise Pahl. A linguagem iconográfica da cerâmica Marajoara: um estudo da arte pré-histórica na Ilha de Marajó, Brasil, AD 400–1300. Porto Alegre, Brazil: EDIPUCRS, 1997. 207 p.: bibl., ill., map. (Col. Arqueologia; 3)

Detailed analysis of motifs on specimens from more than seven sites identifies 52 minimal units of potential iconographic significance.

489 Schmitz, Pedro Ignácio. Serranópolis II: pinturas e gravuras dos abrigos. Colaboração de Fabíola Andréa Silva e Marcus Vinícius Beber. São Leopoldo, Brazil: Instituto Anchietano de Pesquisas/UNISINOS, 1997. 65 p., 97 plates: bibl., ill., maps. (Publicações avulsas; 11)

Detailed illustration of painted and incised figures from 26 rockshelters along the Rio Verde, Goiás, dating from 11000–1000 BP. Includes tabulation by technique, color, abundance, motif, spatial distribution, and comparison with adjacent areas.

490 Tocchetto, Fernanda Bordin. Possibilidades de interpretação do conteúdo simbólico da arte gráfica Guarani. *(Estud. Ibero-Am./Porto Alegre,* 22:1, junho 1996, p. 27–45, bibl., ill.)

Meaning of three motifs on precolumbian painted vessels is inferred from their mythological significance among surviving Guaraní speakers.

491 Whitehead, Neil L. Ethnic transformation and historical discontinuity in Native Amazonia and Guayana, 1500–1900. (*Homme/Paris*, 33 : 126/128, avril/déc. 1993, p. 285–305, bibl.)

Argues that "assumptions" concerning environmental limitations and misuse of historical data have biased recognition of prehistorical cultural complexity and population density.

CHILE

492 Adovasio, J.M. and D.R. Pedler. Monte Verde and the antiquity of humankind in the Americas. (*Antiquity/Cambridge*, 71:273, Sept. 1997, p. 573–580, bibl., ill.)

Personal examination of site and artifacts in 1997 by selected US Paleo-Indian specialists produced unanimous agreement on a minimum antiquity 1,000 years prior to Clovis.

493 Aguilera A., Nelson and Paola Grendi I. Hallazgo de un chenque protoaonikenk en Juni Aike, Magallanes. (*An. Inst. Patagon./Hum.*, 24, 1996, p. 163–175, bibl., ill., map, photos)

Burials representing three successive periods permit reconstructing changes in treatment of the dead since European contact.

494 Arriaza, Bernardo T. Beyond death: the Chinchorro mummies of ancient Chile. Foreword by John W. Verano. Washington: Smithsonian Institution Press, 1995. 176 p.: bibl., ill. (some col.), index.

Comprehensive study of 282 examples permits classification, description, and interpretation of mummification techniques and of details of health, diet, technology, settlement, and society between 5000 and 1700 BC. Argues that mummification was invented in Arica-Camerones region to insure continuity of life in the context of environmental uncertainty. See also item **495** and **496**.

495 Arriaza, Bernardo T. Chinchorro bioarchaeology: chronology and mummy seriation. (*Lat. Am. Antiq.*, 6, 1995, p. 35–55, bibl., ill., tables)

Chronological changes and geographical distribution of Chinchorro mummies indicate emergence in the Arica region ca. 5000 BP in the context of continuous settlement by a maritime-adapted population. See also item **494** and **496**.

496 Arriaza, Bernardo T. Tipología de las momias Chinchorro y evolución de las prácticas de momificación. (*Chungará/Arica*, 26, 1994, p. 11–24, bibl., ill.)

Red, Black, Bandage, Mud-coated, and Natural types correlate positively with chronology and negatively with quantity of associated offerings. See also items **495** and **494**.

497 Cartajena, Isabel. Determinación de restos óseos de camélidos en dos yacimientos del Loa Medio, II Región. (*Estud. Atacameños*, 11, 1994, p. 25–52, bibl., ill., tables)

Criteria for discriminating four species of camelids, defined using contemporary mixed assemblages, are applied to samples from Chiuchiu cemetery and Chiuchiu 200.

498 Congreso Nacional de Arqueología Chilena, 13th, Antofagasta, Chile, 1994. Actas. v. 1–2. Antofagasta, Chile: Univ. de Antofagasta, Instituto de Investigaciones Antropológicas, 1995. 2 v.

Seventy-two articles discuss development of coastal communities, interregional relations, local chronology, and inferences from lithics, textiles, ceramics, basketry, mortuary practices, and faunal remains in northern Chile. *Actas* published in journal *Hombre y Desierto: Una Perspectiva Cultural*, v. 9, 1995 (see item **506**).

499 Costa-Junqueira, María Antonietta and Agustín Llagostera M. Coyo-3: momentos finales del período medio en San Pedro de Atacama. (*Estud. Atacameños*, 11, 1994, p. 73–107, bibl., ill., tables)

Associations of ceramic features in burials imply two moieties, also characterized by quantitative and qualitative differences in occurrence of skull deformation, hallucinogenic paraphernalia, copper and gold objects, and camelid remains.

500 Dillehay, Tom D. Monte Verde: a late Pleistocene settlement in Chile. v. 2, The archaeological context and interpretation. Washington: Smithsonian Institution Press, 1997. 1 v.: appendices, bibl., ill., index, tables. (Smithsonian series in archaeological inquiry)

Detailed descriptions of fieldwork, environment, stratigraphy, radiocarbon chronology, research design, organic preservation, wood assemblage, cordage, microtopography, modern plant use, archaeobotanical identifications, lithics, faunal remains, and activity patterning provide the most comprehensive evidence yet assembled in support of human occupation in South America contemporary with the earliest North American sites. Data are combined to infer diet, activities, land use, foraging strategy, medicinal knowledge, and other components of daily life.

501 Dillehay, Tom D. Vue générale des éléments trouvés pendant la campagne de recherche et implications culturelles dans le site du pléistocène final de Monte Verde, Chile. (*Anthropologie/Paris*, 98, 1994, p. 128–148, bibl., ill., map, tables)

Summarizes stratigraphy, taphonomic, botanical, faunal, and cultural remains dating from 13,000 BP.

502 Falabella, Fernanda *et al.* Nuevos antecedentes sobre los sistemas culturales en Chile central sobre la base de análisis de composición de elementos. (*Rev. Chil. Antropol.*, 13, 1995/96, p. 29–59, bibl., ill., tables)

Compositional analysis of bone and pottery from two sites reveals differences between preceramic and ceramic populations, and between coastal and interior populations, incompatible with a model of transhumance and redistribution of goods.

503 Fedorova, I.K. Doshchechki kokhau rongorongo iz Kunstkamery. [Kohau Rongo-Rongo tablets in the Peter the Great Museum of Anthropology and Ethnography.] Saint Peterburg: Rossiĭskaia akademiia nauk, Muzeĭ antropologii i ėtnografii im. Petra Velikogo, 1995. 155 p.: ill.

The author, a long-time scholar of Rapa Nui culture and ethnohistory, describes her principles for decoding ancient Rongo-Rongo texts. She also provides the texts of the tablets preserved in the museum and a "catalog" of the glyphs or symbols. She identifies the script as hieroglyphic and indigenous. Includes English-language summary and table of contents. [B. Dash]

504 Gallardo I., Francisco; Mauricio Uribe R.; and Patricia Ayala R. Arquitectura inka y poder en el Pukara de Turi, norte de Chile. (*Gac. Arqueol. Andin.*, 24, 1995, p. 151–171, bibl., ill.)

Archaeological and ethnohistoric information are combined to infer ideological and dominance significance of spatial organization and architecture.

505 Graffam, Gray; Mario Rivera; and Alvaro Carevic. Copper smelting in the Atacama: ancient metallurgy at the Ramaditas Site, northern Chile. (*in* Quest of mineral wealth. Baton Rouge: Louisiana State Univ., 1994, p. 75–92, bibl., ill., tables)

Analysis of samples dating ca. 2000 BP indicates a different process than was used at Batán Grande, Peru.

506 *Hombre y Desierto: Una Perspectiva Cultural.* Vol. 9, pts. 1–2, 1995. Antofagasta, Chile: Univ. de Antofagasta, Instituto de Investigaciones Antropológicas.

See item **498**.

507 Jackson Squella, Donald and Antonia Benavente Aninat. Secuencia, cambios y adaptación de los cazadores-recolectores de la microcuenca de Chiu-Chiu, provincia del Loa. (*Chungará/Arica*, 26, 1994, p. 49–64, bibl., ill.)

Changes in lithic assemblages from excavations at three sites permit reconstructing the transition from wild foods to camelid domestication and adoption of pottery ca. 900 BC.

Jornadas de Arqueología de la Patagonia, 2nd, Puerto Madryn, Argentina, 1993. Ponencias. See item **422**.

508 Llagostera M., Agustín. El componente cultural Aguada en San Pedro de Atacama. (*Bol. Mus. Chil. Arte Precolomb.*, 6, 1995, p. 9–34, bibl., ill.)

Associations among textiles, baskets, and wooden objects in 23 tombs imply regional exchange network related to shamanism.

509 Lynch, Thomas F. and Lautaro Núñez A. Nuevas evidencias inkas entre Kollahuasi y Río Frío, I y II Regiones de Chile. (*Estud. Atacameños*, 11, 1994, p. 145–164, bibl., ill., maps)

Identifies the exact route of the Inca road, as well as associated structures and their possible functions.

510 Massone Mezzano, Mauricio; Donald Jackson; and Alfredo Prieto. Perspectiva arqueológica de los selk'nam. Santiago: Dirección de Bibliotecas, Archivos y Museos, Centro de Investigaciones Diego Barros Arana, 1993. 170 p.: bibl., ill., maps. (Col. de antropología; 1)

Stratigraphy, spatial distribution, and characteristics of artifacts, fauna, and other remains in two regions of northern Tierra del Fuego are interpreted in the context of ethnographic data and experimental replication of cooking and flintknapping activities.

511 Molina, Yéssica *et al.* Uso y posible cultivo de coca (Erythroxylum spp.) en época prehispánicas en los valles de Arica. (*Chungará/Arica*, 23, dic. 1989, p. 37–49, bibl., photos, tables)

Anatomical and histological analyses of 57 samples of leaves from Tiwanaku-period tombs suggest coca was cultivated locally, rather than imported, after ca. AD 300.

512 Nami, Hugo Gabriel. Observaciones sobre desechos de talla procedentes de las ocupaciones tempranas de Tres Arroyos—Tierra del Fuego, Chile. (*An. Inst. Patagon./Hum.*, 22, 1993/94, p. 175–180, bibl., ill., graphs, photo, table)

Experimental replication establishes the use of bifacial technology among the earliest populations.

513 Núñez A., Lautaro and **Martin Grosjean.** Cambios ambientales pleistoceno-holocénicos: ocupación humana y uso de recursos en la Puna de Atacama, norte de Chile. (*Estud. Atacameños*, 11, 1994, p. 11–24, bibl., graphs, ill., tables)

Abandonment of high elevations ca. 8500 BP correlates with reduction in subsistence resources attributable to increased aridity.

514 Núñez A., Lautaro and **Francisco Mena.** El caso Monte Verde: ¿hacia un veredicto final? (*Bol. Soc. Chil. Arqueol.*, 24, 1997, p. 38–44)

Gives Chilean perspective on implications of formal recognition of the antiquity of occupation at Monte Verde.

515 Núñez A., Lautaro *et al.* Cuenca de Taquatagua en Chile: el ambiente del Pleistoceno Superior y ocupaciones humanas. (*Rev. Chil. Hist. Nat.*, 67, 1994, p. 503–519, bibl., ill., map, tables)

Reconstruction of environmental and cultural events at two locations dated 10,120

and 9900 BP, in which mastodont remains are associated with fishtail points, suggests hunting of megafauna during increasing aridity.

516 Núñez A., Lautaro. Evolución de la ocupación y organización del espacio Atacameño. (*in* Agua, ocupación del espacio y economía campesina en la región Atacameña: aspectos dinámicos. Antofagasta, Chile: Univ. Católica del Norte; Paris: Institut français de recherche scientifique pour le développement en coopération, ORSTOM, 1995, p. 18–60, bibl., ill., maps, tables)

Changes in subsistence and settlement behavior from 3000 BC to present are inferred from sites along a transect from the shore to the Argentine border.

517 Núñez A., Lautaro *et al.* Reconstrucción multidisciplinaria de la ocupación prehistórica de Quereo, centro de Chile. (*Lat. Am. Antiq.*, 5, 1994, p. 99–118, bibl., ill., maps, tables)

Presents paleontological, sedimentological, climatic, and archaeological evidence for human association with extinct horse, ground sloth, mastodon, and camelid ca. 11,000 BP (six C14 dates).

518 Ocampo E., Carlos and **Pilar Rivas H.** Caracterización arqueológica preliminar del suroeste de la Tierra del Fuego. (*An. Inst. Patagon./Hum.*, 24, 1996, p. 125–151, bibl., maps, tables)

Surface collections from 80 locations centered on Río Condor and Lago Blanco are classified according to inferred site function, associated vegetation, subsistence resources, and artifact concentration. Patterns reflect interactions between canoe and terrestrial groups.

519 Orellana Rodríguez, Mario. Historia de la arqueología en Chile, 1842–1990. Santiago: Bravo y Allende Editores, 1996. 217 p.: bibl., ill., ports. (Col. de ciencias sociales)

Changes in theory and in research emphasis are traced for five periods: pre-1882, 1882–1911, 1911–40, 1940–60, and 1960–90. Illustrated with portraits of the most influential figures.

520 Orellana Rodríguez, Mario. Prehistoria y etnología de Chile. Santiago: Univ. de Chile, 1994. 240 p.: bibl., ill. (Col. de Ciencias Sociales)

History of aboriginal Chileans from Paleo-Indian to present, in the context of environmental change, central Andean and European invasions, and integration into modern Chilean society.

521 Patrimonio arqueológico en áreas silvestres protegidas. Recopilación de Mauricio Massone Mezzano y Roxana Seguel. Santiago: Dirección de Bibliotecas, Archivos y Museos; Centro de Investigaciones Diego Barros Arana, 1994. 174 p.: bibl., ill. (Col. de antropología; 3)

Fieldwork in Campana National Park (V Region), Radal Siete Tazas Protected Area (VII Region), and Conguillío National Park emphasized involvement of local communities in the effort to instill understanding of the importance of cultural patrimony.

522 Rees, Charles; Andrea Seelenfreund; and Catherine Westfall. Patrones de asentamiento prehispánicos en el valle del Río Maule, Región Central-Sur de Chile. (*Gac. Arqueol. Andin.*, 23, 1993, p. 139–159, bibl., ill., maps)

Survey data from 39 sites and 51 TL dates extending from AD 200–1700 define three periods characterized by increase in the variety of ceramic decoration, the number of settlements, and regional differentiation.

523 Santos Varela, Mariela. Posibles evidencias de hornos alfareros en la desembocadura del valle de Camarones: períodos Intermedio Tardío, Tardío. (*Chungará/Arica*, 23, dic. 1989, p. 7–18, appendix, bibl., maps, photos)

Clay composition, camelid guano, polishing stones, poorly fired sherds, concentration of Na and K, dimensions, and ventilation documented in five hearths indicate use for firing pottery.

524 Seelenfreund, Andrea. Análisis de restos botánicos de dos sitios alfareros tempranos in la Bahía de las Cañas, VII Región. (*Rev. Chil. Antropol.*, 13, 1995/96, p. 61–78, bibl., ill., map, tables)

Except for Cucurbita, identifiable plants were used for construction and manufacturing.

525 Standen, Vivien G. Temprana complejidad funeraria de la cultura Chinchorro, norte de Chile. (*Lat. Am. Antiq.*, 8:2, 1997, p. 134–156, bibl., ill., map, tables)

Examines presence of artificial mummification in 134 burials representing three classes of interrments, and finds highest frequency and greatest diversity of techniques among fetuses, neonates, lactating infants, and children.

526 Stehberg Landsberger, Rubén. Instalaciones incaicas en el norte y centro semiárido de Chile. Santiago: Dirección de Bibliotecas, Archivos y Museos; Centro de Investigaciones Diego Barros Arana, 1995. 224 p.: bibl., ill. (Col. de antropología; 2)

Investigations in area between Río Copiapó and Río Rapel suggest Inca impact was earlier and stronger than assumed. The highway network and associated structures are described and illustrated.

527 Van Tilburg, JoAnne. Moving the Moai: transporting the megaliths of Easter Island; how did they do it? (*Archaeology/New York*, 48:1, Jan./Feb. 1995, p. 34–43, ill., maps, photos)

Computer modeling identifies the most efficient method of moving statues, manpower requirements, optimum daily diet, and implications for societal support.

528 Westfall, Catherine. Pipas prehispánicas de Chile: discusión en torno a su distribución y contexto. (*Rev. Chil. Antropol.*, 12, 1993/94, p. 123–161, bibl., ill., maps)

Summary of morphology, provenience, date, and cultural affiliation by general regions, with illustrations of the principal types.

COLOMBIA

529 Arqueología de rescate, Oleoducto Vasconia-Coveñas: un viaje por el tiempo a lo largo del Oleoducto; cazadores-recolectores, agroaleareros y orfebres. Bogotá: Oleoducto de Colombia, 1994. 273 p.: bibl., ill. (some col.).

Provides descriptions of sites, excavations, and lithic and ceramic artifacts for three environmental zones between the Caribbean coast and Bogotá. Correlation with previously documented complexes, detailed maps, and abundant illustrations make this a useful reference.

Arte indígena en Colombia: cultures del món, Castell de Bellver. See item **1123**.

530 **Bioantropología de la Sabana de Bogotá, siglos VIII al XVI DC.** Recopilación de Braida Elena Enciso y Monika Therrien. Bogotá: Instituto Colombiano de Antropología-Colcultura, 1996. 1 v.: bibl., ill., maps, tables. (Recuperación y reinterpretación de datos arqueológicos de la Sabana de Bogotá; 2)

Topics include animals in Muisca society, fauna from three sites, remains of cultigens, diet, dental attrition, and paleopathology.

Bouchard, Jean-François. Los datos de cronología cultural para el litoral del Pacífico nor-ecuatorial: Período Formativo Tardío y Período de Desarrollo Regional, sur de Colombia—norte del Ecuador. See item **562.**

531 **Bruhns, Karen Olsen.** Archaeological investigations in central Colombia. Oxford, England: Tempus Reparatum, 1995 203 p.: bibl., ill. (BAR international series; 606)

Description of 65 sites, lithics, and ceramics in the Department of Quindío, representing the Middle Cauca and Caldas complexes dating ca. AD 800–1300.

532 **Cardale de Schrimpff, Marianne.** Caminos prehispánicos en Calima: el estudio de caminos precolombinos de la cuenca del alto Río Calima, Cordillera Occidental, Valle del Cauca. Bogotá: Fundación de Investigacones Arqueológicas Nacionales, Banco de la República, 1996. 188 p.: bibl., ill., maps.

Provides detailed descriptions and maps of six roads, associated sites, and excavations. Roads are straight, 3–10 m wide and to 1.5 m deep. Dates imply use between 800 BC and AD 800.

533 **Cárdenas-Arroyo, Felipe.** Complex societies in pre-Hispanic Colombia: the Tairona as a case study. (*in* Chieftains, power & trade: regional interaction in the intermediate area of the Americas = Caciques, intercambio y poder: interacción regional en el área intermedia de las Américas. Bogotá: Depto. de Antropología, Univ. de los Andes, 1996, p. 63–74, maps)

Archaeological and historical evidence suggests that comparison of demographic, environmental, and subsistence aspects of Colombian chiefdoms can illuminate processes leading to evolution of complex societies.

534 **Cárdenas-Arroyo, Felipe.** Paleodieta y paleodemografía en poblaciones arqueológicas muiscas. (*Rev. Colomb. Antropol.,* 30, 1993, p. 129–148, bibl., graphs, tables)

Stable isotope ratios in 18 human bone samples imply high consumption of maize and meat. High infant mortality is reflected in 11.7-year life expectancy.

535 **Compilación bibliográfica e informativa de datos arqueológicos de la Sabana de Bogotá, siglos VIII al XVI DC.** Recopilación de Braida Elena Enciso y Monika Therrien. Bogotá: Instituto Colombiano de Antropología-Colcultura, 1996. 1 v: bibl., maps. (Recuperación y reinterpretación de datos arqueológicos de la Sabana de Bogotá; 1)

Annotated bibliography of 129 titles on the Sabana de Bogotá; a list of titles on the Antiplano Cundiboyacense; indices to author, geographic location, and type of document; bibliographic sources of pottery types; and maps locating archaeological sites make this a valuable reference.

536 **Drennan, Robert D.** Chiefdoms in northern South America. (*J. World Prehist.,* 9, 1995, p. 301–340, bibl., map)

Applying four criteria for identifying chiefdoms (warfare, intensive agriculture, centralized storage and local redistribution, and long-distance exchange) to coastal Ecuador and four regions in Colombia reveals wide variation in their occurrence and intensity.

Echeverría Almeida, José and **María Victoria Uribe.** Area septentrional andina norte: arqueología y etnohistoria. See item **574.**

537 **Enciso, Braida Elena.** El ocaso del sol de los venados: arqueología de rescate en la Sabana de Bogotá. (*Rev. Colomb. Antropol.,* 30, 1993, p. 149–182, bibl., graphs, maps, photos, tables)

Analyses of animal bones from a site dated ca. AD 1000 revealed predominance of Odcocoilous, a minority of Mazama, and occasional birds, fish, and small mammals.

538 **Falchetti de Sáenz, Ana María.** El oro del gran Zenu: metalurgia prehispánica en las llanuras del Caribe colombiano. Bogotá: Banco de la República, Museo del Oro, 1995. 354 p., 1 folded leaf of plates: bibl., ill. (some col.), maps. (Col. bibliográfica. Antropología)

Detailed analysis and classification of ca. 5,000 objects from the coastal plain west of Río Magalena based on technology, form, function, and decoration identify five regional styles defined by differences in staff heads, horizontally elongated nose ornaments, filigree earrings, and mammiform pectorals. Important source on precolumbian goldworking.

539   Gnecco, Cristóbal and **Santiago Mora Camargo.** Late Pleistocene/early Holocene tropical forest occupations at San Isidro and Peña Roja, Colombia. (*Antiquity/Cambridge*, 71:273, Sept. 1997, p. 683–690, bibl., ill.)

Lithic assemblages from the Popayán Valley and middle Río Caquetá indicate humans occupied tropical forests since at least the end of the Pleistocene.

540   Gnecco, Cristóbal. Prácticas funerarias como expresiones políticas: una perspectiva desde el suroccidente de Colombia. (*Rev. Colomb. Antropol.*, 32, 1995, p. 85–102)

Evaluates archaeological evidence for four models of social organization inferred from burial practices and concludes none can be eliminated or confirmed.

541   Gnecco, Cristóbal. Relaciones de intercambio y bienes de elite entre los cacicazgos del suroccidente de Colombia. (*in* Chieftains, power & trade: regional interaction in the intermediate area of the Americas = Caciques, intercambio y poder: interacción regional en el área intermedia de las Américas. Bogotá: Depto. de Antropología, Univ. de los Andes, 1996, p. 175–196, map)

Similarities in metal objects encountered in burials imply an extensive network of alliances among elites, rather than cultural homogeneity.

542   Gnecco, Cristóbal and **Amal Mohammed.** Tecnología de cazadores-recolectores subandinos: análisis funcional y organización tecnológica. (*Rev. Colomb. Antropol.*, 31, 1994, p. 5–31, bibl., ill., map, tables)

Functional analysis indicates primary use of lithics for hunting, butchering, and processing bone and hide in spite of tropical forest context favoring concentration on plant resources.

543   Herreman, Frank and **Mireille Holsbeke.** Power of the sun: the gold of Colombia. Antwerp: City of Antwerp; The

Hague: Museum Paleis Lange Voorhout; Snoeck-Ducaju & Zoon, 1993. 187 p.: bibl., ill. (some col.).

Beautiful gold and pottery objects from the principal cultural regions illustrate regional variation in style and manufacture.

544   Lleras Pérez, Roberto. La historia prehispánica tardía del noroeste de Suramérica, 800 a 1500 DC. (*Rev. Arqueol. Am.*, 8, 1995, p. 51–70, bibl., ill.)

Refutes impression that Colombia was marginal to important advances and supports autonomous development during the 700 years prior to European contact.

545   Oyuela-Caycedo, Augusto. The study of collector variability in the transition to sedentary food producers in northern Colombia. (*J. World Prehist.*, 10, 1996, p. 49–93, bibl., ill., tables)

Comparing subsistence strategies in estuarine and inland environments favors the latter as the context for adoption of sedentism and food production ca. 6000 BP.

546   Patiño, Diógenes. El altiplano nariñense, el Valle de Sibundoy y la ceja de montaña andina en el Putumayo: investigaciones de arqueología de rescate. (*Cespedesia/Cali*, 66, 1994/1995, p. 115–179, bibl., ill., map, tables)

First information on sites and ceramics along a transect from the Sibundoy Valley eastward to 500 m elevation.

547   Perspectivas regionales en la arqueología del suroccidente de Colombia y norte del Ecuador. Edición de Cristóbal Gnecco. Popayán, Colombia: Editorial Univ. del Cauca, 1995. 342 p.: bibl., ill., index.

Fifteen articles discuss chronology, settlement pattern, and evidence of interaction among coastal and highland populations during the past two millennia.

548   Pradilla Rueda, Helena; Germán Villate Santander; and **Francisco Ortiz Gómez.** Arqueología del cercado grande de los santuarios. (*Boletín/Bogotá*, 32/33, 1992, p. 20–147, bibl., ill., tables)

Description of 33 burials, ceramics, lithics, and plant and animal remains from a site on the university campus in Tunja occupied during the Herrera and Muisca periods and mentioned in early Spanish accounts.

549 Prehispanic chiefdoms in the Valle de la Plata = Cacicazgos prehispánicos del Valle de la Plata. v. 2, Ceramics—chronology and craft production. Edited by Robert D. Drennan, Mary M. Taft, and Carlos A. Uribe. Pittsburgh, Pa.: Univ. of Pittsburgh, Dept. of Anthropology; Bogotá: Depto. de Antropología, Univ. de los Andes, 1989. 1 v. (University of Pittsburgh memoirs in Latin American archaeology)

Seven pottery types defining three Formative, two Regional Classic, and one Recent Phase were clustered based on mineralogy to estimate population growth and centralized control. Results imply elites were established several centuries prior to economic centralization. For annotation of vol. 1 see *HLAS 53:751.*

550 Rodríguez Bastidas, Edgar Emilio. Fauna precolombina de Nariño. Bogotá: Fundación de Investigaciones Arqueológicas Nacionales; Instituto Colombiano de Antropología, 1992. 122 p.: bibl., ill.

Comparing relative frequencies and geographical origins of invertebrates, fishes, amphibians, reptiles, birds, and mammals depicted on pottery, stone, and metal objects, and on rock art associated with highland (Capulí, Tuza, Piartal) and coastal (Tumaco) cultures, permits inferring their ideological and commercial significances.

551 Romero Picón, Yuri. Hombres cosechadores del bosque pluvial bajo del Chocó, estudio paleoetnobotánico. (*Rev. Colomb. Antropol.*, 32, 1995, p. 197–218, bibl., ill., map, table)

Identification of 21 species representing early and late periods suggests enhanced management of wild plants during the late period. Two races of maize are described.

552 Salgado López, Héctor and **David Michael Stemper.** Cambios en alfarería y agricultura en el centro del litoral pacífico colombiano durante los dos últimos milenios. Bogotá: Fundación de Investigaciones Arqueológicas Nacionales, 1995. 234 p.: bibl., ill., map, tables (Publicación de la Fundación de Investigaciones Arqueológicas Nacionales; 58)

Tumaco/Tolita influence prior to AD 400 was replaced by a less complex culture with different ceramics after AD 800; denies any environmental constraints responsible.

553 Santos Vecino, Gustavo. Las sociedades prehispánicas de Jardín y Riosucio. (*Rev. Colomb. Antropol.*, 32, 1995, p. 245–287, bibl., ill., maps, photos, tables)

Investigation in adjacent portions of the middle Cauca distinguished two periods, the earlier C14 1940–1000 BP and the later 1000–330 BP. Both are characterized by dispersed settlements in the temperate zone and are grouped under chiefdoms integrated by reciprocal exchange of specialized products.

554 Stemper, David Michael and **Héctor Salgado López.** Local histories and global theories in Colombian Pacific Coast archaeology. (*Antiquity/Cambridge*, 69:263, June 1995, p. 248–269, bibl., ill.)

Speculative reconstruction of prehistory is notable for its rejection of environmental factors.

555 Tavera de Téllez, Gladys and **Carmen Urbina Caycedo.** Textiles de las culturas muisca y guane. Quito: IADAP, 1994. 144 p.: bibl., ill. (Col. Textiles)

Descriptions of raw materials, loom and non-loom techniques, and decorations.

556 Uribe, María Alicia. La orfebrería Quimbaya Tardía: una investigación en la colección del Museo del Oro. (*Boletín/Bogotá*, 31, 1991, p. 31–124, bibl., ill., tables)

Grouping of several thousand objects into a dozen categories based on technique, form, and function reveals emphasis on hammering to produce simple flat geometric shapes with relief decoration.

ECUADOR

557 Amerindian signs: 5,000 years of precolumbian art in Ecuador. Edited by Francisco Valdez and Diego Veintimilla. Texts translated by Mercedes Reyes. Quito: Dinediciones, 1992. 214 p.: bibl., col. ill., col. maps.

Essays by D. Lavallee, F. Valdez, and T. Cummins provide context for specimens illustrating exceptional quality and diversity of coastal Ecuadorian ceramic art from Formative, Regional Developmental, and Integration Periods.

558 Arellano, Jorge Eduardo. Análisis preliminar del material cultural lítico del sitio CHM-1, provincia de Chimborazo, Ecuador. (*Sarance/Otavalo*, 20, oct. 1994, p. 155–169, bibl., ill., map, tables)

Raw materials and artifact typology resemble Chobshi Cave and Cubilán.

559 Arellano, Jorge Eduardo. Implicaciones del medioambiente del Pleistoceno Tardío y Holoceno Temprano para la ubicación de ocupaciones humanas precerámicas in la Sierra Central del Ecuador. (*Sarance/Otavalo*, 24, 1997, p. 119–134, bibl., ill., table)

Geological and paleoclimatological evidence supports an ice-free corridor suitable for human occupation connecting the Riobamba and Alausí basins, opening between 19,000–13,000 BP and eliminated by volcanism about 9000 BP.

560 Asaro, Frank *et al*. Ecuadorian obsidian sources used for artifact production and methods for provenience assignments. (*Lat. Am. Antiq.*, 5, 1994, p. 257–277, bibl., tables)

Provides detailed analytic data and statistical calculations used in identifying samples interpreted in article by Burger *et al.* (item **565**).

561 Athens, J. Stephen. Etnicidad y adaptación: el Período Tardío de la ocupación Cara en la sierra norte del Ecuador. (*Sarance/Otavalo*, 24, 1997, bibl., ill.)

Interprets ethnohistorical, linguistic, and archaeological evidence for use of ethnic unity and territorial boundaries as the mechanisms for alliance-building among autonomous chiefdoms for defense against foreign aggression.

562 Bouchard, Jean-François. Los datos de cronología cultural para el litoral del Pacífico nor-ecuatorial: Período Formativo Tardío y Período de Desarrollo Regional, sur de Colombia—norte del Ecuador. (*Andes/Warsaw*, 1, 1996, p. 137–152, bibl.)

Incomplete descriptions of complexes and discrepancies in dates inhibit understanding of cultural development.

563 Bray, Tamara L. El problema Panzaleo: una cerámica no-local en la sierra norte del Ecuador. (*in* Chieftains, power & trade: regional interaction in the intermediate area of the Americas = Caciques, intercambio y poder: interacción regional en el área intermedia de las Américas. Bogotá: Depto. de Antropología, Univ. de los Andes, 1996, p. 197–228, bibl., ill., maps, tables)

Stylistic features and composition of Panzaleo pottery present in minor frequencies in the north Ecuadorian highlands suggest production and trade from the eastern Andean foothills.

564 Bruhns, Karen Olsen; James Burton; and Authur G. Rostoker. La cerámica "incisa en franjas rojas:" evidencia de intercambio entre la sierra y el oriente en el Formativo Tardío del Ecuador. (*in* Tecnología y organización de la producción cerámica prehispánica en los Andes. Lima: Pontificia Univ. Católica del Perú, Fondo Editorial, 1994, p. 53–66, bibl., ill.)

Petrographic analysis of sherds from highland and eastern lowland sites permits differentiating locally manufactured from traded pottery with similar decoration.

565 Burger, Richard L. *et al*. An initial consideration of obsidian procurement and exchange in prehispanic Ecuador. (*Lat. Am. Antiq.*, 5, 1994, p. 228–255, bibl., ill., tables)

Neutron activation and x-ray fluorescence analysis of specimens from 16 sites identify four sources in the Mullimaca Valley near Quito. Analysis implies a limited and sporadic use of this raw material, incompatible with accepted models of intensive exchange during Ecuadorian prehistory. See also item **560**.

566 Byrd, Kathleen M. Subsistence strategies in coastal Ecuador. (*in* Case studies in environmental archaeology. New York: Plenum Press, 1996, p. 305–316, bibl., map, tables)

Faunal remains from five Valdivia Tradition sites reveal radical differences in emphasis on terrestrial and marine fauna.

567 Cordero Iñiguez, Juan and Leonardo Aguirre Tirado. La ciudad de Tomebamba: Museo de Sitio. Cuenca: Banco Central del Ecuador, 1994. 72 p.: bibl., ill. (some col.), maps.

Numerous plans of typical structures, a glossary, and bibliography make this popular synthesis of prehistoric cultural development in the south highlands useful to specialists.

568 Cordero Iñiguez, Juan and Antonio Fresco González. Nueva imagen de Ingapirca. Cuenca: Banco Central del Ecuador, 1995. 95 p.: bibl., col. ill.

Well-illustrated description of structures encountered during restoration procedures following severe damage from torrential rains during 1993.

569 Cummins, Tom. La tradición de figurinas de la costa ecuatoriana: estilo tecnológico y uso de moldes. (*in* Tecnología y organización de la producción cerámica prehispánica en los Andes. Lima: Pontificia Univ. Católica del Perú, Fondo Editorial, 1994, p. 157–171, bibl., ill.)

Reviews elaboration of single-piece molds from Chorrera through coastal Regional Developmental complexes, with emphasis on Jama-Coaque culture.

570 Currie, Elizabeth J. Archaeology, ethnohistory and exchange along the coast of Ecuador. (*Antiquity/Cambridge,* 69:264, Sept. 1995, p. 511–526, bibl., ill., map, photos)

Excavations at López Vieja revealed high frequency of special decorative objects, weaving tools, and debitage implying manufacture of items for trade during the Manteño period.

571 DeBoer, Warren R. Traces behind the Esmeraldas shore: prehistory of the Santiago-Cayapas Region, Ecuador. Tuscaloosa: Univ. of Alabama Press, 1996. 234 p.: bibl., ill., index, maps.

Survey along the lower Cayapas and Santiago rivers located ca. 200 habitation sites. Ceramic distinctions define seven phases, partly sequential and partly regional; 25 C14 dates extend from ca. 400 BC to AD 1400. Settlements become smaller, more dispersed, and culturally isolated after ca. AD 400.

572 *Les derniers incas: civilisations précolombiennes en Écuateur.* Dijon, France: Editions Faton. (Les dossiers d'archéologie; 24)

Authoritative and well-illustrated synthesis of prehistoric cultural development includes brief history of archaeological research.

573 Di Capua, Costanza. Valdivia figurines and puberty rituals: an hypothesis. (*Andean Past,* 4, 1994, p. 229–279, bibl., ill., map)

Correlations between extent of head depilation and presence and prominence of breasts and arms on ceramic figurines suggest pre-puberty, puberty, adolescent, and adult stages of maturation. Examples are provided in 51 figures.

Drennan, Robert D. Chiefdoms in northern South America. See item **536.**

574 Echeverría Almeida, José and **María Victoria Uribe.** Area septentrional andina norte: arqueología y etnohistoria. Otavalo, Ecuador: Instituto Otavaleño de Antropología; Quito: Ediciones del Banco Central del Ecuador, 1995. 458 p. (some folded): bibl., ill. (Col. Pendoneros ; 8)

Eight chapters discuss details of ceramic chronology in Ecuador and metallurgy in Colombia. Particularly useful for abundant illustrations and chronological charts.

575 Encuentro de Investigadores de la Costa Ecuatoriana en Europa, *1st, Barcelona, 1993.* Primer encuentro de investigadores de la Costa Ecuatoriana en Europa: arqueología, etnohistoria, antropología sociocultural Quito: Ediciones Abya-Yala, 1995. 568 p.: bibl., ill.

Topics include ethnoarchaeology in Esmeraldas, regional exchange, preceramic period, northern Guayas basin chronology, and changes in adaptive strategies at the mouth of the Río Esmeraldas.

576 Guillaume-Gentil, M. Nicolas. El fenómeno de las tolas en la cuenca norte del Guayas—Ecuador: nuevas perspectivas. (*Andes/Warsaw,* 1, 1996, p. 153–172, bibl., ill.)

Topographic survey of 471 mounds revealed significant variation; stratigraphy shows multiple occupations during the Regional Development Period, terminating with Integration Period.

577 Idrovo Urigüen, Jaime. Santuários y conchales en la provincia de El Oro: aproximaciones arqueológicas. Machala, Ecuador: Casa de la Cultura Ecuatoriana, Núcleo de El Oro, 1994. 202 p., 1 folded leaf of plates: bibl., ill., map.

Describes extensive terraces associated with the Integration Period site of Guayquichuma and shell middens at the Jambelí Phase site of Guarumales, as well as pottery, stone, and metal objects exhibited in the Banco Central Museum at Machala. Three C14 dates from middens at Guarumales extend from 1960 ± 40 to 1475 ± 30 BP.

578 **Ledergerber-Crespo, Paulina.** Factores geográficos en la localización de sitios arqueológicos: el caso de Morona-Santiago, Ecuador; un informe preliminar. (*in* Cultura y medio ambiente en al area andina septentrional. Quito: Ediciones Abya-Yala, 1995, p. 343–375, bibl., ill.)

Archaeological survey revealed distinct settlement and ceramic complexes above and below ca. 500 m elevation, corresponding to subsistence differences among present-day Shuar groups. Describes utility of several remote-sensing methods for locating sites.

579 **Ledergerber-Crespo, Paulina.** Implicaciones de las ofrendas en un cemeterio Jambelí, en la costa del Ecuador. (*Sarance/Otavalo*, 24, 1997, p. 99–118, bibl., ill., map)

Illustrates pottery, stone, shell, bone, and metal objects from burials, implying trade with contemporary coastal and highland groups.

580 **Lippi, Ronald David.** La primera revolución ecuatoriana: el desarrollo de la vida agrícola en al antiguo Ecuador. Quito: Marka, Instituto de Historia y Antropología Andinas, 1996. 97 p.: bibl., ill. (Antropología e historia para todos; 1)

Overview of cultural development to end of the Formative is useful for recent information on Valdivia Tradition sites.

581 **Lozano Castro, Alfredo.** Cuenca: ciudad prehispana; significado y forma. Quito: Ediciones Abya-Yala; Cuidad; Madrid: Centro de Investigación Urbana y Arquitectura Andina, 1991. 227 p.: bibl., ill., maps.

Architect attempts to reconstruct the symbolic significance of space and the territorial organization of the town of Tumipampa, underlying modern Cuenca.

582 **Marcos Pino, Jorge G.** Ancient Ecuador: coastal societies of the northern Andean region, 300 BC–1500 AD. Guayaquil, Ecuador: Museo Arqueológico, Banco del Pacífico, 1993. 104 p.: bibl., ill. (some col.).

Well-illustrated overview of cultural development incorporates interpretations from author's fieldwork. Bilingual text.

583 **Marcos Pino, Jorge G.** and **Adam Michczyński.** Good dates and bad dates in Ecuador: radiocarbon samples and archaeological excavation; a commentary based on the "Valdivia Absolute Chronology." (*Andes/Warsaw*, 1, 1996, p. 93–114, bibl., tables)

Reviews problems of sample context, and provides calibrations for all existing dates, comparison with TL dates, and refined chronology for Valdivia periods.

584 **Masucci, Maria A.** Marine shell bead production and the role of domestic craft activities in the economy of the Guangala Phase, southwest Ecuador. (*Lat. Am. Antiq.*, 6, 1995, p. 70–84, bibl., ill., tables)

Although only 25 km from the shore, the production of beads from Strombus and Spondylus is attributed to exchange with littoral communities.

Perspectivas regionales en la arqueología del suroccidente de Colombia y norte del Ecuador. See item 547.

585 **Reinoso Hermida, Gustavo.** El período precerámico del Ecuador. Cuenca, Ecuador: Univ. de Cuenca, 1993. 297 p.: bibl., ill. (Publicaciones del Depto. de Difusión Cultural de la Univ. de Cuenca)

General synthesis focuses on El Inga, Chobshi Cave, Cubilán, Punín, and Chalán in the highlands and Las Vegas on the coast.

586 **Rostoker, Arthur G.** An archaeological assemblage from eastern Ecuador. San Francisco: Treganza Anthropology Museum, San Francisco State Univ., 1996 89 p.: bibl., ill. (Treganza Anthropology Museum papers; 18)

Detailed description of 76 rim sherds from Michael Harner's excavation at the Yaunchu Site on the Río Upano.

587 **Sánchez Mosquera, Amelia.** Ecología y sociedad en Jama-Coaque. (*Cuad. Hist. Arqueol.*, 46/47, 1996, p. 38–57, bibl., ill.)

Examination of 64 pottery biomorphic vessels from the Museo del Banco Central shows 40 percent representing a "fantastic creature" and 25 percent depicting molluscs, with the manatee/dolphin as the principal mammal.

588 **Sánchez Mosquera, Amelia.** Las ocupaciones del Guayaquil antiguo: informe final Prospección Arqueológica de Guayaquil; fase I, área noroeste. Guayaquil, Ecuador: s.n., 1995. 215 leaves: bibl., ill., maps (1 col.).

Diagnostic combinations of form and decoration distilled from pottery samples from 140 sites identify previously unrecognized occupations during the Formative, Regional Development, and Integration Periods.

Sandweiss, Daniel H. Mid-Holocene cultural interaction between the north coast of Peru and Ecuador. See item **661**.

589 **Schwartz, Frederick A.** and **J. Scott Raymond.** Formative settlement patterns in the Valdivia Valley, SW coastal Ecuador. (*J. Field Archaeol.*, 23:2, 1996, p. 205–224, bibl., ill.)

Traces settlement behavior and population density from Valdivia through Engoroy Periods based on number and area of sites. Concludes that developments in Mesoamerica and the Central Andes had little impact on Ecuador.

590 **Staller, John Edward.** El sitio Valdivia Tardío de la Emerenciana en la costa sur del Ecuador y su significación del desarrollo de complejidad en la costa oeste de Sudamérica. (*Cuad. Hist. Arqueol.*, 46/47, 1996, p. 14–37, ill.)

Argues that increasing constriction of jar necks during Valdivia 8 (1500–1200 BC) in El Oro represents local evolution of stirrup spouts and transition to the Machalilla Phase.

591 **Van der Merwe, Nikolaas J.; Julia A. Lee-Thorpe;** and **J. Scott Raymond.** Light, stable isotopes and the subsistence base of Formative cultures at Valdivia, Ecuador. (*in* Prehistoric human bone: archaeology at the molecular level. Berlin: Springer-Verlag, 1993, p. 63–97, bibl., ill., map, tables)

Comparison of collagen from modern fauna in marine, riverine, and terrestrial habitats and from human skeletons of all periods indicates unimportance of maize and marine foods during Valdivia, emphasis on marine foods during Machalilla, and consumption of maize during Chorrera, which increased during Guangala.

592 **Vargas A., Marco.** Investigaciones arqueológicas en el sector de Morán, provincia del Carchi. (*Sarance/Otavalo*, 22, oct. 1995, p. 171–207, bibl., ill., map)

Describes ring-shaped dwellings, ridged fields, burials, and ceramics representing an agricultural community.

593 **Zedeño, María Nieves.** Análisis de cerámica chorrera del sitio Peñon del Rio. Guayaquil, Ecuador: Escuela Superior Politécnica del Litoral, Escuela de Arqueología, 1990. 160 p.: bibl., ill. (Tecnología prehispánica)

Describes composition, morphology, decoration, and function of ceramics from habitational contexts on the lower Río Babahoyo.

THE GUIANAS

594 *Archaeology and Anthropology*. No. 11, 1996. The origin, characterization, and chronology of the Mabaruma subseries of the Barrancoid Tradition by Denis Williams. Georgetown, Guyana: Ministry of Education and Cultural Development.

Stratigraphic, C14, and typological evidence support *in situ* development of Barrancoid ceramics in northwestern Guyana ca. 1600 BC.

595 **Meggers, Betty J.** Amazonia on the eve of European contact: ethnohistorical, ecological, and anthropological perspectives. (*Rev. Arqueol. /São Paulo*, 8:2, 1993/95, p. 91–115, bibl., ill.)

Presents ecological, archaeological, ethnographic, and contemporary evidence incompatible with early European accounts of dense, sedentary populations and protostates throughout Amazonia and the Guianas.

596 **Nowacki-Breczewski, Philippe.** Petit-Saut, un progamme de sauvetage archéologique en Guyane: premiers résultats. (*Caribena/Martinique*, 3, 1993, p. 159–173, bibl., graph, ill., maps)

Pottery samples from six sites on the lower Sinnamary with simple vessel shapes and rare red or incised decoration are associated with six C14 dates extending from 1875 ± 80 to 885 ± 50 BP.

597 **Roosevelt, Anna C.** The demise of the Alaka initial ceramic phase has been greatly exaggerated: response to D. Williams. (*Am. Antiq.*, 62:2, April 1997, p. 353–364, bibl., ill.)

Claims proveniences on laboratory submission forms for charcoal samples take precedence over stratigraphic evidence for evaluating C14 dates. See also item **601**.

598 **Rostain, Stéphen.** La céramique amérindienne de Guyane française. (*Schweiz. Amer. Ges.*, 55/56, 1991/92, p. 93–127, bibl., ill.)

Detailed description of pottery making among present-day Palikur of the lower Oyapoque, including clay source, temper, paste preparation, construction, decoration, firing, and function. Useful for interpreting prehistoric ceramics.

599 Rostain, Stéphen. The French Guiana coast: a key area in prehistory between the Orinoco and Amazon Rivers. (*in* Between St. Eustatius and the Guianas: contributions to Caribbean archaeology. Saint Eustatius, Netherlands Antilles: St. Eustatius Historical Foundation, 1994, p. 53–99, bibl., ill.)

A frontier between Aristé-related ceramics in the east and Arauquinoid ceramics in the west reflects expansions ca. AD 600, followed by intrusion of Koriabo-related pottery from the south.

600 Rostain, Stéphen. L'occupation amérindienne ancienne du littoral de Guyane. v. 2. Paris: Univ. de Paris I-Panthéon/Sorbonne, U.F.R. d'art et d'archéologie, Centre de recherche en archéologie précolombienne, 1994. I v.

Expansions of the Koriabo, Aristé, Arauquín, and Polychrome traditions from adjacent regions are documented by ceramics from 50 sites throughout the coast. Fifty-one C14 dates provide the first detailed sequence of precolumbian cultural development.

601 Williams, Denis. Early pottery in the Amazon: a correction. (*Am. Antiq.*, 62:2, April 1997, p. 342–352)

Stratigraphic evidence, additional C14 dates, and paleoenvironmental evidence support a preceramic context for C14 dates attributed by Roosevelt to early pottery. See also item **597.**

PERU

Adamska, Anna and Adam Michczyński. Towards radiocarbon chronology of the Inca State. See item **383.**

602 Alarcón, Marleni M.; Denise Pozzi-Escot; and Cirilo Vivanco. Instrumentos de alfareros de la época Wari. (*Bull. Inst. fr. étud. andin.*, 22:2, 1993, p. 467–496, bibl., ill., map, tables)

Consultation with present-day traditional potters in the Ayacucho region identifies uses of tools and techniques of production by Huari potters.

603 Alva, Walter. Sipán. Lima: Cervecería Backus & Johnston, 1994. 331 p.: bibl., ill. (chiefly col.). (Col. Cultura y artes del Perú)

Copiously illustrated account of the history, principal tombs, architecture, and artifacts associated with one of the most spectacular discoveries in Peruvian archaeology, which documented the reality of individuals and events depicted on Moche vessels.

Andean art at Dumbarton Oaks. See item **385.**

604 Archaeologica Peruana 2: arquitectura y civilización en los Andes prehispánicos. Edición de Elisabeth Bonnier y Henning Bischof. Mannheim, Germany: Sociedad Arqueológica Peruano-Alemana, Reiss Museum, 1997. 234 p.: bibl., graphs, ill., tables.

Eleven chapters deal with aspects of settlement morphology, construction features and materials, architectural analysis, social implications, and chronological changes from preceramic to Inca times.

605 Arsenault, Daniel. Balance de los estudios moche (Mochicas) 1970–1994: primera parte: análisis iconográfico. (*Rev. Andin.*, 13:1, primer semestre 1995, p. 237–270, bibl.)

Comparisons of approaches and results to deciphering Moche iconography by Benson, Donnan, Berezkin, and Hocquengheim are supplemented by other experts who conclude much remains to be learned.

606 Bischof, Henning. Análisis iconográfico y del estilo en la elaboración de cronologías arqueológicas: el caso del Formativo Centroandino. (*Andes/Warsaw*, 1, 1996, p. 61–91, bibl., ill.)

Evaluates relative merits of stylistic analysis and radiometric dates for assessing the origin and dispersal of Chavinoid elements.

607 Bischof, Henning. Toward the definition of pre- and early Chavín art styles in Peru. (*Andean Past*, 4, 1994, p. 169–228, bibl., ill.)

Detailed analysis of iconography on stone and pottery from earlier sites suggests antecedents for Classic Chavín art.

608 Bonavia, Duccio et al. Un sitio precerámico de Huarmey (PV35–6) antes de la introducción del maíz. (*Bull. Inst. fr. étud.*

---

andin., 22:2, 1993, p. 409–442, bibl., ill., photo, tables)

Analysis of botanical remains identifies possible coca and cotton, as well as beans and cucurbits, implying a mixed economy of gathering, incipient agriculture, fishing, shellfish gathering, and hunting of small land mammals.

609   Briceño Rosario, Jesús. El recurso agua y el establecimiento de los cazadores recolectores en el valle de Chicama. (*Rev. Mus. Arqueol. Antropol. Hist.*, 5, 1995, p. 143–161, bibl., ill., map)

Early lithic sites are associated with springs throughout the Andean region.

610   Campana D., Cristobal. La cultura mochica. Lima: Consejo Nacional de Ciencia y Tecnología, 1994. 168 p.: bibl., ill. (some col.).

Readable, well-illustrated overview of Moche architecture, daily life, technology, social organization, ideology, and art includes analysis of proportional constraints guiding painted and modeled decoration on pottery.

611   Canziani Amico, José. Las lomas de Atiquipa: arqueología y problemas de desarrollo regional. (*Gac. Arqueol. Andin.*, 24, 1995, p. 113–133, bibl., ill.)

Describes extensive terracing, large settlements, storage facilities, and corrals on the arid south coast.

612   Cardich, Augusto. L'origine de la civilisation andine. (*Anthropologie/Paris*, 98, 1994, p. 173–189, bibl., map)

Argues for a central highland evolution and dispersal of the foundations of Andean civilization.

613   Castillo Benites, Daniel. Petroglifos de Pamapas de Jaguey. (*Bol. Lima*, 16:91/96, 1994, p. 27–30, bibl., ill., map)

Illustrates abstract and biomorphic motifs from four previously unreported locations in the upper Chicama Valley.

614   Cerro Ñañañique: un établissement monumental de la période formative, en limite de désert, Haut Piura, Pérou. Ouvrage collectif sous la direction de J. Guffroy. Paris: ORSTOM, 1994. 440 p.: bibl., ill., maps. (Col. Etudes et thèses, 0767–2888)

Describes and interprets excavations, structures, plant and animal remains, human remains, lithics, ceramics, iconography.

Twenty C14 dates place occupation between 2920 ± 140 and 2350 ± 150 BP.

615   Chapdelaine, Claude; Greg Kennedy; and Santiago Uceda. Activación neutrónica en el estudio de la producción local de la cerámica ritual en el sitio Moche, Perú. (*Bull. Inst. fr. étud. andin.*, 24:2, 1995, p. 183–212, bibl., graphs, ill., map, tables)

Significantly greater homogeneity among ritual vessels and figurines compared with domestic vessels implies differences in control over production.

616   Chepstow-Lustry, A.J. et. al. 4000 years of human impact and vegetation change in the central Peruvian Andes—with events parallelling the Maya record? (*Antiquity/Cambridge*, 70:270, Dec. 1996, p. 824–833, bibl., graphs, map, photo)

Pollen record from Marcacocha shows sharp changes ca. AD 100 and 1000, implying temperature fluctuations. This phenomenon has also been documented in Yucatán and is possibly related to El Niño.

617   Clarkson, Persis B. and Ronald I. Dorn. New chronometric dates for the *puquios* of Nasca, Peru. (*Lat. Am. Antiq.*, 6, 1995, p. 56–69, bibl., ill., tables)

AMS dates of AD 560 and 600 on organic material from varnish on stone lintels of two *puquios* imply prehistoric construction.

618   Coloma Porcari, César. Los inicios de la arqueología en el Perú, o, *Antigüedades peruanas* de Mariano Eduardo de Rivero. Lima: Instituto Latinoamericano de Cultura y Desarrollo, 1994. 180 p.: bibl., facsims., ill., indexes.

Biographical data on the "Father of Peruvian Archeology" include works published between 1827–57 and sites discovered or described up to 1841. Work also includes facsimilies of four editions of *Antigüedades peruanas*.

619   Coloquio sobre la Cultura Moche, 1st, Trujillo, Peru, 1993. Moche: propuestas y perspectivas; actas. Edición de Santiago Uceda y Elias Mujica B. Trujillo, Peru: Univ. Nacional de la Libertad; Lima: Instituto Francés de Estudios Andinos; Asociación Peruana para el Fomento de las Ciencias Sociales, 1994. 549 p., 16 p. of plates: bibl., ill. (some col.), maps, tables (Travaux de l'Institut français d'études andines, 79)

Chapters discuss osteological evidence, ceramic production, mural tradition, pre-Moche antecedents, and relevance of traditional models of sociopolitical organization and expansion.

620 Costin, Cathy L. and **Melissa B. Hagstrum.** Standardization, labor investment, skill, and the organization of ceramic production in late prehistoric highland Peru. (*Am. Antiq.*, 60:4, October 1995, p. 619–639)

Differential occurrence of intentional and mechanical attributes associated with specialized production suggests Wanka potters worked without centralized control, whereas Inca pottery was made locally under bureaucratic supervision.

621 Davies, Nigel. The Incas. Niwot, Colo.: Univ. Press of Colorado, 1995. 259 p.: bibl., index, maps.

Readable summary of the history, imperial infrastructure, mechanisms of control and integration, and other unique characteristics of the Inca Empire.

622 Donnan, Christopher B. A Chimu-Inka ceramic-manufacturing center from the north coast of Peru. (*Lat. Am. Antiq.*, 8:1, 1997, p. 30–54, bibl., ill., table)

Analysis of molds, wasters, and other evidence demonstrates production of local and Inca-derived forms for use by commoners.

Druc, Isabelle C. De la etnografía hacia la arqueología: aportes de entrevistas con ceramistas de Ancash, Perú, para la caracterización de la cerámica prehispánica. See item **1194.**

623 Eeckhout, Peter. Pirámide con rampa número 3 del Pachacacmac, costa central del Perú: resultados preliminares de la primera temporada de excavaciones, zona 1 y 2. (*Bull. Inst. fr. étud. andin.*, 24:1, 1995, p. 65–106, bibl., maps, photos)

Detailed description of occupational sequences in two locations confirms postulated transition from ceremonial to mortuary to domestic function of Pyramid 3.

624 Erickson, Clark L. Investigación arqueológica del sistema agrícola de los camellones en la cuenca del Lago Titicaca del Perú. [S.l.]: Piwa; P.E.L.T., [1996?] 336 p.: ill. (some col.), maps.

Provides detailed evidence on precolumbian construction, maintenance, and use of raised fields, and on labor investment,

productivity, and advantages observed during experimental replication. TL dates and stratigraphy identify two periods of use: ca. 1000 BC–AD 4000 and AD 1000–1540.

625 Farfán Lovatón, Carlos. Asentamientos prehispánicos de la cuenca alta del Chillón. (*Gac. Arqueol. Andin.*, 24, 1995, p. 31–61, bibl., ill., map)

Survey identified 30 dispersed, agglutinated settlements in strategic locations from 2800–4200 m. elevation, the majority dating in the Late Intermediate Period.

626 Frame, Mary. Las imágenes visuales de estructuras textiles en el arte del antiguo Perú, con comentarios. (*Rev. Andin.*, 12:2, segundo semestre 1994, p. 295–401, bibl., ill., photos)

Spanish version of article published in 1986, in the papers of the Junius B. Bird Conference on Andean Textiles (Washington: 1984), with a brief addition and critical evaluations.

627 Franco Jordán, Regulo G. El centro ceremonial de Pachacamac: nuevas evidencias en el templo viejo. (*Bol. Lima*, 15:86, marzo 1993, p. 45–62, bibl., ill., maps, photos)

Changes in decoration and construction reflect the introduction of a new ideology during the Middle Horizon.

628 González Carré, Enrique and **Denise Pozzi-Escot.** Arqueología regional de Ayacucho: balance y bibliografía básica. (*Gac. Arqueol. Andin.*, 6:21, abril 1992, p. 173–196, bibl., maps)

Brief history of archaeological research includes detailed bibliography listing chronicles and maunscripts as well as books and articles.

Hansen, Barbara C.S. and **Donald T. Rodbell.** A late glaciel/Holocene pollen record from the eastern Andes of northern Peru. See item **2647.**

629 Hecker, Giesela and **Wolfgang Hecker.** Die Grabungen von Heinrich Ubbelohde-Doering in Pacatnamu, Nordperú: Untersuchungen zu den Huacas 31 und 14 sowie Bestattungen und Fundobjekte. Berlin: D. Reimer, 1995. 497 p.: bibl., ill. (some col.).

Extremely detailed descriptions of excavations, structures, and artifacts, ranging from marks on adobes and engravings to ceramics, textiles, and less common items.

630 **Heyerdahl, Thor; Daniel H. Sandweiss; and Alfredo Narváez.** Pyramids of Túcume: the quest for Peru's forgotten city. New York: Thames and Hudson, 1995. 240 p.: bibl., ill. (some col.), index, maps.

Well-illustrated synthesis of multi-year excavations at a city of the Lambayeque culture extending over 220 hectares with 26 major pyramids, and founded ca. AD 1100.

631 **Historia y cultura del Perú.** Edición de Marco Curatola y Fernando Silva-Santisteban. Lima: Univ. de Lima, Facultad de Ciencias Humanas; Banco de Crédito del Perú; Museo de la Nación, Instituto Nacional de Cultura; Organización Internacional para las Migraciones, 1994. 450 p.: bibl., ill.

Twenty-one specialists review aspects of cultural development from human arrival to the present, with emphasis on spatial-temporal continuity.

632 **Hocquenghem, Anne-Marie and Peter Kaulicke.** Estudio de una colección de cerámica de Yacila, extremo norte del Perú. (*Bull. Inst. fr. étud. andin.*, 24:2, 1995, p. 213–243, bibl., ill., maps, photos)

Detailed analysis of a larger sample of pottery resolves chronological disagreements and establishes a close relation between coastal fishermen and agriculturalists of the Piura Valley beginning in the Formative Period.

633 **Hocquenghem, Anne-Marie.** Rutas de entrada del *mullu* en al extremo norte del Perú. (*Bull. Inst. fr. étud. andin.*, 22:3, 1993, p. 701–719, bibl., maps, photos)

Argues that ocean currents would have impeded travel by sea and reviews evidence for terrestrial routes via the highlands or southward from Tumbes.

634 **Hoshower, Lisa M. et al.** Artificial cranial deformation at the Omo M10 site: a Tiwanaku complex from the Moquegua Valley, Peru. (*Lat. Am. Antiq.*, 6, 1995, p. 145–164, bibl., ill., table)

Variations in deformation among six Tiwanaku V cemeteries identify residential descent groups rather than differences in status or ethnicity.

635 **Huarochirí: ocho mil años de historia.** v. 1. Recopilación de Vladimiro Thatar Alvarez. Lima: Municipalidad de Santa Eulalia de Acopaya, 1992. 1 v.

Chapters by various authors summarize archaeological, ethnohistorical, mythical, historical, and ethnographical sources of data.

636 **Huaycochea Núñez de la Torre, Flor de María.** Qolqas, bancos de reserva andinos: almacenes Inkas; arqueología de qolqas. Cusco, Peru: Univ. Nacional de San Antonio Abad del Cusco, 1994. 283 p.: bibl., ill. (some col.).

Detailed inventory of storage facilities in the Ollantaytambo region includes chronology, architecture, topographic location, function, capacity, conservational efficiency, control, and administration.

637 **Investigaciones en la Huaca de la Luna, 1995.** Recopilación de Santiago Uceda, Elias Mujica B. y Ricardo Morales. Trujillo, Peru: Facultad de Ciencias Sociales, Univ. Nacional de la Libertad, 1997. 242 p.: bibl., ill., tables.

Detailed and well-illustrated descriptions of excavations in Huaca de la Luna, Cerro Blanco, and the Area Urbana provide new data on construction, burials, residences, storage facilities, workshops, roads, and artifacts. Chapters discuss conservation of structures and materials.

638 **Kaulicke, Peter.** La cultura Mochica: arqueología, historia y ficción. (*Histórica/Lima*, 17:1, julio 1993, p. 93–107, bibl.)

Moche society consisted of local chiefdoms with different rhythms of growth and small territories; Moche Valley was more powerful but not the capital of a multi-valley State.

639 **Kuntur Wasi y Cerro Blanco: dos sitios del Formativo en el Norte del Perú.** Tokyo: Hokusen, 1995. 217 p.: bibl., ill. (some col.), tables.

Describes excavations, ceremonial architecture, tombs, monoliths, and ceramics defining seven phases extending from 1500–50 BC. Relative chronology and C14 dates are nearly identical to the Cajamarca Valley sequence.

640 **Kuznar, Lawrence A.** Awatimarka: the ethnoarchaeology of an Andean herding community. Fort Worth, Tex.: Harcourt Brace College Publishers, 1995. 141 p.: bibl., ill., index, maps. (Case studies in archaeology)

Associations and distributions of features, artifacts, faunal remains, and structures at sites with different functions among modern camel herders assist in identifying similar behavior in prehistoric sites.

641 Lavalée, Danièle *et al*. Telarmachay: cazadores y pastores prehistóricos de los Andes. Lima: Institut français d'études andines, 1995. 445 p.: bibl., ill., maps, tables.

Detailed description of excavations in a rockshelter occupied ca. 9000–3800 BP includes specialist reports on pollen; chemistry, sedimentology, and petrography of strata; use wear on lithics; spatial distribution of 465 stone tools; and human bones. Work provides the most comprehensive documentation yet of a Peruvian preceramic site.

642 Lumbreras, Luis Guillermo. Chavín de Huántar: excavaciones en la Galería de las Ofrendas. Mainz am Rhein, Germany: P. von Zabern, 1993. 559 p.: bibl., ill. (some col.). (Materialien zur allgemeinen und vergleichenden Archäologie, 0170–9518; 51)

Landmark description of gallery and artifacts recovered during 1966–67 excavations. Pottery is classified into undecorated wares and Chavín and non-Chavín styles, and is described by morphology. Stone, bone, antler, shell, and human and animal remains arc discussed. Non-funeral context, post-deposition fracture, subterranean location, and early date (1100–750 BC) suggest inaugural ceremony. Presence of pottery and artifacts of diverse proveniences and traditions makes assemblage a valuable horizon marker for the Andean region.

643 Makowski Hanula, Krzysztof. La ciudad y el origen de la civilización en los Andes: sobre el imperativo y los límites de la comparación en la prehistoria. Lima: Pontificia Univ. Católica del Perú, Facultad de Letras y Ciencias Humanas, 1996. 37 p.: bibl. (Cuadernos de la Facultad de Letras y Ciencias Humanas; 15)

The universal role of cities in the origin of civilization is a myth that impedes understanding of Andean cultural development.

644 Matos, Ramiro. Los Inka de la sierra central del Perú. (*Rev. Arqueol. Am.*, 8, 1995, p. 159–190, bibl., ill.)

Interprets ruins of eight administrative centers in the context of ethnohistoric accounts of their characteristics and functions.

645 Miller, George R. and **Richard L. Burger.** Our father the cayman, our dinner the llama: animal utilization at Chavín de Huántar, Peru. (*Am. Antiq.*, 60:3, July 1995, p. 421–458, bibl., ill.)

Faunal remains from residential contexts reveal a shift from domestic llama/wild vicuña to domestic llama alone, as well as changes in utilization of carcass parts, procurement, and processing. Implications for social stratification, economic specialization, and other aspects of Chavín culture are discussed.

646 Moore, Jerry D. The archaeology of dual organization in Andean South America: a theoretical review and case study. (*Lat. Am. Antiq.*, 6, 1995, p. 165–181, bibl., tables)

Ethnohistoric and archaeological evidence from the Nepeña Valley suggest dual organization may not be detectable in settlement patterns on the north coast of Peru.

647 Moore, Jerry D. Architecture and power in the ancient Andes: the archaeology of public buildings. Cambridge, England; New York: Cambridge Univ. Press, 1996. 256 p.: bibl., ill., index, maps. (New studies in archaeology)

Compares plans of 22 structures on the Peruvian north coast dating from preceramic to Chimu. Uses objective criteria to assess social purpose (centrality, ubiquity); symbolic intent (scale, permanence); and social control (visibility, access pattern).

648 Mormontoy Atayupanqui, Alfredo. Investigaciones arqueológicas en Sillkinchan, San Jeronimo—Cusco. (*Andes/Cusco*, 1, 1996, p. 77–96, bibl,, ill., tables)

Existing structures are Inca and overlie an earlier Killke occupation.

649 Orefici, Giuseppe. Nuevos enfoques sobre la transición Paracas-Nasca en Cahuachi, Perú. (*Andes/Warsaw*, 1, 1996, p. 173–198, bibl., ill.)

Excavations in Pueblo Viejo and Cahuachi attempt to assess existence of a pre-Nasca ceramic tradition and the regional role of Cahuachi during the Early Horizon.

650 The Pacatnamu papers. v. 2, The Moche occupation. Edited by Christopher B. Donnan and Guillermo A. Cock. Los Angeles: Museum of Cultural History, Univ.

of California, 1997. 1 v. (300 p.): bibl., ills. (some col.)

Specialists describe burials, skeletal remains, textiles, botanical offerings, copper artifacts, fineline ceramics, a cane coffin, and a room filled with offerings.

651 Panaifo Teixeira, Mónica. Evaluación de nuestra arqueología amazónica. (in Amazonia: en busca de su palabra; aportes al desarrollo amazónico como homenaje a los diez años del IIAP, 1982–1991, y al primer centenario de la muerte de Antonio Raimondi, 1891–1991. Iquitos, Peru: IIAP, 1994, p. 167–229, bibl., ill., maps)

Summary of archaeological complexes is based on published sources.

Patterson, Thomas C. Conceptual differences between Mexican and Peruvian archaeology. See item **114.**

652 Peru's south coast: an emerging research frontier. (Andean Past, 4, 1994, p. 9–167, bibl., ill., maps)

Series of articles discusses Initial Period and Inca textiles, Paracas mummy bundles, Nasca pottery, burials, and recent excavations at the Initial Period site of Hacha.

653 Pillsbury, Joanne. Los relieves de Chan Chan: nuevos datos para el estudio de la secuencia y ocupación de la ciudad. (Rev. Mus. Arqueol. Antropol. Hist., 5, 1994, p. 47–79, bibl., ill.)

A change from additive (modeling) to subtractive (outlining and cutting) technique of execution provides a relative chronology.

654 Pillsbury, Joanne. The thorny oyster and the origins of empire: implications of recently uncovered *Spondylus* imagery from Chan Chan, Peru. (Lat. Am. Antiq., 7:4, 1996, p. 313–340, bibl., ill.)

Diving and maritime transport depicted on relief decoration and sharp increase in use during the Chimu period suggest that intentional enhancement of Spondylus acquisition and redistribution was a critical factor in emergence of the Chimu State.

655 Pozorski, Thomas and **Shelia Pozorski.** Ventilated hearth structures in the Casma Valley, Peru. (Lat. Am. Antiq., 7:4, 1996, p. 341–353, bibl., ill.)

Describes Late Preceramic coastal variants of a previously reported highland semi-

subterranean circular structure, and suggests a sweathouse function.

Ramos Vera, Claudio. Rehabilitación, uso y manejo de camellones: propuesta técnica. See item **1218.**

656 Ravines, Rogger. Cerámica arqueológica del Río Tambopata, Madre de Dios. (Bol. Lima, 15:90, nov. 1993, p. 15–20, ill., map, photos)

Describes and illustrates vessels with complicated-incised or red-painted decoration from the vicinity of Laberinto.

657 Reinhard, Johan. Peru's ice maidens: unwrapping the secrets. (Natl. Geogr. Mag., 189:6, June 1996, p. 62–81, ill., photos)

Graphic account of discovery, condition, dress, and offerings asociated with a well-preserved female sacrifice and ritual burial on the summit of Nevado Ampato during the late Inca Period.

658 Rice, Prudence M. The archaeology of wine: the wine and brandy haciendas of Moquegua, Peru. (J. Field Archaeol., 23:2, 1996, p. 187–204, bibl., ill.)

Investigation of 130 wine hacienda sites reveals similarities in technology and organization with earlier Roman practices as well as Spanish models.

659 Ríos, Marcela and **Enrique Retamozo.** Investigaciones sobre la metalurgia Vicús. (Gac. Arqueol. Andin., 23, 1993, p. 33–66, bibl., ill.)

Describes 84 metal ornaments and implements from Tomb II, and identifies two techniques of guilding.

660 Rodríguez López, Luis Francisco. Costa Norte: diez mil años de prehistoria. Lima: Ministerio de la Presidencia, Consejo Nacional de Ciencia y Tecnología, 1994. 409 p.: bibl., ill., maps.

Useful resumé of cultural development exemplified by complexes and sites representing the Preceramic, Formative, Early Regional Developmental, and Late Regional States periods. Includes a tourist circuit for each valley.

661 Sandweiss, Daniel H. Mid-Holocene cultural interaction between the north coast of Peru and Ecuador. (Lat. Am. Antiq., 7:1, 1996, p. 41–50, bibl., ill.)

Resemblance between small elongated

pebbles from the Ostra site and Valdivia stone figurines of similar age suggests migration or interaction during the Holocene Climatic Optimum, when environmental conditions were more similar.

662 **Schreiber, Katharina J.** and **Josué Lancho Rojas.** The *puquios* of Nasca. (*Lat. Am. Antiq.*, 6, 1995, p. 229–254, bibl., ill.)

Provides details on construction and maintenance of 36 subterranean channel systems. Use by Nasca 5 is implied by changes in settlement density, perhaps provoked by prolonged drought between AD 540–610.

663 **Shady Solís, Ruth.** La neolitización en los Andes Centrales y los orígenes del sedentarismo, la domesticación y la distinción social. (*Saguntum/Valencia*, 28, 1995, p. 49–61, bibl., map)

Comparison of cultural development in coastal and highland environments from 8000–3500 BC shows no correlation between intensive agriculture, increasing sedentism, and social complexity.

664 **Shimada, Izumi.** Cultura Sicán: dios, riqueza y poder en la Costa Norte del Perú. Lima: Fundación del Banco Continental para el Fomento de la Educación y la Cultura, Edubanco, 1995. 219 p.: bibl., ill. (some col.).

Popular account of investigations focuses on metalworking, distribution of marked adobes, tombs and offerings *in situ*, and gold ornaments. Well illustrated.

665 **Shimada, Izumi.** Pre-hispanic metallurgy and mining in the Andes: recent advances and future tasks. (*in* In quest of mineral wealth: aboriginal and colonial mining and metallurgy in Spanish America. Baton Rouge: Louisiana State Univ., 1994, p. 37–73, bibl., ill., tables)

Uses recent research at Sicán to argue for a wholistic approach to investigating production, distribution, and use of metals.

666 **Silverman, Helaine.** The Formative Period on the south coast of Peru: a critical review. (*J. World Prehist.*, 10, 1996, p. 95–146, bibl., ill.)

Environmental constraints account for lag in population increase and cultural complexity, compared with regions to the north.

667 **Silverman, Helaine.** Paracas in Nazca: new data on the Early Horizon occupation of the Rio Grande de Nazca drainage,

Peru. (*Lat. Am. Antiq.*, 5, 1994, p. 359–382, bibl., ill., map, tables)

Detailed examination of south coast chronologies indicates that development of Nasca from late Paracas occurred in the Ica Valley.

Stanish, Charles *et al.* Archaeological survey in the southwestern Lake Titicaca Basin. See item **447.**

Stanish, Charles. The hydraulic hypothesis revisited: Lake Titicaca Basin raised fields in theoretical perspective. See item **448.**

668 **Stone-Miller, Rebecca.** Art of the Andes: from Chavín to Inca. New York: Thames & Hudson, 1996. 224 p.: bibl., ill. (some col.), index, maps. (World of art)

Well-illustrated overview of major art styles: Chavín, Paracas and Nasca, Moche, Tiwanaku and Wari, Late Intermediate Period, and Inca.

Tiwanaku and its hinterland: archaeology and paleoecology of an Andean civilization. v. 1, Agroecology. See item **449.**

669 **Treacy, John M.** Las chacras de Coporaque: andenería y riego en el valle del Colca. Lima: IEP, 1994. 298 p.: bibl., ill., maps. (Estudios de la sociedad rural; 12)

Comprehensive description of irrigated terraces includes location, environment, climate, water management, chronology, pre- and post-Spanish use, present agricultural cycle and management, and potential for rehabilitation.

670 **Ulbert, Cornelius.** Die Keramik der formativzeitlichen Siedlung Montegrande, Jequetepequetal, Nord-Peru. Mainz am Rhein, Germany: Verlag P. von Zabern, 1994. 205 p.: bibl., ill. (some col.). (Materialien zur allgemeinen und vergleichenden Archäologie, 0170–9518; 52)

Provides a ceramic typology based on excavated samples of rim sherds. Decoration emphasizing zoned polish, punctate, and incision suggests an early Formative date.

671 **Valdez, Lidio M.** and **Cirilo Vivanco.** Arqueología de la cuenca del Qaracha, Ayacucho, Perú. (*Lat. Am. Antiq.*, 5, 1994, p. 144–157, bibl., ill., map)

Settlement pattern of dispersed villages in fortified locations following fall of the Wari State was transformed under Inca control.

672 **Valencia, Armando Harvey.** Corican-cha: el gran templo del sol. Cusco, Peru: Univ. Nacional de San Antonio Abrad del Cusco, 1994. 253 p.: bibl., ill. (some col.), maps.

Synthesis of appearance, function, and significance aims to inform and inspire secondary-school students to emulate and supersede Inca accomplishments.

673 **Wise, Karen; Niki R. Clark;** and **Sloan R. Williams.** A Late Archaic Period burial from the south-central Andean coast. (*Lat. Am. Antiq.*, 5, 1994, p. 212–227, bibl., ill.)

Well-preserved cotton textiles and bone artifacts suggesting use of hallucinogens are associated with an adult male burial in the Ilo region dated ca. 3750 BP.

674 **Zighelboim, Ari.** Encenas de sacrificio en montañas en la iconografía moche. (*Bol. Mus. Chil. Arte Precolomb.*, 6, 1995, p. 35–70, bibl., ill.)

Classification of vessels by number of peaks (one to five), subdivided by associated actors, reveals four basic schemes that are described in detail.

URUGUAY

675 **Congreso Nacional de Arqueología Uruguaya, 8th, Maldonado, Uruguay, 1994.** Arqueología en el Uruguay: 120 años después. Edición de Mario Consens, José María López Mazz y María del Carmen Curbelo. Montevideo: Banco Comercial, 1995. 484 p.: bibl., ill., index, maps.

Papers concentrate on four themes: archaeology of the Cuenca de la Laguna Merín, historical archaeology, ethnohistory, and specialized forms of analysis. Important source.

676 **Hilbert, Klaus.** Arqueologia pré-histórica do Uruguai: uma revisão. (*Estud. Ibero-Am. /Porto Alegre*, 20: 1, julho 1994, p. 137–161, bibl., maps)

Summarizes principal archeological traditions from Paleo-Indian to European contact periods. For Spanish-language version, see item **677.**

677 **Hilbert, Klaus.** Aspectos de la arqueología en el Uruguay. (*Hoy Hist.*, 11:61, enero/feb. 1994, p. 77–89, bibl.)

Reviews principal traditions from Pa-leo-Indian to European contact as interpreted by various investigators. For Portuguese-language version, see item **676.**

Reunião Científica da Sociedade de Arqueologia Brasileira, 7th, João Pessoa, Brazil, 1993. Actas. See item **484.**

VENEZUELA

678 *Antropológica.* No. 82, 1994/1996. La etnohistoria prehispánica Guaiquerí de Cecilia Ayala Lafée. Caracas: Fundación La Salle de Ciencias Naturales; Instituto Caribe de Antropología y Sociología.

Combining archaeological, paleoenvi-ronmental, linguistic, and ethnohistorical evidence, reconstructs Guaiquerí culture in the context of changing environmental conditions from initial occupation to European contact period on Margarita, Cubagua, and Coche islands and adjacent mainland of eastern Venezuela.

679 **Arvelo, Lilliam.** Modelo de poblamiento para la cuenca del Lago de Maracaibo. (*in* Chieftains, power & trade: regional interaction in the intermediate area of the Americas = Caciques, intercambio y poder: interacción regional en el área intermedia de las Américas. Bogotá: Depto. de Antropología, Univ. de los Andes, 1996, p. 75–106, ill., maps, table)

Temporal and spatial distributions of five ceramic traditions and two independent styles correlate with linguistic and ethnohistoric evidence for heterogeneity, implying repeated immigrations from the east, south, and west since ca. 1500 BC.

680 *Boletin Museo Arqueológico de Quibor.* No. 3, 1994. Homenaje a Erika Wagner. Quibor, Venezuela: Museo Arqueológico de Quibor.

Includes curriculum vitae of Wagner, as well as articles on ethnohistory, ethnobotany, and validity of precolumbian population estimates for the middle Orinoco and interior Guayana.

681 **Durán, Reina.** Una aldea prehispánica en Colinas de Queniquea. (*Bol. Inf. / San Cristóbal*, 10:10, 1993, p. 5–63, bibl., ill.)

Preliminary results of excavations in a settlement consisting of some 30 residential terraces.

682 Sanoja, Mario and **Iraida Vargas Arenas.** Gente de la canoa: economía política de la antigua sociedad apropiadora del noreste de Venezuela. Caracas: Fondo Editorial Tropykos; Comisión Estudios de Postgrado, UCV, 1995. 463 p.: bibl., ill., maps.

Site characteristics, subsistence remains, and artifacts from preceramic sites are interpreted in the context of social anthropological theory to reconstruct responses to changing environmental conditions prior to the first millenium BC.

683 Spencer, Charles S.; Elsa M. Redmond; and **Milagro Rinaldi.** Drained fields at La Tigra, Venezuelan llanos: a regional perspective. (*Lat. Am. Antiq.*, 5, 1994, p. 119–143, bibl., ill., maps)

Discrepancy between estimated food requirements of the nearest settlement and productivity of a drained field complex eliminates demographic pressure as the cause of construction ca. AD 550.

684 Vargas Arenas, Iraida. Historia arqueológica de Caracas. (*in* Seminario de Arqueología del Caribe, *1st, Altos de Chavón, Dominican Republic, 1995.* Ponencias. Altos de Chavón, Dominican Republic: Museo Arqueológico Regional Altos de Chavón; Organization of American States, 1996, p. 129–150, bibl., ill.)

Excavations in five locations to facilitate reconstruction of colonial structures provide data on daily life that supplement traditional historical emphasis on exceptional persons and events.

685 Vargas Arenas, Iraida and **Mario Sanoja.** La selva tropical y las sociedades antiguas en la Cuenca del Caribe. (*Rev. Arqueol. Am.*, 8, 1995, p. 71–89, bibl.)

Review of human exploitation of the riverine ecosystems of eastern Venezuela from earliest evidence to present supports the need to study and preserve the archaeological and natural resources.

ETHNOLOGY
Middle America

JEFFREY H. COHEN, *Assistant Professor of Anthropology, Pennsylvania State University*

THERE WAS A TIME when ethnographers could portray Mesoamerican communities as populations isolated from the influence of global economics, national politics, and the rapid rate of contemporary social change, and expect little argument or disagreement from fellow academicians. Certainly there was little regard for the opinions of the "natives," nor much desire to place village studies into frameworks that might account for unanticipated events like the Zapatista uprising. Recently, however, anthropologists, sociologists, and activists have begun to grapple with, and report upon, the revolutionary changes taking place among the populations with whom they work. This growing trend can be linked to several watershed events including: 1) the Zapatista uprising in Mexico; 2) the signing of peace treaties in Guatemala and El Salvador; 3) open elections in Nicaragua; and 4) transnational migration. Much of the work cited here suggests a rethinking of basic assumptions concerning the awareness that indigenous and peasant communities have of their place and role in global economics.

Some of the most important work of the biennium can be found in two multi-disciplinary volumes that outline the historical antecedents to the Zapatista movement in Chiapas (items **695** and **761**). An important innovation found in *El arreglo de los pueblos Indios* is the translation of each chapter into an indigenous language, fostering a dialogue between local leaders and academics (item **695**). Gossen adds a further dimension to our knowledge of the Zapatistas by defining the movement's roots according to Mayan thought and worldview (item **729**). Moving the discussion of human rights from Mexico to Guatemala is *Maya cultural activism* which brings together essays by Maya and non-Maya activists and anthropologists (item **749**). A trend that I would hope to see continue is the current movement towards a passionate, involved ethnography that not only reports on the struggle for justice in Mesoamerica, but takes an activist role in calling for change. Most outstanding in this respect is Binford's sensitive and thoughtful analysis of the El Mozote massacre in El Salvador (item **702**).

The study of ethnic identity has been perhaps the most active area of research during the biennium and a majority of the articles reviewed for this volume (and many that could not be included) touch upon this issue. Much of the work moves beyond a discussion of the definition of identity to an examination of the politics of ethnicity and the responses of indigenous peoples to ongoing change (see Wilson, item **781** and Carmack, item **709** on Mayan resistance and Campbell's outstanding volume on the Isthmus Zapotec, item **705**). Article-length pieces examine the construction of ethnicity in ethnographic research. Cook and Joo argue that scholars must carefully explain the use of the term *Indian,* taking into account that ethnography's historical assumptions may cloud analysis (item **715**). Watanabe examines how ethnographic constructions inform academic and popular debates (particularly in terms of pan-Mayanism) (item **780**). Finally, Nash suggests that scholars need to account for the ways that glosses of ethnicity may obscure local debates of ethnic meaning and identity (item **758**).

A third important area of growth in the field concerns the study of transnational migration and its profound impact on both sending and receiving communities, as well as on national policies. Altamirano and Hirabayashi's important collection of essays demonstrates the influence of rural to urban migration on identity, politics, and the economy (item **689**). Descriptions of different populations continue to provide important ethnographic data and add to our understanding of migration as a social process chosen by a growing number of Mexicans and Central Americans (items **690, 712,** and **775**).

Exceptional ethnography continues to be written on the region. Much of this work concentrates on gender issues, relations of power, cultural change, and the environment. Alonso and Frye provided community studies that place contemporary populations into rich webs of history (items **692** and **722** respectively). Eber (item **718**) and Gutmann (item **732**) authored strong works on gender and its ties to politics, cultural movements, and development concerns. The outstanding analysis of Kuna plant knowledge by Ventocilla *et al.* stands as an example of the benefits that multidisciplinary, cooperative research projects can offer to both scholars and natives (item **777**). Finally, the three volumes on indigenous medical knowledge and practices by Virginia Mellado-Campos *et al.* are a monumental addition to our basic understanding of the continued role of traditional medical practices among Mexico's native communities (item **751**).

686 Acheson, James M. Household organization and budget structures in a Purepecha pueblo. (*Am. Ethnol.,* 23:2, May 1996, p. 331–351, bibl., graphs)

In-depth analysis of budgeting strategies and household production in a Purepecha furniture-making community. Identifies household types and explores how household differences develop from various investment and budget strategies.

687 Adams, Richard N. Ethnic conflict, governance, and globalization in Latin America, with special attention to Guatemala. (*in* Ethnic conflict and governance in comparative perspective. Washington: Woodrow Wilson International Center for Scholars, 1995, p. 51–69)

Adams discusses the difficult position in which Guatemala's indigenous communities are caught. While increasing media coverage fosters international communication, the issues facing indigenous communities continue to be defined by nation-States and the history of ethnic politics. Solutions must be based on local factors; unfortunately the resolution of ethnic conflict remains unlikely. For related information see item **688.**

688 Adams, Richard N. A report on the political status of the Guatemalan Maya. (*in* Indigenous peoples and democracy in Latin America. New York: St. Martin's Press, 1994, p. 155–186, appendix, tables)

See item **687.**

689 Albó, Xavier et al. Migrants, regional identities and Latin American cities. Edited by Teófilo Altamirano and Lane Ryo Hirabayashi. Foreward by Stephen D. Glazier. Arlington, Va.: American Anthropological Assoc., 1997. 193 p.: bibl., ill., maps. (Society for Latin American Anthropology publication series; 13)

An interesting collection exploring the intersection of such issues as ethnicity, migration, urbanism, and nationalism. The Mesoamerican specialist will find Hirabayashi's discussion of regional identity among Zapotec migrants living in Mexico City and Michael Kearny's discussion of transnationalism particularly interesting.

690 Alcalá Delgado, Elio and Teófilo Reyes Couturier. Migrantes Mixtecos: el proceso migratorio de la Mixteca Baja. México: Instituto Nacional de Antropología e Historia, 1994. 173 p.: bibl., ill., maps. (Serie Antropología/Instituto Nacional de Antropología e Historia. Col. científica; 278)

A comprehensive analysis of migration among the Mixtec of Oaxaca. Reviews various theoretical models and presents qualitative as well as quantitative material. A good discussion of social, economic, and cultural changes brought about by migration from the region.

691 Alejos García, José. Mosojäntel: etnografía del discurso agrarista entre los Ch'oles de Chiapas. México: Univ. Nacional Autónoma de México, 1994. 259 p., 1 folded leaf of plates: bibl., ill. (some col.), index.

Focuses on oral history and the importance locals place on the early-20th century, a period when many Ch'ole men worked as *mozos* on coastal plantations. The stories are a defining feature of local identity and provide a backdrop for understanding current patterns of social change.

692 Alonso, Ana María. Thread of blood: colonialism, revolution, and gender on Mexico's northern frontier. Tucson: Univ. of Arizona Press, 1995. 314 p.: bibl., index, 2 maps. (Hegemony and experience)

This outstanding volume links the analysis of community and social organization with macro-level processes and history. Examines how gender, ethnicity, and local concepts of power relate to national identity, economy, and power. A fascinating discussion of Mexican society and the revolutionary change occuring along Mexico's northern border.

693 Alvarez, Robert R. Changing ideology in a transnational market: *chile* and *chileros* in Mexico and the US. (*Hum. Organ.,* 53:3, Fall 1994, p. 255–262, bibl., map)

An important analysis of entrepreneurial change (and the movement away from patron-client ties) in Mexican and US chile markets in light of NAFTA.

694 Alvarez, Robert R. and George A. Collier. The long haul in Mexican trucking: traversing the borderlands of the north and the south. (*Am. Ethnol.,* 21:3, Aug. 1994, p. 606–627, bibl.)

Authors survey trucking among northern Mexicans and highland Mayas and note the different networks each group depends upon to facilitate business and incorporate themselves into Mexico's growing economy. The northern Mexican group relies on personal networks and patronage while Mayan truckers rely on ethnically based cooperative ties.

695 El arreglo de los pueblos Indios: la incansable tarea de reconstitución. Selección de textos y nota introductoria de Jacinto Arias. Tuxtla Gutiérrez, Mexico: Secretaría de Educación Pública/Gobierno del Estado de

Chiapas, Instituto Chiapaneco de Cultura,
Unidad de Escritores Mayas Zoques, 1994.
463 p.: bibl., ill. (some col.).
    A collection of seven outstanding es-
says covering the history of indigenous movements and rebellion in Mexico. The goal of
the collection is to establish the historical
antecedents to the Zapatista uprising. The
volume includes discussions of Chiapas
(Whiting, Fábregas Puig and Arias Pérez),
Oaxaca (Díaz-Polanco and Burguete), Sonora
and the Yaqui (Hu-DeHart) the border region
(Arrieta), and general changes in indigenous
society (Varese). Each essay has been translated into one of four indigenous languages:
Chol, Zoque, Tzeltal, and Tzotzil, making the
volume an important addition for natives as
well as academics.

Arroyo Mosqueda, Artemio. El mundo multiple: tradición y modernidad en la Huasteca
Hidalguense. See item **4564.**

696   **Babb, Florence E.** After the revolution:
       neoliberal policy and gender in Nicara-
gua. (*Lat. Am. Perspect.,* 23:1, Winter 1996,
p. 27–48, bibl.)
    Important discussion of the effects of
neoliberal economic policies on the roles of
women in the household and the work force.
The author argues for the extended analysis
of the ways in which women are continually
marginalized, made to work harder, and
forced to reorganize (particularly into cooperatives) to cope with programs of structural
adjustment.

697   **Báez Cubero, Lourdes.** La reproducción
       de la identidad de los grupos domésti-
cos Nahuas, a través de la práctica de diversas
alternativas de subsistencia. (*in* Primer anuario de la dirección de etnología y antropología
social del INAH. México: Instituto Nacional
de Antropología e Historia, 1995, p. 169–180,
bibl.)
    Discussion of the ways in which
household production strategies create a
framework for cultural resistance, appropriation, and innovation within Nahua
communities.

698   **Barabas, Alicia M.** El proceso de des-
       identificación étnica de los Chochos
de Oaxaca. (*in* Primer anuario de la dirección
de etnología y antropología social del INAH.
México: Instituto Nacional de Antropología e
Historia, 1995, p. 127–149, bibl., map, table)

    Explores the decline of identity among
the Chocholteca. Suggests the strengths and
weaknesses of geographic and social network
approaches to identify. Argues for a model
that accounts for social change and is sensitive to the relationship of ethnicity, identity,
and globalization.

699   **Baskes, Jeremy.** Coerced or voluntary?:
       the *repartimiento* and market partici-
pation of peasants in late colonial Oaxaca.
(*J. Lat. Am. Stud.,* 28:1, Feb. 1996, p. 1–28)
    An analysis of the *repartimiento* in
Oaxaca as a voluntary system through which
peasants sought loans from their *alcaldes.*
While credit was expensive, this does not
equal exploitation. The expense was, in part,
the *alcalde's* way of surviving in a risky market system, and the credit gained allowed the
peasants to participate more readily in the
market.

700   **Behar, Ruth.** Rage and redemption:
       reading the life story of a Mexican mar-
keting woman. (*in* The dialogic emergence of
culture. Edited by Dennis Tedlock and Bruce
Mannheim. Urbana: Univ. of Illinois Press,
1995, p. 148–178)
    An interesting discussion of gender,
the art of doing life history, and the translation of field experience to text. Making the
article particularly engaging is the way in
which it examines preconceived notions of
peasant women in Mexico. The essay presents the life story of a complex individual
who is both using and responding to these
general notions in her own construction of
self.

701   **Bellon, Mauricio R.** Farmers' knowl-
       edge and sustainable agroecosystem
management: an operational definition and
an example from Chiapas, Mexico. (*Hum.
Organ.,* 54:3, Fall 1995, p. 263–272, bibl.)
    The author shows that sustainable
agriculture is influenced by environmental,
social, and economic constraints that limit
farmers' actions. While some practices may
be sustainable (the maintenance of various
strains of corn by Chiapan farmers), other
practices (plowing, fertilizer misuse) are not.
Bellon suggests that successful development
must combine sustainability with local values and practices.

Berlin, Heinrich; Gonzalo de Balsalobre; and
Diego de Hevia y Valdés. Idolatría y supersti-

ción entre los indios de Oaxaca. See *HLAS* 56:394.

702 Binford, Leigh. The El Mozote massacre: anthropology and human rights. Tucson: Univ. of Arizona Press, 1996. 282 p.: bibl., ill., index, maps. (Hegemony and experience)

Combines personal testimonials with ethnographic and historical detail placing El Mozote within the context of the political economy of the country, the region, and hemisphere. The volume is important for its frank portrayal of El Salvador and the massacre, and for its analysis of human rights reporting and protest in Central America. Proposes an anthropology that engages in the struggle for human rights, rather than simply studying it. For the sociologist's comment see item **4693.**

703 Briseño Guerrero, Juan. Aquí nomás—aquí somos: reproducción de la organización comunal de Ocuiltzapoyo S.L.P. México: Centro de Investigaciones y Estudios Superiores en Antropología Social, 1994. 232 p.: bibl., ill. (Col. Miguel Othón de Mendizábal)

A discussion of the persistence of a Nahua community despite the threats posed by trends in Mexican lawmaking. Through the analysis of oral history and daily life practices, the author demonstrates how the stories people tell create a foundation for community, which is maintained through work, particularly agricultural production.

704 Brittin, Alice A. Close encounters of the third world kind: Rigoberta Menchú and Elisabeth Burgos's *Me llamo Rigoberta Menchú.* (*Lat. Am. Perspect.,* 22:4, Fall 1995, p. 100–114)

According to the author, focusing on the inconsistencies discovered in *testimonios* written by and about indigenous women, questioning the truthfulness of their stories misses the power of the narrative genre and its ability to give a voice to people frequently who are unheard. Truth is not the issue, rather it is understanding the relationships that exist between teller, translator, and the State.

Byland, Bruce E. and **John M.D. Pohl.** In the realm of 8 Deer: the archaeology of the Mixtec codices. See item **302.**

705 Campbell, Howard. Zapotec renaissance: ethnic politics and cultural revivalism in southern Mexico. Albuquerque: Univ. of New Mexico, 1994. 347 p.: bibl., ill., index.

In this outstanding ethnography, Campbell explores how the construction of identity and the politics of ethnicity provide the Zapotec a sense of local power and independence. Focuses on the important role of indigenous intellectuals and the movement for local rule that has long consumed the community and its population.

706 Cancian, Frank. The hamlet as mediator. (*Ethnology/Pittsburgh,* 35:3, Summer 1996, p. 215–228, bibl., map, table)

Cancian explores the nature and meaning of the hamlet in Mesoamerica focusing on its role as a "mediator" for local society and its ongoing adaptation to State pressure. As with so much of his work on Zinacantán, this is an outstanding discussion of the complexities of rural life and the relationship of a local community to the State.

707 Capello, Héctor M. *et al.* Nuevas identidades culturales en México. Coordinación de Guillermo Bonfil Batalla. México: Consejo Nacional para la Cultura y las Artes, 1993. 225 p.: bibl., ill. (Pensar la cultura)

A collection of six essays exploring aspects of cultural identity. Linking the discussion of ethnicity, religion, gender, migration, national character, and new social movements in barrios and among migrants is an appreciation for the hierarchical, political and class-based nature of identity. The collected works are an important addition to our growing understanding of modern Mexico and the dynamics of identity, both its formation and negotiation.

708 Carlsen, Robert S. Social organization and disorganization in Santiago Atitlán, Guatemala. (*Ethnology/Pittsburgh,* 35:2, Spring 1996, p. 141–160, bibl.)

Traces the development of Santiago Atitlán pointing out the ebb and flow of village autonomy and identity in relation to other indigenous villages, Spanish influences, and international politics.

709 Carmack, Robert M. Rebels of highland Guatemala: the Quiché-Mayas of Momostenango. Norman: Univ. of Oklahoma

Press, 1995. 559 p.: bibl., ill., index. (Civilization of the American Indian series; 215)

A powerful ethnohistory/ethnography of the Quiché-Maya. Carmack goes into great detail as he describes 500 years of tense and cyclical sociocultural, economic, and political contact between Maya and Ladino populations. In addition to a complex account of Ladino dominance, the author reveals how the Maya construct powerful responses to their percieved powerlessness.

710   Castañeda, Quetzil E. In the museum of Maya culture: touring Chichén Itzá. Minneapolis: Univ. of Minnesota Press, 1996. 356 p.: bibl., ill., index, maps.

Very interesting discussion of the ways in which anthropology, tourism, archaeology, and popular culture all contribute to the creation of the Maya as a social unit and Chichén Itzá as a place.

711   Chance, John K. The barrios of colonial Tecali: patronage, kinship, and territorial relations in a central Mexican community. (*Ethnology/Pittsburgh,* 35 : 2, Spring 1996, p. 107–139, bibl., tables)

Analysis of the barrio in Mesoamerican studies tends to move too quickly from precolumbian to modern times, resulting in historical gaps in the literature. Using colonial data from Santiago Tecali in the Valley of Puebla, this work helps fill in the gaps as it describes the barrio's development as a dynamic blend of indigenous and colonial structures. For archaeologist's comment, see item **43.**

712   Chavez, Leo Ralph. The power of the imagined community: the settlement of undocumented Mexicans and Central Americans in the United States. (*Am. Anthropol.,* 96 : 1, March 1994, p. 52–73)

A valuable study of migration. Using logistic regressions to test the importance of community among Mexican and Central American immigrants to the US, the author finds that the ability to integrate one's self into a community is often more significant than legal issues.

713   Cojtí Cuxil, Demetrio. Políticas para la reivindicación de los Mayas de hoy: fundamento de los derechos específicos de pueblo Maya. 1. ed., Ed. especial. Guatemala: Editorial Cholsamaj; SPEM, 1994. 86 p.: bibl.

This critique of assimilationist and hybrid approaches to the study of indigenous cultural change (described as internal colonialism) proposes in their place a model based on autonomy and social equality. Proposes nine methods for creating a new Guatemalan society based upon equal rights and cultural plurality.

714   Collier, George A. Structural adjustment and new regional movements: the Zapatista rebellion in Chiapas. (*in* Ethnic conflict and governance in comparative perspective. Washington: Woodrow Wilson International Center for Scholars, 1995, p. 28–50, bibl., maps)

Examination of the Zapatista rebellion as a movement that effectively links disparate, but equally marginal, sectors of Chiapan society. The movement's strength comes from its ability to organize Chiapan poor (ethnic and otherwise) around shared symbols in order to challenge their marginality in relation to the State.

715   Cook, Scott and **Jong-Taick Joo.** Ethnicity and economy in rural Mexico: a critique of the indigenista approach. (*LARR,* 30 : 2, 1995, p. 33–59, bibl.)

This important article that argues it is time to rethink *indigenismo* and our use of the term *indigenous* in descriptions of Mesoamerican populations. According to the authors, the term must be more than an unsubstantiated anthropological marker, especially given the rapid pace of social change in Mesoamerica.

716   Díaz Barriga, Miguel. *Necesidad:* notes on the discourses of urban politics in the Ajusco foothills of Mexico City. (*Am. Ethnol.,* 23 : 2, May 1996, p. 291–310, bibl.)

A detailed and interesting analysis of the meanings that urban poor living on the outskirts of Mexico City associate with the term *necesidad* (meaning, "necessity," as in "the poor are those with necesity"). Díaz-Barriga explores how the use of the term criticizes the State and structures of power, even as it reproduces and reinforces those same structures.

Díaz Polanco, Héctor. Indigenous peoples in Latin America: the quest for self-determination. See item **6.**

717   Dow, James. Ritual prestation, intermediate-level social organization, and Sierra Otomí oratory groups. (*Ethnology/*

Pittsburgh, 35:3, Summer 1996, p. 195–202, bibl.)

This piece explores how the Otomí create themselves through ritual action and how that action mediates social relations between individuals and families, and within the community.

718 Eber, Christine Engla. Women & alcohol in a highland Maya town: water of hope, water of sorrow. Austin: Univ. of Texas Press, 1995. 327 p.: bibl., ill., index.

Eber combines a sensitive, reflexive style of writing, to create a powerful and insightful account of the changing uses of alcohol among Mayan women. The result is a text that is ethnographically rich and theoretically challenging. Alcoholism is much more than a substance abuse issue, it is embedded in social, gender, and ethnic relations.

719 Estado y nación: las demandas de los grupos étnicos en Guatemala. Recopilación de Jorge Solares. Guatemala: FLACSO Guatemala; Fundación Friedrich Ebert, 1993. 468 p.: bibl.

Summarizes four FLACSO-Guatemala conferences (1988–90) that included intellectuals, clergy, and urban and rural leaders. The volume's innovative style mixes dialogues from the seminars with essays on issues of ethnicity, self-identity, perception of the "other," and interethnic relations. The goal is to foster a dialogue on Guatemala's changing landscape, and the place of ethnicity in this process.

720 Fernández Poncela, Anna M. The disruptions of adjustment: women in Nicaragua. (*Lat. Am. Perspect.*, 23:1, Winter 1996, p. 49–66, bibl.)

A strongly-worded critical piece in which the author points out the high costs of structural adjustment for Nicaraguan women. Issues include psychological stress, violence, the breakdown of infrastructural support, and the politics of reproduction.

721 Field, Les W. Constructing local identities in a revolutionary nation: the cultural politics of the artisan class in Nicaragua, 1979–90. (*Am. Ethnol.*, 22:4, Nov. 1995, p. 786–806, bibl.)

Field's discussion of artisan cooperatives in Nicaragua is an excellent account of the dynamic relationship between ethnic identity, class consciousness, and revolutionary State politics.

722 Frye, David. Indians into Mexicans: history and identity in a Mexican town. Austin: Univ. of Texas Press, 1996. 258 p.: bibl., ill., index, map.

An interesting blend of ethnography and history follows the town of Mexquitic, San Luis Potosí, through more than two centuries. Focuses on how identity is negotiated through time, and the roles played by the Church, representatives of the State, and the local population as the community is transformed from a "Republic de los Indios" to a mestizo town.

723 Fuentes etnológicas para el estudio de los pueblos Ayuuk (Mixes) del estado de Oaxaca. Recopilación de Salomón Nahmad Sittón. Oaxaca, Mexico: CIESAS-Oaxaca; Instituto Oaxaqueño de las Culturas, 1994. 636 p.: bibl., ill. (Dishá. Colección Antropología)

An excellent resource on the Mixe that combines new and reprinted ethnographic studies. Includes an extensive bibliography.

724 García Canclini, Néstor. Mexico: cultural globalization in a disintegrating city. (*Am. Ethnol.*, 22:4, Nov. 1995, p. 743–755, bibl.)

Argues that anthropology must embrace an interdisciplinary perspective (drawing on sociology and communication studies) to better explore, understand, and explain urban culture. Anthropology's strength in local analysis combined with an appreciation of global processes will help the discipline move past the babel of urban culture and in the process, become better at representing and understanding social groups.

725 Gledhill, John. Neoliberalism, transnationalization and rural poverty: a case study of Michoacán, Mexico. Boulder, Colo.: Westview Press, 1995. 254 p.: bibl., ill., index, maps.

An analysis of agrarian reform policies and their impact on the rural poor during the Salinas administration (1988–94). Argues that neoliberal policies must be analyzed through the lens of class-based politics, tied to global economic transformations (including migration), and, at the same time, must be specific to Mexico's unique history and relationship to the US.

726   **Godoy, Ricardo.** The effects of rural education on the use of the tropical rain forest by the Sumu Indians of Nicaragua: possible pathways, qualitative findings, and policy options. (*Hum. Organ.*, 53 : 3, Fall 1994, p. 233–244, bibl.)

Uses evidence from local educational programs to suggest that they are worthwhile for more than short-term environmental solutions, and, if administered as part of larger development programs, should afford better environmental protection and management.

727   **Goldin, Liliana R.** Economic mobility strategies among Guatemalan peasants: prospects and limits of nontraditional vegetable cash crops. (*Hum. Organ.*, 55 : 1, Spring 1996, p. 99–107, bibl., tables)

Investigation of the social and economic costs and benefits of shifts in production from traditional to nontraditional crops among Guatemalan peasant farmers.

728   **González Ventura, Josefa Leonarda.** Vida cotidiana de Jicayan. v. 1. Oaxaca de Juárez, Mexico: CELIAC, 1993. v. 1: bibl., ill., map.

A product of the project "Preservación de la Literatura Indígena," this is a sensitive and empowering native ethnography. González-Ventura describes life in Ñuu Savi, and in doing so, is able to defend a local community that is beginning the process of self-preservation and self-documentation.

729   **Gossen, Gary H.** From Olmecs to Zapatistas: a once and future history of souls. (*Am. Anthropol.*, 96 : 3, Sept. 1994, p. 553–570)

Gossen argues the Zapatista revolt is about more than agrarian reform. The author believes that it is also concerned with the construction of a pan-Mayan movement based upon the soul as a coessence tying individuals to each other and to the community. The movement allows the Zapatista to create a following among those sharing their conception of the soul.

730   **Greenberg, James B.** Capital, ritual, and boundaries of the closed corporate community. (*in* Articulating hidden histories: exploring the influence of Eric R. Wolf. Edited by Jane Schneider and Rayna Rapp. Berkeley: Univ. of California Press, 1995, p. 67–81)

A fascinating discussion of Mixe economic practices. Greenberg examines the way in which money and external capitalism are interpreted locally, and the ways in which the Mixe reconstruct the market according to cultural knowledge and local values.

731   **Guionneau-Sinclair, Françoise.** Los Kuna de Panamá y la represa del Bayano, 20 años despúes. (*Tareas/Panamá*, 90, mayo/agosto 1995, 103–117, bibl., tables)

Clear discussion of the development, impact, and status of the Bayano River dam in Panama. The author outlines the environmental, biological, cultural, and social impacts of the project and current actions taken by the Kuna in association with other ethnic groups to counter continued degradation.

732   **Gutmann, Matthew C.** The meanings of macho: being a man in Mexico City. Berkeley: Univ. of California Press, 1996. 344 p.: bibl., ill., index, maps. (Men and masculinity; 3)

An important and interesting volume on gender, focusing on the meaning of manhood in Mexico City. Much more than a discussion of machismo, the text challenges the stereotypes of the Latin male and in their place paints a portrait of rapidly changing gender roles.

733   **Hale, Charles R.** Resistance and contradiction: Miskitu Indians and the Nicaraguan State, 1894–1987. Stanford, Calif.: Stanford Univ. Press, 1994. 296 p.: bibl., ill., index, maps.

This interesting ethnography follows the contradictions of Miskitu ethnicity as the population (caught between US imperialism and the Sandinistas) struggles to become part of the nation while maintaining its identity. Hale explores the politics of nation building, the constitutive role of hegemony among subordinate peoples, and the place of anthropology and the anthropologist in the construction of identity. For the historian's comment see *HLAS 56:1728.*

734   **Hammond, John L.** Popular education in the Salvadoran guerrilla army. (*Hum. Organ.*, 55 : 4, Winter 1996, p. 436–445)

An interesting discussion of the role education played in the development of the FMLN's forces. Author discusses positive impact of popular education among the largely illiterate peasant membership of the army. For sociologist's comment, see item **4717.**

735 **Harris, Max.** Moctezuma's daughter: the role of *la malinche* in Mesoamerican dance. (*J. Am. Folk.*, 109:432, 1996, p. 149–179)

Through analysis of a variety of dances, the author describes the role of the *Malinche*, not in the story of the conquest, but rather as a semidivine figure powerful in her own right and integral to the construction of indigenous cosmology and the negotiation of social space.

736 **Hendrickson, Carol Elaine.** Weaving identities: construction of dress and self in a highland Guatemala town. Austin: Univ. of Texas Press, 1995. 259 p.: bibl., ill., index, maps.

An innovative ethnography of Maya *traje* that describes the social life of cloth, its role in the construction of identity, and its part in the changing structure of regional gender relations. *Traje* empowers, brings women into the global market, and is an enduring of symbol cultural knowledge.

737 **Hernández Castillo, Rosalva Aída.** Invención de tradiciones: encuentros y desencuentros de la población Mame con el indigenismo Mexicano. (*Anuario/Tuxtla Gutiérrez*, 1994, p. 146–171, bibl., maps)

Interesting discussion of contact and dialogue between the Mam and Mexican societies around such important issues as identity, ethnicity, and the meaning of "indigenous." The author effectively shows how the Mam use dialogue with the State to create a framework for resistance.

738 **Heyman, Josiah McConnell.** Changes in house construction materials in border Mexico: four research propositions about commoditization. (*Hum. Organ.*, 53:2, Summer 1994, p. 132–142, tables)

The author suggests changes in the materials used in house construction signal more than economic transitions. The analysis of house types needs to account for the ways time is defined; whether or not the household is an investment; the changing nature of networks; and the analysis of consumption and social inequality.

739 **Hirabayashi, Lane Ryo.** Mountain Zapotec migrants and forms of capital. (*PoLAR/Washington*, 17:2, 1994, p. 105–116)

Interesting application of Pierre Bourdieu's ideas on forms of capital to the discussion of changes in patterns of association and dispute resolution among Zapotec migrants living in Mexico City.

740 **Hofling, Charles Andrew.** Indigenous linguistic revitalization and outsider interaction: the Itzaj Maya case. (*Hum. Organ.*, 55:1, Spring 1996, p. 108–116, bibl.)

A critical discussion of the role anthropologists play in "linguistic revitalization" projects. Hofling asks that we, as outside researchers with our own agendas, carefully consider the scope and impact of our actions as well as the local, state, and international relationships that influence the structure, organization, and possible success of any project.

741 **Howell, Jayne.** This job is harder than it looks: rural Oaxacan women explain why they became teachers. (*Anthropol. Educ. Q.*, 28:2, June 1997, p. 251–279, bibl., map, tables)

Covering a woefully underrepresented area in the ethnographic record, Howell examines the social and economic reasons behind, the ramifications of, and recent declines in the movement of women into teaching careers in rural Oaxaca.

742 **Hu-DeHart, Evelyn.** Adaptación y resistencia en el Yaquimi: los Yaquis durante la colonia. Traducción de Zulai Marcela Fuentes Ortega. Revisión de traducción de Teresa Rojas Rabiela. México: CIESAS; INI, 1995. 124 p.: bibl., ill. (some col.), maps (some col.). (Historia de los pueblos indígenas de México)

An interesting discussion of Yaqui history focusing on the arrival of the Spanish, the impact of Jesuit missionaries, and the indigenous response (in particular the rebellion of 1740). Places Yaqui history into a global perspective and shows the linkages between this isolated region and the Crown, the Church, and extra-local economic forces.

743 **Journal of Latin American Anthropology.** Vol. 2, No. 1, Fall 1996. Mestizaje. Arlington, Va.: Society for Latin American Anthropology, 1996. 182 p.

An important collection of articles exploring the concept of *mestizaje* as used by people of varying and contradictory status through space (primarily Central and South America) and time (historical and current examples). Mesoamericanist contributions follow the development of mestizaje in Nicaragua from the early-20th century through the revolution. Carol Smith and Florencia Mallon add provocative concluding essays.

744 Kearney, Michael. Desde el indigenismo a los derechos humanos: etnicidad y política más allá de la Mixteca. (*Nueva Antropol.*, 14:46, 1994, p. 49–67)

Important discussion of the ways that migration impacts upon the struggle for human rights and the meaning of ethnicity. Kearney shows how the movement of Mixtec to California allows them to escape hegemonic pressures of State bureaucracy, organize at a pan-ethnic level, and gain support for the improvement of civil/human rights in Mexico. For related article, see item **745.**

745 Kearney, Michael. The effects of transnational culture, economy, and migration on Mixtec identity in Oaxacalifornia. (*in* The bubbling cauldron: race, ethnicity, and the urban crisis. Edited by Michael Peter Smith and Joe R. Feagin. Minneapolis: Univ. of Minnesota Press, 1995, p. 226–243)

For related article, see item **744.**

Leal Carretero, Silvia. *Xurawe, o, La ruta de los muertos:* mito huichol en tres actos. See *HLAS 56:4219.*

746 Leatham, Miguel C. Practical religion and peasant recruitment to non-Catholic groups in Latin America. (*Relig. Soc. Order*, 6, 1996, p. 175–190)

A fascinating examination of evangelical conversion in Mexico and Latin America. Author explores how peasants frame new religious practices in a "folk-Catholic" paradigm to meet the challenges of everyday life.

747 Lisbona Guillén, Miguel. Los estudios sobre Zoques de Chiapas: una lectura desde el olvido y la reiteración. (*Anu. Inst. Chiapaneco Cult.*, 1993, p. 78–125b, bibl., maps)

An excellent resource and bibliography on the Zoque covering works that date from the conquest through 1993.

748 Low, Setha M. Spatializing culture: the social production and social construction of public space in Costa Rica. (*Am. Ethnol.*, 23:4, Nov. 1996, p. 861–879, bibl., photos)

Explores how public spaces become the settings for contesting and producing social

meaning. For sociologist's comment, see item **4727.**

749 Maya cultural activism in Guatemala. Edited by Edward F. Fischer and R. Mckenna Brown. Austin: Univ. of Texas Press/Institute of Latin American Studies, 1996. 253 p.: bibl., ill., index, maps. (Critical reflections on Latin America series)

An important collection of essays on Mayan activism. Included are pieces by native and non-native scholars reviewing Guatemalan history, ethnic violence, peasant and indigenous cultural resistance to the State, material culture, development, and literacy. Each article brings to the fore a concern for human rights.

750 Medina, Laurie Kroshus. Development policies and identity politics: class and collectivity in Belize. (*Am. Ethnol.*, 24:1, Feb. 1997, p. 148–169, bibl.)

Medina studies the intersection of class, ethnicity, and identity in the Belizean citrus industry. Focusing on a variety of players, including politicians, business executives and wage laborers, the author examines how class identity is segmented and reformulated in response to social setting and practice. For sociologist's comment, see item **4729.**

751 Mellardo Campos, Virginia et al. La medicina tradicional de los pueblos indígenas de México. Colaboración de Soledad Mata Pinzón et al. Dirección de Carlos Zolla. Coordinación de Virginia Mellado Campos. Revisión de María del Carmen Carrillo Farga. México: Instituto Nacional Indigenista, 1994. 3 v. (977 p.): bibl., ill., maps. (Biblioteca de la medicina tradicional mexicana)

An ambitious and outstanding work on traditional medical practices of Mexico's indigenous peoples. The three volume set is divided into chapters describing indigenous populations. After brief ethnographic sketches, the particular practices of each group are discussed. Issues covered include Western and indigenous diseases and their cures, the resources of each cultural group, and problems that threaten each group's traditional practices.

752 Moberg, Mark. Myths that divide: immigrant labor and class segmentation in the Belizean banana industry. (*Am. Ethnol.*, 23:2, May 1996, p. 311–330, bibl., tables)

Moberg examines the changing structure of the Belizean banana industry as waves of Central American immigrants enter the country. He critiques class segmentation theory and argues that the politics of ethnicity and migration both divide and link workers in much the same fashion as class.

753 Monaghan, John. The covenants with earth and rain: exchange, sacrifice, and revelation in Mixtec sociality. Norman: Univ. of Oklahoma Press, 1995. 310 p.: bibl., ill., index, maps. (The civilization of the American Indian series; 219)

Interesting ethnography explores how Nuyootecos create community through a social life based on fictional relationships that mimic family ties. See also item **754** for a related journal article by the same author.

754 Monaghan, John. The Mesoamerican community as a *great house.* (*Ethnology/Pittsburgh*, 35:3, Summer 1996, p. 181–194, bibl.)

See item **753.**

755 Mulhare, Eileen M. Barrio matters: toward an ethnology of Mesoamerican customary social units. (*Ethnology/Pittsburgh*, 35:2, Spring 1996, p. 93–106, bibl.)

Suggests that the concept of the "barrio" is too often ill-defined in the literature. As she points out in her conclusions, the issue is more than academic. The barrio as a misunderstood model of social organization can have a negative effect on development projects, and may also miss the dynamics of change in peasant and indigenous communities in Mesoamerica.

756 Muñoz Cruz, Héctor and Rossana Podestá Siri. Yancuitlalpan: tradición y discurso ritual. México: Univ. Autónoma Metropolitana, Unidad Iztapalapa, División de Ciencias Sociales y Humanidades, 1994. 205 p.: bibl., ill., maps. (Iztapalapa, texto y contexto; 19)

A rich sociolinguistic account of Nauhautlata ritual and ceremony built around the investigation of Yancuitlapan (Puebla, Mexico) oral tradition. Discussion includes detailed presentation of non-verbal and oral traditions associated with rites of passage, community celebrations, and the village's *mayordomias.*

757 Nab'ab'l qtanam: la memoria colectiva del pueblo mam de Quetzaltenango; una antologia de mitos y leyendas, cuentos, fábulas, historias, relatos de vida, tradiciones religiosas, costumbres y creencias sobre la base de la tradición oral y documentos históricos. Recopilación de Rainer Hostnig y Luis Vásquez Vicente. Quetzaltenango, Guatemala: Centro de Capacitación e Investigación Campesina, 1994. 281 p.: ill. ;

Anthropologists and local leaders joined together to produce this volume documenting local traditions. The result is an excellent collection of myths, rituals, and practices (plus minimal analysis) of the Mam.

758 Nash, June. The reassertion of indigenous identity: Mayan responses to State intervention in Chiapas. (*LARR*, 30:3, 1995, p. 7–41, bibl.)

An important discussion of the positive and negative uses of ethnicity in Maya communities in Chiapas. Nash demonstrates the error of a universalizing model of ethnicity. As an alternative, she explores a range of communities and identities: from those where ethnicity is exploitative (particularly communities where caciques hold power), to those where ethnicity is a tool for resisting State politics and global market forces. For political scientist's comment, see item **3086.**

759 Nutini, Hugo G. Mesoamerican community organization: preliminary remarks. (*Ethnology/Pittsburgh*, 35:2, Spring 1996, p. 81–92, bibl.)

Nutini reviews the contribution of Mesoamerican studies to the theoretical development of ethnology. He argues for renewed emphasis on understanding the place of kinship in Mesoamerican society to foster the studies of community change and social transformation.

760 Ouweneel, Arij. From *tlahtocayotl* to *gobernadoryotl:* a critical examination of indigenous rule in 18th-century central Mexico. (*Am. Ethnol.*, 22:4, Nov. 1995, p. 756–785, bibl., maps)

Using data from the 18th century, the author argues that the indigenous villages of Anáhuac, central Mexico, were stratified communities. Further, the author maintains that the structure of these communities was an adaptation to colonial rule not a mechanism of social control imposed by Spanish officials.

761 **Paisajes rebeldes: una larga noche de rebelión indígena.** Coordinación de Jane-Dale Lloyd y Laura Pérez Rosales. México: Univ. Iberoamericana, Depto. de Historia, 1995. 291 p.: bibl. (Serie Historia y grafía; 1)

Eight important essays by outstanding scholars explore the historical development of the uprising in Chiapas. The essays work to place the events of 1994 and beyond into a framework that takes into account the movement's social and cultural antecedents (Knight, Aoyama, Thomson, Van Young, and Benjamin), as well as more recent trends in Mexican politics (Harvey, de Vos, and Casillas).

762 **People of the peyote: Huichol Indian history, religion & survival.** Edited by Stacy B. Schaefer & Peter T. Furst. Albuquerque: Univ. of New Mexico Press, 1996. 574 p.: bibl., ill., index, map.

An international and multidisciplinary collection on the Huichol. Chapters on contemporary life include the discussion of gender, religion, healing and ceremonial practices, peyotism, and cultural change. Particularly interesting are Nahmad Sitton's piece on Huichol religion and the Mexican State; Shaefer's chapter on peyotism and meaning; and the conclusions co-authored by Furst and Schaefer that offers an excellent illustration of the challenges and dynamism of Huichol contemporary life.

763 **Pitarch Ramón, Pedro.** Animismo, colonialismo y la memoria histórica Tzeltal. (*Rev. Esp. Antropol. Am.*, 26, 1996, p. 183–203, bibl.)

Interesting discussion of the understudied question of selfhood among the Tzeltal. The author shows how Tzeltal ideas concerning the co-essence of souls organizes historical knowledge of self and community.

764 **Re Cruz, Alicia.** Una comunidad Maya de Yucatán: transformación social y expresión simbólica. (*Rev. Esp. Antropol. Am.*, 26, 1996, p. 167–181, bibl.)

Interesting discussion of the growing importance of migration in the reproduction of Chan Kom. Author blends symbolic theory and political economy to unravel the complex issues of identity, cultural knowledge, and social change.

765 **Rubio, Miguel Angel.** Tiempo de peregrinar: el Señor de Tila y la cosmovisión de los Chontales. (*Am. Indíg.*, 54:1/2, enero/junio 1994, p. 119–148, bibl.)

Rich ethnographic discussion of the Chontal religious pilgrimage to the site of Señor de Tila in Chiapas, Mexico. The author explores the rituals associated with the pilgrimage and the syncretism of Chontal and Catholic beliefs.

766 **Sandstrom, Alan R.** Center and periphery in the social organization of contemporary Nahuas of Mexico. (*Ethnology/Pittsburgh*, 35:3, Summer 1996, p. 161–180, bibl., tables)

Valuable piece exploring various mediating structures that exist between local kin and family ties on one hand and macro-State systems on the the other, and which aid villagers in their struggles to cope with a changing world.

767 **Seligson, Mitchell A.** Thirty years of transformation in the agrarian structure of El Salvador, 1961–1991. (*LARR*, 30:3, 1995, p. 43–74, bibl., graphs, tables)

The 1992 peace accords moved El Salvador away from its history of revolution and unprecedented atrocities. However, Seligson points out, the peace accord will do little to solve the continued problem of the landless and land-poor. Rather, the accords will likely diminish concern for the country and inequalities will remain for the foreseeable future. For sociologist's comment, see item **4747** and for economist's comment, see item **1792.**

768 **Semillas de industria: transformaciones de la tecnología indígena en las Américas.** Edición de Mario Humberto Ruz. México: CIESAS; Washington: Smithsonian Institution, 1994. 266 p.: bibl.

Outstanding collection of ethnographic and historical essays, extended commentaries, and summaries that examine changes in technology, markets, and production among Mesoamerican craft makers. Contributions focus on environmental issues, the conquest, the role of anthropological research, and colonial history in the construction of present-day indigenous resistance and agricultural change. Particularly valuable are essays by Nash exploring the contradictions of craft production in Mexico, and by Turok and Morris discussing change and continuity among Chamulan women weavers.

769 Sherzer, Joel. The Kuna and Columbus: encounters and confrontations of discourse. (*Am. Anthropol.*, 96:4, Dec. 1994, p. 902–924)

A traditional chant performed in 1970 is translated with local assistance as a means of exploring the intersection of Kuna and non-Kuna cultural systems. This outstanding piece points out that the goal of anthropology is not necessarily "correct" translation, rather, it should be aimed at understanding the how and why meaning is assigned in different situations.

770 Stanford, Lois. Transitions to free trade: local impacts of changes in Mexican agrarian policy. (*Hum. Organ.*, 53:2, Summer 1994, p. 99–109, bibl., tables)

Analysis of Mexico's new agrarian laws pays attention to their impact upon rural, small scale, agricultural communities. Stanford argues that the government has not succeeded in modernizing the agricultural sector, instead increased foreign investment has led to rising regional competition, declining profits and unstable, unbalanced economic growth that impacts the structure of rural communities. For economist's comment see item **1699.**

771 Suárez-Orozco, Carola and **Marcelo M. Suárez-Orozco.** Transformations: immigration, family life, and achievement motivation among Latino adolescents. Stanford, Calif.: Stanford Univ. Press, 1995. 285 p.: bibl., index.

Explores migration between the US and Mexico and focuses on the differences among adolescent groups. The authors analyze four populations (native Mexican, native North Americans, first generation Latino immigrants, and second generation immigrants) and begin to unravel the difficult issues of cultural differences, social identity, family structure, and personal reasons for migrating.

772 Tice, Karin Elaine. Kuna crafts, gender, and the global economy. Austin: Univ. of Texas Press, 1995. 240 p.: bibl., ill., index, maps.

An informative analysis of craft production among the Kuna. Tice combines rich ethnographic detail and a description of mola

production with an analysis of the impact of global market forces, tourism, and state programs (including the development of craft cooperatives) on local culture.

773 Truex, Gregory F. *Barrio* as a metaphor for Zapotec social structure. (*Ethnology/Pittsburgh*, 35:3, Summer 1996, p. 203–213, bibl., tables)

Explores the meaning and use of the barrio in a rural Zapotec community. The discussion focuses on the complexity of the term as a maker of membership and a symbol of identity.

774 Vásquez Dávila, Marco Antonio. Hábitat y cultura de los Chontales del centro, Tabasco. (*Am. Indíg.*, 54:1/2, enero/junio 1994, p. 91–118, bibl., maps, table)

General introduction to Chontal society and culture emphasizing interethnic relations with mestizo populations and Chontal adaptation to Tabasco's environment.

775 Vásquez Rojas, Edith and **Manlio O. Cobos Orozco.** Un acercamiento a los Choles y Tzeltales de Tenosique, Tabasco. (*Am. Indíg.*, 54:1/2, enero/junio 1994, p. 341–376, bibl.)

The authors document the migration of Choles and Tzeltales from their homelands in Chiapas to Tabasco's southeastern forest. While this movement has taken the Tzeltal and Chol out of highly exploitive situations in Chiapas, the authors suggest that new challenges face their communities.

776 Ventocilla, Jorge et. al Los indígenas Kunas y la conservación ambiental. (*Mesoamérica/Antigua*, 16:29, junio 1995, p. 95–124, bibl., map, photos)

See item **777.**

777 Ventocilla, Jorge; Heraclio Herrera; and **Valerio Núñez.** Plants and animals in the life of the Kuna. Edited by Hans Roeder. Translated by Elisabeth King. Austin: Univ. of Texas Press, 1995. 165 p.: bibl., ill., index. (Translations from Latin America series)

More than an account of Kuna ecology, this book argues for a positive environmental policy. The authors urge the Kuna to consider the potential ecological hazards of pursuing certain business interests, and remind their readers of the reliable, though delicate, relationship that exists between human society and the natural world. For related information, see item **776**.

778 Verbeeck, Lieve. Het spel en de stokjes: mesoamerikaanse bordspelen. The game and the sticks: Mesoamerican board games. (*Wampum/Leiden*, 14, 1996, p. 3–137, bibl., ill, map, photos)

Two-part article: 1) describes *patolli, kolítza, bul,* and their relationship to other Mesoamerican board games; and 2) discusses in more detail the Mayan game of *bul* in the small Mopan community of Santa Cruz in Belize. Focuses on influence of Maya traditional culture on modern life. Based on four months of fieldwork in 1993. [R. Hoefte]

779 Villar, Maria de Lourdes. Hindrances to the development of an ethnic economy among Mexican migrants. (*Hum. Organ.*, 53:3, Fall 1994, p. 263–268, bibl.)

Discussion of Mexican-American entrepreneurs in Chicago demonstrates that patterns of association and employment create an enclave economy lacking ties to regional markets.

780 Watanabe, John M. Unimagining the Maya: anthropologists, others, and the inescapable hubris of authorship. (*Bull. Lat. Am. Res.*, 14:1, Jan. 1995, p. 25–45)

A criticism of naive ethnography and the identity pan-Mayanists construct from that same ethnography. Watanabe challenges this pattern and suggests it is time to consider the role ethnography plays in the process of identity negotiation, and to spend less time on theories and the poetics of reportage.

781 Wilson, Richard. Maya resurgence in Guatemala: Q'eqchi' experiences. Norman: Univ. of Oklahoma Press, 1995. 397 p.: bibl., ill., index, maps.

Important work blends relational and essentialist approaches to the study of ethnicity. The outcome is an analysis of identity, religious conversion, armed insurrection, and State repression that takes into account constrained meanings (material and historical processes, both real and invented) and processual meanings (creatively living and dealing with the exigencies of the moment). For historian's comment see *HLAS 56:1799*.

782 Woodrick, Anne C. A lifetime of mourning: grief work among Yucatec Maya women. (*Ethos/Society*, 23:4, Dec. 1995, p. 401–422, bibl., table)

For related information, see item **783**.

783 Woodrick, Anne C. Mother-daughter conflict and the selection of ritual kin in a peasant community. (*Anthropol. Q.*, 68:4, Oct. 1995, p. 219–233, bibl., tables)

The author argues there is an overemphasis on the role of men in the study of *compadrazgo*. Here the creation of godparent relationships between mothers and daughters is explored in detail as a force mediating the stresses of problematic courtships and estrangements following marriage. For related information, see item **782**.

784 Zapata Martelo, Emma. Modernization, adjustment, and peasant production: a gender analysis. (*Lat. Am. Perspect.*, 23:1, Winter 1996, p. 118–130, bibl.)

The author examines the marginal status of women in rural Mexico and how it influences the structure and success of agrarian development programs. For sociologist's comment, see item **4683**.

West Indies

LAMBROS COMITAS, *Gardner Cowles Professor of Anthropology and Education, Teachers College, Columbia University and Director, Research Institute for the Study of Man*

THIS SECTION INCLUDES annotations of publications on sociocultural dimensions of anthropology that cover the Caribbean archipelago, The Guianas, Belize, and several other West Indian or West Indian-like enclaves located on other parts of the Circum-Caribbean mainland or world. Slightly more than three-quarters of these annotations deal with the following countries or dependencies: Antigua, Barbados, Barbuda, Belize, British Virgin Islands, Colombia, Cuba, Curaçao, Dominica, the Dominican Republic, French Guiana, Ghana, Grenada, Guyana, Haiti, Jamaica, Martinique, Montserrat, Nevis, Puerto Rico, St. Lucia, St. Vincent, Suriname, Trinidad, and Venezuela. The remaining deal with the Caribbean in either regional or subregional terms. The countries, territories, or regional units receiving the most attention during this biennium were Jamaica (supporting, in part, Michael Manley's pungent contention a number of years ago that Jamaica is the most studied and least understood country in the Caribbean), followed by Trinidad, the Caribbean in general, Guyana, and Suriname.

As in the past, the publications cited cover a wide range of subject matter, including a very few examples (of a rapidly growing genre) that deal with migratory experiences of Caribbean folk away from the Caribbean. Therefore, for the reader's convenience, I have categorized most of the works cited into several broad, overlapping topical categories, in order of quantitative importance.

a) Ethnicity and identity. During the past few years, a great deal of the anthropological research on the Caribbean has been focused on questions related to these two linked themes. This biennium is certainly no exception; more than thirty of the citations in this section are devoted to either ethnicity or identity or both including the following four readers or collections of articles: *Across the dark waters: ethnicity and Indian identity in the Caribbean* (item **786**), *Ethnicity in the Caribbean: essays in honor of Harry Hoetink* (item **827**), *Ethnicity, race and nationality in the Caribbean* (item **828**), and *Les Indes antillaises, présence et situation des communautés indiennes* (item **829**). Among other citations, see also Angrosino on the Indo-Caribbeans (item **789**), Austin-Broos on heritable identity in Jamaica (item **791**), Chalifoux on the Hmong in French Guiana (item **817**), Duany on transnational migration from the D.R. (item **825**), Eguchi on the reconstruction of Carib ethnic identity (item **826**), Henry and Tracey on multi-ethnicity in Trinidad (item **844**), Khan on Muslims in Trinidad (item **850**), Koningsbruggen on Trinidad carnival (item **854**), Kumar Misra on a separate East Indian identity in Trinidad (item **876**), Mintz on ethnic difference and plantation sameness (item **875**) and on the concept of ethnicity (item **873**), Oostindie on the Dutch Caribbean predicament (item **883**), Price and Price on museums and ethnicity (item **892**), and Tracey on adaptive responses to race and ethnic conflict in Trinidad (item **907**).

b) Religion. If one includes publications on Rastafari, it would appear that there has been a significant increase in writings about religion-related phenomena during this biennium. Twenty-one citations are listed in this category including the three-volume conference proceedings (one each on cults, voodoo, and Rastafari) entitled *AyBoBo: Afro-Karibische Religionen/African Caribbean religions* (item **902**) and *Rastafari and other African-Caribbean worldviews* (item **819**). See also Austin-Broos on State and religion in Jamaica (item **790**), Bernard on popular religion in Haiti (item **800**), Besson and Chevannes on the continuity-creativity debate (item **803**), Brea and Millet on Africanisms in Cuban carnivals (item **814**), Chevannes on revivalism and identity in Jamaica (item **820**), Glazier on funeral practices in Trinidad (item **834**) and new religious movements in the Caribbean (item **835**), Houk on Orisha in Trinidad (item **847**), Kremser on Kélé in St. Lucia (item **855**), Pollak-Eltz on anima worship in Venezuela (item **888**), and others. For writings on Rastafari, see also Chevannes on a new approach to Rastafari (item **818**) and the symbolism of dreadlocks in Jamaica (item **819**), Savishinsky on the global spread of the Rastafarian movement (item **4922**), Simpson on recollections of 1953 work with Rastafari (item **899**), and Yawney on the appeal of Rastafari religion (item **914**).

c) Aspects of social relations and social organization. See Berleant-Schiller on labor to peasantry (item **797**), Besson on peasant adaptation (item **804**) land, kinship, and community in the Leewards (item **805**) and on a rejoinder to Crichlow (item **802**), Birth on transracial kinship in Trinidad (item **810**), Browne on informal economy in Martinique (item **815**), Drayton on Caribbean textbooks (item **823**), Gmelch on Barbadian return migrants (item **822**), Gmelch and Gmelch on St. Lucy Parish, Barbados (item **836**), Handwerker on domestic violence (item **841**), King on Belizean management of marine resources (item **852**), Lazarus-Black on kinship and family policy in Antigua (item **859**), LeFranc on a re-examination of the Jamaican family system (item **860**), Lowes on decline of Antiguan elites (item **862**), Martinez on the Haitian *bracero* in the D.R. (item **864**), Maurer on common property in the Caribbean (item **867**) and on family land in the British Virgin Islands (item **868**), Mintz on the Caribbean as *oikoumen* (item **873**), Moberg on transnational labor in Belize (item **877**), Phillips on street children in Trinidad (item **887**), Price on a comparison of Martinican and Saramaka Maroon race relations (item **889**), R.T. Smith on racial violence in Guyana (item **901**), and Yelvington on flirting in a Trinidadian factory (item **915**).

d) Women's studies and gender relations. Seventeen citations are listed in this section including the collection entitled *Women and change in the Caribbean: a pan-Caribbean perspective* (item **913**). See Abraham-van der Mark on mating patterns of Curaçaoan Sephardic elites (item **785**), Allen on Curaçaoan women and Cuban migration (item **787**), Barrow on small-scale women farmers in Barbados (item **794**), Berleant-Schiller and Maurer on women's roles in Barbuda and Dominica (item **799**), Besson on reputation and respectability (item **806**), Bolles on women and work in Jamaica (item **812**), LaFont on family courts in Jamaica (item **856**), Lake on Rastafarian women (item **857**), McKay on tourism in Negril, Jamaica (item **870**), Miller Matthei and Smith on Garifuna women (item **866**), Olwig on Nevisian women at home and abroad (item **882**), Parry on gender in the classroom (item **885**), Pereira on violence and sex (item **886**), and Yelvington on gender, ethnicity, and class in a Trinidadian factory (items **916** and **917**).

e) Maroon/Amerindian studies. See Besson on Jamaican Maroon land tenure patterns (item **801**), Bilby on Aluku identity development (item **807**), on oral traditions of Jamaican Maroons and the Aluku of the Guianas (item **808**), and on the meaning of oaths and treaties for Maroons (item **809**), Forte on Guyanese Amerindians for the non-specialist (item **832**) and on Guyanese Amerindian culture, economics, politics, and language (item **830**), Groot on Maroon pacification in Suriname (item **838**), Mentore on the Waiwai and distribution of the hunt (item **871**), Myers on the Makushi Caribs (item **879**), Price on State violence against Surinamese Maroons (item **891**), Sanders on the protected status of Guyanese Amerindians (item **896**), Thoden van Velzen on collective fantasies of the Surinamese Nydukas (item **906**), Vernon on Ndjuka ethnomedicine and Maroon identity (item **910**), and Zips on Jamaican influences on African diasporic discourses (item **918**) and on the history and contemporary situation of Jamaican Maroons (item **919**).

f) Aspects of culture. See Allen on resistance as a creative factor (item **788**), Birth on Trinidadian models of time (item **811**), Crooks on bicultural factors in Belizean school achievement (item **821**), Hoogbergen on resistance (item **846**), Losonczy on African slave beliefs (item **861**), Maynard on the translocation of the Yoruba *esusu* (item **869**), Miller on mass consumption in Trinidad (item **872**), Olwig on the cultural complexity (item **880**) and national culture of Nevis (item **881**), Price and Price on museum openings in Guyane, Spain and Belize (item **890**), Stevens on symbolism of *manje* in Haiti (item **905**), Vargas on Dominican villages (item **908**), and Zips on the "continuity of Black resistance" (item **920**).

I am indebted to Dennis St. George, Lewis Burgess, and Lisa Citron for their generous assistance in compiling this section.

785   Abraham-Van der Mark, Eva. Marriage and concubinage among the Sephardic elite of Curaçao. (*in* Women & change in the Caribbean: a Pan-Caribbean perspective. Kingston: Ian Randle; Bloomington: Indiana Univ. Press; London: J. Currey, 1993, p. 38–49, bibl.)

Focusing on women's role in the survival of Sephardic Jewish community of Curaçao, author deals with issues of marriage, kinship, religion, and caste with reference to means used by the group to maintain its economic and political power despite risks and fluctuations of a trade-based economy. Provides interesting description and analysis of *kerida*, an institutionalized form of concubinage.

786   Across the dark waters: ethnicity and Indian identity in the Caribbean. Edited by David Dabydeen and Brinsley Samaroo. London: Macmillan Caribbean, 1996. 222 p.: bibl., index. (Warwick University Caribbean studies)

Useful collection of essays is derived primarily from 1988 conference on East Indians in the Caribbean. Contributors are not mainly ethnographers; however, their subject matter (race relations, religious and cultural practices, etc.), and their manner of dealing with it, are essentially anthropological. Includes 10 chapters dealing with Trinidad, Jamaica, Guyana, and Suriname.

787   Allen, Rose Mary. Curaçaoan women's role in the migration to Cuba. (*in* Mundu yama sinta mira: womanhood in Curaçao. Curaçao: Fundashon Publikashon, 1992, p. 59–75, bibl.)

Examines direct and indirect participation of Curaçaoan women in the labor migrations to Cuba during first two decades of 20th century. Both women who migrated and those who stayed behind found themselves in male-dominated public spheres as workers and/or spokespersons for their absent men. In both situations, women's activities are seen

as survival strategies and as evidence of increased flexibility in their roles.

788   Allen, Rose Mary. Resistance as a creative factor in Curaçaoan culture. (*in* Born out of resistance: on Caribbean cultural creativity. Utrecht, The Netherlands: ISOR-Publications, 1995, p. 63–74, bibl.)

By describing slaves' expressions of dissatisfaction with their conditions, critically examines idea that slaves were well treated in Curaçao.

789   Angrosino, Michael V. The Indo-Caribbeans: evolution of a group identity. (*Rev. Rev. Interam.*, 26:1/4, enero/dic. 1996, p. 67–108, bibl.)

Reviews social science perspectives on Indo-Caribbeans and relates changes in these views to changes in folk conceptions of identity. Asserts that Indo-Caribbean intellectuals have taken the lead in defining their identity and the nature of their own society.

790   Austin-Broos, Diane J. Politics and the Redeemer: State and religion as ways of being in Jamaica. (*NWIG*, 70:1/2, 1996, p. 59–90, bibl.)

Examines role of "popular" churches in Jamaica, emphasizing the Pentecostal experience, the relationship of that church with the State, and the importance of the Pentecostal transcendental ideology on these issues. Includes case material. For sociologist's comment, see item **4765**.

791   Austin-Broos, Diane J. Race/class: Jamaica's discourse of heritable identity. (*NWIG*, 68:3/4, 1994, p. 213–233, bibl.)

Discusses cultural concepts of race and class in Jamaica, rejecting idea that race encompasses class or that Jamaican culture is definable by reference to a naturalized hierarchy based on race. Argues that race and class are distinct but closely related aspects of a larger "discourse of heritable identity" in which concepts of inherited, internalized environmental influences coincide with biological categories of race. Meaning of discourse will vary according to placement of actor in Jamaican society.

792 Austin-Broos, Diane J. Redefining the moral order: interpretations of Christianity in postemancipation Jamaica. (*in* The meaning of freedom: economics, politics, and culture after slavery. Pittsburgh, Pa.: Univ. of Pittsburgh Press, 1992, p. 221–243, bibl.)

Relates developments in Jamaican Christianity to social and economic conditions since emancipation. Argues that Jamaicans have interpreted Christianity over time in ways which render it meaningful to their experience. Consequently, analysis of religion in Jamaica should not be concerned solely with identifying Africanisms as resistances and European influences as domination; rather, Christianity should be considered as having been localized and reconstructed by Jamaicans. For historian's comment, see *HLAS 54:1969*.

793 Aymer, Paula L. Uprooted women: migrant domestics in the Caribbean. Westport, Conn.: Praeger, 1997. 172 p.: bibl., index, map.

Traces labor migration of women from Eastern Caribbean to oil-producing countries such as Venezuela, Trinidad, Curaçao, and especially Aruba. Discusses women's participation in the labor force, gender relations, domestic service, the social and economic position of the migrants, and motherhood. Argues that US investments are an important factor in the migration of Caribbean women. [R. Hoefte]

794 Barrow, Christine. Small farm food production and gender in Barbados. (*in* Women & change in the Caribbean: a Pan-Caribbean perspective. Kingston: Ian Randle; Bloomington: Indiana Univ. Press; London: J. Currey, 1993, p. 181–193, bibl.)

Study of small-scale female farmers in Barbados focuses on gender distinctions in resource allocation and division of labor. Argues that one legacy of slave plantation system is a cultural arrangement that prescribes total involvement of Afro-Caribbean women in agriculture and other aspects of the economy. In this context, a survey of 111 small farmers, divided equally by sex, found a "remarkable degree" of equality between male and female farmers with regard to access to land and other resources, even though the women farmers did not constitute a homogenous group.

795 Barthélemy, Gérard. Dans la splendeur d'un après-midi d'histoire. Port-au-Prince: Editions Henri Deschamps, 1996. 428 p.: bibl.

Anthropological perspectives on aspects of a political/social/economic history of Haiti include commentary on language, race, agriculture, and religion. Based on author's interpretation of other textual matter as well as on participant observations.

796 Beahrs, Andrew. "Ours alone must needs be Christians": the production of enslaved souls on the Codrington Estates. (*Plant. Soc. Am.*, 4:2/3, Fall 1997, p. 279–310, facsims., map, table)

Analyzes failure of Society for the Propagation of the Gospel to convert the slaves of the Codrington Estates in 18th-century Barbados. Argues that the project was flawed because its conception of slavery differed from that prevailing on the island. Clash of missionary and planter models of slavery did, however, result in new formulation: transition to a racial justification for slavery rendered conversion socially meaningless.

797 Berleant-Schiller, Riva. From labour to peasantry in Montserrat after the end of slavery. (*in* Small islands, large questions: society, culture and resistance in the post-emancipation Caribbean. Edited by Karen Fog Olwig. London; Portland, Or.: F. Cass, 1995, p. 53–72, bibl.)

Traces development of a peasantry in post-emancipation Montserrat. Squatting on abandoned land, purchases of freeholds, and sharecropping contributed to growth of this category despite official policies designed to deny land to freedmen.

798 Berleant-Schiller, Riva. The white minority and the emancipation process in Montserrat, 1807–32. (*NWIG*, 70:3/4, 1996, p. 255–281, bibl.)

Self-defeating behavior of majority of white oligarchy in Montserrat during emancipation process, particularly its contempt for law and the Constitution, significantly contributed to this group's decline.

799 Berleant-Schiller, Riva and Bill Maurer. Women's place is every place: merging domains & women's roles in Barbuda & Dominica. (*in* Women & change in the Caribbean: a Pan-Caribbean perspective. Kingston: Ian Randle; Bloomington: Indiana Univ. Press; London: J. Currey, 1993, p. 65–79, bibl., ill.)

Comparative analysis of women's roles not only examines similarities and differences between the two islands, but also attempts to validate/refute the public-private dichotomy which has characterized the literature on gender-based status differentiation.

800 Bernard, Jean Maxius. Le fêtes champêtres et la religion populaire en Haïti. (*Bull. Bur. natl. ethnol.*, numéro spécial 1987–1992, p. 106–113, bibl.)

Brief analysis and description of Haitian popular religion emphasizes aspects of feasts and festivals celebrating rural life. Reveals syncretisms between Catholicism, patron-saint worship, and voodoo.

801 Besson, Jean. Caribbean common tenures and capitalism: the Accompong Maroons of Jamaica. (*Plant. Soc. Am.*, 4:2/3, Fall 1997, p. 201–232)

Maroons' highly integrated social organization in town of Accompong challenges relevance of "plantation society" models for understanding Caribbean society. Moreover, author argues, Maroon corporate land tenure is not a pre-capitalist "survival;" rather, it is a Creole adaptation to global capitalism.

802 Besson, Jean. Consensus in the family land controversy: rejoinder to Michaeline A. Crichlow. (*NWIG*, 69:3/4, 1995, p. 299–304)

Gives a point-by-point reply to Crichlow's analysis (see *HLAS 55:786*) of family land tenure in the Anglophone Caribbean. Despite Crichlow's criticisms of Besson's work, the latter determines that Crichlow's actual findings "mainly support" her own conclusions.

803 Besson, Jean and **Barry Chevannes.** The continuity-creativity debate: the case of Revival. (*NWIG*, 70:3/4, 1996, p. 209–228, bibl.)

Examines Jamaican religious beliefs and practices since slavery. Authors argue that although Revival has African antecedents, it has been transformed by Jamaicans to meet the challenges of contemporary life. Framing the debate about Jamaican religion in the polarized terms of "African continuity" or "Creole creativity" is not helpful for understanding methods of and reasons for religious expression.

804 Besson, Jean. Free villagers, Rastafarians and modern Maroons: from resistance to identity. (*in* Born out of resistance: on Caribbean cultural creativity. Utrecht, The Netherlands: ISOR-Publications, 1995, p. 301–314, bibl.)

Based on extensive field work in Trelawney, Jamaica, author argues that free villagers, Maroons, and rural Rastafarians represent a tradition of Caribbean peasant adaptation rooted in land as a "focus of domination, resistance, and identity."

805 Besson, Jean. Land, kinship, and community in the post-emancipation Caribbean: a regional view of the Leewards. (*in* Small islands, large questions: society, culture and resistance in the post-emancipation Caribbean. Edited by Karen Fog Olwig. London; Portland, Or.: F. Cass, 1995, p. 73–99, bibl.)

Compares post-emancipation agricultural production in Hispanic and non-Hispanic Caribbean, the latter characterized by "peasantries and their customary tenures." In this context, "land, kinship, and community" are discussed, with special attention paid to the Leewards.

806 Besson, Jean. Reputation & respectability reconsidered: a new perspective on Afro-Caribbean peasant women. (*in* Women & change in the Caribbean: a Pan-Caribbean perspective. Kingston: Ian Randle; Bloomington: Indiana Univ. Press; London: J. Currey, 1993, p. 15–37, bibl.)

Contends that while Peter Wilson's theory of reputation and respectability as a means of understanding Caribbean society (see *HLAS 31:2032* and *HLAS 43:8250*) has much to recommend it, the theory obscures understanding of Afro-Caribbean women. Drawing on data from Jamaica and the Anglophone Caribbean, author argues that, contrary to Wilson's formulation, "Afro-Caribbean peasant women do not subscribe to Eurocentric respectability and . . . they participate in the main dimensions of reputation identified by Wilson." In fact, author places women at the center of "Afro-Caribbean cultures of resistance."

807 Bilby, Kenneth M. The emergence of an ethnic enclave: the Aluku. (*SWI Forum*, 8:2, dec. 1991, p. 48–55)

Briefly describes identity development of the resettled Aluku (Boni) in French Guiana. Argues that "the unique identity the Aluku inhabit (which occupies a space between French Guianese Creole identity at one pole, and Surinamese Maroon identity at the other, while being defined in contrast to both) remains strong."

808 Bilby, Kenneth M. Oral traditions in two Maroon societies: the Windward Maroons of Jamaica and the Aluku Maroons of French Guiana and Surinam. (*in* Born out of resistance: on Caribbean cultural creativity. Utrecht, The Netherlands: ISOR-Publications, 1995, p. 169–180, bibl.)

Traces the "Abandoned Child," the "Miracle Food," and the "Bullet Catching" themes in the oral traditions of two Maroon societies which are said to express a "common Maroon ethos."

809 Bilby, Kenneth M. Swearing by the past, swearing to the future: sacred oaths, alliances, and treaties among the Guianese and Jamaican Maroons. (*Ethnohistory/Society*, 44:4, Fall 1997, p. 655–698, bibl., ill.)

Interprets treaties between colonial authorities and Maroons in Jamaica and Guyana. Author brings to the task contemporary ethnographic data about Maroons and the meaning of oaths among West Africans. Argues that Maroons held the treaties to be sacred and immutable and, therefore, they should be interpreted in that light. The "spirit" of the treaties, with implications for continued self-determination, remains salient for the Maroons.

810 Birth, Kevin K. Most of us are family some of the time: interracial unions and transracial kinship in eastern Trinidad. (*Am. Ethnol.*, 24:3, Aug. 1997, p. 585–601, table)

Uses 15 interracial unions between indigenous peoples and Creoles, and attendant transracial kinship links, to explore naturalizing ideologies tied to conceptions of race in Trinidad. Ideas of race and kinship held by each group take on different meanings when used in the context of transracial relationships. Differing affiliation patterns play a role in determining the relative strength of kinship ties and consequent claims of similarity and difference. Three patterns are discerned: 1) cultural notions of "diluted" Creoles and indigenous peoples; 2) schismogenic interactions that evoke attributions of either differ-

ence or similarity; and 3) influence of longstanding indigenous patrifiliation and Creole matrifiliation patterns on the development of transracial ties.

811 Birth, Kevin K. Trinidadian times: temporal dependency and temporal flexibility on the margins of industrial capitalism. (*Anthropol. Q.*, 69:2, April 1996, p. 79–89, bibl.)

Examines the relationship between unemployment and an inflexible model of time among rural Trinidadians who did not complete secondary school. The more traditional flexible models of time are said to promote adaptability to patterns of occupational multiplicity, but secondary education teaches a model more appropriate for regularized labor. For sociologist's comment, see item **4774.**

812 Bolles, Augusta Lynn. Sister Jamaica: a study of women, work, and households in Kingston. Lanham, Md.: Univ. Press of America, 1996. 129 p.: bibl., ill., map.

Study of working-class factory women at home and in the workplace was carried out during last years of Michael Manley's administration. After reviewing political and economic context of female labor and working conditions, author deals with basic strategies of how women and their households "make do" by analyzing domestic chores and household division of labor by household type.

813 Born out of resistance: on Caribbean cultural creativity. Edited by Wim Hoogbergen. Utrecht, The Netherlands: ISOR-Publications, 1995. 418 p.

Recommended collection. For anthropological contributions see Allen (on resistance and Curaçaoan women), Besson (on free villagers), Bilby (on oral traditions), Chevannes (on Revivalism), Glazier (on new religious movements), Groot (on charting Suriname's Maroons), Hoogbergen (on resistance), and Pollak-Eltz (on *anima* worship).

814 Brea, Rafael and **José Millet.** The African presence in the carnivals of Santiago de Cuba. Translated by Katheryn A. Thompson. (*J. Caribb. Stud.*, 10:1/2, Winter 1994/Spring 1995, p. 30–49, bibl.)

Examines Africanisms in Santiago de Cuba festivals. St. James is said to be associated with the Yoruba deity Oggún and the Dahomeyan Ogoú. Moreover, aspects of the celebration of carnivals are referred to by their African origins. Evolution of carnival is traced from colonial times to present. For sociologist's comment, see item **4784**.

815 Browne, Katherine E. The informal economy in Martinique: insights from the field, implications for development policy. (*Hum. Organ.*, 55:2, Summer 1996, p. 225–234, bibl., graphs)

Cross-class study of informal economy in Martinique suggests that qualitative field studies could substantially inform quantitatively-oriented development planners. Data reveal ties based on undeclared economic activities across class lines that challenge widely held assumption that informal economy is a strategic adaptation of the poor alone. From a planning perspective, the "poor" should be viewed neither as a "discrete, bonded group" nor as "economically isolated."

816 Carlin, Eithene B. Speech community formation: a sociolinguistic profile of the Trio of Suriname. (*NWIG*, 72:1/2, 1998, p. 4–42, bibl.)

Presents historical, economic, sociological, and cultural factors contributing to present-day status of the Trio and their Cariban language as update and context for exploring internal sociolinguistic factors that influence Trio speech choices.

817 Chalifoux, Jean-Jacques; Philippe Isabel; and Raphaël Rizindana. La presse et les hmongs en Guyane Française: stéréotypes et construction idéologique de l'image des hmongs et de la Guyane. (*Etud. créoles*, 16:2, 1993, p. 53–69, bibl.)

Describes and analyzes role of the press during late 1970s in constructing and diffusing stereotypes and images of Hmong immigrants to French Guiana, and ways in which these images were utilized in French Guianese discourse.

818 Chevannes, Barry. New approach to Rastafari. (*in* Rastafari and other African-Caribbean worldviews. Houndmills, England: Macmillan; The Hague: Institute of Social Studies, 1998, p. 20–42)

Reinterpreting Rastafari "in the context of cultural continuity," author argues that Rastafari is the "fulfillment" of Revival and a "worldview movement" rather than a revolutionary millenarian movement.

819 Chevannes, Barry. The phallus and the outcast: the symbolism of the dreadlocks in Jamaica. (*in* Rastafari and other African-Caribbean worldviews. Houndmills, England: Macmillan; The Hague: Institute of Social Studies, 1998, p. 97–126)

Explores meaning of "matted hair among the Rastafari," arguing that it symbolizes both separation from the world and male dominance, and that these meanings are closely related, even identical. Females represent "a force used to contain [men] within society."

820 Chevannes, Barry. Revivalism and identity. (*in* Born out of resistance: on Caribbean cultural creativity. Utrecht, The Netherlands: ISOR-Publications, 1995, p. 245–252, bibl.)

The Revivalist table ritual expresses important social values held widely in Jamaica, even by non-Revivalists. Author deals with three such values—hospitality, ancestor worship, and emotional well-being—as basis for holding that Revivalism and Pentecostalism are variant cultural expressions of the same underlying values.

821 Crooks, Deborah L. Biocultural factors in school achievement for Mopan children in Belize. (*Am. Anthropol.*, 99:3, Sept. 1997, p. 586–601, bibl., ill.)

Examines relationships among nutritional status, household factors, and school performance for 63 Mopan Maya children in the Toledo District. No clear association was found between chronic undernutrition and school performance. Variation in household environment, specifically parenting style and family size, were positively correlated with school performance. Author considers findings to be inconclusive given small sample size and insufficient operationalization and measurement of study variables.

Déita. La légende des loa du vodou haïtien. See item **4810**.

822 Double passage: the lives of Caribbean migrants abroad and back home. Interviews by George Gmelch. Ann Arbor: Univ. of Michigan Press, 1992. 339 p.: bibl., ill., index, map.

Includes 13 oral life histories of Barbadian return migrants from Great Britain and North America, a sample roughly representative of all Barbadian returnees in terms of gender, class, and receiving countries. Histories and commentary treat the entire migration cycle: reasons for departure, experiences abroad, and problems of return. Useful concluding sections on meaning of return migration and on value of oral history for such study.

823 Drayton, Kathleen B. White man's knowledge: sex, race and class in Caribbean English language textbooks. (in Gender: a Caribbean multidisciplinary perspective. Kingston: Ian Randle Publishers; Center for Gender and Development Studies, Univ. of the West Indies; Oxford, England: James Currey, 1997, p. 159–181, bibl.)

Caribbean English-language textbooks used in preparation for the Caribbean Examination are analyzed for gender bias, racial ideology, and references to class. Author concludes that the texts, reflecting the ideology of the dominant group, reproduce sexism and obscure the structural predicates of class differentiation. Moreover, racism is perpetuated by omission of references to black achievements.

824 Duany, Jorge. The creation of a transnational Caribbean identity: Dominican immigrants in San Juan and New York City. (in Ethnicity, race and nationality in the Caribbean. San Juan: Institute of Caribbean Studies, Univ. of Puerto Rico, 1997, p. 195–232, bibl., ill.)

Findings from ethnographic field research in both locales indicate existence of transnational identity among Dominicans.

825 Duany, Jorge. Transnational migration from the Dominican Republic: the cultural redefinition of racial identity. (*Caribb. Stud.*, 29:2, July/Dec. 1996, p. 253–282, bibl.)

In an analysis of racial identity among Dominican migrants to New York and Puerto Rico, author argues that the Iberian-Caribbean three-tiered model (white-mulatto-black or white-black-other) held by migrants conflicts with the two-tiered northwestern European model. Each model has implications for racial attitudes and relations, and the conflict between them is a challenge to migrants' adjustment.

826 Eguchi, Nobukiyo. Ethnic tourism and reconstruction of the Caribs' ethnic identity. (in Ethnicity, race and nationality in

the Caribbean. San Juan: Institute of Caribbean Studies, Univ. of Puerto Rico, 1997, p. 364–380, bibl.)

Discusses Carib ethnic identity within context of tourism and nation-building in Dominica. Argues that a number of aspects of that identity, particularly the "primitive," have been reconstructed as an adaptive strategy to attract tourists. Maintenance of a distinctive Carib identity, however, is not always consistent with the official nation-building efforts of Dominica.

827 Ethnicity in the Caribbean: essays in honor of Harry Hoetink. Edited by Gert Oostindie. London: Macmillan Caribbean, 1996. 239 p.: bibl., index, map, port. (Warwick University Caribbean studies)

Recommended collection. For anthropological contributions see Mintz on ethnic difference (item **875**); Oostindie on Dutch Caribbean predicament (item **883**); Price and Price on museums, ethnicity, and nation-building (item **892**); and Quintero Rivero on the somatology of manners (item **893**).

828 Ethnicity, race and nationality in the Caribbean. Edited by Juan Manuel Carrión. San Juan: Institute of Caribbean Studies, Univ. of Puerto Rico, 1997. 418 p.: bibl., ill., maps.

See items **824, 826,** and **844**.

829 Festival international de l'indianité, 1st, Saint-François, Guadeloupe, 1990. Les Indes antillaises: présence et situation des communautés indiennes en milieu caribéen. Coordination de Roger Toumson. Paris: L'Harmattan, 1994. 263 p.: bibl.

Proceedings of a 1990 intercultural colloquium held in Guadeloupe includes three contributions by anthropologists: 1) "Approche Anthropologique de l'Indianité, Composant de l'Antillanité" by J. Lirus-Galap; 2) "Trois Mythes Tamouls" by Gerry L'Étang; and 3) "Les Darçanas (*points de vue* indiens) de l'Inde à l'Espace Américain" by N. Chevry.

830 Forte, Janette. About Guyanese Amerindians. Georgetown: J. Forte, 1996. 129 p.: bibl.

Collection of author's background papers written for the Amerindian Research Unit of the Univ. of Guyana offers brief, but relatively comprehensive, survey of Guyanese Amerindian cultures, economic issues, subsistence techniques, politics, land claims, and language. Useful bibliography appended.

831 Forte, Janette. The case of *The Barama River Caribs of Guyana* restudied. (*Soc. Econ. Stud.,* 39:1, March 1990, p. 203–217, bibl.)

Critique of "recent" research on Barama River Caribs focuses primarily on Kathleen Adams' 1972 doctoral dissertation. Since it has been virtually impossible since independence to receive official permission to study Guyanese Amerindians, it is argued that data and conclusions drawn from very few, sporadic studies are often flawed because they cannot be crosschecked against parallel studies.

832 Forte, Janette. Thinking about Amerindians. Georgetown: J. Forte, 1996. 113 p.

Collection of author's papers, articles, and addresses about Guyanese Amerindians, intended for non-specialist, includes examination of their need for self-determination, the impact of economic exploitation of their territories, their position on environmental issues, and their strategic placement in Guyana's response to Brazilian regional hegemony.

833 Giraud, Michel. Dialectics of descent and phenotypes in racial classification in Martinique. (*in* French and West Indian: Martinique, Guadeloupe, and French Guiana today. Charlottesville: Univ. Press of Virginia, 1995, p. 75–85)

Discussion of racial typologies identifies several principles by which racial classifications are made: descent (one has the race of one's ancestors); inequality (categories are hierarchical); and stereotypes. Problems implicit in these principles, as well as recent changes in their operation, are also explored.

834 Glazier, Stephen D. Funerals and mourning in the spiritual Baptists and Chango traditions. (*Am. Negra,* 2, dic. 1991, p. 123–134)

Range of funeral practices of both Trinidadian religious groups are based on beliefs and forms drawn from several different sources. However, their unique feature is the extent to which African and European Christian ceremonies have been compartmentalized.

835 Glazier, Stephen D. New religious movements in the Caribbean: identity and resistance. (*in* Born out of resistance: on Caribbean cultural creativity. Utrecht, The Netherlands: ISOR-Publications, 1995, p. 253–262, bibl.)

Broad survey of Caribbean syncretic religious movements supports argument that such movements should not be considered simply as expressions of protest or products of deprivation. Rather, such movements may have accomodationist aspects and other features that would be overlooked in an approach based solely on resistance or deprivation.

836 Gmelch, George and **Sharon Bohn Gmelch.** The parish behind God's back: the changing culture of rural Barbados. Ann Arbor: Univ. of Michigan Press, 1997. 240 p.: ill.

Comprehensive ethnographic portrait of contemporary rural Barbados focuses on patterns of work, gender relations and life cycle, community, and religion in St. Lucy Parish. Recurring theme throughout work is impact of widening social relations—through globalization, tourism, transnationalism, technology, mass media—on village life and values.

837 Goldwasser, Michael. Remembrances of the Warao: the miraculous statue of Siparia, Trinidad. (*Antropológica/Caracas,* 84, 1994/1996, p. 3–41, bibl.)

History and description of the adoration of a statue located in a Catholic church in southern Trinidad. Under different names and with different rites, this statue is venerated by Catholics, Hindus, Moslems, Amerindians, and others. Although each group has its own traditions about statue's origin and significance, author argues that it links the various groups to the Warao aborigines of the island and "embodies the history of the people" of Trinidad.

838 Groot, Silvia W. de. Charting the Suriname Maroons, 1730–1734. (*in* Born out of resistance: on Caribbean cultural creativity. Utrecht, The Netherlands: ISOR-Publications, 1995, p. 142–156, bibl., ill.)

Anthropologist discusses history of Dutch efforts to pacify or eradicate Maroons in 18th-century Suriname. Uses period maps and charts, and circumstances of their creation, to flesh out narrative.

839 **Haiti. Bureau national d'ethnologie.** Le Carnaval dans nos moeurs. (*Bull. Bur. natl. ethnol.*, numéro spécial 1987–1992, p. 82–105, bibl., photos)

Photos, with text, of Haitian costumes and other carnival-associated artifacts displayed at a 1993 exhibition presented by Haiti's Bureau national d'ethnologie.

840 **Hall, Douglas.** A man divided: Michael Garfield Smith; Jamaican poet and anthropologist, 1921–1993. Kingston: Press Univ. of the West Indies, 1997. 174 p.: bibl., ill., index. (The Press UWI biography series, 0799–057X; 1)

Informative biography of the late M.G. Smith, the Jamaican-born social anthropologist whose contributions as Caribbeanist, Africanist, and theoretician will be long valued.

841 **Handwerker, W. Penn.** Why violence?: a test of hypotheses representing three discourses on the roots of domestic violence. (*Hum. Organ.*, 57:2, Summer 1998, p. 200–208, bibl., graphs, table)

Author tests three theories of domestic violence in Antigua and Barbados, finding that such violence is embodied in individuals and social relationships, not in social circumstances.

842 **Hay, Fred J.** Microethnography of a Haitian boutique. (*Soc. Econ. Stud.*, 39:1, March 1990, p. 153–166, bibl.)

Based on a six-week stay, author provides details about the Oasis Restaurante and Bar, a *plaisance boutique* operated by a local politician. Describes the central position of this *boutique*, asserted to be an important Haitian local institution, in the economic, social, and political life of the community.

843 **Heinen, H. Dieter** and **Stanford Zent.** On the interpretation of Raleigh's *Discoverie of Guiana:* a view from the field. (*Curr. Anthropol.*, 37:2, April 1996, p. 339–341, bibl.)

Authors criticize Whitehead (see item 912) on several points of fact and interpretation, and call into question his statement that anthropology is concerned with "intelligibility rather than veracity."

844 **Henry, Andre-Vincent** and **Kenneth Tracey.** Salad, *callaloo* or *pelau*: understanding multi-ethnicity in Trinidad and Tobago. (*in* Ethnicity, race and nationality in the Caribbean. San Juan: Institute of Caribbean Studies, Univ. of Puerto Rico, 1997, p. 401–416, bibl., ill.)

Argues that M.G. Smith's "plural society" model (see *HLAS 29:1542* and *8477*) fails to represent reality and does not account for the fact that elites manipulate ethnic identities for their own purposes. Authors offer their model of Caribbean ethnicity based on "co-equal cultures in a creolizing process." Model centers on genetic and cultural exchanges between Indo-Trinidadians and Afro-Trinidadians and on a form of multiculturalism that valorizes common national interests while minimizing ethnic tensions.

845 **Ho, Christine G.T.** The twin processes of racialization and ethnification among Afro-Trinidadian immigrants in Los Angeles. (*Caribb. Q.*, 41:3/4, Sept./Dec. 1995, p. 99–122, bibl.)

Analyzes how Afro-Trinidadian immigrants in Los Angeles deal with American "biracial" system of social stratification. Migrants are said to confront the process of "racialization" by strategically using their ethnic identity to "offset the liability of their race." For sociologist's comment see item **4847.**

846 **Hoogbergen, Wim.** On resistance. (*in* Born out of resistance: on Caribbean cultural creativity. Utrecht, The Netherlands: ISOR-Publications, 1995, p. 9–22, bibl.)

Editor of collection introduces theme of "resistance" in the Caribbean, arguing that it may be expressed in political, cultural, linguistic, literary, and musical terms rooted in identity, and may encompass acts on a continuum bounded by massive violent revolt on one end and almost invisible expressions of dissent on the other.

847 **Houk, James Titus.** Spirits, blood, and drums: the Orisha religion in Trinidad. Philadelphia: Temple Univ. Press, 1995. 238 p.: bibl., ill., index.

Valuable, well-presented study examines background, rites and ceremonies, and social organization of Orisha religion, "arguably the most purely African cultural practice left on the island." However, worshipers combine, in varying degrees, elements from five traditions—African, Catholic, Hindu, Protestant, and Kabbalah—to form an "Afro-American religious complex."

848 Institute of Social Studies (The Hague). Rastafari and other African-Caribbean worldviews. Edited by Barry Chevannes. Houndmills, England: Macmillan; The Hague: Institute of Social Studies, 1995. 282 p.: bibl., index.

Recommended collection includes selections by editor on native religions of Jamaica, a new approach to Rastafari, and the origin and symbolism of dreadlocks. Also includes articles by: Jean Besson on religion as resistance in Jamaica; by John Homiak on dub history (use of oral testimony by Rastafarians in their ritual discourse); Ellis Cashmore on the Rastafarian de-labeling process; H.U.E. Thoden van Velzen on African-American worldviews in the Caribbean; Wilhelmina van Wetering on Surinamese creole women's discourse on possession and therapy; and Roland Littlewood on problems in the analysis of origins.

849 Jolivet, Marie José. De "l'habitation" en Guyane: éléments de réflexion sur la question identitaire créole. (*in* Jeux d'identités: études comparatives à partir de la Caraïbe. Paris: L'Harmattan, 1993, p. 141–165)

Considers origins of French Guianese creole culture in context of small homesteads established in the wake of emancipation. Author posits the common denominator of creole culture to be the modern notion of individualism in contrast to the tribal holism of neighboring Maroons and Amerindians. Although no rupture between the economic/technological domains and the rest of culture is apparent, creolization is distinguished by the dynamic reappropriation and adaptive use of knowledge and technology from any source in accordance with the constraints imposed by time and place.

850 Khan, Aisha. Homeland, motherland: authenticity, legitimacy, and ideologies of place among Muslims in Trinidad. (*in* Nation and migration: the politics of space in the South Asian diaspora. Philadelphia: Univ. of Pennsylvania Press, 1995, p. 93–131, bibl.)

Explores authenticity and legitimacy in Muslim religious and cultural "expression," and development of transnational identity. Compares and contrasts developments among Indo-Trinidadian and Afro-Trinidadian Muslims. Former are said to manifest a shift from India as "motherland" (denoting "cultural origins") to "homeland" (related to Is-

lamic traditions); the latter are committed to a more universalistic conception of Islam. Argues that "homeland" and "motherland" concepts are instrumental in elaboration of a sense of continuity among diasporic populations.

851 Khan, Aisha. Rurality and "racial" landscapes in Trinidad. (*in* Knowing your place: rural identity and cultural hierarchy. New York: Routledge, 1997, p. 39–69, bibl.)

Concept of "rural/urban opposition" is used to explore development of spatial, racial, gender, and occupational identity in Trinidad, primarily among Indo-Trinidadians. "Opposition" has implications for formation of "cultural hierarchies" which provide an organization of identities, which in turn informs stratification. Argues that rural/urban aspect of identity, associated with the domain of "land," is essential to understanding "race" in the Caribbean.

852 King, Thomas D. Folk management among Belizean lobster fishermen: success and resilience or decline and depletion? (*Hum. Organ.*, 56:4, Winter 1997, p. 418–426)

Investigates paradoxical impact of changing tenure relations, migration of successors, and the tourist industry on Belizean lobster fishermen's management of marine resources.

853 Koningsbruggen, Petrus Hendrikus van. The spirit of Canboulay: the sociocultural autonomy of the Trinidad Carnival. (*Focaal/Nijmegen*, 30/31, 1997, p. 159–177, bibl.)

Describes various components of the Trinidad Carnival, focusing on open character of the festival. Argues that the fading away of boundaries between what were originally class-bound sociocultural spheres provides an opportunity for entirely new forms of exchange and confrontations between opposite orientations. Stresses importance of role of Creole middle class in safeguarding the event from superficiality. [R. Hoefte]

854 Koningsbruggen, Petrus Hendrikus van. Trinidad carnival: a question of national identity. London: Macmillan Caribbean, 1997. 293 p.: bibl., ill., index. (Warwick University Caribbean studies)

Presents multifaceted analysis of Trinidadian carnival, a festival seen by author as a "form of meta-comment on Trinidad within the performance of a kind of collective psychodrama." Useful chapters are devoted to the history of carnival, its development into a national festival, the social elements that influence and impact the contemporary event, social dynamics, and carnival's linkage to national identity.

855 Kremser, Manfred. Kélé in St. Lucia: a minority cult emerging from the underground. (*in* Society of Caribbean Research. International Conference, *1st, Berlin, 1988.* Alternative cultures in the Caribbean. Frankfurt: Vervuert Verlag, 1993, p. 93–101, bibl.)

Traces history of Saint Lucian *Kélé* cult. Part of African heritage of the Djine (free African migrants from the Guinea Coast), cult was practiced underground until recently when changing attitudes about Africanisms enabled free expression.

856 LaFont, Suzanne. The emergence of an Afro-Caribbean legal tradition: gender relations and family courts in Kingston, Jamaica. San Francisco: Austin & Winfield, 1996. 222 p.: bibl., ill., index.

Ethnography of the use of family courts focuses on gender relations and ideology, family structure, and dominant ideology as expressed in the law. Presents findings on gender attitudes, expectations between men and women, and range of discourse between men and women. Describes Jamaican family court as an "arena" for negotiation/contestation of gender relations, and makes convincing argument for laws/processes which are "more relevant to the target population." Argues that promotion of the "nuclear family" in law has not had its intended effects; instead, it has permitted litigants to manipulate official ideology for their own ends rather than leading to its internalization.

857 Lake, Obiagele. The many voices of Rastafarian women: sexual subordination in the midst of liberation. (*NWIG*, 68:3/4, 1994, p. 235–257, bibl.)

Despite Rastafarian rhetoric of liberation and Afrocentric symbolism, work describes de facto relationship of Rasta men to Rasta women in Jamaica as retrogressive. Domestic responsibilities and lack of access to resources reinforces inferior status of these women.

858 Lake, Obiagele. Toward a pan-African identity: diaspora African repatriates in Ghana. (*Anthropol. Q.*, 68:1, Jan. 1995, p. 21–36)

Utilizing life histories of African-American and African-Caribbean migrants to Ghana, author suggests that these individuals maintain transnational ties and have forged a "pan-African identity."

859 Lazarus-Black, Mindie. My mother never fathered me: rethinking kinship and the governing of families. (*Soc. Econ. Stud.*, 44:1, March 1995, p. 49–71, bibl.)

Analyzes kinship, gender, and family policy in Antigua. Argues that policy is promulgated on the basis of hegemonic folk conceptions of kinship with no appreciation for "the complexities of family and gender relations" or power. Criticizes Edith Clarke's *My mother who fathered me* (see HLAS 21:447 and HLAS 29:1473), and asserts that there is a Caribbean idiom of fatherhood, associated with gender ideology, which contrasts with motherhood. Kinship, it is argued, should be examined in terms of events/interactions rather than structural categories. For sociologist's comment see item **4775.**

860 LeFranc, Elsie. The meaning of sexual partnerships: re-examining the Jamaican family system. (*Bull. East. Caribb. Aff.*, 19:4, Dec. 1994, p. 17–29, bibl.)

Re-examines putative notions of development, stability, and longevity of multiple partnerships in Jamaica. Finds that short-term (five years or less) serial partnering characterizes Jamaican mating relations, a factor which contradicts the commonly held idea of simultaneous relationships. Of the three types of union investigated—visiting, common law, marriage—marriage was the least prevalent. Moreover, marriage rates were found to be falling.

861 Losonczy, Anne-Marie. El luto de sí mismo: cuerpo, sombra y muerte entre los negro-colombianos del Chocó. (*Am. Negra*, 1, junio 1991, p. 43–61, bibl.)

Examines beliefs of descendants of African slaves as to interaction between the living and the otherworldly (shadow souls) in different contexts, primarily ritual, festival, and death. Concept of shadow illuminates Afrocolombian views of identity and alternative identity, individuality and multiplicity, silence and speech, life and death.

862 Lowes, Susan. "They couldn't mash ants": the decline of the white and non-white elites in Antigua, 1834–1900. (*in* Small islands, large questions: society, culture and resistance in the post-emancipation Caribbean. Edited by Karen Fog Olweg. London: F. Cass, 1995, p. 31–52, bibl.)

Traces fortunes of elite groups in 19th-century Antigua. A burgeoning non-white middle class saw its opportunities restricted by revival of exclusionary practices when economy contracted. Ultimately both white and non-white elites abandoned the island.

863 Mahabir, Kumar. Whose nation is this?: the struggle over national and ethnic identity in Guyana. (*Caribb. Stud.*, 29:2, July/Dec. 1996, p. 283–302, bibl.)

Analyzes manipulation and negotiation of ethnic and racial identity set against the backdrop of Guyanese nation-building project. Argues that "ethnic communality" rather than integration, which author appears to equate with assimilation, should be respected.

864 Martínez, Samuel. Indifference with indignation: anthropology, human rights, and the Haitian bracero. (*Am. Anthropol.*, 98:1, March 1996, p. 17–25, bibl.)

Critically reviews activist and academic representations of braceros as "slave" or "free." Emphasizes need to consider human and civil rights in conjuction with constraints of crushing individual and structural poverty. Concludes that such poverty makes braceros "not free" and stripped of essential political and civil rights.

865 Martínez, Samuel. The masking of history: popular images of the nation on a Dominican sugar plantation. (*NWIG*, 71:3/4, 1997, p. 227–248, bibl.)

Uses ethnology of a *batey* in southeastern Dominican Republic to study contested nature of hegemony. Focuses on use of images that deny historical role played by Africans and their descendants in founding the Dominican Republic and on how the people are thereby able to preserve memories "of the past that really matter."

866 Matthei, Linda Miller and **David A. Smith.** Women, households, and transnational migration: the Garifuna and global economic restructuring. (*in* Latin America in the world-economy. Westport, Conn.: Greenwood Press, 1996, p. 133–149, bibl.)

Discusses role of Garifuna women as active participants in the creation of transnational networks between Belize and US. Indicates that studies that focus on households mask the contributions of women to those persistent ties and gendered differences in the operation of global forces on transmigration. Argues that Garifuna women in both Belize and Los Angeles are characteristically engaged in a strategic process of network-building which, given the economic instability in both sites, mitigates against the weakening of transnational relationships.

867 Maurer, Bill. Colonial policy and the construction of the commons: an introduction. (*Plant. Soc. Am.*, 4:2/3, Fall 1997, p. 113–133)

Introduction to serial issue deals with salience of Caribbean cases to scholarly debate about common property. Contains review of literature/debate/problems of common tenure and indicates opportunities for comparative study.

868 Maurer, Bill. Fractions of blood on fragments of soil: capitalism, the commons, and kinship in the Caribbean. (*Plant. Soc. Am.*, 4:2/3, Fall 1997, p. 159–171)

Uses case study of dispute over family land in British Virgin Islands to support contention that family land is tied to the concept of "family," which in the Caribbean is embedded in the "liberal model of inequality."

869 Maynard, Edward S. The translocation of a West African banking system: the Yoruba *esusu* rotating credit association in the Anglophone Caribbean. (*Dialect. Anthropol.*, 21, 1996, p. 99–107)

Discusses the *esusu*, or "rotating credit association," found in West Africa, the Caribbean, and among Caribben migrants to the US. Argues that the *esusu* is an African "survival" which has persisted relatively unchanged because of its important "instrumental" and "expressive" functions. Asserts that the *esusu* may have been "stored in the collective memory" of Caribbean slaves and "revived" when it was needed.

870 McKay, Lesley. Women's contribution to tourism in Negril, Jamaica. (*in* Women & change in the Caribbean: a Pan-Caribbean perspective. Kingston: Ian Randle;

Bloomington: Indiana Univ. Press; London: J. Currey, 1993, p. 278–286, bibl.)

Lower-class women in Negril participate directly in the tourist industry and, in fact, can earn relatively substantial income. However, given that their work is an extension of their domestic roles, the income earned is insufficient to change prevailing gender roles, i.e., female subordination.

871 Mentore, George. Peccary meat and power among the Waiwai Indians of Guyana. (*Archaeol. Anthropol.*, 10, 1995, p. 19–35, bibl., ill.)

Using a case study, author argues that kinship rules contain directives about the distribution and consumption of the fruits of the hunt. Through kinship ideology, the group appropriates/allocates the products of surplus labor. Kinship, therefore, is the site of power relations.

872 Miller, Daniel. Modernity, an ethnographic approach: dualism and mass consumption in Trinidad. Oxford, England; Providence, R.I.: Berg, 1994. 340 p.: bibl., index.

Ethnography of Trinidad focuses on processes of mass consumption. Asserts that Trinidadians confront problems of "modernity" (focus on the present as divorced from the past, concomitant need to recreate moral premises, sense of "compression of space-time," sense of instability, desire for subjective experience, "sense of the private"), and construct their "selves" and their culture through consumption. Trinidad manifests "a culture which is self-constructed, in full knowledge that it is in fact self-constructed."

873 Mintz, Sidney W. Cultural difference and social assortment in the Caribbean region. (*in* Ethnic conflict and governance in comparative perspective. Washington: Woodrow Wilson International Center for Scholars, 1995, p. 14–27, bibl.)

In a discussion of the concept of ethnicity, author argues that Caribbean ethnic identity, often associated with phenotypical characteristics, has unique features which are tied to the distinctive socioeconomic histories of the region. Ethnicity is not tied to a "mystical attachment to the land" and is seen more as a personal characteristic, a feature which mitigates the potential for violent ethnic strife.

874 Mintz, Sidney W. Enduring substances, trying theories: the Caribbean region as *oikoumen*. (*J. Royal Anthropol. Inst.*, 2:2, June 1996, p. 289–311, bibl.)

Author, a senior Caribbeanist, explores the recent scholarly attention paid to the Caribbean in light of the popularity of globalization issues. Asserts that anthropological treatments of the region often fail to account for its complex history. The Caribbean has "a modernity that predated the modern."

875 Mintz, Sidney W. Ethnic difference, plantation sameness. (*in* Ethnicity in the Caribbean: essays in honor of Harry Hoetink. London: Macmillan Caribbean, 1996, p. 39–52, bibl.)

Relates formation of racial and ethnic identities in the Caribbean to plantation systems. Similar "structural-processual features" were present in different degrees and at different times in various Caribbean societies; therefore, it is useful to consider identity formation from perspective of group relationships to the plantation economy, particularly for comparative purposes. Argues that identities are less products of the system than aspects of "resistance to its regimen."

876 Misra, Promode Kumar. Cultural design in identity formation in Trinidad. (*East. Anthropol.*, 48:3, July/Sept. 1995, p. 201–226, bibl.)

A "deep cultural design," which tends to organize itself, is responsible for maintenance of a separate East Indian identity in Trinidad. Citing supporting ethnographic evidence of East Indian cultural continuities, author offers the following factors as having contributed to the "emergence" of East Indian identity in Trinidad: population size, control of land, village formation, political action, recognition of rites of passage, films and music, family structure, religious activities, role of the pandit, the *tharia-lota* network, language, and cuisine.

877 Moberg, Mark. Transnational labor and refugee enclaves in a Central American banana industry. (*Hum. Organ.*, 55:4, Winter 1996, p. 425–435, bibl., tables)

Examines formation of Central American immigrant enclaves in Belize and their disenfranchisement. Situation is result of an open border policy and a development strategy based on unfair labor laws and exploitative employment practices. For sociologist's comment see item **4731.**

878   Murray, David A.B. The cultural citizen: negations of race and language in the making of Martiniquais. (*Anthropol. Q.*, 70:2, April 1997, p. 79–90)

Deliberate absences in the official rhetoric that surrounds a Martinican cultural identity (distinct from France's but without an entrenched desire for independence from France) include references to race and language. These absent qualities in the cultural citizen "expose social divisions antithetical to Martinican bureaucratic and political interests" and have the potential for disrupting "the entrenched, privileged discourse of the State."

879   Myers, Iris. The Makushi of the Guiana-Brazilian frontier in 1944: a study in culture contact. (*Antropológica/Caracas*, 80, 1993, p. 3–98, bibl., ill.)

Based on a 1944 description of the Makushi, a Carib group in then British Guiana, and their contact with Europeans and others, argues that effects of this contact led to "disorganization, disintegration and deterioration."

880   Olwig, Karen Fog. Cultural complexity and freedom: Nevis and beyond. (*in* Small islands, large questions: society, culture and resistance in the post-emancipation Caribbean. Edited by Karen Fog Olwig. London: F. Cass, 1995, p. 100–120, bibl.)

Examination of Nevis in the post-emancipation period from the perspective of cultural complexity identifies three "traditions" (plantation system, the "African-Caribbean community," and the "Methodist mission of respectability") which, according to author, reveal the fluid and changing nature of culture. Criticizes approaches that reify "culture as a number of concrete and bounded entities."

881   Olwig, Karen Fog. Defining the national in the transnational: cultural identity in the Afro-Caribbean diaspora. (*Ethnos/Stockholm*, 58:3/4, 1993, p. 361–376, bibl.)

Study of Nevis focuses on problem of defining a national culture (of a very small, poor territory) in a former colonial area. Argues that Afro-Caribbean culture developed in the margins of the colonial regime and,

given internal conditions, this margin has been extended over the past 150 years to include relations with emigrants dispersed worldwide. As a consequence, life on Nevis, the nature of its cultural apparatus, and the cultural context that most clearly "demarcates and unifies Nevisians" are best viewed as transnational.

882   Olwig, Karen Fog. The migration experience: Nevisian women at home & abroad. (*in* Women & change in the Caribbean: a Pan-Caribbean perspective. Kingston: Ian Randle; Bloomington: Indiana Univ. Press; London: J. Currey, 1993, p. 150–166, bibl.)

While emigration constitutes an important break with family networks (which determine a woman's role in Nevis), the tenacity of these networks essentially follows these migrating women abroad, requiring them to maintain relationships via financial support for family back home. Strong obligations back home limit their opportunities to build new networks abroad. Author concludes that the Afro-Caribbean female-centered family form can be seen to persist even where its outward manifestation has changed; it continues to exist as a socially directive ideal, as a socioeconomic reality, and as a vital link to the Caribbean and its heritage.

883   Oostindie, Gert. Ethnicity, nationalism and the exodus: the Dutch Caribbean predicament. (*in* Ethnicity in the Caribbean: essays in honor of Harry Hoetink. London: Macmillan Caribbean, 1996, p. 206–231, bibl.)

In an analysis of race and ethnicity as elements in nation-building projects, particularly in the Dutch Caribbean, author examines process of "decolonization" and resistance to it, migration and its implications, and problems of "viability"—factors that complicate nationalism in the region.

884   *OSO.* Vol. 17, No. 1, 1998. Rituelen rond de dood [Funeral rites]. Edited by Wim Hoogbergen. Nijmegen, The Netherlands: Stichting Instituut ter Bevordering van de Surinamistick te Nijmegen.

Special issue is devoted to funeral rites as practiced among several population groups in Suriname. In nine short articles authors discuss funeral rituals and customs among

Suriname Creoles, Hindus, Muslims, Amerindians, and Ndjuka Maroons. [R. Hoefte]

885 **Parry, Odette.** Equality, gender and the Caribbean classroom. (*21st Century Policy Rev.*, 3 : 1/2, 1996, p. 177–197, bibl.)

Ethnographic study of male underachievement in Jamaican high schools is based on classroom observation and interviews with teachers and counselors. Teachers perceived differences between male and female students in terms of classroom behavior, academic aptitudes, and gender-appropriate behavior. However, the teachers located the source of these gender socialization problems outside the school, and minimized their own roles in reproducing these patterns.

886 **Pereira, Joe.** Gun talk and girls' talk: the DJ clash. (*Caribb. Stud.*, 27 : 3/4, July/Dec. 1994, p. 208–223, bibl.)

Discusses "dancehall" variety of reggae music and its themes of "violence and sex." Argues that "dancehall" expresses gender politics and resistance to dominant culture among the lower class.

887 **Phillips, Daphne.** The family in crisis: explaining the new phenomenon of street children in Trinidad. (*Bull. East. Caribb. Aff.*, 19 : 4, Dec. 1994, p. 1–11, bibl.)

Attempts to explain appearance of an estimated 7,000 Trinidadian street children by pointing to that country's incorporation into global capitalist economy and consequent erosion of its economic, social, cultural, and political practices and institutions. Resultant financial instability, political powerlessness, and social degeneracy of Trinidadian society set the conditions for appearance and increasing numbers of street children.

888 **Pollak-Eltz, Angelina.** Anima worship in Venezuela. (*in* Born out of resistance: on Caribbean cultural creativity. Utrecht, The Netherlands: ISOR-Publications, 1995, p. 238–244, bibl.)

Describes Venezuelan ritual practices and ideology associated with adoration of *animas*, the spirits of the dead "canonized" by ordinary people but not by the Church, through which devotees seek supernatural intervention in their material problems. Phenomenon is seen as a coping mechansim and alternative to revolutionary movements.

889 **Price, Richard.** Duas variantes das relações raciais no Caribe. (*Estud. Afro-Asiát.*, 28, out. 1995, p. 185–202, bibl., table)

The system of Martinican race relations is compared to that of the Saramacca Maroons of Suriname. Martinicans tend "to assimilate French values" and to exhibit a form of "vertical, hierarchized racism." Saramacca Maroons resist "European ideology" and put into practice a more "pluralized, horizontal formula."

890 **Price, Richard** and **Sally Price.** Executing culture: musée, museo, museum. (*Am. Anthropol.*, 97 : 1, March 1995, p. 97–109, bibl.)

Comparative analysis focuses on planned opening of museums in French Guiana, Spain, and Belize. Authors explore ideology behind the museums, their ostensible goals, and their designs relating these aspects to nation-building projects.

891 **Price, Richard.** Executing ethnicity: the killings in Suriname. (*Cult. Anthropol.*, 10 : 4, Nov. 1995, p. 437–471, bibl.)

Vivid description of incidents of brutal State violence in 1980s against Saramacca Maroons and others in Suriname provide context for an account of related proceedings before the Inter-American Court of Human Rights in which author testified *inter alia* about Saramacca culture and customary law. Analysis of Court's handling of "culture difference" suggests that it acted under tacit western cultural assumptions and failed to address "the central legal issue of 'tribal' peoples with nation-states," i.e., their autonomy. For political scientist's comment, see item **3317.**

892 **Price, Richard** and **Sally Price.** Museums, ethnicity and nation-building: reflections from the French Caribbean. (*in* Ethnicity in the Caribbean: essays in honor of Harry Hoetink. London: Macmillan Caribbean, 1996, p. 80–105, bibl.)

Explores representations of ethnic/cultural differences in museums and other officially sanctioned institutions in the French Caribbean, set against the backdrop of assimilationist nation-building projects. Suggests that such exhibitions may serve as a "cage or cemetery," or "a supremely elegant resting place" for differences.

893 **Quintero Rivero, Angel G.** The somatology of manners: class, race and gender in the history of dance etiquette in the
Hispanic Caribbean. (*in* Ethnicity in the Caribbean: essays in honor of Harry Hoetink.
London: Macmillan Caribbean, 1996, p. 152–
181, bibl.)

Analysis of etiquette as "control of the
body" focuses on norms of dancing. Author
interprets a recent revival of "comedies of
manners" as related to the development of an
urban middle class, but insists that "race and
gender must be incorporated" into such an
analysis.

894 **Razak, Victoria M.** Carnival in Aruba:
history and meaning in Aruba's bacchanal. New York: Cenda Publications, 1997
213 p.: appendices, bibl., map, photos.

Sketchy, illustrated history of Aruba's
carnival focuses on its traditions, themes and
events, music, principal characters, and mas-
querade groups. In the last chapters, author
discusses context and meaning of Aruban carnival and representation and the politics of
identity. Includes a carnival chronology and
glossary. [R. Hoefte]

895 **Reddock, Rhoda.** "Douglarisation" and
the politics of gender relations in Trinidad and Tobago: a preliminary exploration.
(*Contemp. Issues Soc. Sci. Caribb. Perspect.*,
1, 1994, p. 98–127, bibl.)

Examines attitudes of ethnic groups
about interethnic marriage and individuals of
mixed Afro-Trinidadian/Indo-Trinidadian an-
cestry. Argues that Indo-Trinidadians, especially Hindus, are the most opposed to ex-
ogamy and relates this viewpoint to ideas
of "caste." Discusses meaning of the term
"douglarisation" as it is understood by various ethnic categories.

896 **Sanders, Andrew.** Protected status and
the Amerindians of Guyana: a comparative examination. (*Soc. Econ. Stud.*, 44:2/3.
June/Sept. 1995, p. 125–141, bibl.)

Comparative analysis studies implications of "protective status" for Guyanese
Amerindians, arguing that this status contributes to "low social standing," conflict, and
powerlessness. Advocates policy changes
with regard to the following problem areas:
consultation, legal "safeguards," and education of the public about Amerindians.

897 **Schiller, Nina Glick; Linda Basch;** and
Cristina Szanton Blanc. From immi-
grant to transmigrant: theorizing migration.
(*Anthropol. Q.*, 68:1, Jan. 1995, p. 48–63)

Discusses transnationalism and
proposes "parameters of an ethnography"
thereof. Explains transnationalism as migrants' response to discrimination and insecurity in the metropole, and as result of "nation building" in both sending and receiving
countries. Recent developments in US immigration policy and American attitudes towards immigrants are interpreted, in part, as
driven by concern over transmigrant loyalties. Much of article's evidence is drawn from
authors' studies of migration from Saint Vincent, Grenada, and Haiti. See also item **4291.**

898 **Sélimé, Jean Claude.** Pour une nouvelle
approche de l'anthropologie haïtienne.
(*Bull. Bur. natl. ethnol.*, 1993–1994, p. 31–38,
bibl.)

Brief sketch of indigenous Haitian anthropology outlines diverging approaches of
Nationalist and Indigenist schools. Argues
that only in the past few decades have Haitian anthropologists begun to embrace the in-
ductive method and to stress explanation of
the Haitian reality over valorization of the
Haitian.

**As senhoras do pássaro da noite: escritos so-
bre a religião dos orixás.** See item **974.**

899 **Simpson, George Eaton.** Some reflections on the Rastafari Movement in
Jamaica: West Kingston in the early 1950s.
(*Jam. J.*, 25:2, Dec. 1994, p. 3–10, bibl., ill.,
photos)

Informative work includes reflections
on initial 1953 fieldwork by the first scholar
to study Rastafarians. State of the Movement
at that time (organization, beliefs, symbols,
activities, etc.) is described and contrasted
with later periods.

900 **Small islands, large questions: society,
culture, and resistance in the post-
emancipation Caribbean.** Edited by Karen Fog
Olwig. London; Portland, Or.: F. Cass, 1995.
200 p.: bibl., index, maps. (Studies in slave
and post-slave societies and cultures)

Recommended collection. For anthropological contributions see Berleant-Schiller
on the shift from labor to peasantry in Montserrat (item **797**); Besson on land, kinship, and

community (item **805**); Lowes on elites in Antigua (item **862**); and Olwig on cultural complexity and freedom in Saint Kitts and Nevis (item **880**).

901 Smith, Raymond T. "Living in the gun mouth": race, class, and political violence in Guyana. (*NWIG*, 69:3/4, 1995, p. 223–252, bibl., table)

Gives anthropological perspectives on the "racial violence" of the 1960s, and on the responses of the public to actions taken by their leaders and their patrons in London, Washington, Havana, or Moscow. Relates differing views of social scientists on these events. For sociologist's comment see item **4925**.

902 Society for Caribbean Research. International Conference, (2nd, Vienna, 1990.) Ay BōBō: afro-karibische Religionen = African-Caribbean religions. v. 1, Kulte/ Cults. Edited by Manfred Kremser. Vienna: WUV Universitätsverlag, 1996. 1 v.: bibl., ill., maps, photos. (Wiener Beiträge zur Ethnologie und Anthropologie; 8 = Vienna contributions to ethnology and anthropology; 8)

Includes four contributions by anthropologists which merit mention: 1) Stephen D. Glazier's "Changes in the Spiritual Baptist Religion, 1966–1990;" 2) Angelina Pollak-Eltz's "The Cult of Maria Lionza in Venezuela;" 3) Silvia W. de Groot's "Opposition to Social Change in a Maroon Society"; and 4) Wilhelmina van Wetering's "Maroon Religious Movements of Suriname." See also items **903** and **904**.

903 Society for Caribbean Research. International Conference, (2nd, Vienna, 1990.) Ay BōBō: afro-karibische Religionen = African-Caribbean religions. v. 2, Voodoo. Edited by Manfred Kremser. Vienna: WUV Universitätsverlag, 1996. 1 v.: bibl., ill., index, photos. (Wiener Beiträge zur Ethnologie und Anthropologie; 8 = Vienna contributions to ethnology and anthropology; 8)

Includes three contributions by anthropologists which merit mention: 1) Gerhard Kubik's "West African and African-American Concepts of Vodu and Òrìsà;" Ulrike Sulikowski's "Hollywoodzombie: Vodou and the Caribbean in Mainstream Cinema;" and 3) Stephanie Schmiderer's "Dancing for the Loas to Make the Loas Dance." See also items **902** and **904**.

904 Society for Caribbean Research. International Conference, (2nd, Vienna, 1990.) Ay BōBō: afro-karibische Religionen = African-Caribbean religions. v. 3, Rastafari. Edited by Manfred Kremser. Vienna: WUV Universitätsverlag, 1994. 1 v.: bibl., index, photos. (Wiener Beiträge zur Ethnologie und Anthropologie; 8 = Vienna contributions to ethnology and anthropology; 8)

Includes three contributions by anthropologists which merit mention: 1) Werner Zips' "Rastafari: eine Kulterrevolution in der Afrikanischen Diaspora;" 2) Carole D. Yawney's "Rastafari Sounds of Cultural Resistance: Amharic Language Training in Trenchtown, Jamaica;" and 3) John P. Homiak's "From Yard to Nation: Rastafari and the Politics of Eldership at Home and Abroad." See also items **902** and **903**.

905 Stevens, Alta Mae. The symbolic significance of *manje* in Haitian culture. (*J. Caribb. Stud.*, 11:1/2, Winter 1995/Spring 1996, p. 135–153, bibl.)

In a discussion of the "symbolic relationships" centered around *manje* (food, eating, etc.), author examines its multiple meanings in a variety of social contexts, literature, and public discourse.

906 Thoden van Velzen, H.U.E. Revenants that cannot be shaken: collective fantasies in a Maroon society. (*Am. Anthropol.*, 97:4, Dec. 1995, p. 722–732, bibl.)

Brief historical review and analysis of selected collective fantasies found among Suriname's Nydukas from 1960s–80s. Suggests that an analysis of the concept, and the creation, dissemination, and adoption of collective fantasies, is a useful medium for understanding mundane changes in, and changing responses to, values and behavior related to resource use, perversity, social stratification, aggression, and conflict.

907 Tracey, Kenneth. Adaptive responses to race and ethnic conflict. (*Caribb. Q.*, 40:3/4, Sept./Dec. 1994, p. 98–108, bibl.)

Taking a Darwinian approach to racial and ethnic conflict in the Caribbean, author attempts to analyze racial/ethnic conflict in Trinidad and Tobago in terms of "adaptiveness" (i.e., the extent to which a cultural condition promotes continuity/survival). Concludes that conflict is maladaptive and that the principle of "co-equal cultures" should be adopted.

908 Vargas, Manuel. Culture, ideology, and dwelling in two Dominican villages. (*NWIG*, 70: 1/2, 1996, p. 5–38, bibl., maps)

Explains how and why two adjacent villages with very similar infrastructures, populated by indigenous groups from two distant geographical regions of the Dominican Republic, acted in "significantly different ways" in the face of "comparable structural constraints" and the same official discourse and pressure. For sociologist's comment, see item **4937.**

909 Verbeck, Geneviève; Peer Scheepers; and Maurits Hassankhan. Etnocentrisme in Suriname [Ethnocentrism in Suriname]. (*OSO/Netherlands*, 19:2, 1997, p. 133–145, bibl., tables)

Important report on ethnic relations in Suriname in the 1990s. Authors studied ethnic prejudices in Paramaribo among the three largest groups: Creoles, British Indians or Hindustani, and Javanese. The Javanese are the most highly valued; the Creoles least valued. Authors conclude that compared to earlier research done by Speckmann (1963) and Van Renselaar (1963), the prejudices of Creoles and Hindustani toward each other have not changed much between 1963 and 1992. Unfortunately, the list of questions asked is not included. [R. Hoefte]

910 Vernon, Diane. Choses de la forêt: identité et thérapie chez les noirs marrons Ndjuka du Surinam. (*in* Juex d'identités: études comparatives à partir de la Caraïbe. Paris: L'Harmattan, 1993, p. 261–281)

Informative study discusses association of Ndjuka ethnomedicine and construction of Maroon identity in Suriname. Both domains are tied to a mystical attachment to land, an attachment that regards traditional medical practices, ethnopharmacopoeia, and the people themselves as "things of the forest."

911 Wetering, Wilhelmina van. Demon in a garbage chute: Surinamese creole women's discourse on possession and therapy. (*in* Rastafari and other African-Caribbean worldviews. Houndmills, England: Macmillan; The Hague: Institute of Social Studies, 1998, p. 211–232)

Analyzes symbolism of demonic possession and evil among female Surinamese migrants in The Netherlands. Relationships with men, rivalry, and status-seeking mark a "field . . . charged with magical dangers." Argues that magical beliefs are related to the social structure and that they will persist when social relations remain substantially unchanged.

912 Whitehead, Neil L. The historical anthropology of text: the interpretation of Ralegh's *Discoverie of Guiana*. (*Curr. Anthropol.*, 36:1, Feb. 1995, p. 53–74, bibl.)

Interpretation of this text in anthropological perspective underscores argument that such readings may help indigenous peoples reconstruct their histories. Author synthesizes "anthropological, historiographic, and literary approaches," and posits that European accounts should not be rejected out of hand as mere "textual exemplars of European credulity and cultural chauvinism." See also item **843.**

913 Women & change in the Caribbean: a Pan-Caribbean perspective. Edited by Janet Henshall Momsen. Kingston: Ian Randle; Bloomington: Indiana Univ. Press; London: J. Currey, 1993. 308 p.: bibl., ill., index, maps.

Very useful collection includes 19 articles. For anthropological contributions see Abraham-Van der Mark on mating patterns of Sephardic elite of Curaçao (item **785**); Berleant-Schiller and Maurer on women's roles in Barbuda and Dominica (item **799**); Besson on the reputation and respectability argument (item **806**); McKay on women and tourism in Negril (item **870**); Olwig on Nevisian women and migration (item **882**); and Yelvington on gender and ethnicity in a Trinidadian factory (item **916**).

914 Yawney, Carole D. *Rasta mek a trod:* symbolic ambiguity in a globalizing religion. (*in* Society of Caribbean Research. International Conference, *1st, Berlin, 1988*. Alternative cultures in the Caribbean. Frankfurt: Vervuert Verlag, 1993, p. 161–168)

Attempts to explain how Rastafarianism has gained adherents worldwide. Argues that in addition to Jamaican migration and the attractiveness of reggae music, the symbolism of the religion has a widespread appeal to oppressed people. Sufficiently ambiguous, the religion can commend itself to people of diverse backgrounds.

915 Yelvington, Kevin A. Flirting in the factory. (*J. Royal Anthropol. Inst.*, 2:2, June 1996, p. 313–333, bibl.)

Analyzes "flirting" between white supervisors and Afro-Trinidadian and Indo-Trinidadian factory workers. Argues that flirting is embedded in power relations and ethnic identity, and is a form of "symbolic violence."

916 Yelvington, Kevin A. Gender & ethnicity at work in a Trinidadian factory. (*in* Women & change in the Caribbean: a Pan-Caribbean perspective. Kingston: Ian Randle; Bloomington: Indiana Univ. Press; London: J. Currey, 1993, p. 263–277, bibl., ill.)

Examines three aspects of gender and ethnicity in social relations in a factory: composition and structural positions of the work force, role and forms of supervision, and social relations between workers. Suggests that gender, ethnicity, and class are socially constructed with reference to each other, and that their interrelationship exists on a symbolic as well as structural level.

917 Yelvington, Kevin A. Producing power: ethnicity, gender, and class in a Caribbean workplace. Philadelphia: Temple Univ. Press, 1995. 286 p.: bibl., ill., index, maps.

Highly detailed and well-argued study focuses on mostly women workers in a Trinidadian factory. Utilizes approach which author claims unites history, culture, structure, and agency. In fact, coherent and theoretically sophisticated analytical framework provides context for the ethnographically rich, multidimensional narratives of women workers "who endure oppression while at the same time reclaiming their dignity." Core argument is that the production process "becomes a site where the meanings of ethnicity, class, and gender are constructed, contested, and consented to."

918 Zips, Werner. "Let's talk about the motherland": Jamaican influences on the African discourses in the diaspora. (*in* Born out of resistance: on Caribbean cultural creativity. Utrecht, The Netherlands: ISOR-Publications, 1995, p. 46–52, bibl.)

Caribbean contributions to discourse about Africa among peoples of the African Diaspora include Maroon society as model for black nationalist aspirations for self-determination, the works of Garvey, Rastafarian ideology, reggae music, and other forms of popular culture. Black Americans and Afro-Caribbeans have influenced one another regarding the significance of Africa as a unifying concept.

919 Zips, Werner. Schwarze Rebellen: Afrikanisch-karibischer Freiheitskamp in Jamaica. Vienna: ProMedia, 1993. 303 p.: appendix, ill.

History of Jamaican Maroons with emphasis on 18th-century Maroon wars is accompanied by descriptions of present situation of Maroon communities on the island. Includes sections on economic patterns, kinship organization, religious practices, and migration. English-language edition forthcoming from UWI Press.

920 Zips, Werner. "Sister Nanny a one a we, brother Kojo a one a we, brother Bob Marley a one a we . . .": the continuity of Black resistance in Jamaica. (*in* Society of Caribbean Research. International Conference, *1st Berlin, 1988*. Alternative cultures in the Caribbean. Frankfurt: Vervuert Verlag, 1993, p. 69–76, bibl.)

Utilizing examples drawn from Jamaican history, author attempts to set out the paradigmatic conditions that should undergird a meaningful use of the term "continuity of Black (Afro-Jamaican) resistance."

South America
Lowlands

SILVIA MARIA HIRSCH, *Professor of Anthropology, Princeton University*
ROBIN M. WRIGHT, *Professor of Anthropology, Universidade Estadual de Campinas (Brazil)*

IN THE LITERATURE REVIEWED for this issue, one characteristic clearly stands out: a large number of edited volumes on various themes which cluster into four main areas: indigenous history, religions, kinship and social organization, and indigenism. The Quincentenary celebrations (1992) and the UN's International Decade of the World's Indigenous People (1995) were important stimuli both for the publication of vast amounts of material on Amazonian native peoples and for the identification of uncovered areas.

One important area receiving attention is history, which has been either neglected or not considered recoverable for a long time. A few pioneering voices in the 1970s and early 1980s called attention to the need for historical research and Latin American anthropologists eventually began organizing this interest through symposia at the international Americanists meetings (item **928**). In the mid-1980s, this research movement was coordinated in Brazil by the Center for Indigenous History in São Paulo, which, in 1991, organized a major international conference on the History of Indians in Brazil (item **962**). The following year, the conference papers were published in a volume which surpassed the two volumes on the conquest of Brazilian Indians by John Hemming, until then virtually the only reference books on the subject (*HLAS 42:1648, 51:877* and *52:2889*).

One result of this conference was the identification of what had yet to be done on Lowland ethnohistory, such as a basic survey of material relevant to indigenous history in Brazilian archives. As a result, the Center published a guide to Brazilian historical archives in 1994 (item **960**). Large areas of Amazonia were not included in the volume, indicating directions for future research. In Northeast Brazil, a number of research projects are currently underway to reconstruct regional indigenous history.

Shortly after reaching a peak of intensity, the research focus on history in Brazil lost steam. Theses continued to be produced in the area, but numerous research questions went unanswered, such as historical demography and images of the Indian in history. These topics will most likely continue to be investigated, but on a smaller-scale and in a less-centralized fashion.

The second area of research is native religions. The noteworthy, systematic publication of collections of myths, particularly by ABYA-YALA Publishers in Quito, has made numerous obscure works available to researchers (item **938**). However, a contextual explanation that would make these myths accessible to unspecialized readers does not exist. One interesting development we may continue to see is collections of myths organized by native narrators (item **971**).

The literature is limited in types of interpretations and analyses of myths and religion. Structuralist analyses continue to appear, although recent critiques of Lévi-Straussian analysis confirm the weakness of its ethnographic base (item **995**). One collection focuses on myth as praxis comparing mythic forms among Lowland and Andean societies (item **924**). Parallels can be drawn between these studies and the more linguistically-oriented discourse-centered approaches of North American anthropology, particularly in the focus on narrative performance and construction of meaning.

Papers from the International Congress of Anthropological and Ethnological Sciences (ICAES) in 1993 focus on the relation of mythic structure to historical praxis—an evident link in millenarian, messianic, and prophetic movements (item **933**). An excellent monograph explores the relation among founding myths, historical narratives, and social structure of the Curripaco of the Guainía River in Colombia (item **987**). A monograph on the Warao of the Orinoco Delta is a beautiful demonstration of how mythic and religious themes are expressed in material existence (item **993**).

A number of studies focus on eschatology, death and the afterlife, and cannibalism in the Lowlands (items **957, 951,** and **980**). Cunha's classic study on the Krahó (HLAS 43:1098) and Castro's brilliant monograph on the Araweté, now translated into English (item **950**), continue to serve as models on the theme. The importance of death to the construction of identity and alterity, and the centrality of predation are key themes in the relations of cosmos to society and society to nature in Lowland South America.

Ethnoaesthetics appears as an important concern in recent publications (items **958** and **1004**). Among other things, these studies explore relations among mythological themes and artistic motifs.

The greatest number of studies in religion have concentrated on shamanism, including both monographs (items **1005** and **966**) and collections of articles (item **982**). The complexity and richness of shamanism are explored through diverse approaches focusing on performance, relations to cosmogony and cosmology, prophetism, Western medical practices, and ecology. A key issue in debate is the basis of shamanic power in ritual reproduction of the cosmos and society (item **988**). One new topic to the study of religion is the relation of Christianity to native cultures. In Brazil, a global and comparative research project explores the diversity of relationships among indigenous religions and Christianity, concentrating on the nature of conversion experiences, prophetic movements, and native churches in the Lowlands.

Kinship and social organization are the areas in which Lowland ethnologists have most clearly been rethinking available analytical models and theoretical presuppositions. One leading figure in this movement, Eduardo Viveiros de Castro, has for nearly a decade undertaken a comparative study of kinship systems in Amazonia, focusing especially on Dravidian systems (item **946**), and has proposed a new model for conceptualizing the notions of affinity and consanguinity and their interrelations in Amazonia. Some articles in the extremely important 1993 issue of *L'Homme* on Amazonia discuss possibilities and implications of new kinship models, demonstrating that dialogue among French, Brazilian, and British anthropologists has a great deal to offer by way of a new synthesis (item **932**).

One area where Lowland Ethnology could advance is by a critical rethinking of the separation between studies of Central Brazil (particularly Gê-speaking societies) and the rest of Amazonia—a distinction produced and reinforced by predominant directions in the field in the 1960s and 1970s. The isolation of Gê studies has prevented a more effective synthesis which may account for the significant differences between Gê models of society and Amazonian patterns (item **932**).

Indigenism provides the greatest diversity in the literature; this 'practical ethnology' addresses the relationship of traditional ethnology to practical and political questions such as land, health, education, development, and movement politics. These concerns have preoccupied indigenous peoples for a long time but ethnology has only recently begun to make theoretical contributions. For example, the new journal *Filhos da terra* offers Brazilian indigenous leaders the opportunity to express their concerns about many of these practical issues (item **955**).

The two predominant concerns in education are educating primary and secondary school teachers and the general population about indigenous peoples, and conversely, rethinking Western pedagogical models to meet indigenous peoples' needs. Brazilian ethnologists and specialists have dedicated substantial attention to these questions (items **977, 954, 963,** and **940**). Some fundamental areas are lacking research: in particular, an encyclopedia of indigenous peoples in Brazil does not yet exist. However, an institute in São Paulo is organizing a collective project to produce a multimedia CD-ROM on the subject.

Health is yet another area where specialists from various areas have come together to explore the possibilities of making Western medical systems more responsive to indigenous needs, while determining the principal concerns of indigenous medical systems (items **973, 935,** and **941**). On the question of land, various collections of articles have been published on recognizing and demarcating indigenous lands. One interesting development is the ethnologist's expert role in preparing legal documents concerning land claims in Brazil, an area in which research on indigenous history has a central role (items **953** and **945**).

Development research in indigenous areas has not advanced significantly in the past few years: outside of critiques of the effects of development projects (items **978, 934,** and **989**), a few studies explore ethnoecology, ethnoagronomy and ethnobotany and propose alternative development models (item **925**). One noteworthy study recommends an approximation between sustainable development and indigenous needs (item **934**).

A number of studies evaluate indigenous movements of resistance (see Turner in item **946**) and revitalization, their relation to cultural constructs, and how past experiences can help to shape strategies for future political moves (item **926**). One relevant article examines ethnogenesis, or "the process of constructing and transforming social identity in changing historical conditions" (Hill, HLAS 53: Introductory Essay), which should be a model for reconsidering the anthropologist's role in political movements of cultural revitalization (item **985**).

Discourse-centered approaches to ethnography continue to produce important results as authors explore limitations and potentialities in life narratives (item **1002**), the relation of expressive performance to cultural transmission (item **959**), the construction and reproduction of power in inter-ethnic relations (items **947** and **948**), and the construction of knowledge and sensibility in social relations (item **979**).

Hill's prediction that ecological studies of Amazonia would continue to diminish in the 1990s (*HLAS 55: Introductory Essay*) has not changed significantly. Despite the English translation of Philippe Descola's classic work on the Achuar (item **998**), his synthesis of ecological and symbolic approaches has unfortunately received little attention. Two studies demonstrate the enormous potential his approach has over more reductionist and pragmatic concerns of 'sustainable development' or 'resource management' (items **990** and **984**). [RW]

PARAGUAY, BOLIVIA, AND ARGENTINA

Research and publications on lowland groups of Bolivia, Paraguay, and Argentina have grown steadily during the last decade. There has been a systematic increase of studies on the large Chaco region which includes these three countries. The largest number of publications have come from Paraguay and Argentina. Growing areas of research include: the struggle for indigenous peoples to claim territorial and legal rights, the impact of new national indigenous legislation, indigenous minorities and the State, and new forms of religiosity.

Articles on the Paraguayan Guaraní groups represent the struggle for land rights and the impact of national legislation on indigenous rights. A case-study analysis illustrates the conflict and contradiction of the national legislation created to protect indigenous rights and the difficulties of implementation (item **1029**). Government agencies in charge of protecting and defending indigenous peoples often express conflicting solidarities and alliances with different social groups. The analysis of the impact of new indigenous law in Misiones, Argentina on the Guaraní communities examines how political parties attempt to co-opt indigenous leaders and how indigenous peoples emerge as political actors involved in organizing and deciding the fate of their communities (item **1030**). Another study documents the conflicts that arise between different forms of leadership in these communities (item **1025**). A thorough analysis of Wichí toponymy, in which indigenous knowledge of the environment has the potential for effecting change in territorial claims, is a seminal contribution to this area of study (item **1027**).

The emergence of a new indigenous political discourse has been an ongoing theme during the last decade. One study examines the Enxet, who are developing an ethnic discourse in response to the challenges they confront in the process of land claims (item **1025**). Another work provides a detailed sociocultural and economic description of indigenous communities in Paraguay, which is useful for scholars interested in the present-day situation and in development projects (item **1020**). A growing interest in legal issues, focusing on folk law is exemplified in a detailed study of Ava-Guaraní social control and folk law (item **1019**). These studies can contribute to effective policy making among native peoples.

The analysis of indigenous people's incorporation into the capitalist economy and their ways of coping with economic changes have focused on adaptive strategies and native resource management (items **1032, 1028,** and **1033**).

The longstanding interest in religiosity, mythology, and shamanism continues to be evident in several studies. The study of Ava-Katu-Eté shamanism is a noteworthy contribution to the vast literature on Guaraní religiosity and mythical narrative (item **1017**). Several articles reflect the growing interest on the conflicts between shamanism and evangelism. Wright's study of Toba evangelical therapeutic practices uses a discursive analysis of death dreams illustrating the complex relationship between evangelical and shamanic practices (item **1035**).

The growing process of urban migration of indigenous peoples is still not a major topic, but recent studies depict new forms of organization, leadership, and linguistic change that have come with the movement to the cities (item **1018**).

The ethnology of Lowland Paraguay, Bolivia, and Argentina has grown in both publications and research but the field is much less explored than the rest of Lowland South America. There are still gaps in ecological oriented research, gender issues and migration and urbanization of indigenous peoples. [SH]

GENERAL

921   Aguiar, Maria Suelí de. Fontes de pesquisa e estudo da família Pano. Campinas, Brazil: Editora da Unicamp, 1994. 282 p.: index. (Série Pesquisas)

Most complete bibliography available on Panobo-speaking peoples of the Brazil/Peru/Bolivia border, who are currently receiving considerable attention from ethnologists. Includes a thorough survey of the literature and archives in all three countries, and provides complete references on obscure items. Organized by historical and linguistic bibliographies, and groups within the Panobo language family. [RW]

922   Alès, Catherine. Chroniques des temps ordinaires: corésidence et fission yanomami. (*Homme/Paris*, 30: 113, jan./mars 1990, p. 73–101, bibl., ill.)

Seeks to interpret the highly fluid territorial organization and residence of the Yanomamo in Brazil and Venezuela. Argues that the system of warfare and conflict—when considered in the context of a system of alliances and relations defined by social and spatial proximity and distance—emerges as a determining element of social structure, accounting for its flexibility and fluidity. [RW]

923   Amérindia. No. 18, 1993. Paris: Association d'ethnolinguistique amérindienne.

Entire issue is dedicated to studies of "le monde arawak"—five Arawak-speaking societies of Central and South America. Essays are written by primarily French anthropologists, linguists, and historians, whose research concentrates on relations among Andean and Lowland South American cultures.

Topics include mythic narratives, kinship terminologies, and linguistics. Given the paucity of studies on lowland Arawak peoples, issue provides a welcome collection. [RW]

924 Bulletin. Nos. 57/58, 1993/94. La parole mythique en Amérique du Sud. Edition de Pierre-Yves Jacopin. Geneva: Sociéte suisse des américanistes.

Entire issue (11 articles) focuses on myth as praxis in Andean and Lowland South America. Topical coverage includes a variety of themes, but articles are centered on mythic speech and its relations to sociocultural contexts—rituals, corpus of myths, narrative performance—through which meaning is constructed. Excellent concluding essay by editor synthesizes diverse approaches to the question of myth as praxis. [RW]

925 Cerón Solarte, Benhur. El manejo indígena de la selva pluvial tropical: orientaciones para un desarrollo sostenido. Quito: Ediciones ABYA-YALA; Rome: Movimiento Laicos para América Latina, 1991. 256 p.: bibl., ill., maps. (Col. 500 años; 43)

Excellent study advocates incorporating indigenous cultural knowledge in sustainable development projects. Encourages an ethnobiological research focus recognizing the indigenous symbolic relationship with the environment, along with knowledge gained through the human and natural sciences. Comparative study focuses mainly on the Awa-Cuaiquer of Colombia and Ecuador. [RW]

926 Chirif Tirado, Alberto; Pedro García Hierro; and Richard Chase Smith. El indígena y su territorio son uno solo: estrategias para la defensa de los pueblos y territorios indígenas en la Cuenca Amazónica. Lima: Oxfam América: Coordinadora de las Organizacones Indígenas de la Cuenca Amazónica, COICA, 1991. 214 p.: bibl., ill.

Synthesizes and evaluates experiences of 15 projects undertaken in the Amazon regions of Brazil, Peru, Ecuador, and Bolivia in defense of indigenous lands and resources over the past decade. Provides guidelines for defining indigenous strategies of territorial defense and consolidation. Serves as a subsidy for indigenous movements and the promotion of alternative models of resource development. [RW]

927 Los espíritus aliados: chamanismo y curación en los pueblos indios de Sudamérica. Recopilación de Emanuele Amodio

y José E. Juncosa. Quito: Ediciones ABYA-YALA; Rome: Movimiento Laicos para América Latina, 1991. 255 p.: bibl., ill. (Col. 500 años; 31)

Five articles on shamanic curing in South America—among the Mapuche of Chile, Embera of Colombia, Macuxi of Brazil, Shuar of Ecuador, and Cametsa of Colombia. Contends that myths and ritual curing practices are dynamic cultural elements and hence adaptable to changes in the societies that sustain them. [RW]

928 Etnohistoria del Amazonas. Coordinación de Peter Jorna, Leonor Malaver, y Menno Oostra. Quito: Ediciones ABYA-YALA; Rome: MLAL, Movimiento Laicos para América Latina, 1991. 288 p.: bibl., maps. (Col. 500 años; 36)

Volume continues Latin American anthropologists' growing interest in indigenous history. Includes an important reinterpretation of an old historical question on the nature of Guarani prophetism; an innovative study of the long-term transformations in native political economy of Amazonia; and studies of the Northwest Amazon based on newly-researched collections of documents and oral histories of contact. [RW]

929 Federarbeiten der Indianer Südamerikas: aus der Studiensammlung Horst Antes; Rautenstrauch-Joest-Museum, 30 September 1994 bis 28; Januar 1995, Reiss-Museum der Stadt Mannheim, 16. März bis 18. Juni 1995. Edited by Gisela Völger and Ursula Dyckerhoff. Photography by Helmut Buchen and Marion Mennicken. Stuttgart, Germany: Oktagon, 1994. 433 p.: bibl., ill. (chiefly col.), maps.

Short descriptions and maps accompany exquisite photographs of feather objects and adornments. [C.K. Converse]

930 Ferguson, R. Brian. Yanomami warfare: a political history. Sante Fe, N.M.: School of American Research Press; Seattle: Univ. of Washington Press, 1995. 449 p.: bibl., index, maps.

Re-evaluation of Yanomamo warfare defends a material motivation hypothesis grounded in an etic behavioral approach. Elaborating a method previously applied to the study of Pacific Northwest warfare patterns, author develops a formal analytic model and applies it to histories of Yanomamo conflicts, political relations among villages, and warfare strategies. Effects of Western contact—especially the introduction of manufactured goods—on warfare patterns are discussed. [RW]

931 Gasché, Jürg. Reflexiones sobre los alcances del desarrollo rural para los pueblos indígenas de la Amazonia. Lima: Univ. Nacional Mayor de San Marcos, Facultad de Ciencias Sociales, Escuela Académico Profesional de Antropología, 1992. 48 p.: bibl. (Lecturas en antropología; 1. Serie Antropología y ecología)

A critical theoretical reflection on the distance between academic studies of ethnoecology and ethnoagronomy, and indigenous—specifically Huitoto (Colombian Amazon)—concepts of traditional agriculture. Crucial question in light of indigenous organizations' growing interest in economic and ecological development. Provides guidelines for a growing approximation. [RW]

932 L'Homme. Vol. 33, Nos. 126–128, avril–sept. 1993. La Remonté de l'Amazone: anthropologie et histoire des sociétés amazoniennes. Paris: Laboratoire d'anthropologie, Collège de France.

Outstanding articles by well-known specialists indicate research directions in contemporary Lowland South American ethnology, including kinship and social organization, political organization and relations to nation-states, indigenous history, ecology, and cosmology and symbolism. Reevaluation of Amazonian and Central Brazilian social structures and models of Dravidian terminologies shed new light on the analysis of kinship structures and related institutions such as warfare. The time-worn distinction between Gê and Amazonian ethnographies is questioned. A major synthesis of Lowland ethnology that will have far-reaching repercussions in the years to come. Extremely useful teaching tool. [RW]

933 International Congress of Anthropological and Ethnological Sciences, 13th, México, 1993. Religiosidad y resistencia indígena hacia el fin del milenio. Organización de Alicia M. Barabas. Quito: Ediciones Abya-Yalla, 1994. 287 p.: bibl. (Col. Biblioteca Abya-Yalla; 11)

Over half of the 11 papers presented at the Symposium on Socioreligious Movements in Latin America refer to millenarian movements in Amazonia and the Chaco. In-

cludes several valuable theoretical overviews, evaluations of directions for research, and proposals for new approaches to the study of millenarianism. [RW]

934 Jornadas Amazónicas Internacionales, 2nd, Quito, 1992. Amazonía, escenarios y conflictos. Coordinación de Lucy Ruiz M. Quito: CEDIME, 1993. 811 p.: bibl., ill., maps.

Wide-ranging collection of short essays analyzes the serious social, economic, and political problems currently affecting Amazonia. Themes include structuring of space and regional economies; environmental policies and sustainable development; indigenous organizations and political movements; education and Amazonian identity; and the "internationalization" of Amazonia (militarization, narcotraffic, and rural violence). [RW]

935 Kroeger, Axel and Françoise Barbira-Freedman. La lucha por la salud en el alto Amazonas y en los Andes. Quito: Abya-Yala, 1992. 404 p.: bibl., ill.

In-depth anthropological and medical study examines health situation in the upper Amazon of Peru/Ecuador, particularly among the Shuar. Studies various types of available formal and informal health resources. In view of the inadequacy of health care, study recommends improvement based on combined traditional and Western medical resources. [RW]

936 Moran, Emilio F. Human adaptive strategies in Amazonian blackwater ecosystems. (*Am. Anthropol.,* 93:2, June 1991, p. 361–382, bibl., graphs, map, tables)

Examines unique environmental conditions of blackwater ecosystems in Northwest Amazonia, and human adaptive strategies—such as hierarchical forms of social organization, land use, and land tenure—associated with the area. Argues the need for more sensitive characterizations of the environment that explain diversity in forms of sociopolitical organization and resource use in comparing Amazonian ecosystems. [RW]

937 Plotkin, Mark J. Tales of a shaman's apprentice: an ethnobotanist searches for new medicines in the Amazon rain forest. New York: Viking, 1993. 318 p., 8 p. of plates: bibl., ill.

Fascinating and highly readable account of an ethnobotanist's research on medicinal plants and hallucinogens among the Trio and Oyana of Surinam/Brazil and the Yanomamo of Venezuela. In view of the declining importance of shamanism and loss of plant knowledge due to rapid cultural change, author encourages research promoting the patenting of indigenous knowledge of medicinal plants, which may also serve as an important revenue source for indigenous-based cultural survival programs. See also item **992**. [RW]

938   Los pueblos indios en sus mitos. Quito: Abya-Yala, 1993– . 17 v: bibl., ill.

Abya-Yala editors translated and published in Spanish a collection of previously published works on the mythologies of native peoples of Latin America, many of which are now out of print or otherwise difficult to obtain, providing an enormous service to both the scholarly and indigenous communities. Some myth descriptions are accompanied by ethnographic introductions and/or annotations. Indigenous-language versions of the myths are sometimes included. [RW]

Saúde e povos indígenas. See item **973**.

939   Seminario sobre Reconocimiento y Demarcación de Territorios Indígenas, Brasília, 1991. Reconocimiento y demarcación de territorios indigenas en la amazonia: la experiencia de los países de la región. Bogotá: Fundación GAIA; CEREC, 1993. 303 p.: bibl., ill., maps. (Serie Amerindia; 4)

Recognized specialists in indigenism of Amazon Basin countries analyze the political, legal, and economic situations of indigenous lands in relation to official recognition and demarcation, and native control over lands and resources. A series of policy recommendations, complemented by those of indigenous leaders, define directions for concrete reforms. [RW]

940   Simpósio Indios e Não Indios—uma Interação Desigual no Limiar do Século XXI, Campinas, Brazil, 1991. Lingüística indígena e educação na América Latina. Organização de Lucy Seki. Campinas, Brazil: Editora da Unicamp, 1993. 408 p.: bibl., ill., maps. (Col. Momento)

The result of a multidisciplinary conference organized by the Instituto de Estudos da Linguagem at UNICAMP in 1991, this collection brings together texts by specialists from various fields and from various Latin

American countries united by a common concern: to discuss theoretical issues related to education and communication, and their practical applications to the preservation and cultural revitalization of indigenous peoples. Intended audiences include students, linguists, educators, anthropologists and other social scientists, and indigenous support organizations. [RW]

941   Simposio Salud y Población Indígena de la Amazonia, 1st, Quito, 1993. Salud y población indígena de la amazonia. v. 1–2. Organización y recopilación de Eduardo Estrella y Antonio Crespo. Quito: Tratado de Cooperación Amazónica; Comisión de las Comunidades Europeas; Museo Nacional de Medicina del Ecuador, 1993. 2 v.: bibl., ill.

Specialists, researchers, and indigenous leaders from diverse areas of Amazonia presented their work at an international symposium on indigenous health. Topics include: food and nutrition, epidemiology and health problems, health assistance programs, traditional medical systems and knowledge of medicinal plants, and the question of intellectual property rights to medical resources. Measures for improving health care and nutritional programs are suggested. [RW]

942   Zerries, Otto. Die Rolle des Tapirs bei außerandinen Indianern. (*in* Circumpacifica: Festschrift für Thomas S. Barthel. Frankfurt: Peter Lang, 1990, v. 1, p. 589–626, bibl., ill., map)

Surveying the importance of the tapir in South American myth, ritual, cosmology, and soul beliefs, key semantic associations of this figure are isolated and contrasted with other animal metaphors and symbolism of the continent. [RW]

BRAZIL

943   Albert, Bruce. A fumaça do metal: história e representações do contato entre os Yanomami. (*Anu. Antropol.*, 89, 1992, p. 151–189, bibl.)

Structural-historical analysis of representations of contact among the Yanomam, a Yanomami subgroup in Brazil. The Yanomami interpret the events and effects of contact through the symbolic filter of their political theory of pathogenic powers (diseases), to which the identity of the white man and the status of manufactured objects have been subsumed. A key article in the growing number of studies of structural history in lowland South America. [RW]

944 Albert, Bruce. L'or cannibale et la chute du ciel: une critique chamanique de l'économie politique de la nature, Yanomami, Brésil. (*Homme/Paris*, 33 : 126/128, avril/déc. 1993, p. 349–378, bibl.)

Discourse analysis of a Yanomami shaman and political leader demonstrates a complex interweaving of symbolic themes derived from traditional cosmology and imposed categories of ethnicity. Indigenous discourse produces critical reflection on non-indigenous cultural constructions of nature, and is not derived from the ecological rhetoric of defense organizations. [RW]

945 Almeida, Alfredo Wagner Berno de. Terra, conflito e cidadania. (*Reforma Agrár.*, 22 : 1, jan./abril 1992, p. 61–86, bibl.)

Document presented to the Permanent Peoples' Forum in Paris in 1990 by a leading expert on agrarian conflicts in rural Brazil and Amazonia. Analyzes role of expert reports in the legal process and structure of State power. Summarizes types of violations of indigenous and peasant rights, and cites numerous cases of violence—invasions of indigenous areas, forced resettlement, slave labor, massacres—that have taken place recently in Amazonia. [RW]

946 Amazônia: etnologia e história indígena. Organização de Eduardo Batalha Viveiros de Castro e Manuela Carneiro da Cunha. São Paulo: Núcleo de História Indígena e do Indigenismo; Fundação de Amparo à Pesquisa do Estado de São Paulo, 1993. 431 p.: bibl., ill., maps. (Série Estudos)

Papers presented at a conference held at the Museu Goeldi in Belém in 1987 serve as an introduction to concepts, methods, and problems in the anthropology and history of indigenous Amazonia. Collection reflects thematic diversity and theoretical dynamics of Amazonian ethnology, consolidating new areas of research such as analyzing historicity in its political and symbolic dimensions, critically rethinking classic areas of study such as kinship and social organization, deepening interpretation of native cosmologies, and evaluating interaction between socio- and biodiversity in Amazonia. [RW]

947 Baines, Stephen Grant. "É a FUNAI que sabe": a Frente de Atração Waimiri-Atroari. Belém, Brazil: SCT/CNPq, Museu Paraense Emílio Goeldi, 1991. 362 p.: bibl., ill., maps. (Col. Eduardo Galvão)

Discourse analysis of domination in the relations between the Fundação Nacional do Indio (FUNAI) and the Waimiri-Atroari indigenous group of northern Brazil. Explores construction of ethnic identity in the contact situation through the FUNAI agents' systematic manipulation, implantation of "total institutions" of domination, and reinforcement of historical stereotypes of contact. A major advance in situational analyses of interethnic relations. [RW]

948 Baines, Stephen Grant. Os Waimiri-Atroari e a invenção social de etnicidade pelo indigenismo empresarial. Brasília: Depto. de Antropologia, Univ. de Brasília, 1995. 27 p.: bibl. (Série Antropologia; 179)

"Social invention of ethnicity" is explored by comparing and distinguishing among various phenomena and contexts: from the ethnic discourse of native peoples of northeastern Brazil used as a political strategy to defend land claims; to ethnicity as a survival strategy under colonialist-type regimes, as in the case of the Waimiri-Atroari where the official indigenous agency supports a large company occupying indigenous lands. [RW]

949 Bastos, Rafael José de Menezes. Indagação sobre os Kamayurá, o Alto-Xingu e outros nomes e coisas: uma etnologia da sociedade xinguara. (*Anu. Antropol.*, 94, 1995, p. 227–269, bibl.)

Interpretation of oral histories of the Kamaiurá, a Tupian people of the upper Xingu who—like the Waiwai of northern Brazil—are descendants of peoples of different language groups. Oral histories refer to a process of drastic reduction and ethnic reconstitution, which author traces through a regional perspective on the complex and shifting political configuration of the upper Xingu over time. [RW]

950 Castro, Eduardo Batalha Viveiros de. From the enemy's point of view: humanity and divinity in an Amazonian society. Translated by Catherine V. Howard. Chicago: Univ. of Chicago Press, 1992. 407 p.: bibl., ill., index.

Translated and revised version of author's 1986 doctoral thesis, one of the most influential monographs in Brazilian ethnology of the last decade. Describes and interprets cosmology and social philosophy of the Araweté, a Tupi-Guarani people of eastern Amazonia, from the perspective of concepts of the person, death and eschatology, divinity, and systems of shamanism and warfare. The theme of divine cannibalism is treated as part of the complex of Tupi-Guarani ritual anthropophagy. [RW]

951 Conklin, Beth A. "Thus are our bodies, thus was our custom": mortuary cannibalism in an Amazonian society. (*Am. Ethnol.*, 22 : 1, Feb. 1995, p. 75–101, bibl.)

Examines cultural logic of mortuary cannibalism among the Wari' (Pakaasnovas) of western Brazil. Rejecting materialist and symbolic interpretations, analysis emphasizes indigenous understanding of the relation of cannibalism to mourning experiences; that is, the body's social significance makes its destruction essential for managing grief and attenuating the memories of the deceased. Cannibalism is a key element in processes of human-animal regeneration and reciprocity, as elaborated in myth, cosmology, and eschatology. [RW]

952 Crocker, Christopher. El hombre-mono con ojos de metal: maneras bororo de apodar a los otros. (*in* De palabra y obra en el Nuevo Mundo. Madrid: Siglo Veintiuno Editores, 1992, v. 1, p. 237–264, map)

Well-known ethnologist of the Bororo of Mato Grosso interprets indigenous view of alterity—specifically, representations of the "white man"—and its codification in nicknames, myth, and ritual, as ways of controlling the Other. Demonstrates how key sociocosmological contrasts are worked out in the situation of interethnic contact. [RW]

953 Direitos indígenas e antropologia: laudos periciais em Mato Grosso. Organização de Denise Maldi. Cuiabá, Brazil: EdUFMT, 1994. 292 p.: bibl., maps.

Four "expert reports" (*perícias*) by anthropologists and historians focus on indigenous peoples of Mato Grosso (Cinta Larga, Paresi, Bakairi, Zoró). Commissioned by the Procuradoria Geral da República and used in land tenure litigation, work contains a wealth of ethnohistoric and ethnological information on these peoples and the history of contact. [RW]

954 Ferreira, Mariana Kawall Leal. Com quantos paus se faz uma canoa!: a matemática na vida cotidiana e na experiência escolar indígena. Brasília: Ministério da Educação e do Desporto, Secretaria de Educação Fundamental, Depto. de Política Educacional, Assessoria de Educação Escolar Indígena, 1994. 59 p.: bibl., ill.

Author relies on her experiences as an educator among various native peoples in Brazil to examine the specific problems of teaching mathematics. Argues for utilizing ethnomathematics approach developed by D'Ambrósio, relating mathematics to native reality. [RW]

955 *Filhos da Terra.* Vol. 1, No. 1, junho 1992. 500 anos de resistência. Rio de Janeiro: Univ. Federal do Rio de Janeiro.

Collection of interviews with indigenous leaders at various intertribal conferences held from 1989–92, including the Primeiro Encontro dos Povos Indígenas do Xingú in 1989, the 1991 formation of the Comitê Intertribal 500 Anos de Resistência in Rio de Janeiro, the Mulher, Direitos Indígenas e Meio Ambiente conference in the same year, and others. Important material for understanding concretely the concerns and complaints of indigenous peoples regarding issues such as education, health, Fundação Nacional do Indio (FUNAI), the Church, and anthropologists. [RW]

956 Fisher, William H. Megadevelopment, environmentalism, and resistance: the institutional context of Kayapó indigenous politics in central Brazil. (*Hum. Organ.*, 53 : 3, Fall 1994, p. 220–232, bibl.)

Analyzes history of Cayapo resistance to external pressures over land and resources as a way of contextualizing and understanding their recent role in environmentalist movements opposing large-scale development projects in the Brazilian Amazon. Rejecting "culturalist" explanations, author links Cayapo actions to a broader political and economic framework and to Cayapo perceptions of this framework as the basis for effective strategies of resistance. [RW]

957 Gonçalves, Marco Antonio. O significado do nome: cosmologia e nominação entre os Pirahã. Rio de Janeiro: Sette Letras, 1993. 170 p.: bibl., ill., map.

The system of personal names among the Mura-Pirahá of southeastern Amazonas, a group little-known in ethnographic literature, is the starting point. Using the logic of this naming system, author elucidates themes in cosmology, sociability, ritual, eschatology, cannibalism, warfare, identity, and alterity. A contribution to structuralist analysis of classification systems. [RW]

958 Grafismo indígena: estudos de antropologia estética. Organização de Lux Boelitz Vidal. São Paulo: Studio Nobel; FAPESP; Edusp, 1992. 296 p.: bibl., ill. (some col.), map.

Beautifully illustrated and well-organized collection of 15 articles by Brazilian ethnologists and specialists deals with such questions as interpretation of prehistoric rock art, artistic expression of mythological themes, hallucinogenic art, body painting and its relation to sociocultural symbolism, and tradition and innovation in the context of historical change. A major theoretical and methodological contribution to the interpretation of indigenous art forms and, more generally, to the anthropology of esthetics. [RW]

959 Graham, Laura R. Performing dreams: discourses of immortality among the Xavante of Central Brazil. Austin: Univ. of Texas Press, 1995. 290 p.: bibl., ill., index, maps.

Discourse-centered approach to Xavante culture focuses on the performance of songs, the telling of dreams, and the transmission of culture. Principal arguments are that the meaning of expressive practices is constructed through performance; that dreams may be seen as communicative and hence social processes; and that discursive practices are essential to the process of cultural transmission. [RW]

960 Guia de fontes para a história indígena e do indigenismo em arquivos brasileiros: acervos das capitais. Coordenação de John Manuel Monteiro. São Paulo: NHII-USP; FAPESP, 1994. 496 p.: indexes. (Série Instrumentos de pesquisa)

Inventory of archives in Brazilian state capitals containing information on indigenous peoples and/or indigenist policy. This major research tool is of fundamental importance for research in Brazilian indigenous history. Organized by state, each entry contains general information on the archive, technical information about the documents, a brief summary of thematic content, and the details about the availability of research tools (indices, manuals, etc.). [RW]

961 Hartmann, Günther. Das Nrówa-Re-Fest der Pau d'Arco-Kayapó, Zentral-Brasilien. (*Z. Ethnol.*, 113:2, 1988, p. 239–260, bibl., photos)

Detailed description of the Nrówa-Re festival among the Pau d'Arco Kayapó of Central Brazil is based on the fieldnotes of Wilhelm Kissenberth, who lived among them in 1908–09; and on an unpublished manuscript of Curt Nimuendajú, the last ethnographer to have visited the Pau d'Arco who ceased to exist as a group in the 1930s. [RW]

962 História dos índios no Brasil. Organização de Manuela Carneiro da Cunha. São Paulo: Fundação de Amparo à Pesquisa do Estado de São Paulo; Companhia das Letras; Secretaria Municipal de Cultura, Prefeitura do Município de São Paulo, 1992. 611 p.: bibl., ill. (some col.), indexes, maps (some col.).

Pioneering collection of articles on Brazilian indigenous history represents state-of-the-art research since topic became a central focus of ethnology in 1980s, and is principal product of the Núcleo de História Indígena e do Indigenismo research group coordinated by Cunha. Includes contributions by 30 leading specialists including archaeologists, linguists, historians, and anthropologists. Organized by region with separate sections on source materials and indigenous policy and legislation. Volume fills a major gap in South American ethnology and proposes new approaches and perspectives to study of ethnohistory. Richly illustrated and handsomely produced. [RW]

963 Indios no Brasil. Organização de Luís Donisete Benzi Grupioni. São Paulo: Secretaria Municipal de Cultura, Prefeitura do Município de São Paulo; Mari-Grupo de Educação Indígena/USP, 1992. 279 p.: bibl., ill., (some col.), maps.

Collection of articles prepared for the 1992 exposition on Brazilian indigenous peoples organized by the Secretaria Municipal de Cultura of São Paulo reflects the principal themes: indigenous peoples in the history of contact; cultural diversity of indigenous societies through cosmologies, art, and language;

and indigenous peoples in the present-day pluricultural situation of Brazil. [RW]

964 Instituto Socioambiental (Brazil). Povos indígenas no Brasil, 1991–1995. São Paulo: Instituto Socioambiental, 1996? 871 p.: bibl., ill., indexes, maps.

Includes compilation of Brazilian news reports and analyses of critical questions in indigenous affairs over a four-year period. Published every four years, these volumes represent the highest quality of professionalism among Brazilian NGOs committed to the indigenous rights movement and are reliable sources of up-to-date information and analyses on indigenous news throughout the country. As in previous volumes, following a section of thematic analyses, work is organized into 19 geographical regions. Numerous new features have been added: bibliographies on indigenous peoples of Amazonia, directories of NGOs, and complete indices of peoples and locations. A most useful sourcebook for scholars and students interested in the present situation of Brazilian indigenous peoples. [RW]

965 Lima, Antonio Carlos de Souza. Um grande cerco de paz: poder tutelar, indianidade e formação do Estado no Brasil. Petrópolis, Brazil: Vozes, 1995. 335 p.: bibl., ill., maps.

Revisionist history of Brazilian indigenous policy at the beginning of the Velha República focuses on the creation of the Serviço de Proteção aos Índios (SPI) and its first director, Cândido Mariano da Silva Rondon. Demythologizes Rondon, and reevaluates SPI's project objectives and place within the apparatus of State power. This study, written by an anthropologist, provides an ethnographic history of the principal elements and processes that constitute a certain modality of State power, i.e., tutelary power, as exercised by the SPI over the indigenous population. [RW]

966 Lukesch, Anton. Schamanen am Rio Xingu: neuentdeckte Indianerstämme im brasilianischen Urwald. Vienna: Böhlau, 1990. 342 p.: bibl., ill., index, maps.

Comparative study of shamanism among the Tupian Asurini and Araweté of the Xingu River region is based on author's fieldwork in mid-1980s. Provides detailed descriptions of shamanic rituals, mythic foundations, and relations to worldview. [RW]

Meggers, Betty J. Amazonia: man and culture in a counterfeit paradise. See item **471.**

967 Mehringer, Jakob and **Jürgen Dieckert.** Die Körper: und Wesensauffassung bei den brasilianischen Canela-Indianern. (*Z. Ethnol.*, 115, 1990, p. 241–259, bibl., ill.)

Semantic analysis of concepts of the body and "spirit" ("entity") among the Canella of northeastern Brazil. Authors argue that the notion of spirit implies unity of the human being, or person, and thus is subject to disintegration or "soul loss" in cases of sickness or extreme emotional states which may provoke "sadness" and death. Log-racing and ritual songs are mechanisms for controlling potential disintegration by promoting "happiness" and unity of the human being. [RW]

968 Monteiro, John Manuel. Negros da terra: índios e bandeirantes nas origens de São Paulo. São Paulo: Companhia das Letras, 1994. 300 p.: bibl., ill. (some col.), index, maps (some col.).

Thorough and well-documented history of 16th- and 17th-century society and economy in São Paulo region analyzes impact of slavery on the indigenous peoples of the region and the formation of a slave-based economy and society. Offers new perspectives in the study of regional economies based on indigenous slavery and in the historiography of *bandeirantismo* (expeditions to the interior). [RW]

969 Nimuendajú, Curt. Etnografia e indigenismo: sobre os Kaingang, os Ofaié-Xavante e os índios do Pará. Organização e apresentação de Marco Antonio Gonçalves. Campinas, Brazil: Editora da Unicamp, 1993. 160 p.: bibl., ill., maps. (Col. Repertórios)

Contains several previously unpublished reports and letters by German ethnographer of Brazilian indigenous peoples. Begins with first ethnographic description of the Kaingangue, including particularly valuable notes on ceremonial organization and symbolism. Second report deals with the ethnohistory and process of extermination of the Opaye. Final entry constitutes letters written from Pará providing information on a series of groups in the region. Excellent biographical introduction. [RW]

970 Nugent, Stephen L. Amazonian caboclo society: an essay on invisibility and peasant economy. Providence, R.I.: Berg, 1993. 278 p.: bibl., ill., index, maps. (Explorations in anthropology)

Important study examines peasant/*caboclo* society of the lower Brazilian Amazon, a largely neglected population in the anthropological literature on Amazonia. After discussing various representations of *caboclos* as "marginal societies," analysis focuses on local community organization, economic processes, and their relation to national development. Finally, author discusses implications of recent proposals for sustainable development for deconstructing the "invisibility" of the *caboclo*. For sociologist's comment see *HLAS 55:5185*. [RW]

971 Pãrõkumu, Umusī and Tõrãmū Kēhíri. Antes o mundo não existia: mitologia dos antigos Desana-Kēhíripõrã. 2a. ed. rev. e ampliada. São João Batista do Rio Tiguié, Brazil: UNIRT; São Gabriel da Cachoeira, Brazil: FOIRN, 1995. 264 p.: ill. (some col.), maps. (Col. Narradores indígenas do Rio Negro; 1)

Revised version of a collection of myths, originally published in 1980 (see *HLAS 47:1363*), of the Desana indigenous group (of the Kenhiripõra descent group) of the northwest Amazon. The first of a projected series of volumes by indigenous narrators of the region, with the support of the Federação das Organizações Indígenas do Rio Negro (FOIRN), volume presents a Portuguese translation of the lengthy Desana creation cycle and other myths (simplified and discussed by the narrator for the purpose of widespread distribution). [RW]

972 Samain, Etienne. Moroneta kamayurá: mitos e aspectos da relidade social dos índios kamayurá, Alto Xingu. Rio de Janeiro: Lidador, 1991. 270 p.: bibl., ill. (some col.).

Focuses on relation of the mythology of the Kamaiurá to specific aspects of their social reality. Presents structuralist analysis of various myths and offers a group of unedited myth texts. A beautifully illustrated volume, rich in historical and ethnographic information on peoples of the upper Xingu. Myth texts are preceded by a lengthy discussion of the importance of the sociocultural context of narration. [RW]

973 Saúde e povos indígenas. Organização de Ricardo Ventura Santos e Carlos Everaldo Alvares Coimbra Júnior. Rio de Janeiro: Editora Fiocruz, 1994. 251 p.: bibl., ill., map.

Innovative collection of 10 articles by anthropologists and medical specialists with experience among South American indigenous peoples, principally in Brazil. Overall objective of volume is to integrate bioecological and sociocultural factors in the understanding of health and sickness in indigenous societies. Articles are thematically organized in three parts: 1) studies of pre-history and contact history, 2) ethnomedicine, and 3) impact of socioeconomic processes on health/sickness profiles. [RW]

974 As senhoras do pássaro da noite: escritos sobre a religião dos orixás. Organização de Carlos Eugênio Marcondes de Moura. Ilustrações de Carybé. São Paulo: AM; Edusp, 1994. 248 p.: bibl., ill.

Collection of essays by specialists on the *orixás* African-American religion describes religion's mythic foundation, traditional institutions, and ritual practices as observed in Africa, Brazil, and Cuba. Includes diverse analyses and interpretations of rituals and beliefs, the history of cults, and an up-to-date bibliography. Useful for specialists and researchers, and for initiates in Afro-Brazilian religions. [RW]

975 Shapiro, Dolores J. Blood, oil, honey, and water: symbolism in spirit possession sects in northeastern Brazil. (*Am. Ethnol.*, 22:4, Nov. 1995, p. 828–847, bibl.)

Comparative description and analysis of key symbols in four spirit-possession religions of northeastern Brazil. Demonstrates how each group utilizes these symbols in different ways to represent or disavow an ideology correlated with a distinct "racial" identity. Situational interpretation of symbolic manipulation enriches the understanding of dynamic religious processes. [RW]

976 Sierra Camacho, María Teresa. La lucha por los derechos indígenas en el Brasil actual. México: CIESAS, 1993. 154 p.: bibl. (Col. Miguel Othón de Mendizábal)

Mexican anthropologist's analysis of emergence of the Brazilian indigenous movement is based on interviews with participants and documentary material, leading up to the major gains in indigenous rights achieved by the 1988 Assembléia Nacional Constituente campaign. Briefly traces historical antecedents of the modern movement, the context of its emergence in the 1970s, the legislative reforms of the 1988 Constitution, and the continuing threats to indigenous rights. [RW]

977   A temática indígena na escola: novos subsídios para professores de 1o. e 2o. graus. Organização de Aracy Lopes da Silva e Luís Donisete Benzi Grupioni. Brasília: MEC; UNESCO; São Paulo: MARI, 1995. 575 p.: bibl., ill., map.

Voluminous collection of 22 articles by Brazilian anthropologists focuses on presentation of thematic materials about Brazilian indigenous peoples in primary and secondary school curricula. Designed as a resource book for rethinking the question, work presents the most up-to-date information on legal and political questions affecting indigenous peoples; critical essays and new perspectives on pre-history, history, and historiography; linguistic and ethnological surveys; and a series of stimulating reflections on, and strategies for, presenting sociocultural diversity in the classroom. [RW]

978   Universidade Federal do Pará (Brazil). Núcleo de Meio Ambiente. Sociedades indígenas e transformações ambientais. Organização de Antônio Carlos Magalhães. Belém, Brazil: Univ. Federal do Pará, Núcleo de Meio Ambiente, 1993. 203 p.: bibl., ill., maps. (Série Universidade e meio ambiente; 6)

Seven articles by Brazilian ethnologists analyze impact of large-scale development projects on the environment and indigenous peoples of Brazil. Covers a diversity of situations from Amazonia, the Northeast, and the South. Includes critical reflections on possibilities of sustainable development and resource use in indigenous areas. [RW]

979   Urban, Greg. Metaphysical community: the interplay of the senses and the intellect. Austin: Univ. of Texas Press, 1996. 288 p.: bibl., ill., index.

Leading exponent of discourse-centered approach examines social organization of the Shokleng, Gê-speaking peoples of southern Brazil. Author suggests a reading in terms of the problematic of knowledge: the theme of intelligibility and sensibility and their interrelations; logical empiricism and its connection to the world; the attachment of circulating discourse to sensible space; the relation of discourse and power relations; and the relation of discourse to reference. [RW]

980   Vilaça, Aparecida. Comendo como gente: formas do canibalismo Wari'. Rio de Janeiro: ANPOCS; Editora UFRJ, 1992. 363 p.: bibl., ill., maps.

Structural analysis of cosmology and social organization of the Wari' (Pakaasnovos), a Txapakuran-speaking people of western Rondônia, presented in extraordinarily rich detail. Investigates mortuary practices, shamanism, and the central importance of cannibalism to Wari' culture. Examination of cannibalism under two aspects, 'exo-' and 'endo-' cannibalism, referring to the domains of cosmos and society respectively, reveals predation as the dominant organizing principle of Wari' worldview. [RW]

981   Wright, Robin M. Guardians of the cosmos: Baniwa shamans and prophets. parts 1–2. (*Hist. Relig.*, 32:1, Aug. 1992, p. 32–58 [and] 32:2, Nov. 1992, p. 126–145)

Two-part study of the religion of the Baniwa of the northwest Amazon. Pt. 1 outlines cosmogony through a summary of the major creation myth cycles, and cosmology through shamanic discourse on the significance of the multi-tiered cosmos. Pt. 2 demonstrates connections of shamanic experience to cosmology and cosmogony through discourse on travels, curing practice, and training. Study focuses on salvific powers of master-shamans, the basis of prophetism and messianic ideologies. [RW]

982   Xamanismo no Brasil: novas perspectivas. Organização de E. Jean Matteson Langdon. Florianópolis, Brazil: Editora da UFSC, 1996. 367 p.: bibl., ill., maps.

Collection of 12 articles on shamanism among various indigenous groups in Brazil, mainly in the northern and western Amazon. Highly useful introduction contextualizes the study of shamanism in the history of anthropology. The "new" perspectives treat shamanism as a cosmological system, grounded in 1) a notion of cosmic energy to which shamanic power is linked; 2) a principle of transformation which characterizes a metaphoric vision of the universe; and 3) shamanic ecstasy as the basis of shamans' power. [RW]

COLOMBIA, VENEZUELA, AND THE GUIANAS

983 Colson, Audrey Butt and **Cesáreo de Armellada.** El rol económico del chamán y su base conceptual entre los Kapones y Pemones septentrionales de las Guayanas. Traducción de Angelina Pollak-Eltz y Fray Cesáreo de Armellada. (*Montalbán/Caracas*, 22, 1990, p. 7–97, bibl.)

Two recognized specialists in Cariban peoples and cultures of the Guayanas present convincing evidence of the economic importance of shamanism in the regulation and control of natural resources among the Acawai. Through analysis of spiritual elements and dynamics of the cosmos, shamanic and collective ritual, and the prophetic Hallelujah religion, authors point to the innumerable ways shamans regulate Acawai relations with their environment. See also items **998** and **984.** [RW]

984 Hammen, Maria Clara van der. El manejo del mundo: naturaleza y sociedad entre los Yukuna de la Amazonia colombiana = Managing the world: nature and society by the Yukuna of the Colombian Amazonia. 2. ed. Bogotá: Tropenbos, 1992. 376 p.: bibl., ill., indexes, maps. (Estudios en la Amazonia colombiana; 4 = Studies on the Colombian Amazonia; 4)

Following recent studies in symbolism and ecology, this ethnography of the Arawak-speaking Yukuna of the Colombian Amazon explores shamanic models for the regulation of human relations to the environment. Through detailed consideration of qualitative (mythic) and quantitative (statistical) aspects of different subsistence activities, author demonstrates both the symbolic and pragmatic construction of Yukuna environmental management, as well as historical influences on native models. See also items **998** and **983.** [RW]

985 Jackson, Jean E. Culture, genuine and spurious: the politics of Indianness in the Vaupés, Colombia. (*Am. Ethnol.*, 22:1, Feb. 1995, p. 3–27, bibl.)

Highly relevant article explores how Tucanoan indigenous peoples of the Colombian Vaupés have adapted notions of their own history and culture to fit into the currently politicized question of indigenous identity. This process involves local and na-

tional indigenous rights organizations and international NGOs. Also addresses question of ethnographic authority, i.e., the confrontation between anthropological and native visions of indigenous culture and history. See also item **986.** [RW]

986 Jackson, Jean E. Preserving Indian culture: shaman schools and ethno-education in the Vaupés, Colombia. (*Cult. Anthropol.*, 10:3, Aug. 1995, p. 302–329, bibl.)

Critically assesses results of an early 1980s indigenist program to create shaman schools among Tucanoan-speaking peoples of the Colombian Vaupés as a way of revitalizing and disseminating shamanic knowledge and practice. The complexities of the Tucanoan situation of contact presented serious difficulties for the project; nevertheless, the experiment succeeded in identifying key questions in the politics of cultural change. See also item **985.** [RW]

987 Journet, Nicolas. La paix des jardins: structures sociales des Indiens curripaco du haut Rio Negro, Colombie. Paris: Institut d'ethnologie, Musée de l'homme, 1995. 384 p.: bibl., ill., index, maps. (Mémoires de l'Institut d'ethnologie, 0768-1380; 31)

Ethnography of the Curripaco, a northern Arawak people of the Colombian Amazon, about whom little has been published. Author presents their vision of society as a continuation of the myth of origin of clans, initiation rites, and agriculture, in contrast to a prior state of war, hunting, and forest-dwelling existence. The Curripaco hold these two mythical visions of life-in-society and their relations with nature. [RW]

988 Losonczy, Anne-Marie. La maîtrise du multiple: corps et espace dans le chamanisme embera du Chocó, Colombie. (*Homme/Paris*, 30:114, avril/juin 1990, p. 75–100, bibl.)

Original study of the Embera (Chocó, Colombia) analyzes shamanic ritual as the construction of a symbolic topography. Shamanic voyages and spirit possession in ritual performances carve out a structure of variously marked signs/spaces that are transposed onto the cosmos, bodily boundaries, and territorial space. This structure may undergo change, redefining spatial and corporeal limits and boundaries. [RW]

989 Morales Méndez, Filadelfo. Del mori- chal a la sabana. Caracas: Univ. Central de Venezuela, Facultad de Ciencias Económicas y Sociales, Escuela de Sociología y Antropología, 1989. 153 p.: bibl., ill.

Critical study analyzes official indigenist policy in Venezuela and its effects on the Cariban Kari'ña (Carib). Brief introduction to Kari'ña social organization is followed by a summary of official indigenist policy concentrating on the Instituto Agrario Nacional program creating indigenous enterprises. The effects of this program—and herein lies the contribution of the study—have been entirely negative for indigenous social, political, and economic organization. Thus, the program represents another form of internal colonialism. [RW]

Myers, Iris. The Makushi of the Guiana-Brazilian frontier in 1944: a study in culture contact. See item **879.**

990 Osborn, Ann. Las cuatro estaciones: mitología y estructura social entre los u'wa. Traducción de Fabricio Cabrera Micolta. Bogotá: Banco de la República, Museo del Oro, 1995. 269 p.: bibl., ill. (Col. bibliográfica. Antropología)

Examines ritual, cosmology, and ecology of the U'wa, a Chibcha-speaking people of the Andean region in northeastern Colombia. Provides a fascinating demonstration of the intimate and consistent relations among U'wa sung mythic narratives, the ritual celebrations of which are determined by seasonal movements, and by human life cycle and subsistence activities in three distinct Andean environments. Extensive use of sung narratives and exegeses. [RW]

Pollak-Eltz, Angelina. Anima worship in Venezuela. See item **888.**

991 Preuss, Konrad Theodor. Religión y mitología de los Uitotos: recopilación de textos y observaciones efectuadas en una tribu indígena de Colombia, Suramérica. v. 1–2. Bogotá: Instituto Colombiano de Cultura; Corporación Colombiana para la Amazonia Araracuara; Editorial Univ. Nacional, 1994. 2 v.: bibl.

Superb Spanish translation of early 20th-century classic in religious ethnography of lowland South America, previously inaccessible to a non-German-reading public.

Translated by two German linguists and a native Witoto. Vol. 1 provides a brief ethnographic presentation and interpretations, followed by summaries of myth texts. Vol. 2 consists of a fully annotated collection of myth texts with juxtalinear and free translations, ritual song texts, and a Witoto-Spanish dictionary. [RW]

992 Schultes, Richard Evans and **Robert Francis Raffauf.** El bejuco del alma: los médicos tradicionales de la Amazonia Colombiana, sus plantas y sus rituales. Prólogo de Ghillean T. Prance. Epílogo de Michael J. Balick. Traducción de Carlos Alberto Uribe Tobón. Bogotá: Ediciones Uniandes; Banco de la República; Medellín, Colombia: Editorial Univ. de Antioquia; 1994. 284 p.: bibl., photos.

This companion volume to Schultes' previous work (see *HLAS 53 : 1137*) is a superb collection of photos taken during 20 years of research in the Colombian Amazon. Thematically organized around the "visionary vines" (*banisteriopsis, ayahuasca*), hallucinogenic plants and snuffs among native peoples, volume ranges widely over ethnobotany, shamanism, art, ritual, and natural phenomena in western Amazonia. Minimal text is accompanied by citations from other ethnographies. See also item **937.** [RW]

Society for Caribbean Research. International Conference, (2nd, Vienna, 1990.) Ay BôBô: afro-karibische Religionen = African-Caribbean religions. v. 1, Kulte/Cults. See item **902.**

Whitehead, Neil L. The historical anthropology of text: the interpretation of Ralegh's *Discoverie of Guiana*. See item **912.**

993 Wilbert, Johannes. Mystic endowment: religious ethnography of the Warao Indians. Cambridge, Mass.: Harvard Univ. Center for the Study of World Religions; Harvard Univ. Press, 1993. 308 p.: bibl., ill., index, maps. (Religions of the world)

Collection includes some of the author's most important essays written during 25 years of research among the Warao of the Orinoco Delta. Focus is on religious life, for which author provides in-depth comparative and historical interpretations of the symbolic values the Warao bestow on environmental, material, and social processes, revealing how Warao experience of life and the material conditions of existence are endowed with religious and mystical significance. This approach, outside of studies of the Guarani, has rarely been explored in South American ethnology.

PERU AND ECUADOR

994   Baer, Gerhard. Cosmología y shamanismo de los matsiguenga: Perú Oriental. Traducción de María Susana Cipolletti. Quito: Ediciones Abya-Yala, 1994. 389 p.: appendix, bibl., ill. (Col. Biblioteca Abya-Yala; 15)

Religious ethnography focuses on the Arawak-speaking Machiguenga of the eastern Peruvian Amazon. Religion is understood as a system of orientation to reality and meaning, and is explored through classification of being, conceptions of sickness and health, and the central role of shamanism. Extensive appendix contains a collection of myth summaries. [RW]

995   Ballón Aguirre, Enrique. Etiología jíbara I: origen de la monogamia, el zapallo, la arcilla y las manchas de la luna. (*Amazonía Peru.*, 12:24, junio 1994, p. 11–76, bibl.)

In pt. 1 of a two-part study, author offers a critique of Lévi-Strauss' analysis of Jivaroan myths linking the potter and jealousy. Utilizing unabridged versions of Jivaroan myths, study adopts a semiotic approach to mythic discourse, demonstrating notional displacement which occurs in the semantic interpretation of texts taken from different Jivaroan groups, thus raising doubts concerning the associations proposed by Lévi-Strauss. See also item **1011**. [RW]

996   Bant, Astrid A. Parentesco, matrimonio e intereses de género en una sociedad amazónica: el caso aguaruna. (*Amazonía Peru.*, 12:24, junio 1994, p. 77–103, bibl, graphs, photos, tables)

Examines Aguaruna kinship and marriage, both as a system of rules and norms and as praxis in the negotiation of gender interests. Author's actor-oriented approach to social relations emphasizes the process of differentiation in gender interests as an important element in planning and implementing development projects, and in highlighting

women's roles in social continuity and change. [RW]

997   Chaumeil, Jean Pierre. Del proyectil al virus: el complejo de dardos-mágicos en el chamanismo del oeste amazónico. (*in* Congreso Nacional de Antropología, 6th, Bogotá, 1992. Cultura y salud en la construcción de las Americas. Bogotá: Instituto Colombiana de Cultura, 1993, p. 261–277, bibl., ill., map)

Studies use of shamanic projectiles (darts) among native peoples of the middle and upper Amazon, and their relation to ethnomodels of sickness and plant therapy. Offers the suggestive hypothesis that such projectiles correspond to an "ethnovirological" complex, the main characteristic of which is the "cultivated" nature of pathogenic agents, and that this complex bears underlying similarities to Western medical models. See also item **1005**. [RW]

Comunidades campesinas y nativas, en el nuevo contexto nacional. See item **1189**.

998   Descola, Philippe. In the society of nature: a native ecology in Amazonia. Translated by Nora Scott. Cambridge, England; New York: Cambridge Univ. Press, 1994. 372 p.: bibl., ill., indexes, maps. (Cambridge studies in social and cultural anthropology; 93)

English translation of author's masterful and important study, originally published in French (Paris: Maison des sciences de l'homme, 1986) and translated into Spanish (1992). Provides ethnographic description and analysis of the symbolic and technical relations of the Achuar to the Amazon environment. This pioneering model of a synthetic ecological/symbolic approach investigates dynamic interactions between techniques used in socializing nature and the symbolic systems that sustain these interactions. Overcomes previous limitations of materialist ecological and conceptual symbolic analyses. The value of this contribution is its understanding of the Achuar process of domesticating nature and of the long-run implications of this process for resource use in the Amazon environment. See also items **984, 999,** and **983**. [RW]

999   Descola, Philippe. Les lances du crépuscule: relations jivaros, Haute Amazonie. Paris: Plon, 1993. 505 p., 32 p. of plates:

bibl., ill., indexes, maps. (Terre humaine, 0492–7915)

The originality and the main contribution of this ethnography of the Achuar, an indigenous group of the Peru/Ecuador border region, is its style, which departs from standard monographic writing to explore the literary possibilities of ethnography. The result is an extraordinarily engaging work in which native thought, emotions, and actions—in short, Achuar culture—is revealed in constant dialogue with the ethnographer and in his reflections. See also item **998**. [RW]

1000 Deshayes, Patrick and **Barbara Keifenheim.** Penser l'autre: chez les Indiens Huni Kuin de l'Amazonie. Préface de Robert Jaulin. Paris: L'Harmattan, 1994. 237 p.: bibl., ill., map. (Recherches & documents. Amériques latines)

Structuralist analysis, inspired by the works of R. Jaulin and P. Clastres, examines system of relations among the Panoan Cashinawa (Huni Kuin) of the Peru/Brazil border. Organized around the central notions of *self* and *other* and their interrelations, which are interwoven through a dynamic system of complementary oppositions that define the parameters of kinship and alliance, gender relations, political economy, ritual and cosmology, and interethnic relations. [RW]

1001 García Tomas, María Dolores. Buscando nuestras raíces: historia y cultura chayahuita. v. 1–6. Lima: Centro Amazónico de Antropología y Aplicación Práctica, 1993– . 6 v.: bibl., ill., maps.

Extraordinary collection of material gathered and organized by Catholic missionaries examines the history, technology, social organization, and religion of the Chayahuitas, an indigenous group of the upper Amazon, Peru. In addition to providing a thorough survey of historical sources, the volumes are rich in native texts and illustrations: myths, songs and chants, and explanations of medical practices, all by native authors/narrators. [RW]

1002 Hendricks, Janet Wall. To drink of death: the narrative of a Shuar warrior. Tucson: Univ. of Arizona Press, 1993. 316 p.: bibl., ill., index.

Discourse-centered approach to Shuar life history presents an autobiography of a Shuar warrior, and provides a discussion of Shuar speech events and their linguistic, cul-

tural, and situational contexts. Given the paucity of anthropological studies of individual life narratives in lowland South America, work is an important contribution. [RW]

1003 Hombre y Ambiente. Vol. 6, No. 21, enero/marzo 1992. La cultura médica de los runas de la región amazónica ecuatoriana de Eduardo Kohn. Quito: Ediciones Abya-Yala.

Analyzes various aspects of the medical system of the Runa (Canelo) of the Ecuadorian Amazon, emphasizing dynamics of the system in relation to external change. Following an analysis of recent studies of ecological symbolism and ethnomedicine, author discusses Runa concepts of sickness and their relation to cosmology, shamanism, and use of medicinal plants. An extensive appendix identifies Runa medicinal plants. [RW]

1004 Illius, Bruno. La "Gran Boa": arte y cosmología de los Shipibo-Conibo. (*Amazonía Peru.*, 12:24, junio 1994, p. 185–212, bibl., photo)

Examines relations of cosmology and art among the Sipibo-Conibo of eastern Peru. In *ayahuasca*-inspired visions, shamans perceive (hear-see-sing) designs—such as the great boa—presented to them by powerful mythical beings and primordial shamans. Designs are transmitted and reproduced by women on textiles, ceramics, and other art forms, and are considered marks of Sipibo-Conibo identity. [RW]

1005 Instituto Normal Bilingüe Intercultural Shuar-Bomboiza (Ecuador). Tséntsak: la experiencia chamánica en el pueblo shuar. Quito: Ediciones ABYA-YALA; Bomboiza, Ecuador: Instituto Normal Bilingüe Intercultural Shuar-Bomboiza, 1991. 145 p.: bibl.

Produced by the Shuar of Ecuador, work focuses on shamanism and shamanic forces (*tsentsak*, darts). Includes biographies and interviews with Shuar shamans, and discussions of the shamans' practice, classes of shamans, initiation and trance experiences, and witchcraft. Particularly valuable insider perspective, with reflections on anthropological interpretations of Shuar shamanism. See also item **997**. [RW]

1006 Kane, Joe. Savages. New York: Knopf; Random House, 1995. 273 p.: bibl., col. ill., map.

Journalist's fascinating and well-written account of the Huao peoples' struggle against North American oil companies and evangelical missionaries resulting from the construction of the oil pipeline in the Ecuadorian Amazon. Provides an insider's view of international NGO politics, indigenous federation politics, missionized indigenous peoples, and the special place occupied by the Huao in Ecuadorian indigenous struggles. For political scientist's comment see item **3429**. [RW]

1007 Kensinger, Kenneth M. How real people ought to live: the Cashinahua of eastern Peru. Prospect Heights, Ill.: Waveland Press, 1995. 305 p.: bibl., ill., index, map.

Collection of author's essays written over the last 25 years on the Cashinawa of the Curanja and upper Purús Rivers in eastern Peru. Includes a sequence of short ethnographies on diverse aspects of Cashinawa society and culture: subsistence activities, gender roles and sexuality, social organization, political organization, religion, and culture change.

1008 Myers, Thomas P. El efecto de las pestes sobre las poblaciones de la Amazonía alta. (*Amazonía Peru.*, 8 : 15, agosto 1988, p. 61–82, bibl., tables)

Contribution to demographic history of the upper Amazon focuses on the consequences of epidemic diseases on the 17th- and 18th-century native populations. A series of tables organizes information on population, region, and ethnic group, providing estimates of the extent of post-contact depopulation. Important for stimulating further work in Amazonian historical demography.

1009 Regan, Jaime. Hacia la tierra sin mal: la religión del pueblo en la Amazonía. 2. ed., corr. Iquitos, Peru: CETA, 1993 456 p.: bibl., photos.

Despite weakness of author's theoretical framework and frank liberation theology perspective, this second, revised edition of his 1983 study (see *HLAS 47 : 1331*) remains an extraordinary ethnography of the popular religiosity of the native peoples of the upper Peruvian Amazon. Following a historical and socioeconomic introduction, author focuses on the spirituality, ritual, and millenarianism that comprise Amazonian popular religion. Of special interest are the lengthy discourses of numerous informants, collections of oral

traditions, and documents left by the Brotherhood of the Cross.

1010 Renard-Casevitz, France Marie and **Olivier Dollfus.** Geografía de algunos mitos y creencias: espacios simbólicos y realidades geográficas de los machiguenga del Alto-Urubamba. (*Amazonía Peru.*, 8 : 16, Dec. 1988, p. 7–39, bibl., map)

Examines Machiguenga geographical knowledge as codified in myths of the origin of place-names or local topographical configurations on the upper Urubamba, Peru. Important study for understanding Machiguenga notions of territoriality. Includes annotated myth texts, list of toponyms, and map. [RW]

1011 Roe, Peter G. Impossible marriages: animal seduction tales among the Shipibo indians of the Peruvian jungle. (*J. Lat. Am. Lore*, 16 : 2, Winter 1990, p. 131–173, bibl., ill., table)

Analysis of Sipibo myths reveals a "system of dynamic dualism" which, author asserts, is widely applicable to other lowland mythologies. This is consistent with Lévi-Strauss' more recent writings on the asymmetry or disequilibrium in Amerindian dualism, demonstrated in Sipibo thought. See also item **995**. [RW]

1012 Rojas Zolezzi, Enrique C. Los Ashaninka, un pueblo tras el Bosque: contribución a la etnología de los campa de la Selva Central Peruana. Lima: Pontificia Univ. Católica del Perú, Fondo Editorial, 1994. 359 p.: bibl., ill.

Ethnography fills a significant gap in the literature on the Ashaninca by presenting a coherent picture of ecology, technology, political and religious organization, and history as a dynamic system both in its internal reproduction and in its transformations. Focus is primarily on demonstrating importance of symmetric exchange in social life, and on the role of myth in the organization of productive activities. Important discussion of recent political changes in Ashaninca territory. [RW]

1013 Santos-Granero, Fernando. Etnohistoria de la Alta Amazonia: siglos XV–XVIII. Quito: Ediciones ABYA-YALA, 1992? 305 p.: bibl., maps. (Col. 500 años; 46)

Collection of author's essays on various interrelated themes and processes in the ethnohistory of the Peruvian Upper Amazon. Volume's overall intent is to contribute to the construction of an indigenous perspective on Amazonian history, a subject largely ignored in Peruvian historiography. Essays include analyses of precolumbian history, of various periods in colonial history, and of present-day indigenous views of history. [RW]

1014 Santos-Granero, Fernando and **Frede-rica Barclay.** Ordenes y desórdenes en la selva central: historia y economía de un espacio regional. Lima: Instituto de Estudios Andinos: IEP Ediciones; Quito: FLACSO, Sede Ecuador, 1995. 365 p.: bibl., ill. (Serie Estudios de la sociedad rural, 1019–4517; 13)

First study written from a regional perspective of economic history of the central Peruvian forest from 17th century to present. The process of constituting regional space and economic articulation involved pioneer colonists, highland colonists, and indigenous peoples (Amuesha and Ashaninca, who had to integrate themselves economically as a strategy of resistance and survival). Metaphor of "order" and "disorder" refers to the contributions to integration and articulation of regional space to national life, bringing together many factors including recent actions of armed revolutionary groups such as the Sendero Luminoso. [RW]

1015 Tizón, Judy. Transformaciones en la Amazonía: estatus, género y cambio entre los Ashaninka. (*Amazonía Peru.*, 12:24, junio 1994, p. 105–123, bibl.)

Systematically assesses generally negative impacts of externally-imposed changes (deforestation, colonization, road construction) on gender relations among the Ashaninca (Campa) of the Peruvian Amazon over past 20 years. This question has received little attention in anthropological literature. [RW]

PARAGUAY, ARGENTINA, AND BOLIVIA

1016 Alvarsson, Jan-Åke. The Mataco of the Gran Chaco: an ethnographic account of change and continuity in Mataco socioeconomic organization. Uppsala, Sweden: Academiae Upsaliensis; Stockholm: Almqvist & Wiksell International, 1988. 314 p.: bibl., ill., index. (Acta Universitatis Upsaliensis. Uppsala studies in cultural anthropology, 0348–5099; 11)

In-depth ethnographic study of the

Mataco of Bolivia focuses on socioeconomic organization, changes, and continuities. Describes impact of historical changes on Mataco cultural practices, and discusses kinship and social organization as forms of identity maintenance. Contributes to the study of economic strategies of lowland groups. [SH]

1017 Bartolomé, Miguel Alberto. Chamanismo y religión entre los ava-katu-ete. 2. ed. Asunción: Centro de Estudios Antropológicos, Univ. Católica, 1991. 176 p.: bibl., ill. (Biblioteca paraguaya de antropología; 11)

Interprets Ava Katu Ete myth cycle and its relation to ritual. Describes author's shamanic initiation and use of chants by shamans. Analyzes shamanic role of healer, healing techniques, and new role as intermediary between the community and the Paraguayan authorities. Important contribution to Guaraní religiosity. [SH]

1018 Bigot, Margot; Graciela Beatriz Rodríguez; and **Héctor Vázquez.** Asentamientos Toba-Qom en la ciudad de Rosario: procesos étnicos identitarios. (*Am. Indíg.*, 51:1, enero/marzo 1991, p. 217–251, bibl.)

General overview of the process of culture and identity change among the Toba who migrated to the city of Rosario, Argentina. Emphasis is on linguistic changes. [SH]

1019 Chase-Sardi, Miguel. El precio de la sangre: Tugüy Ñeë Repy; estudio de la cultura y el control social entre los avá-guaraní. Asunción: Centro de Estudios Antropológicos, Univ. Católica, 1992. 363 p.: bibl., ill. (Biblioteca paraguaya de antropología; 14)

Provides ethnographic description of Ava-Guaraní (Paraguay) folk legal practices and mechanisms for social control. Particular emphasis is on revenge and the administration of justice. Describes role and functioning of the communal assemblies. Includes questionnaire for research on folk law including areas of justice, property inheritance, and leadership. [SH]

1020 Chase-Sardi, Miguel; Augusto Brun; and **Miguel Angel Enciso.** Situación sociocultural, económica, jurídico-política actual de las comunidades indígenas en el Paraguay. Asunción: Centro Interdisciplinario de Derecho Social y Economía Política, Univ. Católica, 1990. 494 p.: bibl. (Serie Investigaciones (CIDSEP); 14)

Provides overview of sociocultural and

economic situation of Ayoreo, Chamacoco, Guana, Angaite, Lengua, Sanapana, Toba-Maskoy, Choroti, Mak'a, Nivacle, Toba-Q'om, Guaraní-Nandeva, Mbya-Guaraní, and Pai Tavytera indigenous groups of Paraguay. Useful updated survey on the situation of each specific community. [SH]

1021 Chiriguano. Recopilación de Jürgen Riester. Santa Cruz de la Sierra, Bolivia: Apoyo para el Campesino Indígena del Oriente Boliviano, 1994. 674 p.: bibl., ill. (Pueblos indígenas de las tierra bajas de Bolivia; 3)

Collection of ethnohistorical essays ranges from analyzing emergence of Chiriguano identity to studying role of missions and messianic movements. Several articles address conflicts created by evangelical churches and their relation with shamanism. Includes important essays on traditional medicine and history of struggle for land titles. For historian's comment see *HLAS 56:2824.* [SH]

1022 Cordeu, Edgardo Jorge. Los chamococo o ishír del Chaco Boreal: algunos aspectos de un proceso de desestructuración étnica. (*Am. Indíg.,* 44:3, julio/sept. 1989, p. 545–580, bibl., ill.)

Overview of process of culture change among the Chamacoco of Paraguay focuses on changes in spatial arrangements, symbolic space, loss of kinship rules, and transformation of mythology. Discusses incorporating symbols and ideas from the national society which are being reinterpreted by the Chamacoco. [SH]

1023 Cruz, Luis María de la. La presencia nivaklé (chulupí) en el territorio formoseño. (*in* Hacia una nueva carta étnica del Gran Chaco: informe de avance, 1990/1991. Las Lomitas, Argentina: Centro del Hombre Antiguo Chaqueño, 1991, p. 87–106)

Traces settlement and distribution of the Nivaklé (Ashluslay) in the Argentine Chaco region by analyzing toponyms, relationship with enemy groups, control over resources, and expeditions conducted to colonize and control the region. Oral history narratives complete this ethnohistory of Nivaklé settlement. [SH]

1024 Idoyaga Molina, Anatilde. La misionización y el surgimiento de nuevas formas terapéuticas y culturales entre los pilagá

(Chaco Central). (*Anthropologica/Lima,* 12:12, 1994, p. 133–157, bibl.)

Examines impact of missionary conversion among the Pilaga and the emergence of syncretic religious and therapeutic practices. Some major cultural changes are the power acquired by evangelical pastors and the loss of power of traditional chiefs. In spite of changes, shamans continue to play a prominent role. [SH]

1025 Kidd, Stephen W. Land, politics and benevolent shamanism: the Enxet Indians in a democratic Paraguay. (*J. Lat. Am. Stud.,* 27:1, Feb. 1995, p. 43–75)

Analyzes Enxet indigenous group during democratic transition period, with special reference to their land struggle. Examines this struggle from a historical perspective, analyzing colonization of their territory and emergence of new indigenous political discourse. [SH]

1026 Palmer, John and **José Braunstein.** Bereavement terminologies in the Chaco. (*in* Hacia una nueva carta étnica del Gran Chaco III: materiales. Las Lomitas, Argentina: Centro del Hombre Antiguo Chaqueño, 1992, p. 7–23)

Bereavement terms among major Chaco groups express differences in social relations and kinship systems, and reflect changes in social processes and relations brought about by death. A distinction is made between bereavement terms as applied to affines and to consaguineal kin. [SH]

1027 Palmer, John. Wichí toponymy. (*in* Hacia una nueva carta étnica del Gran Chaco VI. Las Lomitas, Argentina: Centro del Hombre Antiguo Chaqueño, 1995, p. 3–64)

Detailed study of Wichí toponymic knowledge provides valuable data on environment, flora, fauna, natural resources, illness, bodily functions, and social relations. Includes semantic analysis of Wichí toponymy and in-depth data on Wichí territory used to support claim rights. [SH]

Prieto, Esther. Indigenous peoples in Paraguay. See item **5107.**

1028 Reed, Richard K. Prophets of agroforestry: Guaraní communities and commercial gathering. Austin: Univ. of Texas Press, 1995. 251 p.: bibl., ill., index, maps.

Detailed analysis examines Chiripá economy, ability to maintain identity, and social organization despite contact. Emphasis is on Chiripá agroforestry based on both ecological use of the forests and ability to cope with capitalist expansion. Valuable contribution to study of Chiripá relation with national society. [SH]

1029 Schmidt, Donatella. Legislation, development, and the struggle for land: the case of the Mbya of eastern Paraguay. (*Lat. Am. Anthropol. Rev.*, 6:1, Spring 1994, p. 11–28, appendices, bibl., table)

Examines territorial loss and subsequent struggle among the Mbya. Based on case studies which illustrate and analyze the constraints in applying new indigenous legislation. Examines contradictory and conflictive role of national indigenous institutions in defending indigenous rights. [SH]

1030 Seró, Liliana and Alejandro E. Kowalski. Cuando los cuerpos guaraníes se irguieron sobre el papel. (*in* Después de la piel: 500 años de confusión entre desigualdad y diferencia. Posadas, Argentina: Depto. de Antropología Social, Facultad de Humanidades y Ciencias Sociales, Univ. Nacional de Misiones, 1993, p. 226–261, bibl., ill., photos, tables)

Provides general overview of contemporary Guarani groups in Misiones province. Focuses on legal situation, relationship to the State, and emergence of new leaders. Examines new provincial indigenous legislation, and gives detailed account of the problems it has generated in the Guarani communities. [SH]

1031 Stearman, Allyn MacLean. Yuqui foragers in the Bolivian Amazon: subsistence strategies, prestige, and leadership in an acculturating society. (*J. Anthropol. Res.*, 45:2, Summer 1989, p. 219–245, bibl., tables)

Provides economic and quantitative analysis of Yuqui meat distribution and its relation to prestige. Analyzes hunting skills in relation to leadership and prestige. Describes changes in egalitarian patterns and leadership characteristics resulting from contact. [SH]

1032 Trinchero, Héctor Hugo; Daniel Piccinini; and Gastón Gordillo. Capitalismo y grupos indígenas en el Chaco Centro-Occidental, Salta y Formosa. v. 1–2. Buenos Aires: Centro Editor de América Latina, 1992. 2 v.: bibl., maps. (Biblioteca Política argentina; 371–372)

In-depth analysis of incorporation of the Toba of Argentina to the capitalist economy includes detailed account of transformation of subsistence strategies resulting from incorporation as wage-workers in regional economies. Focus is on historical and ecological changes and on development of new economic and political strategies. [SH]

1033 Wicker, Hans Rudolf. *Yvykytí*—cutting the earth: Indian land rights strategies in eastern Paraguay. (*Bulletin/Geneva*, 53/54, 1989/90, p. 109–124, maps, photos)

Addresses differences between Mbya Ava and Pai Tavytera groups in their relationship with national society and the State. Examines struggle for land titles and use of different strategies in the process of incorporation into market economy. Discusses problems encountered by political and religious leaders as power relations are redefined. [SH]

1034 Wilbert, Johannes and Karin Simoneau. In their own words: introduction, concordance of new motifs, and bibliography. Cambridge, Mass.: Harvard Univ., Center for the Study of World Religions, 1992. 280 p.: bibl., index, map. (Folk literature of South American Indians)

Final volume of a series on folk literature of lowland South American indigenous peoples. Provides a list of contributors, a synthesis of narrative content, themes, and an extensive motif index. Important contribution to the study of folk narrative. Useful for comparative research. [SH]

1035 Wright, Pablo G. La política de la muerte: discurso shamánico y evangélico de los toba argentina. (*in* Congreso Internacional de Americanistas, *47th, New Orleans, 1991*. La muerte y el más allá en las culturas indígenas latinoamericanas. Quito, Ediciones ABYA-YALA, 1992, p. 15–36, bibl., map)

Examines notions and dreams of death, and concept of self among the Toba. Analyzes Toba evangelical therapeutic forms and interpretations of illness and their conflict with shamanic practices and beliefs through discourse analysis. [SH]

Highlands

JOANNE RAPPAPORT, *Professor of Spanish and in the School of Foreign Service, Georgetown University*

SEVERAL SIGNIFICANT and broad themes emerge from this biennium's review of Andean book-length publications. Particularly prominent are various studies of Andean modernity ranging from theoretical approaches to Latin American popular culture using reception of the media as the conceptual pivot (item **13**) to studies of the development of child protective institutions in Bogotá (item **1138**), and from the radicalization of poor urban dwellers in Peru (item **1226**) to the impact of violence at all levels of society (items **1134** and **1050**). Several broad-ranging anthologies reexamine traditional research themes, such as ethnicity, *mestizaje,* and fiestas within the overarching contexts of administrative and political modernization, modernist ideologies, and the transnational flow of people, goods, and ideas (items **1122** and **1227**). Writings on Andean indigenous issues have also recast native studies within a modern context, concentrating on indigenous movements, nationalism, participation in the State apparatus (items **1189, 1091, 1166** and **1041**), development of agrarian communities within larger political and economic contexts (item **1067**), and adaptation of local belief systems to modernization and secularizing social forces (item **1121**). Volumes dedicated to reevaluating Andean gender roles also address the inclusion of various peoples into the modern project, particularly women's participation in modern civil society and their experience with the violence that characterizes Andean modernity (item **1044**).

Integral to Latin American modernity is a focus on rural-urban and international migration. In just over half a century, a predominantly agrarian continent has been transformed into an urban one, and numerous citizens of Andean countries have sought new lives and livelihoods in the US and Europe, so it is surprising to note the scarcity of book-length publications on the ethnography of migration, including studies of population movements within national (items **1087** and **1037**) and international (item **1151**) spheres. This paucity may reflect the still nascent stage of urban and transnational anthropology among Latin Americanist ethnographers.

Another significant feature of Andean modernity and of new trends in Andeanist anthropology is the growing scholarly voice of native Andean peoples. Some of these contributions emanate from the institutions that originally fostered the development of an indigenous intelligentsia, such as the Taller de Historia Oral Andina (THOA) in Bolivia. The latter continues to produce provocative and innovative historical analyses of Aymara society allowing scholars to rethink our conceptual categories and our publications programs in regard to this ethnic group (item **1073**). Other entries spring from indigenous groups that have only recently produced published works on history (item **1161**), traditional medicine (items **1201** and **1087**), popular religion (item **1169**), and technical themes (item **1191**). The expansion of indigenous scholarship has even spurred unschooled and unaffiliated would-be scholars to begin to investigate their own reality (item **1069**). Members of other minority groups, such as Afrolatins, have also participated in this trend (item **1231**). The testimonial genre in Andean anthropology, in which subordinated minorities and members of popular sectors make themselves heard through the literary mediation of an editor, has maintained its vitality alongside these recent developments (items **1190,**

1177, 1054 and 1228). Among the most innovative examples of a recent *testimonio*, is a work by the Taller de Historia Oral Andina. The fact that both narrator and editor are Aymara raises important questions regarding the changing role of editor as arbitrator who prepares an unheard or unheeded testimonial voice for popular consideration (item **1074**).

A number of studies regarding curing practices illustrate that the historical perspective, which has become popular within Andean ethnography, is now becoming central to the research of medical anthropologists. Joralemon and Sharon's study of Peruvian coastal curers (item **1199**), and other research from the same region concerning curing practices over time (item **1196**), combine history and anthropology through a focus on individual life histories. Also represented are historical studies of the combination of Mapuche and Western health systems in the Southern Cone (items **1058** and **1110**). Many studies of Andean medicine have concentrated on health practices that help alleviate animal, as well as human, illnesses; the best example of this current is Genin's excellent interdisciplinary anthology of articles concerning camelid herding (item **1098**).

Various volumes that have appeared in this biennium must be singled out for their outstanding value. Two notable books that examine representation in the Andes are among the most suggestive and innovative. Deborah Poole's exceptional study of Andean photography allows us to see photographs that represent ethnographies, historical monographs, and museum exhibits in a different light (item **1046**). These images may serve as windows to the history of the racial categorization constructed by foreign and national travelers, anthropologists, photographers, and the subjects themselves. Raúl Romero's stunning collection of essays by renowned scholars of Andean music and dance focuses on the representations of inter-ethnic relations by both indigenous and mestizo artists within a modernist world (item **1209**).

Ethnicity is also the central theme of another pivotal publication originating in Colombia, a country not generally perceived as belonging to the Andean ethnic sphere. Myriam Amparo Espinosa's (item **1130**) study of metaphors in the historical narrative of the Quintín Lame Armed Movement, a Páez guerrilla group, marks a new form of research which struggles to reproduce subaltern forms of narrative within Western academic genres. From the other end of the Andes comes Tristan Platt's fascinating excursion into liturgical narratives as interpreted in historical documents and by contemporary peoples (item **1093**), indicating that there are numerous novel approaches to the intersection of documentary historical research and ethnographic observation and description.

Two exemplary works attempt to view ethnicity through multiple lenses—gender and kinship, on the one hand, and economic articulation with the market, on the other. Both edited volumes contain articles by some of the most highly regarded researchers of the second generation of Andean anthropology. Denise Arnold's in-depth analysis of Andean ethnography and family relations offers new approaches to the study of gender roles (item **1042**). Brooke Larson and Olivia Harris' exemplary collection of Andean markets studies shows us that Andean forms of reciprocity and exchange must be analyzed within their respective historical contexts, studied at the interstices of ethnic groups and of gender relations, examined against the backdrop of ethnic and racial ideologies, and questioned in terms of their development within regional and national spheres of market exchange (item **1040**).

Finally, a new kind of Andean study is beginning to replace the "peoples and cultures" anthologies of the past. I refer specifically to Starn, DeGregori and Kirk's *Peru reader: history, culture, and politics*, which combines anthropology with history, political science, and literary studies, and merges analytical academic writing with fictional, poetic, and journalistic genres, to provide a multidisciplinary, multi-genre, and temporally-diverse kind of work (item **1215**). In this reader, Andean ethnology is considered through the perspective of various disciplines, and Andean culture is viewed as a result of the interaction between *lo andino* and European- and African-derived cultures, within historically-derived structures of power.

This is the last of my contributions to *HLAS*. I fondly thank the *HLAS* staff for its collaboration during my six years on board, and wish Linda Seligmann, the new contributing editor, the best in her future contributions to the *Handbook*.

GENERAL

1036 Barrera, Mercedes *et al.* Le travail des femmes à frías: modèle andin et variante régionale. (*Bull. Inst. fr. étud. andin.*, 22:3, 1993, p. 739–761, bibl., map, tables)

Based on ethnographic research in the sierra of Piura and on inter-regional comparison, this interdisciplinary article by Peruvian and French economists and anthropologists suggests that traditional models of gendered labor organization do not consider the tremendous diversity of situations under which Andean peasant women work. The historical reconstruction of the development of farming systems must be taken into account in such an analysis.

Berg, Hans van den. Bibliografía Aymara v. 1–3. See item **4535**.

1037 Ciudades de los Andes: visión histórica y contemporánea. Recopilación de Eduardo Kingman Garcés. Quito: IFEA; CIUDAD, 1992. 480 p.: bibl., ill., maps. (Travaux de l'Institut français d'études andines, 0768–424X; 72)

Anthropologists, historians, and sociologists contribute to this magnificent volume that records the geographic, temporal, and ethnic diversity of Andean cities, focusing on Bolivia, Ecuador, and Peru. Organized into sections on colonial, republican, and modern cities, this comparative study successfully indicates which elements of Andean culture have persisted and which have not. This volume presents new ways of understanding how Andean modernity was forged within an interethnic context.

Desarrollo o descolonización en los Andes? See item **1193**.

1038 Dinámicas del descanso de la tierra en los Andes. Edición científica de Dominique Hervé, Didier Genin y Gilles Rivière.

La Paz: IBTA-ORSTOM, 1994. 356 p.: bibl., ill., maps.

Collection of articles from a broad range of disciplines including linguistics, anthropology, agronomy, zoology, and history are written by foreign, national, and indigenous authors working in Bolivia, Ecuador, and Peru. Contributions include studies of indigenous categories of agricultural activity, various techniques of crop rotation and pastoral intervention, and the relationship between crop rotation and regional market systems.

1039 Encuentro Internacional sobre Situación Actual de la Familia Indígena en la Subregión Andina, *Riobamba, Ecuador, 1993.* Memorias: familia y etnias. Quito: Comisión III del Parlamento Andino, Comisión de la Mujer, el Niño y la Familia del Congreso Nacional; UNICEF, Fundación Mujer y Comunidad, 1993. 336 p.: bibl., ill., photos.

Proceedings of an international congress on problems faced by Andean indigenous families. Ethnic groups from Bolivia, Colombia, Ecuador, Peru, and Venezuela participated. Central working document provides a regional comparison of transformations experienced by the Andean family over the past few decades, taking into account issues such as migration, female agricultural production, poverty levels, and bilingual education.

1040 Ethnicity, markets, and migration in the Andes: at the crossroads of history and anthropology. Edited by Brooke Larson and Olivia Harris, with Enrique Tandeter. Durham, N.C.: Duke Univ. Press, 1995. 428 p.: bibl., ill., index, maps.

Major compilation of historical and anthropological articles focuses on the nature of markets and exchange structures in the Andes. Prominent scholars explore Andean participation in the European market structure, the influence of migration in changing ethnic boundaries and spheres of exchange, and the politics of market exchange during the colonial period. Larson's introduction places articles within the context of Andean economic systems, while Harris concludes with an appreciation of the relationships between mestizo and indigenous ethnic identities in the context of market relations. Both introduction and conclusion lend a greater coherence to this carefully-crafted and monumental volume.

1041 Indigenous peoples and democracy in Latin America. Edited by Donna Lee Van Cott. New York: St. Martin's Press; Washington: Inter-American Dialogue, 1994. 271 p.: bibl., index, map.

Collection of articles resulting from a project of the Inter-American Dialogue, addresses confrontation between indigenous peoples and the State in Latin America. Also examines evolution of contemporary State policies, emphasizing diversity of indigenous experiences in the Andean Region, Mesoamerica, and the SouthernCone. Andean contributions focus on Bolivia (Xavier Albó, items **5078** and **3485**), Colombia (Jesús Avirama and Rayda Marquez, item **1124**), Ecuador (Melina H. Selverston, item **3439**), and Peru (María Isabel Remy, item **5064**).

1042 Más allá del silencio: las fronteras de género en los Andes. v. 1, Parentesco y género en los Andes. Edición de Denise Y. Arnold. La Paz: Instituto de Lengua y Cultural Aymara; Centre for Indigenous American Studies and Exchange, Univ. of St. Andrews, 1997. 583 p.: bibl., plates. (Biblioteca de Estudios Andinos)

Multidisciplinary articles from Chile, Bolivia, Ecuador, and Peru, examine new directions in Andean gender studies. Volume proposes an alternative to traditional essentialist Andean and paternalist feminist research, focusing instead on construction of a processual model based on Andean models of gender. Earlier approaches to gender complementarity and trial marriage in the Andes are also critiqued.

1043 Miranda Luizaga, Jorge and **Ramiro Párraga Chirveches.** Hacia una etnociencia andina: revitalización de formas educativas tradicionales y métodos de enseñanza

como alternativa política y desarrollo de la región andina. (*in* Reunión Anual de Etnología, 6th, La Paz, 1990. Actas. La Paz: MUSEF, 1990, p. 217–230, graphs, tables)

Explores structure of numerical systems in the Uru, Pukina, Aymara, and Quechua languages in order to develop an appropriate ethnomathematics system for use in bilingual education programs.

Mitchell, William P. The transformation of cultural anthropology: the decline of ecology and structure and the rise of political economy and the cultural construction of social reality. See item **1207.**

1044 Mujeres de los Andes: condiciones de vida y salud. Edición de Anne-Claire Defossez, Dedier Fassin y Mara Viveros. Colombia?: Instituto Frances de Estudios Andinos; Univ. Externado de Colombia, 1992. 471 p.: bibl. (Travaux de l'Institut français d'etudes andines; 0768–424X; 65)

Rich collection of articles by anthropologists, economists, historians, physicians, and sociologists reflects on the complexity and diversity of issues associated with women's participation in traditional and non-traditional socio-cultural roles in Bolivia, Colombia, Ecuador, and Peru. Issues addressed include the relationship between illness and pregnancy in different ethnic groups within both urban and rural areas, female participation in civil society, and violence in gender relations.

1045 Ortíz Surco, Jorge. Tecnología agrícola andina: los *waru-waru*, los *wachos* y las *k'ochas*. (*Etnología/La Paz*, 15:20, 1991, p. 23–34, bibl.)

Briefly describes Andean forms of agricultural technology, including *waru-warus*, or raised fields; *wachus*, agricultural terraces; and *k'ochas*, artificial lakes for reed cultivation. The first two are explained in technical terms, focusing on problems of drainage, erosion, etc.

1046 Poole, Deborah. Vision, race, and modernity: a visual economy of the Andean image world. Princeton, N.J.: Princeton Univ. Press, 1997. 263 p.: bibl., ill., index. (Princeton studies in culture/power/history)

Long-awaited work analyzes role of visual images and technologies (particularly photography, painting, and drawing) in shaping modern understandings of race in the Andes. This fascinating work documents various depictions of Andean peoples from the 18th–20th centuries, placing scientific analyses of race within the sphere of the modern visual economy.

1047 Rösing, Ina. La deuda de ofrenda: un concepto central de la religión andina. (*Rev. Andin.*, 12:1, primer semestre 1994, p. 191–216, bibl.)

Analyzes general nature of Andean religion, focusing on notions of debt and offering within the context of salvation and well-being. Asserts that these notions have long persisted across time.

1048 Skar, Sarah Lund. Appropriating pawns: Andean dominance and the manipulation of things. (*J. Royal Anthropol. Inst.*, 1, Dec. 1995, p. 1–17)

Employs theories of exchange developed in Melanesia to consider the Andean *Prenda* system which entails the transfer of an object to ensure reimbursement of goods or services owed. This system articulates relations of dominance and submission and leads author to question egalitarian emphasis in the study of Andean exchange systems.

1049 Vaca Bucheli, Rocío. El problema del tiempo y el espacio en el estudio de las culturas populares andinas. (*Sarance/Otavalo*, 16, agosto 1992, p. 11–30, bibl.)

Suggests that popular Andean cultures be studied through a dual and complementary perspective focusing on spatial development and temporal succession. Redefines popular culture in terms of the processes of production and circulation of objects in multiple, culturally-defined spheres of time and space.

1050 Violencia en la región andina. Recopilación de Felipe E. Mac Gregor. Lima: Asociación Peruana de Estudios e Investigación para la Paz, 1993. 202 p.: bibl. (Serie Violencia en la región andina; 1)

Volume includes scholars from Bolivia, Chile, Colombia, Ecuador, Peru, and Venezuela, who conduct team research on issues related to these countries. General overview of impact of violence within families, in society, and in relation to the State and State institutions. Individual contributors examine relationship of violence to culture, the State, everyday life, drug trafficking, the media, and national pacification plans. A highly coherent volume that provides insights into one of Latin America's most pressing problems.

ARGENTINA

1051 Arrue, Wille and **Beatriz Kalinsky.** De "la médica" y la terapeuta: la gestión intercultural de la salud en el sur de la provincia del Neuquén. Buenos Aires: Centro Editor de América Latina, 1991. 288 p.: bibl., ill., map. (Bibliotecas universitarias. Sociedad y cultura)

Interdisciplinary study by a physician and an anthropologist looks at interpenetration of popular and scientific medicine within a clinical setting in the province of Neuquén. This sophisticated theoretical volume goes beyond a comparative study of curing practices, to examine institutional articulation of medical systems and suggest areas for collaboration.

1052 Balazote Oliver, Alejandro Omar and **Juan Carlos Radovich.** Procesos migratorios en dos reservas mapuche de Río Negro y Neuquén. (*Cuad. Antropol. Pensam. Latinoam.*, 14, 1992/93, p. 23–39, bibl.)

Compares migratory processes of two Mapuche communities from provinces of Río Negro and Neuquén. Utilizes Lourdes Arizpe's parametric method to explain various factors that encourage members of rural indigenous communities to migrate to urban areas.

1053 Barreto, Oscar. Fenomenología de la religiosidad mapuche. Bahía Blanca, Argentina: Archivo Histórico Salesiano de la Patagonia Norte; Buenos Aires: Centro Salesiano de Estudios San Juan Bosco, 1992. 108 p.: bibl. (Documentario patagónico; 3. Estudios proyecto; 7)

Analyses the Mapuches' adoption of Catholisism. Focuses on elements of ritual, myth, and spiritual understanding that characterize traditional Mapuche religion.

1054 Cabral, Gregorio. Gregorio Cabral, un mapuche rionegrino: historia de vida. Presentación de M.E. Pérez Amat y M.M. González Coll. Bahía Blanca, Argentina: Depto. de Humanidades, Univ. Nacional del Sur, 1992. 25 leaves: bibl.

Autobiography of an elderly Mapuche man who translated it from the Mapuche language into Spanish. Particularly valuable as an attempt to record popular memory [by an uneducated member of a subordinated minority]. Examines ritual life and Mapuche participation in the dominant society institutions.

1055 Echeverría Baleta, Mario. Kai ajnun: el milenario arte tehuelche de los quillangos pintados. Argentina: M. Echeverría Baleta, 1991. 80 p., 43 p. of plates: bibl., ill. (some col.).

Studies clan paintings on camelid skins worn as clothing by the Tehuelche that are similar to rock paintings from Patagonia. Most of the book is composed of reproductions and explanations of the abstract designs painted on this medium.

1056 Ginóbili de Tumminello, María Elena. Los Onas o Selk'nam: observaciones etnológicas y etnográficas de la obra inédita del P. Lino Carbajal. Bahía Blanca, Argentina: Instituto Superior Juan XXIII; Viedma, Argentina: Fundación Ameghino, 1994. 70 p.: bibl., ill. (Cuadernos del Instituto Superior Juan XXIII; 17)

Excerpts from the unpublished papers of Father Lino Carbajal, a Salesian missionary who worked among the Ona in the early 20th century. Topics include material culture, curing practices, cosmology, and ritual. Provides valuable (but unfortunately edited) documentary material on historical Tierra del Fuego.

1057 Guber, Rosana. Las manos de la memoria. (*Desarro. Econ.*, 36:141, abril/junio 1996, p. 423–442)

Explores how the vandalization of ex-president Juan Domingo Perón's tomb is understood within the Argentine historical imagination, particularly in the minds of political elites during the democratic administration of Raúl Alfonsín. In this historical vision, the memory of the dead is safeguarded and a return to power is sought.

1058 Hernández, Isabel. La identidad enmascarada: los mapuche de Los Toldos. Buenos Aires: Editorial Universitaria de Buenos Aires, 1993. 388 p.: bibl., ill., maps. (Col. Temas)

Valuable study documents political organization and system of land tenure in the Coliqueo Mapuche of Los Toldos from the 19th–20th centuries. Includes detailed ethnography with extensive data on economic organization, education, and health, as well as analysis of resurgent ethnicity manifested through discourse and ceremony.

1059 Madrazo, Guillermo B. Tiempo y etnicidad en el noroeste argentino. (*Am. Indíg.*, 51:1, enero/marzo 1991, p. 193–216, bibl., table)

Studies spread of mestizaje in northeastern provinces of Argentina—Jujuy, Salta, Catamarca, Tucumán, Santiago del Estero, La Rioja—and economic and sociocultural adaptations to criollo society. Spiritual values, however, mark the persistence over time of the ethnic experience within these communities.

1060 Merlino, Rodolfo J. and Mario Rabey. Resistencia y hegemonía: cultos locales y religíon centralizada en los Andes del Sur. (*Allpanchis/Cusco*, 23:40, segundo semestre, 1992, p. 173–200, bibl.)

Examines confrontation of popular and official religious observance in the Puna of Jujuy (Argentina) and on the warmer slopes of Humahuaca, Jujuy, and Sosocha (Argentina) and Talina (Bolivia). Focuses on rites associated with the cult of Pachamama and on texts and documents from Tilcara to illustrate counterhegemonic resistance in southern Andean communities.

1061 Pereda, Isabel and Elena Perrotta. Junta de hermanos de Sangre: un ensayo de analisis del nguillatun a traves de tiempo y espacio desde una visión Huinca. Buenos Aires: Sociedad Argentina de Antropología, 1994. 174 p.: ill. (some col.).

A history of the Mapuche *Nguillatún* ceremony is followed by descriptions and comparisons of 70 Argentine and Chilean ceremonies. Written by a transnational team of archaeologists, work also includes an ethnomusical analysis of Mapuche ritual chants.

1062 Pérez Bugallo, Rubén. El carnaval de los "indios:" una advertencia sobre el conflicto social. (*Cuad. Antropol. Pensam. Latinoam.*, 14, 1992/93, p. 93–120, bibl., photos)

Study of urban carnival in Salta examines historical evolution of *comparsas* which serve to distinguish indigenous groups. Gives special attention to changes perceived by participants as expressed in quotations from interviews.

1063 Radovich, Juan Carlos and Alejandro Omar Balazote Oliver. La etnicidad Mapuche en un contexto de relocalización: la represa de Piedra del Aguila. (*Am. Indíg.*, 51:1, enero/marzo 1991, p. 277–319, bibl., map, tables)

See item **1064.**

1064 Radovich, Juan Carlos and **Alejandro Omar Balazote Oliver.** "Piedra del Aguila": big dam and the resettlement of the Mapuche population from southern Argentina. (*Bull. Int. Anthropol. Ethnol. Res.*, 34/35, 1992/93, p. 103–115, bibl., maps)

Examines social impact that the construction of Piedra del Aguila dam has had on the Mapuche of Neuquén. Traces resettlement process in the Pilquiniyeu del Limay and Ancatruz reservations over a two-year period and describes resulting economic and social transformations. Also available in Spanish (see item **1063**).

1065 Rubinelli, María Louisa. Reflexiones acerca de la muerte en los Andes del NOA. (*in* Propuestas para una antropología argentina. Buenos Aires: Editorial Biblos, 1994, v. 3, p. 179–205, bibl., graph, ill., tables)

The notion of death as the end of existence is traced within Andean culture, concentrating on two practices from the Quebrada de Humahuaca: mourning rituals and All Saints Day. Structural relationships among symbols in these rituals are analyzed and charted. [The NOA of the title refers to the Argentine Northwest.]

1066 Savigliano, Marta. Tango and the political economy of passion. Boulder, Colo.: Westview Press, 1995. 289 p.: bibl., ill., index. (Institutional structures of feeling)

Innovative historical study of the dance and musical lyrics of Tango. Interweaves tales of sexuality, gender, race, class, and national identity to examine relations between machismo, colonialism, and commodification as manifested in expressive culture.

1067 Sociedad y articulación en las tierras altas jujeñas: crisis terminal de un modelo de desarrollo. Recopilación de Alejandro Raúl Isla. Buenos Aires: MLAL?, 1992. 255 p.: bibl., ill., maps. (Investigación y desarrollo; 2)

Compilation of essays, concerning agrarian structure, peasant-landlord conflict, indigenous rebellions, and the development process of the Andean province of Jujuy. [based on team research]. Volume is significant for its contextualization of indigenous and peasant economic and political structures within the larger regional and national Argentine economy, as well as for its articulation of historical studies with ethnographic examinations of contemporary society.

1068 Torres, Graciela F. Prácticas de crianza infantil en dos comunidades vallisto Calchaquiés del Noroeste Argentino. (*Hombre Desierto*, 6/7, 1992/93, p. 103–121, bibl., tables)

Research on child socialization process in two peasant communities of the Argentine Northwest gives special attention to nursing and weaning, personal hygiene and excretory methods, language, and locomotion.

BOLIVIA

1069 Alba, Juan José and **Lila Tarifa.** Los jampiris de Raqaypampa. Cochabamba, Bolivia: CENDA, 1993. 377 p.: bibl., ill. (some col.).

Interdisciplinary study examines health problems in Raqaypampa, the penetration of western medical techniques, and native medical knowledge. Includes numerous testimonies of traditional medical specialists regarding cure for specific diseases and the use of herbs for medicinal puposes.

1070 Apaza Quispe, Manuel. Costumbres y creencias mitológicas de la antiquísima civilización khana aymara. La Paz: M. Apaza Quispe, 1994. 46 p.: ill. (De la tradición khana-aymara; 1)

Volume by Aymara author focuses on religious and ritual practices in ancient and contemporary Kollasuyu. Provides information on marriage rituals, maleficent beings, and ritual dances. Significant publication insofar as it is written by an unschooled researcher unaffiliated with the numerous native institutes in Bolivia.

1071 Arnold, Denise Y. En el corazón de la plaza tejida: el *wayñu* en Qaqachaka. (*in* Reunión Anual de Etnología, 6th, *La Paz, 1992.* Actas. La Paz: Museo Nacional de Etnografía y Folklore, 1993, t. 2, p. 17–70, bibl., ill., photo, tables)

Explores, as intertexts, analogies between Andean textile traditions and performative arts, with particular emphasis on the *wayñu*. Music and choreography are examined within the context of ritual cycles, while textiles are studied in relation to songs about weaving and clothing. Spatial and structural organization of the two forms are analyzed and compared.

1072 Balboa Valencia, Alfredo and **Julio César Córdova.** La juventud alteña: entre la integración e identificación socio-cultural aymara y occidental y sus formas de relación social. (*in* Reunión Anual de Etnología, *6th, La Paz, 1992.* Actas. La Paz: Museo Nacional de Etnografía y Folklore, 1993, t. 1, p. 75–84, tables)

Brief ethnology of children of Aymara migrants to El Alto analyses the family as locus of cultural transmission and the media's role in cultural transformation.

1073 Choque Canqui, Roberto and **Esteban Ticona Alejo.** Jesús de Machaqa: la marka rebelde. v. 2, Sublevación y masacre de 1921. La Paz: CEDOIN; CIPCA, 1996– . 1 v: appendices, bibl., ill., index, maps. (Col. Historia y documento. Cuadernos de investigación; 46)

Collaborative work by Aymara historians. Volume recounts history of 1921 Jesús de Machaca uprising. Includes detailed analysis of the rebellions context and repercussions and the nature of popular urban opinion surrounding the event. Especially valuable for its detailed documentary and oral history appendices.

1074 Condori Chura, Leandro and **Esteban Ticona Alejo.** El escribano de los caciques apoderados = Kasikinakan purirarunakan qillqiripa. La Paz: Hisbol; THOA, 1992. 284 p.: ill. (Serie Testimonios; 7)

Bilingual (Spanish/Aymara) biography of the Aymara secretary for the early-20th-century Caciques Apoderados movement. Interesting testimony edited by a member of the same ethnic group (Ticona Alejo), which carefully examines urban indigenous life in La Paz and the organization of the movement.

1075 Esch-Jakob, Juliane. Sincretismo religioso de los indigenas de Bolivia. La Paz: HISBOL, 1994. 132 p.: bibl., ill. (some col.). (Serie Religión y sociedad; 6)

Unlike religious syncretism, in which cultures become fused, the encounter between indigenous and Western cultures in Bolivia resulted in a juxtaposition of indigenous and Christian cultural elements. This lack of adaptation, argues this philosophical treatise, is the result of the impossibility of substituting the functions of Christianity for those of traditional religion.

1076 Fernández Juárez, Gerardo. "El banquete aymara": aspectos simbólicos de las mesas rituales aymaras. (*Rev. Andin.,* 12 : 1, primer semestre 1994, p. 155–190, bibl., map, photos)

Examines practice of ritual food offerings to Aymara divinities in exchange for increased productivity and good health. Describes in rich detail the banquet and the symbolic aspect of the ritual table. Focuses on issues such as visual organization of the offering, role of hosts and "guests," and symbolism associated with color, texture, odor, and flavor.

1077 Fernández Juárez, Gerardo El banquete aymara: mesas y yatiris. La Paz: Hisbol, 1995. 570 p.: bibl., ill. (Biblioteca andina; 15)

Extremely rich and detailed study of Aymara commensality and rituals is based on the structure and customs of the banquet table. Includes ethnographic descriptions and classifications of food, types of ritual and non-ritualized meals, and a sophisticated interpretation of relationships between hosts and ritual specialists, everyday and ritual meals, offerings and sacrifice, and indigenous commensality and the Catholic mass.

1078 Fernández Juárez, Gerardo. Las *illas* de San Juan: fuego, agua, *ch'amaka* y mesa de una comunidad aymara. (*Cuad. Prehispánicos,* 15, 1991/1994, p. 85–106, bibl., photos)

Describes celebration of San Juan among Aymaras of Lake Titicaca region, focusing on cattle ritual. Culinary gifts and animal sacrifices are analyzed within a context of reciprocity.

1079 Fernández Juárez, Gerardo. El mundo *abierto:* agosto y Semana Santa en las celebraciones rituales aymaras. (*Rev. Esp. Antropol. Am.,* 26, 1996, p. 205–229, bibl., photos)

The Aymara ceremonial cycle corresponds to August 1 and Holy Week, the two times of the year when the earth opens up and requires sacrifices, petitions, prayers, and requests to the deities. Includes detailed descriptions of the offerings left for the deities during these festivals in the community of Ajllata Grande, La Paz depto.

1080 Fernández Juárez, Gerardo. Ofrenda, ritual y terapia: las mesas aymaras. (*Rev. Esp. Antropol. Am.,* 25, 1995, p. 153–180, bibl., photos)

Studies the therapeutic system of Aymara communities in El Alto. Includes classification of diseases and cures, and describes methods of diagnosis, preparation of the *mesa* and offerings, and culinary process of reciprocity and alimentary responsibility involved in the *mesas.*

1081 Fernández Juárez, Gerardo. Tinku y Taypi: dos recursos culinarios pertinentes en las ofrendas aymaras a la Pachamama. (*Anthropologica/Lima*, 11, enero 1994, p. 49–78, bibl., photos)

Examines how food is used in various Aymara practices to establish a pact of reciprocity (*ayni*) with the Pachamama that ensures agricultural productivity. Focuses on alimentary contents of *mesas de ofrenda* and their preparation in both rural and urban Aymara communities.

1082 Flores, Willer; Jaime López; and Katherine Plicque. Lliqllas chayantaka: textiles en el norte de Potosí. (*in* Reunión Anual de Etnología, 6th, La Paz, 1992. Actas. La Paz: Museo Nacional de Etnografía y Folklore, 1993, t. 1, p. 163–200, appendix, bibl., tables)

Historically situated and ethnographically contextualized description of the classification, production, and use of textiles in Chayantaka, a community of Norte de Potosí. Appendix explains structure and spatial organization of Chayantaka weavings and provides rich detail on terminologies and symbolism.

1083 Gutiérrez Condori, Ramiro. Instrumentos musicales tradicionales en la comunidad artesanal Walata Grande, Bolivia. (*Rev. Mus. Nac. Etnogr. Folk.*, 5, 1995, p. 60–88, bibl., photos)

Historical and ethnographic description of the community. Focuses on production of musical instruments by peasant artisans, types of instruments and the tools used to make them.

1084 Harris, Olivia. El tiempo en la religiosidad aymara: Dios y el inka. (*in* Reunión Anual de Etnología, 4th, La Paz, 1990. Actas. La Paz: MUSEF, 1990, p. 31–48, bibl.)

Explores indigenous notions of history in Norte de Potosí. Uses native terminologies to examine concepts of ruptures between historical epochs and studies beliefs concerning the territory's ancient inhabitants.

1085 Jolicoeur, Luis. El cristianismo aymara: inculturación o culturización. Cochabamba, Bolivia: Univ. Católica Boliviana, 1994. 465 p.: bibl.

Offers theological exploration of "inculturation," the introduction of Christian gospel in to indigenous communities that results in transcultural fusion; and "culturization," the receiving community's creation of a new cultural expression of the gospel. Processes explored primarily at a theoretical level but are framed by appreciation of the Aymara world view.

1086 Langevin, André. Los instrumentos de la orquesta de Kantu. (*Rev. Mus. Nac. Etnogr. Folk.*, 3:3, 1991, p. 11–54, bibl., tables)

Fascinating and detailed typology of musical instruments used by Aymara and Quechua peasants from Bautista Saavedra. Concentrates on instrument production, their registers, associated nomenclature, and the nature of double *zampoñas* (reed pipes).

1087 Llanque, Domingo; Diego Irarrázabal; and Santiago Mendoza. Medicina aymara. La Paz: Hisbol, 1994. 72 p.: bibl. (Breve biblioteca de bolsillo; 15)

In this collection of articles, each author takes a different perspective on Aymara medicine. Llanque focuses on the role of Aymara priests and curers in communicating with the beings that inhabit the three levels of the universe, and these individuals' functions in establishing control over the human community. Irarrázabal compares traditional Aymara and western "scientific" medicine, suggesting new avenues for a complementary relationship between them. Mendoza explores nature of illnesses believed by the Aymara to be caused by spirits.

1088 Loza-Balsa, Gregorio. Enciclopedia de la medicina aymara. v. 2, Etno-medicina; documentos. La Paz: Organización Panamericana de la Salud; La Organización Mundial de la Salud, 1995. 1 v.: appendix, bibl.

A dictionary of Aymara terms which refer to illnesses and their symptoms, medicinal plants, and use of animals and minerals in traditional curing. Aymara terms are translated into Spanish. Includes useful documentary appendix summarizing information on curing practices and medicinal plants contained in colonial chronicle sources.

1089 Máscaras de los Andes bolivianos = Masks of the Bolivian Andes. Edición de Peter McFarren. Fotografías de Peter McFarren y Sixto Choque. La Paz: Editorial Quipus; Banco Mercantil, 1993. 171 p.: ill. (some col.).

Stunning catalog of festival masks from the Bolivian highlands. Includes bilingual articles by Teresa Gisbert and others detailing the making of masks, their symbolism, and their use in fiestas. Striking photos by Aymara photographer Sixto Choque.

Merlino, Rodolfo J. and **Mario Rabey.** Resistencia y hegemonía: cultos locales y religíon centralizada en los Andes del Sur. See item **1060.**

1090 Nuñez, René. La participación indígena en la escuela, 1929–1933: la Escuela Municipal de Challapata. (in Reunión Anual de Etnología, *4th, La Paz, 1990.* Actas. La Paz: MUSEF, 1990, p. 99–110, tables)

Using registration materials as a primary source, this case study from the *departamento* of Oruro compares ethnic and linguistic characteristics of the student body from 1929–42. Includes detailed tables outlining the school children's ages, region of origin, ethnicity, and linguistic attributes.

1091 Pacheco, Diego. El indianismo y los indios contemporáneos en Bolivia. La Paz: HISBOL/MUSEF, 1992. 395 p.: bibl., ill. (Serie Movimientos sociales; 7)

Historical study of the *indianista* movement since 1970. Asks whether *indianismo* is a valid political alternative for Bolivia. Meticulously-researched monograph follows evolution of the movement, examining the espousal and rejection of party politics and the distancing of the leadership from community authorities.

1092 Pacheco Balanza, Diego. Política aymara contemporánea. (*Etnología/La Paz,* 21, 1995, p. 16–31)

Analyzes the transition from sindicalist to ethnic politics in Bolivia. Focuses on the Katarista-Indianista movement, particularly Aymara hegemony as reflected by Aymara in participation in electoral politics.

1093 Platt, Tristán. Los Guerreros de Cristo: cofradías, misa solar, y guerra regenerativa en una doctrina Macha, siglos XVIII–XX. Traducción de Luis H. Antezana. La Paz: ASUR; Plural, 1996. 142 p.: bibl., photos. (Ediciones ASUR; 5)

Cronicles the interpretation of Christian liturgical text associated with Corpus Christi from a traditional Andean religious perspective—particularly of the *tinku*—over three centuries. Analyzes use of Christian doctrine in fiestas, confraternities, and extraliturgical rites in Macha (Potosí dept.). Provides fascinating example of the value of merging ethnographic and historical theories and methodologies.

1094 Portugal M., Pedro. El *khari khari* como explicación de la epidemia de cólera en Huaricana, agosto-octubre de 1991. (in Reunión Anual de Etnología, *6th, La Paz, 1992.* Actas. La Paz: MUSEF, 1993, v. 1, p. 237–249, bibl.)

Using ethnographic interviews and periodical accounts, indigenous author investigates explanation of a cholera epidemic. In interviews, many community members deny presence of cholera, and instead attribute illness and death to the *khari khari*; however, results of a survey conducted in the same community indicate acceptance of the existence of a cholera epidemic. Belief in the *khari khari* reflects the fear of a community destabilized by disaster.

1095 Rösing, Ina. Paraman purina—going for rain: "mute anthropology" versus "speaking anthropology"; lessons from an Andean collective scarcity ritual in the Quechua-speaking Kallawaya and Aymara-speaking Altiplano region (Andes, Bolivia). (*Anthropos/Switzerland,* 90: 1/3, 1995, p. 69–88, bibl., table)

Using a rain-calling ritual as an example, author calls attention to the need for anthropologists to analyze the spoken word in ritual performance in order to grasp the religious substance of the ritual. This approach opens analysis of the ritual to greater heterogeneity and variation in cultural expression than is generally the case. For annotation of Spanish-language version see item **5095.**

Rösing, Ina. Paraman Purina—llamar la lluvia. See item **5095.**

1096 Ströbele-Gregor, Juliana. ¿Seducida?: mujeres en comunidades religiosas evangélicas fundamentalistas; los casos de El Alto y La Paz. (in Reunión Anual de Etnología, *6th, La Paz, 1992.* Actas. La Paz: Museo Nacional de Etnografía y Folklore, 1993, t. 1, p. 121–134, bibl.)

Presents series of hypotheses to explain attraction of evangelical religion to urban women. Conversion to Protestantism is explained in terms of a) a search for security, b) a form of intentional acculturation, c) a non-confrontational means of dealing with the arbitrary actions of the State.

1097 Van Kessel, Juan. La senda de los Kallawayas. Puno, Peru: CIDSA, 1993. 151 p.: bibl., ill.

Five ethnographic essays explore the Callahuaya world view, traditional medicine, a comparison of academic and native discourses on Callahuaya culture, and contrasting western and indigenous views of development.

1098 Waira pampa: un sistema pastoril camélidos-ovinos del altiplano árido boliviano. La Paz: ORSTOM; CONPAC; IBTA, 1995. 299 p.: bibl., ill. (some col.).

Interdisciplinary work attempts to elucidate the complex process of pastoral activity in arid Andes. Problems inherent to the system are identified and grassroots alternatives suggested. This rich series of ethnographic studies by anthropologists, ecologists, zoologists, and agronomists isolates herds' vulnerability to severe climactic changes as a key impediment to this form of economic activity, and proposes alternative schemes for feeding animals and maintaining their health and reproductive activity. All contributors give attention to the sociocultural system within which these herders operate.

CHILE

1099 Bacigalupo, Ana Mariella. Variación del rol de machi dentro de la cultura mapuche: tipología geográfica, adaptiva e iniciática. (*Rev. Chil. Antropol.*, 12, 1993/94, p. 19–43, bibl.)

Focusing on the variable role of the medical and ritual figure of the *machi*, author creates a typology for comprehending the complexities of Mapuche shamanism, taking into account geographic variation, cultural and economic adaptation, and forms of knowledge. Based on research in the central valleys and urban centers of Araucanía.

1100 Bibliografía general de la sociedad y cultura mapuche. Temuco, Chile: Centro de Estudios de la Araucanía, Univ. de la Frontera, 1993. 540 p.: indexes.

Lengthy bibliography of historical and contemporary sources on the Mapuche spans numerous disciplines including anthropology, law, history, linguistics, psychology, education, ecology, agronomy, and demography, among others. While not annotated, this valuable compendium includes useful thematic and authors' summaries of articles published in a variety of international venues.

1101 Carahue, la antigua imperial: visión de su patrimonio cultural; un aporte al V centenario. Producción y edición de Myriam Hernández. Carahue, Chile: Dirección de Administración de Educación Municipal, Ilustre Municipalidad de Carahue, 1992. 257 p.: bibl., ill. (some col.).

Multidisciplinary anthology of brief articles published by the municipality. Details history and prehistory, architecture, ecology, folklore, and literature of Carahue, Araucanía. Articles are of varying quality.

1102 Concha S., Claudia and **Verónica Salas M.** Quinchamalí, cultura urdida entre gredas, arados y cerezos. Santiago: Taller de Acción Cultural, 1994. 226 p.: bibl., ill. (Col. Rescate de la memoria histórica)

Includes series of testimonies collected by the Taller de Acción Cultural in Quinchamalí, a center of Mapuche ceramic production. Narrators detail nature of artisanal production of the past and the reintroduction of ceramics manufacture. Unfortunately narrators are not identified by name in this compilation.

1103 Espinosa Ojeda, Bernarda. Medicina tradicional: función de la machi en comunidades mapuche rurales. (*in* Salud psicosocial, cultura y democracia en América Latina: los autores sociales, salud integral y democracia. Asunción: Editora ATHYHA-IPD, 1993, v. 3, p. 91–108, bibl.)

Comparative study of traditional medicine in eight rural and urban Mapuche communities details names and causes of illnesses, role of the *machi* or mediator between humans and ancestral spirits, and the continued relevance of traditional medicine among contemporary Mapuches.

1104 Foerster G., Rolf. Introducción a la religiosidad mapuche. Santiago: Editorial Universitaria, 1993. 183 p.: bibl. (Col. Imagen de Chile)

Following a historical discussion of missionary reactions to Mapuche religiosity, work examines the Mapuche pantheon, ritual, and religious institutions, as well as relationship between religiosity and ethnic identity. Mapuche millennialism is studied through analysis of examples of millennial movements. Concludes with suggestion to redefine ethnicity through Pentecostalism.

1105 Gacitúa, Estanislao. Hacia un marco interpretativo de las movilizaciones mapuches en los últimos 17 años. (*Nütram/ Santiago*, 8:28, 1992, p. 22–44, bibl., graph, tables)

Social and historical analysis of Mapuche discourse in context of four types of popular resistance: public meetings, protests, land takeovers, and violent strikes. Utilizes indigenous documents and regional newspapers to detail Mapuche strategies in response to interethnic conflict from 1973–90.

1106 Grebe, María Ester. Concepción del tiempo en la cultura aymara: representaciones icónicas, cognición y simbolismo. (*Rev. Chil. Antropol.*, 9, 1990, p. 64–81, bibl., ill.)

Studies Aymara notions of time through examination of iconic representations of 20 native artists of Isluga, Chile, that display patterns related to the daily and annual cycles. The cognitive and symbolic categories exhibit a common pan-Andean cultural ground as well as a mosaic of local and individual transformations.

1107 Grebe, María Ester. El subsistema de los ngen en la religiosidad mapuche. (*Rev. Chil. Antropol.*, 12, 1993/94, p. 45–64, bibl., ill., tables)

Examines Mapuche system of the *ngen*, or "spirit owners of nature," within the context of five subsystems that make up the Mapuche belief system. The *ngen* are associated with hunting and gathering activities. This recapitulation of a Mapuche ethnic model describes origin of the *ngen* and its 10 ethnocategories.

1108 Gundermann Kroll, Hans. Comunidad indígena y ciudadanía: la experiencia aymara en el norte de Chile. (*Allpanchis/ Cusco*, 26:46, segundo semestre 1995, p. 91–130, bibl.)

What does it mean to be an indigenous citizen of Chile? This question is studied historically for the Aymara, and through an examination of ethnic organizations for the Mapuche. Comparative perspective using as examples two communities with distinct adaptations to the Chilean nation.

1109 Matus de la Parra, Ana Isabel. El ceremonial de la limpia de canales en Caspana. (*Rev. Chil. Antropol.*, 12, 1993/94, p. 65–86, bibl.)

Describes cleaning of irrigation canals in a community of northern Chile. Focuses on importance of water in the ritual cleaning. Includes a detailed description of the ceremony and texts of accompanying songs.

1110 Medicinas y culturas en La Araucanía. Recopilación de Luca Citarella. Santiago: Editorial Sudamericana, 1995. 616 p.: bibl., ill.

Encyclopedic, multi-authored work comprehensively relates the history and current forms of Mapuche curing practices, ethnoclassifications of illness and herbal cures, and training of medical specialists. Juxtaposed is a similarly detailed study of popular medicine and another concerning the history of western medicine in Chile. The articulation among the three medical systems is analyzed from sociological, juridical, and cultural standpoints, proposing practical solutions to health planners.

1111 Mitología mapuche. Recopilación de Yosuke Kuramochi y Juan Luis Nass. Traducción de Rosendo Huisca Melinao. Quito: Ediciones ABYA-YALA; Rome: Movimiento Laicos para América Latina, 1991. 264 p.: (Col. 500 años; 40)

Bilingual collection of Mapuche myths collected in a variety of Chilean communities. Includes variants of the Palguín legend and other important narratives. Published in Mapuche as well as Spanish, all myths include ethnographic annotations.

1112 Muñoz, Bernardo. Procesos de cambios sociales en el área de San Pedro de Atacama: pérdida y recuperación de la identidad étnica; una contribución antropológica para el desarrollo. Bonn, Germany: Holos, 1993. 219 p.: bibl., ill., maps. (Mundus Reihe Ethnologie; 66)

Doctoral dissertation examines Atacameño *ayllu*—a nexus of communal labor, ritual, and reciprocity across vertical levels— as a vehicle for resisting dominant Chilean society. Focuses particularly on period of the Pinochet dictatorship and contemporary democratic period. Conclusion reflects on the nature of ethnodevelopment.

1113 **Nakashima Degarrod, Lydia.** Sueños de muerte y de transformación de los mapuche de Chile. (*in* Congreso Internacional de Americanistas, *47th, New Orleans, 1991.* La muerte y el más allá en las culturas indígenas latinoamericanas. Quito: Ediciones ABYA-YALA, 1992, p. 37–51, bibl., ill.)

Narratives of dreams which warn of imminent death or risk are the basis for this exploration of death and dreaming among the Mapuche. Work views dreams as vehicles for communication with the dead.

Orellana Rodríguez, Mario. Prehistoria y etnología de Chile. See item **520.**

1114 **Orlove, Benjamin S.** Meat and strength: the moral economy of a Chilean food riot. (*Cult. Anthropol.,* 12:2, May 1997, p. 234–268, bibl., tables)

Examines 1905 food riot in Santiago, comparing it to similar events in other parts of the world. Inconsistencies in the riot's timing relative to a rise in food prices, the type of foodstuff with increased prices and nature of the ensuing repression lead author to consider ritualized forms of public behavior related to notions of justice as causes of riot. Through historical comparison, the specificities of the moral economy are underlined.

1115 **Oyarce, Ana María** and **Susana Schkolnik.** Los mapuches: una investigación multidisciplinaria en reducciones indígenas de Chile. (*Notas Pobl.,* 23:61, junio 1995, p. 211–240, bibl.)

Multidisciplinary demographic study of indigenous communities of the Araucanía Region focuses primarily on infant mortality in the Temuco area. Argues that the Mapuche population is young and characterized by high migration, low educational level, an agricultural economy, growing incorporation into western cultural norms, and declining infant mortality.

1116 **Parker G., Cristián.** Cultura Mapuche y prácticas médicas tradicionales en la Región del Bio-Bio, Chile. (*Nütram/Santiago,* 7:25, 1991, p. 45–74)

Studies relationship between traditional medical techniques practiced among popular sectors and the cultural and religious beliefs of the Mapuche. Demonstrates influence of Mapuche magico-religious beliefs among the poor.

Pereda, Isabel and **Elena Perrotta.** Junta de hermanos de Sangre: un ensayo de analisis del nguillatun a traves de tiempo y espacio desde una visión Huinca. See item **1061.**

1117 **Resumenes analíticos de la cultura mapuche.** Selección e indización documental de Sylvia Galindo Godoy. Temuco, Chile : Centro de Estudios de la Araucanía, Univ. de la Frontera, 1994. 159 p.: indexes.

Valuable annotated bibliography of legal, anthropological, demographic, agricultural, and ecological works published on the Mapuche since the 1960s. Each entry is described with key words, a list of contents, sources and methods utilized, and brief evaluation of work's importance. Useful author and topical indexes.

1118 **Salas Astrain, Ricardo.** Una interpretación del universo religioso mapuche. (*Nütram/Santiago,* 7:25, 1991, p. 20–44)

Analyzes Mapuche sacred world through a study of its symbolic and ritual language. Concentrates on hermeneutics of ritual speech and telluric symbolism of the *Ngillatun* ritual suggests Christianity is internalized by the Mapuche and not simply imposed upon them.

1119 **Sierra, Malú.** Mapuche, gente de la tierra. Santiago: Editorial Persona, 1992. 280 p.: bibl., ill. (Donde todo es altar)

Monograph in the form of a personal reminiscence interspersed with ethnographic description. Examines Mapuche ritual and cosmology, history, oral tradition, and contemporary efforts at ethnic organizing in popular narrative form.

1120 **Tudela Poblete, Patricio Hernán.** Chilenización y cambio ideológico entre los aymaras de Arica, 1883–1930: intervención religiosa y secularización. (*Rev. Chil. Antropol.,* 12, 1993/94, p. 201–231, bibl., map)

An anthropological study of historical documents of the Arica region. Explores transformation of *ayllus* into Chilean institutions from the late-19th to early-20th centuries. The "Chileanization" campaign developed by the government included both sentiments of citizenship and modernizing ideology, as well as substitution of Aymara religious observance with orthodox Catholic observance.

1121 Tudela Poblete, Patricio Hernán.
Transformación religiosa y desintegración de la comunidad aymara tradicional en el norte de Chile. Bonn, Germany: Holos, 1992. 316 p.: bibl., ill., maps. (Mundus Reihe Ethnologie; 58)

Detailed examination based on archival research of sociocultural transformation among Aymara of northern Chile during 19th and 20th centuries focuses particularly on introduction of new belief systems developed in response to modernization. Also examines how processes of modernization, nationalism, and secularization promoted the loss of traditional forms of community organization and ethnic identity. Significant contribution.

COLOMBIA

1122 Antropología en la modernidad. Recopilación de María Victoria Uribe y Eduardo Restrepo. Bogotá: Instituto Colombiano de Antropología, 1997. 399 p.: bibl.

Multifaceted look at Colombian modernity by Colombian and foreign anthropologists focuses on ethnic identity and national legislation (Gros, Wade, Losonczy, Restrepo, Rappaport, Gow); consumer society (Villaveces); the anthropology of Bogotá politics (Gutiérrez); new social movements (Escobar, Pardo); and indigenous rejections of modernity (Roelens, Bolaños).

1123 Arte indígena en Colombia: cultures del món, Castell de Bellver. Palma de Mallorca: Ajuntament de Palma, 1992. 151 p.: col. ill.

Museum catalog of Tucuna and Cuna art includes archaeological entries on Tumaco and Amazonian petroglyphs. Exquisitely photographed volume includes contributions by major Colombian ethnographers detailing nature of esthetics and myth in these native societies.

1124 Avirama, Jesús and Rayda Márquez.
The indigenous movement in Colombia. (in Indigenous peoples and democracy in Latin America. New York: St. Martin's Press, 1994, p. 83–105, appendices)

Historical appreciation of indigenous rights movement in Colombia examines milestones in the movement, the response of non-indigenous Colombia to the movement, and indigenous/State relations.

1125 Candelier, Henri. Riohacha y los indios guajiros. Traducción de Max Fauconnet. Bogotá: Ecoe Ediciones, 1994. 168 p.: ill., map. (Serie Interés general)

Spanish translation of a work by a late-19th-century travel writer includes rich material on indigenous communities of the Guajira, as well as on indigenous/Colombian relations and urban popular culture of the era. Valuable contribution to the Spanish-language historical literature.

1126 Cepeda Espinosa, Manuel José. Ethnic minorities and constitutional reform in Colombia. (in Ethnic conflict and governance in comparative perspective. Washington: Woodrow Wilson International Center for Scholars, 1995, p. 100–138, appendices)

Evaluates implementation of ethnic reforms included in the 1991 Colombian Constitution. Brief descriptions of judicial procedures (acción de tutela and acción pública) through which communities have forced implementation of minority rights. Concludes that there have been important gains in native rights through judicial implementation of constitutional reforms.

1127 Congreso Nacional de Antropología, 6th, Bogotá, 1992. La construcción de las Américas. Recopilación de Carlos Alberto Uribe Tobón. Bogotá: Univ. de los Andes, Facultad de Humanidades y Ciencias Sociales, Depto. de Antropología, 1993. 287 p.: bibl., ill.

Rich, interdisciplinary volume spanning archaeology, anthropology, political science, literary studies, and history focuses primarily on Colombia but also includes one article on Brazil and several on Peruvian themes. Of ethnographic interest are articles by Jaime Arocha, Nina de Friedmann, Michael Taussig, and Peter Wade on the construction of blackness in Colombia; and works by Hernán Henao, Jean Jackson, and Myriam Jimeno on the nature of indigenous ethnicity. Both of these themes are framed by the codification of ethnic diversity in Colombia's 1991 Constitution.

1128 Ereira, Alan. The elder brothers. New York: Knopf; Random House, 1992. 243 p.: bibl. col. ill., index.

Relates filmmaker's ethnographic voyage to the Kagaba of the Sierra Nevada de Santa Marta. Includes narrative history, developed from secondary sources of Tairona/Spanish relations, discussion of Kagaba relations with State institutions, and examination of Sierra Nevada's involvement in broader Colombian conflicts. Author's personal reminiscences connect these themes.

1129 Escobar, Arturo. Encountering development: the making and unmaking of the Third World. Princeton, N.J.: Princeton Univ. Press, 1995. 290 p.: bibl., index. (Princeton studies in culture/power/history)

Evaluates development enterprise and development discourse from a critical theory perspective. This view of development policies and control mechanisms employs Colombian case studies of the Programa de Desarrollo Rural Integrado and of the local application of the discourse of women in development.

1130 Espinosa, Myriam Amparo. Surgimiento y andar territorial del Quintín Lame. Quito: Ediciones Abya-Yala, 1996. 121 p.: bibl., ill.

Creative rewriting of Cauca history from multiple perspectives and positions focuses on territorial expansion of the Movimiento Quintín Lame, an indigenous guerrilla organization that operated during the 1980s. Important contribution to Colombian anthropology for its use of metaphors created by the protagonists as theoretical vehicles for framing an alternative historical ethnography.

1131 Esquivel Trianot, Ricardo. Indígena o campesino: ¿caminos al desarrollo? (*Cuad. Desarro. Rural*, 35, segundo semestre 1995, p. 83–101, bibl., tables)

Uses 1985 census data to examine indigenous *resguardo* of Cota as it relates to loss of ethnic identity. Uses information on gender, age, population growth, migration, economic activity, land tenancy, and living conditions to illustrate the deindianization process.

1132 Friedemann, Greta. The devil among blacks of the Pacific Littoral and the Cauca Valley in Colombia: cultural constructions. (*Am. Negra*, 8, dic. 1994, p. 99–111, bibl., ill.)

Explores complex notions of the devil in the Pacific Coast and Cauca Valley. Lends ambiguity to the European figure featured in Taussig's *The devil and commodity fetishism in South America* (see *HLAS 43: 255b*). The devil is both good and evil, a trickster and a resistance figure.

1133 Friedemann, Nina S. de. Lumbalú: ritos de la muerte en Palenque de San Basilio, Colombia. (*Am. Negra*, 1, junio 1991, p. 65–84, bibl., maps)

Historic-ethnographic work describes funeral chants in Palenque de San Basilio, a community located on the Pacific Coast descended from maroons. Analyzes chant lyrics and their symbolism through their historical contextualization and place within the worldview of the *palenque* (name given to Colombian communities of slave descendants).

1134 Jimeno, Myriam and **Ismael Roldán.** Las sombras arbitrarias: violencia y autoridad en Colombia. Bogotá: Editorial Univ. Nacional, 1996. 208 p.: bibl., ill.

Interdisciplinary study focuses on violence in popular sectors of Bogotá. This significant work uses both quantitative and ethnographic data to examine mistreatment and violence as understood by the urban poor in terms of sites of violence, scenarios for violence, nature of violent interactions, and cultural representations of violence.

1135 *Journal of Latin American Anthropology*. Vol. 1, No. 2, 1996. Ethnicity reconfigured: indigenous legislators and the Colombian Constitution of 1991. Edited by Joanne Rappaport. Arlington, Va.: American Anthropological Association.

Collection of articles by anthropologists provides general evaluation of the ethnic provisions of the 1991 Colombian Constitution. Studies examine construction of ethnicity by indigenous legislators (Rappaport and Dover), implications of constitutional reform for traditional authorities (Padilla), and differences between indigenous sovereignty in Colombia and Oceania (Linnekin). Case studies from Cauca (Jimeno, Field) and the Vaupés (Jackson) trace implications of decentralization of ethnic administration in specific regions of Colombia.

1136 Llano Restrepo, María Clara and **Marcela Campuzano Cifuentes.** La chicha, una bebida fermentada a través de la historia. Bogotá: Instituto Colombiano de Antropología; CEREC, 1994. 160 p.: bibl., ill. (Serie Amerindia; 9)

Innovative volume, which begins with precolumbian Muiscas and ends in 1940s, inserts history of chicha drinking within broader legislative and medical history of Colombia. Relationship between hygiene, nation-building, urban expansion, and growth of popular culture is explored within this framework.

1137 Muñoz Cordero, Lydia Inés. El carnaval andino de San Juan de Pasto: expresión de la cultura mestiza y de resistencia popular. (*in* Colección nuestra patria es America: la cultura en la historia. Edited by Jorge Nuñez Sánchez. Quito: Editora Nacional, 1992, v. 8, p. 81–103.)

Focuses on celebration's history since 1926, the year it was introduced in its current form. Examines carnival as an expression of mestizo culture and a means of popular resistance. Follows a decade-by-decade account of the festival's elaboration.

1138 Muñoz Vila, Cecilia and Ximena Pachón C. La aventura infantil a mediados de siglo: los niños colombianos enfrentan cambios sociales, educativos y culturales que marcarán su futuro. Bogotá: Planeta, 1996. 352 p.: bibl., ill. (Col. Espejo de Colombia)

Ethnographic study examines infanticide and child abandonment and abuse in 20th-century Bogotá by analyzing consequences of the transfer of child protective services from the private charitable sphere to the public realm. Special focus on institutions dedicated to children's health and education, development of recreational spaces and changes in family structure.

1139 Murillo Sencial, Zakik. Aluna: la conciencia de un cuerpo sin orificios. (*Bol. Antropol./Antioquia*, 10:26, 1996, p. 64–104)

Corrects and builds upon Reichel-Dolmatoff's path breaking 1984 study of Kagaba cosmology (see *HLAS 49:1061* and *HLAS 53:1259*). Examines in copious detail Kagaba epistemology through exegesis with *mamas* of spatial and calendrical relations.

1140 Ocampo, Gloria Isabel. Diversidad étnica y jurisdicción indígena en Colombia. (*Bol. Antropol./Antioquia*, 11:27, 1997, p. 9–33)

Analyzes problems arising as provisions of 1991 Colombian Constitution concerning autonomous indigenous jurisdiction are put into practice. Concentrates on suits in which indigenous and constitutional rights conflict. Argues that contemporary formulations of customary law may provide subtle vehicles for assimilation.

1141 Rappaport, Joanne. Textos legales e interpretación histórica: una etnografía andina de la lectura. (*Iberoam./Frankfurt*, 16:3/4, 1992, p. 67–79)

Study of a southern Highland Pasto community analyzes the coexistence of oral and written models of recounting history. Use of community and personal archival materials in oral narrative, influence of literate metaphors in oral history, and imposition of geographic metaphors for organizing archives are some of the themes discussed.

1142 Streicker, Joel. Spatial reconfigurations, imagined geographies, and social conflicts in Cartagena, Colombia. (*Cult. Anthropol.*, 12:1, Feb. 1997, p. 109–128, bibl.)

Examines struggles for territorial control in the context of recent economic changes in Cartagena. Focuses on how claims of identity and relations of inequality are constructed spatially. Multi-class and multiethnic analysis moves from the urban sphere to the international political economy, to the image of Africa, and to Caribbean tourism.

1143 Taussig, Michael. The sun gives without receiving: an old story. (*Comp. Stud. Soc. Hist.*, 37:2, 1995, p. 368–398)

Far-ranging discussion of a devil's pact that produces riches that can purchase only luxuries. Uses the pact as a way to explore the introduction of herbicides into Colombian cane fields. Also describes several stories of devil pacts and native curing within the context of cocaine and oil production.

1144 Wade, Peter. The language of race, place and nation in Colombia. (*Am. Negra*, 2, dic. 1991, p. 41–67, bibl., ill.)

Innovative exploration of the nature of Colombian nationhood from the perspective of race and mestizaje. Suggests that national ideologies presuppose homogeneity but maintain hierarchical distinctions. Thus Colombian nationhood is built on a system of contrasts in which Afrocolombians are seen as inferior members.

1145 Zuluaga Gómez, Víctor. Vida pasión y muerte de los indígenas de Caldas y Risaralda. Pereira, Colombia: Univ. Tecnológica de Pereira, 1994. 150 p.: bibl. (Col. Universidad Tecnológica de Pereira)

Begins with a discussion of the creation of colonial *resguardos* in what are today the *departamentos* of Caldas and Risaralda.

Continues with examinations of indigenous participation in the Wars of Independence, the recruitment of indigenous soldiers during 19th-century civil wars, and implementation of indigenous legislation in the region from Independence to the present.

ECUADOR

1146 Almeida Vinueza, José. La etnicidad como principio político activo en el urbanismo latinoamericano: el caso de Otavalo, Ecuador. (*Sarance/Otavalo*, 22, oct. 1995, p. 13–27, bibl.)

Reflects on the return of indigenous people to the urban center of Otavalo. Suggests that the urban/rural distinction is no longer a suitable identification of native peoples; that indigenous ethnicity can thrive under conditions of "progress;" and that these conclusions indicate the need to proceed on a national political project such as that proposed by the indigenous movement.

1147 Bourque, Nicole L. Savages and angels: the spiritual, social and physical development of individuals and households in Andean life-cycle festivals. (*Ethnos/Stockholm*, 60:1/2, 1995, p. 99–114, bibl.)

Analyzes role of the household in life-cycle festivals of the Ecuadoran indigenous community of Sucre. Traces changes in household status as individual members move through successive rites of passage. Suggests scholars should pay more attention to complex relationships within households, instead of concentrating exclusively on parent-child relationships. See also item **1148.**

1148 Bourque, Nicole L. Spatial meaning in Andean festivals: Corpus Christi and Octavo. (*Ethnology/Pittsburgh*, 33:3, Summer 1994, p. 229–243, bibl., map)

Examines sociospatial divisions and significance of movement between them during Corpus Christi and Octavo festivals in the Ecuadorian indigenous community of Sucre. During festival time the village becomes a model of the cosmos through an expansion of social boundaries. Includes detailed description of the festival's geographic choreography. See also item **1147.**

1149 Butler, Barbara Y. Espiritualidad y uso del alcohol entre la gente otavaleña. (*Sarance/Otavalo*, 16, agosto 1992, p. 31–63)

Examines spiritual and social value of alcohol (*chicha* and *trago*) in Otavalo community of San Rafael, detailing its spiritual and ritual uses and function in affirming social hierarchies. Also examines influence of economic, political, and religious change on consumption of distilled liquor.

1150 Campesinos del Mira y del Chanchán. v. 1. Quito: Ediciones Abya-Yala; Pontificia Univ. Católica del Ecuador, Depto. de Antropología, 1992- . 1 v.: bibl.

Brief report of a team research project concerning peasant populations in southern Carchi and northern Imbabura provinces. Project included ethnohistorical research on indigenous chiefdoms and on economy of slavery in the colonial and republican periods. Also collected oral histories from deindianized peasant communities, Afro-Ecuadorian districts, and zones of colonization.

1151 Carpio Benalcázar, Patricio. Entre pueblos y metrópolis: la migración internacional en comunidades austroandinas del Ecuador. Quito: ILDIS; Ediciones Abya-Yala, 1992. 220 p.: bibl.

Study of international migration from Azuay and Cañar provinces to US employs methodologies and theory drawn from a range of social sciences. Explores the origins, development, impact, and personal narratives of the migration and concludes that Ecuador's economic crisis has fostered this process.

1152 Chalán Guamán, Luis Aurelio. Sistema de cargos entre los saraguros. (*Pueblos Indíg. Educ.*, 8:33/34, enero/junio 1996, p. 235–250, ill.)

Describes the *cargo* system (which determines an individual's appointment, duties, and obligations) in Saraguro. The symbolism of the steps in the system, the appointment and obligations of *cargo* holders, and the prerequisites for occupying a *cargo* are highlighted. Author is a member of the Saraguro indigenous community. See also item **1169.**

1153 Chango, María and Agustín Jerez. Reis Pishta. (*Pueblos Indíg. Educ.*, 8:33/34, enero/junio 1996, p. 115–130)

Local authors describe the Fiesta de Los Reyes in Salasaca. Emphasizes the *cargo* system (which determines an individual's appointment, duties, and obligations), the mythic and historical personages depicted in the festivities, and the sequence of events which occur during the festival.

1154 Coba Andrade, Carlos Alberto. Persistencias etnoculturales en la fiesta de San Juan en Otavalo. (*Sarance/Otavalo*, 20, oct. 1994, p. 13–36, bibl.)

An "archaeology" of the San Juan fiesta in Otavalo traces elements to the preincaic, incaic, and colonial traditions.

1155 Comisión Ecuménica de Derechos Humanos—CEDHU (Ecuador). Indigenous peoples' rights in Ecuador. (*Beyond Law*, 5:13, Aug. 1995, p. 9–40)

Document prepared by Ecuador's Comisión Ecuménica de Derechos Humanos analyzes platform and proposal of Ecuadorian indigenous organizations. Highlights characteristics of the platform and proposal, the achievements and limitations of the indigenous movement, indigenous reactions to recent changes in agrarian law, and the *levantamiento indígena* of 1990 and a series of political actions that have since occurred.

1156 Compadres y priostes: la fiesta andina como espacio de memoria y resistencia cultural. Recopilación de Luis Fernando Botero. Quito: Ediciones ABYA-YALA, 1991. 148 p.: bibl., ill. (Col. Antropología aplicada; 3)

Collection of student essays from a course on religious anthropology conducted in field sites. Students explore and describe festivals from the liturgical calendar of the Catholic Church such as Christmas, Epiphany, Corpus Christi, All Souls, and various saints' days held in highland indigenous communities. Includes an historical and theoretical introduction by the editor/professor.

1157 Confederación de Nacionalidades Indígenas del Ecuador—CONAIE. Derechos de los pueblos indígenas: situación jurídica y políticas de estado. Recopilación de Ramón Torres Galarza. Quito: CONAIE/CEPLAES; Abya-Yala; s.d. 194 p.

Valuable volume, the result of a workshop organized by la Confederación de Nacionalidades Indígenas del Ecuador, contains individual presentations by indigenous and non-indigenous authors who outline proposals, analyze indigenous issues, and evaluate State policy. Examines topics such as territorial, political, economic, cultural and intellectual property rights, rights of biodiversity, and administration of justice.

1158 Ecuador indígena: espiritualidad, música y artesanía. Quito: Ediciones Abya-Yala; Otavalo, Ecuador: Instituto Otavaleño de Antropología, 1992. 204 p.: bibl., ill.

Articles by Ecuadorian and foreign anthropologists examine a broad range of topics including alcohol consumption, production of hemp handicrafts, historicity and peasant economy, and children's games.

1159 Figueroa, José Antonio. Historización o tiempo fundacional: centralización política chachi y estrategias autonómicas del grupo awa. (*Sarance/Otavalo*, 20, oct. 1994, p. 69–88, bibl.)

Analyzes manipulation of history by contemporary indigenous political actors. Focuses on relationship between historical memory and political centralization among the Chachi (Cayapa) and the erasing of the past by the decentralized Awa (Cuaiquer).

1160 Foro de la Mujer Indígena del Ecuador, Quito, 1994. Nosotras, las mujeres indígenas de diferentes nacionalidades no somos solo el pasado, somos del pasado, presente y del futuro: memorias. Quito: Confederación de Nacionalidades Indígenas del Ecuador, 1994. 121 p.: ill.

Series of reports emanating from national and regional meetings of Ecuadorian indigenous women includes transcripts of speeches by indigenous leaders; resolutions; and discussions of topics such as the role of women in the household, health, and Ecuadorian agrarian reform.

1161 Guaña, Pablo; Pedro Camino; and Quimbia Ulco. Inti Raymi Cayambi: la fiesta sagrada del sol en la mitad del mundo; la Fiesta de San Pedro en Cayambe. Cayambe, Ecuador: CICAY, 1992. 159 p.: bibl., ill.

A native-authored volume written for a native audience. This compendium of songs, newspaper articles, engravings, cultural projects, festival flyers and programs, and ethnographic description attempts to provide readers with the tools necessary to construct an alternative history on the basis of cultural revitalization. Work focuses on the *Inti Raymi*/San Pedro festival which takes place on June 21 in Cayambe. See also item **1162.**

1162 Guandinango, Angel. Fiesta ritual de *Inti Raimi* o Fiesta de San Pedro. (*Pueblos Indíg. Educ.*, 8:33/34, enero/junio 1996, p. 57–63)

Native author examines *Inti Raimi/ San Pedro* festival in Cotacachi. Focuses on festivals preparation and organization and describes events that occur during festivities. See also item **1161**.

1163 Meisch, Lynn A. "We will not dance on the tomb of our grandparents": "500 Years of Resistance" in Ecuador. (*Lat. Am. Anthropol. Rev.*, 4:2, Winter 1992, p. 55–74, bibl., ill., photos)

Historical study of indigenous resistance in Ecuador begins with the 1964 agrarian reform, moves to the creation of the Confederación de Nacionalidades Indígenas del Ecuador (CONAIE), and concludes with events surrounding the 1992 celebration "500 Years of Resistance" by Ecuadorian indigenous organizations.

1164 Minnaar, Renneé. Interacción entre etnicidad y género: ser hombre o mujer indígena en Otavalo, Ecuador. (*Sarance/Otavalo*, 22, oct. 1995, p. 29–63, bibl.)

Against a background of the economic and social changes that have transformed Otavalo into a commercial weaving center, work examines relationship between gender and ethnicity in order to better understand migration, urbanization, and the industrialization of textile production within the context of Andean cultural continuity.

1165 Quiroga, Diego. "Ahora el diablo somos nosotros mismos": religiosidad popular en la Costa Norte de Ecuador. (*Nariz Diablo*, 20, mayo 1994, p. 76–85, photos)

Uses the metaphor "Ahora el diablo somos nosotros mismos," To examine the reintroduction of Catholic images within the structure of a popular religious observance that attempts to ameliorate social tensions and critique socioeconomic transformation. Within the framework of discussion about the devil, funeral ceremonies, *novenarios*, and *arrullos* are analyzed using key images from witchcraft and magic.

1166 Ramón Valarezo, Galo. El regreso de los runas: la potencialidad del proyecto indio en el Ecuador contemporáneo. Quito: COMUNIDEC; Fundación Interamericana, 1993. 349 p.: bibl., maps.

Stimulating collection of Ramón Valarezo's articles focuses on genesis of indigenous nationality in Ecuador, the development of utopian philosophies regarding native peoples, historical forms of indigenous resistance, nature of contemporary indigenous pluralist proposals, and evaluation of development strategies in indigenous communities.

1167 Śniadecka-Kotarska, Magdalena. Ekwador: procesy modernizacji i kształtowania nowej tożsamości na przykładzie Indian Otavalo i Saraguro [Ecuador: the processes of modernization and formation of a new identity using the Otavalo and Saraguro Indians as an example]. Warsaw: Centrum Studiów Latynoamerykańskich (CESLA), Uniwersytet Warszawski, 1997. 57 p.: bibl., ill., maps. (Dokumenty Robocze; 26)

Studies effects of modernization and integration on two Ecuadorian indigenous groups—the Otavalo and Saraguro—Based on *in situ* research conducted by author during 1993 and 1995. [Z. Kantorosinski]

1168 Suremain, Charles-Edouard de. De la coopérative a la communauté: ethnogenèse, organisation sociale et identité d'un groupe de colons, paroisse d'Alluriquín, Équateur. (*Bull. Inst. fr. étud. andin.*, 22:2, 1993, p. 551–584, bibl., maps, tables)

Thirty-year study focuses on a group of colonists in Santo Domingo de los Colorados. Through analysis of ethnogenesis, identity, and social organization examines transformation of unrelated persons into a coherent community with a common identity. Includes examination of land tenure arrangements, labor sharing, and social hierarchies.

1169 Universidad Politécnica Salesiana (Ecuador). Departamento de Antropología Aplicada. Los saraguros: fiesta y ritualidad. Recopilación de Linda Belote y James Belote. Quito: ABYA-YALA: Univ. Politécnica Salesiana, 1994. 257 p.: bibl., ill., map. (Col. de Antropología aplicada; 9)

Series of articles by indigenous students describes major Saraguro community rituals and celebrations, including Christmas, Holy Week, Corpus Christi, marriages, and wakes; and the process of constructing a house and its accompanying ceremonies. Includes numerous drawings by community members. See also item **1152.**

1170 Vásquez B., Teresa. Artesanía de Manabí: mediador de identidad. Quito: Ediciones ABYA-YALA, 1992. 127 p., 2 folded leaves of plates: bibl., ill.

Based on fieldwork in Canton Montecristi, Manabí prov., work describes artesanal production of ceramic, metal, and straw objects for the tourist market. Details social relations as aspect of production. Examines whether artisanry provides a basis for identity formation.

1171 Vokral, Edita V. "Trabajamos de todo, todo el día:" cambios en la división laboral por sexo y relaciones sociales de género originados por la introducción de nuevas estrategias de supervivencia; provincia de Chimborazo, Ecuador. (*Bulletin/Geneva,* 55/56, 1991/92, p. 79–92, bibl.)

Analyzes changes in sexual division of labor brought about by modernization and introduction of new technologies. Focuses on adoption of horticulture and rural-urban migration.

1172 Weismantel, Mary J. Making kin: kinship theory and Zumbagua adoptions. (*Am. Ethnol.,* 22:4, Nov. 1995, p. 685–709)

Neither the functionalist biological definition of the family nor critiques by feminist and symbolic anthropologists adequately explain kinship practices in Zumbagua, Ecuador, where people become parents of children by feeding and caring for them over an extended period of time. Article is followed by a critical commentary by Susan McKinnon and a response by Weismantel.

PERU

1173 Allen, Catherine J. Time, place and narrative in an Andean community. (*Bulletin/Geneva,* 57/58, 1993/94, p. 89–95, bibl.)

Analyzes relationship between place, time, and narrative, in order to understand how Quechua-speaking peasants interpret their environment. Useful discussion of narrative typologies focuses on ambiguities of each tale.

1174 Altamirano, Teófilo. Cuarenta años de antropología en la Pontificia Universidad Católica del Perú. (*Anthropologica/Lima,* 12:12, 1994, p. 263–280)

Descriptive history of the Pontificia Universidad Católica del Perú, one of the most important Andean schools of anthropology. Includes an administrative history of anthropology at the institution; discusses debates held in Lima concerning the relevance

of development to Peruvian anthropology and on the relationship between anthropology and symbolism.

1175 Altamirano, Teófilo. Pastores quechuas en el oeste norteamericano. (*Am. Indíg.,* 51:2/3, abril/sept. 1991, p. 203–222)

About 3,000 Quechuas have settled in the plains states of the US where they tend sheep flocks. This descriptive ethnography details recruitment, labor process, social and cultural life, return migration, and earning investment of Quechua shepherds in Wyoming.

1176 Amodio, Emanuele. Cocacha mamacha: prácticas adivinatorias y mitología de la coca entre los quechuas del Perú. (*Bulletin/Geneva,* 57/58, 1993/94, p. 123–137, bibl., ill., photos)

Detailed description of how coca leaves are used in divination rituals. Considers leaf shape, stains, faults, state of conservation, and relative position. Employs both historical documentation and ethnographic research conducted in La Convención.

Arguedas, José María. Canto kechwa: con un ensayo sobre la capacidad de creación artística del pueblo indio y mestizo. See *HLAS 56:4157.*

1177 Ari, Manuela. Manuela Ari: an Aymara woman's testimony of her life. Edited by Lucy T. Briggs and Sabine Dedenbach-Salazar Sáenz. Bonn: Holos, 1995. 290 p.: bibl. (BAS; 25)

Biography of an Aymara woman, collected from 1940–43 in Chucuito by Harry Tschopik. Presented in Aymara with line-by-line translations into English and Spanish. Significant for being the oldest example of Andean testimonial literature.

1178 Becker, Alton L. and **Bruce Mannheim.** Culture troping: languages, codes, and texts. (*in* The dialogic emergence of culture. Edited by Dennis Tedlock and Bruce Mannheim. Urbana: Univ. of Illinois Press, 1995, p. 237–252)

Article, in dialogue form, argues that we too easily construct analogues for our texts in other cultures, converting these cultures' narratives into a flat, monological style. A conversation among Quechua-speaking women from Peru is analyzed to illustrate the fragmentary, interactive, and context-dependent nature of southern Andean texts.

1179 Bey, Marguerite. La communauté dans l'espace de reproduction des familles paysannes au Pérou. (*Bull. Inst. fr. étud. andin.*, 21 : 1, 1992, p. 327–348, bibl., maps)

Thirty-year study of social change in two rural communities of Yauyos, *departamento* of Lima, details family responses to questions concerning education and economic monetization. Social change has created or redefined certain concepts such as paisano, rural community, and survival strategies.

1180 Brougère, Anne-Marie. Y por qué no quedarse en Laraos?: migración y retorno en una comunidad altoandina. Traducción de Luis Muelle López. Lima: Instituto Francés de Estudios Andinos; Instituto Andino de Estudios en Población y Desarrollo, 1992. 202 p.: bibl., ill., maps

Translated from the original French, valuable monograph examines processes of migration in the Cañete valley, exploring history of migratory movements, and the nature of rural exodus and its impact on community structures. Concludes with a demographic study of return migrants.

1181 Burga, Manuel. Historia y memoria colectiva: violencia e identidad en el ritual andino. (*in* Congreso Nacional de Investigaciónes en Historia, *1st, Lima, 1984.* Actas. Lima, CONCYTEC, 1991, v. 1, p. 201–226, tables)

Ethnography of Peruvian culture using both oral and written historical sources. Studies patterns of violence and identity in rituals performed during patron saint fiestas, and the representation of the Inca-Spanish encounter at Cajamarca to highlight the conflicts involved in the creation of a national consciousness.

1182 Cáceda Díaz, Fernando and **José Rossel Fernández.** Flora medicinal nativa y cosmovisión campesina en comunidades de Puno. Puno, Peru: Univ. Nacional del Altiplano, Escuela de Postgrado, Maestría en Desarrollo Rural, 1993. 253 p.: bibl., ill. (Desarrollo rural)

Botanical description of medicinal plants native to the Puno area situates them within a regional cultural context, with particular regard to their medical use, utility as a human or animal food, and ritual and cosmological importance. Drawings accompany the descriptions.

1183 Cáceres Valdivia, Eduardo. The incorporation of economic, social, cultural, and indigenous people's rights into the agendas of human rights organizations in Peru. (*Beyond Law*, 5 : 13, Aug. 1995, p. 41–63)

A human rights agenda for the coming decade in Peru discusses human rights objectives in terms of globalization and the so-called "democratic transition," the nature of an "integral" view of human rights, and the relationship between human rights and global issues given the current economic and political world system.

1184 Cadena, Marison de la. The political tensions of representations and misrepresentations: intellectuals and *mestizas* in Cuzco, 1919–1990. (*J. Lat. Am. Anthropol.*, 2 : 1, Fall 1996, p. 112–147)

Anthropological analysis of relationship between *cuzqueño indigenista*, *neo-indigenista* intellectuals, and working-class women. *Mestizas* were described by both intellectual groups as erotic beings. However, these women responded by proposing an image of *mujeres de respeto*.

1185 Calvo C., Rossano. Qosqo sociedad e ideología, siglo XX: estudios de antropología del Qosqo. Qosqo, Peru: Municipalidad del Qosqo, 1995. 159 p.: bibl., ill.

Series of essays related to anthropology of Cusco. Includes study of role played by mestizaje in ethnic and social mobility, the history of the official staging of the Inti Raymi festival, and a consideration of the extent to which 19th- and 20th-century intellectual movements have represented Inca history.

1186 Cavero Carrasco, Ranulfo. Imaginario colectivo e identidad en los Andes: a propósito de "Tayta Cáceres"; un heroe cultural. Ayacucho, Peru: Univ. Nacional de San Cristóbal de Huamanga, 1994. 237 p.: bibl.

Fascinating work explores Ayacuchan oral tradition regarding Andrés Avelino Cáceres and Ayacucho's participation in the late-19th-century war with Chile. Analyzes 75 Quechua- and Spanish-language narratives with respect to predominant narrative motifs, transmission of oral knowledge, fidelity of the narratives to notions of historical truth, and role of these narratives in the process of regional identity formation.

1187 Chávez, Fabiola. Iniciación y sueño entre las *parteras* de la sierra de Piura, Ayabaca. (*Anthropologica/Lima*, 14:14, 1996, p. 183–207, bibl.)

Argues that *parteras* of rural Piura communities should provide pediatric care as well as childbirth assistance. Offers a historical comparison of curing metaphors based on colonial texts and narratives of contemporary *parteras*.

1188 Coasaca Núñez, Willver. El arbol y el experimentador campesino: tecnología andina forestal. Lima: Representaciones Ojeda, 1993. 119 p.: bibl.

Brief volume, based on research among tree-growers of the Colca Valley, studies peasants, called *curiosos* here, engaged in agricultural experimentation. Focuses on the agricultural technology they develop and employ, and, specifically on how this body of knowledge is transmitted from generation to generation within traditional Andean patterns of narrative, economic cooperation, and childrearing.

1189 Comunidades campesinas y nativas, en el nuevo contexto nacional. Edición de Máximo Gallo Q. Lima: CAAAP; SER, 1993. 230 p.: bibl.

Fascinating collection analyzes legal relationship of Amazonian and Andean indigenous communities to the Peruvian State, with a special focus on constitutional reform and the legislative process. Analyzes how effectively native communities are served by current legislation in regard to liberal democracy, violence, and development policy. Careful distinction between juridical circumstances of Highland and Lowland native communities.

1190 Condori Mamani, Gregorio and **Asunta Quispe Huamán.** Andean lives. Translated from the Quechua with annotations and revised glossary by Paul H. Gelles and Gabriela Martínez Escobar. Introduction by Paul H. Gelles. Photographs by Eulogio Nishiyama. Austin: Univ. of Texas Press, 1996. 199 p.: bibl., ill., index.

Autobiographies first published in Cusco during the late 1970s in the original language. Sensitive and elegant translation, with detailed annotations, makes these life stories accessible to English-speaking readers.

1191 Crianza andina de la chacra. Lima: Proyecto Andino de Tecnologías Campesinas, 1994. 380 p.: bibl., ill.

Volume compares Andean and Western knowledge systems. Favors the indigenous appreciation of landscape, exploitation of water and soil resources, and reading of meteorological signs. Notable, detailed explanation of the cosmological basis for camelid herding by an indigenous writer, Victor Quiso Choque of Puno.

1192 Damonte V., Gerardo. Componentes de la cultura urbana en el Perú. (*Anthropologica/Lima*, 11, enero 1994, p. 285–307, bibl.)

Historically-based investigation focuses on multiple migrations of European, Afroperuvian, Andean, and Asian populations to Peruvian cities. Analyzes causes of migration and strategies of assimilation into the urban environment. Concludes with a biography of a *cuzqueño* migrant to Lima.

1193 Desarrollo o descolonización en los Andes? Lima: Proyecto Andino de Tecnologías Campesinas, 1993. 328 p.: bibl., ill. (some col.).

Collection of essays argues that four decades of development has not erased poverty in Peru. Instead of praising western development strategies, authors underscore the vitality of Andean culture, contrasting it with western cosmology, agronomy, astronomy, education, economy, and art. Concludes by calling for a decolonization of the Andean world.

1194 Druc, Isabelle C. De la etnografía hacia la arqueología: aportes de entrevistas con ceramistas de Ancash, Perú, para la caracterización de la cerámica prehispánica. (*Bull. Inst. fr. étud. andin.*, 25:1, 1996, p. 17–41, appendix, bibl., maps, photos, tables)

Ethnographic study focuses on work of 25 potters. Examines types of clay used, process of ceramic production, and zones of distribution. Valuable information on constraints influencing ceramic manufacture, an important issue for archaeologists.

1195 Eláez Ramírez, Jerónimo. Visiones, curaciones y arte en el Antisuyo. Qosqo, Peru: Municipalidad del Qosqo, 1994. 110 p.: bibl., ill.

Study of shamanism and use of hallucinogenic drugs in Antisuyo explores nature of shamanic trance, visions, and interpretation of dreams. Analysis is situated within broader anthropological theories of shamanism, finding that neither a social systems nor a cultural approach is sufficient. Instead, Carlos Castañeda's notion of "another reality" is seen as a useful theoretical vehicle.

1196 En el nombre del señor: shamanes, demonios y curanderos del norte del Perú. Edición de Luis Millones y Moisés Lemlij. Lima: Seminario Interdisciplinario de Estudios Andinos, 1994. 330 p.: bibl., ill., map. (Biblioteca peruana de psicoanálisis; 19)

Exceptional volume brings together anthropologists, archaeologists, and ethnohistorians to examine the persistence and emergence of curing traditions, witchcraft, and spirit possession in northern Peru. Contributions include studies of the material culture (Elera), iconography (Makowski Hanula) and functions associated with precolumbian shamanism (Polia Meconi). Also considers colonial-era shamanism as a form of resistance (Mills, Gareis), European examples of colonial-era spirit possession (Blanco, Lemlij), and the persistence of cultural forms in contemporary curing (Topic, Sharon, Yauri Montero, Malengreau).

1197 Gelles, Paul H. Equilibrium and extraction: dual organization in the Andes. (*Am. Ethnol.*, 22:4, Nov. 1995, p. 710–742, bibl., ill.)

Based on ethnographic study from southern Peruvian Andes, work argues that ubiquity of moiety organization arose from an indigenous imperial mode of domination which endured under Spanish rule. Continued use of moieties is explained by role of dualism in ritual action.

1198 Irarrázaval, Diego. Tradición y porvenir andino. Chucuito, Peru: IDEA, Instituto de Estudios Aymaras; Lima: TAREA, Asociación de Publicaciones Educativas, 1992. 296 p.: bibl.

Reflecting upon 11 years of religious work in southern Andean communities, author describes Andean forms of relationship with the earth and human body, symbolic and ritual language, the liberating potential of Andean organization, and pastoral work in the Puno area.

1199 Joralemon, Donald and **Douglas Sharon.** Sorcery and shamanism: curanderos and clients in northern Peru. Salt Lake City: Univ. of Utah Press, 1993. 306 p.: bibl., ill. index.

Unusual study of northern coastal Peruvian curers centers on their lives and shared cultural ideology, the roots of which derive from indigenous cosmology, not folk Catholicism. Studies curers' philosophy by analyzing four patient accounts and examining their role in social and gender-based conflicts.

1200 León Caparó, Raúl. Racionalidad andina en el uso del espacio. Lima: Pontificia Univ. Católica del Perú, Fondo Editorial; Banco Central de Reserva del Peru, 1994. 378 p.: bibl., ill.

Ethnography of social and territorial space, based on fieldwork in Paucartambo, describes characteristics and social functions of socioeconomic units (kinship systems) in the community of Qollana-Wasaq by examining the development of maize and potato cultivation and cattle raising.

1201 Llanque Chana, Andrés. Uywaña: medicina veterinaria andina. Puno, Peru: CIDSA, 1993. 113 p.: bibl., ill.

Study of Andean veterinary medicine by Aymara author focuses on cosmological backdrop of divinatory diagnosis and ritual treatment of supernaturally-caused disease in animals. Classification of diseases caused by physical factors and accompanying pharmacopoeia.

1202 Luerssen, Susan J. Illness and household reproduction in a highly monetized rural economy: a case from the southern Peruvian highlands. (*J. Anthropol. Res.*, 49:3, Fall 1993, p. 255–281, table)

In an economically heterogeneous town of the Peruvian Altiplano, illness reflects income and employment differentiation, is a causal factor in determining an individual's standing within the socioeconomic structure, and ultimately maintains family-based social hierarchies from generation to generation.

1203 Luis-Blanc, François. Médecins et chamanes des Andes: Awankay, l'Esprit-Condor plane, immobile, sur la vallée. Préface de Jean-Pierre Chaumeil. Paris: L'Harmattan,

1994. 202 p., 8 p. of plates: bibl., ill., map. (Recherches & documents. Amériques latines)

Travel monograph by French physician describes healing practices of highland Peru. Details native forms of diagnosis, use of hallucinogenic drugs in curing sessions, and intellectual encounters of Andean and European forms of curing specific illnesses.

1204 Malengreau, Jacques. Trashumancia, migraciones y restructuraciones étnicas entre sierra y selva al norte de Chachapoyas, Perú. (*Bull. Inst. fr. étud. andin.*, 24:2, 1995, p. 295–315, bibl., map)

Defines conditions of maintenance, reproduction, and transformation of ethnic identities and ethnic frontiers within the context of population movements between Highlands and Lowlands. Examines transcommunity migration, social fragmentation, cultural continuity, and ethnic reproduction as forms of collective restructuring across diverse communities.

1205 Marzal, Manuel M. El mito en el mundo andino ayer y hoy. (*Anthropologica/Lima*, 13:13, 1995, p. 7–21, bibl.)

Interdisciplinary reflection on the Andean mythology. Analyzes relationship between myth and cosmos, history, politics, and religion within the context of Peruvian mestizaje.

1206 Mitchell, William P. Algunos son más iguales que otros: oferta de mano de obra, reciprocidad y redistribución en los Andes. (*Anthropologica/Lima*, 11, enero 1994, p. 173–207)

Analyzes hegemonic function of reciprocity and redistribution through study of scarcity of labor, organization of agricultural work, and social stratification in Quinua, Ayacucho. Asymmetrical reciprocity is used to obtain laborers, masking unequal power and access to resources. Provides an antidote to notions of symmetry and equilibrium in the Andean world.

1207 Mitchell, William P. The transformation of cultural anthropology: the decline of ecology and structure and the rise of political economy and the cultural construction of social reality. (*Ecol. Hum.*, 12:2, juin 1994, p. 41–64, bibl.)

Historical appreciation of Andean studies traces movement from ecological and structural approaches to contemporary examinations of the social construction of reality. Appearance of Sendero Luminoso is seen as a turning point in Andean anthropology. Although purporting to deal with Andean studies in general, article concentrates on Peru.

1208 Murguía, Luis. Ritual del matrimonio quechua. Puno, Peru: Facultad de Ciencias Sociales, Univ. Nacional del Altiplano, 1994. 110 p.: bibl., ill. (Antropología. Culturas en desaparición; 1)

Highly detailed description of marriage practices in a Quechua-speaking community. Includes explanations and descriptive summaries of the complex rituals associated with marriage and of the articulation of status within this ceremonial framework. Also discusses forms of post-marital residence.

1209 Música, danzas y máscaras en los Andes. Edición de Raúl R. Romero. Lima: Pontificia Univ. Católica del Perú; Instituto Riva-Aguero, Proyecto de Preservación de la Música Tradicional Andina, 1993. 411 p.: bibl., ill. (some col.), music.

Articles concerning popular music and dance in Peru written by leading scholars in this field: Bigenho, Cánepa Koch, Casas Roque, Mendoza-Walker, Ráez Retamozo, Romero, Turino, and Vreeland. Situate expressive culture within the framework of modernity, providing rich descriptive and analytical insights on mestizo and indigenous artistic expression in a variety of Peruvian communities. Béjar's bibliography provides numerous secondary sources on regional studies of dance and music, historical approaches to expressive culture, and Peruvian classical music.

1210 Nugent, David. From devil pacts to drug deals: commerce, unnatural accumulation, and moral community in "modern" Peru. (*Am. Ethnol.*, 23:2, May 1996, p. 258–290, bibl., map)

Focusing on northern Andean Peru, argues for the historical contextualization of local responses to market expansion, which in Chachapoyas have changed radically since the 1930s. Traces historical development of discourse on the market, from a positive appreciation of integration to rejection of the market as a dangerous and alien presence.

1211 Ortiz Rescaniere, Alejandro. Amores
    bélicos. (*Anthropologica/Lima*, 12:12,
1994, p. 225–258)
    Reflects on scholarly descriptions of
the Andean personality, which confine indigenous people to stereotypes such as the
noble savage, the idyllic peasant, the ecological sage, the generous community member,
or the barbaric primitive. Uses anthropological works from a variety of eras, juxtaposed to
his own analysis of an autobiography of a *cuzqueño* soldier.

1212 Ortiz Rescaniere, Alejandro. Unas imá-
    genes del tiempo. (*Anthropologica/
Lima*, 13:13, 1995, p. 141–166)
    Examines images and experiences of
time in Peruvian indigenous communities of
San Lorenzo de Quinti and Huarochiri. Examines perception of a mediocre present vs. an
idealized past among the Vicosinos, and the
hesitation to embrace cultural change among
the Secoyas.

1213 Oths, Kathryn S. Health care decisions
    of households in economic crisis: an
example from the Peruvian highlands. (*Hum.
Organ.*, 53:3, Fall 1994, p. 245–254, bibl.,
graphs, tables)
    Describes health care treatment
choices available to Andean peasants during a
period of economic crisis. Studies how households make pragmatic decisions about which
illnesses will receive treatment. No evidence
of a turn from biomedical to traditional care;
instead, both are used to a lesser degree.

1214 Paerregaard, Karsten. Más allá del di-
    nero: trueque y economía categorial en
un distrito en el valle del Colca. (*Anthropolo-
gica/Lima*, 11, enero 1994, p. 209–251, bibl.,
graphs)
    Describes ecological, economic, and
institutional features of barter in the Colca
Valley. Analyzes social categories and cultural identities of barter participants, and examines historical articulation of barter with
the monetary economy of Peru.

**1215 The Peru reader: history, culture, poli-
    tics.** Edited by Orin Starn, Carlos Iván
Degregori, and Robin Kirk. Durham, N.C.:
Duke Univ. Press, 1995. 531 p.: bibl., ill.,
index, map.
    Vast, multidisciplinary collection con-
tains previously published articles and excerpts from books on Peruvian themes. Con-

cerns archaeology, history, political systems,
resistance movements, drugs, and cultural
issues. Includes ethnographic contributions
of Peruvianists such as Irene Silverblatt, John
Murra, José María Arguedes, Catherine Allen,
Orin Starn, and others.

1216 Polia, Mario. La *mesa* curanderil y cos-
    mología andina. (*Anthropologica/
Lima*, 13:13, 1995, p. 23–53, bibl., tables)
    Using data gathered in Piura, author
provides clues for "reading" the symbolism of
the *mesa* or altar of traditional medical spe-
cialists.The *mesa* is described as an *imago
mundi* and analyzed through study of its eti-
mology, number symbolism, geographic refer-
ents, and dualistic structure.

1217 Prochaska, Rita. Taquile y sus tejidos:
    version castellano-english. 2. ed. Jesús
María, Peru: Arius, 1990. 127 p.: bibl., ill.
(some col.).
    Second edition of brief ethnographic
description of the island of Taquili provides a
more detailed study of weaving. Examines fi-
bers and techniques, design symbolism, and
contextualization of weaving within the
weavers' life cycle.

1218 Ramos Vera, Claudio. Rehabilitación,
    uso y manejo de camellones: propuesta
técnica. Lima: Lluvia Editores, 1991. 78 p.:
bibl., ill., map.
    Compilation of technical considera-
tions concerning the rehabilitation and use of
raised fields in Puno dept. examines issues of
canal construction, crop rotation, and peasant
participation in such projects.

1219 Rojas Zolezzi, Enrique C. Los ciclos de
    Pachakama, Inka y Sacramento en la
mitología Campa Ashaninka como interpre-
taciones de los procesos de reemplazo tecnológico y subordinación económica surgidos de
la colonización. (*Anthropologica/Lima*, 11,
enero 1994, p. 109–154, bibl., maps)
    Uses oral history to examine how
Campa Ashaninka mythology reflects technological change and economic subordination
since European colonization.

1220 Sánchez Garrafa, Rodolfo. Espacio y
    estructuras religiosas en los mitos de
Awsangate. (*Anthropologica/Lima*, 13:13,
1995, p. 167–185, bibl.)
    Explores relationship among spatial

organization, myth, human activity, and nature as integral parts of Andean cosmology through a study of the mythology associated with the Awsangate and Kayangate *apus* (mountain spirits) in Lawramarka. Includes numerous mythic texts. See also item **1221.**

1221 Sánchez Garrafa, Rodolfo. Los mitos de Awsangate: cuando los apus se reúnen. (*Anthropologica/Lima*, 12:12, 1994, p. 179–192, bibl.)

Based upon research in Lawramarka (Cusco depto.), examines symbolic structure of myths relating to the Awsangate and Kayangate *apus* (mountain spirits), and the relationship between humans, nature, and the supernatural as expressed in the organization of sacred space. See also item **1220.**

1222 Silverman, Gail P. Ch'unchu pallay. Lima: Pontificia Univ. Católica del Perú; Awana Wasi del Cuzco, 1993. 58 p.: ill. (Awana Wasi del Cuzco; 3)

Visual archive compares the Ch'unchu motif in weavings from Cusco area to the Inkarrí myth represented in Quero textiles. Brief explanatory section is followed by photographs and schematic diagrams of various examples. See also item **1223.**

1223 Silverman, Gail P. El tejido andino: un libro de Sabiduría. Lima: Banco Central de Reserva del Perú, Fondo Editorial, 1994. 202 p.: bibl., ill. (some col.), index, maps.

Ethnographic study examines Quero weaving techniques and pictorial motifs. Cosmological knowledge in pictograms are compared to motifs in precolumbian *tocapu* designs and analyzed in the context of notions of space and time. Analyzes various motifs within context of the Inkarrí myth, the story of the first Inca and Quero culture hero. See also item **1222.**

1224 Spier, Fred. San Nicolás de Zurite: religion and daily life of a Peruvian Andean village in a changing world. Amsterdam: VU Univ. Press, 1995. 130 p.: bibl., ill., maps. (Anthropological studies VU; 18)

Analyzes political relationship between Catholicism, Protestantism, and indigenous religion within a Peruvian Andean community. Combines interpretation of historical documents with ethnographic observations to compare modernizing ideologies of both Catholics and Protestants.

1225 Starn, Orin. Maoism in the Andes: The Communist Party of Peru-Shining Path and the refusal of history. (*J. Lat. Am. Stud.*, 27:2, May 1995, p. 399–421, bibl.)

Examines history and ideology of the Partido Comunista del Perú-Sendero Luminoso. Questions whether movement embodied a distinctive Peruvian Marxism and demonstrated a departure from Peruvian culture and traditions.

1226 Stokes, Susan Carol. Cultures in conflict: social movements and the State in Peru. Berkeley: Univ. of California Press, 1995. 183 p.: bibl., ill., index.

Ethnography by a political scientist focuses on how urban poor have changed their perceptions of the State, citizenship, class and gender relations, and democracy and have movilized radical social movements. Analysis includes historical and ethnographic components.

1227 La tradición andina en tiempos modernos. Edición de Hiroyasu Tomoeda y Luis Millones. Osaka, Japan: National Museum of Ethnology, 1996. 212 p.: bibl., photos, plates. (Senri ethnological reports; 5)

Stimulating volume by interdisciplinary team of Japanese and Peruvian scholars, contains articles focusing on Peruvian modernity. Included are a general history of the city of Trujillo (Castañeda), a cultural history of Ayacucho (Gamarra), an illuminating essay on the nature of Andean Spanish (Zavala), an intriguing study of the social classification of mestizas (Rozas and Calderón), and various examinations of Andean fiestas and religious images within the context of modernity (Kato, Nobuoka, Millones, Tomoeda) and tourism (Flores Ochoa).

1228 Valderrama Fernández, Ricardo and Carmen Escalante Gutiérrez. Nosotros los humanos: ñuqanchik runakuna; testimonio de los quechuas del siglo XX. Cusco, Peru: Centro de Estudios Regionales Andinos Bartolomé de Las Casas, 1992. 253 p.: bibl., ill. (Biblioteca de la tradición oral andina; 12)

Remarkable set of bilingual testimonial narratives of Quechua-speaking peasants from Cotabambas, Apurímac dept. Biographies of Victoriano Tarapaki and Lusiku Ankalli, the former a community leader and the latter a thief, provide an exceptional window into social context of rural livestock theft, family structure, cosmology, and music from Cotabambas.

1229 Watters, Raymond Frederick. Poverty and peasantry in Peru's Southern Andes, 1963–90. Pittsburgh, Pa.: Univ. of Pittsburgh Press, 1994. 366 p.: bibl., ill., index, map. (Pitt Latin American series)

Focuses on a production model of the peasantry and their access to resources. Examines historical, economic, social, and political forces shaping the community of Chilca. Considers peasants' problems through study of politics and mobilization, deindianization, migration, and agricultural innovation. For geographer's comment see *HLAS 55:2515.*

1230 Yauri Montero, Marcos E. El Señor de la Soledad de Huarás: discursos de la abundancia y carencia; resistencia andina. Lima: Editorial Ave, 1993. 194 p.: bibl.

Argues that constellation of images and myths surrounding the representation of the Señor de la Soledad indicates an andeanization of Catholicism within which precolumbian ritual is reconfigured to conform to Christianity. Using the discourse surrounding the representation, the history of its multiple restorations following natural disasters, and the apparitions associated with the sanctuary, study explores interweaving of Andean and European cosmologies in a local context.

1231 Zamudio, Delia. Piel de mujer. Recopilación de Maritza González. Lima: Fomento de la Vida-Fovida, 1995. 163 p.: ill.

Biography of an Afro-Peruvian feminist and labor leader in the pharmaceutical industry offers a historical perspective of the Peruvian labor movement over the past two decades. Also contains poignant observations on the meaning of race and gender in urban Peru.

1232 Zecenarro Villalobos, Bernardino. De fiestas, ritos y batallas: algunos comportamientos folk de la sociedad andina de los k'anas y ch'umpiwillcas. (*Allpanchis/Cusco,* 23:40, segundo semestre 1992, p. 147–172, bibl.)

Examines ritual in high provinces of Cuzco, focusing on the agricultural functions of ritual battles among the K'anas and Ch'umpiwillcas, and on how *kasarakuy* and *velakcha* rituals, directed at the Pachamama, ensure fertility. Patron saint fiestas are believed to resynthesize ancient Andean belief systems.

JOURNAL ABBREVIATIONS

Allpanchis/Cusco. Allpanchis. Instituto de Pastoral Andina. Cusco, Peru.

Am. Anthropol. American Anthropologist. American Anthropological Assn., Washington.

Am. Antiq. American Antiquity. The Society for American Archaeology. Washington.

Am. Ethnol. American Ethnologist. American Ethnological Society. Washington.

Am. Indíg. América Indígena. Instituto Indigenista Interamericano. México.

Am. Negra. América Negra. Pontificia Univ. Javeriana. Bogotá.

Amazonía Peru. Amazonía Peruana. Centro Amazónico de Antropología y Aplicación Práctica, Depto. de Documentación y Publicaciones. Lima.

Amérindia/Paris. Amérindia. Association d'Ethnologistique Amérindienne (AEA). Paris.

An. Inst. Patagon./Hum. Anales del Instituto de la Patagonia: Serie Ciencias Humanas. Univ. de Magallanes. Punta Arenas, Chile.

Analecta Praehist. Leiden. Analecta Praehistorica Leidensia. Leiden Univ. Press. Leiden, The Netherlands.

Anc. Mesoam. Ancient Mesoamerica. Cambridge Univ. Press. Cambridge, England.

Andean Past. Andean Past. Latin American Studies Program, Cornell Univ., Ithaca, N.Y.

Andes/Cusco. Andes: Revista de la Facultad de Ciencias Sociales. Univ. Nacional de San Antonio Abad del Cusco, Facultad de Ciencias Sociales. Cusco, Peru.

Andes/Warsaw. Andes: Boletín de la Misión Arqueológica Andina. Univ. of Warsaw. Warsaw, Poland.

Ann. Assoc. Am. Geogr. Annals of the Association of American Geographers. Lawrence, Kan.

Ann. Carnegie Mus. Annals of the Carnegie Museum. Carnegie Museum of Natural History. Pittsburgh, Penn.

Annu. Rev. Anthropol. Annual Review of Anthropology. Annual Reviews, Inc., Palo Alto, Calif.

Anthropol. Educ. Q. Anthropology and Education Quarterly. Council on Anthropology and Education. Washington.

Anthropol. Q. Anthropological Quarterly. Catholic Univ. of America, Catholic Anthropological Conference. Washington.

Anthropologica/Lima. Anthropologica. Depto. de Ciencias Sociales, Pontificia Univ. Católica del Perú. Lima.

Anthropologie/Paris. L'Anthropologie. Institut de paleontologie humaine. Paris.

Anthropos/Switzerland. Anthropos. International Review of Ethnology and Linguistics. Anthropos-Institut. Freiburg, Switzerland.

Antiquity/Cambridge. Antiquity. A Quarterly Review of Archaeology. The Antiquity Trust. Cambridge, England.

Antropológica/Caracas. Antropológica. Fundación La Salle de Ciencias Naturales; Instituto Caribe de Antropología y Sociología. Caracas.

Anu. Antropol. Anuário Antropológico. Tempo Brasileiro. Rio de Janeiro.

Anu. Estud. Am. Anuario de Estudios Americanos. Consejo Superior de Investigaciones Científicas; Univ. de Sevilla, Escuela de Estudios Hispano-Americanos. Sevilla, Spain.

Anu. IEHS. Anuario IEHS. Univ. Nacional del Centro de la Provincia de Buenos Aires, Instituto de Estudios Histórico-Sociales. Tandil, Argentina.

Anu. Inst. Chiapaneco Cult. Anuario Instituto Chiapaneco de Cultura. Instituto Chiapaneco de Cultura. Tuxtla Gutiérrez, Mexico.

Anuario/Tuxtla Gutiérrez. Anuario. Centro de Estudios Superiores de México y Centroamérica, Univ. de Ciencias y Artes del Estado de Chiapas. Tuxtla Gutiérrez, Mexico.

Arch. Völkerkd. Archiv für Völkerkunde. Museum für Völkerkunde in Wien und von Verein Freunde der Völkerkunde. Vienna.

Archaeoastronomy/England. Archaeoastronomy. Science History Publications. Giles, England.

Archaeol. Anthropol. Archaeology and Anthropology. Ministry of Education and Cultural Development. Georgetown, Guyana.

Archaeology/New York. Archaeology. Archaeology Institute of America. New York.

Arq. Mus. Hist. Nat. Arquivos do Museu de História Natural. Univ. Federal de Minas Gerais. Belo Horizonte, Brazil.

Arqueol. Contemp. Arqueología Contemporánea. Programa de Estudios Prehistóricos. Buenos Aires.

Arqueol. Mex. Arqueología Mexicana. Instituto Nacional de Antropología e Historia, Editorial Raíces. México.

Arqueología/México. Arqueología. Instituto Nacional de Antropología e Historia. México.

Beyond Law. Beyond Law = Más Allá del Derecho. Instituto Latinoamericano de Servicios Legales Alternativos. Bogotá.

Biblos/Rio de Janeiro. Biblos: Revista do Departamento de Biblioteconomia e História. Editora da Fundação Univ. do Rio Grande. Rio Grande, Brazil.

Bol. Am. Boletín Americanista. Univ. de Barcelona, Facultad de Geografía e Historia, Depto. de Historia de América. Barcelona.

Bol. Antropol./Antioquia. Boletín de Antropología. Univ. de Antioquia. Medellín, Colombia.

Bol. Inf./San Cristóbal. Boletín Informativo. Museo de Táchira. San Cristóbal, Venezuela.

Bol. Lima. Boletín de Lima. Revista Cultural Científica. Lima.

Bol. Mus. Arqueol. Quibor. Boletín del Museo Arqueológico de Quibor. Museo Arqueológico de Quibor. Quibor, Venezuela.

Bol. Mus. Chil. Arte Precolomb. Boletín del Museo Chileno de Arte Precolombino. Santiago.

Bol. Mus. Para. Goeldi. Boletim do Museu Paraense Emílio Goeldi. Nova série: antropologia. Conselho Nacional de Desenvolvimento Científico e Tecnológico, Instituto Nacional de Pesquisas da Amazônia. Belém, Brazil.

Bol. Soc. Chil. Arqueol. Boletín de la Sociedad Chilena de Arqueología. Sociedad Chilena de Arqueología. Santiago.

Boletín/Bogotá. Boletín del Museo del Oro. Banco de la República. Bogotá.

Bull. Bur. natl. ethnol. Bulletin du Bureau national d'ethnologie. Bureau national d'ethnologie. Port-au-Prince, Haiti.

Bull. East. Caribb. Aff. Bulletin of Eastern Caribbean Affairs. Univ. of West Indies. Cave Hill, Barbados.

Bull. Inst. fr. étud. andin. Bulletin de l'Institut français d'études andines. Lima.

Bull. Int. Anthropol. Ethnol. Res. Bulletin of the International Committee on Urgent Anthropological and Ethnological Research. International Union of Anthropological and Ethnological Sciences. Vienna.

Bull. Lat. Am. Res. Bulletin of Latin American Research. Society for Latin American Studies. Oxford, England.

Bull. Soc. hist. Guadeloupe. Bulletin de la Société d'histoire de la Guadeloupe. Archives départamentales avec le concours du Conseil général de la Guadeloupe. Basse-Terre, Guadeloupe.

Bulletin/Geneva. Bulletin. Société suisse des américanistes; Musée et institut d'éthnographie. Geneva.

CAA/Oxford. Computer Applications and Quantitative Methods in Archaeology. BAR. Oxford.

Camb. Archaeol. J. Cambridge Archaeological Journal. Cambridge Univ. Press. Cambridge, England.

Caribb. J. Sci. Caribbean Journal of Science. Univ. of Puerto Rico. Mayagüez, Puerto Rico.

Caribb. Q. Caribbean Quarterly. Univ. of the West Indies. Mona, Jamaica.

Caribb. Stud. Caribbean Studies. Univ. of Puerto Rico, Institute of Caribbean Studies. Río Piedras.

Caribena/Martinique. Caribena: cahiers d'études américanistes de la Caraïbe. Centre d'études et de recherches archéologiques (CERA). Martinique.

Cerám. Cult. Maya. Cerámica de Cultura Maya. Temple Univ., Dept. of Anthropology. Philadelphia, Penn.

Cespedesia/Cali. Cespedesia. Depto. del Valle del Cauca. Cali, Colombia.

Chungará/Arica. Chungará. Univ. del Norte, Depto. de Antropología. Arica, Chile.

Clio Arqueol./Recife. Clio: Série Arqueológica. Univ. Federal de Pernambuco. Recife, Brazil.

Comp. Stud. Soc. Hist. Comparative Studies in Society and History. Society for the Comparative Study of Society and History; Cambridge Univ. Press. London.

Contemp. Issues. Soc. Sci. Caribb. Perspect. Contemporary Issues in Social Science: a Caribbean Perspective. Univ. of the West Indies, Faculty of Social Sciences, ANSA McAL Psychological Research Centre. St. Augustine, Trinidad.

Cuad. Antropol. Pensam. Latinoam. Cuadernos del Instituto Nacional de Antropología y Pensamiento Latinoamericano. Ministerio de Cultura y Educación. Buenos Aires.

Cuad. Arquit. Mesoam. Cuadernos de Arquitectura Mesoamericana. Facultad de Arquitectura, Univ. Nacional Autónoma de México. México.

Cuad. Desarro. Rural. Cuadernos de Desarrollo Rural. Instituto de Estudios Rurales, Pontificia Univ. Javeriana. Bogotá.

Cuad. Hist. Arqueol. Cuadernos de Historia y Arqueología. Casa de Cultura, Núcleo del Guayas. Guayaquil, Ecuador.

Cuad. Prehispánicos. Cuadernos Prehispánicos. Seminario de Historia de América, Univ. de Valladolid. Spain.

Cult. Anthropol. Cultural Anthropology: Journal of the Society for Cultural Anthropology. American Anthropological Assn.; Society for Cultural Anthropology. Washington.

Curr. Anthropol. Current Anthropology. Univ. of Chicago. Chicago, Ill.

Del Caribe. Del Caribe. Casa del Caribe. Santiago, Cuba.

Desarro. Econ. Desarrollo Económico. Instituto de Desarrollo Económico y Social. Buenos Aires.

Dialect. Anthropol. Dialectical Anthropology. M. Nijhoff. Dordrecht, The Netherlands.

Diálogo Andin. Diálogo Andino. Univ. de Tarapacá. Arica, Chile.

Doss. d'Archéol. Les Dossiers d'Archéologie. Editions Faton. Dijon, France.

East. Anthropol. The Eastern Anthropologist. Ethnographic & Folk Culture Society. Lucknow, India.

Ecol. Hum. Ecologie Humaine. Laboratorie d'écologie humaine. Aix-en-Provence, France.

Espace Caraïbe. Espace Caraïbe. Maison des Pays Ibériques, Univ. M. de Montaigne, Bordeaux, France; Centre d'Études et de Recherches Caraïbéennes, Univ. des Antilles et de la Guyane, Pointe-à-Pitre, Guadeloupe.

Estud. Afro-Asiát. Estudos Afro-Asiáticos. Centro de Estudos Afro-Asiáticos. Rio de Janeiro.

Estud. Atacameños. Estudios Atacameños. Univ. del Norte, Museo de Arqueología. San Pedro de Atacama, Chile.

Estud. Hombre. Estudios del Hombre. Depto. de Estudios del Hombre, Univ. de Guadalajara. Guadalajara, Mexico.

Estud. Ibero-Am./Porto Alegre. Estudos Ibero-Americanos. Pontificia Univ. Católica do Rio Grande do Sul, Depto. de História. Porto Alegre, Brazil.

Estud. Jalisc. Estudios Jaliscienses. Univ. de Guadalajara. Guadalajara, Mexico.

Estud. Leopold. Estudos Leopoldenses. Faculdade de Filosofia, Ciências e Letras. São Leopoldo, Brazil.

Estudios/Guatemala. Estudios. Instituto de Investigaciones Históricas, Antropológicas, y Arqueológicas, Univ. de San Carlos de Guatemala. Guatemala.

Ethnohistory/Society. Ethnohistory. American Society for Ethnohistory. Duke Univ., Durham, N.C.

Ethnology/Pittsburgh. Ethnology: An International Journal of Cultural and Social Anthropology. Univ. of Pittsburgh, Penn.

Ethnos/Stockholm. Ethnos. Statens Etnografiska Museum. Stockholm.

Ethos/Society. Ethos. Society for Psychological Anthropology; Univ. of California, Los Angeles.

Etnología/La Paz. Etnología: Boletín del Museo Nacional de Etnografía y Folklore. La Paz.

Etud. créoles. Etudes créoles. Comité international des études créoles. Montréal.

Expedition/Philadelphia. Expedition. Univ. Museum, Univ. of Pennsylvania. Philadelphia, Penn.

Filhos Terr. Filhos da Terra. Núcleo de Pesquisa e Estudos Históricos, Instituto de Filosofia e Ciências Sociais, Univ. Federal do Rio de Janeiro.

Focaal/Nijmegen. Focaal: Tijdschrift voor Antropolgie. Stichting Focaal.

Gac. Arqueol. Andin. Gaceta Arqueológica Andina. Instituto Andino de Estudios Arqueológicos. Lima.

Geoarchaeology/New York. Geoarchaeology. John Wiley. New York.

Geol. Soc. Am. Bull. The Geological Society of America Bulletin. Geological Society of America. Boulder, Colo.

Hist. Archaeol. Historical Archaeology. Society for Historical Archaeology. Bethlehem, Penn.

Hist. Relig. History of Religions. Univ. of Chicago. Chicago, Ill.

Histórica/Lima. Histórica. Pontificia Univ. Católica del Perú, Depto. de Humanidades. Lima.

Hombre Ambient. Hombre y Ambiente. Ediciones Abya-Yala. Quito.

Hombre Desierto. Hombre y Desierto: Una Perspectiva Cultural. Univ. de Antofagasta, Instituto de Investigaciones Antropológicas. Antofagasta, Chile.

Homme/Paris. L'Homme. Laboratoire d'anthropologie, Collège de France. Paris.

Hoy Hist. Hoy es Historia: Revista Bimestral de Historia Nacional e Iberoamericana. Editorial Raíces. Montevideo.

Hum. Ecol. Human Ecology. Plenum Publishing Corp., New York.

Hum. Organ. Human Organization. Society for Applied Anthropology. New York.

Iberoam./Frankfurt. Iberoamericana. Vervuert Verlagsgesellschaft. Frankfurt.

Información/Campeche. Información. Centro de Estudios Históricos y Sociales, Univ. Autónoma de Campeche. Campeche, Mexico.

J. Am. Folk. Journal of American Folklore. American Folklore Society. Washington.

J. Anthropol. Res. Journal of Anthropological Research. Univ. of New Mexico. Albuquerque, N.M.

J. Archaeol. Method Theory. Journal of Archaeological Method and Theory. Plenum Pub. Corp. New York.

J. Archaeol. Res. Journal of Archaeological Research. Plenum Press. New York.

J. Archaeol. Sci. Journal of Archaeological Science. Academic Press. New York.

J. Caribb. Hist. The Journal of Caribbean History. Caribbean Univ. Press. St. Lawrence, Barbados.

J. Caribb. Stud. Journal of Caribbean Studies. Assn. of Caribbean Studies. Coral Gables, Fla.

J. Ethnobiol. Journal of Ethnobiology. Center for Western Studies. Flagstaff, Ariz.

J. Field Archaeol. Journal of Field Archaeology. Boston Univ., Boston, Mass.

J. Lat. Am. Anthropol. Journal of Latin American Anthropology. American Anthropological Assn. Arlington, Va.

J. Lat. Am. Lore. Journal of Latin American Lore. Univ. of California, Latin American Center. Los Angeles, Calif.

J. Lat. Am. Stud. Journal of Latin American Studies. Centers or Institutes of Latin American Studies at the Universities of Cambridge, Glasgow, Liverpool, London, and Oxford. Cambridge Univ. Press. London.

J. Royal Anthropol. Inst. Journal of the Royal Anthropological Institute. The Royal Anthropological Institute. London.

J. Steward Anthropol. Soc. Journal of the Steward Anthropological Society. Urbana, Ill.

J. World Prehist. Journal of World Prehistory. Plenum Press. New York.

Jam. J. Jamaica Journal. Institute of Jamaica. Kingston.

LARR. Latin American Research Review. Latin American Research Review Board. Univ. of New Mexico, Albuquerque, N.M.

Lat. Am. Anthropol. Rev. The Latin American Anthropology Review. Society for Latin American Anthropology. Fairfax, Va.

Lat. Am. Antiq. Latin American Antiquity. Society for American Archaeology. Washington.

Lat. Am. Indian Lit. J. Latin American Indian Literatures Journal. Geneva College. Beaver Falls, Penn.

Lat. Am. Perspect. Latin American Perspectives. Univ. of California. Newbury Park, Calif.

Mesoamérica/Antigua. Mesoamérica. Centro de Investigaciones Regionales de Mesoamérica. Antigua, Guatemala.

Mexicon/Berlin. Mexicon. K.-F. von Flemming. Berlin, Germany.

Montalbán/Caracas. Montalbán. Univ. Católica Andrés Bello, Facultad de Humanidades y Educación, Institutos Humanísticos de Investigación. Caracas.

Nariz Diablo. Nariz del Diablo. Centro de Investigaciones y Estudios Socio-Económicos. Quito.

Natl. Geogr. Mag. National Geographic Magazine. National Geographic Society. Washington.

Nature/London. Nature: International Weekly Journal of Science. Macmillan Magazines. London.

NewsWARP/Thorverton. NewsWARP. Wetland Archaeology Research Project, Fursdon Mill Cottage. Thorverton, England.

Notas Pobl. Notas de Población. Centro Latinoamericano de Demografía. Santiago.

Nueva Antropol. Nueva Antropología. Nueva Antropología. México.

Nütram/Santiago. Nütram. Centro Ecuménico Diego de Medellín. Santiago.

NWIG. New West Indian Guide/Nieuwe West Indische Gids. KITLV Press. Leiden, The Netherlands.

OSO/Netherlands. OSO. Stichtring Instituut ter Bevordering van de Surinamistick (IBS) te Nijmegen. Nijmegen, The Netherlands.

Pesquisas/São Leopoldo. Pesquisas. Instituto Anchietano de Pesquisas. São Leopoldo, Brazil.

Plant. Soc. Am. Plantation Society in the Americas. Univ. of New Orleans.

PoLAR/Washington. Political and Legal Anthropology. American Anthropological Assn., Assn. for Political and Legal Anthropology (a division of AAA). Washington.

Prehistoria/Buenos Aires. Prehistoria: Revista del Programa de Estudios Prehistóricos. Consejo Nacional de Investigaciones Científicas y Técnicas. Buenos Aires.

Publicaciones/Córdoba. Publicaciones. Univ. Nacional de Córdoba, Facultad de Filosofía y Humanidades. Córdoba, Argentina.

Pueblos Indíg. Educ. Pueblos Indígenas y Educación. Ediciones Abya-Yala. Quito.

Pumapunku/La Paz. Pumapunku. Centro de Investigaciones Antropológicas Tiwanaku. La Paz.

Quat. Res./New York. Quaternary Research. Academic Press. New York.

Reforma Agrár. Reforma Agrária. Asociação Brasileira de Reforma Agraria (ABRA). Campinas, Brazil.

Relig. Soc. Order. Religion and the Social Order. JAI Press; Assn. for the Sociology of Religion. Greenwich, Conn.

Res. Explor. Research & Exploration. National Geographic Society. Washington.

Res/Harvard. Res. Peabody Museum of Archaeology and Ethnology, Harvard Univ., Cambridge, Mass.

Rev. Andin. Revista Andina. Centro Bartolomé de las Casas. Cusco, Peru.

Rev. Arqueol. Am. Revista de Arqueología Americana. Instituto Panamericano de Geografía e Historia. México.

Rev. Arqueol./Madrid. Revista de Arqueología. Zugento Ediciones. Madrid.

Rev. Arqueol./São Paulo. Revista de Arqueologia. Sociedade de Arqueologia Brasileira. São Paulo.

Rev. Cent. Estud. Av. La Revista del Centro de Estudios Avanzados de Puerto Rico y el Caribe. San Juan.

Rev. CEPA. Revista do CEPA. Centro de Ensino e Pesquisas Arqueológicas, Faculdades

Integradas de Santa Cruz do Sul. Santa Cruz do Sul, Brazil.

Rev. Chil. Antropol. Revista Chilena de Antropología. Depto. de Antropología, Univ. de Chile. Santiago.

Rev. Chil. Hist. Nat. Revista Chilena de Historia Natural. Valparaíso, Chile: Sociedad de la Biología de Chile.

Rev. Colomb. Antropol. Revista Colombiana de Antropología. Ministerio de Educación Nacional, Instituto Colombiano de Antropología. Bogotá.

Rev. Esp. Antropol. Am. Revista Española de Antropología Americana. Facultad de Geografía e Historia. Univ. Complutense de Madrid.

Rev. Indias. Revista de Indias. Consejo Superior de Investigaciones Científicas, Instituto Gonzalo Fernández de Oviedo. Madrid.

Rev. Mus. Arqueol. Antropol. Hist. Revista del Museo de Arqueología, Antropología e Historia. Univ. Nacional de Trujillo, Museo de Arqueología. Trujillo, Peru.

Rev. Mus. Arqueol. Etnol. Revista do Museu de Arqueologia e Etnologia. Univ. de São Paulo.

Rev. Mus. Hist. Nat. San Rafael. Revista del Museo de Historia Natural de San Rafael. Mendoza, Argentina.

Rev. Mus. Nac. Etnogr. Folk. Revista del Museo Nacional de Etnografía y Folklore. MUSEF Editores. La Paz.

Rev. Rev. Interam. Revista/Review Interamericana. Inter-American Univ. Press. Hato Rey, Puerto Rico.

Rev. Univ. Nac. Río Cuarto. Revista de la Universidad Nacional de Río Cuarto. Río Cuarto, Argentina.

Rev. Univ. Val. Guatem. Revista de la Universidad del Valle de Guatemala. Univ. del Valle de Guatemala. Guatemala.

Rev. USP. Revista USP. Coordenadoria de Comunicação Social (CCS), Univ. de São Paulo.

Runa/Buenos Aires. Runa. Archivo para las Ciencias del Hombre; Univ. de Buenos Aires, Facultad de Filosofía y Letras, Instituto de Antropología.

Saguntum/Valencia. Saguntum: Papeles del Laboratorio de Arqueología de Valencia. Univ. de València, Facultat de Geografia i Història, Depto. de Prehistòria i Arqueologia. Valencia, Spain.

Sarance/Otavalo. Sarance. Instituto Otavaleño de Antropología. Otavalo, Ecuador.

Schweiz. Amer. Ges. Schweizerische Amerikanisten Gesellschaft. Société suisse des américanistes. Genève.

Science/Washington. Science. American Assn. for the Advancement of Science. Washington.

Soc. Econ. Stud. Social and Economic Studies. Univ. of the West Indies, Institute of Social and Economic Research. Mona, Jamaica.

SWI Forum. SWI Forum voor Kunst, Kultuur en Wetenschop. De Stichting. Paramaribo, Suriname.

Tareas/Panamá. Tareas. Centro de Estudios Latinoamericanos (CELA). Panamá.

Vínculos/San José. Vínculos. Museo Nacional de Costa Rica. San José.

Wampum/Leiden. Wampum. Archeologisch Centrum. Leiden, The Netherlands.

World Archaeol. World Archaeology. Routledge & Kegan Paul. London.

Z. Ethnol. Zeitschrift für Ethnologie. Deutschen Gesellschaft für Völkerkunde. Verlag Albert Limbach. Braunschweig, Germany.

21st Century Policy Rev. 21st Century Policy Review. I.A.A.S. Publishers. Langley Park, Md.

ECONOMICS

GENERAL

JAMES W. FOLEY, *Associate Dean, School of Business Administration, University of Miami, Coral Gables*

A REVIEW OF THE LITERATURE issued this biennium reveals a striking shift in focus among scholars of Latin American economics. Topics at the forefront as recently as Vol. 55 of the *Handbook*, particularly 1) the causes of the debt crisis and appropriate policy responses, 2) agrarian reform, and 3) radical solutions to the region's problems, have ceded primacy to a different set of research concerns. Questions dominating the current literature include the impact of market reforms on income distribution and poverty, regional integration and regional labor markets, and privatization.

The quantitative decline in literature regarding the debt crisis is likely due to the two decades that have elapsed since this issue first emerged; scholars have simply exhausted the subject. Instead, economists are focusing on the impact of existing reform policies on the economies of the region. Those with an abiding interest in the debt crisis, however, will benefit from William R. Cline's volume, *International Debt Reexamined* (item **1283**).

The relationship between the role of the State and economic policy helps to explain the paucity of literature on agrarian reform. Market liberalization programs, currently in place in almost all nations of the region, call for a smaller, less intrusive role for the government, while agrarian reform generally requires a more activist role for the State. Nevertheless, agrarian specialists will find useful a work by William C. Thiesenhusen evaluating the successes and failures of agrarian reform efforts in various countries of the region (item **1471**).

Finally, the relative lack of radical tracts is perhaps best explained by the fall of communism in Eastern Europe, and the ascendency of free-market policies in both developed and underdeveloped areas of the world.

Highly welcome among the current list of new works are studies examining income distribution and poverty. Twenty years ago, data on income distribution was sparse and of questionable validity. Undoubtedly, market liberalization and its impact on income distribution has sparked the intellectual fires of Latin American specialists, and as a result, there has occurred a quantum leap in the quantity and quality of literature on this subject. Indeed, it is difficult to choose among the many fine works on this topic. Of particular interest is a work by Samuel A. Morely (item **1402**), and volumes edited by Victor Bulmer-Thomas (item **1408**), Nora Lustig (item **1288**), Herman Sautter (item **1349**), and George Psacharopoulos (item **1424**). Also valuable are articles by Werner Baer and William Maloney (item **1251**), Albert Berry (item **1261**), and William Glade (item **1330**). A multidisciplinary volume edited by William C. Smith, Carlos H. Acuna and Eduardo A. Gamarra that analyzes the impact of market reforms on democracy and political systems is also noteworthy (item **1373**).

Not surprisingly, privatization continues as an area of interest for regional specialists. However, whereas earlier work studied the financing and implementation of privatization, most recent literature has considered its impact on economic efficiency. Particularly noteworthy are books edited by William Glade (item **1264**) and Werner Baer and Melissa H. Birch (item **1252**), and an article by David Felix (item **1318**). Two econometric exercises by Frank Sader quantifying the impact of privatization on foreign investment (item **1441**), and Armando Castelar Pinheiro and Ben Ross Schneider's work on government fiscal impact of privatization in four Latin American countries (item **1420**) also deserve mention. Other exceptional works on this general area include articles by Jose L. Carvalho on the role of property rights in the achievement of economic growth and efficiency (item **1280**), and by Paul Holden and Sareth Rajapatirana on the necessary economic factors and institutions for a successful private sector (item **1346**).

As stated in the previous volume, the formation of Mercosur and NAFTA, as well as the potential creation of WHFTA (Western Hemisphere Free Trade Area), have contributed to a renewed interest in regional integration. Particularly interesting are the volumes edited by Weine Karlsson and Akhil Malaki (item **1352**) and Elsie L. Echerri-Carrol (item **1406**). A useful article by Jeffrey Frankel, Ernesto Stein, and Shang-jin Wei uses econometric techniques to analyze the welfare and efficiency effects of preferential trade agreements (item **1324**).

Literature pertaining to Latin American labor markets has become highly specialized in recent years, with the role of women and the informal sector receiving varying degrees of attention. Particularly provocative works are those by UNIFEM on the feminization of poverty (item **1291**); Irma Arriagada's article regarding the changing nature of urban female labor markets (item **1248**); and Alexandria Cox Edwards and Judith Roberts' work on the macroeconomic determinants of female labor participation rates (item **1307**). Studies on the informal sector, once a major focus of labor market analysis, are rare. Scholars continue to argue about the appropriate definition of this admittedly elusive concept frequently rehashing previously discussed issues. However, exceptions exist. Edward Funkhouser's article analyzes employment patterns and wage structures in the informal sector (item **1739**). Douglas Marcouiller, Verónica Ruiz de Castilla, and Christopher Woodruff use econometric techniques to determine informal sector-formal sector wage differentials (item **1386**).

Finally, a few comments about miscellaneous works. Victor Bulmer-Thomas' major contribution, *The economic history of Latin America since independence*, uses modern analytical techniques to describe the economic history of the region from the early 1800s to the early 1900s (item **1269**). Robert E. Grosse has written a highly competent work on foreign exchange black markets, a subject which until now has not been studied with any great depth (item **1338**). Suitable for use in a course dealing with Latin American economic issues is a volume edited by James L. Dietz, *Latin America's economic development* (item **1375**). Fabian Echegaray wrote an intriguing article in which econometric techniques are used to analyze the determinants of Latin American presidential elections (items **1304** and **1304**). Finally, the growing concern with environmental issues among scholars is particularly noteworthy. Of interest is John O. Browder's review essay that examines the environmental impact of regional deforestation (item **2389**).

1233 La academia va al mercado: relaciones de científicos académicos con clientes externos. Recopilación de Hebe M.C. Vessuri. Caracas: Fondo Editorial FINTEC; Monte Avila Editores Latinoamericana, 1995. 378 p.: bibl., ill.

Collection of essays examines relationship between academic sector, business, and government in Venezuela and Brazil. Focuses on sociological, institutional, and ethical aspects of technological transfer between these entities.

1234 Administración de reservas internacionales en la banca central. México: Centro de Estudios Monetarios Latinoamericanos, 1994. 151 p.: bibl., ill. (Reuniones y seminarios)

Reviews theoretical background and highlights some major developments in management of central bank reserves over the last five years. Draws primarily from the experience and contracts of the Bank for International Settlements. [R. Looney]

1235 Agosin, Manuel R. A tale of two regions: investment in Latin America and East Asia. (*Estud. Econ./Santiago*, 22:1, junio 1995, p. 45–71, bibl., tables)

Uses an econometric model to analyze reasons that East Asian investment rates are higher than in Latin American rates. Concludes that Latin America's poorer performance is due to 1) the impact of the debt crisis, 2) domestic credit constraints, and 3) the region's slower economic growth.

1236 Agosin, Manuel R. and **Ricardo Ffrench-Davis.** Trade liberalization and growth: recent experience in Latin America. (*J. Interam. Stud. World Aff.*, 37:3, Fall 1995, p. 9–58, bibl., tables)

Examines "radical" change in trade policies implemented by Latin American countries during 1990s. Discusses current and likely future results of these programs. Draws applicable lessons export-oriented economies in Asia and puts forth policy recommendation designed to ensure that trade liberalization will result in long-term economic growth.

1237 Aguinis, Ana María Meirovich de. Empresas e inversiones en el Mercosur: sociedades y joint ventures; establecimiento de sucursal y filial; inversiones extranjeras; impuestos. Buenos Aires: Abeledo-Perrot, 1992. 572 p.: bibl.

Compares legal procedures necessary to form a business in each of the four Mercosur countries. Informative and practical, volume benefits from a consistent conceptual focus. Useful comparisons to European Union rules and offers suggestions for harmonization. [M. Birch]

1238 Aitken, Brian; Ann Harrison; and **Robert E. Lipsey.** Wages and foreign ownership: a comparative study of Mexico, Venezuela, and the United States. (*J. Int. Econ.*, 40:3/4, May 1996, p. 345–371)

Examines whether high levels of direct foreign investment are correlated with higher wages. Empirically confirms this hypothesis. In Mexico and Venezuela, higher wages are paid only by foreign-owned firms, whereas in the US higher wages in one company will lead to spillover effect causing generally higher wages throughout an industry.

1239 Ajustes, políticas sociales y fondos de inversión en América Latina. San José: Asociación Latinoamericana de Organismos de Promoción, 1994. 143 p.

Examines social policies and quality of life in Latin America, historically and at present. Specific cases are cited for Chile, Colombia, Costa Rica, and Peru. Also examines role of NGOs in decreasing poverty and improving quality of life.

1240 Alameda Ospina, Raúl. Las políticas macroeconómicas en América Latina: mercantilismo, librecambio, proteccionismo, apertura. Bogotá: Ecoe Editores, 1994. 87 p.: bibl. (Textos universitarios)

Short, readable history of Latin American macroeconomic policies from mercantilism to liberalization. Emphasizes trade policies.

1241 Altimir, Oscar. Economic development and social equity: a Latin American perspective. (*J. Interam. Stud. World Aff.*, 38:2/3, Summer/Fall 1996, p. 47–71, bibl., graph, tables)

Analyzes income distribution changes during 1970s, particularly from 1980–93, in Argentina, Brazil, Chile, Colombia, Costa Rica, Mexico, Peru, Uruguay, and Venezuela. Focus is on improving income distribution.

1242 Altimir, Oscar. Income distribution and poverty through crisis and adjustment. (*CEPAL Rev.*, 52, April 1994, p. 7–31, bibl., tables)

Examines impact of 1980s stabilization programs on income distribution and poverty in Argentina, Brazil, Chile, Colombia, Costa Rica, Mexico, Panama, Peru, Uruguay, and Venezuela. Based on current policies, author concludes that future income distribution may become even more unequal.

1243 Análisis de coyuntura económica: métodos aplicados en América Latina. Coordinación de Eduardo Lora y Joaquín Vial. Bogotá: FEDESARROLLO; CIEPLAN; TM Editores, 1995. 335 p.: bibl. (Académica; Económica)

Empirical macroeconomic analysis of various aspects of economic performance for 11 largest Latin American countries. Includes articles on balance of payments, labor markets, monetary and fiscal policy, and inflation.

1244 Los Andes en cifras. Quito: FLACSO, Sede Ecuador; IICA, Oficina Ecuador, 1994. 226 p.: bibl., ill. (Serie Publicaciones misceláneos, 0534–5391; A3/EC-94–01. Serie Colecciones y documentos. Economía)

Comparative statistics from Bolivia, Colombia, Ecuador, Peru, and Venezuela. Most cover the period 1970–90. Principally socioeconomic data, but includes information on the military and environment. [D. Schodt]

1245 Antecedentes estadísticos de la distribución del ingreso en los años ochenta. v. 1, Argentina, Bolivia y Brasil. Santiago: Comisión Económica para América Latina y el Caribe, 1993. 1 v. (Serie Distribución del ingreso ; 10–17)

Collection of recent statistical data on income distribution in Argentina, Bolivia, and Brazil is based on household surveys. Includes information for principal urban areas.

1246 Arditi, Nessim. Europa y América Latina: un vínculo de cooperación para el desarrollo. Madrid: Instituto Latinoamericano y del Caribe de Planificación Economica y Social; Centro de Comunicación, Investigación y Documentación entre Europa, España y América Latina, 1994. 103 p.: bibl., tables.

Overview of European development aid to Latin American countries provides analysis of objectives, priorities, and aid mechanisms, organized by donor country. Describes aid agreements currently in place and allocation of aid among countries, geographic regions, economic sectors, and institutions. Many statistical charts.

1247 Arnove, Robert F. et al. A political sociology of education and development in Latin America: the conditioned State, neoliberalism, and educational policy. (*Int. J. Comp. Sociol.*, 37 : 1/2, June 1996, p. 140–158, bibl., tables)

Focuses primarily on ways in which structural adjustment policies of various international agencies (World Bank, IMF, USAID) have affected government financing of, and policies for the provision of, education.

1248 Arriagada, Irma. Changes in the urban female labour market. (*CEPAL Rev.*, 53, Aug. 1995, p. 91–110, bibl., tables)

Uses 1980 and 1990 household surveys for 13 Latin American countries to describe and analyze the changing structure and nature of female urban labor markets during 1980s. Sets forth policy recommendations to improve the welfare of female workers and increase their productivity.

1249 Asociación Latinoamericana de Integración (Montevideo). Estructura y evolución del comercio regional, 1985–1991. Montevideo: ALADI, 1992. 123 p.: bibl., col. ill.

Compilation of trade statistics for the 11 member countries of the Asociación Latinoamericana de Integración (ALADI) for 1985–91. Includes statistics on imports and exports, classified by product groups and trading partners.

1250 Baer, Werner and Kent Hargis. Forms of external capital and economic development in Latin America, 1820–1997. (*World Dev.*, 25 : 11, Nov. 1997, p. 1805–1820)

Describes the changing nature, structure, and characteristics of capital inflows from 1820–1997. Discusses advantages and disadvantages of differing types (portfolio, equity, etc.). A must read for economic historians of the region.

1251 Baer, Werner and William F. Maloney. Neoliberalism and income distribution in Latin America. (*World Dev.*, 25 : 3, March 1997, p. 311–327, tables)

Examines regressiveness of recently implemented neoliberal policies. Emphasizes empirical difficulty of measuring their impact. Concludes that worsening of region's income distribution may not be due to neoliberal policies per se, but rather to the stabilization policies that accompanied them.

1252 Baer, Werner. Privatization in Latin America. (*World Econ.*, 17:4, July 1994, p. 509–529)

Explores privatization process in Argentina, Brazil, Chile, and Mexico. Raises questions about the ultimate impact on income distribution and economic efficiency. Concludes that outcome is by no means certain.

1253 Bagella, Michele. Integrazione finanziaria, movimento dei capitali e debito estero: lezioni dall'America Latina. (*Econ. Int./Genova*, 49:3, agosto 1996, p. 347–372, appendix, bibl., graphs, tables)

To ensure stability in international financial markets, author proposes that the IMF establish a "special fund" to help countries with balance of payments problems when such problems are *not* the result of internal economic policies.

1254 Bekerman, Marta and **Pablo Sirlin.** Trade policy and international linkages: a Latin American perspective. (*CEPAL Rev.*, 55, April 1995, p. 65–79, appendix, bibl.)

Analyzes ways in which government intervention can be used to increase Latin America's international economic linkages. Analysis is based on a review of theoretical literature on the subject, as well as on successful examples from specific countries.

1255 Bellod Redondo, José Francisco. Ahorro e inversión en el largo plazo: el caso de la América Latina. (*Trimest. Econ.*, 63:251, julio/sept. 1996, p. 1113–1137, bibl., tables)

Highly technical econometric analysis of the long-term saving/investment relationship in Latin America. Examines 1960–90. Of special interest to growth theorists.

1256 Benevente, José Miguel *et al.* Changes in the industrial development of Latin America. (*CEPAL Rev.*, 60, Dec. 1996, p. 133–156)

Analyzes how liberalization has affected region's industrial structure. Notes decrease in industry relative to GDP. Describes

changing role of transnational corporations, domestically-owned conglomerates, small and medium-sized firms, etc. Discusses productivity gap between Latin American industry and that of other parts of the world.

1257 Bernal-Meza, Raúl. América Latina en la economía política mundial. Buenos Aires: Grupo Editor Latinoamericano; Emecé Editores, 1994. 305 p.: bibl. (Col. Estudios internacionales)

Discusses Latin America's current and potential role in the world economy. Analyzes feasibility of implementing various strategies to increase region's importance in world trade and the global order.

1258 Berríos, Rubén. Economic transition in Poland: the relevance of the Latin American experience. (*Rev. Econ. Polít.*, 15:4, oct./dez. 1995, p. 112–133, bibl., tables)

Since the fall of the Soviet Union, Poland has implemented reforms similar to those enacted in Latin America: market and trade liberalization, stabilization, and privatization. Reviews outcomes of these reforms and outlines lessons that Poland could have learned from the Latin American experience.

1259 Berry, Albert. The challenge of decimating poverty in Latin America by 2010. (*Front. Norte*, 6, número especial, 1994, p. 101–119, tables)

Analyzes impact of structural adjustment on income distribution in seven Latin American countries. Notes that worsening of income distribution occurred in countries pursuing open trade policies with devaluation, whereas countries that adopted gradual trade reform have seen an improvement in income distribution.

1260 Berry, Albert. El contexto macroeconómico de las políticas, proyectos y programas para promover el desarrollo social y combatir la probreza en América Latina y el Caribe. Quito: Corporación de Estudios para el Desarrollo; New York: United Nations Development Programme, 1997. 47 p.: bibl., tables. (Apunte técnico; 32)

Discusses impact of region's macroeconomic policies on social development and poverty reduction.

1261 Berry, Albert. The income distribution threat in Latin America. (*LARR*, 32:2, 1997, p. 3–40)

Analyzes causes of "worsening" distribution of income in Argentina, Chile, Colombia, Costa Rica, Dominican Republic, Ecuador, Mexico, and Uruguay. Concludes that economic policy reforms are the primary culprit.

1262 Bielschowsky, Ricardo. The Taiwanese experience with small and medium-sized enterprises (SMEs): possible lessons for Latin America and the Caribbean. Santiago: Comisión Económica para América Latina y el Caribe, 1995. 44 p.: bibl., tables. (Serie Desarrollo productivo; 28)

Describes Taiwan's success with small and medium-sized enterprises (SMEs). Explains factors (government policies, cultural, institutions) responsible for this success, and draws conclusions regarding their utility in Latin America.

1263 Bielschowsky, Ricardo and **Giovanni Stumpo.** Transnational corporations and structural changes in industry in Argentina, Brazil, Chile and Mexico. (*CEPAL Rev.*, 55, April 1995, p. 143–169, bibl., tables)

Focuses on changes in the manufacturing sector since 1973 in Chile, 1978 in Argentina, 1981 in Brazil, and 1982 in Mexico. Found significant differences in structure and impact, which were attributable to differences in macroeconomic policy and in structural and institutional characteristics.

1264 Bigger economies, smaller governments: privatization in Latin America. Edited by William P. Glade with Rossana Corona. Boulder, Colo.: Westview Press, 1996. 407 p.: bibl., ill.

Provides empirical analysis of impact of privatization on fiscal sector, capital flows, technology, business efficiency, banking, and national savings. Includes articles on Argentina, Chile, and Mexico. A timely and important work.

Birle, Peter *et al.* Dos estudios sobre los empresarios y la integración regional. See item **2221.**

1265 Boltvinik, Julio. Poverty in Latin America: a critical analysis of three studies. (*Int. Soc. Sci. J.*, 48:148, June 1996, p. 245–260, bibl., photo, tables)

Interesting critical evaluation of methodology used in three studies to measure regional poverty. Studies were prepared by

ECLAC, the World Bank, and the UNDP Regional Project for Overcoming Poverty.

1266 Bradford, Colin I. The new paradigm of systemic competitiveness: toward more integrated policies in Latin America. Paris: Organisation for Economic Co-operation and Development, 1994. 269 p.: bibl., ill.

A "new paradigm" for growth that attempts to integrate sectoral analysis, trade, and macroeconomic and microeconomic theory. Goal is to develop most of policies to supportive of technological innovation, which authors believe is crucial for international competitiveness and growth.

1267 Browder, John O. Deforestation and the environmental crisis in Latin America. (*LARR*, 30:3, 1995, p. 123–137, bibl.)

Review essay assesses six books that examine reasons for regional deforestation and the resulting environmental impact. For geographer's comment, see item **2389.**

1268 Bulmer-Thomas, Victor and **Pablo Rodas-Martini.** Databases for large Latin American companies. (*LARR*, 31:3, 1996, p. 151–159)

Describes strengths and weaknesses of a new database (ECONOMATICA, in São Paulo) for over 700 companies in Argentina, Brazil, Chile, Mexico, and Peru.

1269 Bulmer-Thomas, Victor. The economic history of Latin America since independence. Cambridge, England; New York: Cambridge Univ. Press, 1994. 485 p.: bibl., ill., index, maps. (Cambridge Latin American studies; 77)

Uses modern analytical techniques to describe Latin American economic history from early 1800s–early 1990s. Highly empirical work. Includes a superb bibliography. A major contribution. For historian's comment see *HLAS 56:1052.*

1270 Burki, Shahid Javed and **Sebastian Edwards.** Consolidating economic reforms in Latin America and the Caribbean. (*Financ. Dev.*, 32:1, March 1995, p. 6–9, tables)

Authors propose policies for accelerating economic growth and reduced poverty. Growth policies include increasing savings rates, improving export competitiveness, and infrastructure investment. Poverty reduction policy includes more educational programs and a decrease in payroll taxes to stimulate job growth and enhance international competitiveness.

1271 Burki, Shahid Javed and **Sebastian Edwards.** Dismantling the populist State: the unfinished revolution in Latin America and the Caribbean. Washington: World Bank, 1996. 38 p.: bibl. (World Bank Latin American and Caribbean studies. Viewpoints)

Well-written paper discusses institutional reforms needed for dismantling the populist State. Contends that such reforms, no matter how painful, must be made immediately to consolidate gains from earlier reforms.

1272 Burki, Shahid Javed and **Sebastian Edwards.** Latin America after Mexico: quickening the pace. Washington: World Bank, 1996. 32 p.: bibl., ill. (World Bank Latin American and Caribbean studies)

Analyzes Mexico's Dec. 1994 currency devaluation and impact of resulting crisis on other countries in the region. Contends that crisis acted as a "wake-up call," prompting many countries to implement policy reforms.

1273 Burki, Shahid Javed and **Guillermo E. Perry.** The long march: a reform agenda for Latin America and the Caribbean in the next decade. Washington: World Bank, 1997. 115 p.: bibl., ill. (World Bank Latin American and Caribbean studies)

Detailed discussion of reforms necessary to accelerate economic growth and reduce poverty in the region. Reforms include equity market development, civil service reform, in health and education investment, labor market liberalization, and greater trade openness.

1274 Bustelo, Pablo. La industrialización en América Latina y Asia Oriental: un estudio comparado de Brasil y Taiwán. Madrid: Editorial Complutense, 1994. 203 p.: bibl.

Compares historical industrialization process in Latin American and East Asian countries. Specifically, compares cases of Brazil and Taiwan for the period 1890–1980.

1275 Bustos, Raúl. Reforma a los sistemas de pensiones: peligros de los programas opcionales en América Latina. (*Estud. Públicos*, 58, otoño 1995, p. 319–335, graphs, table)

Analyzes pension system reforms mod-

eled after the Chilean system which were implemented in Argentina, Colombia, and Peru.

1276 Calvo, Guillermo A.; Carmen M. Reinhart; and **Carlos A. Vegh.** Targeting the real exchange rate: theory and evidence. (*J. Dev. Econ.*, 47:1, June 1995, p. 97–133)

Mathematical model that predicts that undervalued real exchange rates are correlated with high rates of inflation. Empirical tests for Brazil, Chile, and Colombia support this contention.

1277 Campodónico, Humberto. Ajuste estructural, pobreza y participación popular. (*Ecuad. Deb.*, 37, abril 1996, p. 104–130, tables)

Highly critical analysis of the adverse distributional and social effects of orthodox and neoliberal reforms implemented by Latin American governments since the 1980s.

Carmona, Fernando. Una alternativa al neoliberalismo: México y Latinoamérica 94. See item **4572.**

1278 Cartas, José María. Institucionalización de la economía de mercado en América Latina. (*Contribuciones/Buenos Aires*, 12:4, oct./dic. 1995, p. 193–206, bibl.)

Contends that neoliberal policies will be successful only if governments strengthen civil rights and promote economic integration of marginalized social groups. Discusses necessary institutional changes.

1279 Carter, Michael R.; Bradford L. Barham; and **Dina Mesbah.** Agricultural export booms and the rural poor in Chile, Guatemala, and Paraguay. (*LARR*, 31:1, 1996, p. 33–65, appendix, bibl., graph, tables)

Analyzes impact of agricultural export booms on overall economic growth and income distribution. Uses examples of Chilean orchard fruit, Guatemalan vegetables, and Paraguayan grain to conclude that distributional incomes vary, i.e., the rural poor may either be helped or hurt depending on the specific export crop.

1280 Carvalho, José L. Private sector development and property rights in Latin America. (*Rev. Bras. Econ.*, 50:3, julho/set. 1996, p. 351–377, bibl.)

Highly sophisticated study discusses role of private property rights in Latin America as they affect economic development and economic efficiency. Uses Chile and Peru as examples. Excellent.

1281 Centro de Estudios Monetarios Latino-americanos (Mexico). Reformas y re-estructuración de los sistemas financieros en los países de América Latina. México: Centro de Estudios Monetarios Latinoamericanos, 1994. 153 p.: bibl. (Reuniones y seminarios)

Studies financial reforms in the region and devotes special attention to the changing role and function of central banks and the financial system. Detailed examination of this process in Chile, Mexico, and Peru.

1282 Cintra, Marcos Antonio Macedo. Financial repression and the Latin American finance pattern. (*CEPAL Rev.*, 53, Aug. 1995, p. 31–47, bibl.)

Technical critique of the theory of financial repression, a term which refers to financial markets rendered inefficient by institutional and policy obstacles. Contends that simply deregulating markets will not guarantee growth, and that State intervention in financial markets is necessary for industrial growth.

1283 Cline, William R. International debt reexamined. Washington: Institute for International Economics, 1994. 535 p.: bibl., ill., index. (Policy analyses in international economics; 40)

Impressive study includes an historical review of causes of 1980s crisis, the various policy responses, and resulting impact. Extensive survey of debt crisis literature. Draws lessons from the past to be used for future policy formulation. Likely to be the definitive study on international debt. For international relations specialist's comment see *HLAS* 55:3795.

1284 Colclough, Christopher. Education and the market: which parts of the neoliberal solution are correct? (*World Dev.*, 24:4, April 1996, p. 589–610)

Examines neoliberal position that eduction in developing countries should be financed privately, rather than by the government. Using data from 63 countries, 22 in Latin America, concludes that such a policy would be inefficient and inequitable.

1285 Collins, Susan M. On becoming more flexible: exchange rate regimes in Latin America and the Caribbean. (*J. Dev. Econ.*, 51:1, Oct. 1996, p. 117–138)

Describes experiences of 24 Latin American countries as they changed from fixed to flexible exchange rate regimes between 1978–92.

1286 Cominetti, Rossella. El gasto social en América Latina: un examen cuantitativo y cualitativo. Santiago: Comisión Económica para América Latina y el Caribe, 1994. 167 p.: ill. (Cuadernos de la CEPAL: 0252–2195; 73)

Quantitative description of social government expenditures focuses on education, health, welfare, housing, and social security spending in 12 Latin American countries from 1980–93. Emphasizes efficiency, fiscal impact, and redistributive effects of spending policies.

1287 Cooperation or rivalry?: regional integration in the Americas and the Pacific Rim. Edited by Shōji Nishijima and Peter H. Smith. Boulder, Colo.: Westview Press, 1996. 302 p.: bibl., index. (Latin America in global perspective)

Articles study impact of inter-American economic integration on Pacific Rim countries. Examine NAFTA as well as potential effect of the yet-to-be-established Western Hemisphere Free Trade Area (WHFTA). For political scientist's comment see item **3994.**

1288 Coping with austerity: poverty and inequality in Latin America. Edited by Nora Lustig. Washington: Brookings Institution, 1995. 460 p.: bibl., index, tables.

Series of well-written articles examines regional poverty and income distribution. Includes separate articles on Argentina, Brazil, Chile, Mexico, Peru, and Venezuela, as well as over 150 tables. Valuable contribution.

1289 Correa, Carlos M. Strategies for software exports from developing countries. (*World Dev.*, 24:1, Jan. 1996, p. 171–182)

Comparative study focuses on three Latin American countries (Argentina, Brazil, and Chile) and on Asian countries that have successfully developed export-software industries. Discusses problems the countries faced and strategies that firms and governments used to overcome them.

1290 Cortés, Fernando. The metamorphosis of the marginal: the debate over the informal sector in Latin America. (*Curr. Sociol.*, 45:1, Jan. 1997, p. 71–90)

Theoretical paper examines definitional, methodological, and theoretical issues associated with research and analysis of the informal sector. Laments the heterogeneity of the various meanings given to the term, *informal sector.*

1291 Cuánto cuesta la pobreza de las mujeres?: una perspectiva de América Latina y el Caribe = The human cost of women's poverty: perspectives from Latin America and the Caribbean. México: UNIFEM, 1995. 161 p.: bibl., ill., index.

Series of articles examines feminization of poverty in the region. Includes case studies for Brazil, Mexico, Barbados, and the Caribbean. Contains policy recommendations for alleviating poverty among women. Required reading for the specialist in women's studies.

1292 Damill, Mario; José María Fanelli; and Roberto Frenkel. De México a México: el desempeño de América Latina en los noventa. (*Desarro. Econ.*, 36, no. especial, verano 1996, p. 51–85, bibl., tables)

Discusses three types of macroeconomic policies adopted by Latin American countries using Argentina and Mexico; Chile and Colombia; and Brazil as examples. Also analyzes impact on these countries by the Mexican crisis of Dec. 1994.

1293 De Geyndt, Willy. Social development and absolute poverty in Asia and Latin America. Washington: World Bank, 1996. 54 p.: bibl. (World Bank technical paper: 0253-7494; 328)

Using econometric techniques analyzes causes of widespread poverty in Latin America and the 10 largest East and South Asian countries. Concludes that slow economic growth is not the only explanatory variable, and cites importance of schools and health care.

1294 Desarrollo de productos de raíces y tubérculos: América Latina. Lima: Centro Internacional de la Papa, 1992 375 p.: appendices, bibl., graphs, tables. (Product development for root and tuber crops; 2)

Examines current and potential uses of root and tuber crops in Latin America with primary emphasis on various potential commercial uses (e.g., flour, mixes, animal feed, etc.). Individual papers discuss research underway in Colombia, Costa, Rica, Cuba,

Ecuador, Guatemala, Mexico, Panama, and Peru.

1295 La descentralización fiscal en América Latina: problemas y perspectivas. Edición de Ricardo López Murphy. Buenos Aires: Fundación de Investigaciones Económicas Latinoamericanas; Washington: Banco Interamericano de Desarrollo, 1995. 333 p.: bibl., ill.

Describes fiscal decentralization experience of Argentina, Chile, Colombia, and Peru. Examines regulation, information collection, transfer mechanisms, technical assistance, regional development, and income distribution.

1296 La deuda pública en América Latina en perspectiva histórica = The public debt in Latin America in historical perspective. Edición de Reinhard Liehr. Frankfurt: Vervuert; Madrid: Iberoamericana, 1995. 527 p.: bibl., ill., index. (Bibliotheca Ibero-Americana; 58)

Includes 14 papers on evolution of Latin American public debt from independence to 1930s with an emphasis on foreign debt. Discusses Argentina, Brazil, Chile, Mexico, Peru, and Venezuela, focusing primarily on period before World War I.

1297 Devereux, John and Michael Connolly. Commercial policy, the terms of trade, and the real exchange rate revisited. (*J. Dev. Econ.*, 50:1, June 1996, p. 81–99)

Uses econometric techniques to analyze how commercial policy and changes in the external terms of trade impact real exchange rates in Argentina, Colombia, Ecuador, and Venezuela.

1298 Devlin, Robert and Ricardo Ffrench-Davis. The great Latin America debt crisis: a decade of asymmetric adjustment. (*Rev. Econ. Polít.*, 15:3, julho/set. 1995, p. 117–142, bibl., tables)

Notes that abundance of capital inflows in 1990s is similar to pattern that occurred in 1970s leading ultimately to 1980s debt crisis. Draws lessons from 1970s and suggests policies for prevention of another debt crisis.

1299 Di Filippo, Armando. Transnationalization and integration of production in Latin America. (*CEPAL Rev.*, 57, Dec. 1995, p. 133–149, bibl., tables)

Discusses role of transnational corporations in producing goods (machinery and equipment, metal and chemical products) that account for the preponderance of regional intra-industry trade. Provides brief case studies for Argentina, Brazil, Chile, Colombia, and Venezuela.

1300 Díaz Fuentes, Daniel. Crisis y cambios estructurales en América Latina: Argentina, Brasil y México durante el periodo de entreguerras. México: Fondo de Cultura Económica, 1994. 425 p.: bibl., ill. (Economía latinoamericana)

Describes structural changes that occurred in Argentina, Brazil, and Mexico from 1920–40. Excellent source of historical data.

1301 Dirven, Martine. Youth expectations and rural development. (*CEPAL Rev.*, 55, April 1995, p. 127–141, bibl., tables)

Analyzes causes of migration of youth from rural/agricultural areas. Notes that only half of the people born in rural areas during the 1960s still reside there. Discusses implications for economic growth and the rural sector.

1302 Dourojeanni, Axel. Water management and river basins in Latin America. (*CEPAL Rev.*, 53, Aug. 1995, p. 111–128, bibl.)

Examines feasibility of establishing management boards to ensure environmentally appropriate water management policies. Sets forth policy recommendations to achieve these goals.

1303 Durand, Francisco. Incertidumbre y soledad: reflexiones sobre los grandes empresarios de América Latina. Lima: Friedrich Ebert, 1996. 222 p.: bibl., ill.

Durand examines the complex relations between Latin American economic groups and the market, the State, and the society. Demonstrates that governmental efforts to control powerful economic groups ("financial oligarchs") have historically only resulted in further strengthening those very groups. [C. Rabinovich]

1304 Echegaray, Fabián. ¿Voto económico o referendum político?: los determinantes de las elecciones presidenciales en América Latina, 1982–1994. (*Desarro. Econ.*, 36:142, julio/sept. 1996, p. 603–619, bibl., graphs, tables)

Interesting econometric analysis of the determinants of Latin American presidential elections. Uses data from 30 elections to conclude that inflation, GDP growth rates, and unemployment levels have no statistically significant impact. Instead, the "approval rating" of the president is the critical variable in determining outcome.

1305 Economic and Social Progress in Latin America. 1994. Fiscal decentralization: the search for equity and efficiency. Washington: Inter-American Development Bank.

Reviews economic policy and performance for each Latin American country during 1993. Includes a special section on fiscal decentralization, with case studies for Argentina, Chile, Colombia, and Peru. Appendix contains 75 tables containing useful data from each country.

1306 Economic and Social Progress in Latin America. 1995. Overcoming volatility. Washington: Inter-American Development Bank; Baltimore, Md.: Johns Hopkins Univ. Press, 1995.

Comprehensive overview of economic and social conditions in Latin America. Includes individual country profiles and extensive analysis of factors causing region's economic volatility and of policies that could reduce such volatility. Excellent source of data.

1307 Edwards, Alejandra Cox and **Judith Roberts.** Macroeconomic influences on female labor force participation: the Latin American evidence. (*Estud. Econ./Santiago*, 20:1, junio 1993, p. 87–106, bibl., tables)

Analyzes impact of macroeconomic conditions on female labor markets. Reviews literature on women's labor force participation. Finds that in low income countries, as economic conditions worsen, participation rates for women increase and are higher than in normal economic times.

1308 Edwards, Sebastian. Why are Latin America's savings rates so low?: an international comparative analysis. (*J. Dev. Econ.*, 51:1, Oct. 1996, p. 5–44)

Econometric analysis of determinants of savings rates concludes that growth rate of per capita income is primary determinant of public and private savings. Also concludes that political instability causes lower savings rates and that public savings crowd out private savings.

Los empresarios ante la globalización. See item **4587.**

1309 The environmental dimension in development planning. v. 1. Santiago: Comisión Económica para América Latina y el Caribe, 1990- . 1 v: bibl., ill.

Series of essays examines problems and issues involved in facturing environmental concerns into development plans. Finds that in most Latin American countries development planners virtually ignore environmental issues.

1310 La equidad en el panorama social de América Latina durante los años ochenta. Santiago: Comisión Económica para América Latina y el Caribe, 1991. 148 p.: bibl.

Discusses the unequal access to economic and employment opportunities for different age groups during 1980s. Statistics on employment, income distribution, and poverty.

Estrategias de desarrollo: intentando cambiar la vida. See item **4542.**

1311 Europe and Latin America in the world economy. Edited by Susan Kaufman Purcell and Françoise Simon. Foreword by Gonzalo de Las Heras. Boulder, Colo.: Lynne Rienner Publishers, 1994. 215 p.: bibl., ill., index.

Series of articles on changing nature of economic relations between Latin America and Europe includes separate chapters on region's economic interation with 1) Germany, 2) Eastern Europe, 3) Spain, and 4) Europe in general. Also includes chapter on impact of Latin American and European integration. For political scientist's comment see item **4004.**

1312 Fairlie Reinoso, Alan. América Latina: nuevos retos, viejos problemas. (*Probl. Desarro.*, 25:99, oct./dic. 1994, p. 77–102)

Critical analysis of neoliberal economic policies. Presents alternatives that aim to reconcile growth, stability, and fairness.

1313 Familia y futuro: un programa regional en América Latina y el Caribe. Santiago: Comisión Económica para América Latina y el Caribe, 1994. 137 p.: bibl.

Examines the family in Latin America with discussions with urban and rural families, and women's roles. Proposes policies to alleviate poverty.

1314 Fanelli, José María and **Gary McMahon.** Economic lessons for Eastern Europe from Latin America. Buenos Aires: CEDES, 1994. 43 p.: bibl. (Documento CEDES; 107. Serie Economía)

Draws lessons from recent economic events in Latin America that may be useful to countries of Eastern Europe as they transform their economies. Topics include monetary policy and stabilization, external trade and finance, fiscal policy, and privatization.

1315 Farné, Stefano. Apertura comercial y distribución del ingreso: la teoría y las experiencias de Chile, México y Uruguay. (*Univ. Econ.*, 9:1, feb. 1994, p. 71–104, bibl., graphs, tables)

Compares actual impact of trade liberalization to theoretically predicted outcomes in Chile, Mexico, and Uruguay. Finds that while liberalization increases economic efficiency, real wages have not increased and income distribution has not improved.

1316 Feinsilver, Julie M. Biodiversity prospecting: a new panacea for development. (*CEPAL Rev.*, 60, Dec. 1996, p. 115–132)

Analyzes possible implications for Latin America of biodiversity prospecting, which is defined as "the exploration of biological resources in search of active compounds for pharmaceutical development, agriculture, and industry." Describes several projects currently underway in the region.

1317 Felipe, Jesus and **Marcelo Resende.** A multivariate approach to the measurement of development: Asia and Latin America. (*J. Dev. Areas*, 30:2, Jan. 1996, p. 183–218, tables)

Analyzes 39 development indicators for 21 Latin American and 14 Asian countries. Concludes that underdevelopment is multidimensional and cannot be measured by economic variables alone. Health, education, and demographic indicators, which are highly correlated with economic variables, must also be considered.

1318 Felix, David. Sisyphus among the neoliberals: on privatization and rolling back the Latin American State. (*in* The State, markets and development: beyond the neoclassical dichotomy. Edited by Amitava Krishan Dutt *et al.* Brookfield, Vt.: Edward Elgar Publishing Company, 1994, p. 85–106, tables)

Argues that theorists have overstated

potential benefits of privatization. Contends that State intervention in the economy, which has decreased since mid-1980s, will increase in the future as failures of privatization become evident.

1319 Feliz, Raúl Aníbal and John H. Welch.
Cointegration and tests of a classical model of inflation in Argentina, Bolivia, Brazil, Mexico, and Peru. (*J. Dev. Econ.*, 52 : 1, Feb. 1997, p. 189–219)
Uses a classical model *cum* rational expectations to analyze the inflationary process. Concludes that economic agents act on their rational expectations, particularly as they anticipate future monetary growth. Sophisticated analysis.

1320 Financial sector reforms, economic growth, and stability: experiences in selected Asian and Latin American countries. Edited by Shakil Faruqi. Washington: World Bank, 1994. 274 p.: bibl., ill. (EDI seminar series)
Compares financial sector reforms and their impact on economic growth and stability in selected countries of Latin America and Asia. Articles range from the quite specific (e.g., securities regulation in Thailand), to more general.

1321 Finkman, Javier and Maximiliano Montenegro. Vientos de cambio: los nuevos temas centrales sobre las empresas transnacionales. Buenos Aires: CEPAL, Oficina de Buenos Aires, 1995. 67 leaves: bibl., ill. (Documento de trabajo; 63)
Describes Latin American governments' changing attitudes toward transnational enterprises. Government policies which previously discouraged transnational enterprises are now structured to maximize direct foreign investment. Analyzes impact of these policies.

1322 Fleury, Sônia. Estado sem cidadãos: seguridade social na América Latina. Rio de Janeiro: Editora Fiocruz, 1994. 251 p.: bibl.
Describes impact of institutional and political environment on the quality and structure of a country's social security system. Uses case studies of Great Britain, Germany, and US to draw parallels and conclusions that can be applied to Argentina, Brazil, Chile, and Uruguay.

1323 Foreign direct investment in Latin America in the 1990s. Madrid: Institute for European-Latin American Relations; Washington: Inter-American Development Bank, 1996. 149 p.: bibl., ill.
Concise, highly empirical work summarizes direct foreign investment flows to the region. Provides data on foreign investment by major economic powers (UK, Germany, Japan, US, etc.) in specific Latin American countries. For international relations specialist's comment see item **4006.**

1324 Frankel, Jeffrey; Ernesto Stein; and Shang-jin Wei. Trading blocks and the Americas: the natural, the unnatural, and the supernatural. (*J. Dev. Econ.*, 47 : 1, June 1995, p. 61–95)
Uses econometric analysis to examine two issues: 1) whether preferential trade agreements (e.g., the Andean Pact, Mercosur, NAFTA, etc.) cause trade to become more regionalized; and 2) whether this is good or bad in terms of welfare and efficiency.

1325 Frediani, Ramón O. La economía del medio ambiente. (*Bol. Inf. Techint*, 286, abril/junio 1996, p. 33–58, bibl., tables)
Brief survey of basic concepts and most relevant conclusions of current debates on environmental economics. Includes examples and statistics from Argentina and other Mercosur countries.

1326 Frediani, Ramón O. Planes de estabilización y reforma estructural en América Latina: una síntesis. Buenos Aires: CIEDLA; Bonn: Konrad-Adenauer-Stiftung, 1996. 109 p.: bibl.
Examines eight Latin American countries (Argentina, Brazil, Chile, Colombia, Mexico, Peru, Uruguay, and Venezuela) in light of adjustment policies and market reforms.

1327 Frenkel, Roberto. Strengthening the financial sector in the adjustment process: an overview. (*in* Strengthening the financial sector in the adjustment process. Washington: Inter-American Development Bank, 1994, p. 1–38, bibl.)
Analyzes the financial sector's contribution to the development process in Argentina, Brazil, Colombia, and Uruguay. Focuses on factors that prevent the financial sector from efficiently intermediating at low cost a

large perecentage of the savings generated in a given country.

1328 Garriga, Marcelo and **Pablo Sanguinetti.** The determinants of regional exchange in Mercosur: geography and trade liberalization. (*An. Asoc. Argent. Econ. Polít.*, 3, 1995, p. 431–452, bibl., tables)

Provides evidence that among Mercosur countries, trade is driven by exploitation of comparative advantages coupled with geographical proximity. Argues that once these two factors and the unilateral trade liberalization reforms pursued by each nation are taken into account, the contribution to trade from preferential reduction in tariffs is rather modest. [G. Cañonero]

1329 Girón, Alicia. Fin de siglo y deuda externa: historia sin fin; Argentina, Brasil y México. México: Instituto de Investigaciones Económicas, Univ. Nacional Autónoma de México; Cambio XXI, 1995. 191 p.: bibl. (México y América)

Describes 1980s debt crisis, subsequent debt renegotiation and restructuring process, and implementation of market-oriented policies during 1990s in Argentina, Brazil, and Mexico.

1330 Glade, William P. Institutions and inequality in Latin America: text and subtext. (*J. Interam. Stud. World Aff.*, 38:3/2, Summer/Fall 1996, p. 159–179, bibl.)

Examines historical causes of income inequality, and reasons for its persistence. Worth reading.

1331 Gligo, Nicolo. The present state and future prospects of the environment in Latin America and the Caribbean. (*CEPAL Rev.*, 55, April 1995, p. 109–126, bibl., tables)

Highly critical view of prevailing development policies concludes that they are not environmentally sustainable.

1332 Goldstein, Daniel J. Third World biotechnology, Latin American development, and the foreign debt problem. (*in* Biotechnology in Latin America: politics, impacts, and risks. Wilmington, Del.: Scholarly Resources, 1995, p. 37–56)

Highly sophisticated article discusses differing definitions of the term "biotechnology" in the Third World and the US. Provides an agenda for development of biotechnology in Latin America.

Gonçalves Júnior, Carlos Augusto and **João Paulo Cândia Veiga.** A indústria automotiva brasileira no MERCOSUL. See item **2353.**

1333 Gontijo, Cláudio. Política de estabilização e abertura externa: uma análise comparativa das experiências do Chile, da Argentina e do México. (*Rev. Econ. Polít.*, 15:1, jan./março 1995, p. 41–57, bibl., tables)

Comparative study of stabilization programs in Argentina (1987–92), Chile (1976–81), and Mexico (1982–92). Concludes that simultaneous external and internal equilibria are difficult to achieve and that a trade-off exists between the two.

1334 Government responses to the Latin American debt problem. Edited by Robert E. Grosse. Coral Gables, Fla.: North-South Center Press, Univ. of Miami; Boulder, Colo.: Lynne Rienner Publishers, 1995. 217 p.: bibl., ill., index.

Within editor's insightful "introduction and overview" (and follow-up conclusions), he and seven specialists analyze actions of five countries (Chile, Brazil, Peru, Bolivia, and Mexico), the Brady Plan for commercial bank relief, and government creditworthiness. Commentaries and statistics are appended to each chapter. Highly useful set of studies. [P. Atkins]

1335 Govindaraj, Ramesh; Christopher J.L. Murray; and **Gnanaraj Chellaraj.** Health expenditures in Latin America. Washington: World Bank, 1995. 51 p.: bibl. (World Bank technical paper: 0253–7494; 274)

Uses econometric techniques to estimate determinants of health expenditures in the region. Also includes useful review of the literature on regional health expenditures. Focuses particularly on estimates of private health care spending, for which data is generally inadequate.

1336 Green, Duncan. Latin America: neoliberal failure and the search for alternatives. (*Third World Q.*, 17:1, March 1996, p. 109–122)

Highly critical discussion of neoliberal policies. Compares neoliberal and CEPAL models of development.

1337 Green, Duncan. Silent revolution: the rise of market economies in Latin America. London: Duncan Green; Cassell; Latin America Bureau; New York: Monthly Review Press, 1995. 1 v.

Contends that 1980s International Monetary Fund austerity programs, in context of the Latin American debt crisis, are the principal contributors to failure of statist economic systems. Acknowledges modest successes of neoliberal economic policies but emphasizes their crushing effect on poor socioeconomic sectors unable to participate. [P. Atkins]

1338 Grosse, Robert E. and **Clarice Pechman.** Foreign exchange black markets in Latin America. Westport, Conn.: Praeger, 1994. 224 p.: bibl., ill, index, maps.

Examines how and why foreign exchange black (i.e., parallel) markets function, as well as their economic impact. Includes case studies for Argentina, Brazil, Colombia, Jamaica, and Peru. Valuable contribution represents one of the few in-depth studies of this topic.

1339 Gutiérrez, Mario A. Observaciones respecto a las economías pequeñas en el proceso de integración económica del Hemisferio Occidental. (*Trimest. Econ.*, 63:251, julio/sept. 1996, p. 1171–1227, bibl., graphs, tables)

Examines problems and advantages for small countries that enter into integration schemes with large countries.

1340 Haya de la Torre, Agustín. La restauración neoliberal: un modelo excluyente. Lima: Fundación Andina, 1994. 131 p.: bibl.

Highly critical analysis of recent neoliberal reforms in Latin America blames failure of import substitution on opposition from local oligarchies and on the failure to implement comprehensive agrarian reforms.

1341 Helwege, Ann. Poverty in Latin America: back to the abyss? (*J. Interam. Stud. World Aff.*, 37:3, Fall 1995, p. 99–123, bibl., table)

Examines recent poverty trends in the region. Argues for greater emphasis on redistributive policies contending that their contribution to human capital development will result in greater growth.

1342 Hernández-Ledezma, José Juan and **Valentine Solyman-Golpashini.** Manipulation of gametes and embryos in animal biotechnology's impact on livestock production in Latin America. (*in* Biotechnology in Latin America: politics, impacts, and risks.

Wilmington, Del.: Scholarly Resources, 1995, p. 147–172)

Reviews various reproductive biotechnologies and ways in which they can be used in Latin America to increase livestock production. Of particular interest for agricultural economists.

1343 Hesse, Milton von. Public policies and the competitiveness of agricultural exports. (*CEPAL Rev.*, 53, Aug. 1995, p. 129–146, bibl., graphs, tables)

Sophisticated, empirical analysis of changes and trends in region's agricultural export sector. Contends that government intervention is needed to make corrections to flaws in the internal market (e.g., imperfect information, lack of financing and technology).

1344 Hewitt, W.E. Canada-Latin America municipal exchange as a strategy for regional development: some observations on the cost-benefit balance sheet. (*J. Dev. Areas*, 30:4, July 1996, p. 447–461)

Describes a new form of development assistance known as the international municipal exchange (IME). Such a program exists between Canada and six Latin American countries (Brazil, Chile, Ecuador, El Salvador, Mexico, and Peru).

1345 Hicks, Norman L. Adjustments during crisis: government expenditures and revenues in Latin America, 1975–1988. (*Estud. Econ./Santiago*, 21:1, junio 1994, p. 1–21, bibl., graphs, tables)

Examines changes in region's public finances and government expenditures from 1975–88. Finds that social spending increased both per capita and as a percentage of GDP. Capital spending, however, declined.

1346 Holden, Paul and **Sarath Rajapatirana.** Unshackling the private sector: a Latin American story. Washington: World Bank, 1995. 108 p.: bibl. (Directions in development)

Summarizes recent studies of region's private sector, focusing on key variables, both institutional and economic, that create the incentives and economic environment favorable to growth of private business sector.

Huber, Evelyne and **John D. Stephens.** Conclusion: agrarian structure and political power in comparative perspective. See item **2951.**

1347 Huddle, Donald L. Post-1982 effects of neoliberalism on Latin American development and poverty: two conflicting views. (*Econ. Dev. Cult. Change*, 45:4, July 1997, p. 881–897)

Essay reviews two books. Sebastian Edwards' *Crisis and reform in Latin America: from hope to despair* (Oxford Univ. Press, 1995) concludes that neoliberal market reforms have had a beneficial impact. Duncan Green, in *Silent revolution: the rise of market economies in Latin America* (see item **1337**), concludes that market reforms have had a "devastating" impact.

1348 Implicaciones estadísticas de los procesos de integración: primer seminario interamericano. Santiago: Centro Interamericano de Enseñanza de Estadística (CIENES), 1992. 157 p.: bibl., ill.

Series of papers examines implications of regional integration policies on data collection and analysis. Major focus is on comparability of international statistics.

1349 Indebtedness, economic reforms, and poverty. Edited by Hermann Sautter. Frankfurt: Vervuert Verlag; Madrid: Iberoamericana, 1995. 213 p.: bibl., graphs, tables. (Göttinger Studien zur Entwicklungsökonomie; 2)

Six articles analyze reasons for increase in poverty in the years following implementation of adjustment programs. Also discusses policies that could lessen the region's poverty.

1350 La industria y la integración en los 90: resultados de una encuesta a los industriales latinoamericanos. Encuesta de Jaime Campos y Alejandra Herrera. Coordinación de Guillermo R. Ondarts. Buenos Aires: Banco Interamericano de Desarrollo, Instituto para la Integración de América Latina, 1992. 183 p.: bibl. ill. (Publ.; 395)

Examines growth of Latin American manufactured exports under the new integration schemes. Specific chapters are devoted to Venezuela and the Andean Group nations.

1351 Integrating the Americas: shaping future trade policy. Edited by Sidney Weintraub. New Brunswick, N.J.: Transaction Publishers, 1994. 197 p.: bibl., ill.

Eight well-written essays for Latin America. Outlines policies appropriate for accelerating process of hemispheric free trade and integration.

1352 International Congress of Americanists, *48th, Stockholm/Uppsala, 1994*. Growth, trade, and integration in Latin America: proceedings. Edited by Weine Karlsson and Akhil Malaki. Stockholm: Institute of Latin American Studies, Stockholm Univ., 1996. 329 p.: bibl., ill.

Evaluations of recent economic reforms and integration efforts in the region. Emphasizes success of outward-oriented policies and regional cooperation schemes such as Mercosur and NAFTA.

1353 International Federation of Building and Wood Workers (Geneva). Economic integration in the Americas: Mercosur and NAFTA. Geneva: International Federation of Building and Wood Workers, 1994. 31 p.: bibl., ill. (An IFBWW discussion paper)

Analyzes impact of Mercosur and NAFTA on issues of importance to labor, e.g., protection against discrimination and forced labor, right to bargain collectively, minimum employment standards, and child labor laws. Gives special emphasis to impact of Mercosur and NAFTA on those employed in the construction and wood and forestry sectors.

1354 Investing and selling in Latin America. Edited by Shirley Christian. Shawnee Mission, Kan.: Hemisphere Business, 1995. 358 p.: bibl., ill., index.

Off-beat, somewhat chatty discussion of how to sell and invest in Latin America. Although occasionally anecdotal, contains much useful advice on doing business in Latin America.

1355 Ippolito-O'Donnell, Gabriela and **Brenda Markovitz.** Poverty in Latin America: a rapporteurs' report. Notre Dame, Indiana: The Helen Kellogg Institute for International Studies, Univ. of Notre Dame, 1996. 39 p. (Working paper; 219)

Series of articles examines extent of and trends in poverty, role of education and job creation in alleviating poverty, and changing role of the State in dealing with poverty.

1356 Jiang, Shixue. Lamei Fazhan Moshi Yanjiu. [Studies on development models of Latin America.] Beijing: Economic Management Press, 1996. 321 p.: tables.

Argues that since mid-1980s Latin American countries followed a new post-import substitution development model. Compares Latin America's development model with that of East Asia, and traces causes of former's "failure" and latter's "success." Also discusses four sets of relationships in Latin American development models: 1) economic development and stabilization, 2) industralization and agricultural development, 3) economic growth and income distribution, and 4) State intervention and market regulation. [M. Xianglin]

Josling, Tim. Agricultural trade policies in the Andean Group: issues and options. See item **2042.**

1357 *Journal of Interamerican Studies and World Affairs.* Vol. 37, No. 3, Fall 1995. Report on neoliberal restructuring. Edited by Elena H. Alvarez. Coral Gables, Fla.: Univ. of Miami, 1995.

Issue devoted to articles on neoliberal economic policies in Latin America.

1358 Joyce, Joseph P. and **Linda Kamas.** The relative importance of foreign and domestic shocks to output and prices in Mexico and Colombia. (*Weltwirtsch. Arch.*, 133:3, 1997, p. 458–478)

Uses econometric analysis to examine relative importance of foreign shocks (e.g., US interest rates) and domestic shocks (e.g., domestic money supply) on output and prices in Mexico and Colombia.

Kaplan, Marcos. Integración internacional de América Latina: aspectos sociopolíticos. See item **4021.**

1359 Karlsson, Weine; Joakim Olofsson; and **David Wirmark.** Latin America and East Asia: comparing regional development. (*in* Current developments in Asia Pacific. Stockholm: Center for Pacific Asia Studies, Stockholm Univ., 1994, p. 121–164, bibl., tables)

Compares development in Latin America and East Asia. Describes economic relations between the two, and outlines prospects for increased economic cooperation in terms of trade and direct investment.

1360 Katada, Saori N. Two aid hegemons: Japanese-U.S. interaction and aid allocation to Latin America and the Caribbean. (*World Dev.*, 25:6, June 1997, p. 931–945)

Empirically analyzes determinants of Japanese aid allocation to the region for pe-

riod 1971–91. Determinants include 1) economic and political self interest, 2) support of US power, and 3) improvement of US/Japanese relations via support of US policy goals.

1361 Kiguel, Miguel Alberto. Exchange rate policy, the real exchange rate, and inflation: lessons from Latin America. (*Cuad. Econ./Santiago*, 31:93, agosto 1994, p. 229–249, appendix, bibl., graphs, tables)

Uses data and examples from various Latin American countries to analyze effectiveness of alternative exchange rate policies for achieving more competitive real exchange rates and low inflation. Concludes that exchange rate policies have little effect on real exchange rate.

1362 Kosacoff, Bernardo P. Nuevas bases de la política industrial en América Latina. Buenos Aires: CEPAL, Oficina de Buenos Aires, 1995. 24 leaves: bibl. (Documento de trabajo; 60)

Describes status of current debate on industrialization policy in Latin America following the demise of the traditional import substitution paradigm.

1363 Kunicka-Michalska, Barbara. La deuda externa latinoamericana: problemas escogidos. Warszawa: Centro de Estudios Latinoamericanos, Univ. Varsovia, 1994. 31 p.: bibl., tables. (Documentos de trabajo; 13)

Brief overview of external debt literature. Extensive bibliography.

1364 Kuwayama, Mikio. Recent economic trends in China and their implications for trade with Latin America and the Caribbean. (*CEPAL Rev.*, 56, Aug. 1995, p. 61–82, bibl., tables)

Empirical description of China's global trade structure. Although the country currently has little economic interaction with Latin America, author uses Chinese trade data to explore feasibility of increased trade and investment between Latin America and China.

1365 Labarca, Guillermo. How much can we spend on education? (*CEPAL Rev.*, 56, Aug. 1996, p. 169–184, bibl., tables)

Argues that Latin American educational system is inefficient because it is highly labor-intensive. Contends that significant improvements in education can be achieved only if region adopts capital-intensive educational technologies.

1366 Labor and economic reforms in Latin America and the Caribbean. Washington: World Bank, 1995. 28 p.: bibl., ill. (Regional perspectives on world development report 1995, 1020–3648)

Discusses impact of economic policy and performance on well-being of region's workers. Focuses on impact of policy reforms on labor markets in 1980s-90s. Concludes that countries with well-established reforms will experience significant gains for their workers.

1367 Lacarte Muró, Julio A. Ronda Uruguay del GATT: la globalización del comercio mundial. Montevideo: Fundación de Cultura Universitaria, 1994. 426 p.

Author is a Uruguayan diplomat who actively participated in the Uruguay Round trade negotiations. Describes in detail the eight-year process, its background, and its conclusions. Describes final agreements, including creation of the World Trade Organization.

1368 Lahera, Eugenio; Ernesto Ottone; and Osvaldo Rosales. A summary of the ECLAC proposals. (*CEPAL Rev.*, 55, April 1995, p. 7–25)

Summarizes agenda of Economic Commission for Latin America and the Caribbean (ECLAC) on public policy reform. Convenient and concise discussion of ECLAC's position on major development issues and policies.

1369 Latin America and the Caribbean: policies to improve linkages with the global economy. Santiago: Comisión Económica para América Latina y el Caribe, 1994. 301 p.: bibl., ill.

Documents increase in linkages that occurred between Latin America and the world economy during 1990s. Focuses on three issues: 1) trade policy; 2) productivity improvement policies; and 3) macroeconomic policies to promote stability. Examines impact of policies on international capital flows.

1370 Latin America in graphs: demographic, economic and social trends; 1994– 1995 edition. Washington: Inter-American Development Bank, 1995. 200 p.: chiefly graphs.

Exhaustive (over 1,000 charts) graphical presentation of demographic and macroeconomic data for 26 Latin American countries, for period 1974–94. Covers national income, balance of payments, energy, debt, labor force, and population statistics.

1371 Latin American capital flows: living with volatility; a study group report. Washington: Group of Thirty, 1994. 152 p.: bibl.

Examines capital flows to Latin America during 1980s-90s, discussing reasons for such flows and their impact on the region. Major emphasis on policy and structural reforms that must be implemented to increase capital flows.

1372 Latin American finance. (*Economist/ London*, 337:7944, Dec. 9–15, 1995, p. 1–22 (and insert between p. 54–55), graphs, photos, table)

Analyzes region's financial boom during 1990s, current banking system structure, efforts to develop domestic capital markets, reasons for low national savings rates, strategies to reduce volatility of financial markets, and current structural reforms.

1373 Latin American political economy in the age of neoliberal reform: theoretical and comparative perspectives for the 1990s. Edited by William C. Smith, Carlos H. Acuña, and Eduardo A. Gamarra. Coral Gables, Fla.: North-South Center, Univ. of Miami; New Brunswick, N.J.: Transaction Publishers, 1994. 218 p.: bibl., ill.

Series of well-written, multidisciplinary articles examines market-oriented reforms instituted by most Latin American countries during 1980s-90s. Emphasizes impact of market reforms on political system and democratization.

1374 Latin America's competitive position in the enlarged European market. Edited by Bernard Fischer, Albrecht von Gleich, and Wolf Grabendorff. Baden-Baden, Germany: Nomos Verlagsgesellschaft, 1994. 404 p.: bibl., ill., maps. (Veröffentlichungen des HWWA-Institut für Wirtschaftsforschung-Hamburg)

Series of articles examines impact of recent Latin American reforms on the region's competitiveness within European markets. Documents increase in goods and capital flows, and outlines programs necessary for increased trade and investment.

1375 Latin America's economic development: confronting crisis. Edited by James L. Dietz. 2nd ed. Boulder, Colo.: Lynne

Rienner Publishers, 1995. 401 p.: bibl., ill., index, map.

Twenty articles on a wide range of major economic issues facing the region. Includes sections on economic history, inflation, balance of payments, transnational corporations, development strategies (e.g., import substitution, export-led growth), income distribution, labor markets, and the role of women. Excellent for classroom use.

1376 Li, He. Sino-Latin American Economic Relations: recent trends and future prospects. Amherst: Latin American Studies Program, Univ. of Massachusetts at Amherst, 1990. 26 p.: appendices. (Program in Latin American Studies Occasional Papers Series; 25)

Outlines changes in economic relations between China and Latin America during late 1970s-80s. Discusses China's exports to and imports from Latin America, as well as China's direct investment in the region.

1377 Littler, Graeme. The growth of Latin America's equity markets. (*Financ. Dev.*, 32:1, March 1995, p. 22–23)

Empirically illustrates the impressive growth in Latin American equity markets during the period 1990–94. Data provided for Argentina, Brazil, Chile, Colombia, Mexico, Peru, and Venezuela.

1378 Londero, Elio and **Simón Teitel.** Industrialization and the factor content of Latin American export of manufactures. (*J. Dev. Stud.*, 32:4, April 1996, p. 581–601)

Documents growth of Latin American manufactured exports. Empirically demonstrates that growth is due to either natural or government-induced (i.e., import substitution industrialization) comparative advantage. Case studies for Argentina, Colombia, and Uruguay.

1379 Londoño de la Cuesta, Juan Luis. Poverty, inequality, and human capital development in Latin America, 1950–2025. Washington: World Bank, 1996. 38 p.: bibl., ill. (World Bank Latin American and Caribbean studies; 2)

Presents and analyzes data on extent of and trends in poverty from 1950–94. Uses these trends to project poverty to 2025. Concludes that rapid decreases in poverty will occur only if region devotes significantly more resources to education.

1380 López, Fabiana and **Raúl Dichiara.** Integración comercial: el caso de la industria química y petroquímica en el Mercosur. (*An. Asoc. Argent. Econ. Polít.*, 3, 1995, p. 527–544, appendix, bibl., tables)

Reports the effect of trade liberalization within Mercosur on two manufacturing sectors: chemistry and petrochemistry. [G. Cañonero]

1381 Loza Tellería, Gabriel. Integración y apertura externa. La Paz: G. Loza Tellería, 1992. 132 p.: bibl., ill.

Discusses Latin American effort aimed at regional economic integration. Reviews different forms of economic integration from preferential tariff areas to common markets. Argues that there have been waves of enthusiasm for regional economic integration, erroneously seeing it as a panacea for economic development problems. Full economic union is not feasible, nor will it solve major problems. Cogently written and clearly argued. [J. Franks]

1382 Mackenzie, G.A. Reforming Latin America's old-age pension systems. (*Financ. Dev.*, 32:1, March 1995, p. 10–13)

Concisely states problems facing region's pension plans. Discusses pros and cons of various reform proposals. Also describes Chile's defined contribution plan, implemented in 1991.

1383 Mamalakis, Markos J. Poverty and inequality in Latin America. (*J. Interam. Stud. World Aff.*, 38:2/3, Summer/Fall 1996, p. 1–13, bibl., tables)

Presents alternative methodologies for measuring: 1) welfare, 2) poverty, 3) relative distribution of income and consumption, 4) distributive justice, and 5) entitlements.

Mancero Samán, Alfredo. Seguridad social y vejez: la privatización de los fondos de pensiones. See item **2045.**

1384 Manrique Campos, Irma. América Latina: reestructuración financiera y autonomía de la banca central. (*Probl. Desarro.*, 25:99, oct./dic. 1994, p. 171–190)

Examines central banks' role in, and reactions to, financial liberalization programs of 1970s-80s in Chile, Colombia, and Mexico.

1385 Marchand, Marianne H. Latin American women speak on development: are we listening yet? (*in* Feminism, postmodernism, development. New York: Routledge, 1995, p. 56–72)

Excellent review of recent feminist literature pertaining to Third World women. Special emphasis on neocolonial discourses. Important work.

1386 Marcouiller, Douglas; Verónica Ruiz de Castilla; and Christopher Woodruff. Formal measures of the informal sector wage gap in Mexico, El Salvador, and Peru. (*Econ. Dev. Cult. Change*, 45:2, Jan. 1997, p. 367–392)

Uses econometric techniques to test hypothesis that workers in the informal sector earn less than those employed in the formal sector. Hypothesis was borne out for El Salvador and Peru, but not for Mexico where informal sector workers earn more.

1387 Maredia, Mywish K. and Carl K. Eicher. The economics of wheat research in developing countries: the one hundred million dollar puzzle. (*World Dev.*, 23:3, March 1995, p. 401–412, bibl., graph, tables)

Analyzes the optimum size and program type of 71 wheat research programs in 35 developing countries. Concludes that roughly one-half are inefficient, and suggests policies for increasing efficiency.

1388 Mattos, Carlos A. de. Nuevas estrategias empresariales y mutaciones territoriales en los procesos de reestructuración en América Latina. (*in* Territorios en transformación: análisis y propuestas. Madrid: Fondo Europeo de Desarrollo Regional; Consejo Superior de Investigaciones Científicas, 1994, p. 3–35, bibl.)

Analyzes impact of structural adjustment policies on regional development within the various Latin American countries. Focuses on decision-making impact of these policies for business, as well as effect on domestic and international capital flows.

1389 Maza Zavala, D.F. Políticas de estabilización y de ajuste en la América Latina. (*Nueva Econ./Caracas*, 4:4, marzo 1995, p. 1–64, tables)

Surveys various Latin American stabilization and adjustment policies, classifying them into two categories: neoliberal and structuralist. Presents five case studies based on experiences of Argentina, Brazil, Chile, Mexico, and Venezuela.

1390 Meeting the infrastructure challenge in Latin America and the Caribbean. Washington: World Bank, 1994. 55 p. (Directions in development)

Summarizes argument that increased infrastructure expenditures are critically needed to accelerate regional growth. Discusses power, telecommunication, transportation, water and sewerage facilities, etc. Emphasizes means of financing these projects.

1391 Mena Keymer, Hugo. Acerca de la viabilidad de la investigación empírica macroeconométrica en la América Latina. (*Trimest. Econ.*, 61:244, oct./dic. 1994, p. 641–677, bibl., tables)

Examines reliability of national accounts time series for econometric models. Concludes that Latin America is "statistically underdeveloped," and, accordingly, validity of macroeconomic econometric research on Latin America should be questioned.

1392 El Mercosur: aspectos institucionales y económicos. Coordinación de Augusto Mario Morello. La Plata, Argentina: Librería Editora Platense, 1993. 282 p.: bibl.

Series of essays on institutional and economic aspects of Mercosur. Topics discussed are: international law in the member countries, labor market and enviromental legislation, educational systems, dispute resolution mechanisms, Mercosur's compatibility with pre-existing preferential trade arrangements in the region, and a comprehensive analysis of the Asunción treaty. [G. Cañonero]

1393 Mercosur y Comunidad Europea. Coordinación de Eve I. Rimoldi de Ladmann. Buenos Aires: Facultad de Derecho y Ciencias Sociales, Univ. de Buenos Aires; Ediciones Ciudad Argentina, 1995. 235 p.: bibl. (Monografías jurídicas/Ediciones Ciudad Argentina)

Proceedings from a meeting regarding Mercosur and the European Community. Historical, regional, political, and legal differences between the two preferential trade agreements are the main focus. Other issues include: regional cooperation, the environment, and scientific development. [G. Cañonero]

1394 Mesa-Lago, Carmelo. Pension system reforms in Latin America: the position of the international organizations. (*CEPAL Rev.*, 60, Dec. 1996, p. 133–156)

Outlines and compares positions taken by various international organizations (World Bank, International Labour Organization, ECLAC, Inter-American Social Security Association, Inter-American Development Bank) concerning the appropriate reforms to be made in the region's pension and social security systems.

1395 Mesa-Lago, Carmelo. La reforma de la seguridad social en América Latina y el Caribe: hacia una disminución del costo social del ajuste estructural. Santiago: Corporación de Investigación, Estudio y Desarrollo de la Seguridad Social, 1994. 265 p.: tables.

Highly detailed discussion of recent reforms in regional social security programs. Examines various approaches for ameliorating hardships caused by these reforms.

1396 Mesa-Lago, Carmelo. La reforma de la seguridad social y las pensiones en América Latina: importancia y evaluación de las alternativas de privatización. 2. ed. Quito: INCAE, 1994. 80 p.: bibl.

Survey, by the definitive scholar in this area, of recent and proposed reforms in Latin American social security and pension systems. Focuses on privatization.

1397 Mesa-Lago, Carmelo. Social welfare reform in the context of economic-political liberalization: Latin American cases. (*World Dev.*, 25:4, April 1997, p. 497–517)

Examines impact of economic reform on social security, health care, and pensions. Separate segments devoted to Argentina, Chile, Colombia, Costa Rica, Cuba, Mexico, Peru, and Uruguay.

1398 Meyer, Carrie A. Opportunism and the NGOs: entrepreneurship and green north-south transfers. (*World Dev.*, 23:8, Aug. 1995, p. 1277–1289)

Describes political and economic role of two environmental NGOs: Fundación Natura in Ecuador and Instituto Nacional de Biodiversidad (INBio) in Costa Rica.

1399 Meyer, Carrie A. The political economy of NGOs and information sharing. (*World Dev.*, 25:7, July 1997, p. 1127–1140)

Argues that sharing information is a primary function of NGOs. Analyzes implications of declining information costs for information-intensive NGOs. Provides examples from Latin America.

1400 Moguillansky, Graciela. The impact of exchange-rate and trade policy on export performance in the 1980s. (*CEPAL Rev.*, 55, April 1995, p. 95–108, bibl., graphs, tables)

Analyzes impact of a drop in exchange rates on short- or long-term export growth. Concludes that exports in general are little affected by long-term changes in exchange rates, although certain products may be. Also concludes that volatile exchange rates discourage export sector investment.

1401 Morici, Peter. Free trade in the Americas. New York: Twentieth Century Fund Press, 1994. 39 p.: bibl.

Highly succinct discussion of NAFTA focuses on the policies and procedures that current members must adopt in order to attract new Latin American members.

1402 Morley, Samuel A. Poverty and inequality in Latin America: the impact of adjustment and recovery in the 1980s. Baltimore, Md.: Johns Hopkins Univ. Press, 1995. 222 p.: bibl., index.

Analyzes impact of economic events of the 1980s (e.g., debt crisis, readjustment policies) on poverty and inequality. Case studies provided for Argentina and Venezuela, which suffered greatly; and for Colombia and Costa Rica, which were able to decrease poverty and improve income distribution. Valuable contribution.

1403 Mujer y crisis: respuestas ante la recesión. Coordinación de Neuma Aguiar. Río de Janeiro: Mujeres por un Desarrollo Alternativo; Caracas: Editorial Nueva Sociedad, 1990. 131 p.: bibl.

Essays examine various issues affecting women in Latin America today. Topics include work opportunities and the family. [R. Looney]

1404 The multilateral development banks. v. 4, Inter-American Development Bank by Diana Tussie. Boulder, Colo.: Lynne Rienner, 1995– . 1 v.

Examines history, structure, functioning, and development of the Inter-American Development Bank (IDB). Major focus is on evaluating IDB's effectiveness in promoting economic growth, reducing poverty, and improving social (i.e., welfare) indicators.

1405 Myers, David L. Latin American cities: internationally embedded but nationally influential. (*LARR*, 32:1, 1997, p. 109–123)

Review essay examines 11 books that study the growth of key Latin American cities.

1406 NAFTA and trade liberalization in the Americas. [Edited by] Elsie L. Echeverri-Carroll. Austin: Bureau of Business Research, Graduate School of Business; IC² Institute, Univ. of Texas at Austin, 1995. 309 p.: bibl., ill.

Includes 10 highly technical articles on regional trade liberalization. Three articles assess macroeconomic impact of NAFTA on Canada, Mexico and the US; three others assess NAFTA's impact on specific sectors (e.g., banking, agriculture). The remaining four examine trade liberalization in Argentina, Brazil, Chile, and Colombia.

1407 Naím, Moisés. Latin America the morning after. (*Foreign Aff.*, 74:4, July/Aug. 1995, p. 45–61, graphs)

Reviews upcoming challenges for regional governments as they attempt to implement 1990s reforms. Concludes that the greatest challenge is building the institutions necessary for more rapid social reform.

1408 The new economic model in Latin America and its impact on income distribution and poverty. Edited by Victor Bulmer-Thomas. New York: St. Martin's Press; London: Institute of Latin American Studies, Univ. of London, 1996. 370 p.: bibl., ill., index. (Institute of Latin American Studies series)

Analyzes impact of free market, trade liberalization, and export promotion policies on income distribution. Case studies of Brazil, Chile, Honduras, and Mexico. Contains a wealth of data. Valuable contribution.

1409 Novaes, Walter and Sergio Werland. Inflationary bias and State-owned financial institutions. (*J. Dev. Econ.*, 47:1, June 1995, p. 135–154)

Mathematical model that demonstrates why State-owned financial institutions frequently run deficits. Deficits are "covered" by the central government, thereby

causing budget deficits, which in turn lead to inflation.

1410 Novara, Juan. Integración económica, comercio internacional y medio ambiente: enseñanzas para el Mercosur. (*Estudios/Fundación Mediterránea*, 17:72, enero/marzo 1995, p. 3–32, bibl., graphs, tables)

Analyzes effects of trade on the environment. Also discusses policy differences regarding environmental issues among Mercosur countries and the need to harmonize these provisions with NAFTA in order to facilitate further regional integration. [G. Cañonero]

1411 La nueva visión de América en el siglo XXI: unidad o diversidad. Buenos Aires: Ediciones Univ. del Salvador, 1993. 269 p. (Col. Actas)

Series of papers considers likely regional trade patterns for 21st century. Topics include regional integration, environmental protection, cultural integration, relationship between nations and transnational corporations, and relationship between Southern Cone countries and Northern Hemisphere.

1412 Ocampo, José Antonio and Roberto Steiner. Foreign capital in Latin America: an overview. (*in* Foreign capital in Latin America. Edited by José Antonio Ocampo and Robert Steiner. Washington: Inter-American Development Bank, 1994, p. 1–34, tables)

Discusses factors responsible for increase in foreign capital inflows that occurred from 1990–92. Capital inflows in this period were more than four times greater than for the previous three years, with Argentina, Chile, Colombia, Mexico, and Venezuela receiving the preponderance.

Open regionalism in Latin America and the Caribbean: economic integration as a contribution to changing production patterns with social equity. See item **1856.**

1413 Owens, Trudy and Adrian Woods. Export-oriented industrialization through primary processing. (*World Dev.*, 25:9, Sept. 1997, p. 1453–1470)

Econometrically analyzes whether exporting primary products can eventually lead to export-oriented industrialization in countries which currently do not have a comparative advantage in manufacturing. Concludes that this could occur in regions having at least a moderately skilled labor force, such as Latin America.

1414 Panagariya, Arvind. The Free Trade Area of the Americas: good for Latin America? (*World Econ.*, 19:5, Sept. 1996, p. 485–515)

Examines potential costs and benefits of formation of a Free Trade Area of the Americas (FTAA), in which Latin American countries would join with the members of NAFTA to form a free trade area. Concludes that such an association would have a generally negative impact on Latin America.

1415 Paredes M., Ricardo and **Luis A. Riveros.** Human resources and the adjustment process: an overview. (*in* Human resources and the adjustment process. Edited by Ricardo Paredes and Luis A. Riveros Washington: Inter-American Development Bank, 1994, p. 1–12, bibl.)

Analyzes extent to which human resources have adapted to structural changes in the economies of Brazil, Chile, Colombia, and Uruguay. Concludes that education and training increase mobility and adaptability of human resources.

1416 Paredes M., Ricardo; José Miguel Sánchez C.; and **Arturo Fernández.** Privatización y regulación en Latinoamérica. (*Rev. Anál. Econ.*, 10:2, nov. 1995, p. 3–19, bibl.)

Describes recent economic issues regarding regulation. Specifies institutional factors that determine quality, effectiveness, and scope of regulation in a country. These include the legal and regulatory environment and the existence of policies that provide incentives for private sector competition.

1417 Park, James William. Latin American underdevelopment: a history of perspectives in the United States, 1870–1965. Baton Rouge: Louisiana State Univ. Press, 1995. 274 p.: bibl., ill., index.

Discusses explanations commonly given in US for Latin American underdevelopment from 1870–1965. Explanations were based primarily on perceptions, and more often misperceptions, of the culture, people, and environment of the region. Interesting.

1418 Payne, Leigh A. and **Ernest Bartell.** Bringing business back in business-State relations and democratic stability in Latin America. (*in* Business and democracy in Latin America. Pittsburgh, Pa.: Univ. of Pittsburgh Press, 1995, p. 257–290)

Historically, Latin American business leaders have been politically and economically weak, and dependent upon State intervention for their survival. Author contends that this is changing, with favorable implication for democracy.

1419 Pichón, Francisco J. and **Jorge E. Uquillas.** Agricultural intensification and poverty reduction in Latin America's risk-prone areas: opportunities and challenges. (*J. Dev. Areas*, 31:4, Summer 1997, p. 479–514)

Specifies programs that must be implemented in poor, environmentally degraded areas in order to achieve sustainable growth. Places primary emphasis on technological improvements and innovations.

1420 Pinheiro, Armando Castelar and **Ben Ross Schneider.** The fiscal impact of privatization in Latin America. Brasília: Instituto Pesquisa Econômica Aplicada, 1994. 41 p.: bibl., tables. (Texto para discussão; 354)

Empirical analysis of recent privatization programs in Argentina, Brazil, Chile, and Mexico and their fiscal impact. Concludes that revenues from privatization are too small to have a significant impact on fiscal crises.

1421 Plá, Juan Algorta. O sector agropecuário frente a instalação do Mercosul. (*Cad. Sociol.*, número especial, out. 1994, p. 97–107, bibl.)

Mercosur offers opportunities for complementarity in production among member countries which, if properly exploited, will improve conditions in all countries and restore the balance of trade among them. However, initial conditions in the countries are so different that an equitable outcome is not assured; article traces probable impact of integration on various sectors of each country. [M. Birch]

1422 Pobreza y modelos de desarrollo en América Latina. Recopilación de Felix Bombarolo y Horacio E. Caride. Buenos Aires: FICONG; Washington: Economic Development Institute of the World Bank, 1994. 348 p.: bibl., ill.

Series of articles analyzes causes of Latin American poverty, and outlines policies for reducing it. Case studies for Chile, Colombia, Ecuador, and Nicaragua.

1423 Posada, Marcelo Germán; Mariano Martínez de Ibarreta; and Pablo Alfredo Pucciarelli. Agroindustria y cambio tecnológico: elementos para su análisis en América Latina. (*Probl. Desarro.*, 27:105, abril/junio 1996, p. 81–105)

Describes growth of agroindustry (agribusiness) since 1950s. Discusses social and economic processes of agribusiness complexes, as well as nature and dynamics of technological progress in this area.

1424 Poverty and income distribution in Latin America: the story of the 1980s. Washington: World Bank, 1996. 307 p.: bibl., ill., maps. (World Bank technical paper: 0253–7494; 351)

Highly empirical analysis documents increase in poverty and worsening of income distribution during 1980s. Demonstrates that low levels of education increase incidence of poverty and income inequality. Data provided for individual countries. Valuable data reference source.

1425 Privatization in Latin America: new roles for the public and private sectors. Edited by Werner Baer and Melissa H. Birch. Westport, Conn.: Praeger, 1994. 215 p.: bibl., ill., index.

Series of well-written articles on regional privatization efforts. Separate chapters on Argentina, Brazil, Chile, and Mexico. Other topics include: 1) changing roles of the State and business, 2) recent trends in direct foreign investment, and 3) changes in Latin American equity markets. Valuable contribution.

1426 Public finances, stabilization, and structural reform in Latin America. Edited by Guillermo E. Perry and Ana María Herrera. Washington: Inter-American Development Bank, 1994. 133 p.: bibl., graphs, index, tables.

Summarizes recent changes in Latin American public finances and tax structures. Primary focus on Argentina, Chile, Colombia, and Mexico. Describes impact of fiscal decentralization, privatization, and trade liberalization, as well as various types of tax reforms.

1427 Queisser, Monika; Osvald Larrañaga; and Mónica Panadeiros. Adjustment and social development in Latin America

during the 1980s: education, health care, and social security, München, Germany: Weltforum, 1993. 394 p.: bibl. (Ifo-Studien zur Entwicklungsforschung; 25)

Detailed examination of impact of recent stabilization and adjustment policies on health, education, and social security in Argentina, Bolivia, Chile, Peru, and Uruguay. Good source of data. Highly competent work.

1428 Rakowski, Cathy A. Convergence and divergence in the informal sector debate: a focus on Latin America, 1984–92. (*World Dev.*, 22:4, April 1994, p. 501–516, bibl.)

Discusses various meanings given to term "informal sector" since its inception approximately two decades ago. Outlines the gradual, yet incomplete, development of a consensus as to term's meaning.

1429 Ramírez López, Berenice Patricia and Saúl Osorio. Hechos y perspectivas del financiamiento en América Latina. (*Probl. Desarro.*, 25:99, oct./dic. 1994, p. 191–204, tables)

Analyzes changing nature of growth financing during last 10 years.

1430 Ramos, Joseph R. Poverty and inequality in Latin America: a neostructural perspective. (*J. Interam. Stud. World Aff.*, 38:2/3, Summer/Fall 1996, p. 141–157, bibl., graph, tables)

Notes that Latin America has achieved an income level at which, when compared with the historical standards of other countries, one would expect a more equal distribution of income. Asks why such a transformation has not occurred, and presents an explanation.

1431 Ranis, Gustav. Will Latin America now put a stop to *stop-and-go?* (*J. Interam. Stud. World Aff.*, 38:3/2, Summer/Fall 1996, p. 127–140, bibl.)

Historically, Latin America has grown by "stop-and-go" cycles, usually based on the availability of foreign exchange. Article examines whether the recently implemented economic reforms and policies will stop this phenomenon. Inconclusive.

1432 Reform, recovery, and growth: Latin America and the Middle East. Edited by Rudiger Dornbusch and Sebastian Edwards. Chicago: Univ. of Chicago Press, 1995.

426 p.: bibl., ill., indexes. (A National Bureau of Economic Research project report)

Series of well-written articles analyzes elements that comprise successful stabilization programs, as well as impact of deregulation, privatization, tax reform, and trade liberalization. Discusses reform efforts in Argentina, Bolivia, Brazil, Chile, Israel, Mexico, Peru, and Turkey.

1433 Reilly, Charles A.; Elisavinda Echeverri-Gent; and Laura Mullahy. Selected bibliography. (*in* New paths to democratic development in Latin America. Edited by Charles A. Reilly. Boulder, Colo.: Lynne Rienner Publishers, 1995, p. 273–302)

Bibliography on literature pertaining to transition of South American and southern European countries from corporate, bureaucratic authoritarian States to democratic forms of government. Includes a general bibliography with separate sections for Argentina, Brazil, Chile, Colombia, Mexico, and Peru.

1434 Reynolds, Lloyd G. Some sources of income inequality in Latin America. (*J. Interam. Stud. World Aff.*, 38:2/3, Summer/Fall 1996, p. 39–46, bibl.)

Examines determinants of income inequality in the region, including unequal distribution of land ownership, regressive tax systems, impact of rapid industrialization (e.g., the Kuznets effect), and lack of government redistributive programs. Examples from Brazil and Mexico.

1435 Riveros, Luis A. Labor markets, economic restructuring and human resource development in Latin America in the 1980s. (*Rev. Econ. Trab.*, 2:4, julio/dic. 1994, p. 27–49, bibl., tables)

Analyzes role of labor market in adjustment process. Concludes that Latin American labor mobility is a critical determinant of the impact of adjustment policies. Argues that region's governments should implement policies (e.g., training) to increase labor mobility.

1436 Rodríguez, Alfredo and Lucy Winchester. Cities, democracy and governance in Latin America. (*Int. Soc. Sci. J.*, 147, March 1996, p. 73–83, bibl., photo, tables)

Describes economic, social, and political changes taking place in Latin American cities as a result of the transformation of the

world economy and the transition to democracy. Examines implications on these changes for the manner in which these cities are governed.

1437 La Ronda Uruguay y el desarrollo de América Latina. Edición de Patricio Leiva Lavalle. Santiago: CLEPI, 1994. 446 p.: bibl.

Leading authorities assess consequences of the Uruguay GATT Round for Latin America. Topics include intellectual property, trade dispute procedures, agricultural trade, protectionism, new commercial opportunities, and textiles. [R. Looney]

1438 Rosenbluth, Guillermo. The informal sector and poverty in Latin America. (*CEPAL Rev.*, 52, April 1994, p. 155–175, bibl., tables)

Discusses origins and extent of informal sector in Latin America. Concludes that most, but not all, of the people in informal sector are poor. Provides data for Argentina, Brazil, Guatemala, Mexico, Panama, Paraguay, Uruguay, and Venezuela.

1439 Rosenthal, Gert. On poverty and inequality in Latin America. (*J. Interam. Stud. World Aff.*, 38:2/3, Summer/Fall 1996, p. 15–37, bibl., graphs, tables)

Empirically demonstrates the widening of income distribution from 1980–92. Shows that in all likelihood, Latin America has the most skewed distribution in the world. Concludes that no single policy will help; rather, a combination of economic growth, expanded education, and income redistributive policies is needed.

1440 Sachs, Jeffrey. Alternative approaches to financial crises in emerging markets. (*Rev. Econ. Polít.*, 16:2, abril/junho 1996, p. 40–52, bibl.)

Reviews lessons to be drawn from problems Latin American countries face during 1980s-early 1990s. Focuses on three types of financial crises: 1) fiscal crises, particularly with foreign debt; 2) foreign exchange crises; and 3) banking crises.

1441 Sader, Frank. Privatizing public enterprises and foreign investment in developing countries, 1988–93. Washington: The World Bank, 1995. 46 p.: bibl., ill. (Occasional paper/Foreign Investment Advisory Service; 5)

Analyzes impact of privatization programs on direct foreign investment (DFI). Uses econometric techniques to demonstrate that infrastructure privatization is highly correlated with higher levels of subsequent DFI capital inflows.

1442 Safa, Helen Icken and **María de los Angeles Crummett.** The magic of the market and the price women pay: examples from Latin America and the Caribbean. (*in* Economic development and women in the world community. Westport, Conn.: Praeger, 1996, p. 183–196)

Documents women's entry into the labor force. Questions whether result is an increase in gender consciousness and greater autonomy, or exploitation. Concludes that labor force participation increases gender consciousness.

1443 Sagasti, Francisco. El desarrollo en la transición al siglo XXI: una perspectiva latinoamericana. (*Estud. Int. /Santiago,* 28:109, enero/marzo 1995, p. 25–36)

Calls for a new development paradigm based on recent innovations in science and technology.

1444 Salama, Pierre. Flexibilidad laboral y globalización financiera en América Latina. (*Rev. Ciclos,* 12, 1997, p. 59–76, tables)

Analyzes impact of financial globalization on organization and function of Latin American labor markets. Notes worsening of income distribution and increase in unemployment.

1445 Sanguinetti, Julio Luis. Mercosur: las alternativas del diseño institucional definitivo. (*Integr. Latinoam.,* 19:201, junio 1994, p. 3–21, bibl.)

Provides rich discussion, from a legal perspective, of the provisions of the Treaty of Asunción and some subsequent protocols. Also discusses concept of supranationality. [M. Birch]

1446 Scheman, L. Ronald. Banking on growth: the role of the Inter-American Development Bank. (*J. Interam. Stud. World Aff.,* 39:1, Spring 1997, p. 85–100)

Presents concise summary of goals, operation, and priorities of the IDB. Discusses Bank's increasing importance during 1980s and 1990s.

1447 Schuldt, Jürgen. Repensando el desarrollo: hacia una concepción alternativa para los países andinos. Quito: Centro Andino de Acción Popular, 1995. 356 p.: bibl. (Estudios y análisis)

Argument for a rethinking of development that is neither the "Washington consensus" nor the view argued by CEPAL, but which is both popular and grounded in the Andean experience. Useful. [D. Schodt]

1448 Seminario Taller Internacional El Desarrollo Rural en América Latina Hacia el Siglo XXI, *Bogotá, 1994.* Memorias. v. 1–2. Bogotá: Pontificia Univ. Javeriana, Maestría en Desarrollo Rural e Instituto de Estudios Rurales, 1994. 2 v.: bibl.

Discusses rural development within context of neoliberal economic policies. Examines family farms, commercial agriculture, and role of rural women. Case studies for Brazil and Colombia.

1449 Sheahan, John. Effects of liberalization programs on poverty and inequality: Chile, Mexico, and Peru. (*LARR,* 32:3, 1997, p. 7–37)

Analyzes and discusses impact of three different types of liberalization models, implemented in Chile, Mexico, and Peru respectively.

1450 Sherraden, Margaret S. Social policy in Latin America: questions of growth, equality, and political freedom. (*LARR,* 30:1, 1995, p. 176–190)

Review essay covers 18 books that focus primarily on the current state of pensions, health care, and social security in the region.

1451 Shirley, Mary M. Privatization in Latin America: lessons for transitional Europe. (*World Dev.,* 22:9, Sept. 1994, p. 1313–1323, bibl., graphs, tables)

Outlines five "lessons" from the Latin American privatization experience that could benefit transitional European countries initiating privatization efforts.

1452 Shome, Parthasarathi. Tax reform in Latin America. (*Financ. Dev.,* 32:1, March 1995, p. 14–17)

Outlines recent tax reforms in the region. The most significant changes occurred in 1) the personal income tax, 2) corporate taxes, 3) consumption taxes, and 4) international trade taxes.

1453 Siddique, Saud. Financing private power in Latin America and the Caribbean. (*Financ. Dev.*, 32:1, March 1995, p. 18–21)

Outlines challenge of financing the region's electric power needs. Discusses the various sources of financing for independent power producers.

1454 Sierra, Gerónimo de. Los pequeños países de América Latina en la hora neoliberal. (*Rev. Cienc. Soc./Montevideo*, 8:9, nov. 1993, p. 16–28, bibl., tables)

Examines impact of 1980s orthodox stabilization policies on seven of region's smallest countries: Bolivia, Costa Rica, Dominican Republic, Ecuador, El Salvador, Haiti, and Uruguay. Concludes by explaining that negative impact of these policies was greater in these countries than in the region's larger countries.

1455 Singh, Ajit. Asia y América Latina comparados: divergencias económicas en los años '80. (*Desarro. Econ.*, 34:136, enero/marzo 1995, p. 513–532, bibl., tables)

Analyzes reasons for Asia's development success and Latin America's collapse during 1980s. Emphasizes the differing long-term development strategies of the two regions.

1456 Siri, Gabriel. Social investment funds in Latin America. (*CEPAL Rev.*, 59, Aug. 1996, p. 73–82)

Describes recent use of social investment funds to relieve regional poverty. These funds, first used in Bolivia in 1986, typically create temporary jobs for social and infrastructure projects. Also examines the financing of these funds.

1457 Smith Perera, Roberto. Economic relations between Latin America and the European Union. (*CEPAL Rev.*, 56, Aug. 1995, p. 97–110, bibl., graphs, tables)

Notes that Latin America's trade surplus with the European Union has steadily declined and became a deficit, for the first time in four decades, in 1993. Presents various proposals to reverse this trend.

1458 Soares, Guido F.S. A compatibilização da ALADI e do Mercosul com o GATT. (*Bol. Integr. Lat.-Am.*, 16, jan./abril 1995, p. 18–39, appendix)

Written by a professional diplomat and international lawyer, article provides a precise discussion of the treatment of Latin American integration, particularly ALADI and Mercosul, in the context of GATT, the global, multilateral trade agreement. [M. Birch]

1459 Social security systems in Latin America. Edited by Francisco E. Barreto de Oliveira. Washington: Inter-American Development Bank; Baltimore, Md.: Johns Hopkins Univ. Press, 1994. 227 p.: bibl., ill., index.

Comparative study of social security systems in Argentina, Brazil, Chile, and Venezuela. Of primary interest for specialists in social security.

1460 Sprout, Ronald. Economic relations between Latin America and the high-performing Asian developing countries. (*CEPAL Rev.*, 56, Aug. 1995, p. 83–96, bibl., tables)

Describes investment and trade trends between three Latin American countries (Brazil, Mexico, and Venezuela) and seven Asian countries (China, Indonesia, Korea, Malaysia, Singapore, Taiwan, and Thailand).

1461 The state of world rural poverty: a profile of Latin America and the Caribbean. Rome: IFAD, 1993. 92 p.: bibl., ill. (some col.).

Discusses rural poverty, including lack of food security and basic needs. Examines factors causing this poverty, and suggests programs for ameliorating the situation.

1462 Stolovich, Luis. El impacto de la integración económica regional sobre el mundo de trabajo: el caso del MERCOSUR. Montevideo: Depto. de Asesoramiento Técnico, Económico y Social, Centro Interdisciplinario de Estudios sobre el Desarrollo-Uruguay, 1994. 120 p.: bibl., ill. (Cuadernos de información popular; 13)

A work designed to help union leaders understand the potential implications of regional integration for workers. In spite of its relative simplicity, book organizes in a convenient way a significant amount of information on industrial relations in Mercosur countries. [M. Rama]

1463 Stolovich, Luis. El poder económico en el Mercosur. Montevideo: Centro Uruguay Independiente, 1994? 453 p.: bibl., ill. (Serie Los Poderosos; 6)

Analyzes link between Mercosur and the consolidation of "economic groups" (conglomerates characterized by a wide sectoral diversification) in Argentina, Brazil, and Uruguay. Based on analysis of 149 such groups, this polemic essay assesses how they have fared in a context of increased reliance on market mechanisms. [M. Rama]

1464 Strategie rozwojowe i polityka przemysłowa wybranych krajów Azji i Ameryki Łacińskiej: praca zbiorowa. Edited by Joanna Żabińska. Katowice, Poland: Akademia Ekonomiczna im. Karola Adamieckiego, 1995. 137 p.: bibl. (Prace naukowe)

Analyzes development strategies and industrial policies pursued from 1960–92 by select countries of Latin America and Asia. Reveals that in early stages of industrialization, all countries, to a certain degree, resort to a policy of import substitution. [Z. Kantorosinski]

1465 Strategies to combat poverty in Latin America. Edited by Dagmar Raczynski. Washington: Inter-American Development Bank; Baltimore, Md: The Johns Hopkins Univ. Press, 1995. 274 p.: bibl., ill., index.

Provides individual case studies of poverty programs in Argentina, Brazil, Chile, and Costa Rica. Documents shift in anti-poverty strategies from "universal" programs, such as general subsidies and price controls, to targeted programs where government spending is channeled to poorest sectors.

1466 Szasz Pianta, Ivonne and **Edith Pacheco.** Mercados de trabajo en América Latina. (*Perf. Latinoam.,* 4:6, junio 1995, p. 49–69, bibl., tables)

Overview of labor market conditions in Latin America emphasizes two issues: 1) the impact of labor market liberalization; and 2) the increasingly precarious nature of working conditions resulting from the growing importance of the informal sector.

1467 Tanner, Evan. The effect of government spending on the current account, output, and expenditures: evidence from Latin America. (*J. Dev. Econ.,* 44:2, Aug. 1994, p. 287–310)

Uses econometric techniques to conclude that *temporary* increases in government spending induce larger increases in the current account deficit than does a *permanent* increase.

1468 Taylor, Alan M. Debt, dependence, and the demographic transition: Latin America in the next century. (*World Dev.,* 23:5, May 1995, p. 869–879)

Observes that Latin American "dependency rates" (i.e., the proportion of the population that is not working) will decline in the late-20th and early-21st centuries. Latin American countries therefore will rely less on foreign borrowing.

1469 Teitel, Simón. Crecimiento, decadencia y encrucijada: ¿qué estrategia de desarrollo debe adoptar la América Latina? (*Trimest. Econ.,* 62:247, julio/sept. 1995, p. 337–380, ibl., tables)

After a decade of stagnation, the 1990s represent a critical crossroads for regional policy formulation. Author outlines three policies to ensure development: 1) an industrial development policy oriented toward exports; 2) support for technological innovation in these industries; and 3) a less ambitious governmental role.

Tellechea de Arca, Mireya. Paraguay socioeconómico y cultural: hidrovía-MERCOSUR. See item **2848.**

1470 Teubal, Miguel. Globalización y expansión agroindustrial: superación de la pobreza en América Latina. Buenos Aires: Corregidor, 1995. 268 p.: bibl. ill. (Economía, política y sociedad)

Ten essays and case studies examine impact of economic globalization and neoliberal reforms on Latin American agricultural sector. Describes process of agricultural modernization and its impact on urban and rural lower-income groups.

1471 Thiesenhusen, William C. Broken promises: agrarian reform and the Latin American campesino. Boulder, Colo.: Westview Press, 1995. 226 p.:

Critically examines successes and failures of agrarian reform efforts in Bolivia, Chile, El Salvador, Guatemala, Nicaragua, and Mexico. Concludes that agrarian reform has done little to reduce poverty or to create employment opportunities and a more equal distribution of resources. Worth reading.

Thrupp, Lori Ann; Gilles Bergeron; and **William F. Waters.** Bittersweet harvests for global supermarkets: challenges in Latin America's agricultural export boom. See item **2061.**

Tokman, Víctor E. *et al.* Globalización y empleo: cambios en el empleo en Perú y América Latina, y en la vida laboral de hombres y mujeres. See item **2177.**

Tomassini, Luciano. La reforma del Estado y las políticas públicas. See item **2989.**

Touraine, Alain. Latinoamérica, punto cero. See item **2990.**

1472 Tsunekawa, Keiichi. Japanese investment in liberalizing Latin American economies: current pattern and possible impacts of FTA initiatives. (*Rev. Econ. Polít.*, 15:3, julho/set. 1995, p. 97–116, bibl., tables)

Describes changes in sectoral distribution of Japanese investments in Latin America. As a result of regional liberalization, the importance of Japanese investment in manufacturing is diminishing as Japanese investors become importers of finished products. Specifically analyzes trends in Argentina, Brazil, Chile, Mexico, and Venezuela.

1473 Uribe-Echevarría, Francisco. La reforma de las políticas públicas y las regiones: nuevas tareas y nuevas formas de gestión del desarrollo. (*in* Territorios en transformación: análisis y propuestas. Madrid: Fondo Europeo de Desarrollo Regional; Consejo Superior de Investigaciones Científicas, 1994, p. 391–421, bibl., table)

Outlines new policies for regional development in light of economic liberalization and new role of government. Policies include transferring power to local authorities, expanding private sector participation, and changing from an objective-oriented planning framework to a process-oriented management framework.

1474 Vargas, Víctor and Juan Rafael Vargas. Perspectivas latinoamericanas en mercados mundiales de productos tropicales. (*Cienc. Econ./San José*, 14:1, 1994, p. 159–175, appendices, bibl., map, tables)

Describes SIMBAD (Simulación Básica de la Agricultura y el Desarrollo), an agricultural model used to simulate effects of trade liberalization in the context of the Uruguay Round trade negotiations.

1475 Vera-Vassalo, Alejandro C. Foreign investment and competitive development in Latin America and the Caribbean. (*CEPAL Rev.*, 60, Dec. 1996, p. 133–156)

Describes new foreign investment strategies of regional governments. Outlines changes in forms of foreign investment (i.e., direct vs. portfolio), and its sectoral distribution. Concludes that region's challenge is to develop a policy framework that will maximize transfer of technological know-how.

1476 Vigevani, Tullo and João Paulo Cândia Veiga. Mercosul: interesses e mobilização. São Paulo: Univ. de São Paulo, Instituto de Estudos Avançados, 1995. 29 p.: bibl., graph. (Col. documentos. Série assuntos internacionais; 38)

Discusses motivation of union movements in Mercosur countries to participate in the regional integration process, and examines role of "innovation militancy." Concludes that if unions are successful in opening a political space for labor issues, the Mercosur process may resemble developments in Europe more than NAFTA. [M. Birch]

1477 Vilas, Carlos María. De ambulancias, bomberos y policias: la política social del neoliberalismo. (*Desarro. Econ.*, 36:144, enero/marzo 1997, p. 931–952, bibl.)

Interesting *interdisciplinary* critical view and evaluation of neoliberal economic policies. Concludes that social costs of such programs are greater than the resulting benefits.

Wiarda, Howard J. After Miami: the summit, the peso crisis, and the future of US-Latin American relations. See item **4058.**

1478 World Bank Conference on Development in Latin America and the Caribbean, 1st, Rio de Janeiro, 1995. Proceedings. Edited by Shahid Javed Burki and Sri-Ram Aiyer. Washington: World Bank, 1997. 1 v: bibl. (World Bank Latin American and Caribbean studies)

Series of articles, most with comments, on challenge of regional reform. Includes articles on increasing savings rates, reducing poverty and inequality, and increasing educational opportunities.

1479 *World Development.* Vol. 24, No. 2, Feb. 1996. Sustainable development: macroeconomic, environmental, and political dimensions. Edited by Lance Taylor. Oxford, England: Pergamon Press.

This issue focuses on sustainable development. Includes separate articles on Argentina, Brazil, Chile, Mexico, and Nicaragua.

1480 Zuvekas, Clarence. Latin America's struggle for equitable economic adjustment. (*LARR*, 32:2, 1997, p. 152–169)

Review essay covers 11 books that examine equity impact of various reform policies and programs.

MEXICO

ROBERT E. LOONEY, *Professor of National Security Affairs, Naval Postgraduate School*

MUCH OF THE RECENT LITERATURE on the Mexican economy focuses on the events and consequences of the disastrous devaluation of December 1994. The economy contracted by seven percent in 1995. While overall growth was restored in 1996, wages of many groups will require a much longer period to recover (item **1542**). Even worse, unofficial estimates suggest open and hidden unemployment combined may still amount to one quarter of the work force.

Clearly, the economy that is emerging after two years of shock therapy and a crippling recession is very different from that of Mexico when it joined the North American Free Trade Area in January 1994. Gone are the high expectations (item **1622**) that characterized much of the economic writing on the country during the early days of NAFTA membership.

The main objective of economic policy since the devaluation of the currency has been to restore credibility and regain investor confidence. The government therefore has been following an austere fiscal policy and is expected to continue to do so. The IMF-linked austerity program, introduced by President Zedillo and Finance Minister Ortiz in March 1995 as part of a US-led international financial rescue package, has had mixed results. The economy has stabilized: inflation shows signs of improvement and the currency has remained fairly stable within the floating regime established in 1995. However, there are significant questions concerning the success of the austerity program in dealing with the underlying causes of the peso crisis (item **1560**).

This pattern of collapse and resurrection is not new to Mexico. Three of the last four presidential election years were followed by an economic crisis—high inflation, recession, and devaluation. In a growing world economy, Mexico's per capita real income (in US dollars) has fallen to about half its 1980 peak. On average, Mexico has less real income today than it did 20 years ago. In June 1997, the government announced a three-year economic plan designed to speed growth, boost investment, and prevent a recurrence of the financial crises which have plagued the country at the end of each six-year government term.

Why does Mexico keep dashing hopes? How can the cycle be broken? The works cited in this section provide interpretations that vary across a wide spectrum.

The writings of those on the left (item **1547**) emphasize the connection between economic and political factors and maintain that three fundamental facts can be learned from the crisis: 1) the neoliberal economic model has been a failure; 2) Mexico cannot make the necessary decisions within the framework of the current corrupt political system; and 3) the nation is well on its way to losing its identity. In general, these authors stress solutions that redefine the economic strategy to regain an option of real growth and fair income distribution based on the expansion of the internal market; open up the political system (elections, media, disclosure of political party funding) to real competition, establish mechanisms for accountability in the management of public affairs, and create checks and balances between the State powers; and establish a new consensus over the "national interest" which in practical terms, means defining a clearer and more sovereign relationship with the rest of the world.

Here the critical issue in economic terms is to promote a dynamic and growing internal market. This requires that Mexico examine its basic needs: how to feed, clothe, house, and educate its people; and then determine how to insure jobs for all. The left stresses that the government has abandoned the internal market to its fate; basic agricultural production has plummeted and there is no existing industrial policy. The only way to solve the Mexico-US migratory problem is to create jobs within Mexico. The necessary resources will come from the drastic renegotiation of Mexico's foreign debt; a redefinition of the NAFTA agreement, including the temporary suspension of some of its sectorial effects; and a political negotiation with Washington to suspend the effects of the February 1995 accords.

The centrist view is more difficult to summarize. Here writers give varying degrees of emphasis to government incompetence, corruption, and the authorities' mistaken assumptions concerning the implications of globalization (item **1529**). A common theme is that the Mexican economic reforms followed "the Washington consensus"—that is, policy goals of fiscal discipline, tax reform, financial liberalization, a single competitive exchange rate, liberalization of trade and foreign investment, privatization, and deregulation. A boom in foreign portfolio investment, induced mainly by transient economic conditions abroad, initially helped, but eventually undermined Mexican reforms. Portfolio flows—investment in Mexican stocks and bonds—initially masked the gravity of Mexico's current account deficit. Then, even when it should have been evident that the country was importing more than was prudent and that its currency was overvalued, foreign investors continued to pump dollars into the economy, exacerbating the peso's overvaluation, stimulating imports, and constraining the government's policy options.

Centrist writings point out that the Mexican government was not a passive spectator in the unfolding drama, rather it was the central actor performing a tightly scripted role that greatly constrained its flexibility. The government needed to rid the economy of its legacy of instability and inefficiency; domestic political restrictions made that task more difficult, while powerful and volatile external forces clouded the government's vision and compromised its policies.

The writings of those on the right are less numerous and often confined to the editorial pages of the conservative press and business publications (item **1540**). Among these works, the emphasis is usually on the incompleteness of the economic reform process and the reform trap into which the country seems to have fallen. These authors contend that in Mexico political leaders don't engage as deeply as is really needed into radical reforms, thus the reforms are short-sighted, limited by political correctness and ambiguous language. Suggested reforms include restructuring the tax system to create greater investment incentives; reforming monetary policy through, for example, the creation of a currency board system; reducing public spending; completing the deregulation process, including deregulation of strategic industries such as oil and energy (necessary to generate net reserves for the currency board); and, finally, social reforms, such as privatizing the social security system.

More narrowly focused writings concentrate on aspects of the peso crisis, such as the increased instability brought about by volatile capital flows (item **1511**). Also of concern is the marked shift in patterns of ownership and control. Investment-starved Mexican companies are increasingly accepting "strategic foreign partners"—the standard euphemism for selling out to a multinational. These arrangements have brought hundreds of millions of dollars into the country, making Mexico a more open economy today than at any previous time in its history. Such openness, however, makes the country vulnerable to external shocks (item **1517**).

The most dramatic change has taken place in Mexico's external sector. In fewer than five years, exports have doubled. Most of this growth has taken place since the peso devaluation as manufacturers sought foreign buyers for goods they could no longer sell at home. By 1996 there were approximately 31,000 Mexican companies directly involved in export activities compared with 15,000 in 1993. In short, Mexico's economic recovery has been driven by the export sector. Unfortunately, this recovery has been very uneven.

The peso crisis accentuated the divide between Mexico's modern export-oriented economy, which now accounts for almost 30 percent of the national output, and the deeply depressed local economy. The latter contracted by 15 percent during the 1995 recession, and only recovered an estimated one percent of lost output in 1996.

Many writers are worried about the poor linkages between the dynamic export sector and the backward local economy (item **1554**). This situation makes Mexico vulnerable since it has only a limited ability to substitute imports. Export industries are overdependent on imported inputs, while imports of consumer goods tend to surge as soon as there is a modest recovery in real income.

Rapid increases in imports are due, in part, to the poor management and low productivity that plague the country's small- and medium-sized companies. Many hope that technical assistance provided by State development banks, universities, and business councils will begin to remedy these shortcomings. The government is trying to persuade large exporters to increase local sourcing, particularly within the maquiladora (in bond) industry on the US border, which draws less than three percent of its inputs from within Mexico.

The country's recent crisis and export boom are also causing regional frictions (item **1691**). Southern states such as Chiapas, Oaxaca, and Guerrero have been left behind as the rest of the country races to integrate with the US. The gap between Mexico's industrial north and more backward south has widened with the dollar economy's concentration of resources. Average labor wages in the northern state of Nuevo Leon are three times the level in Chiapas, a state that borders Guatemala. Per capita consumption in Baja California, another northern state, is five times higher than in Oaxaca, which lies 3,000 km. further south. Life expectancy is 20 years higher in northern Mexico than it is in the sough. One quarter of the population is illiterate in southern Mexico, compared with less than six percent of the population on the US border. Not surprisingly, the two guerrilla uprisings that since 1994 have shaken Mexico erupted in Chiapas and Guerrero.

Even within regions, inequalities are growing (items **1486** and **1487**): real incomes have lost one-fifth of their purchasing power since the devaluation, while more than 50 percent of urban families subsist on less than two minimum wages—the equivalent of 52 pesos or $6.50 a day.

The squeeze on incomes is unlikely to lead to a surge in wage demands—Mexico's labor movement is too subservient to protest. But growing economic hardships are fueling a smoldering popular anger that some economists fear could explode without warning.

1481 Agroeconomía de la papa en México. Coordinación de Anne Biarnès, Jean-Philippe Colin y María de Jesús Santiago Cruz. México City: ORSTOM; Colegio de Postgraduados, 1995. 190 p.: bibl., ill., maps.

Provides an overview of the country's potato industry. Leading experts contribute papers on topics such as regional production patterns, demand for potatoes, and the competition faced by this crop.

1482 Aguascalientes en los noventas: estrategias para el cambio. Coordinación de Claudio H. Vargas. Aguascalientes, Mexico: Instituto Cultural de Aguascalientes, 1993. 455 p.: bibl., ill., col. map, tables. (Contemporáneos)

Series of papers on the economy of Aguascalientes. Emphasis is on problems confronting the rural sector; however, there is a useful discussion of all facets of the regional economy. Numerous tables present hard to find information on the local economy.

1483 Aguilar Barajas, Ismael. Descentralización industrial y desarrollo regional en México: una evaluación del programa de parques y ciudades industriales, 1970–1986. México: Colegio de México, Centro de Estudios Demográficos y de Desarrollo Urbano, 1993. 398 p.: bibl., ill., maps.

Excellent description of the government's attempts at regional decentralization of industry covers the period 1970–88. Focus is on Morelia and Aguascalientes.

1484 Aguilar Monteverde, Alonso. La economía mexicana: cambios, nuevos problemas, perspectivas. (*Probl. Desarro.*, 26:100, enero/marzo 1995, p. 97–123)

The author analyzes the Mexican economy for the last 25 years, focusing on the most significant international changes; also he reflects upon neo-liberal change and its repercussions in underdeveloped countries, which in the Mexican case has meant economical stagnation, falling investment, debilitation of agricultural activities, privatization, and increasing external debt. The essay ends with a series of perspectives, stressing the need for elaborating an "alternative strategy" based on the action of a wide democratic front.

1485 Ajustes y desajustes regionales: el caso de Jalisco a fines del sexenio salinista. Recopilación de Jesús Arroyo Alejandre y Da-

vid E. Lorey. Guadalajara, Mexico: Univ. de Guadalajara, Centro de Ciencias Económico Administrativas; Los Angeles: UCLA Program on Mexico, 1995. 480 p.: bibl., ill., maps. (Serie Ciclos y tendencias en el México del siglo XX ; t. 11)

Wide-ranging series of essays with Jalisco as the focus. Topics include trade with NAFTA and Latin America, the changing production structure of Jalisco state, the impact of the government's neo-liberal economic reforms and the problems associated with increased migration to the US.

1486 Alarcón González, Diana. Changes in the distribution of income in Mexico and trade liberalization. Tijuana, Mexico: El Colegio de la Frontera Norte, 1994. 170 p.: bibl.

Study examines trends in income distribution in Mexico during the period of trade and economic liberalization. Makes the obvious but often ignored point that the prediction of orthodox theory can turn out to be false if its assumptions are not fulfilled and if offsetting forces are at work. The study's detailed analysis of the effective protection rates in 1989 shows how inadequate reforms have been as far as the promotion of efficient resource allocation.

1487 Alarcón González, Diana. La evolución de la pobreza en México durante la década de los ochenta. (*Front. Norte*, 6, número especial, 1994, p. 133–140, bibl., tables)

Argues that the economic restructuring and reform of the 1980s carried a high social cost. The worsening distribution of income produced a considerable increase in poverty levels. This conclusion is based on a comparative analysis of the 1984 and 1989 Surveys of Household Income and Expenditures. These surveys also show that the greatest increase in poverty was in the country's small rural areas.

1488 Alarcón González, Diana and Terry McKinley. Gender differences in wages and human capital: case study of female and male urban workers in Mexico from 1984 to 1992. (*Front. Norte*, 6:12, julio/dic. 1994, p. 41–50, tables)

This paper investigates the wage differential between female and male urban workers in Mexico from 1984–92. The objective is to determine how the wage differential has changed during the period of structural adjustment in Mexico and how this change has been related to differences in endowment of human capital. Using data from the income-expenditure surveys for 1989, 1992, and 1994, they conclude that women workers should have benefited little from structural adjustment. In general, wage inequality has increased substantially during the period of adjustment and it has worsened the relative wages of female workers.

1489 Alarcón González, Diana. Libre comercio y homologación arancelaria en las zonas libres y franjas fronterizas de México. (*Front. Norte*, 7:14, julio/dic. 1995, p. 63–79, appendix, bibl., tables)

Through the use of simulation, this study offers an examination of the quantitative impact that a changing tariff schedule (to comply with NAFTA) will have on commercial and industrial enterprises located in Mexico's free trade zones and border corridors. It argues that although the proposal to equalize tariffs minimizes the costs of this transition in tariff structure, the process itself will provoke a short-term increase in tariffs on certain imports, in addition to a more restrictive fiscal regime for imports from third countries.

1490 Alarcón González, Diana and Terry McKinley. A poverty profile of Mexico in 1989. (*Front. Norte*, 6, número especial, 1994, p. 141–154, tables)

Absolute poverty increased in Mexico between 1984–89, with most of this increase concentrated in rural areas. This paper attempts to provide a profile of the poor based on the 1989 data from INEGI's Income Expenditure Survey. Concludes that rural wage workers and campesinos are the most numerous among the poor and face the greatest depths and severity of poverty. On the other hand, the poor self-employed in non-agricultural sectors are consistently worse off than poor workers. These factors help to explain why inequality among the poor is significant and targeting poverty alleviation at the most severely poor is necessary, especially the poorest of the agricultural sector.

1491 Alegría Olazábal, Tito. Condiciones espaciales de la pobreza urbana y una propuesta para su disminución. (*Front. Norte*, 6, número especial, 1994, p. 61–76, bibl., graphs, tables)

Paper advances a proposal for a program of government intervention that would decrease poverty levels in Mexican cities which have benefited from the internationalization of capital. Tijuana is used as an example. Argues that since poverty is centralized in extended pockets within the urban area, government interventions should focus on modifying the features of these locales; living standards of the population would improve as a result. The inverse option (privileging policies directed toward people over those directed toward place) is the approach that has generally been tried at the various levels of government, but with little savings in the costs for equipment, services, and jobs that are associated with spatial segregation.

1492 Alford, Alan et al. Integración financiera y TLC: retos y perspectivas. Recopilación de Alicia Girón, Edgar Ortiz y Eugenia Correa. Mexico: Siglo Veintiuno Editores; Instituto de Investigaciones Económicas, UNAM, 1995. 447 p.: bibl., ill. (Economía y demografía)

Leading authorities contribute papers on a wide variety of topics related to recent developments in the country's financial system. Topics include integration with the new global markets, effects of financial reform on the macroeconomy, deregulation, and reforms in the country's stock market.

1493 Alternativas para el desarrollo agroindustrial. Coordinación de Vinicio Horacio Santoyo Cortés y Manrrubio Muñoz Rodríguez. Chapingo, Mexico: Univ. Autónoma Chapingo, Centro de Investigaciones Económicas, Sociales y Tecnológicas de la Agroindustria y de la Agricultura Mundial; Programa Interdepartamental Integración Agricultura-Industria, 1993. 351 p.: bibl.

Series of essays by leading Mexican authorities covering all aspects of agribusiness: technology and technological change, producer associations, education, regional problems, and alternatives.

1494 Alvarez C., Jesús et al. Aspectos tecnológicos de la modernización industrial de México. Coordinación de Pablo Mulás del Pozo. México: Academia de la Investigación Científica; Academia Nacional de Ingeniería; Fondo de Cultura Económica, 1995. 404 p.: bibl. (Sección de obras de ciencia y tecnología)

Leading authorities discuss all aspects of industrial technology in Mexico. International comparisons are made with the newly industrialized countries in East Asia. The special circumstance of the *maquiladora* industries is also examined.

1495 Análisis de la crisis mexicana y su impacto en América Latina: foro internacional, ESAN, 9 de febrero de 1995. Exposición de Isaac Katz *et al.* Panelistas, Susana de la Puente *et al.* Lima: Escuela de Administración de Negocios para Graduados, Instituto de Desarrollo Económico, 1995. 156 p.: ill.

Series of essays presented at a conference examining the post-1982 Mexican economic crisis. Focus is on the impact of the crisis on other Latin American economies. There is extensive analysis of the more recent 1994–95 crisis, especially of the devaluation of the peso.

1496 Análisis de las exportaciones de Baja California, 1991–1994. Mexicali?: Gobierno del Estado de Baja California, Secretaría de Desarrollo Económico, 1995. 57 p.: graphs, ill.

Detailed examination of Baja California's exports. Contains detailed description of the region's main exports. For each product data is graphed to show trends and changes over the last several years.

1497 Anda Gutiérrez, Cuauhtémoc. Jalisco: modernidad y futuro. México: s.n., 1995. 237 p., 40 p. of plates: bibl., col. ill.

General overview of the economy of the state of Jalisco. Sections cover the economies of the major towns such as Guadalajara, Zapopan, and Tlaquepaque. Other chapters examine the resource base of the region, the historical evolution of the economy, the region's expanding external trade, and new industries. The final sections speculate as to the region's future prosperity.

1498 Los años del esfuerzo colectivo: la obra pública en Zapopan, 1992–1995. Zapopan, Mexico: Dirección de Obras Públicas, H. Ayuntamiento de Zapopan, 1995. 165 p.: ill., maps.

Provides a detailed description of the public works program for the city of Zapopan in the early 1990s. Contains a number of maps showing the location of projects, together with a description of the contribution made by each to the city's welfare.

1499 Antología de la planeación en México. v. 24, Tres años de ejecución del Plan Nacional de Desarrollo, 1989–1994. México: Secretaría de Programación y Presupuesto : Fondo de Cultura Económica, 1994. v. 1–9, 11–20, 22–24: bibl., ill.

Detailed documentation of the implementation of the Plan Nacional de Desarrollo for the years 1989–94. Contains sections on the goals of the plan, the methods of implementation, and an assessment of accomplishments. Also includes the extensive legislation surrounding the plan.

1500 Apertura económica y perspectivas del sector agropecuario mexicano hacia el año 2000. Coordinación de Emilio Romero Polanco, Felipe Torres Torres y María del Carmen del Valle. México: Instituto de Investigaciones Económicas, Univ. Nacional Autónoma de México, 1994. 488 p.: bibl., ill. (Libros de la revista Problemas del desarrollo)

Leading authorities examine the many problems facing the country's agricultural sector. Emphasis is on government policy, its failures, and potential for stimulating improved rural income growth. Topics include land reform, transportation, free trade and agricultural profitability, and the conditions for sustainable growth.

1501 Arellano Cadena, Rogelio and **Eduardo González Castañon.** Dinámica de la inflación: un análisis econométrico del ajuste heterodoxo mexicano. (*Estud. Econ./México*, 8:2, julio/dic. 1993, p. 249–261, bibl., graphs, tables)

The authors examine the recent inflationary process of the Mexican economy using two complementary approaches that avoid the restrictions imposed by structural models. The first approach applies a vector autoregressive process, while the second applies multivariate cointegration.

1502 Arias, Patricia. Planificación agraria en contexto de riesgo, mediante los modelos MOTAD y de Markowitz: una aplicación a la comarca de La Campiña, Guadalajara. (*Invest. Agrar.*, 9:3, dic. 1994, p. 393–409, bibl., graphs, tables)

Analyzes the risk of choosing efficient crop plans through application of the MOTAD model using quadratic programming. The model is applied to the irrigated area of La Campina, Guadalajara.

1503 **Aroche Reyes, Fidel.** Cambio técnico y cambio estructural: la hipótesis de coeficientes decrecientes; pruebas estadísticas con datos para México. (*Estud. Econ./México*, 10:2, julio/dic. 1995, p. 147–162, appendix, bibl., tables)

Examines several controversies concerning the stability of Mexico's input/output coefficients. One hypothesis is that technical coefficient change is basically due to technological change, except when there are price differences. On the other hand, there are models maintaining that differences between coefficients over time will be negative. Finds that Mexican data provides evidence for such a statement over long periods, but evidence for short periods is not always consistent.

1504 **Avalos Huertas, Antonio** and **Fausto Hernández Trillo.** Comportamiento del tipo de cambio real y desempeño económico en México. (*Econ. Mex.*, 4:2, segundo semestre 1995, p. 239–263, appendices, bibl., tables)

An ARCH (Autoregressive Conditional Heteroscedasticity) model is used to obtain the variances over time for the real exchange rate (RER) (peso/dollar) in Mexico. A model is then constructed to establish the relationship between the RER variability and exports and Mexican GDP, respectively. A negative relationship is found which suggests that not only the level, but the stability of the RER is important in explaining economic performance in an open economy.

1505 **Banco de México.** Bibliografía sobre la economía mexicana, 1992–1994. México: Dirección de Investigación Económica, Oficina de Servicios Bibliotecarios, 1992– .

Excellent selected bibliography on the Mexican economy compiled by Banco de Mexico.

1506 **Bannister, Geoffrey J.** Rent sharing in the multi-fibre arrangement: the case of Mexico. (*Weltwirtsch. Arch.*, 130:4, 1994, p. 800–827, bibl., graphs, tables)

Looks at the implications of imposing voluntary export restrictions (VERs) in imperfectly competitive markets.

1507 **Barbosa Cano, Fabio.** Recursos petroleros de México, 1974–1994: estudios e informes de México y Estados Unidos. México: Instituto de Investigaciones Económi-

cas, Univ. Nacional Autónoma de México, 1994. 115 p.: bibl.

Useful description of exploration and resource discovery in the country's petroleum sector. An extensive bibliography lists nearly all the published research on the topic.

1508 **Barbosa Cano, Manlio.** El crecimiento industrial del estado de Puebla: caracteres económicos e implicaciones sociales en cien años de industrialización. México: Instituto Nacional de Antropología e Historia, 1993. 167 p.: appendix, bibl. (Col. Científica; 260; Serie Historia)

Takes a long run view of the process of development in Puebla, with much of the data going back to 1900. Traces the evolution of the work force, as well as the changing structure of industrialization in the region. Contains a very complete appendix with numerous original tables depicting economic change in the area.

1509 **Batta González, José de Jesús.** Perfil de las organizaciones económicas de León y su área de influencia. León, Mexico: Univ. Iberoamericana León, Comité Editorial, 1994. 156 p.: bibl., tables. (Aportes; 4)

Detailed examination of industrialization in León and surrounding areas. Numerous tables present hard to find data on the economy. Of interest is the development of a comprehensive model to identify the needs of the region.

1510 **Becker, Guillermo.** Retos para la modernización industrial de México. México: Nacional Financiera; Fondo de Cultura Económica, 1995. 161 p. (Nueva cultura económica)

Brief outline of the country's industrial policies. Provides overview of the industrial labor force, its productivity, and competitive position in the world economy. The study concludes with a number of useful recommendations on how the country might improve its industrial productivity.

Blanton, Richard E. *et al.* A dual-processual theory for the evolution of Mesoamerican civilization. See item **34**.

1511 **Bonilla Sánchez, Arturo.** México: la primera gran crisis en la globalización financiera. (*Probl. Desarro.*, 26:102, julio/sept. 1995, p. 85–108, table)

Analyzes the way in which Mexico's

access to the growing process of financial globalization from a position of disadvantage reached a crisis as a result of negative effects of production and openness to short-term, speculative foreign capital. The reduction of the gross domestic product, the excessive increase in the current account deficit, and political problems led to the crisis. The resulting international impact forced Mexico to agree to a huge credit which, according to the author, will aggravate and prolong the crisis.

1512 Borja, Arturo. El estado y el desarrollo industrial: la política mexicana de cómputo en una perspectiva comparada. México: Centro de Investigación y Docencia Económicas; Miguel Angel Porrúa Grupo Editorial, 1995. 301 p.: bibl. (Las Ciencias sociales)

Interesting analysis of the origins and growth of the computer industry in Mexico. Takes a political economy approach towards assessing the role of the government in the development of the industry.

1513 Bouchain Galicia, Rafael C. El déficit en cuenta corriente: la crisis de divisas y el programa de ajuste económico. (*Probl. Desarro.*, 26:102, julio/sept. 1995, p. 109–145, bibl., graphs, tables)

Analyzes the causes and development of the foreign exchange crisis which led to the macro-devaluation of Dec. 1994. The central hypothesis is that the main cause of the breakdown of the neo-liberal financial strategy was the explosive growth of the current account deficit produced during the Salinas Administration, financed by massive capital inflow via portfolio investments which reacted to the violent political events of 1994.

1514 Brachet-Márquez, Viviane de and **Margaret S. Sherraden.** Political change and the welfare state: the case of health and food policies in Mexico, 1970–93. (*World Dev.*, 22:9, Sept. 1994, p. 1295–1312, bibl., tables)

This paper addresses recent changes in Mexico's welfare policy and government strategies to retain popular support in the midst of economic deterioration. In the first part, the authors discuss major interpretations of welfare policy development. In the second part, they review food and health policy changes since 1980. They conclude that contrary to popular conception, social policies were not eliminated. The period pattern was one of initial cut back, followed by stagnation, and later growth.

Burki, Shahid Javed and **Sebastian Edwards.** Latin America after Mexico: quickening the pace. See item **1272.**

1515 Buscaglia, Edgardo. Legal and economic development in Mexico: the steps ahead. (*J. Interam. Stud. World Aff.*, 36:2, Summer 1994, p. 191–205, bibl.)

Argues that in order to promote stability within Mexican society, improvement in the distribution of income and wealth must be addressed by more than just government public spending. The legal framework and the administration of justice must also provide the requisite access to the courts and make enforcement of property rights predictable. Additionally, believes that some of the legal mechanisms recommended in this essay would also help ameliorate the unstable social situation in Mexico.

1516 Calderón, Alvaro; Michael Mortimore; and Wilson Peres. Mexico's incorporation into the new industrial order: foreign investment as a source of international competitiveness. Santiago: Economic Commission for Latin America and the Caribbean (ECLAC), United Nations, 1995. 43 p.: bibl., graphs, tables. (Desarrollo productivo; 21)

Concludes that transnational corporations have been central to the improvement of Mexico's international competitiveness and its closer integration into the new international industrial order. That integration is limited to the North American regional trading group. In the case of Mexico there exist both high-tech (automobile industry) and low-tech (in-bond assembly) variants and both are externally generated.

1517 Calva, Guillermo A. and **Enrique G. Mendoza.** Petty crime and cruel punishment: lessons from the Mexican debacle. (*Am. Econ. Rev.*, 86:2, May 1996, p. 170–175, bibl., graph)

Argues that the harsh punishment that the world capital markets dealt Mexico (and emerging markets in general) following the country's attempt at a modest devaluation reflect the substantial risks embodied in the volatile capital flows characteristic of the global world economy. Despite conventional-wisdom arguments favoring the devaluation as the best policy for dealing with a large current-account deficit and an overvalued real exchange rate, and despite devaluation's effectiveness at addressing these problems, the attempt at correcting the misalignment of the exchange rate triggered a deep and protracted economic crisis and caused continued weakness in Mexico's currency and stock markets.

1518   Calva, José Luis. El modelo neoliberal mexicano: costos, vulnerabilidad, alternativas. México: Fundación Friedrich Ebert, Representación en México; Distribuciones Fontamara, 1993. 199 p.: bibl. (Col. Economía y sociedad)

Assesses the relevance of the neoliberal economic policies for Mexico. After developing the neo-liberal model of stabilization and growth, an assessment is made of the applicability of this model to the Mexican context.

1519   Calva, José Luis. El nudo macroeconómico de México: la pesada herencia de Ernesto Zedillo. (*Probl. Desarro.*, 26 : 100, enero/marzo 1995, p. 63–95, tables)

Starting from a well-documented argument, the author shows the inadequacies of neo-liberal politics in solving the economic and social problems of the country; also he questions the validity of models based on macroeconomic adjustments that were unable to overcome the difficulties they were intended to solve. Proposes specific steps for redesigning the failed neo-liberal scheme.

1520   Calva, José Luis. La reforma del regimen agrario. Texcoco, Mexico: CIESTAAM, 1993. 24 leaves, 1 leaf: bibl. (Reporte de investigación; 17)

Examines the ramifications of a new model for the agricultural sector. Focuses on the consequences of Article 27 in the new Ley Agraria. Particular emphasis on farm size and its impact on incomes and production.

1521   Campos, Ricardo. La participación del sector público en la vivienda. Toluca, Mexico: Univ. Autónoma del Estado de México, 1993. 269 p.: bibl. (Col. Textos y apuntes; 46)

Examines the country's housing policy. Of particular interest is an in-depth assessment of the National Housing Program, 1990–94.

1522   Campos Aragón, Leticia. El ciclo largo de la caída salarial en México. (*Probl. Desarro.*, 26 : 102, julio/sept. 1995, p. 147–171, graphs, tables)

This article explains how, in the course of 18 years, neoliberalism in Mexico has steadily worsened the working conditions of the country's salaried workers by three means: 1) imposing wage ceilings almost always below inflation levels; 2) weakening the fundamental bases of trade union law, such as the right to strike, trade unions's formation, and collective hiring; and 3) imposing new and more intensive work methods for those who have managed to preserve their jobs, together with unemployment and the threat of the technological reorganization of production.

1523   Carabias, Julia *et al.* Manejo de recursos naturales y pobreza rural. México: Univ. Nacional Autónoma de México; Fondo de Cultura Económica, 1994. 138 p.: bibl., ill. (some col.). (Sección de obras de ciencia y tecnología)

Wide-ranging examination of the country's rural economy and resource problems. Extensive discussion of income patterns in different regions, as well as an assessment of the effects of growth on the natural environment.

Carmona, Fernando. Una alternativa al neoliberalismo: México y Latinoamérica 94. See item **4572.**

1524   Carstens, Catherine Mansell. Las finanzas populares en México: el redescubrimiento de un sistema financiero olvidado. México: Centro de Estudios Monetarios Latinoamericanos; Editorial Milenio; Instituto Tecnológico Autónomo de México, 1995. 306 p.: bibl., ill., index.

Excellent overview of financial reform in Mexico. Covers all facets of the system from large commercial banks to smaller peasant establishments in rural areas.

1525   Cartas, José María. Estabilización macroeconómica y reforma estructural en el contexto político y social: el caso de México. Buenos Aires: Fundación Konrad Adenauer, Centro Interdisciplinario de Estudios sobre el Desarrollo Latinoamericano, 1993. 200 p.: bibl., ill. (Serie Estabilización y reforma estructural)

Overview of Mexican attempts at stabilization during the 1980s. Comprehensive examination of the various facets of reforms including the external sector, public finances, and privatization. The study concludes with an excellent assessment of the various impacts and consequences of the reforms.

1526 Casas Guzmán, Francisco Javier. La modernización de la empresa pública en México: logros y resultados, 1988–1994. México: Fondo de Cultura Económica, 1994. 249 p.: ill. (Una visión de la modernización de México)

Excellent study documenting the government's attempts at reforming the country's public enterprises. The first sections describe the government's attempts at reforming the system, with the latter sections assessing the outcome of these programs.

1527 Castañeda, Gonzalo. La demanda por crédito hipotecario en un sistema con índices duales. (*Econ. Mex.*, 4:2, segundo semestre 1995, p. 301–312, bibl.)

Offers an explanation for the observed interest rate inelasticity for mortgage demand between 1989–93 in Mexico. The Dual Index Mortgages offered many individuals access to credit and the possibility of having their own housing, with relatively small installments. These mortgages allowed greater flexibility in the intertemporal choice of consumption, and hence individuals became indifferent to certain changes in interest rates.

1528 Castañeda, Gonzalo. La restricción empresarial en la política fiscal: el caso mexicano de 1972–1976. (*Estud. Econ. /México*, 8:2, julio/dic. 1993, p. 213–247, bibl., graphs)

This paper presents a model grounded on game theory with incomplete information to explain some economic events that took place in Mexico during the Echeverría Administration. Specifically, the aborted fiscal reform of 1972 and the deterioration of the relationship between the government and the private sector from 1973–76 (represented by excessive government expenditures, capital flight, inflation, and low investment).

1529 Castañeda, Gonzalo. El tipo de cambio de equilibrio, expectativas y sucesos polítos: un análisis teórico con base en la experiencia mexicana reciente. (*Trimest. Econ.*, 62:248, oct./dic. 1995, p. 495–521, graphs)

In order to explain the drop in international reserves and the subsequent devaluation in Dec. 1994, the author assumes that investors were aware of the peso overvaluation and the likelihood of a balance of payments

crisis. At the same time, these investors were aware that individual decisions taken together might, in the short run, be enough to keep the Mexican economy functioning, regardless of the long run implausibility of the huge current account deficit. By means of a simple analytical model, the author then shows that political events in 1994 made evident that the overvaluation would produce a speculative attack on the peso, validating the expectations.

1530 Castillejos Bedwell, Simón. El campo ante el futuro de México. México: Distribuciones Fontamara, 1995. 123 p. (Fontamara; 177)

A critical assessment of the government's recent policies towards the agricultural sector. Offers a number of innovative ideas for improving the lot of the rural poor. A particularly useful section presents and critiques the Plan Nacional de Desarrollo, 1995–2000.

1531 Castro Meléndrez, Feliciano. Modernización y ejido: expansión del capital y ruptura política; un estudio regional. Fresnillo, Mexico: Unión de Ejidos Guillermo A. Cabrera, 1992. 238 p.: bibl., ill., maps.

Examination of problems facing ejidos, especially those in the state of Zacatecas. Topics include investment, credit, and shifting government policy towards the sector. Contains much original data.

Cerda, Luis. Causas ecónomicas de la revolución mexicana. See *HLAS 56:1440.*

1532 Cernea, Michael M. The building blocks of participation: testing bottom-up planning. Washington: World Bank, 1992. 71 p.: bibl. (World Bank discussion papers; 166)

Examines how a capacity for mobilizing community participation can be built into a project's design and staffing. This paper answers that question by analyzing, step-by-step, one case rich in experience: the decentralization project in Mexico and its predecessor, the PIDER (Programa Integral para el Desarollo Rural) program. The time span of this series of projects stretches from the early 1970s to the early 1990s.

1533 Chullén, Jorge. La industria azucarera mexicana. (*Debate Agrar.*, 21, mayo 1995, p. 115–134)

Good overview of the problems facing the country's sugar industry.

1534 Cienfuegos Velasco, Francisco *et al.* Sonora hacia el 2000: tendencias y desafíos. Coordinación de Miguel Angel Vázquez Ruiz. Hermosillo, Mexico: SINO, 1993. 341 p.: bibl., ill.

Papers from a seminar held on May 8–9, 1991. The main theme of this seminar was Sonora in the year 2000, with emphasis on reforms and modernization. Papers examine all aspects of the Sonoran economy, assessing current problems and proposing constructive solutions.

1535 Claessens, Stijn and Sweder van Wijnbergen. Secondary market prices and Mexico's Brady deal. (*Q.J. Econ.*, 108:4, Nov. 1993, p. 965–982, bibl., graphs, tables)

The use of official funds in debt reduction packages has been widely argued to amount to a creditor bailout. Authors analyze this question using Mexico's 1989 Brady deal as a case study. Using an option-based pricing model, they obtain pre- and postmarket values for Mexico's commercial debt and find that the market value, inclusive of official funds, went up only marginally. Consequently, Mexico obtained a large share of the benefits of the official funds and struck a favorable deal. The Brady debt reduction formula thus seems to offer an efficient framework for debt workouts.

1536 Clavijo, Fernando *et al.* La política industrial en México. Coordinación de Adalberto García Rocha,. México: Secretaría de Comercio y Fomento Industrial; Colegio de México, Centro de Estudios Económicos, 1994. 234 p.: bibl., ill.

Papers from a seminar presented on April 25–26, 1994 at the Centro de Estudios Económicos. Discuss the major problems currently confronting the country's industrial development. A number of innovative ideas are put forth by some of the country's leading academic experts on the country's industrialization.

Collier, George A. The rebellion in Chiapas and the legacy of energy development. See *HLAS 56:1444.*

1537 La competitividad de la industria mexicana frente a la concurrencia internacional. Recopilación de Antonio Argüelles y José Antonio Gómez Mandujano. México: Nacional Financiera; Fondo de Cultura Económica, 1994. 329 p.: bibl., ill. (Estructura económica y social de México—los noventa)

Compilation of papers presented at a conference on industrial competitiveness and productivity in Puerto Vallarta on Dec. 1–4, 1992. Focus is on the pressures placed on Mexican industry by increasing contact with the rest of the world. Interesting section places many of these issues in a regional setting within Mexico.

1538 Contreras, Oscar *et al.* Mercado de trabajo en la industria maquiladora de exportación : síntesis del reporte de investigación. Coordinación de Jorge Carrillo Viveros. México: Secretaría del Trabajo y Previsión Social, Subsecretaría B, Dirección General de Empleo; Colegio de la Frontera Norte, Dirección General Académica, 1991. 95 p.: ill., tables.

Summary of a detailed study of employment and wage conditions in *maquiladoras* in Tijuana, Cuidad Juárez, and Monterrey. Numerous tables present detailed information not available from other sources.

1539 Contreras Pissón, Carlos Guillermo; Rybén López Malo Lorenzana; and Raúl Vázquez Osorio. El sector social de la economía en México. Coordinación de Hugo Esteve. México: Instituto de Proposiciones Estratégicas, 1991. 158 p.: bibl., ill.

Series of essays by leading authorities on the various facets of Mexico's economic/social arrangements. Essays vary from philosophical discussions of Marx and Marxists to comparisons with the situation in other countries. Several of the essays discuss the evolution of government programs, while several stress the country's legal and institutional structure.

1540 Corona, Rossana. Impact of privatization in Mexico on economic efficiency and market structure: analysis of five companies. (*in* Bigger economies, smaller governments: privatization in Latin America. Boulder, Colo.: Westview Press, 1996, p. 247–275, bibl., tables)

Argues that the importance of analyzing the effect of privatization on production efficiency and market structure lies in the implications both factors have for social wellbeing. On the one hand, an increase in labor production efficiency translates into real wage growth and greater expansion of the economy as a whole. On the other, more competitive market structures beneficially affect the distribution of income between consumers and business. Finally, if the government optimizes and allocates its resources to activities that contribute the most to social welfare, the greater tax receipts accruing from economic growth will also have contributed in a positive way to social welfare.

1541 Cortés Cáceres, Fernando and **Rosa María Rubalcava.** El ingreso de los hogares. Aguascalientes, Mexico: Instituto Nacional de Estadística, Geografía e Informática; El Colegio de México; Instituto de Investigaciones Sociales, UNAM, 1994. 66 p.: bibl., ill.

Excellent analysis of the 1990 census data. Contains extensive summaries of household incomes by region, occupation, etc. A strong point of the study is its illustration of changes in income distribution that have occurred in recent years.

1542 Crisis económica, pobreza y política social. Coordinación de Enrique Valencia Lomelí. Guadalajara, Mexico: IDEA; ITESO; Centro Universitario de Ciencias Sociales y Humanidades, Univ. de Guadalajara, 1995. 165 p.: bibl., ill.

Six essays on the growing problem of poverty in Mexico. Authors attempt to measure poverty and determine its more important causes, including inflation, lagging wages, shifts in productive structure, etc. Essays end with speculation about the government's ability to alleviate poverty in the future.

1543 Cuevas Rodríguez, Enrique. El desarrollo de la crisis en México y la estrategia de cambio estructural, 1970-1988. Guadalajara, Mexico: Univ. de Guadalajara, 1993. 111 p.: bibl. (Cuadernos de difusión científica; 36)

A detailed examination of the origins of the 1982 economic crisis.

1544 Cultura regional y apertura económica. Recopilación de Miguel Manríquez Durán. Hermosillo, Mexico: Colegio de Sonora, 1994. 153 p.: bibl.

Based on a 1992 forum on the trade treaties with Canada. Several interesting papers examine the more important trade issues

confronting the country; topics include the role of education in structuring trade patterns and the transfer of technology.

Damill, Mario; José María Fanelli; and **Roberto Frenkel.** De México a México: el desempeño de América Latina en los noventa. See item **1292.**

1545 Damm Arnal, Arturo. Las dos caras de la moneda: de la vieja a la nueva economía mexicana. México: Editorial MiNos, 1992. 114 p.

Puts forth suggestions for improving the country's economic system. Includes proposals for reforming the monetary system, macroeconomic liberalization, as well as macroeconomic reforms.

1546 Damm Arnal, Arturo. La revolución fiscal en México: una cuestión pendiente; razones en contra de los muchos, y muy elevados, impuestos. México: Panorama Editorial, 1995. 93 p. (Col. Desarrollo gerencial)

Outlines the case for fiscal reform in Mexico and then proposes a number of constructive changes to the existing system.

1547 Dávila Aldás, Francisco R. La crisis económica de México y los nuevos retos en el futuro escenario internacional. (*Relac. Int./México*, 67, julio/sept. 1995, p. 45-61)

Describes and characterizes the economic crisis in Mexico after the devaluation of Dec. 20, 1994. Concludes that this crisis is the first manifestation of Mexico's formal membership in the North American Free Trade Agreement. It is a demonstration of the structural crisis that the country has been experiencing for many years.

1548 Dávila Aldás, Francisco R. Del milagro a la crisis: la ilusión, el miedo, y la nueva esperanza; análisis de la política económica mexicana, 1954-1994. México: Distribuciones Fontamara, 1995. 429 p.: bibl. (Fontamara, col.; 166)

Interesting analysis of Mexico's political economy. Beginning in 1910, the study traces the government's approach to policy making and shows how past mistakes have led to the country's current problems.

1549 Dávila Flores, Mario. La economía de Coahuila en el año 2000. Saltillo, Mexico: Univ. Autónoma de Coahuila, Coordinación General de Estudios de Postgrado e Investigación, 1994. 105 p.: bibl., ill.

Examines the growth potential of Coahuila for the rest of the 1990s. The study begins with a macroeconomic overview of the economy followed by an analysis of the region's balance of payments, pattern of industrialization, and finally the government's financial situation.

1550 De Janvry, Alain; Elizabeth Sadoulet; and Gustavo Gordillo de Anda. NAFTA and Mexico's maize producers. (*World Dev.*, 23:8, Aug. 1995, p. 1349–1362, bibl., graph, tables)

The fall in the producer price of maize that will accompany implementation of trade liberalization and NAFTA has led to dire predictions of falling incomes and labor displacement in Mexican agriculture. The authors use a household survey of the ejido sector to show that a majority of maize producers are in fact not producing for the market and will consequently not be directly affected as producers by a drop in the price of maize, while a significant share will benefit as consumers. For the net sellers, the authors explore determinants of two solutions to a falling maize price: diversification toward high value crops and modernization of maize production. For both, results show the fundamental importance of reconstruction-supportive institutions for marketing, credit, and technical assistance to replace services formerly offered by government and subsequently discontinued under State contraction.

1551 Democracia y política económica alternativa. Coordinación de Enrique de la Garza Toledo. México: La Jornada Ediciones; Centro de Investigaciones Interdisciplinarias en Humanidades, UNAM, 1994. 345 p.: bibl., ill. (Col. La democracia en México)

Leading authorities assess recent developments in a number of relevant economic areas. Topics include trends in the international economy, the debate between Monetarists and the Keynesians, evolution of the financial system, and privatization.

1552 Desarrollo agropecuario en Yucatán de 1958 a 1982: siendo gobernadores del Estado los señores Agustín Franco Aguilar, Luis Torres Mesías, Carlos Loret de Mola y el Dr. Francisco Luna Kan. Recopilación de Paulino Romero Conde. Mérida, Mexico: Talleres Gráficos del Sudeste, 1995. 207 p.

Good overview of developments in Yucatán's agricultural sector. Leading experts contribute essays mainly concerned with that state's policies toward the sector.

1553 Desarrollo sustentable: retos y prioridades. Recopilación de Eugenia Olguín *et al.* Xalapa, Mexico: Instituto de Ecología, 1994. 129 p.: bibl.

Some of the country's leading authorities offer thoughts on importance of achieving sustainable growth in Mexico. The first essay by former President Miguel de la Madrid outlines the concept of sustainable development. This is followed by papers examining the political, social, and ecological impediments to sustainable development.

1554 El desarrollo urbano de México a fines del siglo XX. Coordinación de Adrián Guillermo Aguilar, Luis Javier Castro Castro y Eduardo Juárez Aguirre. Monterrey, Mexico: Instituto de Estudios Urbanos de Nuevo León; Sociedad Mexicana de Demografía, 1995. 225 p.: bibl., ill.

Essays cover wide variety of topics related to urbanization and migration. The volume begins with a detailed examination of the patterns of urbanization over the 1960–90 period. Other essays cover the government's attempts to decentralize the country's economic activity, problems created by Mexico City's urban sprawl, problems associated with the migration to northern states, and water shortage.

1555 El dinero de plástico: historia del crédito al consumidor y de los nuevos sistemas de pago en México. México: J.R. Fortson Editores; CARNET, 1990. 153 p.: bibl., col. ill.

Popular description of the development of bank cards/credit cards in Mexico.

1556 DRI/McGraw-Hill and SRI International. Chihuahua, Mexico's first 21st century economy: working report, March 1994. Chihuahua, Mexico: Proyecto Chihuahua Siglo XXI, 1994. 1 v. (various pagings): ill.

The Chihuahua Siglo XXI Project is a long-term, comprehensive effort to design and implement new economic development strategies for Chihuahua. In 1993, DRI/McGraw-Hill and SRI International examined the external and internal economic environment for the state, developed a new economic vision to guide the decisions of policymakers and leaders in the private sector, and developed strategies and tactics for moving the economy in new directions. This report summarizes the plan.

1557 Dutrénit, Gabriela and **Mario Capdevielle.** El perfil tecnológico de la industria mexicana y su dinámica innovadora en la década de los ochenta. (*Trimest. Econ.*, 60: 239, julio/sept. 1993, p. 643–674, bibl., graphs, tables)

This paper presents the results of an empirical estimation of the technological taxonomy proposed by K. Pavitt for the Mexican industry. This approach allows the authors to analyze the technological profile of the manufacturing sector, its evolution in the 1980s, and its export pattern. A comparison is made with the estimated technological profile of the US manufacturing industry. Results show a specialization of Mexican manufactures in the sectors of low technological dynamism.

1558 La economía mexicana en el umbral del siglo XXI: antología. Recopilación de María Luisa González Marín y Lucía Alvarez Mosso. México: Ediciones Quinto Sol; H. Cámara de Diputados, LV Legislatura; Instituto de Investigaciones Económicas, UNAM, 1994. 287 p.: bibl.

Series of papers stressing various aspects of free trade. Topics include changes in the international financial system, *maquiladoras*, NAFTA, public sector finances, and trade conflicts between Mexico, the US, and other Latin American countries.

1559 Economía y democracia: una propuesta alternativa. Recopilación de Ifigenia Martínez. México: Grijalbo, 1995. 484 p.: bibl., ill.

Wide-ranging set of papers dealing with most aspects of the economy. Topics include: the transition to democracy, economic reforms, sustainable production, agriculture, industry, education and technology, productivity and competition, and employment.

1560 Edwards, Sebastian. Exchange-rate anchors, credibility, and inertia: a tale of two crises, Chile and Mexico. (*Am. Econ. Rev.*, 86:2, May 1996, p. 176–180, bibl., graphs, tables)

Argues that both the Mexican (1980s) and Mexican and Chilean (1970s) structural reforms were characterized by drastic openings of the economy, sweeping privatization programs, and major deregulation efforts. In both cases the authorities used a predetermined nominal exchange-rate anchor to reduce inflation, disregarding the real-side consequences of this policy. These stabilization programs—combined with very large capital inflows—were undermined by a weak banking system and generated a situation of exchange rate overvaluation, a vulnerable financial sector, and eventually, the collapse of the currency.

1561 Eggerstedt, Harald; Rebecca Brideau Hall; and **Sweder van Wijnbergen.** Measuring capital flight: a case study of Mexico. (*World Dev.*, 23:2, Feb. 1995, p. 211–232, graphs, tables)

The authors show how various methods commonly used to measure capital flight produce vastly different estimates. Choosing an inadequate measurement concept can lead to distorted quantitative results. The paper argues in favor of the residual approach, which assumes that capital inflows in the form of increases in external indebtedness and foreign investment should finance either the current account or reserve accumulation; shortfalls in reported use can be attributed to capital flight. Several important adjustments, however, are required to avoid distortions. The paper includes a new set of capital flight estimates for Mexico.

1562 El ejecutivo mexicano en el entorno de competitividad internacional. Monterrey, Mexico: Centro de Estudios Estratégicos, Centro de Estudios sobre Educación; Instituto Tecnológico y de Estudios Superiores de Monterrey, 1995. 61 p.: bibl., graphs, tables.

Presents the results of a survey of Mexican executives. Topics include levels of education, international experience, areas of expertise, etc. Extensive tables and graphs make the main points of the report easy to grasp.

1563 Elizondo, Carlos. The making of a new alliance: the privatization of the banks in Mexico. México: Centro de Investigación y Docencia Económicas, 1993. 27 p. (Documento de trabajo, 0185–3384; 5. Estudios políticos)

Examines the prevarication of the Mexican banks that started in May of 1990. Finds that in the process of privatization the government showed its relative autonomy from the former bankers whose assets were nationalized in 1982. In fact, the government has shown that it was not at the mercy of specific private financiers. The banks were not sold back to their previous owners, but to the highest bidder.

1564 Empresa, crisis y desarrollo. México: Univ. Autónoma Metropolitana, Unidad Iztapalapa, División de Ciencias Sociales y Humanidades, Depto. de Economía, 1991. 219 p.: bibl., ill. (Serie de investigación; 4)

Series of essays on economic problems currently facing Mexico and other Latin American countries. Topics include antiinflationary policies, determinants of balance of payments problems, industrial concentration, technology, dependence, multinational corporations, and exports of non-traditional products.

1565 Ensayos sobre la economía de la Ciudad de México. Recopilación de Ricardo Samaniego. México: Ciudad de México Librería y Editora, Pórtico de la Ciudad de México, 1992. 302 p.: bibl., ill.

Leading experts provide papers on the economy of Mexico City. Topics include the city's demographics, educational system, public finances, water availability, and industrial development.

1566 Eskeland, Gunnar S. Attacking air pollution in Mexico City. (*Financ. Dev.*, 29:4, Dec. 1992, p. 28–30, graph, photo)

Describes a program whereby Mexico City is trying to economize on tasks that cause pollution as well as make cars and fuels cleaner. The program combines pricing and regulatory measures to stimulate these changes.

1567 Espinoza Valle, Víctor Alejandro. Reforma del estado y empleo público: el conflicto laboral en el sector público de Baja California. México: Instituto Nacional de Administración Pública, 1993. 380 p.: bibl.

Excellent study of public employment in Baja California. Detailed data on patterns of employment, wages, and other benefits of public employees in the region. Identifies numerous problems and provides recommendations for reform of the system.

1568 Estado de México: perspectivas para la década de los 90. Coordinación de Roberto Blancarte. Zinacantepec, Mexico: El Colegio Mexiquense; Instituto Mexiquense de Cultura, 1994. 705 p.: bibl., ill., maps.

An extensive series of essays by leading economic authorities. Topics covered include the agricultural sector, industrialization, labor and employment, education, industrial development, and the country's demographic evolution.

1569 Exposición sobre la política monetaria: para el lapso 1°. de enero de 1995–31 de diciembre de 1995. México: Banco de México, 1995. 59 p.: ill.

Report from the Bank of Mexico on the current economic conditions as of the end of 1995. Topics include production and employment, the external sector, inflation, public finances, and the country's monetary situation.

1570 Feliz, Raúl Aníbal and **John H. Welch.** Un análisis de la credibilidad y del comportamiento de las bandas unilaterales de los tipos de cambio en México y Chile. (*Econ. Mex.*, 3:1, enero/junio 1994, p. 5–30, bibl., graphs, tables)

The purpose of this study is to gauge the performance of unilateral target zones arrangements in Mexico and Chile. The authors look at the institutional and historical evolution of these exchange rate regimes: they then deal with performance in a more formal fashion by looking at the stochastic behavior of the exchange rates and the credibility of the target zones. Their results indicate that both the Chilean and Mexican arrangements have been credible.

1571 Feliz, Raúl Aníbal and **Laura Vargas.** Una prueba econométrica del enfoque moderno de la cuenta corriente en México. (*Estud. Econ./México*, 9:2, julio/dic. 1994, p. 189–207, bibl., graphs, tables)

Derives and evaluates the observable implications of the new view of the current account of the balance of payments in Mexico, during the period 1950–91. According to this view, the current account is a result of the optimal decisions towards saving and investing from economic agents. The results arising from econometric tests applied to Mexico are consistent with the observable implications of this new view.

1572 Feltenstein, Andrew and **Jiming Ha.** The role of infrastructure in Mexican economic reform. (*World Bank Econ. Rev.,* 9: 2, May 1995, p. 287–304, graphs, tables)

This article estimates the relationship between the provision of public infrastructure and private output in 16 sectors in Mexico. The sector specific cost functions depend on wages, the cost of capital, and the nominal values of the stocks of three types of infrastructure: electricity, transport, and communications. The article concludes that infrastructure in electricity and communications generally reduces the cost of sectoral production, but transportation infrastructure tends to increase cost of sectoral production.

Fernández Jilberto, Alex E. and **Barbara Hogenboom.** Mexico's integration in NAFTA: neoliberal restructuring and changing political alliances. See item **4082.**

1573 Flores Osorio, Jorge Mario *et al.* Estudios regionales: ensayos sobre cinco estados de la República. Tlaxcala, Mexico: Consejo Nacional de Ciencia y Tecnología, 1994. 136 p.: bibl., ill., maps. (Col. Textos de apoyo académico)

Essays on the economies of Guerrero, Hidalgo, Morelos, Querétaro, and Tlaxcala. Topics include political developments, the educational systems, and the unique characteristics of these five important states.

Franco, Gabriel Ascencio. Neoliberalismo y usura. See item **2543.**

1574 Friedmann, Santiago; Nora Lustig; and **Arianna Legovini.** Mexico: social spending and food subsidies during adjustment in the 1980s. (*in* Coping with austerity: poverty and inequality in Latin America. Washington: The Brookings Institution, 1995, p. 334–374, bibl., tables)

Focuses on how changes in social spending and the reform of food subsidies affected living standards during adjustment. Specifically the authors address the size of social spending cuts and the nature of food subsidy reform, as well as the government's efforts to mitigate the impact on the poor; the extent to which spending cuts limited human and physical resources in institutions providing public education and health care; and the deterioration in social indicators.

1575 Galindo, Luis M. La hipótesis de expectativas en el mercado de cetes en México, 1990–1995. (*Estud. Econ./México,* 10:1, enero/junio 1995, p. 67–88, appendices, bibl., tables)

The objective of this essay is to analyze the expectations hypothesis under the assumption of rational expectations for the public bond market in Mexico. The results indicate that the expectations hypothesis with rational expectations is rejected. The empirical evidence also indicates there is a stable long-term relationship between short- and long-term interest rates and that the term structure and the changes in the short-term interest rates contain information with which future changes in interest rates can be forecasted.

1576 Galve-Peritore, Ana Karina and **N. Patrick Peritore.** Mexican biotechnology policy and decision makers' attitudes toward technology policy. (*in* Biotechnology in Latin America: politics, impacts, and risks. Wilmington, Del.: Scholarly Resources, 1995, p. 69–95, table)

Reports findings from extensive survey of attitudes towards biotechnology policy in Mexico. Find that three levels of analysis are pertinent to biotechnology policy in the country: theory, policy, and decision makers' attitudes.

1577 García-Hernández, Francisco and **Rosa Claudia Hernández Cavazos.** La politica económica y la crisis de México : nueva crisis, viejos problemas. México: Centro de Estudios Estratégicos, ITESM, 1995. 97 p.: bibl., ill.

The authors assess several of the economy's chronic problem areas, including investment and external debt, employment, and the *maquiladoras.* The analysis is original and more insightful than other volumes addressing these themes.

1578 García Zamora, Rodolfo. Crisis y modernización del agro en México, 1940–1990. México: Univ. Autónoma Chapingo, Dirección de Difusión Cultural, 1993. 335 p.: bibl., ill., map.

Examination of various government programs intended to improve the agricultural sector. Emphasis is on PIDER, SAM, PRONAL, and PRONADRI.

1579 Garrido, Celso. National private groups in Mexico, 1987–1993. (*CEPAL Rev.*, 53, Aug. 1995, p. 159–175, bibl., tables)

In the author's view, an important result of the economic reforms begun in Mexico in 1983, especially in the period after 1987, is that national private groups have assumed a leading place in the new economic model. These are not only traditional groups which were restructured in the course of those reforms, but also new groups formed or developed in that period which have come to have decisive weight in the national economy.

1580 Garza, Gustavo and **Salvador Rivera.** Dinámica macroeconómica de las ciudades en México. Aguascalientes, Mexico: Instituto Nacional de Estadística, Geografía e Informática; México: ECM; IIS- UNAM, 1994. 120 p.: bibl., graphs, ill., tables.

Excellent compilation of all facets of economic activity in the country's leading cities. Numerous tables and graphs present difficult to find data on the evolution of the urban centers during the last several decades.

1581 Gasca Neri, Rogelio. Foro Global México-Aspen: desarrollo de la infraestructura en México, Acapulco, febrero 1994. México?: Secretaría de Comunicaciones y Transportes, 1994. 1 v. (various pagings): ill. (some col.), maps.

Overview of the existing condition of Mexican infrastructure. Oriented toward identifying areas that need further investment and expansion.

1582 Gil-Díaz, Francisco and **Agustín Carstens.** One year of solitude: some pilgrim tales about Mexico's 1994–1995 crisis. (*Am. Econ. Rev.*, 86:2, May 1996, p. 164–169, bibl., graph, tables)

Paper addresses the following question: how could Mexico's fiscal, supply-side, and trade reforms lead it into the crisis caused by the Dec. 1994 devaluation. The authors analyze the hypotheses that have been proposed to explain the crisis and conclude that it had a political origin and that some of the financial disequilibria, including the maintenance of a fixed nominal exchange rate in the face of the recent explosion in international transactions, contributed to the crisis.

1583 Globalización, economía y proyecto neoliberal en México. Coordinación de Ernesto Soto Reyes, Mario Alejandro Carrillo y Andrea Revueltas. México: Univ. Nacional Autónoma Metropolitana, Unidad Xochimilco; France: GRESAL, Univ. Pierre Mendes France de Grenoble, 1995. 337 p.: bibl., ill. (Col. Ensayos)

Papers focus on problems associated with the implementation of neoliberal economic policies in Mexico under the Salinas Administration. Concern is with labor conditions, and the ability of firms to face foreign competition.

1584 Gollás, Manuel and **Oscar Fernández.** El subempleo sectorial en México. (*Trimest. Econ.*, 60:240, oct./dic. 1993, p. 909–926, bibl., tables)

The authors measure the degree of disguised unemployment in 18 sectors. They also develop a method of estimation that can be applied to any country with reliable input-output tables.

1585 Gómez Flores, Ramiro. Sinaloa: el reto de la modernización productiva y social. Culiacán, Mexico: Univ. Autónoma de Sinaloa, 1993. 230 p.: bibl., ill., maps.

Comprehensive description of the current economic conditions in the state of Sinaloa. Focus is on regional planning and the government's efforts at expanding the region's economy.

Gonçalves Júnior, Carlos Augusto and **João Paulo Cândia Veiga.** A indústria automotiva brasileira no MERCOSUL. See item **2353.**

1586 González de la Rocha, Mercedes. The resources of poverty: women and survival in a Mexican city. Oxford, UK; Cambridge, USA: Blackwell, 1994. 311 p.: bibl., index, map. (Studies in urban and social change)

Examination of problems faced by working-class families in Guadalajara. Bringing women and children to the center of her analysis, the author explores the effects of an uneven labor market on the structure and organization of households, revealing a highly homogenous working class, united in its survival instinct and in its dependence upon the women of the family for the defense of its standards of living.

Gould, David M. Mexico's crisis: looking back to assess the future. See item **3057.**

1587 Gutiérrez Arriola, Angelina. Reflexiones sobre la reestructuración del capital y del trabajo en México. (*Probl. Desarro.*, 26:101, abril/junio 1995, p. 173–204)

Between 1980–94 Mexico's large firms, as well as their workers, have undergone a continuous process of restructuring. Integrated into the production chain at the world level, they have modified their corporate strategies through the development of a network of alliances, mergers, and contracts, at the same time they have remodeled their production processes, attempting to rationalize them by means of a new organization of work based on quality, productivity, and the multifunctional worker.

Heath, Hilarie J. British merchant houses in Mexico, 1821–1860: conforming business practices and ethics. See *HLAS 56:1335.*

Heredia, Blanca. Estructura política y reforma económica: el caso de México. See item **3059.**

1588 Heredia, Blanca. Mexican business and the State: the political economy of a muddled transition. (*in* Business and democracy in Latin America. Pittsburgh, Pa.: Univ. of Pittsburgh Press, 1995, p. 179–216, tables)

The author first examines the conditions that led to conflict in State-private sector relations and the growing politicization of Mexican business leaders during 1970–82. This is followed by an analysis of how the government rapidly undermined business opposition after 1982.

1589 Hernández Trillo, Fausto. Crecimiento y liberalización económica: un análisis de series de tiempo para México. (*Estud. Econ./México*, 8:1, enero/junio 1993, p. 65–85, graphs, tables)

This paper presents a methodology to measure the long-term impact of economic liberalization and deregulation on economic growth in Mexico. The methodology determines whether there has been a permanent change in the growth rate. The results show that in the Mexican case the increase has been transitory, and change has been in the level of growth rather than in the rate. This suggests that technology and labor productivity has not changed substantially, and hence growth is explained by the use of idle capacity.

1590 Holt, Richard P.F. The 1982 reforms and the employment conditions of Mexican women. (*in* Women in the age of economic transformation: gender impact of reforms in post-socialist and developing countries. New York: Routledge, 1994, p. 178–191, tables)

Analyzes the impact of post-1982 economic reforms on the employment conditions of Mexican women. Special attention is given to changes in the rural and urban sectors as well as in the *maquila* industry. Finds that declining wages and the high unemployment rates forced women to increase their work force participation rates faster than their male counterparts. Unlike the more developed countries, however, higher female work force participation has not greatly benefited Mexican women. They have been forced to migrate to the urban areas in order to protect their family incomes. In addition, while married women have been working more, they have been pushed into the less desirable jobs of the informal sector.

1591 Huerta González, Arturo. Riesgos del modelo neoliberal mexicano: tratado de libre comercio, tipo de cambio, bolsa de valores. México: Editorial Diana, 1992. 149 p.: bibl.

Focuses on the government's liberalization of trade, particularly that with North America. Concludes with an excellent assessment of the pros and cons of the external sector reforms.

1592 Hueth, B.M.; G.T. O'Mara; and R.E. Just. NAFTA: repercusiones del Tratado de Libre Comercio entre EE.UU. y Mejico en el sector agrícola y ganadero. (*Invest. Agrar.*, 10:1, abril 1995, p. 125–148, bibl., tables)

Provides an analysis of the effects of NAFTA on US and Mexican markets for various agricultural products. Simulations are carried out under four alternative scenarios. The results show that impacts are significantly attenuated under the transition specified in the agreement and major estimated effects are on corn-related variables.

1593 Ibarra Escobar, Guillermo. Economía terciaria y desarrollo regional en México: el caso de Sinaloa. Culiacán Rosales, Mexico: Univ. Autónoma de Sinaloa; Instituto de Estudios Urbanos de Nuevo León, 1995. 378 p.: bibl., ill., maps, tables.

Examines the changing economic structure of Mexico, with emphasis on the shift of production toward the tertiary or service sector. While the study covers the whole country and its regions, emphasis is on the state of Sinaloa. Contains numerous tables of hard to find data on regional economies.

1594 La industria mexicana en el mercado mundial: elementos para una política industrial. Recopilación de Fernando Clavijo y José I. Casar Pérez. México: Fondo de Cultura Económica, 1994. 2 v.: bibl. (Lecturas/El Trimestre económico; 80)

Part 2 of a major study of the competitiveness of Mexican industry. This volume covers agro-industry, textiles, automobiles, and electronics. The essays are by leading authorities on each industry.

1595 Instituto Nacional de Estadística, Geografía e Informática (Mexico). Una visión de la modernización de México en cifras. México: Fondo de Cultura Económica, 1994. 416 p.: graphs, tables. (Una visión de la modernización de México)

Exhaustive compilation of data on the Mexican economy. Book consists exclusively of tables and graphics covering all facets of the economy and the country's population. Topics include demographics, employment, earnings, education, the public sector, agriculture and the other major sectors, regional income, etc.

1596 Integración comercial Nuevo León-Texas. Coordinación de Sylvia Adriana Pinal. Monterrey, Mexico: Centro de Estudios México-Estados Unidos-Canadá, 1994. 295 p.: bibl., ill., tables.

Detailed examination of the changing pattern of trade between Nuevo León and Texas. Contains many original tables with data not easily obtainable from other sources.

1597 Izquierdo, Rafael. Política hacendaria del desarrollo estabilizador, 1958–1970. México: El Colegio de México, Fondo de Cultura Económica; Fideicomiso Historia de las Américas, 1994. 309 p.: bibl., index. (Serie Hacienda. Sección de obras de historia)

Historical examination of key areas of economic policy in Mexico. In addition to documenting the major trends in policy, the book contains a wealth of detailed data on the economy.

1598 Jarquín Sánchez, María Elena. La producción del calzado en Tepito. México: Univ. Nacional Autónoma de México, Centro de Investigaciones Interdisciplinarias en Humanidades, 1994. 174 p.: bibl., ill., tables. (Col. Alternativas)

Carefully documented study of footwear production. Contains many original tables listing employment, output, and other relevant statistics.

1599 Jesús Silva Herzog: universitario ejemplar; homenaje en el centenario de su natalicio. Recopilación de Benito Rey Romay y Georgina Naufal Tuena. Prólogo de Miguel de la Madrid H. México: Instituto de Investigaciones Económicas/UNAM; Fondo de Cultura Económica, 1994. 183 p.: bibl. (Obras de economía latinoamericana)

Series of papers discussing the life and contributions of former Finance Minister Jesus Silva Herzog. Includes a forward by Miguel de la Madrid, who was president during the 1982 debt crisis when Silva Herzog acted as the country's main negotiator with the creditor countries.

1600 Jusidman de Bialostozky, Clara and **Marcela Eternod.** La participación de la población en la actividad económica en México. Aguascalientes, Mexico: Instituto Nacional de Estadística, Geografía e Informática, 1994. 214 p.: bibl., ill.

Provides an excellent statistical account of the country's labor force. Detailed tables contain a wealth of information concerning the occupational composition of the work force, labor trends, and location of the major occupations.

1601 Klein-Robbenhaar, John F.I. Agro-industry and the environment: the case of Mexico in the 1990s. (*Agric. Hist.*, 69:3, Summer 1995, p. 395–412, tables)

Concludes that the modernization of Mexican agriculture imposes capitalist-style development over indigenous modes of production. Argues that for the vast majority of rural Mexicans, agro-industry represents further rural misery and hunger and a deteriorating quality of life.

1602 Kraemer Bayer, Gabriela. Utopía en el agro mexicano: cuarenta proyectos de desarrollo en áreas marginadas. Chapingo, Mexico: Dirección de Difusión Cultural,

CIESTAAM (Diagnóstico Externo), Univ. Autónoma Chapingo, 1993. 582 p.: bibl., ill.

Explores ways in which the country can improve the lives of rural people in Mexico. Covers all facets of agricultural improvement including technology, reorganization of producer groups, and government policy.

1603 Krugman, Paul. Dutch tulips and emerging markets. (*Foreign Aff.*, 74:4, July/Aug. 1995, p. 28–44, ill.)

Argues that because the 1990–95 euphoria about developing countries was so overdrawn, the Mexican crisis is likely to trigger a reversal. That is, the rest of the decade will probably be marked by falling expectations. Markets will no longer pour vast amounts of capital into countries whose leaders espouse free markets and sound money on the assumption that such policies will necessarily produce vigorous growth; investors will want hard evidence of such growth. This new reluctance will be self-perpetuating, in that the huge capital gains in emerging markets equities will not continue.

1604 Leiderman, Leonardo; Nissan Liviatan; and Alfredo Thorne. Shifting nominal anchors: the experience of Mexico. (*Econ. Mex.*, 4:2, segundo semestre 1995, p. 197–237, bibl., graph, tables)

This paper discusses the role of exchange rate policy as a nominal anchor in Mexico and develops the inflation target as the monetary framework for anchoring prices. Describes how Mexico is applying this framework while shifting to a more flexible exchange regime, and also discusses the role of the newly independent central bank and monetary policy in keeping inflation under control while shifting nominal anchors. Describes the situations as seen in early 1994, but makes no attempt to describe the events that led to the 1994 crisis and its aftermath.

Liehr, Reinhard. La función crediticia de los comerciantes en la ciudad de Puebla, México en la época anterior a los bancos, 1821–1864. See *HLAS 56:1346*.

Loaeza, Soledad. La experiencia mexicana de liberalización. See item **4613.**

1605 Loedl, Peter and Mark A. Martínez. El Banco de México y la política monetaria: la lucha por la independencia y la credibilidad política. (*Probl. Desarro.*, 26:101, abril/junio 1995, p. 91–124)

Based on a detailed examination of the relationship between the Central Bank's level of independence, its ability to carry out a noninflationary monetary policy and the credibility given to its policies, the authors make a comparative analysis between the Mexican Central Bank and the Bundesbank (the Central Bank of Germany). Having shown that Banco de Mexico's autonomy is conditioned by the presidentialist regime, the essay concludes that the State should adopt a different type of economic culture and policies.

1606 López G., Julio *et al*. Mercado, desempleo y política de empleo. México: Nuevo Horizonte Editores; Centro de Estudios para un Proyecto Nacional, 1996. 183 p.: bibl.

A number of leading authorities present essays focused on the country's labor supply and employment problems. The essays contain a number of interesting observations backed up in many cases with sound empirical analysis. Techniques, such as input-output analysis, produce valuable insights into factors underlying the country's pattern of employment.

1607 López G., Julio. The potential of Mexican agriculture and options for the future. (*CEPAL Rev.*, 47, Aug. 1992, p. 137–148, bibl., tables)

Suggests that the potential of Mexican agriculture is enormous. In the short run, the sector's potential can be increased through recapitalization and other institutional measures. In order to stimulate supply, the author feels it would be necessary to provide suitable incentives for producers, such as selective subsidies. These should be short-term subsidies and should be differentiated by product, type of producer and, possibly, by region.

1608 López Rangel, Rafael. Problemas metropolitanos y desarrollo nacional. México: Univ. Autónoma Metropolitana, Unidad Azcapotzalco, 1992. 191 p.: bibl., ill., maps. (Col. Libro de texto)

Begins by tracing the urbanization process in Latin America, then contrasts that process with the situation in Mexico. Detailed account provided of the growth of Mexico City from 1930–94. The study ends with a good discussion of the problem of financing the growing costs of providing public services in the country's capital.

1609 Loría Díaz, Eduardo. Estilos de crecimiento y salarios manufactureros en México. Toluca, México: Univ. Autónoma del Estado de México, 1994. 333 p.: bibl.

Uses an economic modeling approach to determine factors affecting manufacturing remuneration.

1610 Lustig, Nora *et al*. México: evolución macroeconómica, financiación externa y cambio político en la década de los 80. Madrid: Fundación CEDEAL, 1992. 172 p.: bibl., ill. (Situación latinoamericana. Serie Estudios América Latina en la década de los 80)

Essays examine the causes and consequences of Mexico's crisis during the 1980s. Topics include the external debt situation, macroeconomic stabilization, and government attempts to buffer the country from the effects of the disruptions.

1611 Lustig, Nora. México, hacia la reconstrucción de una economía. Traducción de Eduardo L. Suárez. México: El Colegio de México; Fondo de Cultura Económica, 1994. 200 p.: bibl., index. (Sección de obras de economía latinoamericana)

Seeks to describe and interpret Mexico's economic experience during the 1980s. Emphasizes the shift in development strategy from import substitution, State-controlled economy to an open economy in which the State's intervention is limited by a new legal and institutional framework. Also of interest is an examination of the social costs of the economic crisis and adjustment during the 1980s. Speculates about why adjustment and reform in the 1980s may have been easier for Mexico than for other debt-ridden countries.

1612 Lustig, Nora and Ann Mitchell. Poverty in Mexico: the effects of adjusting survey data for under-reporting. (*Estud. Econ./México*, 10:1, enero/junio 1995, p. 3–28, appendix, bibl., graphs, tables)

Estimates changes in poverty in Mexico between 1984–89 using uncorrected data from household surveys. Estimate is repeated after the data is adjusted for underreporting using National Accounts totals as benchmarks. The paper illustrates the sensitivity of poverty estimates in Mexico regarding both the adjustment itself and the specific procedure used to adjust the survey data for underreporting.

1613 Mancera, Miguel. No easy recipe: one year after the Mexican financial crisis, the Governor of Banco de México Miguel Mancera talks to *The Banker*. (*Banker/London*, 146:840, Feb. 1996, p. 66–68, photos)

Interview with Miguel Mancera, governor of the Bank of Mexico. In this article Mancera addresses the questions: 1) What has been the level of government financial assistance to the banks over the past year and how much will it need to allocate to support programs in 1996?; and 2) what factors characterize the government's current policy on bank intervention, especially in light of recent moves regulating Inverlat and Banamex?

1614 Mansell-Carstens, Catherine. The impact of the Mexican bank reprivatizations. (*in* Bigger economies, smaller governments: privatization in Latin America. Boulder, Colo.: Westview Press, 1996, p. 277–316, bibl., graphs, tables)

Examines several interrelated issues. First is an assessment of the nationalization of the banks and economic conditions in the early 1980s. This is followed by an analysis of the essential bank reprivatization policies as pursued by the De la Madrid and Salinas Administrations. Concludes with an examination of the social and economic impact of the bank reprivatizations. The latter is examined from a macroeconomic view, detailing the impact on the structure of the financial services industry.

1615 Márquez Padilla, Carlos. Los sistemas de relaciones industriales de México, Canadá y Estados Unidos. (*Trimest. Econ.*, 61:243, julio/sept. 1994, p. 433–465, bibl., table)

This paper carries out a comparative analysis of the system of industrial relations in Mexico, Canada, and the US. The aim is to identify the constraints each country faces in the adjustment process needed to efficiently adapt the employment relationships to the present economic conditions. The article concludes that on the whole, none of the three industrial systems is superior. In each case there exists particular dimensions in which one country has a disadvantage and therefore there is a space that could justify government intervention.

Martin, Cheryl English. Modes of production in colonial Mexico: the case of Morelos. See *HLAS 56:1184.*

1616 Martínez, Gabriel and **Guillermo Fárber.** Desregulación económica, 1989–1993. México: Fondo de Cultura Económica, 1994. 356 p. (Una visión de la modernización de México)

Documents the government's attempt at economic deregulation during the latter part of the Salinas Administration (1989–93). Areas covered include the transport sector, industry, telecommunications, and a number of agricultural products.

1617 Martínez de Ita, María Eugenia *et al.* El proceso de reestructuración en México: análisis de ramas. Puebla, Mexico: Benemérita Univ. Autónoma de Puebla, 1993. 243 p.: bibl., ill.

Marxist interpretation of the problems currently facing the country's leading industries. In particular, the difficulties firms are having with increased competition from foreign products stemming from the government's liberalization policies. Industries include textiles, automobiles, telecommunications, steel, and tobacco with case studies of the auto companies in Puebla.

Martínez de Vega, María Elisa. Los mercaderes novohispanos: control virreinal y fraude fiscal en el primer tercio del siglo XVII. See *HLAS 56:1186.*

1618 McKinniss, Candace Bancroft and **Arthur A. Natella.** Business in Mexico: managerial behavior, protocol, and etiquette. New York: Haworth Press, 1994. 156 p.: bibl., index. (Haworth marketing resources)

Intended to provide foreign business people with an overview of the Mexican psychology as well as an understanding of the complexity of Mexican culture. The aim of the book is to impart a level of sensitivity and true cultural awareness of the country.

1619 Memorias: segundo simposio estatal; la investigación y el desarrollo tecnológico en Aguascalientes 1995; 4 al 6 de octubre; sede, Instituto Tecnológico de Aguascalientes. Aguascalientes, Mexico: Instituto Tecnológico de Aguascalientes, 1995. 100 p.: bibl., ill.

Series of scientific conference papers, many in abstract form. Studies deal with all aspects of the life sciences, with many focused on the situation in Aguascalientes state. Many of the papers reflect state-of-the-art information on the various crops grown in the region.

1620 Méndez Morales, José Silvestre. Pasado, presente y futuro de la economía mexicana: 100 preguntas y respuestas. México: Panorama Editorial, 1995. 140 p.: bibl.

Asks and answers 100 frequently asked questions concerning the functioning of the country's economy.

1621 Mercado, Alfonso and **José Alberto Godínez.** El comercio intraindustrial de bienes en la frontera norte de México: el caso de Baja California. (*Front. Norte,* 7:14, julio/dic. 1995, p. 9–22, bibl., tables)

The structure of foreign trade in Mexico's northern border region is examined at two levels: by sector and by type of trade relationship (inter-industry and intra-industry). Finds that the border's distinct trade pattern is explained by a combination of factors: 1) the very limited development of non-maquila industry; 2) the high proportion of border transactions (facilitated by the proximity to the US consumer market); and 3) the minimal backward linkages between the export-oriented *maquiladora* industry and local suppliers of industrial inputs.

1622 Mexico: the promise of NAFTA. London: Economist Intelligence Unit for the United Nations Industrial Development Organization, 1993. 224 p.: bibl., ill., index. (Industrial development review series)

Comprehensive examination of the North American Free Trade Agreement (NAFTA) and the likely impact of this treaty on the Mexican economy. The first part of the study examines the economic and industrial policies adopted since the mid-1980s and their impact on economic growth. The study then looks at likely developments in each of the country's major sectors—agriculture, industry, energy, etc.

1623 Mexico, economic and financial statistics: data book, September 30, 1993. Mexico: Secretaría de Hacienda y Crédito Público, 1993. 42 p.

Presentation of the country's basic economic and financial statistics. Excellent details presented in areas of federal finances, inflation indices, and State enterprise finances.

1624 México en los noventa: globalización y reestructuración productiva. Coordinación de Ernesto H. Turner Barragán, Guillermo Vargas Uribe y Alfredo Sánchez Daza. México: Univ. Autónoma Metropolitana,

Azcapotzalco, Depto. de Economía, Area de Teoría y Análisis Económico; Morelia, Mexico: Univ. Michoacana de San Nicolás de Hidalgo, Escuela de Economía, 1994. 320 p.: bibl., map.

Leading scholars and authorities examine the main issues confronting the Mexican economy. Topics include liberalization and deregulation, regionalization, debt, agricultural transformation, and external trade.

1625 México, hacia el desarrollo sustentable: bases de la transición. México: SEMARNAP, 1996. 76 p.: bibl., ill.

Examines the steps necessary to put Mexico on a path of sustainable growth. The study develops a comprehensive framework, integrating the country's natural resource base with programs that strike a balance between growth and environmental decline.

1626 México, hacia la globalización: lecturas seleccionadas de economía internacional. Recopilación de Federico Rubli Kasier y Benito Solís Mendoza. Prólogo de Jesús Silva Herzog Flores. México: Editorial Diana, 1992. 491 p.: bibl., ill.

Series of important papers on all facets of Mexico's integration with the world economy. Topics vary from the price of petroleum, to *maquiladoras*, NAFTA, external debt, etc. Of particular interest is the introduction contributed by former finance minister Jesús Silva Herzog F.

1627 Mexico, la nueva macroeconomía. Coordinación de Julio López G. México: Centro de Estudios para un Proyecto Nacional; Nuevo Horizonte Editores, 1994. 324 p.: bibl., ill.

Series of papers assessing Mexico's recent macroeconomic performance. Chapters cover the process of adjustment from the crisis of 1982 to 1992, the potential of the agricultural sector, structural problems in manufacturing, the service sector, and problems of semi-industrialized economies within the new world economy.

1628 Miller, Simon. The agrarian question in Mexico: debate in a cul-de-sac. (*J. Peasant Stud.*, 22:1, Oct. 1994, p. 164–174)

Review essay of four recent books on the Mexican peasantry. Argues that our understanding of the agrarian question in Mexico continues to be bogged down by unfo-

cused monographs on the one hand and schematic assumptions on the other; and that much research needs to be done. Research is needed to appraise two frequent assumptions: 1) that the hacienda economy was pre-capitalist; and 2) that the agrarian program in Mexico ushered in the rural transition to capitalism.

1629 Minello, Nelson *et al.* El desarrollo de una industria básica: Altos Hornos de México, 1942–1988. Monclova, Mexico: Arte y Cultura Monclova, 1995. 260 p.: bibl., ill.

Traces this history from 1942–88 of one of Mexico's largest steel ventures, Altos Hornos de Mexico. All facets of the industry are covered, including the firm's links with the local economy, labor, production problems, administration, finances, and government policies towards the sector.

Miño Grijalva, Manuel. Estructura económica y crecimiento: la historiografía económica colonial mexicana. See *HLAS 56: 1193.*

1630 La modernización del sector eléctrico, 1988–1994. México: Secretaría de Energía, Minas e Industria Paraestatal; Centro de Investigación y Docencia Económicas, 1994. 211 p.: bibl., ill.

Leading authorities contribute sections on different aspects of the changes taking place in the electric utility sector. Topics include: government policy, private sector participation, regulation, implications of NAFTA, and the legal framework.

1631 Moguel, Julio and Armando Bartra. El sector agropecuario mexicano: un balance sobre el desastre, 1988–1994. (*Probl. Desarro.*, 26:102, julio/sept. 1995, p. 173–197, tables)

Following a relative upturn during the 1970s, Mexican agriculture entered a phase of stagnation and decapitalization during what was known as the lost decade. The sector resumed its negative trend during a new, lengthy cycle of overall economic crisis, announced in 1982 and triggered by the fall in oil prices; neoliberal adjustment policies helped to complete the agricultural sector's financial collapse. The article makes a general assessment of the period, with particular emphasis on the Salinas Administration's policies.

Molina Jiménez, Iván. Protocolos y mortuales: fuentes para la historia económica de Centroamérica, siglos XVI-XIX. See *HLAS 56: 1635.*

1632 Moreira Rodríguez, Héctor; Bárbara Valle Torres; and Antonio Serrano Camarena. Una visión del futuro de Nuevo León Monterrey, Mexico: ITESM, Centro de Estudios Estratégicos, 1994. 244 p.: bibl., ill.

After providing a detailed description of Nuevo León, the author goes on to offer an interesting picture of the region's future.

1633 Moreno, Juan Carlos and Jaime Ros. Market reform and the changing role of the State in Mexico: a historical perspective. (*in* The State, markets and development: beyond the neoclassical dichotomy. Edited by Amitava Krishan Dutt *et al.* Brookfield, Vt.: Edward Elgar Publishing Company, 1994, p. 107–143, bibl., graph, tables)

Examines Mexico's current development problems from a historical perspective. Reviews long-term economic development trends focusing on radical shifts in development strategy and changes in the role of markets and the State. Changes over last ten years are given particular attention. A major theme of the study is that the real obstacles to economic development have often been misperceived. In contrast to the optimism which currently dominates perceptions of Mexico's economic prospects, the authors argue that downward cycles may happen again.

1634 Moreno Uriegas, María de los Angeles and Romeo R. Flores Caballero. Evolución de la deuda pública externa de México, 1950–1993. Monterrey, Mexico: Castillo, 1995. 266 p.: bibl., ill.

Uses a historical approach to document the factors that have contributed to the growth of Mexico's external debt. Emphasizes the economic conditions that led to the accumulation of debt and the institutions that facilitated the government's external borrowing.

1635 Mortimore, Michael. Transforming sitting ducks into flying geese: the Mexican automobile industry. Santiago: ECLAC, 1995. 74 p.: bibl., graphs, tables. (Desarrollo productivo; 26)

Discusses the transformation of industries from an import-substitution orientation to an internationally competitive orientation. Uses the Mexican automobile industry to demonstrate that industries can be restructured, thus altering the structural nature of a country's integration into the international production system.

1636 Muench Navarro, Pablo E. *et al.* La producción agrícola en el estado de Colima. Colima, Mexico?: Univ. Autónoma Chapingo, Dirección de Centros Regionales, 1992. 285 p.: bibl., ill., maps.

Extremely detailed documentation of Colima's agricultural sector. Contains a large amount of original data.

1637 Mungaray Lagarda, Alejandro. Organización industrial a través de redes de subcontratación: una alternativa a las actividades mexicanas de maquila. (*Estud. Front.*, 30, enero/abril 1993, p. 9–32, bibl.)

Discusses basic aspects of the institutional organization of the economy. Describes a system of flexible industrial organization and its potential implementation among small businesses that manage reduced-optimum scales. Specifically, proposes the formation of a network of subcontractors as an alternative to the *maquiladora* system currently operating in northern Mexico.

1638 Musalem, Alberto R.; Dimitri Vittas; and Asli Demirgüç-Kunt. North American Free Trade Agreement: issues on trade in financial services from Mexico. Washington: Financial Sector Development Dept., World Bank, 1993. 58 p.: bibl. (Policy research working papers; WPS 1153)

Analyzes the implications of NAFTA for the Mexican financial sector. Examines differences in sector development, banking regulations, insurance and securities markets, constraints to capital mobility involving direct foreign investment (DFI) regulations, and taxation of financial assets. In each case, existing regulations are compared and contrasted, transitional problems are discussed, and recommendations are made.

1639 The NAFTA debate: grappling with unconventional trade issues. Edited by M. Delal Baer and Sidney Weintraub. Boulder, Colo.: Lynne Rienner Publishers, 1994. 211 p.: bibl., ill., index.

Examines the merits of including three non-traditional areas in the NAFTA agreement: 1) environmental and labor standards;

2) social issues such as human rights and health care; and 3) issues arising due to the integration of low wage and high wage countries. Leading authorities also address issues such as Mexican nationalism, political reform, and transition mechanisms.

1640 Navarro, Jaime. The economic effects of emigration: Mexico. (*in* Emigration and its effects on the sending country. Santa Monica, Calif.: Rand, 1994, p. 185–203, bibl., tables)

Reviews the potential socioeconomic impacts of emigration on Mexico, particularly in light of the cyclical nature of Mexican international migration, as opposed to permanent migration. The available research seems to suggest that the net economic benefits to Mexico are positive, providing higher living standards for the migrants and their immediate families. On the other hand, the Mexican government appears politically powerless to influence a binational policy dealing with international flows.

Los negocios y las ganancias de la colonia al México moderno. See *HLAS 56:1365.*

1641 Nichols, Nancy A. From complacency to competitiveness: an interview with Vitro's Ernesto Martens. (*Harv. Bus. Rev.*, 93, Sept./Oct. 1993, p. 162–171, ill., photo)

Interviews with Ernesto Martens to determine the extent to which NAFTA is providing opportunities for trade and investment.

1642 Novelo Urdanivia, Federico and **José Flores Salgado.** El TLC de Norteamérica y la persistente incertidumbre. México: Univ. Autónoma Metropolitana, Unidad Xochimilco, 1993. 99 p.: bibl., tables. (Col. Libros de texto)

Examines the significant patterns of trade among Mexico, the US, and Canada. Contains many useful tables.

1643 Las nuevas políticas de ajuste en América Latina. Guadalajara, Mexico: Univ. de Guadalajara; Paris: CEMCA, 1995. v. 1: bibl., ill. (Col. Jornadas académicas. Serie Coloquios)

First in a series assessing the effects of globalization on Latin American economies. This volume examines the impact of increased integration and competition on the Mexican economy. Leading authorities examine such issues as the implementation of neoliberal policies, job security and the union movement, and volatile capital flows.

1644 Nuevo León, Mexico (state). Secretaría de Desarrollo Urbano y Obras Públicas. Plan multidimensional de desarrollo urbano de Nuevo León, 1995–2020: documento para la consulta pública; versión abreviada. Monterrey, Mexico: Gobierno del Estado, Secretaría de Desarrollo Urbano y Obras Públicas, 1995. 157 p., 15 leaves of plates: bibl., ill., col. maps.

Provides long-term plan for the growth and development of the state of Nuevo León. After a detailed examination of the current situation, the plan outlines steps that can be taken to assure the state's rapid development to the year 2020. Offers a wealth of data not readily available from other sources.

1645 Las oportunidades de la industria [name of industry] de Baja California en el Tratado de Libre Comercio. Mexicali: Gobierno del Estado de Baja California, Secretaría de Desarrollo Económico, Dirección de Asesoría y Gestoría, 1993–94. 6 v.: ill.

Six volume set of statistics and information concerning trade and investment opportunities trade and investment in Mexican firms. Provides detailed data and forecasts of exports to the US and Canada of major Mexican industries.

1646 Ornelas Delgado, Jaime. Neoliberalismo y ocupación del territorio en México. (*Probl. Desarro.*, 25:99, oct./dic. 1994, p. 55–75, tables)

Analyzes the background and characteristics of regional politics from 1989–94. Points out that the neoliberal policy includes comparative advantages that are exploited to facilitate the location of in-bond industries in the north of the country. Also analyzes the unequal distribution of public investment benefitting states with higher income levels to the detriment of those with high indexes of marginalization.

1647 Ortiz Hernán, Sergio. Caminos y transportes en México: una aproximación socioeconómica; fines de la colonia y principios de la vida independiente. México: Secretaría de Comunicaciones y Transportes : Fondo de Cultura Económica, 1994. 214 p.: bibl., map. (Estructura económica y social de México—los noventa)

Excellent study of the country's early economy. Using largely primary sources, the author provides a vivid picture of the economy and transportation patterns of Mexico up to the time of Independence.

1648 Ortíz Wadgymar, Arturo. Política económica de México, 1982–1994: dos sexenios neoliberales. 2. ed. corr. y aum. México: Editorial Nuestro Tiempo, 1994. 165 p.: bibl.

Examination of the neoliberal policies undertaken by the government during the de la Madrid and Salinas Administrations. Concludes that these policies, while appearing to be effective, have a number of serious limitations.

1649 Ortíz Wadgymar, Arturo. Reflexiones acerca de los procesos devaluatorios recientes en México, 1982–1994. (*Probl. Desarro.*, 26:101, abril/junio 1995, p. 125–144, graph, tables)

In order examine the features of recent devaluation processes in Mexico, including that of 1994, the article posits various hypotheses on the relationship between devaluations and the structural crisis, external debt, neoliberal adjustment programs, the current account deficit, and alternative means of meeting the debt: a moratorium or debtors' club. The author concludes by indicating the problems with these solutions, such as social costs and increased external debt.

1650 Ovalle Muñoz, Pedro de Jesús. Ganadería intensiva en la costa de Chiapas. Tuxtla Gutiérrez, Mexico: Facultad de Ciencias Sociales, Univ. Autónoma de Chiapas, 1995. 115 p.: appendix, bibl., map.

Takes a historical approach towards assessing the cattle trade in the state of Chiapas. Provides an especially useful and a detailed statistical appendix of the trends and main facets surrounding the production and trade of beef.

1651 El pacto: las premisas políticas de una estrategia económica. Centro de Estudios Industriales, Subdirección de Análisis. México: Confederación de Cámaras Industriales de los Estados Unidos Mexicanos, 1990. 47 p. (Reporte mensual de análisis de coyuntura)

Assessment of the goals and accomplishments of *El Pacto* between the government and the public to prevent inflation. Topics include the pact's macroeconomic impact, effects on industry, and the social ramifications. An excellent chapter speculates on the future of *El Pacto*.

1652 Panagides, Alexis. Mexico. (*in* Indigenous people and poverty in Latin America: an empirical analysis. Edited by George Psacharopoulos and Harry Anthony Patrinos. Washington: The World Bank, 1994, p. 127–163, graphs, map, tables)

Combines information from the literature on indigenous peoples and a new analysis of a 1989 household survey. Examines topics such as income, earnings, education, and child labor. The earnings differential between indigenous and non-indigenous workers is broken down into its explained and unexplained components. Additionally, the determinants of poverty are estimated and policy simulations are conducted. The results show that more education would reduce overall poverty and decrease the earnings gap between workers in indigenous areas and workers in non-indigenous areas.

1653 Pastor, Manuel. Mexican trade liberalization and NAFTA. (*LARR*, 29:3, 1994, p. 153–173, bibl.)

Review essay of 15 recent books on the Mexican economy, the liberalization process, and NAFTA. Concludes that although several of the works are flawed, most of them constitute building blocks for constructing a complete analysis of the contemporary Mexican economy and the prospects for North American economic integration.

1654 Pastor, Manuel and **Carol Wise.** The origins and sustainability of Mexico's free trade policy. (*Int. Organ.*, 48:3, Summer 1994, p. 459–489, graph, table)

Combines political and economic analysis in an attempt to account more fully for the origins and sustainability of Mexico's commercial opening during the 1980s. Contends that the political sustainability of free trade is still questionable due to increasing macroeconomic fragility, the ideological rigidity of local policymakers, and mounting pressures for the democratization of information and decision making.

1655 Paz Sánchez, Fernando. El campo y el desarrollo económico de México. México: Editorial Nuestro Tiempo, 1995. 321 p.: bibl. (Col. Los grandes problemas nacionales)

Examines the evolution of the agricultural sector since around 1970. Good general survey of government programs in that sector as well as an assessment of developments such as land reform.

1656 Pazos, Luis. Devaluación: ¿por qué, qué viene, qué hacer? México: Editorial Diana, 1995. 156 p.: bibl.

Leading authority presents a non-technical explanation of the events leading up to the ill-fated 1994 devaluation of the peso, together with the ensuing financial crisis.

1657 Pazos, Luis. Libre comercio, México-E.U.A.: mitos y hechos = Free trade, Mexico-U.S.A.: myths and facts. 2. ed. actualizada. México: Editorial Diana, 1993. 330 p.: bibl., ill.

Analyzes the pros and cons of a free trade zone between Mexico, the US, and Canada. Argues that free trade has inspired myths in both US and Mexico of decapitalization, deterioration in the trade terms, dependency, and invasion of labor and merchandise. Demonstrates the falsity of these myths with logical arguments and empirical data. Maintains that a free trade agreement and the free flow of investment is the best way for Mexico to reach higher levels of socioeconomic growth.

1658 Peñaloza Webb, Miguel. La conformación de una nueva banca: retos y oportunidades para la banca en México. México; Nueva York: McGraw-Hill, 1995. 185 p.: ill., tables.

Good overview of important changes taking place in the country's banking system. Provides numerous original tables on the changing composition of the system and the different financial groups. The study ends with a critical evaluation of public policy toward the industry.

1659 Peñaloza Webb, Miguel and Tomás Peñaloza Webb. ¡Crisis 95!: una explicación clara del problema y cómo superarlo. México: McGraw-Hill, 1995. 105 p.: ill.

Leading authority presents a non-technical explanation of the events leading up to the ill-fated 1994 devaluation of the peso and the ensuing financial crisis.

1660 Peniche Patrón, Noé Antonio. Riesgos y oportunidades para el campo yucateco. Mérida, Mexico: Gobierno del Estado de Yucatán, 1994. 400 p.: ill. (some col.), maps (some col.).

An examination of Yucatán's economy to determine the potential of the sector for developing exports. Provides a wide variety of data not available from other sources.

Pérez Acevedo, Martín. Empresarios y empresas en Morelia, 1860–1910. See *HLAS 56: 1371.*

1661 Pérez López, Emma Paulina. Ganadería y campesinado en Sonora: los poquiteros de la Sierra Norte. México: Consejo Nacional para la Cultura y las Artes, 1993. 241 p.: bibl. (Regiones)

Traces the historical development of cattle raising in the Sonora region from the early 1920s to the mid-1980s. Interesting conclusions concerning the future of the rural economy in the Sierra Norte.

1662 Philippatos, George C. and K.G. Viswanathan. The Mexican debt moratorium and its effect upon U.S. bank stock values: empirical tests on major event windows. (*Glob. Financ. J.*, 5:1, Summer 1994, p. 75–101, appendix, bibl., tables)

Paper tests the effects of the Mexican foreign debt moratorium. Finds that the announcement of the debt moratorium conveyed a negative signal to the market and forced bank stock prices downward—both Mexican-loan exposed and non-exposed banks. High loan-exposure banks were penalized more and for a longer period of time than low-exposure banks—the latter group's effects being virtually indistinguishable from those of the non-exposed banks.

1663 Piñón Antillón, Rosa María. México, inmerso en la crisis financiera: de lo conyuntural a lo estructural. (*Relac. Int./México*, 67, julio/sept. 1995, p. 33–43, bibl., graphs, tables)

Examines the recent (Dec. 1994–Jan. 1995) economic crisis and concludes that it had an even broader impact than the 1984 debt crisis. The crisis has affected the entire Mexican industrial sector and has hurt all social groups. Concludes that the cause of this crisis was the abrupt devaluation of the peso by more than 100 percent. This in turn was caused by the enormous uncertainty generated by the Chiapas rebellion, the Mexican political murders, and trade balance deficits.

Piñón Antillón, Rosa María. El reto de México: desarrollo y mercados externos. See item **4105.**

1664 Plan Pátzcuaro 2000: investigación multidisciplinaria para el desarrollo sostenido. Recopilación de Víctor M. Toledo, Pedro Alvarez-Icaza y Patricia Avila. México: Fundación Friedrich Ebert, Representación en México, 1992. 320 p.: bibl., ill., maps.

Papers from various authorities outline a development plan for the region around Lake Pátzcuaro. Chapters describe the natural resources of the region, development patterns, and demographic trends. Drawing on this background, a development strategy for the local economy is outlined.

1665 Pozos Ponce, Fernando. Metrópolis en reestructuración: Guadalajara y Monterrey, 1980–1989. Guadalajara, Mexico: Univ. de Guadalajara, 1996. 237 p.: bibl. (Libros de tiempos de ciencia; 10)

Focusing on the changing urban structure of Monterrey and Guadalajara, the authors trace the changing economic conditions that have led to expanded urbanization and rural-urban migration. One interesting feature is a discussion of the impact of the economic crisis of the early 1980s in each city.

1666 Programa de apoyo y fortalecimiento a la economía guanajuatense. Guanajuato: Gobierno del Estado de Guanajuato, Secretaría de Desarrollo Económico, 1995. 103 p.: tables.

Outlines the economic plans and policies for Guanajuato. Numerous tables describe the major programs for Guanajuato. These, in turn, are linked to the agencies responsible for their implementation.

1667 Rabellotti, Roberta. Is there an "Industrial District Model?": footwear districts in Italy and Mexico compared. (*World Dev.*, 23 : 1, Jan. 1995, p. 29–41, bibl.)

Presents results of empirical research carried out in two footwear clusters located in Italy, the "land of industrial districts," and two clusters of footwear enterprises in Mexico. The aim is to compare the "ideal-type industrial district," as it is defined in the literature, and the case studies in Mexico and Italy. Material from a survey reveals how clusters in both countries differ from the textbook model. Similarities and differences are investigated in some detail, with attention given to the intensity and quality of backward and forward linkages, the existence of an industrial atmosphere, and the nature of the institutional press.

1668 Ramírez, Miguel D. Public and private investment in Mexico, 1950–90: an empirical analysis. (*South. Econ. J.*, 61 : 1, July 1994, p. 1–17, bibl., graph, tables)

Investigates whether public investment complements or displaces private capital formation in Mexico. Uses sophisticated statistical analysis to show that public investment stimulates private sector capital formation.

1669 Reestructuración de la economía mexicana: integración a la economía mundial y la Cuenca del Pacífico. Coordinación de Alfredo Sánchez Daza y Juan González García. México: Univ. Autónoma Metropolitana, Unidad Azcapotzalco; Univ. de Colima; RNICP, 1995. 434 p.: bibl., ill.

Collection of essays examining Mexico's changing position in the world trade system. Emphasis is on trade with other North American countries and those in the Pacific Basin. Subjects include NAFTA, new exports, telecommunications, trade with Japan, competitiveness of Mexican exports, tourism, automotive and agricultural trade, and problems of trade negotiation.

1670 Reinoso, Eduardo D. La competitividad de los Estados Unidos Mexicanos. 2a. ed. Monterrey, Mexico: Centro de Estudios Estratégicos, Instituto Tecnológico y de Estudios Superiores de Monterrey, 1995. 259 p.: bibl., ill., tables.

Develops a detailed method of determining the competitiveness of a wide range of products. Uses this measure to rank the Mexican states on each product. Extensive set of detailed tables.

1671 Renard, María Cristina. La comercialización internacional del café. Chapingo, Mexico: Univ. Autónoma Chapingo, Dirección de Difusión Cultural, Depto. PIIAI Subdirección de Investigación, 1993. 90 p.: bibl. (Col. Cuadernos universitarios. Serie Ciencias sociales; 11)

Examination of the international coffee industry. Traces production expansion in the major growing regions and assesses the implications of such expansion for Mexican growers and producers.

1672 Renard, María Cristina. El Soconusco: una economía cafetalera. México: Univ. Autónoma Chapingo, Dirección de Difusión Cultural, 1993. 99 p.: bibl., maps.

Examination of the country's coffee industry includes an excellent history of its origins and development. Also discussed are some of the government policies towards the sector, as well as the impact of the sector on the regional economy.

1673 Revenga, Ana; Michelle Riboud; and Hong Tan. The impact of Mexico's retraining program on employment and wages. (*World Bank Econ. Rev.*, 8:2, May 1994, p. 247–277, bibl., graphs, tables)

Analyzes the impact and effectiveness of the Mexican labor retraining program for unemployed and displaced workers—Programa de Becas de Capacitación para Trabajadores (PROBECAT). Findings suggest that participation in PROBECAT reduced the mean duration of unemployment for both men and women trainees, and increased the monthly earnings of men, but not those of women.

1674 Rey Romay, Benito. México: el neoliberalismo fracasa y la apertura comercial estalla. (*Probl. Desarro.*, 26:100, enero/marzo 1995, p. 125–135)

Argues that the present serious situation of the Mexican economy originates from two simultaneous crises: 1) the neoliberal model established 12 years ago and its hardening during the last six years; and 2) the new form of insertion of the country into the international system of commerce. The author proposes corrective steps, some of them drastic and contrary to the anti-crisis government program. Cautions against the slow and perverse separation of the government models from the rest of the country's economic agents.

1675 Reyes-Ortega, Pedro and Haydee Muñoz. La estructura productiva salarial en México. México: Centro de Investigación y Docencia Económicas, 1993. 45 p.: bibl., ill. (Documento de trabajo, 0185-3384; 11. Economía)

Offers a sophisticated mathematical model of the country's production function to identifying productivity trends. Uses the Chow test to examine whether the economy has undergone any major structural changes with regard to sources of growth.

1676 Rivera, Salvador. El desarrollo económico en Nuevo León, 1970–1993. Monterrey, Mexico: Instituto de Estudios Urbanos de Nuevo León, 1995. 54 p.: bibl., ill.

(Documentos de investigación aplicada; v. 1, no. 2 = 2)

Examines the evolution of the economy of Nuevo León state from 1970–93. Of particular interest is the impact of increased globalization on the regional economy. Develops a macroeconomic framework and examines changes in industrial production. Provides an excellent set of recommendations for strengthening the state's economy.

1677 Rodríguez, Armando E. and Mark D. Williams. Economic liberalization and antitrust in Mexico. (*Rev. Anál. Econ.*, 10:2, nov. 1995, p. 165–181, bibl., graphs, table)

The theoretical framework proposed in this paper suggests that dedicating resources to traditional antitrust enforcement may not be an appropriate policy for a liberalizing economy. Instead, the agency should devote its resources to competition advocacy—especially during Mexico's transition to a more open economy—and limit its enforcement activities to unambiguously anti-competitive horizontal restraints on competition.

1678 Rodríguez Hernández, Francisco. Condiciones de vida en el Estado de México: evolución en la década de los ochenta. Zinacantepec, Mexico: Colegio Mexiquense, 1994. 87 p.: bibl., maps, tables. (Investigaciones/El Colegio Mexiquense; 6)

Assesses the changes in quality of life of households in the state of Mexico during the 1980s. Focus is on access to basic needs such as water, electricity, education, sanitation, and so forth. Numerous useful tables compiled from surveys.

1679 Rogozinski, Jacques. La privatización de empresas paraestatales. México: Fondo de Cultura Económica, 1993. 206 p.: bibl., ill. (Una Visión de la modernización de México)

Traces the development of parastatal enterprises in Mexico and examines the government's current approach to their privatization.

1680 Ros, Jaime. Financial markets and capital flows in Mexico. (*in* Foreign capital in Latin America. Edited by José Antonio Ocampo and Roberto Steiner. Washington: Inter-American Development Bank, 1994, p. 193–239, bibl., graphs, tables)

Examines recent developments involving foreign capital flows and financial market development in Mexico. Concludes that the massive capital inflows since 1989 were caused by a variety of factors or, more specifically, by the fact that nearly all of the determinants of capital flows, both external and internal, have almost without exception had a positive effect on these flows.

1681 Ros, Jaime. Mercados financieros, flujos de capital y tipo de cambio en México. (*Econ. Mex.*, 4:1, primer semestre 1995, p. 5–67, appendices, bibl., graphs, tables)

Examines the nature and determinants of the surge in capital flows to Mexico between 1990–93 and the resulting macroeconomic adjustments in the financial and goods markets. Argues that this episode of massive capital inflows led to an over-valuation of the real exchange rate with respect to its long term equilibrium value. As a result, by mid-1992 the Mexican economy was facing a macroeconomic adjustment problem which necessitated a real devaluation of the peso. Also compares the recent episode with the previous episode of capital inflows associated with the oil boom of the late 1970s and early 1980s.

1682 Rubio, Luis. Mexico, NAFTA, and the Pacific Basin. (*in* Cooperation or rivalry: regional integration in the Americas and the Pacific Rim. Boulder, Colo.: Westview Press, 1996, p. 76–93)

Paper consists of four main areas: 1) establishes the context for Mexico's decision to negotiate NAFTA and analyzes its political objectives; 2) examines Mexican trade policy discussing trade diversification versus concentration; 3) explores the potential expansion of NAFTA to include new members; and 4) assesses Mexico's aims with respect to the Pacific Basin.

1683 Rueda Peiro, Isabel. La industria manufacturera mexicana y la crisis actual. (*Probl. Desarro.*, 26:101, abril/junio 1995, p. 145–172, tables)

This essay studies the development of Mexican industry over the past 12 years, particularly the manufacturing sector, which began with one crisis and ended with another deeper crisis. The process of production and foreign trade is characterized by inequality, particularly regarding the retrogression of growing commercial deficits of those manu-

facturing firms that export a portion of their production. At the same time as rising unemployment and the reduction of real salaries has reduced domestic demand, the abrupt commercial opening has increased competition and turned several industrialists into businessmen. The author points out the risks of continuing the dominant neo-liberal policy and proposes a number of alternatives.

1684 Ryan, Leo. Good health is good business: capacity building for marketing integrated health services to the business community in northern Mexico. (*in* Drug lessons & education programs in developing countries. New Brunswick, N.J.: Transaction Publishers, 1995, p. 117–137, bibl., photo, tables)

Illustrates the use of a transfer partnership framework to structure a ten-month training program administered by the Mexican Federation of Private Associations for Health and Community Development (FEMAP) in Ciudad Juárez, Mexico. The transfer partnership, is based on state-of-the-art research on learning transfer, and has shown promise for drug abuse prevention training in a variety of cultural settings in the US.

Salvucci, Richard J. The origins and progress of U.S.-Mexican Trade, 1825–1884: "hoc opus, hic labor est." See *HLAS 56:1377.*

1685 Sánchez González, Manuel. Fiscal impact of privatization in Mexico. (*in* Bigger economies, smaller governments: privatization in Latin America. Boulder, Colo.: Westview Press, 1996, p. 163–188, tables)

Examines a number of issues associated with the sale of State enterprises in Mexico. First, develops theoretical framework that serves as a reference for interpreting the determinants and economic implications of the fiscal impact of privatization. Concludes by presenting lessons and recommendations derived from a number of case studies.

1686 Sánchez-Ugarte, Fernando J.; Manuel Fernández Pérez; and Eduardo Pérez Motta. La política industrial ante la apertura. México: Secretaría de Comercio y Fomento Industrial; Nacional Financiera; Fondo de Cultura Económica, 1994. 318 p.: bibl., graphs, ill., tables. (Nueva cultura económica)

Provides a detailed examination of industrial growth in Mexico. Numerous tables and graphs provide excellent documentation of the sector's evolution.

1687 Santa Cruz Díaz Santana, Arturo. El proceso de internacionalización del sector servicios. Guadalajara, Mexico: Univ. de Guadalajara, 1994. 82 p.: bibl., ill. (Cuadernos de difusión científica; 45)

Three chapters introduce the reader to new developments in Mexico's service sector. Emphasizes telecommunications and financial services. Considers the competitiveness of Mexico's services in the new international environment.

1688 Santos Llorente, Javier *et al.* El petróleo en Veracruz. Ed. conmemorativa 1988. México: Petróleos Mexicanos, 1988. 226 p.: bibl., ill.

Series of papers in celebration of the 50th anniversary of the expropriation of foreign petroleum companies and the establishment of PEMEX. The papers are mainly historical, dealing with the early years of the industry and its impact on Veracruz.

1689 Schettino, Macario. El costo del miedo: la devaluación de 1994. México: Grupo Editorial Iberoamérica, 1995. 155 p.: bibl., ill.

Assessment of the 1994 devaluation of the Mexican peso. Emphasizes factors leading up to the devaluation and the subsequent impact on the economy and standards of living. The study closes with an assessment of the emergency plan put in place after the devaluation.

1690 Schettino, Macario. Economía contemporánea: un enfoque para México y América Latina. México: Grupo Editorial Iberoamérica, 1994. 404 p.: bibl., ill., index.

Uses basic economic analysis to shed light on the country's current economic policies and plans. Largely intended for those with no economics background, this study does an excellent job of showing the relevance of economic theory for understanding the country's current economic situation.

1691 Seminario Nacional sobre Alternativas para la Economía Mexicana, *Mexico City, Mexico?, 1993.* Desarrollo regional y urbano: tendencias y alternativas. Coordinación general de José Luis Calva. Coordinación modular de Adrián Guillermo Aguilar. Gua-

dalajara, Mexico: Centro Universitario de Ciencias Sociales y Humanidades, Univ. de Guadalajara; México: Instituto de Geografía, UNAM: Juan Pablos Editor, 1995. 2 v.: bibl., ill.

Series of papers examining the changing patterns of regional and urban incomes. Emphasis is on the underlying causes of the patterns and the effectiveness of government measures intended to stem the tendency toward greater concentration of income.

1692 Seminario Nacional sobre Alternativas para la Economía Mexicana, *Mexico City, Mexico?, 1993.* Globalización y bloques económicos: realidades y mitos. Coordinación general de José Luis Calva. Coordinación modular de Jesús Rivera de la Rosa y Jaime Preciado Coronado. Guadalajara, Mexico: Centro Universitario de Ciencias Sociales; Puebla, Mexico: Programa de Estudios de Economía Internacional; México: Juan Pablos Editor, 1995. 333 p.: bibl.

Papers from a seminar on economic alternatives for Mexico. This volume contains papers on various aspects of globalization, with emphasis on regional trade groups. Of particular interest are the papers dealing with financial issues and the manner in which changing world capital markets are affecting investment patterns in Mexico.

1693 Serra Puche, Jaime. La nueva política industrial de México. México: SECOFI, 1994. 78 p.: ill.

Discusses some recent developments related to the increasing internationalization of the country's industries. Assesses such problems as increased rates of dumping and the development of new exports. The final sections outline the main changes in industrial legislation during the last several years.

1694 Siembieda, William J. Looking for a place to live: transforming the urban *ejido.* (*Bull. Lat. Am. Res.,* 15:3, Sept. 1996, p. 371–385, bibl., map, tables)

Examines the process of ejido alienation and transformation in light of the 1992 changes to Article 27 of the Mexican constitution, and discusses the future impact on these remaining urban ejidos.

1695 Silvers, Arthur L. and **Cameron E. Rookley.** Salarios y tecnología en los patrones regionales del tratado comercial Estados Unidos-México. (*Probl. Desarro.*, 25:99, oct./dic. 1994, p. 35–53, tables)

This paper analyzes recent data to identify emerging trends in the sectorial mix of imports and exports between Mexico and the US. Attempts to determine whether or not low-wage, low-technology industries produce the majority of Mexican exports to the US and concomitantly, whether high-salary, high-technology industries account for most US exports to Mexico.

1696 Sinaloa: una visión de futuro. Dirección de David Rendón Velarde. 3. ed. Culiacán, Mexico: ITESM Campus Sinaloa, Centro de Estudios Estratégicos; Fundación Desarrollo Económico de Sinaloa, 1995. 331 p.

Looks at the potential of the Sinaloan economy. Tries to identify advantages to the State of expanding its international trade. Assesses the region's infrastructure and other resources necessary for expansion of exports and industrial production. The study concludes with a discussion of the ecological implications of expanded economic activity.

1697 Los sistemas de abasto alimentario en México frente al reto de la globalización de los mercados. Recopilación de Javier Delgadillo Macías, Luis Fuentes Aguilar y Felipe Torres Torres. México: Univ. Nacional Autónoma de México, 1993. 264 p.: bibl., ill., tables.

Overview of the changes taking place in Mexico's food supply system. Contains numerous tables documenting trade patterns, transportation, and regional flows within Mexico.

1698 Springer, Gary L. and Jorge L. Molina. The Mexican financial crisis: genesis, impact, and implications. (*J. Interam. Stud. World Aff.*, 37:2, Summer 1995, p. 57–81)

Concludes that the economic opening, the introduction of NAFTA, and the current economic crisis have created a political space in Mexico that is quickly being occupied by new elements: emerging interest groups, the private sector, and opposition parties. This situation provides political and social challenges for the government over and above the need to restore economic growth.

1699 Stanford, Lois. Transitions to free trade: local impacts of changes in Mexican agrarian policy. (*Hum. Organ.*, 53:2, Summer 1994, p. 99–109, bibl., tables)

An examination of Michoacán's cantaloupe export industry finds that US companies no longer offer financial credit to peasant organizations and instead work exclusively with wealthy commercial producers. From 1987–90, the local agricultural industry declined overall and the market structure became more concentrated. A statistical measure of market structure for three seasons (1987–88, 1988–89, and 1989–90) shows an increasing concentration of local industry in the hands of private commercial farms. Demonstrates the need for local-level studies that examine the linkages between macro-level policy changes and local economies. Concludes that the impact of Mexico's capitalization of the agricultural sector and NAFTA will vary across different regions and different commodity systems. For the ethnologist's comment see item **770.**

1700 Steele, Diane. Women's participation decisions and earnings in Mexico. (*in* Case studies on women's employment and pay in Latin America. Washington: World Bank, 1992, p. 339–348, bibl., tables)

Examines the factors influencing women's decisions to participate in the labor force in Mexico. Findings suggest that participation rates are positively influenced by education and urban residence. The presence of teenage children in the household does not appear to influence women's decision to work.

1701 Suárez Aguilar, Estela and Miguel Angel Rivera Ríos. Pequeña empresa y modernización: análisis de dos dimensiones. Cuernavaca, Mexico: Univ. Nacional Autónoma de México, Centro Regional de Investigaciones Multidisciplinarias, 1994. 263 p.: bibl., ill.

Provides many ideas on how small Mexican manufacturing companies can increase their productivity and profitability.

1702 Székely, Gabriel; Jaime del Palacio; and Peter F. Cowhey. Teléfonos de México: una empresa privada. México: Grupo Editorial Planeta, 1995. 177 p.: bibl., ill. (Espejo de México)

Traces the privatization of Teléfonos

de Mexico. Covers factors leading up to privatization, restructuring of the company, and legal problems involved in privatization. An important section examines the initial results of privatization (1991–93), with a final section assessing the likely performance of the company over the 1994–2000 period.

1703 Szekely, Miguel. Aspectos de la desigualdad en México. (*Trimest. Econ.*, 62:246, abril/junio 1995, p. 201–243, appendix, bibl., graphs, tables)

Analyzes the changes in inequality registered in Mexico during the 1984–92 period of stabilization and economic liberalization. Concludes that in macroeconomic terms, economic policy had both progressive and regressive outcomes which although in some cases cancelled each other out, ultimately provoked a sharp deterioration in income distribution. Believes that economic reforms have played an important role in current outcomes and, moreover, that some measures such as privatization and financial liberalization, have contributed to the increased concentration of ownership of resources. Sees grave consequences for the future.

1704 Szekely, Miguel. Estabilización y ajuste con desigualdad y pobreza: el caso de México. (*Trimest. Econ.*, 61:241, enero/marzo 1994, p. 135–175, bibl., graphs, tables)

Analyzes the relationship between adjustment, poverty, and inequality in Mexico during the 1980s. Results suggest that adjustment and stabilization were accompanied by greater inequality and poverty. Concludes that an important change in the structure of the economy took place, and as a result, despite high growth rates, considerable reductions in inequality are necessary for the eradication of poverty.

1705 Taller de Identificación de Proyectos Productivos para el Programa de Desarrollo Regional Sustentable de las Zonas Ixtleras y Candelilleras, *Univ. Autónoma Agraria Antonio Narro, Buenavista, Saltillo, Coahuila, marzo 23, 1995*. Memoria. Buenavista, Mexico: Univ. Autónoma Agraria Antonio Narro, 1995. 153 p.

Focusing on the agricultural potential of the region. Study outlines the government's programs and plans for stimulating the economy and overcoming many of the social and environmental constraints to development.

1706 Tamayo, Jesús. Breve balance y perspectivas de la industria maquiladora de exportación. (*Estud. Front.*, 27/28, enero/abril y mayo/agosto 1992, p. 28, bibl., tables)

Offers a general overview of the *maquiladora* industry, analyzing its development from its origins to the present. Stresses links between the *maquiladoras* and urbanization of Mexico's northern border and the resulting challenges facing both Mexico and the US.

1707 Tapia Gómez, José Carmen. Economía y movimiento cafetalero: del Inmecafé a la autogestión en la Sierra de Atoyac de Alvarez, 1970–1984. Chilpancingo, Mexico: Univ. Autónoma de Guerrero, Dirección de Investigación Científica, Inst. de Inv. Cient., Area Humanístico Social, 1996. 351 p.: bibl., ill., tables. (Serie Economía y sociedad; 2)

Examines the region's coffee industry from the early 1970s to the early 1980s. Very comprehensive analysis with numerous tables of original data on production, acreage and primary markets.

Teichman, Judith A. Privatization and political change in Mexico. See item **3119.**

1708 Testimonios sobre el TLC. Recopilación de Carlos Arriola. México: Miguel Angel Porrúa; Diana [distributor], 1994. 294 p.: bibl.

Papers focus on the implications of integration into a North American trade agreement for Mexico. Leading authorities, such as Victor Urquidi and Carlos Urentes, assess such issues as the legal obstacles to economic integration, the effect on companies, and the future of the integration process.

1709 Tijerina Guajardo, José Alfredo. Efecto de la inversión pública en los estados federativos de México sobre el crecimiento económico. Monterrey, Mexico: Univ. Autónoma de Nuevo León, Facultad de Economía, Centro de Investigaciones Económicas, 1995. 20 p.: bibl. (Documento de trabajo)

Focuses on the public sector's investments in the Federal District during the period 1970–93. Analytical analysis similar to that of Robert Barro of Harvard Univ. Main thrust of the study is an assessment of the productivity of the government's capital program for the region.

1710 Toro Vázquez, Juan José. La balanza de pagos de México: su importancia en el análisis económico. 2. ed. actualizada y ampliada. San Luis Potosí, Mexico: Facultad de Economía, Univ. Autónoma de San Luis Potosí, 1995. 58 p.: bibl.

Describes in detail the conventions underlying Mexico's balance-of-payment statement, as well as the methods of compilation. Demonstrates how changes to various components of balance of payments would impact Mexican economy.

1711 Torres Bautista, Mariano Enrique. El origen de la industrialización de Puebla. México: Claves Latinoamericanas; Puebla: El Colegio de Puebla, 1995. 246 p.: bibl., 2 maps.

Excellent history of industrialization in the Puebla region. Focuses on the pre-1870 period, with an extensive analysis of the colonial period. Emphasis is on the economic and political institutions that have structured the direction of economic development.

1712 Vázquez Pallares, Natalio. En defensa de nuestro petróleo: artículos periodísticos de 1952 denunciando una conducta antimexicana. 2. ed. Morelia, Mexico: Univ. Michoacana de San Nicolás de Hidalgo, Instituto de Investigaciones Históricas, Depto. de Historia de México, 1994. 137 p.: ill. (Estudios de historia mexicana; 3)

Interesting analysis of 20 articles on the petroleum industry published in *El Popular* in 1952. Emphasizes the nationalization of the petroleum industry in 1938, as well as government legislation enacted in the 1940s.

1713 Vela Sosa, Raúl. Yucatán, eje de la región maya ante la integración económica del continente. Mérida, Mexico?: Colegio de Economistas de Yucatán, 1995. 151 p.: bibl., ill.

Examines the economic conditions in Yucatán with emphasis on the state's trade with Central America. Good descriptions of the Central American countries, with observations on their comparative advantages and potential as markets for Yucatán products.

1714 Verduzco Chávez, Basilio; Nora L. Bringas; and M. Basilia Valenzuela Varela. La ciudad compartida: desarrollo urbano,

comercio y turismo en la región Tijuana-San Diego. Guadalajara, Mexico: Univ. de Guadalajara, Coordinación Editorial; Tijuana, Mexico: El Colegio de la Frontera Norte, 1995. 278 p.: bibl., ill.

Examines the Tijuana/San Diego regional economy. Since this region crosses an international border, an extensive discussion is given of the cultural and sociological linkages on both sides of the border. An important contribution of this study is the presentation of original data on the extent of commerce and tourism between the two main cities in the region.

1715 Villafuerte Solís, Daniel. Desarrollo económico y diferenciación productiva en el Soconusco. San Cristóbal de las Casas, Mexico: Centro de Investigaciones Ecológicas del Sureste, Unidad de Estudios Económicos y Sociales, 1992. 122 p.: bibl., tables.

Excellent overview of the agriculture and ecology of the Soconusco Region. Numerous tables present data that is extremely difficult to find in other sources.

1716 Villanueva Mukul, Eric. Crisis henequenera, reconversión económica y movimientos campesinos en Yucatán, 1983–1992. Yucatán, Mexico: Maldonado Editores; Univ. Autónoma de Yucatán; CEDRAC, 1993. 133 p.

Examines the disruption of the region's agricultural economy by the economic reforms initiated in 1982 and reinforced during the Salinas administration.

1717 Villavicencio, Daniel; Rigas Arvanitis; and Liliana Minsberg. Aprendizaje tecnológico en la industria química mexicana. (*Perf. Latinoam.*, 4:7, dic. 1995, p. 121–148, bibl., graphs, tables)

Authors contend that the increasing globalization of the marketplace and technological advances have created a competitive framework for businesses that tests their capacity for innovation and their ability to interact with an environment that is itself an engine for innovation. To demonstrate this theory, the article presents research on the Mexican chemical industry, studying the capacity of various firms in this sector for accumulating technical know-how. Concludes by speculating on the likelihood that the firms will become more innovative.

1718 Villegas H., Eduardo and Rosa María Ortega O. El nuevo sistema financiero mexicano. 2. ed., 1. reimp. México: Editorial PAC, 1994. 377 p.: bibl., ill.

Useful description of the country's financial system. Includes details about the primary banks and institutions, together with data on changing financial instruments and laws.

1719 Weintraub, Sidney. The depth of economic integration between Mexico and the United States. (*Wash. Q.*, 18:4, Autumn 1995, p. 173–184)

Looks at the causes and nature of the Dec. 1990 financial crisis in Mexico. The crisis is then placed in the context of US/Mexican integration. The author draws two competing conclusions: 1) the existence of NAFTA made a marked difference in how Mexico and the US reacted to the crisis, or put differently, that NAFTA added much depth to the integration of the two economies; and 2) even this extra depth is insufficient. For international relations specialist's comment, see item **4132.**

1720 Weiss, John. Trade liberalization in Mexico in the 1980's: concepts, measures and short-run effects. (*Weltwirtsch. Arch.*, 128:4, 1992, p. 711–726, bibl., tables)

Trade liberalization has been introduced in many developing countries over the last decade, often as part of structural adjustment programs. This paper discusses the recent experience of Mexico, which introduced a major trade reform in the mid-1980s. The paper begins by considering alternative definitions and measures of trade liberalization, before examining some of the consequences of liberalization in Mexico, focusing on the manufacturing sector.

1721 Wilcox Young, Linda. Free trade or fair trade? NAFTA and agricultural labor. (*Lat. Am. Perspect.*, 22:1, Winter 1995, p. 49–58, bibl., tables)

Argues that the focus on the aggregate employment estimates associated with the introduction of NAFTA is misdirected. Even if there is the potential for net employment gains in the long run, the real issue is whether the adjustments necessary to realize that potential are achievable within a realistic time frame.

1722 Zamora Millán, Fernando. Concertación económica: planeación caso México. México: Instituto Politecnico Nacional, Dirección de Bibliotecas y Publicaciones, 1991. 169 p.

Overview of the country's attempts at avoiding regional concentration of economic activity. Surveys the manner in which the government has planned regional decentralization.

1723 Zapata, Francisco. Mexican labor in a context of political and economic crisis. (*in* Changing structure of Mexico: political, social, and economic prospects. Armonk, N.Y.: M.E. Sharpe, 1996, p. 127–136, tables)

Argues that profound changes are taking place in the historic relationship between labor and the Mexican State. As a result of both the internationalization of the national productive and financial apparatus and tensions within a political alliance representing diverse social interests, a tough period lies ahead in which neither the new economic model nor the modifications of the corporatist arrangement have a guaranteed future.

1724 Zapata, Francisco; Taeko Hoshino; and Linda Hanono. La restructuración industrial en México: el caso de la industria de las autopartes. México: El Colegio de México, Centro de Estudios Sociológicos, 1994. 142 p.: bibl., ill., tables. (Cuadernos del CES; 37)

Good assessment of the country's industrial development, especially after 1982. Study focuses on the problems facing the automotive industry. Many tables contain difficult to find data on the industry.

1725 Zepeda Miramontes, Eduardo. La captación bancaria en la frontera norte en la década de los ochenta. (*Front. Norte*, 7:14, julio/dic. 1995, p. 45–61, tables)

According to the author, during the 1980s Mexico's prior advances in strengthening its banking system were reversed, and problems without easy solutions emerged, especially within specific regional contexts. This study analyzes the banking sector's ability to attract deposits in selected border cities. Highlights include the various factors that handicapped the national banking system during this period, the role played by a loss of confidence, and the organization and operation of the nationalized banking system, as it influenced the ability of border city banks to attract deposits.

CENTRAL AMERICA

CLARENCE ZUVEKAS, JR., *Consulting Economist, Annandale, Virginia*
DEREKA RUSHBROOK, *Independent Consultant, Tucson, Arizona*

REGION-WIDE STUDIES in this section are dominated by the theme of international trade. Many Central American and other researchers continue to support stronger regional economic integration, but increasingly as part of a broader, outward-oriented strategy called "open regionalism." Thus, even a notable long-time critic of outward-oriented trade strategies currently views globalization as inevitable and argues that stronger regional integration is important for strengthening Central America's ability to compete internationally (item **1742**). A collection of essays by a distinguished Costa Rican economist with a longer commitment to open regionalism provides good insights on regional integration (item **1745**).

The effect of NAFTA on Central American trade with the US is receiving much attention. One work provides a thorough discussion of issues and policy options (item **1740**). A study by CEPAL finds few negative effects of NAFTA on Central America in the short run; but preliminary data for 1996 suggest that some production for the US market may be shifting from Central America to Mexico (item **1731**). This topic merits more detailed investigation in order to strengthen the growing policy debate on NAFTA's implications for macroeconomic and trade policies in Central America.

EL SALVADOR

El Salvador has experienced a strong economic rebound since adopting significant policy reforms in 1989 and signing the Peace Accords in January 1992. The recovery, however, has had little impact on the distribution of income and wealth. Rapid economic growth and large-scale remittances from abroad (a large portion of which goes to poor families) have reduced the incidence of poverty, but not as much as suggested by household survey data. Observers regarding the pattern of economic recovery as a threat to the consolidation of peace are rightfully concerned.

A good starting point for understanding recent economic performance in El Salvador, and the reasons for concern about equity issues, is the introduction to the special section in the December 1995 issue of *World Development* (item **1778**; individual articles annotated separately). One collection of seminar papers presents different sides of the economic policy debate (item **1783**). A representative critique of orthodox policies offers a pro-poor strategic vision combining valid suggestions with a strong utopian outlook and an unwillingness to eschew well-intentioned State interventions that have failed to help the poor in the past (item **1780**).

Other noteworthy studies include a regional study of the urban informal sector (item **1739**); a study on El Salvador's social security system (item **1785**); and a review of changes in El Salvador's agrarian structure (item **1792**).

More research is needed on poverty and income distribution and how they are affected by alternative economic policies. Solid analytical work is hampered by the lack of a consistent database: El Salvador's household survey instrument continues to have major weaknesses. Costa Rica is the only Central American country that has adequate household survey data.

GENERAL

1726 Antecedentes estadísticos de la distribución del ingreso en los años ochenta. v. 3, Costa Rica. v. 4, Guatemala. v. 5, Honduras. Santiago: Naciones Unidas, Comisión Económica para América Latina y el Caribe, 1993. 3 v. (Serie Distribución del ingreso; 12–14)

Useful compilation of income-distribution data from household surveys in Costa Rica (1981–90), Guatemala (1986–90), and Honduras (1986–90). Includes Gini coefficients. Notes that data have limitations for analytical purposes but does not discuss these data problems in detail.

1727 Bastiaensen, Johan *et al.* Ajuste estructural y economía campesina: Nicaragua, El Salvador, Centroamérica. Edición de Jan P. de Groot y Max Spoor. Managua: Escuela de Economía Agrícola, UNAN, 1995. 308 p.: bibl.

Essays on Nicaragua, El Salvador, and Central America argue that structural adjustment has not stimulated basic-grains production or production for export by small farmers. Argues that supply-side measures to stimulate small-farmer production are essential for structural adjustment programs to be economically sustainable. Includes policy recommendations.

1728 Bulmer-Thomas, Victor and **Fernando Rueda-Junquera.** The cooperation agreement between Central America and the European Union: a case study of the special GSP scheme. (*Bull. Lat. Am. Res.*, 15:3, Sept. 1996, p. 323–340, bibl., tables)

Analyzes initial impact (through 1992) of the European Union's special trade benefits for Central America. The impact was greatest in Costa Rica and Guatemala, and least in Nicaragua and Panama. Authors conclude that differential impact is largely related to appropriateness of macroeconomic and microeconomic policies.

1729 Cáceres, Luis René. Costos y beneficios de la integración centroamericana. (*CEPAL Rev.*, 54, Dec. 1994, p. 111–128, bibl., graphs, tables)

Shows that benefits of integration are concentrated in Costa Rica and Guatemala. Presents and constructively analyzes data on intra-industry trade. Conducts statistical tests explaining intraregional trade patterns,

but underlying data are sometimes weak and some results seem implausible. Calls for regional coordination beyond macroeconomic policy.

1730 Centro América: obstáculos y perspectivas del desarrollo. Coordinación de Salvador Arias Peñate, Juan Jované y Luis Ng. San José: Depto. Ecuménico de Investigaciones, 1993. 630 p.: bibl., ill. (Col. universitaria)

Country-by-country description of ambitious construction of relatively uniform, policy-oriented economic model (MOCECA), which links social accounting matrix with econometric models of final demand and monetary demand. Data problems for most countries restrict the model's applicability, and utility is limited because of rapidly changing economic structures.

1731 Centroamérica y el TLC: efectos inmediatos e implicaciones futuras. Santiago: Naciones Unidas, Comisión Económica para América Latina el el Caribe, 1996. 164 p.: bibl. (Cuadernos de la CEPAL, 0252–2195; 78)

Detailed examination of effects of NAFTA on Central American trade. Finds few short-run negative effects. Likely long-run effects can be countered by macroeconomic policy reforms. Economic integration with North America is seen as desirable, either through accession to NAFTA or participation in the proposed Free Trade Area of the Americas.

1732 Competitividad de los sectores productivos de Centroamérica y Panamá. Coordinación general de Helio Fallas. Panamá: FEDEPRICAP, 1993–1994. 16 v.: bibl.

Descriptive, analytical, and policy-oriented papers on factors affecting competitiveness of Central American exports. As measured by its share in imports by industrial countries, Central America (except for Costa Rica) experienced a significant decline in competitiveness in 1979 and 1989. Market shares increased for some sectors, including clothing, fish and seafood, and vegetables.

1733 Current, Dean and **Sara J. Scherr.** Farmer costs and benefits from agroforestry and farm forestry projects in Central America and the Caribbean: implications for policy. (*Agrofor. Syst.*, 30:1/2, 1995, p. 87–103)

Analyzes 56 activities in 21 small-farmer projects. Financial analysis shows 75 percent of activities were profitable to farmers, with positive net present value. Not clear, however, whether economic analysis with full costs and shadow pricing would show positive results. Includes policy recommendations to improve project outcomes.

1734 De Franco, Mario A. Evaluación y recomendaciones sobre la nueva integración centroamericana: un enfoque de equilibrio general. (*Rev. Integr. Desarro. Centroam.*, 50, Jan./June 1996, p. 27–156)

Computable general equilibrium model simulates economic effects of reducing tariffs and other barriers to intra-Central American trade. Effects on balance are positive, although current-account deficits widen and benefits are highly unequal among countries. Generally sound policy recommendations address negative impacts.

1735 Del trabajo no remunerado al trabajo productivo: la participación de la mujer en el sector informal urbano (SIU). San José: Fundación Arias para la Paz y el Progreso Humano; OIT, PREALC, 1993. 326 p.: bibl.

Mainly includes descriptive chapters on Costa Rica, El Salvador, Guatemala, Honduras, and Panama based on household survey data of varying quality. Also presents regional summaries and gender-related policy and research recommendations. Useful source for data on informal sector.

1736 El desarrollo sostenible: un desafío a la política económica agroalimentaria. Recopilación de Pablo Araya, Rafael Díaz y Luis Fernando Fernández. San José: Depto. Ecuménico de Investigaciones, 1995. 248 p.: bibl., ill. (Col. Ecología-teología)

Geographic focus of essays varies from Latin America to Central America to Costa Rica. "Sustainability," not always defined, usually refers to environmental concerns. Most discussions of environmental issues are general, with little attention to detailed measures for addressing specific problems. Some essays on trade policy discuss economic rather than environmental sustainability.

1737 Escaith, Hubert and Claudia Schatan. Central America: inflation and stabilization in the crisis and post-crisis eras. (*CEPAL Rev.*, 58, April 1996, p. 35–51, bibl., tables)

Describes and analyzes inflationary trends. Models pooling time-series data for four countries provide an eclectic explanation of inflation, with changes in external prices and foreign exchange flows, monetary expansion, and inertial inflation related to market imperfections and segmentation all found to play a significant role.

Fallas, Helio et al. Apertura externa y competitividad. See item **1761.**

1738 Funkhouser, Edward. Remittances from international migration: a comparison of El Salvador and Nicaragua. (*Rev. Econ. Stat.*, 77:1, Feb. 1995, p. 137–146)

Statistically examines differences in remittance behavior. Emigrants in the US from El Salvador are twice as likely to send money home as those from Nicaragua, and they send about twice as much. Observable household characteristics explain less of the difference in remittance behavior than differences in self-selection patterns and behavioral coefficients.

1739 Funkhouser, Edward. The urban informal sector in Central America: household survey evidence. (*World Dev.*, 24:11, Nov. 1996, p. 1737–1751)

Valuable comparative study, including statistical analysis of wage determinants, of differences in labor force characteristics between formal and informal sectors, based on household surveys at two or more points in time. Finds significant returns to education in both sectors. Also finds many common patterns, especially among El Salvador, Guatemala, and Honduras.

1740 Gitli, Eduardo. Consideraciones estratégicas para Centroamérica en sus negociaciones post-NAFTA con Estados Unidos. S.l.: s.n., 1994. 33 leaves: bibl.

Good summary of US trade preferences for Central American exports; potential effects of NAFTA on Central American exports; and options for trade negotiations with the US. Appropriately advises Central Americans to regard trade agreements with the US as a natural outcome of—not starting point for—economic policy reforms.

1741 Globalización y fuerza laboral en Centroamérica. Coordinación de Juan Pablo Pérez Sáinz. San José: FLACSO, Programa Costa Rica, 1994. 291 p.: bibl.

Informative study of labor force characteristics, labor relations, and work environment in *maquila* plants in Costa Rica, Guatemala, and Honduras. Based on interviews with managers and workers in firms selected on the basis of availability rather than randomly. Editor and contributors discuss theoretical issues regarding *maquila* employment.

1742 Guerra-Borges, Alfredo. La integración centroamericana ante el reto de la globalización: antología. Managua: Coordinadora Regional de Investigaciones Económicas y Sociales, CRIES, 1996. 192 p.: bibl.

Recent essays by longtime analyst and proponent of Central American integration. Historically skeptical about the potential benefits of worldwide trade liberalization, author accepts reality of globalization and argues that stronger regional integration (including with the rest of Latin America) will better prepare Central American countries for participation in global markets.

1743 Kaimowitz, David. El apoyo tecnológico necesario para promover las exportaciones agrícolas no tradicionales en América Central. San José: Instituto Interamericano de Cooperación para la Agricultura, Programa de Generación y Transferencia de Tecnología, 1992. 102 p.

Good review of strengths and weaknesses of various technology-transfer agents, based on literature review, interviews, and case studies. Emphasizes importance of postharvest as well as production technology. Stresses that imported technology must be supplemented with local technological development. Provides data on area and export value by crop and country.

1744 Kreft, Heinrich. El desarrollo de Centroamérica desde una perspectiva alemana. (*Contribuciones/Buenos Aires*, 13:3, julio/sept. 1996, p. 187–204, table)

Useful review of increased European involvement in Central America following outbreak of armed hostilities in the late 1970s. Argues that Europeans viewed these events in North-South, not East-West terms, and sought to help eliminate internal causes of the conflicts in order to protect their own geopolitical interests. Includes a table of annual European economic assistance commitments.

1745 Lizano Fait, Eduardo. Integración y desarrollo en Centroamérica. Tegucigalpa: Banco Centroamericano de Integración Económica, 1994. 378 p.: bibl.

Collection of mostly policy-oriented essays written between 1960–94 by a leading Central American economist and active participant in discussions on regional economic integration. In addition to sound economic analysis, the author contributes perceptively to analysis of institutional arrangements and political context.

1746 Morales G., Abelardo. Integración y apertura: nuevos escenarios de cooperación y conflicto en Centroamérica. (*Centroam. Int.*, 11, 1994, p. 2–11, graphs, tables)

Useful review of recent developments in Central American economic integration, including formation of the Sistema de Integración Centroamericana (1991) and signing of the Protocol of Guatemala (1993). Discusses Costa Rica's unwillingness to advance the integration process as far or as fast as desired by its neighbors.

1747 Proyecto de formación sobre el tema de la integración regional e inserción de las economías centroamericanas en el mercado mundial: convenio FEDEPRICAP/U.E. v. 3, La movilidad laboral en Centroamérica. v. 4, Impacto fiscal de las políticas comerciales regionales y mecanismos de compensación. v. 6, Superación de obstáculos al comercio intraregional. Coordinación técnica de Anabelle Ulate Q. Panama: FEDEPRICAP, 1995. 3 v.: ill.

Informative studies on costs and benefits of labor mobility, fiscal impacts of regional trade policies, and obstacles to intraregional trade. The project also includes four other studies.

1748 El regionalismo abierto en América Central: los desafíos de profundizar y ampliar la integración. (*Rev. Integr. Desarro. Centroam.*, 50, Jan./June 1996, p. 295–303)

Advocates measures to integrate more closely the Central American economies through an "open regionalism" strategy stressing generalized trade liberalization and deregulation. Provides detailed, wide-ranging policy recommendations for stimulating intraregional trade in both goods and services. Suggests that the integration process be expanded, first to Panama and then to Mexico.

1749 Rodríguez, Ennio. Centroamérica: mercado común, liberalización comercial y acuerdos de comercio. (*Presencia/San Salvador*, 5:19, 1993, p. 74–93, ill., tables)

Good analysis of interrelationships among economic integration in Central America, the region's free trade negotiations with other Latin American countries, and NAFTA. Argues that regional integration within Central America should be consolidated before new free trade agreements with other countries are negotiated.

1750 Sanahuja, José Antonio. Relaciones Europa-Centroamérica: ¿continuidad o cambio? San José: Programa Costa Rica, Facultad Latinoamericana de Ciencias Sociales, FLACSO, 1994. 98 p. (Cuaderno de ciencias sociales; 70)

Valuable review of the political and economic discussions between the European Union and Central American governments, particularly through the "Diálogo de San José" beginning in 1984. Offers thoughtful suggestions for strengthening the dialogue.

1751 Trade, industrialization, and integration in twentieth-century Central America. Edited by Irma Tirado de Alonso. Westport, Conn.: Praeger, 1994. 303 p.: bibl., ill., index, map.

Useful but uneven collection of essays on topics that receive little detailed attention elsewhere. Valuable mainly for the wealth of data and for essays on assembly operations, Mexican-Central American trade, and integration options for Panama. Covers trends since 1960, concentrating on 1980–91. Some essays are long on description but short on analysis.

BELIZE

1752 Gabb, Anthony A. A history of banking in Belize. (*in* Belize: selected proceedings from the second interdisciplinary conference. Lanham, Md.: Univ. Press of America, 1996, p. 65–85, bibl., table)

Starting with the Maya, descriptive essay traces the evolution of capital accumulation in Belize with a focus on the development of the banking system over the past 100 years, broken into three distinct periods. The bulk of the essay considers monetary independence and the role of the Central Bank in regulating the commercial banking system and responding to balance-of-payments deficits from 1982–89.

1753 1991 population census: major findings. Belmopan, Belize: Central Statistical Office, Ministry of Finance, 1991. 27 p.: ill., tables.

Compendium of statistical tables presents census results by district. Text is primarily descriptive, with some explanation of rationale for changes and perceived remaining weaknesses in the census questionnaires. The study takes issue with "common beliefs" contradicted in the data.

1754 Woods, Louis A. *et al.* International migration and the ruralization of Belize, 1970–1991. (*in* Belize: selected proceedings from the second interdisciplinary conference. Lanham, Md.: Univ. Press of America, 1996, p. 173–198, bibl., tables)

Examines the urban-to-rural redistribution of population in Belize with particular attention to the roles of immigration/emigration flows, ethnic mix, and economic activity. The costs of this shift include provision of social services and infrastructure to a more dispersed population, erosion of human capital, and adaptation to a new demographic structure.

COSTA RICA

1755 Clark, Mary A. Nontraditional export promotion in Costa Rica: sustaining export-led growth. (*J. Interam. Stud. World Aff.*, 37:2, Summer 1995, p. 181–223, bibl., graphs, tables)

Assesses the variables shaping export-led growth strategies and the likely impact of the withdrawal of external assistance on these programs' sustainability as US aid fell in the 1990s. The policy environment remains favorable to nontraditional exporters, despite the decline of institutional support and the elimination of fiscally unsustainable tax rebates (CATs). Provides a general overview and tentative framework for assessing sustainability of such programs.

1756 Comercio y ambiente: perspectivas desde la actividad bananera. Recopilación de Roxana Salazar Cambronero *et al.* 1. ed. San José: Fundación Ambio, 1994. 104 p.; bibl. (Serie Ambiente y Derecho)

Three articles on banana production and environment focus on economic imperatives, ecological risks, and the importance of the European importation system.

1757 Corrales, Jorge. Al bienestar por el liberalismo. San José: Impresos C.Q.M., 1994. 273 p.

Collection of about 70 short articles previously published in *La Nacion*. Half offer commentary on contemporary economic policies and phenomena. Fails to note essays' publication dates, making this collection less useful than it might otherwise be.

1758 Cruz, María Concepción et al. Population growth, poverty, and environmental stress: frontier migration in the Philippines and Costa Rica. Washington: World Resources Institute, 1992. 100 p.: bibl., ill. (World Resources Institute report)

Stresses links of demographic and environmental strains to larger issues of land tenure institutions and economic policies. The Costa Rican government's grants of provisional rights to squatters has led to more degradation/migration in Costa Rica and fueled the expansion of cattle ranching. Economic crisis merely added to other socioeconomic factors leading to a net migration from deforested into forested areas. Standard policy recommendations.

1759 Desarrollo rural integrado: ¿concepto o finalidad?; una experiencia en Costa Rica; el Proyecto CEE NA/82–12. San José: Comisión de las Comunidades Europeas, 1990? 268 p.: bibl., col. ill., maps.

Extremely detailed overview of a European Community sponsored rural development project in the Central Pacific region during 1984–90. Information is organized by community, institution, or project, and thus may be difficult to synthesize. Describes how locally identified needs and local institutions were incorporated into the process.

1760 Doorman, Frans et al. La situación agraria en Coto Sur: análisis y recomendaciones para el desarrollo de la pequeña finca. Heredia, Costa Rica: Univ. Nacional; Utrecht, Holland: Univ. Estatal de Utrecht, 1992. 410 p.: bibl.

Thoughtful and exhaustive analysis of the socioeconomic structure in the region, placing a detailed interdisciplinary case study in the context of changing agricultural policies. Compares risks and returns to investment in and marketing of various products, from corn to palm oil, with special attention to yields, technology, and farm characteristics.

1761 Fallas, Helio et al. Apertura externa y competitividad. Recopilación de Leiner Alberto Vargas Alfaro. Heredia, Costa Rica: Univ. Nacional, Maestría en Política Económica; Editorial Fundación UNA, 1994. 309 p.: bibl., ill.

Includes several essays on Costa Rican competitiveness. The more interesting essays focus on growing competitiveness in the 1990s, with an export structure shifting towards dynamic sectors and new markets; on the role of tax incentives in increasing nontraditional exports; and on the roles of inefficient ports and monopolistic shipping lines in reducing exports.

1762 Financiamiento de la microempresa rural: FINCA-Costa Rica. Edición de Claudio González Vega, Ronulfo Jiménez Rodríguez, Rodolfo Quirós Rodríguez. San José: Proyecto Servicios Financieros, Ohio State Univ., Academia de Centroamérica y Fundación Interamericana, 1993. 307 p.: bibl., ill., maps.

Focuses on the successful evolution of and remaining weaknesses in FINCA's policies in offering efficient financial services, and emphasizes the organization's need to secure its own long-term future and financial viability to offer better services to its clients. Provides detailed institutional information and a clear analysis of credit as a development tool.

Franco, Eliana and **Carlos Sojo.** Gobierno, empresarios y políticas de ajuste. See item **3153.**

1763 Gindling, T.H. and **Katherine Terrell.** The nature of minimum wages and their effectiveness as a wage floor in Costa Rica, 1976–91. (*World Dev.*, 23:8, Aug. 1995, p. 1439–1458, graphs, tables)

Survey of eight broadly defined industries finds the minimum wage does not serve as an effective wage floor; one-third of the labor force earns less than the minimum wage. Demographic characteristics of those earning less are similar to those in other countries. Recent simplification of regulations did not increase compliance due to weak enforcement and the exclusion of part-time workers from the code.

1764 Guardia Quirós, Jorge. Del cambio fijo a la liberalización cambiaria: colección de ensayos. San José: Litografía e Imprenta Lil, 1993. 246 p.: ill.

Collection of essays, most previously published in *La Nación* from 1981–92, advocating a liberalized exchange-rate regime. Clear commentary on contemporary events and the fiscal impact of exchange-rate policies.

1765 Hamilton, Nora and **Carol Thompson.** Export promotion in a regional context: Central America and Southern Africa. (*World Dev.*, 22:9, Sept. 1994, p. 1379–1392, bibl.)

Examines the history of economic policy and export promotion in Costa Rica and Zimbabwe. Authors question potential for success of trade liberalization and nontraditional export strategies if the policies are not placed in the context of a broader development strategy and increased regional cooperation to increase bargaining power.

1766 Hilje Quirós, Brunilda; Carlos Naranjo; and **Mario Samper K.** "Entonces ya vinieron otras variedades, otros sistemas:" testimonios sobre la caficultura en el valle central de Costa Rica. 1. ed. San José : Convenio ICAFE-UNA, 1995. 193 p. : ill.

Interviews with a cross section of Costa Rica's coffee producers focus on changing agricultural practices, technological advances, and demands of the international market.

1767 Jiménez Gómez, Roberto. Globalización y desarrollo. San José: Editorial Asiade, 1994. 42 p.: bibl., ill.

Examines Costa Rica's entrance into the world economy and its impact on social equity and the conservation of natural resources. Advocates a larger State role in promoting increased international competitiveness based on greater human capital and adopted technology, as well as in ensuring access to basic needs.

1768 Monge González, Ricardo and **Claudio González Vega.** Economía política, proteccionismo, y apertura en Costa Rica. San José: Academia de Centroamérica, 1995. 208 p.: bibl., ill.

Uses simultaneous equation model to examine the determinants of the protectionist structure. Employs a general equilibrium approach to estimate social costs of protectionism during 1986–92. High losses associated with rent-seeking activities lead the au-

thors to advocate a rapid transition to a more open trading system.

1769 Nowalski, Jorge; Pedro A. Morales C.; and **Gregorio Berliavsky.** Impacto de la maquila en la economía costarricense. San José: Friedrich Ebert Stiftung, 1994. 105 p.: bibl.

Overview of *maquila* policy with an optimistic focus on net employment generation (particularly for women and in secondary regions) and foreign exchange earnings. Studies of textile firms indicate inferior working conditions and scant opportunities for technology transfer or accumulation of human capital. Despite the sector's short-run dynamic nature, low productivity levels limit its potential as a basis for promoting long-term growth.

1770 Persson, Annika and **Mohan Munasinghe.** Natural resource management and economywide policies in Costa Rica: a computable general equilibrium (CGE) modeling approach. (*World Bank Econ. Rev.*, 9:2, May 1995, p. 259–285, graphs, tables)

A standard CGE model incorporating markets for cleared land and logs is used to analyze impact of broad macro policies and introduction of property rights on the rate of deforestation. Most results reflect those of earlier partial-equilibrium models, but illuminate the intersectoral effects of tax and subsidy policies leading to shifts in resources between agriculture and industry. Results differ from those offered by partial-equilibrium studies.

1771 Programa de ajuste y la reforma estructural entre la necesidad político-económico [sic] y la viabilidad político-social [sic]. San José: Fundación Konrad Adenauer; CIEDLA; INDEP, 1992. 89 leaves.

Collection of essays from a one-day seminar evaluating structural adjustment in Costa Rica. Divergent viewpoints unified by recognition of need for reform and consolidation of market competition, but critical of neoliberal policies implemented without regard for social cohesion, the role of human capital (social spending), and income distribution.

1772 Reforma financiera en Costa Rica: perspectivas y propuestas. Edición de Claudio González Vega y Thelmo Vargas Madrigal. San José: Academia de Centroamérica, 1993. 475 p.: bibl. (Serie Proyecto Servicios Financieros)

Comprehensive overview of the regulatory history and structure of the banking system. Provides a cross-section of proposals for reforming the banking system, as well as a coherent exposition of the necessity for continued reform. Particular attention is given to the inherent difficulties of establishing an effective development bank.

1773   La seguridad social en Costa Rica: problemas y perspectivas. Edición de Elías Jiménez Fonseca. San José: Editorial Nacional de Salud y Seguridad Social, 1994. 277 p.: bibl., ill.

Includes essays describing the history of the government's involvement in providing health care, and proposals for reforming medical coverage and health services. Suggested changes include decentralization, increased transparency, redistribution of medical resources, and improved evaluation/quality control mechanisms.

1774   Solís Fallas, Ottón. Experiencia de Costa Rica con los ajustes estructurales y la apertura de mercados. Panamá: Sindicato de Industriales de Panamá, 1995. 24 p. (Col. Almuerzo industrial)

Former Planning Minister ascribes increasing inflation and growing trade and fiscal deficits to indiscriminate policies guiding Costa Rica's liberalization. Argues that the primary obstacle to development is resource quality; thus, rather than directing loans toward export credits, the government should invest heavily in education, health, and public infrastructure while maintaining monetary and fiscal discipline.

1775   Torres, Oscar and Hernán Alvarado. Los efectos de la política macroeconómica en la agricultura y la seguridad alimentaria: caso, Costa Rica. Panama: CADESCA, 1990. 78 p.: bibl., ill.

Overview of structural adjustment's impact on output of and trade in basic grains and traditional and nontraditional exports. Emphasizes need for regional coordination of policies, and the difficulty of evaluating export-promotion programs that may enjoy initial "easy" phases, like those seen in import-substitution industrialization after a short period in existence.

1776   Vargas Alfaro, Leiner Alberto. Apertura comercial, productividad y recomposición industrial: el caso de Costa Rica. Heredia, Costa Rica: Editorial Fundación UNA, 1993. 79 p.: bibl., ill. (Serie Política económica; 7)

Econometric study of the impact of liberalization on total factor productivity and Costa Rican competitiveness in international trade. Attributes slow lowering of tariffs to fiscal rigidity and the need to sustain debt payments while following anti-inflationary policies. Advocates more consistent and rapid lowering of trade barriers.

EL SALVADOR

1777   Acevedo, Carlos; Deborah Barry; and Herman Rosa. El Salvador's agricultural sector: macroeconomic policy, agrarian change and the environment. (*World Dev.*, 23:12, Dec. 1995, p. 2153–2172)

Argues that macroeconomic policies have contributed to falling relative domestic agricultural prices, and that policies and current landholding patterns cause major environmental damage. Advocates currency devaluation, price supports to move toward self-sufficiency in basic grains, additional agrarian reform, and environmental programs. Little consideration of potential economic and financial costs.

1778   Boyce, James K. Adjustment toward peace: an introduction. (*World Dev.*, 23:12, Dec. 1995, p. 2067–2077)

Regards both macroeconomic and political stabilization as necessary for consolidating peace. Financing immediate costs of peace will require overcoming some political obstacles. In the long run, economic growth, greater income equality, and peace appropriately viewed as mutually reinforcing. Underestimates external donors' efforts to promote these complementarities yet exaggerates their ability to effect change.

1779   Boyce, James K. External assistance and the peace process in El Salvador. (*World Dev.*, 23:12, Dec. 1995, p. 2101–2116)

Quantifies and disaggregates external-donor and government commitments to Peace Accords programs through early 1994. Argues that some external donors—especially international financial institutions—

failed to exercise peace conditionality. Maintains that the government could have done more to reallocate expenditures and raise additional revenues, but understates achievements in these areas.

1780 Crecimiento estéril o desarrollo: bases para la construcción de un nuevo proyecto económico en El Salvador. Recopilación de Roberto Rubio Fabián, Joaquín Arriola Palomares y José Víctor Aguilar. San Salvador: Fundación Nacional para el Desarrollo; Equipo de Educación Maíz, 1996. 218 p.: ill.

Important work argues that current policies depend excessively on external resources, focus on consumption rather than investment, and exacerbate inequalities. Details ambitious, alternative strategy that includes much direction by the State. Some policy suggestions are worthwhile, but many would repeat past mistakes and are incompatible with stated goal of sustainable, equitable growth. Costs are not considered.

1781 Dada Sánchez, Héctor. El sector manufacturero en El Salvador: competitividad y potencial de expansión de las exportaciones. San Salvador: Centro de Investigaciones Tecnológicas y Científicas, Dirección de Investigaciones Económicas y Sociales, 1994. 28 p.: graphs, tables. (Política Económica; 22, enero/feb. 1994)

Good review of analytical data on competitiveness of El Salvador's exports, particularly of manufactured products. Argues that differences in sector- and firm-level competitiveness are explained more by firm-level technical capacity than by relative factor intensity. Recommends that government take steps beyond trade liberalization to strengthen this capacity.

1782 Danby, Colin. Challenges and opportunities in El Salvador's financial sector. (World Dev., 23:12, Dec. 1995, p. 2133–2152)

Comprehensive review of various components of financial sector. Argues that financial liberalization was premature and that growth of small-scale institutions has been discouraged. Correctly stresses deposit mobilization is essential for sustaining financial institutions that serve lower-income borrowers. Tends to overstate monetary consequences of large capital inflows.

El Salvador a fin de siglo. See item **4706.**

1783 El Salvador hacia el año 2000: una plataforma de política económica y social de consenso. San Salvador? Centro Internacional para el Desarrollo Económico; Centro de Estudios Democráticos, s.d. 1 v.

Seminar papers by members of four think tanks, representing different political persuasions, on the role of the State in society, poverty, social policy, and macroeconomic policy, with comments by noted non-Salvadoran economists. Also includes statements by three vice-presidential candidates. An important contribution to the economic policy debate.

1784 López, José Roberto. El tratado de libre comercio México-El Salvador. San Salvador: FUSADES, 1993. 236 p.: bibl. (Documento de trabajo/Fundación Salvadoreña para el Desarrollo Económico y Social (FUSADES), Depto. de Estudios Económicos y Sociales (DEES); 34)

Argues that free trade agreement with Mexico would benefit El Salvador. Recommends detailed negotiation strategy, based on lessons from Chilean, US, and Costa Rican negotiations with Mexico. Includes results of surveys of Salvadoran exporting and importing firms trading with Mexico. Finds El Salvador's economy to be more open than Mexico's.

1785 Mesa-Lago, Carmelo; Ricardo Córdova Macías; and Carlos Mauricio López Grande. El Salvador: diagnóstico y propuesta de reforma de la seguridad social. San Salvador: Centro Internacional para el Desarrollo Económico; FundaUngo; Friedrich Ebert Stiftung, 1994. 92 p.: bibl.

Excellent, detailed description and analysis of social security in El Salvador, where coverage rate is among lowest in Latin America. Negative real yields on investment, overgenerous benefits, and high administrative costs have weakened financial structures. Discusses options for reform. Advocates mixed public-private pension system and complementary private health program.

1786 Murray, Kevin et al. Rescuing reconstruction: the debate on post-war economic recovery in El Salvador. Cambridge, Mass.; San Salvador: Hemisphere Initiatives; Washington: Washington Office on Latin America, 1994. 57 p.: map, tables.

Critical evaluation of mixed initial results (1992–94) of the government's National Reconstruction Plan. Examines roles of donor agencies, NGOs, and national and local governments. Notes relatively low level of popular participation. Some expectations, especially those for the land transfer program, seem too high. Offers many sound recommendations.

1787 Pastor, Manuel and Michael Conroy.
Distributional implications of macroeconomic policy: theory and applications to El Salvador. (*World Dev.*, 23:12, Dec. 1995, p. 2117–2131)
Discusses complex theoretical issues—both generally and for El Salvador—of relationship between income distribution and macroeconomic performance. Cites research showing complementarities between greater equality and economic efficiency/growth. Proposes alternative macroeconomic policy framework for El Salvador that would further reduce both short-run and long-run inequality.

1788 Paus, Eva. Exports, economic growth and the consolidation of peace in El Salvador. (*World Dev.*, 23:12, Dec. 1995, p. 2173–2193)
Excellent analysis of export competitiveness, emphasizing real exchange-rate overvaluation and the countering effects of falling real wages. Proposes numerous measures to stimulate faster export growth. Argues that continued real-wage declines are incompatible with consolidating peace and with long-term competitiveness.

1789 Restrepo, Carlos. Políticas de desarrollo científico y tecnológico: recomendaciones para el caso de El Salvador. San Salvador: Depto. de Estudios Económicos y Sociales de FUSADES, 1995. 149 p.: ill. (Documento de trabajo; 39)
Argues that the State plays an important role in promoting international competitiveness through policies and programs to develop local scientific and technological capacities. Usefully reviews existing policies and institutions; discusses experiences of Costa Rica and Mexico; and offers policy recommendations. Regards intra-institutional cooperation as very weak.

1790 Riveros, Luis A. and Felipe Balmaceda.
Discriminación en un mercado del trabajo segmentado: diferencias salariales por gé-

nero en El Salvador. (*Estud. Econ./Santiago*, 21:2, dic. 1994, p. 277–299, bibl., tables)
Econometric analysis shows that apparent male-female wage gap narrows when corrected for selection bias resulting from overrepresentation of women in the low-wage informal sector. The labor-market structure explains much of the gap. Also, differences in human-capital endowments explain more of the gap than does "pure" discrimination.

1791 Rodríguez, América. Inversión en recursos humanos y nuevas modalidades de la política social en El Salvador: el programa EDUCO. San Salvador: Centro de Investigaciones Tecnológicas y Científicas, Dirección de Investigaciones Económicas y Sociales, 1994. 28 p. (Política Económica; No. 19, julio/agosto 1993)
Preliminary evaluation of important experiment in educational decentralization, targeting poor rural communities and focusing on both pre-primary education and the first few primary grades. Community organizations are being empowered to hire teachers and purchase supplies. Author finds less decentralizing in practice than in theory; however experiment remains promising.

1792 Seligson, Mitchell A. Thirty years of transformation in the agrarian structure of El Salvador, 1961–1991. (*LARR*, 30:3, 1995, p. 43–74, bibl., graphs, tables)
Thorough examination of 1961–1971 agricultural census data, secondary data sources, and 1991–92 multipurpose household survey results. Argues that most estimates of landless and land-poor populations around 1980, including those based on the 1971 census, were inaccurate. Still, these categories represented 51 percent of the economically active population in 1991, compared with 60 percent in 1971. For the ethnologist's comment see item **767** and for the sociologist's comment see item **4747.**

1793 Wood, Elizabeth and Alexander Segovia. Macroeconomic policy and the Salvadoran peace accords. (*World Dev.*, 23:12, Dec. 1995, p. 2079–2099)
Insightful analysis of weak relationship between macroeconomic policy and implementation of peace accords suggests that problems resulted more from weak government commitment than from funding constraints, despite lower-than-expected external

funding and overstated short-run potential for tax-revenue increases. Appropriately suggests dependence on remittances and overvalued exchange rate will endanger long-term growth.

GUATEMALA

1794 Agricultura y campesinado en Guatemala: una aproximación. Guatemala: Asociación para el Avance de las Ciencias Sociales en Guatemala (AVANCSO), 1993. 29 p. (Texto para debate; 1)

Brief overview of agriculture's importance in the national economy. Primary focus is on the unequal distribution of land, credit, and technology, reflecting the concentrated and exclusionary nature of the traditional model. Little information on nontraditional exports.

1795 Asamblea de la Sociedad Civil (Guatemala). Esperanza de paz: una propuesta para el desarrollo integral de Guatemala. Guatemala: Centro de Investigaciones Económicas Nacionales, 1994. 35 p.: ill.

Criticizes the inequitable mercantilist economic model and proposes development based on ensuring basic needs and equal-opportunity access while restricting the role of the State, decentralizing the economy, and relying on market mechanisms. Brief analysis of problems in social and macroeconomic areas, but little attention to how proposed solutions might be implemented.

1796 Barham, Bradford L.; Stephen Boucher; and Michael R. Carter. Credit constraints, credit unions, and small-scale producers in Guatemala. (*World Dev.*, 24:5, May 1996, p. 793–806, bibl., graphs, tables)

Important contribution to literature on the role of credit unions and financial markets in promoting equitable development. Focus is on local markets and small-scale, lower-wealth producers. Advocates short-term support to create decentralized, market-oriented credit unions that will be self-sustaining while enhancing financial-market efficiency as they expand services to credit-constrained low-income households.

1797 Garst, Rachel. FIS y FONAPAZ en Guatemala: una nueva relación ONG-Estado. Guatemala: Consejo de Instituciones de Desarrollo de Guatemala, 1993. 123 p.: bibl.

Compares and contrasts the history and structure of FONAPAZ and FIS and their relationships with the IMF, World Bank, NGOs and the national government. Fairly complete descriptive overview. Does not offer an evaluation of the institutions' operations.

1798 Guatemala: ONG's y desarrollo; el caso del altiplano central. México: CEIDEC, 1993. 155 p.: bibl., map.

Investigates NGO role in implementing rural development programs, primarily agricultural export diversification. Provides a careful review of USAID's proposals and the Sanford commission review in particular. Gives detailed information on horticultural production in the context of the socioeconomic structure of the region. Mainly concerned with NGOs' perceived neglect of the need for food security, access to land, and political participation, as well as emphasizing exporting for exporting's sake.

1799 Katz, Elizabeth G. Gender and trade within the household: observations from rural Guatemala. (*World Dev.*, 23:2, Feb. 1995, p. 327–342, bibl., tables)

Uses a household model to estimate demographic and village-level determinants of women's participation in new male income-generating activities. Examines impact of work choices and income transfers on purchases of male goods versus food and domestic technology, distinguishing between household types. Intra-household resource allocation should be considered when evaluating policy interventions.

1800 Política económica y social del gobierno de Guatemala para el período 1991–1996: hacia una democracia económica y social. Guatemala: Lito Van Color, 1991. 88 p.

Overview of general social and economic objectives outlined at the beginning of Serrano's term, designed in concordance with the UN's view of the changes necessary to strengthen human rights and the legal system while ending armed conflict. Little attempt to unify the lists presented.

1801 Rodas, Isabel. Inserción de una comunidad agraria al mercado de agroexportación, Joya Grande, Chimaltenango. (*Estudios/Guatemala*, 1, 1994, p. 81–102, bibl., map)

Traces history of the introduction of

horticultural products into a small altiplano community. The way in which small farmers were assimilated into the production chain depended upon land tenure, access to credit, and the specific crop. Touches upon effect on seasonal migration, gender impacts, and forming cooperatives. Some attention given to criteria necessary for success. General applicability is unclear.

1802 Samayoa Urrea, Otto. Bases para la elaboración de una política de desarrollo económico a través de las exportaciones. Guatemala: Gremial de Exportadores de Productos No Tradicionales, 1994. 34 p.: bibl., ill.

Traces evolution of nontraditional exports to markets outside Central America from 1970 onwards. Evaluates multiplier effects, employment, and value added created by these exports. Identifies factors limiting exports, including macroeconomic policy, infrastructure, and general market structures, and proposes solutions to these constraints.

1803 Steele, Diane. Guatemala. (*in* Indigenous people and poverty in Latin America: an empirical analysis. Edited by George Psacharopoulos and Harry Anthony Patrinos. Washington: The World Bank, 1994, p. 97–126, graphs, tables)

Uses extensive data from a 1989 national household survey to compare the situations of indigenous and non-indigenous peoples, with an emphasis on poverty, income-distribution inequality, and labor markets. Employs regression analysis to examine the impact of gender, ethnicity, and age on school attendance and literacy. Thorough empirical overview.

HONDURAS

1804 Actividad económica de las empresas maquiladoras ubicadas en las zonas libres y zonas de procesamiento industrial, año 1993. Tegucigalpa: Banco Central de Honduras, Depto. de Estudios Económicos, 1994. 23 leaves.

Provides an overview of the legal background and incentives for firms operating in these areas of Honduras, and a statistical review of their macroeconomic and socioeconomic impact. Little analysis or coverage of the evolution of these programs. See also item **1805.**

1805 Actividad económica de las zonas libres y zonas de procesamiento industrial. Tegucigalpa: Banco Central de Honduras, Depto. de Estudios Económicos, Sección Cuentas Nacionales, 1993. 15 leaves.

For review see item **1804.**

1806 Castro Rubio, Angel Augusto. Un plan de desarrollo regional: el Bajo Aguán en Honduras. México: Univ. Iberoamericana, 1994. 146 p.: bibl., maps. (Col. Estudios regionales)

Examines introduction of palm oil production in agricultural cooperatives from 1970s onward in a region previously dominated by banana plantations controlled by foreign capital. Summarizes project-specific and national land reform policies, and analyzes resulting changes in the labor market and the organization of production and exchange.

1807 Dewalt, Billie R.; Philippe Vergne; and **Mark Hardin.** Shrimp aquaculture development and the environment: people, mangroves and fisheries on the Gulf of Fonseca, Honduras. (*World Dev.*, 24:7, July 1996, p. 1193–1208, bibl., map, tables)

Significant contribution to research on the possibilities aquaculture offers for sustainable development, with particular attention to environmental degradation and mangrove depletion. Focus is on the socioeconomic implications of continued growth in the industry and the importance of promoting cooperation among stakeholders in the region if positive benefits are to be realized. Suggests that regulation must recognize protected areas, multiple users, and overlapping scales of government.

1808 Honduras: informe económico de coyuntura 1993 y perspectivas 1994. Tegucigalpa?: Consejo hondureño de la empresa privada (COHEP), 1994. 70 p.: ill., tables.

Examines national economic policies and goals. Attributes comparatively weak economic performance within the region to the government deviating from strict structural adjustment policies and lack of fiscal discipline.

1809 Honduras. Secretaría de Planificación, Coordinación y Presupuesto. Lineamientos generales de estratégia para el desarrollo social y productivo, 1994–1998. Tegucigalpa: Gobierno de Honduras, Secretaría de

Planificación, Coordinación y Presupuesto, 1994. 52 leaves.

Consists of lists of sector-specific strategies, objectives, and plans of action to be considered by the government during the five-year period. May be useful as an indication of government aims, but offers little context, statistical support or analysis, and no explanation of how implementation may occur.

1810 Honduras, libro Q: pobreza, potencialidad y focalización municipal. 2. ed. rev. Tegucigalpa: Secretaría de Planificación, Coordinación y Presupuesto, 1994. 226 p.

Rich source of data on poverty and social problems, including socioeconomic and cultural characteristics of households, cost of living, and extensive information at the municipal and departmental level. Offers a logit model of poverty. Solid foundation for future policy studies.

1811 Isaula, Roger. Honduras: el ajuste en el sector agrícola y la seguridad alimentaria. Tegucigalpa: CEDOH, 1996. 85 p.: bibl.

Critique of 1992 agricultural modernization laws substituting market mechanisms for agrarian reform that would provide the poor with access to land. Emphasizes negative impact of structural adjustment on the agricultural sector to convince international financial institutions of the need to address the link between poverty, hunger, unequal land distribution and an export-oriented sector.

1812 Martin, Michael J. and Timothy G. Taylor. Evaluation of a multimedia extension program in Honduras. (*Econ. Dev. Cult. Change*, 43:4, July 1995, p. 821–834, tables)

Farmers' decisions to adopt new agricultural technologies depend primarily on demographic characteristics and extension services; these factors are incorporated into a single-equation model. In Comayagua, personal contacts developed through training and visiting programs were more effective for promoting technology diffusion, but also more costly, than were tailored multimedia approaches.

1813 El mercado de tierras en Honduras. Coordinación de Ramón Salgado *et al.* Tegucigalpa: Centro de Documentación de Honduras, 1994. 274 p.: bibl.

Detailed investigation of supply and demand characteristics in land markets in two agricultural regions, referencing to impact of 1992 agricultural reforms. Imperfections in the land market, including the titling process, can not be treated in isolation; imperfections in related markets must also be resolved.

1814 Noé Pino, Hugo and Rodulio Perdomo. Efectos de la política macroeconómica en la agricultura y la seguridad alimentaria: caso, Honduras. Panama: CADESCA, 1990. 93 p.: bibl., ill.

Explores structural adjustment's impact on the output of basic grains and traditional agricultural exports. Unlike prior import-substitution policies that discriminated against exporters, new policies exclude small producers oriented towards the domestic market, exacerbating the problem of food security while the government advocates a perceived comparative advantage in the global agricultural market.

1815 Plan agrícola para el desarrollo del campo, 1995–1998, PROAGRO. Tegucigalpa: Secretaría de Recursos Naturales SRN, 1995. vii, 68 leaves: bibl.

Analyzes negative effect of macroeconomic policies on agricultural sector. Proposes detailed sectoral programs and support services with reference to specific product groups. Fails to discuss how resources to implement proposals and stated goals might be secured.

1816 Rivera Rodil, Rodil. El neoliberalismo en Honduras y una alternativa de cambio. Tegucigalpa?: Editorial Millenium, 1993. 85 p.

Examines economic crisis and structural adjustment policies in Honduras, and offers suggestions for a broad restructuring of the government and macroeconomic policies. Lacks empirical analysis, and provides scant theoretical underpinnings for the suggested reforms.

1817 Wattel, Cor J. et al. Financiamiento rural alternativo: experiencias con el crédito no-bancario en Honduras. Tegucigalpa: Editorial Guaymuras; Cooperación Suiza al Desarrollo, 1994. 214 p.: bibl. (Col. Puerta abierta. Cultura y educación popular)

Surveys 94 families and 10 credit providers in various regions to determine financing use and needs. Analyzes factors affecting the success of loan programs under varying conditions. Recommends action based on existing debt levels, economic activity, and institutional framework.

1818 Webb, Anna Kathryn Vandever; Kye Woo Lee; and Anna Maria Sant'Anna. The participation of nongovernmental organizations in poverty alleviation: a case study of the Honduras Social Investment Fund Project. Washington: World Bank, 1995. xvii, 40 p.: bibl. (World Bank discussion papers, 0259–210x; 295)

Analyzes how relative strengths and resources of NGOs and the public sector may complement each other to offer services more effectively. After highlighting typical problems, authors offer recommendations for improving collaboration among governmental and implementing agencies, NGOs, and the World Bank.

NICARAGUA

1819 Acevedo Vogl, Adolfo José. Algunas implicaciones de los acuerdos con el FMI y el Banco Mundial (ESAF y ERC-II) para el país y la sociedad nicaraguense: quince puntos críticos sobre el ESAF y ERC-II. Managua: Coordinadora Regional de Investigaciones Económicas y Sociales, 1994. 32 p. (Documento de trabajo; 94/3)

Criticizes contractionary adjustment policies for excluding small and medium firms, which leads to a reconcentration of income and wealth and reduced access to credit, and for using external resources for consumer goods, imports, and debt service rather than domestic investment. Advocates some form of continued wage indexation, price controls, and protection for simple manufactured goods.

1820 Acevedo Vogl, Adolfo José. Nicaragua y el FMI, Fondo Monetario Internacional: el pozo sin fondo del ajuste. Managua: Latino Editores, 1993. 177 p.: bibl.

Criticizes structural adjustment policies for their restrictive and monetarist nature resulting in "overkill." Advocates reactivating internal demand, slowly opening to the world market, and offering credit to stimulate export sectors in the short run. Focuses on redirecting external resources towards production and poverty relief rather than debt reduction.

1821 Aguilar O., Carlos et al. Mercados de granos básicos en Nicaragua: hacia una nueva visión sobre producción y comercialización. Recopilación de Harry Clemens, Duty Greene y Max Spoor. Managua: Escuela de Economía Agrícola, 1994. 320 p.: bibl., ill.

Includes essays about specific product markets, certain government agencies and policies, on liberalization, and problems some regions face. Concludes that the government must devote resources to modernizing markets, particularly in the areas of transportation and credit infrastructures, the dissemination of information, and legal support. Also encourages reforming macroeconomic policies.

1822 Alemán, Estela and Isolda Espinoza. Viabilidad económica del cooperativismo agrario en Nicaragua: período 1979–1991. Managua: Univ. Nacional Autónoma de Nicaragua, Facultad de Ciencias Económicas, Escuela de Economía Agrícola, CIES-ESECA, 1993. 94 p.: bibl.

Concludes that Sandinista macroeconomic policies favoring cooperatives generated inefficiencies and underutilized resources, and that excessive State support led to dependency and a lack of autonomy which undermined the cooperatives' ability to attain economic goals. Less favorable policies initiated in 1990 forced adjustments that increased efficiency and generated competitive advantages.

Babb, Florence E. After the revolution: neoliberal policy and gender in Nicaragua. See item **696.**

1823 Clemens, Harry. Competitividad de Nicaragua en la producción agrícola. Managua: Univ. Nacional Autónoma de Nicaragua, Facultad de Ciencias Económicas, Escuela de Economía Agrícola, 1994. 56 p.: bibl., maps. (Serie CIES/ESECA; 94.1)

Provides overview of the evolution of production of specific agricultural commodities from 1960 onwards, with attention to domestic versus international factors, regional variations, and macroeconomic and sectoral policies. Nicaragua shows high potential competitiveness in sectors with few inputs (such as beef, beans, and coffee), but is not competitive in processed products or those requiring irrigation.

1824 Dijkstra, A. Geske. The impact of structural adjustment programs on manufacturing: lessons from Nicaragua. (*World Dev.*, 24:3, March 1996, p. 535–547, bibl., tables)

Considers how lack of investment and non-market environment in the 1980s contributed to low adaptability and low supply elasticities of manufacturing under structural adjustment policies. Trade liberalization did not lead to competitive markets, exacerbating problems of inflation, unemployment, and dampened output. Supports neostructuralist government policies.

1825 Estudio de la pobreza en Nicaragua: documento de trabajo. Managua: Gobierno de la República de Nicaragua, Ministerio de Acción Social, Gabinete Social, 1994. 80 leaves: bibl., ill., maps.

Using 1993 survey data on household capacity to satisfy basic needs, the study provides a preliminary overview of the magnitude, distribution, and intensity of poverty, and of the related characteristics and conditions of households in poverty. Utilizes different criteria for urban and rural poverty. Finds that extreme poverty is concentrated among the young and in rural areas. Summary data only.

Everingham, Mark. Revolution and the multiclass coalition in Nicaragua. See item **4709.**

1826 Franco, Silvio de. Sobrevivencia y espíritu empresarial: el sector informal en Managua 1977–1978. Traducción de Caspar Pick. Managua: Fondo Editorial, Banco Central de Nicaragua, 1993. 167 p.: bibl., ill.

Using a survey of 650 families, thorough study compares worker and firm characteristics in the informal sector to those found in the formal sector and in other nations' urban informal sectors. Finds that problems in the sector are aggravated by migration into Managua encouraged by greater employment opportunities and income possibilities. National policies to reduce underemployment in the agricultural sector, combined with increased access to education and credit in the informal sector, may alleviate these problems.

1827 Ghysels, Joris. El empleo en Nicaragua: como la crisis actual se generaliza para el año 2000. Managua: Nitlapán, UCA: Fundación Friedrich Ebert, Representación en Nicaragua, 1995. 72 p.: bibl., ill. (Materials de estudio y trabajo; 17)

Attributes increasing open urban unemployment shown in annual surveys (1992–94) to the saturation of the informal sector and to the increase of labor force participation rates in response to economic crisis. Disaggregates results based on salary, age, education, sex, and underemployment by sector and occupational status. Advocates employment-generating public projects (particularly those aimed at women), increased emphasis on basic education, and expanded social welfare programs.

1828 Hacia un acuerdo nacional contra la pobreza. Managua: Instituto Nicaragüense de Estudios Sociopolíticos, 1993. 88 p.: ill. (Ediciones INESP; 11)

Five essays detail the extent and causes of rapid growth in extreme poverty and offer proposals to combat deprivation. The authors, representing the Chamorro government, the Catholic Church, PNUD, and PDC, disagree regarding necessary additional resources and structural transformations, but share some social investment targets.

1829 Jonakin, Jon. The impact of structural adjustment and property rights conflicts on Nicaraguan agrarian reform beneficiaries. (*World Dev.*, 24:7, July 1996, p. 1179–1191, bibl., tables)

Important study of changes in land tenure leading to restratification in post-Sandinista Nicaragua. Reduced government-support programs, particularly agricultural credit and insecure property rights, have contributed to land sales at below-market prices by small-scale producers who had received land collectivized in the 1980s. Includes regional and sectoral analyses based on crop mixes and asset ownership.

1830 López, Mario and Max Spoor. Cambios estructurales en el mercado de granos básicos en Nicaragua. Managua: Univ. Nacional Autónoma de Nicaragua, Facultad de Ciencias Económicas, Escuela de Economía Agrícola, 1993. 27 p.: bibl. (Serie CIES/ESACA; 93.1)

Includes Jalapa and Nueva Guinea case studies. Analyzes adjustments in production and marketing strategies in the wake of both privatization and a reduced State role, and the impact these adjustments had in product and input markets. Producers and consumers are likely to be adversely affected by increasing monopolization and the short-run outlook of intermediaries.

1831 Medal, José Luis. Nicaragua: políticas de estabilización y ajuste; su interrelación con la estrategia de desarrollo. Managua?: s.n., 1993. 183 p.: bibl.

Argues that negative impact of structural adjustment was a result not only of prior monetary policies, but also of structural characteristics imposed by the import-substitution industrialization of the common market and the agroexport model. Advocates heterodox policies to stimulate exports while retaining orthodox measures of restrictive monetary and fiscal policies, without overly constricting aggregate demand.

1832 Núñez Soto, Orlando. Desarrollo sostenible y economía campesina. Managua: Centro para la Investigación, la Promoción y el Desarrollo Rural y Social, CIPRES, 1993. 85 p.: bibl. (Cuadernos del CIPRES; 14)

Seeks to explain relationship among capitalist agriculture, environmental degradation, and the socioeconomic conditions of rural areas in Nicaragua. Offers proposals for alternative systems of production, including organic agriculture, and encourages the supporting role of NGOs.

1833 ¿Qué hace la mujer nicaragüense ante la crisis económica? Recopilación de María Rosa Renzi y Sonia Agurto Vílchez. Managua: Fundación Internacional para el Desafío Económico Global, 1994. 235 p.: bibl., ill.

Critiques impact of structural adjustment on household composition and women in the labor market and at home. Argues that the policies' effects on women's access to basic needs ensure long-term poverty and violence. Examines household and market survival strategies, and male-female differences in unemployment and income trends.

1834 Ramírez Rodríguez, Aníbal. En torno a una estrategia de desarrollo para la reconversión del modelo productivo: caso de Nicaragua; ensayo preliminar. Managua: Multiformas R.L., 1993. 223 p.: bibl., maps (some col.).

Considers impact of various development models on land use and degradation. Proposes a detailed development plan to preserve and utilize ecosystems to their full-

est while relieving social inequities. Strong analysis of potential problems but lacks suggestions for solutions.

1835 Rodríguez, Luís; Orlando Mendoza; and Raúl Rubén. Nicaragua, evolución de la estructura agrária, 1960–1985. Managua: Proyecto CSUCA/CDR-ULA, Desarrollo de la Estructura Agraria en Centroamerica, 1992. 104 p.: appendix, bibl.

Examines institutional factors affecting land holdings, accumulation and production during the Somoza and Sandinista eras. Provides Kaleckian analysis of the relationship between traditional export and subsistence sectors. Gives significant attention to exchange rate policies. Offers useful statistical appendix.

1836 Spoor, Max. Neo-liberalism and institutional reform in post 1990 Nicaragua: the impact on grain markets. (*Bull. Lat. Am. Res.*, 13:2, May 1994, p. 186–202, bibl., tables)

Provides useful overview of Sandinista interventionist and UNO "laissez-faire" agricultural policies as they affected peasant producers in the grain markets. Considers impact of both macroeconomic and market-specific reforms leading to the stagnation of the early 1990s and the restructuring of input markets and marketing channels. Suggests that market fragmentation continues to create marginalization.

1837 Utting, Peter. Economic adjustment under the Sandinistas: policy reform, food security, and livelihood in Nicaragua. Geneva: UNRISD, 1991. 115 p.: bibl., ill. (UNRISD report; 91.1)

Reports that the reform process of the late 1980s negatively impacted urban families, particularly those engaged in informal sector activities. Notes that rural families experienced less severe declines in protein and calorie intake, as well as fewer negative changes in the composition of their diets. Provides a detailed view of survival strategies, market responses, and the organization of social and producer relations.

Weisskoff, Richard. Forty-one years of structural continuity and social change in Nicaragua, 1950–1991. See item **4213.**

1838 Wiegersma, Nan. State policy and the restructuring of women's industries in Nicaragua. (*in* Women in the age of economic transformation: gender impact of reforms in post-socialist and developing countries. New York: Routledge, 1994, p. 192–205, tables)

Focuses primarily on the garment and textile industry, investigating impact of neoliberal policies implemented during 1991–93 on employment opportunities for Nicaraguan women. Provides overview of the evolution of female participation in the work force prior to and during the Sandinista Administration. Finds that characteristics of hiring in the free trade zone, gender bias in the labor unions, and the contraction of the textile industry have led to a reversal of prior gains in women's job opportunities, particularly for the middle-aged.

PANAMA

Amado Burgos, David. Los panameños hacia el siglo XXI. See item **3227**.

González, Simeón. Panamá, 1968–1990: ensayos de sociología política. See item **4715**.

1839 Herrera, Ligia. Regiones de desarrollo socioeconómico de Panamá 1980–1990: transformaciones ocurridas en la década. Panamá: CELA, 1994. 140 p.: bibl., ill.

Primarily focuses on regional levels of urbanization, education, sanitation and health care, and household income and nutrition. Maps show clear levels of regional variation. Concludes that the majority of the population experienced a notable deterioration in its socioeconomic situation during the decade.

1840 Jované, Juan. Los desafíos de la economía panameña: hacia una agenda nacional. Panamá: CECADES, 1994. 53 p.: bibl. (Serie Alternativas)

Suggests that Panama must pursue sustainable development with equity while reasserting its sovereignty amidst declining export growth and a changing international division of labor shaped by new technologies. Proposes debt reduction without conditionality, while abandoning structural adjustment for temporary protectionist barriers to stimulate export diversification in high value-added, high-wage, dynamic service sectors to generate foreign exchange and promote stability. Unfortunately, no empirical evidence identifies these promising industries.

1841 Lachman Varela, Rubén. Fundamentos teóricos y prácticos de la macroeconomía: hacia un modelo de desarrollo para Panamá. Panamá: Centro de Estudios Económicos, Asociación Panameña de Ejecutivos de Empresa, 1993. 151 p.: bibl., ill.

Provides brief overview of (primarily Keynesian) macroeconomic theory as it relates to Panama's development. Advocates market liberalization, with intervention necessary due to the lack of truly free markets. Recommends State direction for successful deregulation. Stresses that Panama's comparative advantage in the global economy is its location, from which the country can not profit while economic power continues to be highly concentrated.

1842 Panamá: niveles de satisfacción de las necesidades básicas; mapa de la pobreza. Panamá: República de Panamá, Ministerio de Planificación y Política Económica, Dirección de Planificación Económica y Social, Depto. de Planificación Social, Sección de Análisis Social, 1993. 100 leaves.: appendix, bibl. (Documento de trabajo; 44)

Compares regional 1990 census information to 1980 data. Includes useful statistical appendix with information on basic needs by district. Concludes that although the number of people whose basic needs were not attained had risen, the percentage of this population fell during the decade. For a more complete version see item **1839**.

1843 Pinilla, Silma and **Wim Dierckxsens.** Cooperativismo de Panamá en cifras. San José: Confederación de Cooperativas del Caribe y Centro América (CCC-CA), 1993? 108 p.: bibl., ill., maps.

Reviews employment, financial, and administrative structures of cooperatives based on a 1992 census. Concludes with a comparative assessment of how structural adjustment has affected cooperatives. Determines that needs are greatest in the human resource areas of administration and entrepreneurship.

1844 Quintero, Iván. ¿Quienes son los dueños de la tierra en Panamá?: Veraguas, Coclé y Chiriquí. Panamá: COPODEHUPA, 1993. 128 p.: bibl.

Provides historical background to the evolution of land use and accumulation in these regions. Consists primarily of lists of landowners and summaries of their involvement in politics and the economy. Offers relatively little analysis, but does attempt to link the structure of land ownership with the impact of structural adjustment.

THE CARIBBEAN AND THE GUIANAS (EXCEPT CUBA AND PUERTO RICO)

RANSFORD W. PALMER, *Professor of Economics, Howard University*

THE LITERATURE REVIEWED FOR *HLAS* 57 reflects a preoccupation with three major issues: structural adjustment, economic integration, and privatization. The 1980s was the decade of structural adjustment. This process was and is driven by the rationale that these small foreign trade-dependent Caribbean countries must become more competitive if they are to survive in an increasingly competitive world. It has been an agonizing process for both policy makers and the people.

The books reviewed seem to be unanimous in their conclusion that structural adjustment has had a negative effect on the welfare of the region's population (items **1852, 1871, 1875, 1894, 1909,** and **1899**). Yet it could be argued that the absence of structural adjustment would have had an even more devastating effect as the main commodity exports of the region are replaced by skill-intensive products from more efficient producers. The resentment engendered by those whose welfare has been negatively affected has been heightened by the externally imposed character of the adjustment and the apparent loss of national sovereignty to the international arbiters of structural adjustment: the International Monetary Fund and the World Bank.

While structural adjustment is viewed as having a negative impact on welfare, privatization, which is part of the adjustment process, is viewed positively as an engine of growth (items **1845, 1859, 1870, 1860, 1862,** and **1908**). It is reasonable to say that the growth in the number of publications analyzing the role of the private sector is itself a measure of the progress of structural adjustment.

Among the Commonwealth Caribbean countries the subject of economic integration has received a great deal of attention. Although this topic has been a part of the literature for the past 30 years, today it has acquired a tone of urgency in the face of rapid changes in the world economy such as the creation of large trading blocs and the changing technology of the production process (items **1847, 1849, 1856,** and **1887**). Despite this urgency, some member countries continue to vascillate because of the uncertain impact on their economies of a common external tariff.

The principal objective of regional integration is to improve efficiency and, therefore, competitiveness. Central to this objective is the improvement of worker productivity requiring greater investment in human and physical capital. It is argued that monetary integration could play an important role by improving efficiency of regional allocation of capital (item **1850**). But if labor productivity is to benefit fully from capital mobility, labor must also be able to move freely. Unfortunately, labor mobility remains largely an issue of debate, and has yet to make the passage to the realm of policy. As a consequence, there is a tendency for workers to move to the US where they can be more productive.

GENERAL

1845 Adam, Christopher; William Cavendish; and Percy S. Mistry. Adjusting privatization: case studies from developing countries. London: J. Currey; Portsmouth, N.H.: Heinemann; Kingston: Ian Randle, 1992. 400 p.: bibl., ill., index.

An examination of privatization from an economic perspective. The authors evaluate the effects of ownership transfer on economic performance and market structure in seven developing countries: Jamaica, Trinidad and Tobago, Malaysia, Papua New Guinea, Sri Lanka, Kenya, and Malawi.

1846 Augustine, C.; W. Sandiford; and W. Samuel. Financial integration and efficiency of the financial sector in the ECCB area. (*Soc. Econ. Stud.*, 44: special issue, 1995, p. 87–110, bibl., tables)

Argues that even though the Eastern Caribbean Central Bank area is serviced by a single currency and a common central bank, an integration of financial markets does not exist; that the establishment of a monetary union has been prevented due to a number of factors, including indirect restrictions on capital movement and gaps in the financial infrastructure; and that, in essence, the inability to achieve integration can be attributed to an unwillingness of financial institutions to expand outside of their country. Authors point out that efforts are being made to bring about financial integration through the implementation of new financial services.

1847 Axline, W. Andrew. From CARIFTA to CARICOM: deepening Caribbean integration. (*in* Caribbean freedom: society and economy from emancipation to the present. Kingston, Jamaica: Randle, 1993, p. 476–487)

An examination of the expansive and distributive character of the stages of economic integration in the Caribbean since the Caribbean Free Trade Area came into operation in 1968.

1848 Capital transnacional y trabajo en el Caribe. Recopilación de Gérard Pierre-Charles. México: Plaza y Valdés; Univ. Nacional Autónoma d. México, Instituto de Investigaciones Sociales, 1988. 281 p. bibl. (Col. Folios universitarios)

A collection of papers from a conference held at the Instituto de Investigaciones Sociales de la UNAM, Mexico. The papers discuss two aspects of the evolution of the Caribbean over the past two decades: the penetration of transnational capital and its consequences for social and economic development of the region and the phenomenon of population migration to the metropole.

1849 Caribbean economic development: the first generation. Edited by Stanley Lalta and Marie Freckleton. Kingston: Ian Randle Publishers, 1993. 400 p.: bibl., index.

A collection of essays by Caribbean scholars on the development experience of the English-speaking Caribbean countries, with an emphasis on policy-oriented analyses and alternative development strategies. Explores such issues as import substitution, regional integration, self-reliance and State-led development, and structural adjustment.

1850 Caribbean monetary integration. Edited by Terrence Farrell and DeLisle Worrell. Port of Spain: Caribbean Information Systems and Services, 1994. 267 p.: bibl.

A collection of essays explores alternative strategies for sound regional monetary integration and their implications for the labor market and the individual member countries. Discusses ways in which monetary union can reduce capital flight, the cost of doing business, and the risk associated with a change of exchange rate strategies.

1851 Circuits monétaires et financiers dans les économies antillaises. Seminaire des 25 et 26 mai 1990, Salle Bellan—CCI de Pointe-à-Pitre. Guadeloupe: Société des économistes de la Guadeloupe; ADESC, Association des dîplomes d'écoles supérieures de commerce, 1991. 110 p.

A collection of papers on monetary and financial policies in the Caribbean and their implications for growth and development. Covers Martinique, Guadeloupe, Trinidad and Tobago, Barbados, and Jamaica. Discusses the important role of the social security system in Guadeloupe and the structure of the financial sector in the Antilles. Recommends that the banking system become more localized, that deposit insurance be given priority, and that credit be made more available to targeted sectors.

1852 Conference of Caribbean Economists, 3rd, Santo Domingo, 1991. Reestructuración, crisis y crecimiento: la experiencia caribeña: trabajos seleccionados de la Tercera

Conferencia de Economistas del Caribe. Recopilación de Pedro Juan Rivera Guzmán. Kingston: Asociación de Economistas del Caribe, 1993. 272 p.: bibl.

Includes papers from the Third Conference of Caribbean Economists held in Santo Domingo in 1991. The papers cover analyses of the economic experience of Guyana, Dominica, St. Lucia, Barbados, the Dominican Republic, and Cuba during the decade of the 1980s. There is also discussion of economic cooperation between Haiti and the Dominican Republic.

Conway, Dennis. Rethinking the consequences of remittances for Eastern Caribbean development. See item **2458.**

Douzant-Rosenfeld, Denise. Approvisionnement de deux métropoles caraïbes: Santo Domingo et La Havane. See item **2459.**

1853 Griffith, Winston H. Caribbean countries and the twenty-first century. (*Can. J. Lat. Am. Caribb. Stud.,* 18:36, 1993, p. 25–57)

Argues that if Caribbean countries restructure their economies at the regional level, and if they can create an appropriate supply of knowledge skills, which must be at the heart of the restructuring process in the region, they can develop new products and services, become internationally competitive, and experience higher rates of growth and development.

1854 Hardy, Chandra. The Caribbean Development Bank. Boulder, Colo.: Lynne Rienner Publishers, 1995. 133 p. (Multilateral development banks; 3)

A study of the history of the operations of the Caribbean Development Bank and its agenda for development. Author argues that "the CDB has matured as a financial and development institution. It now needs to rise to a higher level of lending, play a larger role in policy dialogue, exercise intellectual leadership, and deepen its involvement in the region's development" (p. 111).

1855 Méndez, Mario. Reformas y lucha de intereses. Santo Domingo: s.n., 1993. 201 p.: ill.

An examination of the political aspects of economic reforms in the 1980s in three small developing countries: the Dominican Republic, Jamaica, and Costa Rica.

1856 Open regionalism in Latin America and the Caribbean: economic integration as a contribution to changing production patterns with social equity. Santiago: United Nations, Economic Commission for Latin America and the Caribbean, 1994. 103 p.: bibl.

An attempt to answer some general and specific questions regarding regional integration, such as: Why should integration be encouraged? What kind of integration should be encouraged? Which mechanisms and instruments are most suitable for integrating economies at this point? How do the new integration plans differ from those of the 1960s and 1970s? The answers to these and other questions "are based on the core premise that recent integration efforts have generally involved the interaction of two types of phenomena:" trade liberalization and deregulation policies introduced at the national level; and explicit agreements or policies which entail certain preferences with respect to the treatment accorded other nations.

1857 Potter, Robert B. Low-income housing and the State in the eastern Caribbean. Kingston: The Press Univ. of the West Indies, 1994. 79 p.: bibl., ill., index.

The first comprehensive analysis of housing conditions and State policies in three countries of the eastern Caribbean: Grenada, St. Lucia, and St. Vincent and the Grenadines. The study focuses on the interrelationships between the poor, low-income housing, and the policies of the State. The author concludes that "in the realm of State housing policy and provision, the efforts of low-income groups to house themselves have been almost totally neglected as a socio-cultural resource of major importance." (p.72).

1858 Seerattan, Dave Arnold. Financial regulation and reform: the theoretical basis, lessons from experience and appropriate strategies for Caribbean policy-makers. (*Soc. Econ. Stud.,* 44:special issue, 1995, p. 155–196, bibl., tables)

Paper outlines types of financial reforms and their objectives, and examines their impact on the regulatory system. Author sees changes in the financial sector as increasing the effectiveness of the monetary and financial policy instruments needed for structural adjustment.

1859 **Worrell, DeLisle.** Investment in the Caribbean. (*Soc. Econ. Stud.*, 42:2/3, June/Sept. 1993, p. 243–259, bibl., graphs, tables)

Examines the factors which influence investment in the Caribbean and suggests policies which would accelerate the rate of investment in non-tradables and create new areas of comparative advantage.

DOMINICAN REPUBLIC

Burac, Maurice. Les zones franches industrielles en République Dominicaine. See item 2456.

1860 **Cabal, Miguel.** Microempresas y pequeñas empresas en la República Dominicana: resultados de una encuesta nacional; informe preliminar. Santo Domingo: Fondo para el Financiamiento de la Microempresa, 1992. 158 p.: bibl., ill.

A survey of small businesses in the Dominican Republic and an analysis of their quantitative profile, the causes of their success and failure, their access to credit, and their relationship to other social, economic, and cultural factors in the country.

1861 **Ceara Hatton, Miguel; Edwin Croes; and Omar Arias.** El gasto público social de la República Dominicana en la década de los ochenta. Santo Domingo: Centro de Investigación Económica para el Caribe; Fondo de las Naciones Unidas para la Infancia, 1993. 233 p.: bibl., ill.

An examination of the implications for human development and economic growth of the low share of social public spending in the Dominican Republic in the 1980s.

1862 **Fundación Economía y Desarrollo.** Impacto del sector privado en la economía dominicana. 2. ed. Santo Domingo: Acción Empresarial, 1990. 264 p.: ill.

Argues that the private sector is the engine of growth in the Dominican Republic. Reviews the political economy of the three reformist administrations from 1966–90. Ends with an examination of the impact of taxes and subsidies on the private sector.

1863 **Montás, Juan Temístocles.** Energía, política y economía en la República Dominicana: los problemas de la década de los ochenta. Santo Domingo: Editora Alfa y Omega, 1993. 252 p.: bibl., ill., map.

Examines the relationship between the energy sector and the Dominican economy over the period 1980–90. The author concludes, among other things, that the Dominican Republic should establish a petroleum policy to determine the amount of commercial petroleum reserves in the country.

1864 **Ramírez, Nelson.** La fuerza de trabajo en República Dominicana: análisis de los resultados del cuestionario de hogar ampliado, encuesta demográfica de salud 1991, Endesa-91. Santo Domingo: Instituto de Estudios de Población y Desarrollo, 1993. 36 leaves: bibl., ill. (Serie monográfica; 03)

A study of the demographic and economic characteristics of the labor force of the Dominican Republic based on data from questionnaires distributed to households.

1865 **Santana, Isidoro** and **Magdalena Rathe.** Reforma social: una agenda para combatir la pobreza. Santo Domingo: Ediciones de la Fundación Siglo 21, 1993. 277 p.: bibl.

A study of the provision of education, health, and social security in the Dominican Republic. Recommends a program for institutional reform that includes decentralization of government bureaucracies and community and private sector participation.

COMMONWEALTH CARIBBEAN AND GUYANA

1866 **Augustin, Gurulf.** Plantation economy and land reform: the Jamaican example, 1972–1980. (*in* Society of Caribbean Research. International Conference, *1st, Berlin, 1988*. Alternative cultures in the Caribbean. Frankfurt: Vervuert Verlag, 1993, p. 279–291)

A critical assessment of land distribution in Jamaica under the first Michael Manley government based on interviews with small farmers. Author concludes that although some land distribution took place, there was no real land reform. Suggests that "a far reaching programme would have required a combination of legal and constitutional changes in land tenure and land ownership in addition to massive financial resources to develop the infrastructure and to set up a small-scale agroindustry" (p. 291).

1867 **Bennett, Karl M.** An analysis of the performance of the financial sector in Barbados, Jamaica and Trinidad and Tobago.

(*Soc. Econ. Stud.*, 44:special issue, 1995, p. 69–85, bibl., tables)

Paper examines the role played by private institutions within the financial sector in the mobilization and allocation of savings in Barbados, Jamaica, and Trinidad and Tobago. Focuses on the role of commercial banks in order to ascertain the extent to which financial institutions changed their pattern of lending and investment at a time when governments were encouraging domestic firms to engage in non-traditional production.

1868 Best, Lloyd and Deryck R. Brown.
Trinidad and Tobago Unit Trust Corporation: 10 years of success. Port of Spain: Published for the Trinidad and Tobago Unit Trust Corp. by the Trinidad and Tobago Institute of the West Indies, 1992. 83 p.: ill. (some col.).

Mainly a report on the achievements and future endeavors of the Unit Trust Company (UTC). Examines the performance of the UTC as an agency for mobilizing local savings into investment and its future role as a specialized financial intermediary in the domestic, regional, and international markets.

1869 Carey, Kathleen. Optimal hotel capacity: the case of Barbados. (*Soc. Econ. Stud.*, 41:2, June 1992, p. 103–126, appendices, bibl., tables)

Proposes a theory and empirical methodology for determination of optimal hotel capacity. Applied to the Barbados luxury hotel sector for 1978–84, the results suggest that Barbados has excess hotel capacity.

1870 Chaderton, Robertine. The failure of Barbadian businesses in the 1980s: lessons for the decade of the 90s. Cave Hill, Barbados: Institute of Social and Economic Research (Eastern Caribbean), Univ. of the West Indies, 1993. 59 p.: bibl.

Investigates the large number of business failures in Barbados in the 1980s. Attributes these failures primarily to poor financial information. Concludes with an assessment of the lessons that might prevent future failures.

1871 Consequences of structural adjustment: a review of the Jamaican experience. Edited by Elsie LeFranc. Kingston: Canoe Press, 1994. 225 p.: bibl., index.

Examines the extent to which structural adjustment in Jamaica has been induced by stabilization and structural adjustment policies of the 1980s. Concludes that the social and economic cost of those policies has been high.

1872 Coppin, Addington. Sectoral labor employment in a Caribbean economy: the case of Barbados. (*Rev. Black Polit. Econ.*, 23:1, Summer 1994, p. 49–66)

Examines the demand for labor in five sectors of the Barbados economy. Results of empirical analysis suggest that employers in the major sectors are more likely to alter their demand for labor based on expectations of the economy's performance, rather than in response to labor cost factors denominated in producer prices.

1873 Craigwell, Roland. A dynamic consumption function for Trinidad and Tobago. (*Soc. Econ. Stud.*, 44:1, March 1995, p. 117–144, bibl., graphs, tables)

Paper focuses on the derivation of a consumption function—a key macroeconomic relationship—for Trinidad and Tobago for the period 1955–90. Argues that previous attempts to derive the function failed because they ignored dynamic issues. Concludes that traditional as well as non-traditional variables influence consumption behavior, including anticipated income; government spending that complements private consumption; and inflation.

1874 Danielson, Anders. The economic surplus: formation, distribution and role in economic growth. (*Soc. Econ. Stud.*, 39:1, March 1990, p. 127–152, appendix, bibl., tables)

Discusses the concept of surplus in development economics, its classic heritage, and its modern empirically oriented approaches. Estimates the surplus in Jamaica during 1962–84 and suggests that the distribution and disposal of the surplus are important factors in Jamaica's stagnation.

1875 Douglas, Seymour. The I.M.F. and the Jamaican labour sector, 1977–1990: a study of the impact of wage guidelines. Kingston: Joint Trade Unions Research Development Centre, 1993. 58 leaves. (Occasional paper/Joint Trade Union Research Development Centre, Research Department)

Traces the effects of the IMF's adjustment related policies; identifies the negative impact of wage guidelines on the welfare of

Jamaican workers; and provides many reasons why these guidelines should not be used.

1876 Downes, Andrew S.; Carlos Holder; and Hyginus Leon. The wage-price-productivity relationship in a small developing country: the case of Barbados. (*Soc. Econ. Stud.*, 39:2, June 1990, p. 49–77, appendix, bibl., graphs, tables)

Application of cointegration theory to the wage-price productivity relationship in Barbados shows that the rate of inflation increases with factor costs and that productivity has a positive impact on real wages and offsets price inflation.

1877 Ethnicity and employment practices in the public and private sectors in Trinidad and Tobago. St. Augustine: Univ. of the West Indies, Centre for Ethnic Studies, 1994? v. 1: bibl., ill.

Investigation of the ethnic composition of employment in the public sector of Trinidad and Tobago and the differences in the rate of mobility among ethnic groups. Finds that Indians were "heavily underrepresented in the higher reaches of the public sector" but "adequately represented" in the judicial and professional sectors.

1878 An evaluation of government's subsidy and incentive programmes in relation to the dairy and meat industries in Trinidad and Tobago: a report submitted to the cabinet appointed Commission of Enquiry into the Meat and Dairy Industry of Trinidad and Tobago. Dept. of Agricultural Economics and Farm Management, Faculty of Agriculture, the University of the West Indies, St. Augustine, Trinidad and Tobago. St. Augustine, Trinidad and Tobago: Dept. of Agricultural Economics and Farm Management, Faculty of Agriculture, the Univ. of the West Indies, 1983. 2 v. (319 p.).: bibl.

An assessment of the effectiveness of the government's incentive programs for poultry and livestock development with special emphasis on pasture management. Proposes a new system for the administration of agricultural subsidies and incentive programs.

1879 Gershenberg, Irving. Gender, training, and the creation of a managerial elite: multinationals and other firms in Jamaica. (*J. Dev. Areas*, 28:3, April 1994, p. 313–324, tables)

An analysis of how women have fared as managers; how long it has taken them to attain promotions; how much training they have received while employed; the kinds of managerial posts they fill, that is, production, sales, personnel, and so on; and the role of transnational corporations in promoting women in management. Concludes that while women in Jamaica have been successful in attaining training and promotion to top- and middle-level management positions and in managerial areas not generally considered "female," there is little evidence that multinational firms played any singular role.

1880 Grosse, Robert E. Jamaica's foreign exchange black market. (*J. Dev. Stud.*, 31:1, Oct. 1994, p. 17–43, bibl., graphs, tables)

Explains the structure and function of the black market in foreign exchange. Argues that the black market contributed importantly to the operation of Jamaica's underground economy during the 1980s, and that this market was undermined by the liberalization of the foreign exchange market and the elimination of capital controls in 1991–92.

1881 Handa, Sudhanshu. The determinants of female headship in Jamaica: results from a structural model. (*Econ. Dev. Cult. Change*, 44:4, July 1996, p. 793–815, tables)

Argues that the formation of female-headed-households (FHH) in Jamaica is a response to local social and economic conditions. Author uses a bargaining model to explain how alternative prospects influence a woman's choice of residence. The model assumes that a person's willingness to form a household with a partner depends on the level of utility to be derived from the union. Results show that external opportunities influence the household formation decisions of adult women in Jamaica.

1882 Hewan, Clinton G. Jamaica and the United States Caribbean Basin Initiative: showpiece or failure? New York: Peter Lang, 1994. 153 p.: bibl. (American university studies. Series X, Political science; 44)

An analysis of US foreign policy in the Caribbean and Central America in general, and Jamaica in particular, with special emphasis on the Caribbean Basin Initiative and its impact on economic and socio-political conditions. Concludes that the primary objective of the CBI for US policy was military security, political loyalty, and advantages for US economic interests.

1883 Huber, Evelyne and **John D. Stephens.** Changing development models in small economies: the case of Jamaica from the 1950s to the 1990s. (*Stud. Comp. Int. Dev.*, 27:3, Fall 1992, p. 57–92, bibl., tables)

From a detailed examination of the successes and failures of the different models of development embraced by Jamaica from the 1950s–90s, the authors attempt to sketch a model of development for small developing countries as an alternative to the neoliberal model advocated by the International Monetary Fund.

1884 Koot, Ronald S. and **Prasad Padmanabhan.** Stock market liberalization and the distribution of returns on the Jamaican stock market. (*Glob. Financ. J.*, 4:2, Fall 1993, p. 171–188, bibl., graphs, tables)

Examines the relative importance of economic and political factors as determinants of stock returns in Jamaica, using monthly stock returns data for the period 1969–90. Results of empirical analysis suggest that the information arrival process governing stock market movements may be induced in part by government policies and by structural changes resulting from privatization and market liberalization.

1885 Lue Lim, Gail. Jamaica's financial system: its historical development. Kingston: Bank of Jamaica, 1991. 54 p.: bibl.

A survey of the structure of Jamaica's financial system divided into three periods: 1) the transition from the Currency Board as the monetary authority to the creation of the central bank (before the 1970s); 2) the rise of such new institutions as the Jamaica Development Bank and the Jamaica Mortgage Bank (1970s–80s); and 3) an expansion of commercial banks, trust companies, and other financial institutions in the current period.

1886 Marston, David. Jamaica's experience with indirect instruments: lessons for the Caribbean. (*Soc. Econ. Stud.*, 44:special issue, 1995, p. 111–138, bibl., graphs, tables)

Evaluates Jamaica's experience with indirect monetary instruments, their efficiency in monetary control, and their impact on intermediation and competition in the financial system. One lesson arising from the Jamaican experience is that indirect instruments serve to achieve intermediate monetary targets and facilitate the development of money markets.

1887 Mascoll, Clyde A. and **Nadine Harding.** The effects of changing Common External Tariff (CET) rates: the Barbados case. (*Soc. Econ. Stud.*, 42:4, Dec. 1993, p. 185–215, bibl., graph, tables)

Analyzes the empirical implications of changing the existing Common External Tariff (CET) rates on sectoral protection, government revenue, and the cost of living in Barbados. Concludes that lowering the CET rates will reduce protection for the manufacturing sector and may reduce government revenues and the cost of living.

1888 McCoy, James P. Bauxite processing and employment: a case study. (*Soc. Econ. Stud.*, 39:2, June 1990, p. 1–48, appendices, bibl., tables)

Uses static input-output analysis to estimate the effects of increased domestic processing of bauxite on sectoral and aggregate employment in Jamaica.

1889 McElroy Jerome L. and **Klaus de Albuquerque.** The economic impact of retirement tourism in Montserrat: some provisional evidence. (*Soc. Econ. Stud.*, 41:2, June 1992, p. 127–152, bibl., tables)

Examines the extent to which retirement tourism has transformed the economy of Montserrat. Suggests that North American retirement tourists account for over 20 percent of the country's gross tourist spending.

1890 Modeste, N.C. The impact of growth in the tourism sector on economic development: the experience of selected Caribbean countries. (*Econ. Int. /Genova*, 48:3, agosto 1995, p. 375–385, bibl., graph, tables)

Constructs a model to explain the effect of growth in the tourism sector on overall economic development, using data from Barbados, Antigua and Barbuda, and Anguilla. Concludes that the growth of the tourism sector has a positive effect on economic development and a negative effect on the agricultural sector as resources are transferred from agriculture to tourism.

1891 Nwanna, G.I. Currency devaluation and growth: the case of a tourism-based economy. (*Econ. Int. /Genova*, 49:2, maggio 1996, p. 261–273, bibl., tables)

Study examines the effect of devaluation on short-term growth of output in the tourism-based economy of the Bahamas. Concludes that devaluation has a positive impact in the short run; that devaluation can be beneficial to LDC's that depend on tourism; and that the impact of devaluation depends on the economic structure and government policies.

1892 Panton, David. Dual labour markets and unemployment in Jamaica: a modern synthesis. (*Soc. Econ. Stud.*, 42:1, March 1993, p. 75–118, appendices, bibl.)

A reformulation of the dualistic model of the Jamaican labor market to include regional (rural/urban), organizational (formal/informal), agricultural (farm/nonfarm), and government variables in the labor market segmentation theory (primary/secondary). Author argues that any policy aimed at increasing employment must be based on an accurate analytical model of the Jamaican labor market.

1893 Peart, Kenloy. Financial reform and financial sector development in Jamaica. (*Soc. Econ. Stud.*, 44:special issue, 1995, p. 1–22, bibl., tables)

Paper examines financial reform programs and their effects for Jamaica. Finds that reform in the financial system led, among other things, to the creation of a more competitive environment, a reduced role for government in directly allocating financial resources, and a rapid expansion in the activities of near-bank institutions that provide services similar to those of commercial banks, but which operate within a different regulatory framework.

1894 Ramsaran, Ramesh F. Growth and adjustment in a petroleum-based economy: some aspects of the Trinidad and Tobago experience since the 1970s. (*Soc. Econ. Stud.*, 42:4, Dec. 1993, p. 217–240, bibl., tables)

Describes the rapid decline of the Trinidad and Tobago economy, the deterioration of its social sectors, and the policy responses to arrest the decline.

Regulation and the informal economy: microenterprises in Chile, Ecuador, and Jamaica. See item **2053.**

1895 Scott, Katherine MacKinnon. Female labor force participation and earnings: the case of Jamaica. (*in* Case studies on women's employment and pay in Latin America. Washington: World Bank, 1992, p. 323–338, bibl., tables)

Investigation of gender-based wage differentials in Jamaica. Focuses on the extent to which differences between male and female earnings are a function of different human characteristics or the different values placed on male and female labor in the labor market. Concludes that gender-based discrimination in Jamaica is high and that "this is a critical issue that must be addressed if women are to be equal partners with men in the Jamaican economy."

1896 Smith, Courtney A. Socialist transformation in peripheral economies: lessons from Grenada. Aldershot; Brookfield USA: Avebury, c1995. 282 p.: bibl.

Explores the path of reform taken by Grenada after it was invaded by the US. Examines the role of the Peoples Revolutionary Government (PRG) as the main instrument of change and its main policy measures which included the opening of the international airport, expansion of the export base, and diversification of international economic relations.

1897 Sustainable development in the Guianas. Edited by Henry Jeffrey and Renate Tjon Lim Sang. Georgetown: Univ. of Guyana, 1993. 128 p.: bibl., ill.

A collection of papers from a conference held at the Univ. of Guyana focusing on the relationship between economic development and the environment. Among the issues discussed are the exploitation of such indigenous resources as fish and timber and the search for alternative technologies.

1898 Taylor, B.E.; J.B. Morison; and E.M. Fleming. The economic impact of food import substitution in the Bahamas. (*Soc. Econ. Stud.*, 40:2, June 1991, p. 45–62, bibl., tables)

Examines the foreign exchange leakage through the importation of foodstuffs into the Bahamas and assesses the impact of a significant reduction of food imports on the economy. Uses input/output methodology to estimate the indirect effects of import substitution, which are significant increases in output and employment.

1899 Thomas, Clive Y. Lessons from experience: structural adjustment and poverty in Guyana. (*Soc. Econ. Stud.*, 42:4, Dec. 1993, p. 133–184, bibl., tables)

Reviews the development experience of Guyana and the relationship between macroeconomic adjustment and its devastating impact on the people perceived as subjects of such adjustment.

1900 Worrell, DeLisle. Open market operations in small open economies with fixed and flexible exchange rates. (*Soc. Econ. Stud.*, 44:special issue, 1995, p. 139–154, graphs, tables)

Paper seeks to determine how much scope capital market imperfections allow for autonomous monetary policy under fixed and flexible exchange rate regimes illustrated by the experiences of Barbados (fixed) and Jamaica (flexible).

FRENCH CARIBBEAN AND FRENCH GUIANA

1901 Jiha, Jacques and **Gray Orphee.** A note on Haiti: evidence from cointegration analysis. (*Soc. Econ. Stud.*, 44:1, March 1995, p. 95–115, bibl., tables)

Study focuses on inflation in Haiti between 1953–83. Authors challenge the established methodology of analyzing inflation in log-level and first difference forms because of errors arising from poor cointegration of unit root variables and misspecification bias in nonstationary variables that are cointegrated. They conclude that in the short run, inflation in Haiti is affected by imported inflation and inflation inertia.

1902 Lumarque, J. Le secteur informel dans l'économie haitienne. (*Conjonction/Port-au-Prince*, 49:199, 1995, p. 53–69, bibl., tables)

Paper examines the characteristics of the informal sector such as barriers to entry, number of people employed, technology required, products sold, factors of production, availability of credit, as well as competition faced by producers. Highlights the advancements possible in this sector and how they may be integrated with the rest of economy.

1903 Paysans, systèmes et crise: travaux sur l'agraire haïtien. v. 1, Histoire agraire et développement. v. 2, Stratégies et logiques sociales. Pointe-à-Pitre, Guadeloupe: S.A.C.A.D., Groupe de recherche/formation Systèmes agraires caribéens et alternatives de séveloppement, Univ. des Antilles et de la Guyane; Port-au-Prince: F.A.M.V., Faculté d'agronomie et de médecine vétérinaire, Univ. d'Etat d'Haïti, 1993. 2 v.: bibl., ill., maps.

Vol. 1 examines the economic and social conditions of Haitian agriculture with an emphasis on the production and marketing of agricultural products by peasants, the distribution of land, and the extent of artisan activities among the peasantry. Vol. 2 examines the social aspect of Haitian agriculture. Studies the relationship between farmers and the markets and discusses the special bond between the Haitian farmer and the land. Enumerates problems faced by the Haitian farmer, such as farm fragmentation, the lack of technical and mechanical skills, and the seasonality of prices. A third and final volume is planned. For geographer's comment see item **2468.**

1904 Sam, Pierre D. Gérer le réel haïtien: une nouvelle dimension. Port-au-Prince: Impr. Henri Deschamps, 1993. 256 p.: bibl.

Attempts to portray the "real Haitian" against the background of the cultural evolution of African and other Caribbean societies. Author attributes the economic failure in Haiti to the absence of economic dualism or the existence of a state of permanent discordance between the rural and urban populations, in contrast to the situation in such countries as Cote d'Ivoire, Nigeria, and Korea, where economic dualism has been an engine for economic growth and development. Author also argues that economic development is hampered by the failure of the Haitian to develop a nationalist sentiment, by excessive pride in the past, and lack of objectivity in decision making.

1905 Tardieu, Jerry. Embargo sur Haïti: les premières conséquences; suggestions pour l'après-crise. Haïti: J. Tardieu, 1992. 229 p.: bibl., ill.

Evaluates the adverse impact of the recent international embargo on the Haitian economy. Argues that the embargo drove the population into hunger and misery and that, in a struggle to survive, inflicted great damage on the natural environment. The authors think that the national economy can recover quickly and even grow significantly if the international community awards massive financial aid to the country. Concludes that the transformation of the behaviors and attitudes of Haitians themselves remains the most important determinant of economic growth and development of the country.

1906 Victor, Jean Andre. Les petits métiers de l'environment dans la plaine du cul-de-sac. (*Conjonction/Port-au-Prince*, 49:199, 1995, p. 30–52, bibl., tables)

A study of the characteristics, problems, and potential of petty traders in Haiti, and their overall integration into the local economy. Argues that petty traders facilitate the livelihood of many people by providing jobs as well as essentials needed by the consuming public and that their success stems from their strategic location in the plains of Haiti.

1907 White, T. Anderson and **Carlisle Ford Runge.** Common property and collective action: lessons from cooperative watershed management in Haiti. (*Econ. Dev. Cult. Change*, 43:1, Oct. 1994, p. 1–41, graphs, map, tables)

An empirical analysis of the effectiveness of voluntary collective action for watershed management in rural Haiti. Authors conclude that free riding is not a "dominant strategy" and that "individuals within and beyond the watersheds flocked to cooperate in the new collective activity." Behaviors and attitudes of Haitians themselves remain the most important determinant of economic growth and development of the country.

DUTCH CARIBBEAN AND SURINAME

1908 Free enterprise in Curaçao. Edited by Macklenan F. Hasham and Dennis V. Dare. Curaçao: Curaçao Chamber of Commerce and Industry; Univ. of the Netherlands Antilles, 1992? 229 p.: bibl., ill., index.

Examines the characteristics of free enterprise in Curaçao focusing on the interchange between government and private enterprise, the factors limiting free enterprise, and privatization. Among the observations made is that "government is seen as having the most important role to play in establishing policy that works in favor of unobstructed development of entrepreneurship."

1909 Mhango, Baijah Hunderson Philip.
Economic development and structural adjustment: fundamental issues; inaugural lecture delivered at the occasion of the acceptance of the appointment as professor of economics at the Anton de Kom Univ. of Suriname on Thursday, December 17, 1992. Paramaribo: Anton de Kom Univ. of Suriname, 1993. 112 p.: bibl.

Author focuses on the issue of structural adjustment and international financial institutions especially as they relate to the economy of Suriname.

CUBA

JORGE PEREZ-LOPEZ, *Bureau of International Labor Affairs, United States Department of Labor*

THE ECONOMIC SLOWDOWN that began over a decade ago, and intensified during the 1990s, continues to batter Cuba. While the economic free-fall of the early 1990s apparently ended in 1994, positive economic growth recorded since has not markedly improved the population's standard of living. Modest economic improvement in 1994–96 permitted *Economía y Desarrollo*, the most important economic journal, to resume publication in 1995. Annual reports by the Banco Nacional de

Cuba (item **1925**) and some economics monographs (item **1923**) also became available once again during this time. Publication of economic statistical compendia, however, has not resumed.

Cuba's experimentation with economic reforms in 1993–94 spawned a significant amount of literature that either described and evaluated reforms that had been implemented (items **1930, 1934, 1917, 1920, 1913,** and **1927**) or proposed new ones (items **1912,** and **1932**). The reform process slowed considerably after 1994. No meaningful reforms have been implemented since, the exception being those that affect the external sector (items **1934, 1938, 1916, 1940, 1924, 1927,** and **1918**), particularly those that concern the promotion of incoming foreign investment (items **1926, 1914, 1919, 1929,** and **1933**).

1910 Alvarez, José and **Ricardo A. Puerta.** State intervention in Cuban agriculture: impact on organization and performance. (*World Dev.*, 22:11, Nov. 1994, p. 1663–1675, tables)

Very thoughtful and well-documented essay. Concludes that despite preferential access to inputs, State farms lag behind non-State producers (cooperatives and small private farmers) in productivity.

1911 Betancourt, Roger R. Growth capabilities and development: implications for transition processes in Cuba. (*Econ. Dev. Cult. Change*, 44:2, Jan. 1996, p. 315–331, graph)

Provocative article examining Cuba's recent performance and prospects in a broad context of economic and social indicators.

1912 Carranza, Julio; Luis Gutiérrez Urdaneta; and **Pedro M. Monreal González.** Cuba, la restructuración de la economía: una propuesta para el debate. La Habana: Editorial de Ciencias Sociales, 1995. 219 p.: bibl. (Economía)

Important proposal to restructure Cuba's economy into a more efficient system (by economist associated with Cuba's Centro de Estudios sobre América (CEA)). Although the proposal contains some market-oriented mechanisms, it is framed within a socialist system and preserves a large role for the government. This modest proposal was too radical for the Cuban government. (Raúl Castro criticized the CEA as a "fifth column" working against the revolution in his March 1996 speech on revolutionary purity.) Cuban edition is out of print; a slightly updated version is available as *Cuba, la restructuración de la economía; una propuesta para el debate* (Caracas: Editorial Nueva Sociedad, 1997, 188 p.).

Caunedo, Silvia. La siempre fiel isla de Cuba: la realidad del cambio. See item **3331.**

1913 Cuba: apertura y reforma económica; perfil de un debate. Edición de Bert Hoffmann. Caracas: Instituto de Estudios Iberoamericanos de Hamburgo; Editorial Nueva Sociedad, 1995. 168 p.: bibl.

Essays, official documents, and protest songs related to Cuba's economic reforms of the 1990s. Well-balanced collection, including speeches by Fidel Castro and assessments by domestic and foreign observers. In an insightful essay ("¿El fin de las 'medidas a medias'?"), Hoffman wonders whether the reforms had run their course by the end of 1994.

1914 Cuba: inversiones y negocios, 1995–1996. La Habana: Consultores Asociados (CONAS), 1995. 1 v.

Glossy monograph aimed at potential foreign investors in Cuba. Despite its promotional character, monograph contains useful sectoral analyses, developments in commercial law and regulations, and economic statistics. Interestingly, although CONAS professes to be a private consulting firm, many of the report's contributors are affiliated with the Cuban government. A similar monograph for 1994–95 has also been published.

1915 *Cuba, Handbook of Trade Statistics.* 1996. Washington: Central Intelligence Agency, Directorate of Intelligence.

Latest edition of useful annual compendium on Cuban foreign trade statistics. Provides compilation of partner country data and statistics on sugar and nickel exports supplied by Cuba to international commodity organizations. Most series run through 1995, although there are some statistics for the first quarter of 1996. Earlier editions are also available.

1916 Cuba in the international system: normalization and integration. Edited by Archibald R.M. Ritter and John M. Kirk. New York: St. Martin's Press, 1995. 312 p.: bibl., index, 2 maps. (International political economy series)

Important collection of 16 essays by Cuban and foreign specialists emerging from the symposium "Cuba in the International System: Normalization and Integration" held at Carleton Univ., Ottawa, in Sept. 1993. Articles on external sector reforms (by Pedro Monreal and Manuel Rúa), remittances (by Carmelo Mesa-Lago), commercial relations with Latin America (by Francisco León), US subsidiaries' trade with Cuba (by Donna Rich Kaplowitz), and compensation issues in US-Cuba normalization of relations (by Archibald R.M. Ritter) have significant economic content and are quite valuable. [Spanish language versions of the papers appeared in a special edition of the journal *Estudios Internacionales* (Santiago) 27 : 107/108 (julio–sept. /oct.–dic. 1994).]

1917 *Cuba in Transition: Papers and Proceedings of the Annual Meeting of the Association for the Study of the Cuban Economy (ASCE).* v. 6, 1991– .

Over 40 papers plus commentaries on a variety of topics related to the Cuban economy; economic performance, agriculture, transition strategies, foreign economic relations, legal framework, environment, etc. Collection emphasizes Cuba's transition to a market economy. Meeting was held in August 1996. Volumes for earlier meetings of the Association have also been published.

1918 Cuba's ties to a changing world. Edited by Donna Rich Kaplowitz. Boulder, Colo.: Lynne Rienner Publishers, 1993. 275 p.: bibl., ill., maps.

Collection of 14 essays by specialists on Cuba's economic and political ties with China, Japan, the Middle East, the United Kingdom, the European Community, the former Soviet Union, Brazil, Canada, Mexico, Central America, the Caribbean, and the US. Essays on relations with China (by Damián Fernández), Japan (by Kanako Yamaoka), the United Kingdom (by Gareth Jenkins) and the US (by Michael D. Kaplowitz and Donna Rich Kaplowitz) have significant economic content.

1919 Dávalos Fernández, Rodolfo. Las empresas mixtas: regulación jurídica. Madrid: Consultoría Jurídica Internacional, 1993. 205 p.

Legal analysis and commentary on Cuban laws and regulations governing foreign joint ventures up to 1993.

1920 Deere, Carmen Diana; Niurka Pérez; and Ernel Gonzales. The view from below: Cuban agriculture in the "Special Period in Peacetime." (*J. Peasant Stud.*, 21 : 2, Jan. 1994, p. 194–234, bibl., maps, tables)

Analysis of changes made in the agricultural sector to adapt to special period stringencies. Presages conversion of inefficient State farms into production cooperatives, and the establishment of agricultural markets.

1921 Feinsilver, Julie M. Cuban biotechnology: the strategic success and commercial limits of a first world approach to development. (*in* Biotechnology in Latin America: politics, impacts, and risks. Wilmington, Del.: Scholarly Resources, 1995, p. 97–125)

Well-documented essay on achievements and problems faced by Cuba's incipient biotechnology industry.

1922 Fernández Font, Marcelo. Perspectivas del mercado mundial azucarero hasta el año 2000: participación de Cuba. (*Rev. Bimest. Cuba.*, 78, enero/junio 1995, p. 109–141, bibl., tables)

Sobering assessment of the world sugar market through the year 2000 and of Cuba's participation in it. Author is a former Cuban Minister of International Trade.

1923 Figueras, Miguel Alejandro. Aspectos estructurales de la economía cubana. La Habana: Editorial de Ciencias Sociales, 1994. 181 p.: bibl., ill. (Economía)

Very important study by Cuban government economist and academic. Inventories Cuba's human and natural resource base and analyzes recent performance and problems in the agricultural, sugar, and manufacturing sectors. Also examines the application of science and technology, and foreign economic relations. Essential reading for understanding Cuba's current economic situation and prospects.

1924 González, Zoila. Retos y dificultades del comercio de Cuba con el Mercado Europeo. (*Rev. Estud. Euro.*, 7:27/28, julio/dic. 1993, p. 65–88, appendix, tables)

Informative overview of Cuban economic relations with the European Community. Emphasis on Spain.

1925 *Informe Económico: 1995.* Mayo 1996. Habana: Banco Nacional de Cuba.

Brief report of Cuban economic performance during 1994–95 and prospects for 1996 prepared by the Banco Nacional de Cuba (BNC). Resumes publication of BNC reports discontinued during the economic crisis. Time series data on the gross domestic product, international trade, and the government budget are particularly important since no official statistical compendium has been published since 1989. A similar report for 1994 (issued in Aug. 1995) has also been published.

1926 Investing in Cuba: problems and prospects. Edited by Jaime Suchlicki and Antonio Jorge. New Brunswick, N.J.: Transaction Publishers, 1994. 185 p.: appendices, bibl., ill.

Collection of essays identifying problems and risks associated with foreign investment in Cuba. Appendices reproduce the foreign investment law of 1982 (since replaced by a new foreign investment law passed in 1995) and accompanying regulations.

1927 Jenkins, Gareth and Lila Haines. Cuba: prospects for reform, trade and investment. New York: The Economist Intelligence Unit, 1994. 173 p.

Well-informed analysis of the Cuban economic condition and prospects for reform. Emphasis on sectors of the economy that are open to foreign trade and investment. Generally balanced, although a bit too upbeat in certain areas. Volume is particularly useful because authors have had access to Cuban government officials and statistics usually not available to researchers.

1928 Klinger Pevida, Eduardo. Cuba y la integración de América Latina y el Caribe: génesis del pensamiento integracionista. Santo Domingo: Organización para la Promoción de la Lectura y el Libro, 1995. 168 p.: bibl.

Chapter IV describes Cuban economic relations with Latin American and Caribbean countries during the last three decades. Chapter VI offers a very optimistic assessment of Cuba's role in hemispheric economic integration.

1929 Lessmann, Robert. Empresas mixtas en Cuba. Versión al castellano de Nora López. Caracas: Fundación Friedrich Ebert; Editorial Nueva Sociedad, 1994. 103 p.: bibl.

Very informative account of foreign joint ventures in Cuba.

1930 Mesa-Lago, Carmelo. Are economic reforms propelling Cuba to the market? Miami: Univ. of Miami North-South Center, 1994. 85 p.

Excellent and very readable review of Cuba's economic reforms of 1993–94. Essential reading for all students of the Cuban economy.

1931 Mesa-Lago, Carmelo. Historia económica de la Cuba socialista. Madrid: Alianza Editorial, 1994. 246 p.: tables.

The best economic history of socialist Cuba to date, written by an authority on the subject. Contains sound analysis supported by 25 statistical tables. Updates and significantly expands earlier work by the author. Includes excellent assessments of the rectification process and the special period.

1932 Miranda Parrondo, Mauricio de. Cuba ante el reto de los cambios. (*Economía/Cali*, 19, primer semestre 1995, p. 41–73, tables)

Very general proposal for reforms—including political reforms—by a Cuban economist residing in Colombia.

1933 Molina Díaz, Elda. Ley 77: nueva ley de inversiones extranjeras en Cuba; estudio comparativo con las experiencias de China y Vietnam. (*Econ. Desarro./Habana*, 25:119, marzo 1996, p. 39–56, bibl., tables)

Compares Cuba's new foreign investment law (Law No. 77 of 1995) with similar instruments in China and Vietnam. Concludes that Cuba's difficulties in attracting investment are a function of the lack of broader-based economic reforms.

1934 Monreal González, Pedro M. and Manuel Rúa. Apertura y reforma de la economía cubana: las transformaciones institucionales, 1990–1993. (*Estud. Int./Santiago*, 27:107/108, julio–sept./oct.–dic. 1994, p. 542–569)

Useful review of Cuban external sector reforms: 1) liberalization of foreign investment; 2) efforts to diversify foreign trade; and 3) encouragement of foreign tourism. Understates difficulty of reforming the external sector due to the lack of meaningful economic reforms. [An English version under the title "'Apertura' and Reform of the Cuban Economy: The Institutional Transformations, 1990–93" is available in *Cuba in the International System: Normalization and Integration*, edited by Archibald R.M. Ritter and John M. Kirk (eds.) (New York: St. Martin's Press, 1995)].

1935 Pérez-López, Jorge F. Odd couples: joint ventures between foreign capitalists and Cuban socialists. Miami: North-South Center Press, Univ. of Miami, 1995. 38 p. (The North-South Agenda Papers; 16)

Detailed, informative discussion of announced foreign joint ventures in Cuba. Actual foreign investments are unknown, but are probably less than half (perhaps much less) than the government's announced $2.1 billion figure. Good discussion of obstacles to foreign investment and the 1995 foreign investment law, which introduced few significant changes.

1936 Pérez Villanueva, Omar Everleny and Hiram Marquetti Nodarse. La economía cubana: actualidad y tendencias. (*Econ. Desarro./Habana*, 25:117, sept. 1995, p. 33–53, appendix, graph, tables)

Assessment of economic performance in 1994 by two analysts associated with the Center of Studies of the Cuban Economy. Argues that in 1994, the Cuban economy arrested the free fall that began in 1989.

1937 Pollitt, Brian H. The Cuban sugar economy: collapse, reform and prospects for recovery. (*J. Lat. Am. Stud.*, 29:1, Feb. 1997, p. 171–210)

Well-documented essay on the status and prospects of the Cuban sugar industry. Skeptical about the likelihood of the Cuban sugar industry's recovery, and questions the economic rationale for attempting such recovery.

1938 Ritter, Archibald R.M. La dualidad del tipo de cambio en la economía cubana de los noventa. (*CEPAL Rev.*, 57, Dec. 1995, p. 113–131)

Thoughtfully analyzes causes and effects of the dollarization of the Cuban economy. Outlines ambitious reform program that would unify the dollar and peso sectors of the economy.

1939 Roca, Sergio G. Reflections on economic policy: Cuba's food program. (*in* Cuba at a crossroads: politics and economics after the Fourth Party Congress. Gainesville: Univ. Press of Florida, 1994, p. 94–117, bibl., tables)

Challenging essay by recently-deceased specialist on the Cuban economy. Concludes that the food production program cannot succeed in the absence of broad economic reforms and the cessation of Fidel Castro's meddling in economic policymaking.

1940 Sandoval González, Raúl A. Cuba: "dolarización," endeudamiento externo, proceso de ajuste y otras reflexiones. (*Econ. Desarro./Habana*, 25:118, dic. 1995, p. 49–63, bibl., tables)

Good exposition of Cuba's principal monetary/financial problems. Short on meaningful solutions.

1941 Zimbalist, Andrew. Dateline Cuba: hanging on in Havana. (*Foreign Policy*, 92, Fall 1993, p. 151–167)

Analyzes critical condition of the Cuban economy in 1993, emphasizing damage inflicted by US policies.

VENEZUELA

ROBERT PALACIOS, *Economist, World Bank*

THE ECONOMIC AND POLITICAL TURBULENCE beginning in 1989 set Venezuelan social scientists on a path of criticism toward both public and private spheres that continues in this selection of economic literature. The attack on business practices in Venezuela is the focal point of a series of sectoral studies, the most comprehensive being the IESA-based work (item **1957**). Highlights from the series of industry-specific studies include the examination of the textile industry (item **1952**) and an analysis of pulp and paper production (item **1951**). The analysis of manufacturers provides interesting descriptive data across many sectors which complements the specific industry analyses (item **1942**). An insightful account of the early years of the second Pérez Administration connects the critiques of the private and public sectors (item **1967**). In particular, the banking crisis, illustrates the Government's failure as regulator.

Not surprisingly, several studies focus on social policy issues, including housing, nutrition, poverty and labor markets. Housing is well covered in a collection of essays (item **1947**), although there is significant variation in the quality of the contributions. Analysis of the labor market and related public programs is provided by two IESA studies (items **1955** and **1943**). Empirical work on poverty continues to be weak as evidenced in the scarce data found in the conference proceedings of the Fundación Adenauer (item **1958**). The report on nutrition and poverty is a welcome exception (item **1965**).

Finally, there have been more studies on decentralization and regional economic development since the political reforms of the late 1980s increased the autonomy of state governors. More broadly, the literature reflects a growing trend in Latin America toward fiscal federalism. Gueron provides a solid case for this trend in the Venezuelan context (item **1963**) and regional studies attest to the increasing interest in individual regions as economic entities (items **1972** and **1970**).

1942 Avalos Gutiérrez, Ignacio *et al.* Estudio de la capacidad tecnológica de la industria manufacturera venezolana. Coordinación de Horacio Viana. Caracas: Fondo Editorial FINTEC, 1994. 198 p.: bibl., ill.

Using a representative sample of 600 small, medium, and large Venezuelan industrial firms and three rounds of interviews, the survey team investigates these firms' strategies and business practices in areas ranging from technology transfer to personnel training and management. Interesting descriptive information despite a shallow analytical framework.

1943 Betancourt, Keila and Samuel Freije. Sector informal. Caracas: Instituto de Estudios Superiores de Administración, 1994. 80 p.: bibl., ill., tables.

In-depth look at informal labor markets in Venezuela following up on previous work by Gustavo Márquez and others which use OCEI survey data. Unfortunately, past studies are not updated with more recent survey results. Useful data tables.

1944 Carvallo, Gastón. El proceso histórico de la agricultura venezolana. Presentación, compilación y revisión de textos de Jo-

sefina Ríos de Hernández. Caracas: CENDES; Fondo Editorial Tropykos, 1995. 178 p.: bibl. (Serie Agricultura y sociedad; 6)

Although historical and descriptive, author relies on secondary material and does not provide new insights to the topic.

1945 Concha Vergara, Mario H. Neoliberalismo: ¿prosperidad o miseria? Caracas?: Ediciones Los Heraldos Negros, 1995. 150 p.: bibl.

Populist tract attacks neoliberal agenda during the early 1990s. Argues that privatization and liberalization of trade rules are among the World Bank/IMF policies which will lead to poverty and inequity. No serious analytical discussion.

1946 Coronel, Gustavo. Una perspectiva gerencial de la Corporación Venezolana de Guayana: la visión, los desastres y las soluciones. Sabana del Medio, Venezuela: G. Coronel, 1995. 193 p.

A recent historical account of the Corporación Venezolana de Guayana (CVG), including decision-making structure and interaction between State enterprise managers and society. Includes interesting anecdotal material for research-oriented public sector firms and the incentives which drive them.

1947 La cuestión de los barrios: homenaje a Paul Henry Chombart de Lauwe. Recopilación de Teolinda Bolívar y Josefina Baldó. Caracas: Monte Avila Editores Latinoamericana; Fundación Polar; Univ. Central de Venezuela, 1996. 491 p.: bibl., ill. (Perspectiva actual)

Volume consists of short papers by experts on urban housing and the question of the barrios, including several international experts. While quality varies somewhat, papers represent the best thinking on policies dealing with informal housing in Venezuela. Concrete proposals included.

De Janvry, Alain *et al.* The political feasibility of adjustment in Ecuador and Venezuela. See item **2028.**

1948 De la Venezuela rentista a la Venezuela productiva: programa de estabilización y recuperación económica. Caracas?: CORDIPLAN, 1994. 95 p.

Government document outlining the policies which would guide the nation.

1949 Dehollain, Paulina L. El consumo de alimentos en Venezuela, 1940–1987. Caracas: Fundación Polar, Area Economía Agr-alimentaria, 1993. 195 p.: bibl., ill., tables. (Sistema alimentario venezolano. Estudios especiales)

Detailed study of food consumption patterns makes only slight references to the 1940–80 period and instead presents and discusses hundreds of tables covering the 1980s. Of special interest are consumption patterns of different income strata which may be useful to poverty specialists.

1950 Díaz Bruzual, Leopoldo. Potencia Zuliana. Venezuela: s.n., 1990. 224 p.: bibl.

Regional expert presents data and description of both petro- and agrochemical developments and general economic and social situation in Zulia through 1988.

1951 Documentos de base: Proyecto Venezuela Competitiva. v. 7, Industria de pulpa y papel de Magín Briceño. Caracas: Ediciones IESA, 1994. 1 v.: bibl., ill.

Industry closeup applies Harvard business school analytical framework made popular by Michael Porter. Includes useful data

and some comparisons with overall Latin American competition. Concludes that wood and paper industry is not competitive and that State intervention has been deleterious.

1952 Documentos de base: Proyecto Venezuela Competitiva. v. 8, Industria textil de Ramón Rosales. Caracas: Ediciones IESA, 1994. 1 v.: bibl., ill.

Detailed study of textile industry in Venezuela includes international comparisons of labor costs and data on investment, capacity, and other indicators.

1953 Documentos de base: Proyecto Venezuela Competitiva. v. 17, Educación de Juan Carlos Navarro. Caracas: Ediciones IESA, 1994. 1 v.: bibl., ill.

Interesting analysis of education data, most of which is 1991 or earlier. However, connection to business competitiveness and the Proyecto Competitiva is weak.

1954 Documentos de base: Proyecto Venezuela Competitiva. v. 24, Formación de nuevas empresas de Henry Gómez-Samper y Carlos Suárez. Caracas: Ediciones IESA, 1994. 1 v.: bibl., ill.

Anecdotal analysis of the challenges entrepreneurs face when attempting to start new businesses in Venezuela.

1955 Documentos de base: Proyecto Venezuela Competitiva. v. 25, Formación de recursos humanos de Elena Granell y Matilde Parra. Caracas: Ediciones IESA, 1994. 1 v.: bibl., ill.

Reviews active labor market strategies and relationship of private and public sectors in worker training programs. Authors suggest relationship is largely ineffective and recommend policies to improve the outcome.

1956 Echevarría Salvat, Oscar A. La economía venezolana, 1944–1994. Prólogo del Dr. Antonio Casas González. 3. ed. actualizada. Caracas: Federación Venezolana de Cámaras y Asociaciones de Comercio y Producción, 1995. 416 p.: bibl.

Description of the Venezuelan economy from 1944 to 1994. Coverage is weakest for the first two decades. Extensive array of data should prove useful to researchers with specific and cross-sectoral interests despite lack of analytical framework. Covers post-1988 crisis period through the early part of the banking crisis.

1957 Enright, Michael J.; Antonio Francés; and Edith Scott Saavedra. Venezuela, el reto de la competitividad. Caracas: Ediciones IESA, 1994. 733 p.: bibl.

Editors draw on two years of work by 80 academics and specialists and 36 case studies to produce a comprehensive, policy-oriented guidebook for making Venezuela more competitive. The study has more of a business school orientation than an underlying economic framework and, as such, provides an excellent background for anyone understanding why being competitive continues to be so difficult for Venezuela's private sector.

1958 Estrategias para superar la pobreza: seminario aniversario, Caracas, 29 al 31 de enero de 1996. Caracas: Fundación Konrad Adenauer; CEDICE; Fundación Pensamiento y Acción, 1996. 234 p.: bibl., ill.

Proceedings of a conference of better-known scholars in the social areas. While informative and indicative of the state of thinking on poverty in Venezuelan academic circles, only a few of the chapters present new analysis. Much of the empirical reference is not referenced, limiting its usefulness. One exception is Sabino's table tracking poverty estimates from a variety of sources between 1970–95.

1959 Faraco, Francisco José and Romano Suprani Marotta. La crisis bancaria venezolana: análisis preliminar. Caracas: Editorial Panapo, 1995. 162 p.: bibl., ill.

Preliminary analysis of this important economic event in recent Venezuelan history. Provides useful background on the banking sector, monetary policy, and the initial reactions of the government. Presents relevant data through 1993, including first estimates of the costs of the bailout.

1960 Fontiveros, Domingo. Tendencias del gasto fiscal en Venezuela y sus implicaciones. (*Temas Coyunt./Caracas*, 33, junio 1996, p. 87–144, appendix, bibl., graphs, tables)

Presentation of evidence of worsening structural fiscal deficits even as debt servicing obligations become less of a constraint, five years into the adjustment which began in 1989. Not surprisingly, author suggests that politically driven expenditures were favored during the period.

1961 Gasto público y distribución del ingreso en Venezuela. Recopilación de Gustavo Márquez. Caracas: Ediciones IESA, 1993. xvi, 147 p.: bibl., ill.

Translation and revision of the English, originally published by the Interamerican Development Bank (see *HLAS 55:1737*).

1962 Gómez, Emeterio. La economía de mercado: selección de escritos y ensayos, 1985–1991. Caracas: Banco Central de Venezuela, 1992. 224 p. (Col. de estudios economicos, 0798–5584; 15)

Collection of essays and a colorful series of newspaper articles on Venezuelan economic history during the difficult years leading up to and during the early years of the market-oriented Pérez Administration.

1963 Gueron, Gabrielle. La descentralización fiscal en Venezuela: análisis del situado constitucional. (*Politeia/Caracas*, 17, 1994, p. 119–171, bibl., tables)

Excellent, thorough analysis of the overcentralized fiscal situation and the weaknesses of the *situado constitucional* method of resource allocation resources at the state level. The well-rounded discussion of the situation in the early 1990s and proposals that would make the system more redistributive and encourage fiscal responsibility at the local level are useful starting points. The main recommendation to improve regional and local databases for fiscal accounts, while mundane, is undoubtedly a precondition for improving policy in the future.

1964 Gutiérrez, Alejandro. La agricultura venezolana durante el período de ajustes. Caracas: Fundación Polar, Area Economía Agroalimentaria, 1995. 118 p.: bibl. (Sistema alimentario venezolano. Estudios especiales, 1316–029X)

Detailed overview of the recent evolution of the agricultural sector in the context of the macroeconomic changes and adjustment policies of the early 1990s. Includes good description of government policy and the position of the multilateral institutions. Presentation of data and figures useful for nonspecialists with basic knowledge. Lacks clear advisable policies for the future.

1965 Jaén, María Helena. Nutrición y pobreza. Caracas: Ediciones Cavendes, 1994. 92 p.: bibl., ill. (Nutrición, base del desarrollo, 1315–3420; 7)

Postcrisis evaluation of nutrition and poverty. Includes useful data on targeted social programs, regional poverty, and nutritional status.

1966 Lugo, Luis. La singular historia de la OPEP. Caracas: Ediciones CEPET, Centro de Formación y Adiestramiento de Petróleos de Venezuela y sus Filiales, 1994. 263 p.: appendices, bibl., ill.

Interesting review of OPEC's history, focusing on the institutional mechanisms which produced the cartel's agreements. Detailed appendices of pricing and other agreements are of special interest to oil sector analysts using time series data.

1967 Naím, Moisés and Antonio Francés. The Venezuelan private sector: from courting the State to courting the market. (in Lessons of the Venezuelan experience. Edited by Louis W. Goodman et al. Washington: Woodrow Wilson Center Press, 1995, p. 165–192, graph, tables)

A familiar but well-told story by leading authorities on the Venezuelan private sector and its reaction to the reforms which began in 1989. The description of the first years of reform downplays mistakes made by the Pérez Administration. Authors conclude that there are dangers lurking for the new market-oriented economy as a result of the weak regulatory environment which characterized Venezuela in the mid-1990s.

1968 Olavarría, Jorge. El efecto Venezuela. 3. ed. Caracas: J. Olavarría; Editorial Panapo de Venezuela, 1996. 165 p.: ill.

Vitriolic attack on the misuse of oil wealth in Venezuela. Author puts into perspective the scale of wasted opportunity by comparing revenue and expenditure figures throughout the century. Comparison is juxtaposed with quotes from Juan Pablo Pérez Alfonzo, criticizing the exploitation of the country's resources over several decades. Charges of incompetence and corruption are not surprising. Focus is on political economy.

1969 Olavarría, Jorge. No, señor Presidente! no!: artículos publicados en "El Universal" 1994. Caracas: J. Olavarría, 1994. 226 p.: index.

Collection of articles published in the Caracas daily paper focus on the financial crisis of 1994. Comparison made with US Savings and Loan crisis. Deregulation of banking

activities supported by the Pérez Administration blamed. Author claims the policies were inspired by "IESA technocrats" (IESA professors who occupied ministerial positions in Pérez cabinet) who overlooked the negative consequences of similar policies in the US. [R. Salgado]

Pantin, Guillermo. Latino Mafia: crónica de la corrupción del sistema. See item **3475.**

1970 Parra Luzardo, Gastón. De la nacionalización a la apertura petrolera: derrumbe de una esperanza. Maracaibo, Venezuela: Univ. del Zulia, Vicerrectorado Académico, Centro Experimental de Estudios Latinoamericanos, 1995. 359 p.: bibl.

Analysis does not offer an economic diagnosis of the recent movements towards opening the oil sector to foreign participation. Nevertheless, the author provides valuable context for such an analysis concentrating on institutional and legal evolution. Most interesting section is an account of the mixed experience of the Cristóbal Colón project.

Perry, William. Political assessment. See item **3476.**

Rodríguez-Valdés, Angel. Latino, pecado capital. See item **3477.**

1971 Rojas, Reinaldo. La economía de Lara en cinco siglos: una aproximación a su estudio. Barquisimeto, Venezuela: Asamblea Legislativa del Estado Lara; Asociacion Pro Venezuela, Seccional Lara, 1996. 112 p.: bibl., ill.

Descriptive overview of economic development in this Venezuelan state recounts the experience of European explorers in the 16th and 17th centuries, the expansion of cocoa trade in the 19th century, and the rise and decline of the coffee trade. Modern period description does not make use of all available data.

Serbín, Andrés. A new approach to the world? the gran viraje and Venezuelan policy. See item **4456.**

1972 Thula Rangel, Benjamín. Guayana en el desarrollo nacional y global, 1993–2000. Caracas: Imprenta Universitaria de la Univ. Central de Venezuela, 1994. 215 p.: bibl., ill. (some col.).

Regional study focuses on large industries of the CVG and reads more like a business plan than an economic analysis of this troubled area. Includes useful data and information on the interaction between the State and the productive sectors in the utilities and big industries such as aluminum. More promotional than critical assessment of performance with few answers for the future.

1973 Vega Febres, Cecilia; María A. Bellorín; and Edgar Abreu Olivo. Bibliografía agroalimentaria, Fundación Polar. Caracas: Area Economía Agroalimentaria, Fundación Polar, 1995. 130 p.: bibl., indexes.

Indexed and well-annotated bibliography of use to scholars doing research on agricultural policy in Venezuela.

COLOMBIA

NOHRA REY DE MARULANDA, *Manager of Integration and Regional Programs Department, Inter-American Development Bank*

FOLLOWING AN ESTABLISHED TREND, discussions of the fundamental economic reforms of the last decade, particularly those related to the external sector, continue to dominate the economic literature of Latin America. This is certainly true for Colombia as the works reviewed for *HLAS 57* amply demonstrate; approximately one-third of the works annotated examine economic reforms.

Several works, for example, assess the impact of liberalization or "apertura" on the agricultural sector (items **1985, 1992,** and **2003**). Various other works examine the end of the International Coffee Agreement, analyzing the affect on coffee exports and the sector in general (items **1998, 2000,** and **1984**). In keeping with the Colombian tradition of prudent macroeconomic management and fiscal discipline, many works reviewed this biennium anticipate the Cusiana oil boom, and propose policies to avoid a case of "Dutch Disease" (items **1991, 1987** and **2011**). A small number of articles study the relatively unexplored topics of women's employment (items **2012, 1997,** and **2014**) and child labor (item **1989**).

As noted in previous *HLAS* volumes, analyses of the impact of the narcotics trade on the Colombian economy and society continue to have a surprisingly small place in the literature of the field. Although given mention in several works, only one book reviewed this biennium is dedicated to an exploration of the Colombian narcotics trade (item **2013**).

Finally, it seems once again necessary to remark on the paucity of theoretical works, the limited number of studies by non-Colombian authors, and the concentration of well-conceived articles within a very limited number of journals.

1974 Acevedo Bohórquez, Jorge; Juan Carlos Salazar; and Wigberto Castañeda H. El metro de Medellín: una ilusión costeada por todos los colombianos. Bogotá: FONADE; Instituto SER de Investigación, 1993. 167 p.: bibl., ill., maps.

Study of the chronology of the construction of Medellín's light rail system, based on direct interviews, tracking of press releases, and official documents. Presents innumerable strategic and executional barriers that plagued the project. The author's stated intention is to generate discussion about the role of the State and its institutions in projects such as this one, and to explain lessons learned to avoid committing similar mistakes in the future.

1975 La apertura económica en Colombia: agenda de un proceso. Prólogo de César Gaviria Trujillo. Bogotá: Cámara de Comercio

de Bogotá; Tercer Mundo Editores, 1993.
340 p.: bibl., ill.

Analyzes the structural process of the economic opening begun in 1990. Unlike past economic liberalizations, this process is not contingent upon availability of hard currency, but obeys a long-term economic strategy designed to stimulate growth. The process is deployed across several fronts in addition to international trade, among them, renewed exchange rate and fiscal policy, financial and tax reform, foreign investment incentives and new labor laws. The book offers background for sector and industry leaders, and a complete bibliography.

1976 Ardila Gómez, Arturo. Control de la congestión vehicular en Bogotá con herramientas microeconómicas. (*Desarro. Soc.*, 35, marzo 1995, p. 7–26, bibl., maps, tables)

Proposes and analyzes four alternatives to deal with the enourmous problem of automobile congestion which has attained exceedingly high levels in Bogotá.

1977 Arias Jiménez, Enrique *et al.* Alternativas de privatización para el sector público colombiano. Bogotá: Univ. Externado de Colombia, 1993. 182 p.: bibl.

Discussion by academics, government officials, and private sector leaders on the virtues of reducing the role of the Colombian State in favor of private interests, with the objective of increasing economic efficiency. Although a selective process of privatization has long been praised as beneficial for economies such as Colombia's, major sales of nationalized industries have not yet been achieved and successive governments have failed to elaborate a comprehensive privatization plan. The authors describe the benefits of moving in this direction and point out that the new Constitution opens the way for a process of privatization that includes even primary services.

1978 La autonomía del Banco de la República: economía política de la reforma. Recopilación de Roberto Steiner. Bogotá: Tercer Mundo Editores; FEDESARROLLO, 1995. 315 p.: bibl. (Economía colombiana)

This volume traces the history of the 1991 reorganization of Colombia's central bank, resulting from constitutional changes. Perspectives from then Finance Minister

R. Hommes, key constitution framers, and central bank technocrats make evident the different interests at stake in the process, the debate that arose around them, and the compromises that were struck to broker an agreement. Although some critics argue that the new bank will not do enough to curb inflation, the general consensus is that it is a modern, efficient institution that stands in solid balance vis-à-vis the government, and that it will improve the country's ability to face new economic challenges.

1979 Avella Gómez, Mauricio. Pensamiento y política monetaria en Colombia, 1886–1945. Bogotá: Contraloría General de la República, Ediciones Especiales, 1987. 388 p.: bibl., ill.

Very comprehensive examination of the evolution of monetary policy in Colombia, from the debated adoption of paper currency to the economic maturity of the second half of this century. The author uses extensive historical data to track political attitudes and changes, and to generate an economic analysis of the impact of adopted policies.

1980 Barajas, Adolfo. La eficacia de la política monetaria en Colombia: un estudio de la relación entre inflación y encajes bancarios. (*Ens. Polít. Econ.*, 23, junio 1993, p. 7–36, bibl., graphs, tables)

Seeks to determine the critical reserve requirement level for banks in Colombia over an extended period of time. The author argues that in both the post-coffee boom era and in the 1991–93 period, reserves exceeded the critical level, which is counterproductive to the effort to reduce inflation.

1981 Bucheli, Marcelo. Sindicalismo y prensa entre los contratos petroleros: estudio histórico para Colombia. (*Desarro. Soc.*, 35, marzo 1995, p. 27–52, bibl.)

Historical analysis of the behavior of the press and trade unions in responding to deals made by the Colombian government and diverse multinationals for oil exploration.

1982 Carrasquilla B., Alberto. Bandas cambiarias y modificaciones a la política de estabilización: lecciones de la experiencia colombiana. (*Rev. Banco Repúb./Bogotá*, 68:807, enero 1995, p. 22–47, bibl., graphs)

This article traces the Colombian switch from a crawling peg exchange policy to a band fluctuation policy. The Colombian experience is unique, since all other countries that have adopted a policy of band fluctuation were previously in a fixed exchange rate system.

1983 Colombia ante la economía mundial. Recopilación de Miguel Urrutia. Bogotá: T.M. Editores; FEDESARROLLO, 1993. 263 p.: bibl., charts, ill. (Académica; Economía colombiana)

Collection of articles by well-respected academics, researchers, and policymakers assesses Colombia's position in a globalized economy. The 1990s mark the decisive integration of Colombia's economy with the rest of the world. So far the process has been seen as largely beneficial: it is argued that currency liberalization has promoted not only a repatriation of national capital and an increase in foreign investment, but also has made it inevitable for government to pursue fiscal discipline. However, to gain legitimacy as a player in the world market, Colombia needs to advance its policies in the areas of environment, human rights, and drug trafficking. Moreover, the economy can only move forward insofar as progress is made in education, science, and technology, and in the development of a social policy that allows all citizens to participate in the country's progress.

1984 El comercio exterior y la política internacional del café. Coordinación de Roberto Junguito Bonnet y Diego Pizano Salazar. Bogotá: FEDESARROLLO, Fondo Cultural Cafetero, 1993. 405 p.: bibl., ill., index.

Vol. 2 of a very comprehensive study of trends in the coffee sector by two economic experts in the field (see *HLAS 55:1781.*) The book systematically tracks the development of the international coffee market, including Colombia's participation. Cautiously attempts to project the behavior of the coffee trade during the 1990s, after the dissolution of the International Coffee Agreement; predictions include a price recovery, a moderate increase in demand, and profitable production shifting to those countries and regions that can increase productivity.

1985 Competitividad sin pobreza: estudios para el desarrollo del campo en Colombia. Coordinación de Clara González y Carlos Felipe Jaramillo. Con la colaboración de Ministerio de Hacienda y Crédito Público *et al.*

Bogotá: FONADE; TM Editores, 1993. 530 p. (Economía agraria)

Series of papers commissioned by the Colombian National Planning Dept. Contains recommendations for agricultural policy in the 1990s and beyond, based on three major strategies: 1) a prudent macroeconomic policy; 2) an increase in competitiveness fueled by infrastructural investment and the strengthening of mechanisms to generate and transfer technology; and 3) social investment to improve human capital and reduce poverty. Several technical articles by field experts substantiate these recommendations.

1986 Echeverry, Juan Carlos. Indicadores de política y canales de transmisión monetaria: Colombia, 1975–1991. (*Ens. Polít. Econ.*, 24, dic. 1993, p. 7–41, bibl., graphs, tables)

Uses a battery of macroeconomic tests to isolate the best indicator of Colombian monetary policy. Leads to the (intuitive) conclusion that the interest rate with its high predictive character best carries the message of monetary policy to the economy.

1987 Estabilización y crecimiento: nuevas lecturas de macroeconomía colombiana. Recopilación de Roberto Steiner. Bogotá: TM Editores; FEDESARROLLO, 1994. 249 p.: bibl., ill. (Economía colombiana)

Compilation of scholarly articles study the behavior of the main macroeconomic variables in the face of important external and internal perturbations. Building on the findings from these studies, the book develops a second major theme anticipating the dangers and magnitude of the imminent Cusiana oil boom, and then makes some policy suggestions to correctly handle the boom.

1988 Fernández, Diego E. Análisis de la equidad del sistema de transferencia del impuesto al valor agregado en Colombia. Buenos Aires: Centro de Investigaciones Económicos; Instituto Torcuato Di Tella, 1994. 31 p.: bibl., tables. (Serie Documentos de trabajo)

Careful study of the expedience of the current laws governing the allocation of proceeds from the value-added tax across Colombian municipalities. The author argues that the current laws could be improved upon based on considerations of efficiency and equality.

1989 Flórez, Carmen Elisa; Felicia Marie Knaul; and Regina Méndez. Un análisis cuantitativo del trabajo infantil y juvenil en Colombia. (*Desarro. Soc.*, 34, sept. 1994, p. 179–224, bibl., graphs, tables)

Based on information from household surveys, authors analyze child and juvenile work both in the labor market and in the household. Findings show many children work long hours and demonstrate a negative relationship between work and school attendance.

1990 Flórez E., Luis Bernardo. Gestión económica estatal de los ochentas: del ajuste al cambio institucional. v. 1–2. Dirección de Luis Bernardo Flórez E. Coordinación técnica de Ricardo Bonilla González. Bogotá: Univ. Nacional de Colombia, Centro de Investigaciones para el Desarrollo, 1995. 2 v.: bibl., ill.

Two volumes of very comprehensive work in which academic researchers carefully plot five main themes of Colombian economic policy from 1980–94: 1) the process of institutional adaptation, from the definition of strategies to confront the crisis of the early 1980s to the constitutional changes of 1991 and their effects; 2) the macroeconomic agenda, including an analysis of fiscal policy and foreign debt; 3) the social agenda, with emphasis on education, health, and decentralization; 4) policies adapted in the industrial, agricultural, energy, and public services sectors; and 5) an analysis of changes in the development model, including the redefinition of the role of the State and the resulting shift in interaction between public and private sectors.

1991 Garay, Luis J. Descentralización, bonanza petrolera y estabilización: la economía colombiana en los años noventa. Bogotá: FESCOL; CEREC, 1994. 273 p.: bibl. (CEREC: Serie Textos; 24)

In-depth study of the effects that the expected revenue from the exploitation of the Cusiana oil fields will have on the Colombian economy. Based on both theoretical and empirical analysis of similar national and international phenomena, the author considers ways in which the revenue from the boom can be exploited to benefit other sectors of the economy, promote growth with equity, and avoid inflation and Dutch disease. Emphasizes the process of decentralization underway in Colombia. This is important since, as a result of this process, close to half of the revenue generated by the oil boom will not be received by the central government, but by the regions from which the oil is extracted.

1992 Jaramillo, Carlos Felipe. Apertura, crisis y recuperación: la agricultura colombiana entre 1990 y 1994. Bogotá: FONADE; TM Editores, 1994. 253 p.: bibl., ill. (Académica; Economía agraria)

This book covers the performance of the agricultural sector during the Gaviria Administration, and purports to offer a dispassionate account of the extent to which Gaviria's economic policy of opening markets to globalization led to the sector's 1992 crisis. Production statistics and international studies are used to argue that the agricultural policy did not precipitate the 1992 crisis; other factors such as the fall of international prices and the severe drought that occurred during that year need to be considered. Also asserts that beginning in 1993, the agricultural sector entered a period of recuperation.

1993 Kalmanovitz, Salomón. Economía y nación: una breve historia de Colombia. 4. ed. corr. y aum. Bogotá: Tercer Mundo Editores, 1994. 576 p.: bibl. (Historia económica)

A new edition of the 1985 Colombian economic history (see *HLAS 51:2148*). New material covers Colombia's performance during the 1980s, Latin America's "lost decade," when economic growth declined but was not negative as elsewhere across the region. Also considers Colombia's possibilities and expectations for the new millennium: added to the positive fact that constitutional reforms have pluralized the country, the author—who has traditionally argued from the left—accepts that neoliberal policies implemented in the 1990s have increased competitiveness, favorably positioning the country to develop agricultural and manufacturing export niches leading to sustainable growth. This will be coupled with the imminent boom of the mining industry. However, economic growth and social cohesion will be hurt by the seemingly unresolvable problem posed by drug trafficking.

1994 Londoño de la Cuesta, Juan Luis. Distribución del ingreso y desarrollo económico: Colombia en el siglo XX. Bogotá:

TM Editores; FEDESARROLLO; Banco de la República, 1995. 261 p.: bibl., ill. (Economía colombiana)

Examines historical evolution of income distribution in Colombia from mid-1930s to late 1980s. Uses econometric techniques to analyze relative importance of the major determinants of income distribution. [J. Foley]

1995 López Castaño, Hugo. Contexto macroeconómico colombiano, mercado laboral y urbano y retos para una política de empleo. Bogotá: Fundación Friedrich Ebert de Colombia, 1993. 62 p.: bibl., ill. (Documentos de trabajo)

Working paper uses extensive statistical data to describe labor market performance from a crisis period of 1980–85 to a recovery in 1986–89, and up to 1993. The balance is mixed: unemployment has ceased being cyclical and has become structural, informal employment is on the decline but is still significant, and workers have lost purchasing power due to inflation. The author closes by considering some possible future employment strategies in terms of volume and quality, such as job retraining and unemployment insurance.

1996 Lora, Eduardo *et al.* Colombia: evolución macroeconómica, financiación externa y cambio político en la década de los 80. Madrid: Fundación CEDEAL, 1993. 218 p.: bibl., ill. (Situación latinoamericana; Serie Estudios América Latina en la década de los 80)

Traces the main tendencies of the Colombian economy during the 1980s. A solid macroeconomic review and an analysis of the handling of foreign debt explain how Colombia escaped the "lost decade." This examination is coupled by an overview of the decade's political swings, marked especially by successive government's handling of the guerrillas and the increasingly violent drug trafficking groups. The book is rounded off by a balance of the decade's social change: although some progress was achieved, it was not necessarily equitable.

1997 Magnac, Thierry. Female labor market participation and wages in Colombia. (*in* Case studies on women's employment and pay in Latin America. Washington: World Bank, 1992, p. 169–195, bibl., graphs, tables)

Data from household surveys are used in a macroeconometric model of female participation in Colombian labor markets in an attempt to explain a dramatic increase in participation rates. The author detects a positive effect of income on labor participation of married women, but finds limitations to the descriptions provided by the model.

1998 Montenegro, Armando. Café, dinero y macroeconomía en Colombia: ensayos. Bogotá: FESCOL, 1993. 394 p.

Collection of essays written between 1984–89 that present elaborate macroeconomic models adjusted to approximate the behavior of the Colombian economy during its long period of dependency on coffee exports. These models were mainly used to back up policy proposals and to advise the government on sound economic action given the variations of the International Coffee Agreement. The final analysis suggests that the coffee trade will have a decreasing role in the Colombian economy.

1999 Moss, Diana L. and **James R. Tybout.** The scope for fuel substitution in manufacturing industries: a case study of Chile and Colombia. (*World Bank Econ. Rev.*, 8:1, Jan. 1994, p. 49–74, bibl., tables)

Since effective, direct strategies for emissions control are difficult to implement in countries like Chile or Colombia, the authors set out to analyze if the government can influence fuel substitution through fiscal policy without severely hurting productive sectors with limited flexibility in obtaining energy. The article analyzes plant-level data from manufacturing industries in Chile and Colombia to conclude that fiscal policies can significantly influence the mixture of energy usage among manufacturers, even though the effect of these policies will be heterogenous and can be hurtful to some manufacturing subsectors.

2000 El negocio cafetero ante el mercado libre: informe de la Comisión Mixta para el Estudio del Café. Recopilación de Sergio Clavijo, José Leibovich, Carlos Felipe Jaramillo con la colaboración de Ministerio de Hacienda y Crédito Público, Depto. Nacional de Planeación. Bogotá: Tercer Mundo Editores, 1994. 459 p.: bibl., ill. (Académica; Economía agraria)

Report of a study commissioned by the government to assess the coffee sector crisis, accentuated in this decade after the dissolution of the International Coffee Agreement. The report was prepared by a group of experts in the field, and substantiated by studies subcontracted to special consultants. Concludes that coffee exports are and will continue to be viable and important for the Colombian economy, but that the sector has to increase its competitiveness and the institutions that govern it need to undergo reform to adapt to new market conditions. However, a renewed increase of relative importance of coffee exports, or a major change in the export structure (i.e., from a basic product to a more finished product) is not foreseen.

2001 Ocampo, José Antonio *et al.* Ensayos de historia monetaria y bancaria de Colombia. Recopilación de Fabio Sánchez. Bogotá: Tercer Mundo Editores, 1994. 331 p.: bibl., ill. (Historia económica; Economía agraria)

This volume incorporates seven articles on monetary and banking history in Colombia in the 19th and early 20th centuries. Uses archival documents as input for macroeconomic analysis.

2002 Ocampo, José Antonio. La internacionalización de la economía colombiana. Bogotá: CLADEI; FESCOL, 1993. 54 p.: bibl., ill. (Serie Documentos CLADEI-FESCOL; 5)

Monograph by an influential academic researcher and policymaker on the opening of the Colombian economy. The author presents a history of the relationship between economic development and protectionism in Colombia, describes the current process of economic opening, and makes a projection about its impact. Asserts that the Colombian economy was already turning to new exports and private investment prior to the Gaviria Administration non-gradual opening process. Predicts that the effects of this process in terms of growth will be moderate for the existing productive sectors, but that the new model precludes incentives for the development of new areas of production.

2003 Ocampo, José Antonio; Gabriel Turbay M.; and Juan Manuel Ospina Restrepo. Situación actual y perspectivas del sector agropecuario colombiano. Bogotá: CLADEI; FESCOL, 1994. 50 p.: ill. (Documentos CLADEI-FESCOL; 6)

Technical articles by then Agriculture Minister Ocampo and two sector leaders. Analyzes different possibilities for achieving the internationalization of Colombian agriculture and/or rural development. Favors strategy based on improving sector's credit structure.

2004 Poverty in Colombia. Washington: World Bank, 1994. 306 p.: bibl., col. map., ill. (A World Bank country study, 0253–2123)

This report by World Bank economists and Colombian consultants maps out a strategy for poverty reduction in Colombia by concentrating efforts on rural development, social and infrastructural services, and decentralization strengthening. Expenditures would be financed by revenues generated by oil exports, presupposing macroeconomic health and increased government efficiency and accountability.

2005 Ramírez Gómez, Manuel. El impacto de la política cambiaria sobre la estructura industrial. (*Desarro. Soc.*, 32, sept. 1993, p. 79–106, graph, tables)

Examines the impact of the real exchange rate on economic activity. The author tracks the evolution of the exchange rate and finds a significant revaluation of at least 10 percent over the short period between 1991–93, after the opening of the economy. This has had a negative effect on relative prices of Colombian goods which affects international trade but not internal consumption.

2006 Reyes Posada, Alvaro. El impacto de las regulaciones laborales sobre el mercado de trabajo: el caso colombiano. (*in* Regulación del mercado de trabajo en América Latina. Panamá Zona 9, Panamá; San Francisco, Calif.: Centro International para el Desarrollo Económico, 1994, p. 123–156, bibl., tables)

Author presents main aspects of Colombian labor legislation and the reforms introduced in 1990. In analyzing the structure of employment in the Colombian economy, he tentatively proposes the possible impact of labor legislation on the structure of the labor market.

2007 Ritchey-Vance, Marion. The art of association: NGOs and civil society in Colombia. Rosslyn, Va.: Inter-American Foundation, 1991. 176 p.: bibl., ill. (Country focus series; 2)

A study of the large number of non-governmental organizations that operate in Colombia, describing the different kinds of NGOs that have been formed in the past two decades, their objectives, their level of participation in society, and their impact. The author, a senior representative of the Inter-American Foundation, draws on experience gained by working with the numerous NGOs the foundation has supported.

2008 Sanclemente, Carlos. Desarrollo y crisis del sector eléctrico colombiano, 1890–1993. Bogotá: Empresa Editorial Univ. Nacional, 1993. 138 p.: bibl.

Tracks the century-long history of the development of the electric sector in Colombia. Of interest is the analysis of the factors that led to the 1992 national energy shortage and the policy lessons that are inferred from that incident.

2009 Sarmiento Anzola, Libardo. Una nueva oleada de modernismo. (*Cuad. Econ. / Bogotá*, 14:22, primer semestre 1995, p. 239–252, bibl., graphs)

Preliminary analysis of the Samper Administration Development Plan, and its purported goal of a "social jump." The author considers the elements of the program to be insufficient to confront the serious structural problems that the country and the economy face. The assumption that increased social spending will translate into the creation of a new, just society is naive, especially amidst the problems generated by the illegal drug trade, which is largely overlooked by the plan.

2010 Sarmiento Palacio, Eduardo. Fallas de mercado y motores de crecimiento económico. Bogotá: Ediciones Uniandes; Educar Cultural Recreativa, 1993. 246 p.: bibl., ill. (Economía colombiana)

This volume challenges the validity of the application of free market models of economic development to an economy such as the Colombian one. Using a methodology that combines expectations from macroeconomic theory with empirical facts and observations, the author argues that in the Colombian economy, the forces of supply and demand do not necessarily meet in all markets, and that developing countries do not benefit from adopting the same policies as industrialized ones.

2011 Seminario Cusiana y la Economía Colombiana en los Años Noventa, *Bogotá, 1993*. Cusiana: un reto de política económica; documentos presentados en el Seminario Cusiana y la Económia Colombiana en los Años Noventa, julio 7–8 de 1993, Bogotá. Coordinación de Armando Montenegro y Miguel Kiguel. Bogotá: Depto. Nacional de Planeación; Banco Mundial, 1993. 439 p.: bibl., ill.

Compilation of documents presented at a 1993 seminar on sound ways for the Colombian State to handle revenues earned from the exploitation of the newly discovered oil fields of Cusiana. Participants included President Gaviria, his economic team, members of the Central Bank Board, senior economists from international institutions, and worldwide academic experts. The documents recognize the widely held consensus that without sufficient planning, the flux of revenue generated by new oil exports will create inflation and Dutch disease. To avoid problems, fiscal discipline and social investment are diagnosed.

2012 Tenjo, Jaime. Labor markets, the wage gap and gender discrimination: the case of Colombia. (*in* Case studies on women's employment and pay in Latin America. Washington: World Bank, 1992, p. 149–168, bibl., tables)

An attempt to analyze the wage gap between men and women in Colombia. Concludes that the wage gap in Colombia is lower than the one in developed countries (below 30 percent), and that if certain "female ghettos" such as domestic service are excluded from the comparison, the gap is further diminished. For sociologist's comment see item **4982.**

2013 Thoumi, Francisco E. Economía política y narcotráfico. Traducción de Pedro Valenzuela. Bogotá: TM Editores, 1994. 339 p.: bibl., index.

Very thoughtful study of a problem of the utmost importance for Colombia. The author analyzes the country's economic and political development since the post-war to better understand the profound changes it has undergone; he then proceeds to survey the known facts about the illegal drug industry. Within this context, Thoumi attempts to determine why Colombia developed, since the 1970s, a marijuana, and subsequently a cocaine, industry. Further, he evaluates the effects of the drug trade on the Colombian economy and social order. The final analysis suggests that Colombia's chances of reducing the negative impact of the drug trade are slim.

2014 Veléz, Eduardo and **Carolyn Winter.** Women's labor force participation and earnings in Colombia. (*in* Case studies on women's employment and pay in Latin America. Washington: World Bank, 1992, p. 197–207, bibl., tables)

Although female participation in the labor market is generally taken as an indicator of sex equality stemming from increased education and lower fertility rates, the authors examine whether equality is really at the root of women's increased levels of participation in Colombia. Their conclusions indicate that labor market participation is in fact positively influenced by education, although female labor is concentrated in low paying positions with fewer possibilities for advancement.

ECUADOR

DAVID W. SCHODT, *Professor of Economics, St. Olaf College*

SINCE THE MID-1980S, debate surrounding stabilization and structural adjustment policies and their social and economic consequences has been a prominent feature of the literature in Ecuador and throughout Latin America. Based on the impressive monetary and national accounts statistics produced by Ecuador's Central Bank, macroeconomic performance is readily measured, and several inflation studies have tapped this source. Social indicators are much less well-developed; however, two publications offer a detailed analysis of current conditions and track future trends. An review of the World Bank's 1994 Ecuador Living Standard Measurement Survey determines an important baseline for measuring poverty (item **2030**), and INEC's survey provides data for examining basic needs satisfaction (item **2024**).

As usual, there are a number of solid general economic history works. Two sources are distinguished by their careful use of archival data: Pineo's rich social history of Guayaquil during the cacao boom draws on previously unexploited archival resources (item **2051**), and nicely complements Arosemena's history of the Ecuadorian cacao and chocolate industries (item **2018**). This type of research has not yet been applied to the more recent period of the banana boom.

Survey data collected from settlement areas in the Ecuadorian Amazon region have allowed for empirical analysis of agriculture within the region. Pichón's work is notable among several that draw on these data for an empirical analysis of the determinants of deforestation (item **2050**).

In general economists studying Ecuador have not focused on comparative work, although recent economic integration efforts may stimulate more. Ironically, the 1995 border war between Ecuador and Peru provided the impetus for a comparative economic history of the two countries (item **2057**). Although somewhat superficial, this symbolic book may lead to more work in this area.

2015 Acosta, Alberto. Breve historia económica del Ecuador. Quito: Corporación Editora Nacional, 1995. 262 p.: bibl., ill. (Biblioteca general de cultura; 7)

General economic history valuable as introduction. Includes glossary of economic terms and chronology of economic events.

2016 Albornoz Guarderas, Vicente. Análisis de la inflación ecuatoriana, 1980–1993, en base a la técnica de vectores autorregresivos. Quito: Corporación de Estudios para el Desarrollo (CORDES), 1994. 40 p.: bibl., tables.

Five-variable estimation with monthly data finds major cause of inflation is exchange rate changes, followed by net internal credit. Does not find M1 significant.

2017 Análisis de cadenas agroindustriales en Ecuador y Perú. Santiago: Naciones Unidas, Comisión Económica para América Latina y el Caribe, 1993. 294 p.: bibl., ill. (Estudios e informes de la CEPAL; 87)

Detailed studies, sponsored by the UN, of quinoa and maracuya industries in Ecuador and frozen asparagus in Peru. Possibly valuable for those interested in non-traditional exports. See also items **2061** and **2055.**

2018 Arosemena, Guillermo. El fruto de los dioses. v. 1–2. Guayaquil, Ecuador: Editorial Graba de Guayaquil, 1991. 2 v. (855 p.): bibl., ill.

Valuable history of the Ecuadorian cacao industry from 1600–83. Includes previously unavailable information on local chocolate industry. See also Crawford de Roberts, *El Ecuador en la época cacaotera* (Quito: Editorial Universitaria, 1980, *HLAS 44:2904, 47:3448, and 48:2995*) and Guererro, *Los Oligarchas de Cacao* (Quito: Editorial El Conejo, 1983, and *HLAS 44:2899*).

2019 Arosemena, Guillermo. Nuestros males crónicos: las crisis económicas en el Ecuador. Guayaquil, Ecuador: s.n., 1994. 400 p.: bibl., ill.

Survey of economic crises from 1550–1991. Not much theoretical grounding, but may be useful as a historical account.

2020 Arteta Villavicencio, Gustavo. Efectos de las instituciones democráticas en la política y la economía. Quito: Corporación de Estudios para el Desarrollo, 1997. 44 p.: appendices, bibl., graphs, tables. (Documento de trabajo; 6)

Applies public choice theory to the Ecuadorian Congress. Finds number of laws adopted is more a function of structure than of the party in power or the personalities of the country's political leaders.

2021 Baydas, Mayada M.; Richard L. Mayer; and Nelson Aguilera-Alfred. Credit rationing in small-scale enterprises: special microenterprise programmes in Ecuador. (*J. Dev. Stud.*, 31:2, Dec. 1994, p. 279–288, tables)

Supply and demand model is estimated to analyze factors used by lenders to ration credit. Uses 1990 small enterprise survey. Finds that less profitable enterprises and entrepreneurs with less education have less demand for credit and that supply factors are relatively unimportant.

2022 Carrasco, Hernán. Campesinos y mercado de tierras en la costa ecuatoriana. Roma: Organización de las Naciones Unidas para la Agricultura y la Alimentación, 1994. 148 p.: bibl., maps.

Study sponsored by FAO of agricultural land markets in three coastal provinces. Emphasizes roles of the small producer and landless campesino.

2023 Chiriboga Zambrano, Galo A. and **Vjekoslav Darlić Mardešić.** Contratos colectivos, 1974–1992. Quito: ILDIS, 1993. 117 p.: bibl., ill. (Estadísticas laborales del Ecuador; 1)

Provides valuable statistics on organized labor in Ecuador during this period.

2024 Compendio de las necesidades básicas insatisfechas de la población ecuatoriana: mapa de la pobreza. Guayaquil, Ecuador: Instituto Nacional de Estadística y Censos (INEC), 1995. 847 p.: ill. (some col.), col. maps. (Serie descentralización; 1, Pobreza)

Valuable survey of basic needs satisfaction based on 1990 census of population and housing. Contains a wealth of data disaggregated by province, canton, and parish (rural only).

2025 Corsino Cárdenas, José. Ensayo histórico de la economía ecuatoriana. Quito: Banco Central del Ecuador, 1995. 208 p.: bibl. (Biblioteca de historia económica; 6)

Economic history by distinguished Ecuadorian economist and policymaker. Includes interesting material on the banana boom by one of its architects.

2026 Creamer, Germán. The Ecuadorean participation in the Andean Pact: macroeconomic and sectoral impact. Notre Dame, Indiana: Kellogg Institute, Univ. of Notre Dame, 1996. 28 p.: bibl., tables. (Working paper; 226)

Applies neostructuralist macroeconomic model to question of whether Ecuador's participation in the Andean Group will stimulate basic goods sector. Identifies net gains for Ecuador.

2027 De Janvry, Alain and **Pablo Glikman.** Encadenamientos de producción en la economía campesina en el Ecuador. San José: Fondo Internacional de Desarrollo Agrícola (FIDA); Instituto Interamericano de Cooperación para la Agricultura (IICA), 1991. 562 p.: bibl., ill., map. (Estrategias para mitigar la pobreza rural en América Latina y El Caribe; 1. Serie FIDA/IICA; 1)

This valuable resource focuses on microeconomic and macroeconomic determinants of rural poverty in Ecuador. Compare with Whitaker and Colyer, *Agriculture and economic survival HLAS 53:2166.*

2028 De Janvry, Alain *et al.* The political feasibility of adjustment in Ecuador and Venezuela. Paris: Development Centre of the Organisation for Economic Co-operation and Development, 1994. 155 p.: bibl. (Political feasibility of adjustment. Development Centre studies)

This OECD study builds on De Janvry's earlier simulations for Ecuador (see *HLAS 55:1799*). Spurrier adds in-depth knowledge of Ecuadorian politics. Little comparison with Venezuela, but valuable for the analysis of Ecuador. Explicitly links income changes to sectors and groups.

2029 Desafíos en la agroexportación no tradicional: impactos ambientales y sociales. Edited by William F. Waters. Washington: World Resources Institute; Quito: Univ. San Francisco de Quito, 1993. 220 p.: bibl.

Report of two workshops examines socioeconomic and environmental effects of nontraditional agriculture. Useful primarily for range of opinions represented, from academics to small producers.

2030 Ecuador poverty report. Washington: World Bank, 1996. 353 p.: bibl., ill. (A World Bank country study)

Valuable report based on the Ecuador Living Standard Measurement Survey (1994). Uses total consumption expenditures. Provides a baseline reference for future work. Contrast with INEC's basic needs survey (item **2024**).

2031 Empleo, cuello de botella del ajuste. Edición de Rafael Urriola. Quito: CEPLAES-CEOSL, 1994. 194 p.: bibl.

Proceedings from a 1993 conference sponsored by CEPLAES, CEOSL, and the ILO. Presents wide range of views on deteriorating employment opportunities during last 15 years.

2032 García de Véliz, Graciela and **Gaitán Villavicencio.** La transportación urbana en Guayaquil, 1985–1990: realidad y perspectivas. Guayaquil, Ecuador: Instituto de Investigaciones Económicas y Políticas; Quito: ILDIS, 1993. 95 p.: bibl. (Guayaquil futuro; 6)

Description and statistics on urban transport in Guayaquil, partially based on 1985 survey of drivers.

2033 Godard, Henry and **Fabián Peralta.** L'évolution des messages publicitaires des entreprises financièrs installées en Èquateur: un indicateur de la mondialisation de la communication, 1960–1991. (*Bull. Inst. fr. étud. andin.*, 22:3, 1993, p. 791–838, bibl., ill., graphs, maps, tables)

Interesting analysis of advertising messages by financial institutions from 1960–91. Shows increased use of regional and national personalities in recent years.

2034 Grindle, Merilee S. and **Francisco E. Thoumi.** Muddling toward adjustment: the political economy of policy change in Ecuador. (*in* Political and economic interactions in economic policy reform: evidence from eight countries. Oxford, UK: Cambridge, Mass.: Blackwell, 1993, p. 124–178)

Analyzes adjustment policies in 1982–83, 1984–86, and 1988–90-periods during which the introduction of reforms was followed by "a notable amount of slippage." Rich discussion of economic reform in the context of weak democratic institutions.

2035 Gylbert, Cécil. Destino Galápagos: la explotación comercial de un espacio protegido. Quito: Fundación Charles Darwin para las Islas Galápagos; ORSTOM, 1993. 101 p.: bibl. (Fundación Charles Darwin contribución; 516)

For review see item **2048**. See also item **2049.**

2036 Hofman, André A. and **Rudolf M. Buitelaar.** Ventajas comparativas extraordinarias y crecimiento a largo plazo: el caso de Ecuador. (*CEPAL Rev.*, 54, Dec. 1994, p. 149–166, bibl., graphs, tables)

Dutch Disease analysis of economic growth in Ecuador during the 20th century. Argues that, to avoid previous problems, economic liberalization requires sound public policy.

2037 Hurtado, Osvaldo. Perspectivas económicas y políticas del Ecuador. Quito: Corporación de Estudios para el Desarrollo (CORDES), 1997. 47 p.: bibl., ill., tables. (Serie Temas de economía y política, 1)

First publication of a new series by CORDES. Includes three timely and thoughtful presentations by Osvaldo Hurtado, Luis Jácome, and Mario Ribadeneira on politics, economics, and business, respectively, during the Alarcón presidency.

2038 Jácome, Luis Ignacio. Ecuador: the country's progress from chronic to moderate inflation. (*CEPAL Rev.*, 52, April 1994, p. 115–128, bibl., graphs, tables)

An English-language version of item **2039,** focusing on the 1992 stabilization.

2039 Jácome, Luis Ignacio. La experiencia de estabilización en el Ecuador. Quito: Corporación de Estudios para el Desarrollo, 1994. 54 p.: bibl. (Apunte técnico; 28)

Analyzes three episodes of stabilization policies adopted in 1982, 1988, and 1992. Deems most recent attempt, undertaken by the Durán-Ballén administration, as the most successful. Complements item **2028.**

2040 Jakubson, George and **George Psacharopoulos.** The effect of education on female labor force participation and earnings in Ecuador. (*in* Case studies on women's employment and pay in Latin America. Washington: World Bank, 1992, p. 255–271, bibl., tables)

Explores why women with similar levels of education and experience continue to earn less than men. Finds differences in labor market structure most important.

2041 Jameson, Kenneth P. Higher education in a vacuum: stress and reform in Ecuador. (*High. Educ.*, 33, April 1997, p. 265–281, bibl.)

Useful survey of higher education in Ecuador includes statistics on institutions and enrollment. Highlights reforms taking place at the institutional level despite the

absence of central government policy initiatives.

2042 Josling, Tim. Agricultural trade policies in the Andean Group: issues and options. Washington: World Bank, 1997. iv, 35 p.: bibl. (World Bank technical paper, 0253–7494; 364)

Chapter on Ecuador offers a comparison with other Andean Pact countries. Argues that Ecuador is most in need of stability and security offered by regional market access.

2043 Lucio-Paredes, Pablo *et al.* Paquetazo: las medidas de Sixto y Dahik. Quito: Editorial El Conejo, 1992. 148 p. (Col. Ecuador/hoy)

Collection of articles critical of 1992 economic policies of the Sixto Durán-Ballén administration (1992–96). Useful principally for overview of policies.

2044 Luna Osorio, Luis. Competir en el mundo y exportar. Quito: ITSA, 1995. 229 p.: bibl. (Col. ITSA; 1)

Overview of Ecuador's foreign trade sector written as a text. Useful introduction to basic trade statistics and institutional arrangements.

Luna Tamayo, Milton. Las trampas históricas de la industria ecuatoriana: su frustrada constitución como clase. See item **5030.**

Maiguashca, Juan. Los sectores subalternos en los años 30 y el aparecimiento del velasquismo. See *HLAS 56:2745.*

2045 Mancero Samán, Alfredo. Seguridad social y vejez: la privatización de los fondos de pensiones. Quito: CORDES, 1994. 292 p.: bibl.

Solid analysis of reform proposals for Ecuadorian social security system in context of theory and experience of other countries. Argues against privatization based on Chilean model. See also item **2047.**

2046 Mapa de necesidades básicas insatisfechas del Ecuador. Dirección técnica de Consuelo Aguinaga C. Colaboración de Marlene Haro I. Procesamiento de Mario Herrera. Edición y revisión de estructura y contenido de Galo Arias V. y Raúl Sosa. Ecuador: República del Ecuador, Vicepresidencia de la República, Instituto Nacional de Estadística y Censos (INEC), 1994. 128 p.: bibl., ill.

INEC publication based on 1990 population census. Useful to compare with 1982 census. Finds population with unsatisfied basic needs from 1982–90 increased for rural areas, and declined for urban areas, with the net result that national rates fell slightly over this period.

2047 Mesa-Lago, Carmelo. Instituto Ecuatoriano de Seguridad Social (IESS): evaluación económica y opciones para reforma. Quito: INCAE, 1993. 127 p.: bibl.

Solid study by a leading authority. Predicts a severe financial crisis by 1995 and suggests creation of a combined public/private system as a possible solution.

2048 Miras, Claude de; Christophe Grenier; and Marco Andrade. Censo de los establecimientos comerciales urbanos (1993) de Puerto Ayora (Isla Santa Cruz), Puerto Baquerizo Moreno (Isla San Cristóbal), Puerto Villamil (Isla Esabela), Provincias de Galápagos, Ecuador. Quito: Fundación Charles Darwin para las Islas Galápagos; ORSTOM, 1994. 39 p.: ill. (Fundación Charles Darwin contribución; 515)

One of a three-volume study of commercial activity in the Galápagos Islands. Useful data on growth in tourism industry and conflicts with environmental sustainability in an ecologically fragile region. See also items **2049** and **2035.**

2049 Miras, Claude de. Las Islas Galápagos—un reto económico: tres contradicciones básicas. Simposio: perspectivas científicas y de manejo para las Islas Galápagos. Quito: Fundación Charles Darwin para las Islas Galápagos; ORSTOM, 1995. 16 p.: ill. (Fundación Charles Darwin contribución; 513)

For review see item **2048.** See also item **2035.**

2050 Pichón, Francisco J. Colonist land-allocation decisions, land use, and deforestation in the Ecuadorian Amazon frontier. (*Econ. Dev. Cult. Change,* 45:4, July 1997, p. 707–744, tables)

Uses 1990 survey data from Napo and Sucumbios provinces for empirical analysis. Concludes that deforestation depends on roads, claim size, and land tenure policies. Discusses policy alternatives. Useful. See also item **2060.**

2051 Pineo, Ronn F. Social and economic reform in Ecuador: life and work in Guayaquil. Gainesville: Univ. Press of Florida, 1996. 245 p.: bibl., ill., index, map.

Important, empirically grounded portrait of life in Guayaquil at the turn of the century. Situates social changes in context of cacao boom. Notes the cacao industry did not contribute to the development of a significant middle class (who might lobby for urban reform), nor to the emergence of an organized lower class.

2052 Potencial impacto ambiental de las industrias en el Ecuador: exploración preliminar y soluciones. Dirección general y recopilación de Marco A. Encalada Reyes. Quito: Fundación Natura, 1991. 651 p.: ill.

Catalog of production processes, environmental impacts, and alternative technologies to reduce environmental damage for 39 industries.

2053 Regulation and the informal economy: microenterprises in Chile, Ecuador, and Jamaica. Edited by Víctor E. Tokman and Emilio Klein. Boulder, Colo.: Lynne Rienner Publishers, 1996. 217 p.: bibl., ill., index.

Surveys enterprises with less than 10 employees and low capitalization. Describes tax and labor laws and finds common patterns across the three countries: males predominate among owners, women among workers and self-employed; and higher education is associated with larger, better-capitalized firms.

2054 Robalino, César; Ana Lucía Armijos; and Augusto de la Torre. The Brady Ecuador deal. Washington: The World Bank, 1994. 18 p.: graphs, tables.

Solid analysis of the 1994 Brady Plan agreement for Ecuador's external debt by high-level economic policymakers. Useful background on an important topic.

2055 Rosero Bixby, Luis. La diversificación de las exportaciones agrícolas: el caso del mango. (*Ecuad. Deb.,* 30, dic. 1993, p. 125–140, photo, tables)

Case study of mango export industry development in context of Ecuador's non-traditional agricultural exports. In contrast to other studies of non-traditionals, this focuses on a coastal crop. Complements item **2061.**

2056 Salgado Peñaherrera, Germánico. Del desarrollo al espejismo: el tránsito de la economía ecuatoriana en los años 60 y 70. Quito: Corporación Editora Nacional, 1995. 194 p.: bibl. (Biblioteca de ciencias sociales; 45)

General economic history of the 1960s–70s by a noted analyst and policymaker.

2057 Salgado Peñaherrera, Germánico; Luis Ignacio Jácome; and Mauricio Pozo. Ecuador y Perú: economía y desarrollo. Quito: CORDES, 1995. 132 p.: bibl., ill.

Comparative survey of Ecuadorian and Peruvian economic development from 1950 to present written in aftermath of 1995 conflict. A noteworthy comparison despite its solely Ecuadorian authorship.

2058 Tassara Sancho, Alberto. Ecuador: conyuntura 1995; primer semestre. Quito: CORDES, 1995. 37 p.: graphs, tables. (Apunte técnico; 29)

Typical solid survey of Ecuadorian economic performance from CORDES. A valuable reference. See also item **2059.**

2059 Tassara Sancho, Alberto. Ecuador: conyuntura 1995; segundo semestre. Quito: CORDES, 1995. 30 p.: graphs, tables. (Apunte técnico; 31)

For review see item **2058.**

2060 Thapa, Keshari K.; Richard E. Bilsborrow; and Laura L. Murphy. Deforestation, land use, and women's agricultural activities in the Ecuadorian Amazon. (*World Dev.,* 24:8, Aug. 1996, p. 1317–1332, bibl., graph, map, tables)

Uses 1990 household survey data in a recursive model to test women's participation in agriculture as a function of land use and land area cleared. Finds pasture places fewer burdens on women than coffee, but contributes more to deforestation.

2061 Thrupp, Lori Ann; Gilles Bergeron; and William F. Waters. Bittersweet harvests for global supermarkets: challenges in Latin America's agricultural export boom. Washington: World Resources Institute, 1995. 214 p.: bibl., ill., map.

Critical analysis of non-traditional agricultural exports in Latin America with many examples from Ecuador. Helps put Ecuadorian industry in a broader context.

Valenzuela G., Jaime. Actividades urbanas y control de los usos del suelo: hacia una zonificación del centro metropolitano. See item **2841.**

2062 Vicuña Izquierdo, Leonardo. Crisis, ajustes y renegociación. Guayaquil, Ecuador: Univ. de Guayaquil, Facultad de Ciencias Económicas, Depto. de Publicaciones, 1994. 191 p.: bibl., ill.

Overview of economic policy in 1992–93, with discussion of 1994 debt renegotiation. See also item **2043.**

CHILE

MARKOS J. MAMALAKIS, *Professor of Economics, University of Wisconsin-Milwaukee*

ON NOVEMBER 18, 1996, Chile and Canada signed a free trade agreement in Ottawa, Canada. After growing 8.5 percent in 1995, Chilean total output grew at about 7.0 percent in 1996. Economic institutionality under President Eduardo Frei is in harmony with the successful framework created during Gen. Pinochet's presidency and reinforced during the democratic rule of President Aylwin. Political, social and economic freedoms are increasingly enjoyed within the post-Pinochet democratic regime. Environmental issues are receiving increased, but nevertheless inadequate, attention.

Chilean average per capita income in 1993, measured in purchasing power parity (PPP) dollars, was $8,400, compared to $24,240 for the US in the same year. Per capita income of the poorest 20 percent of households was (PPP) $1,386 in Chile, compared to $5,814 in the US. A profound, largely non-polemic, constructive debate is permeating Chile regarding implementing fundamental strategies for accelerating growth, reducing poverty and inequality, and ultimately, permitting Chile to compete as a developed nation. However, the promising research in this area remains largely incomplete.

Most issues and dimensions of the Chilean economy have been rigorously reviewed and analyzed. The quantity and quality of studies examining such topics as privatization, the social security system, agriculture, industry, mining, education, banking, trade relationships, education and the nonprofit sector are impressive. Macro and micro studies abound. Mesoanalysis of groups and sectors remains limited, if not inadequate.

Although well-researched studies of the relative distribution of private income and consumption and a few focusing on the relative distribution of semipublic (intermediate) consumption and income exist, overall there are major gaps in the knowledge of the nature, causes and cures of inequality and poverty. More research is necessary for understanding the distribution of income among classes (labor and capital), sectors, regions, by gender, and within the labor and property income groups. The relationship between various dimensions of inequality of distribution and poverty on the one hand, and output growth and welfare on the other hand requires attention. Improved statistics on poverty, distribution and inequality are also needed.

All studies reviewed in this section make important contributions to our understanding of the historical evolution of the Chilean economy. The following works stand out in terms of their singular quality: 1) Juan Gabriel Valdes examines the profound impact of the Chicago School on Chile during the Pinochet presidency and beyond (item **2137**); 2) Hojman studies education, health, labor markets, foreign trade, and saving and investment (item **2100**); 3) Foxley discusses causes of President Aylwin's successful democratic government (item **2092**); 4) MIDEPLAN, guided by Sergio Molina, describes Aylwin's strategy of growth with equity (item **2121**); and 5) CIEDESS provides a comprehensive study of the Chilean social security system (item **2111**).

2063 **Acevedo A., Roberto** *et al.* Chile hacia el 2000: ideas para el desarrollo. Edición de Felipe Larraín B. Santiago: Centro de Estudios Públicos, 1994. 562 p.: bibl., ill.

A group of distinguished scholars and policymakers presents detailed views covering all major aspects of Chile's future economic development.

2064 **Aedo, Cristián** and **Osvaldo Larrañaga.** The Chilean experience. (*in* Social service delivery systems: an agenda for reform. Washington: Inter-American Development Bank, 1994, p. 13–49, bibl., tables)

Describes Chile's social programs in health, education, financial assistance, and nutrition, and discusses the results of an econometric evaluation of quality and de-

mand in Chile's elementary education. Economic policy lessons are drawn from Chile's experience with such social policy issues as targeting, decentralization, private delivery, and cost recovery for over a decade.

2065 **Agacino, Rafael; Gonzalo Rivas;** and **Enrique Román.** Apertura y eficiencia productiva: la experiencia chilena, 1975–1989. Washington: Depto. de Desarrollo Económico y Social, Banco Interamericano de Desarrollo, 1992. 153 p.: bibl. (Serie de documentos de trabajo; 113)

An evaluation of the adjustment of the Chilean economy, in particular the industrial sector, to the post-1973 foreign trade liberalization. Examines the impact of liberalization on production, the nature of institutional reforms, and macroeconomic achievements. Suggests that participation of labor in the design of adjustment policies could reduce social tensions and facilitate the transition toward greater competitiveness. Recommends a more aggressive State role as an agent of technological and financial transfers.

2066 Agosin, Manuel R.; J. Rodrigo Fuentes; and Leonardo Letelier. Chile: the origins and consequences of external capital. (*in* Foreign capital in Latin America. Edited by José Antonio Ocampo and Roberto Steiner. Washington: Inter-American Development Bank, 1994, p. 103–142, appendix, bibl., graphs, tables)

Analyzes the determinants, macroeconomic management, and effects of external capital inflows on the Chilean economy. Suggests that pragmatic policies could make a significant contribution to economic growth.

2067 Agosin, Manuel R. El retorno de los capitales extranjeros privados a Chile. (*Trimest. Econ.*, 62:248, oct./dic. 1995, p. 467–494, bibl., graphs, tables)

An evaluation of the magnitude, composition, determinants, and effects of the huge capital inflows into the Chilean economy since 1987. The large share of this capital inflow, in the form of foreign direct investment, has contributed to an increase in the rate of investment. The most important determinant of short-term capital flows has been the interest rate differential between Chile and the US, corrected for devaluation expectations. Heterodox exchange rate policies have successfully discouraged volatile short-term and portfolio capital inflows which had reduced the effectiveness of macroeconomic policy and led to exchange rate appreciation.

2068 Antecedentes estadísticos de la distribución del ingreso en los años ochenta. v. 6, Chile y México. Santiago: Naciones Unidas, Comisión Económica para América Latina y el Caribe, 1993. 8 v. (Serie Distribución del ingreso; 10–17)

Statistics of the relative distribution of household income in 1989–90 at the national level, in Greater Santiago, and in other urban areas.

2069 Arbeláez Martínez, Beatriz. La privatización como alternativa para el sector público de países en desarrollo. Bogotá: Univ. Externado de Colombia, 1993. 195 p.: bibl.

Comprehensive discussion of privatization process in developing countries provides case studies for Chile, Malaysia, and Nigeria. [J. Foley]

2070 Arrizabalo Montoro, Xabier. Milagro o quimera: la economía chilena durante la dictadura. Madrid: Libros de la Catarata, 1995. 319 p.: bibl. (Los libros de la catarata)

A critical examination of Chile's neoliberal experiment during the Presidency of Gen. Augusto Pinochet Ugarte from a Marxist-structuralist perspective.

2071 Auge exportador chileno: lecciones y desafíos futuros. Edición de Patricio Meller y Raúl Sáez. Santiago: CIEPLAN; Dolmen Ediciones, 1995. 243 p.: bibl., ill.

A comprehensive review of the Chilean export sector between 1960–94. Presents lessons that can be derived from this experience and examines future challenges.

2072 Avanzando en equidad: un proceso de integración al desarrollo, 1990–1992. Santiago: Ministerio de Planificación y Cooperación (MIDEPLAN), 1992. 151 p.: ill.

The fruits of Chilean development have rarely been shared by the masses of the poor. This important report by Sergio Molina Silva, Minister of Planning and Cooperation, presents the anti-poverty policies of integration, participation, modernization, and development carried out during the first two years of the Aylwin presidency. Post-Pinochet democratic Chile faces the dual challenge of becoming and remaining competitive in the global economy and achieving growth with equity. The democratically elected government of President Patricio Aylwin delegated the primary responsibility of improving equity and distribution of income to Molina Silva. The present document contains a detailed account of the Ministry's (MIDEPLAN's) efforts to achieve the goal of growth with justice and equity.

2073 Baraona Urzúa, Pablo; Martín Costabal Llona; and Alvaro Vial. Mil días, mil por ciento: la economía chilena durante el gobierno de Allende. Santiago: Univ. Finis Terrae, 1993. xii, 97 p.: bibl. (Col. Univ. Finis Terrae. Economía)

Authors document the rise and fall of Chile's socialist experiment under President Salvador Allende. They aim to remind Chileans of the chaos created by the revolutionary, communist strategies. On the 20th anniversary of President Salvador Allende's and the Popular Unity's fall, a description of Allende's thousand days in power is presented. The authors focus on the major events, forces and consequences of Allende's reign.

2074 Bardón M., Alvaro. Una experiencia económica fallida: crónicas económicas (1971–1973) sobre el gobierno de la Unidad Popular. Santiago: Univ. Finis Terrae, 1993. 158 p.: bibl. (Col. Univ. Finis Terrae. Economía)

A valuable collection of previously published newspaper and other articles on basic economic policy issues by Alvaro Bardón Muñoz, former president of the Central Bank of Chile, Undersecretary of the Ministry of Economy, President of the State Bank of Chile, and major architect of Chile's post-1973 neoliberal paradigm during the Pinochet presidency.

2075 Bartell, Ernest. Perceptions by business leaders and the transition to democracy in Chile. (*in* Business and democracy in Latin America. Pittsburgh, Pa.: Univ. of Pittsburgh Press, 1995, p. 49–103)

A masterful examination of the attitudes of business leaders in Chile who had survived the Marxist attacks under Allende and the merciless forces of foreign competition, depression, and financial crises during the subsequent neoliberal experiment. Argues that the personal self-confidence of Chilean leaders interviewed in 1988 contributed to the subsequent economic growth, which in turn has reinforced the sense of stability and continuity that justifies further optimism.

2076 Basch, Miguel and Carlos Budnevich. Volatilidad y eficiencia en el mercado accionario: evidencia reciente para el caso chileno. (*Cuad. Econ./Santiago*, 31:92, abril 1994, p. 59–85, bibl., tables)

Observed Chilean stock market prices seem to be far more volatile than economic fundamentals seem to suggest. Detailed statistical tests support the hypothesis of some sort of fad behavior.

2077 Braun, Juan et al. Desafíos de la descentralización: propuestas para consolidar la autonomía y el financiamiento local y regional. Recopilación de Ignacio Irarrázaval Llona. Santiago: Centro de Estudios Públicos, 1993. 416 p.: bibl.

A collection of significant essays analyzing the multifaceted process of decentralization. Contains detailed proposals for the consolidation of local and regional autonomy and finance.

Bustos, Raúl. Reforma a los sistemas de pensiones: peligros de los programas opcionales en América Latina. See item **1275.**

2078 Cáceres, Carlos F. et al. Las tareas de hoy: políticas sociales y económicas para una sociedad libre. Recopilación de Cristián Larroulet. Santiago: Zig-Zag; Libertad y Desarrollo, 1994. 502 p.: bibl., ill. (Col. Temas de hoy)

Christián Larroulet, Juan Andrés Fontaine, Andrés Concha, Patricia Matte, Rosa Camhi, Antonio Sancho, Mercedes Cifuentes, Claudio Osorio, Juan Eduardo Errázuriz, and Rosanna Costa describe the macroeconomic policies, the reforms in education, health and justice, the infrastructure requirements, the new export phase, and the policies to remove poverty and establish an efficient State, which are necessary to advance a free society during the new era of Chilean democracy.

2079 Castro, Sergio de. Un camino de crecimiento para Chile. (*Estud. Públicos*, 53, verano 1994, p. 13–35)

Sergio de Castro, who shaped Chile's economic destiny and institutional, liberal reform as Minister of Economics (1974–76) and Minister of Finance (1976–82) during the Pinochet presidency, proposes further monetary, budgetary, educational, and health reforms, and privatization of public enterprises and CODELCO (Copper Company) as a means of raising Chile's annual income growth rate to 8–9 percent.

2080 Chacón, Boris; Berta Teitelboim G.; and Marcelo Albornoz D. Situación y características del empleo en Chile en 1990. Santiago: MIDEPLAN, División de Planificación, Estudios e Inversión [sic], Depto. de Planificación y Estudios Sociales, 1991? 51 leaves. (Documentos/sociales)

A detailed report on formal and informal employment in Chile in 1987 and 1990 both in non-agricultural and agricultural activities. Also contains information of employment by region, age, gender, level of income, indigenous and non-indigenous population, etc.

2081 Chile: subnational government finance. Washington: World Bank, 1993. 137 p.: ill., map. (A World Bank country study, 0253–2123)

Without significant and lasting sociopolitical change, Chile is not expected to join the club of developed nations. The present essay contains a thorough examination of the subnational government reforms that are needed to increase efficiency in the provision of basic health, education, housing, and other semipublic or public services.

2082 Coeymans A., Juan Eduardo and Felipe Larraín B. Efectos de un acuerdo de libre comercio entre Chile y Estados Unidos: un enfoque de equilibrio general. (*Cuad. Econ./Santiago*, 31:94, dic. 1994, p. 357–399, appendices, bibl., tables)

From an exclusive reliance on unilateral integration since the mid 1970s, Chile's trade strategy has shifted emphasis in the 1990's towards bilateral and regional integration within the American continents. In the past few years Chile has signed free trade agreements with Mexico, Colombia and Venezuela, and is now evaluating options with NAFTA and Mercosur. This paper examines the macroeconomic effects of a potential FTA (Free Trade Agreement) between Chile and the US using a computable general equilibrium model (CGE). It evaluates only the elimination of trade barriers between Chile and the US. The paper finds that potential gains from such a FTA would not be uniformly distributed across economic sectors. Sectors benefitting the most would be those that, in the initial position, face higher trade barriers in the US and have less competition from imports. The most important effect of this trade agreement, however, would be an increase in foreign investment into Chile, as a consequence of lower perceived country risk, of up to an additional two percent of GDP per year.

2083 Collins, Joseph and John Lear. Chile's free market: a second look. Foreword by Walden Bello. Epilogue by Stephanie Rosenfeld. Oakland, Calif.: Food First, 1995. 331 p.: bibl., index, map.

This polemic treatise attempts to prove that Chile's post-Allende neoliberal experiment cannot and should not be considered a "miracle." It contains a frontal attack against the free market, privatization, and

trade liberalization principles of Chile's neoliberal paradigm.

2084 Coloma C., Fernando. Subsidio de cesantía: antecedentes y propuesta. Santiago: Pontificia Univ. Católica de Chile, Instituto de Economía, 1993. 74 p.: bibl. (Documento de trabajo, 0716–7334; 159)

An examination of the background of unemployment subsidies and a proposal for reform.

2085 Corbo, Vittorio. Las reformas económicas en Chile: una síntesis. (*Economía/Lima*, 17:33/34, julio/dic. 1994, p. 9–42, bibl., tables)

Careful review of the nature of the economic reforms in Chile between 1973–92 and the lessons that can be derived.

2086 Cuentas financieras de la economía chilena, 1986–1990. Santiago: Banco Central de Chile, 1995. 86 p.: tables.

A valuable presentation of Chile's financial accounts during 1986–90.

Díaz, Alvaro. Tendencias de la reestructuración económica y social en Latinoamérica. See item **2942.**

Edwards, Sebastian. Exchange-rate anchors, credibility, and inertia: a tale of two crises, Chile and Mexico. See item **1560.**

2087 Elter, Doris. El desmonte de los sistemas de seguridad social del Estado y su efecto en los derechos humanos en Chile. (*Otro derecho*, 7:1, 1995, p. 17–108, bibl., graph, tables)

An extensive analysis and evaluation of the Chilean social security system during the 1980–93 period.

2088 Falaha Lumi, Boris. Una evaluación crítica de los programas de transferencia tecnológica en el agro chileno. (*Rev. Sociol./Santiago*, 6/7, p. 135–150, table)

The transfer of technology to the agricultural sector can be successful only if it facilitates the complete integration and participation of farmers in the economy by assisting in the formulation and implementation of specific small scale production projects.

2089 Feliú, Manuel. Los desafíos de la empresa moderna: la batalla del capital humano. Santiago: Editorial Renacimiento, 1994. 218 p.

Manuel Feliú provides detailed arguments in favor of the role of private incentives, private ownership of means of production, and competitive markets as basic means of achieving both growth and equity.

2090 Fontaine, Juan Andrés. Inversiones extranjeras por fondos de pensiones: efectos sobre la política macroeconómica. (*Cuad. Econ./Santiago*, 31:93, agosto 1994, p. 161–183, bibl., graphs, table)

Chile has had a long experience with exchange controls. This paper reviews the macroeconomic arguments for capital controls, with special focus on those restricting international diversification by pension funds. It points out that progress has been slow in allowing pension funds to invest abroad and in removing certain restrictions to capital inflows.

2091 Fontaine, Juan Andrés. Transición económica y política en Chile: 1970–1990. (*Estud. Públicos*, 50, otoño 1993, p. 229–279, bibl., tables)

A systematic, careful examination of the economic and political transformations in Chile between 1970–90.

2092 Foxley, Alejandro. La economía política de la transición: el camino del diálógo. Santiago: Ediciones Dolmen, 1993. 245 p.: ill. (Col. Economía y gestión)

The Chilean transition to democracy has been, in spite of many problems, most successful. The present volume contains dialogues between Alejandro Foxley, a major architect of that process, and labor, business, the poor, political leaders, parliamentarians, and other economic agents and social organizations. These dialogues enhance our understanding of the success of President Aylwin's democratic government.

2093 Gill, Indermit S. Is there sex discrimination in Chile?: evidence from the CASEN survey. (*in* Case studies on women's employment and pay in Latin America. Washington: World Bank, 1992, p. 119–147, bibl., graphs, tables)

Examines the extent of and components of the earnings differential between men and women in Chile's formal economy. Reveals the existence of significant male-female earnings differentials across all schooling, age, and tenure levels. The statistical findings can be interpreted to mean that the Chilean labor market discriminates against

women. The results can also be explained in terms of intrinsic differences between female and male human capital. Collection and analysis of more refined work experience data would provide a better understanding of labor market phenomena, especially for women, than concentration on the issue of sampling bias of observed work histories.

2094 Godoy Arcaya, Oscar and **Salvador Valdés Prieto.** Democracia y previsión en Chile: experiencia con dos sistemas. (*Cuad. Econ./Santiago*, 31:93, agosto 1994, p. 135–161, appendix, table)

An excellent discussion of the evolution of Chile's social security system during the "old" and "new" democracies. Argues that the independence of the social security system from the political manipulations that were typical under the old democracy has created a more equitable system under the new democracy.

2095 Guardia, Alexis. Distribución del ingreso en Chile, 1990–1993, según la encuesta de hogares. (*Estad. Econ.*, 10, junio 1995, p. 7–32, bibl., tables)

A thorough, comprehensive examination of the distribution of income in Chile between 1990–93 according to the household survey.

2096 Guerrini, Owen. ¿Contango?: un relato personal; el affaire Codelco. Santiago: Emérida Ediciones, 1994. 127 p.

An extensive, valuable personal account of major aspects and circumstances of Chile's infamous 1994 "Davilazo" scandal, the "loss" of hundreds of millions of dollars by CODELCO (Chile's state-owned copper company) through actions involving Juan Pablo Dávila, Chief of the Dept. of Futures Markets of its sales office.

2097 Hachette, Dominique. Argentina: ¿socio posible? (*Cuad. Econ./Santiago*, 31:94, dic. 1994, p. 319–355, appendix, bibl., tables)

This article presents the main characteristics of bilateral trade between Chile and Argentina, summarizes a cost-benefit analysis of a possible integration, highlights significant problems that need to be solved before reaching complete integration, and presents some conclusions. Integration benefits are estimated to be small. Integration with Argentina could benefit Chile only if it is complete, the neighbor's macroeconomic stability is ensured, and if gross distortions (e.g. subsidy on oil derivatives) fade out in Argentina. A full integration scheme with Argentina (and NAFTA as well) would face resistance from farmers because it would stimulate significant transfers from wheat and vegetable oil input producers, and perhaps sugar too, to Chilean consumers. Because integration acts as a catalyst, solutions to these problems should be found quickly.

2098 Hachette, Dominique; Rolf J. Lüders; and **Guillermo Tagle.** Five cases of privatization in Chile. (*in* Privatization in Latin America. Edited by Manuel Sánchez and Rossana Corona. Washington: Inter-American Development Bank, 1993, p.41–100, bibl., tables)

Excellent analysis of six cases of privatization in Chile. The political objective of privatizations was to foster the dilution of power to ensure a lasting democratic regime. The economic objective was to turn the private sector, which was considered more efficient than the public one, into the engine of development. During the first round of privatizations they were also used by government to increase its revenues and reduce its deficit. Discusses methods, shortcomings, and lessons from the first and second round of privatizations.

Hey, Jeanne A.K. Ecuadorean foreign policy since 1979: ideological cycles or a trend towards neoliberalism? See item **4414.**

2099 Hofman, André A. Chile's economic performance in the 20th century: a comparative perspective. (*Estud. Econ./Santiago,* 20:1, junio 1993, p. 107–140, bibl., tables)

An excellent assessment of Chile's economic performance in the 20th century in a comparative perspective. First, economic performance is explained by quantifying such "proximate" causes of output and productivity growth as labor and capital services inputs, availability of natural resources and factors affecting the efficiency of resource use. Second, the role of such "ultimate" causes as institutions, interest groups, historical accidents, and external forces is examined.

2100 Hojman, D.E. Chile: the political economy of development and democracy in the 1990s. Pittsburgh, Pa.: Univ. of Pittsburgh

Press, 1993. 256 p.: bibl., index. (Pitt Latin American series)

This excellent, comprehensive study of education, health, labor markets, income distribution, the role of the State, copper, foreign trade, savings, investment, etc. until 1991, makes a significant contribution to our understanding of the Chilean development process. Hojman concludes "that all the technical and political conditions are there to solve any remaining or foreseeable problems, and that future government mistakes . . . . are likely to be small and swiftly corrected." (p. 203)

Hojman, D.E. Chile under Frei (again): the first Latin American tiger—or just another cat? See item **3628.**

2101 Hojman, D.E. Rent-seeking and corruption in a successful Latin American economy: Chile in the 1990s. (*in* International Congress of Americanists, *48th, Stockholm, 1994.* Problems of democracy in Latin America. Stockholm, Sweden: Institute of Latin American Studies, Stockholm Univ., 1996, p. 35–51, bibl.)

Argues that Chile could accelerate its income growth and reduce inequalities by eliminating rent-seeking and related corruption.

2102 Informe de coyuntura: evolución del empleo femenino, 1990–1993. Santiago: Servicio Nacional de la Mujer Depto. Planificación y Estudios, 1994. 18 p.: tables.

A statistical overview of the labor market of females during 1990–93.

Instituto Geográfico Militar (Chile). Atlas del desarrollo económico y social de Chile. See item **2815.**

Integración económica Argentino-Chilena. See item **2289.**

2103 Irarrázaval Llona, Ignacio. The role of community organizations in fighting poverty in Chile. (*in* Community organizations in Latin America. Edited by Juan Carlos Navarro. Washington: Inter-American Development Bank, 1994, p. 23–65, appendix, bibl., tables)

Systematic, highly informative, thorough examination of the size, nature, sources of finance, legal organization, goals, and efficiency of operation of the community organizations (OPC = organizaciones de participación comunitaria) that came into existence shortly after the military coup in 1973 and gained strength in the 1980s.

2104 Johansen, Oscar et al. Perspectivas económicas de Chile. Recopilación de Guillermo E. Martínez. Santiago: Corporación Libertas, 1992. 190 p.: ill.

Fifteen leading political figures, businessmen and academicians present, in brief essays, their diverse, pluralistic views about the economic prospects of democratic Chile. All major policy issues (from investment to improved distribution of income to elimination of poverty) are carefully examined.

2105 Kaufmann, Friedrich. La política de la pequeña y mediana empresa en Chile. (*Contribuciones/Buenos Aires*, 12:2, abril/junio 1995, p. 137–147, bibl., table)

Micro enterprises accounted for 8.3 percent of all enterprises in Chile in 1992. They created 40 percent of all jobs. Small enterprises accounted for 14 percent of all enterprises and created 34 percent of all jobs. This essay examines the conditions, problems, and the vital role played by micro, small, and medium-sized enterprises in eradicating poverty, strengthening democracy, and contributing to development. It suggests the need for a renewed climate of confidence between the State, enterprises, and individuals.

2106 Larroulet, Cristián. Impact of privatization on welfare: the Chilean case, 1985–1989. (*in* Bigger economies, smaller governments: privatization in Latin America. Boulder, Colo.: Westview Press, 1996, p. 369–395, bibl., tables)

Convincingly demonstrates that the transfer of property to private sectors in the second half of the 1980s was decisive in contributing to economic recovery by increasing efficiency, investment, creating thousands of new direct proprietors, and convincing the democratically elected government, which took office in March 1990, of the validity of the development strategy based on free markets and free trade.

2107 Levine Bawden, Flavián et al. Historias personales, políticas públicas: entrevistas de Margarita Serrano y Marcia Scantlebury. Recopilación de Oscar Muñoz Gomá. Santiago: Editorial Los Andes; Corporación de Investigaciones Económicas para Latinoamérica, 1993. 187 p.: ill. (Serie Diálogos)

Interviews of eight men who played leading roles in the debates and developments that defined Chile's economic life from the late 1930s-60s. Among the more interesting are those of Jorge Marshall, head of the Central Bank; Aníbal Pinto of CEPAL; entrepreneur Eugenio Heiremans; and Sergio Molina, who held important policy-making positions in the Ibáñez, Alessandri, and Frei governments. [M. Fleet]

2108 Lüders, Rolf J. Did privatization raise enterprise efficiency in Chile? (*in* Bigger economies, smaller governments: privatization in Latin America. Boulder, Colo.: Westview Press, 1996, p. 219–246, appendices, bibl., graphs, tables)

In the 1980s, private firms did not on average perform more efficiently than public sector firms. This happened because the military government established the same nondiscriminatory rules and regulations for private and public sector firms, and imposed strict self-financing policies and professional management for State-owned enterprises. In the long run, however, without privatization, authorities would have been induced to gain political support by granting rents to certain sectors of the population.

2109 Maloney, William F. Privatization with share diffusion: popular capitalism in Chile, 1985–1988. (*in* Privatization in Latin America: new roles for the public and private sectors. Westport, Conn.: Praeger, 1994 p. 135–161, bibl., graphs, tables)

A masterful examination of the Chilean paradigm of popular capitalism, including the accompanying policies of indirect popular capitalism and worker capitalism, as implemented during the far-reaching privatizations of 1985–88.

Mancero Samán, Alfredo. Seguridad social y vejez: la privatización de los fondos de pensiones. See item **2045.**

2110 Meller, Patricio. La apertura comercial chilena: enseñanzas de política. Washington: Depto. de Desarrollo Económico y Social, Banco Interamericano de Desarrollo, c1992. 56 p.: bibl., ill. (Serie de documentos de trabajo; 109)

Trade liberalization contributed to a more efficient allocation of resources and an improvement in welfare by lowering prices and increasing the variety of products available to the consumer. According to the Chilean experience of exports based on natural resources, significant benefits have also been derived by other activities and regions that add value to these composite commodities.

2111 Modernización de la seguridad social en Chile: resultados y tendencias. Santiago: Corporación de Investigación, Estudio y Desarrollo de la Seguridad Social (CIEDESS), 1994. 435 p.: graphs, tables.

Outstanding, comprehensive study describes the profound changes to the social security system that materialized during 1980–94. In addition to examining the historical evolution and present status of social security, services provided, institutions, evaluation, and projections, and containing detailed statistics, it also covers the institutionality and legal norms of social security of the Armed, Social Security, and Order Forces.

2112 Montecinos, Verónica. Economists, politics and the State: Chile 1958–1994. Amsterdam: CEDLA, 1988. 151 p.: appendix, bibl., ill. (CEDLA Latin America studies; 80)

Studies ascent of professional economists to high positions in government during last five administrations in Chile. Initially, economists were in control of economic policymaking, but gradually have increased their influence by occupying top positions throughout the State bureaucracy. Also looks at economists' role during and after Chile's transition to democratic rule. Research is based on more than 100 interviews with high-ranking government officials. The interviewees are listed in the appendix. [R. Hoefte]

Moss, Diana L. and **James R. Tybout.** The scope for fuel substitution in manufacturing industries: a case study of Chile and Colombia. See item **1999.**

2113 Muñoz Gomá, Oscar. Economy and society in Chile: frustration and change in the historical process. (*Int. Soc. Sci. J.,* 134, Nov. 1992, p. 487–501, photos)

A comprehensive review of the long-term process of economic development and change in Chile.

2114 Muñoz Gomá, Oscar and **Carmen Celedon.** Chile en transición: estrategia económica y política. (*in* La política económica en la transición a la democracia: lec-

ciones de Argentina, Bolivia, Chile, Uruguay. Santiago: CIEPLAN, 1993, p. 119–147, bibl., tables)

A solid, pragmatic review and analysis of the economic and political strategies of transition adopted during the first two years of the presidency of Patricio Aylwin. Also, a broad examination of many remaining challenges and a presentation of policies necessary to meet them.

2115 Nauriyal, Bharat B. Measures of cost economies in Chilean banking, 1984–1991. (*Rev. Anál. Econ.,* 10:1, junio 1995, p. 71–99, bibl., tables)

Presented are measures of cost economies in Chilean banking following the many regulatory and structural changes implemented by Chilean authorities in the aftermath of the 1981–83 financial system crisis. The findings suggest the presence of persistent and significant economies of scale. Weaker evidence on the presence of economies of scope is also detected.

2116 Parada D., J. Rigoberto. El FONDECYT y la investigación en economía. (*Estud. Soc./Santiago,* 85, trimestre 3, 1995, p. 49–82, bibl., graphs, tables)

Concludes that the development of the Fondo Nacional de Desarrollo Científico y Tecnológico (FONDECYT) has been a fundamental factor for the promotion of research in Chile. Its efficiency is evaluated by analyzing the project selection processes, the allocation of resources, and the actual distribution of funds, with particular emphasis on economic research.

2117 Paredes M., Ricardo and **Luis A. Riveros.** Chile. (*in* Human resources and the adjustment process. Edited by Ricardo Paredes and Luis A. Riveros. Washington: Inter-American Development Bank, 1994, p. 63–108, appendices, bibl., tables)

Claims that labor mobility has been limited because of the inappropriate enactment of human resource development programs. Recommends creation of flexible institutional and legal mechanisms that would promote labor mobility and closer links between labor costs and productivity.

2118 Paredes M., Ricardo. Jurisprudencia de las comisiones antimonopolios en Chile. (*Estud. Públicos,* 58, otoño 1995, p. 227–317, appendix, tables)

Claims that the impressive success of antimonopoly legislation in Chile since 1973 resulted from favorable structural change that centered on markets as the mechanism for allocating resources.

2119 Passicot Callier, Andrés. La situación de la economía nacional frente a la coyuntura internacional. (*Polít. Estrateg.*, 60, mayo/agosto 1993, p. 38–45)

Reviews challenges faced by the Chilean economy in the international environment and suggests a multi-pronged strategy to meet them. Concludes that Chile must, above all, preserve the new institutional framework created between 1973–93.

2120 Peña, Julio and Javier Núñez. On the regulation of marine industrial fisheries: the case of Chile. (*Estud. Econ. /Santiago*, 21:1, junio 1994, p. 125–162, bibl., tables)

For more than 50 years Chilean marine fisheries were ruled by "historical rights" in the issuance of fishing permits. From 1988–91, there arose a strong debate about the efficiency of the prevailing regulatory framework. After prolonged discussions, a political agreement was reached whereby only a partial, and non-compulsory, use of Individual Transferrable (Catch) Quotas is allowed, provided that a consensus concerning biological overfishing is reached. This important paper reviews the process of reforms and negotiations that led to this outcome.

2121 Población, educación, vivienda, salud, empleo y pobreza: CASEN 1990. Santiago: MIDEPLAN, 1992. 445 p.: bibl., ill.

A primary goal of the Aylwin presidency has been achievement of growth with equity. Chile, as well as most of Latin America, has experienced high levels of poverty and welfare inequality for as long as statistical information is available. This volume contains the best survey data (1990) demonstrating the redistributive impact of public expenditures between 1987–90. It also identifies the poor, their incomes, and other features, and proposes detailed anti-poverty programs. Includes an introduction by Sergio Molina Silva, Minister of Planning and Cooperation, who has spearheaded the anti-poverty campaign.

Pressaco, Carlos Fabián. Partidos políticos y rol del Estado en la economía: acuerdos e intereses. See item **3650.**

2122 Raczynski, Dagmar. Políticas sociales y programas de combate a la pobreza en Chile: balance y desafíos. (*Colecc. Estud. CIEPLAN*, 39, junio 1994, p. 9–73, bibl., tables)

An excellent analysis of the social policies and programs attacking poverty in Chile. After a review of the historical evolution of social policies, it focuses on three specific programs related to the quality of education, the exclusion of poor youth from labor markets, and increased voice, information, and participation of social organizations in poor areas. Describes progress as well as much unfinished business.

2123 Ramírez, Apolonia. Empresa de FFCC del Estado: un caso de privatización en democracia. Santiago: Ediciones Janequeo; Programa de Economía del Trabajo, 1993. 173 p.: bibl.

A contribution to the ongoing debate about the role of State railroads in Chilean economic development within the overall transportation activity.

2124 Ramos, Joseph R. El problema del empleo: enfoques ortodoxos y estructurales. (*Cuad. Econ. /Santiago*, 30:90, agosto 1993, p. 225–246, graphs)

Contrasts the orthodox approach, which sees the roots of the employment problem primarily in the rigidities and imperfections of the labor market, to the structural approach, which attributes the bulk under- and unemployment problems in developing countries to failures in markets complementary to the labor market, such as those of human capital, physical capital, technology, and goods. Examines in detail the principal sources of "structural" under- and unemployment in an effort to demonstrate the greater relevance and policy richness of this approach.

Regulation and the informal economy: microenterprises in Chile, Ecuador, and Jamaica. See item **2053.**

2125 Riquelme, Silvia. Cómo ganar dinero en Chile: empresarios revelan el secreto de su éxito. Santiago: Zig-Zag, 1994. 222 p.: ill. (Col. Temas de hoy)

Entrepreneurs played a pivotal role in Chilean economic development, especially after 1973. This fascinating volume contains the stories of 34 successful Chilean entrepreneurs, revealing the dynamic, human side of Chile's process of privatization, liberalization, and deregulation.

2126 Robbins, Donald J. Relative wage structure in Chile, 1957–1992: changes in the structure of demand for schooling. (*Estud. Econ./Santiago,* 21, no. especial, nov. 1994, p. 49–78, bibl., tables)

Movement from protectionism to trade liberalization, it has been hypothesized, will decrease the relative wages of skilled versus unskilled labor (or "relative wages"). Paper argues that this did not happen in Chile. Between-industry demand changes were small. Changes in the relative demand for differing schooling levels inside industries or "within-industry" demand changes caused relative wages to rise. Results suggest that for trade liberalizations to be successful and equitable, high and growing levels of university educated workers may be needed.

2127 Robbins, Donald J. Should educational spending be redistributed from higher to primary education in LDC's?: a note with application to Chile. (*Rev. Anál. Econ.,* 10:1, junio 1995, p. 37–51, bibl., graphs, tables)

The reduction in Chile of relative spending on education at a time when wage dispersion was growing rapidly due to skill-based demand, does not appear to have been justified on efficiency grounds. This redistribution exacerbated the rising relative wages, contributed to the rising inequality of earnings, and, in combination with the growth of private universities, may have worsened one dimension of inter-generational inequality.

2128 Román, Enrique. La pequeña industria ante el reto de la modernización: reestructuración industrial chilena, 1975–1989. Santiago: Ediciones del Ornitorrinco; Friedrich Ebert Stiftung, 1991. 240 p.: bibl., ill.

A comprehensive examination of Chile's industrial sector during 1975–89. Combines empirical, historical, and analytical approaches to provide valuable insights into recent industrialization process.

2129 Rosende R., Francisco. La autonomía del Banco Central de Chile: una evaluación preliminar. (*Cuad. Econ./Santiago,* 30:91, dic. 1993, p. 293–325, bibl., tables)

Reviews discussion on Chile's Central Bank independence and evaluates the bank's performance under its new (since Dec. 1989)

legal status. Concludes that its autonomy has achieved an important degree of public acceptance, in spite of some initial, mainly politically motivated, difficulties. The bank's achievement of reduced inflation has been painless in terms of income growth and unemployment thanks to a strong real exchange rate depreciation.

2130 Saavedra-Rivano, Neantro. Chile and regional integration. (*in* Cooperation or rivalry: regional integration in the Americas and the Pacific Rim. Boulder, Colo.: Westview Press, 1996, p. 97–111, tables)

Systematic review of Chile's international trade relationships with the US, Mexico, Canada (NAFTA), Latin America, the Pacific Rim countries, and Europe.

Silva, Eduardo. From dictatorship to democracy: the business-State nexus in Chile's economic transformation, 1975–1994. See item **3667.**

2131 Silva, Eduardo. The State and capital in Chile: business elites, technocrats, and market economics. Boulder, Colo.: Westview Press, 1996. 282 p.: bibl.

In this book-length extension of an earlier article on economic policy under Pinochet, Silva analyzes the interplay of social groups (principally capitalists and landowners), state structure, economic ideas, and international factors in affecting economic policy agenda setting, formulation, and implementation. He stresses the importance of shifting coalitions of economic elites, challenging the view that the regime's technocratic advisers were either of a single mind or immune to outside pressures. [M. Fleet]

2132 Statistical synthesis of Chile, 1988–1992. Santiago: Gerencia de División Estudios, Banco Central de Chile, 1993. 54 p.: graphs, tables.

Excellent collection of basic statistics for the 1988–92 period.

2133 Sunkel, Osvaldo. Is the Chilean "miracle" sustainable? (*J. Interam. Stud. World Aff.,* 37:3, Fall 1995, p. 1–7)

If Chile is to increase the growth rate of its exports and output to the extent necessary to become a developed economy, and if it is to eliminate poverty and reduce inequality, it must improve the utilization and conservation of its natural resources. This is a necessary condition for the transition from an unsustainable to an environmentally sustainable economic growth path that is in harmony with social equity and democracy.

2134 Too good to be true. (*Banker/London*, 145:837, Nov. 1995, p. 86–87, table)
Brief but balanced evaluation of Chile's economic and financial strengths and weaknesses in 1995.

2135 La transformación de la producción en Chile : cuatro ensayos de interpretación. Santiago: Naciones Unidas, Comisión Económica para America Latina y el Caribe, 1993. 372 p.: bibl., ill. (Estudios e informes de la CEPAL, 0256–9795 ; 84)
These four essays provide a detailed analysis of Chile's structural transformation of production during 1948–88. Special emphasis is placed on the relationship between structural transformation and international competitiveness. Carefully examines the role of the Chilean Development Corporation, copper mining, and export diversification.

2136 Valdés, Alberto and **Barry Schaeffer.** Surveillance of agricultural price and trade policies: a handbook for Chile. Washington: The World Bank, 1995. xi, 71 p.: bibl., ill. (World Bank technical paper; 291)
Presents and discusses the methodology and results of calculating the Nominal Protection Rate (NPR), Effective Protection Rate (EPR), Effective Rate of Assistance (ERA), and Producer Subsidy Equivalent (PSE) for Chile on apples, grapes, beef, maize, milk, sugar beets, and wheat for 1984–93.

2137 Valdés, Juan Gabriel. Pinochet's economists: the Chicago school of economics in Chile. Cambridge; New York:

Cambridge Univ. Press, 1995. 347 p.: bibl., index. (Historical perspectives on modern economics)
A fascinating, masterful, generally objective, critical examination of Chilean economic development primarily between 1973–94. Focuses on the role of the Chicago School in reshaping the economic structure and destiny of Chile during the Pinochet, Aylwin, and Frei presidencies. Describes the rise to prominence of the Chicago School actors in the Pinochet government, the implantation of the Chicago School in Chile, the two phases of power of the Chicago School actors, the progress towards a stable economy, and the return to democracy. Concludes "that the Chicago revolution has left an indelible stamp on Chilean society's complex route towards modernity" (p. 280).

Valenzuela G., Jaime. Actividades urbanas y control de los usos del suelo: hacia una zonificación del centro metropolitano. See item **2841.**

2138 Vicuña P., Ricardo. La política de acuerdos de libre comercio de Chile. (*Cuad. Econ./Santiago*, 31:94, dic. 1994, p. 305–317, bibl.)
This paper examines Chile's "new trade strategy" since 1990 which involves negotiating free trade agreements with several regional partners and an invitation to be a member of NAFTA and to negotiate its association with Mercosur. This strategy is a departure from its old, exclusively unilateral, tariff reduction approach. It presents the economic rationale behind this "new strategy" and the challenges that it imposes for the future.

PERU

CATALINA RABINOVICH, *Consultant, Hispanic Division, Library of Congress, Washington, D.C.*

AS OF THE MID-1990S IN PERU, Fujimori had been reelected and the dramatic economic shifts that had gripped the country ceased. The liberalization process which started at the beginning of the decade continues, however the implementation of the remaining privatizations has slowed considerably. Macroeconomics are no longer of interest. Some signs of populism are beginning to appear, even within economic policies. Nevertheless, the essential goals of the first Fujimori Administration continue to define the current term: the end of terrorism, the control of inflation, and Peru's reconnection to international economic institutions. Despite the enormous economic and social problems that remain, including the need to strengthen democratic institutions, peace and stability have gained a foothold. Within this relative calm, professionals and researchers are no longer forced to play the role of fire-fighters as they had for the past three decades. Instead of devoting all their energy to managing crises and dowsing panic, they now have the time and space to think, be creative, and develop specific economic and social programs. The works annotated in this section reflect this new-found freedom. Many of the studies incorporate current issues, such as gender, ecology, globalization, agriculture and agribusiness, and last but not least, analyses of a fascinating Peruvian phenomenon, Gamarra. It is a pleasure to evaluate issues as important as the ones dealt with during this biennium, leaving to others the role of extinguishing fires.

2139 Agreda Ugas, Víctor *et al.* Comerciali-zación agrícola en el Perú. Edición de Javier Escobal. Lima: Grupo de Análisis para el Desarrollo (GRADE); Agencia para el Desarrollo Internacional (AID), 1994. 329 p.: bibl.

Until recently there has been limited discussion about agricultural marketing in Peru. Despite elimination of certain restrictions, the market's efficiency has not improved. This work analyzes market imperfections due to both existing noncompetitive structures and the presence of externalities.

2140 Aguilar, Víctor; Leonith Hinojosa; and Carlos Milla. Turismo y desarrollo: po-sibilidades en la región Inka. Colaboración de Werner Nordt. Cusco: CARTUC; Centro de Estudios Regionales Andinos Bartolomé de Las Casas, 1992. 108 p.: ill. (Estudios y debates regionales andinos)

Examines Cusco's tourist infrastructure as of 1992, before the capture of Abimael Guzmán. Proposes strategies for development of tourism within the framework of national development.

Alvarez, Elena H. Economic development, restructuring and the illicit drug sector in Bolivia and Peru: current policies. See item **2181.**

Análisis de cadenas agroindustriales en Ecuador y Perú. See item **2017.**

2141 Anderson, Jeanine *et al.* Pobreza y polí-ticas sociales en el Perú. Lima: Univ. del Pacífico, Centro de Investigación; Taller de Políticas y Desarrollo Social, 1994. 433 p.: bibl., ill.

Gathers documentation on poverty produced by four research centers during 1991–92. Fernández Baca and Seinfeld conclude, for example, that "the empirical evidence suggests that the quality of the stock of human capital . . . may turn out to be a key factor for an economic take-off." Very thorough work.

2142 Arroyo Ferreyros, Juan Carlos. Babel: antecedentes, interrogantes y alternati-vas para el transporte público de Lima. Lima?: Talleres Gráficos de Editorial San Marcos, 1991? 221 p.: bibl., ill.

Offers technical suggestions for the chaotic public transportation system in Lima.

2143 Beltrán, Pedro G. Pensamiento y ac-ción: selección de textos. Lima: Instituto de Economía de Libre Mercado, 1994. 472 p.: bibl., facsims., ill.

Reissue of Beltrán's writings from 1946–79. Topcis remain current since policies similar to those he espoused as Minister of Economics (1959–61) are once again being implemented.

2144 Botteri, Giancarlo *et al.* Ensayos sobre la realidad económica peruana. v. 1. Lima: Univ. del Pacífico, Centro de Investigación, 1993. 1 v.: ill. (Serie Cuadernos de investigación; 19)

High quality analysis of important economic topics by senior undergraduates from the Univ. del Pacífico.

2145 Brush, Stephen B. *et al.* La chacra de papa: economía y ecología. Recopilación de Enrique Mayor. Lima: CEPES, 1992. 294 p.: ill., maps.

A creative interdisciplinary study on the peasant economy. Contains three sections: 1) a profitability analysis of the potato crop that traces the transition from consumer subsidies to "liberalization," with its current price distortions; 2) an analysis of the persistence of *aparceria* in peasant communities, a topic that has been taboo since the 1969 agrarian reform; and 3) a review of widely prevailing idea that the introduction of modern crops diminishes biological diversity.

2146 Caminos entrelazados: la realidad del empleo urbano en el Perú. Edición de Gustavo Yamada Fukusaki. Lima: Univ. del Pacífico, Centro de Investigación, 1996. 450 p.: bibl., ill.

Yamada and a group of young economists apply novel labor economics theories to the current economic situation. Conclude that within the labor market, more than half of the self-employed or micro-enterprise workers earn more than their cost of opportunity in the formal sector, casting aside prevailing pessimistic views.

2147 Cannock, Geoffrey and **Alberto Gonzales-Zúñiga.** Economía agraria. Lima: Univ. del Pacífico, 1994. 514 p.: bibl., ill. (Biblioteca universitaria; 22. Agroempresa)

Didactic study of the principles of agrarian economics incorporating Peruvian case studies.

2148 Convención Nacional del Agro Peruano, *1st, Lima, 1994.* CONVEAGRO '94: I Convención Nacional del Agro Peruano, Huampani 13–15 julio de 1994, Lima, Peru; exposiciones, principales acuerdos, conclusiones, recomendaciones. Lima: Asociación de Promoción Agraria, 1994. 203 p.: ill.

After the various phases of agrarian reform which have occurred in Peru since the 1960s, CONVEAGRO gathered representatives of the current agrarian institutions from all over the country. Topics discussed included agricultural development, liberalization of the economy, and the diminishing of the role of the State.

2149 Cornejo Ramírez, Enrique. La fuga invisible: fuga de capitales y comercio exterior en el Perú. Lima: Univ. de Lima, Facultad de Economía, 1993. 696 p.: bibl.

Analysis of the loss of foreign exchange through capital flight. Concludes that "an important part of this flight is not registered on the balance of payments, not even under 'errors and omissions,' but it is there . . . it is, then, an invisible flight."

Eguren, Fernando. Sociedad rural: el nuevo escenario. See item **5045.**

2150 Elías, Lidia and **Cecilia Garavito.** La mujer en el mercado de trabajo. Lima: Asociación Laboral para el Desarrollo ADEC-ATC, 1994. 106 p.: bibl., ill.

After analyzing impact of macroeconomic policy measures on the labor market, authors examine women's involvement in Lima's labor market. Although the level of women's involvement has increased during the last ten years, a significant gap in real income due to gender remains.

2151 Figueroa, Adolfo. Crisis distributiva en el Perú. Lima: Pontificia Univ. Católica del Perú, Fondo Editorial, 1993. 202 p.: bibl.

To conventional macroeconomic disequilibriums, such as fiscal and external crises, Figueroa adds the idea of a distributive crisis. After a theoretical discussion, Figueroa applies his model to the Peruvian crisis, which he assumes is based on a distributive crisis. Concludes that the country will not solve its economic problems until the distributive crisis is resolved. "But, as Keynes used to say . . . by then we might all be dead . . ."

2152 Foro Económico (Peru), *7th, Lima, 1993.* El costo del crédito en el Perú. Recopilación de Javier Portocarrero Maisch. Lima: Fundación Friedrich Ebert, 1994. 85 p.: ill.

Various experts analyze the reasons for Peru's high interest rate; three years after the 1990 economic shock, the interest rate remained double that of the industrial world. Otero and Naranjo suggest that "the main reason for these high rates of real interest is the reduced size of financial intermediation . . . the banks must accept competition as a mechanism of progress."

2153 Foro Económico (Peru), *8th, Lima?, 1993.* Ataque a la pobreza en el Perú. Edición de Javier Portocarrero Maisch. Lima: Fundación Friedrich Ebert, 1994. 95 p.: bibl.

Analyzes poverty in Peru during Fujimori's first administration both before and after macroeconomic stabilization.

García Belaúnde, José Antonio. El Perú en el Grupo Andino, 1992–1997: los años difíciles. See item **3561**.

García Núñez, Gonzalo. Perú: la visión de los peruanos excluidos; balance y perspectivas, 1950–1995. See item **5047**.

2154 Garrido-Lecca, Hernán. Economía y ecología: encuentros y desencuentros. Lima: Fundación Friedrich Ebert, 1994. 141 p.: bibl., ill.

Offers an alternative approach to environmental preservation based on Latin American realities. Attempts to avoid usual conflict between environmental goals and all other public policies. "Development is not an enemy of the environment, neither the opposite is true."

2155 Ginocchio, Luis. Agroindustria. Piura, Perú: Sietevientos Editores, 1993. 225 p.: bibl.

Sees agriculture development as a necessity. Provides numerous examples of modern export-oriented agriculture.

Gonzales de Olarte, Efraín. El ajuste estructural y los campesinos. See item **5048**.

2156 Gonzales de Olarte, Efraín. En las fronteras del mercado: economía política del campesinado en el Perú. Lima: IEP, 1994. 371 p.: bibl., ill. (Serie Análisis económico, 1019–4509; 16)

Gonzales says that ". . . the development of the peasants follows the path of regional and urban development, and, perhaps would bring about a change in their status. That is to say, through development . . . they would stop being peasants." This conclusion is based on an in-depth analysis demonstrating that sectors on the frontiers of the market have remained untouched by economic development during the last 40 years.

2157 Irigoyen Alvizuri, Marina and **María del Carmen Bastos R.** Exportaciones de la micro y pequeña industria: un reto para las ONGs; experiencias y reflexiones. Lima: PAMIS Fondo Editorial, 1992. 162 p.: bibl., ill.

Focuses on two trends: 1) State abandonment of certain functions and their adoption by the private sector; and 2) NGO dominance in filling the social welfare vacuum.

Authors use two analytical approaches: the micro and small enterprises as export generators, and NGOs as tools to help promote the new role as exporters. Provides interesting examples.

2158 Kervyn, Bruno. La economía campesina en el Perú: teorías y políticas. Cusco, Perú: Centro de Estudios Rurales Andinos Bartolomé de las Casas, 1988. 92 p.: bibl. (Debates andinos; 14)

Discusses the main issues of the Peruvian peasant economy, debating the underlying theories while examining its consequences for economic policy. "We do not need to look for new theoretical models for the Andean peasant . . . because his outlook would be much like peasants from other regions of the world. Nonetheless . . . on a macroeconomic level, the Andean peasant is in fact a specific case."

2159 Lajo, Manuel. El pan nuestro: ¿cómo interpretar y resolver el problema alimentario del Perú? Lima: Centro de Estudios Nueva Economía y Sociedad; Escuela de Administración de Negocios para Graduados; Fundación Friedrich Ebert, 1992. 395 p.: bibl., ill.

According to the author, Peruvian agriculture is stagnating as result of having lost its natural market to imported foodstuffs. Rather than protecting farmers and Andean peasants, Peruvian governments have, for the last 50 years, subsidized food imports. He proposes a reversal of this situation.

2160 Leone Russo, Marco. Riesgos y oportunidades de los procesos de reforma estructural: un análisis para el caso peruano. Lima: Univ. de Lima, Facultad de Economía, Centro de Investigaciones Económicas y Sociales, 1993. 278 p.: bibl., ill. (Serie Documentos; 10)

A young Italian economist—the author—arrives in Peru and observes the economy at its worse point (1991–92). He returns again after the implementation of structural reforms, and is surprised by the changes.

2161 Marthans León, Juan José. La banca en los programas de estabilización: tres años de política financiera en el Perú. Lima: Univ. de Lima, Facultad de Economía, 1993. 242 p.: bibl., ill.

Outlines economic policy suggestions for correcting the imperfections of the liberalization strategy followed from 1990–93. Concentrates on the performance of financial markets, especially commercial banks.

2162 Perú: crisis y desafío. Lima: CONFIEP, 1992. 406 p.: ports.

Report from a conference held immediately following the capture of Abimael Guzmán, the head of Shining Path. Paper topics reflect concern for Peru, but greater hope in the future. As engineer Carlos Tapia expresses on p. 105, "many of the things we used to think were impossible have now become possible."

2163 The Peruvian economy and structural adjustment: past, present, and future. Edited by Efraín Gonzales de Olarte. Coral Gables, Fla.: North-South Center Press, Univ. of Miami; Boulder, Colo.: distributed by Lynne Rienner Publishers, 1996. 373 p.: bibl., index.

Eleven well-known economists (Peruvians as well as experts on Peru) such as Hunt, Schydlowsky, and Thorp, discuss critical ideas on the Peruvian economic situation in the 1990s, sharing their suggestions for the future.

2164 Ponce Monteza, Carlos Ramón. Gamarra: formación, estructura y perspectivas. Lima: Fundación Friedrich Ebert, 1994. 161 p.: bibl., ill., maps.

Lucid essay about the commercial and manufacturing dressmaking conglomerate known to Lima's population as Gamarra— the most succesful and extensive sectorial conglomerate of Peruvian enterprises.

2165 Portocarrero S., Felipe and Luis Torrejón M. Modernización y atraso en las haciendas de la élite económica: Perú, 1916–1932. Lima: Univ. del Pacífico, Centro de Investigación; Consorcio de Investigación Económica, 1992. 109 p.: bibl., ill. (Serie Cuaderno de investigación; 16)

What was the economic and entrepreneurial rationale of Peruvian landowners at the beginning of the century? By examining the structure and the size of their haciendas, the authors explain the relative importance of those assets as well as the entrepreneurial rationale of their owners. They identify two coexisting groups: the "modernizers" and the "rentiers."

2166 Rejas Salazar, José. El campesino y su inserción en el mercado: recursos productivos, mercado de bienes e ingreso. Cusco: Centro de Estudios Regionales Andinos Bartolomé de las Casas, 1992. 170 p. (Trabajos del Colegio Andino; 10)

Researching peasant families in two Bolivian communities, author explores how peasants relate to the market. For example, finds evidence of low quality of seed use coupled with use of chemical products—an indicator of their market involvement. Also finds vast differences in agricultural output among families. Confirms interaction and interdependence between market and production.

2167 Rodríguez Cuba, Javier. De profesional a taxista: el mercado laboral de técnicos y profesionales en los 90. Lima: Asociación Laboral para el Desarrollo, 1995. 160 p.: bibl., ill.

Explains dissonance between job training and employment in Peru: half of employed professionals and three-fourths of technicians in Lima do not work in careers for which they were trained.

2168 Rojas, Jorge. Las políticas comerciales y cambiarias en el Perú, 1960–1995. Lima: Pontificia Univ. Católica del Perú, Fondo Editorial, 1996. 290 p.: bibl.

With the goal of understanding achievements and failures of protectionism in Peru, Rojas analyzes the impact of economic policies in the country during the last 35 years. Helps explain how the common citizen has been able to accept such strong neoliberal reform in the 1990s.

2169 Rojas Senisse, Hugo. Perú: de exportador a importador de azúcar. Lima: Instituto Peruano del Azúcar, 1993. 94 p.: bibl.

Examines Peruvian sugar industry from dependency perspective. Traces country's evolution from exporter to importer. While author does mention the crisis in the sugar cooperatives, he does not fully explain the reasons for the crisis, attributing all failures to dependency.

2170 Saba, Daniel. Memorias de un confeccionista: historia del proceso de privatización de PETROPERU. Lima: D. Saba de Andrea, 1995. 239 p.

In this fascinating memoir, Saba offers a personal, journalistic account of the controversial privatization of PETROPERU. Admits that mistakes were made, and some decisions were at best haphazard and at worst irresponsible.

Salgado Peñaherrera, Germánico; Luis Ignacio Jácome; and Mauricio Pozo. Ecuador y Perú: economía y desarrollo. See item **2057.**

2171 Samamé Boggio, Mario. Desarrollo y minería. Lima: Fondo Editorial, Banco Central de Reserva del Perú, 1994. 248 p.: bibl., ill., maps.

Samamé asserts "mining is a decentralized activity par excellence . . . so much so that by promoting the develoment of mining, geographical development is being promoted." Presents a variety of mining projects to be developed by the year 2010, with corresponding estimates of economic benefits for the country.

2172 Sánchez Enríquez, Rodrigo. Ecología, producción y desarrollo campesino: tipologías, impactos y factibilidad; aportes para una metodología de investigación y seguimiento. Lima: Taller de Investigación en Tecnologías Agroecológicas, 1993. 267 p.: bibl., ill.

A thoroughly researched study of peasant agri-ecological technologies. Concludes that despite short-term trend toward agricultural depression, there are long-term possibilities for agro-ecological development.

2173 Schuldt, Jürgen. La enfermedad holandesa y otros virus de la economía peruana. Lima: Univ. del Pacífico, Centro de Investigación, 1994. 84 p.: bibl. (Documento de trabajo; 20)

"The most uncommon type of Dutch Disease has infected the Peruvian economy," says the author in this study of economic policy and conditions in Peru.

2174 Seminario Permanente de Investigación Agraria, 5th, Arequipa, Peru, 1993. Perú, el problema agrario en debate. Recopilación de Oscar Dancourt, Enrique Mayer y Carlos Monge. Lima: SEPIA; CAPODA, 1994. 757 p.: bibl., ill., maps.

Offers a wealth of information on Peruvian agricultural sector. Includes impact of adjustment policies on sector, discussion of Rondas Campesinas, labor market changes, cultural impact on rural society, ecological issues, and discussion of agro-exports. Topics reveal magnitude of change in sector during last several decades.

Stokes, Susan Carol. Democratic accountability and policy change: economic policy in Fujimori's Peru. See item **3593.**

Stokes, Susan Carol. Economic reform and public opinion in Peru, 1990–1995. See item **3594.**

2175 Távara M., José I. Cooperando para competir: redes de producción en la pequeña industria peruana. Lima: DESCO, 1994. 223 p.

Based on research in two districts, the author examines small enterprise networks, assessing their contribution to regional development and the alleviation of urban poverty in Peru. Interesting and enriching work.

2176 Tello, Mario Delfín. Mecanismos hacia el crecimiento económico: el enfoque de la organización industrial en el sector manufacturero peruano, 1970–1987. Lima: Consorcio de Investigación Económica; Pontificia Univ. Católica del Perú, Fondo Editorial, 1993. 284 p.: bibl., ill.

Analyzes and explains failure of Peru's import substitution plan (1970–90). Discusses concerns with shift toward market liberalization beginning in Aug. 1990.

2177 Tokman, Víctor E. *et al.* Globalización y empleo: cambios en el empleo en Perú y América Latina, y en la vida laboral de hombres y mujeres. Recopilación de Griselda Tello Vigil. Lima: ADEC-ATC Asociación Laboral para el Desarrollo, 1995. 242 p.: bibl., ill.

Economic globalization has led to tremendous social changes, particularly regarding employment. This work examines the impact of these changes in Peru and Latin America.

2178 Toledo Segura, Rafael. El programa de estabilización y las reformas estructurales en el Perú en 1993. Buenos Aires: CIEDLA, 1993. 195 p.: bibl., ill. (Serie Estabilización y reforma estructural)

Assesses Fujimori's economic program during his administration's first three years, concluding with some interesting suggestions.

2179 Valle, Delma del. Migración y empleo femenino. Lima: ADEC-ATC, Asociación Laboral para el Desarrollo, 1992? 106 p.: bibl.

Important work on gender and Peruvian migration during the bloody decade of the 1980s. Finds that most women who are heads of households work in the informal sector, and therefore, have lower incomes. Not surprisingly, households where only women or children are employed show greater levels of poverty.

2180 Yamada Fukusaki, Gustavo. Autoempleo e informalidad urbana: teoría y evidencia empírica de Lima metropolitana, 1985–86 y 1990. Lima: Univ. del Pacifico, Centro de Investigación, 1994. 73 p.: bibl., ill. (Serie Cuaderno de investigación; 22)

Theoretical and empirical analysis of informal urban sector. Among the work's conclusions: "there is a certain neutrality in the policies affecting informal self-employment in developing countries."

BOLIVIA

JEFFREY FRANKS, *Economist, International Monetary Fund*

WHILE THE PAST FEW YEARS have seen the publication of an increasing number of works on Bolivian economics, the quality of the writings remains uneven. The advent of desktop publishing has made it easier for Bolivian organizations to produce a greater quantity of monographic studies, as well as seminar and conference proceedings. A small number of gems can be found among the proceedings, but they are few and far between. The most consistently high quality work inside Bolivia has been that published in the journal *Análisis Económico,* and that produced by UDAPE (Unit for Economic Policy Analysis) and the think-tank CEDLA (Center for Agrarian and Labor Studies).

The stabilization and structural adjustment programs initiated in Bolivia since 1985 continue to dominate macroeconomic writings. There is little new being said in these works with the exception of a few interesting studies on the political aspects of economic reforms (items **2196** and **2201**). CEDLA has issued a valuable series of book-length studies on different aspects of stabilization and structural adjustment, including works examining the impact of adjustment on the labor market and industry (items **2184** and **2200** respectively).

Urquiola's study on poverty may be the best among many works tackling this issue (item **2208**). Questions of gender and race have begun to figure more prominently in economic studies, including excellent works on the economic costs incurred by indigenous peoples by Wood and Patrinos (item **2210**) and Patrinos and Psacharopoulos (item **5093**). The informal sector of the economy remains a popular subject, but one where the quality of output varies widely. As would be expected given its economic importance, there are several works on the role of coca and cocaine in the Bolivian economy, though here again, quality is uneven.

2181 Alvarez, Elena H. Economic development, restructuring and the illicit drug sector in Bolivia and Peru: current policies. (*J. Interam. Stud. World Aff.,* 37:3, Fall 1995, p. 125–149, bibl., tables)

Interesting but superficial overview of the coca-cocaine market in Peru and Bolivia, and its role in the economic stabilization process. The drug market's importance in these countries has declined recently. Cocaine's influence on the economy may have provided a cushion against costs of economic stabilization policies, but also may have complicated adjustment by increasing the exchange rate.

2182 Blanes Jiménez, José. Crisis y ajuste en el mercado de trabajo. La Paz: Centro Boliviano de Estudios Multidisciplinarios (CEBEM), 1993. 133 p.: bibl.

Overly lengthy discussion of political economy of Bolivian labor market. Argues that economic reform has produced profound changes in employment, wages, and labor relations. Now, trade unions do not know how to behave as social—rather than political—agents. Current labor legislation is entirely inadequate and irrelevant in regard to actual labor relations. Business, labor, and government must work together in order to establish traditional collective bargaining relationships.

2183 Castedo Franco, Eliana and H.C.F. Mansilla. Economía informal y desarrollo socio-político en Bolivia: transformaciones socio-culturales, erosionamiento de la legitimidad estatal y perspectivas de lo informal. La Paz: Centro Boliviano de Estudios Multidisciplinarios (CEBEM), 1993. 349 p.: bibl.

Good discussion of characteristics and evolution of informal sector. Focuses on sociopolitical implications of the sector's rise, including its effect on party politics and the trade union movement. Also discusses how the economic crisis, political problems, and demographic shifts have impacted the sector. Competent and well-written, with useful information based on original research.

2184 CEDLA (Organization). Empleo y salarios: el círculo de la pobreza. La Paz: CEDLA, 1993. 356 p.: bibl., ill. (Programa de ajuste estructural. Serie Estudios e investigaciones; 5)

Fifth book in the CEDLA series on the structural adjustment program. Focuses on its impact on the urban labor market. Argues that underemployment is widespread and that wages have not kept up with inflation. Labor market is too laissez-faire to boost wages and guarantee reasonable working conditions. Provocative and well-written analysis.

2185 CEDLA (Organization). The Bolivian experiment: structural adjustment and poverty alleviation. Edited by Pitou van Dijck. Amsterdam: CEDLA, 1998. 270 p. (Latin America Studies; 84)

Eleven essays, plus editor's introduc-

tion and conclusion analyze the benefits and shortcomings of the neoliberal reform program, New Economic Policy (NEP). Authors examine economic and social transition caused by NEP's framework of rules, and the changed relationship between central government and market. Empirical essays discuss specific dimensions of the NEP and the transition process since 1985. [R. Hoefte]

2186 Centro de Estudios de la Realidad Económica y Social (Bolivia). El consumo alimentario en Bolivia. Cochabamba, Bolivia: CERES; Ediciones Runa, 1992. 222 p.: bibl. (Col. CERES; 1)

Comprehensive look at food production, processing, commercialization and consumption in Bolivia. Sections on agricultural evolution and consumption patterns and strategies of different social groups, based on a 1988–89 survey. Raw data is of some use, but analytical sections are very weak.

2187 Centro Interdisciplinario de Estudios sobre el Desarrollo Latinoamericano. Ajuste estructural y crecimiento económico: evaluación y perspectivas del caso boliviano. Buenos Aires: Fundación Konrad Adenauer, Centro Interdisciplinario de Estudios sobre el Desarrollo Lationoamericano, 1993. 119 p.: bibl. (Serie Estabilización y reforma estructural)

Workmanlike review of Bolivia's experience with macroeconomic stabilization and reform from 1985–92. Discusses political environment in which reforms were undertaken; explores economic deterioration before 1985; and discusses stabilization policies and their results.

2188 Cossío Muñoz Reyes, Fernando and María Félix Delgadillo. Estimación de la evasión en el impuesto al valor agregado (IVA). (*Anál. Econ./La Paz*, 9, nov. 1994, p. 89–112, bibl., graphs, tables)

Uses input-output matrix and VAT revenue information to estimate VAT tax evasion. Finds evasion has declined steadily since 1987 tax reform but remains high by Latin America standards, particularly in domestic activity: agriculture, restaurants and foods, metals, machinery, and chemicals.

2189 Cupé Clemente, Ernesto et al. Estimación del acervo del capital físico en Bolivia: 1992–1998. (*Anál. Econ./La Paz*, 13, junio 1995, p. 191–219, bibl., graphs, tables)

Attempts to create a time series of capital stock estimates by economic sector and type of capital. Finds that capital-output ratio declined after 1988; capital stock rose significantly. Largest capital increase came from a construction boom, reflected in a rising capital-output ratio in housing sector.

2190 Fernández Saavedra, Gustavo. La transformación del Estado: tendencias y desafíos; la experiencia boliviana. La Paz: ILDIS; Müller y Asociados, 1995. 185 p.: bibl. (Serie Democracia y sociedad)

Examines economic role of Bolivian State in relation to global trends toward political democratization, increased economic openness, and the technological revolution. Argues that changes in the economic structure imply an increasing concentration of wealth—both within industrial countries and between the industrial countries and the Third World.

2191 Gisbert, María Elena; Michael Painter; and **Mery Quitón.** Gender issues associated with labor migration and dependence on off-farm income in rural Bolivia. (*Hum. Organ.*, 53:2, Summer 1994, p. 110–122, bibl.)

Discusses off-farm male employment in the Bolivian Altiplano and its impact on women. Argues that a vicious cycle results, whereby agricultural income falls, forcing men to seek outside employment, which in turn raises women's workload, lowers agricultural productivity, and increases environmental degradation. Includes policy recommendations directed at NGOs for improving conditions for women by facilitating collective action and redirecting development projects specifically, to target women more directly. Interesting, but economic reasoning is somewhat muddled.

2192 Instituto Latinoamericano de Investigaciones Sociales. La apuesta al futuro: reflexiones en torno a la tecnología. Recopilación y edición de Rodolfo Eróstegui T. La Paz?: ILDIS, 1990? 170 p.: bibl., ill.

Discusses technological development in Bolivia. Includes papers on R+D investment in Latin America, government technology policies, technological status of Bolivia's physical capital, and agricultural technology. Concludes with a grandiose call for industrial reconversion. Covers a topic not previously

studied in Bolivia, but contributions are of uneven quality.

2193 Instituto Latinoamericano de Investigaciones Sociales. Bolivia—dependencia monetaria, el obstáculo para su desarrollo. Recopilación de Carlos Gustavo Jahnsen Gutiérrez. Berlín: Fundación Alemana para el Desarrollo Internacional, Centro para el Desarrollo Económico y Social; La Paz: Instituto Latinoamericano de Investigaciones Sociales, 1994. 226 p.: bibl. (Dok; 1705 C/c)

Presenting a new angle on dependency theory, papers argue that dependency is imposed by forcing peripheral countries to accept weak currencies. Such countries are condemned to a cycle of balance of payments and debt crises, addressed by tight monetary policy together with devaluation, which further weakens the currency while squashing domestic investments and growth. Recommends a type of modern mercantilism: undervalued currency, selective tariffs, balance of payments surpluses, along with fiscal balance and lax monetary policy.

2194 Jemio Mollinedo, Luis Carlos and **Ernesto Cupé Clemente.** Modelo de evaluación de impactos en precios. (*Anál. Econ. / La Paz*, 14, mayo 1996, p. 7–28, bibl., tables)

Uses Leontieff input-output matrix technique to estimate price effects of wage increases, devaluations, and petroleum price hikes. Provides insights on the transmission mechanisms from policy changes to consumer prices, but neglects secondary effects and does not incorporate inflationary expectations.

2195 Jordán Pozo, Rolando. Colapso de la minería tradicional y surgimiento de la nueva minería. (*in* Bolivia en la hora de su modernización. México: Univ. Nacional Autónoma de México, 1993, p.63–79, graphs, tables)

Describes 1980's mining crisis in Bolivia which follows a pattern similar to periodic collapses dating from late 16th century. Bolivian mining has been characterized by low investment and high costs, which expose it to price fluctuations and bad macroeconomic policies. Response to collapse has been to reorient and modernize production.

2196 Lazarte, Jorge and **Mario Napoleón Pacheco T.** Bolivia, economía y sociedad, 1982–1985. La Paz: CEDLA, 1992. 173 p.:

bibl. (Programa de ajuste estructural. Serie Estudios e investigaciones; 2)

Analyzes political economy of the descent into hyperinflation from 1982–85. Includes a nice discussion of the political and economic background to the revolution of 1952. Also discusses the country's economic model from 1952–85 and how its political and economic collapse precipitated the move to democracy and free market economics. Well-organized and insightful.

2197 Medina, Javier. Del alivio a la pobreza al desarrollo humano: buscando la Bolivia del próximo milenio. La Paz: HISBOL, 1994. 253 p.: bibl., ill. (Ensayos para repensar el país; 4)

Well-written but eccentric essays focus on rural development and education policy. Emphasize need to respect and incorporate indigenous institutions and ways of thinking in development policy. Offering a "new age" environmentalism and holistic approaches to development, work is critical of official development agencies. Includes both obscure philosophical pieces and very practical commentaries on specific Bolivian development projects.

2198 La microempresa productiva en Bolivia. Investigación y recopilación de Isabel Arauco L., José Baldivia Urdininea, y M. Inés Pérez Oropeza. La Paz: Fundación para Alternativas de Desarrollo, 1991. 121 p.: bibl., ill.

Describes size, status, and principal difficulties facing microindustry in Bolivia. Provides information on the work of NGOs in this sector and contains policy recommendations. Descriptive material is useful, but policy recommendations are clichéd and not well integrated.

2199 Molina Díaz, Germán. Las reformas de las finanzas públicas en Bolivia. (Contribuciones/Buenos Aires, 12:2, abril/junio 1995, p. 73–86, bibl., tables)

Describes Bolivian tax system since the 1985 New Economic Policy, including 1994 modifications. Also briefly discusses fiscal performance in early 1990s. A succinct, well-written summary offering little analysis.

2200 Montaño Ordóñez, Gary and **Carlos Villegas Qurioga.** Industria boliviana: entre los resabios del pasado y la lógica del mercado. La Paz: CEDLA, 1993. 337 p.: bibl.

(Programa de ajuste estructural. Serie Estudios e investigaciones; 4)

Fourth book from CEDLA analyzes Bolivian structural adjustment program. Examines evolution of Bolivian industry from pre-hyperinflation through crisis and structural adjustment. From 1987 onward, industrial growth was fairly robust, but concentrated in light industry and oriented toward the domestic market. Large enterprises have grown the most, while real wages have fallen and working hours have risen. Well-researched and well-written volume.

2201 Morales, Juan Antonio. Política económica después de la transición a la democracia. (in Bolivia en la hora de su modernización. México: Univ. Nacional Autónoma de México, 1993, p.129–157, bibl., tables)

Focuses on political economy of Bolivian stabilization and structural adjustment programs. Argues that return of democracy in 1982 unleashed long-repressed demands by major social actors unaccustomed to rules of democratic discourse. Stabilization was possible only after major groups became convinced there was no alternative. Much reform remains to be done.

2202 Scott, Katherine MacKinnon. Women in the labor force in Bolivia: participation and earnings. (in Case studies on women's employment and pay in Latin America. Washington: World Bank, 1992, p. 21–38, bibl., tables)

Uses regression analysis on household survey data to examine gender discrimination in the Bolivian labor market. Women's participation in labor force is low, and working women earn only 62 percent of the wages of their male counterparts. This discrepancy is in part accounted for by the fact that women work fewer hours. However, a substantial gender gap remains, which may be due to discrimination. Interesting, but ignores some important variables.

2203 Seminario Internacional sobre el Financiamiento de Iniciativas Comunitarias en Asentamientos Urbanos, *Santa Cruz, Bolivia, 1992.* Pobreza urbana y desafíos actuales: financiamiento de las inic[i]ativas de base. Coordinación de José Blanes Jiménez y Rolando Carrazana Rocha. La Paz: Centro Boliviano de Estudios Multidisciplinarios (CEBEM), 1993. 231 p.: bibl.

Proceedings from an international conference on support for small enterprise and base community programs. Includes four presentations and summaries of two others. Examines numerous case studies of microcredit, housing finance, and poverty alleviation projects, offers recommendations.

2204 Seminario Regional Plan de Desarrollo del Trópico, 1st, Cochambaba, Bolivia, 1992. Desarrollo alternativo: utopias y realidades. Coordinación de Mario Arrieta Abdalla. La Paz: Instituto Latinoamericano de Investigaciones Sociales (ILDIS), 1993. 177 p.: ill.

Discussions from a conference on alternative development for Bolivian coca-growing regions. Participants included peasant representatives, NGO professionals, and academics. The affected peasants feel they have not been adequately consulted regarding alternative development strategies and that projects are subject to favoritism. The unedited voices of peasant coca growers are interesting, but offer more opinion than factual information.

2205 Toranzo Roca, Carlos F. and Gonzalo Chávez Alvarez. Claves y problemas de la economía boliviana. La Paz: ILDIS, 1993. 261 p.: bibl.

Toranzo examines Bolivian stabilization and structural adjustment through 1991, focusing on social issues. Argues that the government attempted to use social spending to cushion effects of economic stabilization, but failed to make such spending a real focus. Chávez presents a formal structuralist model of Bolivia's hyperinflation. Argues that public prices, the exchange rate, and an underlying distributional conflict among social actors played key roles in generating hyperinflation.

2206 Truett, Dale B. and Lila J. Truett. Trade preferences and exports of manufactures: a case study of Bolivia and Brazil. (*Weltwirtsch. Arch.*, 129:3, 1993, p. 573–590, bibl., tables)

Briefly explores impact of US General System of Preferences (GSP) on Bolivian and Brazilian exports. Bolivia had a much higher share of US imports covered by the GSP than Brazil. Presents simple regression results on export demand which show that the GSP had a significant impact only on exports of Bolivian manufactures, supporting the hypothesis that lower-income GSP-eligible countries are most likely to benefit.

2207 Unión Nacional de Instituciones para el Trabajo de Acción Social (Bolivia). Aspectos de la inseguridad alimentaria en Bolivia. La Paz: UNITAS, 1993. 132 p.: bibl., ill.

Four papers on food policy in Bolivia address food production and consumption patterns, the milk industry, and external trade in food and food products. General view is that food situation in Bolivia has worsened in recent years; that food aid has had detrimental effects; and that the free market is not a positive influence in food security.

2208 Urquiola Soux, Miguel. Participando en el crecimiento: expansión económica, distribución del ingreso y pobreza en el área urbana de Bolivia; 1989–1992 y proyecciones. La Paz: UDAPSO, Unidad de Analisis de Políticas Sociales, 1994. 94 p.: bibl., ill. (Cuadernos de investigación; 2)

Intelligent analysis of poverty and income distribution in Bolivia during late 1980s-early 1990s. Includes simulations of the evolution of poverty under different future growth scenarios. Poverty rates fell between 1989–92 among all socioeconomic strata, but income distribution worsened because of the tendency for the educated to benefit more.

2209 Villegas Quiroga, Carlos. La industria manufacturera privada en el marco del ajuste estructural. (*Umbrales/La Paz*, 1, 1993, p. 69–89, tables)

Descriptive portrait of Bolivian industrial sector. Microenterprises constitute 89 percent of enterprises and account for 38 percent of employment, but only 17 percent of value added. By contrast, 207 large enterprises (1.7 percent) generate 38 percent of employment and 66 percent of value added. Industrial output is concentrated in food processing, textiles, wood processing, and metal products.

2210 Wood, Bill and Harry Anthony Patrinos. Urban Bolivia. (*in* Indigenous people and poverty in Latin America: an empirical analysis. Edited by George Psacharopoulos and Harry Anthony Patrinos. Washington: The World Bank, 1994, p. 55–96, graphs, tables)

Uses survey data to study poverty among indigenous people. Poverty rates are much higher among indigenous groups. Lower human capital and other explained factors account for 78 percent of this discrepancy, while the remaining 22 percent is unexplained and possibly reflects discrimination. Concludes that increased education for indigenous people (perhaps including bilingual education) could produce substantial reductions in indigenous poverty, as well as an important drop in birth rates.

2211 Zeballos Hurtado, Hernán. Agricultura y desarrollo económico II. La Paz: Centro de Información para el Desarrollo, 1993. 302 p.: bibl., ill.

Comprehensive examination of the Bolivian agricultural sector originally produced in 1988 (see *HLAS 55:2001*). This version contains an updated review of the evolution of the sector covering the years after stabilization through 1992. Also includes satellite maps in an expanded discussion of the geography of Bolivian agriculture, and a detailed chapter on the livestock industry. Solid, but undistinguished reference work.

PARAGUAY AND URUGUAY

MARTIN RAMA, *Senior Economist, World Bank*

OVER THE LAST TWO YEARS, new themes have emerged in Uruguayan economic literature. Among them, the analysis of the corporation occupies an important place. Indeed, several of the studies reviewed this biennium use a variety of statistical sources to describe the features and performances of different groups of businesses, ranging from small and medium enterprises to powerful "economic groups." Other studies trace the development of State-owned enterprises, from their ownership by British capital (item **2226**) to their nationalization earlier in this century (item **2231**), and, finally, to the first serious attempts at modernization in recent years. Still other works focus on collective action by employers' associations and trade unions, particularly in relation to Mercosur. In a similar vein, several studies analyze other forms of collective action, including cooperative health-care providers and neighborhood associations. In most cases there is an effort to firmly ground the study on data analysis.

Mercosur remains, of course, an important topic in the reviewed literature. However, unlike previous years, there are now several studies which do not merely describe the agreements and the challenges they pose to a small country such as Uruguay. Recent studies focus on more specific topics, ranging from the impact of increased regional integration on industrial relations to the consequences of geographic location of production at the regional level. One study reviewed here represents one of the most competently executed studies of the Uruguayan economy yet written; this work goes beyond regional integration to evaluate the overall implications of the Uruguayan trade regime on a variety of economic outcomes (item **2225**).

A few other topics have received considerable attention in recent years. Among them, as in other years, is the labor market. Some of the studies reviewed in this edition of *HLAS* demonstrate interesting applications of econometric techniques to microeconomic labor market data. Other labor market and human resource studies are more descriptive. One frequently covered topic is the historic analysis of government expenditures, revenue, and debt from independence until relatively early in this century. Finally, several studies have a strong statisticalbias, which is enough to exclude them from a review of economic literature. Such is the case with studies of seasonality or common trends in aggregate economic time series. Studies dealing with poverty and its measurement, on the other hand, were included in this volume.

PARAGUAY

Compared to the more sociological or philosophical orientation of Paraguayan economic literature in previous years, this edition of *HLAS* includes studies with significant empirical content. Several deal with agricultural production, a welcome development for a largely agricultural country. Specifically, the link between public policies, farming revenues and rural poverty is competently analyzed more than once (especially, in item **2216**). Other studies deal with specific agricultural activities, such as cotton production. Finally, this edition of *HLAS* includes studies on economic history, as well as on sectoral and macroeconomic policies. It should be noted, however, that there continues to be a dearth of published studies on topics related to the Paraguayan economy.

PARAGUAY

2212 Ferreira Falcón, Magno. El complejo hidroeléctrico Yacyretá: histórico y polémico Proyecto Binacional. Asunción: Colegio de Graduados en Ciencias Económicas del Paraguay, Fundación de Graduados en Ciencias Económicas, 1990. 230 p.: bibl., ill.

Upbeat narration of the process leading to the construction of the huge hydroelectric dam on the Paraná River, on the border between Argentina and Paraguay. Documents technical and legal aspects of the project, and analyzes its cost and financing. Discusses its implications in terms of population displacement.

2213 Lariño Noia, Felipe. Tres proyectos de viviendas en Paraguay: análisis comparativo de costos. Asunción: Ediciones HELVETAS, 1995. 156 p.: bibl., ill. (some col.), index.

Assesses three building projects which cover the full range of low-cost housing currently supported by the government in Paraguay. Characteristics of the dwellings and their costs are carefully documented, thus contributing in a very practical way to more effective public policies.

2214 Nikiphoroff, Basilio. El subdesarrollo rural paraguayo: la problemática algodonera; estrategias para el desarrollo. Asunción: Fundación Moisés Bertoni; Intercontinental Editora, 1994. 244 p.: ill. (some col.), map. (Col. Futuro verde)

Most Paraguayan cotton is produced in small family plots, with much lower productivity than in other countries. Based on a series of surveys of farmers and traders, this study reviews several aspects of cotton growing including agricultural practices, profitability levels, peasant institutions, technical assistance, credit availability, and trading.

2215 Ocampos, Lorraine. Paraguay, tipos de cambio y proceso de integración. Asunción: CEPPRO, 1993. 76 p.: bibl., ill. (Serie Estudios; 4)

Overview of Paraguayan exchange rate policies compared to other Mercosur countries, in light of an eventual coordination of macroeconomic policies in the region. Proficient analysis of aggregate data.

2216 Paolino, Carlos. Políticas públicas e ingresos campesinos en el Paraguay. Asunción: Centro Paraguay de Estudios Sociológicos, 1994. 99 p.: bibl., ill.

Clever use of existing household surveys and previous studies of the land market to infer how public policies affect the earnings and consumption patterns of small farmers across different regions in Paraguay. Examines the implications for rural poverty given further market liberalization of product and land market.

2217 Pastore, Mario. State-industrialisation: the evidence on Paraguay, 1852–1870. (*J. Lat. Am. Stud.*, 26:2, May 1994, p. 295–324, tables)

Reviews and rejects the hypothesis that State intervention in Paraguay led to a spectacular industrialization effort in the second half of the 19th century. Although the agricultural export boom furnished more resources to the government than was originally thought, government measures of mercantilist inspiration clearly fell short of the mark.

2218 Villalobos, Ruy de and **Gary N. Howe.** Hacia una estrategia de desarrollo campesino en el Paraguay. San José: FIDA; IICA, 1992. 502 p.: bibl., ill. (Estrategias para mitigar la pobreza rural en América Latina y el Caribe; 2. Serie FIDA-IICA; 2)

Diagnosis of the problems of the agricultural sector in Paraguay, focusing on the potential of different policies for alleviating poverty. Covers a large variety of topics using mainly a monographic approach.

URUGUAY

2219 Arbeletche, Pedro. Los efectos de la regulación en el mercado de lácteos en Uruguay. Buenos Aires?: Instituto Torcuato Di Tella; Centro de Investigaciones Económicas, 1994. 42 p.: appendix, bibl., graphs, tables. (Serie Documentos de Trabajo)

This report applies the standard tools of partial equilibrium analysis to the dairy sector in Uruguay. This sector is characterized by heterogeneous producers confronting two different prices for fresh milk. Represents a commendable attempt to ground sectoral policies on sound microeconomic analysis.

2220 Arends, Mary. Women's labor force participation and earnings: the case of Uruguay. (*in* Case studies on women's employment and pay in Latin America. Washington: World Bank, 1992, p. 431–449, bibl., tables)

Uses household survey data to investigate reasons explaining the approximately 25 percent earnings differential observed between men and women in Uruguay. Uruguay is particularly interesting in this respect, because of the high participation rates and the high educational attainment of women.

2221 Birle, Peter *et al.* Dos estudios sobre los empresarios y la integración regional. Montevideo: FESUR; CIESU; EPPAL, 1994. 165 p.: bibl.

First essay addresses the role played by entrepreneurs from Argentina, Brazil, Uruguay, and Paraguay in the creation and even-

tual consolidation of Mercosur, highlighting their lack of participation in previous regional integration endeavors. Second essay presents the views of Uruguayan entrepreneurs on Mercosur, as indicated by a survey of employees of the largest manufacturing firms.

2222 Bucheli, Marisa *et al.* Recursos humanos en el proceso de ajuste: el caso uruguayo. (*Rev. Econ./Uruguay*, 1:1, mayo 1994, p. 87–154, bibl., graphs, tables)

Uses household survey data to assess the changes in participation rates, occupational structure, and unemployment rates during the period 1974–92. Careful empirical work focuses on youth, women, and the elderly, the three most vulnerable groups in the face of significant economic restructuring.

2223 Buxedas, Martín *et al.* Micro y pequeña empresa: las MYPES en el Uruguay; desempeño y perspectivas. Montevideo: Centro Interdisciplinario de Estudios sobre el Desarrollo, Uruguay, 1995. 99 p.: bibl., ill.

Uses a variety of statistical sources to describe the characteristics and performance of private urban firms with a personnel of 20 or less. Analyzes the institutional context in which these firms operate. The most novel part reports on a survey of managers of these small firms.

2224 Caño-Guiral, Maira. La estructura industrial en el Uruguay y el proceso de apertura ecónomica. (*Rev. Econ./Uruguay*, 1:2, nov. 1994, p. 123–169, appendix, bibl., tables)

Analyzes the impact of trade liberalization on the market orientation of 38 manufacturing sectors during 1988–92. A significant trend towards lower export orientation is evident in most sectors, but the underlying reasons are unclear.

Del PIT al PIT-CNT: ¿réquiem para el movimiento sindical? See item **3821.**

2225 The effects of protectionism on a small country: the case of Uruguay. Edited by Michael Connolly and Jaime de Melo. Washington: World Bank, 1994. 172 p.: bibl., ill. (World Bank regional and sectoral studies)

Competently executed series of studies on the distorted trade regime of Uruguay until the late 1980s and the effect of protectionism on a variety of economic outcomes. Topics covered range from the political economy of trade distortions to the sectoral impact of specific regulations. Worth reading.

2226 Finch, Martin Henry John. Economía y sociedad en el Uruguay del siglo XX. Montevideo: Univ. de la República, Facultad de Humanidades y Ciencias de la Educación, Depto. de Publicaciones, 1992. 66 p.

Interesting series of lectures by a British historian who has worked extensively on Uruguay. The lectures deal with the relationship between the government and British utilities at the beginning of the 20th century, and with the role played by the working class establishing social legislation, among other topics.

Gans, Paul. Desarrollo económico y sector informal en América Latina: el ejemplo del comercio ambulante en Montevideo. See item **2855.**

2227 Kruse, Herman C. Los orígenes del mutualismo uruguayo. Montevideo: Ediciones Populares para América Latina, 1994. 85 p.: bibl., col. ill.

Interesting although somewhat anecdotal history of the cooperative health-care movement in Uruguay. Discusses how various communities of immigrants used different philosophical approaches, ranging from anarchist to Catholic, to shape these cooperatives in the late-19th and early-20th centuries.

2228 Martín, Oscar and Elsa López Esteves. Administración y cambio organizacional en empresas públicas: el caso del proyecto de mejora de la gestión de UTE. (*Quantum/Montevideo*, 2:4, verano 1995, p. 91–116, tables)

Based on the particular experience of UTE, the company in charge of generating and distributing electricity in Uruguay, lessons are learned about reorganizing a State-owned enterprise. Documents the reform process in UTE from a managerial perspective.

2229 Mieres, Pablo. Las comisiones barriales en el norte y noreste del país. Montevideo: Centro Latinoamericano de Economía Humana, 1992. 180 p.: bibl., ill. (Serie Investigaciones; 63)

Careful study of collective action through neighborhood associations in seven provincial cities. Based on a survey of association leaders and focus group discussions. Social composition of associations, decision-making processes, and interactions with government and political parties are discussed.

2230 Millot, Julio and Magdalena Bertino. Las finanzas del Estado Oriental de 1830 a 1876. (*Quantum/Montevideo*, 2:4, verano 1995, p. 117–141, tables)

Organizes in a consistent way the available data from government accounts from the first half-century after independence from Spain. Results are comparable series on expenditures, revenue, and debt over the years. Shows the significance of import taxes in spite of the free trade rhetoric of the time.

2231 Nahum, Benjamín. Empresas públicas uruguayas: origen y gestión. Montevideo: Ediciones de la Banda Oriental, 1993. 118 p.: bibl., ill. (Serie Escritos de historia económica; 1)

This study first reviews the reasons brandished early in this century to justify the creation of State-owned enterprises in Uruguay. Then analyzes the performance of these enterprises during the first two decades of their existence, and predicts their ultimate decline. Carefully executed work contains a wealth of information.

2232 Nahum, Benjamín. La evolución de la deuda externa del Uruguay, 1875–1939. Montevideo: Ediciones de la Banda Oriental, 1995. 168 p.: bibl. (Serie documental; 2)

Meticulously documented analysis of foreign borrowing by successive Uruguayan governments, attempts to distinguish between foreign pressures and domestic initiatives. Relies on previously unpublished sources, including a series of notes exchanged between the Uruguayan governments and their British and French creditors.

2233 Notaro, Jorge. El tránsito al Mercosur y sus impactos en las relaciones de trabajo: el escenario regional y las economías pequeñas. (*Cuad. CLAEH*, 69, junio 1994, p. 93–107)

Predicts the consequences of Mercosur on industrial relations in Uruguay. After describing the labor market institutions, it reviews the attitudes of the labor movement towards regional integration and identifies the trade-offs to be faced in the near future.

2234 Noya, Nelson and Daniel Dominioni.
El fortalecimiento del sector financiero en el proceso de ajuste: liberalización y
regulación; el caso uruguayo. (*in* El fortalecimiento del sector financiero en el proceso de
ajuste: liberalización y regulación. Buenos
Aires: Centro de Estudios de Estado y Sociedad; Washington: Banco Interamericano de
Desarrollo, 1994, p. 207–252, bibl., graphs,
tables)
Thorough examination of the Uruguayan financial sector during the 1980s–90s.
Emphasizes the distinctive features of this
system, including the prevalence of dollar-
denominated assets, the significant market
share of State-owned banks and the absence
of any large, private domestic banking group.
The policy implications of the analysis are
drawn.

2235 Pascale, Ricardo. Crisis financiera y
finanzas empresariales: el caso uruguayo. (*Quantum*/Montevideo, 1:1, dic.
1993, p. 47–76, tables)
Based on a financial survey of the largest manufacturing firms in Uruguay, carried
out in 1982–84 and 1990–91. After describing
the sources and uses of funds in both periods,
this work evaluates the profitability of these
firms and identifies their reactions to macroeconomic crises.

2236 Rama, Germán W. Los jóvenes y el
mundo del trabajo en Uruguay. Montevideo: Arca, 1994. 144 p.: bibl. (Col. Nuevas
fronteras)
Description of the educational attainment, labor force participation, and occupational structure of Uruguayans aged 15 to 29.
Mostly based on a national survey of youth
carried out in 1989–90. Also reviews the legal
obstacles to increased economic activity in
this age group.

**2237 Santos Granero, Alvaro and Ernesto
González Posse.** Evaluación económica
y social del proyecto de mejora de gestión de
UTE. (*Quantum*/Montevideo, 2:4, verano
1995, p. 73–89, bibl., table)
UTE, a large company in charge of generating and distributing electricity, was one
of the first State-owned enterprises to experience a significant restructuring. This article
attempts to appraise this restructuring using
the tools applied to investment projects. The
results indicate substantial returns.

2238 Schonebohm, Dieter. Mercosur: ¿desafío o amenaza? Montevideo: FESUR;
Ediciones de Ciencias Sociales, 1994. 134 p.:
bibl.
Reviews the policy debate in the Uruguayan press and parliament surrounding the
creation of Mercosur. The first part focuses
on partisan views at different stages of the
process. The second, and most interesting
part, deals with the reactions of business associations and trade unions throughout this
process.

**2239 Seminario sobre Medición e Investigación de la Pobreza en Argentina, Brasil
y Uruguay, *Montevideo, 1988*.** Pobreza y necesidades básicas en el Uruguay: indicadores
y resultados preliminares. Montevideo: Arca;
Dirección General de Estadística y Censos,
Comisión Económica para América Latina
y el Caribe, 1989. 100 p.: bibl.
Three methodological papers on how
to measure, characterize, and monitor poverty in Uruguay. The first one describes the
criteria used to construct an index of unfulfilled basic needs. The second paper details
each of the indicators used to construct the
index. The final paper emphasizes the distinction between permanent and temporary
poverty.

2240 Silveira, Sara and Gloria Fanta. Los
caminos de la formación del capital humano en la industria exportadora uruguaya.
Montevideo: Comisión Económica para América Latina y el Caribe, Oficina de Montevideo, 1994. 142 p.: bibl.
Summarizes the results of a survey of
export-oriented firms in the textile, leather,
garment, and chemical sectors. Describes the
educational attainment and work experience
of their labor force, including on-the-job
training. There is a wealth of information in
this study, although the analysis is relatively
unsophisticated.

2241 Terra, María Inés and Adriana Gigliotti. Mercosur: localización de la
producción; un modelo de geografía económica. (*Rev. Econ.*/Uruguay, 2:1, mayo 1995,
p. 73–111, bibl., graphs, tables)
Elaborate analysis of Mercosur using
methodological tools of economic geography.
Based on a general equilibrium model with
monopolistic competition, economies of
scale, and transport costs, the article predicts

the location of economic activities as trade barriers are removed. A primer.

2242 Torello, Mariella and **Gabriel Arimón.** Incertidumbre macroeconómica e inversión en Uruguay. Montevideo: Comisión Económica para América Latina y el Caribe, Oficina de Montevideo, 1993. 73 p.: bibl., ill.

Careful study of reasons for low investment rates in Uruguay. After describing the principle trends of capital accumulation from 1974–92, constructs a series of indicators of macroeconomic uncertainty and assesses their impact—as well as that of other aggregate variables—on private investment decisions.

ARGENTINA

GUSTAVO ENRIQUE CANOÑERO, *Consulting Economist, Argentina*

THE CONSOLIDATION OF THE CONVERTIBILITY PLAN, albeit the critical period following the Mexican crises, has generated research with a longer horizon than before. Topics such as the effect of trade liberalization on productive sectors and the environment, industrial policies, productivity and growth prospects, regional economies, labor market reform, poverty, and income distribution are now at the core of research activities in Argentina, replacing inflation, hyperinflation, stabilization plans, the international debt crisis and others.

The adjustment process to a more market-oriented environment in Argentina has attracted much attention; many papers discuss this transition process in the agriculture, services and other manufacturing sectors. All of the literature encompasses one essential topic—the role of industrial policy. Two studies on this topic are of particular interest: one describes and analyzes government industrial policy (item **2299**); the other, a study by a group of leading Argentine economists, analyzes the case of Argentina in light of existent international experiences (item **2316**).

Related to the country's economic transformation, significant research efforts explore new prospects for economic growth. Specifically, productivity growth is the subject of an illuminating analysis presented at the 1994 meeting of Argentine private banks (item **2272**). Similarly, the prospects of an export-oriented strategy motivated a number of worthwhile studies. Two books provide a comprehensive view of the effect of trade openness on the manufacturing sector and its current and expected performance (items **2293** and **2244**).

After being neglected for years, regional economies were the subject of intensive analysis. Three papers stand out for their depth and appeal. Two of the works provide a set of indicators on regional development in Argentina (items **2292** and **2295**), and the third offers an overview of the challenges facing these regions (item **2283**).

Research has been devoted to remaining issues in the area of structural reforms, particularly the labor market and public administration. One highly recommended paper presents a comprehensive study of the Argentine labor market (item **2268**). Two studies presented at the 1994 meeting of Argentine private banks are fundamental to understanding the Argentine labor market and evaluating related policies: one typifies unemployment during 1990–94 and another examines education in the labor force (item **2272**). On reforming the central administration, there is a very enticing proposal for an integral reform in a book by the Consejo Empresario

Argentino (item **2246**). Unfortunately, public administration reform in the provinces remains largely unexplored.

Existing studies on poverty and income distribution are worth mentioning as they contribute to understanding the social effect of the reform process. Three entries on this topic should be highlighted: one from the Secretary of Economic Programming containing basic data (item **2300**), another by Martinez Nogueira studying the government policies to combat poverty (item **2302**), and the third by Minujin providing an analytical view of the poverty issue (item **2305**).

Additionally, some basic references of economic research in Argentina include proceedings from three important conferences in economics in recent years: the 1994 Annual Conference of Private Banks (item **2272**), the 1995 Annual Meeting of the Argentine Association of Political Economy (item **2248**), and the 1996 First Meetings in Economic Research (item **2275**). These proceedings showcase research work representing the new agenda and exist alongside some pioneering and stimulating research. On the issue of regulation, the two reports by the World Bank on public utilities and transportation are noteworthy (items **2249** and **2250**).

2243 Abdala, Manuel Angel *et al.* Elasticidades de demanda de servicio telefónico básico en Argentina. (*An. Asoc. Argent. Econ. Polít.*, 2, 1995, p. 7–33, bibl., tables)

Estimates demand elasticity of basic phone services in Argentina for the period 1990–93.

2244 Ablin, Eduardo R. *et al.* Hacia una nueva estrategia exportadora: la experiencia argentina, el marco regional y las reglas multilaterales. Edición de Bernardo P. Kosacoff. Buenos Aires: Univ. Nacional de Quilmes, 1995. 423 p.: bibl., ill.

Series of essays on the export strategy followed in Argentina since 1974, with special emphasis on the most recent changes. Exports by small and medium enterprises, internationalization of manufacturing firms, trade withing Mercosur, and the increasing importance of multilateral agreements are the main subjects examined.

2245 Adelman, Jeremy. Post-populist Argentina. (*New Left Rev.*, 203, Jan./Feb. 1994, p. 65–91)

Beginning with Perón's first presidency in 1946, the author charts the changes in economic policy up to the present and concludes that nowadays the capitalists are plundering the people. [P. Lewis]

2246 La administración pública nacional: propuesta para su reestructuración.
Trabajo realizado por Fundación de Investigaciones Económicas Latinoamericanas. Buenos Aires: Consejo Empresario Argentino, 1996. 277 p.: bibl.

Presents a proposal for a comprehensive reform of the central administration in Argentina. This inquiry, carried out by the Fundación de Investigaciones Económicas Latinoamericanas (FIEL) under the supervision of Manuel A. Solanet, provides a possible solution to one of the unfinished matters in structural reforms in Argentina.

2247 Alsogaray, Alvaro. Experiencias de cincuenta años de política y economía argentina. Buenos Aires: Planeta, 1993. 414 p.

The former finance minister addresses economic policy in the last 50 years in Argentina and his efforts to make economic liberalism—political conservatism in Latin America—the prevailing order.

2248 *Anales de la Asociación de Economía Política.* No. 30, 1995. Mendoza, Argentina: Univ. Nacional de Cuyo, Facultad de Ciencias Económicas.

Proceedings from the annual meeting of the Argentine Association of Political Economy. Includes papers on a wide range of topics in economics.

2249 Argentina: reforming provincial utilities. Washington: World Bank, 1996. 51 p.

Analyzes the reform needs and options in electricity distribution, and water and sanitation services in Argentina's provinces. The main focus is on the regulation of private operators.

2250 **Argentina: transport privatization and regulation.** Washington: The World Bank, 1996. 63 p.

Identifies the main issues the Argentine provinces face and options they have in carrying out their new expanded responsibilities in the transport sector. Draws some lessons from the national reforms in railways, roads, ports, and waterways.

2251 **Argentina. Ministerio de Economía y Obras y Servícios Públicos.** Economic Report 1995. Buenos Aires: Ministerio de Economía y Obras y Servícios Públicos, 1996. 212 p.: appendix, tables.

Government report on 1995 economic performance. Contains a statistical appendix.

2252 *Argentina: a Country for Investment and Growth.* 1995. Buenos Aires: Ministerio de Economía y Obras y Servicios Públicos.

Presents a comprehensive analysis of reforms introduced in Argentina since 1990. Constitutes an important source of historical data and projections.

2253 **Artana, Daniel et al.** Reforma y convergencia: ensayos sobre la transformación de la economía argentina. Recopilación de Felipe A.M. de la Balze. Buenos Aires: Ediciones Manantial, 1993. 366 p.: bibl., ill.

Essays on economic reforms for sustainable growth in Argentina. Includes a background study on growth in Argentina since 1870 and essays on external trade, capital markets, privatization, the tax system, and State reform. One chapter discusses the social legitimacy of the adjustment policy.

2254 **Azpiazu, Daniel and Hugo Nochteff.** El desarrollo ausente. Buenos Aires: Tesis Grupo Editorial Norma, 1994. 233 p.: bibl.

Two critical essays about the diagnosis and recommendations coming from the "Washington consensus" (name used by J. Williamson to describe the basic beliefs and recommendations of mainstream economists in Washington). Studies based on the Argentine experience up to 1991.

2255 **Azpiazu, Daniel and Eduardo M. Basualdo.** La indústria siderúrgica argentina en un contexto de privatizaciones y transformaciones estructurales. Buenos Aires: Asociación Trabajadores del Estado, 1993. 185 p.: bibl.

Examines the effect of deregulation and privatization on the steel industry in Argentina and draws policy recommendations.

Back in the saddle: a survey of Argentina. See item 3682.

2256 **Barbeito, Alberto C. and Rubén M. Lo Vuolo.** La modernización excluyente: transformación económica y estado de bienestar en Argentina. Buenos Aires: UNICEF; CIEPP; LOSADA, 1992. 221 p.: bibl., ill.

Provides a critical view of the process of economic reform.

2257 **Basualdo, Eduardo M.; Claudio Lozano; and Joon Bang.** La producción industrial en las provincias: principales empresas en los bloques productivos del azúcar, el arroz, el tabaco, el té, el vino y la yerba mate. Buenos Aires: Instituto de Estudios sobre Estado y Participación; Asociación Trabajadores del Estado, 1994. 52 p. (Cuaderno; 31. Informe; 4)

Analyzes the dominant enterprises and industrial establishments in six agroindustrial productive clusters: sugar, rice, tobacco, tea, wine, and yerba; all of them fundamental for the regional economies.

2258 **Basualdo, Eduardo M. and Pedro Castillo.** Provincia de Misiones: características productivas. Buenos Aires: Instituto de Estudios sobre Estado y Participación; Asociación Trabajadores del Estado, 1995. 52 p.: bibl., ill. (Cuaderno; 36. Estudios provinciales)

Describes the productive characteristics of the province of Misiones. Detailed information on economic activity is organized by product and geographic location.

2259 **Beccaria, Luis and Ricardo Carciofi.** Argentina: social policy and adjustment during the 1980s. (in Coping with austerity: poverty and inequality in Latin America. Washington: The Brookings Institution, 1995, p. 187–236, appendix, bibl., tables)

Traces the evolution of poverty for greater Buenos Aires during the 1980s, and analyzes the parallel evolution of government social expenditures and policies during that decade.

2260 **Beccaria, Luis and Aida Quintar.** Reconversión productiva y mercado de trabajo: reflexiones a partir de la experiencia de Somisa. (*Desarro. Econ.*, 35:139, oct./dic. 1995, p. 401–418, bibl., tables)

Presents a characterization of the restructuring process being observed in the Argentine economy. Focuses on the social consequences of the privatization of one of the country's biggest steel plants, Somisa.

2261 Bekerman, Marta and **Pablo Sirlin.** Patrón de especialización y política comercial en la Argentina de los noventa. Comentarios de Osvaldo Kacef y Gabriel Yoguel. (*Desarro. Econ.*, 36, no. especial, verano 1996, p. 115–154, appendix, graphs, tables)
Analyzes Argentine economic specialization pattern during 1986–94. In this context, evaluates prospects of sustainable growth and proposes additional commercial policies.

Beliz, Gustavo. Vale la pena: adiós a la vieja política. See item **3683.**

2262 Bercovich, Néstor and **Martina Chidiak.** Reestructuración industrial y gestión ambiental en el sector de celulosa y papel en Argentina. Buenos Aires: Centro de Investigaciones para la Transformación, 1994. 94 p.: bibl. (Documentos de trabajo; DT16)
Looks at the preceding and current characteristics of the restructuring process of cellulose and paper industry. Effects of macroeconomic and regulatory changes are emphasized, especially those concerning the environment.

2263 Berlinski, Julio. Post trade liberalization institutional issues in Argentina. Buenos Aires: Instituto Torcuato Di Tella; Centro de Investigaciones Económicas, 1994. 49 p.: bibl. (Serie documentos de trabajo; DTE 182)
Presents legislative sequences regarding trade policy devices for the period 1988–93. Provides an inside look at the way trade policy is created in Argentina, using laws, decrees, and administrative decisions, all with different implications as to the degree of commitment of the government and the opposition.

2264 Berlinski, Julio. Trade policies in Argentina. Buenos Aires: Instituto Torcuato Di Tella; Centro de Investigaciones Económicas, 1993. 397 p.: bibl., tables. (Serie Documentos de Trabajo)
Provides an overview of the trade regime in Argentina between 1969–88. Describes aggregate indicators regarding the current account, terms of trade and trade policies, the factor contents of exports and imports, and the instruments of protection and the anti-export bias of the trade regime between 1969–88, including preliminary estimates of the 1988 tariff reform.

2265 Bianchi, Eduardo and **Jorge Robbio.**
Tratado de Libre Comercio de América del Norte: desviación comercial en perjuicio de Argentina y Brasil. (*Econ. Mex.*, 3:1, enero/junio 1994, p. 93–169, bibl., tables)
Discusses the expected effect of NAFTA on Argentine and Brazilian exports to the US market. Estimates trade diversion using a trade policy simulation model.

2266 Bisang, Roberto and **Bernard Kosacoff.**
Tres etapas en la búsqueda de una especialización sustentable: exportaciones industriales argentinas, 1974–1993. Buenos Aires: CEPAL, 1995. 45 leaves: ill. (Documento de trabajo; 59)
Analyzes industrial exports since 1973, from the period of import substitution to the present days of openness.

Blutman, Gustavo. Orden y desorden en la reforma del Estado argentino, 1989–1992. See item **3686.**

2267 Bogo, Jorge. La regulación de la actividad pesquera: una propuesta de cambio de política. (*Desarro. Econ.*, 33:132, enero/marzo 1994, p. 541–563, bibl., graphs, tables)
Evaluates the current regulatory scheme of the Argentine fishing industry, and investigates the introduction of individual quotas as an alternative.

2268 Bour, Juan Luis. Regulaciones laborales y funcionamiento del mercado de trabajo en América Latina: el caso argentino. (*in* Regulación del mercado de trabajo en América Latina. Panamá Zona 9, Panamá; San Francisco, Calif.: Centro International para el Desarrollo Económico, 1994, p. 33–75, appendix, graph, tables)
Comprehensive study of the Argentine labor market. Contains history, analysis of legislation and labor taxes, labor cost estimates, and an overall evaluation.

2269 Cetrángolo, Oscar and **Laura Golbert.**
Desempleo y política en las provincias argentinas. Buenos Aires: Centro de Estudios para el Cambio Estructural, 1995. 13 p.: ill. (Serie Notas; 4, julio 1995)

Describes the implementation of existing employment in all districts of the country.

2270 Chudnovsky, Daniel and **Martina Chidiak.** Apertura, reestructuración productiva y gestión ambiental: las industrias básicas en la Argentina. Comentarios de Enrique A. Bour y Martín González Rozada. (*Desarro. Econ.*, 36, no. especial, verano 1996, p. 155–186, bibl., tables)

Evaluates effects of pro-market reforms in Argentina by looking at three manufacturing sectors: paper, petrochemistry, and steel. These sectors were among those heavily protected in the past. They contribute an important share of manufacturing exports, and have a significant effect on the environment.

2271 Ciccolella, Pablo. Transformaciones recientes del territorio fueguino argentino. (*in* Territorios en transformación: análisis y propuestas. Madrid: Fondo Europeo de Desarrollo Regional; Consejo Superior de Investigaciones Científicas, 1994, p. 135–153, bibl.)

Analyzes the effect on the province of Tierra del Fuego of the so-called "Regime de promoción industrial," a promotion scheme that benefited the province between 1978–85.

2272 Convención de Bancos Privados, *10th, Buenos Aires, 1994.* Desafíos y opciones para crecer: actas y documentos técnicos. Buenos Aires: Asociación de Bancos Argentinos, 1994. 612 p.: bibl., ill.

Pending challenges to sustainable growth such as the reform of the judiciary power, employment policies, education and the labor market, and external policies are the center of this publication. Presents the point of view of both the policymaker and the academic for each topic.

2273 Dabús, Carlos A. Precios relativos y no neutralidad de la inflación: el caso argentino. (*Estud. Econ./Bahía Blanca*, 9:21/22, enero/dic. 1993, p. 1–21, appendix, bibl., graph, tables)

Tests the positive relationship between inflation and changes in relative prices using Argentina as a case study.

2274 Damill, Mario and **Saúl Keifman.** Liberalización del comercio en una economía de alta inflación: Argentina, 1989–91. Buenos Aires: CEDES, 1991. 34 p.: bibl., tables. (Documento CEDES; 72)

Highlights the links between stabilization policies and openness in Argentina between 1989–91. Compares the relative importance of changes in external trade regulations to changes in relative prices experienced with the introduction of the convertibility plan.

2275 *Desarrollo Económico.* Vol. 36, no. especial, verano 1996. Buenos Aires: Instituto de Desarrollo Económico y Social.

Proceedings of a meeting of the ten leading research groups in Argentina provide a good guide to the dominant economic agenda. Papers examine issues such as real effective exchange rates, regionalism in the Western hemisphere, trade liberalization and industrial restructuring, unemployment, health insurance, and the performance of the pension fund's administrators.

Díaz Bessone, Ramón Genaro. El futuro de la Argentina. See item **2723.**

2276 La economía internacional: temas de estudio en la Argentina. Ministerio de Relaciones Exteriores, Comercio Internacional y Culto, Secretaría de Relaciones Económicas Internacionales, Centro de Economía Internacional. Buenos Aires: Centro de Economía, 1994. 188 p.: bibl., ill.

Contains three essays related to international trade focusing on the environment, the potential of the fishing industry, and dumping devices.

2277 Eggers, Francisco and **Karina Smolej.** Evolución de las finanzas públicas de la provincia de Buenos Aires, 1970–1993. La Plata: Ministerio de Economía de la Provincia de Buenos Aires, 1994. 171 p.: ill. (Cuadernos de economía; 1)

Provides historical analysis of public finances in Argentina's largest province.

2278 Estudios argentinos para la integración del Mercosur. Ministerio de Relaciones Exteriores y Culto, Secretaría de Relaciones Económicas Internacionales, Centro de Economía Internacional. Buenos Aires: Centro de Economía Internacional, 1993. 571 p.: bibl., ill.

Essays on a variety of subjects associated with regional integration within Mercosur. Topics examined range from tax harmonization and macroeconomic interdependence to the importance of regional integration for the energy sector.

2279 Evolución reciente de la pobreza en el Gran Buenos Aires, 1988–1992. Ministerio de Economía y Obras y Servicios Públicos, Secretaría de Programación Económica. Argentina: Comité Ejecutivo para el Estudio de la Pobreza en la Argentina, 1993. 39 p.: bibl. (Documento de trabajo; 2)

Examines poverty in Buenos Aires province based on a definition of the poverty line determined by a basket of goods and services.

2280 Fanelli, José María and José Luis Machinea. Capital movements in Argentina. Buenos Aires: CEDES, 1994. 47 p.: bibl., tables. (Documento CEDES; 99. Serie Economía)

Looking at the Argentine case, this paper examines the effect of a sudden and exogenous change in the amount and characteristics of capital inflows on macrostability and in the financial and real structures of the domestic economy.

Ferreira Falcón, Magno. El complejo hidroeléctrico Yacyretá: histórico y polémico Proyecto Binacional. See item **2212.**

2281 Figueras, Alberto José and Alberto M. Díaz Cafferata. Cambios estructurales y desocupación regional: la provincia de Catamarca. (*Rev. Econ. /Argentina*, 45:75, oct./dic. 1994, p. 51–107, bibl., graphs, tables)

Reports on structural reforms in the province of Catamarca. In particular, investigates the effect of reforms on the labor market.

2282 Frenkel, Roberto and Guillermo Rozenwurcel. The multiple roles of privatization in Argentina. (*in* Institutional design in new democracies: Eastern Europe and Latin America. Boulder, Colo.: Westview Press, 1996, p. 219–233, tables)

This paper takes a different look at the Argentine privatization process: it aims to ascertain the motives guiding the Menem administration's drive toward privatization.

2283 Gatto, Francisco. Nuevos elementos para la discusión de la problemática regional en Argentina en los años 90: la transformación macroeconómica y el proceso subregional de integración económica. (*in* Territorios en transformación: análisis y propuestas. Madrid: Fondo Europeo de Desarrollo Regional; Consejo Superior de Investigaciones Científicas, 1994, p. 71–99, bibl.)

Provides an overview of the new regional environment shaped by macroecomic discipline, structural reforms, and the process of regional integration. In this context, alternative policies regarding the Argentine provinces are discussed.

2284 Gorenstein, Sylvia. Reestructuración del capitalismo argentino y repercusiones territoriales: reflexiones en torno al "modelo neuquino." (*EURE/Santiago*, 20:60, agosto 1994, p. 43–61, bibl., tables)

Analyzes the particularities of Neuquén, a province with a successful economic performance despite the strong intervention of the provincial government.

2285 Harriague, M. Marcela; Leonardo Gasparini; and Benigno Vélez. El gasto público social y su impacto redistributivo. Coordinación de María C.V. de Flood. Buenos Aires: Ministerio de Economía y Obras y Servicios Públicos, Secretaría de Programación Económica, 1994. vii, 180 p.: bibl., tables.

Offers a detailed analysis of the public social expenditure and its effect on income distribution. Includes historical data.

2286 Hogares con necesidades básicas insatisfechas (NBI): 1980 y 1991. Argentina: Ministerio de Economía y Obras y Servicios Públicos. Secretaría de Programación Económica, 1993. 71 p.: bibl., ill., tables. (Documento de trabajo/CEPA, Comité Ejecutivo para el Estudio de la Pobreza en la Argentina; 3)

This is third report by the Executive Committee for the Study of Poverty. Provides information on unsatisfied basic needs among households by county and in the country as a whole.

2287 El horizonte de complementación de la Argentina con la región Asia Pacífico. v. 1–3. Ministerio de Economía y Obras y Servicios Públicos, Secretaría de Programación Económica. Buenos Aires: Ministerio de Economía y Obras y Servicios Públicos, Secretaría de Programación Económica, 1994. 3 v.: bibl., ill., maps.

Extensive study on the prospects of trade between Argentina and Pacific Asia. Provides background information on goods and investment flows between Argentina and

China, Hong Kong, Taiwan, Malaysia, Korea, and Singapore, and analyzes the prospects of different economic sectors.

2288 Huici, Néstor and Jorge Schvarzer. Situación de la industria alimentaria en Argentina y Brasil en el contexto del Mercosur. Buenos Aires: Banco Interamericano de Desarrollo, Instituto para la Integración de América Latina, BID-INTAL, 1993. 124 p.: ill. (Publ.; 410)

Evaluates prospects of the food industry in Argentina and Brazil given the promising trends in trade observed within the preferential arrangement. Provides detailed data by sector.

2289 Integración económica Argentino-Chilena. Ministerio de Relaciones Exteriores, Comercio Internacional y Culto, Secretaría de Relaciones Económicas Internacionales, Centro de Economía Internacional. Buenos Aires: Centro de Economía Internacional, 1993. 231 p.: bibl.

Series of essays addresses potential for economic integration between Argentina and Chile. Analyzes agricultural and energy production and transmission sectors. Also examines transportation between the two countries, tax systems, and protection devices.

2290 Isuani, Ernesto Aldo; Rafael Rofman; and Jorge Antonio San Martino. Las jubilaciones del siglo XXI: ¿podemos gastar a cuenta? (Bol. Inf. Techint, 286, abril/junio 1996, p. 79–104, graphs, tables)

Examines Argentina's experience with its new pension system.

2291 Jornadas Internacionales: Argentina y Brasil en el Mercosur, Univ. de Buenos Aires, 1994. Argentina y Brasil en el Mercosur: políticas comunes y alianzas regionales. Recopilación de Mario Rapoport. Buenos Aires: Grupo Editor Latinoaméricano, 1995. 176 p.: bibl. (Col. Estudios internacionales)

In light of the prospects for regional integration, the proceedings of this conference analyze Argentina and Brazil's policies on issues such as external relationships, stabilization, trade and regional integration, education, science and technology, and development.

2292 Juri, María de la Esperanza et al. Las economías de las provincias desde inicios de la década. (Noved. Econ., 17:172/173, abril/mayo 1995, p. 28–93, tables)

Series of essays provides a comprehensive view of regional economies in Argentina for the period 1990–94. The degree of development of economic activities, investment performance, external trade participation, public finance, the degree of regulation, the tax structure, and economic infrastructure supply are the main indicators examined.

2293 Kosacoff, Bernardo P. et al. El desafío de la competitividad: la industria argentina en transformación. Buenos Aires: Alianza Editorial, 1993. 421 p.: bibl. (Alianza estudio; 21)

Essays focus on the transformation of the Argentine industrial sector in response to trade liberalization. Topics discussed include global trends, issues of industrial organization and public policies, labor market aspects, and the experience of multinational and medium and small enterprises.

2294 Kozulj, Roberto. La evolución del sector petrolero desde la desregulación: inversión pública y rentabilidad privada. (Desarro. Energ., 3:5, marzo 1994, p. 95–116, bibl., graphs, tables)

Provides an incisive explanation of two facts observed in the oil sector during the first three years of deregulation policies: 1) the rapid increase in production levels; and 2) the reduction in user's prices.

Krantzer, Guillermo and Jorge Sánchez. Regulaciones en el transporte urbano: el caso de Buenos Aires. See item **3738.**

2295 El libro azul de las provincias: las economías regionales en la transformación económica de la República Argentina. Buenos Aires: Instituto de Investigaciones Económicas y Financieras de la Confederación General Económica, 1993. 389 p.: bibl., ill.

Analyzes the economic and social situation of 14 Argentine provinces and the Federal District.

2296 Lifschitz, Edgardo and Eugenia Crespo Armengol. Evolución de la protección arancelaria nominal y efectiva, 1990–2001. (Bol. Inf. Techint, 283, julio/sept. 1995, p. 91–116, tables)

Using an input-output table with 1989 data on tariffs and prospect tariff levels according to the Mercosur agreements, the authors provide an estimate of the level of nominal and effective protection for Argentina for the period 1990–2001.

2297 López, Andrés F. Ajuste estructural y estrategias empresarias en la industria petroquímica argentina. (*Desarro. Econ.,* 33 : 132, enero/marzo 1994, p. 515–540, bibl., tables)

Analyzes the evolution of the oil industry in the last two decades. In particular, explores the response to economic deregulation in the 1990s.

2298 López, Néstor and Alfredo Monza. Un intento de estimación del sector informal urbano en la Argentina. (*Desarro. Econ.,* 35 : 139, oct./dic. 1995, p. 467–474, tables)

Methodological exercise estimates the size and characteristics of the Argentine informal economy for the period 1990–94.

2299 Magariños, Carlos; José Luis Díaz Pérez; and Pablo Sierra. Política industrial en los años '90. (*Bol. Inf. Techint,* 282, abril/junio 1995, p. 17–32, appendix, graphs, tables)

Describes the government industrial policy since 1990. Four components are highlighted: a specialization and restructuring policy, an automobile industry policy, a three-year incentive plan for development of small and medium-sized enterprises, and a development program for industrial suppliers.

2300 Mapas de la pobreza en la Argentina. Comité Ejecutivo para el Estudio de la Pobreza en la Argentina. Buenos Aires: Ministerio de Economía y Obras y Servicios Públicos, Secretaría de Programación Económica, Instituto Nacional de Estadísticas y Censos, 1994. 357 p.: maps, tables. (Documento de trabajo/CEPA; 4)

Major comprehensive study of poverty based on the National Census of Households of 1991. Provides different measures of poverty in Argentina by counties.

2301 Marshall, Adriana. Regímenes institucionales de determinación salarial y estructura de los salarios: Argentina, 1976–1993. (*Desarro. Econ.,* 35 : 138, julio/sept. 1995, p. 275–288, appendix, bibl., graphs, tables)

Analyzes the effects on labor compensation of changes in the labor market legislation in Argentina. Focuses on the wage structure by economic sector and manufacturing activity.

2302 Martínez Nogueira, Roberto. Devising new approaches to poverty in Argentina. (*in* Strategies to combat poverty in Latin America. Washington: Inter-American Development Bank; Baltimore: John Hopkins Univ. Press, 1995, p. 33–85, appendices, bibl., tables)

Studies programs designed to fight poverty, focusing on maternal and child nutrition programs, the development of production among rural poor, and the eradication of squatter settlements on government land.

2303 Martínez Nogueira, Roberto. Negotiated interactions: NGOs and local government in Rosario, Argentina. (*in* New paths to democratic development in Latin America. Edited by Charles A. Reilly. Boulder, Colo.: Lynne Rienner Publishers, 1995, p. 45–70, table)

Examines the relations among the four actors involved in the workings of NGOs: NGOs, neighborhood organizations, local governments, and political parties. The case study is Rosario, where these institutions have been particularly important since the economic crisis of the late 1980s.

2304 Martirena Mantel, Ana María. El tipo de cambio en Argentina de los años noventa y la globalización de la economía mundial. Buenos Aires: Instituto Torcuato Di Tella; Centro de Investigaciones Económicas, 1995. 28 p.: bibl. (Serie Documentos de Trabajo)

Analyzes effect of financial innovation on the equilibrium exchange rate. Within that framework, presents an evaluation of Argentina's exchange rate up to 1992.

2305 Minujin Z., Alberto and Nestor López. Sobre pobres y vulnerables: el caso argentino. Buenos Aires: UNICEF, 1993. 18 leaves: bibl., ill. (Documento de trabajo/UNICEF Argentina; 18)

Presents an analysis of poverty dynamics for 1986–92, focusing on the impact of changes in the labor market through the different social levels.

2306 Mitnik, Oscar and Silvia Montoya. Pobreza y distribución del ingreso: dinámica y características; Gran Buenos Aires, 1974–1994. (*Estudios/Fundación Mediterránea,* 18 : 74, julio/sept. 1995, p. 70–94, bibl., graph, tables)

Reviews the evolution of poverty and income distribution levels for greater Buenos Aires by comparing five years: 1974, 1986, 1989, 1991, and 1994. Poverty line methodology is used, applying three measurements:

head count index, poverty gap, and seriousness of poverty.

2307 Montoya, Silvia. Capacitación y reentrenamiento laboral: Argentina durante la transición. Córdoba, Argentina: Instituto de Estudios Económicos sobre la Realidad Argentina y Latinoamericana; Fundación Mediterránea, 1996. 60 p.: bibl., graphs, tables. (Estudios/Fundación Mediterránea; vol. 19, no. 76, enero/marzo 1996)

Analyzes the importance of training and related policies in Argentina, and evaluates them in light of international experience. Draws some recommendations for policies aimed to facilitate the transition of a changing economy.

2308 Montoya, Silvia and **Marcela Perticara.** Los migrantes en el mercado de trabajo urbano: el caso del Gran Buenos Aires. (*An. Asoc. Argent. Econ. Polít.*, 3, 1995, p. 667–686, bibl., graph, tables)

Evaluates the role of migration from neighboring countries to the labor market of greater Buenos Aires using data for the period 1974–94.

Moreno, Omar. La última oportunidad del sindicalismo argentino. See item **3751.**

2309 Müller, Alberto E.G. Tras la privatización: las perspectivas del medio ferroviario argentino. (*Desarro. Econ.*, 34:134, julio/sept. 1994, p. 243–262, bibl., tables)

Evaluates prospects for rail cargo in Argentina after the privatization process.

2310 Obschatko, Edith S. de; Eduardo Sguiglia; and **Ricardo Delgado.** Efectos de la desregulación sobre la competitividad de la producción argentina. Buenos Aires: Grupo Editor Latinoamericano, 1994. 232 p.: bibl., ill. (Col. Estudios políticos y sociales)

Two essays on the effect of deregulation on competitiveness. The first essay provides indicators of the impact on agriculture. The second essay takes a more general approach, though it offers a detailed list of factors affecting different sectors.

2311 Pablo, Juan Carlos de. Quién hubiera dicho: la transformación que lideraron Menem y Cavallo. Buenos Aires: Planeta, 1994. 303 p.: bibl., ill. (Espejo de la Argentina)

Contains a detailed analysis of the stages of the Argentine transformation since 1989. Discusses privatization of public enterprises, liberalization of trade, the new monetary and social security system, and institutional adjustments to increase market competition.

2312 Pérez Barrero, María Delia. Tendencias recientes del desarrollo regional argentino. (*Rev. Ciclos*, 3:5, segundo semestre 1993, p. 3–42, maps, tables)

Applying the analysis of clusters on 68 variables related to production, employment and population, attempts to provide a description of economic development trends in the various regions of the country.

2313 Pessino, Carola. From aggregate shocks to labor market adjustments: shifting of wage profiles under hyperinflation in Argentina. Buenos Aires: Centro de Estudios Macroeconómicos de Argentina, 1993. 58 p.: bibl., ill. (Serie Documentos de trabajo; 95)

Examines the impact of inflation on the structure and inequality of wages. A cross section of microdata on wage profiles are compared between 1987–89, before and after the episode of hyperinflation.

2314 Plan quinquenal, 1995–1999: Argentina en crecimiento, 1995–1999. Buenos Aires: Ministerio de Economía; Presidencia de la Nación, 1995. 47 p.: col. ill., col. maps.

Presents the government economic program for 1995–2000.

2315 Pucci, Roberto. Ajuste y crisis en el NOA: el caso de Tucumán. (*Real. Econ./Buenos Aires*, 127, oct./nov. 1994, p. 100–115, tables)

Provides an analytical view of economic adjustment in Tucumán, taking into account prospects for development under the new pro-market rules.

Ratliff, William E. and **Roger Fontaine.** Argentina's capitalist revolution revisited: confronting the social costs of statist mistakes. See item **3763.**

2316 Reconversión y estímulo a las actividades productivas. Buenos Aires: Fundación de Investigaciones Económicas Latinoamericanas; Fundación Konrad Adenauer, 1993. 66 p.: bibl., ill.

Evaluates alternative policies aimed at facilitating industrial restructuring. After discussing the experience in Spain, Japan, and Korea, as well as the past Argentine experience, the study provides some specific recommendations. Additionally, analyzes the recent experiences of the automobile and wine industries.

Richard Jorba, Rodolfo A. and **Eduardo E. Pérez Romagnoli.** La década de 1870 en Mendoza: etapa de reorientación de la economía y el espacio hacia el dominio vitivinícola. See item **2768.**

Richard Jorba, Rodolfo A. Modelo vitivinícola en Mendoza: las acciones de la élite y los cambios espaciales resultantes, 1875–1895. See item **2769.**

2317 Rozenwurcel, Guillermo and **Raúl Fernández.** El fortalecimiento del sector financiero en el proceso de ajuste: el caso argentino. (*in* El fortalecimiento del sector financiero en el proceso de ajuste: liberalización y regulación. Buenos Aires: Centro de Estudios de Estado y Sociedad; Washington: Banco Interamericano de Desarrollo, 1994, p. 41–85, bibl., tables)

Examines the Argentine financial sector before the Dec. 1994 crisis. Present evidence that the strong dependence on external funds, low levels of financial intermediation, a short horizon of assets and liabilities, and solvency problems in the provincial public banks were already matters of concern.

2318 Schilder, E.D. and **B.E. Bravo-Ureta.** Análisis de costos en explotaciones lecheras de la región central argentina con algunas comparaciones internacionales. (*Invest. Agrar.*, 9:2, agosto 1994, p. 199–214, bibl., graphs, tables)

By looking at 84 farms in the center of the country, the authors estimate unit costs and scale economies in the Argentine milk industry, and make comparisons with international prices.

2319 Schvarzer, Jorge. La industria que supimos conseguir. Buenos Aires: Planeta, 1996. 370 p.: bibl. (Historia argentina)

Provides a rich history of the manufacturing sector in Argentina. Concludes with a critical view of current policies.

Schwartz, Gilson. Brazil, Mercosur, and SAFTA: destructive restructuring or Pan-American integration? See item **2374.**

2320 Seminario Regional de Economía y Empleo en el Norte Argentino, *Salta, Argentina, 1994.* Seminario: julio 1994, Salta.

Contribuciones de Roberto Augusto Ulloa *et al.* Buenos Aires?: MTSS, 1994. 197 p.: ill., maps.

Examines the characteristics of the economy of the northern region. Topics addressed include communication with the rest of the country, natural resources, allocation incentives, and particularly, the labor market.

Tellechea de Arca, Mireya. Paraguay socioeconómico y cultural: hidrovía-MERCOSUR. See item **2848.**

2321 Torres, Clemencia. Regulatory schemes and investment behavior in transmission of electricity: the case of Argentina. (*Rev. Anál. Econ.*, 10:2, nov. 1995, p. 203–235, bibl., map, tables)

Analyzes the impact of regulation on the expansion of the network for high voltage electricity. In particular, attempts to explain the lack of new investment—necessary to eliminate local bottlenecks in the transmission system—despite the seemingly favorable new regulation.

2322 Tussie, Diana. Bargaining at a crossroads: Argentina. (*in* The developing countries in world trade: policies and bargaining strategies. Edited by Diana Tussie and David Glover. Boulder, Colo.: Lynne Rienner Publishers, 1993, p. 119–136, tables)

Describes and assesses the strategy and procedures that Argentina used to bargain in the Uruguay Round. Different from the past during the Uruguay Round, Argentina used unilateral liberalization both as a goodwill gesture and a moral argument to push for increased access to markets.

2323 Weinschelbaum, Federico. La inversión en investigación y desarrollo: funciones objetivo sociales y privadas y formas de mercado con una aplicación a la industria farmacéutica argentina. Buenos Aires: Instituto Torcuato di Tella; Centro de Investigaciones Económicas, 1994. 38 p.: bibl. (Serie documentos de trabajo; DTE 185)

Analyzes use of property rights as a device to limit the effect of market failures on research and development. More importantly, applies this theoretical framework to the drug industry in Argentina to provide specific recommendations.

BRAZIL

MELISSA H. BIRCH, *School of Business, University of Kansas*
RUSSELL E. SMITH, *School of Business, Washburn University*

THE OPENING OF THE BRAZILIAN ECONOMY, beginning in 1990 with the Collor government's neoliberal reforms, the apparent victory of the Real Plan of 1994 over (hyper)inflation, and the established pattern of economic growth within a relatively open economy shifted the focus of Brazilian economic literature from a preoccupation with macroeconomic stabilization to a broad consideration of emerging, as well as, traditional themes. Emerging themes include the impact of the open economy (including the common market of the South, Mercosul), increased international competitive pressure following forty years of import-substitution-industrialization, and the reform of the Brazilian State. More traditional themes include regional development, income distribution, labor policies and labor markets, agriculture, and Brazilian economic history.

The creation of Mercosul, the regional economic integration project negotiated between 1991 and 1994 with Argentina, Paraguay, and Uruguay, has spawned a considerable amount of new, increasingly complex literature that covers nearly all areas of economic activity and regulation. The more general works examine Mercosul in relation to other international trade treaties such as GATT and ALADI (item **1458**). More focused studies examine Brazil's relations with its South American and North American neighbors within this new regional context (items **2331** and **2374**). In addition, Mercosul's impact on already existing Brazilian regional disparities is also studied (item **2381**). The construction of Mercosul's legal framework is analyzed (items **1445** and **2382**), as is the impacts on specific sectors, including agriculture (items **2338** and **1421**) and the automobile industry (item **2353**).

The post-1990 open economy was accompanied by a heightened concern with productivity issues, as reflected in broad analyses of the competitive position of Brazilian industries within the world economy (items **2345** and **2354**), and industrial distribution and productivity changes in the state of São Paulo (item **2351**). The open economy impacted regional development by increasing international linkages (item **2340**) and by assigning a role for Mercosul in the reconcentration of economic activities in southeastern and southern Brazil (item **2341**). Reform of the State, which paralleled the economic opening, is evident in analyses of economic stabilization and public policy in general (item **2359**), the Real Plan (item **2348**), tax policy (items **2366** and **2336**), social security reform (item **2328**), privatization (item **2355**), and the role of the State investment banks (item **2362**). Other policy issues are studied in the context of the post-1950 import-substitution-industrialization period, including US investment (item **2349**), indexation (item **2379**), the relationship between public and private sectors (item **2378**), the ethanol program (items **2364** and **2370**), and the Carajas project (item **2372**). Some works provide especially valuable data on exchange rates (item **2325**) and recent economic and social conditions (item **2342**).

Income distribution inequality is one of the most durable themes in Brazilian economic development. Studies for Brazil as a whole (items **2373** and **2330**) and for the Rio de Janeiro and São Paulo metropolitan areas in particular (item **2360**), indicate that income distribution worsens, or at best stays the same, regardless of macroeconomic conditions. The minimum wage is found to have limited use as a tool to counter poverty and income inequality (item **2369**). Other labor market themes considered include labor market flexibility and adjustment (items **2347** and **2324**), agricultural labor (items **2350** and **2357**), and wage determination (items **2367** and **2329**). Numerous studies examine various aspects of the household labor-supply decision, often based on household data from the Pesquisa Nacional por Amostra de Domicilios (items **2368, 2356, 2358** and **2337**). Historical analyses consider technology, infrastructure, and industrialization (item **2380**), and the Japanese role in Brazilian economic development (item **2334**).

2324 Amadeo, Edward *et al.* Brazil. (*in* Human resources and the adjustment process. Edited by Ricardo Paredes and Luis A. Riveros. Washington: Inter-American Development Bank, 1994, p. 13–61, bibl., graphs, tables)

Chapter reports on Brazil's structural adjustment process since the 1970s and its impact on employment, wages, and incomes. Also reports on the educational system, the population's educational attainment, and the vocational educational system. Offers conclusions in terms of training and costs of structural adjustment.

Andrade, Manuel Correia de Oliveira. A cassiterita nas regiões norte e nordeste do Brasil. See item **2860**.

2325 Associação Nacional das Instituições do Mercado Aberto (Brazil). Câmbio. Rio de Janeiro: Associação Nacional das Instituições do Mercado Aberto, 1994?. 339 p.: bibl., ill., tables. (Séries históricas)

Examines Brazilian exchange rates from 1889 to 1994. Brief historical overview, followed by detailed tables of real nominal exchange rates between the US dollar and Brazilian currency. Monthly data is provided for the period after 1930, and daily quotations of official and parallel dollar rates are available for more recent years.

2326 Associação Nacional das Instituições do Mercado Aberto (Brazil). Dívida pública. Rio de Janeiro: Associação Nacional das Instituições do Mercado Aberto, 1994? 176 p.: bibl., ill., tables. (Séries históricas)

Examines public debt in Brazil. Precise definitions of various instruments and associated financial terms are followed by exceedingly detailed tables ranging from annual data beginning in 1887 to monthly or quarterly coverage of debt composition (by instrument or holder) during the 1980s.

2327 Baer, Werner and **Charles Mueller.** Environmental aspects of Brazil's economic development. pt. 1. (*Luso-Braz. Rev.*, 32:1, Summer 1995, p. 83–99, bibl.)

Chronicles accumulating environmental damage associated with Brazilian economic development which occurred without adequate planning for appropriate handling of industrial waste. Discusses air, water, and soil pollution associated with industrial development and agricultural expansion. Examines how poverty and inadequate social services contribute to environmental degradation.

2328 Barbosa, Fernando de Holanda and **Guillermo Mondino.** El sistema de seguridad social en Brasil: por qué es importante reformarlo. (*Estudios/Fundación Mediterránea*, 17:71, oct./dic. 1994, p. 155–173, bibl., graphs, tables)

Begins with an accessible theoretical discussion of social security systems, savings rates, and distribution, then introduces the Argentine and Chilean cases, and presents a detailed description of the Brazilian social security system. Identifies seven principal problems and suggests reforms.

2329 Barros, Alexandre Rands. O papel dos salários reais na determinação da renda: um teste empírico para o Brasil com dados para o período 1971–86. (*Rev. Bras. Econ.*, 48:3, julho/set. 1994, p. 325–353, bibl., graphs, tables)

Uses monthly industry data from 1971–86 to contrast Keynesian and neoclassical perspectives on the impact of real wage shocks on aggregate income. Results support Keynesian view that real wage increases permanently raise aggregate real income, while inflationary impact is not long term.

2330 Barros, Ricardo Paes de and **Rosane Mendoça.** A evolução do bem-estar, pobreza e desigualdade no Brasil ao longo das últimas três décadas, 1960–1990. (*Pesqui. Planej. Econ.*, 25 : 1, abril 1995, p. 115–164, appendices, bibl., graphs, tables)

Analyzes effect of changes in average income and inequality on poverty and social well-being throughout the 1960–90s. Finds that inequality increased continuously, while changes in poverty and well-being followed the business cycle.

2331 Bekerman, Marta. Que vantagens econômicas traz para o Brasil a integração no Cono Sul? (*Rev. Bras. Comér. Exter.*, 11 : 42, jan./março 1995, p. 41–49, bibl., photo)

Despite its position as the largest market in Mercosur, Brazil achieves considerable gains from regional integration in the Southern Cone, including profits from expanding market size as well as competitive advantages in third markets. Potential technological cooperation within leading sectors and enhanced negotiating power in international fora also constitute important benefits.

2332 Bêrni, Duilio de Avila. Análise contrafactual da distribuição da renda no Brasil. (*Rev. Econ. Polít.*, 15 : 3, julho/set. 1995, p. 66–83, bibl., tables)

Uses an input-output framework to speculate on impact on employment and wages if income in Brazil between 1970–80 had been redistributed from high-income households to low-income households or to the government, based on expenditure patterns of the three groups. Redistribution to low-income households would have favored rural, agricultural, and labor-intensive activities and a decline in average wages, while redistribution to the government would generate more employment in urban services and possible wage increases.

Bianchi, Eduardo and **Jorge Robbio.** Tratado de Libre Comercio de América del Norte: desviación comercial en perjuicio de Argentina y Brasil. See item **2265.**

Bustelo, Pablo. La industrialización en América Latina y Asia Oriental: un estudio comparado de Brasil y Taiwán. See item **1274.**

2333 Cacciamali, Maria Cristina et al. Crescimento econômico e geração de empregos: considerações sobre políticas públicas. (*Planej. Polít. Públicas*, 12, junho/dez.

1995, p. 167–197, appendixes, bibl., tables)

Analyzes changes in the operation of Brazilian labor markets during the 1980s. Summarizes technological changes in labor markets worldwide. Evaluates effectiveness of various existing and proposed public labor-market policies and argues for active policies to meet challenges brought by technological and macroeconomic changes.

2334 Câmara de Comércio e Indústria Japonesa do Brasil. Concurso de monografia: a contribuição japonesa no desenvolvimento econômico do Brasil. São Paulo: Forja Editora, 1989? 70 p.: bibl., ill.

Four papers document and analyze the experience, participation, and contribution of Japanese immigrants in the Brazilian economy from 1908–88. Examines immigration process, geographical and sectoral participation, demographic characteristics and human capital attainments, role in specific companies, and Brazilian-Japanese relations.

2335 Canuto, Otaviano. Brasil e Coréia do Sul: os (des)caminhos da industrialização tardia. São Paulo: Nobel, 1994. 178 p.: bibl.

One of few scholarly comparisons of Asian and Latin American economic policy performance. Examines Brazil and South Korea in the context of late-industrializing peripheral countries and as models of NICs (newly industrialized countries). Finds important differences in their experiences and indicates how Brazil might learn from South Korea especially regarding importance of education, agrarian reform, and of large companies in acquisition and development of technology.

2336 Comissão Executiva de Reforma Fiscal (Brazil). Reforma fiscal: coletânea de estudos técnicos. v. 1–2. Coordenação de Ary Oswaldo Mattos Filho. São Paulo: Dórea Books and Art, 1993?. 2 v.

Technical studies that formed the basis for the 1992 tax reform proposed to Congress by the Collor Government. Prepared over an intense five-month period, individual papers discuss income and consumption taxes (including some discussion of a flat tax), as well as taxes on property, assets, and business transactions. Other chapters cover assignment of revenues, budgeting, decentralization, social security, and education.

2337 Connelly, Rachel; Deborah S. DeGraff; and **Deborah Levison.** Women's employment and child care in Brazil. (*Econ. Dev. Cult. Change*, 44:3, April 1996, p. 619–656, appendix, tables)

Uses detailed data from the 1985 Pesquisa Nacional por Amostra de Domicílios to analyze relationship between women's labor force activity and child-care choices in Brazil. Results are consistent with economic theory and indicate that mother's employment is influenced by the presence of children and potential alternative caregivers. Both employment and use of nonparental child care are positively influenced by level of education.

Cordeiro, Helena Kohn. A circulação da informação no espaço brasileiro e o sistema bancário. See item **2872.**

2338 Delgado, Nelson Giordano. Política ativa para a agricultura e MERCOSUL: observações a partir do caso brasileiro. (*Estud. Soc. Agríc.*, 5, nov. 1995, p. 103–113, bibl.)

Notes that Brazil historically has had an "active" agricultural policy that promotes modernization and provides economic benefits. Economic integration will limit the government's ability to continue such "active" sectoral policy and will require, instead, greater examination of the role of agriculture in the economy and society.

2339 Desenvolvimento e natureza: estudos para uma sociedade sustentável. Organização de Clóvis de Vasconcelos Cavalcanti. São Paulo: Cortez Editora; Recife, Brazil: Fundação Joaquim Nabuco, 1995. 429 p.: bibl., ill.

Collection of essays on sustainable development in Brazil. Includes conceptual pieces and chapters focusing on examples of sustainable development techniques.

2340 Desigualdades regionais e desenvolvimento. Organização de Rui de Britto Alvares Affonso e Pedro Luiz Barros Silva. São Paulo: FUNDAP; Editora Unesp, 1995? 340 p.: (Federalismo no Brasil)

First volume in a series on Brazilian federalism analyzes the increased spatial deconcentration of economic activity between regions, within regions, and within states. Also addresses the new and increased international economic links of the regions, the impact of deconcentration on the labor market,

living conditions, heterogeneity and inequality, the division of labor, and center-periphery relations.

2341 Diniz, Clélio Campolina. Reversión de la polarización y reconcentración regional en Brasil. (*in* Territorios en transformación: análisis y propuestas. Madrid: Fondo Europeo de Desarrollo Regional; Consejo Superior de Investigaciones Científicas, 1994, p. 239–266, bibl., maps, tables)

Examines processes of regional polarization in Brazil through 1970, the subsequent apparent decentralization and reversal of polarization of the 1980s, and later reconcentration. Argues that powerful forces, including the market, the existing industrial base, the location of research activities, and the professional labor market, support the reconcentration of activities within Brazil's most developed region, from Minas Gerais to Rio Grande do Sul and the state of São Paulo. This process will be accentuated by regional integration under Mercosur.

2342 A economia brasileira em gráficos = The Brazilian economy in graphs. Rio de Janeiro: Fundação Getulio Vargas; Brasília: Fundação Alexandre de Gusmão, 1996? 130 p.: bibl., ill.

Graphic representations of macroeconomic variables, social indicators, labor and financial market data, and sectoral performance (including agricultural, external, and public sectors). Useful guide.

2343 Encontro Nacional de Economia, 22nd, Florianópolis, Brazil, 1994. Anais. v. 1–2. São Paulo: Associação Nacional de Centros de Pos-Graduação em Economia, 1995? 2 v.

Vol. 1 includes 33 papers organized into sections on issues such as the independence of central banks, economics of technology, economic theory, regional and urban economics, macroeconomics, international economics, history and economic development, growth and distribution, labor economics, and economic methodology. Vol. 2 includes 27 papers. Sections cover economic demography, open-economy macroeconomics, industrial economics, history of economic thought, agricultural economics, economics of the public sector, labor economics, Brazilian economic history, and the environment.

2344 Federação das Indústrias do Estado de Rondônia (Brazil). Rondônia: perfil e diretrizes de desenvolvimento industrial e de infra-estrutura. Porto Velho, Brazil: FIERO, 1995. 471 p.: ill., map.

Analyzes the economy of Rondônia state during 1994. Includes detailed chapters on the geopolitical, economic, and social history of the state, industrial profile, electrical energy, transportation, the free trade area of Guaraja-Mirim, access to several regional markets (including Asia and North America), lines of credit and fiscal incentives, industrial policy and state incentives, and training programs.

2345 Ferraz, João Carlos; David Kupfer; and Lia Haguenauer. Made in Brazil: desafios competitivos para a indústria. Rio de Janeiro: Editora Campus, 1996. 386 p.: bibl., ill.

Examines competitive position of Brazilian industry within world economy and its determinants, including managerial and firm innovation, productivity, and human resource characteristics; market and industry structure; and macroeconomic, political, regulatory, infrastructural, and social factors. Analysis and results are provided by industries in four product groups: commodities, durable goods manufacturing and its suppliers, traditional manufactures, and technology-intensive import-substitution industries.

2346 Ferreira, Alcides and Nilton Horita. BM&F: a história do mercado futuro no Brasil. Prefácio de Ari Oswaldo Mattos Filho. São Paulo: Cultura Editores Associados, 1996. 474 p.: bibl., ill., index, photos.

An informal history of first 10 years of the futures market in Brazil based on interviews with many of the founding players. Includes photographs of the BM&F and of many people associated with it.

2347 Flexibilidade do mercado de trabalho no Brasil. Organização de José Márcio Camargo. Rio de Janeiro: Fundação Getulio Vargas Editora, 1996. 243 p.: bibl., ill.

Five separately authored chapters present substantial information and analyses of flexibility in manufacturing employment from the mid-1980s through early 1990s. Considers role of labor institutions, including the law of labor contracts, labor courts, and systems of indemnification for job loss, as well as macroeconomic conditions. Con-

cludes that labor markets are very flexible and that flexibility creates disincentives to investment in training and human capital.

2348 Fórum Nacional Os Grandes Desafios do Novo Governo, Rio de Janeiro, 1995. O real e o futuro da economia. Coordenação de João Paulo dos Reis Velloso. Rio de Janeiro: J. Olympio Editora, 1995. 246 p.: bibl., ill.

Volume considers impact of Plano Real on stabilization and growth. Reviews future industrial and labor market policies in post-inflationary Brazil.

2349 Freitas Júnior, Norton Ribeiro de. O capital norte-americano e investimento no Brasil: características e perspectivas de um relacionamento econômico, 1950 a 1990. Rio de Janeiro: Editora Record, 1994. 430 p.: appendices, bibl., index.

Traces evolution of US investment in Brazil from 1950–90. Discusses its role in creation of the Brazilian business environment. Contains a chapter on American English expressions that have contributed to the "language of business" in Brazil, and appendices that include lists of US firms conducting business in Brazil between 1869 and the 1920s, and as of 1992.

2350 Fundação Sistema Estadual de Análise de Dados (São Paulo). Força de trabalho na agricultura paulista. São Paulo: SEADE, 1996. 101 p.: bibl., ill. (Análises & ensaios)

Results of study estimating the agricultural labor demands associated with 46 specific crops in São Paulo state. Substantial attention given to detailing the methodology. Sugarcane accounts for 40 percent of labor demand, while sugarcane, coffee, oranges, eucalyptus, beans, and cotton make up 75 percent of total demand.

2351 Fundação Sistema Estadual de Análise de Dados (São Paulo). Produtividade e ajuste na indústria paulista. São Paulo: SEADE, 1995. 119 p.: bibl., ill. (Análises & ensaios)

Analyzes productivity changes in manufacturing in São Paulo state between 1986–94. Finds that productivity was constant during the earlier years and increased after 1990 as a result of economic opening and reorganization of production within the firm. Concludes that low levels of investment in human capital may constitute an obstacle to attaining international levels of competitiveness.

2352 Gareis, Maria da Guia Santos. Industrialização no Nordeste, 1880–1920. Rio de Janeiro: Notrya Editora, 1994. 142 p.: bibl., ill. (Col. História, política & sociedade)

Examines emergence and growth of manufacturing in Brazil's Northeast from 1880–1920, which was most evident in the textile industries of Pernambuco and Bahia. Contrasts manufacturing growth stimulated by export activities, such as coffee production, with growth stimulated by the internal market. Argues that greater emphasis should be put on the latter.

2353 Gonçalves Júnior, Carlos Augusto and João Paulo Cândia Veiga. A indústria automotiva brasileira no MERCOSUL. (*São Paulo Perspect.*, 9:1, jan./março 1995, p. 111–127, bibl., tables)

Discusses potential for consolidation of automobile manufacturing in the Southern Cone within the context of global changes in the automobile industry. Reviews Mexican experience to draw lessons for Brazil and Mercosur.

2354 Hollanda Filho, Sergio Buarque de. A crise da indústria automobilística brasileira sob a perspectiva da evolução mundial do setor. (*Estud. Econ./São Paulo*, 23:1, jan./abril 1993, p. 67–124, bibl.)

Analyzes performance of Brazilian automobile industry since early 1980s. Examines factors related to the recession in the internal market and the failure of an export solution to emerge. Particular attention is paid to impact of protectionism on the industry's response to the crisis, as well as the reaction of multinational subsidiaries in Brazil to advances of Japanese competitors.

2355 Instituto de Economia do Setor Público (São Paulo). Processo de privatização no Brasil: a experiência dos anos 1990–92. São Paulo: Instituto de Economia do Setor Público, FUNDAP, 1993. 322 p.: bibl., ill. (Relatório de pesquisa; 11)

Overview of Brazilian privatization in the context of regional trends. Reviews major privatizations between 1990–92 including steel and petrochemicals. Discusses various policy aspects of privatization. One chapter considers acceptable forms of payment (*moedas*).

2356 Jatobá, Jorge. A família brasileira na força de trabalho: um estudo de oferta de trabalho, 1978/88. (*Pesqui. Planej. Econ.*, 24:1, abril 1994, p. 1–34, bibl., tables)

Study of labor supply decisions in a family context is based on data from the Pesquisa Nacional por Amostra de Domicílios for metropolitan areas of the Northeast and Southeast. Concludes that the labor supply of all family members increases when the income of the head of the family declines (income effect) and when unemployment among family members increases (unemployment effect). Income effect is stronger in the Southeast and declines as incomes rise. Unemployment effect is more important in the Northeast and affects all income groups, though less so as income of the head rises.

Jornadas Internacionales: Argentina y Brasil en el Mercosur, Univ. de Buenos Aires, 1994. Argentina y Brasil en el Mercosur: políticas comunes y alianzas regionales. See item **2291.**

2357 Kageyama, Angela and Paulo Rehder. Condições de trabalho e de vida nas principais atividades agrícolas no Brasil em 1990. (*Estud. Econ./São Paulo*, 25:2, maio/agôsto 1995, p. 174–188, bibl., tables)

Uses factor analysis to investigate differences in working and living conditions among various agricultural activities. Results suggest existence of five types of activity: large-scale modern, traditional, large-scale traditional, family operations, and backward and subsistence. The first two have good working conditions, while first and fourth have good living conditions.

2358 Lam, David and Robert F. Schoeni. Effects of family background on earnings and returns to schooling: evidence from Brazil. (*J. Polit. Econ.*, 101:4, Aug. 1993, p. 710–740, bibl., graphs, tables)

Analyzes the high return-to-schooling rate for married men in Brazil, controlling for family background as represented by father's and father-in-law's education. Finds that father-in-law's education has a higher association with earnings than father's education, and that the measured return to education by the father, though reduced, is still high. Authors attribute results to a process of assortive mating where father-in-law's education is correlated with unmeasured worker characteristics rather than to family connections. For sociologist's comment see item **5265.**

2359 Longo, Carlos Alberto. A economia brasileira de 1985 a 1994: a transição inacabada. São Paulo: Editora Atlas, 1994. 247 p. (Publicação Atlas)

Collection of newspaper columns written between 1983–94. Informed commentary on policy issues of the period and the evolution of economic ideas. The Cruzado, Bresser, Summer, and Collor Plans are covered, along with some discussion of Mercosur and the tax reform of the 1988 constitution. Concludes with an evaluation of Fernando Henrique Cardoso's term as finance minister.

2360 Mattos, Fernando Augusto M. Estrutura ocupacional e distribuição de renda: regiões metropolitanas de São Paulo e do Rio de Janeiro. (*São Paulo Perspect.*, 9:2, abril/junho 1995, p. 91–99, bibl., tables)

Uses data from the Pesquisa Nacional por Amostra de Domicílios (PNAD) for 1981 and 1989 to analyze changes in personal income distribution for the metropolitan areas of São Paulo and Rio de Janeiro. Finds that distribution of income worsened in both regions, while average income rose in São Paulo and fell in Rio de Janeiro. Only two out of five occupational groups in Rio de Janeiro experienced gains in real income. Gains in São Paulo were higher.

2361 Mattoso, Jorge. A desordem do trabalho. São Paulo: Scritta, 1995. 210 p.: bibl. (Pensieri)

Compares evolution of 20th-century industrial production and work in the developed world and Brazil. "Disorder of work" refers to the breakdown of the mass production model and the consequent insecurities workers face because of industrial restructuring, which in turn was the result of technological and production systems of a Third Industrial Revolution during last third of the century. Largely theoretical.

2362 Medeiros, Cezar. O banco universal contemporâneo: uma estratégia para financiar os investimentos; o papel do Banco do Brasil, dos demais bancos oficiais e dos fundos de pensão. Rio de Janeiro: INsight Editorial, 1996. 213 p.: bibl., ill.

Analyzes Brazilian financial system. Focuses on the central role of the Banco do

Brasil and other State banks. In contrast to neoliberal analyses, affirms the economic development role of State banks in credit creation and allocation. Argues for a strong, reorganized State financial sector.

2363 Moguillansky, Graciela. Factores determinantes de las exportaciones industriales brasileñas durante la decada de 1980. (*Cuad. Econ./Santiago*, 31:92, abril 1994, p. 3–25, bibl. graphs, tables)

Using a simultaneous error correction model to evaluate impact of trade and exchange rate policies on Brazilian manufactured exports, study finds that manufactured and semi-manufactured exports respond differently. Only manufactured exports are guided by long-term profitability, competitivity, and internal and external demand conditions. While both sectors respond to price, this factor is more important for manufactured exports. Semi-manufactures are more sensitive to immediate economic conditions.

2364 Nitsch, Manfred. The biofuel programme PROALCOOL within the Brazilian energy strategy. (*in* Science, development and environment in Brazil: experiences and options for the future. Stockholm: Institute of Latin American Studies, Stockholm Univ., 1995, p. 43–63, bibl., graphs, tables)

Reports most recent results of ongoing German study of PROALCOOL, the world's most extensive effort to substitute fossil fuel with renewable biofuel. Generally critical in its evaluation. Concludes that program's success can be attributed only to "very special dynamics of coinciding political, social, technological, commercial, and ideological factors."

2365 Okuneva, Liudmila Semenovna. Na putiakh modernizatsii: opyt Brazilii dlia Rossii. [On the road to modernization: what Russia can learn from Brazil's experience.] Moscow: Russian Academy of Sciences, Institute of Latin American Studies, 1992. 63 p.: bibl.

Brief monograph attempts to derive some lessons for the new Russia from Brazil's recent experiences with democratization, anti-inflationary policies, and privatization (i.e., "shock therapy"). Compares social aspects of modernization in Brazil and Russia and their social psychology as exemplified by the 1989 Brazilian elections. [B. Dash]

2366 Oliveira, Fabrício Augusto de. Crise, reforma e desordem do sistema tributário nacional. Campinas, Brazil: Editora da Unicamp, 1995. 157 p.: bibl. (Col. Momento)

Describes Brazilian fiscal system that emerged from the Fiscal Reform of 1966, and traces its development up to the 1980s crisis. Carefully examines structure, coverage, equity, and efficiency of tax system established by the new constitution of 1988. Discusses budgeting and fiscal federalism and decentralization. Concludes with a look at current issues and prospects for further reform.

2367 Pinheiro, Armando Castelar and **Lauro Ramos.** Diferenciais intersetoriais de salários no Brasil. (*Rev. BNDES*, 3, junho 1995, p. 197–219, bibl., tables)

Asks whether labor market segmentation exists in Brazil by analyzing wage differentials by industry, holding human capital and job characteristics constant. Finds that industry differentials exist and that they increase overall inequality because industries with positive wage differentials also employ higher skilled workers. Positive differentials are also associated with less competitive market structures, the presence of State firms, and export activities which suggests that Brazilian exports are not based on social dumping.

2368 Ramos, Lauro and **Ana Lúcia Soares.** Participação da mulher na força de trabalho e pobreza no Brasil. (*Rev. Econ. Polít.*, 15:3, julho/set. 1995, p. 84–95, graphs, tables)

Paper analyzes labor force participation of married women as a function of per capita household income, and finds a direct relationship. Further analysis suggests that both are positively associated with educational attainment and negatively associated with number of preschool-age children at home, suggesting that the solution to poverty would be found in education and childcare services.

2369 Ramos, Lauro and **José Guilherme Almeida Reis.** Salário mínimo, distribução de renda e probreza. (*Pesqui. Planej. Econ.*, 25:1, abril 1995, p. 99–114, bibl.)

Analyzes potential effect of a 25 percent real value minimum wage increase in narrowing the distribution of income and decreasing poverty rate. Finds limited potential impact on either variable because the real value of the minimum wage is low, and many who receive the minimum wage are secondary workers in non-poor households.

2370 Rask, Kevin. The social costs of ethanol production in Brazil: 1978–1987. (*Econ. Dev. Cult. Change*, 43:3, April 1995, p. 627–649, graphs, map, tables)

Evaluates long-term performance of ethanol industry from a social cost/benefit perspective. Concludes that ethanol production has been a viable substitute for oil imports only in the early 1980s and only in the center-south region. Costs of production in the Northeast are extremely high and can be understood only in the context of social and distributional concerns.

2371 Reis, Bruno Pinheiro W. Conflito distributivo em sociedades pretorianas: uma interpretação teórica da inflação brasileira. (*Nova Econ.*, 4:1, nov. 1994, p. 107–129, bibl.)

Analyzes systemic inflation and hyperinflation as a function of the weakness or fragility of democratic institutions. Draws from public choice literature in the US and the concept of pretorian societies (those with institutions ineffective in moderating group actions). Finds that 1980s Brazil presented a case of inflation based on non-regulated distributive conflict.

2372 Roberts, J. Timmons. Trickling down and scrambling up: the informal sector, food provisions and local benefits of the Carajás mining "growth pole" in the Brazilian Amazon. (*World Dev.*, 23:3, March 1995, p. 385–400, bibl., maps)

Reports findings of the first empirical field study on the local impact of Carajás mining project. Finds that while Carajás continued in the tradition of enclave economies, the local government and the informal sector of the satellite boom-town played an important role in capturing trickle-down benefits. Ranchers and middlemen receive the greatest share of benefits, while small farmers benefit little.

2373 Romão, Maurício Costa. Distribuição de renda, pobreza e desigualdades regionais no Brasil. (*Rev. Econ. Nordeste*, 25:3, julho/set. 1994, p. 331–384, bibl., tables)

Examines personal distribution of income, poverty, and regional differences for the period 1960–88. Concludes that both economic growth and recession increased or maintained income concentration. Poverty declined with growth and increased in times of recession.

2374 Schwartz, Gilson. Brazil, Mercosur, and SAFTA: destructive restructuring or Pan-American integration? (*in* Cooperation or rivalry: regional integration in the Americas and the Pacific Rim. Boulder, Colo.: Westview Press, 1996, p. 129–149, tables)

Focuses on distinctiveness of Brazilian experience with economic reform and stabilization. Suggests that the future of Mercosur lies in the successful management of key differences between Brazil and Argentina. These differences translate into two competing views of integration, characterized by the author as "neo-colonial rivalry" vs. US-led Pan-American integration.

2375 Seminário Internacional de Política Agrícola, *4th, Viçosa, Brazil, 1992*. Desenvolvimento agrícola na década de 90 e no século XXI. Redação de Erly Cardoso Teixeira. Viçosa, Brazil: Univ. Federal de Viçosa, 1993. 219 p.: bibl., ill.

Collection of 12 papers from a conference on agricultural policy. Organized into four themes: sustainable agricultural development, human capital and development, agricultural policy and technological change, and macroeconomic policy and development. Considers Brazilian agriculture in the context of the demand for food, international trade and the open economy, inflation, technological change, and resource availability.

2376 Seminário sobre Aspectos Ambientais de Projetos Co-financiados pelo Banco Mundial, *Brasília, 1993*. Aspectos ambientais de projetos co-financiados pelo Banco Mundial: lições para o futuro. Organização de Alencar Soares de Freitas e Pedro Ribeiro Soares. Brasília: Instituto de Pesquisa Econômica Aplicada, 1994. 153 p.: bibl. (Série IPEA; 146)

Uses reports from World Bank analysts and Brazilian consultants to review environmental impact of World Bank-financed projects in Brazilian cities of São Francisco, Carajás, Polonoroeste, and Procop. Concludes with section on lessons learned from past experiences and recommendations regarding importance of ongoing project management and assessments.

2377 Serviço Nacional de Aprendizagem Industrial (Brazil). Departamento Regional de São Paulo. A indústria em São Paulo: sua evolução e distribuição espacial. São Paulo: SENAI São Paulo, 1992. 197 p.: bibl., col. maps.

Presents and analyzes data on changes in the geographical distribution of industrial employment and output within São Paulo state between 1970–88 within regional- and *municipio*-level groups. Details the spread of industrial activity outside of Greater São Paulo, and finds that state's share in the national total is declining.

2378 Shapiro, Helen. The public-private interface: Brazil's business-government relations in historical perspective, 1950–1990. (*in* The State, markets and development: beyond the neoclassical dichotomy. Edited by Amitava Krishan Dutt *et al.* Brookfield, Vt.: Edward Elgar Publishing Company, 1994, p. 144–168, bibl.)

Describes set of economic policies and institutional arrangements established during 1950s that generated the Brazilian miracle. Explores why policies were ineffective in responding to challenges of 1980s. Posits that fiscal crisis made previously successful policies unsustainable. Argues for importance of institutional arrangements in understanding Brazilian postwar development.

2379 Simonsen, Mario Henrique. 30 anos de indexação. Rio de Janeiro: Fundação Getúlio Vargas Editora, 1995. 167 p.: bibl., ill.

Traces Brazilian experience with indexation, from its inception in 1964 until its end in 1994 with the implementation of the Plano Real. Examines use of indexation on taxes, salaries, exchange rates, and in monetary correction. Discusses previous attempts at de-indexation, the role of indexation in inertial inflation, and the use of a foreign exchange rate anchor in place of indexation.

2380 Tecnologia e industrialização no Brasil: uma perspectiva histórica. Organização de Shozo Motoyama. São Paulo: Editora Unesp, Fundação para o Desenvolvimemto da UNESP; Centro Estadual de Educação Tecnológica Paula Souza, 1994. 450 p.: bibl. (Col. Biblioteca básica)

Collection of 15 chapters on the role of technology in industrialization and development in Brazil. Section on construction includes chapters on railroads, ports, waterworks and sewer systems, buildings and urban works, highways, and hydroelectricity. Sections on industry include chapters on steel, electricity, chemicals, metal-mechanical products, biotechnology, informatics, and new technologies.

Tellechea de Arca, Mireya. Paraguay socioeconómico y cultural: hidrovía-MERCOSUR. See item **2848.**

Truett, Dale B. and **Lila J. Truett.** Trade preferences and exports of manufactures: a case study of Bolivia and Brazil. See item **2206.**

2381 Valente Júnior, Airon Saboya and **Antônio de Castro Queiroz Serra.** O nordeste brasiliero frente ao MERCOSUL. (*Rev. Econ. Nordeste*, 25:3, julho/set. 1994, p. 439–464, bibl., table)

Evaluation of regional integration trends finds that Mercosur's orientation has been exceptionally mercantilist, giving economic development issues too little attention. Concludes that while there are sectors within the Northeast that stand to benefit from market expansion, the region as a whole stands to lose investment and resources, thereby increasing regional inequality in Brazil and Mercosur.

2382 Veiga, Pedro da Motta. Mercosul: a agenda de consolidação interna e os dilemas da ampliação. (*São Paulo Perspect.*, 9:1, jan./março 1995, p. 15–27, bibl., tables)

Written by the president of Brazil's Banco Nacional de Desenvolvimento Econômico e Social (BNDES). Describes developments in the evolution of Mercosur from 1990–94, and Brazil's proposal for creation of SAFTA—South American Free Trade Area. Discusses trade-offs implicit in geographic expansion vs. consolidation and extension of liberalization within Mercosur.

2383 Winograd, Carlos D. Learning from failed stabilisation: high inflation and the Cruzado Plan in Brazil. London: Institute of Latin American Studies, 1995. 60 p.: appendix, bibl. (Research papers/University of London, Institute of Latin American Studies, 0957–7947; 38)

Short volume provides concise review of economic conditions that led to the Cruzado Plan. Discusses its impact on inflation and the lessons that can be derived from the experience. A statistical appendix provides useful macroeconomic data for the 1980s, especially 1983–87.

Zeferino, Augusto César. Análise da localização espacial dos investimentos multinacionais no Brasil. See item **2926.**

JOURNAL ABBREVIATIONS

Agric. Hist. Agricultural History. Agricultural History Society. Univ. of Calif. Press. Berkeley.

Agrofor. Syst. Agroforestry Systems. Kluwer Academic Publishers. Dordrecht, The Netherlands.

Am. Econ. Rev. The American Economic Review. American Economic Assn., Evanston, Ill.

An. Asoc. Argent. Econ. Polít. Anales de la Asociación Argentina de Economía Política. Facultad de Ciencias Económicas, Univ. Nacional de Cuyo. Mendoza, Argentina.

Anál. Econ./La Paz. Análisis Económico. Ediciones UDAPE (Unidad de Análisis de Políticas Económicas). La Paz.

Argent. Ctry. Investm. Growth. Argentina: a country for investment and growth. Ministerio de Economía y Obras y Servicios Públicos. Buenos Aires.

Banker/London. The Banker. Financial Times Business Publishing Ltd., London.

Bol. Inf. Techint. Boletín Informativo Techint. Organización Techint. Buenos Aires.

Bol. Integr. Lat.-Am. Boletim de Integração Latino-Americana. Ministério das Relações Exteriores, Subsecretaria-Geral de Assuntos de Integração, Econômicos e de Comercio Exterior, Grupo de Estudos Técnicos. Brasília.

Bull. Inst. fr. étud. andin. Bulletin de l'Institut français d'études andines. Lima.

Bull. Lat. Am. Res. Bulletin of Latin American Research. Society for Latin American Studies. Oxford, England.

Cad. Sociol. Cadernos de Sociologia. Univ. Federal do Rio Grande do Sul, Programa de Pós-Graduação em Sociologia. Porto Alegre, Brazil.

Can. J. Lat. Am. Caribb. Stud. Canadian Journal of Latin American and Caribbean Studies. Univ. of Ottawa. Ontario, Canada.

Centroam. Int. Centroamérica Internacional. Facultad Latinoamericana de Ciencias Sociales (FLACSO). San José.

CEPAL Rev.   CEPAL Review/Revista de la CEPAL. Naciones Unidas, Comisión Económica para América Latina. Santiago.

Cienc. Econ./San José.   Ciencias Económicas. Instituto de Investigaciones en Ciencias Ecónomicas, Univ. de Costa Rica. San José.

Colecc. Estud. CIEPLAN.   Colección Estudios CIEPLAN. Corporación de Investigaciones Económicas para Latinoamérica. Santiago.

Conjonction/Port-au-Prince.   Conjonction. Bulletin de l'Institut français d'Haïti. Port-au-Prince.

Contribuciones/Buenos Aires.   Contribuciones. Estudios Interdisciplinarios sobre Desarrollo y Cooperación Internacional. Konrad-Adenauer-Stiftung; Centro Interdisciplinario de Estudios Sobre el Desarrollo Latinoamericano (CIEDLA). Buenos Aires.

Cuad. CLAEH.   Cuadernos del CLAEH. Centro Latinoamericano de Economía Humana. Montevideo.

Cuad. Econ./Bogotá.   Cuadernos de Economía. Univ. Nacional de Colombia. Bogotá.

Cuad. Econ./Santiago.   Cuadernos de Economía. Pontificia Univ. Católica de Chile, Instituto de Economía. Santiago.

Cuba Handb. Trade Stat.   Cuba: Handbook of Trade Statistics. Central Intelligence Agency, Directorate of Intelligence. Washington.

Cuba Transit.   Cuba in Transition: Papers and Proceedings of the . . . Annual Meeting of the Association for the Study of the Cuban Economy. Florida International Univ. Miami; Assn. for the Study of the Cuban Economy. Washington.

Curr. Sociol.   Current Sociology/La Sociologie Contemporaine. International Sociological Assn. Sage Publications. Thousand Oaks, Calif.

Debate Agrar.   Debate Agrario. Centro Peruano de Estudios Sociales (CEPES). Lima.

Desarro. Econ.   Desarrollo Económico. Instituto de Desarrollo Económico y Social. Buenos Aires.

Desarro. Energ.   Desarrollo y Energía. Instituto de Economía Energética. Río Negro, Argentina.

Desarro. Soc.   Desarrollo y Sociedad. Univ. de los Andes, Facultad de Economía, Centro de Estudios sobre el Desarrollo Económico (CEDE). Bogotá.

Econ. Desarro./Habana.   Economía y Desarrollo. Univ. de La Habana, Instituto de Economía. La Habana.

Econ. Dev. Cult. Change.   Economic Development and Cultural Change. Univ. of Chicago, Research Center in Economic Development and Cultural Change. Chicago, Ill.

Econ. Int./Genova.   Economia Internazionale. Instituto di Economia Internazionale. Genova, Italy.

Econ. Mex.   Economía Mexicana. Centro de Investigación y Docencia Económicas. México.

Econ. Soc. Prog. Lat. Am.   Economic and Social Progress in Latin America. Inter-American Development Bank. Washington.

Economía/Cali.   Economía. Univ. de San Buenaventura. Cali, Colombia.

Economía/Lima.   Economía. Depto. de Economía, Pontificia Univ. Católica del Perú. Lima.

Economist/London.   The Economist. London.

Ecuad. Deb.   Ecuador Debate. Centro Andino de Acción Popular (CAAP). Quito.

Ens. Polít. Econ.   Ensayos sobre Política Económica. Banco de la República, Depto. de Investigaciones Económicas. Bogotá.

Estad. Econ.   Estadística & Economía. Instituto Nacional de Estadísticas. Santiago.

Estud. Econ./Bahía Blanca.   Estudios Económicos. Univ. Nacional del Sur. Bahía Blanca, Argentina.

Estud. Econ./México.   Estudios Económicos. El Colegio de México. México.

Estud. Econ./Santiago.   Estudios de Economía. Depto. de Economía, Univ. de Chile. Santiago.

Estud. Econ./São Paulo.   Estudos Econômicos. Univ. de São Paulo, Instituto de Pesquisas Econômicas. São Paulo.

Estud. Front.   Estudios Fronterizos. Instituto de Investigaciones Sociales, Univ. Autónoma de Baja California. Mexicali, Mexico.

Estud. Int./Santiago. Estudios Internacionales. Instituto de Estudios Internacionales, Univ. de Chile. Santiago.

Estud. Públicos. Estudios Públicos. Centro de Estudios Públicos. Santiago.

Estud. Soc. Agric. Estudos Sociedade e Agricultura. Depto. de Letras e Ciências Sociais, Curso de Pós-graduação em Desenvolvimento, Agricultura e Sociedade, Instituto de Ciências Humanas e Sociais, Univ. Federal Ruaral do Rio de Janeiro.

Estud. Soc./Santiago. Estudios Sociales. Corporación de Promoción Universitaria. Santiago.

Estudios/Fundación Mediterránea. Estudios. Instituto de Estudios Económicos sobre la Realidad Argentina y Latinoamericana; Fundación Mediterránea. Córdoba, Argentina.

Estudios/Guatemala. Estudios. Instituto de Investigaciones Históricas, Antropológicas, y Arqueológicas, Univ. de San Carlos de Guatemala. Guatemala.

EURE/Santiago. EURE: Revista Latinoamericana de Estudios Urbanos Regionales. Centro de Desarrollo Urbano y Regional, Univ. Católica de Chile. Santiago.

Financ. Dev. Finance and Development. International Monetary Fund; The World Bank. Washington.

Foreign Aff. Foreign Affairs. Council on Foreign Relations, Inc. New York.

Foreign Policy. Foreign Policy. National Affairs Inc.; Carnegie Endowment for International Peace. New York.

Front. Norte. Frontera Norte. Colegio de la Frontera Norte. Tijuana, Mexico.

Glob. Financ. J. Global Finance Journal. JAI Press, Greenwich, Conn.

Harv. Bus. Rev. Harvard Business Review. Graduate School of Business Administration, Harvard Univ., Boston.

High. Educ. Higher Education. Kluwer Academic Publishers. Dordrecht, Netherlands.

Hum. Organ. Human Organization. Society for Applied Anthropology. New York.

Inf. Econ./Habana. Informe Económico. Banco Nacional de Cuba. La Habana.

Int. J. Comp. Sociol. International Journal of Comparative Sociology. York Univ., Dept. of Sociology and Anthropology. Toronto, Canada.

Int. Organ. International Organization. World Peace Foundation; Univ. of Wisconsin Press. Madison.

Int. Soc. Sci. J. International Social Science Journal. Blackwell Publishers. Oxford, England.

Integr. Latinoam. Integración Latinoamericana. Instituto para la Integración de América Latina. Buenos Aires.

Invest. Agrar. Investigación Agraria: Economía. Instituto Nacional de Investigaciones Agrarias. Madrid.

J. Dev. Areas. The Journal of Developing Areas. Western Illinois Univ. Press. Macomb, Ill.

J. Dev. Econ. Journal of Development Economics. North-Holland Publishing Co., Amsterdam, The Netherlands.

J. Dev. Stud. The Journal of Development Studies. Frank Cass. London.

J. Int. Econ. Journal of International Economics. Amsterdam.

J. Interam. Stud. World Aff. Journal of Interamerican Studies and World Affairs. Institute of Interamerican Studies, Univ. of Miami. Coral Gables, Fla.

J. Lat. Am. Stud. Journal of Latin American Studies. Centers or Institutes of Latin American Studies at the Universities of Cambridge, Glasgow, Liverpool, London, and Oxford. Cambridge Univ. Press. London.

J. Peasant Stud. The Journal of Peasant Studies. Frank Cass & Co., London.

J. Polit. Econ. Journal of Political Economy. Univ. of Chicago. Chicago, Ill.

LARR. Latin American Research Review. Latin American Research Review Board. Univ. of New Mexico, Albuquerque, N.M.

Lat. Am. Perspect. Latin American Perspectives. Univ. of California. Newbury Park, Calif.

Luso-Braz. Rev. Luso-Brazilian Review. Univ. of Wisconsin Press. Madison, Wis.

New Left Rev. New Left Review. New Left Review, Ltd., London.

Nova Econ. Nova Economia. Depto. de Ciências Econômicas, Univ. Federal de Minas Gerais. Belo Horizonte, Brazil.

Noved. Econ. Novedades Económicas. Fundación Mediterránea. Córdoba, Argentina.

Nueva Econ./Caracas. Nueva Economía. Academia Nacional de Ciencias Económicas. Caracas.

Otro Derecho. El Otro Derecho. Instituto Latinoamericano de Servicios Legales Alternativos (ILSA). Bogotá.

Perf. Latinoam. Perfiles Latinoamericanos. Facultad Latinoamericana de Ciencias Sociales. México.

Pesqui. Planej. Econ. Pesquisa e Planejamento Econômico. Instituto de Planejamento Econômico e Social. Rio de Janeiro.

Planej. Polít. Públicas. Planejamento e Políticas Públicas. Instituto de Pesquisa Econômica Aplicada (IPEA). Brasília.

Polít. Estrateg. Política y Estrategia. Academia Nacional de Estudios Políticos y Estratégicos. Santiago.

Politeia/Caracas. Politeia. Instituto de Estudios Políticos, Univ. Central de Venezuela. Caracas.

Presencia/San Salvador. Presencia. Centro de Investigaciones Tecnológicas y Científicas. San Salvador.

Probl. Desarro. Problemas del Desarrollo: Revista Latinoamericana de Economía. Instituto de Investigaciones Económicas, UNAM. México.

Q. J. Econ. The Quarterly Journal of Economics. Cambridge, Mass.

Quantum/Montevideo. Quantum. Facultad de Ciencias Económicas y de Administración. Montevideo.

Real. Econ./Buenos Aires. Realidad Económica. Instituto Argentino para el Desarrollo Económico (IADE). Buenos Aires.

Relac. Int./México. Relaciones Internacionales. Centro de Relaciones Internacionales. Facultad de Ciencias Políticas y Sociales, Univ. Nacional Autónoma de México. México.

Rev. Anál. Econ. Revista de Análisis Económico. Programa de Postgrado en Economía, ILADES/Georgetown Univ., Santiago.

Rev. Banco Repúb./Bogotá. Revista del Banco de la República. Bogotá.

Rev. Bimest. Cuba. Revista Bimestre Cubana. Sociedad Económica de Amigos del País. La Habana.

Rev. Black Polit. Econ. The Review of Black Political Economy. National Economic Assn.; Atlanta Univ. Center. Atlanta, Ga.

Rev. BNDES. Revista do BNDES. Banco Nacional de Desenvolvimento Econômico e Social. Rio de Janeiro.

Rev. Bras. Comér. Exter. Revista Brasileira de Comércio Exterior. Fundação Centro de Estudos do Comércio Exterior. Rio de Janeiro.

Rev. Bras. Econ. Revista Brasileira de Economia. Fundação Getúlio Vargas, Instituto Brasileiro de Economia. Rio de Janeiro.

Rev. Ciclos. Revista Ciclos en la Historia, Economía y la Sociedad. Fundación de Investigaciones Históricas, Económicas y Sociales, Facultad de Ciencias Económicas, Univ. de Buenos Aires. Buenos Aires.

Rev. Cienc. Soc./Montevideo. Revista de Ciencias Sociales. Facultad de Ciencias, Depto. de Sociología, Fundación de Cultura Universitaria. Montevideo.

Rev. Econ./Argentina. Revista de Economía. Banco de la Provincia de Córdoba. Córdoba, Argentina.

Rev. Econ. Nordeste. Revista Econômica do Nordeste. Banco do Nordeste do Brasil, Depto. de Estudos Econômicos do Nordeste. Fortaleza, Brazil.

Rev. Econ. Polít. Revista de Economia Política. Centro de Economia Política. São Paulo.

Rev. Econ. Stat. The Review of Economics and Statistics. Elsvier Science Publishers BV. Amsterdam.

Rev. Econ. Trab. Revista de Economía y Trabajo. Programa de Economía del Trabajo. Santiago.

Rev. Econ./Uruguay. Revista de Economía. Banco Central de Uruguay. Montevideo.

Rev. Estud. Euro. Revista de Estudios Europeos. Centro de Estudios sobre Europa Occidental. La Habana.

Rev. Integr. Desarro. Centroam. Revista de la Integración y el Desarrollo de Centroamérica. Banco Centroamericano de Integración Económica. Tegucigalpa.

Rev. Sociol./Santiago. Revista de Sociología. Depto. de Sociología, Facultad de Ciencias Sociales, Univ. de Chile. Santiago.

São Paulo Perspect. São Paulo em Perspectiva. Fundação SEADE. São Paulo.

Soc. Econ. Stud. Social and Economic Studies. Univ. of the West Indies, Institute of Social and Economic Research. Mona, Jamaica.

South. Econ. J. Southern Economic Journal. Chapel Hill, N.C.

Stud. Comp. Int. Dev. Studies in Comparative International Development. Transaction Periodicals Consortium, Rutgers Univ., New Brunswick, N.J.

Temas Coyunt./Caracas. Temas de Coyuntura. Instituto de Investigaciones Económicas y Sociales, Univ. Católica Andrés Bello. Caracas.

Third World Q. Third World Quarterly. Third World Foundation; New Zealand House. London.

Trimest. Econ. El Trimestre Económico. Fondo de Cultura Económica. México.

Umbrales/La Paz. Umbrales. Univ. Mayor de San Andrés. La Paz, Bolivia.

Univ. Econ. Universitas Económica. Pontificia Univ. Javeriana, Facultad de Ciencias Económicas y Administrativas. Bogotá.

Wash. Q. The Washington Quarterly. Georgetown Univ., The Center for Strategic and International Studies. Washington.

Weltwirtsch. Arch. Weltwirtschaftliches Archiv. Zeitschrift des Institut für Weltwirtschaft an der Christians-Albrechts-Univ. Kiel. Kiel, Germany.

World Bank Econ. Rev. The World Bank Economic Review. World Bank. Washington.

World Dev. World Development. Pergamon Press. Oxford, England.

World Econ. The World Economy. Basil Blackwell. London.

GEOGRAPHY

GENERAL

WILLIAM VAN DAVIDSON, *Associate Professor and Chair, Department of Geography and Anthropology, Louisiana State University*

GEOGRAPHICAL PUBLICATIONS RESULTING FROM THE CELEBRATION of the 500th anniversary of Columbus' voyage to America have flooded the scene during the last biennium. Colorful reproductions of maps and other illustrations that date from the period surrounding the Age of Discovery fill these works. Volumes on Spanish engineering in the New World and nautical cartography are especially valuable (items **2418** and **2394** respectively).

The second major concentration of materials focuses on the interrelation of natural regions, ecological changes, and conservation. Many of these investigations may have been prompted by the 1st Latin American Congress on Ecology (Montevideo, 1989) (item **2400**) or by the 25th UN Conference on Environment and Development (Rio de Janeiro, 1992). Notable are Dinerstein's sweeping report on Latin American "ecoregions" and the status of conservation efforts therein (item **2408**) and Gallopín's two-volume compilation of the classification of major ecosystems and specific studies on the consequences of environmental change (item **2412**).

The impressive growth of urban centers in Latin America continues to attract research interest (items **2451** and **2429**), as does the movement of population to, from, and within Latin America. The final recurring theme concerns natural catastrophes such as volcanos, earthquakes, and, of course, El Niño (item **2427**).

One promising new journal has appeared: *Meridiano: Revista de Geografía,* is produced by the Centro de Estudios Alexander von Humboldt in Buenos Aires, under the direction of Omar Horacio Gejo. The most important recent gatherings of geographers interested in Latin America are those of the Conference of Latin Americanist Geographers (CLAG)—in Juárez, Mexico (Sept. 1994), Tegucigalpa, Honduras (Jan. 1996), and Arequipa, Peru (July 1997). CLAG activities are publicized through CLAGNET, a listserve efficiently organized by David J. Robinson, Syracuse University.

2384 Adams, R.D. and **W.P. Richardson.**
A view of South and Central America from the International Seismological Centre. (*Geofís. Int.,* 35:3, July/Sept. 1996, p. 193–203, bibl., maps, tables)

Series of maps both with seismograph stations and earthquakes by magnitude in Central and South America, 1980–1992.

2385 Amado, Janaína and **Luiz Carlos Figueiredo.** No tempo das caravelas. São Paulo: Editora Contexto; Goiânia, Brazil: Cegraf, UFG, 1992. 161 p.: bibl., ill., maps. (Col. Caminhos da história. História Contexto. Publicação; 194)

Two Brazilian scholars discuss popular perspectives on the contact period. Topics include new views of the discovery, cartography, navigation, 16th-century images, impact of Spanish horses and war dogs, and dispersal of the potato.

2386 Amaya, María Teresa *et al.* Medio ambiente y desarrollo. Recopilación de Ernesto Guhl. 2a. ed. Bogotá: Ediciones Uniandes; Tercer Mundo, 1992. 289 p.: bibl., ill., maps.

Twenty presentations on development and natural environments, mostly about Colombia. Parsons' early ridged field study is revisited (see *HLAS 31:5618*). One exceptional paper, by geographer Sandner, emphasizes the importance of involvement on several scales, and presents evidence from Costa Rica and Central America to illustrate this notion.

Aragón, Luis E. The Amazon as a study object: building regional capacity for sustainable development. See item **2864.**

2387 Belluzzo, Ana Maria de Moraes. O Brasil dos viajantes. v. 1, Imaginário do novo mundo. São Paulo: Metalivros; Rio de Janeiro: Odebrecht, 1994. 1 v.: bibl., ill. (some col.), col. maps.

Elegant reproductions of the earliest European illustrations of the New World, especially Brazil. Explanation of real and imaginary images offered. Bibliography and biographical notes on travellers, artists, and cartographers are contributions.

2388 Bromley, Rosemary D.F. and Gareth A. Jones. Identifying the inner city in Latin America. (*Geogr. J.*, 162:2, July 1996, p. 179–190)

Using data from Quito the 1970s–80s, authors argue that the inner city in Latin America has undergone population loss and socioeconomic decline, and experiences a predominance of rental occupance—the same trends that occurred in North American and European inner cities in the 1960s–70s. [D. Gade]

2389 Browder, John O. Deforestation and the environmental crisis in Latin America. (*LARR*, 30:3, 1995, p. 123–137, bibl.)

A review of six books on the environmental impact of deforestation. A multitude of factors influence forest clearing, and to understand processes and consequences both the local scene and qualitative ethnographical

inquiries are often useful. The middle players—between the local and global scales—are deemed as most important, particularly for political ecologists. For economist's comment, see item **1267.**

2390 Budyko, Mikhail Ivanovich *et al.* Cambios antropogénicos del clima en América del Sur. Buenos Aires: Academia Nacional de Agronomía y Veterinaria, 1994. 223 p.: bibl. (Serie de la Academia Nacional de Agronomía y Veterinaria; 19)

Russian climatologists study past and present climate changes in South America, and indicate that future studies will reveal enormous impacts on hydrology and agricultural productivity.

2391 Castillo G., Manuel Angel. Tendencias recientes de la migración en América Latina. (*Perf. Latinoam.*, 4:6, junio 1995, p. 71–119, bibl., tables)

Migration in Latin America has increased and become more complex. The simple model of rural-urban migration is now joined by rural-rural, urban-urban, and variations of international mobility. Movements to the US have become a dominant feature. Several tables indicate changes by country, 1950–90.

2392 Caviedes, César N. Estudios sobre la variabilidad espacial del voto en América Latina. (*Rev. Interam. Bibliogr.*, 43:2, 1993, p. 257–267, bibl.)

Review and brief commentary on the electoral geography and geographical factors involved in Latin American voting patterns, with emphasis on Chile.

2393 CELADE. América Latina y el Caribe: dinámica de población y desarrollo; un perfil sintético. (*Notas Pobl.*, 21:58, dic. 1993, p. 265–294, tables)

Population statistics by country, 1950–2000. Total population, annual increases, natural growth rates, life expectancy, infant mortality, urbanization, international migration, and relationships of these features to the demographic transition model are mentioned.

2394 Cerezo Martínez, Ricardo. La cartografía náutica española en los siglos XIV, XV y XVI. Madrid: C.S.I.C., 1994. 319 p., 12 leaves of plates: appendix, bibl., ill. (some col.), index, col. maps.

Reproductions of 82 maps show the progress in cartography during the Age of Discovery. The author, a former director of the Museo Naval in Madrid, relates nicely the history of major expeditions and the cartographic changes that followed. Valuable bibliography and chronological list of maps for the period included in appendix.

2395 Christofoletti, Antonio. A inserção da geografia física na política de desenvolvimento sustentável. (*Geografia/Rio Claro*, 18 : 1, abril 1993, p. 1–22, bibl.)

Stresses contributions of physical geography to sustainable development. [K. Muller]

2396 Las ciudades de América Latina: problemas y oportunidades. Edición de Alfonso Puncel Chornet. València, Spain: Univ. de València, 1994. 170 p.: bibl., ill., maps. (Col. oberta)

Ten brief papers on urban studies, including recent growth, administration, planning, downtown renewal, settlement forms, poverty, and legal status. Lima, Buenos Aires, Havana, and São Paulo are most studied.

2397 Comisión Amazónica de Desarrollo y Medio Ambiente. Amazonia sin mitos. Washington: Banco Interamericano de Desarrollo; New York: Programa de las Naciones Unidas para el Desarrollo, 1992? xvii, 111 p.: bibl., ill.

A straightforward look at modern Amazonia. Some interesting details are that the region is settled and is not homogeneous; Amazonia displays enormous biodiversity and many natural resources. Despite strategies for sustainable development of the basin, there has been a considerable impact on nature and society to date. Detailed maps show native populations, reserves, and parks. Concludes with an appeal for the development of the region.

2398 Conferência Latinoamericana sobre Sistemas de Informação Geográfica, *4th, São Paulo, 1993.* Anais. São Paulo: Escola Politécnica da Univ. de São Paulo?, 1993. 771 p.: bibl., ill., maps.

Abstracts of 40 presentations on Geographic Information Systems (GIS). [K. Muller]

2399 Conferencia y Curso Iberoamericano— S.I.G., *5th, Mendoza, Argentina, 1995.* Actas. Mendoza, Argentina: Univ. Nacional

de Cuyo, Facultad de Filosofía y Letras, 1995. 548 p.: bibl., ill., maps.

Handbook for a course on geographic information systems that demonstrates the advantages of studying conservation, natural resource evaluations, changes in rural and urban landscapes, cartographic analysis, and environmental and catastrophic alterations.

2400 Congreso Latino Americano de Ecología, *1st, Montevideo, 1989.* Actas: 10–17 de diciembre de 1989. Recopilación de Eduardo Gudynas y Ricardo Xalambrí. Montevideo: CIPFE, 1992. 325 p.: bibl., ill. (some col.), maps.

Three introductory essays and 175 abstracts, primarily of a biological nature, from congress participants.

2401 Conocimiento y sustentabilidad ambiental del desarrollo en América Latina y el Caribe. Recopilación de Francisco León. Santiago: Dolmen Ediciones, 1994. 325 p.: bibl., ill.

Eight substantial papers that examine environmental change in Latin America and the Caribbean. Considers how development is affected by agriculture, biodiversity, drainage basins, coastal and semi-arid ecosystems, and urbanization. Lacks contribution of geographers.

2402 Cunill, Pedro. Las transformaciones del espacio geohistórico latinoamericano, 1930–1990. México: Colegio de México, Fideicomiso Historia de las Américas; Fondo de Cultura Económica, 1995. 198 p.: bibl. (Serie Ensayos/Fideicomiso Historia de las Américas. Sección de obras de historia)

Essay on the major changes in Latin American "space" between 1930–90 focuses on environmental alterations, geographical catastrophies, the expansion of violence, over-exploitation of energy and mineral resources, ramifications of the law of the seas, agricultural landscapes, and urban centers.

2403 De bosques y gente: aspectos sociales de la desforestación en América Latina. Coordinación de María Fernanda Paz. Cuernavaca, Mexico: Univ. Nacional Autónoma de México, Centro Regional de Investigaciones Multidisciplinarias, 1995. 271 p.: bibl., ill.

Seven articles on the socioeconomic aspects of deforestation occurring in Mexico, Costa Rica, Honduras, and Bolivia.

O desafio das florestas neotropicais = The challenge of neotropical forests. See item 2875.

2404 El desarrollo del transporte público urbano en América Latina y el mundo. Santiago: Naciones Unidas, Comisión Económica Para América Latina y el Caribe, 1994. 72 p.: bibl., ill.

This small pamphlet, well-illustrated with modern photographs, contains information on the evolution of mass transit in Latin America, from horse-drawn omnibus to metro. Brief economic analysis of efficiency needed.

2405 D'Hollander, Raymond. La connaissance de la géographie du globe à l'époque de Christophe Colomb. (*Acta geogr.*, 101, mars 1995, p. 19–53, bibl., ill., graphs)

Overview of geographical knowledge, primarily Greek and Arabic, that preceded Columbus' voyage to America.

2406 Diario de Don Francisco de Paula Martínez y Sáez: miembro de la Comisión Científica del Pacífico 1862–1865. Edición crítica de María de los Ángeles Calatayud Arinero. Prólogo de Miguel Ángel Puig-Samper. Madrid: Consejo Superior de Investigaciones Científicas, 1994. 334 p.: ill. (Col. Biblioteca de Historia de América; 11)

A personal diary from the Aug. 1862–June 1865 Spanish scientific expedition that circumnavigated South America. Description of trips down the Amazon, into central California, and others. Mostly personal activities, with some natural history and local descriptions included. Does not discuss the scientific results of the trip.

2407 Dickenson, John. A neglected *seed of change:* a bibliographic note on the history and geography of viticulture in Latin America. (*Rev. Interam. Bibliogr.*, 43 : 3, 1993, p. 403–411, bibl.)

A brief review of the bibliography on wine in Latin America. Because of the importance of wine in the culture of Spain and Spanish America, much remains to be studied on viticulture in Latin America.

2408 Dinerstein, Eric *et al.* A conservation assessment of the terrestrial ecoregions of Latin America and the Caribbean. Washington: World Bank, 1995. xvii, 129 p.: appendices, bibl., ill., col. maps (1 fold. in pocket).

Important report on the status of conservation efforts in Latin America. This biogeographical approach delimited five major ecosystems, 11 major habitat types, and 191 ecoregions. Appendices provide extensive database on the ecoregions, and nine well-constructed maps of Latin America illustrate the bioregions, major habitats, ecoregions, mangrove, conservation status, biological distinctiveness, and conservation priorities. The foldout map of "Ecoregions of Latin America and the Caribbean" is a major contribution.

2409 Emigracja, Polonia, Ameryka Łacińska: procesy emigracji i osadnictwa Polaków w Ameryce Łacińskiej i ich odzwierciedlenie w świadomości społecznej. [Emigration, Poland, Latin America: the processes of emigration and Polish settlement in Latin America and their image in the social consciousness.] Edited by Tadeusz Paleczny. Warsaw: Centrum Studiów Latynoamerykańskich, Uniw. Warszawski, 1996. 256 p.: bibl. (Seria Polska a Świat Iberoamerykański)

Collection of essays by 10 distinguished Polish scholars on the Poles' awareness of emigration and the Polish community's presence in Latin America. Book includes possibly the most extensive bibliography of research material. [Z. Kantorosinski]

The environmental dimension in development planning. v. 1. See item 1309.

2410 Ferrer Regales, Manuel and Antonio Peláez López. Población, ecología y medio ambiente. Pamplona, Spain: Univ. de Navarra, 1996. 284 p.: bibl., ill. (Col. Geografía; 7)

A good overview of these interrelated themes, including methodologies and major practitioners. Potential college text cites a variety of works published worldwide. Spain is used as an example for some of the data.

2411 The fragile tropics of Latin America: sustainable management of changing environments. Edited by Toshie Nishizawa and Juha I. Uitto. Tokyo; New York: United Nations Univ. Press, 1995. 335 p.: bibl., ill., maps.

Amazonia and adjacent lands have tremendous environmental variations, and approaches to the sustainable management of these fragile lands must be different. Geographers Hiraoka, Nishizawa, Sternberg, and Yagasaki have important contributions among the 14 articles. See items 2886, 2900, and 2922 for annotations of individual chapters.

2412 El futuro ecológico de un continente: una visión prospectiva de la América Latina. v. 1–2. Recopilación de Gilberto C. Gallopín *et al.* Tokyo; New York: Editorial de la Univ. de las Naciones Unidas; México: Fondo de Cultura Económica, 1995. 2 v.: bibl., ill. (Lecturas; 79)

Vol. 1 of these large volumes classifies major ecosystems in Latin America. Presentations in vol. 2 address such as the productivity of varying ecosystems, development and environment, protected areas, the social consequences of ecological changes, and other themes.

2413 García Zarza, Eugenio. La emigración española a Iberoamérica, 1946–90: estudio geográfico. (*in* Jornadas de Estudios Geográficos Iberoamericanos, *2nd, Salamanca, Spain, 1990. Las migraciones en Iberoamérica.* Salamanca: Instituto de Iberoamérica y Portugal, 1992, p. 23–54, bibl., graphs, maps, tables)

Since WWII almost three million Spaniards have left Spain. A third moved to Spanish America, mostly before 1961; the others migrated into central Europe, mostly after 1961. Galicia was the leading province of emigration; Argentina and Venezuela were major countries of immigration. A nice map shows that Andean and Central American countries have few Spanish migrants.

2414 García Zarza, Eugenio. Importancia geográfica de las migraciones en Iberoamérica. (*in* Jornadas de Estudios Geográficos Iberoamericanos, *2nd, Salamanca, Spain, 1990. Las migraciones en Iberoamérica.* Salamanca: Instituto de Iberoamérica y Portugal, 1992, p. 11–21, graphs, tables)

A broad look at Latin American population changes, with little direct reference to migration. Interesting primarily for an attempt at determining proportions of racial groups by country for 1991 (table 5).

2415 Geografía del medio ambiente: una alternativa del ordenamiento ecológico. Edición de Miriam I. Arcia Rodríguez. México: Univ. Autónoma del Estado de México, 1994. 289 p.: bibl., ill., maps. (Col. Ciencias y técnicas; 24)

A basic, well-organized academic presentation on using the methodology of geography in environmental research. Examples mostly from Cuba.

2416 *Geoistmo.* Vol. 6/7, Nos. 1/2, Una invitación a la geografía de la salud. Edición de Connie Weil. San José: Asociación de Profesionales en Geografía de Costa Rica.

Four articles, previously published in English, are presented in Spanish as an issue of the major Costa Rican geographical journal. Addresses health problems and colonization, the crisis of public health in Latin America, and distributional aspects of squistosomiasis. Extensive bibliography.

2417 Georgescu-Pipera, Paul and **Constantino Georgescu-Pipera.** Integración fluvial suramericana = South American river integration. Caracas: Fundación ORIAMPLA, 1993. 115 p.: bibl., ill. (some col.), maps.

Advocates the expansion of navigability and waterborn commerce in interior South America. Concludes that connecting the three dominant river systems—Orinoco, Amazon, Paraná—would increase trade possibilities. Includes a useful collection of maps and macro-scale statistics on major tributaries.

2418 González Tascón, Ignacio. Ingeniería española en Ultramar: siglos XVI–XIX. v. 1–2. Madrid: CEHOPU; CEDEX; MOPT; Colegio de Ingenieros de Caminos, Canales y Puertos, 1992. 2 v.: bibl., ill. (some col.), index. (Col. de Ciencias, Humanidades e Ingeniería; 42)

Detailed description of Spanish engineering feats in the New World. Hundreds of maps, plans, and drawings, mostly from Spanish archives, illustrate the construction techniques of ports, aqueducts, roads, canals, bridges, and other public works. Despite a lack of analysis, these volumes are valuable for the historical geography of colonial Spanish America. Ample citations and bibliography.

2419 Guallart Martínez, José María. Grupos nativos en los territorios eclesiasticos de Latinoamérica. Lima: Centro Amazónico de Antropología y Aplicación Práctica (CAAAP), 1992. 170 p.: ill.

A listing of indigenous groups in Latin America, either "etnias tribales" or "etnias campesinas," by country and church district. Information on population, names, and locations is inadequate for Mexico and Central America, and slightly better for South America. The ethnogeographical atlas lags behind current knowledge.

2420 Hébert, John R. and **Anthony P. Mullen.** The Luso-Hispanic world in maps: a selective guide to manuscript maps to 1900 in the collections of the Library of Congress. Washington: Library of Congress, 1999. 282 p. bibl., maps

This is a selective compilation of 1011 citations of maps held in three divisions of the Library of Congress: Geography and Map, Manuscripts and Rare Books, and Special Collections. The period covered is roughly mid-16th century–1900. Areal extent is primarily the Americas (920 items), but 9 atlases, 6 world maps, and 76 maps from the Old World are also presented. Thirty-nine are reproduced herein, including prominent examples from Maggs, Howe, and Squier map collections. References typically include title, location, cartographer's name, date, size, scale, LC call number, and brief description of the map's content. The compilers, both of the Library of Congress, have produced an extremely useful cartographical guide—one that provides an enticement to delve further into the vast collections of the LC.

2421 Iberoamérica desde el espacio. Coordinación técnica de José Sancho Comíns y Emilio Chuvieco Salinero. Spain: Sociedad Estatal Quinto Centenario; Univ. de Alcalá; Instituto Geográfico Nacional; Lunwerg Editores, 1992. 303 p.: col. ill., maps.

This tremendous photo album includes beautiful and often startling color views of Latin America taken from satellites, 1985–90. Images, organized by natural areas, urban centers, and agriculture and mining zones, and are accompanied by general texts without citations. Each of the almost 100 sites has a location map, a color landscape photograph, and an image, mostly LANDSAT, from space.

2422 Kent, Robert B. Homenaje a la patria: Latin American national atlases. (*LARR*, 30:1, 1995, p. 256–265)

A nice review of six national atlases: Bolivia (1985), Panama (1988), Cuba (1989), Peru (1989), Mexico (1990), and Colombia (1992). Produced by national geographical institutes, the atlases vary greatly in quality, but all have value to geographers interested in those countries.

2423 Laguna Sanz, Eduardo. El ganado español: un descubrimiento para América. Madrid: Ministerio de Agricultura, Pesca y

Alimentación, Secretaría General Técnica, 1991. 237 p.: bibl., col. ill. (Publicaciones del Ministerio de Agricultura, Pesca y Alimentación, Secretaría General Técnica)

A general history on the distribution of livestock in Spain since ancient times, and on the introduction of animals into America. Rich in illustrations, including photographs, maps, reproductions of Spanish archival documents, and drawings, but often without details of scholarly citation. Notes on horses, mules, cattle, sheep, pigs, goats, chickens, and bees.

2424 Li, Yuan and **Dazhang Chen.** Haiwai Huaren Jiqi Juzhudi Gaikuang. [A survey of overseas Chinese and their lands of residence.] Beijing: China Overseas Chinese Publishing Company, 1991. 507 p.: maps, tables.

General survey of overseas Chinese throughout the world includes entries for 22 Latin American countries and regions. Each entry contains information on population distribution, "Chinatowns," history of Chinese immigration, ancestral dialects, occupations and employment, economic achievements, prominent figures, and culture and education. Authors are either relatives of overseas Chinese or officials involved in administration of overseas Chinese affairs. [M. Xianglin]

2425 Marchena Gómez, Manuel J. El espacio regional latinoamericano. (*Rábida/Huelva*, 9, marzo 1991, p. 51–68, graph, maps, photo, tables)

An attempt to map and to briefly explain GNP disparity, efforts at agricultural reform, industrialization, and urbanization, by country.

2426 Marchena Gómez, Manuel J. Una nueva geografía de América Latina: ¿un descubrimiento geográfico? (*Invest. Geogr./Murcia*, 14, julio/dic. 1995, p. 5–30, bibl., maps)

Latin America is experiencing a dichotomy between developing and poverty-stricken regions, even within countries. Maps show levels of development, emerging areas, regional economic integration, and areas of extreme poverty.

2427 Martin, Louis et al. Perturbaciones del régimen de las lluvias y condiciones de tipo El Niño en América del Sur tropical desde hace 7000 años. (*Bull. Inst. fr. étud.*

andin., 24:3, 1995, p. 595–605, bibl., graphs, maps)

The fascination with the climatological phenomenon, El Niño, continues. Paleoecological records from Brazil and Bolivia indicate several short dry periods over 7000 years. Variations were apparently related to strong El Niño events in the past.

2428 Martín Lou, María Asunción and **Merten Sievers.** Latinoamérica y desarrollo, perspectivas y progresos a través de artículos en revistas geográficas alemanas y estadounidenses, 1980–1994. (*Estud. Geogr./ Madrid*, 57:222, enero/marzo 1996, p. 93–123, bibl., tables)

A review of eight major German and US geographical journals for their coverage on Latin American development issues, 1980–1994.

2429 Martín Lou, María Asunción and **Eduardo Múscar Benasayag.** Proceso de urbanización en América del Sur: modelos de ocupación del espacio. Madrid: Editorial MAPFRE, 1992. 315 p.: bibl., ill., index, maps. (Col. MAPFRE 1492. Col. Ciudades de Iberoamérica; 10)

A chronological presentation and description of the urban centers of South America during the precolumbian, colonial, and modern periods.

2430 El medio ambiente como factor de desarrollo: prefactibilidad de proyectos de importancia ambiental y de interés económico. Santiago: Naciones Unidas, Comisión Económica para América Latina y el Caribe/ PNUMA, 1989. 123 p.: maps. (Estudios e informes de la CEPAL; 75)

Brief summaries of feasibility studies on economic development as related to environmental factors. Topics include conservation efforts in northwestern Argentina, frontier ranching in eastern Colombia, forest burning for pasture in extreme southern Chile, oil production in eastern Ecuador, agroforestry in southern Honduras, and agricultural production in Andean Peru.

2431 A mining strategy for Latin America and the Caribbean. Industry and Mining Division, Industry and Energy Department. Washington: World Bank, Industry and Mining Division, Industry and Energy Dept., 1996. 129 p.: ill. (World Bank technical paper, 0253–7494; 345)

Technical papers that assess the current state of mining in parts of Latin America, and propose a framework for growth in the mineral sector. Specific coverage for four country groups: Mexico/Venezuela, Chile, Bolivia/Peru, and Argentina/Ecuador/Panama. [T. Martinson]

2432 Montagnini, Florencia *et al.* Sistemas agroforestales: principios y aplicaciones en los trópicas. 2. ed. San José: Organización para Estudios Tropicales, 1992. 622 p.: bibl., ill. (some col.), index, maps.

A complete handbook on agroforestry. Beginning with definitions and classifications, presents all perspectives on agroforestry, including planning, ecological aspects, management, diffusion, and case studies from Costa Rica and Brazil. Worldwide sources of information on the topic are listed.

2433 Navarro, Juan Carlos. Historia natural, o, jardín americano: manuscrito de 1801. México: Univ. Nacional Autónoma de México; Instituto Mexicano del Seguro Social; Instituto de Seguridad y Servicios Sociales de los Trabajadores del Estado, 1992. 314 p.: col. ill.

Facsimiles of almost 500 color illustrations of useful Mexican plants as originally presented by Fray Navarro in 1801. Modern text includes Náhuatl, Spanish, and scientific names, medicinal uses; and in some cases, plant habitats of the plants.

2434 Las nuevas formas de movilidad de las poblaciones urbanas en América Latina: memorias del Taller CEDE ORSTOM, Bogotá, 7–11 de diciembre de 1992. Edición científica de Françoise Dureau *et al.* Bogotá: CEDE, 1995. 201 p.: bibl., ill. (Documento CEDE; 097)

Twenty-two brief papers, primarily from Colombian demographers and geographers, focus on internal migration, urban movements, and the resulting conditions in Colombia, especially Bogotá. Other studies on Ecuador, Mexico, Venezuela, and Uruguay included.

2435 Ordorica Mellado, Manuel. La población futura de América Latina. (*Perf. Latinoam.*, 4:6, junio 1995, p. 149–179, tables)

Tables of population estimates by country, 1985–2025. Includes total population, growth rates, life expectancy, infant mortality, death rates, age and sex structure, urban growth, and others.

2436 Ornig, Joseph R. My last chance to be a boy: Theodore Roosevelt's South American expedition of 1913–1914. Mechanicsburg, Pa.: Stackpole Books, 1994. 272 p.: bibl., ill., index, maps.

Perhaps because of his love of birds, Teddy Roosevelt went to South America five years after leaving the White House. His adventures down a southern tributary of the Amazon appeared in *Through the Brazilian wilderness* (1914) (see *HLAS 32:2973*). In 1992, Ornig, Roosevelt's great-grandson, retraced the route and described his experiences in this version of the President's trip. Interesting for field geographers who want to know just how tough it used to be to travel down the Amazon.

2437 Petroleum basins of South America. Edited by A.J. Tankard, Ramiro Suárez Soruco and Herman J. Welsink. Tulsa, Okla.: American Association of Petroleum Geologists, Yacimientos Petrolíferos Fiscales Bolivianos, and Academia Nacional de Ciencias de Bolivia, 1995. 805 p.: bibl., ill. (some col.), index, maps. (AAPG memoir; 62)

State-of-the-art geology of the oil-producing regions of South America. Presented in 41 very well-illustrated scholarly articles.

2438 Romeiro, Ademar Ribeiro et al. Ecologia e desenvolvimento. Coordenação editorial de Dália Maimon. Rio de Janeiro: Associação de Pesquisa e Ensino em Ecologia e Desenvolvimento, 1992. 278 p.: bibl., ill.

Conference papers examine topics such as the environment, policy questions, energy, and agriculture. [K. Muller]

2439 Rozanski, Kazimierz and Luis Araguás Araguás. Spatial and temporal variability of stable isotope composition of precipitation over the South American continent. (*Bull. Inst. fr. étud. andin.*, 24:3, 1995, p. 379–390, bibl., graphs, map)

Information from 60 stations in Argentina, Brazil, Chile, Ecuador, and Peru regarding the isotope composition of precipitation shows variations according to location, altitude, and seasonality.

2440 Rubio Recio, José Manuel et al. Ambientes y fauna iberoamericana: una muestra. La Rábida, Spain: Univ. Hispano-

americana Santa María de La Rábida; Seville, Spain: Univ. de Sevilla, 1991. 132 p.: ill. (some col.), maps. (Serie Catálogos)

A collection of 72 photos of animals and various landscapes in Latin America. Venezuela, Bolivia, and Mexico prominent.

2441 Silgado Ferro, Enrique. Investigaciones de sísmicidad histórica en la América del Sur en los siglos XVI, XVII, XVIII, y XIX. Lima: CONCYTEC; CERESIS, 1992? 108 p.: ill.

A compilation of archival information on earthquakes and tsunamis, primarily in western South America, 1541–1894. Some attempt to determine their intensities.

2442 Small towns and beyond: rural transformation and small urban centres in Latin America. Amsterdam: Thela, 1997. 145 p.: bibl., map, table.

Collection of nine empirically based studies of urbanization and development outside large metropolises. Authors explore the nature, direction, and impact of urban-rural linkages resulting from the flow of goods, services, information, capital, and labor. First essay discusses smaller Latin American towns in general while the others cover Brazil, Costa Rica, Ecuador, Peru, Bolivia, and Mexico. [R. Hoefte]

2443 Sternberg, Hilgard O'Reilly. Proposals for a South American waterway. (*in* International Congress of Americanists, *48th, Stockholm, 1994.* Threatened peoples and environments in the Americas = Pueblos y medios ambientes amenazados en las Américas. Stockholm: Institute of Latin American Studies, Stockholm Univ., 1996, v. 1, p. 99–125, bibl., maps)

Examines historical and contemporary plans to link the Caribbean to the Río de la Plata by connecting the Orinoco/Amazon/Paraná/Paraguay drainage systems.

2444 Terra ignota: la geografía de América Latina a través de cronistas de los siglos XVI y XVII. Presentación y selección de textos de Josefina Oliva de Coll. México: Editorial Trillas, 1986. 210 p.: bibl., ill., maps. (Linterna mágica; 3)

Random selection of 16th- and 17th-century descriptions of physical geography in the New World, including seas and rivers, climate and winds, mountains and volcanos, plants, animals, and fabled creatures.

2445 Território: globalização e fragmenta-ção. Organização de Mílton Santos, Maria Adélia Aparecida de Souza e Maria Laura Silveira. São Paulo: Editora Hucitec; Associação Nacional de Pós-Graduação e Pesquisa em Planejamento Urbano e Regional, 1994. 332 p.: bibl., maps. (Geografia, teoria e realidade; 30)

More than thirty authors examine spatial context, especially in reference to globalization, often from a Marxist perspective. Sections include transnationalization, urbanization, and territoriality within the limits of national and local power.

2446 Trópico em movimento: alternativas contra a pobreza e a destruição ambiental no trópico úmido. Organização de Heliana Brito Franco. Belém, Brazil: POEMA, 1994. 312 p.: bibl., ill., maps. (Série POEMA; 2)

Documents some sustainable development projects. Ten authors examine Brazil, five look at other Latin American countries, three focus on Africa, and two on Asia.

2447 Los trópicos latinoamericanos: ecosistemas fundamentales para la producción de alimentos y materias primas en el siglo XXI; memorias; Bogotá, 18 y 19 de agosto de 1992. Bogotá: Instituto Colombiano Agropecuario, 1994. 206 p.: bibl., ill.

Three theoretical presentations on agricultural development, followed by specific considerations of savannas, coastal zones, and Amazonia for agricultural productivity. Examples from Colombia and Brazil.

2448 Urteaga, Luis et al. El bosque ilustrado: estudios sobre la política forestal española en America. Edición de Manuel Lucena Giraldo. Spain?: Instituto Nacional para la Conservación de la Naturaleza; Instituto de la Ingeniería de España, 1991. 241 p.: bibl., ill. (some col.), maps (some col.).

Eleven wonderfully illustrated chapters by Spanish geographers and historians on Spanish forestry policy in America, primarily 18th century. Specific regional coverage of Cuba, Dominican Republic, Guayana, Paraguay, and Peru. Logwood, rubber, and quinine highlighted.

2449 Valorando a natureza: análise econômica para o desenvolvimento sustentável. Organização de Peter Herman May e Ronaldo Serôa da Motta. Rio de Janeiro: Editora Campus, 1994. 195 p.: bibl., ill.

Eleven authors from Brazil and other Latin American countries, the US, and Asia collaborate to examine environmental topics such as damage, costs, global warming, sustainability, and political support from an economic perspective. [K. Muller]

2450 Vernet Ginés, Juan et al. El Tratado de Tordesillas en la cartografía histórica. Coordinación de Jesús Varela Marcos. Valladolid, Spain: Junta de Castilla y León; V Centenario Tratado de Tordesillas, 1994. 167 p.: bibl., ill. (some col.), maps (some col.)

Seven articles on the historical cartography of the period surrounding the 1494 delimitation of the Treaty of Tordesillas. A nice compilation, but only one study focuses on the cartography of the treaty.

2451 Villa Soto, Miguel. Población, espacio y ciudad en el Nuevo Mundo: perfiles demográficos de la urbanización de América Latina. (*Rábida/Huelva*, 12, oct. 1992, p. 52–81, bibl., tables)

A compilation and review of data on urbanization and urban places for aboriginal, colonial, and modern periods. Tenochtitlán/Mexico City has always been large. Shows when colonial ports and mining centers became important. Today, in the late 1990s, two-thirds of the million-plus cities are in Brazil, Colombia, Mexico, and Argentina.

MIDDLE AMERICA

TOM L. MARTINSON, *Professor of Geography, Auburn University, Alabama*
GARY S. ELBOW, *Professor of Geography, Texas Tech University*

ISSUES OF ENVIRONMENTAL degradation highlight the contributions this biennium to the section on Middle American geography: Eyre on Jamaica (item **2460**);

González (item **2461**), Mendoza (item **2466**), Russell (item **2470**), and Schorgmayer and del Rosario on the Dominican Republic (item **2474**), Vargas on Central America (item **2484**), and Morgner (item **2494**), Sánchez-Azofeifa and Quesada-Mateo (item **2495**) on Costa Rica. There is a special focus on Central American border zones, as seen in Girot and Granados (item **2480**), Pujol i Caussa and Pujadasi Tort (item **2510**), and Arias and Nations (item **2477**). Umaña and Brandon (item **2497**) review Costa Rica's successful environmental resource management. Environmental issues related to the Canal's devolution to Panama are discussed in Fernández, Riba, and Cardoze F. (item **2511**) and Manfredo (item **2512**). Herlihy shows how establishing indigenous biosphere reserves and *comarcas* is an effective conservation strategy (item **2481**).

Also included are various studies in population geography, migration, settlement, and urban geography: Davidson on Honduras (item **2508**), Higgins on Nicaragua (item **2509**), Amaya H. on Cuba (item **2452**), Collins on Belize (item **2487**), Douzant-Rosenfeld on Santo Domingo and Havana (item **2459**), Pérez Romagnoli on Panama (item **2513**), Sagawe on Hispanola, Puerto Rico, and Cuba (item **2472**), and Sansonetti on the Italian colonization of San Vito in the highlands of southwestern Costa Rica (item **2496**).

Works on agricultural issues include the *Atlas agropecuario de Costa Rica* (item **2489**), Grossman's study of the effect of export agriculture on local food production in St. Vincent (item **2462**), and Sluyter's review of wetlands agriculture in early Mesoamerica (item **2483**).

The materials for Mexico this biennium are dominated by works on regional and urban development. Studies range in geographic scale from national-level surveys to works on individual urban areas. Among the more interesting national-scale studies is Ornelas Delgado's study of Mexican regional development policy from 1940 to 1982 (item **2565**). This book discusses planning for rural and urban development, including integrated river basin projects, arid zone development, industrial decentralization, housing and urban improvement plans, and a variety of other government-sponsored infrastructure and social improvement programs. Intermediate in scale is Alegría Olazábal's study of urban processes on the Mexico-US border (item **2515**). She views the frontier as an integrated transition zone uniting the two countries economically and socially, while also comprising a unique area of regional development within each country. At the local scale, two books on Puebla stand out. Virginia Cabrera Becerra (item **2528**) examines the impact of national policies on the expansion of the city, and Patrice Melé follows a similar approach, but focuses on industrial location policies and residential planning processes that affect the spatial structure of Puebla (item **2562**).

Other items of special interest on Mexican geography include a detailed analysis of the Plano en Papel Maguey, a 16th-century map of a portion of Tenochtitlán (item **2547**); a lengthy, illustrated guide to 1000 medicinal plants found in Mexico likely to become an indispensable reference for biogeographers and ethnobotanists (item **2519**); a case study particularly interesting for rural development specialists that examines the changing relationship between rural areas and small cities in the Rincón de Guanajuato, the southwestern part of the state (item **2516**); and a theoretically-oriented article on cultural geography that proposes a new model to explain development of irrigation technology in precolumbian Mexico (item **2540**). Finally, Jones' excellent monograph on the impact of migration on sending communities in Coahuila and Zacatecas should be noted (item **2555**). This work presents data that challenges assumptions regarding migrant characteristics and the impact of migration on families and communities in Mexico.

Two studies regarding urban development processes are of special interest within the body of work on Guatemala. Gellert's history of Guatemala City's urban expansion provides valuable information on the city's spatial development through time (item **2502**). Pérez Sáinz discusses the city's development during the 1980s, a time when Guatemala faced economic and political crisis (item **2507**).

CARIBBEAN AND THE GUIANAS

2452 Amaya H., Carlos A. Crecimiento de los asentamientos urbanos en Cuba, 1970–1981. (*Rev. Geogr./Mérida,* 31, 1990, p. 95–116, bibl., graph, map, tables)

Small and medium-sized towns grew while large centers such as Havana declined as decentralization progressed during the 1970–81 era.

2453 Arbona, Sonia I. and **John M. Hunter.** Economic development threatens groundwater in Puerto Rico: results of a field study. (*J. Geogr.,* 94:6, Nov./Dec. 1995, p. 558–569, appendix, bibl., maps, tables)

Seven wells that provide over one-third of the public water supply for four *municipios* showed signs of pollution by heavy metals, noxious chemicals, and organic compounds.

2454 Borsdorf, Axel. Kuba, 100 Prozant Kubanisch?: Anspruch und Wirklichkeit der Entwicklungsstrategie Castros. [Cuba, 100 percent Cuba?: the promises and realities of Castro's development program]. (*Mitt. Österr. Geogr. Ges.,* 135, 1993, p. 191–202, bibl., table)

Contemporary trends reveal a weakness in the Cuban economy that has increased the country's dependency.

2455 Boswell, Thomas D. Characteristics and processes of urbanization in the Caribbean. (*Yearbook/CLAG,* 17/18, 1990, p. 67–90, bibl., graph, map, tables)

Review article concludes that Caribbean cities differ from North American cities, especially in their high rate of natural population increase and rural-to-urban migration.

2456 Burac, Maurice. Les zones franches industrielles en République Dominicaine. (*Cah. Outre-Mer,* 48:189, jan./mars 1995, p. 5–20, graphs, map, table)

Outlines economic contributions of the country's free trade zones, where products, particularly leather goods, are produced for export.

2457 Congrès régional de l'environnement, 2nd, Cayenne, 1990. Gestion de l'écosystème forestier et aménagement de l'espace régional: actes du IIème Congrès régional de l'environnement. Organisation de la Sépanguy avec la participation du Conseil de la culture, de l'éducation et de l'environnement, Cayenne, Chambre de commerce et d'industrie de la Guyane, 16–17 février 1990. Cayenne: Conseil de la culture, de l'éducation et de l'environnement-Conseil régional de Guyane; Societé pour l'étude, la protection et l'aménagement de la nature en Guyane, Collection "Nature guyanaise", 1994. 248 p.: ill. (some col.), maps.

Focuses on the forest of French Guiana, which has one of the most diverse environments in the world. Records presentations of the Second Regional Congress on Environment concerning natural environment, vegetation, flora, fauna, human interaction and management, and conservation issues.

2458 Conway, Dennis. Rethinking the consequences of remittances for Eastern Caribbean development. (*Caribb. Geogr.,* 4:2, Sept. 1994, p. 116–130, graph, map, bibl.)

Asserts that remittances are economically sufficient for households but do not support national development.

2459 Douzant-Rosenfeld, Denise. Approvisionnement de deux métropoles caraïbes: Santo Domingo et La Havane. (*in* Nourrir les métropoles d'Amérique Latine: approvisionnement et distribution. Paris: Editions L'Harmattan, 1995, p. 91–120, bibl., map, tables)

Explores food distribution systems in Havana and Santo Domingo. Examines efficiency and fairness of market prices.

2460 Eyre, L. Alan. The tropical rainforests of Jamaica. (*Jam. J.,* 26:1, June 1996, p. 26–37, bibl., graphs, photos, table)

Summarizes abuses and prescriptions for change in an environment on the edge of destruction.

Geografía del medio ambiente: una alternativa del ordenamiento ecológico. See item 2415.

2461 González, Zoila and **William Gutiérrez.** Diagnóstico del estado ecológico del Río Ozama. (*Rev. UNIBE,* 2:2/3, mayo/dic. 1990, p. 1–35, bibl., graphs, maps)

Offers the Río Ozama in Santo Domingo as an example of how the Dominican Republic can organize its resources to establish environmental norms.

2462 Grossman, Lawrence S. The political ecology of banana exports and local food production in St. Vincent, Eastern Caribbean. (*Ann. Assoc. Am. Geogr.,* 83:2, June 1993, p. 347–367, bibl., graphs, maps, photos, tables)

Village-level study reveals that export agriculture is not the primary cause of decline in local food production.

2463 Guadeloupe, Martinique et Guyane dans le monde américain: réalités d'hier, mutations d'aujourd'hui, perspectives 2000. Direction de Maurice Burac. Paris: Karthala; Schoelcher, Martinique: GEODE Caraïbe, Univ. des Antilles et de la Guyane, 1994. 391 p.: bibl., ill., maps.

Edited by head of Dept. of Geography at the Univ. of the French Antilles and Guyana, contributions explore historical and political dimensions of contemporary issues examined by geographers in the French Caribbean—degradation of the environment, recurrent hurricanes, and changing forms of human migration and diasporas. [A. Pérotin-Dumon]

Huyghues-Belrose, Vincent. Le littoral de la Guyane Française: perspectives historiques. See *HLAS 56:1831.*

2464 Mansingh, Ajai. Stewards of creation covenant: Hinduism and the environment. (*Caribb. Q.,* 41:1, March 1995, p. 59–75, bibl.)

Proposes that understanding and management of the environment must be based on spiritual values.

2465 Marchena Gómez, Manuel J. and **Angel R. Velasco Martín.** La región caribe como espacio turístico. (*Estud. Perspect. Turismo,* 2:2, abril 1993, p. 130–149, bibl., graphs, tables)

Proposes that contemporary Caribbean tourism is similar to Mediterranean tourism in the 1960s.

2466 Mendoza G., Leticia *et al.* Contaminación por monoxido de carbono en la ciudad de Santo Domingo. (*Cienc. Soc./Santo Domingo,* 18:1, enero/marzo 1993, p. 40–48, bibl., graph, table)

Using new system of measuring devices, study confirms the presence of carbon monoxide poisoning in Santo Domingo, with highest concentrations at two city locations.

2467 Miller, Mark M.; Tim W. Hudson; and **Joseph L. Scarpaci.** Cuban geography in higher education: survival in the "special period." (*J. Geogr.,* 95:2, March/April 1996, p. 59–65, bibl., tables)

Overview of the programs and personnel of the Facultad de Geografía at the Univ. de Havana includes a list of black market prices for selected food items in contemporary Cuba.

2468 Paysans, systèmes et crise: travaux sur l'agraire haïtien. v. 1, Histoire agraire et développement. v. 2, Stratégies et logiques sociales. Pointe-à-Pitre, Guadeloupe: S.A.C.A.D., Groupe de recherche/formation Systèmes agraires caribéens et alternatives de séveloppement, Univ. des Antilles et de la Guyane; Port-au-Prince: F.A.M.V., Faculté d'agronomie et de médecine vétérinaire, Univ. d'Etat d'Haïti, 1993. 2 v.: bibl., ill., maps.

Places agriculture in the context of Haiti's economic, social, and political life. Complete three-part study will include historical development from Indian heritage through independence, transformation of rural space, and traditional systems of agricultural production. Two volumes have been issued to date. For political scientist's comment, see item **1903.**

2469 Richardson, Bonham C. Detrimental determinists: applied environmentalism as bureaucratic self-interest in the *fin-de-siècle* British Caribbean. (*Ann. Assoc. Am. Geogr.,* 86:2, June 1996, p. 213–234, graph, map, photos)

Reviews flawed tenets of environmental determinism in light of British colonial experience in the West Indies.

2470 Russell, Fernando Arturo and **Louis Fournier.** Análisis de los cambios de la cobertura del suelo en la zona occidental de la República Dominicana. (*Rev. Eme-Eme,* 18:86/88, mayo 1990/abril 1991, p. 53–62, bibl., map, tables)

Uses satellite technology to chart change in land cover, particularly the effects of deforestation, in the Dominican Republic.

2471 Ryder, Roy. Point score analysis of agricultural decision-making in the Dominican Republic. (*Caribb. Geogr.*, 4:1, March 1993, p. 2–14, bibl., map, tables)

Studies 18 factors that determine agricultural decisions in the Las Cuevas River watershed of the Cordillera Central.

2472 Sagawe, Thorsten. Algunos datos sobre el origen de los centros urbanos en La Española, Puerto Rico y Cuba. (*Rev. Eme-Eme*, 18:86/88, mayo 1990/abril 1991, p. 33–52, appendix, graphs, maps, tables)

Since suburbanization has begun to affect large Caribbean cities, few studies on the growth of these urban centers have been conducted.

2473 Sanité, Léon P. Conservation et gestion du patrimoine naturel guyanais. Cayenne: CCEE-Conseil régional Guyane; DIREN Guyane; SEPANGUY, 1995. 34 p.: bibl., ill., maps.

Contains current information on physical and settlement geography of French Guiana. Fills some information gaps on this little-known part of South America.

2474 Schorgmayer, Helmut and **Pedro Juan del Rosario.** Medio ambiente y sociedad en el espacio rural dominicano. (*Rev. Eme-Eme*, 16:85, enero/abril 1990, p. 85–110, bibl., tables)

Attempts to bridge gap between techno-theoretical knowledge concerning environment and development interactions and actual practices of Dominican farmers.

Seguinot Barbosa, José. La ecología urbana de San Juan: una interpretación geográfico-social. See item **4923.**

Wing, Elizabeth S. and **Stephen R. Wing.** Prehistoric ceramic age adaptation to varying diversity of animal resources along the West Indian archipelago. See item **381.**

CENTRAL AMERICA
General

2475 Alonso Santos, José Luis. Migraciones y desplazamientos forzados de población en América Central durante la crisis de los ochenta. (*in* Jornadas de Estudios Geográficos Iberoamericanos, *2nd, Salamanca,*

Spain, 1990. Las migraciones en Iberoamérica. Salamanca: Instituto de Iberoamérica y Portugal, 1992, p. 133–161, bibl., maps, tables)

Investigates causes and effects of Central American population movement during the 1980s, particularly migration to the US.

2476 Annis, Sheldon et al. Poverty, natural resources, and public policy in Central America. New Brunswick, N.J.: Transaction Publishers, 1992. 208 p.: bibl., ill., maps. (U.S.-Third World policy perspectives; 17)

Suggests specific guidelines for linking responsible environmental management and economic development. Includes proposals for international peace parks, fostering conservation institutions, and modifying nontraditional agricultural exports.

2477 Arias, Oscar and **James D. Nations.** A call for Central American peace parks. (*in* Poverty, natural resources, and public policy in Central America. Edited by Sheldon Annis. New Brunswick, N.J.: Transaction Publishers, 1992, p. 43–58, maps)

Proposes that peace parks represent cooperative regional solutions to environmental problems.

2478 Caldentey Albert, Pedro and **René Antonio Rivera Magaña.** Agricultura y seguridad alimentaria en Centroamérica. (*in* Coloquio de Geografía Rural, *7th, Córdoba, Spain, 1994.* Actas. Córdoba, Spain: Servicio de Publicaciones de la Univ. de Córdoba, p. 481–485, bibl., table)

Suggests that dependence on external markets and loss of local economic control during the 1980s should lead to new, alternative approaches in agricultural land use in Central America at the end of the 1990s.

2479 La estructuración de las capitales centroamericanas. Recopilación de Rodrigo Fernández Vásquez y Mario Lungo. San José: Editorial Universitaria Centroamericana, 1988. 344 p.: bibl., ill., maps. (Col. Rueda del tiempo)

Review of development of Central America's capital cities includes historical urban maps.

2480 Girot, Pascal O. and **Carlos Granados.** La integración centroamericana y las regiones fronterizas: ¿competir o compartir? (*Presencia/San Salvador*, 5:19, 1993, p. 13–37, bibl., ill., maps)

Suggests that border zones between Central American nations must play a vital role in development and can be zones of environmental and cultural protection.

2481 Herlihy, Peter H. *Wildlands* conservation in Central America during the 1980s: a geographical perspective. (*Yearbook/CLAG*, 17/18, 1990, p. 31–43, bibl., maps, tables)

Conservation of unaltered terrestrial and aquatic environments has been achieved through three main approaches: 1) establishment of biosphere resources; 2) establishment of comarcas; and 3) the obtaining of legal land title by indigenous groups.

Historia general de Centroamérica. v. 1., Historia antigua. Edición de Robert M. Carmack. See item **84.**

2482 Jiménez, José A. Los manglares del Pacífico centroamericano. Ilustraciones de Silvia Troyo y Zeidy Angulo. Heredia, Costa Rica: Editorial Fundación UNA, 1994. 336 p.: bibl., ill. (some col.).

Complete reference work on Central American mangroves includes their ecology, structure, management, flora, and associated fauna. Color and black-and-white illustrations.

2483 Sluyter, Andrew. Intensive wetland agriculture in Mesoamerica: space, time, and form. (*Ann. Assoc. Am. Geogr.*, 84:4, Dec. 1994, p. 557–584, bibl., ill., maps, photo)

Reviews recent literature on wetlands agriculture from four perspectives: the emergence of urbanization and settlement; other agroecosystems; ecological parameters; and comparison of contemporary and antecedent systems.

2484 Vargas, Gilbert. Estudio del uso actual y capacidad de uso de la tierra en América Central. (*Anu. Estud. Centroam.*, 18:2, 1992, p. 7–20, bibl., maps, table)

Concludes that most Central American land use is not appropriate to its environment, causing degradation.

Belize

2485 Allender, Darrell. The impact of expatriates on the development of resorts in Western Cayo district, Belize. (*Yearbook/CLAG*, 21, 1995, p. 67–76)

Case study of the shift of hotel ownership from Belizean nationals to foreign immigrants (expatriates). Finds that change in ownership accompanies a transition in the function of these facilities from simple lodging facilities to integrated resorts which offer food, lodging, tours, and recreational activities.

2486 Chomitz, Kenneth M. and **David A. Gray.** Roads, land use, and deforestation: a spatial model applied to Belize. (*World Bank Econ. Rev.*, 10:3, Sept. 1996, p. 487–512, bibl., graphs, tables)

Von Thunen's model and GIS technology offer assistance to planners wishing to determine the development impact of road extension.

2487 Collins, Charles O. Refugee resettlement in Belize. (*Geogr. Rev.*, 85:1, Jan. 1995, p. 20–30, bibl., map, photos)

Compares two refugee settlements, Valley of Peace, which is sponsored, and Las Flores, a squatter settlement, which are both occupied primarily by Salvadorean-origin population. Concludes that the squatter settlement is in a better location and has superior amenities, but interviews with refugees indicate greater satisfaction with the sponsored settlement.

2488 Los impactos del turismo y sus alternativas: el caso de San Pedro, Ambergris, Belize. Edición de Alfredo A. César Dachary, Stella Maris Arnáiz Burne y Daniel Navarro L. Chetumal, Mexico: Centro de Investigación de Quintana Roo, 1991. 116 p.: bibl., ill., index.

Programmatic study conducted in 1990 at the request of Belizean national and local authorities includes socioeconomic and ecological data that may be of interest to scholars. Analysis may be useful for students of tourism.

Costa Rica

2489 Atlas agropecuario de Costa Rica. Edición de Gonzalo Cortés Enríquez. San José: Florica Instituto; Editorial Univ. Estatal a Distancia, 1994. 529 p.: bibl., ill. (some col.), maps (some col.).

Maps are secondary to text in this atlas, which includes major agricultural crops and cultivated plants of Costa Rica. Each section includes information on the origin and development of the cultivated plant, its evolution in the country, its importance in the national economy, distribution of its cultivation, and technical aspects of its production.

2490 Barrientos Llosa, Zaidett and **Julián Monge-Nájera.** La biodiversidad de Costa Rica = The biodiversity of Costa Rica. 1. ed. Heredia, Costa Rica: Instituto Nacional de Biodiversidad, Costa Rica, 1995. 79 p., 32 p. of plates : bibl., col. ill.

Excellent overview of Costa Rica's ecosystems and wildlife, with color photos on quality stock.

2491 Béneker, Tine. *Buscar mejor ambiente:* migratie naar, uit en langs een kleine stad in Costa Rica. Utrecht: Koninklijk Nederlands Aardrijkskundig Genootschap; Faculteit Ruimtelijke Wetenschappen Universiteit Utrecht, 1997. 199 p.: bibl., ill., maps. (Nederlandse geografische studies, 0169-4839; 216)

Studies the role of San Isidro in the migration processes of Costa Rica. Focuses on the town's role vis-à-vis the surrounding rural expulsion area. Describes the center's settlement and social and professional integration of migrants. Also looks at young, often-skilled people who leave in search of better opportunities. However, permanent outmigration from the countryside is far greater than outmigration from San Isidro. Includes summaries in English and Spanish. [R. Höefte]

2492 Carriere, Jean. The crisis in Costa Rica: an ecological perspective. (*in* Environment and development in Latin America: the politics of sustainability. Edited by David Goodman and Michael Redclift. Manchester, U.K.: Manchester Univ. Press; New York: St. Martin's Press, 1991, p. 184–204, bibl., maps, tables)

Attempts to link ecological deterioration and exhaustion of the natural resource base and economic and political constraints, leading to irreversible ecological breakdown.

2493 Coffey, Brian. Investment incentives as a means of encouraging tourism development: the case of Costa Rica. (*Bull. Lat. Am. Res.*, 12:1, Jan. 1993, p. 83–90, bibl., map, tables)

Evaluates potential of the Tourism Investment Incentives Law (1985) to increase development of the tourist industry, mainly

by instituting tariff and surcharge exemptions on imported goods.

2494 Morgner, Fred G. Poisoning the garden: Costa Rica's ecological crisis. (*in* Seminar on the Acquisition of Latin American Library Materials (SALALM), *36th, San Diego, Calif., 1991.* Latin American studies into the twenty-first century: new focus, new formats, new challenges. Albuquerque: SALALM Secretariat General Library, Univ. of New Mexico, 1993, p. 77–87)

Uses the worst environmental abuses (deforestation and pesticide use) to illustrate the point that restrictive measures must be applied to suppliers and consumers alike.

2495 Sánchez-Azofeifa, G. Arturo and **Carlos Quesada-Mateo.** Deforestation, carbon dynamics, and sustainable mitigation measures in Costa Rica: the Puerto Viejo de Sarapiquí case study. (*Interciencia/Caracas*, 20:6, Nov./Dec. 1995, p. 396–400, bibl., maps)

Forest depletion in Costa Rica is accelerating, and the virtual disappearance of commercial forest in the Sarapiquí area is symptomatic of tendencies throughout Central America.

2496 Sansonetti, Vito. Quemé mis naves en estas montañas: la colonización de la altiplanicie de Coto Brus y la fundación de San Vito de Java. San José: Jiménez & Tanzi, 1995. 99 p.: ill. (some col.).

Historical account of the founding and early years of one of the most interesting colonies in the Americas, San Vito de Java in the highlands of southwestern Costa Rica.

2497 Umaña, Alvaro and **Katrina Brandon.** Inventing institutions for conservation: lessons from Costa Rica. (*in* Poverty, natural resources, and public policy in Central America. Edited by Sheldon Annis. New Brunswick, N.J.: Transaction Publishers, 1992, p. 85–107, maps, table)

Describes how Costa Rica was able to establish, consolidate, and coordinate government agencies to promote natural resource management.

2498 Vargas, Gilbert. Contaminación y deterioro de la calidad de vida en Costa Rica. (*Herencia/San José*, 6:1/2, 1994, p. 117–138, bibl., maps, photos, tables)

Documents places where contaminated water is consumed by people or used for irrigation of crops in Costa Rica's Valle Central, and how this water is causing beach contamination, especially near Puntareans.

2499 Yoder, Michael S. Cattle production, global markets, and the transformation of a small-farm community in Costa Rica's Nicoya Peninsula. (*SECOLAS Ann.*, 27, March 1996, p. 5–16, bibl., map, tables)

Illustrates how one small community adjusts to a changing global economy.

El Salvador

2500 Bommer, J.J. et al. Seismic hazard assessments for El Salvador. (*Geofís. Int.*, 35:3, July/Sept. 1996, p. 227–244, bibl., graphs, maps, tables)

Differences in seismic prediction models lead to strikingly different outcomes in the event of earthquake activity in El Salvador.

2501 Tálice, Rodolfo V. Eto-ecología salvadora: planeta en decadencia, humanidad en peligro. v. 1–2. Montevideo: Asociación Eto-ecologista del Uruguay, 1990–1991. 2 v.: bibl.

Small two volume work contains basic considerations about the human role in the environmental deterioration. Emphasizes the "ethos" of the situation. [C. Caviedes]

Guatemala

2502 Gellert, Gisela. Ciudad de Guatemala: factores determinantes en su desarrollo urbano, 1775 hasta la actualidad. (*Mesoamérica/Antigua*, 15:27, junio 1994, p. 1–68, maps, tables)

Detailed description of Guatemala City's development since its founding. Identifies three developmental periods: "colonial" (1775–1871), "liberal" (1871–1944), and "modern" (1944-present). Essential article for study of Guatemalan urbanization.

2503 Horst, Oscar H. 1902, año de caos: el impacto político y socioeconómico de las catástrofes naturales en Guatemala. (*Mesoamérica/Antigua*, 16:30, dic. 1995, p. 309–326, map, photos)

Describes multiple natural catastrophes which struck Guatemala in 1902 and their impact on the national economy and political life. The impact of earthquakes, a vol-

canic eruption, a tsunami, and floods was complicated by Guatemala's status as an international debtor nation, which had to negotiate loan extensions with European nations. Contains many interesting photographs.

2504 Hostnig, Rainer. Monografía del municipio de Ostuncalco. Colaboración de Luis Vásquez. Quetzaltenango, Guatemala: CCIC, 1991. xxxii, 192 p.: appendices, bibl., ill., maps.

Offers compendium of information on the history and physical, economic, and cultural conditions of a much-studied Guatemalan *municipio*. The text is accompanied by approximately 80 pages of appendices which contain copies or transcriptions of historical documents, data, maps, and other useful information.

2505 Lovell, William George. A beauty that hurts: life and death in Guatemala. Toronto, Canada: Between the Lines, 1995. 174 p.: bibl., map.

Personal testimonial of the impact of the 1954–96 Guatemalan civil war, written by an historical geographer with years of research experience in the country. Beautifully written book focuses on the destruction wrought upon Indian communities by a war between guerrilla and government forces.

2506 Payeras, Mario. Latitud de la flor y el granizo: y otros escritos sobre el medio ambiente mesoamericano. 2. ed. Tuxtla Gutiérrez, Mexico: Gobierno del Estado de Chiapas, Consejo Estatal de Fomento a la Investigación y Difusión de la Cultura, DIF-Chiapas, Instituto Chiapaneco de Cultura, 1993. 131 p.: bibl., maps. (Serie Centroamericana)

An environmental history of Guatemala, written from a Marxist perspective by a former guerrilla fighter who before his death was one of Guatemala's most creative writers, is of both literary and scholarly interest.

2507 Pérez Sáinz, Juan Pablo. Ciudad de Guatemala en la década de los ochenta: crisis y urbanización. Guatemala: FLACSO; Fundación Friedrich Ebert, 1991. 75 p.: bibl., map. (Debate; 10.)

Examines processes of social and structural change in Guatemala City based on Alejandro Portes' research concerning impacts of Guatemala's economic decline and the violence that shook rural areas during the 1980s. Discusses spatial polarization of the population, growth of the informal labor market, and urban development policies. Also examines Guatemalan urban hierarchy. Welcome addition to the small collection of current studies of Guatemala City.

Honduras

2508 Davidson, William van. Honduras. (in Latin American urbanization: historical profiles of major cities. Edited by Gerald Michael Greenfield. Westport, Conn.: Greenwood Press, 1994, p. 313–330, bibl., maps)
Survey of urbanization in Honduras concentrates on founding and early development of the country's two major cities, Tegucigalpa and San Pedro Sula.

Dewalt, Billie R.; Philippe Vergne; and Mark Hardin. Shrimp aquaculture development and the environment: people, mangroves and fisheries on the Gulf of Fonseca, Honduras. See item **1807.**

Nicaragua

2509 Higgins, Bryan. Nicaragua. (in Latin American urbanization: historical profiles of major cities. Edited by Gerald Michael Greenfield. Westport, Conn.: Greenwood Press, 1994, p. 396–415, bibl., maps, tables)
Review of urbanization in Nicaragua includes information on pre-Conquest communities and the role of the Somoza family in the rise and fall of Managua.

2510 Pujol i Caussa, Pere and Montserrat Pujadasi Tort. Usos del sòl i fronter agrària al sud-est de Nicaragua. (Doc. Anàl. Geogr., 28, 1996, p. 79–98, bibl., maps, tables)
Uses geographic information systems to illustrate changing land use in Nicaragua along the Costa Rican border.

Panama

2511 El Canal y la posición geográfica de Panamá: seminario-taller celebrado los días 8 y 9 de septiembre de 1990, en el Hotel Riande de Tocumen, Panamá. Exposición de Marco Fernández, Jorge Riba y Fernando Cardoze F. Moderación de Woodrow de Castro. Panamá: Instituto Latinoamericano de Estudios Avanzados, 1991. 47 p. (Seminario-taller; 90/2)
Round table discussion of Canal issues

as Panama prepares to assume complete administration responsibility. Analyzes land use problems.

2512 Manfredo, Fernando. La contaminación ambiental en las bases militares. (Tareas/Panamá, 90, mayo/agosto 1995, p. 119–128)
Estimates cost of environmental cleanup at US military bases devolving to Panama.

2513 Pérez Romagnoli, Eduardo E. Colonización espontánea de tierras nuevas en América Latina: el caso de Panamá y el aporte de investigaciones nacionales. (Bol. Estud. Geogr., 26/27, 1990/91, p. 9–30, bibl., maps)
Migration to the lowlands of northern Panama has caused deforestation and environmental degradation.

MEXICO

2514 Aguilera Ortega, Jesús and Alma Delia Corral Fernández. La producción de suelo urbano a través de fraccionamientos en el Estado de México, 1946–1992. México: Univ. Autónoma del Estado de México, 1993. 305 p.: bibl., ill., maps. (Col. Textos y apuntes; 45)
The state of Mexico has created legal urban subdivisions since 1951 that currently occupy 30 percent of urban land. Discusses legal bases for creating subdivisions and analyzes their impact on service provision to the urban population. Of interest to researchers of urban development in Mexico's core.

2515 Alegría Olazábal, Tito. Desarrollo urbano en la frontera México-Estados Unidos: una interpretación y algunos resultados. México: Consejo Nacional para la Cultura y las Artes, 1992. 285 p.: bibl., ill., map. (Regiones)
Interesting study analyzes processes of frontier development from a Mexican perspective. Divided into two sections: 1) analysis of border area urban growth and 2) review of three frontier-related activities (temporary and long-term migration to the border and the placement of maquiladora plants in Mexican border cities). Extensive data on the border region from the late 1980s.

2516 Arias, Patricia. Nueva rusticidad mexicana. México: Consejo Nacional para la Cultura y las Artes, 1992. 311 p.: bibl. (Regiones)

Research based on El Rincón de Guanajuato, an area that includes parts of Guanajuato, Jalisco, and Michoacán states, examines changes in the relationship between small/mid-sized cities and rural areas between 1970–90. Women entered the labor market as workers in local industry and as vendors of imported products; men increasingly depended on earnings as migrant laborers, either in Mexico or, more frequently, in the US to augment farm earnings. Well-researched study sheds light on trends in the Mexican rural economy.

2517 Arreola, Daniel David and **James R. Curtis.** Ciudad Chihuahua: its changing morphology and landscape. (*Yearbook/CLAG*, 20, 1994, p. 73–85, bibl., maps, photos, tables)

Authors of a recent book on Mexican border cities (see *HLAS 55:2358*) examine the country's interior. Study argues that changes affecting the urban structure of Chihuahua are similar to those in border cities. Suggests that similar urban development processes are operating throughout northern Mexico.

2518 Arreola Ayala, Alvaro et al. Votos y mapas: estudios de geografía electoral en México. Coordinación de Gustavo Ernesto Emmerich. Toluca, Mexico: UAEM, 1993. 340 p.: bibl., ill., maps.

Ten studies of regional voting results, subdivided by political party for several Mexican states (Federal District, Nayarit, Puebla, Mexico State, Michoacán, Sonora, Guanajuato, and others). The most recent elections covered are 1989 and 1991; the oldest from 1946, for the Federal District. Interesting addition to the growing literature on Mexican electoral geography (see *HLAS 55:2399*).

2519 Atlas de las plantas de la medicina tradicional mexicana. v. 1. Coordinación general de Arturo Argueta Villamar. Subcoordinación de Leticia M. Cano Asseleih. Asistencia a la coordinación de María Elena Rodarte. Responsabilidad para la etnobotánica de María Concepción Gallardo Vázquez et al. México: Instituto Nacional Indigenista, 1994. 3 v. (1786 p.): bibl., ill., maps. (Biblioteca de la medicina tradicional mexicana)

Extremely valuable reference work on Mexican ethnobotany. One thousand species of medicinal plants are illustrated, referenced by popular name, and classified botanically,

pharmacologically, and chemically. Provides information on their history and traditional uses. Lists locations of herbarium samples. Part of proposed series on Mexican traditional medicine to be published by INI. Likely to become the definitive work for many years to come. Bibliography.

2520 Banzo, Mayté. Approvisionnement de Mexico et marginalisation des producteurs péri-urbains. (*in* Nourrir les métropoles d'Amérique Latine: approvisionnement et distribution. Paris: Editions L'Harmattan, 1995, p. 69–90, bibl., maps)

Case study of farming in the Chalco-Amecameca Basin in Mexico City's southern periphery finds that the major constraints to agricultural development are marketing inefficiency and low prices, which keep farmer income low. These factors pave the way for subdivision and urbanization of agricultural land in the urban periphery.

2521 Bataillon, Claude. Mexico, au début du XXIe siècle. (*in* Le Mexique à l'aube du troisième millénaire. Paris: Editions de l'Institut des hautes études de l'Amérique latine, 1993, p. 41–48, map)

Speculates Mexico City's growth and development during the the 1990s. Offers several scenarios for population growth and the changing national political status of the Federal District.

2522 Bellon, Mauricio R. Landholding fragmentation: are folk soil taxonomy and equity important?; a case study from Mexico. (*Hum. Ecol.*, 24:3, Sept. 1996, p. 373–393)

Presents peasant farmers' rationale for maintaining fragmentation of land holdings. Allows for the equal distribution of land with varying degrees of soil quality. Useful contribution.

2523 Biotic communities: southwestern United States and northwestern Mexico. Edited by David Earl Brown. Salt Lake City: Univ. of Utah Press, 1994. 342 p.: bibl., ill., index, maps.

Encyclopedic listing of biotic communities comments on factors that account for change in these communities over time. Of ecological and biogeographical interest.

2524 Borges Contreras, José J. and **Graziella Sánchez Mota.** Santa Rosalía y Guerrero Negro: cobre y sal en el desierto. México: Instituto de Seguridad y Servicios Sociales de los Trabajadores del Estado, 1992. 132 p.: bibl., ill. (some col.), maps.

Brief, general history of two towns in Baja California Sur that developed during the latter part of the 19th century to house workers in copper (Santa Rosalía) and salt (Guerrero Negro) mines. Utilizes archival and oral sources.

2525 Burwell, Trevor. Bootlegging on a desert mountain: the political ecology of agave (*Agave* spp.); demographic change in the Sonora River Valley, Sonora, Mexico. (*Hum. Ecol.*, 23:3, Sept. 1995, p. 407–432)

Neo-Malthusian approaches do not explain the decline of wild agave in Sonora. Argues situation is complex and better explained through a political ecological approach. Programs to preserve existing agave stands or promote re-establishment must consider ecological relationships among those who exploit the plants at the family and community level.

2526 Cabeza, Gregorio Z. Las islas de México. Mexico: Confederación de Asociaciones de Agentes Aduanales de la República Mexicana, 1993. 101 p.: bibl., ill., maps.

Contains descriptions and anecdotal information on Mexico's oceanic and coastal island territories, collected from various sources dating from the colonial period to the 20th century.

2527 Cabrales Barajas, Luis Felipe. Un siglo de urbanización mexicana. (*Meridiano Rev. Geogr.*, 2, marzo 1996, p. 19–28, bibl., graph, maps, photos, tables)

Identifies three periods of 20th-century urbanization, corresponding roughly to a sigmoid growth curve: moderate growth (1900–40); rapid growth (1940–70); and reduced rate of growth (1970–90). Also discusses regional patterns of recent urban growth. Presents a succinct review of Mexican urbanization.

2528 Cabrera Becerra, Virginia. Políticas regionales y configuración espacial de la región centro de Puebla, 1970–1990. Puebla, Mexico: Univ. Nacional Autónoma de México; Benemérita Univ. Autónoma de Puebla, 1994. 332 p.: bibl., ill.

Theoretically oriented study of the expansion of the urban influence of the city of Puebla, Mexico. The relative importance of the city center has declined with respect to the periphery. Concludes that national-level policies have been important influences on changes in the spatial configuration of the city during the period of study.

2529 Cabrera Hernández, Hugo Martín. Cambio tecnológico en la agricultura maicera de un pueblo chontal de Tabasco. (*Am. Indíg.*, 54:1/2, enero/junio 1994, p. 223–255, bibl., maps, table)

Case study concludes that Chontal Indians of the Tabasco lowlands have maintained traditional agricultural practices, but adapted them to changing ecological conditions, and have selectively adopted new agricultural techniques, including cattle raising and planting of introduced soil building cover crops.

2530 Cambios en el uso del suelo agrícola en México. Coordinación de Luis Fuentes Aguilar. México: Univ. Nacional Autónoma de México, Instituto de Geografía, 1992. 211 p.: bibl., ill., maps.

Twelve case studies on Mexican agricultural land use. Topics include agricultural land use change, both locally and at the national level; attempts to reestablish productive activities on degraded soils; colonization in tropical zones; and agricultural land uses in metropolitan Mexico City.

2531 Cambrezy, Luc; Bernal Lascuráin; and **Jean-Yves Marchal.** Crónicas de un territorio fraccionado: de la hacienda al ejido, Centro de Veracruz. Prólogo de Jean Meyer. Fotografías de Miguel Fematt Enríquez. Archivos fotográficos de Juan Carlos Reyes Romero. México: Larousse; ORSTOM; Centro de Estudios Mexicanos y Centroamericanos, 1992. 180 p.: bibl., ill. (some col.), maps

Eclectic history of haciendas in the state of Veracruz from late-19th century to 1940 includes useful photographs, maps, and architectural drawings of haciendas near the turn of the century. Provides interesting and thought-provoking text.

2532 Canales Cerón, Alejandro. El poblamiento de Baja California, 1848–1950. (*Front. Norte*, 7:13, enero/junio 1995, p. 5–23, bibl., graphs, tables)

Argues that modern demographic patterns of Baja California began to form during the second half of the 19th century. Since there was no pre-existing colonial settlement structure, an independent settlement pattern based on proximity to the US and shaped by national government policies evolved in the region.

2533 Casas, Alejandro *et al.* Plant management among the Nahua and the Mixtec in the Balsas River Basin, Mexico: an ethnobotanical approach to the study of plant domestication. (*Hum. Ecol.*, 24:4, Dec. 1996, p. 455–478)

Field study among Mexican Indians discusses strategies for domesticating various plants. Useful study of plant domestication.

2534 Cisneros Sosa, Armando. La ciudad que construimos: registro de la expansión de la ciudad de México, 1920–1976. México: Univ. Autónoma Metropolitana, Unidad Iztapalapa, División de Ciencias Sociales y Humanidades, 1993. 228 p.: bibl., ill. (Texto y contexto; 13)

Descriptive history of post-revolutionary Mexico City. Following the Calles Administration (1934), chapters are organized by six-year presidential administrations, which accurately reflects the importance of national government policies in shaping the city's development.

2535 Comrie, Andrew C. An all-season synoptic climatology of air pollution in the U.S.-Mexico border region. (*Prof. Geogr.*, 48:3, Aug. 1996, p. 237–251, bibl., graphs, maps, table)

Ozone pollution levels of four border cities (San Diego, Tucson, El Paso, and San Antonio) are correlated with regional climate conditions. Results indicate a characteristic ozone pollution pattern associated with certain climate conditions. Argues climate conditions reflect general ozone pollution potential where actual pollution data are unavailable. Technical study of interest to specialists.

2536 Conferencia Nacional sobre el Henequén y la Zona Henequenera de Yucatán, *Mérida, Mexico, 1992.* Memorias. Recopilación de Piedad Peniche Rivero y Felipe Santamaría Basulto. Mérida, Mexico: Gobierno del Estado; CONACYT, 1993. 590 p.: bibl., ill.

Mexico's henequen (sisal) production dropped to nearly 1/3 its 1970 level by 1990. This volume contains information on the impact of this diminishing production for Yuca-

tán. Includes papers on technical aspects of production and on alternative crops.

2537 Curtis, James R. Mexicali's Chinatown. (*Geogr. Rev.*, 85:3, July 1995, p. 335–348, bibl., map)

Speculates on factors that drew Chinese migrants to the Mexicali Valley into business during the first quarter of the 20th century. Compares the physical character of the Chinese district in 1925 with its current condition.

2538 Delaunay, Daniel and Carole Brugeilles. Los espacios de la fecundidad en el norte de México de 1970 a 1990. (*Trace/México*, 24, déc. 1993, p. 87–106, bibl., maps, tables)

Statistical analysis of fecundity in the northern states of Mexico. Concludes that border area urban fecundity is lower than most areas of the country and that there is a slight decrease in fecundity with proximity to the border. Of interest to demographers and population geographers. Relevant for similar studies of other frontier areas.

2539 Delgadillo Macías, Javier. Economía y migración: la nueva geografía de la movilidad poblacional en México. (*Probl. Desarro.*, 24:94, julio/sept. 1993, p. 113–132, graphs, tables)

Based largely on the 1990 census, studies migration by state. Identifies regional and intraregional migration flows, which are attributed largely to economic factors. Concludes that NAFTA will intensify pre-existing tendencies for a general south-to-north migration flow, and will increase population pressure on the northern cities.

2540 Doolittle, William E. Indigenous development of Mesoamerican irrigation. (*Geogr. Rev.*, 85:3, July 1995, p. 301–323, bibl., map, photos)

Attempts to explain technological innovation by proposing a new framework of indigenous development to replace traditional models of independent invention and diffusion. Examples of precolumbian water management from central Mexico support the argument. Theoretical aspects attract cultural geographers and anthropologists; photographs and discussion of technology will be of interest to historical geographers and ethnohistorians.

2541 Estrella Valenzuela, Gabriel. Movilidad de población y comportamiento reproductivo: el caso de Baja California. (*Estud. Front.*, 29, sept./dic. 1992, p. 57–89, bibl., tables)

Interesting study of fecundity among migrants and native-born residents of Baja California from 1986–90. Concludes that migrant women have higher rates of fecundity because of a greater number of births out of wedlock, larger numbers of informal unions, lower rates of birth control use among women in informal unions, and longer lactation periods.

2542 Estudio integral de la frontera México-Belice. v. 1, Análisis socioeconómico. v. 2, Monografías de México. v. 3, Monografías de Belice. v. 4., Recursos naturales. Chetumal, Mexico: Centro de Investigaciones de Quintana Roo, 1994. 4 v.: ill. (some col.), maps.

Expresses Mexico's continued concern with its southern border. Presents an account of border region economic development, settlements, and resources. Presents considerable information on Belize, including street maps for each border area settlement.

2543 Franco, Gabriel Ascencio. Neoliberalismo y usura. (*Relaciones/Zamora*, 54, primavera 1993, p. 103–116, bibl., maps)

Article 27 of the Mexican Constitution changed the status of ejidos and made it possible for large land holders and peasant producers to cooperate economically through credit relationships. Loans from large to small producers are paid off from harvest proceeds. Small producers are becoming subordinated to larger operators. An interesting study of the impact of neoliberal policies in southern Chiapas.

2544 Gamboa de Buen, Jorge. Ciudad de México. México: Fondo de Cultura Económica, 1994. 261 p.: bibl., ill. (Una Visión de la modernización de México)

Presents a brief history of the growth and development of Mexico City. Serves as background for discussion of plans and programs developed by the Salinas de Gortari Administration to address the city's serious problems such as lack of housing, environmental pollution, transportation, and public security and safety. Written for a general audience.

García Barrios, Raúl; Luis García Barrios; and **Elena Alvarez-Buylla.** Lagunas: deterioro ambiental y tecnológico en el campo semiproletarizado. See item **4594.**

2545 García de Fuentes, Ana and **Angel Navarro Madrid.** El desarrollo de la ganadería bovina tropical en Yucatán, México: la lucha por el espacio agrario. (*in* Coloquio de Geografía Rural, 7th, Córdoba, Spain, 1994. Actas. Córdoba, Spain: Servicio de Publicaciones de la Univ. de Córdoba, 1994, p. 547–552, bibl., tables)

The increased importance of Yucatán cattle raising since 1950 has paralleled the decline of henequen production. Approximately 70 percent of the state's cattle are raised in 10 Northeastern *municipios*, where Tizimín is the major center.

2546 Garcia Quiñones, Rolando. Análisis comparativo de un tipo singular de retorno: el caso de los mexicanos indocumentados devueltos. (*Probl. Desarro.*, 24:93, abril/junio 1993, p. 121–151, tables)

Uses comparative statistics from previously published studies and two Mexican surveys of returned migrants (1977 and 1984) to analyze trends in socioeconomic characteristics of migrants. Concludes with a Marxist-oriented discussion of labor markets in the US and Mexico.

2547 González Aragón, Jorge. La urbanización indígena de la ciudad de México: el caso del Plano en papel maguey. México: Univ. Autónoma Metropolitana, Unidad Xochimilco, 1993. 77 p.: bibl., ill. (some col.). (Biblioteca Memoria mexicana; 1)

Analyzes the *Plano en Papel Maguey*, an early colonial Indian map of a section of Tenochtitlán, to better understand the city's 16th-century urban structure. Well-illustrated monograph and valuable document for study of the early development of Mexico City and Spanish colonial influence on pre-existing urban structure.

2548 Gutiérrez Haces, Teresa and **Daniel Hiernaux Nicolas.** Reorganización territorial en el norte de México y pacto federal. (*Probl. Desarro.*, 26:100, enero/marzo 1995, p. 191–222, tables)

Argues that globalization of the Mexican economy has made it imperative that the central government decentralize power and resources to the states and *municipios*. Suggests this is especially urgent in the northern frontier, where rapid growth of urban centers, industry, and population calls for locally-based responses.

2549 Heineberg, Heinz; Jorge Camberos Garibi; and Christoph Schäfers. Verstädterung in Mexiko: das Beispiel des Bundesstaates Jalisco und des Metropolitangebietes Guadalajara [Urbanization in Mexico: the example of the state of Jalisco and the metropolitan area of Guadalajara]. (*Geogr. Rundsch.*, 7/8, Juli/Aug. 1993, p. 400–408, bibl., graphs, maps, tables)

Reviews Mexican urban planning with emphasis on coordination between city, metropolitan area, and state, using the example of Jalisco state and the city of Guadalajara. The sewer explosion of 1992 is an example of the need for greater planning coordination.

2550 Hoffmann, Odile. Rumbos y paisajes de Xico: geografía de un municipio de la sierra veracruzana. México: ORSTOM; Xalapa, Veracruz: Instituto de Ecología, 1993. 130 p.: bibl., ill., maps.

Conventional microregional study in the French tradition includes chapters on land use, physical landscape (ecology), settlement history, and contemporary land use and rural life.

2551 Hoffmann, Odile. Territorios antiguos, percepciones renovadas: tres visiones para un mismo espacio municipal, en México. (*in* International Congress of Americanists, *48th, Stockholm, Sweden, 1994*. El lugar y el espacio en la tradición de las culturas latinoamericanas. Stockholm: Institute of Latin American Studies, Stockholm Univ., 1996, p. 27–56, bibl., maps, tables)

Physical limits of the dominantly Indian *municipio* of Xico (Veracruz) have remained fixed since the conquest, but psychological configurations of this space have changed markedly over time. Attributes change to differing valuations of territory over time and among different groups. Interesting study in territoriality and spatial perception.

2552 Icazuriaga, Carmen. La metropolización de la Ciudad de México a través de la instalación industrial. México: Ediciones de la Casa Chata; CIESAS, 1992. 217 p.: bibl., ill.

Case study of the *municipio* de Tultit-lán, an industrializing zone at the northern limit of Mexico City's metropolitan area. Changes in Tultitlán reflect general development characteristics for the metropolitan area. Important study for those with an interest in Mexico City and urbanization.

2553 Jauregui, Ernesto. Rainfall fluctuations and tropical storm activity in Mexico. (*Erdkunde/Bonn*, 49:1, Jan./März 1995, p. 39–48)

Mexico's foremost climatologist analyzes link between El Niño activity and drought occurrence since colonial times and notes reduction of hurricane frequency for the period 1961–90 on both the Pacific and Gulf Coasts during El Niño events.

2554 Jiménez Pelayo, Agueda; Jaime Olveda; and Beatriz Núñez Miranda. El crecimiento urbano de Guadalajara. Zapopan, Mexico: Colegio de Jalisco; H. Ayuntamiento de Guadalajara; CONACYT, 1995. 325 p., 6 folded leaves of plates: bibl., ill., maps.

An urban history of Guadalajara is divided into three independently authored parts, each dealing with a separate historical period. Describes the city's development from its founding in 1542–1990. Illustrated with photographs and maps. Treasury of information on the history and urban geography of Mexico's second largest city.

2555 Jones, Richard C. Ambivalent journey: U.S. migration and economic mobility in north-central Mexico. Tucson: Univ. of Arizona Press, 1995. 172 p.: bibl., ill., index, maps.

Compares impact of US migration on *municipios* in the states of Coahuila and Zacatecas. Findings suggest there are important differences in the socioeconomic characteristics of migrants of the two areas and that the remittance of funds by migrants impacted the receiving communities in different ways. Concludes with an interesting speculation on possible impacts of free trade initiatives for rural *municipios*.

2556 Jones, Richard C. Immigration reform and migrant flows: compositional and spatial changes in Mexican migration after the Immigration Reform Act of 1986. (*Ann. Assoc. Am. Geogr.*, 85:4, Dec. 1995, p. 715–730, bibl., graph, maps, tables)

Study based on INS data from apprehended Mexican illegal immigrants indicates that the 1985 legislation reduced illegal immigration and shifted immigrant source points toward the center of the country and away from the northern states.

2557 Lambert, Dean P. Crop diversity and fallow management in a tropical deciduous forest shifting cultivation system. (*Hum. Ecol.*, 24:4, Dec. 1996, p. 427–454)

Examines shifting cultivation practices among small farmers in the seasonally dry forest of Guerrero state, Mexico. Contrasts shifts with those reported in the literature for humid tropical forest regions. Describes subtle but important differences in practices, including highly seasonable labor allocation, varying fallow cycle periods, and occasional use of chemical fertilizers and pesticides.

2558 Lambert, Dean P. Regional core-periphery imbalance: the case of Guerrero, Mexico, since 1821. (*Yearbook/CLAG*, 20, 1994, p. 59–71)

Reviews the historical development of one of Mexico's most isolated states to better understand the emergence of scattered core areas during the past 50 years or so as communication with Mexico City has improved.

2559 Limas Hernández, Alfredo and **Mario Armando Vázquez Soriano.** México como conjunto de espacios regionales. Ciudad Juárez, Mexico: Unidad de Estudios Regionales, Univ. Autónoma de Ciudad Juárez, 1994. 28 p. (Cuadernos de Trabajo; 22)

Brief history of regional development in Mexico since the conquest suggests that Mexican regional structure will change as a result of recent trade agreements, but does not speculate on the exact form of those changes.

López Piñero, José María and **José Pardo Tomás.** Nuevos materiales y noticias sobre la *Historia de las plantas de Nueva España* de Francisco Hernández. See *HLAS 56:1181.*

2560 Luna Morales, César del C. Cambios en el aprovechamiento de los recursos naturales de la antigua ciénega de Tlaxcala. Tlaxcala, Mexico: Univ. Autónoma Chapingo, 1993. 190 p.: bibl., ill. (Col. Cuadernos universitarios. Serie Agronomía; 24)

Detailed account of changing resource use in an area of southwestern Tlaxcala state. Concludes that major changes, most of which have taken place over the last century, include: replacement of pasture by cultivated land, the drying up of lakes and wetlands, and a reduction in biogical diversity.

2561 Malmström, Vincent H. Geographical origins of the Tarascans. (*Geogr. Rev.*, 85:1, Jan. 1995, p. 31–40, bibl., maps)

Relies on linguistic, technological, and ethnohistorical evidence to propose an Andean origin for the Purépecha, believed to have arrived in Michoacán state in Mexico around AD 800. A controversial proposal likely to generate lively debate among historical geographers, ethnohistorians, and archaeologists.

2562 Mele, Patrice. Puebla, urbanización y políticas urbanas. Puebla, Mexico: Benemérita Univ. Autónoma de Puebla, Instituto de Ciencias; México: Univ. Autónoma Metropolitana, Azcapotzalco, 1994. 229 p.: bibl., ill., maps.

Case study in Mexican urban development focuses on industrial location processes and the contrasts between formal and informal housing within the city and its hinterland. (The distinction between formal and informal housing is inconsequential given the rapid integration of informal housing into the urban fabric.) Concludes that industries have not transformed rural areas, rather they have created extensions of urban influence beyond the traditional city limits.

2563 Mühlenpfordt, Eduard. Ensayo de una descripción fiel de la República de Méjico, con especial referencia a su geografía, etnografía y estadística, el estado de Oajaca. Traducción de María del Carmen Salinas y Elisabeth Siefer. México: Codex Editores; Librería Madero, 1993. 116 p.: bibl., index. (Tule)

Reprint of an 1844 book originally published in German, contains descriptions of the state and city of Oaxaca and numerous smaller Oaxacan towns and villages of the time. Also offers some social and economic data.

2564 Navarro B., Bernardo. El metro y sus usuarios: Ciudad de México. México: Univ. Autónoma Metropolitana, Unidad Xochimilco; Univ. Nacional Autónoma de México, Depto. del Distrito Federal, 1993. 221 p.: bibl., ill.

The Mexico City metro system differs from others in Latin America due to the high proportion of poor and working-class commuters. This study, based on 1986 surveys of four working-class colonias of the Mexico City metropolitan area, compares public transportation use among communities with differing levels of service.

2565 Ornelas Delgado, Jaime. Estructuración del territorio y política regional en México. Tlaxcala, Mexico: Univ. Autónoma de Tlaxcala, 1993. 203 p.: bibl., maps. (Col. Textos de apoyo académico)

Careful study of Mexican regionalization policy and its results between 1940–82. Concludes that long-term government policies have failed to promote successful decentralization or to counter tendencies toward unequal distribution of wealth.

2566 Ortega, Sylvia and Paz Trigueros. La migración interna e internacional en México: una perspectiva histórica. (*in* Jornadas de Estudios Geográficos Iberoamericanos, 2nd, *Salamanca, Spain, 1990.* Las migraciones en Iberoamérica. Salamanca: Instituto de Iberoamérica y Portugal, 1992, p. 87–131, bibl., graphs, maps, tables)

General review of the history of Mexican migration emphasizes the second half of the 20th century. Includes detailed maps offering a graphic view of the origin and destination of internal migrants by state for the 1960s.

2567 Popp, Kilian. Urbanización de terrenos por iniciativa privada como proceso parcial del desarrollo urbano en México: el caso de la ciudad de Puebla. (*Anu. Estud. Soc.,* 1993, p. 189–228, bibl., graphs, maps, tables)

Using Puebla as an example, the paper attempts to determine the role of residential subdivisions (*fraccionamientos*) in Mexican urban development. Finds that the practice of land subdivison creates residential segregation, generally benefitting elites or government officials, and reflects lack of adequate planning strategies.

2568 Preciado Coronado, Jaime. Por una geografía del poder: la inversión pública en la Federación y en Jalisco. Guadalajara, Mexico: Univ. de Guadalajara, Dirección General Académica, 1992. 133 p.: bibl., ill., maps. (Cuadernos de difusión científica; 31. Difusión científica.)

Examines the role of public investment in Mexican decentralization at the national, state (Jalisco), and local (*municipio*) levels.

Studies spatial pattern of public investment in Mexico with many graphs, maps, and commentary on the politics of public investment.

2569 Producción forestal de México. VII censo agropecuario, 1991. Aguascalientes, Mexico: Instituto Nacional de Estadística, Geografía e Informática; Colegio de Postgraduados, c1995. xxv, 170 p.: bibl., ill., maps.

Based on a 1991 census, collection of statistics and maps details Mexican forest production by state.

2570 Romero Lankao, Patricia. Impacto socioambiental, en Xochimilco y Lerma, de las obras de abastecimiento de la Ciudad de México. México: Univ. Autónoma Metropolitana, Unidad Xochimilco, 1993. 151 p.: bibl., ill. (some col.).

Case study of the mostly negative impact of Mexico City's water supply projects on the largely agricultural communities at Xochimilco (begun in 1912) and Lerma River (1951 and after). Examines impacts of urban infrastructure projects on surrounding areas.

2571 Tamayo, Jesús. Tiraderos o depósitos de desechos tóxicos y radioactivos en la frontera noreste: cronología y notas de una experiencia reciente. (*Estud. Front.,* 30, enero/abril 1993, p. 125–139, bibl., map)

Offers commentary on US waste dumps situated near the Mexican border. Discusses Mexican official and public reaction. Presents a Mexican perspective on the problem.

2572 Toledo, Víctor M. et al. La selva útil: etnobotánica cuantitativa de los grupos indígenas del trópico húmedo de México. (*Interciencia/Caracas,* 20:4, July/Aug. 1995, p. 177–187, bibl., graphs, map, tables)

Identifies over 1300 species of useful plants from the humid tropical lowlands of Mexico. Finds that there is a wide gulf between Western ideas of the rainforest as an obstacle to development and the Native American concept of the forest as resource rich, which rationalizes their tendency to preserve areas of forest within their domain. Interestingly, the study concludes that secondary forest is more productive in useful plants than primary forest.

2573 Van Young, Eric. Doing regional history: a theoretical discussion and some Mexican cases. (*Yearbook/CLAG,* 20, 1994, p. 21–34)

Noted historian of Mexico applies regional theory to the identification of historical regions in that country. Thought-provoking piece is of interest to geographers and historians working in areas beyond the article's area of focus.

2574 Vos, Jan de. Las fronteras de la frontera sur: reseña de los proyectos de expansión que figuraron la frontera entre México y Centroamérica. Villahermosa, Mexico: Univ.

Juárez Autónoma de Tabasco, Centro de Investigaciones y Estudios Superiores en Antropología Social, 1993. 177 p.: appendix, bibl., maps.

Historical study of international boundary development on the Mexican Gulf coast from precolumbian times to the end of the 19th century. Appendix contains 22 documents regarding the establishment of Mexico's southern limit.

WESTERN SOUTH AMERICA

DANIEL W. GADE, *Professor Emeritus of Geography, The University of Vermont*

ENVIRONMENTAL AND CONSERVATION ISSUES have taken center stage this biennium as the stars of geographical published works on Andean countries. Urbanization as a spatial and ecological process has received less attention from geographers during the 1990s than in previous decades. On the other hand, regions of tropical forest, which all five western South American countries possess, have attracted much interest in recent years. Good work in biogeography, including the study of vegetation, and on past physical landscapes and processes is also more common.

Four monographs that analyze primary data also suggest the range of subject matter within contemporary geography. Newson presents archival-based conclusions on colonial Ecuadoran population decline (item **2629**). Radcliffe and Westwood offer a post-structuralism glimpse at governmental development in contemporary Ecuador (item **2631**). Tracy produced an illuminating dissertation on agricultural terraces (item **2661**). Foremost among this chapter's contributions is Zimmerer's excellent field-based study, organized within a political-ecological framework, of peasant crop diversity (item **2664**).

Much of the best Andeanist work mentioned here has been produced by North American and European, rather than Latin American, scholars. However, that gap continues to narrow. Four fine studies from South Americans focus on the Colombian Caribbean (item **2607**); premodern land transportation in Colombia (item **2598**); the cultural landscape of Azuay (item **2619**); and the historical geography of settlement in Piura (item **2650**).

Two serials merit mention as prime outlets for works on Andean geography. Since its debut 17 years ago, the quarterly *Mountain Research and Development* has published many articles on the physical and/or human aspects of the Andean highlands. Though edited in North America, a Swiss government agency largely funds this journal. Also underwritten from Europe is the *Bulletin de l'Institut français d'Etudes andines*, an important source of new knowledge on western South America thanks to its steady publication, in Spanish and French, of primary research results. Much of this research has been sponsored by ORSTOM, a French agency. Through the combined efforts of ORSTOM and the *Bulletin*, the French currently lead the way in the production of innovative Andean geographic studies.

GENERAL

2575 Abele, Gerhard. Modelle zur Entwicklung des Hochgebirgsreliefs und ihre Anwendung am Beispiel der Anden. (*Mitt. Österr. Geogr. Ges.*, 135, 1993, p. 41–60, bibl., graph, map)

Asserts that aridity reduced erosion and preserved the unusual crustal thickness reported for the Central Andes following Cenozoic uplift.

2576 The Andean countries by satellite.
Direction, design and edition by Benjamin Villegas. Texts by L. Enrique Garcia, Gustavo Wilches-Chaux, and Olivier Bernard. Bogotá: Villegas Editores, 1995. 239 p.: bibl., col. ill., index, col. maps.

Colored plates of satellite imagery using the SPOT system show land configurations from Venezuela to Argentina.

Bromley, Rosemary D.F. and **Gareth A. Jones.** Identifying the inner city in Latin America. See item **2388.**

2577 Coca and cocaine: an Andean perspective. Edited by Felipe E. Mac Gregor. Foreword by Giuseppe di Gennaro. Westport, Conn.: Greenwood Press, 1993. 155 p.: bibl., index. (Contributions in criminology and penology, 0732–4464; 37)

Political and economic aspects of cocaine in Peru, Colombia, and Bolivia from the perspective of individuals from those countries.

2578 Deler, Jean-Paul. Une urbanisation andine. (*in* L'Amérique du Sud aux XIXe et XXe siècles: héritages et territoires. Sous la direction de H. Rivière d'Arc. Paris: Armand Colin Editeur, 1993, p. 137–157, ill.)

Examines the physical urban developmental process of Andean cities from the colonial period to the late-20th century.

2579 Enfoque integral de la salud humana en la Amazonia. Edición de Luis Yarzábal, Carlos Espinal y Luis E. Aragón. Caracas: Asociación de Univ. Amazónicas; Univ. Central de Venezuela, 1992. 559 p.: bibl., ill. (Serie Cooperación amazónica; 10)

Thirteen papers from a symposium held in Caracas use disease data from the late 1980s to assess the health conditions in the Amazon portions of eight countries.

2580 Gade, Daniel W. Carl Troll on nature and culture in the Andes. (*Erdkunde/ Bonn,* 50:4, Okt./Dez. 1996, p. 301–315)

Critical assessment of the Andean work of Carl Troll (1899–1975), European geographer whose field research on vegetation, climate, and land use in highland Bolivia and Peru led to early formulations of the concept of verticality and theories regarding the ecological bases of Inca civilization.

2581 International Workshop on the Andean Agroecosystem, *Lima, 1992.* El agroecosistema andino: problemas, limitaciones, perspectivas; anales del Taller Internacional sobre el Agroecosistema Andino, Lima, marzo 30- abril 2, 1992. Edición de Luis Hernán Rincón R. Lima: Centro Internacional de la Papa, 1993. 363 p.: bibl., ill. (some col.).

Papers indicate that Andean agricultural studies have shifted focus from issues relating to modern technology, yield maximization, and foreign models of agropastoral development to concerns revolving around genetic erosion, underexploited Andean crops, regional agroecology, and alternative uses for agricultural products.

2582 Jett, Stephen C. Cairn trail shrines in Middle and South America. (*Yearbook/ CLAG,* 20, 1994, p. 1–8)

Though widespread in highland Latin America, cairns are especially common and ritually significant in the Andes.

2583 Neotropical Montane Forest Biodiversity and Conservation Symposium, *New York Botanical Garden, 1993.* Biodiversity and conservation of neotropical montane forests. Edited by Steven P. Churchill *et al.* Bronx, N.Y.: New York Botanical Garden, 1995. 716 p.: bibl., ill., index, maps.

Uneven collection of 60 papers; most concern Andean mountain flora, forests, and habitats. Several papers focus on human modifications.

2584 Páramo: an Andean ecosystem under human influence. Edited by H. Balslev and J.L. Luteyn. London; San Diego: Academic Press, 1992. 296 p.: bibl., ill., index, maps.

Twenty papers resulting from a 1991 symposium in Denmark on the páramo ecosystem that extends from western Venezuela,

Colombia, Ecuador and northern Peru. Rather than adaptations to climate, as previously believed, these high-altitude grasslands are now clearly seen as artefacts of human intervention.

2585 Seltzer, Geoffrey O.; Donald T. Rodbell; and Mark R. Abbott. Andean glacial lakes and climate variability since the last glacial maximum. (*Bull. Inst. fr. étud. andin.*, 24:3, 1995, p. 539–549, bibl., graphs, maps, table)

Sediment cores from the Central Andes suggest that the last glacial maximum predated 20,000 BP and that glaciers had retreated to their present limits by 10,000 BP.

VENEZUELA

2586 Cervigón, Fernando. Las dependencias federales. Caracas: Biblioteca de la Academia Nacional de la Historia, 1995. 170 p.: bibl., ill. (Serie Historias regionales)

Physical and human survey of Caribbean Islands claimed by Venezuela, both oceanic and those on the continental shelf (excluding Margarita).

2587 Chiossone, Tulio. Diccionario toponímico de Venezuela. Caracas: Monte Avila Editores, 1992. 509 p.: bibl. (Col. Manuales)

Descriptions of the origins of Venezuelan place names. Includes cartographic references to historical places.

2588 Delgado, Luis; Hugo Marín Márquez; and Alicia Apitz de Parra. El Zulia: su espacio geográfico. Caracas: Academia Nacional de la Historia; Maracaibo, Venezuela: Univ. del Zulia; Gobernación del Estado Zulia; Banco Maracaibo, 1992. 479 p.: bibl., ill. (some col.), index, maps.

Well-produced synthesis of information on natural resources, settlement, and socioeconomic factors in the oil-rich state of Zulia.

2589 Flora of the Venezuelan Guayana. Vol. 1 edited by Paul E. Berry, Bruce K. Holst, and Kay Yatskievych. Series edited by Julian A. Steyermark, Paul E. Berry, and Bruce K. Holst. St. Louis: Missouri Botanical Garden; Portland, Or.: Timber Press, 1995– . 1 v.: bibl., ill. , indexes, maps (some col.).

Much broader than title suggests, volume is comprised of authoritative and superbly illustrated chapters on geographical and physical features, history of botanical exploration, vegetation, phytogeography, and conservation. Otto Huber is the author of 90 percent of this volume which covers this region covering three states: Amazonas, Bolívar, and Delta Amacuro.

2590 El macizo del Chimantá: escuedo de Guayana Venezuela, un esayo ecológico tepuyano. Edición scientífico de Otto Huber. Caracas: O. Todtmann, 1992. 343 p.: bibl., ill. (some col.), maps.

Describes climate, geology, geomorphology, soils, pollen analysis, flora and vegetation, and fauna of Chimantá, a massif in Bolívar state whose highest elevations reach 2700 m above sea level.

2591 Pérez, Jesús. Aspects géographiques et historiques des llanos vénézuéliens: une contribution à leur êtude. (*Bol. Am.*, 34:44, 1994, p. 179–195, bibl., tables)

Lucid overview of the physical, historical, and economic aspects of this distinctive region of Venezuela.

2592 Rivero Santos, Angelo A. Neighborhood associations in Venezuela: "los vecinos" voice their dissent. (*Yearbook/CLAG*, 21, 1995, p. 1–12)

Case study of struggle for power in Venezuelan civil society. Local groups in Caracas demand a share of the decision-making process from the old centralized elite.

2593 Salazar-Quijada, Adolfo. El origen de los nombres de los estados y de los municipios de Venezuela. Caracas: Cartografía Nacional; Univ. Central de Venezuela, 1994. 426 p.: bibl. (Ediciones de la Comisión Nacional de Nombres Geográficos; no. 1)

Origins of Venezuelan state and municipio names. Useful bibliographies.

2594 Sebastiani, Mirady et al. Large-scale shrimp farming in coastal wetlands of Venezuela, South America: causes and consequences of land-use conflicts. (*Environ. Manag.*, 18:5, Sept./Oct. 1994, p. 647–661)

Case study of conflicts between industrial-scale shrimp farming businesses and nongovernmental organizations in a bird-rich lagoon near Nuevo Unare in the state of Anzoátegui.

2595 Silva Léon, Gustavo A. Nevada media anual en los Andes merideños. (*Rev. Geogr. Venez.*, 33, 1992, p. 245–259, bibl., graphs, maps, tables)

Data on snowfall quantity and density in three chains of the Sierra de Mérida where the snowline begins at 3,800 m.

Vargas Arenas, Iraida and **Mario Sanoja.** La selva tropical y las sociedades antiguas en la Cuenca del Caribe. See item **685.**

2596 Yerena, Edgard. Corredores ecológicos en los Andes de Venezuela. Caracas: Editorial Torino, 1994. 87 p.: bibl., ill., maps (some col.). (Parques nacionales y conservación ambiental, 0798-2887; 4)

Describes proposal to employ concept of "corridors" to connect existing nature reserves, in this case in the Cordillera de Mérida. This corridor would help protect the rare spectacled bear.

COLOMBIA

Amaya, María Teresa *et al.* Medio ambiente y desarrollo. See item **2386.**

2597 Amazonia colombiana: diversidad y conflicto. Recopilación de Germán I. Andrade, Adriana Hurtado Guerra y Ricardo Torres. Bogotá: Centro de Estudios Ganaderos y Agrícolas, 1992. 404 p., 2 leaves of plates: bibl., ill. (some col.), maps.

Excellent collection of 15 papers by different authors concerning the natural environment and human agency, population and resources, and policies and management.

2598 Caminos reales de Colombia. Dirección de Pilar Moreno de Angel y Jorge Orlando Melo González. Recopilación académico de Mariano Useche Losada. Fotografía y reproducciones de Alberto Sierra Restrepo. Bogotá: Fondo FEN Colombia, 1995. 317 p.: bibl., ill. (some col.), index, maps.

Lavish retrospective of roads and travel in all major regions of Colombia before the automobile. Reproductions of many archival colonial maps.

Coca and cocaine: an Andean perspective. See item **2577.**

2599 Colombia pacífico. Recopilación de Pablo Leyva Franco. Bogotá: Fondo para la Protección del Medio Ambiente José Celes-

tino Mutis, 1993. 2 v. (854 p.): bibl., ill. (some col.), maps (some col.).

Well-illustrated, multi-authored collection on the Pacific region of Colombia. Useful essays on mining, fishing, agriculture, population, Afro-Colombian culture, rural dwellings, and health.

2600 Contaminación industrial en Colombia. Recopilación de Ernesto Sánchez Triana y Eduardo Uribe Botero. Bogotá?: Depto. Nacional de Planeación, 1994. 303 p.: bibl., ill.

Multi-authored work on Colombian industrial pollution includes the following themes: state of the environment, manufacturing, water contamination, solid wastes, air pollution, financial structure and legal aspects of pollution and pollution control, and compliance with environmental regulations.

2601 Garcés Guerrero, Diego Miguel and **Susana de la Zerda Lerner.** Gran libro de los parques nacionales de Colombia. Bogotá: Intermedio Editores, 1994. 230 p.: bibl., col. ill.

Useful information on more than 40 protected national parks. Many magnificent photographs.

2602 Hernández Camacho, Jorge *et al.* Sabanas naturales de Colombia. Bogotá: Banco de Occidente, 1994. 207 p.: bibl., col., ill., col. maps.

Beautifully illustrated introduction to the Colombian savanna that covers most of the Orinoco drainage east of the Andes. Discusses vegetation, flora, fauna, and people—past and present.

2603 Herrera Angel, Marta. Population, territory and power in eighteenth century New Granada: *pueblos de indios* and authorities in the province of Santafe. (*Yearbook/CLAG*, 21, 1995, p. 121–131)

Archival documents from Boyacá and Cundinamarca reveal an 18th-century trend that resulted in the displacement of traditional authorities, and the loss of Indian communal lands and their village sites.

2604 Hofstede, Robert G.M.; M. Ximena Mondragón Castillo; and **Constanza M. Rocha Osorio.** Biomass of grazed, burned, and undisturbed páramo grasslands, Colombia: aboveground vegetation. (*Arctic Alpine Res.*, 27:1, 1995, p. 1–12)

Experiments on intensive burning and grazing of the páramo which caused a decrease of up to 66 percent in the total biomass.

2605 Jimeno, Myriam; María Lucía Sotomayor; and Luz María Valderrama. Chocó: diversidad cultural y medio ambiente. Bogotá: Fondo FEN Colombia, 1995. 189 p.: bibl., ill. (some col.), maps.

Good description of the Chocó region, an area marginalized by its poor accessibility and eternal rains. Main topics include its demographic racial-ethnic character, economic activities, and social and environmental problems.

2606 Luciani, Jérôme. Le transport aérien en Colombie: historique et problèmes actuels. (*Bull. Inst. fr. étud. andin.*, 22:2, 1993, p. 611–632, graph, maps, tables)

Analyzes Colombian commercial aviation, focusing on internal passenger flows and problems of the post-protectionist era.

2607 Mapa cultural del Caribe colombiano. Dirección regional de Anuar Yaver Cortés. Santa Marta, Colombia: Consejo Regional de Planificación de la Costa Atlántica, 1993. 201 p.: bibl., maps.

Excellent cultural geographic study of the territory from San Jorge to La Guajira that exemplifies Caribbean influences in northern Colombia. Imaginative maps accompany crafted text.

2608 Mejía Gutiérrez, Mario. Amazonia colombiana: historia del uso de la tierra. Florencia, Colombia: Consejo Regional de Planificación Corpes de la Amazonia, 1993. 191 p.: bibl., ill. (some col.).

Historical-geographical perspective on resource use and settlement in the Colombian Amazon. Remarkable for the range of topics discussed.

2609 Monroy Cabra, Marco Gerardo. Delimitación terrestre y marítima entre Colombia y Venezuela. Bogotá: Univ. Santo Tomás, Facultad de Derecho, 1989. 228 p.: maps (some folded). (Col. Fray Antón de Montesinos)

Colombian law professor's perspective on the international boundary dispute in the Gulf of Venezuela.

2610 O'Brien, Philip J. Participation and sustainable development in Colombia. (*Rev. Eur.*, 59, Dec. 1995, p. 7–35, bibl.)

Superb essay on the formation of new political relationships among members of Colombian civil society as they negotiated with the State on questions of the environment and sustainable development.

2611 Parsons, James Jerome. Las regiones tropicales americanas: visión geográfica de James J. Parsons. Recopilación de Joaquín Molano Barrero. Bogotá: Fondo FEN Colombia, 1992. 454 p.: bibl., ill., maps.

Magnificent edition of articles translated into Spanish, by the late Berkeley geographer, James J. Parsons (1914–97). Approximately half are studies on Colombia. Parsons was known for his masterful ability to understand, from direct observation, the interaction between nature and culture.

2612 La política ambiental del fin de siglo: una agenda para Colombia. Edición de Manuel Rodríguez Becerra. Bogotá: Cerec, 1994. 398 p.: bibl., ill. (Serie ecológica; 8)

Collectively, 15 essays illustrate Colombia's environmental objectives.

2613 Restrepo Forero, Olga. La expedición botánica y la comisión corográfica: una mirada comparativa. (*Senderos/Bogotá*, 5:25/26, agosto 1993, p. 535–563, bibl., ill., maps)

Insightful comparison of three scientists (Mutis, Codazzi, and Caldas) and their contributions to Colombian natural history and geography.

2614 Reyes Zambrano, Pedro et al. El páramo: un ecosistema de alta montaña. Bogotá: ECOAN, 1995. 168 p.: bibl., ill. (some col.), maps. (Serie Montañas tropoandinas; 1)

Excellent description of the landscape, glaciation, soils, and vegetation in the Boyacán páramo of the Sierra Nevada del Cocoy.

2615 Simposio Internacional Investigación y Manejo de la Amazonia, *Leticia, Colombia, 1989.* Memorias del Simposio Internacional Investigación y Manejo de la Amazonia. Bogotá: República de Colombia, Ministerio de Agricultura, Instituto Nacional de los Recursos Naturales Renovables y del Ambiente, 1989. 165 p. (Biblioteca Andrés Posada Arango. Serie de Publicaciones Especiales del INDERENA; 1)

Diverse papers discuss the agriculture, botany, archaeology, forest and park management, geopolitics, soils, and the Ticuna people of the Colombian Amazon.

2616 Zambrano Pantoja, Fabio and **Olivier Bernard.** Ciudad y territorio: el proceso de poblamiento en Colombia. Bogotá: Academia de Historia de Bogotá, 1993. 297 p.: bibl., ill., maps. (Travaux de l'Institut français d'études andines, 0768–424X; 64)

Historical geography of Colombian settlement focusing on changing distributions of urban areas.

ECUADOR

2617 Acciones de desarrollo en zonas de influencia de áreas protegidas. Quito: Fundación Natura, 1992. 333 p.: bibl., maps (some col.).

Information on Ecuador's 14 protected areas: political status, human pressures, social context, institutions involved, and support projects.

2618 Bebbington, Anthony. Peasant federations, development institutions, and technological change in the Andes. (*in* Inquiry at the grassroots. Edited by William Glade and Charles A. Reilly. Arlington, Va.: Inter-American Foundation, 1993, p. 153–176, tables)

Field research on rural development in Chimborazo province led to this critical analysis of farmer organizations and grassroots support groups. Provides research findings useful to peasants.

2619 Borrero Vega, Ana Luz. El paisaje rural en el Azuay. Cuenca: Banco Central del Ecuador, Centro de Investigación y Cultura, 1989. 270 p.: bibl., ill., maps. (Biblioteca de geografía ecuatoriana; 5)

Richly illustrated monograph uses a cultural landscape approach to illustrate agricultural and settlement differences in this small but diverse province of Azuay.

Bromley, Rosemary D.F. and **Gareth A. Jones.** Identifying the inner city in Latin America. See item **2388**.

2620 Brown, Lawrence A. *et al.* Urban-system evolution in frontier settings. (*Geogr. Rev.*, 84:3, 1994, p. 249–265)

Examines Ecuadorian Oriente through universal models of urban development in frontier areas.

2621 La ciudad del Tena y su proyección al sector *la isla* en el contexto de la provincia de Napo. (*Paisajes Geogr.*, 14:28, 1994, p. 4–72)

Socioeconomic analysis of the Amazon boom town of Tena, capital of Napo province.

2622 El contexto geológico del espacio físico ecuatoriano: neotectónica, geodinámica, volcanismo, cuencas sedimentarias, riesgo sísmico. Coordinación de René Marocco. Quito: Corporación Editora Nacional; Colegio de Geógrafos del Ecuador, 1994. 113 p.: bibl., ill., maps. (Estudios de geografía; 6)

Particularly illuminating among the seven papers included here are those dealing with the following topics: tectonics of highland Ecuador; volcanic ash in the Interandean valley; history of seismic activity in Quito; and seismic risk in Quito.

2623 Dehn, Martin. An evaluation of soil conservation techniques in the Ecuadorian Andes. (*Mt. Res. Dev.*, 15:2, 1995, p. 175–182)

Argues that bench terraces are not an appropriate solution to soil erosion on sloping land in Ecuador.

2624 Elbow, Gary S. Territorial loss and national image: the case of Ecuador. (*Yearbook/CLAG*, 22, 1996, p. 93–105)

Maps, monuments, and slogans remind Ecuadorians of the national territory after the 1941 conflict with Peru. The loss remains within the national conciousness, and Ecuadorians maintain hope that the land will someday be regained.

2625 Escuela Politécnica Nacional Proyecto para manejo del riesgo sísmico de Quito: síntesis. Quito?: GeoHazards International, 1996. 41 p.: ill. (some col.), col. maps. (Quito metropolitano; 4)

Interdisciplinary project estimates impact of earthquake hits in Quito, a city with high seismic risk. Provides strategy for managing risk.

2626 La gestión ambiental en el Ecuador. Quito?: Ministerio de Relaciones Exteriores del Ecuador, 1993. 271 p.: bibl., ill., maps.

Useful source on more than 20 topics of environmental concern in Ecuador, including atmospheric pollution, health, and quality of life.

2627 Harden, Carol P. Interrelationships between land abandonment and land degradation: a case from the Ecuadorian Andes. (*Mt. Res. Dev.*, 16:3, 1996, p. 274–280)

Contrary to conventional belief, abandoned cropping fields used for grazing have high rates of runoff and erosion.

2628 Lavenu, Alain; Roger Baudino; and Frédéric Égo. Stratigraphie des dépôts tertiaires et quaternaires de la dépression interandine d'équateur (entre 0° et 2°15' S). (*Bull. Inst. fr. étud. andin.*, 25:1, 1996, p. 1–15, bibl., maps)

Stratigraphy and sedimentology show certain similarities in three zones studied (Ambato-Latacunga, Alausi-Riobamba, and Quito-Guayllabamba), all part of a fault graben of Miocene age filled with volcanic material.

2629 Newson, Linda A. Life and death in early colonial Ecuador. Norman: Univ. of Oklahoma Press, 1995. 517 p.: bibl., index, maps. (The civilization of the American Indian series; v. 214)

Historical demography for 16th- and 17th-century Ecuador. The book's regional framework reveals major differences in mortality rates. Calculates that depopulation in the Sierra during the 16th century was four times that of the Coast.

2630 Perreault, Thomas. Nature preserves and community conflict: a case study in highland Ecuador. (*Mt. Res. Dev.*, 16:2, 1996, p. 167–175)

Examines management strategies for a nature preserve by (1) an NGO (Bosque Pasochoa e. of Quito) and (2) the local community (Bosque Mindo w. of Quito).

Pichón, Francisco J. Colonist land-allocation decisions, land use, and deforestation in the Ecuadorian Amazon frontier. See item **2050.**

2631 Radcliffe, Sarah A. and Sallie Westwood. Remaking the nation: place, identity and politics in Latin America. London; New York: Routledge, 1996. 203 p.: bibl., ill., index, maps.

Predictable postmodernist analysis of Ecuador's national identity. Examines gender, race, ethnicity, and religion. Case study of nation's development out of inchoate space.

2632 Rodríguez Rojas, José. Las islas Galápagos: estructura geográfica y propuesta de gestión territorial. Quito: Ediciones Abya-Yala, 1993. 276 p.: bibl., ill., maps.

Data and ideas on economic activities, especially tourism, and territorial administration of the archipelago. Many original maps.

2633 Sampedro V., Francisco. El espacio territorial ecuatoriano de 1830 a 1995, con la Guerra del Cenepa desatada por el Perú: auténtica historia de límites. Quito: DIMAXI, 1995? 98 p.: ill. (some col.), col. maps.

Analyzes from a nationalistic perspective the events of early 1990s in light of Ecuador's simmering border conflict with Peru.

2634 Stern, Margaret J. An inter-Andean forest relict: vegetation change in Pasochoa volcano, Ecuador. (*Mt. Res. Dev.*, 15:4, 1995, p. 339–348)

Time sequence aerial photography of Pasochoa volcano, 34 km east of Quito. Shows changes since the 1950's, in relative proportion of cloud forest, bamboo thickets, fields and páramo. Human activity, past and present, is important in understanding Andean ecology.

2635 Suremain, Charles-Édouard de. Les systèmes de plantation d'un système d'hacienda: étude sur la diversité des cultures et des mains-d'œuvre dans trois grandes exploitations agricoles de la côte équatorienne; région de Santo Domingo de Los Colorados. (*Bull. Inst. fr. étud. andin.*, 21:1, 1992, p. 349–374, bibl., map, tables)

Description and analysis of agropastoral production and labor force of three haciendas near Santo Domingo de los Colorados.

2636 Swyngedouw, Erik A. The contradictions of urban water provision: a study of Guayaquil, Ecuador. (*Third World Plan. Rev.*, 17:4, Nov. 1995, p. 387–405, bibl., photos, tables)

Raises basic questions about Guayaquil where 35 percent of residents, mostly poor, do not have access to the city water supply and must therefore depend on private vendors who charge high prices.

Valenzuela G., Jaime. Actividades urbanas y control de los usos del suelo: hacia una zonificación del centro metropolitano. See item **2841.**

2637 Wunder, Sven. Deforestation and the uses of wood in the Ecuadorian Andes. (*Mt. Res. Dev.*, 16:4, 1996, p. 367–382)
Finds that deforestation in highland Ecuador results from a need for agricultural and grazing land, not a need for fuel wood.

PERU

2638 Alarcón Aliaga, Carlos. Catástrofe ecológica en la Sierra Central del Perú: incidencia de la actividad minero-metalúrgica en el medio ambiente. Lima: IPEMIN, 1994. 84 p.: bibl., ill. (Serie Desarrollo y medio ambiente)
Documents the serious air and water pollution from mining and smelting operations particularly affecting the town of La Oroya, Lake Chinchaycocha, and the Mantaro River.

2639 Ames Márquez, Alcides and **Bernard Francou.** Cordillera Blanca: glaciares en la historia. (*Bull. Inst. fr. étud. andin.*, 24:1, 1995, p. 37–64, bibl., graph, maps, photos, table)
Cordillera Blanca (Ancash dept.) contains 26 percent of the world's glaciers within the tropical zone. Reviews advancement of scientific knowledge about the glaciers and their movement, and presents a history of human catastrophes associated with them.

2640 Balvín Díaz, Doris; Juan Tejedo Huamán; and **Humberto Lozada Castro.** Agua, minería y contaminación: el caso Southern Perú. Ilo, Peru: Ediciones Labor, 1995. 346, civ p.: bibl., ill.
Carefully prepared indictment of Southern Peruvian Copper Corporation activities in Tacna and Moquegua depts. The firm has usurped scarce water resources and polluted them and the air in its quest for mining profits.

2641 Bouchard, Jean-François; V. Carlotto; and **P. Usselman.** Machu Picchu: problemas de conservación de un sitio Inca de ceja de selva. (*Bull. Inst. fr. étud. andin.*, 21:3, 1992, p. 905–927, bibl., ill., maps, photos)
Solifluction and water infiltration, caused by heavy rainfall, is largely responsible for the deterioration of indigenous constructions of Machu Picchu. Site needs a drainage system.

Bouysse-Cassagne, Thérèse. Le Lac Titicaca: histoire perdue d'une mer intérieure. See item **2667.**

Coca and cocaine: an Andean perspective. See item **2577.**

2642 Coomes, Oliver T. A century of rainforest use in western Amazonia: lessons for extraction-based conservation of tropical forest resources. (*For. Conserv. Hist.*, 39:3, July 1995, p. 108–120)
Environmental history of the Tahuayo River basin (near Iquitos, Peru), a region characterized by four economic cycles since 1850.

2643 Coomes, Oliver T. Income formation among Amazonian peasant households in northeastern Peru: empirical observations and implications for market-oriented conservation. (*Yearbook/CLAG*, 22, 1996, p. 51–64)
Systematic interview survey of rural households along an Amazon tributary near Iquitos. Examines family income and degree of dependence on diverse local resources. Results provide an empirical base for understanding peasant livelihood and a sound foundation for conservation initiatives.

2644 Dumont, Jean-François. Rasgos morfoestructurales de la llanura amázonica del Perú: efecto de la neotéctonica sobre los cambios fluviales y la delimitación de las provincias. (*Bull. Inst. fr. étud. andin.*, 21:3, 1992, p. 801–833, bibl., maps)
Cenozoic folding and faulting had a major impact on river drainage in Amazonian Peru.

Encuentro Binacional Perú-Bolivia, La Paz, 1991. El Lago Titicaca: análisis peruano-boliviano de las relaciones entre el ambiente y el desarrollo social; memorias. See item **5085.**

2645 Giddings, John Calvin. Demon river Apurímac: the first navigation of upper Amazon canyons. Salt Lake City: Univ. of Utah Press, 1996. 300 p.: ill., maps.
Well-written, first-person account of the author's 1970s kayaking adventure through the Apurimac River gorge, from near its source above 4000 m to the jungle far below. Interspersed are descriptive accounts of the still little known canyon and its indigenous inhabitants.

2646 Grupo Permanente de Estudio sobre Riego (Peru). Gestión del agua y crisis institucional: un análisis multidisciplinario del riego en el Perú. Lima: Tecnología Intermedia (ITDG); Servicio Holandés de Cooperación Técnica (SNV), 1993. 317 p.: bibl., ill.

Ten essays by different authors on Peruvian irrigation from different disciplinary perspectives: inventory, politics, projects, social organization, administration, irrigation methods, water rates, education, and research.

2647 Hansen, Barbara C.S. and Donald T. Rodbell. A late glaciel/Holocene pollen record from the eastern Andes of northern Peru. (*Quat. Res./New York*, 44:1, July 1995, p. 216–227)

A pollen record from a lake at 3575 m near Pataz suggests increased human activities ca. 4,000 years BP had a greater impact on vegetation than did climate.

2648 Hays-Mitchell, Maureen. Streetvending in Peruvian cities: the spatio-temporal behavior of *ambulantes*. (*Prof. Geogr.*, 46:4, Nov. 1994, p. 425–438, bibl., maps, tables)

Studies six mid-size Peruvian cities to reveal the spatial and temporal distributions of street vendors, the locational constraints of these entrepreneurs, and the vendors' attempts to limit competition.

2649 Hocquenghem, Anne-Marie and Luc Ortlieb. Eventos El Niño y lluvias anormales en la costa del Perú: siglos XVI–XIX. (*Bull. Inst. fr. étud. andin.*, 21:1, 1992, p. 197–278, bibl., ill., maps, tables)

Important historical sources written between 1532–1891 reconstruct El Niño activity, characterized by heavy rains and flooding on the Peruvian coast. Conclusions are at odds with other reconstructions published during the 1980s.

2650 Huertas V., Lorenzo. Patrones de asentamiento poblacional en Piura, 1532–1850. (*Bull. Inst. fr. étud. andin.*, 25:1, 1996, p. 91–124, appendices, bibl., maps, tables)

Rural settlement in Piura underwent two phases of nucleation: 1572–1600 and 1782–1850. Both involved coercive Hispanic policies but differed in several ways. A fine archival-based study.

2651 Humboldt, Alexander von. Humboldt en el Perú: diario de Alejandro de Humboldt durante su permanencia en el Perú, agosto a diciembre de 1802. Traducido del francés por Manuel Vegas Vélez. Piura, Peru: Centro de Investigación y Promoción del Campesinado, 1991. 96 p., 10 leaves of plates: bibl., ill., map.

Good Spanish translation of Humboldt's 1802 Peruvian journal.

2652 Hurtado, Isabel *et al.* Exodo o redistribución: tendencias demográficas en la región Inka, 1961–1993. Cusco: Centro de Estudios Regionales Andinos Bartolomé de Las Casas, 1993. 148 p.: bibl., ill., maps. (Documentos regionales, 1022–0909; 5)

Summaries of the 1993 census data for the Inca region (Depts. Cuzco, Madre de Dios, and most of Apurimac) are compared to four previous censuses dating back to 1940. Total population growth for this region since 1981 is only 2 percent, while 53 other districts have lost population.

2653 Kent, Robert B. Spatial and temporal variations of sound in an Andean city: Cajamarca, Peru. (*GeoJournal/Boston*, 33:4, 1994, p. 453–458)

Sound profiles based on 6am–12pm readings from four neighborhoods in Cajamarca, each having unique daily auditory rhythm. Imaginative approach; conclusions are tentative.

2654 Llosa, Héctor and María A. Benavides. Arquitectura y vivienda campesina en tres pueblos andinos: Yanque, Lari y Coporaque en el valle del Río Colca, Arequipa. (*Bull. Inst. fr. étud. andin.*, 23:1, 1994, p. 105–150)

Physical layouts and architectural characteristics of three Indian villages located in the Colca valley during the 1570s. Illustrates and beautifully describes how the Hispanic vision of space, designs, and material use was tempered by indigenous solutions.

2655 Maché, José, and Luc Ortlieb. Registros del fenómeno El Niño en el Perú. (*Bull. Inst. fr. étud. andin.*, 22:1, 1993, p. 35–52, charts, graph)

Critically assesses evidence for past El Niño events. Examines paleoclimatic indicators (glaciation, flood deposits, beach-ridge sequences), archaeological findings, historical archives, and instrumental records of this century.

2656 Machupicchu: devenir histórico y cultural. Editorial, selección y notas de Efraín Chevarría Huarcaya. Cusco?: E. Chevarría Huarcaya, 1992? 250 p.: bibl., ill. (some col.), maps.

Collection of articles by eminent scholars on the geography, geology, biota, discovery and exploration, ethnohistory, archaeology, architecture, poetry, and tourism of South America's most visited archaeological site. Many photographs.

2657 Mesclier, Evelyne. Pérou: vers une redistribution des populations rurales andines?; changements dans la société paysanne et évolution de l'organisation de l'espace. (*Bull. Inst. fr. étud. andin.*, 22:3, 1993, p. 763–789, bibl., graphs, maps)

Examines the 1993 census data to document geographical changes in population. Agricultural society in rural Peru has declined.

2658 Morlon, Pierre. De las relaciones entre clima de altura y agricultura de la sierra del Perú en los textos de los siglos XVI y XVII. (*Bull. Inst. fr. étud. andin.*, 21:3, 1992, p. 929–959, bibl., maps)

Compilation and commentary on highland agriculture and climate from a dozen colonial chronicles. Demonstrates chroniclers' scientific insights into the Sierran environment. For historian's comment see *HLAS* 56:2439.

2659 Pérez Ruiz, Wilfredo. La saga de la vicuña. Lima: W. Perez Ruiz, 1994. 408 p.: bibl., ill. (some col.).

Evolution of vicuña policy in Peru from conservation of endangered species in 1965 to rational use by peasant communities in 1979.

2660 Riofrío, Gustavo; Luis Olivera Cárdenas; and Juan Carlos Callirgos. ¿Basura o desechos?: el destino de lo que botamos en Lima. Lima: Centro de Estudios y Promoción del Desarrollo, 1994. 165 p.: ill.;

Studies trash, recycling, and waste disposal in metro Lima.

2661 Treacy, John M. Las chacras de Coporaque: andenería y riego en el valle del Colca. Editado por Maria A. Benavides, Blenda Femenías, William M. Denevan. Traducción de Aroma de la Cadena y Eloy Neira. Lima: IEP, 1994. 298 p.: bibl., ill., maps. (Estudios de la sociedad rural; 12)

Superb field-based study concludes that stone-faced terraces in the Colca Valley (Arequipa dept.) are of pre-Inca origin. Need for water management, not soil conservation, explains their construction. Terrace abandonment during the historic period was driven more by social-historical factors than by environmental change.

2662 Vereau, Walter Marcelo. Región Nor-Oriental del Marañón: problemas y desafíos. Chiclayo, Peru: Centro de Estudios Sociales Solidaridad, 1994. 280 p.: bibl., maps.

Spatial analysis of agriculture and pastoralism in the Marañon region (from the coast at Chiclayo, highlands at Cajamarca, and selva). Emphasis on changes wrought by agrarian reform and the commercial functioning of six sub-regions.

2663 Villanueva Sotomayor, Julio. El Perú y el mundo: atlas geográfico histórico. Lima: A.F.A. Editores e Importadores, 1995? 624 p.: ill. (some col.), maps (some col.), photos, tables.

Polychromatic compendium of geographical and historical information. Mostly text, photos, and tables with some maps.

2664 Zimmerer, Karl S. Changing fortunes: biodiversity and peasant livelihood in the Peruvian Andes. Berkeley: Univ. of California Press, 1996. 319 p.: bibl., ill., index, maps. (California studies in critical human geography; 1)

Brilliant study of the relationship between crop plant biodiversity, peasant behavior, and the larger society dispells some long held assertions about Andean farming. Based on fieldwork conducted during the 1980s in the highland portion of Paucartambo prov. (Cusco).

BOLIVIA

2665 Angulo Cabrera, Gildo. Al mar: por las hidrovías y corredores de la integración sudamericana. La Paz: s.n., 1993. 228 p.: bibl., ill. (some col.), maps.

Assessment by a Bolivian navy rear admiral of inland river navigation during the century-long quest to unlock Bolivian trade eastward into the Amazon and Paraná-La Plata systems.

2666 Argollo, Jaime and Philippe Mourguiart. Paleohidrología de los últimos 25.000 años en los Andes bolivianos. (*Bull.*

Inst. fr. étud. andin., 24:3, 1995, p. 551–562, bibl., graphs, map)

Changing water levels in lakes of the Bolivian Altiplano (Titicaca, Poopó, Salar de Coipasa) over the last 25,000 yrs are connected to temperature and rainfall variations.

Assies, Willem. The extraction of non-timber forest products as a conservation strategy in Amazonia. See item **2865.**

2667 Bouysse-Cassagne, Thérèse. Le Lac Titicaca: histoire perdue d'une mer intérieure. (*Bull. Inst. fr. étud. andin.*, 21:1, 1992, p. 89–159, bibl., maps, tables)

Astute reconstruction of an aboriginal settlement, derived from colonial chronicles that describe the lacustrine environment around Lake Titicaca.

Coca and cocaine: an Andean perspective. See item **2577.**

2668 Conservación de la diversidad biológica en Bolivia. Edición de María Marconi. La Paz: Centro de Datos para la Conservación: United States AID Mission to Bolivia, 1992. 443 p.: bibl., ill., col. maps.

Multi-authored study of Bolivia's biological diversity, use of biological resources, and instruments of conservation. Bolivia has over the past 25 years made enormous efforts to inventory its fauna and flora to determine what can be saved.

Dockweiler Cárdenas, Jorge. La Paz en emergencia. See item **3500.**

Encuentro Binacional Perú-Bolivia, *La Paz, 1991.* El Lago Titicaca: análisis peruano-boliviano de las relaciones entre el ambiente y el desarrollo social; memorias. See item **5085.**

2669 Finsterwalder, Rüdiger. Moderne Hochgebirgsdarstellung-gezeigt am Beispiel der Alpenvereinskarte *Cordillera Real Süd 1:50 000.* (*Erdkunde/Bonn*, 49:1, Jan./März 1995, p. 32–38, map)

Discussion and presentation of a gorgeous piece of mountain cartography centered on the Mt. Illimani zone southeast of La Paz.

2670 Francou, Bernard and **Pierre Ribstein.** Glaciers et évolution climatique dans les Andes boliviennes: glacier de Zongo et glacier de Chacaltaya, Cordillère Royale, 16°S. (*Bull. Inst. fr. étud. andin.*, 24:1, 1995, p. 23–36, bibl., graphs, map, table)

Further evidence of dramatic glacier retreat in the Central Andes since the 1980s, due, in part, to global warming.

Galindo Soza, Mario. Políticas y estrategias del medio ambiente urbano. See item **3505.**

2671 Guardia Butrón, Fernando and **David R. Mercado Burgoa.** Procesos históricos de conformación de la red urbana del Valle Alto de Cochabamba: asentamientos rurales, villas coloniales, ciudades republicanas. Cochabamba, Bolivia: Colegio de Arquitectos de Cochabamba; Fondo Nacional de Vivienda Social, 1995. 158 p.: bibl., ill. (some col.), maps.

Cultural-historical landscape perspective on seven small towns in Cochabamba dept. that had greater importance during the colonial period than they do today.

2672 Hanagarth, Werner. Acerca de la geoecología de las sabanas del Beni en el noreste de Bolivia. La Paz: Instituto de Ecología, 1993. 188 p.: bibl., ill. (some col.), plans.

Most detailed study published to date on the Beni grasslands and the biophysical factors said to control them. Anthropogenic causation is more plausible but not discussed.

2673 Huaraco, comunidad de la puna. Edición de Cecile B. de Morales. La Paz: Instituto de Ecología, Univ. Mayor de San Andrés, 1994. 266 p.: bibl., ill.

Resources, livelihood, and natural history of a Quechua-speaking community with strong emphasis on plants, animals, and soils. Not a balanced treatment, but provides some detailed information of the ecology of the Bolivian Altiplano.

2674 Kent, Robert B. *et al.* Centros de mercadeo y jerarquía urbana en el valle alto y distrito sur, Departamento de Cochabamba, Bolivia. (*Rev. Geogr./México*, 120, julio/dic. 1994, p. 133–157)

Analysis of commerce in six market towns of Cochabamba Dept. shows that Punata clearly dominates by all trading criteria used.

2675 Klein, Andrew G.; Bryan L. Isacks; and **Arthur L. Bloom.** Modern and last glacial maximum snowline in Peru and Bolivia: implications for regional climatic change. (*Bull. Inst. fr. étud. andin.*, 24:3, 1995, p. 607–617, bibl., maps, tables)

Comparison indicates that the snowline was approximately 1200m lower during the last glacial maximum (14,000 yrs. BP) than during the present one.

2676 Lake Titicaca: a synthesis of limno-logical knowledge. Edited by C. Dejoux and A. Iltis. Dordrecht, the Netherlands; Boston: Kluwer Academic Publishers, 1992. 597 p.: bibl., ill. (some col.), indexes, maps. (Monographiae biologicae; 68)

Represents more than a century of research on this extraordinary lake. Includes chapters on origins, morphology, sedimentation, hydrology, climatology, physical chemistry, plankton, fish and other fauna, ethnology, fishery potential, water resources, and contamination.

2677 Libermann Cruz, Máximo et al. La desertificación en Bolivia. La Paz: LIDEMA, 1994. 126 p.: bibl., ill. (some col.), maps.

Human impact on Bolivia's vegetation, compounded by sub-humid rainfall, has converted parts of the highlands and southeastern lowlands into man-made deserts. Good introduction to this serious environmental problem.

2678 McGlade, Michael S.; Ray Henkel; and Randall S. Cerveny. The impact of rainfall frequency on coca (Erythroxylon coca) production in the Chaparé region of Bolivia. (Yearbook/CLAG, 20, 1994, p. 97–105)

Coca leaf production in the Chaparé requires adequate drying time; heavy and continuous rains hinder that phase. Production estimates do not take this factor into account.

2679 Mendizábal de Finot, Marthadina. Oruro: del desastre a la esperanza ambiental. La Paz: ILDIS, 1993. 278 p.: bibl., ill.

Population of economically precarious Oruro has continued to increase even as mining in the region has declined. Environmental contamination of air, soil, and water plague the city, one of Bolivia's six largest.

2680 Mourguiart, Philippe; Jaime Argollo; and Denis Wirrmann. Evolución paleohidrológica de la cuenca del Lago Titicaca durante el Holoceno. (Bull. Inst. fr. étud. andin., 24:3, 1995, p. 573–583, bibl., graphs, maps)

Evidence from ostracoid fossils suggests that the water depth of Lake Titicaca between ca. 8,000–3,900 BP was shallower than at present.

2681 Rafiqpoor, M. Daud. Geomorphologische Kartierung in der Apolobamba-Kordillere, Bolivien: Anwendung des Lengendenkonzepts der GMK 100 um einem randtropischen Hochgebirge. (Erdkunde/Bonn, 48:4, Okt./Dez. 1994, p. 241–258, maps)

Application of a recently developed methodology of mapping the Apolobamba Cordillera in northern La Paz Dept. at a scale of 1:100,000.

2682 Reuter, Gerhard et al. Eigenschaften, Entwicklungstendenzen und Alterunderschiede von Moränenböden in den bolivianischen Anden. (Petermanns Geogr. Mitt., 139:5/6, 1995, p. 259–282)

Thirty moraine sites between 3720 and 4840 m in the La Paz Dept. provide data on soil types, horizons, weathering, and Pleistocene and Holocene sequences.

2683 Schlaifer, Michel. Las especies nativas y la deforestación en los Andes: una visión histórica, social y cultural en Cochabamba, Bolivia. (Bull. Inst. fr. étud. andin., 22:2, 1993, p. 585–610, bibl., ill.)

Discusses pressures that have led to the clearing of native tree vegetation in the Andean highlands since the colonial period. Focuses on the Cochabamba valley.

2684 Seibert, Paul. The vegetation of the settlement area of the Callaway people and the Ulla-Ulla highlands in the Bolivian Andes with vegetation map. (Mt. Res. Dev., 14:3, 1994, p. 189–211, map)

Plant communities of the Ulla-Ulla and Charazani zones are shown on accompanying map at a scale of 1:50,000. Discussion of site factors and human impact on vegetation from altitudes above 5,000 m to 2,700 m.

2685 Seminario Nacional sobre Recursos Hídricos y Medio Ambiente, 1st, Cochabamba, Bolivia, 1992. Los recursos hídricos en Bolivia y su dimensión ambiental: políticas, planificación, aspectos legales aprovechamiento y calidad de aguas, manejo de cuencas, degradación, contaminación y estudios; 58 trabajos técnicos presentados en el I Seminario Nacional sobre Recursos Hídricos y Medio Ambiente. Edición de Víctor Ricaldi R., Carlos Flores M. y Leonardo Anaya J. Cochabamba, Bolivia: Editorial AROL, 1992. 597 p.: bibl., ill. (AGID geoscience series; 20)

Collection of 58 technical reports on

water resources, grouped into sections on use, water quality, contamination, watershed management, and strategies.

2686 Villarías-Robles, Juan J.R. and **David M. Pereira Herrera.** El emplazamiento de Canata y la fundación de la villa de Oropesa: una contribución a la geografía histórica del valle de Cochabamba, Bolivia en los siglos XV y XVI. (*Rev. Andin.*, 13:1, primer semestre 1995, p. 199–236, bibl., maps)

Reconstructs the indigenous settlement of Canata, first visited by Spaniards in 1540. Nearby Cochabamba, founded in 1571, eventually superseded it in importance.

2687 Zimmerer, Karl S. Soil erosion and social (dis)courses in Cochabamba, Bolivia: perceiving the nature of environmental degradation. (*Econ. Geogr.*, 69, 1993, p. 312–327)

Who or what is responsible for soil erosion? Unlike governmental and international aid agencies, peasants and rural trade unions in Cochabamba Dept. assess its causation in both local and extra-local terms.

THE SOUTHERN CONE

CESAR N. CAVIEDES, *Professor of Geography, University of Florida, Gainesville*

AFTER YEARS DURING WHICH GEOPOLITICS and the Falklands/Malvinas War dominated the bibliography about the Southern Cone, the emphasis has shifted to concern over the quality of the environment. Several entries from Argentina and Chile demonstrate this current preoccupation. Journalistic treatments that dwell on the dark aspects of this problem abound subtracting value from the serious situation. Works on subjects concerning urban and regional planning, particularly in Argentina and Chile are clearer and less-biased (items **2809, 2818, 2765,** and **2775**).

The controversy in Southern Cone countries about the long-lasting economic advantages and environmental impact of forestry is growing. The development of this sector of extractive resources began in Chile under the rule of Gen. Pinochet. Since Chile has considerable potential in this sector, the economic project of Pinochet's government was to promote the planting of pine and eucalyptus and the controlled exploitation of natural forests for timber, pulp, and wood chips. After more than a decade of expansion, forest products have become an important component of the Chilean export economy. Numerous entries document the controversy over this controlled development. The expansion is praised by entrepreneurs but decried by conservationists. A similar trend is emerging in Uruguay. Conservationists who do not approve of the successful Chilean model are opposing forestation projects since the country's natural forests are all but gone and the soil is seriously eroded.

Works of truly geographical character are scarce. In Argentina there is some high quality geographical production, particularly one book of economic geography (item **2704**), articles about communications systems and squatter settlements edited by Furlani di Civit (items **2727** and **2726**), an innovative paper synthesizing the geography of the country (item **2711**), and a noteworthy monograph on San Luis (item **2732**). In Chile the most notable geographic works have been produced on the demographic characteristics and development of the country (items **2797, 2802,** and **2805**).

Continuing a trend established in the 1980s, works on Southern Cone countries written by North American geographers are totally absent. This neglect mirrors the interest of US and Canadian governments and development agencies toward this area of Latin America now that authoritarian regimes are gone and the threat of Communism has vanished. Contributions by French researchers are also rare, but German research is better represented, especially on Argentine and Uruguayan subjects.

GENERAL

2688 Abadie-Aicardi, Oscar. La geografía y los comienzos de la colonización del litoral atlántico sudamericano: algunas reflexiones comparativas. (*Am. Merid.*, 8, julio 1988, p. 45–58, map)

To a large degree, the colonization of Atlantic South America was due to constant competition between Portugal and Spain over the control of the Atlantic sea routes.

Dascal, Guillermo. Ordenamiento del territorio y agricultura metropolitanos: reflexiones aplicables al caso latinoamericano. See item **2800.**

Galimberti, Diana. Antarctica: an introductory guide. See item **2729.**

2689 Gallez, Paul. Cristóbal de Haro: banqueros y pimenteros en busca del Estrecho Magallánico. Bahía Blanca, Argentina: Instituto Patagónico, 1991. 112 p.: bibl., ill., index, maps.

Cristóbal de Haro, a Sephardic merchant from Anvers, sponsored several expeditions to the Americas to trade spices. This brief work details an alleged voyage of the discovery of the Strait of Magellan in 1514, which was financed by Haro and conducted by the Portuguese Nuno Manuel. It also contends that Haro was the promotor and supporter of the voyage of Fernão de Magalhães, the official discoverer of the strait in 1520.

2690 Hepple, Leslie W. Metáfora, discurso geopolítica y los militares en América del Sur. (*Geopolítica/Buenos Aires*, 18:45, 1992, p. 45–50)

Extremely broad discourse about the relationship between the military establishment and the dominating elites in South America and the practice of geopolitical doctrines.

2691 Klink, Amyr. Paratii: entre dois pólos. São Paulo: Companhia das Letras, 1992. 228 p.: bibl., ill. (some col.), col. maps.

Account of the 22-month voyage by Brazilian navigator Klink on a sailboat from Rio de Janeiro to the Antarctic Peninsula and on to the northern Spitsbergen Islands through Capetown. Excellent photographs.

2692 Lauer, Wilhelm. Human development and environment in the Andes: a geo-ecological overview. (*Mt. Res. Dev.*, 13:2, 1993, p. 157–166, bibl., graphs, maps)

Excellent summary of the current conditions of geo-ecological zones in the Andes recognized in recent studies. Increased human occupation of the fragile mountain environments is believed to be causing substantial changes in Andean ecosystems.

2693 Messerli, Bruno *et al.* Climate change and natural resource dynamics of the Atacama altiplano during the last 18,000 years: a preliminary synthesis. (*Mt. Res. Dev.*, 13:2, 1993, p. 117–121, bibl., graphs, maps, photos)

Paleorecords in the Chilean/Argentine altiplano climate over the past 18,000 years reveal that the last cold period in the subtropical Andes was 7° colder than today. That period was succeeded by a humid period (17,000 to 11,000 BP) which kept montane lakes at high levels. A subsequent humid but warmer period followed between 11,000 to 7,000 BP. Around 3,000 BP the present dry conditions set in.

2694 El reto ambiental del desarrollo en América Latina y el Caribe. Santiago?: Comisión Económica para América Latina y El Caribe, Unidad Conjunta CEPAL/PNUMA de Desarrollo y Medio Ambiente; Programa de las Naciones Unidas para el Medio Ambiente, Oficina Regional para América Latina y el Caribe, 1990. 124 p.: bibl., ill.

After a summary of the major ecosystems of South and Central America, this booklet outlines the major problems faced by these systems such as deforestation and environmental deterioration.

2695 Sanguinetti, Jorge. Conferencia sobre aspectos socio-políticos y económicos de la hidrovía. (*Rev. Geogr./México*, 113, julio/dic. 1991, p. 73–90, tables)

General considerations about the social, geopolitical, and economic advantages of opening an international waterway along the Paraguay, Paraná, and Uruguay rivers.

Tellechea de Arca, Mireya. Paraguay socioeconómico y cultural: hidrovía-MERCOSUR. See item **2848.**

ARGENTINA

2696 Agricultura orgánica: experiencias de cultivo ecológico en la Argentina. Recopilación de Guillermo Schnitman y Pipo Lernoud. Buenos Aires?: Eco Agro, 1992. 350 p.: bibl., ill. (some col.). (Planeta Tierra)

Helpful textbook on the relationship between soil ecology and agricultural production. Examples for differentiating a fertile from a barren, environment included.

2697 Agua y medio ambiente en Buenos Aires. Coordinación y recopilación de Antonio Elio Brailovsky y Dina Foguelman. Buenos Aires: Editorial Fraterna, 1992. 161 p.: bibl., ill. (Serie ecología y medio ambiente)

Basic outline of the problems associated with tap water for Buenos Aires and the contamination of its surface hydrology.

2698 Alpinistas de Lecco en la Patagonia. Milan: Ediciones Scode; Argentina: Boletín Informativo Techint, 1989. 31 p.: col. ill., maps. (Cuadernos patagónicos; 1)

Historical overview of expeditions to the Patagonian Andes undertaken between 1970–88 by climbers from Lecco, Lago di Como, Italy.

2699 Amable, María Angélica and **Liliana Mirta Rojas.** Historia de la yerba mate en Misiones. v. 1. Posadas, Argentina: Ediciones Montoya, 1989. 1 v.: bibl., ill.

Brief work on the origins of *yerba mate* cultivation, processing, and consumption in Misiones. Contains rare quotations from Aimé Bonpland, and legislation governing the production phases of this beverage.

2700 Anastasi, Atilio B. La Mendoza del desierto: poblados y pobladores entre la resistencia y el abandono. (*Rev. Geogr. Norte Gd.*, 18, 1991, p. 67–74, map)

The dry belt of Mendoza in western Argentina is characterized by its settlements and inhabitants. Good presentation of this less-glamorous face of the province of Mendoza.

2701 Argentina como desafío ambiental. Buenos Aires?: Fundación Integración, 1991. 78 p.: bibl., ill., maps.

Main conclusions of a colloquium convened in 1991 to assess the country's energy resources, climate, fisheries, industrial pollution, and environmental laws. Excellent primer on these subjects.

2702 Arquez, Graciela S. La contaminación acuática en Argentina. Buenos Aires: Greenpeace Argentina, 1988. 93 p.: bibl., ill.

Several examples of water contamination in Argentine rivers and lakes are exposed in this document sponsored by Greenpeace. Based on solid scientific observations, this is a valid first approximation to pollution sources in Argentina.

2703 Arroyo, Mónica. Ajuste económico y sector agrario: particularidades de esta relación en la Argentina de los ochenta. (*Rev. Geogr./México*, 118, julio/dic. 1993, p. 43–50, bibl.)

General paper about the deteriorating economic situation in Argentina, focusing on foreign debt and its impact on agricultural sector development. The rising internal distribution of agricultural commodities is viewed as a positive effect of the general contraction.

Azara, Félix de. Apuntamientos para la historia natural de los páxaros del Paraguay y del Río de la Plata. See item **2843.**

2704 Ballistrieri, Carlos A. et al. Geografía económica argentina: temas. Coordinación de Juan Roccatagliata. Buenos Aires: Librería El Ateneo Editorial, 1993. 367 p.: maps.

Selection of themes on the spatial components of the Argentine economy. Although treatment is exhaustive, approach it somewhat dated. One notable chapter is Jofre's demographic analysis. Fails to address the country's economic regionalization.

2705 Beccaceci, Marcelo D. and **Bonnie J. Hayskar.** Patagonia wilderness. St. Paul, Minn.: Pangaea, 1991. 126 p.: bibl., col. ill., index, map.

Lavish pictorial guide to the natural treasures of Argentine Patagonia, published in Minnesota. Compare with similar productions from Chile (items **2787, 2792,** and **2810**).

2706 Borello, José Antonio. The territorial dimension of manufacturing restructuring: the transformation of places in contemporary Argentina. (*Yearbook/CLAG*, 16, 1990, p. 41–55, bibl., graphs, map, table)

Solidly based study of the relocation and restructuring of the manufacturing sector in Argentina, focusing on La Rioja and greater Buenos Aires. Critical evaluation of the positive effects of such policies, and emphasis on the negative aspects of deconcentration: back to square one?

2707 Borrini, Héctor R. La colonización como fundamento de la organización territorial del Chaco, 1930–1953. Resistencia, Argentina: Instituto de Investigaciones Geohistóricas, Conicet, Fundanord, 1987. 93 p., 6 p. of plates: bibl., ill., maps. (Cuadernos de geohistoria regional, 0325–8246; 19)

Historical and geographical account of the colonization phases of the Chaco Territory from 1930–53; interesting insights into land-opening procedures, production, and settlement plans. Bibliography is incomplete.

2708 Boscovich, Nicolás. Tres ejes geoestratégicos claves para la integración física de la Argentina en el Cono Sur. (*Geopolítica/Buenos Aires*, 18:47, 1992, p. 23–35, bibl., maps)

Utilizing the dated notion of "geostrategic axes," author details the formation of fluvial axes along the estuary of Rio de la Plata, the lower Uruguay River, and the middle course of the Bermejo River. Concepts are based on fluvial circulation assumptions.

2709 Briano, Héctor A. El ferrocarril de Puerto Deseado al Lago Nahuel Huapi: tramo Puerto Deseado-Cerro Blanco, Provincia de Santa Cruz. Buenos Aires: Gráfica Integral Olivos, 1991. 68 p.: ill., map.

Diary and notes of the engineer Juan Briano, constructor of the railway from Puerto Deseado to Cerro Blanco, northern Argentine Patagonia, in 1909.

2710 Brondolo, Margarita et al. Geografía de Bahía Blanca. Bahía Blanca, Argentina: Ediciones Encestando, 1994. 199 p.: bibl., ill., maps.

Conventional presentation of the city of Bahía Blanca conceived to educate students in the techniques of geographical analysis. Good illustrations.

2711 Bruniard, Enrique; Lilia J. Osuna; and Clelia Moro. Geografía del nordeste argentino. Buenos Aires: SENOC, Asociación para la Promoción de Sistemas Educativos no Convencionales, 1987. 161 p.: bibl., ill., maps. (PROMEC geografía; 18)

Reputed authority on northeast Argentina presents a convincing synthesis of the region. A pioneer work of great style, quality, and substance. Physical landscapes, human activities, population and regional policies are clearly outlined.

2712 Burkart, Rodolfo. Nuestros bosques norteños: desvaloración y deterioro. (*Real. Econ./Buenos Aires*, 114/115, feb./mayo 1993, p. 54–73, bibl., ill., tables)

Deforestation in northern Argentina is serious. In 1985, 26–59 percent of tree stands were lost compared to 1970. Author exposes causes of this loss and outlines steps to reverse this negative trend.

2713 Bustos Cara, Roberto N.; Francisca C. González; and Nélida S. Marenco. Comportamiento socio-demográfico y organización territorial en un área de secano del Partido de Villarino. (*Rev. Univ. Geogr.*, 4:1/2, 1989/90, p. 99–130, bibl., graphs, maps, tables)

Population decrease in a rural semi-dry area of the province of La Pampa is explained as a function of dependent infrastructural conditions. Lack of access to services and job opportunities in the countryside forces rural workers to seek employment in towns.

2714 Caillou de Sierra, Martha and **Ana Teresa Cusa.** El crecimiento urbano y los servicios de saneamiento básico en San Miguel de Tucumán, 1960–91. (*Rev. Geogr./México*, 118, julio/dic. 1993, p. 23–42, graphs, maps, tables)

Cursory description of the supply of essential services (water, sewage) during the city of Tucumán's westward expansion throughout the period considered in this study.

2715 El Cerro Torre. Milan: Ediciones Scode; Argentina: Boletín Informativo Techint, 1990. 32 p.: col. ill. (Cuadernos patagónicos; 3)

Account of several expeditions from Lecco (Italy) climbing Cerro Torre. Excellent and dramatic photographs.

2716 Claraz, Jorge. Diario de viaje de exploración al Chubut, 1865–1866. Estudio preliminar y mapa de Rodolfo M. Casamiquela. Traducción del vocabulario y apéndice, bibliografía y epílogo de Meinrado Hux. Buenos Aires: Ediciones Marymar, 1988. 189 p., 1 folded leaf of plates: map. (Col. Patagonia)

The author, a Swiss immigrant to Argentina, conducted a reconnaissance expedition to the northern reaches of Patagonia in 1865–66. Insightful descriptions of the landscapes, fauna, and Indian tribes encountered.

2717 Codes de Palomo, Maria Isabel and **Silvia Beatriz Robledo.** Percepción de la contaminación industrial en el departamento de Guaymallen, provincia de Mendoza. (*Bol. Estud. Geogr.*, 24:87, 1991, p. 303–351, graphs, maps, tables)

Collective perception of water and air contamination in a suburb of Mendoza reveals acute awareness among low income residents. Industrial expansion is seen as the major contributor to environmental deterioration.

2718 Colombres, Diego and **Jorge Gavilán.** El daño ecológico y social que provocó La Forestal. (*Todo es Hist.*, 306, enero 1993, p. 42–47, photos)

Documents deforestation in the Chaco region affected by the timber company La Forestal from 1906–71. *Quebracho* stands were depleted to obtain tannin.

2719 Congreso Geológico Argentino, 12th, Mendoza, Argentina, 1993. Geología y recursos naturales de Mendoza. Recopilación de Víctor A. Ramos. Buenos Aires: Comisión de Exploración del Instituto Argentino del Petroleo; Asociación Geológica de Mendoza, 1993. 762 p.: bibl., ill.

This volume—supported with an impressive bibliography and pertinent graphics—details the structural geology, paleontology, and fuel deposits of Mendoza, a province famed for its mineral resources.

2720 Crisis ambiental y desarrollo económico: aportes a la discusión en la Argentina. Buenos Aires: Centro Latinoamericano de Estudios Ambientales; Fundación Friedrich Ebert, 1991. 122 p.: bibl.

The environmental deterioration of the country raises serious doubts about the wisdom of implementing acceptable policies of environmental conservation.

2721 Daguerre, Celia; Diana Durán; and **Albina L. Lara.** Argentina, mitos y realidades. Buenos Aires: Lugar Editorial, 1992. 155 p.: bibl., ill., col. maps.

Excellent analysis of many Argentine myths pertaining to the country's place in Latin America and the world. With grace, humor, and caustic criticism the authors demolish false assumptions and present a realistic and sober image of the country.

2722 De Marco, Graciela M. and **Darío C. Sánchez.** Inmigrantes limítrofes en el Gran Buenos Aires: un análisis socioeconómico espacial. (*Rev. Geogr./México*, 117, enero/junio 1993, p. 19–48, bibl., graphs, map, tables)

Locational analysis of immigrants from Uruguay, Paraguay, Bolivia, and Chile and their residential patterns in greater Buenos Aires. The professional-economic profiles of these immigrants are also examined. Numerous tables. Lacks definitive conclusion.

2723 Díaz Bessone, Ramón Genaro. El futuro de la Argentina. Buenos Aires: Grupo Editor Latinoamericano, 1994. 436 p.: bibl. (Col. Estudios políticos y sociales)

Author recognizes four periods in Argentine history and forecasts a better future based on an economy recovery, demographic growth, and superation of the moral crisis that has upset the country since 1930. Interesting interpretation downplays the global significance of the country.

2724 Foschiatti de dell'Orto, Ana María H. El desarrollo urbano y las particularidades demográficas del Chaco y su capital entre 1960 y 1990. (*Rev. Geogr./México*, 115, enero/junio 1992, p. 37–54, bibl., maps, tables)

The internal migration flows in this northern province are reviewed using basic tools and scant bibliographic resources. The resulting maps are, however, of remarkably good quality.

2725 Foschiatti de dell'Orto, Ana María H. and **Alfredo S. Bolsi.** La población de la ciudad de Corrientes entre 1588 y 1988: análisis desde la perspectiva geográfica. (*Rev. Geogr./México*, 118, julio/dic. 1993, p. 65–116, graphs, maps)

Useful and well-illustrated outline of the growth of Corrientes, from colonial times to the present. This solid study is backed by an exemplary methodology.

2726 Furlani de Civit, María E. *et al.* Los asentamientos ilegales en ciudades intermedias: provincia de Mendoza. (*Leguas/ Mendoza*, 2, 1992, p. 67–109, bibl., maps, tables)

Squatter settlements have proliferated in the large- and medium-size centers of the province of Mendoza. Squatters come from other provinces and from Bolivia and Chile seeking harvest work in Mendoza.

2727 Furlani de Civit, María E. *et al.* Las comunicaciones en las provincias de la frontera oeste argentina. (*Bol. Estud. Geogr.*, 24:87, 1991, p. 167–201, graphs, maps, tables)

Communication systems used in northwest Argentina since Inca times are analyzed by a team of geographers. The typology of the networks established over four centuries of human occupation are highly original.

2728 Furlani de Civit, María E. and María J. Gutiérrez. Dinámica agraria en un oasis de especialización vitícola. (*Rev. Geogr./ México*, 115, enero/junio 1992, p. 85–137, bibl., maps, tables)

Solid work—using quantitative data analysis—on land utilization in the surroundings of Mendoza, detailing the costs and yields of viticulture.

2729 Galimberti, Diana. Antarctica: an introductory guide. Miami Beach: Zagier & Urruty Publications, 1991. 143 p.: bibl., ill.

A guide to the Antarctic written without bias by an Argentine naturalist.

2730 Gans, Paul. Dinámica de la utilización del espacio en el centro urbano: el caso de Buenos Aires, 1960–1980. (*Leguas/Mendoza*, 2, 1992, p. 111–138, bibl., maps, tables)

Functional structure of Buenos Aires is studied for the period 1960–80. The tertiary sector activities and detail trade outlets dominated the central urban space.

2731 Garro, Cristóbal R. Sarmiento y los estudios geográficos. Buenos Aires: Academia Nacional de Geografía, 1988. 99 p.: bibl., ill., index. (Publicación especial; 1)

By listing the numerous works on natural sciences published during the presidency of Gen. Sarmiento, the author attempts to prove that Sarmiento was also a geographer.

2732 Geografía de San Luis: el hombre y la tierra. v. 1–2. San Luis, Argentina: Gobierno de la Provincia de San Luis, Ministerio de Cultura y Educación, 1989? 2 v. (477 p.): bibl., ill. (some col.), col. maps.

Two volumes and a folder with color maps describe the physical environment, economic development, and settlements of this province of western Argentina. The style is agile, the presentation attractive, and the illustrations pertinent, revealing the craftsmanship of Ricardo Capitanelli, a born *puntano* and long-time professor at the Univ. of Cuyo. A beautiful tribute to his native province.

2733 Giudice, Luis A. Planificación del sistema de parques nacionales. Buenos Aires: Administración de Parques Nacionales; s.l.: Organización de las Naciones Unidas para la Agricultura y la Alimentación; s.l.: Programa de las Naciones Unidas para el Desarrollo, 1988. 26 leaves: ill., maps.

Concise outline of the rationale and laws applied to establishing natural parks in Argentina. Illustrated with several useful maps.

2734 Gómez Fuentealba, Raúl. Una provincia llamada Neuquén. Buenos Aires: A-Z Editora, 1992. 285 p.: bibl., col. ill., col. maps. (Serie Nosotros)

Excellent illustrated guide to geography and activities of the province of Neuquén and integration attempts with southern Chile which should provide the interior of Argentina with access to the markets of the Pacific.

2735 González Arzac, Ricardo; José Luis Díaz; and Boris Calvetty Amboni. Geohidrología del área noreste provincia de Santa Cruz: síntesis. Buenos Aires: Consejo Federal de Inversiones, 1991. 39 p.: bibl., graphs, maps, tables. (Serie Investigaciones aplicadas. Col. Hidrología subterranea; 1)

The freatic water reserves of the region north of Santa Cruz (Patagonia) might constitute a viable water supply for the expanding city of Santa Cruz.

2736 Gudiño de Muñoz, Maria Elina. Problemática de la agricultura periurbana actual: el caso del oasis del río Mendoza. (*Bol. Estud. Geogr.*, 24:87, 1991, p. 239–265, graphs, maps, tables)

Agricultural production in Mendoza's outskirts battles inefficiency and increasing pressure for land from urban sprawl. Growing subdivision of rural properties is a sign of the agrarian decline.

2737 Guzmán, Yuyú. Las estancias del Tandil. v. 1. Buenos Aires: Librería Sarmiento, 1988. 1 v.: bibl., ill., maps. (Col. El País de las estancias)

Description of the landed estates (estancias) spread throughout the rural municipality of Tandil, province of Buenos Aires. Good basic materials for an investigation of the origin of landed aristocracies in Argentina.

2738 Jornadas Platenses de Geografía, *1st*, *La Plata, Argentina, 1993.* Primeras Jornadas Platenses de Geografía: actas. v. 1–2. La Plata: Univ. Nacional de La Plata, Facultad de Humanidades y Ciencias de la Educación, Depto. de Geografía, 1995. 2 v.: bibl., ill.

Proceedings of a national meeting of geographers at the Univ. de la Plata that allows the reader to gauge the development of scientific geography in the country and become aware of little-known contributions of members from the host department.

2739 Juan Plate: un pionero patagónico. Recopilación de Joaquín Hardt. Argentina: Univ. Nacional del Comahue, 1992. 208 p.: ill., maps.

Exciting diary of German colonist Hans (Juan) Plate, who established a flourishing agricultural settlement in the upper Chubut Valley in 1900–01.

Krantzer, Guillermo and **Jorge Sánchez.** Regulaciones en el transporte urbano: el caso de Buenos Aires. See item **3738.**

2740 Lemus, Jorge D. Características epidemiológico-ambientales del suicidio en la ciudad de Buenos Aires. (*Signos Univ.*, 11:22, julio/dic. 1992, p. 23–80, bibl., graphs, tables)

Suicide in greater Buenos Aires is studied from an ecological perspective. A sense of isolation and abandonment explains suicide among young individuals, while progressive depression is the main culprit among the elderly. Maps show higher suicide rates in high population density areas.

2741 Loqui, Teófilo de. Una expedición al Cabo Vírgenes. Introducción y notas de Antonio E. Serrano Redonnet. Referencias geográficas de Federico A. Daus. Buenos Aires: Marymar Ediciones, 1992. 122 p.: bibl., ill., index. (Col. Patagonia)

In 1887, this young lieutenant of the Argentine navy conducted an expedition from Santa Cruz to Cabo Virgenes (eastern entrance of the Strait of Magellan). His travel notes are reproduced in this well-written account.

2742 Lucioni, María Carmen *et al.* Epidemiología de los accidentes de tránsito en la ciudad de Buenos Aires. (*Signos Univ.*, 11:22, julio/dic. 1992, p. 101–124, graphs, maps, tables)

Revealing study of the locations with the highest frequency of traffic accidents in the city of Buenos Aires.

2743 Lucioni, María Carmen *et al.* Vigilancia epidemiológica ambiental en la ciudad de Buenos Aires: análisis de la prevalencia de factores de riesgo biológico en areneros infantiles. (*Signos Univ.*, 11:22, julio/dic. 1992, p. 81–100, bibl., graphs, tables)

Highly interesting study of parasite contamination in the urban playgrounds of Buenos Aires. A warning for urban mothers.

2744 Maeder, Ernesto J.A. and **Ramón Gutiérrez.** Atlas histórico y urbano del nordeste argentino. Ed. preliminar Chaco, Argentina: Instituto de Investigaciones Geohistóricas, Conicet-Fundanord, 1994. 1 atlas (83 p.): bibl., maps.

Thorough documentation on the conquest and development of settlements in "historical" Misiones from its origins to the present, done with erudition and good sense in the use of cartographic representations.

2745 Mannino, Maria Elena. Diagnóstico de la contaminación ambiental en la ciudad de Mendoza. (*Bol. Estud. Geogr.*, 25:88, 1992, p. 153–184, graphs, maps, tables)

A study of air contamination, noise, and smoke pollution in greater Mendoza conducted at street level reveals a serious situation for the city's poor neighborhoods.

2746 Mansilla, Sandra Liliana. Del conventillo a la villa de emergencia: segregación residencial y migraciones intraurbanas en San Miguel de Tucumán. (*Rev. Geogr. / México*, 118, julio/dic. 1993, p. 51–63, bibl., map, table)

Good modeling of rural migrants moving from internal slums to peripheral emergency settlements, resulting in a virtual improvement of their housing conditions.

2747 Mascitti, Virginia. Flamencos: los caminos de la convivencia. (*Cienc. Hoy*, 4:24, mayo/junio 1993, p. 25–33, graphs, photos)

The social habits of flamingos in Mar Chiquita, Cordoba prov., are closely investigated. Migration from Bolivia, Paraguay, and Chile rules the flamingo population.

2748 Mastrangelo, Fabiana and **Rolando Esteban Schmid.** Godoy Cruz: pasado y presente. Mendoza, Argentina: Ediciones Culturales de Mendoza; Godoy Cruz, Argentina: Municipalidad de Godoy Cruz, 1991. 130 p.: bibl., ill., maps.

Godoy Cruz, a county on the outskirts of Mendoza, has risen to great relevance due to its development as a viticultural center and suburban residential area.

2749 Mata Olmo, Rafael. Aportación al estudio del problema de la tierra en las zonas áridas de la provincia de Mendoza: Malargüe, 1874–1988. (*Bol. Estud. Geogr.*, 25:88, 1992, p. 55–89, bibl., maps)

Colonization of Malargüe, a dry region at the northern edge of Patagonia, began in 1874. Although latifundia were mainly developed at first, in recent years *puestos* (small pastoral estates) have become common.

2750 Molinillo, Marcelo F. Is traditional pastoralism the cause of erosive processes in mountain environments?: the case of the Cumbres Calchaquies in Argentina. (*Mt. Res. Dev.*, 13:2, 1993, p. 189–202, bibl., graphs, maps, tables)

Author investigates if observed soil erosion in the uplands of northwestern Argentina is due to intense grazing or natural processes. His answer is mixed: pastoralism has worsened an already poor situation caused by aridity and slope instability.

2751 Moncaut, Carlos Antonio. Travesías de antaño: por caminos reales, postas y mensajerías. City Bell, Argentina: Editorial El Aljibe, 1993. 272 p.: bibl., ill., maps.

Valuable compilation of historical narrations pertaining to the routes and composition of the mule trains and cart caravans (*carretas*) departing from Buenos Aires to the interior during early republican times.

2752 Moreno, Carlos; Lucio V. García Ledesma; and **Diana Borejko.** Patrimonio de la producción rural: en el antiguo partido de Cañuelas. Buenos Aires: Fundación Arquitectura y Patrimonio; Patrimonio Rural, 1991. 224 p.: bibl., ill.

Historical notes on the last architectural remnants of Argentina's colonial past are supported with excellent hand-drafted illustrations.

2753 Ockier, Cecilia. El barrio Villa Mitre: una singularidad dentro de la trama urbana bahiense. (*Rev. Univ. Geogr.*, 4:1/2, 1989/90, p. 1–37, bibl., maps)

A survey of the functions in a Bahía Blanca peripheral borough reveals evolution from warehousing and storage functions into a middle-class neighborhood of peddlers.

2754 El padre de Agostini y la Patagonia. Milan, Italy: Ediciones Scode; Argentina: Boletín Informativo Techint, 1990. 31 p.: ill. (Cuadernos patagónicos; 2)

Excellent fascicle on the expeditions undertaken by Father Agostini, an Italian Salesian priest, who contributed greatly to the exploration and dissemination of the natural beauty of Patagonia.

2755 Parra de Juri, Graciela Maria. La inmigración española e italiana en los departamentos de Mendoza entre 1895 y 1914: españoles e italianos; propietarios de bienes. (*Bol. Estud. Geogr.*, 24:87, 1991, p. 265–284, graphs, tables)

Spaniards and Italians moved to Mendoza around 1895, taking jobs as blue-collar workers for traditional agrarian elites. Their rapid socioeconomic rise is documented through urban property titles.

2756 Peña, Martín Rodolfo de la. Nidos y huevos de aves argentinas. Santa Fe, Argentina: Tall. Gráf. de Impr. LUX, 1987. 229 p., 30 p. of plates: ill. (some col.), indexes.

Nature guide of birds, including morphology and location of the nest, and shape and color of the eggs. A fascinating specialty of avian biology.

2757 Perucca, Clorinda. Diagnostic paysager des systèmes de production paysans de la province de Misiones, Argentine. Montpellier, France: Institut agronomique méditerranéen de Montpellier, Centre international de hautes études agronomiques méditerranéennes, 1992. 137 p.: bibl., ill., maps. (Col. Théses et masters; 14)

Detailed study of the utilization of the agrarian landscape in Misiones. The economy is mostly based on yerba mate, vegetables, cotton, maize, and the exploitation of natural forests.

2758 Petagna de del Río, Ana María. La complejidad geográfica en la transición ciudad-campo: el sector Aldea Romana en el partido de Bahía Blanca. (*Rev. Univ. Geogr.*, 4 : 1/2, 1989/90, p. 55–78, bibl., graphs, maps, tables)

Criteria for discerning city and countryside in the urban-rural area of Bahía Blanca. Many selected indicators are of qualitative rather than accurate quantitative measures.

2759 Piergentili, Decio. El Ombú: arbol gaucho de discutida historia. (*Todo es Hist.*, 298, abril 1992, p. 63–69, bibl., ill.)

Ombú (*Phytolacca dioica*), a typical tree of the pampas, seems to have originated in the riverine areas of Laguna de Iberá; from there it was introduced into the grasslands to provide shade for humans and animals.

2760 Pino, Diego A. del. El barrio de Villa Ortúzar. Buenos Aires: Municipalidad de la Ciudad de Buenos Aires, 1990. 101 p.: bibl., ill. (Cuadernos de Buenos Aires; 60)

Historical vignettes from prominent residents of the Villa Ortúzar borough in Buenos Aires, written for journalistic purposes.

2761 Problemas urbanísticos de Buenos Aires. Recopilación de Patricio H. Randle. Buenos Aires: OIKOS Asociación para la Promoción de los Estudios Territoriales y Ambientales, 1994. 117 p.: bibl., ill.

Good selection of monographs dealing with urban problems in Buenos Aires, such as green areas, thoroughfares, public transportation, and urban planning.

2762 Quaranta de Errecaborde, Ana María. Historia de la provincialización de Misiones. Argentina: Ediciones Montoya, 1987. 249 p.: bibl., ill.

In 1953, the former Territory of Misiones became a province of Argentina. The historical development of this event is detailed and accompanied by extensive legal documentation.

2763 Quiroga, Dígno Raúl. Apuntes de un viaje por la Patagonia: situación general; problemas conspiración contra la integri-

dad territorial. Córdoba, Argentina: Editorial Pampa de Olaen, 1993. 198 p.: ill.

Collection of vignettes pertaining to Patagonia and Tierra del Fuego that makes reference to the Falkland Islands conflict and to boundary disputes with Chile.

2764 Raimondi, Carlos H. Hacia una argentina marítima. Buenos Aires: Instituto de Publicaciones Navales, Centro Naval, 1991. 253 p.: bibl., ill., maps. (Ediciones del Instituto de Publicaciones Navales; 93. Col. Estrategia; 28)

Revisitation of dated doctrines on South Atlantic hegemony does not consider the modernization of geostrategic premises imposed by air-space dominance and missile deployment.

2765 Randle, Patricio H. *et al.* Ciudades intermedias: su reactivación en la región pampeana; bases para una política. Buenos Aires: Fundación Banco de Boston, 1992. 144 p.: bibl., ill., maps (some col.).

Simple yet enlightening treatment of "secondary urban centers" in Argentina, outlining enormous challenges these centers face as they compete with the attraction and power of Buenos Aires.

2766 Recchi, Enrique and Olga Quitarrá. La población y los consumos eléctricos en el sur bonaerense. (*Rev. Univ. Geogr.*, 4 : 1/2, 1989/90, p. 131–156, bibl., maps, tables)

Electrical energy consumption in the southern part of the Buenos Aires prov. is used as an indicator of rank and size of towns and rural settlements. Interesting approach.

2767 Rey Balmaceda, Raúl C. Testimonios cartográficos del expansionismo territorial chileno. (*Geopolítica/Buenos Aires*, 18 : 45, 1992, p. 35–44, maps)

Author contends that "Chilean expansionism" surfaces in several contemporary historical works whose authors depict the limits of the former Governancy of Chile spreading across the Andes into Argentine territory.

2768 Richard Jorba, Rodolfo A. and Eduardo E. Pérez Romagnoli. La década de 1870 en Mendoza: etapa de reorientación de la economía y el espacio hacia el dominio vitivinícola. (*Bol. Estud. Geogr.*, 25 : 88, 1992, p. 27–53, bibl., table)

The introduction of vineyards into the

oasis of the Mendoza River is documented from 1870–90. The resulting transition from grazing activities (export of cattle to Chile) to a highly specialized viticulture led to a transformation of the local agrarian elites. For the second part of this study see item **2769.**

2769 Richard Jorba, Rodolfo A. Modelo vitivinícola en Mendoza: las acciones de la élite y los cambios espaciales resultantes, 1875–1895. (*Bol. Estud. Geogr.*, 25 : 89, 1993, p. 227–265, bibl., graph, tables)

Continuation of the previous study (see item **2768**). The arrival of immigrants led to a change in mid-sized establishments for viticulture. State liberalization policy favored the emergence of a powerful landowner and wine exporter elite that continues to dominate Mendoza. Well-analyzed and beautifully illustrated, both papers are models of good historical-geographical investigations.

2770 San Carlos (Mendoza, Argentina). San Carlos es futuro. Recopilación de María Eugenia Buttini. Municipalidad de San Carlos, Provincia de Mendoza, Argentina: La Municipalidad, 1987. 231 p.: ill., maps (some col.).

Pertinent description of the natural conditions, resources, and human development of San Carlos dept. in western Argentina. Excellent illustrations and solid information enrich this explanatory volume.

2771 Santos Biloni, José. Arboles autóctonos argentinos. Edición de Carlos Alberto Guastavino. Buenos Aires: Tip. Editora Argentina, 1990. 345 p.: bibl., col. ill., index.

Systematic treatment of arboreal vegetation of Argentina, enhanced by figures and accurate descriptions of habitats and taxonomy.

2772 Schmidt, Margarita. Diferenciación espacial del área central de la ciudad de Mendoza. (*Bol. Estud. Geogr.*, 24 : 87, 1991, p. 203–237, ill., graphs, maps)

The core of the city of Mendoza is typified using land value and building height and function as indicators.

2773 Seca, Mirta Ana. Introducción a la geografía histórica de la Quebrada de Humahuaca: con especial referencia al pueblo de Tilcara. Tilcara, Argentina: Univ. de Buenos Aires, Facultad de Filosofía y Letras, Instituto Interdisciplinario Tilcara, 1989. 148 p.: bibl., ill. (Cuadernos de investigación; 1)

The archaeologically famous Quebrada de Humahuaca (northwestern Argentina) is presented from a geographical and anthropological perspective. The focus is pertinent as the author tries to integrate man and nature with varied success.

2774 Secor, R.J. Aconcagua: a climbing guide. Seattle: Mountaineers, 1994. 138 p.: ill., index, maps.

Useful guide to climbing the Aconcagua mountain with practical advice for the prospective climber.

2775 Sociedades humanas y equilibrio ecológico. Recopilación de María Cristina Zeballos de Sisto *et al.* Buenos Aires: Ediciones Letra Buena, 1992. 312 p.: bibl. (Col. Pensamiento científico)

Interesting compilation of papers on the relations between societies and their natural environments in Argentina. The background in psychology of some of the authors enhances the perceptive components of these rapports. An enlightening contribution.

2776 Stefañuk, Miguel Angel. Evolución de la cartografía de Misiones. Buenos Aires?: Ediciones Montoya, 1991. 235 p.: maps.

Collection of maps showing the colonization phases of the territory of Misiones. Regrettably, a rather low-quality printing job.

2777 Suriano, José Maria and **Luis Humberto Ferpozzi.** Los cambios climáticos en la pampa también son historia. (*Todo es Hist.*, 306, enero 1993, p. 8–25, bibl., maps, photos)

Climatic oscillations in the Pampa suggest that the region was more humid during its colonization but became dry during the 1930s. A renewed period of humidity began in the 1960s, with floods being more erratic and dangerous.

Tellechea de Arca, Mireya. Paraguay socioeconómico y cultural: hidrovía-MERCOSUR. See item **2848.**

2778 Toselli, Claudia. Importancia de la protección del medio ambiente para el desarrollo turístico. (*Signos Univ.*, 11 : 22, julio/dic. 1992, p. 143–162, bibl., map)

Lack of consideration for the preservation of natural environments has led to the deterioration of several tourist locations in the country.

2779 **Vasconi, Mónica A.** and **Víctor H. Villauso.** Migraciones, urbanización y transporte de pasajeros en el eje de crecimiento O.-N.O. del Conurbano Bonaerense. (*Cuad. Geogr./Cádiz,* 3, 1992, p. 123–146, bibl., graphs, maps, tables)

Population flows from and into greater Buenos Aires intensified during the 1970s. Recently, this trend has been halted.

2780 **Videla, María Alejandrina** and **Jorge Suárez.** Mendoza andina: precordillera, alta cordillera. Mendoza, Argentina: Editorial Adalid, 1991. 149 p.: bibl., ill. (some col.), maps.

Excellent description of the geology and surface forms of the cordillera of Mendoza, culminating in Mount Aconcagua. Superb pictures.

2781 **Zamorano, Mariano.** La geografía argentina hasta la primera mitad del siglo XX: vinculaciones científicas y tendencias. (*Bol. Estud. Geogr.,* 25:88, 1992, p. 11–26, graphs)

Lucid essay on the trends in Argentine geographic research based on analysis of articles in two Argentine geographical journals.

2782 **Zinger de Bilhé, Alicia S.; Olga M. del Pozo de Moraes;** and **Rosa de Gaetano de Oroz.** Bahía Blanca: análisis de la aptitud del medio natural para la expansión urbana. (*Rev. Univ. Geogr.,* 4:1/2, 1989/90, p. 79–98, bibl., maps, tables)

After studying the physical characteristics of the site of Bahía Blanca, the authors outline the possibilities for expansion of this bustling city.

CHILE

2783 **La actividad forestal en Chile a 1988: importancia del sector forestal en la actividad económica del país, producción y comercialización forestal, legislación.** Santiago: Instituto Forestal, División Estudios Económicos; Corporación de Fomento de la Producción, Gerencia de Desarrollo, 1989. 59 p.: bibl., ill.

Forestry and wood production reached high levels in the country around 1988. This short pamphlet offers some statistical data in support of this development.

Alpinistas de Lecco en la Patagonia. See item 2698.

2784 **Andrade J., Belisario** and **Consuelo Castro A.** Ensayo de evaluación del impacto de un eventual ascenso del nivel marino inducido por el efecto de invernadero en la zona costera de la región de Valparaíso. (*Rev. Geogr. Norte Gd.,* 19, 1992, p. 53–57, bibl., maps, photos)

Authors hypothesize that some 446 hectares of coastal Valparaíso would be submerged should the sea level rise by two meters due to the greenhouse effect.

2785 **Apey Rivera, María Angélica** *et al.* Fundición y territorio: reflexiones históricas sobre los orígenes de la Fundición Paipote. Recopilación de Juan O'Brien. Santiago: ENAMI, 1992. 258 p.: ill., index, maps (some col.).

Superb presentation of the history of Paipote—Chile's largest state-owned copper melt up to 1970—written by authoritative scholars. Also addressed is the history of mid-level copper mining in Chile, a stratum that rarely receives scholarly attention. Beautifully illustrated. One of the best volumes ever written on copper mining in the country.

2786 **Araya, Braulio** and **Guillermo Millie Holman.** Guía de campo de las aves de Chile. Dibujos de Mariano Bernal Morales. 2. ed. Santiago: Editorial Universitaria, 1988. 405 p., 16 p. of plates: bibl., ill. (some col.). (Col. Fuera de serie)

Valuable inventory of birds in Chilean territory detailing taxonomy and body morphology. Contains excellent color plates.

2787 **Araya Uribe, Baldo.** Aysén siglo XXI. Santiago: Imprenta de Carabineros de Chile, 1991. 195 p.: bibl., ill.

Historical vignettes and notes on curiosities of the natural environment in this southern province of Chile.

2788 **Arenas, Federico.** La estructuración territorial de la región del Biobío: otro desafío pendiente. (*Rev. Geogr. Norte Gd.,* 19, 1992, p. 83–88, table)

Rapid population growth and good job opportunities have led to overcrowding in the coastal fringe of Concepción. Other urban centers in that region are creating their own agricultural hinterlands along the Central Valley.

2789 **Bertrand, Maria S.; Roberto Figueroa M.;** and **Patricio Larraín N.** Renovación urbana en la intercomuna de Santiago: respuesta a la Ley 18.595 durante el período

1987–1990. (*Rev. Geogr. Norte Gd.*, 18, 1991, p. 27–36, bibl., maps, tables)

Urban renewal in Santiago after passing of a special law in 1987 is reviewed. This legal step elicited some initial action but has proven rather ineffective thereafter.

2790 Boldrini, Gustavo. Chiloé: andanzas y palabra escrita. Santiago: Mar Interior, 1990. 116 p.: bibl., ill.

Anecdotal accounts of picturesque places and local customs on the island of Chiloé in southern Chile.

2791 Börgel Olivares, Reinaldo. Evidencias del llamado efecto invernadero en las regiones australes de Chile. (*Rev. Geogr. Norte Gd.*, 19, 1992, p. 97–103, bibl., photos, tables)

The greenhouse effect in southern Chile is reflected in desiccation of shallow lakes, reduction of forest stands, withdrawal of glaciers, and increase in summer precipitation.

2792 Börgel Olivares, Reinaldo et al. Geografía física y humana de la XI Región de Chile y sus zonas pantanosas: perspectivas de ordenamiento ambiental. (*Rev. Geogr. Norte Gd.*, 19, 1992, p. 105–119, bibl., maps, photos, tables)

General characterization of the landform features of the southern region of Aysén. Volcanoes, soils, settlements, and activities of the region are also summarily outlined.

2793 Börgel Olivares, Reinaldo. La Laguna del Desierto y su proyección geográfica en los problemas de límites con Argentina. (*Rev. Geogr. Norte Gd.*, 18, 1991, p. 19–26, bibl., maps)

Laguna del Desierto is a disputed depression of 450 km² that has led repeatedly to border disputes between Chile and Argentina. The author tries to prove that this area belongs to Chile. In 1994, the government of Chile renounced its claims over this territory.

2794 Brahm, Luis. Estructura espacial del desarrollo humano del Gran Santiago. (*EURE/Santiago*, 17:52/53, oct./dic. 1991, p. 87–105, bibl., graph, maps, tables)

Principal component analysis is used to determine socioeconomic factors that distinguish "social sectors" in Santiago. Findings confirm the results of qualitative surveys of the city's socioeconomic structure.

2795 Bruce, James S. and **Mayme Lou S. Bruce.** Alexander Selkirk: the real Robinson Crusoe. (*Explor. J.*, 71:1, Spring 1993, p. 15–21, photos)

Alexander Selkirk, a sailor who was disciplined by his captain and left behind on Juan Fernández Island in 1704, served as model for Daniel Defoe's "Robinson Crusoe." Selkirk survived on the island until 1709.

2796 Candia, Walter B. Mariángel. Aplicación al pie de monte de la comuna de La Reina, de un parámetro primordial para la expansión urbana: el riesgo físico. (*Rev. Geogr. Chile*, 32, 1990, p. 51–71, bibl., maps, tables)

Landslides, flash floods, and mudflows are some of the natural hazards the inhabitants of La Reina, a suburb to the east of Santiago, cope with in humid winters.

2797 Castro J., Abel and **Ana María Errázuriz K.** Indicadores de población y vivienda para la confección de un atlas urbano de las capitales regionales de Chile. (*Rev. Geogr. Norte Gd.*, 19, 1992, p. 35–45, bibl., maps, table)

Indicators pertinent to occupation, age structure, population density, quality of housing, and household equipment are utilized to produce map samples for an urban atlas of Chile's main urban centers.

Caviedes, César N. Estudios sobre la variabilidad espacial del voto en América Latina. See item **2392.**

2798 Chile, a country study. Edited by Rex A. Hudson. 3rd ed. Washington: Federal Research Division, Library of Congress, 1994. 508 p.: bibl., ill., index, maps (some folded). (Area handbook series, 1057–5294. DA pam; 550–77)

Compendium of Chile's history, social conditions, economic trends, and education written by knowledgeable scholars. Indicated as a basic reading source for academics, military, and travellers. Good bibliography.

2799 Contreras Moncada, Rodolfo. Más allá del bosque: la explotación forestal en Chile. Santiago: Editorial Amerinda, 1989. 252 p.: bibl., ill. (Amerinda estudios)

Author espouses optimistic conservation views about the expansion of planted forests in Chile.

2800 Dascal, Guillermo. Ordenamiento del territorio y agricultura metropolitanos: reflexiones aplicables al caso latinoamericano. (*Rev. Geogr. Norte Gd.*, 19, 1992, p. 89–95, bibl.)

Urban sprawl is encroaching valuable agricultural land in Santiago de Chile. Author compares Santiago with other Latin American cities, such as Panama City, Managua, and Buenos Aires.

2801 Donoso Zegers, Claudio. Ecología forestal: el bosque y su medio ambiente. 3. ed. Santiago: Editorial Universitaria; Valdivia: Univ. Austral de Chile, 1992. 368 p.: bibl., ill., index, maps. (Col. Nueva técnica)

Acceptable treatise of the vegetal formations of Chile from an ecological viewpoint. Author does not consider important contributions from Chilean biogeographers.

2802 Errázuriz K., Ana María. Análisis espacial de la natalidad en Chile: 1952–1989. (*Rev. Geogr. Norte Gd.*, 19, 1992, p. 15–21, bibl., graphs, maps)

Birth rates for 1952, 1960, 1972, 1982, and 1989 are analyzed. Results show a remarkable decline across the nation, with the exception of the agrarian-mining region of Atacama.

2803 Ferrer Fougá, Hernán. Proceso de conformación territorial de Chile, 1536–1881: análisis comparado en relación a la Argentina. v. 1. v. 2, Cartapacio de mapas. Santiago: Instituto de Investigaciones del Patrimonio Territorial de Chile, Univ. de Santiago de Chile, 1990. 2 v.: bibl., ill., facsims., maps. (Col. Terra nostra; 19–20)

Interesting presentation of the legal texts by which the Spanish crown granted administrative rights to the conquerors of the Río de la Plata and Chile. Chile's and Argentina's claims over territories in Patagonia are based on these documents. Documents from republican times comparing Argentine and Chilean boundary drawings are also analyzed. This highly scientific work contains skilled sketches and a folio with reproductions of maps from those times.

2804 Figueroa Salas, Jonás. Las ciudades lineales chilenas, 1910–1930. (*Rev. Indias*, 53:198, mayo/agosto 1993, p. 651–662, ill., maps)

The conspicuous expansion of Santiago along major boulevards at the beginning of this century is tied to European influences, particularly those of urbanists from Madrid.

Galimberti, Diana. Antarctica: an introductory guide. See item **2729.**

2805 Gangas Geisse, Mónica. El descenso de la mortalidad en Chile: 1952–1989. (*Rev. Geogr. Norte Gd.*, 19, 1992, p. 23–33, bibl., maps, tables)

An aspect of the modernization of Chile's demography is the decrease of the death rate. The lowest rate is in Santiago and the relative high is in Biobío.

2806 Gangas Geisse, Mónica and Ana María Errázuriz K. Diferenciación interna de la fuerza de trabajo en la provincia de San Antonio. (*Rev. Geogr. Norte Gd.*, 18, 1991, p. 38–43, bibl., graphs, tables)

Labor force in a secondary coastal city of central Chile reveals a high male component, and concentration in construction and industrial activities.

2807 Garayar C., Miguel and Alfredo Sánchez M. Areas metropolitanas y migraciones: aspectos teóricos. Concepción, Chile: Editorial de la Univ. de Concepción, 1989. 66 p.: ill., maps.

Authors outline spatial expansion in three major areas of population concentration. Population flows are rudimentarily analyzed, revealing unfamiliarity with the method pioneered by Jürgen Bähr in Chile.

2808 González Celis, Fernando. Ensayo histórico sobre la noción de estado en Chile, del historiador Mario Góngora. (*Rev. Chil. Hist. Geogr.*, 158, 1990, p. 149–159)

In 1986, the late historian Mario Góngora published an essay purporting that the roots of "Chilean nationality" lie in the identification of a territorial state—a concept of undeniable Spanish origin.

2809 Gross, Patricio. Santiago de Chile, 1925–1990: planificación urbana y modelos políticos. (*EURE/Santiago*, 17:52/53, oct./dic. 1991, p. 27–52, bibl.)

Urban remodeling in Santiago between 1925–90 is reviewed in light of the dominating political tendencies and social priorities during those years. The impact of politics on urban planning is addressed.

2810 Grosse Ickler, Juan Augusto. Expediciones en la Patagonia Occidental: hacia la carretera austral. Traducción del alemán de Lydia Miquel. Santiago: Editorial Andrés Bello, 1990. 360 p.: ill., maps.

Collection of notes written by Juan A. Grosse, a young German colonist who, from 1940–58, traveled the islands of the Province of Aysén, explored the Patagonian Icefields, and ventured onto numerous Patagonian streams. He is credited with being one of the inspirational pioneers for the construction of the Carretera Austral.

2811 Hartwig C., Fernando. Chile, desarrollo forestal sustentable: ensayo de política forestal. Santiago: Editorial Los Andes, 1991. 185 p.: ill. (some col.), maps (some col.). (Serie Medio ambiente y desarrollo)

Lucid study about Chile's forest stands and future marketing strategies. The country is already the number one lumber exporter of South America.

2812 Hartwig C., Fernando. Visión del desarrollo forestal de Chile. Santiago: Proasec, 1989. 105 p.: bibl., ill.

Convincing outline of the present state and future prospects of Chile's forest resources, produced by a revered figure in Chilean forest sciences.

2813 Hurtado Guerrero, Miguel. Memoria sobre el límite septentrional de la República de Chile. Reedición presentada por Hernán Ferrer Fougá. Santiago: Instituto de Investigaciones del Patrimonio Territorial de Chile, Univ. de Santiago, 1987. 95 p.: ill., maps. (Col. Veritas; 2)

Monograph on the historical documents upon which Chile bases her claims to the desert tract north of parallel 25°S, written in 1859 by a naval officer. Also an important document for justifying Chile's occupation of the Bolivian Pacific coast.

2814 Illanes, Juan Pablo et al. Medio ambiente en desarrollo: bases sociales, económicas, biológicas y jurídicas para abordar los problemas de contaminación ambiental en Chile. Recopilación de Ricardo Katz B. y Gabriel del Fávero V. Santiago: Centro de Estudios Públicos, 1993. 507 p.: bibl., ill.

This collection represents a declaration of principles of the Center for Public Studies, an economic and scientific elite that governs studies and problem-solving apparatus about environmental protection in Chile.

2815 Instituto Geográfico Militar (Chile). Atlas del desarrollo económico y social de Chile. Santiago: Instituto Geográfico Militar, 1988. 1 atlas (187 p.): col. ill., col. maps.

Profusely illustrated atlas of Chile's economic development, produced in the last year of Gen. Pinochet's rule.

2816 Jornadas Nacionales de Regionalización, 6th, Concepción, Chile, 1989. Gestión política y desarrollo armónico de Chile. VI Jornadas Nacionales de Regionalización; Concepción 4–5 de mayo 1989, Región del Biobío; CORCHILE-CORBIOBIO. Concepción, Chile: Banco Concepción, 1990. 110 p.: ill.

Critical analysis of regionalization policies implemented in Chile by civilian and authoritarian regimes reveals that neither system has produced the desired decongestion of population and resources in the Santiago-Valparaíso macroregion.

2817 Jornadas Territoriales, 5th, Santiago and Los Angeles, Biobío, Chile, 1989. La región del Biobío: V Jornadas Territoriales. Expositores Isidoro Vázquez de Acuña et al. Santiago: Instituto de Investigaciones del Patrimonio Territorial de Chile, Univ. de Santiago de Chile, 1990. 324 p.: bibl., ill., index, maps. (Col. Terra nostra, 0716–1026; 18)

Another volume in a series destined to present the history and main types of economy of the major regions of Chile. Biobío— a region fiercely fought over by Araucanians and Spaniards/Chileans—is remarkably variegated: plenty of hydroelectric power, rich coal deposits, solid industrial bases, and abundant agricultural production, make this a competitor of Santiago and Valparaíso-Aconcagua.

2818 Larraín, Patricio. El sistema natural en la planificación urbana chilena. (*Rev. Geogr. Norte Gd.*, 19, 1992, p. 59–68, bibl., map, graph)

Physical characteristics of city sites have not been taken seriously in Chile's urban planning. Frequently flood prone areas, landslide slopes, and seismically sensitive areas are considered habitable by urban planners.

2819 Larraín Barros, Horacio. El paisaje fitogeográfico del Norte Chico y Zona Central. (*Rev. Chil. Hist. Geogr.*, 158, 1990, p. 271–291, bibl.)

Interesting work on the landscape perceptions of Indians and early Spanish travellers extracted from the colonial chronicler Gerónimo de Bibar (1558).

2820 López Rubio, Sergio E. El General Ramón Cañas Montalva: sus concepciones geopolíticas magallanico-antárticas. (*Rev. Chil. Hist. Geogr.*, 158, 1990, p. 29–86, ill., maps, photo)

Gen. Ramón Cañas Montalva's (1896–1976) unrealistic views on Chile's geopolitical significance in the South Pacific.

2821 Mardones Flores, María. Geomorfología del curso superior de la hoya del Biobío. (*Rev. Geogr. Chile*, 34, 1991, p. 69–76, bibl., maps)

A noted geomorphologist surveys the upper reaches of the Biobío river where the water is stored in several lakes of late-glacial origin. No chronological dating is offered.

Mascitti, Virginia. Flamencos: los caminos de la convivencia. See item **2747.**

2822 El mercado forestal interno. Santiago: Instituto Forestal, Gerencia Técnica; Corporación de Fomento de la Producción, Gerencia de Desarrollo, 1987. 138 p.: bibl. (Informe técnico; 106)

Financial study of the major lumber varieties used in the country, revealing the importance of spruce and southern beech.

2823 Muñoz, Francisco. La mortalidad en Chile, 1865–1940: tendencias, niveles y estructura. (*in* Congreso sobre a História da População da América Latina, *1st, Ouro Preto, Brazil, 1989.* Actas. São Paulo: Fundação SEADE, 1990, p. 51–63, bibl., graphs, tables)

Mortality rates in Chile (1865–1940) have been declining, which seems to be connected with control of tuberculosis and a decrease in digestive system infections due to improved hygiene.

2824 Núñez Pinto, Jorge and **Pedro Labra Araya.** Cartografía urbana histórica de Talca. (*Universum/Talca*, 7, 1992, p. 65–80, bibl., maps)

City plans from 1844, 1858, 1872, 1904, 1929, 1965, and 1990 are used to trace the growth phases of Talca, in the agrarian core of central Chile.

2825 Peralta Toro, Fernando. Ideas para la discusión de una política de riego: su aplicación al caso de Chile. Santiago: Ediciones Tacora, 1987. 107 p.: ill.

Outline of legislation and principles regulating water management in the semiarid tracts of the country.

2826 Protección del medio ambiente: seminario AIC-TECNIBERIA, 1990. Edición de Herman Schwember. Santiago: CEPAL, 1991. 422 p.: ill.

Another in a series of booklets and pamphlets published in Chile about environmental protection. This reviewer has doubts about the applicability of many of the measures discussed in this setting.

2827 Quintanilla Pérez, Victor and **Carla Reyes Casanova.** Antecedentes sobre la distribución de la vegetación en una subcuenca andina del Río Mapocho. (*Rev. Geogr. Chile*, 35, 1991, p. 19–33, bibl., graphs, maps, photos)

The montane vegetation in a tributary of the Mapocho River is dominated by shrubs, seasonal herbs and grasses, and green summer meadows near the snowline. Water availability and temperature are the main controls.

2828 Quintanilla Pérez, Victor. Problemas y consecuencias ambientales sobre el Bosque de Alerce, (*Fitzroya Cupressoides* (Mol) Johnst), debido a la explotación de la cordillera costera de Chile austral. (*Rev. Geogr./México*, 114, julio/dic. 1991, p. 55–72, bibl., graph, map, photos)

The export of wood chips to Japan has accelerated the contraction of the last stands of alerce (*Fitzroya Cupressoides* (Mol) Johnst) in the southern extreme of continental Chile. Author urges protecting native trees from foreign exploitation.

2829 Ramírez Morales, Fernando. Apuntes para una historia ecológica de Chile. (*Cuad. Hist./Santiago*, 1, dic. 1991, p. 149–198, tables)

Author looks at debates from the early 1900s in the Chilean Congress to trace the origin of initial laws protecting the native animals of Chile. Unfortunately, these laws were rarely followed.

2830 Romero Aravena, Hugo. Patrones espaciales de la modernización agrícola en el Norte de Chile: una perspectiva basada en los sistemas de información geográfica. (*Rev. Geogr. Chile,* 32, 1990, p. 165–196, bibl., graphs, photos, tables)

Application of geographic information systems to the study of vineyard location in the Limari Valley, in the Norte Chico of Chile.

2831 Rottmann, Jürgen and **Nicolás Piwonka.** El Altiplano chileno. Fotografías de Nicolás Piwonka Santiago: UNISYS, 1990? 100 p.: col. ill., col. map.

Beautiful pictorial guide to the western border of the Altiplano. Snow-capped volcanoes, frigid lakes, volcanoes, geysers, and dry vegetation are splendidly illustrated.

2832 Sabatini, Francisco. Santiago: tendencias y posibilidades de desconcentracíon de la industria en la macro región central. (*EURE/Santiago,* 17:52/53, oct./dic. 1991, p. 75–86, bibl.)

A proposal of areas to which the excessive concentration of industries in and around Santiago should be relocated.

2833 Sánchez, Alfredo and **Roberto Morales.** Las regiones de Chile: espacio físico y humano-económico. Santiago: Editorial Universitaria, 1993. 262 p.: bibl., ill. (some col.), maps. (Col. Imagen de Chile)

Conventional presentation of the geography of the 13 administrative regions of Chile illustrated with photographs. Bibliographic sources are scant.

2834 Santis Arenas, Hernán. Los cambios en el uso del suelo en comunas litorales. (*Rev. Geogr. Norte Gd.,* 19, 1992, p. 47–52, maps)

Author detects an excessive number of lots occupied by temporary tenants (summer seaside vacationers) in a tract of coastal land not far from Santiago.

2835 II Región Antofagasta. Santiago: Editorial Kactus, 1989. 96 p.: col. ill., maps.

Vol. 2 in a collection of illustrated guides to the different regions of the country. The beautiful photographs and eloquent maps will entice reader to go and see for themselves.

2836 Simposio Estado de Conservación de la Fauna de Vertebrados Terrestres de Chile, *Santiago, 1987.* Libro rojo de los vertebrados terrestres de Chile: corresponde a las actas del Simposio Estado de Conservación de la Fauna de Vertebrados Terrestres de Chile.

Organizado por la Corporación Nacional Forestal y realizado entre el 21 y 24 de abril de 1987 en Santiago, Chile. Recopilación de Alfonso A. Glade. Santiago: Corporación Nacional Forestal, 1988. 65 p., 1 folded leaf of plates: col. ill., map.

Excellent inventory of species in danger of extinction in different regions of the country. The photographs are beautiful and revealing.

2837 Squeo, Francisco *et al.* Spatial heterogeneity of high mountain vegetation in the Andean desert zone of Chile. (*Mt. Res. Dev.,* 13:2, 1993, p. 203–209, bibl., graphs, tables)

Vegetation in the semi-arid mountains of the Norte Chico attests to a differential adaptation due to low temperatures, chemical soil attributes, slope orientation, and soil moisture.

2838 Teniente Merino, el héroe de Laguna del Desierto. Santiago: Red Internacional del Libro, 1992. 167 p.: ill., maps.

In 1965, a Chilean police patrol ventured into territory claimed by Argentina. In a skirmish with Argentine border patrols, Lieutenant Hernán Merino was shot. The incident created great tension between Chile and Argentina and soured relations for years to come. The details of the incident are retold in this booklet.

2839 Urrutia M., Rosario and **Belisario Andrade J.** Impacto de la actividad de camping sobre unidades medioambientales sensibles de la zona costera entre Llolleo y Algarrobo: Chile Central. (*Rev. Geogr. Norte Gd.,* 18, 1991, p. 9–17, maps, photos, tables)

Camping on the dunes of a coastal strip, not far from Santiago, has led to environmental degradation and garbage accumulation.

2840 Valdés, Ximena. Mujer, trabajo y medio ambiente: los nudos de la modernización agraria. Santiago: Centro de Estudios para el Desarrollo de la Mujer, 1992. 250 p.: bibl., ill., maps.

Pathbreaking study of women in Chilean agriculture that reveals the large involvement of females in harvest-related activities in central Chile.

2841 Valenzuela G., Jaime. Actividades urbanas y control de los usos del suelo: hacia una zonificación del centro metropolitano. (*EURE/Santiago*, 18:55, oct. 1992, p. 61–78, graphs, maps, table)

A comparison of urban land use in the core of Santiago de Chile and Quito leads to the conclusion that the important financial institutions are concentrated in the center of the city, while retail trade is found in peripheral locations.

2842 Veit, Heinz. Upper quarternary landscape and climate evolution in the Norte Chico (northern Chile): an overview. (*Mt. Res. Dev.*, 13:2, 1993, p. 139–144, bibl., tables)

The Andes of Chile's Norte Chico are critically located between the dry "norte" and the winter-rainy "south." This review paper documents climate changes, from cool and humid at about 30,000 BP, over cold and dry around 19,000 BP, to the characteristic semi-aridity of the region we know today, since 3,000 BP.

PARAGUAY

2843 Azara, Félix de. Apuntamientos para la historia natural de los páxaros del Paraguay y del Río de la Plata. Recopilación de Joaquín Fernández Pérez. Spain: Secretaría General del Plan Nacional de I y D, Comisión Interministerial de Ciencia y Tecnología, 1992. 619 p.: bibl., ill. (some col.), indexes.

New printing of this famous work by the Spanish naturalist Félix de Azara (1802) celebrating the scientific depth and artistic value of his observations on the birds of the Río de la Plata lowlands.

2844 Bosio, Juan José; Mabel Causarano; and **Beatriz Chase.** Aproximación a un proyecto del ambiente: La Chacarita; documento de trabajo, avance técnico, metodológico. Asunción: Centro Paraguayo de Estudios Sociológicos, 1989. 79 p., 26 folded leaves of plates: bibl., ill., maps.

Study on site and topography in the Chacarita borough of Asunción with the purpose of protecting dwellings from floods caused by the high waters of Río Paraguay.

2845 El desarrollo sostenible y el conocimiento tradicional. Recopilación de Ramón B. Fogel. Asunción: CERI; Fundación Moisés Bertoni para la Conservación de la Naturaleza, 1993. 132 p.: bibl., ill.

Collection of papers on sustainable

development in Paraguay. Natural resources management, indigenous exploitation, agroforestry, and human diseases are outlined. Considering the scarcity of published materials on the subject, these essays are valuable, even though their quality could be better.

Mascitti, Virginia. Flamencos: los caminos de la convivencia. See item **2747.**

2846 Oportunidades empresariales en la hidrovía Paraguay-Paraná. (*Integr. Latinoam.*, 16:168, junio 1991, p. 3–20, maps, tables)

Outline and projections of the advantages of implementing a regulated waterway along the Paraguay River into the lower course of the Paraná River.

2847 Reed, Richard K. Developing the Mbaracayú Biosphere Reserve, Paraguay: Chiripá Indians and sustainable economies. (*Yearbook/CLAG*, 16, 1990, p. 34–40, bibl., map)

Chiripá Indian nature conservation practices, particularly the exploitation of *yerba mate*, in the Mbaracayú biosphere reserve are hailed as an example of sustainable forest resources extraction.

2848 Tellechea de Arca, Mireya. Paraguay socio-económico y cultural: hidrovía-MERCOSUR. Asunción: J. Ortiz, 1991. 75 p.: bibl., maps. (Estudios sociales)

Pamphlet details the advantage of a possible economic integration of Paraguay and its watercourses with Brazil and Argentina in the MERCOSUR.

URUGUAY

Azara, Félix de. Apuntamientos para la historia natural de los páxaros del Paraguay y del Río de la Plata. See item **2843.**

2849 Barrios Pintos, Aníbal and **Washington Reyes Abadie.** Los barrios de Montevideo. v. 3, Villa Colón y su entorno. Montevideo: Intendencia Municipal de Montevideo, 1992. 1 v.: bibl., ill. (some col.), maps.

Short book depicts Villa Colón, a prosperous neighborhood in the interior of Montevideo.

2850 Barrios Pintos, Aníbal and **Washington Reyes Abadie.** Los barrios de Montevideo. v. 4, Paso Molino, El Prado y sus alrededores. Montevideo: Intendencia Municipal de Montevideo, 1993. 1 v.: bibl., ill. (some col.), maps.

Volume deals with the boroughs of Paso Molino and El Prado, noted for their recreational sites and the historical residences of affluent families.

2851 Barrios Pintos, Aníbal. De San Servando a Río Branco, proyectada capital de un propuesto 20° departamento uruguayo. (*Rev. Nac./Montevideo*, 237, sept. 1991, p. 75–99, bibl., maps, tables)

Historical vignette of San Servando, on the border with Brazil, proposed to be the capital of the future dept. of Manuel Oribe (Río Branco).

2852 Caffera, Rubén *et al.* Desarrollo forestal y medio ambiente. Recopilación de Carlos Pérez Arrarte. Montevideo: CIEDUR; Hemisferio Sur, 1993. 336 p.: bibl., ill., maps.

Collection of position papers on forest conservation and exploitation in Uruguay detailing the extent of deforestation and neglect of conservation practices in the country.

2853 Díaz, José Pedro; Jorge García Ramón; and **Hugo Machín.** El Uruguay impactado: investigación periodística sobre nosotros y el medio ambiente. Montevideo: Editorial Fin de Siglo, 1993. 262 p.: ill., maps. (Col. Reporte)

Collection of essays on controversial environmental conservation issues in Uruguay. Subjects addressed include environmental hazards resulting from the construction of a nuclear plant, expanding rice fields in Rocha, constructing a bridge across the estuary, coal mining in open pits, and a law on environmental protection.

2854 Estudio ambiental nacional. v. 1, Plan de acción ambiental. v. 2, Resumen ejecutivo. Washington: Secretaría Ejecutiva para Asuntos Económicos y Sociales, Departamento de Desarrollo Regional y Medio Ambiente, 1992. 2 v.: bibl., ill., maps.

Outline of the country's main geographical areas describing problems of soil erosion, vegetal degradation, lack of infrastructures, and water pollution. The small volume provides a summary presentation of a plan for environmental improvements.

2855 Gans, Paul. Desarrollo económico y sector informal en América Latina: el ejemplo del comercio ambulante en Montevideo. (*Rev. Geogr./México*, 114, enero/junio 1991, p. 203–223, bibl., maps, tables)

Locations commonly chosen by peddlers to sell their wares and the structural reasons for their existence are studied, using Montevideo's Avenida 18 de Julio as an example.

Mascitti, Virginia. Flamencos: los caminos de la convivencia. See item **2747.**

Sierra, Gerónimo de. Elecciones uruguayas: cambios en el sistema de partidos y bloqueos emergentes. See item **3845.**

BRAZIL

KEITH D. MULLER, *Associate Professor of Geography, Kent State University*

NOT SURPRISINGLY, topics related to Amazonia dominate the literature on Brazilian geography. One work in this category, *The fragile tropics of Latin America,* edited by Toshie Nishizawa and Juha I. Uitto, warrants special mention (item **2411**). Three chapters within this work are especially worthy of consideration. Hilgard O'Reilly Sternberg contemplates the uncertain future of Amazonia wetlands (item **2922**); Emilio F. Moran considers ecosystem management (item **2900**); and Mario Hiraoka discusses non-agricultural economic activities (item **2886**). Four additional chapters deal with the Brazilian Northeast examining white sand soils, drought-deciduous vegetation, characteristics and utilization of tree species, and land-use changes in regard to irrigation.

T. Nishizawa, one of the editors of *The fragile tropics,* was awarded the distinguished Order of Rio Branco, the highest civilian award granted for service to Brazil. This honor pays tribute to his work in Amazonia and the state of Rio de Janeiro, as well as recognizing his leadership of the University of Tsukuba (Japan) research team expeditions in the Northeast of Brazil in the 1980s. These expeditions resulted in numerous articles in English and Japanese, particularly in the interdisciplinary journal *Latin American Studies,* which Nishizawa founded. Professor Nishizawa has also served since 1993 as the Japanese advisor to G-7's Pilot Program to Conserve the Brazilian Rainforest.

Nigel Smith *et al.* provide a balanced study of causal factors behind land-use changes (item **2920**). J.H.C. Gash *et al.* offer a collection of technical chapters concerning the impact of deforestation on climate (item **2859**). Browder and Godfrey present a valuable study of Amazonia's urbanization (item **2868**). Leonel's work critically analyzes the proposed extension of Highway BR-364 from Rondonia state to Peru and the Pacific (item **2893**).

Relevant journals, many first-time additions to the *Handbook,* include *Geografia, Revista do Departamento de Geografia, Secolas* (item **2918**), *Boletím de Geografia Teorética, Ciência & Ambiente,* and *Ciência Hoje. Boletím de Geografia Teorética* includes many climate studies. *Ciência & Ambiente* mostly features local case studies from Rio Grande do Sul. *Ciência Hoje,* in a format similar to *Scientific America,* includes geographical topics, such as (item **2923**).

An article by Mario Hiraoka examines sustainable development options for traditional and changing land-use patterns related to riverine agroforestry along the Tocantíns River, near the mouth of the Amazon (item **2887**).

Norman D. Johns Jr.'s PhD dissertation, "Brazil's Chocolate Forest: Environmental and Economic Role of Conservation in Bahia's Cocoa Agroecosystem," also deserves mention. According to Johns, farmers often avoid the government policy of shade tree removal, and thus help preserve endangered trees and other flora.

2856 Abers, Rebecca and **Alberto Lourenço.** Gold, geo-politics and hyper-urbanization in the Brazilian Amazon: the case of Boa Vista, Roraima. (*in* La urbe latinoamericana: balance y perspectivas a las puertas del tercer milenio. Recopilación de Giuletta Fadda. Caracas: Univ. Central de Venezuela, 1993, p. 65–88, bibl., table)

Considers role played by cities in the conflict between gold mining and preservation of indigenous territory. Examines relationship between urban growth of Boa Vista and region's political economy.

2857 Ab'Sáber, Aziz Nacib. A revanche dos ventos: derruição de solos areníticos e formação de areais na Campanha Gaúcha. (*Ciênc. Amb.,* 11, julho 1995, p. 7–31)

Summarizes previous identification and analyses of these sandy soils.

2858 Allegretti, Mary Helena. Reservas extrativistas: parâmetros para uma política de desenvolvimento sustentável na Amazônia. (*Rev. Bras. Geogr.,* 54:1, jan./março 1993, p. 5–23, bibl., tables)

Suggests that both development and conservation are reconcilable with sustainability. Thoroughly develops historical and conceptual aspects, presents a development methodology for Amazônia, analyzes economic alternatives, and discusses opposing arguments.

Amazônia: desenvolvimento ou retrocesso. See item **4466.**

2859 Amazonian deforestation and climate. Edited by J.H.C. Gash *et al.* Chichester, England; New York: John Wiley, 1996. 611 p.: bibl., ill. (some col.), index, maps.

Results of Anglo-Brazilian Climate Observation Study (ABRACOS), which sought to improve climate model predictions. Significant 29 chapter contribution provides a technical examination of the multifaceted environmental topics: soils, water storage, pastures, forest canopy, leaf dynamics, biomass, radiation, and carbon dioxide.

2860 Andrade, Manuel Correia de Oliveira.
A cassiterita nas regiões norte e nordeste do Brasil. Rio de Janeiro?: CNPq, CETEM, 1991. 115 p., 7 folded leaves: bibl., ill., maps. (Estudos e documentos; 9)
Analyzes production and industrialization of tin, especially with reference to role of multinationals and national integration.

2861 Andrade, Manuel Correia de Oliveira.
Modernização e pobreza: a expansão da agroindústria canavieira e seu impacto ecológico e social. São Paulo: Editora UNESP, Fundação para o Desenvolvimento da UNESP, 1994. 250 p.: bibl., maps. (Col. Biblioteca básica)
Historical survey of sugarcane industry and its ecological and social impact on Brazil.

2862 Andrade, Manuel Correia de Oliveira.
Pierre Monbeig e o pensamento geográfico no Brasil. (*Bol. Paul. Geogr.*, 72, 1994, p. 63–82, bibl.)
Describes contribution of French geographer to Brazil.

2863 Anijos, Rafael Sanzio Araújo dos. Dinâmica da expansão urbana no Distrito Federal do Brasil e sua região do entorno imediato, 1964–1990: monitoramento por meio de dados de sensoriamento remoto. (*Geografia/Rio Claro*, 16:2, out. 1991, p. 115–136, bibl., maps)
Analysis aided by remote sensing media technologies including Landsat images. Results indicate unequal growth due to urban expansion along main highways.

2864 Aragón, Luis E. The Amazon as a study object: building regional capacity for sustainable development. Stockholm: Stockholm Univ., Institute of Latin American Studies, 1994 156 p.: bibl., graphs, maps, tables. (Institute of Latin American Studies; 28)
Describes major research and administrative agencies working in the region. Compares institutions, research, and human resources of each Amazon country. Calls for new theoretical framework of development, worldwide expansion of scholarship, and a strengthening of local institutions and human resources.

2865 Assies, Willem. The extraction of non-timber forest products as a conservation strategy in Amazonia. (*Rev. Eur.*, 62, 1997, p. 33–53, bibl.)
Studies dynamics of extractive economies and their potential for sustainable strategies in northern Bolivia and the Brazilian state of Acre. Focuses on production and marketing of Brazil nuts. Concludes that Brazil cannot profit from these extractive products. Seriously questions the effectiveness of market-based strategies for rainforest conservation. [R. Hoefte.]

2866 Bähr, Jürgen and Rainer Wehrhahn. *Polarization reversal* in der Entwicklung brasilianischer Metropolen?: eine Analyse anhand demographischer Indikatoren am Beispiel von São Paulo. (*Erdkunde/Bonn*, 49:3, Juli/Sept. 1995, p. 213–231, bibl., graphs, maps, tables)
Suggests that peripheralized interior of the country tends to profit more from population increases than do coastal areas. However, concludes that economic dominance of the south and southeast will persist.

Barbosa, Luiz C. The people of the forest against international capitalism: systemic and anti-systemic forces in the battle for the preservation of the Brazilian Amazon rainforest. See item **5213.**

Belluzzo, Ana Maria de Moraes. O Brasil dos viajantes. v. 1, Imaginário do novo mundo. See item **2387.**

2867 Brannstrom, Christian. Brazilian county-level juridical documents as sources for historical geography: a case study from western São Paulo state. (*Yearbook/CLAG*, 23, 1997, p. 41–50)
Calls for serious research of legal documents to provide watershed agricultural and environmental data. Documents analyzed include land survey and subdivision records, probate cases, land use and tenure litigation, and labor complaints.

2868 Browder, John O. and Brian J. Godfrey.
Rainforest cities: urbanization, development, and globalization of the Brazilian Amazonia. New York: Columbia Univ. Press, 1997. 429 p.: bibl., ill., indexes, maps.
Comprehensive and useful analysis of region's urbanization process. Compares east-

ern and western segments, and illustrates heterogeneity of urban frontier. Concludes that current theories of urbanization are inappropriate for Amazonian cities. See also *HLAS 55:2638*.

2869 Os caminhos da reflexão sobre a cidade e o urbano. Organização de Ana Fani Alessandri Carlos. São Paulo: Edusp, 1994. 390 p.: bibl., maps.

Includes 14 conference papers on urban topics, focusing primarily on Recife, Brasília, and São Paulo. Conference explored a number of research topics with the goal of demonstrating the theories and practice of urban studies within discipline of geography in Brazil.

2870 Carney, Judith and **Mário Hiraoka.** *Raphia taedigera* in the Amazon Estuary. (*Principes/Lawrence*, 41:3, 1997, p. 125–130)

Discusses this useful palm's role in peasant communities. Describes its geographical range, ecological features, and use in shrimp traps and fishing weirs.

2871 Carvalho Filho, José Juliano de and **Silvia Maria Schor.** Floresta tropical, desenvolvimento econômico, e equilíbrio sócio-ambiental: o caso de ocupação do Noroeste da Amazônia Brasileira. (*Archè/Rio de Janeiro*, 3:9, 1994, p. 29–44)

Criticizes World Bank funding of, and policies that favor, infrastructure development rather than projects for small farmers and indigenous peoples.

2872 Cordeiro, Helena Kohn. A circulação da informação no espaço brasileiro e o sistema bancário. (*Geografia/Rio Claro*, 16:1, abril 1991, p. 23–36, bibl.)

Integration of telecommunications and concentration of information, especially under dominance of São Paulo, Brasília, and Rio, help to internationalize Brazilian economy.

2873 Davis, Wade. One river: explorations and discoveries in the Amazon rain forest. New York: Simon & Schuster, 1996. 537 p.: bibl., ill., index.

Enjoyable and insightful work was written as a tribute to the scientific achievements of Richard Evans Schultes, an Amazonia explorer active during 1940s-50s. Also relates explorations of the author and of Timothy Plowman, both Schultes' students. Intended for a popular audience.

2874 Dawsey, Cyrus B. An American colony in Brazil, revisited. (*Geografia/Rio Claro*, 18:1, abril 1993, p. 23–35, bibl., map)

Describes three geographical processes regarding migration to and settlement in Brazil of US southerners following the Civil War: 1) initial migration and consolidation of colonies; 2) diffusion of US southern culture; and 3) preservation of the culture.

2875 O desafio das florestas neotropicais = The challenge of neotropical forests. Curitiba, Brazil?: Univ. Federal do Paraná?, 1991? 430 p.: bibl., ill., map.

Articles from an international conference emphasize technical aspects of forestry. Discussions of various regions of Brazil cover topics such as sustainability, soil development, deforestation, mechanized lumbering, and alternative forestry.

2876 Diniz, Alexandre. Occupation and urbanization of Roraima state, Brazil. (*Yearbook/CLAG*, 23, 1997, p. 51–62)

Information obtained from nearly 150 personal interviews relates migrant histories and characteristics. Analyzes major migrant groups: first-time movers, professionals, repeat urban movers, peasants, and miners. Criticizes government's lack of initiative in resolving conflicts and providing infrastructure, and calls for actions which would lessen volatility of pioneer settlement process.

2877 Faissol, Speridão. O espaço, território, sociedade e desenvolvimento brasileiro. Rio de Janeiro: Secretaria de Planejamento, Orçamento e Coordenação, Fundação Instituto Brasileiro de Geografia e Estatística, 1994. 308 p.: bibl.

Examines geographical theory and methodology in a Brazilian context.

2878 Figueiredo, Adma Hamam de. Crédito rural e mudança tecnológica no oeste de Paraná. (*Rev. Bras. Geogr.*, 54:2, abril/junho 1992, p. 83–117, appendix, bibl., maps, tables)

Analyzes rural credit policies for small farm soybean production during second half of 1970s.

The fragile tropics of Latin America: sustainable management of changing environments. See item **2411.**

2879 Geografia e meio ambiente no Brasil.
São Paulo: Editora Hucitec; Rio de Janeiro: Comissão Nacional do Brasil da União Geográfica Internacional, 1995. 397 p.: bibl., ill., maps. (Geografia, teoria e realidade; 28)

Essays examine issues related to global perspective, urbanization, and national territoriality. Despite title, few works concern the environment.

2880 Goulding, Michael; Nigel J.H. Smith; and Dennis J. Mahar. Floods of fortune: ecology and economy along the Amazon. New York: Columbia Univ. Press, 1996. 193 p.: bibl., ill. (some col.), index, maps (some col.).

Excellent photos accompany text that connects cultural and natural landscapes. Nine chapters examine problems and opportunities, settlement history, modern economic risks, and wildlife. Analyses concerning fish, plants, and floodplain agriculture are especially noteworthy. Excellent overview useful for both professionals and general public.

2881 Grabois, José; Mauro José da Silva; and Caio Augusto Amorim Maciel. Reordenação espacial e evolução da ecomomia agrária: o caso das terras altas da transição agreste-mata do norte de Pernambuco. (*Rev. Bras. Geogr.*, 54:1, jan./março 1993, p. 121–177, bibl., maps, photos)

Case study of transitional region between the Agreste and the Zona da Mata, where the spread of sugarcane affects banana, cattle, vineyard, and traditional food crop production.

2882 Grandjean, Pernette. Recife, le marché de gros: reflet d'une région-problème du Brésil. (*in* Nourrir les métropoles d'Amérique Latine: approvisionnement et distribution. Paris: Editions L'Harmattan, 1995, p. 165–189, bibl., graph, map, table)

Describes the functioning of the Centrais de Abastecimento Sociedade Anônima (regional wholesale fresh fruit and vegetable distribution center) in Recife. See also items **2892** and **2914.**

2883 Guidugli, Odeibler Santo. Espacialização da população no vazio demográfico do estado do Amazonas: problemas e perspectivas. (*Geografia/Rio Claro*, 18:2, out. 1993, p. 69–95, bibl., graphs, maps, tables)

Examines demographic evolution in the context of urban growth (especially for Manaus), internal migration, and distribution in rural and urban populations. Persistent lack of settlement in Amazonas has serious implications for both region and nation.

2884 Henkel, Karl. Agrarstrukturwandel und Migration im östlichen Amazonien: Pará, Brasilien. Tübingen, Germany: Im Selbstverlag des Geographischen Instituts der Univ. Tübingen, 1994. 474 p.: bibl., ill., index. (Tübinger Beiträge zur geographischen Lateinamerika-Forschung; 11. Tübinger geographische Studien: 0932–1438; 112)

Valuable, detailed analysis of agriculture and migration in eastern Amazonia.

2885 Herrmann, Maria Lucia de Paula; Magaly Mendonça; and Nazareno José de Campos. São José-SC: Avaliação das enchentes e deslizamentos ocorridos em novembro de 1991 e fevereiro de 1994. (*Geosul/Florianópolis*, 8:16, segundo semestre 1993, p. 46–78, bibl., graphs, photos, tables)

Points to lack of urban flood disaster planning.

2886 Hiraoka, Mário. Aquatic and land fauna management among the floodplain ribereños of the Peruvian Amazon. (*in* The fragile tropics of Latin America: sustainable management of changing environments. Tokyo: United Nations Univ. Press, 1995, p. 201–225, bibl., chart, map, photos, table)

This admirable account illustrates importance of non-agricultural activities in the overall livelihood of Amazonian peasant communities.

2887 Hiraoka, Mário. Land use changes in the Amazon Estuary. (*Glob. Environ. Change*, 5:4, 1995, p. 323–336)

Floodplain inhabitants near Belém are changing from swidden cultivation, with sugarcane as a cash crop, to a permanent farming system based on palm agroforests. Thus, proximity to major urban center has not led to intensified land use as expected, but rather to a change from crop cultivation to agroforestry. Argues that, unlike Boserup's single factor hypothesis, labor and land use changes are multifaceted and difficult to explain.

2888 An inventory of Brazilian wetlands.
Edited by Antônio Carlos Sant'ana Diegues. Gland, Switzerland: IUCN, 1994. 215 p.: bibl., maps.

Useful overview of seven major river and coastal basins. Includes summaries of regions' socioeconomic and environmental conditions.

2889 Jesús, Gilmar Mascarenhas de. O lugar da feira livre na grande cidade capitalista: Rio de Janeiro, 1964–1989. (*Rev. Bras. Geogr.*, 54:1, jan./março 1993, p. 95–120, bibl., maps, photo, tables)

Examines spatial changes and decreasing numbers of periodic outdoor markets caused by competing supermarkets.

2890 Kowarick, Marcos. Amazônia-Carajás: na trilha do saque. São Luís, Brazil: Editora Anita, 1995. 333 p.: bibl., ill., maps.

Discusses how large corporations have harmed natural resources of Amazonia and the Programa Grande Carajás.

2891 Lacerda, Luís Drude de and Willem Salomons. Mercúrio na Amazônia: uma bomba relógio química? Rio de Janeiro: CETEM/CNPq, 1992? 78 p.: bibl., ill., maps. (Tecnologia ambiental: 0103–7374; 3)

Discusses origin and impact of mercury contamination on fish and the ecosystem. Last chapter speculates on long-term effects.

2892 Ladefroux, Raymonde. Disparités sociales et approvisionnement alimentaire au Brésil: analyse aux échelles nationale et micro-régionale; Brasília et son district. (*in* Nourrir les métropoles d'Amérique Latine: approvisionnement et distribution. Paris: Editions L'Harmattan, 1995, p. 147–164, bibl., tables)

Uses Brasília as an example for explaining variations in food processing and distribution throughout Brazil. See also items **2882** and **2914**.

2893 Leonel, Mauro. Roads, Indians and the environment in the Amazon: from central Brazil to the Pacific Ocean. Translated by Edda Frost and Sam Poole. Copenhagen: IWGIA, 1992. 155 p.: bibl., ill., maps. (IWGIA document: 0105–6387; 72)

Highway BR-364 to the state of Rondônia and the proposed Pacific Highway to a Peruvian port are viewed as both conquering space and as weapons of conquest against indigenous peoples. Suggests mediation with independent interdisciplinary advisors prior to highway construction in hopes that the various cultural groups and the environment will be respected.

2894 Loureiro, Violeta Refkalefsky. Amazônia: estado, homem, natureza. Belém, Brazil: Edições CEJUP, 1992. 367 p.: bibl., maps. (Col. Amazoniana; 1)

Adequate overview of basic issues affecting the region with emphasis on land conflicts.

2895 Machado, Lia. A fronteira agrícola na Amazônia brasileira. (*Rev. Bras. Geogr.*, 54:2, abril/junho 1992, p. 27–55, bibl., graphs, maps)

Concludes that the country's discriminatory economic structure is exacerbated in a frontier region.

2896 McGrath, David G.; Fábio de Castro; and Célia Futemma. Reservas de lago e o manejo comunitário da pesca no Baixo Amazonas: uma avaliação preliminar. (*in* Amazônia e a crise da modernização. Belém, Brazil: Museu Paraense Emílio Goeldi, 1994, p. 389–402, bibl., graphs, map, tables)

Calls for a methodology to quantitatively evaluate the ecological and economic viability of fish stock reserves in the lowlands (*várzea*) of Baixo Amazonas, for both the benefit of riverine families and the establishment of a regional fishing policy.

2897 Medeiros, Rosa Maria Vieira. Les *assentamentos:* manifestations de la lutte pour la terre au Bresil. (*Cah. Outre-Mer*, 49:193, jan./mars 1996, p. 95–108, bibl., map, tables)

Examines the "landless movement" (Movimento dos Trabalhadores sem Terra), associated with rural social disturbances.

2898 Montagnini, Florencia; Anna Fanzares; and Sérgio Guimarães da Vinha. Studies on restoration ecology in the Atlantic forest region of Bahia, Brazil. (*Interciencia/Caracas*, 19:6, nov./dic. 1994, p. 323–330, graphs, tables)

Gives results of species/site relationship for 20 native tree species of about 15 years of age from the Estação Ecológica Pau-Brasil.

2899 Montenegro, Ana Maria. Le tourisme international au Brésil. (*Inf. Géogr./ Paris*, 58, 1994, p. 199–210, bibl., graphs, ill., maps, tables)

General overview of Brazil's tourist industry.

2900 Moran, Emilio F. Rich and poor ecosystems of Amazonia: an approach to management. (*in* The fragile tropics of Latin America: sustainable management of changing environments. Tokyo: United Nations Univ. Press, 1995, p. 45–67, bibl., graphs, maps, table)

Assessment based not only on nutrient availability and pH of soils, but also on other environmental and social processes relevant to future development and management. Two extremes are examined—the oligotrophic black-water basins and the anthropogenic forests with rich soils. Concludes that intensive agriculture in Amazonia is possible if restricted to eutrophic areas, especially in areas of anthropogenic forests and soils.

2901 Muller, Keith D.; Paulo R. Palhano Silva; and Baltazar M. de Souza. The *Sem Terra* (Without Land) Movement, Northeast Brazil. (*Pap. Proc. Appl. Geogr. Conf.*, 18, 1995, p. 155–158)

Examines land conflicts which ensue when landless peasants invade underutilized rural holdings, forcing reaction from landowners and authorities.

2902 Muñiz-Miret, Nuria et al. The economic value of managing the *açaí* palm—*Euterpe olerace* Mart.—in the floodplains of the Amazon Estuary, Pará, Brazil. (*For. Ecol. Manage.*, 87, 1996, p. 163–173)

Evaluates productivity, revenues, and cost feasibility of income generated from non-timber forest products produced under traditional household management in secondary forests and home gardens. Concludes that *açaí* is profitable within the well-established market for secondary forest products.

2903 Muricy, Carmen M. Environment in Brazil: a checklist of current serials. (*in* Seminar on the Acquisition of Latin American Library Materials (SALALM), *38th, Guadalajara, Mexico, 1993.* Technology, the environment, and social change. Albuquerque: SALALM Secretariat, Univ. of New Mexico, 1995, p. 135–158)

Updated list compiled by the Rio office of the Library of Congress.

2904 Nogueira, Marcos José et al. Condições geo-ambientais do semi-árido brasileiro. (*Ciênc. Tróp.*, 20:1, jan./junho 1992, p. 173–198, bibl., maps, tables)

Examines characteristics, environmental problems, and settlement influences in semi-arid regions of Brazil. Relies more on agricultural extension (EMBRAPA) data than on census data or radar (RADAMBRASIL) images.

2905 O novo Brasil urbano: impasses, dilemas, perspectivas. Organização de Maria Flora Gonçalves. Porto Alegre, Brazil: Mercado Aberto, [1995?] 358 p.: bibl., ill. (Série Novas perspectivas; 40)

Over 20 authors examine urban issues relative to the future of Brazilian cities. Topics include contemporary trends, national integration or fragmentation, and global integration.

2906 Pellerin, Joel et al. Metodologia de utilização de dados espaciais Landsat MSS e TM no estudo do uso do solo: região de Marília, SP. (*Geosul/Florianópolis*, 8:16, segundo semestre 1993, p. 79–98, bibl., graphs, maps, tables)

Includes local land survey from Landsat data.

2907 Plano estratégico de desenvolvimento do Amazonas: Planamazonas. Manaus, Brazil: Governo do Estado do Amazonas, 1994. 143 p.: col. ill., maps (some col.).

Development plan for the state of Amazonas, prepared by the state government and Superintendência do Desenvolvimento da Amazônia.

2908 Plano metropolitano da Grande São Paulo, 1994/2010. São Paulo: EMPLASA, 1994. 227 p.: ill., maps (some col.).

General overview of São Paulo state government's development plan for metropolitan São Paulo.

2909 Povos das águas: realidade e perspectivas na Amazônia. Organização de Lourdes Gonçalves Furtado, Wilma Leitão e Alex Fiuza de Mello. Belém, Brazil: PR/MCT/CNPq, Museu Paraense Emílio Goeldi, 1993. 292 p.: bibl., ill., maps. (Col. Eduardo Galvão)

Thirteen authors consider fishing as a viable economic activity. Examines changes in fishing societies, ecological impact, legislation and government policy, social movements, and possible establishment of fishing reserves—especially for the state of Pará. See *HLAS 55:2673* for annotation of a chapter in this work discussing traditional practices and their importance as viable ecological and economic models for sustainability.

2910 Roberts, J. Timmons. Expansion of television in eastern Amazonia. *(Geogr. Rev.,* 85:1, Jan. 1995, p. 41–49, bibl., maps)

Questions whether Amazonia can maintain a distinct identity despite media influences portraying cultural norms and values of Brazil's southeast.

2911 Rodrigues, Ivete Oliveira; Josinaldo dos Santos; and **Tereza Maria Ramos de Oliveira.** Médio vale do Paraíba do Sul: estado, políticas públicas e organização do espaço, 1930/1980. *(Rev. Bras. Geogr.,* 54:2, abril/junho 1992, p. 57–82, bibl., tables)

Discusses evolution of urban/industrial development in the Paraíba do Sul River Valley, which centers on São José dos Campos and Barra Mansa/Volta Redonda.

2912 Santos, Mílton. Por uma economia política da cidade: o caso de São Paulo. São Paulo: Editora HUCITEC; EDUC-Editora da PUC-SP, 1994. 145 p.: bibl., maps. (Estudos urbanos; 6)

Despite growth of metropolitan São Paulo, the area's portion of the GNP is diminished as other parts of the country develop.

2913 Santos, Mílton. A urbanização brasileira. São Paulo: Editora Hucitec, 1993. 157 p.: bibl., index, maps. (Estudos urbanos; 5)

Marxist examination of theoretical framework for study of urbanization.

2914 Santos, Roseli Rocha dos and **Marcos Roberto Vasconcelos.** Les changements dans la grande distribution au Brésil: l'exemple de la région sud. *(in* Nourrir les métropoles d'Amérique Latine: approvisionnement et distribution. Paris: Editions L'Harmattan, 1995, p. 257–272, bibl., map, tables)

Discusses changes in food distribution over last decade in Brazil, with focus on the south. See also items **2882** and **2892.**

2915 Schlüter, Heinz. Mensch und Gesellschaft, Natur und Umwelt in Brasilien. *(Lat.am. Stud./Nürnberg,* 33, 1994, p. 163–224, bibl.)

Methodological research uses interdisciplinary approach to examine Brazilian development strategies and their impact on the population and environment. Includes outline of government measures and organizational efforts directed toward fostering environmentally balanced development. [C.K. Converse]

2916 Schmidt, Heike. Die bedeutung der Mangroven für tropische Küstengewässer: Beispiel Brasilien. *(Geogr. Rundsch.,* 47:2, Feb. 1995, p. 128–132, photos)

Shrimp aquaculture is minimally developed and some pristine mangroves in the north still survive. In the south, mangroves are threatened by human activity.

2917 Schroeder, Paul and **Jack K. Winjum.** Brazil's carbon budget for 1990. *(Interciencia/Caracas,* 20:2, marzo/abril 1995, p. 68–75, bibl., tables)

Presents carbon dioxide release and uptake data for Brazil, demonstrating higher rates in Amazonia. Utilizes available published data and considers all known vegetation types.

2918 Sills, Erin O. and **Vitória Yamada Müller.** Domestic nature tourism in Brazil's protected areas: can Brazilian tourists save the Brazilian rain forest? *(SECOLAS Ann.,* 27, March 1996, p. 68–80, bibl., tables)

Case studies of 21 protected areas in seven states. Argues that public/private partnership is the most beneficial avenue for both ecotourism and forest conservation efforts.

2919 Silva, Ciléa Souza de. Saneamento básico e problemas ambientais na região metropolitana de Belém. *(Rev. Bras. Geogr.,* 54:1, jan./março 1993, p. 25–73, bibl., graphs, maps, photos, tables)

Extensive overview of Belém's metropolitan sanitation systems. Examines individual *bairros* to identify correlations between these systems and preventable diseases.

2920 Smith, Nigel J.H. *et al.* Amazonia: resiliency and dynamism of the land and its people. Toyko; New York: United Nations Univ. Press, 1995. 253 p: bibl., ill., maps. (UNU studies on critical environmental regions)

Balanced, worthwhile book includes chapters on threats to the environment, change and societal response, conservation and management, plantation crops, agroforestry, ranching, floodplain dynamics, and trends and opportunities.

2921 Smith, Nigel J.H. The enchanted Amazon rain forest: stories from a vanishing world. Gainesville: Univ. Press of Florida, 1996. 194 p.: bibl., ill., index, maps.

Insightful work, written for a popular audience, offers reader a general understanding of the region.

2922 Sternberg, Hilgard O'Reilly. Waters and wetlands of Brazilian Amazonia: an uncertain future. (*in* The fragile tropics of Latin America: sustainable management of changing environments. Tokyo: United Nations Univ. Press, 1995, p. 113–179, bibl., facsims., graph, maps, photos)

Comprehensive overview includes extensive background description and highlights the deterioration of the aquatic ecosystems. Discusses future uncertainties and extraregional linkages. Calls for a conceptual framework to identify and evaluate the numerous uncertainties before unmanageable crises result.

Tellechea de Arca, Mireya. Paraguay socioeconómico y cultural: hidrovía-MERCOSUR. See item **2848.**

2923 Viera, Ima Célia Guimarães *et al.* O renascimento da floresta no rastro da agricultura. (*Ciênc. Hoje,* 20:119, abril 1996, p. 38–44, graphs, map, photos)

Detailed study of a region near mouth of the Amazon where slash-and-burn agriculture was practiced. The region has undergone five to eight cycles of deforestation and regrowth.

2924 Voeks, Robert A. Sacred leaves of Candomblé: African magic, medicine, and religion in Brazil. Austin: Univ. of Texas Press, 1997. 236 p.: bibl., ill., index, maps.

Thorough ethnobotanical study of the origin, diffusion, use, classification, and cultural significance of Afro-Brazilian sacred plants.

2925 Wehrhahn, Rainer. São Paulo: umweltprobleme einer Megastadt. (*Geogr. Rundsch.,* 46:6, Juni 1994, p. 359–366, bibl., graphs, map, photos, tables)

Descriptive overview of environmental conditions in São Paulo state. Suggests protective measures.

Xavier, Renato. O gerenciamento costeiro no Brasil e a cooperação internacional. See item **4532.**

2926 Zeferino, Augusto César. Análise da localização espacial dos investimentos multinacionais no Brasil. (*Geografia/Rio Claro,* 16:2, out. 1991, p. 75–92, bibl., tables)

Concludes that capital investments will remain concentrated in the southeast, primarily in metropolitan São Paulo, unless industrial and regional policies become more favorable for other regions.

JOURNAL ABBREVIATIONS

Acta geogr. Acta geographica. Société de Géographie. Paris.

Am. Indíg. América Indígena. Instituto Indigenista Interamericano. México.

Am. Merid. América Meridional. Sociedad Regional de Ciencias Humanas. Montevideo.

Ann. Assoc. Am. Geogr. Annals of the Association of American Geographers. Lawrence, Kan.

Anu. Estud. Centroam. Anuario de Estudios Centroamericanos. Univ. de Costa Rica. San José.

Anu. Estud. Soc. Anuario Estudios Sociales. El Colegio de Puebla. México.

Archè/Rio de Janeiro. Archè. Faculdades Integradas Candido Mendes, Ipanema. Rio de Janeiro.

Arctic Alpine Res. Arctic and Alpine Research. Institute of Arctic and Alpine Research, Univ. of Colorado. Boulder.

Bol. Am. Boletín Americanista. Univ. de Barcelona, Facultad de Geografía e Historia, Depto. de Historia de América. Barcelona.

Bol. Estud. Geogr. Boletín de Estudios Geográficos. Univ. Nacional de Cuyo. Mendoza, Argentina.

Bol. Paul. Geogr. Boletim Paulista de Geografia. Associação dos Geógrafos Brasileiros. Seção Regional de São Paulo. São Paulo.

Bull. Inst. fr. étud. andin. Bulletin de l'Institut français d'études andines. Lima.

Bull. Lat. Am. Res. Bulletin of Latin American Research. Society for Latin American Studies. Oxford, England.

Cah. Outre-Mer. Les Cahiers d'Outre-Mer. Institut de géographie de la Faculté des lettres de Bordeaux; Institut de la France d'Outre-Mer; Société de géographie de Bordeaux. Bordeaux, France.

Caribb. Geogr. Caribbean Geography. Univ. of the West Indies, Dept. of Geography. Kingston, Jamaica.

Caribb. Q. Caribbean Quarterly. Univ. of the West Indies. Mona, Jamaica.

Ciênc. Amb. Ciência & Ambiente. Univ. Federal de Santa Maria. Santa Maria, Brazil.

Ciênc. Hoje. Ciência Hoje. Sociedade Brasileira para o Progresso da Ciência. Rio de Janeiro.

Cienc. Hoy. Ciencia Hoy. Asociación Ciencia Hoy; Morgan Antártica. Buenos Aires.

Cienc. Soc./Santo Domingo. Ciencia y Sociedad. Instituto Tecnológico de Santo Domingo.

Ciênc. Tróp. Ciência & Trópico. Fundação Joaquim Nabuco; Editora Massangana. Recife, Brazil.

Cuad. Geogr./Cádiz. Cuadernos de Geografía. Univ. de Cádiz. Cádiz, Spain.

Cuad. Hist./Santiago. Cuadernos de Historia. Univ. de Chile, Facultad de Humanidades y Educación, Depto. de Ciencias Históricas. Santiago.

Doc. Anàl. Geogr. Documents D'Anàlisi Geogràfica. Dept. de Geografia, Univ. Autònoma de Barcelona. Bellaterra, Spain.

Econ. Geogr. Economic Geography. Clark Univ., Worcester, Mass.

Environ. Manag. Environmental Management. Springer-Verlag New York, Inc. New York.

Erdkunde/Bonn. Erdkunde. Archiv für Wissenschaftliche Geographie. Univ. Bonn, Geographisches Institut. Bonn, Germany.

Estud. Front. Estudios Fronterizos. Instituto de Investigaciones Sociales, Univ. Autónoma de Baja California. Mexicali, Mexico.

Estud. Geogr./Madrid. Estudios Geográficos. Instituto de Economía y Geografía Aplicadas, Consejo Superior de Investigaciones Científicas. Madrid.

Estud. Perspect. Turismo. Estudios y Perspectivas en Turismo. Centro de Investigaciones, Estudios Turísticos. Buenos Aires.

EURE/Santiago. EURE: Revista Latinoamericana de Estudios Urbanos Regionales. Centro de Desarrollo Urbano y Regional, Univ. Católica de Chile. Santiago.

Explor. J. The Explorers Journal. New York.

For. Conserv. Hist. Forest & Conservation History. Forest History Society; Duke Univ. Press. Durham, N.C.

For. Ecol. Manage. Forest Ecology and Management. Elsevier Scientific Publishing Company. Amsterdam.

Front. Norte. Frontera Norte. Colegio de la Frontera Norte. Tijuana, Mexico.

Geofís. Int. Geofísica Internacional. Univ. Nacional Autónoma de México, Instituto de Geofísica. México.

Geogr. J. The Geographical Journal. The Royal Geographical Society. London.

Geogr. Rev. The Geographical Review. American Geographical Society. New York.

Geogr. Rundsch. Geographische Rundschau. Zeitschrift für Schulgeographie. Georg Westermann Verlag. Braunschweig, Germany.

Geografia/Rio Claro. Geografia. Associação de Geografia Teorética. Rio Claro, Brazil.

Geoistmo/San José. Geoistmo. Asociación de Profesionales en Geografía de Costa Rica. San José.

GeoJournal/Boston. GeoJournal. D. Reidel Publishing Co., Boston, Mass.

Geopolítica/Buenos Aires. Geopolítica. Instituto de Estudios Geopolíticos. Buenos Aires.

Geosul/Florianópolis. Geosul. Depto. de Geociências, Univ. Federal de Santa Catarina. Florianópolis, Brazil.

Glob. Environ. Change. Global Environmental Change: Human and Policy Dimensions. Butterworth-Heinemann. Guildford, England.

Herencia/San José. Herencia. Programa de Rescate y Revitalización del Patrimonio Cultural. San José.

Hum. Ecol. Human Ecology. Plenum Publishing Corp., New York.

Inf. géogr./Paris. L'information géographique. Paris.

Integr. Latinoam. Integración Latinoamericana. Instituto para la Integración de América Latina. Buenos Aires.

Interciencia/Caracas. Interciencia. Asociación Interciencia. Caracas.

Invest. Geogr./Murcia. Investigaciones Geográficas. Instituto Universitario de Geografía, Univ. de Alicante. Murcia, Spain.

J. Geogr. Journal of Geography. National Council of Geographic Education. Menasha, Wis.

Jam. J. Jamaica Journal. Institute of Jamaica. Kingston.

LARR. Latin American Research Review. Latin American Research Review Board. Univ. of New Mexico, Albuquerque, N.M.

Lat.am. Stud./Nürnberg. Lateinamerika Studien. Univ. Erlangen-Nürnberg, Sektion Lateinamerika. Nürnberg, Germany.

Leguas/Mendoza. Leguas: Revista Argentina de Geografía. Univ. Nacional de Cuyo, Facultad de Filosofía y Letras. Mendoza, Argentina.

Meridiano Rev. Geogr. Meridiano: Revista de Geografía. Centro de Estudios Alexander von Humboldt. Buenos Aires.

Mesoamérica/Antigua. Mesoamérica. Centro de Investigaciones Regionales de Mesoamérica. Antigua, Guatemala.

Mitt. österr. Geogr. Ges. Mitteilungen der österreichischen Geographischen Gesellschaft. Verleger, Herausgeber und Eigentümer. Vienna.

Mt. Res. Dev. Mountain Research and Development. International Mountain Society. Boulder, Colo.

Notas Pobl. Notas de Población. Centro Latinoamericano de Demografía. Santiago.

Paisajes Geogr. Paisajes Geográficos. Centro Panamericano de Estudios e Investigaciones Geográficas. Quito.

Pap. Proc. Appl. Geogr. Conf. Papers and Proceedings of the Applied Geography Conferences. Dept. of Geography, Kent State Univ.; State Univ. of New York (SUNY) at Binghamton.

Perf. Latinoam. Perfiles Latinoamericanos. Facultad Latinoamericana de Ciencias Sociales. México.

Petermanns Geogr. Mitt. Petermanns Geographische Mitteilungen. Justus Perthes. Gotha, Germany.

Presencia/San Salvador. Presencia. Centro de Investigaciones Tecnológicas y Científicas. San Salvador.

Principes/Lawrence. Principes. International Palm Society. Lawrence, Kan.

Probl. Desarro. Problemas del Desarrollo: Revista Latinoamericana de Economía. Instituto de Investigaciones Económicas, UNAM. México.

Prof. Geogr. The Professional Geographer. Assn. of American Geographers. Washington.

Quat. Res./New York. Quaternary Research. Academic Press. New York.

Rábida/Huelva. Rábida. Patronato Provincial del V Centenario del Descubrimiento. Huelva, Spain.

Real. Econ./Buenos Aires. Realidad Económica. Instituto Argentino para el Desarrollo Económico (IADE). Buenos Aires.

Relaciones/Zamora. Relaciones. El Colegio de Michoacán. Zamora, Mexico.

Rev. Andin. Revista Andina. Centro Bartolomé de las Casas. Cusco, Peru.

Rev. Bras. Geogr. Revista Brasileira de Geografia. Conselho Nacional de Geografia, Instituto Brasileiro de Geografia e Estatística. Rio de Janeiro.

Rev. Chil. Hist. Geogr. Revista Chilena de Historia y Geografía. Sociedad Chilena de Historia y Geografía. Santiago.

Rev. Eme-Eme. Revista Eme-Eme. Univ. Católica Madre y Maestra. Santiago de los Caballeros, Dominican Republic.

Rev. Eur. Revista Europea de Estudios Latinoamericanos y del Caribe = European Review of Latin American and Caribbean Studies. Center for Latin American Research and Documentation; Royal Institute of Linguistics and Anthropology. Amsterdam.

Rev. Geogr. Chile. Revista Geográfica de Chile. Instituto Geográfico Militar. Santiago.

Rev. Geogr./Mérida. Revista Geográfica. Univ. de Los Andes. Mérida, Venezuela.

Rev. Geogr./México. Revista Geográfica. Instituto Panamericano de Geografía e Historia, Comisión de Geografía. México.

Rev. Geogr. Norte Gd. Revista de Geografía Norte Grande. Pontificia Univ. Católica de Chile. Santiago.

Rev. Geogr. Venez. Revista Geográfica Venezolana. Univ. de los Andes. Mérida, Venezuela.

Rev. Indias. Revista de Indias. Consejo Superior de Investigaciones Científicas, Instituto Gonzalo Fernández de Oviedo. Madrid.

Rev. Interam. Bibliogr. Revista Interamericana de Bibliografía. Organization of American States. Washington.

Rev. Nac./Montevideo. Revista Nacional. Ministerio de Instrucción Pública. Montevideo.

Rev. UNIBE. Revista UNIBE de Ciencia y Cultura. Univ. Iberoamericana. Santo Domingo.

Rev. Univ. Geogr. Revista Universitaria de Geografía. Univ. Nacional del Sur. Bahía Blanca, Argentina.

SECOLAS Ann. SECOLAS Annals. Southeastern Conference on Latin American Studies; Thomasson Printing Co. Carrollton, Ga.

Senderos/Bogotá. Senderos. Biblioteca Nacional de Colombia. Bogotá.

Signos Univ. Signos Universitarios: Revista de la Universidad del Salvador. Univ. del Salvador. Buenos Aires.

Tareas/Panamá. Tareas. Centro de Estudios Latinoamericanos (CELA). Panamá.

Third World Plan. Rev. Third World Planning Review. Liverpool Univ. Press. Liverpool, England.

Todo es Hist. Todo es Historia. Buenos Aires.

Trace/México. Trace. Centre d'études mexicaines et centraméricaines. México.

Universum/Talca. Universum. Univ. de Talca. Talca, Chile.

World Bank Econ. Rev. The World Bank Economic Review. World Bank. Washington.

Yearbook/CLAG. Yearbook. Conference of Latin Americanist Geographers; Ball State Univ., Muncie, Ind.

GOVERNMENT AND POLITICS

GENERAL

DAVID DENT, *Professor of Political Science, Towson University*
PAUL C. SONDROL, *Associate Professor of Political Science, University of Colorado, Colorado Springs*

SCHOLARLY LITERATURE ON THE GOVERNMENT and politics of Latin America continues to flourish, offering interesting research questions and cross-national comparisons touching on a variety of themes from the recent past. While there continues to be little agreement on specific variables, theories or characteristics that are most essential for understanding the political landscape, a vibrant eclecticism in the research agenda continues to offer interesting observations on politics and social change in Latin America. The following themes and recent works illuminate the major research trends in the literature since *HLAS 55*.

Democratization and Transitology. The process of institutionalizing democracy continues as the crux of current scholarship, but remains a difficult topic of study given the enormous range of structures and practices across the region. Taking the long view, Huber and Stephens' "Agrarian structure and political power in comparative perspective" stresses the importance of historical contingencies and multiple paths to development, and illustrates how landlords, peasants, and class-State constellations interact and inform different, but largely authoritarian, political trajectories in Latin America (item **2951**). More optimistically, Remmer's "The process of democratization in Latin America" summarizes much of the democratization literature over the past decade and argues that the current polyarchic cycle is a distinct phase in which broad electoral participation and respect for opposition rights have become durable features of politics (item **2977**). Press freedom may be seen as a common and indispensable element of democracy, but Salwen's *Latin American journalism* breaks new ground in examining government-press relations and describing impediments to democracy within the context of mass communications (item **2982**).

Institutional Design. Monographs on State reformation and political structures or institutions continue apace as Latin American governments attempt to blend and reconcile workable elements of both tradition and modernity. Mauceri's excellent case study "State reform, coalitions and the neoliberal *Autogolpe* in Peru" argues the *Fujimorazo* of 1992 was an elite attempt to refashion the Peruvian State and its relations with society via economic reform and repression (item **3577**). Loveman's "'Protected democracies' and military guardianship" notes how consolidating democracies vest residual authority (constitutional or supraconstitutional) in military "political guardians" (item **2963**). The old "presidential versus parliamentary" debate regarding system-type as efficacious for democracy receives renewed attention in Thibaut's "Presidencialismo, parlamentarismo y el problema de la consolidación democrática en América Latina" (item **2988**). Often overlooked in the analysis of consolidating democracies is political decentralization at the community or municipal level. Palma Carvajal's "Decentralization and democracy" examines this nexus and urges political subdivisions to take on new functions and responsibilities in these difficult transitions (item **2972**). Finally, Mainwaring and Scully's *Building democratic institutions* focuses on the degree to which political party systems in Latin America are institutionalized, and examines consequences for sustained democracy derived from differing party systems (item **2966**). Using a comparative perspective, Lijphart and Waisman find many similarities in the institutional design of democratization in Eastern Europe and Latin America (item **2952**). Tulchin's edited volume, *The consolidation of democracy in Latin America*, includes a chapter arguing that multilateral diplomacy and international organizations have helped to consolidate democracy by pressuring the remaining authoritarian and recidivist democracies in Latin America (item **2938**).

Social Movements. The interaction of social movements and elite reformers in shaping newer democracies permeates scholarly discourse on Latin America. Numerous works demonstrate that rumors of the death of the Latin American left with the collapse of communism are greatly exaggerated. Among many, Rénique's "The Latin American left: epitaph or new beginning?" suggests that the left, while marginalized, remains alive, dynamic and adaptive (item **2978**). More pessimistic is Haber's "Recent trends in the study of Latin American social movements," revealing limited successes of movement-sponsored reforms in shaping the policy process throughout most of Latin America (item **2957**). The relationship between social movements and nongovernmental organizations is presented in Reilly's *New paths to development in Latin America* where comparative analysis reveals that democracy depends on binding the organizations of civil society through grassroots collective action (item **2971**).

Women and Politics. Interest in the role of women and politics in Latin America continues to increase for social scientists. Jaquette's *The women's movement in Latin America* analyzes women's roles in diverse transitions to democracy in which they played a part, and the distances that remain for women's equality (item **2954**). In Marks' edited volume *Women and grass roots democracy in the Americas*, the contributors focus on how women leaders can take a more effective role in the political and civic life of their respective countries (item **2993**). Gender relations are also included among the numerous themes dealing with the rapidly growing Pentecostal movement examined in Cleary and Steward-Gambino's *Power, politics, and Pentecostals in Latin America* (item **2975**).

Religion and Politics. Though never entirely ignored in the past, Christianity—as a source of inspiration and legitimation of ideas, ideologies, social movements, and regimes—now commands substantial scholarly attention. Sigmund's "Christian democracy, Liberation Theology, and political culture in Latin America" argues that mainstream Catholicism in Latin America contributes to the democratic consensus in Latin American civil society today (item **2983**). Berryman's "Is Latin America turning pluralist?: recent writings on religion" emphasizes Protestant expansion, Catholic self-assessments, and the status of Liberation Theology (item **2930**). On the darker side, Gutierrez's "Iglesia Catolica, estado y democracia" highlights the distinctive institutional conduct, attitudes and complicity in State terrorism of the Argentine Church during the military regime of 1976–83 (item **3728**).

Privatizing Politics. New efforts at institutional design and shrinkage of the

State apparatus have placed greater emphasis on privatizing politics through the use of nongovernmental organizations. In *Building the third sector: Latin America's private research centers and nonprofit development*, Levy examines the growing importance of private research centers in the process of development of nongovernmental policy-making (item **2960**). This theme will receive greater attention as new economic formulas foster development options that place greater demands on private, rather than public, solutions.

2927 Arraztoa Jaimerena, María Teresa.
Las mujeres en los parlamentos latinoamericanos. Investigación de Tirza Rivera-Cira *et al.* Valparaíso, Chile: Univ. Católica de Valparaíso, Centro de Estudios y Asistencia Legislativa, 1993. 86 p.: bibl., ill.

Quantitative and analytical results of standard surveys of female political participation in Latin America over the past 20 years. Includes a scholarly historical overview of women and politics, profiles of women in Latin American legislatures, and a concise synthesis of the impact women have made on specific policy outcomes. Documentation reveals an uphill battle against resistant patriarchal societies.

2928 Bejarano Avila, Jesús Antonio. Una agenda para la paz: aproximaciones desde la teoría de la resolución de conflictos. Bogotá: TM Editores, 1995. 268 p.: bibl. (Sociología y política. Académica)

Presents several essays on theories of conflict resolution and on differences and similarities of the peace processes in Colombia and Central America. Author, who served as presidential peace advisor during the Gaviria Administration and as ambassador in El Salvador and Guatemala, was uniquely positioned to observe these processes and has developed some key insights into the difficult challenge of ending armed conflicts. Essential reading for anyone interested in these issues. [M. Chernick]

Benedetti, Mario. Perplejidades de fin de siglo. See *HLAS 56:3863*.

2929 Benegas Lynch, Alberto. Hacia el autogobierno: una crítica al poder político. Prólogo del premio nobel en economía James M. Buchanan. Buenos Aires: Emecé Editores, 1993. 516 p.: bibl., index.

The author is perhaps Argentina's leading exponent of the Austrian School of Economics. He argues for a minimal State that would leave most social decisions up to freely contractiong adults. Nobel laureate James Buchanan contributes a brief prologue. [P. Lewis]

2930 Berryman, Phillip. Is Latin America turning pluralist?: recent writings on religion. (*LARR*, 30:3, 1995, p. 107–122, bibl.)

Excellent review essay (17 books) discusses current religious developments with emphasis on Protestant expansion, Catholic self-assessments, and the status of liberation theology. Argues that with increasing democratization the identity of the "oppressor" is more diffuse at grass-roots level.

2931 Bronstein, Arturo S. Societal change and industrial relations in Latin America: trends and prospects. (*Int. Labour Rev.*, 134:2, 1995, p. 163–186)

Describes the far-reaching evolution of industrial relations in Latin America over the past 10–15 years. Democratization and a resulting opening to autonomous collective bargaining, the blurring of ideological lines, and new labor legislation all bode well for organized labor. Are these tendencies indicative of structural change, or merely an isolated interlude prior to a return to the traditional pattern of high levels of State intervention and corporate regulation of labor? Author is skeptical.

2932 Buchanan, Paul G. State, labor, capital: democratizing class relations in the Southern Cone. Pittsburgh, Pa.: Univ. of Pittsburgh Press, 1995. 414 p.: bibl., index. (Pitt Latin American series)

Comparative examination of the institutional networks that help to sustain new democracies in Argentina, Brazil, and Uruguay. In a discussion of the role played by labor, capital, and the State in democratizing regimes, author argues that class compromise between working classes and capitalists that is mediated by State institutions (national labor administrations) is the most important variable for institutionalizing democratic capitalist rule. Useful treatment of the role of organized labor and institutional networks in regime transition with an excellent bibliography and index.

2933 Building democracy with women: reflecting on experience in Latin America and the Caribbean. Edited by Ana Maria Brasileiro. New York: United Nations Development Fund for Women, 1996. 81 p.

Articles in this small book are uneven in quality and lightly documented, but they illustrate the practical ways that women throughout Latin America and the Caribbean have organized to promote democracy, rights, and citizenship in a gender-sensitive fashion. Grass-roots projects—from Brazil and Paraguay to Trinidad and Tobago—range from work with parliamentarians and judges on gender sensitization to empowering women to participate in national elections and the policy-planning processes.

Burki, Shahid Javed and **Sebastian Edwards.** Dismantling the populist State: the unfinished revolution in Latin America and the Caribbean. See item **1271.**

2934 Castro Escudero, Teresa. El problema militar y la consolidación de la democracia en América Latina. (*Estud. Latinoam. / México*, 2:3, enero/junio 1995, p. 33–54)

Sweeping generalizations regarding "the role of supervision and control of the armed forces over the whole [democratization] process." Article's provocative treatment of the effects of neoliberalism and "new interventionist American policies" on Latin American militaries is valuable despite glaring weaknesses in analysis.

Caviedes, César N. Estudios sobre la variabilidad espacial del voto en América Latina. See item **2392.**

2935 Child Vélez, Jorge *et al.* Rompiendo la corriente: un debate al neoliberalismo. Recopilación de Jairo Estrada Alvarez y Jesús Gualdrón Sandoval. Prólogo de Darío Fajardo Montaña. Bogotá: Centro de Estudios e Investigaciones Sociales, 1992. 339 p.: bibl. (Serie Crítica y alternativa)

Humanistic critique of neoliberal economic thinking by Colombian social scientists who argue that neoliberalism is much more than a theory of economic development. In the debate assembled in this volume, authors' attack the principal postulates of the economic doctrine of neoliberalism emphasizing its internal contradictions and the absence of an historical perspective on the human situation.

2936 Ciclo de conferencias. México: Instituto Federal Electoral, 1992. 427 p.: ports. (Serie Formación y desarrollo)

Collection based on conference sponsored by Mexico's Instituto Federal Electoral includes essays by some of Mexico's leading intellectuals such as Carlos Monsiváis, and students of electoral processes including Silva Gómez Tagle. Contributors provide a policy-oriented, rather than scholarly-oriented, view of electoral change in 1991–92. [R. Camp]

2937 Collier, Ruth Berins. Labor politics and regime change: internal trajectories versus external influences. (*in* Latin America in the 1940s: war and postwar transitions. Edited by David Rock. Berkeley: Univ. of California Press, 1994, p. 59–88, tables)

Impressive symbiosis of theory and data. Author introduces idea of ". . . critical junctures or historic watershed—particular 'moments' or transitions of fundamental political reorientation" and argues that the 1940s represent precisely such a historic moment. Utilizing two analytic perspectives: the influence of international events (World War II, the Cold War) and internal events (the trajectory of change deriving from the initial incorporation of labor), Collier masterfully combines these perspectives via a comparative analysis of Brazil, Chile, Mexico, and Venezuela. A major contribution.

Collier, Ruth Berins and **David Collier.** Shaping the political arena: critical junctures, the labor movement, and regime dynamics in Latin America. See *HLAS 56:1053.*

2938 The consolidation of democracy in Latin America. Edited by Joseph L. Tulchin with Bernice Romero. Boulder, Colo.: Lynne Rienner Publishers, 1995. 187 p.: bibl., index. (Woodrow Wilson Center current studies on Latin America)

Series of eight papers on the prospects for consolidated democracy in Latin America prepared in 1993 by the Latin American Program of the Woodrow Wilson International Center in conjunction with the Olof Palme International Foundation. Selected essays focus on: 1) obstacles to the democratization process; 2) the political consequences of economic reform programs; and 3) the external context for democratization. In a perceptive chapter on "transitology," Schmitter argues that the increased reliance on multilateral diplomacy and international organizations in the aftermath of the Cold War has brought pressure to bear on the remaining non-democracies and recidivist democracies in the region. Authors express concern about the negative impact of some economic reforms on democratic consolidation.

2939 Constructing culture and power in Latin America. Edited by Daniel H. Levine. Ann Arbor: Univ. of Michigan Press, 1993. 479 p.: bibl., 2 ill. (The Comparative studies in society and history book series)

A notable collection of complementary essays, largely culled from the pages of *Comparative studies in society and history*, examine the ways in which power (exerted by capital, markets, peasants, women, elites, and States) and culture (expressed in official policy, institutions, and communal life) have been constructed out of ordinary experience. Excellent bibliographies accompany all of the articles.

Corporación de Estudios para el Desarrollo (Ecuador). Descentralización y gobiernos municipales. See item **3424.**

2940 Dakolias, Maria. The judicial sector in Latin America and the Caribbean: elements of reform. Washington: World Bank, 1996. xvi, 79 p.: bibl., ill. (World Bank technical paper, 0253-7494; 319)

Professional analysis of essential elements of judicial reform, as provided in any country-specific review by the World Bank. As political and economic development continue, greater attention needs to be given to judicial reform. Basic elements of judicial reform include: guaranteeing judicial independence through changes in judicial budgeting, judicial appointment, and disciplinary systems; adopting procedural reforms; enhancing public access to justice; incorporating gender issues in the reform process; and redefining/expanding legal education and training.

2941 Democracy in Latin America: patterns and cycles. Edited by Roderic Ai Camp. Wilmington, Del.: Scholarly Resources, 1995. 309 p.: bibl., ill. (Jaguar books on Latin America; 10)

Collection of some of the best articles previously published by political scientists on the problems of democracy and development in Latin America highlight the nature of intellectual debate on the subject. Brief introduction by Mattiace and Camp examines the scholarly work on the conditions and variables—political culture and structure, grassroots democratic practices, and economic crisis management—that are essential to constructing and consolidating a democratic regime. Although useful for providing a historical context on the nature of democracy and development in Latin America, the overall value of the volume is hampered by the absence of an index.

2942 Díaz, Alvaro. Tendencias de la reestructuración económica y social en Latinoamérica. (*Síntesis/Madrid,* 22, julio/dic. 1994, p. 99–130, bibl.)

Analysis concentrates on Mexico and Chile, two countries where neoliberal economic reforms and liberalizing political openings advanced significantly between 1983–93. Díaz correlates, somewhat illogically, expanding markets (modes of decentralized coordination based on price systems) with political liberalization (hierarchies based upon "authority and command"). Article is nebulous and thought-provoking at the same time.

2943 Dix, Robert H. Military coups and military rule in Latin America. (*Armed Forces Soc.,* 20:3, Spring 1994, p. 439–456, tables)

Useful article on the incidence of military interventions/rule over the last quarter-century. Dix marshals evidence from the 1980s that generally contradicts the expectations of scholars (Fossum, Nordlinger, Wiarda) writing a generation ago, that military coups would continue to be frequent and normal in Latin America. Concludes that, while coups and military rule have diminished in the 1980s and early 1990s, we may be witnessing the emergence of a more institutionalized form of military involvement than in the past, creating hybrid regimes falling short of either direct military dictatorships or crypto-military democracies.

Echegaray, Fabián. ¿Voto económico o referendum político?: los determinantes de las elecciones presidenciales en América Latina, 1982–1994. See item **1304.**

2944 Elecciones y sistemas de partidos en América Latina. Edited by Dieter Nohlen. San José: IIDH, Instituto Interamericano de Derechos Humanos; CAPEL, Centro de Asesoría y Promoción Electoral, 1993. 516 p.: bibl.

A collaborative effort by analysts associated with the Interamerican Human Rights Institute in San José, Costa Rica and the Center of Electoral Assessment and Promotion on electoral systems, political parties, and party systems and the relationship between elections and democratic consolidation. Examples are drawn primarily from Colombia, Ecuador, Venezuela, Argentina, Costa Rica, Chile, Dominican Republic, Nicaragua, Mexico, Guatemala, El Salvador, and Brazil. Value of work stems from its multinational contributors and its interdisciplinary approach to the subject of political parties and elections in Latin America.

Estrategias de desarrollo: intentando cambiar la vida. See item **4542**.

Fernández Alberté, María Felisa. Descentralización política, o, dimensiones de la libertad. See item **3710**.

2945 Galindo, Florencio. El "fenómeno de las sectas" fundamentalistas: la conquista evangélica de América Latina. 2. ed. Navarra, España: Editorial Verbo Divino, 1994. 463 p.: bibl,. index.

With little pretense to scholarly objectivity, Galindo (Colombian priest) nevertheless renders a profoundly poignant, philosophical, spiritual work analyzing the reasons behind the onslaught of Evangelical Protestantism in Latin America, and the seeming decline of Spanish Roman Catholicism. Excellent documentation.

2946 Godio, Julio. Economía de mercado, Estado regulador y sindicatos. Buenos Aires: Editorial Legasa, 1993. 219 p.: bibl.

The author is a labor lawyer for various unions. He argues for a "mixed" economy that will allow the government and the workers to balance off the power of capital, which is becoming too great under neoliberalism. [P. Lewis]

2947 Gross, Liza. Handbook of leftist guerrilla groups in Latin America and the Caribbean. In collaboration with the Council

on Hemispheric Affairs. Boulder, Colo.: Westview Press, 1995. 165 p.: bibl., ill.

Concise treatment of leftist guerrilla groups—Marxist-Leninist, Trotskyist, Maoist, Guevaraist, Castroist—in 19 countries includes important information on each organization's date of origin, its principal leadership, and its core ideology. The historical and political context is provided for each movement, together with details of the organization's primary activities and its present status. Well-written and useful reference source on the subject includes bibliography organized by country. However, lack of an index makes the data somewhat difficult to access.

2948 Guillermoprieto, Alma. The heart that bleeds: Latin America now. New York: Knopf, 1994. 353 p.

Poignant stories capturing the essence of everyday life for average Latin Americans. This *New Yorker* essayist and Mexican-born journalist perspicaciously covers topics from violence, inequality, and survival to the faithless politicians and the faithful perseverance with which people strive to believe. Beautifully written vignettes of life in Bogotá, Managua, Mexico City, Lima, Buenos Aires, and La Paz illuminate both constants and differences in the political cultures of Latin America.

2949 Hensel, Paul R. One thing leads to another: recurrent militarized disputes in Latin America, 1816–1986. (*J. Peace Res.*, 31 : 3, Aug. 1994, p. 281–297, bibl., tables)

Ambitious article on three specific aspects of recurrent militarized interstate conflict with emphasis on the likelihood of a subsequent dispute, interval between conflicts, and the characteristics of initiators of disputes. A solid article, but in sore need of a good comparativist to provide context and perceptive analysis.

2950 Huang, Wendeng. Zhongguo Gongchandang yu Lamei Zhendang Guanxide Xianzhuang yu Qianjing [Present situation of, and prospects for, relations between the Chinese Communist Party and Latin American political parties]. (*Lat. Am. Stud. / Beijing,* 3, 1996, p. 49–53)

This article, one of the few works published in China on this topic, emphasizes the importance of Latin America to the Chinese Communist Party (CCP) in its efforts to develop ties with other political parties. At present, more than 90 Latin American parties have various forms of contact with the CCP. Discusses present situation and predicts that relations will continue to develop steadily in the future. Author is a CCP researcher. [M. Xianglin]

2951 Huber, Evelyne and **John D. Stephens.**
Conclusion: agrarian structure and political power in comparative perspective. (*in* Agrarian structure & political power: landlord & peasant in the making of Latin America. Pittsburgh, Pa.: Univ. of Pittsburgh Press, 1995, p. 183–232)
Articulate and compelling attempt to provide a more general evaluation of Barrington Moore's seminal *Social origins of dictatorship and democracy.* Analysis demonstrates that landlords, peasants, class-State constellations, and a country's position in the world economy all interacted to spur different (largely authoritarian) political trajectories in Latin America. An excellent work highlighting the importance of historical contingencies and multiple paths to development.

2952 Institutional design in new democracies. Edited by Arend Lijphart and Carlos Waisman. Boulder, Colo.: Westview Press, 1996. 276 p.: bibl., ill., index.
Excellent treatment of the problems involved in the institutional design of democratization. Using a comparative perspective, authors examine the relationship between the tasks of institutional design and the policy outcomes of economic and political liberalization in Latin America and in Central and Eastern Europe. Focuses on how institutions serve a market economy, the design of electoral laws, and executive-legislative relations. Although differences do exist, authors find that "Eastern Europe and Latin America are conceptual and theoretical neighbors rather than distant strangers" to the process of democratization.

2953 Jaquette, Jane S. Conclusion: women's political participation and the prospects for democracy. (*in* The women's movement in Latin America: participation and democracy. Edited by Jane S. Jaquette. Boulder, Colo.: Westview Press, 1994, p. 223–238)
See item **2954.**

2954 Jaquette, Jane S. Introduction: from transition to participation—women's movements and democratic politics. (*in* The women's movement in Latin America: participation and democracy. Edited by Jane S. Jaquette. Boulder, Colo.: Westview Press, 1994, p. 1–11)
Taken together, introduction and conclusion (item **2953**) of this volume illustrate the vitality and complexity of women's (and feminist) movements in Latin America since 1989. By analyzing women's roles in very diverse democratic transitions (Brazil, Chile, Argentina, Uruguay, Peru, Nicaragua, and Mexico), goals and strategies in consolidating democracies that women helped bring to power, Jaquette demonstrates the distance women's movements in Latin America have travelled, and that much terrain remains to be covered.

Latin American political economy in the age of neoliberal reform: theoretical and comparative perspectives for the 1990s. See item **1373.**

2955 Latin American politics and development. Edited by Howard J. Wiarda and Harvey F. Kline. 4th ed., fully rev. and updated. Boulder, Colo.: Westview Press, 1996. 1 v.: bibl., index.
Most recent edition of popular text on the government and politics of Latin America, revised and updated with emphasis on recent developments since 1990. Leading specialists on the region provide an overview of Latin American development and policy processes and a detailed treatment of each country. Volume contains no bibliography but each chapter contains a recent list of suggested readings for those who want to probe the subject further. Not all the chapters devote some discussion to the "international arena," or "foreign policy," and those that do are often quite brief and devoid of the important role of inter-American organizations.

2956 Lavrin, Asunción. Suffrage in South America: arguing a difficult cause. (*in* Suffrage and beyond: international feminist perspectives. Edited by Caroline Daley and Melanie Nolan. New York: New York Univ. Press, 1995, p. 184–209)
The struggle for women's suffrage was difficult and remains an important but largely ignored chapter in Latin American political

history. This well-documented chapter analyzes Uruguay, Chile, Argentina, and Colombia, the first discussions of feminist ideas, the organization of women's parties, and the full participation of women in national politics during the first half of the 20th century.

2957 Lawrence Haber, Paul. Identity and political process: recent trends in the study of Latin American social movements. (*LARR*, 31:1, 1996, p. 171–188, bibl.)

Provides succinct explanation of the (uneven) evolution of social movements in Latin America and corresponding corpus of scholarship. From the heady 1980s transitions to democracy to the present neoliberal, consolidative phase, Haber urges scholars to stop romanticizing what has happened to social movements, revealing the limited successes of movement-sponsored reforms in shaping the policy process in most countries in Latin America.

2958 Leff, Enrique. Ecología y capital: raciodidad ambiental, democracia participativa y desarrollo sustentable. 2. ed., corr. y aum. México: Siglo Veintiuno Editores, 1994. 437 p.: bibl., index. (Sociología y política)

Second edition criticizes the prevailing discourse regarding sustainable development, analyzes the multiple connections between economy and ecology, and philosophizes utopian futures for Latin America. A thought-provoking treatise of the brutal excesses (on man and nature) of political and economic development.

2959 Legislatures and the new democracies in Latin America. Edited by David Close. Boulder, Colo.: Lynne Rienner Publishers, 1995. 182 p.: bibl., index.

What role will legislatures have in the efforts to consolidate democracy in Latin America? Seven case-studies (Mexico, El Salvador, Nicaragua, Argentina, Brazil, Chile, and Uruguay) focus on "the conditions under which legislatures work in Latin America's transitional polities." Needler suggests that the current trend toward democratic rule—"the most democratic in Latin American history"—may usher in a greater role for legislatures in promoting governments free of military intervention, authoritarian dictatorships, and intrusive US foreign policymaking. Legislatures now merit much more attention than in past studies of government and politics.

2960 Levy, Daniel C. Building the third sector: Latin America's private research centers and nonprofit development. Pittsburgh, Pa.: Univ. of Pittsburgh Press, 1996. 368 p.: bibl., index. (Pitt Latin American series)

A trailblazing account of the transformation of Latin American society and politics by nongovernmental organizations over the past quarter century. This examination of the nonprofit sector, and its interaction with the for-profit and public sectors, highlights the importance of private research centers (PRCs) within the nexus of higher education and nonprofit privatization policies. Author argues that PRCs perform many important tasks in the process of development, particularly in the areas of private finance, international philanthropy, market mechanisms, and nongovernmental policymaking. Well researched with a useful bibliography on the subject.

2961 Levy, Daniel C. Latin America's think tanks: the roots of nonprofit privatization. (*Stud. Comp. Int. Dev.*, 30:2, Summer 1995, p. 3–25, appendix, bibl.)

Noted Mexican specialist's important analysis of nonprofit private research centers, which have ". . . largely displaced public universities and achieved a leadership sometimes bordering on monopoly in social research . . ." in most of Latin America. Article identifies and examines the key factors (State repression, State weakness, public university problems, and finance) accelerating the massive growth of nonprofit private activity. Excellent comparative study and scholarly references.

2962 Linz, Juan José; Arend Lijphart; and Arturo Valenzuela. A opção parlamentarista. Organização de Bolivar Lamounier. Prefácio de Carlos Eduardo Lins da Silva. São Paulo: IDESP; Editora Sumaré, 1991? 191 p.: bibl.

Collection of essays by leading political scientists who champion the advantages of parliamentarism over presidentialism. Mostly translations of essays that had great impact in the comparative politics subfield in the late 1980s-early 1990s. Another attempt to sway opinion in advance of the plebiscite of 1993, in which parliamentarism was roundly rejected by Brazilian voters. [T. Power]

2963 Loveman, Brian. Protected democracies and military guardianship: political transactions in Latin America, 1978–1993. (*J. Interam. Stud. World Aff.*, 36:2, Summer 1994, p. 105–189, bibl.)

Excellent comparative study (culture, institutions, content analysis of constitutions) of consolidating democracies vesting residual authority (constitutional or supraconstitutional) in military "political guardians." Despite the halcyon days following the breakdown of authoritarian regimes in the 1980s, author notes that there has been little erosion of the underlying impediments to democracy—both social and economic—afflicting Latin America since colonial times (racism, labor repression, maldistribution of wealth, and politicized militaries). Well-documented for further research.

2964 Mahan, Elizabeth. Media, politics, and society in Latin America. (*LARR*, 30:3, 1995, p. 138–162, bibl.)

Review essay highlighting the impact of globalization on the organization, financing, and regulation of mass media systems and on the production of information and entertainment programming. Several themes are discussed: media dependence on foreign information, technology, and capital; predominance of private capital in establishing the operational norms and programming policies; the impact of advertising on program content; and the role of new technologies. A valuable contribution, integrating history, case studies, politics, and culture.

2965 Mainwaring, Scott. Democracy in Brazil and the Southern Cone: achievements and problems. (*J. Interam. Stud. World Aff.*, 37:1, Spring 1995, p. 113–179, bibl., tables)

Exhaustive comparative work analyzes the new democracies in Argentina, Brazil, Uruguay, and Chile. Focuses on governance, performance, and democratic statecraft, rather than on civil society. Compares achievements and failures while pointing to remaining obstacles to democratic consolidation. Empirically rich and theoretically well-informed, helpful bibliography. Recommended. [T. Power]

2966 Mainwaring, Scott and **Timothy R. Scully.** Introduction: party systems in Latin America. (*in* Building democratic institutions: party systems in Latin America. Edited by Scott Mainwaring and Timothy R. Scully. Stanford: Stanford Univ. Press, 1995, p. 1–34, tables)

Chapter offers a "beginning point for a new comparative study of Latin American parties and party systems." The focus is on one crucial issue: the degree to which party systems in Latin America are institutionalized and consequences for sustained democracy. The authors discuss variations in the numbers of parties and the ideological distance among them, arguing that limited or moderate ideological polarization enhances the prospects for stable party competition and democracy.

2967 Maiztegui, Humberto. Memorias políticas del Secretario Latinoamericano de la Internacional Socialista, 1956–1970. Buenos Aires: Centro Editor de América Latina, 1992. 121 p.: bibl. (Biblioteca Política argentina; 355)

The author was secretary to the Latin American Bureau of the Second (Democratic) International, ever since its founding in 1956. This is a history of the Bureau's 40-year fight to establish social democracy in Latin America, which has brought it into conflict with Peronism, neoliberalism, and every variety of communism: no easy task, nor one that has gained a mass following for the Socialists. [P. Lewis]

2968 Martínez Escamilla, Ramón. Latinoamérica: Estado y política de desarrollo; hacia una tipología del Estado y la política de desarrollo. (*Probl. Desarro.*, 25:99, oct./dic. 1994, p. 143–169)

Interesting article on two central features of the State: as society's highest political organization and as an economic agent. Author highlights the varying levels of political and economic development distinguishing Latin American nations, the concomitant divergent distances between the many political actors who give life to and carry out the functions of the modern State, and the ways in which these variables inform the developmental process.

2969 Meeks, Brian. Caribbean revolutions and revolutionary theory: an assessment of Cuba, Nicaragua and Grenada. London: Macmillan Caribbean, 1993. 219 p.: bibl., index. (Warwick Univ. Caribbean studies)

A good comparison of Caribbean revolutions, focusing on ideology, history, leadership, and the international situation. Best analysis is on the Grenadian revolution. [J. del Aguila]

2970 Meza, Rubén Ariel. El triángulo de la opresión. Paraguay?: R.A. Meza, 1990. 206 p.: bibl.

Short, insightful comparative examination of the machinery of dictatorship in three Latin American personalist despotisms of the first rank: Trujillo's Dominican Republic, Perón's Argentina, and Stroessner's Paraguay.

2971 New paths to democratic development in Latin America: the rise of NGO-municipal collaboration. Edited by Charles A. Reilly. Boulder, Colo.: Lynne Rienner Publishers, 1995. 1 v.: bibl., index.

Comparative case-study approach to the relationship between municipal-NGO (nongovernmental development organizations) joint ventures and democratization and development in Argentina, Brazil, Chile, Colombia, Mexico, and Peru in the early 1990s. Authors analyze collaborative ventures among municipal governments, social movements, and NGOs dealing with housing, health care, waste disposal, urban environmental protection, and education. The case studies illustrate how grassroots collective action can stimulate important change in service delivery systems as the size of the State shrinks and privatization efforts expand. The authors hypothesize that democratization and sustainable development will depend on binding the organizations of civil society to one another, and ultimately to the municipal governments. Greater public-private collaboration may be a critical variable for achieving democratic development, but the path is likely to be a rocky one if past efforts have any bearing on the future.

2972 Palma Carvajal, Eduardo. Decentralization and democracy: the new Latin American municipality. (*CEPAL Rev.*, 55, April 1995, p. 39–53, bibl., table)

The corpus of literature on reforming the State in Latin America often overlooks political decentralization at the community or municipal level. This UN technical advisor examines the nexus between decentralization and democratization in Latin America and that the end of centralization means that communal or municipal subdivisions must take on new functions, capacities, and responsibilities in this difficult and often conflictual transfer of power.

2973 Pereyra, Daniel. Del Moncada a Chiapas: historia de la lucha armada en América Latina. Madrid: Los Libros de la Catarata, 1994. 254 p.: bibl. (Los libros de la catarata; 24)

Argentine leftist provides a short but useful comparative study of guerrilla insurgency in Latin America. Contends, not surprisingly, that armed struggle will continue as a result of the poverty and powerlessness with which the majority of Latin Americans live. Good references.

2974 Pion-Berlin, David. The armed forces and politics: gains and snares in recent scholarship. (*LARR*, 30:1, 1995, p. 147–162)

Crisp, clear review essay integrating the best recent scholarship on the diffuse topic of militarism in Latin America. Insights clarify the persistence of "La cuestión militar" in Latin American scholarship. The transition to democracy has only intensified this interest, since "civilian control of the armed forces must become as integral a component to any definition of democratic society as the traditional hallmarks of participation and contestation."

2975 Power, politics, and Pentecostals in Latin America. Edited by Edward L. Cleary and Hannah W. Stewart-Gambino. Boulder, Colo.: Westview Press, 1997. 261 p.: index, tables.

A carefully crafted volume dealing with broad issues of concern to the rapidly growing Pentecostal movement in Latin America. The major themes in the study include gender relations, political power and organization, and inter-Pentecostal and ecumenical relations. Case studies from Brazil, Chile, Guatemala, Venezuela, and Puerto Ricans in New York examine the historical foundations, patterns of and explanations for Pentecostal growth, and the political and social consequences of the movement. Chapters are well-documented but the volume lacks a reference bibliography on the subject.

2976 Prieto, Alberto. Guerrillas contemporáneas en América Latina. La Habana: Editorial de Ciencias Sociales, 1990. 351 p.: bibl. (Ediciones políticas)

Marxist account of the history of national liberation movements in Latin America from Augusto Sandino in Nicaragua to the 1980s. The character and strategy of close to 100 guerrilla movements in 15 countries are examined for their historical contribution to the cause of revolutionary struggle.

2977 Remmer, Karen L. The process of democratization in Latin America. (*Stud. Comp. Int. Dev.*, 27:4, Winter 1992/93, p. 3–24, bibl.)

An examination of the past decade of democratization in Latin America reveals that the current episode is distinct (which periods are not?) from previous cycles of democratic and authoritarian alternations. Argues that 1990s democratization is a distinct historical phase in which broad electoral participation and respect for opposition rights have become widespread and relatively durable features of the political landscape. The origins of this transformation are contained in the interaction between domestic and international forces. The work's strength is a parsimonious synthesis and integration, summarizing much of the democratization literature over the past decade.

2978 Rénique, José L. The Latin American left: epitaph or new beginning? (*LARR*, 30:2, 1995, p. 177–194)

Has the Latin American left died with the collapse of communism in Eastern Europe and the former USSR? Excellent review essay suggests that the Latin American left, while marginalized, remains alive, dynamic, diverse, and adaptive. Author finds a common pattern within from the diversity of leftist experiences in the region: the displacement of the importance of revolution by democracy as the main topic in the left's current political and intellectual debate.

2979 Rial, Juan. Elecciones y democracia en el Cono Sur y Brasil: análisis proyectivo. (*in* Una tarea inconclusa: elecciones y democracia en América Latina, 1988–1991. San José: Instituto Interamericano de Derechos Humanos, Centro de Asesoría y Promoción Electoral, 1992, p. 647–660)

Brazil and the Southern Cone nations have escaped from harsh military dictatorships and seem to have embraced democracy, if for no other reason than their recent experiences have frightened them into behaving

with moderation. Nevertheless, economics and technology are forcing painful changes upon them which eventually may swing them back toward authoritarianism. The key to the future is whether the middle class will accept an erosion of living standards and whether neoliberalism will bring about prosperity soon enough to avoid a political explosion. [P. Lewis]

Rodríguez, Alfredo and **Lucy Winchester.** Cities, democracy and governance in Latin America. See item **1436.**

2980 Roxborough, Ian. Labor control and the postwar growth model in Latin America. (*in* Latin America in the 1940s: war and postwar transitions. Edited by David Rock. Berkeley: Univ. of California Press, 1994, p. 248–264)

Excellent essay emphasizes that the years 1944–48 contributed to the institutional foundations of the postwar growth model based on import-substituting industrialization (ISI), and to growth of corporatist models of labor control to quell rising leftism and attract foreign capital.

Roxborough, Ian. Labor control and the postwar growth model in Latin America. See item **2980.**

2981 Salinas de Gortari, Carlos *et al.* Libertad y justicia en las sociedades modernas. México: M.A. Porrúa Grupo Editorial, 1994. 518 p.

Contains some 50 essays dealing with ideological change, social welfare, individualism, liberty and justice, citizenship, governability, and political economy, presented at a conference funded by the Mexican Government. Authors include both leading Mexican and internationally distinguished scholars and intellectuals. [R. Camp]

2982 Salwen, Michael Brian and **Bruce Garrison.** Latin American journalism. Hillsdale, N.J.: L. Erlbaum Associates, 1991. 239 p.: bibl., index.

This remarkable and timely book examines the news in Latin American during the early 1990s, emphasizing government-press relations, the contemporary practice of journalism, and the role of regional, national, and international news agencies. The authors capture the complexity and variety of traditions and cultures in Latin America, describing and explaining all of this within the context of mass communications. A major contribution to the study of democracy.

2983 Sigmund, Paul E. Christian Democracy, liberation theology, and political culture in Latin America. (*in* Political culture and democracy in developing countries. Boulder, Colo.: Lynne Rienner Publishers, 1993, p. 329–346)

Sigmund argues that the revival of scholarship on the Roman Catholic Church and social change in Latin America results from the continuing importance of Christianity as a source of inspiration and legitimation of political ideas, ideologies, and social movements. Primary thesis is that mainstream Catholicism in Latin America now supports democracy and has contributed to democratic consensus in civil society, and that the extremes of left (revolutionary liberationists) and right (integralist authoritarians) are today much weaker than in the past.

2984 Sondrol, Paul C. Los intelectuales, la cultura política y las raíces de la presidencia autoritaria en América Latina. (*Rev. Parag. Sociol.*, 30:88, sept./dic. 1993, p. 49–67, bibl.)

Analyzes the diffusion/distortion of the North American model of presidentialism in Latin America. Utilizing original writings of early 19th-century *pensadores*, author argues that a clash of values occurred between the importation of a new, alien, liberal, and secular constitutional arrangement, juxtaposed to the feudalistic, organic, aristocratic, and Catholic sociocultural values of 19th-century Latin America. From this clash emerged the particular brand of Latin American presidentialism; a powerful and more culturally congruent alternative model of rule, rather than merely an historical aberration, as some have argued.

2985 Sosa Elízaga, Raquel. Historia y actualidad de la violencia política en América Latina. (*Estud. Latinoam./México*, 2:3, enero/junio 1995, p. 21–32)

Polemical piece analyzing the historical and sociological roots of political violence (State terrorism and popular insurrection) in Latin America. The crux of the problem appears to be the incapacity of regimes to guarantee order and security; regime inability to establish fair, minimum distribution of

goods; and a generalized lack of political institutionalization due to the "domination of externally dependent oligarchies." Re-hashed dependency theory and the paucity of sources cited diminishes the value of the article.

2986 Stewart-Gambino, Hannah W. Church and State in Latin America. (*Curr. Hist.*, 93:581, March 1994, p. 129–133)

Democratic developments have left a number of national churches with the difficult task of redefining church roles. This brief article captures the flavor of Latin American religious life in the midst of tumultuous change, emphasizing the close links between religion and politics.

2987 Tarragó, Rafael E. Recent reference works on Latin American politics. (*LARR*, 31:1, 1996, p. 267–272)

Excellent review essay (7 books) of useful reference guides for research on Latin America. Author critiques specialized reference works such as Roderic Camp's *Mexican Political Biographies* (HLAS 55:2836) and David Dent's *Handbook of Political Science Research on Latin America* (HLAS 53:3230). Useful reference works on Latin American politics should be given top priority in acquisitions decisions for academic libraries since they save users vast amounts of research time.

2988 Thibaut, Bernhard. Presidencialismo, parlamentarismo y el problema de la consolidación democrática en América Latina. (*Estud. Int./Santiago*, 26:102, abril/junio 1993, p. 216–252, bibl.)

A rather novel, well-written, and compelling re-hashing of the old "presidential versus parliamentary" debate regarding which type of system is efficacious for democracy in Latin America. Compares historical experiences of presidential, semi-presidential, and parliamentary systems in the Southern Cone. Concludes that presidential democracies will remain the norm in Latin America.

2989 Tomassini, Luciano. La reforma del Estado y las políticas públicas. Santiago: Univ. de Chile, Centro de Análisis de Políticas Públicas, 1994. 147 p.: bibl.

Tomassini, formerly of ECLA and the Inter-American Development Bank, and now Executive Secretary of the Univ. of Chile's Center for the Analysis of Public Policy, argues that Latin American countries need leaner, more dynamic, and more responsive state structures to match their more open, competitive, and productive economies. He links durable economic growth and efficiency to both social equity and political stability, and argues that structures and processes that facilitate access to capital and technology for all can make decisive contributions in these areas. [M. Fleet]

2990 Touraine, Alain. Latinoamérica, punto cero. (*Cienc. Polít.*, 25, cuarto trimestre 1991, p. 27–37)

A wide-ranging, thought-provoking discourse on economics, politics, and narco-trafficking in Latin America by French sociologist for a conference on the 500th-year "discovery" anniversary.

2991 Vargas Llosa, Mario. La opción liberal en América Latina. (*Cienc. Polít.*, 25, cuarto trimestre 1991, p. 11–25)

Famous Peruvian author/*político* argues that liberalism as an ideology and program of action remains important and relevant in Latin America's new democracies as a bulwark against the radical right. Author asserts a revolution has occurred in self-conceptions of Latin leftists: "away from connotations of blood, death, demagoguery and dogmatism . . . [towards] creativity, ratio-nality, free markets, and political and legal pluralism." An insightful and philosophical essay.

2992 Walton, Carol G. Latin American women in the political process: a bibliography. Monticello, Ill.: Vance Bibliographies, 1990. 17 p. (Public administration series—bibliography, 0193–970X ; P 2854)

Although somewhat dated, a useful bibliography on women in Latin American politics divided by country and region. Most of the 192 non-annotated citations are from articles and books published in the 1970s–80s.

2993 Women and grass roots democracy in the Americas. Edited by Dorrit Marks. Carolyn Glynn, rapporteur. New Brunswick, N.J.: Transaction Publishers, 1993. 245 p.: ill.

Results of the Consolidation of Democracy in the Americas workshop in 1992 organized jointly by the North-South Center and League of Women Voters. Summaries from 16 papers are included from the 30 Latin American and Caribbean civic leaders who attended, focusing on how women leaders can play a more effective role in the political and civic life of their respective countries. Lists of civic organizations by country and contact persons in each country are also included with useful descriptive information.

MEXICO

RODERIC A. CAMP, *Professor of Government, Claremont-McKenna College*

TWO THEMES, THE ZAPATISTA UPRISING in Chiapas and its aftermath, and the development and consequences of political and economic reforms from the early 1980s through 1994, dominate the literature reviewed this biennium. Given their recent development, events in Chiapas cannot yet be expected to have resulted in a major analytical work. Most political literature on the subject is neither insightful nor balanced. However, some very fine articles and compilations have appeared. Among the best of these is George A. Collier's, "The new politics of exclusion: antecedents to the rebellion in Mexico," written from an anthropological point of view and based on field experience, offering both insightful background information and a clear appraisal of the issues (item **3022**). Though perhaps not as well-developed substantively, but an excellent interpretation nonetheless, is Andrés Fábregas Puig's "Una reflexión sobre el conflicto chiapaneco" (item **3041**). The essays in *Chiapas: los problemas de fondo* examine a variety of interrelated issues (item **3021**). One of the most objective and helpful analyses of civil-military relations stemming from

the region, is "Civil military relations in Mexico: the Zapatista revolt and its implications" by Stephen J. Wager and Donald E. Schulz (item **3128**).

Controversy over the progress of and interrelationships between economic and
political reforms has piqued the interest of scholars in Mexico and the US. Although
most of the literature still fails to draw comparisons with other Latin American
states, or even Asian and European examples, several excellent monographs lay the
groundwork for future studies. Among these is Julie A. Erfani's *The paradox of the
Mexican State: rereading sovereignty from independence to NAFTA*, which provides a general analysis of the evolution of State reform and national sovereignty
since the 1820s (item **3039**). Stephen D. Morris' *Political reformism in Mexico: an
overview of contemporary Mexican politics* offers a detailed analysis of changes
under the presidencies of Miguel de la Madrid and Carlos Salinas, as well as a case
study of Jalisco (item **3083**). The most outstanding work, focused primarily on technocratic leadership, is that of Miguel A. Centeno, *Democracy within reason: technocratic revolution in Mexico* (item **3017**). Guy Poitras and Raymond Robinson's,
"The Politics of NAFTA in Mexico" is an excellent study of the trade agreement's
impact (item **3099**).

The consequences of economic and political reforms have received less attention. One significant result of the reforms -decentralization of decision-making, specifically in the fiscal realm—is analyzed effectively, using historical statistics, in
Alberto Díaz Cayeros', "Desarrollo económico e inequidad regional" (item **3030**).
Jonathan Fox examines a second important outcome of the reforms in his sophisticated theoretical and substantive study on State paternalism (item **3046**).

As noted in previous volumes, electoral processes and analyses have assumed
primary importance for political analysts, and some serious literature concerning
the 1991 congressional elections has begun to appear. Among the best work on election issues is Silvia Gómez Tagle's edited collection, *Elecciones de 1991: la recuperación oficial* (item **3054**), and her monograph, *La frágil democracia mexicana:
partidos políticos y elecciones* (item **3055**). Both provide perceptive insights and
important election data. Studies have already been published on the critical 1994
presidential elections, including the intellectual insights of Octavio Paz in "Las
elecciones de 1994 doble mandato" (item **3097**), and the analysis of the Washington
Office on Latin America in *The 1994 Mexican election: a question of credibility*, a
study of structural weaknesses (item **3087**).

Political parties, unlike electoral issues, continue to receive attention, but
the quality of current work is much less impressive. Nikki Craske's, "Corporatism
Revisited: Salinas and the Reform of the Popular Sector," is the best recent analysis
of a subsidiary organization under the PRI umbrella (item **3027**). A second, Juan
Reyes del Campillo's "Presidencialismo y representación funcional en el PRI," provides information on the party's legislative representation (item **3107**). Luis Javier
Garrido's excellent "La ruptura: la corriente democrática del PRI," is the first comprehensive analysis of the "Democratic Current" *encisión* which began before the
1988 presidential campaign (item **3052**). Notable work has also been conducted on
the National Action Party (PAN). The importance of its legislative branch is evaluated by Alonso Lujambo in "De la hegemonía a las alternativas" (item **3073**). Irma
Campuzano Montoya, explores contributing factors to PAN's first gubernatorial
victory in Mexican political history (item **3013**).

State-group relations, particularly between organized labor and the private sector, continue to be a scholarly focus. The most significant work to appear in this
field is Kevin J. Middlebrook's *The paradox of revolution: labor, the State, and au-*

thoritarianism in Mexico (item **3081**). Two important essays place labor within the context of NAFTA: "Mexican State-labor relations and the political implications of free trade" by Maria Lorena Cook (item **3025**) and "El sindicalismo mexicano frente a la restructuración" by Francisco Zapata (item **3131**). Blanca Heredia's "Mexican business and the State" provides perhaps the best analysis of State-business relations before the Salinas years (item **3060**).

Literature concerning relations between the State and interest groups has incorporated discussions of new topics such as NGOs and the political roles of women. Some of the best work is offered by Luis Hernández and Jonathan Fox in, "Mexico's difficult democracy: grassroots movements, NGOs, and local government" (item **3061**). Graciela Freyermuth Enciso and Mariana Fernández Guerrero focus on women's groups in their work on Chiapas, "Migration, organization, and identity: the case of a women's group from San Cristóbal de las Casas" (item **3048**). Women, as distinct from female-oriented NGOs, have not received much attention within the discipline, and the literature remains analytically and quanititatively sparse. Mexican scholars continue to offer the best work, including that of Carmen Ramos Escandón, "Women's movements, feminism, and Mexican politics" (item **3103**), Gina Zabludovsky, "Mujeres empresarias y participación política en México" (item **3130**), and Marta Lamas, "Algunas características del movimiento feminista en Ciudad de México" (item **3066**).

The media and public opinion polling continue to draw insufficient attention from scholars. Miguel Basáñez, an academic and pollster, provides a useful overview in "Public opinion research in Mexico" (item **3001**). Lucila Vargas, in "Social uses and radio practices," focuses her analysis on communications literature in order to assesses the impact of electronic media on Mexican culture (item **3124**). A more comprehensive study is José Luis Ortiz Garza's examination of the historical political impact of the media, *La guerra de las ondas* (item **3091**).

Three topics, the political role of the Catholic Church and religion generally, the human rights situation in Mexico, and state and local political analyses, continue to be neglected. Miguel Concha Malo's edited collection, *Los derechos políticos como derechos humanos* (item **3029**), provides some appraisals of abuses, while Carlos Fazio's biography of Chiapas' bishop-negotiator, *Samuel Ruiz, el caminante,* sheds new light on the perspective of this leading Catholic figure (item **3042**). Finally, Pablo González Casanova, one of Mexico's leading political scientists, and Jorge Cadena Roa collected descriptive data and difficult-to-obtain statistics from all the Mexican states during the transitional 1980s to compile their three-volume reference work, *La República Mexicana: modernización y democracia de Aguascalientes a Zacatecas* (item **3106**).

2994 Aceves Bravo, Félix Andrés. Diccionario electoral mexicano. Guadalajara, Mexico: Univ. de Guadalajara, Dirección de Publicaciones, 1994. 156 p.: bibl. (Col. Fin de milenio. Serie Códigos y leyes)

Dictionary of electoral institutions and their responsibilities. Given Mexico's continuing electoral reforms, work's utility may be short-lived.

Aguilar, Adrián Guillermo; Boris Graizbord; and **Alvaro Sánchez Crispín.** Las ciudades intermedias y el desarrollo regional en México. See item **4558**.

Alonso, Jorge. Por una alternativa a la inequidad: el Movimiento de Acción y Unidad Socialista. See item **4560**.

2995 Arriola, Carlos. Ensayos sobre el PAN. México: Miguel Angel Porrúa Grupo Editorial, 1994. 349 p.: bibl., index. (Las Ciencias sociales)

Addresses recent changes in the Partido Acción Nacional (PAN), Mexico's second most important electoral force. Insightful examination of the contributions of the party's leadership to the changing Mexican electoral process, and most importantly, of the party's internal divisions.

2996 Aziz Nassif, Alberto. Chihuahua: historia de una alternativa. Prólogo de Lorenzo Meyer. México: Centro de Investigaciones y Estudios Superiores en Antropología Social; La Jornada, 1994. 148 p.: bibl. (Serie Disidencias)

Analyzes a significant case of electoral conflict and fraud in Chihuahua. Concludes that although the 1986 events did not threaten national politics, they did strike a blow to the political elite.

2997 Barragán Barragán, José. Los derechos humanos en México. Guadalajara, Mexico: Univ. de Guadalajara, Dirección de Publicaciones, 1994. 421 p. (Col. Fin de Milenio. Serie Códigos y leyes)

Administrative and legal description of all governmental agencies, civilian and military, relating to the administration of justice and civil rights.

2998 Barrera Bassols, Dalia and **Lilia Venegas Aguilera.** Testimonios de participación popular femenina en la defensa del voto: Ciudad Juárez, Chihuahua, 1982–1986. México: Instituto Nacional de Antropología e Historia, 1992. 134 p.: bibl. (Col. Divulgación)

Brief set of 1988 interviews with female residents of Ciudad Juárez. Interviews attempt to measure women's political involvement and level of participation in a rapidly changing local political environment. Not well-developed, but includes useful information on politicized women, an understudied phenomenon in Mexico.

2999 Barros Sierra, Javier. Javier Barros Sierra, 1968: conversaciones con Gastón García Cantú. Fotografías de Héctor García. 7. ed. corregida y aumentada (nuevo formato). México; Madrid: Siglo Veintiuno Editores, 1993. 253 p., 16 p. of plates: ill.

Seventh edition of a work containing interviews of Javier Barros Sierra, a distinguished public servant and rector of the Univ. Nacional Autónoma de México, conducted by Gaston García Cantú, a leading intellectual. Barros Sierra gives his views on the 1968 stu-

dent strike and subsequent killing of students and bystanders by government officials in Mexico City. An essential source for understanding the complexities of the student movement. For annotation of 2nd edition see *HLAS 37:8152.*

3000 Basáñez, Miguel. Problems in interpreting electoral polls in authoritarian countries: lessons from the 1994 Mexican election. (*Int. Soc. Sci. J.,* 146, Dec. 1995, p. 643–650, graphs, photos, tables)

Basáñez, a major analyst and producer of public opinion polls in Mexico, provides a cogent overview of the value and utility of politically-oriented polls in the Mexican context. Describes what pollsters learned from the 1994 presidential elections, and concludes that to improve the accuracy of electoral forecasting much remains to be learned.

3001 Basáñez, Miguel. Public opinion research in Mexico. (*in* Latin America in comparative perspective: new approaches to methods and analysis. Edited by Peter H. Smith. Boulder, Colo.: Westview Press, 1995, p. 257–273, tables)

One of the most significant developments in Mexican elections is the use of public opinion polls. One of Mexico's leading independent pollsters describes the use of polls in the Mexican context, and the methodological and political issues this practice raises.

3002 Beltrán del Río, Pacal. Michoacán, ni un paso atrás. México: Libros de Proceso, 1993. 397 p.: ill.

A reporter's detailed account, with considerable political insight, of the conflicts between the PRI and the opposition in the state of Michoacán, an intense microcosm of Mexico's political frustrations and electoral fraud occurring from 1886–1993.

3003 Benítez Manaut, Raúl. Las fuerzas armadas mexicanas a fin de siglo: su relación con el estado, el sistema político y la sociedad. (*in* Reconversión militar en América Latina. Coordinación de Gabriel Aguilera Peralta. Guatemala: FLACSO, 1994, p. 63–89, graphs, tables)

Broad, interpretative essay on civil-military relations through 1993. Argues that the dynamic of national security is changing; that the US and Mexico increasingly are in agreement on their conceptualization of national security issues and potential consequences; and that a decreased US military presence in the region will favor Mexico.

3004 Borge, Tomás. Salinas: los dilemas de la modernidad. México: Siglo Vientiuno, 1993. 230 p.: bibl., ill., index. (Historia inmediata)

Notable Sandinista examines the life of Carlos Salinas. Brief but oddly insightful work explores Salinas' childhood, parents, and career. One of the few published sources of useful information about the president's family and early life.

3005 Brachet-Márquez, Viviane de and **Margaret S. Sherraden.** Austérité budgétaire, état de bien-être et changement politique: le cas des politiques de santé et d'alimentation au Mexique, 1970–1990. (*Cah. Am. lat.*, 15, 1993, p. 89–108)

Argues that Mexican social welfare policy, built on provisions of the 1917 Constitution and steadily developed after 1943, strengthened the State. The move away from this approach during the 1990s is a major factor in determining a different political future and redefined State role. [A. Pérotin-Dumon]

3006 Brachet-Márquez, Viviane de. Mexico: the search for new parameters. (*LARR*, 30:3, 1995, p. 163–176, bibl.)

Review essay of recent works on State/labor relations and working-class conditions in Mexico concludes that much of this literature remains observational rather than academic, and that social movements are discounted and looked on as exceptional events. Some of the new works under review address these deficiencies.

3007 Burbach, Roger. Roots of the postmodern rebellion in Chiapas. (*New Left Rev.*, 205, May/June 1994, p. 113–124)

Useful summary of major social and economic conditions which led to the Jan. 1994 Zapatista uprising in Chiapas. Argues that many other Mexican communities share similar fundamental conditions.

3008 Caballero, Alejandro. Salvador Nava: las últimas batallas. Prólogo de Carlos Monsiváis. Mexico: La Jornada, 1992. 207 p. (Serie Disidencias)

Helpful insights into the final political campaign of Salvador Nava Martínez, the independent opposition leader who generated a civic alliance and electoral movement unmatched in provincial Mexico. Focuses on the period shortly before his death and on his gubernatorial candidacy in San Luis Potosí.

3009 Calderón Mólgora, Marco Antonio. Poder y autoridad: elecciones municipales en Michoacán. (*Relaciones/Zamora*, 53, invierno 1993, p. 197–218, bibl.)

Analysis of elections held in this politically conflicted state (home of Cuauhtémoc Cárdenas) from 1988–92. Concludes that attempts to democratize the PRI's internal selection process created more difficulties than they resolved; yet the traditional means of local control by typical interest groups has substantially eroded.

3010 Calderón Mólgora, Marco Antonio. Violencia política y elecciones municipales. Zamora, Mexico: El Colegio de Michoacán; México: Instituto Mora, 1994. 170 p.: bibl. (Col. Investigaciones)

Serious attempt, with some theoretical grounding, to analyze the role of municipal elections in Mexican politics. Focuses specifically on Guerrero and Michoacán where elections have been hotly contested since 1988. Describes the consequences of violence before, during, and after these contests.

3011 Calderón Rodríguez, José María. El sistema político mexicano entre inercia e innovación. (*Iztapalapa/México*, 14:34, julio/dic. 1994, p. 29–44, ill.)

Thoughtful analysis goes beyond treatment of electoral data to argue that two elements are essential for a successful, pluralistic political system: institutional development that promotes organizations advocating equality, and a political culture that stresses equal rights and obligations.

3012 Camp, Roderic Ai. Striving for Mexican democracy: the PRI and the opposition. (*in* Mexico faces the 21st century. Westport, Conn.: Greenwood Press, 1995, p. 29–44)

Noteworthy chapter examines the collective, semi-permanent, second-class status of opposition parties in Mexico. Argues strongly that opposition parties reinforce democratization in a turbulent Mexican sociopolitical arena. The prognosis offered for democracy is somewhat pessimistic given Mexico's unique semi-authoritarian political environment. [D. Dent]

3013 Campuzano Montoya, Irma. Baja California en tiempos del PAN. México: La Jornada Ediciones, 1995. 261 p.: bibl. (Serie Disidencias)

First serious analysis of the topic provides explanation for the 1989 victory of the Partido Acción Nacional (PAN) in Baja California. Author attributes PAN success to errors of the incumbent governor, weaknesses in the campaign of Partido Revolucionario Institucional (PRI) candidate Margarita Ortega Villa, the President's willingness to accept an opposition victory, and the PRI candidate's overconfidence.

3014 Cansino, César. Construir la democracia: límites y perspectivas de la transición en México. México: M.A. Porrúa, 1995. 213 p.: bibl. (Las Ciencias sociales)

Broad overview of transition process in Mexico's political development covers various issues ranging from political culture to the electoral process. Summarizes seven arguments which may either foster or hinder political change. Brief postscript incorporates events in Chiapas into the work's larger context.

3015 Castañeda, Jorge G. Can NAFTA change Mexico? (*Foreign Aff.*, 72:4, Sept./Oct. 1993, p. 66–80)

Author is one of the severest critics of Salinas' international economic strategies. He nevertheless provides a perceptive explanation of NAFTA's pros and cons, and concludes that Mexico, given the choice between the status quo and risk-laden change, must opt for change.

3016 Castañeda, Jorge G. La casa por la ventana. México: Cal y Arena, 1993. 268 p.: bibl.

Outstanding compendium of essays on post-Cold War Mexico and Latin America by well-known Mexican academic. Argues that, for a variety of reasons, the end of the ideological Cold War does not necessarily benefit Latin America. Very informative for students of inter-American relations, Mexican politics, and US-Mexican relations from a Mexican perspective. [P.C. Sondrol]

3017 Centeno, Miguel Angel. Democracy within reason: technocratic revolution in Mexico. University Park: Pennsylvania State Univ. Press, 1994. 272 p.: bibl., ill., index.

Excellent analysis of bureaucratic developments and the technocratic revolution within Mexico. Includes assessments of short-term trends in Mexican leadership. Based on extensive field research and a survey of executive-branch department heads who provide the pool for future national-level political elites. Essential reading for Mexicanists.

3018 Chabat, Jorge. Seguridad nacional y narcotráfico: vínculos reales e imaginarios. (*Polít. Gob.*, 1:1, enero/junio 1994, p. 97–123)

Leading student of US/Mexico national security issues delineates important arguments about the impact of drug trafficking on Mexican national security. Argues that narcotics issue directly influences national political and economic processes. For international relations specialist's comment, see item **3989.**

3019 The challenge of institutional reform in Mexico. Edited by Riordan Roett. Boulder, Colo.: Lynne Rienner Publishers, 1995. 197 p.: bibl., index.

Leading group of Mexican and US specialists assesses changes occurring in Mexican social and political institutions, as well as the policy reforms of the Salinas administration. Examines the Catholic Church, civil-military relations, and electoral reform.

3020 Chanes Nieto, José. La designación del presidente de la República. Mexico: Plaza y Valdés Editores, 1993. 275 p.: bibl. (Col. Folios)

Work's value lies in its compilation of considerable information on presidential succession from 1928–88.

3021 Chiapas: los problemas de fondo. Coordinación de David Moctezuma Navarro. Cuernavaca, Mexico: Univ. Nacional Autónoma de México, Centro Regional de Investigaciones Multidisciplinarias, 1994. 167 p.: bibl.

One of the few serious academic works on the Zapatista movement in Chiapas published in Mexico. Collection focuses on a number of interrelated issues including historical context, social situation, role of the Catholic Church, impact of illiteracy, the indigenous culture, divisions within the native communities, and structural problems.

Ciclo de conferencias. See item **2936.**

3022 Collier, George A. The new politics of exclusion: antecedents to the rebellion in Mexico. (*Dialect. Anthropol.,* 19:1, May 1994, p. 1–44, maps)

Essential, detailed, anthropology-based account of the fundamental causes of the Jan. 1994 Chiapas uprising. Relies heavily on personal field experience. Provides insights unavailable in any other contemporary published account. Outstanding formulation of many relevant issues. For ethnologist's comment see *HLAS 55:724.*

3023 Colosio: un candidato en la transición; frente al México nuevo. Edición de Jaime González Graf. México: Grijalbo; IMEP, 1994. 262 p.: ill.

Campaign biography and evaluation of the assassinated PRI presidential candidate Luis Donaldo Colosio. Useful description of the historical political context of 1994. Excellent detailed appendix on the backgrounds of individuals who would have formed his political *camarilla.*

3024 Conger, Lucy. Mexico: Zapatista thunder. (*Curr. Hist.,* 93:581, March 1994, p. 115–120)

Brief but knowledgeable overview of background and initial phase of the Jan. 1994 Ejército Zapatista de Liberación Nacional uprising in Chiapas.

3025 Cook, Maria Lorena. Mexican State-labor relations and the political implications of free trade. (*Lat. Am. Perspect.,* 22:1, Winter 1995, p. 77–94, bibl.)

Explores potential impact of NAFTA on the future of labor. Concludes that NAFTA will further narrow trade union options at a time when these are already limited. Also suggests that NAFTA may disrupt status-quo economic and political arrangements which have governed the context in which trade unions operate, and will thus change State/union relations and the strategies labor organizations have pursued.

3026 Craig, Ann L. and **Wayne A. Cornelius.** Houses divided: parties and political reform in Mexico. (*in* Building democratic institutions: party systems in Latin America. Edited by Scott Mainwaring and Timothy R. Scully. Stanford, Calif.: Stanford Univ. Press, 1995, p. 249–297, graphs, tables)

Two leading experts provide a balanced and complete overview of the changing roles of the country's three major parties (Partido Revolucionario Institucional, Partido Acción Nacional, Partido de la Revolución Democrática), and the consequences of the changes on their electoral fortunes. Appendix includes a brief but useful summary of the major electoral laws (1918, 1946, 1977, 1986, 1990) and the various amendments enacted between 1946–77.

3027 Craske, Nikki. Corporatism revisited: Salinas and the reform of the popular sector. London: Univ. of London, Institute of Latin American Studies, 1994. 56 p.: bibl., ill. (Research papers/Univ. of London, Institute of Latin American Studies: 0957-7947; 37)

First analysis of the changes in the Confederación Nacional de Organizaciones Populares, the long-standing "popular sector" of the Partido Revolucionario Institucional (PRI). Brief but excellent work also provides considerable insight into the impact of the Programa Nacional de Solidaridad (PRONASOL) on the popular sector, and notes that the PRI repressed its own study which indicated that PRONASOL groups were adversely affecting its electoral fortunes.

3028 Crespo, José Antonio. PRI: de la hegemonía revolucionaria a la dominación democrática. (*Polít. Gob.,* 1:1, enero/junio 1994, p. 47–77, graph)

Careful and thorough theoretical exploration of Mexico's transition to pluralism. Compares similarities and differences to situation in South Korea, Germany, Poland, and Nicaragua. Describes conditions the author considers most auspicious for peaceful change with a dominant party in power.

3029 Los derechos políticos como derechos humanos. Coordinación de Miguel Concha Malo. México: La Jornada Ediciones; Centro de Investigaciones Interdisciplinarias en Humanidades, UNAM, 1994. 152 p.: bibl., ill. (Col. La democracia en México)

Collection of essays, many authored by leading Mexican secular and religious human rights advocates, covers various topics including conceptual issues, political/civil rights, and serious abuses against indigenous populations.

Díaz, Alvaro. Tendencias de la reestructuración económica y social en Latinoamérica. See item **2942.**

3030 Díaz Cayeros, Alberto. Desarrollo económico e inequidad regional: hacia un nuevo pacto federal en México. México: M.A. Porrúa Grupo Editorial, 1995. 126 p.: bibl. (Las Ciencias sociales)

Fiscal decentralization, though poorly studied, is among the most important Mexican political topics. Excellent introduction to some of the most significant political issues involving transfer of revenues from federal to state and local control. Also provides important historical statistical data on distributive patterns over time.

3031 Dinero y partidos: propuestas para regular los ingresos y gastos de los partidos políticos. Coordinación de la Investigación de Jean François Prud'homme. Compilación de Jorge Alcocer V. México; CEPNA; Nuevo Horizonte Editores; Fundación Friedrich Ebert, 1993. 239 p.: bibl.

Regulation of campaign financing is one of the most important reforms proposed for the Mexican electoral party process. This collection of essays analyzes various approaches for accomplishing this reform, and more importantly, provides some of the first analyses of hard data.

3032 Domínguez, Moisés. Observadores electorales, ¿problema de seguridad nacional? (*Memoria/CEMOS*, 67, junio 1994, p. 14–19, ill.)

The presence of international observers was a highly controversial issue during the 1994 Mexican elections. Concerns arose regarding potential inaccuracy of observers' perceptions and reports, and also regarding degree to which their presence constituted an infringement of national sovereignty. Incorporates much of the recent literature on Mexican national security. A useful perspective.

3033 Eguía, Colilá. A quemarropa. Mexicali, Baja California : BusCa Libros, 1994. 194 p.: ill.;

Analysis of motives and possible architects of the assassination of Luis Donaldo Colosio in Baja California, March, 1994, by a respected Baja journalist covering the presidential campaign at the time of the murder.

3034 Ejército Zapatista de Liberación Nacional (Mexico) EZLN: documentos y comunicados; 1° de enero-8 de agosto de 1994. v. 1. Prólogo de Antonio García de León. Crónicas de Carlos Monsiváis y Elena Poniatowska. Fotografías de Paula Haro. México: Ediciones Era, 1994. 332 p.: ill. (Col. Problemas de México)

Collection of numerous published documents from the Ejército Zapatista de Liberación Nacional provides primary research source on this organization. Includes an introduction and several brief editorial commentaries by intellectuals, but primary value is the republished documents themselves.

3035 Elecciones con alternativas: algunas experiencias en la República Mexicana. Coordinación de Jorge Alonso y Jaime Tamayo. México: La Jornada Ediciones; Centro de Investigaciones Interdisciplinarias en Humanidades, UNAM, 1994. 301 p.: bibl., ill., maps. (La democracia en México)

Excellent collection of works regarding local and state elections. Focuses on highly competitive or conflictual electoral contests within important regions in the 1990s: Chihuahua, Baja California, and Michoacán in 1992; San Luis Potosí and Tabasco in 1991; the city elections of Mazatlán in 1989 and Mérida in 1990; and local elections in states of Michoacán and Guerrero. Editors argue that grass-roots resistance is prompting the democratic transformation reflected in these cases.

3036 Elecciones de 1991: la recuperación oficial. Coordinación de Silvia Gómez Tagle. México: La Jornada Ediciones; GV Editores, 1993. 534 p.: bibl., ill. (Serie Disidencias)

One of the best analyses of the 1991 Mexican congressional elections. The editor, one of the country's leading election analysts, places local contests within the larger setting of national politics. Includes detailed essays on 16 states and valuable state and national election data.

3037 Las elecciones de Salinas: un balance crítico a 1991. Recopilación de Arturo Sánchez Gutiérrez. México: FLACSO; Plaza y Valdés, 1992. 239 p.: bibl., ill.

Collection of essays of varying quality, some by Mexico's leading electoral scholars, focuses on the 1991 elections. José Woldenberg, a citizen member of the Comisión Federal Electoral, provides one of the most interesting, offering an account of the selection and nomination process for voting booth directors.

3038 Entre la guerra y la estabilidad política: el México de los 40. Coordinación de Rafael Loyola Díaz. México: Grijalbo; Consejo Nacional para la Cultura y las Artes, 1990. 396 p.: (Los Noventa; 9)

Important contribution for understanding the crucial transitional regime of Manuel Avila Camacho (1940–46). Series of detailed essays explores Mexico's public policy during the period, particularly its international linkages to and role in hemispheric defense. Also examines development of important labor movements and the composition of corporatist interest groups. Includes an imaginative interpretation of cultural contributions by Carlos Monsiváis.

3039 Erfani, Julie A. The paradox of the Mexican State: rereading sovereignty from independence to NAFTA. Boulder, Colo.: Lynne Rienner Publishers, 1994. 238 p.: bibl., ill., index.

Helpful explanation of the evolution of Mexican national sovereignty and the interrelationship between the role of the State and the development of political nationalism from the 1820s through 1994. Explores economic integration and technocratic leadership within this larger political context.

3040 Esteve, Hugo. Las armas de la utopía: la tercera ola de los movimientos guerrilleros en México. México: Instituto de Proposiciones Estratégicas, 1996? 192 p.: bibl., ill.

Extremely useful compilation of essays concerns the poorly studied Mexican political left, including the guerrilla left. Examines relationships among the various factions and groups, and for the first time provides a helpful context for understanding them. Includes information on the Partido Revolucionario Obrero Clandestino Unión del Pueblo (PROCUP), the source of the newly emerging Ejercito Popular Revolucionario (EPR).

3041 Fábregas Puig, Andrés. Una reflexión sobre el conflicto chiapaneco. (*Anu. Inst. Chiapaneco Cult.*, 1993, p. 9–20, bibl.)

Excellent exploration of the background and dominant issues affecting the rise of the Ejército Zapatista de Liberación Nacional and its conflict with the State. Concludes that negotiation between the government and the Zapatistas is insufficient. Author focuses on three broad areas of social conflict that he believes must be addressed:

the power structure, relations between mestizos and indigenous peoples, and relations between the State and indigenous peoples.

3042 Fazio, Carlos. Samuel Ruiz, el caminante. México: Espasa Calpe, 1994. 328 p. (Espasa hoy)

Biography of the bishop whose diocese is home to the Zapatista uprising. Discusses his early life, Catholic upbringing, and socialization experiences in Guanajuato and Rome before becoming a bishop in Chiapas.

3043 Fernández, Nuria. Las desventuras del padrón electoral. (*Memoria/CEMOS*, 69, agosto 1994, p. 13–21, graphs, ill., tables)

Provides some interesting arguments, as well as empirical evidence, for existence of large-scale, sophisticated electoral fraud, directed primarily at the Partido de la Revolución Democrática from 1988–91. Written in a journalistic style that tends to waver between analysis and polemic.

3044 Foley, Michael W. Privatizing the countryside: the Mexican peasant movement and neoliberal reform. (*Lat. Am. Perspect.*, 22:1, Winter 1995, p. 59–76)

Argues that Salinas' agrarian reforms were designed primarily to alter State-group relations and to change the legitimacy of revolutionary agrarian principles, rather than to eliminate obstacles to rural economic growth. Foresees economic hardship and sizeable outmigration from the rural sector, a pattern associated with the Chiapas uprising.

3045 Fox, Jonathan. The difficult transition from clientelism to citizenship: lessons from Mexico. (*World Polit.*, 46:2, Jan. 1994, p. 151–184)

Excellent theoretical and substantive work examines impact of Mexican liberalization on State paternalism, focusing on mass groups affected by the Programa Nacional de Solidaridad. Concludes that electoral competition can either strengthen or weaken coercive clientelism, which in turn can affect electoral competition. Draws broad comparative conclusions.

3046 Fox, Jonathan. Governance and rural development in Mexico: State intervention and public accountability. (*J. Dev. Stud.*, 32:1, Oct. 1995, p. 1–30, bibl., tables)

Fox, who has contributed some of the most insightful literature on NGOs in Mexico, provides an excellent administrative analysis of the impact of Mexico's rural economic policy under the Salinas administration. Identifies some important issues and demonstrates the complexity of decentralization.

3047 Fregoso Peralta, Gilberto. Prensa regional y elecciones. Guadalajara, Mexico: Univ. de Guadalajara, Centro de Estudios de la Información y la Comunicación, 1993. 167 p.: bibl., ill. (Col. Textos de comunicación y sociedad. Serie Cuadernos)

Although analysis is not fully developed or placed in the larger context of general media and politics in Mexico, this brief study examines role of print media, specifically local newspapers, on elections in two important states: Jalisco and Nuevo León.

3048 Freyermuth Enciso, Graciela and **Mariana Fernández Guerrero.** Migration, organization, and identity: the case of a women's group from San Cristóbal de las Casas. (*Signs/Chicago*, 20:4, Summer 1995, p. 970–995, bibl.)

Outstanding piece of research studies the impact of Mexican NGOs and women on grassroots civic action and interest group formation. Work is particularly revealing given the regional political context in which title group operates. Most importantly, work outlines a number of issues and processes of potential concern to other groups making the transition to larger political issues.

3049 El futuro de la izquierda en México. México: Fundación Friedrich Ebert, Representación en México; Centro de Estudios para un Proyecto Nacional, 1992. 327 p.: bibl.

Collection of "think pieces" by leading Mexican leftist intellectuals on the future of the political left in that country. Also includes works by independents and Carlos Castillo Peraza of the Partido Acción Nacional. Based on a 1992 conference.

3050 Galve-Peritore, Ana Karina and **N. Patrick Peritore.** Mexican biotechnology policy and decision makers' attitudes toward technology policy. (*in* Biotechnology in Latin America: politics, impacts, and risks. Wilmington, Del.: Scholarly Resources, 1995, p. 69–95, table)

Authors conducted over 60 interviews with biotechnology decision makers in Mexico concerning their attitudes toward this

new science. While fairly esoteric, article provides a sound mix of methodology and theory. [D. Story]

3051 Garduño Valero, Guillermo J.R. El ejército mexicano, el poder incógnito. (*Iztapalapa/México*, 14:34, julio/dic. 1994, p. 91–106, bibl., graphs, ill.)

Poorly researched essay on an underresearched institution. Author's views, while accurate, add little to the available literature on the Mexican military.

3052 Garrido, Luis Javier. La ruptura: la Corriente Democrática del PRI. México: Grijalbo, 1993. 224 p.: bibl., ill., index. (La intransición mexicana)

Garrido, author of an outstanding historical study of the founding and early years of the Partido Revolucionario Institucional (see *HLAS 53:3323*), offers the first booklength analysis of the most important internal development within the party's structure: the Corriente Democrática. Analyzes party divisions which produced the Cuauhtémoc Cárdenas presidential candidacy in 1988.

3053 Gibson, Edward L. The populist road to market reform: policy and electoral coalitions in Mexico and Argentina. (*World Polit.*, 49:3, April 1997, p. 339–370, tables)

Rare comparative historical analysis of Mexican and Argentine politics focuses on Peronism and the PRI. Argues that more attention needs to be paid to role of regional differences and alliances in shaping political behavior. Foresees declining importance of this theme.

3054 Gómez Tagle, Silvia. Balance de las elecciones de 1991 en México. (*Rev. Mex. Sociol.*, 54:1, enero/marzo 1992, p. 253–287, appendix, graphs, tables)

Focuses on remarkable PRI comeback in 1991 congressional elections following its 1988 debacle. Argues that the appeals to the electoral tribunal demonstrate the different criteria under which the three major parties operate.

3055 Gómez Tagle, Silvia. La frágil democracia mexicana: partidos políticos y elecciones. Mexico: GV Editores; Mujeres en Lucha por la Democracia; Mediodía, 1993. 216 p.: bibl., ill., maps.

Excellent collection of previously published and unpublished articles on election fraud. Includes interesting comparative piece on electoral trends from 1961–88, revealing the level of misinformation being published about electoral fraud in Mexico.

3056 González González, Fernando M. and **Carlos Alba Vega.** Cúpulas empresariales y poderes regionales en Jalisco. Guadalajara, Mexico: Univ. de Guadalajara, 1989. 111 p: bibl. (Cuadernos de difusión científica; 14. Serie Estudios sociales; 1)

Work looks at Guadalajara, one of Mexico's most important industrial centers, in context of Mexican business/government relations. Although it fails to develop fully many essential points, work provides a good basis for understanding the peculiarities of the Guadalajara case.

3057 Gould, David M. Mexico's crisis: looking back to assess the future. (*in* Changing structure of Mexico: political, social, and economic prospects. Armonk, N.Y.: M.E. Sharpe, 1996, p. 15–39, bibl., graphs, tables)

Economist describes antecedents to the Dec. 1994 Mexico peso crisis as perceived by the US Federal Reserve Bank. Clear analysis of the link between economic variables and the more "political" variable of credibility in Mexico's macro-economic policy.

3058 Hellman, Judith Adler. Mexican popular movements, clientelism, and the process of democratization. (*Lat. Am. Perspect.*, 21:2, Spring 1994, p. 124–142, bibl.)

Argues that popular movements deserve attention for their role in the formation of new regional and national identities, the expansion of civil society, and the mobilization of new sectors. Many analysts would dispute conclusion that Mexico is less democratic at present (1994) than at any time in the recent past.

3059 Heredia, Blanca. Estructura política y reforma económica: el caso de México. (*Polít. Gob.*, 1:1, enero/junio 1994, p. 5–46, tables)

Detailed study of important issues concerning Mexican economic development. Examines distribution of federal revenues to individual states from 1977–88. Uses data to evaluate the relationship between high levels of federal investment and political support for the opposition. Tabasco and Chiapas were the states lowest in revenue distribution per capita.

3060 Heredia, Blanca. Mexican business and the State: the political economy of a muddled transition. (*in* Business and democracy in Latin America. Pittsburgh, Pa.: Univ. of Pittsburgh Press, 1995, p. 179–216, tables)

Translated work summarizing author's earlier research focuses on relationship between the State and business enterprises primarily under De la Madrid administration. Also includes short commentary on State/business relations during Salinas administration and on impact of PAN electoral victories.

3061 Hernández, Luis and **Jonathan Fox.** Mexico's difficult democracy: grassroots movements, NGOs, and local government. (*in* New paths to democratic development in Latin America. Edited by Charles A. Reilly. Boulder, Colo.: Lynne Rienner Publishers, 1995, p. 179–210)

Excellent analysis of NGOs' role in Mexico's political development and their potential as political actors. Concludes that NGOs have played an important role in local democratization patterns, while at the same time creating obstacles to local development plans and alternative public policies.

Hernández Chávez, Alicia. Mexican presidentialism: a historical and institutional overview. See *HLAS 56:1492.*

Hernández Rodríguez, Rogelio. Inestabilidad política y presidencialismo en México. See *HLAS 56:1495.*

3062 Los hombres sin rostro: dossier sobre Chiapas; cronología, comunicados, entrevistas, acuerdos de paz y artículos de opinión en torno al conflicto chiapaneco, de enero a abril de 1994. Mexico: CEE; SIPRO, 1994. 298 p.: ill.

Detailed, descriptive chronology of events in Chiapas from Jan. to April 1994. Useful compilation of Zapatista documents, and numerous articles, editorials, and interviews which appeared in the media. Valuable sourcebook for research on the Zapatista movement.

3063 Human Rights Watch/Americas. Human rights and the Chiapas rebellion. (*Curr. Hist.*, 93:581, March 1994, p. 121–123)

Excerpts from the testimony of the Executive Director of Human Rights Watch before the US House Foreign Affairs Subcommittee in 1994 provide details of executions, disappearances, and arbitrary arrests in Chiapas. [D. Story]

3064 Informe sobre el problema de las expulsiones en las comunidades indígenas de los altos de Chiapas y los derechos humanos. México: Comisión Nacional de Derechos Humanos, 1992. 37 p.: bibl.

Brief work provides useful background information on the 1994 Chiapas conflict. Identifies human rights abuses in the region from 1990–92.

3065 Knight, Alan. Populism and neopopulism in Latin America, especially Mexico. (*J. Lat. Am. Stud.*, 30:2, May 1998, p. 223–248)

In-depth exploration, both eclectic in substance and speculative in tone, about the value of populism as an intellectual term, and its utility for understanding Mexican politics. Views Salinas period as one of economic neopopulism through PRONASOL, and sees the potential for the development, under Mexican neoliberalism, of other forms of populism including a popular wing of PAN.

3066 Lamas, Marta. Algunas características del movimiento feminista en Ciudad de México. (*in* Mujeres y participación política: avances y desafíos en América Latina. Bogotá: TM Editores, 1994, p. 143–166, bibl.)

Leading feminist and writer on the expanding role of women in Mexican life provides helpful overview of women's groups' organizational efforts during 1970s, 1980s, and 1990s. Argues that such groups can offer an alternative interpretation of Mexican policy, but that only by joining with parallel domestic and international organizations will they strengthen their potential for effecting political change.

3067 Lamas, Marta; Alicia Martínez; María Luisa Tarrés; and Esperanza Tuñon. Building bridges: the growth of popular feminism in Mexico. (*in* The challenge of local feminisms: women's movements in global perspective. Boulder, Colo.: Westview Press, 1995, p. 324–347, photos)

Briefly but clearly summarizes development of women's political activity both within the context of the Mexican political system and in a comparative context.

3068 Langston, Joy. Japón y México: dos casos de ruptura del partido dominante. (*Polít. Gob.*, 1:1, enero/junio 1994, p. 139–153)

Pays insufficient attention to significant theoretical issues to provide useful comparison of one-party systems in Japan and Mexico. Nevertheless, briefly explores causes and potential consequences of divisions within the ruling parties, including the birth of new splinter parties.

3069 La larga marcha a la modernidad en materia religiosa. Coordinación de José Luis Lamadrid Sauza. México: Fondo de Cultura Económica, 1994. 387 p.: bibl., ill. (Una Visión de la modernización de México)

A prominent PRI politician draws together useful information on the Catholic Church in the context of the 1992 constitutional reforms. Especially valuable are the polling data utilized by the Office of the President. Although data were compiled over an extended period of time, they provide considerable insight into popular views during the reform year.

3070 Lindau, Juan David. Los tecnócratas y la élite gobernante mexicana. México: Editorial J. Mortiz, 1993. 164 p.: bibl. (Cuadernos de Joaquín Mortiz)

Brief work examines controversial issue of technocrats versus politicians in Mexico's leadership. Argues that technocrats do not have many of the characteristics attributed to them.

3071 Loaeza, Soledad. La experiencia mexicana de liberalización. (*Foro Int.*, 34:2, abril/junio 1994, p. 221–251, bibl.)

Alternative interpretation argues that Mexican liberalization differs from experiences elsewhere, since political direction during 1990s has been toward an increased level of authoritarianism and State control rather than the contrary. See also item **4613.**

3072 Logan, Kathleen. Women's participation in democratic transformation: Yucatán. (*SECOLAS Ann.*, 26, March 1995, p. 77–89, bibl.)

Very brief but insightful study of women political activists and successful female leaders (including a governor and a mayor) in Yucatán, a state where the opposition Partido Acción Nacional has long been a major force. Concludes that the success of women in Mexican politics is linked to their ability to keep gender-focused issues out of the political discourse.

3073 Lujambio, Alonso. De la hegemonía a las alternativas: diseños institucionales y el futuro de los partidos políticos en México. (*Polít. Gob.*, 2:1, 1995, p. 43–71)

Well-researched study of the future of opposition parties in Mexico. Examines changes in the legislative branch election law and their impact on the opposition. Unlike most Mexican political research, this work places the Mexican case effectively within the larger body of theoretical literature.

3074 Luna Ledesma, Matilde. Los empresarios y el cambio político: México, 1970–1987. México: Ediciones Era; Instituto de Investigaciones Sociales, UNAM, 1992. 132 p.: bibl. (Col. Problemas de México)

Analyzes private sector's impact on Mexican political developments during crucial period between 1970–87. Argues that future political analyses must consider a new radical tendency toward concern with social issues. That is now apparent within the entrepreneurial community.

3075 Magaloni Kerpel, Beatriz. Elección recional y voto estratégico: algunas aplicaciones para el caso mexicano. (*Polít. Gob.*, 1:2, 1994, p. 309–344, tables)

First sophisticated research into "strategic voting," i.e., the order in which the potential voter might cast a ballot for party alternatives. Concludes that until 1994 Mexicans did not seriously consider such alternative choices for president, and that the 1988 vote for Cárdenas reflected a punishment vote directed toward the PRI rather than the decision to exercise a viable alternative.

3076 Maldonado Sánchez, Braulio. Baja California: comentarios políticos. Prólogo de Gabriel Trujillo Muñoz. México: SEP; Mexicali, Mexico: Univ. Autónoma de Baja California, 1993. 169 p.: bibl., ill. (Col. Baja California, nuestra historia; 4)

Reprint (1st ed.: México: Costa-Amic, 1960) of a valuable autobiography by first governor of Baja California, an important political dissident of the 1960s. Provides insider's view of state and national politics and their relationship to each other during the 1940s and 1950s.

3077 Martínez Rodríguez, Antonia. Transformaciones económicas y cambio político en México. (*Rev. Int. Sociol.*, 7, 1994, p. 107–130)

Thoughtful and balanced overview of Mexico's economic and political transformation in the 1990s. Suggests various scenarios beyond 1992, concluding that the Zapatistas have decidedly altered the political scene, ensuring continued uncertainty beyond 1994.

3078 Medina Peña, Luis. Hacia el nuevo estado: México, 1920–1993. Prólogo de Luis González. México: Fondo de Cultura Económica, 1994. 338 p.: bibl., index. (Sección de obras de política y derecho)

Medina Peña, who moved from academia into government positions in the Salinas Administration, provides a scholarly examination informed by practical experience of the changing nature of the Mexican State. Concludes that a smaller State is not a weaker entity, and that the State must continue to perform, even under neoliberalism. Argues that the State must undergo further changes, which he outlines concretely in this work.

3079 México, el voto por la democracia. Coordinación de Antonio Argüelles y Manuel Villa Aguilera. 2. ed. México: M.A. Porrúa, 1994. 293 p.: bibl. (Los libros de Textos para el cambio)

Collection of essays, some written by Mexico's leading analysts, explores Mexican electoral politics during the 1990s. Topics include the impact of violence, NGOs, public opinion polls, reforms within the PRI, and the electoral process itself. Very useful election data from 1988–94.

3080 Meyer, Lorenzo. La segunda muerte de la Revolución Mexicana. México: Cal y Arena, 1992. 274 p.: bibl.

Collection of essays reflecting author's historical perspectives and criticism of political and economic reforms. Range of interrelated topics, concentrated primarily on Mexico/US relations and political modernization.

3081 Middlebrook, Kevin J. The paradox of revolution: labor, the State, and authoritarianism in Mexico. Baltimore: Johns Hopkins Univ. Press, 1995. 463 p.: bibl., index.

First major comprehensive analysis in English of the post-revolutionary evolution of organized labor from 1920 to present. Argues that before labor plays a major role in Mexico's political and economic future, it must democratize internally; the State also must end direct manipulation of unions. See also item **3114.**

3082 Moctezuma Barragán, Pablo. México, dependencia y autoritarismo. México: MS Editores, 1994. 162 p.: bibl.

Collection of essays explores process leading to Mexico's acceptance of a free trade agreement. Examines influence of organized labor on the political-economic structure and importance of indigenous cultural influences on contemporary Mexican traditions.

3083 Morris, Stephen D. Political reformism in Mexico: an overview of contemporary Mexican politics. Boulder, Colo.: Lynne Rienner Publishers, 1995. 262 p.: bibl., index.

Morris, whose earlier study on corruption provided valuable insights into Mexican political culture (see *HLAS 53:3368*), provides a useful, broad overview of political change in Mexico, the first work of its scope to appear. Includes an excellent case study of Jalisco, a major western state, and pays considerable attention to US influence. Extremely important for understanding trends from 1982–94.

3084 Morris, Stephen D. The struggle of the PRD in Mexico. (*SECOLAS Ann.*, 26, March 1995, p. 26–41)

Brief overview of the rise and decline of Cardenismo in general and of the Partido de la Revolución Democrática specifically. Identifies many patterns which have characterized leftist factionalism through 1993 in Mexico and elsewhere in Latin America.

3085 Nacif, Benito. La no reelección legislativa: disciplina de partido y subordinación al Ejecutivo en la Cámara de Diputados de México. (*Diálogo Debate,* 1:2, julio/sept. 1997, p. 149–167, bibl., ill.)

Examines the legislative branch and the structural features which have affected its role or will affect its future impact on policy-making. Although not an in-depth analysis, this essay in particular explores the significant historical and contemporary of issue of "no reelection."

3086 Nash, June. The reassertion of indigenous identity: Mayan responses to State intervention in Chiapas. (*LARR,* 30:3, 1995, p. 7–41, bibl.)

Detailed analysis of State treatment of indigenous peoples in Chiapas extending back to the 1950s, but particularly from the 1970s through 1993. Contributes to understanding the internal complex evolution of the Zapatista movement during the Salinas administration. For ethnologist's comment see item **758.**

3087 The 1994 Mexican election: a question of credibility. Washington: Washington Office on Latin America; México: Academia Mexicana de Derechos Humanos, 1994. 42 p.: appendix.

Careful appraisal of the structural weaknesses of electoral mechanisms preceding the 1994 presidential elections. Also discusses abuses that occurred during the campaign: fraud, media favoritism, intimidation, and traditional human rights abuses.

El nuevo estado mexicano. v. 4, Estado y sociedad. See item **4638.**

3088 Núñez Jiménez, Arturo. La reforma electoral de 1989–1990. México: Fondo de Cultura Económica, 1993. 194 p.: bibl. (Una Visión de la modernización de México)

Presents the government's perspective on electoral change in a balanced manner. Valuable statistical data on complaints registered against parties for violations, alleged and real.

3089 Obligado a matar: fusilamiento de civiles en México. Mexico: Libros de Proceso, 1993. 323 p.: ill.

Complete testimony of Zacarías Osorio Cruz, a Mexican soldier who sought asylum in Canada. Osorio Cruz testified to having participated in the execution of numerous civilians in Campo Militar Número Uno, which according to critics has been a center of torture and human rights violations for many years. Considerable insight into the Mexican military from an ordinary soldier's point of view.

3090 Ortega Lomelín, Roberto. Federalismo y municipio. México: Fondo de Cultura Económica, 1994. 203 p.: appendices, bibl. (Una Visión de la modernización de México)

Work's value lies in the appendices which contain data on social development expenditures during the transitional years of 1985–92. Analysis mirrors much of the traditional literature on local-national administrative issues.

3091 Ortiz Garza, José Luis. La guerra de las ondas. México: Planeta, 1992. 279 p.: bibl., ill. (Espejo de México; 10)

Explores the role of radio and influence of international politics, particularly from the US, during the crucial years of 1939–45. Given the increasing impact of foreign and domestic media on Mexican politics, work is valuable for historical information and for examination of cultural influences on communications technology.

3092 Osorio Marbán, Miguel. El Partido de la Revolución Mexicana. 4. ed. México: Comité Ejecutivo Nacional del Partido Nacional Revolucionario, 1990. 3 v.: bibl., ill., indexes.

Three-volume "official" history of the PRI from its 1929 founding through 1990. Also provides detailed information on leadership and changes in party statutes, as well as internal documents. Valuable source of documentary information about the party.

3093 Osorio Marbán, Miguel. Presidentes de México y dirigentes del Partido. México: Coordinación de Estudios Históricos y Sociales del CEN del PRI, 1993. 464 p.: bibl., ill.

Descriptive history of the PRI is valuable primarily for information about party leaders and internal structural developments.

3094 Páramo Fernández, Carmen and **Jacqueline Martínez Uriarte.** Partidos de izquierda y elecciones en México. (Cuad. Am., 46:4, julio/agosto 1994, p. 96–110, bibl., tables)

A strategy of electoral alliances is a recent phenomenon in Mexico's increasingly pluralistic electoral process. Work examines eight different alliances formed during the 1988 elections. Concludes that the left did not take advantage of this concept, and that the Partido Mexicano Socialista employed the strategy most successfully, winning 50 percent of joint candidacies.

3095 Paternostro, Silvana. Mexico as a narco-democracy: reportage. (World Policy J., 12:1, Spring 1995, p. 41–47)

Brief overview of events through 1994 related to the US/Mexican agenda on the illegal drug trade. Useful given the dearth of serious academic examination of drug trafficking and its consequences for Mexican social and political security.

3096 Paz, Octavio; Alejandro Rossi; and Enrique Krauze. Chiapas: días de prueba. (Vuelta/México, 18:207, feb. 1994, suplemento extraordinario, p. B-X)

Reflections on the situation in Chiapas by three of Vuelta's distinguished intellectuals (Octavio Paz, Enrique Krauze, and Alejandro Rossi). Also includes several dozen other commentaries by leading intellectuals originally published elsewhere.

3097 Paz, Octavio. Las elecciones de 1994: doble mandato. (Vuelta/México, 18:215, oct. 1994, p. 8–13)

Mexico's Noble Prize winner offers five major recommendations from his analysis of the 1994 presidential elections: an independent legislative branch, a strong judicial authority, a definitive separation between the PRI and the State, expressed renunciation by the incumbent president to nominate his successor, and transformation of centralism to authentic federalism.

3098 Pineda Pablos, Nicolás. La descentralización fiscal en México. (Foro Int., 34:2, abril/junio 1994, p. 252–268, bibl., tables)

Control over economic resources, i.e., fiscal decentralization, is one of the most critical issues facing Mexico's political liberalization strategy. This work only briefly examines the consequences of fiscal decentralization, but provides worthwhile data and raises important questions.

3099 Poitras, Guy and **Raymond Robinson.** The politics of NAFTA in Mexico. (J. Interam. Stud. World Aff., 36:1, Spring 1994, 1–35, bibl.)

Excellent piece explores NAFTA's impact on political liberalization. Concludes that NAFTA was imposed according to the traditional authoritarian features of the Mexican model, and that economic liberalization likely will not foster further democratization.

3100 The political violence in Mexico: a human rights affair. México: Human Rights Comission [and] Parlamentary Group, PRD, 1992. 121 p.: ill.

English-language version of work annotated in item **3125.**

3101 Polling for democracy: public opinion and political liberalization in Mexico. Edited by Roderic Ai Camp. Wilmington, Del.: SR Books, 1996. 194 p.: bibl., ill., index. (Latin American silhouettes)

Recognizing heightened significance of Mexican public survey research, series of essays illuminates the state of Mexican polling and its impact on political liberalization. Well-integrated volume. [D. Story]

3102 Programa Nacional de Solidaridad (Mexico). Consejo Consultivo. El Programa Nacional de Solidaridad. México: Fondo de Cultura Económico, 1994. 271 p.: bibl., ill. (Una Visión de la modernización de México)

Description by the Programa Nacional de Solidaridad, Mexico's social development agency, of its programs and policies. Includes comparative economic data from 1989–94. Useful for measuring the organization's social and political impact.

3103 Ramos Escandón, Carmen. Women's movements, feminism, and Mexican politics. (in The women's movement in Latin America: participation and democracy. Edited by Jane S. Jaquette. Boulder, Colo.: Westview Press, 1994, p. 199–221)

Perhaps the most carefully researched article in English on women's participation in Mexican politics. Examines the role of women's political organizations, specifically in Chihuahua and Mexico City. Also studies impact of this type of organization on Mexican politics. Concludes that women's groups are having and will continue to have a greater impact on political discourse and participation.

3104 The reform of Article 27 and urbanisation of the *ejido* in Mexico. (*Bull. Lat. Am. Res.*, 13:3, Sept. 1994, p. 327–335)

Succinct, clear presentation of the Salinas administration's land reforms, specifically regarding the *ejido*. Outlines major actors involved, the consequences for land tenure and politics generally, and the potential institutional developments subsequent to its implementation.

3105 Reforma electoral para la democracia. México: Grupo Parlamentario Partido de la Revolución Democrática, H. Cámara de Diputados, LV Legislatura, 1992. 67 p. (Col. Propuesta alternativa)

Detailed, article-by-article review of the constitutional reform of the electoral process proposed by the Partido de la Revolución Democrática in 1992.

3106 La República Mexicana: modernización y democracia de Aguascalientes a Zacatecas. Coordinación de Pablo González Casanova y Jorge Cadena Roa. México: La Jornada Ediciones; Centro de Investigaciones Interdisciplinarias en Humanidades, UNAM, 1994. 3 v.: bibl., ill. (Col. La democracia en México)

Three-volume, state by state, descriptive analysis of Mexico's economic, social, and political changes from 1980s through 1991. Although sophistication varies considerably, this difficult-to-obtain material is useful for a local, as distinct from a national, focus.

3107 Reyes del Campillo, Juan. Presidencialismo y representación funcional en el PRI. (*Iztapalapa/México*, 14:34, julio/dic. 1994, p. 123–134, bibl., tables)

Analyzes the representation of the PRI popular sector in 1979–91 federal legislatures. Provides statistical data on committee assignments and career backgrounds of individual legislators. Examines consequences of these data.

3108 Ross, John. Rebellion from the roots: Indian uprising in Chiapas. Monroe, Me.: Common Courage Press, 1995. 424 p.: ill., index.

Helpful journalistic exploration of events leading up to and during the Zapatista uprising in Chiapas. Discusses domestic and international political contexts of the rebellion. Reports day-to-day activities of the Ejército Zapatista de Liberación Nacional. Covers period through the 1994 elections.

3109 Ruíz García, Samuel. Redefinición necesaria: indios y sociedad. (*Memoria/CEMOS*, 67, junio 1994, p. 32–35, ill.)

Author, a leading Catholic personage, mediator, and long-time advocate for indigenous populations in Chiapas, answers questions about his highly controversial role both before and during the Zapatista uprising. One of the few sources providing an opportunity for the bishop to present his own story.

3110 Ruiz Massieu, Armando. El Gabinete en México: revision histórica y propuestas de discusión. México: Oceano, 1996. 378 p.: bibl., index. (Tiempo de México. Con una cierta mirada)

Valuable, one-of-a-kind reference source describes the history of the Mexican

Cabinet since the 1820s. Provides a complete list of Cabinet members for each presidential administration, and indexes the name of each office-holder.

3111 Ruiz Massieu, Mario. Yo acuso: denuncia de un crimen político. México: Grijalbo, 1995. 179 p.: ill.

Polemic by the former assistant attorney general in charge of the investigation of his brother's assassination. Author believes that his brother was murdered by members of the PRI. Some useful documentation.

3112 Salinas de Gortari, Carlos. Entrevistas concedidas por el Lic. Carlos Salinas de Gortari. v. 1. México: PRI; Cambio XXI, Fundación Mexicana, 1994? 1 v.

Complete, well-organized arrangement of President Carlos Salinas' media interviews from Dec. 1, 1988 to Dec. 10, 1990.

Salinas de Gortari, Carlos et al. Libertad y justicia en las sociedades modernas. See item **2981.**

3113 Salinas de Gortari, Carlos. México es mas fuerte: discursos del Presidente Carlos Salinas de Gortari; antología. México: Secretaría de Gobernación, Dirección General de Gobierno, 1993. 263 p.: ill.

Valuable collection of key speeches by President Carlos Salinas de Gortari concerning foreign policy, economic reform, political liberalization, and social justice. Includes his first five *Informes de Gobierno.*

3114 Santos Azuela, Héctor. El sindicalismo en México. México: Editorial Porrúa, 1994. 336 p.: bibl..

Concludes that Mexico has not developed an adequate level of labor consciousness, and that the labor movement's lack of success in bringing about a higher minimum wage will produce social consequences similar to those that occurred in Chiapas during 1994. Provides a partial counterpart to Kevin Middlebrook's English-language work on organized labor (see item **3081**).

3115 Sucesión pactada: la ingeniería política del salinismo. Coordinación de Alejandro Ramos Esquivel. México: Plaza y Valdés Editores, 1993. 230 p.: bibl., ill.

Compiled by the Unidad de Análisis Prospectivo of the newspaper *El Financiero* and written in journalistic style, short work contains considerable background informa-

tion about the Salinas coterie and potential successors to Zedillo.

3116 La sucesión presidencial en México, 1928–1988. Coordinación de Carlos R. Martínez Assad. 2. ed. corr. y aum. México: Nueva Imagen, 1992. 372 p.: bibl.

Examines Mexican presidential transitions since 1928, with subsquent chapters on every presidential campaign from Lázaro Cárdenas (1934) to Carlos Salinas (1988). Useful for historical comparisons.

3117 Taibo, Paco Ignacio. Cárdenas de cerca: una entrevista biográfica. México: Grupo Editorial Planeta, 1994. 157 p.: ill. (Col. México vivo)

This interview provides excellent insights into the life of Cuauhtémoc Cárdenas Solórzano, leader of the Partido de la Revolución Democrática. Discusses his personal and political motivations, his experience as the son of a Mexican president, and the consequences of this upbringing.

3118 Tamayo, Jaime. Del neocardenismo al PRD. (*Iztapalapa/México*, 14:34, julio/dic. 1994, p. 135–150, photo)

An important analyst of the democratic left sheds light on the internal, ideological conflicts within the Partido de la Revolución Democrática and the changing direction of the Cárdenas leadership. Concludes that internal instability has promoted heavy reliance on NGOs as primary sources of political and social influence during elections.

La tarea de gobernar: gobiernos locales y demandas ciudadanas. See item **4673.**

3119 Teichman, Judith A. Privatization and political change in Mexico. Pittsburgh, Pa.: Univ. of Pittsburgh Press, 1995. 291 p.: bibl., index. (Pitt Latin American series)

Major study explores antecedents to privatization strategies in Mexico, and impact of those choices on economic development and political liberalization. Offers controversial interpretations of the consequences of privatization, while also providing many insights into the background and rationale for pursuing this strategy.

3120 Tello Díaz, Carlos. La rebelión de las Cañadas. México: Aguilar, León y Cal, 1995. 247 p.: bibl., ill., index, maps. (Cal y arena)

Discusses social and historical background of the Zapatista uprising and the local and national consequences of the movement. Useful insights into major actors and their motivations.

3121 Tierra adentro: hablan 14 gobernadores. Entrevistas realizadas por Beatriz Reyes Nevares. Mexico: Publicaciones Mexicanas, S.C.L., 1989. 208 p. (El Día en libros; 30. Sección Testimonios y documentos)

Series of interviews with 14 sitting governors held in 1988, a critical time in Mexico's democratic transition. Interviewees include the late José Francisco Ruiz Massieu; Beatriz Paredes, a leading political figure in the Zedillo administration; and Fernando Gutiérrez Barrios, Salinas' first Secretario de Gobernación.

3122 La transición interrumpida: México 1968–1988. México: Depto. de Historia, Univ. Iberoamericana; Nueva Imagen, 1993. 237 p.: bibl.

Essays by leading Mexican and foreign intellectuals, including several interesting contributions which attempt to link political events surrounding the 1968 student massacre with the surprising political consequences of the 1988 presidential election.

3123 Urroz Kanan, Eloy. El hombre del tucán: Jorge González Torres y el Partido Verde Ecologista de México. México: Grupo Editorial Planeta de México, 1994. 158 p.: ill. (Col. México vivo)

Detailed, descriptive account of presidential campaign of Jorge González Torres, candidate of the Partido Verde Ecologista de México. Reprints conversations that took place during his campaign.

3124 Vargas, Lucila. Social uses and radio practices. Boulder, Colo.: Westview Press, 1995. 309 p.: bibl., ill., maps. (International communication and popular culture)

Utilizing communications/anthropological theory, focuses on social effects of "participatory" radio use by ethnic minorities. Case study material has implications for the impact of electronic media on culture.

3125 La violencia política en México: un asunto de derechos humanos. México: Comisión de Derechos Humanos [y] Grupo Parlamentario, PRD, 1992. 141 p.: ill.

A state-by-state, person-by-person listing of individuals who have "disappeared" or been physically abused, according to complaints lodged and investigated by the Comisión de Derechos Humanos of the opposition Partido de la Revolución Democrática. Covers primarily 1989–92. For annotation of English-language version see item **3100**

3126 Vizcaíno, Fernando. Biografía política de Octavio Paz, o, La razón ardiente. Málaga, Spain: Editorial Algazara, 1993. 246 p.: bibl., ill. (Col. Nueva crónica; 4)

Octavio Paz, the Nobel Prize winner and sometimes political analyst, deserves greater biographical attention as a politically-influential intellectual. This work examines Octavio Paz's political interests as a youth and his resignation as Ambassador to India after the student massacre. Excellent bibliography.

3127 Voice of fire: communiqués and interviews from the Zapatista National Liberation Army. Edited by Ben Clarke and Clifton Ross. Translated by Clifton Ross et al. Berkeley, Calif.: New Earth Publications, 1994. 127 p.: ill., maps.

Sourcebook on Chiapas. Translations of EZLN communiques, interviews, and letters from Jan.–June 1994.

3128 Wager, Stephen J. and **Donald E. Schulz.** Civil-military relations in Mexico: the Zapatista revolt and its implications. (*J. Interam. Stud. World Aff.*, 37:1, Spring 1995, p. 1–42, bibl.)

Outstanding evaluation and interpretation of events that led to the Zapatista uprising. Examines movement's potential impact for Mexico's domestic politics and for national and international security issues.

3129 Yáñez Maldonado, Matilde. La alianza PAN-gobierno en la aprobación de las reformas constitucionales en materia electoral, 1988–1989. (*Estud. Polít./México*, 3:12, oct./dic. 1992, p. 23–39)

Information on PAN's internal disagreements over electoral reform, the level of internal dissention, and the individuals involved. Discusses impact of reforms on the 1988–89 elections.

3130 Zabludovsky, Gina. Mujeres empresarias y participación política en México. (*Estud. Polít./México*, 4:1, oct./dic. 1993, p. 173–196, bibl.)

Although women play a significant role in several major economic sectors in Mexico, the literature on female entrepreneurs and their political participation is scant. This essay describes a small pilot study that measures the involvement of female entrepreneurs in interest-group activities.

Zabludovsky, Gina. Sociología y política, el debate clásico y contemporáneo. See item **4682.**

3131 Zapata, Francisco. El sindicalismo mexicano frente a la restructuración. México: El Colegio de México, Centro de Estudios Sociológicos; Instituto de Investigaciones de las Naciones Unidas para el Desarrollo Social, 1995. 179 p.: bibl.

Thoughtful analysis by one of Mexico's leading scholars on the labor movement explores changing role of labor within Mexico's economic model. Raises important questions about labor's position in the new economic environment, and more specifically since the initiation of NAFTA.

3132 Zavala, Iván. Reacomodos electorales del PAN y del PRI, 1985–1991. (*Estud. Polít./México*, 1, oct./dic. 1993, p. 121–171, graphs, tables)

Examines 260 federal electoral districts (omitting the 40 from the Distrito Federal), comparing the vote percentages received by the Partido Acción Nacional (PAN) and the PRI during the 1985 and 1991 national legislative elections. Uses regression analysis to study relationship between voter occupation and party support. Demonstrates significant peasant support for the PAN.

3133 Zea, Leopoldo. Chiapas, yunque de México para Latinoamérica. (*Cuad. Am.*, 8:43, enero/feb. 1994, p. 11–42)

Discusses a broad range of intellectual/historical issues within the framework of Latin America/US relations. Examines situation in Chiapas and the role of the Mexican military. Argues that the PRI must become a real political party rather than a machine for political control.

CENTRAL AMERICA

JOSE Z. GARCIA, *Associate Professor, New Mexico State University*

DURING THE MID-1990S, political writing on Central America benefitted from three trends. First, Central Americans, sometimes funded by private foundations, increased their coverage of elections, political parties and institutions, often explicitly within democratic frameworks. These efforts helped to create a richer empirical and contextual foundation for understanding Central American politics, and increased the level of political writing in the region to be commensurate with writings by scholars outside the region. Some outstanding examples are works by Cerdas Cruz (item **3136**), Vallejo (item **3211**), Aguilera Peralta (item **3186**), Nobel prize-winner Rigoberta Menchú (item **3192**), and Herrera (item **3220**).

Second, the improvement of analytical efforts explaining political crises in Central America during the late 1970s and early 1980s provided a stronger theoretical basis for scholarly discussion and research. Noteworthy entries are those by Spalding (item **3224**), Velázquez (item **3225**), Grenier (item **3169**), and Anderson (item **3134**). The latter article and a collection of six essays edited by Doyle *et al.* (item **3172**) study UN action in El Salvador and Cambodia, proving excellent examples of a third trend, an increase in the number and quality of comparative case studies.

GENERAL

Aguilera Peralta, Gabriel Edgardo. Seguridad, función militar y democracia. See item **3186.**

3134 Anderson, Leslie E. The political ecology of the modern peasant: calculation and community. Baltimore, Md.: Johns Hopkins Univ. Press, 1994. 223 p.: bibl., ill., index, maps.

Why do some peasants rebel while others are quiescent? This comparative study of six peasant villages in Nicaragua and Costa Rica asserts a theory of "political ecology" by which individual and community interests sometimes reach beyond the village boundary and combine in the selection of political choices. Strong theoretical approach, rich contextual backdrop, sound methodology. Major contribution.

3135 Bataillon, Gilles et al. Centroamérica entre democracia y desorganización: análisis de los actores y de los sistemas de acción en los años 1990. Guatemala: FLACSO, 1994. 236 p.: bibl.

Papers of a 1993 colloquium covering parties in Costa Rica, the formation of ARENA in El Salvador, problems of governability, the armed forces, indigenous groups in Guatemala, and others.

Bejarano Avila, Jesús Antonio. Una agenda para la paz: aproximaciones desde la teoría de la resolución de conflictos. See item **2928.**

3136 Cerdas Cruz, Rodolfo. El desencanto democrático: crisis de partidos y transición democrática en Centro América y Panamá. San José: Red Editorial Iberoamericana Centroamérica (REI), 1993. 195 p.: bibl.

Excellent interpretive introduction to contemporary politics in Central America. Chapters on parties, militarism, political systems, the international dimension, and problems facing parties in the transition to democracy.

3137 Cordero, Martha E. and **Fernando Zeledón.** Gasto militar en Centro América: apuntes para entender su discusión nacional en los recientes procesos políticos, 1990–1993. Costa Rica: Univ. de Costa Rica, Instituto de Investigaciones en Ciencias Económicas, 1994. 53 p.: ill. (Documentos de Trabajo; 185)

Study of military expenditures during the late 1980s and early 1990s.

3138 Los derechos humanos, el desarrollo y la dependencia: memoria del foro centroamericano celebrado en El Salvador en mayo de 1991. San José: CODEHUCA, 1991? 93 p.

Thirteenth annual forum of the Commission for the Defense of Human Rights in Central America. Essay by Hinkelammert argues neoliberalism is antistatist, in opposition to popular movements, and reduces the State to a defense of the economic marketplace. Discussion by representatives of each country.

3139 Erbsen de Maldonado, Karin. Desarrollo, desafíos electorales y rediseño de los partidos demócrata cristianos. (*Panorama Centroam. Pensam.*, 36, oct./dic. 1994, p. 47–65, graph, tables)

Strong summary of the fate of Christian Democratic parties in Central America.

3140 Paige, Jeffery M. Coffee and power: revolution and the rise of democracy in Central America. Cambridge, Mass.: Harvard Univ. Press, 1997. 447 p.: bibl., index.

Outstanding comparative study of coffee elites and their distinct ideologies in Costa Rica, El Salvador, and Nicaragua, and the crisis of the 1980s. Well contextualized historically. Major contribution. For sociologist's comment see item **4733.**

3141 Periodismo, Derechos Humanos y Control del Poder Político en Centroamérica (Seminar), San José, 1993. Periodismo, derechos humanos y control del poder político en Centroamérica. Recopilación de Jaime Ordóñez. Textos de Marta Altolaguirre et al. Prólogo de Antonio A. Cançado Trindade. San José: Instituto Interamericano de Derechos Humanos, 1994. 135 p.: bibl.

Proceedings of a conference on the news media in Central America.

3142 ¿Qué será de Centroamérica?: gobernabilidad, legitimidad electoral y sociedad civil. Recopilación de Günther Maihold y Manuel Carballo Quintana. San José: Fundación Friedrich Ebert, 1994. 345 p.: bibl.

Proceedings of a meeting organized by the Fundacion Friedrich Ebert and the Centro de Estudios Democráticos de America Latina in 1993.

3143 Sojo, Carlos. Defensa y crisis fiscal: gasto militar en Centroamérica. (*in* Reconversión militar en América Latina. Coordinación de Gabriel Aguilera Peralta. Guatemala: FLACSO, 1994, p. 161–182, bibl., graphs)

Brief study of military expenditures during the 1980s.

3144 Taller Centroamericano de Educación para la Vida y la Paz, 2nd, San Salvador, 1992. Memoria. II Taller Centroamericano de Educación para la Vida y la Paz, San Salvador, El Salvador, 17–20 agosto 1992. San José: ACAFADE, 1992? 102 p.: ill.

Proceedings of workshop sponsored by the human rights group Central American Association of Families of the Detained and Disappeared. Includes remarks on reconciliation by Salvadoran theologian Jon Sobrino.

3145 Torres-Rivas, Edelberto. Los alcances de la paz en Guatemala y El Salvador. (*Cuad. Hispanoam.*, 564, junio 1997, p. 75–86)

Compares advances toward peace in domestic conflicts in Guatemala and El Salvador. While identifying historical similarities, author also cites differences such as longevity of the struggles. [D. Story]

3146 Torres-Rivas, Edelberto. Dilemas de la postguerra en Centroamérica: la política, lo político, la sociedad. (*Rev. Eur.*, 58, June 1995, p. 7–21)

Discusses possibilities of a political opening in Central America as the region hopefully emerges from a long period of political, economic, and military turmoil. [D. Story]

3147 Yashar, Deborah J. Rehaciendo la política: Costa Rica y Guatemala a mediados del siglo XX. (*Mesoamérica/Antigua*, 17:31, junio 1996, p. 57–98, table)

Excellent article comparing multiclass reformist coalitions from 1944–65, a period when contemporary regimes in Costa Rica and Guatemala were founded. Examines differences in civil society, organizational capacity, and ideology.

BELIZE

3148 Ashdown, Peter David. Garveyism in Belize. Belize City: Society for the Promotion of Education and Research (SPEAR), 1990. 34 p. (SPEAReports; 5)

Interesting article about the impact in Belize of Jamaican-born Marcus Garvey and

the organization he founded in 1914, the United Negro Improvement Association.

3149 Nelken-Terner, Antoninette. Urnas sí, sangre no: cuando en Belice las elecciones generales de 1994 se efectuarón en 1993. (*Trace/México*, 27, juin 1995, p. 81–89, bibl., maps)

Well-written article summarizing the results of the parliamentary "snap elections" of June 30, 1993, and municipal elections of 1994, in historical context.

3150 Palacio, Joseph. Frontiers within and without: the case of Belize. (*Caribb. Q.*, 41:3/4, Sept./Dec. 1995, p. 78–84, bibl.)

Brief explanation of some of the political, geographical, and cultural aspects of contemporary Belize, noting some of the implications for migration. [I. Griffith]

3151 Palacio, Myrtle. Who and what in Belizean elections: 1954–1993. Belize: Glessima Research, 1993. 98 p.

Description of three decades of voting patterns in Belize along with the results of a 1993 voter-attitudes survey containing useful multivariable elections data. [I. Griffith]

COSTA RICA

Anderson, Leslie E. The political ecology of the modern peasant: calculation and community. See item **3134**.

3152 Dabène, Olivier. Costa Rica: juicio a la democracia. San José: FLACSO, 1992. 434 p.: bibl., ill.

Excellent introduction to the Costa Rican political system in the late 1980s written by a French doctoral candidate.

3153 Franco, Eliana and **Carlos Sojo.** Gobierno, empresarios y políticas de ajuste. San José: FLACSO, 1992. 202 p.: bibl.

The Costa Rican government enacted monetary, fiscal, tariff, and other reforms during the latter half of the 1980s in a successful effort to improve exports to non-Central American countries. Analyzes interest group responses during this period of adjustment.

3154 Jiménez Castro, Wilburg. Conceptos sobre desconcentración y descentralización. San José: Centro de Investigación y Capacitación en Administración Pública, 1992. 77 p.: bibl. (Cuadernos del CICAP. Serie Material didáctico; 4)

Experienced public administrator distinguishes between decentralization (relatively full autonomy) and deconcentration (relative lack of hierarchy within an organization). Argues excessive decentralization in some areas after 1949 is now being reversed through privatization, but in other areas, such as the municipal system, there is a need for deconcentration.

3155 Lehoucq, Fabrice Edouard. The institutional foundations of democratic cooperation in Costa Rica. (*J. Lat. Am. Stud.*, 28:2, May 1996, p. 329–355, graphs, tables)

Argues democracy was consolidated in Costa Rica only after the preponderance of power held by the president was reduced gradually in the 20th century.

3156 Morales Alvarez, Miguel. Región Brunca: hacia una síntesis regional y de reflexión sobre descentralización del Estado. Versión preliminar. San José: Fundación Friedrich Ebert, Representación en Costa Rica, 1991. 41 p.: bibl., ill., maps.

Description of the Southern Pacific ("Region Brunca") region of Costa Rica.

3157 Ponsati, Arturo; Enrique Pérez Olivares; y Juan Ricardo Ramírez. Hacia un partido moderno. San José: Instituto de Estudios Políticos, 1991. 83 p. (Cuadernos INDEP. Serie Análisis; 1)

Three somewhat abstract essays sponsored by the Partido Unidad Social Cristiana, including a discussion of desirable functions of parties, problems of translating party victory into effective government, and an analysis of recent Central American experience with internal party divisions.

3158 Seminario Democracia y Descentralización, *Puntarenas, Costa Rica, 1993.* Seminario: Hotel Fiesta, 1–3 de octubre 1993. Puntarenas, Costa Rica: Federación de Municipios del Istmo Centroamericano; Federación de Entidades Privadas de Centroamérica y Panamá, 1993. 192 p.: bibl., ill.

Presentations made at a seminar on decentralization and improvement of Costa Rica's municipal system.

3159 Valverde Castillo, Jorge. Las pensiones y otros beneficios en la seguridad social costarricense. San José: Editorial Nacional de Salud y Seguridad Social, 1994. 80 p.: bibl., ill.

An examination of the social security

system of Costa Rica, with attention paid to the development, organization, and operation of pensions, health insurance, and other social programs. [I. Griffith]

3160 Valverde Rojas, Jaime. Coexistencia solidarismo-sindicalismo en el sector público de Costa Rica: un caso de pragmatismo laboral. San José: Fundación Friedrich Ebert, 1993. 93 p.: bibl. (Foro sindical; 3)

Discussion about the growth of the "solidarism" movement, wherein employees become part-owners of firms. Concludes solidarism benefits owners more than workers, and splinters the trade union movement.

Yashar, Deborah J. Rehaciendo la política: Costa Rica y Guatemala a mediados del siglo XX. See item **3147.**

EL SALVADOR

3161 La amenaza a la soberanía y la destrucción del Estado. 2a ed. San Salvador?: Fuerza Armada de El Salvador, Ministerio de la Defensa Nacional, 1993. 95 p.: ill.

Interesting booklet written apparently in anticipation of the Truth Commission Report, arguing that Marxists in El Salvador intended to destroy the armed forces. Documents of overall strategic plans by the FMLN and armed forces during the mid-1980s.

Boyce, James K. Adjustment toward peace: an introduction. See item **1778.**

Boyce, James K. External assistance and the peace process in El Salvador. See item **1779.**

3162 Byrne, Hugh. El Salvador's civil war: a study of revolution. Boulder, Colo.: Lynne Rienner Publishers, 1996. 255 p.: bibl., index, map.

Study of strategies employed by the two sides in the recent civil war. Argues neither side was able to integrate economic, political, and military strategies into a grand strategy.

3163 Cienfuegos, Fermán. En borrador: apuntes sobre el movimiento de liberación nacional y la construcción de la república democrática en El Salvador. San Salvador?: Ediciones Roque Dalton, 1989. 60 p. (Col. Patria)

A collection of notes about the international system written in 1985 by the FMLN commander.

3164 Cienfuegos, Fermán *et al.* Visiones alternativas sobre la transición. San Salvador: Editorial Sombrero Azul, 1993. 183 p.

Former guerrilla leaders discuss the democratic option prior to presidential elections in 1994. Mostly optimistic viewpoints.

3165 Conversatorio con los hijos del siglo: El Salvador del siglo XX al siglo XXI. Entrevistas de Stefan Ueltzen. San Salvador?: Editorial III Milenio, 1994. 274 p.: ill.

Interviews of various personages allied with the left, including Rubén Zamora, Salvador Samayoa, David Rodríguez (a priest who joined the guerrillas in 1980), and Marcelo Cruz Cruz, an officer in the armed forces who joined the guerrillas.

3166 Diagnóstico-evaluación de la situación actual de la educación en derechos humanos en El Salvador. Diseño académico de Gonzalo Elizondo. Coordinación y edición de Angela Scaperlanda. Equipo investigativo de Mario Nochéz *et al.* San José: Instituto Interamericano de Derechos Humanos, 1994. 98 p.: bibl., col. ill., forms.

Results of a public opinion poll of educators in El Salvador, with recommendations on how best to incorporate human rights education into the country's educational system.

3167 Los escuadrones de la muerte en El Salvador. San Salvador?: Editorial Jaraguá, 1994. 300 p.: ill.

Translations of US newspaper and periodical articles published for the first time in El Salvador, and an article written by anonymous Salvadoran military intelligence officers.

3168 González, Leonel. La estrategia de la victoria: entrevi[s]tas a los comandantes del FMLN, Leonel González, Jesús Rojas, Ricardo Gutiérrez. Por Iosu Perales y Marta Harnecker. San Salvador?: Ediciones Farabundo Martí, 1989. 183 p.: ill.

Interviews with three prominent FPL strategists near the end of the war; particularly revealing when covering FMLN strategy during the early 1980s.

3169 Grenier, Yvon. Guerre et pouvoir au Salvador: idéologies du changement et changement idéologique. Sainte-Foy, Canada: Presses de l'Univ. Laval, 1994. 372 p.: bibl., index. (Sociétés et mutations)

Excellent analysis of power relations

in El Salvador from 1977–79—the period in which the old regime in El Salvador collapsed, and from 1979–82—the period when the political system transitioned to a "point of no-return."

3170 Handal, Schafik Jorge. "No habrá democracia en nuestro país, si no se somete el ejército a la autoridad civil." San Salvador?: Ediciones Liberación, 1990. 72 p.: ill.

Brief history of the Communist Party's Fuerzas Armadas de Liberación (FAL).

3171 Herbert Anaya, su voz no la callarán nunca. San Salvador?: CODEHUCA, 1988. 1 v.

Pamphlet on the 1987 death of Herbert Anaya Sanabria, killed by a death squad after the minister of communication accused him of being a guerrilla. He was coordinator of the nongovernmental CDHES, an organization attached to CODEHUCA.

3172 Keeping the peace: multidimensional UN operations in Cambodia and El Salvador. Edited by Michael W. Doyle, Ian Johnstone, and Robert Cameron Orr. New York: Cambridge Univ. Press, 1997. 448 p.: bibl., index.

Six essays on the UN role in El Salvador, with a chapter comparing UN activity in El Salvador and Cambodia.

3173 Lazo M., Francisco. El sistema político salvadoreño y sus perspectivas: notas para la discusión. San Salvador: CINAS, 1992. 144 p.: bibl., ill.

Brief, simple introduction to the Salvadoran political system since 1970. Special emphasis on the period after 1989.

3174 Lungo, Mario. Perspectivas, obstáculos, retos: el ejercicio del gobierno municipal por el FMLN. (*ECA/San Salvador*, 50:563, sept. 1995, p. 863–869, photos)

Sketch of challenges facing the FMLN within municipalities over which it has gained control through elections.

3175 Medrano, Juan Ramón and Walter Raudales. Ni militar ni sacerdote. San Salvador: Ediciones ARCOIRIS, 1994. 267 p.: ill.

Excellent autobiography by "Balta," an ERP officer who recounts his travels abroad seeking help for the FMLN, his relationships with other ERP commanders such as Rafael Arce Zablah, his stint at Radio Venceremos, and other assignments.

3176 **Montgomery, Tommie Sue.** Getting to peace in El Salvador: the roles of the United Nations Secretariat and ONUSAL. (*J. Interam. Stud. World Aff.*, 37:4, Winter 1995, p. 139–172, bibl., table)

Excellent assessment.

Montgomery, Tommie Sue. Revolution in El Salvador: from civil strife to civil peace. See *HLAS 56:1750*.

3177 **Moroni Bracamonte, José Angel and David E. Spencer.** Strategy and tactics of the Salvadoran FMLN guerrillas: last battle of the Cold War, blueprint for future conflicts. Westport, Conn.: Praeger, 1995. 212 p.: bibl., ill., index, maps.

Excellent description and analysis.

3178 **Perspectivas de las relaciones civiles militares en El Salvador: San Salvador, 7 de octubre de 1993.** San Salvador: Centro de Investigaciones Tecnológicas y Científicas, Dirección de Seminarios; Miami: North-South Center, Univ. of Miami, 1993. 120 p. (Seminarios; 22)

Unusual discussion of desirable outcomes for postwar civil-military relations, with brief presentations by the Salvadoran minister of defense, the UN military advisor, Rubén Zamora, Fidel Chávez Mena, and other leaders.

3179 **Popkin, Margaret; Jack Spence; and George Vickers.** Justice delayed: the slow pace of judicial reform in El Salvador. Washington: Washington Office on Latin America; Cambridge, Mass.: Hemisphere Initiatives, 1994. 18 p.

Brief summary of post-war judicial institution-building in El Salvador.

3180 **Roeder, Guillermo A.** El chivo expiatorio—vive: un testimonio auténtico sobre torturas, intrigas políticas y otras violaciones a los derechos humanos en El Salvador. San José: J. Cárdenas & Asociados, 1988. 224 p.

Insightful eyewitness account about the intersection of military, criminal, political, and business networks which led to the arrest and torture of a former officer in the Salvadoran armed forces.

3181 **Salgado Mina, Kirio Waldo.** De Lenin a Chapultepec: crítica a la *revolución democrática* del FMLN. San Salvador: Editorial ILYD, Instituto Libertad y Democracia, 1993. 100 p.: ill.

Anti-FMLN sketch of recent Salvadoran history. The author fears the FMLN may yet impose Marxism on Salvadoran society through its doctrine of "Democratic Revolution."

3182 **Seminario La Participación Política del FMLN, San Salvador, 1992.** Seminario, 3 de febrero de 1992. San Salvador: Centro de Investigaciones Tecnológicas y Científicas, Dirección de Seminarios, 1992. 56 p. (Seminarios; 16)

Brief essays by Romero Ventura, Schafik Handal, and Fidel Chávez Mena written close to the time of the peace accords.

Torres-Rivas, Edelberto. Los alcances de la paz en Guatemala y El Salvador. See item 3145.

3183 **United Nations. Commission on the Truth.** De la locura a la esperanza: la guerra de 12 años en El Salvador; informe de la Comisión de la Verdad para El Salvador, 1992–1993. San Salvador: Editorial Arcoiris, 1993. 272 p.

The Truth Commission report on human rights violations during the civil war. Important document.

GUATEMALA

3184 **Aguilar de León, Juan de Dios.** Los cuarteles de Guatemala. Guatemala: s.n., 1993. 234 p.: ill.

This book updates, and at times goes beyond, *Nuestros Cuarteles*, written by military historian (Gen.) Pedro Zamora Castellano, in 1932. History of major garrisons, fortresses, biographies of commanders, and some general military history. Important for students of the armed forces in Guatemala.

3185 **Aguilera Peralta, Gabriel Edgardo.** Guatemala: la larga búsqueda de la paz. (*Anu. Cienc. Soc.*, 1:2, mayo 1996, p. 61–77, bibl.)

Citing Guatemalan domestic conflict as one of the most violent in Latin America in the last 35 years, author cites conditions (such as eliminating the possibility of military success) for achieving peace. [D. Story]

3186 **Aguilera Peralta, Gabriel Edgardo.** Seguridad, función militar y democracia. Guatemala: FLACSO, 1994. 105 p.: bibl.

A somewhat abstract essay funded by the Friedrich Ebert Foundation. Discusses the

Central American postwar attempt to reformulate national security agendas, redefine military roles, and downsize the armed forces. Special emphasis on a negotiated settlement of Guatemala's internal war.

3187 Bruno Bologna, Alfredo. Los autogolpes en América Latina: el caso de Guatemala, 1993. (*Estud. Int./Santiago*, 29:113, enero/marzo 1996, p. 3–18)

Summary of events surrounding the dissolution of the National Congress by President Jorge Serrano in May 1993. Culminates in the selection of Ramiro de León Carpio as president by the National Congress on June 5, 1993.

3188 Foro Centroamericano de Derechos Humanos, *Guatemala City, 1993.* El sol es posible: memoria, 1993. San José: CODEHUCA, 1994. 108 p.: ill.

Proceedings of 1993 human rights forum held in Guatemala which primarily concerned Guatemalan indigenous population.

3189 Guatemala: impunity—a question of political will. New York: Amnesty International, 1993. 46 p.

Summary of human rights violations in 1993 and institutional efforts to curtail them.

3190 Guatemala. Procurador de los Derechos Humanos. Los derechos humanos, un compromiso por la justicia y la paz. Guatemala: Procurador de los Derechos Humanos, 1992. 103 p.

The government-sponsored human rights prosecutor's office analyzes its first five years of activities. Statistical breakdown of complaints by year.

3191 Guatemala, la búsqueda de la verdad. Guatemala: Publicaciones CIEPRODH; Editorial TUCUR, 1994. 105 p.: bibl., ill., map. (Col. Estudios; 3)

Pamphlet arguing in favor of the creation of a Truth Commission modeled after the Salvadoran one that functioned from 1992–93.

3192 Menchú, Rigoberta. El clamor de la tierra: luchas campesinas en la historia reciente de Guatemala. 2a. ed. Donostia, Spain: Tercera Prensa, 1992. 127 p.: ill. (Gakoa liburuak; 14)

Lucid, contextually rich narration of the organization, rise, fall, and renewal of the Comité de Unidad Campesina of Highland Guatemala. Written by the Nobel Prize-winning human rights activist.

3193 Pellecer, Carlos Manuel. Algunas cuestiones de la tierra en Guatemala: tres ensayos. Guatemala: Serviprensa Centroamericana, 1990. 112 p.

Brief essays written by an activist who helped create the Guatemalan agrarian reform program of the mid-1940s. Insightful review of agrarian policy.

3194 Scientists and human rights in Guatemala: report of a delegation. Washington: National Academy Press, 1992. 80 p.: bibl.

Report on the Committee on Human Rights of the National Academy of Sciences and the Committee on Health and Human Rights of the Institute of Medicine, recording a trip made to Guatemala in 1992 that investigated the murder of anthropologist Myra Mack and focused attention on human rights problems in the country. Informative and well written.

Torres-Rivas, Edelberto. Los alcances de la paz en Guatemala y El Salvador. See item **3145.**

3195 Valladares de Ruiz, Mayra. Los partidos políticos en Guatemala, julio–diciembre de 1944. (*Estudios/Guatemala*, 2, 1994, p. 77–104, bibl.)

Brief study of the many political parties that formed during the months following President Jorge Ubico's July 1944 resignation.

Yashar, Deborah J. Rehaciendo la política: Costa Rica y Guatemala a mediados del siglo XX. See item **3147.**

HONDURAS

3196 Amaro, Nelson. Descentralización, gobierno local y participación: América Latina y Honduras. Tegucigalpa: Editorial Guaymuras, 1994. 206 p.: bibl.

Handbook on how to make communities more democratic as a result of the national reorganization of municipal government. Strong focus on creating a "culture" of participation. Originally written for USAID project.

3197 Becerra, Longino. El poder político. v. 1. Tegucigalpa: Baktun, 1994. 1 v.: bibl., ill.

Political science textbook includes chapter on the history of Honduran elections.

3198 Carías, Marcos. Vernon & James: vidas paralelas. Tegucigalpa: Acción Cultural Popular Hondureña; Centro de Estudios Históricos de Honduras, 1992. 164 p. (Tierra nuestra; 1)

Parallel biographies of two contemporaries: Vernon Walters, US military officer and diplomat; and James Carney, Jesuit priest who organized peasants in Honduras and after his expulsion from Honduras in late 1979, fought for the Sandinista cause in Nicaragua. Ironic contrast.

3199 Documento sobre la violencia institucional en Honduras. Tegucigalpa: CODEH, 1992. 20 leaves: bibl.

Statistical summary of human rights violations during 1991 broken down by type of violation and perpetrator. General discussion.

3200 Funes H., Matías. Vicisitudes y posibilidades de la izquierda hondureña. (*Rev. Centroam. Econ.*, 1:45, enero/abril 1996, p. 7–34)

Rare discussion of the origins, evolution, and future of the political left in Honduras.

3201 Honduras: informe de la situación derechos humanos, 1995. Tegucigalpa?: Comité para la Defensa de los Derechos Humanos en Honduras (CODEH), 1995? 62 p.: appendices, facsims., graphs, tables.

Annual report.

3202 Juventud Liberal de Honduras. Congreso, 1st, Tegucigalpa, 1991. Ponencias de prominentes liberales en el I Congreso. Tegucigalpa: Instituto de Educación Política Popular del Partido Liberal de Honduras, 1991. 202 p.: ill. (Serie Cuadernos liberales; 7)

Presentations by major Liberal Party figures (including future president Carlos Roberto Reina) outlining party principles, history, factions, and options, prior to the party's resumption of the presidency after 1993 elections.

3203 Partido Liberal de Honduras. Ideario y estatutos. Tegucigalpa: Partido Liberal de Honduras, Instituto de Educación Política Popular; Graficentro Editores, 1990. 70 p.: port.

By-laws of the Liberal Party enacted in 1988.

3204 Pastor Fasquelle, Rodolfo. Perfil de un nuevo discurso político. San Pedro Sula, Honduras: Centro Editorial, 1992. 289 p.

Reprints of newpaper columns written between 1986–91 by a Liberal party activist. Organized loosely by subject; e.g., public administration, education, agrarian reform, human rights, foreign policy, etc.

3205 Posas, Mario et al. Puntos de vista: temas políticos. Tegucigalpa: Centro de Documentación de Honduras, 1992. 140 p.: bibl.

Six somewhat pessimistic essays and an interview discuss neoliberalism, labor unions, the armed forces, and democratization. Includes a strong analytical essay by Posas on political regimes from 1950s–1989.

3206 Reina, Carlos Roberto. El agora y el aula. Tegucigalpa: Alin Editora, 1992. 224 p.: bibl.

Policy preferences of Liberal Party candidate Carlos Roberto Reina, written shortly before his election to the presidency. Outstanding chapter on the history of the Liberal Party internal divisions.

3207 Ruhl, J. Mark. Redefining civil-military relations in Honduras. (*J. Interam. Stud. World Aff.*, 38:1, Spring 1996, p. 33–66, bibl.)

Examines how the absence of credible security threats in the post-Cold War period, reversals in US foreign policy, and changes within civil society have combined to alter the correlates of military power as the nation undergoes democratization. [I. Griffith]

3208 Ruiz, Elias. El Astillero: masacre y justicia. Tegucigalpa: Editorial Guaymuras, 1992. 161 p. (Col. Talanquera)

A Spanish priest provides names and narrates efforts to bring to justice those responsible for the massacre of five peasants involved in a land dispute with a colonel of the Honduran armed forces. Widows received compensation.

3209 Sieder, Rachel. Honduras: the politics of exception and military reformism, 1972–78. (*in* Authoritarianism in Latin America since independence. Westport, Conn.: Greenwood Press, 1996, p. 109–132)

Argues that the relative stability of

Honduras during the 1980s was accomplished through cooptation policies achieved by military rule during the 1970s. Solid contribution.

3210 **Sindicalismo: crisis y perspectivas; experiencia caso STENEE.** Tegucigalpa?: Federación Unitaria de Trabajadores de Honduras; Friedrich Ebert Stiftung, 1992. 97 p.

In May 1991 electrical workers protesting privatization plans went on strike, winning concessions from the government. In November, claiming the government had reneged on promises, they struck again. This time union leadership was destroyed. Chronology of events, and self-critical analysis, written by the union's federation. Exceptionally lucid case study. Funded by Friedrich Ebert.

3211 **Vallejo H., Hilario René.** Crisis histórica del poder político en Honduras. Comayagüela, Honduras: Ultra-Graph, 1990. 101 p.: bibl.

Summary histories of the Liberal and National parties in Honduras.

NICARAGUA

3212 **Alvarado Martínez, Enrique.** ¿Ha muerto el Partido Conservador de Nicaragua? Managua: Editorial UCA, 1994. 79 p. (Col. Alternativa. Serie Debate; 1)

Brief sketch of the Conservative Party in Nicaragua. Emphasizes the 1960s–70s, when Fernando Aguero engineered a pact with Liberal President Somoza.

Anderson, Leslie E. The political ecology of the modern peasant: calculation and community. See item **3134.**

3213 **Argüello, Roberto J.** La vida secreta de los sandinistas. Miami: Ahora Printing, 1996. 187 p.: facsims., photos.

Irreverant, gossipy collection of anti-Sandinista and anti-pro-Sandinista stories, with extensive quotations from other works, written by the nephew of a murdered private enterprise leader in Nicaragua.

3214 **Caldera T., Hilda.** Nacimiento de la democracia cristiana nicaragüense. Managua: Instituto Nicaragüense de Estudios Socio Políticos, 1994. 26 p.: bibl., ill. (Ediciones INESP; 23)

Brief history of the Partido Social Cristiano Nicaraguense.

3215 **Castillo Rivas, Donald.** Gringos, contras y sandinistas: testimonio de la guerra civil en Nicaragua. Bogotá: TM Editores, 1993. 333 p.: bibl., ill., map. (Temas de actualidad)

Outstanding summary of the origins, international connections, and development of what became known as the "contras," a disparate set of groups including ARDE (Eden Pastora and Alfonso Robelo) the Atlantic Front (Miskito groups), the FDN (Enrique Bermúdez), the ill-fated US-inspired FDN-UNO alliance (Robelo, Calero, Bermúdez), and the Southern Front (the regrouping of ARDE by Alfredo César and Donald Castillo).

3216 **Chamorro Cardenal, Pedro Joaquín.** Diario político. Managua: Editorial Nueva Nicaragua, 1990. 341 p.: ill.

Notations (146 total) written from Feb. 1975–Dec. 1977 by the owner of *La Prensa* just before he was assassinated. Navigates the complex labyrinth of Nicaraguan and US-Nicaraguan politics as Chamorro attempted to guide a pluralist political movement toward ousting Somoza. Includes a useful introduction and clarifying footnotes.

3217 **Dye, David R.** *et al.* Contesting everything, winning nothing: the search for consensus in Nicaragua, 1990–1995. Cambridge, Mass.: Hemisphere Initiatives; Washington: Washington Office on Latin America, 1995. 48 p.: graphs, tables.

Excellent, but brief, summary of major policy issues from the post-war period to 1995.

Everingham, Mark. Revolution and the multiclass coalition in Nicaragua. See item **4709.**

3218 **Foro de Política Nacional La Nicaragua Posible, *3rd, Managua, 1991*.** La Nicaragua Posible III: primer encuentro intersindical; 14–15 de febrero de 1991. Managua: UNAN, 1992. 75 p.

Discussions about privatization and labor, *concertación* within the labor movement, and other issues. Sponsored by the International Labor Organization.

3219 **FSLN: del vanguardismo al acuerdo nacional; el debate interno.** 2a ed. Managua: Fundación Friedrich Ebert; Instituto de Estudios Nicaragüenses, 1994. 230 p. ill. (Materiales de estudio y trabajo; 10)

Prominent Sandinista party leaders, including Sergio Ramírez (prior to his defection from the party), Víctor Tirado, Dora Maria Tellez Arguello, and Ernesto Castillo Martínez, discuss and debate the viability of forming a governing consensus ("Acuerdo Nacional") with other parties in light of the 1990 electoral defeat.

3220 Herrera, René. Nicaragua, el derrumbe negociado: los avatares de un cambio de régimen. México: El Colegio de México, Centro de Estudios Internacionales, 1994. 199 p.: bibl.

Outstanding analysis of the slow defeat of Sandinismo in Nicaragua, comparing it to the literature on transitions. Argues that to defeat authoritarian rule adversarial parties in most transactions will create a pact within the framework of an agreed-upon soon-to-be established regime; in Nicaragua adversarial parties negotiated the end of the regime itself. Major contribution.

3221 Linkogle, Stephanie. Nicaragua since 1990: the revolution in a new context. (*Race Cl.*, 37:4, April/June 1996, p. 31–44)

Brief summary of Nicaraguan politics from 1990–96. Strong sociological perspective.

3222 La otra cara de la paz. Managua: ANPDH, 1990. 38 p.

Geographic summary of human rights violations committed in 1988–89 by members of the Sandinista armed forces or other security agencies.

3223 Petrie, Henry Alexander. Jóvenes de Nicaragua: una historia que contar. Prólogo de Daniel Ortega S. Managua: Fundación Movilización Social, 1993. 282 p.: bibl., ill.

Unusually detailed description of efforts supported by the Sandinista government during the 1980s to mobilize young persons (ages 14–28) through literacy and coffee-harvesting campaigns, military service, construction projects, sports associations, young women's organizations, and other activities.

3224 Spalding, Rose J. Capitalists and revolution in Nicaragua: opposition and accommodation, 1979–1993. Chapel Hill: Univ. of North Carolina Press, 1994. 332 p.: bibl., index, map.

Exceptionally lucid description of elite composition, organization, and behavior as it evolved before, during, and after the Sandinista period. Well-informed by elite theory and by a comparative perspective, using Chilean, Peruvian, Salvadoran, and Mexican examples. Major contribution.

3225 Velázquez P., José Luis. La formación del Estado en Nicaragua, 1860–1930. Managua: Fondo Editorial, Banco Central de Nicaragua, 1992. 161 p.: bibl., ill. (Serie Ciencias sociales)

Studies the changes in the Nicaraguan State's role as the economy shifted from indigo to coffee and displaced elite groups. Argues US intervention in 1912, in alliance with non-coffee producing plantation elites in Granada, delayed the consolidation of power by coffee-growing elites until 1926, and fragmented an already weak national oligarchy. Highly suggestive work.

3226 Williams, Harvey. Violeta Barrios de Chamorro. (*in* Women in world politics: an introduction. Edited by Francine D'Amico and Peter R. Beckman. Westport, Conn.: Bergin and Garvey, 1995, p. 31–43, photo)

Brief biography.

PANAMA

3227 Amado Burgos, David. Los panameños hacia el siglo XXI. Bogotá: Editorial Presencia, 1992. 324 p.: bibl., ill., map.

US-trained expert, experienced in international public administration and planning, discusses major social and economic challenges facing Panama. Offers recommendations.

3228 Ben-Yair, Eleazar. Sala 8: Panamá territorio por liberar. Panamá: s.n., 1992. 64 p.

Anectdotes of the action in a Panamanian hospital during the 1989 invasion.

Las clases sociales en Panamá: grupos humanos, clases medias, elites y oligarquía. See item **4699.**

3229 Espino Z., Darinel. El ojo de la tormenta: Panamá, nación o colonia. Panamá: Ediciones de El Canal, 1989. 112 p.: bibl.

Pro-Noriega author situates Panama's problems with the US government in the context of the Central American crisis of the

1980s. Suggests that a nationalist defense of the Panama Canal Treaties underlies Noriega's actions. Published in April 1989, shortly before the fraudulent May elections.

3230 Figueroa Navarro, Alfredo. Juventud y voto: las elecciones presidenciales panameñas de 1989; estudio exploratorio. Panamá: Impresora Roysa, 1990. 51 p. (Avances de sociología política y electoral)

Published results of two polls taken prior to the elections in 1988–89. Nearly half of the more than 900 university students surveyed expressed no party preference. Gen. Noriega was the "most admired" politician among less than four percent of the sample. Bush was preferred over Dukakis. Some demographic data.

González, Simeón. Panamá, 1968–1990: ensayos de sociología política. See item **4715.**

3231 Materno Vásquez, Juan. Mi amigo, Omar Torrijos: su pensamiento vivo. Panamá: Ediciones Olga Elena, 1989. 333 p.: bibl.

Homage to the thinking of Omar Torrijos, the enigmatic ruler of Panama who called himself "a dictator with heart," written by a friend shortly before the US invasion.

3232 Panamá, testimonio de un proceso electoral. Comité de Apoyo a los Observadores Internacionales; Recopilación de Jairo Mora F. Panamá?: s.n., 1989? 308 p.: ill. (some col.).

Reports by international observation teams on the fraudulent 1989 elections held prior to the invasion.

3233 Pérez, Brittmarie Janson. En nuestras propias voces: Panamá protesta, 1968–1989. Traducción de Frank Pérez. Panamá: Editorial La Prensa, 1993. 321 p.: bibl.

Superb study of political protest occurring against each government from 1968 until the invasion. The author, an anthropologist, includes political jokes, slogans, songs and rumors. Concludes political culture has made protest both non-violent and non-ideological.

3234 Ricord, Humberto E. Noriega y Panamá: orgía y aplastamiento de la narcodictadura. México: Impr. Eficiencia, 1991. 694 p.: ill., maps.

Well-researched, lengthy, and balanced account of the fraudulent 1989 elections, the

actions of the OAS, the rebellion of Major Giroldi, and the US invasion of Panama. Rich contextual background. Excellent reference.

3235 Scranton, Margaret E. Panama's first post-transition election. (*J. Interam. Stud. World Aff.*, 37:1, Spring 1995, p. 69–100, bibl.)

Summary of Panama's 1994 presidential elections.

3236 Suárez, Luis Gaspar. Panamá: la lucha gigantesca de un pequeño-gran país. Buenos Aires?: Verum et Militia, 1990. 591 p.: ill., index.

Voluminous autobiography of a Panamanian armed forces member, and a self-professed admirer of Omar Khadaffi. Suárez began as an Arnulfista, joined the Torrijos government, and formed a political party to support the Noriega regime.

3237 Trejos, María Eugenia. Calidad total en Panamá: nuevo desafío para el sindicalismo. San José: ASEPROLA, 1995. 62 p.: bibl.

Results of a study that gauged the impact Total Quality Control had on labor union strength within ten Panamanian businesses.

3238 Velásquez, Osvaldo. Historia de una dictadura: de Torrijos a Noriega. Panamá: Litho Editorial Chen, 1993. 274 p.

The author, a physician, human rights activist, and diplomat, recounts highlights of the period from Torrijos through the 1989 US invasion. Defends invasion.

3239 Yo acuso. Recopilación de Dagoberto Franco. Panama?: Pérez y Pérez, 1990? 98 p.

Franco apparently interviewed an insider, probably a former member of the National Guard, who recounted more than two dozen anecdotes of atrocities (mostly murders) committed under the Torrijos regime and later under the Guard controlled by Gen. Noreiga. The author provides names and context, but not enough evidence to be considered fully reliable.

3240 Zárate P., Manuel F. El destino militar: América Latina, año 2000—; cuatro estudios monográficos. Panama?: Ediciones Panamá, 1993. 74 p.: bibl.

Brief pro-Torrijos view of the Panamanian armed forces in a global context.

THE CARIBBEAN AND THE GUIANAS (EXCEPT CUBA)

IVELAW L. GRIFFITH, *Associate Dean, College of Arts and Sciences, Florida International University*

THIS CHAPTER REFLECTS the reality that Caribbean politics is a multidisciplinary and cross-disciplinary intellectual enterprise by definition, highlighting an accepted feature of area studies. Moreover, understanding the political dynamics of the region requires appreciation of the individual and complementary value of several fields, including history, sociology, economics, anthropology, political economy, and political science, which itself includes a convergence of the subfields of comparative politics and international politics.

The works are descriptive and analytic in nature, and the spectrum ranges from assessing single leaders, countries and issues, to examining subregional concerns by analyzing both regional developments and international desiderata. There is a rich mixture of works at all levels of analysis—unit, group, State, and systemic. Works are single-authored, edited volumes, reports from government agencies and nongovernmental organizations (NGOs), and conference proceedings.

In terms of substance, the entries have three general features. First, they describe, analyze, and (some) attempt to predict the vicissitudes of Caribbean power politics—in both the domestic and international arenas—of the 1980s and the early 1990s. Second, they examine the antecedents, pros and cons, and prospects for political and institutional change in both national and subregional contexts (items **3306, 3307,** and **3303**). Third, there is an effort to address some of the critical issues of the drama of politics throughout the 1970s-90s. Noteworthy topics are democratic governance, corruption, human rights, and geopolitics. While these four issues converge at times (items **3257** and **3283**), most examinations address them individually, focusing on complex matrixes which most of them entail. The matter of governance, for instance, obliges writers to raise questions related to political stability. As several authors discuss, both democratic governance and political stability require attention, among other things, to show how power is organized and contested and explain how political participation is structured and utilized. Transparent elections and civil and political rights such as free speech, press, and assembly are central themes.

Many studies focus on these matters in relation to the pursuit and practice of democratic governance. Due to the way in which political power was exercised in the region, especially during the 1980s, political dysfunctionality is examined, including topics such as bureaucratic and political corruption (both ad hoc and institutionalized), human rights violations, and governmental lethargy and inefficiency (items **3269, 3261, 3278,** and **3291**). Some studies look at cases of functional and slightly malfunctional democratic governance, showcasing laudable exercise of political power and advocating modifications in the organization and use of that power (items **3251** and **3254**).

Some works reflect an appreciation that political legitimacy is no longer merely a function of political participation, free and fair elections, and the prudent use of domestic political authority. It is also increasingly dependent on the interests and pursuits of constituencies and actors outside the country, such as exile communities, electoral monitors, international agencies such as the OAS and the UN, and countries such as the US, Spain, Britain, and Canada (item **3279**). Thus, the role of external actors is increasing, and this is critical to the conferment of legitimacy and the consequent pursuit of political stability.

Questions of democratic governance, political contestation, corruption, and governmental inefficiency require attention to the organization and workings of political units. However, they also dramatize the importance of political leadership. Several studies focus on leadership, some analyzing only the politics, policies, and performance of specific leaders (items **3292, 3264,** and **3273**). Most assessments strive to be objective, while others tend to be unflattering in their discourse.

GENERAL

3241 Alcántara Saez, Manuel. El difícil equilibrio de los regímenes políticos del
Caribe. Madrid: Ediciones Akal, 1992. 46 p.:
bibl., ill. (some col.). (Las Américas; 63. Poli-
tología; 3)

Work describes sociopolitical dynamics of the archipelagic Caribbean by examining the region in terms of its English, French,
Dutch, and Spanish sociocultural groupings.
Efforts to provide summaries of the various
groupings result in information gaps and
vacuums.

**3242 Conference on Improving Prison Con-
ditions in the Caribbean,** *Port-of-
Spain, 1991.* Improving prison conditions in
the Caribbean. St. Michael, Barbados: Caribbean Rights; London: Penal Reform International, 1991. 144 p.: bibl.

1991 conference report on prison conditions and penal reform in the Caribbean includes startling revelations about prison conditions and criminal justice in the Caribbean
and Brazil.

**3243 Democracy and human rights in the
Caribbean.** Edited by Ivelaw L. Griffith
and Betty Nelly Sedoc-Dahlberg. Boulder,
Colo.: Westview Press, 1997. 278 p.: bibl.,
index, tables.

Using case studies and issue analysis,
work addresses challenges to human rights
and democracy confronting the Caribbean region. Focuses on obvious challenges facing
countries such as Cuba, Haiti, and Suriname.
Also examines legal, social, and economic dilemmas confronting the longer-lived democracies of the English-speaking Caribbean.
Chapters on international law, role of the
OAS, and the activity of NGOs are particularly useful for international relations scholars. [J. Braveboy-Wagner]

3244 Eeuwen, Daniel van and **Yolande Pi-
zetty-van Eeuwen.** ¿Existen estados en
el Caribe? (*Nueva Soc.,* 135, enero/feb. 1995,
p. 52–62)

Examines historical, social, and geopolitical circumstances surrounding formation
of States in the Caribbean, and sociopolitical
and other difficulties encountered.

3245 Emmanuel, Patrick A.M. Governance
and democracy in the Commonwealth
Caribbean: an introduction. Cave Hill, Barbados: Institute of Social and Economic Research, Univ. of the West Indies, Cave Hill
Campus, 1993. 118 p. bibl. (Monograph series; 3)

Cursory examination of basic parameters of government and politics in English-
speaking Caribbean.

3246 Griffith, Ivelaw L. Caribbean security:
retrospect and prospect. (*LARR,* 30:2,
1995, p. 3–32)

Perceptive survey and analysis focuses
on the future of Caribbean security. Domestic, regional, and international realities present different challenges for the next century,
including internal instability, reduction or
loss of US economic assistance/investment,
drug trafficking, corruption, tourism, debt,
and sustainable development. Argues for a
"reconceptualization of security" as part of
post-Cold War research agenda. [D. Dent]

3247 Griffith, Ivelaw L. and **Trevor Munroe.**
Drugs and democracy in the Carib-
bean. (*J. Commonw. Comp. Polit.,* 33:3, Nov.
1995, p. 357–376)

Detailed analysis of the Caribbean
drug phenomenon (production, consumption
and abuse, trafficking, and money laundering), and of the consequent multidimensional, region-wide ripple-effects on almost

all aspects of life. Assesses critical challenges to democracy presented by drugs and the corresponding violence and corruption. An important article. [D. Dent]

3248 Hunt, Gary T. and **Marilyn D. Hunt.** The Caribbean in the news: analyzing recent news coverage of the region in the U.S. media. (*J. Caribb. Stud.*, 10:3, Summer/Fall 1995, p. 218–234, tables)

Examines dynamics of select print media coverage of the Caribbean during April–June 1993. Analyzes articles from *The New York Times, The Christian Science Monitor, Newsweek,* and *Time.*

3249 Issues and problems in Caribbean public administration. Edited by Selwyn D. Ryan and Deryck R. Brown. 2nd ed. St. Augustine, Trinidad: Institute of Social and Economic Research (ISER), Univ. of the West Indies, 1992. 373 p.: bibl.

Comprehensive reader on Caribbean public management covers public enterprise control and regulation, planning and development, budgeting and financial management, public corporations, administrative reform, the ombudsman, and other areas.

3250 Jagan, Cheddi. Caribbean community: cross-roads to the future. (*Caribb. Q.*, 40:3/4, Sept./Dec. 1994, p. 1–14, bibl.)

Geopolitical and historical overview of relations between the developed and the developing world, and of the economic and political challenges facing the contemporary Caribbean. Part of a plea for a New Global Humanitarian Order.

3251 Mohamed, S.Y. Fundamental rights and freedoms of the Commonwealth Caribbean. Georgetown: S.Y. Mohamed, 1993. 207 p.: bibl., index.

Examines civil and political rights in the English-speaking Caribbean, and how constitutional mandates and judicial action have protected those rights.

3252 Ragoonath, Bishnu. Decentralization via local government in the Commonwealth Caribbean. (*Lat. Am. Stud./Japan*, 13, 1994, p. 1–21)

Discusses decentralization of government authority in the English-speaking Caribbean. Investigates evolution, development, and constraints of local government operations.

3253 Ryan, Selwyn D. Gobernabilidad democrática y condiciones sociales en el Caribe angolófono. (*in* Gobernabilidad y desarrollo democrático en América Latina y el Caribe. New York: Programa de las Naciones Unidas para el Desarrollo, 1997, p. 44–71)

Examines economic, political, and social constraints to "good governance" of a structural and operational nature, and challenges to formulating and executing social policy in the English-speaking Caribbean. Specifically discusses role of structural adjustment, drugs, corruption, poverty, and youth.

3254 Symposium on the Role of the Ombudsman in the Commonwealth Caribbean, *Barbados, 1989.* The ombudsman: Caribbean and international perspectives. Edited by Patrick A.M. Emmanuel. Cave Hill, Barbados: Institute of Social and Economic Research, Univ. of the West Indies, 1993. 288 p.: bibl.

Proceedings of a conference appraising role and status of the ombudsman in the English-speaking Caribbean. Noted scholars and jurists examine constitutional and political dynamics of the ombudsman in Guyana, Trinidad and Tobago, Jamaica, Barbados, and Saint Lucia. Offers a comparative perspective on those dynamics by providing assessments on Britain, Canada, and Scandinavia. Also explores conceptual aspects of the issue. Includes a short but useful bibliography on the ombudsman in the Caribbean.

Torres-Rivas, Edelberto. Para entender El Caribe. See item **4931.**

3255 Williams, Gwendoline. The effectiveness of newly established agencies and institutions: Caribbean public sector. (*Soc. Econ. Stud.*, 39:2, June 1990, p. 105–133, appendix, bibl.)

Probes institutional, economic, and political factors affecting the organizational efficiency of regional institutions in the Commonwealth Caribbean.

DOMINICAN REPUBLIC

3256 Abinader, José Rafael. La corrupción administrativa en América Latina: el caso de la República Dominicana. Santo Domingo: Editora Panamericana, 1992. 61 p.: bibl.

Assesses legal, fiscal, and political

bases for administrative corruption in the Dominican Republic. Offers suggestions for reform to curtail governmental and quasi-governmental malpractice.

3257 Betances, Emelio. State and society in the Dominican Republic. Foreword by Hobart Spalding. Boulder, Colo.: Westview Press, 1995. 162 p.: bibl., index, maps. (Latin American perspectives series; 15)

Cogent analysis of rulership in the Dominican Republic that offers historical backdrop of political rule, and examines the structural-functional aspects of governance, political economy of State power, and role of domestic and foreign actors in contemporary political development of the nation.

3258 Bolívar Díaz, Juan. El proceso electoral de 1996: algunas interrogantes. (*Estud. Soc./Santo Domingo*, 29:104, abril/junio 1996, p. 7–16)

Examines transparency of 1996 presidential elections, including role of civil society and international observers.

3259 Gautreaux Piñeyro, Bonaparte. El tiempo de la tormenta: Bosch, Caamaño y el PRD. Santo Domingo: Editora de Colores, 1994. 141 p.

Offers a commentary on the nature, influences on, and results of political rule in the Dominican Republic during the 1960s, and on the role of the US and hemispheric geopolitics in the Juan Bosch affair.

3260 Grimaldi, Víctor. Crisis en 1990 y una agenda nacional más allá de 1994. Santo Domingo: Amigo del Hogar, 1993. 167 p.

Assesses causes, outcomes, and role of domestic and international actors in 1990 political crisis. Offers recommendations for political adaptations in several political and economic arenas to avoid a repetition of 1990. See also item **3261.**

3261 Hartlyn, Jonathan. Crisis-ridden elections (again) in the Dominican Republic: neopatrimonialism, presidentialism, and weak electoral oversight. (*J. Interam. Stud. World Aff.*, 36:4, Winter 1994, p. 91–144, bibl., tables)

Examines how institutional, political, economic, and other domestic and international factors shape electoral politics. Argues for reforms in political culture and institu-

tions, and for a greater role for civil society in the electoral process. See also item **3260.**

3262 Maríñez, Pablo A. Democracia y procesos electorales en República Dominicana. Santo Domingo: Editora Alfa y Omega, 1994. 271 p.: bibl.

Collection of some of the author's previously published work provides valuable insight into institutional, political, and economic vicissitudes of power and politics in the Dominican Republic.

Meza, Rubén Ariel. El triángulo de la opresión. See item **2970.**

3263 Peña Gómez, José Francisco and Fernando Alvarez Bogaert. Anatomía del fraude electoral: testimonio prelimina. Santo Domingo: Editorial Gente, 1994. 201 p.: ill.

Two losing candidates for the presidency and vice presidency provide copious documentation of electoral malpractice in the 1994 elections.

3264 Ramírez Morillo, Belarminio. Joaquín Balaguer: estudio de un liderazgo. Santo Domingo: Fundación de Estudios Sociopolíticos, Jurídicos y Económicos, 1994. 185 p.: bibl., ill.

Wide-ranging biographical discussion of the life and times of Joaquín Balaguer examines his roles as scholar, charismatic politician, diplomat, and political mentor. Also examines ways in which he shaped national development of contemporary Dominican Republic.

3265 Ramírez Morillo, Belarminio. El populismo en la República Dominicana. Santo Domingo: Editora Cumbre, 1991. 148 p.: bibl.

Offers insights into nature of populism in the Dominican Republic. Looks at dynamics of political culture and institutional and organizational expressions of populism, along with some of its consequences. Includes a comparative perspective on populism elsewhere in the Americas.

3266 Seminario sobre Reforma Institucional y Democracia, *Santiago de los Caballeros, Dominican Republic, 1991*. Actas. Recopilación de Adriano Miguel Tejada. Santiago, Dominican Republic: PUCMM, 1993. 151 p.: bibl. (Col. Documentos; 169)

Collection of papers from a conference on democracy, institutional reform, and civil society in the Dominican Republic that includes probing commentaries by analysts, some of whom later rose to positions of prominence in the government of President Leonel Fernández.

3267 Taveras Guzmán, Juan Arístides. Algunas vivencias. Santo Domingo: Editora Corripio, 1993. 472 p.: ill. (some col.).

Rich collection of speeches on political, economic, social, and international issues by a distinguished diplomat and public servant spanning more than three decades.

3268 Tejera, Eduardo J. Las reformas estructurales dominicanas: la nueva agenda. Santo Domingo: Editora Alfa y Omega, 1993. 240 p.

Examination of economic and fiscal situation of the Dominican Republic offers suggestions for fiscal, economic, and monetary reform.

3269 Velázquez-Mainardi, M.A. Corrupción e impunidad. Santo Domingo: Editora Tele-3, 1993. 365 p.

Journalist discloses the institutional, political, economic, and legal aspects of corruption in the Dominican Republic. Suggests that exposure of fraud is necessary for national rehabilitation.

3270 Wucker, Michele. Democracy comes to Hispaniola. (*World Policy J.*, 13:3, Fall 1996, p. 80–88)

Discusses the travails of democracy in Haiti and the Dominican Republic, the race factor in Dominican politics and its impact on relations with Haiti, and the mid-1980s rapprochement between the leadership of the two countries.

GRENADA

3271 Collins, Merle. Grenada ten years and more: memory and collective responsibility. (*Caribb. Q.*, 41:2, June 1995, p. 71–78, bibl.)

Balanced retrospective on Grenada a decade after 1983 US intervention. Explains some of the consequences of the 1983 internal power struggle and the "roller-coaster to disaster."

Henry, Paget. Grenada and the theory of peripheral transformation. See item **4843**.

Meeks, Brian. Caribbean insurrections. See item **3324**.

3272 Noguera, Pedro A. Adult literacy and participation democracy in revolutionary Grenada. (*Caribb. Q.*, 41:2, June 1995, p. 38–56, bibl., table)

Examines attempts to use literacy as a key symbolic and substantive instrument of sociopolitical transformation in Grenada during the period of the People's Revolutionary Government.

3273 Noguera, Pedro A. Charismatic leadership and popular support: a comparison of the leadership styles of Eric Gairy and Maurice Bishop. (*Soc. Econ. Stud.*, 44:1, March 1995, p. 1–29, bibl., tables)

Comparative assessment of leadership styles of Eric Gairy and Maurice Bishop are part of a larger examination of the efficacy of charismatic leadership in post-colonial political rule in Grenada.

GUYANA

3274 Grant, Rudolph W. Politics, religion and education: the Canadian Presbyterian Church and the struggle over schools in Guyana. (*J. Caribb. Hist.*, 27:2, 1993, p. 176–196)

Examines role of religion in the education sector in British Guiana, the change in role as the colony approached independence, and factors explaining the abandonment by the Canadian Presbyterian Church of its educational partnership with the government.

3275 Mars, Perry. State intervention and ethnic conflict resolution: Guyana and the Caribbean experience. (*Comp. Polit.*, 27:2, Jan. 1995, p. 167–186, tables)

Studies the sociological and political underpinnings of ethnic conflict in Guyana and modes of conflict resolution adopted by State and nonstate entities.

3276 Rodney, Walter. The birth of the Guyanese working class and the first sugar strikes, 1840/41 and 1847. Georgetown: Working People's Alliance, 1989. 24 p.

Analyzes circumstances precipitating labor protests in mid–19th-century British Guiana and the consequences for political consciousness and activism.

3277 Sallahuddin. Labour at the crossroads. Georgetown: New Guyana Co., 1992. 316 p.

Provides copious documentation and cogent analysis of the travails of the labor movement in Guyana and the manner in which political rule both helped and hindered the pursuit of workers' rights.

HAITI

Averill, Gage. *Aranje* to *Angaje:* carnival politics and music in Haiti. See *HLAS 56:4721.*

3278 Avril, Prosper. Vérités et révélations. v. 1, Le silence rompu, 16 septembre 1988 au 17 septembre 1991. Port-au-Prince: Bibliothèque nationale d'Haiti, 1993. 1 v: appendices.

"Insider's account" of the dynamics of political-military rule in Haiti from Sept. 1988–Sept. 1991 includes 33 appendixes that give valuable insight into Haiti's political drama during that period.

3279 Bazin, Marc L. Haïti 92: democratie sous pression. Port-au-Prince: Editions H. Deschamps, 1995. 274 p.: bibl., ill.

Documents political economy and political institutional aspects of contemporary Haiti, and discusses the role of several Haitian and foreign actors in political conflict resolution efforts in early 1990s.

3280 Bien-Aimé, Wilfrid. Fonction publique et démocratie. (*Forum Libre,* 11, 1992, p. 13–32, bibl., photo)

Explores nature of democracy in practice, considers requirements for functional democracy in Haiti, and outlines some tasks facing public servants operating in a democratic Haiti.

3281 Castor, Suzy. Les femmes haïtiennes aux élections de 1990. Port-au-Prince: CRESFED, 1994. 160 p.: ill.

Examines role of gender in Haitian politics. Also looks at status and activism of women as leaders and followers in Haitian politics since 1986 and in various areas of political and civil life.

3282 Dabel, Verly. La crise haïtienne: quelle(s) issue(s). Port-au-Prince: Arnegraph, 1993. 278 p.: bibl.

Surveys history and sociopolitical dimensions of political and socioeconomic plight of Haiti, and spotlights some changes necessary for improving conditions.

3283 Delince, Kern. Les forces politiques en Haïti: manuel d'histoire contemporaine. Paris: Editions Karthala; Plantation, Fla.: Pegasus Books, 1993. 323 p.: bibl., map.

Examination of the political sociology of Haiti places political governance of the nation in historical and geopolitical context.

3284 Etheart, Bernard. La democracia participativa en Haití: la experiencia de las organizaciones no gubernamentales. (*Estud. Latinoam./México,* 2:3, enero/junio 1995, p. 103–122)

Briefly examines how authoritarian politics and political economy in Haiti helped to shape role and experiences of nongovernmental organizations.

3285 The human rights record of the Haitian national police. Washington: Human Rights Watch/Americas; National Coalition for Haitian Refugees; Washington Office on Latin America, 1997. 40 p.

Documents actions of the new civilian law enforcement agency, showing how a combination of poor attitudes, resource limitations, incompetence, and misguided action have resulted in violation of citizens' rights and undermining of confidence both in the new agents of public order and in government generally. See also item **3291.**

3286 Maesschalck, Marc. La filosofía política de los derechos del hombre: una mirada desde Haiti. (*Estud. Soc./Santo Domingo,* 27:96, abril/junio 1994, p. 9–25)

Places struggle for human rights in Haiti in international context, noting factors such as imperialism and international public opinion. Considers both civil/political and economic/social rights.

3287 Moïse, Claude. La Constitución de 1987, en la transición política haitiana. (*Cienc. Soc./Santo Domingo,* 18:3, julio/sept. 1993, p. 319–335)

Discusses political and constitutional contexts of the 1987 Haitian constitutional amendment. See also items **3288** and **3289.**

3288 Moïse, Claude. Constitución y luchas políticas en Haití. (*Cienc. Soc./Santo Domingo,* 18:3, julio/sept. 1993, p. 247–253)

Cursory examination of historical backdrop of constitutional change in Haiti. See also items **3287** and **3289**.

3289 Moïse, Claude. Une constitution dans la tourmente: le nouveau régime politique haïtien et la crise nationale, 1987–1993, Montréal: Editions Images, 1994. 196 p.

Examines constitutional architecture of governance in Haiti and analyzes legal and constitutional aspects of efforts to resolve the political crisis that followed the ejection of Jean-Bertrand Aristide from the presidency. See also items **3287** and **3288**.

3290 Organization of American States (OAS). Report on the situation of human rights in Haiti. Washington: General Secretariat, Organization of American States, 1993. 56 p. (OAS official records; OEA/Ser.L/V/II.83, doc. 18, May 9, 1993, Original: Spanish)

Human rights status report for period Feb. 1992–Feb. 1993 places the situation in larger political context and addresses consequent refugee plight.

3291 Silencing a people: the destruction of civil society in Haiti. New York: Human Rights Watch Americas, 1993. 136 p.: bibl.

Close-up report reveals repression meted out to religious, political, economic, human rights, and other interest groups and individuals in Haiti in early 1990s. Discusses ways in which civil society has been affected. See also item **3285.**

Verger, Jean-Claude de. Haïti: vive la démocratie! See item **4940.**

Wucker, Michele. Democracy comes to Hispaniola. See item **3270.**

JAMAICA

3292 Ashby, Timothy. Missed opportunities: the rise and fall of Jamaica's Edward Seaga. Indianapolis: Hudson Institute, 1989. 40 p.

Effort to explain political victory and defeat of Edward Seaga fails to examine adequately those events in the context of the sociopolitical situation of the nation and the existing geopolitical milieu.

3293 Mills, Gladstone E. Grist for the Mills: reflections on a life. Kingston: Ian Randle, 1994. 204 p.: ill., index.

Autobiographically oriented account by a distinguished Jamaican scholar-public servant focuses on the politics of change in Jamaica and, to a lesser extent, in the Commonwealth Caribbean. Work is more sociological than political.

3294 Payne, Anthony J. Politics in Jamaica. New York: St. Martin's Press, 1995. 223 p.: bibl., index, maps.

Assessment of post-independence political landscape of Jamaica examines ideological, economic, foreign policy, political organizational, and sociocultural dynamics of the Jamaican polity.

3295 Stone, Carl. Carl Stone on Jamaican politics, economics & society. Kingston: Gleaner Co., 1989. 118 p.

Collection of 49 newspaper columns published in the Jamaican newspaper *Gleaner* from 1987–89 covers national and international political, economic, and social issues. Offers valuable insights into Jamaican political sociology during one of the most challenging periods of the country's contemporary history. See also item **3296.**

3296 Stone, Carl. The Stone columns: the last year's work; a selection of Carl Stone's *Gleaner* articles, January 1992 to February 1993. Edited by Rosemarie Stone. Kingston: Sangster's Book Stores, 1994. 200 p.

Collection of the 65 newspaper articles written by distinguished political sociologist Carl Stone during the year preceding his death in Feb. 1993. Includes some tributes to him. See also item **3295.**

LESSER ANTILLES
British Commonwealth

3297 Irish, J.A. George. Life in a colonial crucible: labor and social change in Montserrat, 1946–present. Plymouth, Montserrat: JAGPI Productions; Brooklyn, N.Y.: Caribbean Research Center, Medgar Evers College (CUNY), 1991. 178 p.

Outlines dynamics of the politics of labor reform in the context of sociopolitical life in Montserrat and the politics of change in the region.

3298 Moree, Lowell A. The black Bahamian: his indomitable quest for metaphysical, ontological, and political balance. New York: Vantage Press, 1990. 100 p.

Philosophical and autobiographical commentary on the sociopolitical dynamics of race, culture, and society in the Bahamas.

3299 Saint Lucia. Electoral Dept. Report on general elections, 27th April 1992. Castries: Electoral Office, 1992. 121 p.: ill., maps.

Official report of the April 1992 general elections includes details on voter turnout, election results, and demographic changes.

Dutch

3300 Croese, Koen. Interventie op afspraak: Nederlandse mariniers op Curaçao [Intervention by agreement: Dutch marines in Curaçao]. Zutphen, The Netherlands: Walburg, 1998. 136 p.: bibl., ill., map.

Provides detailed reconstruction of and background to the developments of May 30, 1969, the date on which an industrial strike escalated into major socioeconomic unrest. In accordance with the Charter of the Kingdom, the Curaçaoan government called in the Dutch military to restore order. Despite book's title, author argues that this assistance cannot be labeled an intervention. Also claims that there were secret plans to transfer sovereignty over the Netherlands Antilles to Venezuela, but hypothesis lacks substantial proof. [R. Hoefte]

3301 Hoefnagels, Peter. Three countries in one kingdom: the Netherlands Antilles and the paradox of independence. (*Low Countries/Rekkem*, 1997/1998, p. 46–54, bibl., photos)

Describes clash of Dutch and Antillean cultures regarding future of Dutch/Antillean relations. Suggests Antilleans exploit Dutch post-colonial feelings of guilt to retain a Dutch passport and Dutch "development aid, Antillean style," which leads only to greater dependence on The Netherlands. However, the Antilles and Aruba are a headache for the Dutch, if only because of the complicated and often inefficient administrative structure of the islands. [R. Hoefte]

3302 Lampe, Armando. A favor de la autonomía de las islas holandesas. (*Caribb. Stud.*, 26:3/4, July/Dec. 1993, p. 335–346)

Examines colonization experience of the Dutch Caribbean islands and the prospects for decolonization.

3303 Lampe, Armando. La descolonización interrumpida: el caso de las islas holandesas en el Caribe. Aruba: Charuba, 1992. 68 p.

Briefly analyzes ambivalence of the Netherlands Antilles over pursuing independence. Reviews attempts to strike a balance between full control and relative autonomy.

3304 Oostindie, Gert and **Peter Verton.** Ki sorto di Reino?: visies en verwachtingen van Antillianen en Arubanen omtrent het Koninkrijk [What kind of Kingdom?: Antillean and Aruban views and expectations of the Kingdom of The Netherlands]. The Hague: Sdu, 1998. 217 p.: appendix, bibl., tables.

Presents outcome of opinion poll from the six Dutch Caribbean islands in 1997–98. Survey covers views and expectations of Antilleans and Arubans with regard to the Kingdom and to The Netherlands in particular. Themes covered include constitutional structure, residence and passport, protection of national territory, democracy and constitutional rule, economic support, respect, and education. Includes summaries in English and Papiamentu. [R. Hoefte]

French

3305 Daniel, Justin. Political constraints of economic dependency: the case of Guadeloupe and Martinique. (*Caribb. Stud.*, 26: 3/4, July/Dec. 1993, p. 311–334)

Examines multiple dynamics of the dependency and clientilistic relationship between France and some of its territories in the Caribbean.

PUERTO RICO

3306 Berríos Martínez, Rubén. Puerto Rico: nacionalidad y plebiscito. Prólogo por Fernando Martín García. Puerto Nuevo, P.R.: Editorial Libertad, 1993. 167 p.

Sociopolitical analysis of the prospects for change in Puerto Rico's status includes examination of potential costs and consequences of pursuing the various options, especially independence.

3307 Colonial dilemma: critical perspectives on contemporary Puerto Rico. Edited by Edwin Meléndez and Edgardo Meléndez. Boston: South End Press, 1993. 255 p.: bibl., index.

Comprehensive, inter-disciplinary work examines social, political, and economic life in Puerto Rico in the context of the island's political and geopolitical milieu.

3308 Cruz Hernández, Eduardo Luis. El plebiscito de 1967: origen, desarrollo y consecuencias en la política puertorriqueña. Río Piedras, P.R.: Editorial Edil, 1993. 315 p.: bibl., ill.

Historically-informed description and analysis of the 1967 plebiscite examines origin, development, and consequences of that vote for the political-constitutional direction of Puerto Rico's future status.

3309 Díaz, José O. Puerto Rico, the United States, and the 1993 referendum on political status. (*LARR*, 30:1, 1995, p. 203–211)

Reviews seven books examining the historical and contemporary political and sociocultural dynamics of Puerto Rican politics specifically and as part of larger examination of Caribbean foreign and domestic politics.

3310 Encuentro de Historiadores en Puerto Rico, *Río Piedras, P.R., 1990.* Del nacionalismo al populismo: cultura y política en Puerto Rico. Recopilación de Silvia Alvarez-Curbelo y María Elena Rodríguez Castro. Río Piedras, P.R.: Decanato de Estudios Graduados e Investigación, Recinto de Río Piedras, Univ. de Puerto Rico; Ediciones Huracán, 1993. 205 p.: bibl.

Papers offer historical insights into the search for cultural and political identity in Puerto Rico. '

3311 Meléndez, Edgardo. El estudio de los partidos políticos en Puerto Rico. (*Rev. Cienc. Soc./Río Piedras*, 30:3/4, 1995, p. 49–100)

Study of political parties in Puerto Rico goes beyond examination of the structural and functional aspects of the parties to examine the dynamics of political party operation in the context of elite and class analysis.

3312 Puerto Rico Federal Affairs Administration. Proceso plebiscitario, 1989–1991 = Political status referendum, 1989–1991. v. 1–3. Washington: Puerto Rico Federal Affairs Administration; Hato Rey, P.R.: Ramallo Bros., 1992 3 v.

Vol. 1 is a compendium of official communications among Puerto Rican political officials, and between governmental officials in Puerto Rico and Washington, on political, economic, and other considerations relating to status change. Also includes copies of San Juan and Washington legislative documents dealing with status questions. Vol. 2 includes studies by primarily Congresional Research Service specialists pertaining to the tax, economic, trade, welfare, citizenship, language, and other implications of a status change for Puerto Rico. Vol. 3 contains General Accounting Office reports and Congressional briefing papers on various aspects and implications of a status change for Puerto Rico.

3313 Samoiloff, Louise Cripps. Puerto Rico: the case for independence. Foreword by Gordon K. Lewis. 2nd ed. Dorado, P.R.: Borinquen Books, 1993. 161 p.: bibl.

Well-written assessment of pros and cons of Puerto Rico's status options. Supports independence, but comments on some of the risks involved in pursuing this option. Cites historical, cultural, and economic examples in advancing a political science appraisal and statement.

3314 Seda Bonilla, Eduardo. Los derechos civiles en la cultura puertorriqueña. 5ta ed. rev. Rio Piedras, P.R.: Ediciones Bayoan, 1991. 256 p.: bibl., ill.

Examines civil, political, economic, social, and cultural rights in Puerto Rico, and analyzes some of the dynamics of race and culture on the island.

SURINAME

3315 Derveld, Ferdy E.R. Ethnicity, spoils, politics, migration and nation building, 1965–1985. (*J. Soc. Sci./Paramaribo*, 3:1/2, 1996, p. 65–90, appendix, bibl., tables)

Discusses relationship between political changes in Suriname and migration from that country to The Netherlands. Presents overview of Dutch literature on migration from Suriname; then looks at political developments and elections in Suriname from 1963–80. Concludes that spoils, ethnicity, and politics have had some influence on migration from Suriname to The Netherlands, especially after 1973. [R. Hoefte]

Groot, Silvia W. de. Changing attitudes: politics of Maroons versus politics of the government in Surinam. See *HLAS 56:1825.*

3316 Haakmat, André. Herinneringen aan de toekomst van Suriname: ervaringen en beschouwingen. [Memories of the future of Suriname: experiences and opinions.] Amsterdam: Arbeiderspers, 1996. 202 p.

Memoirs of former "super minister" and political commentator discuss past and future of Suriname politics. Written before May 1996 elections, Haakmat predicts end of ethnic politics and increasing importance of former military leader Desi Bouterse. Volume has been interpreted generally as Haakmat's attempt to return to the center of Surinamese politics. [R. Hoefte]

3317 Price, Richard. Executing ethnicity: the killings in Suriname. *(Cult. Anthropol.,* 10:4, Nov. 1995, p. 437–471, bibl.)

Detailed study examines sociological and political antecedents to, and consequences of, the late 1980s ethnic strife in Suriname. For anthropologist's comment, see item **891.**

3318 Sedney, Jules. De toekomst van ons verleden: democratie, etniciteit en politieke machtsvorming in Suriname. [The future of our past: democracy, ethnicity and political powerbuilding in Suriname]. Paramaribo: Vaco, 1997. 238 p.: appendix, tables.

Useful study of political developments in Suriname from 1948–96 by former prime minister. Successfully interweaves political analysis and personal experiences. Valuable appendix provides overviews of elections and participating parties, development of the electoral system, and a list of cabinet ministers and parliamentarians in each term. Annotations are minimal. [R. Hoefte]

3319 Sedoc-Dahlberg, Betty Nelly. Democracy and human rights in Suriname. *(in* Democracy and human rights in the Caribbean. Boulder, Colo.: Westview Press, 1997, p. 212–229)

Examines civil and economic/social rights, in search of a balance to prevent repeated authoritarian interruptions in Suriname. Assesses connections among regime instability, economic stagnation, and decrease of State security. Shows that progress has been made in civil and political rights,

but that success in economic and social rights has been jeopardized by government's focus on economic reforms such as adjustment programs. [R. Hoefte]

TRINIDAD AND TOBAGO

3320 Bloeser, Charles. Deprivation, rationality, and rebellion: the case of Trinidad and Tobago. *(Caribb. Stud.,* 25:3/4, 1992, p. 277–304, tables)

Uses relative deprivation and rational actor theory to examine 1990 Jamaat-al-Muslimeen coup attempt in Trinidad. Concludes that a sense of relative deprivation existed among the Jamaat, but that rational choice calculations also marked the attempt to seize State power. See also item **3321.**

3321 Deosaran, Ramesh. A society under siege: a study of political confusion and legal mysticism. Port of Spain: McAl Psychological Research Centre, Univ. of the West Indies, 1993. 270 p.: bibl., ill., index, maps.

In a psychological analysis of the contemporary political drama of Trinidad and Tobago, author uses 1990 coup attempt as a starting point to examine the sociopathology of political rule and the dynamics of formal and informal conflict resolution in the twin-island republic. See also item **3320.**

3322 Inamete, Ufot. Politics and governance in Trinidad and Tobago: major issues and developments. *(Caribb. Stud.,* 25:3/4, 1992, p. 305–324, bibl.)

Examines cultural diversity, party politics, governmental structure, economic performance, and other domestic dynamics allied with regional action in the political life of Trinidad and Tobago.

3323 Joseph, George. Diary of a candidate. Port of Spain: Umbala International Pub., 1993. 352 p.

Portrays drama of electoral politics in Trinidad and Tobago from the vantage point of a candidate. Provides insights into the campaign bacchanal and the institutional and political factors dictating the political modus operandi of the twin-island republic.

3324 Meeks, Brian. Caribbean insurrections. *(Caribb. Q.,* 41:2, June 1995, p. 1–23, bibl.)

Explores sociopolitical and ideological contexts and precipitants of the challenges to the established political order in Trinidad and Tobago in 1970 and 1990, and in Grenada in 1979.

3325 Ryan, Selwyn D. The disillusioned electorate: the politics of succession in Trinidad and Tobago. Port of Spain: Inprint Caribbean, 1989. 344 p.: bibl., ill.

Richly detailed study examines nature and influence of popular participation in electoral continuity and change in Trinidad and Tobago. Focuses on the economic, racial, personality, and organizational dynamics of politics in the country.

3326 Williams, Eric Eustace. Eric E. Williams speaks: essays on colonialism and independence. Edited by Selwyn Reginald Cudjoe. Wellesley, Mass.: Calaloux Publications; Amherst: Univ. of Massachusetts Press, 1993. 436 p.: bibl., ill., index.

Collection of speeches and articles by the late Eric Williams, along with a few other contributions, reveals Williams to be a consummate scholar and politician as well as a charismatic leader who pursued politics of change in the Caribbean.

CUBA

JUAN M. DEL AGUILA, *Associate Professor of Political Science, Emory University*

THE ISSUES DOMINATING MUCH OF CONTEMPORARY PUBLISHING in Cuba concern processes of change that are slowly and (some authors contend) inexorably reshaping the nation's political system, economy and society. Without evidence of a transition away from command socialism, or of an authentic expansion of political rights and freedoms, authors speculate about the forces that finally may bring about radically different conditions.

For instance, electoral changes dating from the mid-1990s presumably have expanded the pool of candidates from which voters choose, though the Communist Party closely monitors elections and anti-system candidates are forbidden. Still, the process expands the political opportunities of pro-system candidates and contributes to the rotation of loyal elites. Writing on the Cuban Communist Party itself has declined, suggesting that scholars are less willing to repeat the findings of earlier research.

Alternatively, the fact that rotation takes place has neither altered the Party's hegemonic position nor changed the character of ancillary and subordinate institutions such as the National Assembly of People's Power. Genuine democratization of governance at any level is as incompatible with the leadership's wishes in the 1990s as was the case in the 1960s, and Castro's central role remains undiminished. In short, rotation stems from a need to satisfy the shifting political demands of different constituencies inside the ruling coalition, but it is not intended to change the fundamental dynamics of governance.

The process of economic reform slowed considerably in the mid-1990s due to the leadership's reluctance to proceed with measures that would undermine social control. However, continued deterioration suggests that the economy's poor performance is acceptable to a government that is not willing to introduce fundamental structural reforms nor grant greater individual or social freedoms.

Although the need for dramatic change has become evident to scholars who are either critical or still marginally sympathetic to the revolution, the political leadership categorically rejects that option. At the policy level, paralysis is increasingly apparent due to the power conflicts among pro-system reformers, orthodox policymakers, and those marking time.

Silvia Caunedo's article "La siempre fiel isla de Cuba: la realidad del cambio" indicates that this unresolved tension is the basic theme of some of the literature of the 1990s (item **3331**). She maintains that the regime's "commitment to immobilism and control of society" is at the root of a crisis of legitimacy affecting the relationship between government and society.

However, the growth of "civil society" and the proliferation of pro-democracy dissident groups continues to generate changes in the nation's cultural climate, encouraged perhaps by public manifestations from the Catholic Church on moral and religious matters (item **3332**). A palpable desire for moral renovation is evident in works published both in and outside of Cuba which challenge the prevailing official view that the revolutionary value system remains strong and credible.

In sum, the literature for this period reflects the ambivalence (and for a dwindling few, melancholy) with which scholars tend to view Cuba in the post-Communist world. Minimal expectations for either economic regeneration or political liberalization form the basis for an expanding scholarly consensus. Stasis and decay, rather than dynamism or new policies, are the recurring themes in much of the academic literature surveyed, indicating that Cuba no longer excites the intellectual passions of a bygone era.

3327 Asambleas provinciales de balance del Partido Comunista de Cuba: 5 de enero al 24 de febrero de 1991. Edición de Iraida Aguirrechu, Dalia Ramos y María Cristina Zamora. La Habana: Editora Política, 1991. 314 p.: ill.

Official account of discussions sponsored by Communist Party during provincial assemblies in 1991. Includes information on local, provincial and national leaders; emphasis is on political-ideological work and on the need to understand what "the special period in peacetime" means for individuals, institutions, and the whole country.

3328 Bengelsdorf, Carollee. The problem of democracy in Cuba: between vision and reality. New York: Oxford Univ. Press, 1994. 247 p.: bibl., index.

A belated, but nontheless very good effort to explore the irreconocilable tension between democracy and authoritarian, paternalist socialism in revolutionary Cuba. Informed by critical Marxism, book challenges the notion that Cuba is an excellent case of "direct democracy," laying responsibility for the absence of freedom and accountability squarely on Castro's dictatorial vocation and the Communist party's hegemony. In a surprising departure, author concludes that "to the degree the (Cuban) leadership continues to insist

upon defining the boundaries of civil society, it *must* in the end fail" (p. 178).

3329 Bunck, Julie Marie. Fidel Castro and the quest for a revolutionary culture in Cuba. University Park: Pennsylvania State Univ. Press, 1994. 252 p.: bibl., index.

An excellent study of political culture, emphasizing cultural and normative resistance to revolutionary values, norms, and goals. Challenges much of the scholarship that maintained that revolution permanently transformed Cuba's traditional culture, and finds that "most Cuban workers rejected many of the revolutionary requirements of the Castro government" (p. 184). Highly recommended.

3330 Los cambios en la constitución cubana. (*Cuad. Nuestra Am.*, 10:20, julio/dic. 1993, p. 180–192)

A short summary of changes to the Cuban constitution that went into effect in 1992, including direct election of deputies to the National Assembly. Includes redefinition of "social property" and discussion of judicial and economic reforms.

3331 Caunedo, Silvia. La siempre fiel isla de Cuba: la realidad del cambio. (*Razón Fe*, 230, sept./oct. 1994, p. 183–196)

A very good analysis of limited economic and political changes through the mid-1990s by a Cuban journalist and historian. Argues that there is no political will to get at the root of the problems and that the regime remains committed to "immobilism and control of society" (p. 192). Concludes with the notion "that the myth of defending socialism's achievements has collapsed," but that Castro's obstinacy means a permanent crisis and general misery.

Cuadra, Angel. Angel Cuadra: the poet in socialist Cuba. See *HLAS 56:3964.*

3332 Cuba: voices from within. (*Hemisphere/Miami*, 5:3, Summer/Fall 1993, p. 2–6)
Edited excerpts from the Cuban bishops' message in 1993, with brief response from sympathizers and "official" spokesmen. The contrast demonstrates just how far apart Church and State remain on matters of morality, doctrine, and the country's future.

3333 Cuba's transition to democracy: lessons from the former Soviet bloc; a conference. Miami: Cuban American National Foundation's Endowment for Cuban American Studies, 1992. 243 p.
This book is a compilation of statements and brief presentations on the subject of a future transition to democracy and market economics in post-communist Cuba. Participants in the conference included exiled academics, the business community, journalists, and former officials from Eastern European countries. Works of this genre common in the early 1990s, when expectations of Cuba's collapse ran amok in some groups and institutions of the exile community.

3334 Dilla Alfonso, Haroldo. Cuba: la agenda democrática y la rearticulación del consenso político. (*Rev. Rev. Interam.*, 22:3/4, otoño/invierno 1992, p. 99–124)
A thoughtful analysis of why socialism remains Cuba's only real option, though calling for political reforms and a "new consensus." Takes issue with arguments of liberal proponents of reform on the grounds that, ideologically and politically, Cuban socialism is not exhausted. Calls for renovation through a Party of the Cuban Nation based on new doctrines and programs.

3335 Dilla Alfonso, Haroldo. Municipios y construcción democrática en Cuba. (*Perf. Latinoam.*, 5:8, enero/junio 1996, p. 79–95, bibl.)

An evaluation of the system of local government, said to be successful in "tasks related to regional development," less so in "conciliating interests in local societies becoming more complex." Good primary data, and devoid of ideological cant.

3336 Domínguez, Jorge I. Cuba en la comunidad internacional en los noventa: soberanía, derechos humanos y democracia. (*Estud. Int. /Santiago*, 27:107/108, julio-sept./oct.–dic. 1994, p. 281–306)
A somewhat optimistic analysis of how a combination of international pressures and changes in US policy could induce moderation and partial liberalization in Cuba. Argues that Cuban government's absolutist view of sovereignty may be an obstacle to internal reforms, but that Cuba must abide by new interpretations of democracy and human rights if it is to re-enter the regional mainstream.

3337 Domínguez, Jorge I. Twenty-five years of Cuban studies. (*Cuba. Stud.*, 25, 1995, p. 3–26)
Summary and synthesis of Cuban studies as a field of study, showing the evolution of the field and the themes that drive scholarly research on domestic and foreign policy issues. A very good reference piece, well-written, and comprehensive.

3338 Edelstein, Joel C. The future of democracy in Cuba. (*Lat. Am. Perspect.*, 22:4, Fall 1995, p. 7–42, bibl.)
An interesting effort from a leftist perspective on the dilemmas and contradictions of democratizing a highly centralized system in the midst of economic difficulties and external pressures. Raises issues of mass-elite relationships, of democracy and socialism, and of pluralism and equity. Part of an ongoing critical debate in sectors of the academic left, some still sympathetic to Cuba; others, much more critical.

3339 Feinsilver, Julie M. Healing the masses: Cuban health politics at home and abroad. Foreword by David E. Apter. Berkeley: Univ. of California Press, 1993. 327 p.: bibl., index.
An excellent, balanced study of the Cuban health system, based on good data, interviews, and the author's recognized expertise on the subject. Good study of how resources can improve public health, while at the same time acknowledging the difficulties

that stem from a planned economy. Overall, a very good analysis, particularly of how the health system of the 1990s is increasingly inadequate.

3340 Fogel, Jean-François and Bertrand Rosenthal. Fin de siglo a la Habana. Traducido del francés por Helena Uribe de Lemoine. Madrid: Anaya & Mario Muchnik, 1995. 679 p.: bibl., index, maps. (Pruebas al canto)

An indispensable book for anyone seeking to understand the reasons for Castroism's failures in the 1990s. Likely to be the definitive investigation of the Ochoa trial and its consequences; larger issues confronting Cuban communism make up the balance of the book. In the end, Cuba drifts (*sin ataduras*), and authors claim that since 1992, Cuba lives its paradoxical independence.

3341 Foro Internacional Cuba y la Transición a la Democracia, *Madrid, 1991.* Foro internacional Cuba y la transición a la democracia: Madrid, 26 y 27 de noviembre de 1991. Madrid: Comité Cubano Pro Derechos Humanos, España, 1992. 190 p.

A series of brief commentaries, testimonials, and accounts of Cuba's present dilemmas, with a view to projecting a democratic transition. The forum included intellectuals, European political figures, writers, and human rights activists. Part of an effort to compare transitions in Eastern Europe with possible future developments in Cuba.

3342 García Reyes, Miguel and María Guadalupe López de Llergo y Cornejo. Cuba después de la era soviética. Dirección del proyecto de Humberto Garza Elizondo. México: Colegio de México, Centro de Estudios Internacionales, 1994. 300 p.: bibl.

An assessment of Cuba's development strategies since the 1960s, and of the tradeoffs of its dependent relationship on the former communist world. Economic openings of the 1990s alongside efforts to maintain single-party political system could prove untenable in today's global context; recommends that Communist party move to the sidelines and compete for power and support.

3343 Gonzalez, Edward and David F. Ronfeldt. Storm warnings for Cuba. Santa Monica, Calif.: RAND, National Defense Research Institute, 1994. xxiii, 159 p.: bibl.

An excellent analysis of the various scenarios developing in Cuba, focusing on how US policy can either influence them or simply stand aside and let the situation simmer. Advocates a "two track policy," with limited engagement but no unilateral concessions to Castro.

3344 González González, Miroslava. La perestroika como una de las principales causas de la crisis del sistema socialista cubano. Puebla, Mexico: Benemérita Univ. Autónoma de Puebla, Dirección General de Fomento Editorial, 1994. 202 p.: bibl.

An evaluation of perestroika's impact on Cuba's economy, society, government, and culture. Concludes that inevitable fundamental changes will lead to socialism's disappearence.

3345 Halperin, Maurice. Return to Havana: the decline of Cuban society under Castro. Nashville, Tenn.: Vanderbilt Univ. Press, 1994. 209 p.: bibl., index.

A personal account from a prominent intellectual whose writings on Cuba have become a mixture of disillusionment and fatalism. This book is based on an account of Halperin's visit in 1989, which left him less optimistic than ever about Cuba's future. He found "the popular mood one of deep discouragement" (p. 190) and could not imagine "any young Cuban, or even older ones, prepared to die for socialism."

3346 Hidalgo, Ariel. Disidencia: ¿segunda revolución cubana? Miami: Ediciones Universal, 1994. 411 p.: bibl., ill., index. (Col. Cuba y sus jueces)

Personal account by one of Cuba's more prominent academic dissidents of how and why he broke with the system, went to prison, and joined the community of "civic dissidents." Now in exile, Hidalgo provides profiles of dissident leaders in Cuba and in exile, raises important questions regarding the effectiveness of civic resistance, documents instances of abuse, harrassment, and repression of human rights activists by governments, and concludes that Cuba's politics of hatred and intolerance are a recurring historical nightmare.

3347 Hofmeister, Wilhelm. Cuba: reforma sin cambios. (*Contribuciones/Buenos Aires*, 11:2, abril/junio 1994, p. 207–223)

A good summary of some aspects of political, economic, and social changes in the 1990s, based on a visit from delegates belonging to the Konrad Adenauer foundation. Concludes that the regime's principal aim is to "maintain itself in power" (p. 220), but that growing misery makes broader economic reforms inevitable. In the end, "reforms without change" will create perilous and uncertain situation.

Irish, J.A. George. Nicolás Guillén: growth of a revolutionary consciousness. See *HLAS 56: 4142.*

3348 Kapcia, Antoni. The politics of change in Cuba: retrenchment, reform or redefinition? (*in* International Congress of Americanists, *48th, Stockholm, 1994.* Problems of democracy in Latin America. Stockholm, Sweden: Institute of Latin American Studies, Stockholm Univ., 1996, p. 124–158)

A highly-detailed and useful account and interpretation of reformist options and measures, including policy changes. Some discussion of Cuban exile politics as well, and of Castro's still-commanding role as top decision-maker. On the whole, a very solid piece.

3349 Lage, Carlos et al. ¿Cuba? sí, cómo no: no nos resignemos a vivir sin patria. Madrid: P.C.P.E., 1993. 241 p.

Interviews with several Cuban leaders, including Juan Escalona, Carlos Lage, Roberto Robaina, and others. They all take the official line on various subjects, but provide useful primary material. Book based on a visit to Cuba by members of Spain's Communist Party of the Peoples of Spain (PCPE).

3350 Liss, Sheldon B. Fidel!: Castro's political and social thought. Boulder, Colo.: Westview Press, 1994. 261 p.: bibl., index. (Latin American perspectives series; 13)

Little more than a hagiography from a prominent scholar, written from a less-than-critical perspective. Book emphasizes Castro's "political and social thoughts," and author states that "fundamentally, my worldview and Castro's coincide" (p. xii). Still, book is useful because it shows how Marxism, Castro's ambitions, and the international context shaped the Cuban Revolution. Good notes and bibliography included.

3351 Los que se quedaron: conversaciones con Luis Báez. La Habana: Editora Política, 1993. 387 p.: bibl., ill.

Interesting as a brief historical document, particularly because it includes interviews with Dulce Ma. Loynaz and Fernando

Ortiz. Other lesser known individuals tend to the sycophantic.

3352 Lutjens, Sheryl L. Remaking the public sphere: women and revolution in Cuba. (*in* Women and revolution in Africa, Asia, and the New World. Edited by Mary Ann Tétreault. Columbia, S.C.: Univ. of South Carolina Press, 1994, p. 366–393)

A thoughtful critique of the public roles and private lives of Cuban women under socialism, written from a feminist-activist perspective. Still subjected to State paternalism and top-down authority, Cuban women are found to emphasize private life in the midst of intense politization. Concludes that some of the gains of socialism still available to women, but new definitions of the public-private domains will reshape their future roles. For sociologist's comment see item **4863.**

3353 Mallin, Jay. Covering Castro: rise and decline of Cuba's communist dictator. New Brunswick, N.J.: Transaction Publishers; Washington: U.S.-Cuba Institute Press, 1994. 208 p.: index.

A good account of the vicissitudes, fascination, and dangers of covering Fidel Castro; author says, in the end, "it has been highly satisfying." Book contains good material on Cuba's foreign adventures, its espionage network, behind-the-scenes accounts of major decisions, and other information.

3354 Martínez Heredia, Fernando. Desconexión, reinserción y socialismo en Cuba. (*Estud. Latinoam./México,* 1:1, 1994, p. 79–97, bibl.)

Driven by international pressures and internal discontent and disillusionment, Cubans seek to re-interpret the viability of socialism by reinforcing its nationalist roots and aspects of cultural pride. Author argues that "the people defend socialism" because it preserves memories of a glorious past and is capable of reforming itself. Warns of the dangers of "dollarization" and of eroding legitimacy, but concludes somewhat incredulously that "Cuba is a laboratory" (p. 96) for other peoples still wondering about socialism.

3355 Medrano, Mignon. Todo lo dieron por Cuba. Miami: Endowment for Cuban American Studies, 1994. 1 v.

An account of early resistance to the revolution by women, written by a prominent

Cuban-American activist. Relies on testimonies and recollections of underground activities and of life and conditions in prisons.

3356 Miranda, Olivia. El marxismo en el ideal emancipador cubano durante la República neocolonial. (*Temas/Habana*, 3, julio/sept. 1995, p. 44–57)

A somewhat turgid effort to fuse Martí's classical republican philosophy with Marxist-Leninist ideology, in order to interpret the revolution in conventional terms. Repetitive of basic themes articulated in "official history" of last 40 years.

3357 Newey, Adam et al. Cuba redux. (*Index Censorsh.*, 24:4, July/Aug. 1995, p. 114–153, ill., photos)

A good update on emerging, independent groups and organizations that challenge the State's monopoly on information of social and economic conditions. Interviews with known human rights activists like Gustavo Arcos.

3358 Partido Comunista de Cuba. Congreso, 4th, Santiago de Cuba, Cuba, 1991. Island in the storm: the Cuban Communist Party's Fourth Congress. Edited by Gail Reed. Melbourne, Australia: Ocean; New York: Center for Cuban Studies, 1992. 200 p., 8 p. of plates: bibl., ill.

A self-indulgent and uninformed account of the Communist Party's Fourth Congress in 1991, riddled with triumphalism and superficiality. Author claims that "social justice remains the centerpiece of Cuban socialism" (p. 22) and that the party "will stay at the helm all the way" (p. 23) despite multiplying difficulties on all fronts. Disregard the author's opinions and judgements and use this book for the bibliographical information provided on leading cadres.

3359 Pastor, Manuel. Cuba and Cuban studies: crossing boundaries during a "special period." (*LARR*, 31:3, 1996, p. 218–234, bibl.)

Critical review essay of recent literature on Cuba, focusing on historical issues and those related to the current crisis. Pastor's criticisms of some of the literature make sense, but are at times off-base. Concludes with the pious view that "we can begin to offer transitional strategies that make sense and preserve the mantle of social justice" sought by the revolution.

3360 Pérez-Stable, Marifeli. The Cuban Revolution: origins, course, and legacy. New York: Oxford Univ. Press, 1993. 252 p.: bibl., index.

A very good and thoughtful account of the Cuban Revolution, rooted in historical analysis with a solid understanding of the discontinuities shaping revolutionary Cuba. Sees the basic drive as "radical nationalism" in the context of institution and nation building.

3361 Radu, Michael. Cuba's transition: institutional lessons from Eastern Europe. (*J. Interam. Stud. World Aff.*, 37:2, Summer 1995, p. 83–111, bibl.)

A very good comparison of the Cuban and Eastern European cases, focusing on why the differences between Cuba and its former partners in the communist world sustain the Cuban system. Concludes that "resistance to decay leads to militarization" and that accounts for the system's survival.

3362 Rodríguez, Ana and Glenn Garvin. Diary of a survivor: nineteen years in a Cuban women's prison. New York: St. Martin's Press, 1995. 325 p.: index.

A personal account of life in prison by an early opponent of the Castro regime. Written as a testimonial and memoir, it documents the sordid abuses visited upon female prisoners in Castro's jails. One of the very few accounts of its kind, it is part of a genre that probes resistance to dictatorship. Offers details of how Castro's propaganda machine attempts to turn opponents of communism into outcasts.

3363 Rojas, Rafael. Insularidad y exilio de los intelectuales cubanos. (*Estud. Filos. Hist. Let.*, 11:43, invierno 1995/96, p. 69–83)

A very sophisticated account of culture and politics since colonial times, focusing on how exile (*exilio*) and *insilio, entierro,* and *destierro* (banishment) limit the public role of Cuban intellectuals. Argues that in Cuba, cultures appear and disappear in a context where "there is little historical density" and where insularity serves as the foundation for utopian speculation. Worth reading. For sociologist's comment, see item **4915.**

3364 Roman, Peter. Workers' parliaments in Cuba. (*Lat. Am. Perspect.*, 22:4, Fall 1995, p. 43–58, bibl.)

A very good account of what goes on in workers' assemblies in Cuba, including revealing statements from ordinary workers and local leaders on the difficulties of daily life. Good primary research, though interpretation and conclusion are soft and unimaginative.

3365 Salazar Valiente, Mario. El dilema cubano. (*Estud. Latinoam./México,* 1:1, 1994, p. 99–117)

Somewhat dogmatic and unimaginative analysis of Cuba's dilemmas, ending with the view that external pressures are decisive in shaping Cuba's future course. Argues that national independence can only be safe-guarded with authoritarian socialism, and that the Cuban system contains "social and economic" rights without being democratic.

3366 Short, Margaret I. Law and religion in Marxist Cuba: a human rights inquiry. Coral Gables, Fla.: North-South Center, Univ. of Miami; New Brunswick: Transaction Publishers, 1993. 216 p.: bibl.

A critical analysis of religious freedom in Marxist Cuba, and of wider human rights violations. Also examines ethics, law, and morality under Marxism, pointing out contradictions between principles and practices. Interesting and worth reading.

COLOMBIA AND ECUADOR

MARC CHERNICK, *Visiting Associate Professor, Department of Government and Center for Latin American Studies, Georgetown University*

COLOMBIA AND ECUADOR ARE KEY REGIONS for social science research related to the emerging issues of post-Cold War, late-20th-century scholarship, including drug-trafficking, indigenous movements, democratic consolidation, decentralization, violence, and peace.

In Colombia, first-rate studies are being published on political violence, drug-trafficking, human rights violations, and the impact of corruption. Scholars continue to contemplate the escalation of violence in the country. Especially noteworthy studies on this topic include Daniel Pecaut's, "Presente, pasado y futuro de la violencia en Colombia" (item **3397**), Camilo Granada and Leonardo Rojas' "Los costos del conflicto armado, 1990–1994" (item **3389**), and *Colombia: inseguridad, violencia y desempeño en las areas rurales* (item **3377**). For discussions of peace processes, see Jesus Antonio Bejarano, *Una agenda para la paz* (item **2928**), and the special edition of *Colombia Internacional* "Seminario sobre procesos de negociación y paz" (item **3404**). A seminal work on drug trafficking sponsored by the United Nations Development Program, *Drogas ilícitas en Colombia: su impacto económico, político y social,* clarifies issues, provides data and dispels certain myths (item **3378**). For a Colombian perspective on the US anti-narcotics war, see Juan Gabriel Tokatlian's *En el límite: la (torpe) norteamericanización de la guerra contra las drogas* (item **3407**).

Many studies have focused on the Gaviria presidential administration's (1990–94) efforts to alleviate the country's political crisis, particularly in regard to the Constituent Assembly (items **3390** and **3412**). The allegations of illegal drug fund use during the 1994 presidential elections, which paralyzed the Samper Administration, have also been well-analyzed: See works by Francisco Leal (item **3408**), Ingrid Betancourt Pulecio (item **3372**), and Chernick (item **3375**). Significant works among the growing body of literature on human rights violations are *Enterrar y callar: las masacres en Colombia, 1980–1993* (item **3409**), publications by the Colombian Commission of Jurists (items **3380** and **3381**), and works by other national and international human rights organizations (items **3379** and **3395**).

In Ecuador, the surprising election of populist leader Abdalá Bucaram, followed only months later by his extraordinary removal from office by Congress has escalated the debate regarding causal factors of the country's inability to consolidate a democratic regime. For the Bucaram crisis and "congressional coup," refer to *Y ahora que?* (item **3444**). *Un solo toque: populismo y cultura política en Ecuador* provides a broader sociological analysis of Bucaram and populism (item **3442**). In regard to the unconsolidated democratic system, refer to Catherine Conaghan's, "Politicians against Parties: Discord and Disconnection in Ecuador's Party System" (item **3423**). Jorge Leon-Trujillo argues that there is evidence of democratic consolidation, but that it is threatened by a growing concentration of political power and economic wealth (item **3431**).

Other scholars have focused on the rise of indigenous movements, and the escalating conflicts among different actors regarding the environment, indigenous rights, multinational investments, and political sovereignty. Articles by Melina Selverston, (items **3439** and **3440**), and Joe Kane, (item **3429**) offer insights on these topics.

Scholars continue to produce significant government and political analyses of Colombia and Ecuador allowing for a better understanding of the individual countries, and also providing useful comparative research on drug-trafficking, violence, democratic consolidation, and other issues. Although economic crisis has caused a slight decline in academic output from Ecuador, there is a growing community of social scientists, and an even larger group of foreign political analysts, examining key issues affecting the country. In Colombia, meanwhile, the growing numbers of works being published demonstrate a correspondingly high quality level. As the works reviewed in this section underscore, the international social science community is increasingly turning their attention toward this region with fine result.

COLOMBIA

3367 Afanador Ulloa, Miguel Angel. Amnistías e indultos: la historia reciente, 1948–1992. Bogotá: República de Colombia, Depto. Administrativo de la Función Pública, 1993. 198 p.: bibl. (Documentos ESAP)

Comprehensively analyzes how government used amnesties and pardons to confront armed movements from 1948–92. Argues that different events have overwhelmed the cycles of pacification policies and amnesties, leading governments to pursue inconsistent and ineffective policies.

3368 Archer, Ronald P. Party strength and weakness in Colombia's beseiged democracy. (*in* Building democratic institutions: party systems in Latin America. Edited by Scott Mainwaring and Timothy R. Scully. Stanford, Calif.: Stanford Univ. Press, 1995, p. 164–199, graph, tables)

Thoughtful analysis outlines state of Colombia's party system, and factors precipi-

tating decline of traditional parties. Analyzes electoral, affective, organizational, and representative dimensions of the parties to conclude that traditional parties have not adapted to country's rapid transformations.

3369 Arias Londoño, Melba. Mujer, sexualidad y ley. Bogotá: Unidad de Psicoterapia y Sexualidad Humana, 1988. 459 p.: bibl.

Feminist perspective on human sexuality examines general aspects of human sexuality (biological, psychological, and social); and Colombian law (civil, penal, labor, and family) as it applies to aspects of sexuality. Critical of laws that do not sufficiently address sexual violence against and social repression of women. An important work for understanding sexual politics and the Colombian law. [D. Dent]

3370 Bateman, Jaime. Jaime Bateman: profeta de la paz. Recopilación de Darío Villamizar Herrera. Bogotá: Compañía Nacional para la Paz, 1995. 421 p.

Tribute to Jaime Bateman, leader and founder of the April 19th Movement (M-19), a major guerrilla group founded in the 1970s. Includes series of interviews with Bateman, and commentaries he wrote before his death in a 1983 plane crash, a time when the M-19 was engaged in direct negotiations with the government. Fascinating insight into the views of M-19's key ideologue on revolution, democracy, and peace negotiations.

3371 Bejarano, Ana María and **Renata Segura Bonnett.** El fortalecimiento selectivo del Estado durante el Frente Nacional. (*Controversia/Bogotá*, 169, nov. 1996, p. 9–35, bibl., tables)

Important article reassesses State development during Frente Nacional period (1958–78). Argues that because of special need to pacify the country in late 1950s–early 1960s, and the continuation of violence into the 1970s–1980s, the country selectively strengthened elements of the traditionally weak State. During this time, congress lost authority to the executive branch and the judicial apparatus lost power to the coercive State apparatus.

Bejarano Avila, Jesús Antonio. Una agenda para la paz: aproximaciones desde la teoría de la resolución de conflictos. See item **2928.**

3372 Betancourt Pulecio, Ingrid. Sí sabía: viaje a través del expediente de Ernesto Samper. Bogotá: Ediciones Temas de Hoy, 1996. 413 p. (Grandes temas; 2)

Strongly-written denunciation by a congresswoman of the Partido Liberal of President Samper. Good account of the corruption charges brought against the president and the atmosphere of political crisis prevailing throughout much of his administration. Argues that Samper was guilty as charged.

3373 Blanquer, Jean Michel. El marco político e institucional de la democracia local en Colombia. (*in* Democracia, etnicidad y violencia política en los países andinos. Lima: Instituto Francés de Estudios Andinos; Instituto de Estudios Peruanos, 1993, p. 193–203, bibl.)

Outlines theoretical model for analyzing development of local democracy in Colombia. Examines interaction of local actors within the institutional framework provided by the new constitution, the current international context, the economy, and the trend toward decentralization.

3374 Castillo, Fabio. Los nuevos jinetes de la cocaína. Bogotá: Oveja Negra, 1996. 231 p., 16 p. of plates: bibl., ill., index, maps.

A decade afte Castillo published *Los jinetes de la cocaina* (see *HLAS 51:3689*), he now returns to identify the new drug entrepreneurs who have emerged since the destruction or weakening of the Medellin and Cali cartels. Rather than finding a decrease in trafficking, this award-winning journalist uncovers a broader, more decentralized industry that continues to be rooted in Colombia.

3375 Chernick, Marc W. Colombia's fault lines. (*Curr. Hist.*, 95:598, Feb. 1996, p. 76–81)

Analyzes separate but overlapping arenas of political, social, criminal, and drug-related violence. Examines drug-related presidential crisis during Samper Administration. Argues that weakening of presidency led to a reversal of trend toward democratic reforms and increased all forms of violence.

3376 Chernick, Marc W. The paramilitarization of the war in Colombia. (*NACLA*, 21:5, March/April 1998, p. 28–33.)

Analyzes paramilitaries' growing involvement in Colombia's internal conflict. Asserts that new investments in rural lands, particularly by drug traffickers, have motivated rise of paramilitary forces that forcibly displace peasant populations and further concentrate landholdings.

3377 Colombia: inseguridad, violencia y desempeño económico en las áreas rurales. Dirección de investigación de Jesús Antonio Bejarano Avila. Bogotá: Fondo Financiero de Proyectos de Desarrollo; Univ. Externado de Colombia, 1997. 255 p.: bibl., ill.

Detailed statistical analysis of evolution of political and economic conflict in Colombia. Details homicides per municipality, land conflicts, guerrilla activity, kidnapping, paramilitary activity, etc. Essential reference source for analysts of Colombian rural violence during 1980s–1990s.

3378 Colombia. Ministerio de Justicia y del Derecho. Dirección Nacional de Estupefacientes. Drogas ilícitas en Colombia: su impacto económico, político y social. Bogotá: PNUD; Editorial Ariel; Ministerio de Justicia y del Derecho, Dirección Nacional de Estupefacientes, 1997. 700 p.: bibl., ill. (Ariel ciencia política)

Exhaustive study analyzes how drug trade has impacted Colombia's economy, rural land purchases, rainforest colonization and deforestation, violence, international commercial and financial relations, and other key areas. The most complete and unbiased study to date.

3379 Colombia y el derecho internacional de los derechos humanos. v. 1, Obligaciones convencionales de Colombia en materia de derecho internacional humanitario. Recopilación de Mario Alejandro Quintero B. y Federico Andrés Torres G. Coordinación de Juan José Quintana Aranguren. Bogotá: Centro de Investigaciones y Proyectos Especiales, Univ. Externado de Colombia, 1994. 1 v.

Collection of major treaties ratified by Colombia in the area of international humanitarian law, specifically body of law that addresses rights of victims of armed conflicts. Treaties include Protocol II of the 1949 Geneva Convention, which addresses rights of victims of internal conflicts. Each treaty is introduced by a short table depicting passage, ratification, status, and any special conditions amended by Colombia. Useful primary documents.

3380 Comisión Andina de Juristas. Seccional Colombiana. Urabá. Bogotá: Comisión Andina de Juristas, Seccional Colombiana, 1994. 185 p.: bibl., maps. (Serie Informes Regionales de Derechos Humanos)

Detailed, informative description of human rights violations in Urabá, a poor banana-producing region with one of the highest levels of violence in the country. Describes complex conflicts among guerrillas, paramilitaries, local populations, government officials, and drug traffickers. Asserts that government is unable to devise an effective strategy to combat human rights violations.

3381 Comisión Colombiana de Juristas. Colombia, derechos humanos y derecho humanitario, 1995. Bogotá: Comisión Colombiana de Juristas, 1996. 255 p.: bibl. (Serie Informes anuales)

Annual human rights report by one of Colombia's most respected human rights organizations. Documents rising levels of violence and human rights violations, growing strength of paramilitary forces and guerrilla organizations, responses of key State human rights institutions to national and international denunciations of official abuses, and actions by national and international NGOs to confront human rights crisis.

3382 Descentralización y corrupción. Bogotá?: FESCOL; MILENIO, 1996. 109 p.: bibl.

Collection of papers from a seminar on decentralization and corruption examines clientelism relationships, direct election of mayors, new forms of corruption, and varous government strategies to confront corruption. Innovative first step in analyzing and conceptualizing a complex problem made more difficult by factors such as endemic violence and guerrilla warfare.

3383 Díaz Ceballos, Ventura. Kunta, un líder para un pueblo. Bogotá?: V. Díaz Ceballos, 1994. 176 p.

Testimonies about Kunta Kinte (1949–91), an Afro-Colombian leader from the *departamento* of Chocó who founded the Movimiento Nacional Cimarrón and led the M-19 guerrillas in Chocó. Work reflects emerging interest in Afro-Colombian political movements.

3384 Dimensiones político-económicas del nuevo orden constitucional. Bogotá: Univ. Nacional de Colombia, Facultad de Derecho, Ciencias Políticas y Sociales, 1996. 272 p.: bibl.

Exceptional studies on implications of specific reforms which followed adoption of 1991 constitution. Issues include waging of war and right to peace, Andean commercial integration, private property, and political reform.

3385 Escobar H., Guillerno León. La descentralización en Colombia o la distancia entre un propósito y la realidad. (*Contribuciones/Buenos Aires*, 10:4, oct./dic. 1993, p. 77–88)

Examines crucial role of municipalities in Colombia's political system, and ways in which decentralization has affected democratization. Argues that many proposed political reforms have not been implemented, and that further efforts are needed to encourage citizen and community participation.

3386 García, Alejandro. Hijos de la violencia: campesinos de Colombia sobreviven a "golpes" de paz. Madrid: Libros de la Catarata, 1996. 319 p.: bibl., ill. (Los libros de la catarata; 44)

Fascinating book narrates history of a peasant group residing along the Carare River that has attempted to create a zone of peace, free from the violence imposed by guerrillas, paramilitaries, and the armed forces. As nonviolent activists, they attempted to bargain with armed groups, and despite innumerable challenges, have managed to impose an uncertain and often violated peace. In 1990 the peasant association won the "Alternative Nobel Peace Prize."

3387 Gilhodes, Pierre. Raíz auge y decadencia del bipartidismo colombiano. (*in* Democracia, etnicidad y violencia política en los países andinos. Lima: Instituto de Estudios Peruanos; Instituto Francés de Estudios Andinos, 1993, p. 17–28)

Examines nature of current bipartisan political system in Colombia. Argues that the country's political crisis is a result of conflicts between the two traditional parties, and problems within the political system as a whole. Proposed solution is to liberate the electorate by modernizing Colombia's political institutions.

3388 Giraldo, Javier. Colombia: the genocidal democracy. Monroe, Me.: Common Courage Press, 1996. 125 p.: index, map.

Father Giraldo, director of a leading Colombian human rights organization, carefully explains Colombia's human rights crisis, citing statistics on political violence and relating eyewitness accounts of extrajudicial assassinations and massacres. Directly implicates the Colombian State in these actions, calling the political regime a "democratatorship," a government based on the rule of impunity rather than the rule of law.

3389 Granada, Camilo and Leonardo Rojas. Los costos del conflicto armado, 1990–1994. (*Planeac. Desarro.*, 26:4, oct./dic. 1995, p. 119–151, bibl., tables)

Interesting study assesses cost of internal conflict in Colombia. Calculates that between 1990–94, the economic cost of the war—including attacks against national infrastructure, kidnappings, and destruction

of oil pipelines—was approximately 12 billion dollars. State expenditures related to the internal war exceeded 4 billion dollars and lost human capital exceeded 6 billion dollars.

3390 Hernández Benavides, Manuel. Una agenda con futuro: testimonios del cuatrienio Gaviria. Bogotá: Presidencia de la República, 1994. 502 p.: bibl., ill.

Interviews with senior officials of the Gaviria Administration, including the President. Focuses on factors leading up to 1991 constitutional reforms and discusses internal governmental struggles.

3391 López, José Ignacio. El Estado como núcleo vital: el caso colombiano. (*Rev. Univ. EAFIT*, 92, oct./dic. 1993, p. 79–90, maps)

Argues that present political troubles and State's inability to solve the guerrilla conflict are due to Colombia's difficulties in forging an adequate relationship among its heartland, hinterland, and frontiers. The country's problems can be better addressed by pursuing strategies for connecting these three areas. Includes good maps.

3392 Losada Lora, Rodrigo. Incidencia de los sentimientos en las preferencias por candidatos. (*Rev. Javer.*, 120:608, sept. 1994, p. 189–199, tables)

Uses 1992 poll data to determine the emotional feelings and attachments that most influence voter behavior.

3393 Martz, John D. The politics of clientelism: democracy & the State in Colombia. New Brunswick, N.J.: Transaction Publishers, 1997. 358 p.: bibl., index.

Integrates social science literature on clientelism with a sharp narrative of Colombian politics during and after the Frente Nacional. Argues that as the Colombian State developed in the second half of 20th century, traditional forms of clientelism were modernized and incorporated into State practices, a process that presented a major barrier to regime democratization.

3394 Molano Cruz, Giovanni. La acción política bajo el Frente Nacional. (*Rev. Colomb. Sociol.*, 2:2, 1995, p. 59–88)

Examines groups formed in opposition to the Frente Nacional, including their agendas, and influence on the political dialogue.

3395 Nationaal Centrum voor Ontwikke-lingssamenwerking (Belgium). Tras los pasos perdidos de la guerra sucia: paramilitarismo y operaciones encubiertas en Colombia. Brusssels: NCOS, 1995. 151 p.: bibl., ill., index, maps.

Report by European human rights organization details rise of Colombian paramilitary movements and their ties to the armed forces. Provides names, describes specific incidents, and directly accuses the State of complicity in the dirty war.

3396 Pécaut, Daniel. ¿Es posible aún una interpretación global de los fenómenos recientes de violencia en Colombia? (*Bol. Socioecon.*, 27, junio 1994, p. 3–14, ill.)

Argues that violence in Colombia should be interpreted as part of a global trend. Focuses on strategies of the principal protagonists arguing that their traditionally understood causes, such as the struggle to control economic resources.

3397 Pécaut, Daniel. Presente, pasado y futuro de la violencia en Colombia. (*Desarro. Econ.*, 36 : 144, enero/marzo 1997, p. 891–930, graph, table)

Provocative article compares different periods in Colombian history in an effort to locate origins of nation's endemic armed conflicts. Concludes that by examining discourses and operations of the various armed actors—particularly guerrillas and paramilitaries—it becomes clear that the sociopolitical context is not the cause of the violence. Rather, violent actors take advantage of collective memories of past periods of violence to construct a social imagery falsely linking current movements to earlier ones, and thereby legitimize essentially territorial conflicts.

3398 Pérez Guzmán, Diego. Desplazamiento interno en Colombia: las otras víctimas de las de la guerra. (*in* Consulta sobre Desplazamiento y Refugio en la Región Andina, *Lima?, 1993*. Desplazados. Lima: Instituto de Defensa Legal, 1995, p. 27–72)

One of the first articles to address an emerging social and political crisis in Colombia: the forced displacement of peasant populations. Since mid-1980s the number of peasants expelled from their lands has risen dramatically, primarily because of paramilitary activity, but also due to the spread of guerrilla activity and counterinsurgency operations. Argues that the government and NGOs have not sufficiently addressed the needs of the displaced.

3399 Pizarro, Eduardo. Colombia: ¿hacia una salida democrática a la crisis nacional? (*in* Democracia, etnicidad y violencia política en los países andinos. Lima: Instituto Francés de Estudios Andinos; Instituto de Estudios Peruanos, 1993, p. 137–166, tables)

Argues that Colombia's progress toward democracy faces serious obstacles: internal guerrilla warfare, drug trafficking, high crime rates, and a contentious transition to a more market-based economy. Projects various political futures for Colombia, depending on different interactions and conflicts among political elites, ordinary citizens, and the military, and on the chosen strategies of conflict resolution and democratic transition.

3400 Reveiz Roldán, Edgar; Javier Torres Velasco; and Mónica Hurtado Lozano. Reforma política y proceso de decisión sobre el gasto en seguridad en Colombia: una economía para la paz, 1990–1993. (*in* Gasto militar en América Latina: procesos de decisiones y actores claves. Santiago?: Centro Internacional para el Desarrollo Económico (CINDE); FLACSO, 1994, p. 205–237)

Outlines transformation of the military's role and the country's national security needs during the 1990s. Provides unique and critical perspective on decision-making process for the allocation of military resources and budgets during Gaviria Administration.

3401 Roll, David. El continuismo político como obstáculo para la profundización democrática en Colombia. (*in* International Congress of Americanists, *48th, Stockholm, 1994.* Problems of democracy in Latin America. Stockholm: Institute of Latin American Studies, Stockholm Univ., 1996, p. 90–105)

Examines Colombia as model for understanding the strengthening of democracy following initial transitory phase. Argues that principal obstacle to Colombian democratization is the persistence of the traditional bipartisan system and its restrictions against a more participatory and inclusive political regime.

3402 Ruiz, Emilio Juan. Cuarto poder: cómo el poder económico se inserta en los medios de comunicación colombianos. Bogotá: Castillo Editorial, 1996. 300 p.: bibl. (Col. rotativa)

Demonstrates how Colombia's major economic groups and political families control the principal print and broadcasting media, following similar trends in many other world regions.

3403 Sánchez, Ricardo. Las izquierdas en Colombia. Bogotá: Facultad de Derecho Ciencias Políticas Sociales, Univ. Nacional de Colombia, 1996. 181 p.: bibl.

Important book analyzes historical development of various leftist movements from legal parties, such as the Partido Comunista de Colombia, to labor unions and armed guerrilla organizations. Proposes that a dialogue among contemporary political theorists, such as Norberto Bobbio, Eric Hobsbawm, and Perry Anderson, could contribute to a reconstruction of the Colombian left.

3404 Seminario Internacional Procesos de Negociación y Paz, *Bogotá, 1996*. Procesos de paz y negociación en Colombia: relatoría. Washington: Woodrow Wilson International Center for Scholars; Bogotá: Fundación Friedrich Ebert de Colombia; Centro de Estudios Internacionales, Univ. de los Andes, 1996. 75 p.

Insightful analysis of Colombian peace originally presented at seminar uniting peace advisors who had experience in Colombia during previous 12 years.

3405 Sociedad civil: control social y democracia participativa. Bogotá: Fescol, 1997. 105 p.: bibl.

Small but significant volume explores participatory democracy and civil society, two concepts increasingly important to Colombian political debate. Essays analyze how theories are both enriched by and illuminate the Colombian experience.

3406 Taller sobre Sistemas de Ordenamiento Territorial, Autonomía y Descentralización, *Bogotá, 1993*. Colombia hacia el milenio: memorias. Bogotá: Comisión de Ordenamiento Territorial; Instituto Geográfico Agustín Codazzi, 1994. 267 p.

Colombia's 1991 constitution mandated formation of a commission to study the possibility of reorganizing national territorial divisions to create political units more representative of the country's social, economic, and cultural diversity. Based on a workshop convened to recommend the best ways to adjust the nation's political map to meet the requirements of decentralization, development, democracy, and social diversity.

3407 Tokatlian, Juan Gabriel. En el límite: la (torpe) norteamericanización de la guerra contra las drogas. Bogotá: CEREC; Grupo Editorial Norma, 1997. 182 p.: bibl.

Six essays analyze Colombia/US relations in post-Cold War period and challenges facing Colombia as US seeks to impose an ill-conceived anti-narcotics policy. Discusses policy options (including drug legalization), alternatives to extradition, and US certification requirements.

3408 Tras las huellas de la crisis política. Edición de Francisco Leal Buitrago. Bogotá: TM Editores; FESCOL; IEPRI, 1996. 298 p.: bibl.

As the Samper government was rocked by allegations of drug-related corruption in the presidential campaign of 1994, Colombia's endemic crisis of governability, violence, and political participation took a dramatic turn for the worse. Moreover, Colombia/US bilateral relations degenerated into mutual accusations and recriminations. In this book, several of Colombia's leading political analysts assess this crisis and its implications for the maintainance of political stability and consolidation of democracy.

3409 Uribe, María Victoria and **Teófilo Vásquez.** Enterrar y callar: las masacres en Colombia, 1980–1993. v. 1. Bogotá: Comité Permanente por la Defensa de los Derechos Humanos; Fundación Terres des Hommes, 1995. 1 v.: bibl., ill., maps.

Hair-raising account of rising incidence of massacres—the killing of four or more persons—as a form of internal warfare or social cleansing in Colombia. Killings continue even as the country has embraced multiple peace processes and signed international treaties on humanitarian law. Documents urban, rural, and regional variants of the practice, and includes survivor and witness testimony.

3410 Uricoechea, Fernando. Colombia: antecedentes y actualidad de la dinámica política. (*in* Los partidos políticos en el inicio de los noventa: seis casos latinoamericanos. Santiago: Ediciones FLACSO, 1992, p. 49–59, bibl.)

Short article analyzes methodologies used to describe political change in Colombia. Concludes that a structural framework yields more insights than a charismatic actor or class conflict explanation.

3411 Vargas, Mauricio; Jorge Lesmes; and Edgar Téllez. El presidente que se iba a caer: diario secreto de tres periodistas sobre el 8,000. Bogotá Planeta, 1996 462 p.: bibl. (Primera plana)

Detailed report on crisis that overwhelmed the Samper presidency. Examines the famous "narco-cassettes" that appeared following 1994 elections and connected Samper with the Cali cartel, the "8000 process" initiated by the Ministro de Justicia y del Derecho against corrupt politicians, the imprisonment of the President's former campaign manager and first Ministro de Defensa Nacional, and the vote in Congress that suspended prosecution of the president.

3412 Vélez Ramírez, Humberto. Lo constitucional, lo real y lo imaginario del Estado: doce ensayos sobre el Estado y la democracia en Colombia Cali, Colombia: Univ. del Valle, 1992. 205 p.: bibl. (Col. Edición previa. Serie Investigaciones)

Twelve informative essays discuss topics such as democracy, the political regime, violence, neoliberalism, State intervention in social life, and the 1991 constituent assembly. Essays together provide valuable insight on the political environment in early 1990s when democratic movements appeared to be growing, while violence continued to escalate.

3413 Villamizar Herrera, Darío. Un adiós a la guerra. Bogotá: Planeta, 1997. 427 p.: bibl., ill. (Documento)

Invaluable account of negotiations with and reincorporation of several guerrilla groups in 1990–91. Thorough history of settlement negotiated with M-19 guerrillas, and reports on parallel negotiations with the Ejército Popular de Liberación, Movimiento Quintín Lame, Partido Revolucionario de Trabajadores, and urban militias of Medellín. Good addition to the large and growing body of literature on guerrillas and peace processes in Colombia.

3414 Villamizar Herrera, Darío. Aquel 19 será. Bogotá: Planeta, 1995. 615 p.: bibl. (Documento)

Complete history of the April 19th Movement (M-19), from its inception in early 1970s to its surrender of arms on March 9, 1990. Includes copies of original documents and testimonies. Valuable resource for analysts of armed conflict in Colombia.

3415 Zuluaga Nieto, Jaime. Cuando la corupción invade el tejido social. (*Nueva Soc.*, 145, sept./oct. 1996, p. 148–159, ill.)

Solid analysis argues that corruption involves more than just the impact of narcodollars on politics. Rather, most corruption stems from individual and collective behaviors deeply rooted in Colombia's bipartisan political system.

ECUADOR

3416 Arias Rendón, Natalia. Partidos políticos: ¿héroes o villanos? (*Ecuad. Deb.*, 36, dic. 1995, p. 49–61, tables)

Closely analyzes level of institutionalization of Ecuadorian party system since country's return to democracy in 1979. Examines ability of parties to channel participation, represent interests, and serve as a vital link between State and society. Finds Ecuador's parties in crisis, unable to influence State decisions—particularly with respect to the economy—and unable to process demands.

3417 Bedoya J., Francisco. Desregulación de la política y elecciones. (*Ecuad. Deb.*, 32, agosto 1994, p. 101–109)

Asserts that instead of promoting democracy, deregulation of the media in Ecuador has corrupted political discourse, replaced ideology, and defined programs with slogans and shallow symbolism. Examination of 1992 election campaigns is used to support argument.

3418 Cabezas Castillo, Tito. Partidos y organismos electorales: una relación que debe mejorarse; el caso de Ecuador. (*in* Partidos y clase política en América Latina en los 90. San José: Instituto Interamericano de Derechos Humanos (IIDH); Centro de Asesoría y Promoción Electoral (CAPEL), 1995, p. 455–473)

Examines relationship between Ecuadorian political parties and the country's electoral institutions, focusing on their budgets and the laws that govern them. Concludes with concrete suggestions for improving the Tribuno Supremo Electoral as a step toward consolidating Ecuadorian democracy.

3419 Carrión, Andrés. Ecuador, la memoria de los otros: entrevistas. Quito: Eskeletra, 1996. 378 p.

Interviews with leading politicians and political figures including ex-presidents, former generals, and former guerrillas; and with leaders of the Church, indigenous movements, and other key areas of national life. Interviews originally broadcast on television during Rodrigo Borja's 1988–92 presidential term.

3420 Centro Andino de Acción Popular (Ecuador). Equipo de Coyuntura. Aspecto políticos de la coyuntura en la primer semestre de 1994. (*Ecuad. Deb.*, 32, agosto 1994, p. 44–51)

Describes key political problems faced by Ecuador during first half of 1994, including economic adjustment, actions of the Partido Social Cristiano, privatization, agrarian reform, and elections.

3421 Centro Andino de Acción Popular (Ecuador). Equipo de Coyuntura. Conflictividad: el conflicto socio-político, febrero–mayo de 1995. (*Ecuad. Deb.*, 35, agosto 1995, p. 21–27, tables)

Statistical analysis of composition and frequency of Ecuadorian social conflicts during first quarter of 1995. Concludes that majority of conflicts stemmed not from unions or other organized groups, but from a heterogeneous array of the unorganized poor who suffer the effects of economic adjustment programs.

3422 Chiriboga Zambrano, Galo A. Neoliberalismo y sindicalismo en Latinoamérica: el caso ecuatoriano. (*in* Modelo neoliberal y sindicatos en América Latina. México: Fundación Friedrich Ebert, 1993, p. 149–163)

Argues that unions have been negligent in their response to neoliberalism, and urges them to develop new paradigms to promote development and reestablish their economic and the political influence.

3423 Conaghan, Catherine M. Politicians against parties: discord and disconnection in Ecuador's party system. (*in* Building democratic institutions: party systems in Latin America. Edited by Scott Mainwaring and Timothy R. Scully. Stanford, Calif.: Stanford Univ. Press, 1995, p. 434–458, tables)

Outlines development of Ecuador's unconsolidated party system since the end of military rule. Describes system as having extreme multipartism, and an electorate with shifting party allegiances. As a result, political parties lack a strong voice in the policy-making process and major decisions gain little support from the electorate. Warns that the future could hold a Peru-style breach of the constitution.

3424 Corporación de Estudios para el Desarrollo (Ecuador). Descentralización y gobiernos municipales. Quito?: CORDES; Banco del Estado, 1993. 289 p.

Papers discuss need for decentralization of Ecuadorian government in order to promote greater economic development, enhance participatory democracy, and provide a more efficient means of delivering basic services to the population. Also offers specific examples of decentralization efforts elsewhere in Latin America.

3425 Echeverría, Julio. Crisis y democracia en el Ecuador. (*in* Hacia la consolidación democrática andina: transición o desestabilización. Bogotá: Depto. de Ciencia Política, Uniandes, 1993, p. 165–204, bibl., tables)

Argues that although Ecuador's political crisis is less severe than that of other Andean nations, major barriers to democratization exist. Principal barrier is the legacy of State-dominated development, originally institutionalized under military rule, which impedes both the economy and political participation.

3426 García Gallegos, Bertha. Las dimensiones societales de la reconversión militar en América Latina: el caso ecuatoriano. (*in* Reconversión militar en América Latina. Coordinación de Gabriel Aguilera Peralta. Guatemala: FLACSO, 1994, p. 141–159)

Claims that transition of armed forces in 1990s resulted not only from fiscal pressures and liberalization of the State, but also from normalization of domestic politics. Focuses on changing social demands and internal pressures, and on how these have influenced military's role in politics.

García Sayán, Diego; Jorge Morelli Pando; and Sinesio Jarama. Perú-Ecuador: las cartas sobre la mesa. See item **3562.**

3427 Ibarra, Hernán. Las elecciones de 1996 o la costeñización de la política ecuatoriana. (*Ecuad. Deb.*, 38, agosto 1996, p. 23–31)

During 1996 presidential elections, two candidates, Jaime Nebot and Abdalá Bucaram Ortiz, from Ecuador's coastal region reached the second round of voting. Although the candidates represented social extremes, with Nebot favored by upper classes and entrepreneurs and Bucaram Ortiz by middle and lower classes, results showed a remarkable consolidation of political power on the coast at the expense of the Sierra.

3428 Instituto Latinoamericano de Investigaciones Sociales. Fuerzas armadas, desarrollo y democracia. Quito: ILDIS; CELA, 1996. 194 p.: bibl.

Papers and panel discussions focus lingering political and economic influence of Ecuadorian armed forces despite their return to the barracks over two decades ago. Papers help define military's singular role in Ecuador, which combines a high level of legitimacy with levels of military prerogatives rivaling those of any other military institution in the hemisphere.

3429 Kane, Joe. Savages. New York: Knopf; Random House, 1995. 273 p.: bibl., col. ill., map.

Fascinating account of the Huao, a small group of nomadic indigenous people of Ecuador's oil-rich Amazon, and their struggle with multinational oil companies and international environmental NGOs. Oil companies have exploited indigenous lands for decades. The Huao want better treatment and compensation for environmental damage from multinationals, but reject environmental deals made in their name by foreign NGOs. Superb journalistic coverage of the emergence of indigenous power and rise of new conflicts, as non-State actors move into national and foreign policy arenas. For ethnologist's comment see item **1006.**

3430 Lamm, Edgar. Las elecciones de 1994 en el Ecuador. (*Contribuciones/Buenos Aires*, 11:2, abril/junio 1994, p. 233–237, table)

Briefly analyzes 1994 Ecuadorian congressional elections and their implications for the principal parties and key players.

3431 León-Trujillo, Jorge. Cambios estructurales y escena política en el Ecuador, 1978–1988: un ciclo político. (*in* Democracia, etnicidad y violencia política en los países andinos. Lima: Instituto Francés de Estudios Andinos; Instituto de Estudios Peruanos, 1993, p. 205–242, graphs)

Argues that modern Ecuadorian politics can be divided into distinct periods: government instability during 1960s, dictatorship after 1972, and a return to constitutional order along with a sustained economic crisis after 1979. Latter period has witnessed election of presidents from the center, left, and right, revealing a seemingly unconsolidated electorate. Yet data show a core of support for each party, which could lead to a more stable democratic order. Trends toward greater concentrations of wealth and political power could undermine this stability.

Maiguashca, Juan. Los sectores subalternos en los años 30 y el aparecimiento del velasquismo. See *HLAS 56:2745.*

3432 McKenzie, Merylyn. La política y la gestión de la energía rural: la experiencia del Ecuador. Quito: Facultad Latinoamericana de Ciencias Sociales, Sede Ecuador, 1994. 368 p.: bibl., ill. (Serie Estudios—Economía)

Extremely detailed and comprehensive analysis of distribution and use of energy in Ecuador's rural sectors. Considers why government policy has failed to provide cost-effective energy resources to rural areas. Provides recommendations for meeting these needs.

3433 Naranjo, Alexis. Las cámaras de la producción y la política: Ecuador, 1980–1990. (*Ecuad. Deb.*, 30, dic. 1993, p. 155–168, graph, tables)

Argues that Ecuador's weak political system and heterogeneous society leads to rejection of parties to mediate conflicts. Asserts that industry associations in economic production centers, such as Quito and Guayaquil, are able to establish crucial blocks of power, influence political decision-making, and take on functions usually reserved for political parties.

3434 Política en caricaturas, 1979–1993.
Recopilación de Gerardo Ruiz Navas.
Quito: Editorial Voluntad, 1993. 878 p.: ill., index.

Collection of 2,300 political cartoons drawn for major newspapers by six Ecuadorian artists between 1979–93. Divided into 26 chapters separating caricaturists' works into various important Ecuadorian political themes inlcuding political parties, presidents, congress, corruption, bureaucracy, the Andean Group, and State modernization. Two- to three-sentence explanation provided for each drawing. Chapter on international affairs captures some interesting interpretations of world events from a Latin American perspective. [D. Dent]

3435 Rangles Lara, Rodrigo. Venturas y desventuras del poder. Quito: Carvajal, 1995. 421 p.

Memoir by press secretary of former president Rodrigo Borja gives eyewitness account of challenges faced by the administration, and its inability to implement a reformist, social democratic agenda in favor of the poor due to national and international pressure to adopt a neoliberal economic agenda.

3436 Romero, Marco. Incertidumbre y estancamiento en medio del ciclo político. (*Ecuad. Deb.*, 38, agosto 1996, p. 7–21)

Notes that the economic decision-making process comes to a halt during the election cycle, both at State level and among industry leaders and entrepreneurs. Represents another symptom of the costs of unconsolidated democracy and lack of a strong civil society and citizen participation. Serious economic repercussions of 1996 were as a result of a more extensive than usual lack of economic leadership. See also item **3438.**

3437 Sánchez Parga, José. Conflicto y democracia en Ecuador. Quito: Centro Andino de Acción Popular, 1995. 165 p.: bibl. (Diálogos)

Leading Ecuadorian analysts and politicians analyze roots of the democratic crisis, problems of governability, impact of political violence, economic decline, and regional and sectoral sources of conflicts. Poignant analyses, and a good scholarly introduction to the debate.

3438 Schuldt, Jürgen. Elecciones y política económica en el Ecuador, 1983–1994. Quito: Instituto Latinoamericano de Investigaciones Sociales, 1994. 128 p.: bibl., ill.

Analyzes economic policymaking during pre- and post-election periods in Ecuador. Demonstrates how past and present governments have manipulated economic situation to gain re-election. Argues that in so doing, governments jeopardize well-being of citizens and democracy. See also item **3436.**

3439 Selverston, Melina H. The politics of culture: indigenous peoples and the State in Ecuador. (*in* Indigenous peoples and democracy in Latin America. New York: St. Martin's Press, 1994, p. 131–152)

Excellent article argues that emergence of indigenous movement has significantly affected Ecuadorian politics. Notes that in Ecuador global trend toward ethnic-centered politics and away from class-centered politics coincided with redemocratization. The indigenous fight for land and cultural pluralism have been catapulted into the forefront of a broader popular struggle for democracy. Essential reading for understanding rise of indigenous politics in 1990s.

3440 Selverston, Melina H. The politics of identity reconstruction: Indians and democracy in Ecuador. (*in* The new politics of inequality in Latin America: rethinking participation and representation. Oxford, England; New York: Oxford Univ. Press, 1997, p. 170–191)

Explores identity-based politics in Ecuador, noting that indigenous leaders were influenced overwhelmingly by the bilingual literacy campaigns of the 1970s–80s. By 1990s, in both the Sierra and the Amazon, indigenous movements were able to mobilize communities around political, social, and cultural issues, and thus proved more effective than earlier class-based peasant organizations. Indigenous movements have been significantly affected the major political system, and have led national strikes in 1990 and 1994. They have overturned agrarian modernization policies prejudicial to indigenous farmers, and have shaped national policies regarding education and political and cultural rights.

3441 Terán, Juan Fernando. AVC: revelaciones y reflexiones sobre una guerrilla inconclusa? Quito: Casa de la Cultura Ecuatoriana Benjamín Carrión, 1994. 250 p.: bibl. (Col. Pensamiento vivo; 1)

Good analysis of Ecuadorian guerrilla movement Alfaro Vive, Carajo!, which was active during 1980s. Author, a former member, describes group's ideology and actions as well as government's response to the guerrilla challenge.

3442 Torre, Carlos de la. Un solo toque: populismo y cultura política en Ecuador. Quito: Centro Andino de Acción Popular, 1996. 79 p.: bibl. (Estudios y análisis)

Analyzes political rise of Abdalá Bucaram Ortiz within the long tradition of Ecuadorian populism pioneered by Velasco Ibarra. Insightful discussions of Bucarám's campaign, political alliances, speeches, style, and political enemies. Concludes with discussion of "new" populism in Ecuador. Essential analysis for understanding subsequent events that led to Bucarám's fall a year after this work was published.

3443 Velasco Ibarra, José María. Pensamiento político. Estudio introductorio y selección de Enrique Ayala Mora. Quito: Banco Central del Ecuador; Corporación Editora Nacional, 1996. 527 p.: bibl. (Biblioteca básica del pensamiento ecuatoriano; 38)

Introduces and explains some of the principal writings of Ecuador's longtime populist leader. Underscores many Ecuadorians' continued fascination with the five-term president. Good introductory essay by Enrique Ayala Mora.

3444 Y ahora qué?—: una contribución al análisis histórico-político del país. Quito: Eskeletra Editorial, 1997. 306 p.: bibl.

Early attempt to explain "congressional coup" of Feb. 5, 1997, when President Abdalá Bucaram Ortiz was removed from office by an act of congress and then replaced by the president of the legislative branch. Helps explain events surrounding Bucaram's presidency and the country's continued political instability.

VENEZUELA

RENE SALGADO, *Independent Consultant, Gaithersburg, Maryland*

THE LAST FEW YEARS of Venezuela's political life have been marked by a changing political mood and increasing economic challenges. Rafael Caldera, Venezuela's president from 1969–73 under a center-right Christian Democratic party platform, took the oath of office again on February 1994. This time, with support from an improvised grouping called "Convergencia" and supplemental support from the old-left Movimiento al Socialismo (MAS), he promised a government of austerity and integrity.

Caldera has faced an unprecedented situation in the national Congress. Venezuela's stable two-party system has severely eroded. Its historical protagonists, AD and COPEI, no longer dominate the political process; some of their most prominent leaders have fallen in disrepute. Caldera's congressional support has been led by his Convergencia-MAS block, but it controls only some 25 percent of the seats and the president can not necessarily expect an enduring coalition with any of the rival congressional delegations. In spite of this, Caldera has enjoyed the support of congressional parties. A representative of Convergencia assumed the presidency of the Senate, and AD and COPEI acquiesced to the passage of most of the legislation requested by the president.

During his early months in office, Caldera reversed some liberalization policies enacted by his predecessor, Carlos A. Pérez. He also revived some practices of State-directed capitalism, giving the government broad authority to control prices and foreign exchange transactions. While Pérez faced a complex political situation, further complicated by coup attempts and formidable opposition by the political class, Caldera had to deal with adverse economic conditions, including high inflation and a severe banking crisis. During the short economic boom in the early 1990s, banks expanded while lax supervision allowed lenders to run wild. Many bank insiders benefitted from soft loans. The boom ended in the second half of 1993 and the economic situation deteriorated rapidly. In January 1994, less than a month before Rafael Caldera's inauguration, the second largest bank in Venezuela, Banco Latino, failed and was taken over by the government.

As of October 1994, the government had seized more than ten failed banks. This accounted for more than one-half of the banking assets in the country. The government guaranteed some $6.1 billion to depositors, which represented roughly 75 percent of the annual budget and a distressing 13 percent of the gross domestic product. In addition, about $3 billion of foreign reserves were lost in the first half of 1994. Additional bank failures continued through the year and on into 1995. Partly in response to the rapidly deteriorating situation, the government imposed blanket foreign exchange controls, with the exchange rate fixed at Bs. 170 to the dollar. Price controls were also placed on about 100 items.

Economic conditions became almost unsustainable during the first two years of Caldera's government. The government, however, only altered its policy course after the December 1995 state and local elections had taken place. Widespread perception that previous reforms had led to a severe political crisis may have prompted Caldera to choose a more cautious conservative approach.

During the first quarter of 1996, the government significantly shifted its interventionist policy, and started to prepare a major stabilization program in consultation with the International Monetary Fund (IMF). The authorities increased domestic fuel prices, liberalized interest rates, unified the exchange rate system under a temporary float, abolished controls on current and capital transactions, eliminated price controls (except for medicines), and started strengthening the social safety net. The policy shift paved the way for a 12-month standby agreement with the IMF and its subsequent loan of approximately $1.4 billion with an additional $2 to $3 billion in loans coming from other multilateral institutions.

Privatization also gained support among policymakers. Although there are as yet no plans to reverse the nationalization of the oil industry, the government is eager for foreign investment, especially for exploration. Starting in 1997, the government announced plans for further privatization of the telecommunication monopoly, the sale of electric and metal sectors, including several aluminum companies, and the auction of the country's banking system.

The current trends in Venezuela's political life are to some extent reflected in the recent political science and political sociology literature. Thus, while discussions of elections, political actors and processes, parties and social participation continue to have prominence, there is growing interest in presidential politics, governmental transparency, decentralization and regulatory policies. In spite of this, much remains to be done to achieve a better understanding of these policy areas as well as the processes and impacts of Caldera's recent economic and political policy shift.

Using documentary analysis and survey research, Agudelo Cáceres provides a useful treatment of electoral processes from 1959–93, including electoral reforms (item **3445**). Other treatments offering useful insights include: Marcotulio and Velandría on congressional electoral campaigns (item **3464**), Codetta on the evolution of political preferences during the 1960s, 1970s, and 1980s (item **3452**), and Hernández on substantive aspects of the personalized proportional representation system introduced in 1993 (item **3460**). Castillo Lara has written a useful collection of articles on behavioral and legal aspects of electoral and party politics at the national and local levels (item **3478**), while *Back to the ballot box,* produced by the Woodrow Wilson Center, offers an analysis of the December 1995 state and local elections, and their impact on the political balance of power and the stability of the political system (item **3449**).

Several discussions and analyses of political actors and political democracy are particularly useful. Giordani offers an empirically based treatment of the evolution of the party ideology and fundamental tenets of Movimiento al Socialismo (item **3458**). Yepes Salas provides a useful overview of Causa R party's evolution, platform, and organization, also empirically based (item **3484**). Molina, Pereira, and Vaivads analyze the role of political parties in the context of the 1990s political crisis, suggesting that party democratization is the key for democratic maintenance (item **3470**). Moleiro *et al.,* a work coauthored by members of Movimiento al Socialismo, critiques emerging party trends, notably, neoliberalism and alliances with other parties for electoral gain (item **3469**). Last, but not least, Ellner's discussion on Venezuelan trade unionism, offers an excellent analysis of the relationships between trade unions, political parties, and State policy vis-à-vis unions, and contains a wealth of information on their internal structures, financial interests, and long-term strategy (item **3455**).

Recent studies on civil-military relations take a historical turn. Arceneaux discusses the relationships between the transmission of military doctrine and institutional fragmentation in the context of the early 1960s unsuccessful military coups (item **3447**). Meanwhile, Krispin thoroughly examines the motivation, planning, execution, and outcomes of the 1945 and 1948 coups (item **3462**).

Examples of interesting discussions of broad historical or contemporary political trends are Ellner's well-researched critique of the portraits of governments (1908–58) painted by political parties and revisionist historians of the period (item **3447**), and Urbaneja's dense analysis of Venezuela's 19th-century liberalism and 20th-century positivist and democratic programs (item **3479**). *Venezuela, del siglo XX al siglo XXI: un proyecto para construirla* is a useful collection of articles organized under the coordination of Carlos Blanco (item **3483**). It addresses issues pertaining to Venezuela's contemporary sociopolitical life. *Venezuela: la democracia bajo presión,* edited by Serbin *et al.,* focuses on current economic policies and emergent political actors (item **3481**), while McCoy and Smith offer a discussion of future potential avenues for Venezuela's political system (item **3467**).

The issue of transparency in government is gaining importance. Chitty La Roche comments on governmental corruption in such areas as management of customs and procurement (item **3451**). Capriles Mendez suggests several policy-oriented mechanisms to curve corruption and/or prevent inappropriate interference of vested interests in the policy process (item **3450**). Pantín and Rodriguez Valdez offer journalistic accounts of the links between money, finance, and political power in the context of the 1994 bankruptcy of Banco Latino (items **3475** and **3477**). A contrasting view of anti-corruption efforts is expressed by Miranda who praises attempts of Venezuelan authorities to eradicate money-laundering and drug-trafficking (item **3468**). Olavarría, on the other hand, argues that corruption in the banking system resulted from banking deregulation policies supported by former President Pérez (item **1969**).

Presidential politics has started to attract the attention of political writers. Escalante, a press secretary during the Perez and Velásquez presidencies, offers insider information on presidential politics (item **3457**). Lovera de Sola and Morón provide brief historical accounts of heads of government during the 19th and 20th centuries (items **3463** and **3472**), while Quirós Corradi's collection of articles contains favorable opinions about Carlos A Pérez and his policies (item **3474**). Finally, Ordóñez has written a hilarious book about power and everyday life in the Palacio de Miraflores, Venezuela's presidential residence (item **3473**).

On decentralization policies there is, as indicated above, growing interest and the issue is studied from different perspectives. A very useful treatment is *Descentralización, gobernabilidad, democracia*, coordinated by Cruz (item **3453**). Alfaro Montaro looks at some actual and potential impacts of decentralization on the relationships between political parties and elected state governors and legislators (item **3446**). A useful collection of articles entitled *Venezuela: centrelisme, régionalisme et pouvoir local*, coordinated by Revel-Mouroz, examines Venezuela's regionalization and decentralization, including a discussion of Zulia's regionalism and the importance of state universities in regional development (item **3480**). *La distribución del poder*, coordinated by Chalbaud, supplies an interesting historical overview of the country's centralist-federalist tendencies, current decentralization law and practices, and the successful governance experiences of several municipal governments (item **3454**). In a collection of essays, Márquez focuses on issues pertaining to decentralization, public administration reform, and policies on internal poverty problems (item **3465**). Finally, an interesting policy-oriented discussion of social policy is offered in *Una política social para la afirmación de la democracia* by the Venezuela Comisión para la Reforma del Estado (item **3482**).

3445 **Agudelo Cáceres, Lilian.** Imagen y poder: la caída de los grandes partidos. Caracas: EDUVEN, 1993. 309 p.: bibl., ill.
Examines electoral politics from 1959–93, including electoral reforms. Emphasizes images of parties, presidential candidates, and prominent politicians. Based on documentary analysis and survey research.

3446 **Alfaro Montaro, Petra.** Los partidos políticos venezolanos y la descentralización política. (*Mundo Nuevo/Caracas*, 17:3/4, julio/dic. 1994, p. 237–251)
Examines impacts of decentralization on the relationships between political parties and elected state governors and legislators. Suggests that decentralization reduces the influence of central party machineries.

Angell, Alan and **Carol Graham.** Can social sector reform make adjustment sustainable and equitable?: lessons from Chile and Venezuela. See item **3607.**

3447 **Arceneaux, Craig.** Democratic consolidation or deconsolidation?: military doctrine and the 1992 military unrest in Venezuela. (*J. Polit. Mil. Sociol.*, 24:1, Summer 1996, p. 57–82, bibl., table)
Discusses notion that transmission of military doctrine is affected by the institutional fragmentation of the military examined in the context of unsuccessful military coups.

3448 **Arenas, Nelly.** El sistema político venezolano: principales ejes de discusión, 1989–1994. (*Cuest. Polít.*, 15, 1995, p. 51–65, bibl.)
Appraises several proposals dealing with the crisis of the Venezuelan political system. Focuses on writings by Venezuelan analysts from 1989–92. Useful.

Arteta Villavicencio, Gustavo. Efectos de las instituciones democráticas en la política y la economía. See item **2020.**

Azócar, Héctor C. La politica de cooperación de Venezuela con el Caribe, perspectivas ante los nuevos procesos de integración subregional: la asociación de estados del Caribe. See item **4218.**

3449 **Back to the ballot box: evaluating Venezuela's 1995 state and local elections.** Washington: Woodrow Wilson International Center for Scholars; 1996. 54 p.: appendix, graphs, maps. (Woodrow Wilson International

Center for Scholars, Latin American Program; 218)

Summary of a Woodrow Wilson Center seminar designed to analyze the Dec. 1995 state and local elections and gauge their impact on the political balance of power and the stability of the political system. Framed around three issues: the stakes of the elections, the relationship between the elections and the economy, and the future of the two-party system. Useful and interesting.

3450 Capriles Méndez, Ruth. Racionalidad de la corrupción en Venezuela. (*Politeia/Caracas*, 16, 1993, p. 207–240)

Suggests mechanisms to curve political corruption including effective control of public expenditures, control of party financing, improved procurement and bidding systems, and preventing inappropriate interference of vested interests in the policy process.

3451 Chitty La Roche, Nelson. 250 millones: la historia secreta. 2da. ed. Caracas: Editorial Pomaire, 1993. 317 p.: ill.

Former president of Chamber of Deputies Comptroller Committees. Describes cases of governmental corruption, in areas such as management of customs and procurement (including transactions in the Ministry of Interior) during Carlos A. Pérez government.

3452 Coddetta, Carolina. La ideologia política del venezolano. Caracas: Coediciones Univ. Simón Bolívar, Congresso de la República, 1990. 148 p.: bibl., ill.

Useful analysis of the evolution of political preferences in Venezuela during the 1960s, 1970s, and 1980s. Based on documentary data and information and survey research.

3453 Descentralización, gobernabilidad, democracia. Coordinación de Rafael de la Cruz. Caracas: Comisión Presidencial para la Reforma del Estado; Programa de las Naciones Unidas para el Desarrollo; Editorial Nueva Sociedad, 1992. 417 p.: bibl., ill., maps. (Serie Venezuela, la reforma del futuro)

Serious analysis of decentralization. Contains a wealth of information on the legal, fiscal, institutional, and service delivery aspects of decentralization in education, health, agriculture, technological research, energy, environment, and public works. Adequate balance between description and prescription;

sectoral studies are well-documented and clearly written.

3454 La distribución del poder. v. 2, Descentralización del ordenamiento urbano y experiencias municipales exitosas. Coordinación de Gabriela Chalbaud. Caracas: Editorial Nueva Sociedad, 1994. 1 v.: bibl., ill. (Serie Venezuela, la reforma del futuro)

Very interesting look at decentralization and urban development. Organized in three parts: 1) historical overview of centralist-federalist tendencies in the country; 2) current decentralization law and practices; and 3) examination of the relatively successful governance experiences of such municipalities as Caroní, Libertador, Los Salias, and Maracaibo.

3455 Ellner, Steve. El sindicalismo en Venezuela en el contexto democrático, 1958–1994. Traducido del inglés por Simón Molina. Caracas: Fondo Editorial Tropykos; Univ. de Oriente, 1995. 351 p.: bibl.

Well-balanced account of the relationships between trade unions, political parties, and State policy vis-à-vis unions. Also examines the internal structures, financial interests, and long-term strategy of organized trade unions, as well as relationships with similar international organizations. Mostly based on primary sources, notably, interviews, archive material, and written press.

3456 Ellner, Steve. Venezuelan revisionist political history, 1908–1958: new motives and criteria for analyzing the past. (*LARR*, 30:2, 1995, p. 91–121, bibl.)

Focuses on portraits of governments between 1908–58 painted by both political parties and revisionist historians, particularly perceptions of political continuity and change during each governmental period. Includes discussion of methodological and conceptual implications of revisionism and its shortcomings. Well researched and interesting.

3457 Escalante, Ricardo. De la caída de Pérez a la del Banco Latino: temores e intereses de Ramón Jota. Caracas: Vadell Hermanos Editores, 1994. 209 p.: ill.

Author became Venezuela's Press Secretary shortly before the impeachment of President Pérez and continued in that position until the end of Ramón J. Velásquez interim presidency. Book offers insider information not available anywhere else on Presidential Politics for a critical period in the evolution of Venezuelan democracy.

3458 Giordani, Jorge. La propuesta del MAS. Caracas: Univ. Central de Venezuela, Centro de Estudios del Desarrollo, Facultad de Ciencias Económicas y Sociales, 1992. 316 p.: bibl.

Discusses the evolution of the (Movimiento al Socialismo) Party ideology and fundamental tenets. Based upon writings of key leaders, interviews of party members, and writings by political analysts.

3459 González, Rosa Amelia and Juan Carlos Navarro. Building public-private cooperation in Venezuela. (*in* Community organizations in Latin America. Edited by Juan Carlos Navarro. Washington: Inter-American Development Bank, 1994, p. 103–150, appendix, bibl., graphs, table)

Pioneering work on nonprofit nongovernmental organizations (NGOs) in Venezuela. Through a discussion of their legal and political contexts, provides a better understanding of grassroots and intermediary NGOs. Also summarizes the work of five NGOs that deliver social services in the country.

3460 Hernández M., Janeth. Efectos políticos del sistema de representación proporcional personalizada en la elección de diputados al Congreso Nacional. (*Cuest. Polít.*, 15, 1995, p. 37–50, bibl., tables)

Discusses substantive aspects and political impacts of the personalized proportional representation system introduced by the electoral reform of 1993.

3461 Kornblith, Miriam. Reforma constitucional: crisis política y estabilidad de la democracia en Venezuela. (*Politeia/Caracas*, 15, 1992, p. 121–169, bibl., table)

Discusses the 1992 constitutional reform attempts. Contains information on the political processes and debates in relevant congressional committees and chambers.

3462 Krispin, Karl. Golpe de estado: Venezuela, 1945–1948. Caracas: Editorial Panapo, 1994. 147 p.: bibl.

Interesting and modern analysis of the 1945 and 1948 coups. Examines issues pertaining to motivation for planning, execution, and outcomes. Well written.

3463 Lovera De-Sola, R.J. Crónica sobre los presidentes de Venezuela: de Cristóbal Hurtado de Mendoza, 1811, a Carlos Andrés Pérez, 1989. Caracas: RJLDS Editor, 1993. 76 p.: bibl.

Brief historical account of heads of government during the 19th and 20th centuries. Acción Democrática presidents get low performance ratings.

3464 Marcotulio, Roberta and Haidée Velandria. Diseño de metodología para promocionar un candidato a diputado. Caracas: Fundación Carlos Eduardo Frias, 1992. 123 p.: bibl. (Col. Canícula; 2)

Offers basic guidelines for congressional electoral campaigns. Discusses candidates' images, platforms, and campaign strategies.

3465 Márquez, Trino. El estado en Venezuela: descentralización, reforma de la administración pública y políticas contra la pobreza. Caracas: Editorial Panapo, 1996. 208 p.: bibl., ill.

Collection of essays on decentralization, public administration reform, and policies poverty policies in Venezuela, some originally presented at international events sponsored by such organizations as the UN or the World Health Organization. Useful data and information.

3466 Mayobre, José Antonio. La labor de Sísifo: los intentos de reformar la televisión en Venezuela. Caracas: Monte Avila Editores Latinoamericana, 1993. 151 p.: bibl. (Documentos)

Identifies and appraises some policy proposals aimed at modifying the regulatory environment of Venezuelan TV during the 1970s.

3467 McCoy, Jennifer L. and William C. Smith. Democratic disequilibrium in Venezuela. (*J. Interam. Stud. World Aff.*, 37:2, Summer 1995, p. 113–179, bibl., tables)

Argues that current challenges for Venezuela are those of a deconsolidation of an established democratic regime. Suggests three possible future scenarios: 1) a revival of State intervention; 2) intensification of social unrest and economic deterioration; and 3) democratic renewal and economic recovery. Interesting.

3468 Miranda M., Pedro N. Venezuela invadida: la diosa blanca en el Caribe. Caracas: Ediciones Sextante, 1995. 166 p.: ill.

Despite preponderance of material on Colombian cartels, this work by a journalist offers a rare look at money laundering and drug trafficking in Venezuela. Praises efforts of Venezuelan authorities to eradicate both of those problems. Describes structures, processes, and activities drug groups adopt to launder and invest their profits.

3469 Moleiro, Moisés et al. El MAS: un proyecto político para el cambio o la conservación. Caracas: Fondo Editorial Tropykos, 1993. 155 p.: bibl.

Members of the Movimiento al Socialismo party critique neoliberalism, internal party organization, and alliances with other parties for electoral gains. Interesting.

3470 Molina Vega, José Enrique; Valia Pereira; and Henry Vaivads. ¿Puede superar la democracia venezolana su crisis?: el papel de los partidos políticos. (*in* Partidos y clase política en América Latina en los 90. San José: Instituto Interamericano de Derechos Humanos (IIDH); Centro de Asesoría y Promoción Electoral (CAPEL), 1995, p. 143–159, tables)

Discusses outcomes of Venezuela's political crisis during the 1990s, especially the role of political parties. Suggests that party democratization is critical for democratic maintenance.

3471 Molina Vega, José Enrique. Sistemas electorales y consolidación de la democracia. (*Politeia/Caracas*, 16, 1993, p. 255–267, bibl.)

Reflects on the relationships between electoral systems and democratic consolidation. Argues that the adoption of a specific system should be weighed according to its capacity to consolidate the democratic process.

Morales Benítez, Otto. Rómulo Gallegos: identidad del escritor y del político. See *HLAS 56:3651.*

3472 Morón, Guillermo. Los presidentes de Venezuela, 1811–1994. Caracas: Planeta, 1993. 335 p.: bibl., ill. (Col. Voces de la historia)

Brief and useful biographical accounts of heads of government during the 19th and 20th centuries, from Cristóbal Mendoza (1811) to Ramón J. Velásquez (1992–4).

Olavarría, Jorge. No, señor Presidente! no!: artículos publicados en "El Universal" 1994. See item **1969.**

3473 Ordóñez, Rosana. La casa del odio. Caracas: Planeta, 1994. 209 p.: ill. (Voces del presente)

Hilarious account of power and everyday life in the *Palacio de Miraflores*, Venezuela's presidential residence. Written by a well-known Venezuelan journalist who became head of official presidential propaganda during the interim presidency of Ramón J. Velásquez. Fun reading.

3474 Otros juicios sobre el proceso al ex presidente Carlos Andrés Pérez: escritos sin pasión y sin odio. Edición de José Agustín Catalá. Caracas: Centauro, 1994. 292 p.: bibl.

Collection of articles containing favorable opinions about Carlos A Pérez and his policies. Includes writings of politicians and political analysts from the left, center, and right and appeared earlier in the pages of Venezuelan newspapers. Several of them question the substance and/or procedures leading to the incarceration of the former president. Interesting.

3475 Pantin, Guillermo. Latino Mafia: crónica de la corrupción del sistema. Caracas: Pomaire, 1994. 189 p.: ill.

Written by a journalist with a long career in political reporting. Harshly criticizes the strong link between money and politics. Argues that the cultivation of political connections was key to the early financial success of Banco Latino. The Latino declared bankruptcy in 1994.

3476 Perry, William. Political assessment. (*in* Venezuela 1994: challenges for the Caldera Administration. Washington: Center for Strategic and International Studies, 1994, p. 1–12)

Very useful overview of the economic and political challenges faced by Caldera's government at the start of his presidential period. Useful information on congressional politics and congressional-presidential relations. Well written.

3477 Rodríguez-Valdés, Angel. Latino, pecado capital. Caracas: Pomaire, 1994. 156 p.: ill., index.

Account of the relationships between

political power and private finance in the case of Banco Latino. Provides a list of businesses linked to the bank.

3478 Stambouli, Andrés et al. Innovación democrática, mitos políticos y organización electoral. Presentación de Lucas Castillo Lara. Coordinación de Manuel Vicente Magallanes. Caracas: Consejo Supremo Electoral, 1988. 276 p.: bibl. (Col. del cincuentenario; 4)

Useful collection of articles on behavioral and legal aspects of electoral and party politics. Covers national and local levels.

Toro Hardy, Alfredo. Bajo el signo de la incertidumbre. See item **4458.**

3479 Urbaneja, Diego Bautista. Pueblo y petróleo en la política venezolana del siglo XX. Caracas: Centro de Formación y Adiestramiento de Petróleos de Venezuela y sus Filiales, 1992. 456 p.: bibl.

Dense analysis of Venezuela's political evolution during the 19th and 20th centuries. Focuses on three broad themes: the 19th century liberal program, the positivist and the democratic programs during the 20th.

3480 Venezuela: centralisme, régionalisme et pouvoir local. Coordination de Jean Revel-Mouroz. Paris: EST-IHEAL, 1988. 235 p.: bibl., maps. (Col. Travaux & mémoires de l'IHEAL; 43. Série Essai; no 3)

Useful collection of articles on Venezuela's regionalization and decentralization. Contains discussion of the importance of state universities in regional development.

3481 Venezuela: la democracia bajo presión. Recopilación de Andrés Serbín et al. Caracas: Instituto Venezolano de Estudios Sociales y Políticos; Editorial Nueva Sociedad, 1993. 218 p.: bibl., ill.

Collection of papers from North-South Center of Univ. of Miami and Venezuela's INVESP seminar held in Caracas in 1992. Focuses on the 1992–93 political crisis, economic policies, and emergent political actors.

3482 Venezuela. Comisión Presidencial para la Reforma del Estado. Una política social para la afirmación de la democracia. Caracas: Comisión Presidencial para la Reforma del Estado, 1989. 194 p. (Col. Reforma del estado; 8)

Interesting policy-oriented discussion of social policy in Venezuela (i.e. health, education, housing, sanitation, and poverty). Covers program and policy strategy as well as institutional aspects. Also provides useful contemporary data and information on performance.

3483 Venezuela, del siglo XX al siglo XXI: un proyecto para constuirla. Coordinación de Carlos Blanco. Caracas: COPRE; PNUD; Editorial Nueva Sociedad, 1993. 478 p.: bibl., ill. (Serie Venezuela, la reforma del futuro)

Useful collection of articles by prominent policy analysts, most of them Venezuelan. Focuses on issues pertaining to Venezuela's contemporary sociopolitical life, including historical evolution, political parties, the role of the State, domestic politics, and international relations. Article by Capriles contains an interesting typology of political corruption.

3484 Yépez Salas, Guillermo. Causa R: origen y poder. Caracas: Fondo Editorial Tropykos, 1993. 198 p.: bibl., ill.

Useful discussion of Causa R party's evolution, platform, and organization. Based on documentary data and survey research.

BOLIVIA

EDUARDO A. GAMARRA, *Associate Professor of Political Science, and Acting Director, Latin American and Caribbean Center, Florida International University, University Park Campus, Miami*

THE EARLY 1990S SAW THE PUBLICATION of a large body of literature on Bolivian government and politics. With few exceptions, the material reviewed for this volume of *HLAS* lacks methodological rigor and sophistication. The level of scholarly output reflects both a lack of social science training among many authors, and the general state of political science as a discipline in Bolivia. A new generation of university-trained social scientists will soon enter the field and the new millennium should witness an improvement in the quality of studies addressing political and government issues. Meanwhile, few US- and European-based scholars focus on the country, adding to the general dearth of good material on Bolivian politics.

The books and articles reviewed this biennium fall into the following basic categories: narcotics trade; democracy and political parties; electoral studies; civil-military relations; indigenous groups and politics; administrative decentralization; institutional analyses; recent political history; and biographies and general surveys. Most remarkable is the proliferation of studies on local politics, owing mainly to approval of the 1994 law decentralizing the Bolivian State.

The drug trade continues to receive much attention. As noted, the quality of the work continues to be quite poor given that the nature of the drug trade inhibits any serious academic inquiry. Therefore, a serious examination of the Bolivian narcotics trade and its impact on the country's political system continues to be wanting. Even less is known about the economic implications of the coca-cocaine economy. Noteworthy among the works included in this volume are the transcripts of a congressional hearing which examined alleged links between political party members and narcotics traffickers (item **3508**). Another important contribution is Mendoza's investigative work on Bolivian organized crime and its political connections (item **3520**).

Civil-military relations issues in Bolivia are generally overlooked by the scholarly community because few civilians take this topic seriously. Nevertheless, a few analysts such as Barrios Morón and Mayorga in *La cuestión militar en cuestión: democracia y fuerzas armadas* have made significant contributions to this area of study (item **3490**).

During the 1990s more emphasis was placed on the study of Bolivian political institutions, and political parties continue to capture attention. The more noteworthy interpretations of Bolivia's party system are Lazarte's essays (item **3516**) and Sandoval's book (item **3529**). The quantity of electoral studies has also increased in recent years, unfortunately outnumbered only by the number of elections themselves. San Martín (item **3527**) and Romero Ballivián (item **3526**) present studies of this genre. A few works reviewed in this volume also analyze municipal elections.

The literature on elections has been well supplemented by a number of essays on the nature of Bolivia's presidential system. Jost (item **3515**) and Fundación Milenio (item **3503**) provide a good overview of the debate surrounding this issue. These studies focus on the characteristics of executive-legislative relations and ponder the viability of a parliamentary alternative to the current system. Despite the literature's institutional focus, the scarcity of studies on the Bolivian National Congress and the judiciary leaves a significant void in Bolivian political science scholarship.

One of the most important topics this biennium concerns the Popular Participation Law, enacted in 1994 during the government of former president Gonzalo Sánchez de Lozada, which has received international attention. The World Bank and other international organizations have adopted it as a model. As a result, the law has had widespread repercussions in Latin America, the Caribbean, and Africa, and its architects have become sought-after consultants. The studies reviewed here provide historical background to the Popular Participation Law; a few attempt to assess its impact. Because the law is less than five years old, all assessments are tentative.

The most interesting of the works reviewed are those by Dabdoub (item **3499**) and Molina (item **3522**).

While not within the decentralization genre, a number of studies have begun to examine local politics and the significance of key actors. Among the more innovative and controversial are works that explore the influence of lodges, masonic and otherwise, on local governments. Ferreira's portrayal of the secret Santa Cruz *logias*, for example, provides fascinating insights into the nature of local Bolivian politics (item **3502**).

Bolivians have produced a long list of political biographies. These biographies, however, are generally homages to party leaders and other politicians, written primarily by partisans rather than social scientists. One example is Sanabria's biography of current president Gen. Hugo Banzer Suárez (item **3528**). A less partisan, and more seriously social scientific, portrait is the biography of Jaime Paz Zamora by Peñaranda and Chávez Zamorano (item **3495**). The scarcity of solid, scholarly biographies is unfortunate. Still lacking are objective social scientific studies of great 20th-century leaders such as Victor Paz Estenssoro, Hernán Siles Zuazo, Walter Guevara Anaya, and others. Exceptions are the very excellent works by Mayorga on the political discourse of emerging leaders in Bolivia (item **3519**). Mayorga, a political sociologist, is likely to become the country's leading social scientist within the decade.

3485 Albó, Xavier. And from Kataristas to MNRistas?: the surprising and bold alliance between Aymaras and neoliberals in Bolivia. (*in* Indigenous peoples and democracy in Latin America. New York: St. Martin's Press, 1994, p. 55–79, bibl., ill.)

Excellent essay attempts to interpret the surprising alliance between Víctor Hugo Cárdenas, leader of the Movimiento Revolucionario Tupac Katari de Liberación; and Gonzalo Sánchez de Lozada, chief of the Movimiento Nacionalista Revolucionario (MNR), author of Bolivia's neoliberal stabilization measures, and one of the country's wealthiest men. Cárdenas ran on the MNR ticket in 1993 and was elected vice president, the first Aymara to hold such a high political office. His election, however, stirred a debate between those who believed his position would enable him to contribute something to his community and those who believed he had been co-opted. Work also available in Spanish (see item **3486**). For sociologist's comment see item **5078**.

3486 Albó, Xavier. — y de kataristas a mnristas?: la sorprendente y audaz alianza entre aymaras y neoliberales en Bolivia. La Paz: Unitas; Cedoin, 1993. 80 p.: bibl., ill.

Spanish-language version of item **3485**.

3487 Ameller Gatica, Agustín. El manejo del poder: MNR-UDP. La Paz: MNR-UDP, 1988. 201 p.: ill.

Author includes several speeches he delivered over the course of a decade in the Cámara de Diputados. Provides interesting first-hand account of the intense political battles that characterized Bolivia's democratization experience, and a unique insight into the functioning of the Congreso Nacional.

3488 Andrade Salmón, Lupe. Los caminos de la corrupción. La Paz: Vaca Sagrada, 1992. 115 p.: ill. (Ediciones La Vaca Sagrada; 1)

Series of articles by conservative columnist for the daily *Ultimo Hora* bemoan lack of public outcry against ubiquitous signs of corruption. Notes that even the act of becoming a lawyer involves many layers of corruption, including bribing university admissions officials, faculty, and others. Offers a particularly interesting set of essays on the problems facing Bolivia's justice system.

3489 Asociación de Instituciones de Promoción y Educación (Bolivia). Descentralización, poder local y rol de las IPDS. La Paz: Asociación de Instituciones de Promoción y Educación, 1993. 194 p.

Essays written before implementation of Bolivia's Ley de Participación Popular analyze role of private social development institutions in decentralization of political power. Many of the authors concur that private institutions should play a key role in the process of decentralization, but they also note that they were excluded from discussions. Includes text of the Proyecto de Ley de Descentralización Administrativa. See also items **3499, 3494,** and **3522.**

3490 Barrios Morón, Raúl and **René Antonio Mayorga.** La cuestión militar en cuestión: democracia y fuerzas armadas. La Paz: Centro Boliviano de Estudios Multidisciplinarios (CEBEM), 1994. 159 p.: bibl.

Good collection of essays on civil-military relations by two leading Bolivian social scientists. Mayorga provides an excellent historical context. Barrios Morón offers two interpretations of how the military and police have fared under democracy and neoliberal reforms.

3491 Blanes Jiménez, José and **H.C.F. Mansilla.** Cinco tesis sobre el trasfondo del complejo coca/cocaína en Bolivia. (*Nueva Soc.*, 142, marzo/abril 1996, p. 65–69)

Argues that Bolivia, in addressing the coca/cocaine issue, should consider alternative strategies to law enforcement. Presents hypotheses which suggest that current strategies will fail: 1) efforts to date have been unsuccessful because social actors have embraced a legitimizing ideology that covers up their respective behaviors; 2) most Bolivians believe that the cocaine trade is a policy issue that does not affect them directly; 3) certain ideas (e.g., that poverty in the countryside is the motivating force behind the coca economy) have taken on the quality of truth and are reinforced by actions of progressive intellectuals; 4) the coca/cocaine complex is likely supported by a majority of the population. Also indicates that failure to find an alternative policy could lead to a delegitimation of the Bolivian State and an emergence of violent, extremist groups.

3492 Blanes Jiménez, José and **Mario Galindo Soza.** Las regiones hoy: desequilibrios institucionales y financieros. La Paz: Centro Boliviano de Estudios Multidisciplinarios (CEBEM), 1993. 101 p.

Two essays explore role of the State and formation of Bolivian regions (Blanes Jiménez), and financial resources assigned to specific regions in 1987–88 (Galindo Soza). Blanes Jiménez provides a good historical overview pointing to an incomplete national integration strategy, extreme structural-regional heterogeneity, and institutional and financial weakness as the principal ob-

stacles to an administrative decentralization program.

3493 Canelas, Demetrio. Dictadura y democracia en Bolivia. Cochabamba, Bolivia: Editorial Canelas, 1992. 588 p.

Compilation of editorials written by the founder of the daily *Los Tiempos* from 1908–early 1950s. Valuable primarily for historians interested in the editorial viewpoint of one of Bolivia's oldest newpapers.

3494 Castro Arze, Miguel and **Mauricio Lea Plaza.** La hora de lo local en Bolivia. (*Nueva Soc.*, 142, marzo/abril 1996, p. 116–125, ill.)

Short history of Bolivian movement toward administrative decentralization that culminated with 1994 law transferring responsibilities to municipal governments. Article reflects important new body of Bolivian social science literature on this topic. Mainly descriptive; few analytical insights. See also items **3489, 3499,** and **3522.**

3495 Chávez Zamorano, Omar and **Susana Peñaranda de Del Granado.** Jaime Paz Zamora: un político de raza. La Paz: S. Peñaranda y O. Chávez, 1997. 400 p.: bibl., ill. (some col.).

A unique look at complex life of Paz Zamora, President of Bolivia from 1989–93. Traces his life from brush with death as a Catholic priest to his ascent to power in late 1980s. Also provides interesting view of internal dynamics of the Movimiento de Izquierda Revolucionaria (MIR), the party founded and guided into political prominence by Paz Zamora. Unfortunately, final chapters gloss over accusations of Zamora's and MIR's involvement with Bolivian narcotics trafficker, which cost the former president and the party's leadership US entry visas.

3496 Comisión Andina de Juristas (Lima). Bolivia: administración de justicia y derechos humanos. Lima: Comisión Andina de Juristas, 1993. 189 p.: bibl. (Serie Informes sobre derechos humanos; 6)

This second report on Bolivia provides valuable overview of judicial system and human rights issues. Concludes that most serious problems in justice sector include lack of judiciary autonomy, long delays in the resolution of cases, and lack of access to justice by most sectors of Bolivian society. Useful section on drug war's impact on Bolivia's justice system.

3497 Conciencia de Patria (Bolivia). El libro del modelo endógeno. La Paz: CONDEPA, 1993. 633 p.: ill.

Good summary of principal beliefs and platform of Conciencia de Patria (CONDEPA), a political party founded in 1988 and headed by radio and television talk show host Carlos Palenque Aviles. In-depth presentation of the *modelo endógeno,* which refers to a nationalist strategy of development conceived by Palenque Aviles and a group of intellectuals from both the right and the left. Also includes history of CONDEPA, an historical interpretation of Bolivian political development over last 50 years, and a critique of current development strategies emphasizing market-oriented reforms and trade liberalization.

3498 Condo Riveros, Freddy. La agresión: así sentimos los cocaleros; testimonios de Guido Tarqui, Andrés Zurita, Juan de la Cruz Villca, Modesto Condori, y el pueblo. La Paz: Ediciones Alkhamari, 1994. 75 p.: ill.

Brief collection of testimonies by four coca growers from the Chaparé, Bolivia's principal coca-producing area. Interesting views on impact of joint US/Bolivian anti-narcotics policies. Includes allegations of widespread violations of human rights by US-trained Bolivian counternarcotics police.

3499 Dabdoub Arrien, Carlos. Descentralización—ya!! Santa Cruz de la Sierra, Bolivia: Impr. Landivar, 1994. 233 p.: bibl.

Summarizes arguments and presents a plan for administrative decentralization in Bolivia, a long-held aspiration of the elite in the easternmost *departamento* of Santa Cruz. Presents familiar arguments for stronger municipal- and departmental-level government while decreasing central government's responsibilities. Chapter 9 is particularly interesting as it discusses attempt by the government in which author served to decentralize Bolivia's health system. See also items **3489, 3494,** and **3522.**

3500 Dockweiler Cárdenas, Jorge. La Paz en emergencia. La Paz: Sagitario Artes Gráficas, 1993. 209 p., 8 leaves of plates: bibl., ill.

Examines range of problems affecting La Paz, from stray dogs to pollution, with the intention of highlighting issues the city

should address in the immediate future. In a broader context, La Paz suffers from ills afflicting most large Latin American cities that have grown in unplanned, disorderly ways over the past two decades.

3501 Dómich Ruiz, Marcos. Militares en la revolución y en la contrarrevolución. La Paz: Instituto de Investigaciones Sociológicas, U.M.S.A., 1993. 82 p.: bibl. (Serie Ensayos. Militarismo, política e ideología; 1)

Reproduces 1980 essay by author, a leading member of the Partido Comunista de Bolivia (PCB), with addition of a short final section from 1983 discussing role of armed forces after Bolivia's transition to democracy. Ideological interpretation adds little to knowledge of the period. Concludes that Bolivian armed forces have respected the Constitution, but are still a very significant power broker.

3502 Ferreira, Reymi. Las logias en Santa Cruz. Santa Cruz: Fondo de Ediciones Municipales, 1994. 248 p.: bibl., ill.

Since late 1980s a significant debate has developed in Bolivia over the presence of *logias* or secret organizations that allegedly control important sectors of political and economic life in the city of Santa Cruz; this book is the first attempt to compile material published between 1988–93 regarding these organizations. The most significant part of the book traces history of masonic movements in the city, documenting their illicit activities. Concludes that the Santa Cruz *logias* control the hiring and firing practices of public sector institutions in that city, thereby functioning as employment vehicles for their members and enabling them to divide local government functions among themselves.

3503 Ferrufino, Alfonso; José Ortiz Mercado; and Juan Cristobal Urioste. ¿Parlamentarismo o presidencialismo?: propuestas para el debate. La Paz: Fundación Milenio, 1995. 126 p.: bibl. (Serie Las instituciones de la democracia)

Includes essays by a noted politician (Ferrufino), a former politician turned political analyst (Ortiz Mercado), and a lawyer who writes opinion columns (Cristobal Urioste). Each tackles the feasibility of replacing Bolivia's presidential system with parliamentarism. While none suggests adopting parliamentarism, all agree that presidentialism is flawed and requires reform. Ortiz Mercado suggests abolishing the vice presidency and establishing a unicameral system, while Ferrufino notes that Bolivia's problems lie in the political parties more than in the presidential nature of the system. Offers succinct analysis of institutional problems facing Bolivia.

3504 Foro político electoral 1993: los programas de los partidos. La Paz: Centro Boliviano de Estudios Multidisciplinarios (CEBEM); ILDIS, 1993. 130 p.

Transcription of debate among political parties, including the Movimiento Nacionalista Revolucionario and the Acuerdo Patriótico, on four key issues: economic policy, labor policy, rural development policy, and State reform.

3505 Galindo Soza, Mario. Políticas y estrategias del medio ambiente urbano. La Paz: Centro Boliviano de Estudios Multidisciplinarios (CEBEM), 1993. 186 p.: bibl.

Useful diagnosis of Bolivia's urban environment. Discusses numerous problems that affect cities of various sizes, and provides strategy for environmental improvement. Also provides a comparative framework by examining urban environment in Venezuela. Concludes that strengthening municipalities through decentralization programs will enhance environmental efforts.

3506 Gamarra, Eduardo A. and **James M. Malloy.** The patrimonial dynamics of party politics in Bolivia. (*in* Building democratic institutions: party systems in Latin America. Edited by Scott Mainwaring and Timothy R. Scully. Stanford, Calif.: Stanford Univ. Press, 1995, p. 399–433, tables)

Definitive analysis of political party activity from 1880–1993. Examines civil-military interactions and the personalities involved. Includes a complete list of parties and their internal dynamics, 1982–92. Argues that as of 1993 the party system was functioning well. Also expresses optimism about Bolivia's democratic future. [D.S. Palmer]

3507 García Argañaras, Fernando. Razón de estado y el empate histórico boliviano: 1952–1982. La Paz: Editorial Los Amigos del Libro; Mala Yerba Editores, 1993. 296 p.: bibl. (Col. Política; 887)

Interesting theoretical chapter analyzes historical processes that brought about

Bolivia's 1952 revolution, and the internal and external contradictions that characterized politics there until 1982. Concludes that any historical process is subject to conflicting tendencies which result from specific economic, ethnic, social, and political contexts.

3508 Granado Cosío, Juan del. Informe dictamen: vinculación de dirigentes del MIR con el narcotráfico. La Paz: Comisión de Constitución, Justicia y Policía Judicial, 1994. 82 p.: ill.

Remarkable document presents findings of a congressional commission that investigated charges against former president Jaime Paz Zamora and the leadership of his party, the Movimiento de Izquierda Revolucionaria (MIR). Commission concluded that the evidence warranted an indictment of Zamora and three other MIR leaders. As a result of this report, Oscar Eid Franco, one of the MIR's principal leaders, was tried and sentenced to a four-year jail term.

3509 Gutiérrez Rojas, Edith. De las arenas del Chaco al valle de Tolata: movilizaciones campesinas. La Paz: Editorial Mensaje Urgente, 1993? 127 p.: bibl.

Published undergraduate thesis written in late 1970s provides a very good history of *campesino* mobilization and resistance from 1930s-70s. Especially useful as a retrospective sociological examination, with statistical data, of *campesino* mobilizations during 1971–78 Banzer dictatorship. Includes description of the so-called "Tolata Massacre," the result of an air force strike launched by the government in response to peasant protests of a stabilization package. See also item **3535.**

3510 Guzmán Arze, Humberto. La integración del Estado boliviano: imagen del país que cabalga sobre los Andes. Buenos Aires: Libros de Hispanoamérica, 1989. 132 p.: ill.

Short book on Bolivian geography, ecology, and ethnic groups. Based on historical analysis, author offers a strategy for Bolivian national integration in the context of a pluricultural/multicultural environment.

3511 Instituto Latinoamericano de Investigaciones Sociales. Balance de las elecciones municipales. Recopilación de Carlos F. Toranzo Roca. La Paz: ILDIS; PAT, 1992? 144 p.

Transcripts of analysis of Dec. 1992 municipal elections. Jorge Lazarte, the country's leading sociologist, notes the high level of voter absenteeism, inability of the left to reconstitute itself, and the commendable transparency of the process. Carlos Meza, historian and Bolivia's leading television anchor, provides a good comparative view of three municipal elections and notes characteristics of political parties.

3512 Instituto Latinoamericano de Investigaciones Sociales. Diversidad étnica y cultural. Edición de Carlos F. Toranzo Roca. La Paz: ILDIS, 1992. 115 p.: bibl.

Transcribes roundtable discussion among leading Bolivian academics and policymakers. Of particular interest is transcription of debate regarding relationship between political parties and Bolivia's distinct ethnic groups.

3513 Instituto Latinoamericano de Investigaciones Sociales. La visión política para el desarrollo agropecuario nacional. Bolivia: Cámara Agropecuaria de Cochabamba; Cámara Agropecuaria del Oriente; Instituto Latinoamericano de Investigaciones Sociales (ILDIS), 1993. 182 p.

Speeches from 1993 conference in which presidential candidates and others offered proposals for development of Bolivia's agricultural sector. Contains speeches of all major candidates including Gen. Hugo Banzer Suárez, Gonzalo Sánchez de Lozada, and Max Fernández Rojas.

3514 Irusta Medrano, Gerardo. Espionaje y servicios secretos en Bolivia: 1930–1980. La Paz: Todo Arte Servicio Gráfico, 1995. 384 p.: bibl., ill.

Interesting history of espionage in Bolivia from Chaco War to military governments of 1970s. Useful information based on interviews with former intelligence officers and a review of classified Bolivian documents. Most interesting section concerns the Cold War exercise "Operación Condor," revealing extent to which right-wing military dictatorships of the Southern Cone, Brazil, and Bolivia shared intelligence and exchanged prisoners.

3515 Jost, Stefan. Relación entre sistema político, régimen electoral y partidos: el caso Bolivia. (*Contribuciones/Buenos*

Aires, 13:2, abril-junio 1996, p. 179–220, bibl., tables)

Good descriptive survey of Bolivia's presidential election system. As a result of the constitutional provision requiring 50 percent plus 1 of the popular vote to win, all Bolivian presidents since 1980 have been elected by the Congreso Nacional. The system therefore can be characterized as "semipresidential" or "parliamentarized presidentialism." Argues that political reforms carried out in mid-1990s will make system more representative.

3516 Lazarte, Jorge. Bolivia, certezas e incertidumbres de la democracia. v. 1–3. Cochabamba, Bolivia: ILDIS; Los Amigos del Libro, 1993. 3 v.: bibl. (Col. Política; 881–883)

In Vol. 1 Lazarte focuses on crises faced by leftist parties in Bolivia, from the Movimiento de Izquierda Revolucionaria and the Partido Comunista Boliviana during Siles Zuazo's 1982–85 government to the crisis of the left during late 1980s-early 1990s. Vol. 2, the best of the series, examines political parties and problems of representative democracy. Vol. 3 compiles a wonderful set of short essays on the basic written and verbal norms of Bolivian democracy developed in the post-hyperinflation context and in the period of economic stabilization. Particularly useful and insightful is "Palenquismo y Neopopulismo," an incisive description and analysis of the rise to political prominence, during late 1980s, of Conciencia de Patria (CONDEPA) and the late Carlos Palenque Aviles.

3517 Mancilla, Felipe. La Confederación de Empresarios Privados de Bolivia (CEPB) y el Estado boliviano. (*Rev. Cienc. Polít./Santiago,* 17:1/2, 1995, p. 103–119)

Argues that Bolivian social science has not adequately studied the social significance of Bolivian private elites and bureaucracies. Claims that the Confederación de Empresarios Privados de Bolivia (CEPB), the private sector's premier association, is the principal supporter of State modernization, especially through the cooperation of several key members in the Movimiento Nacionalista Revolucionario (MNR) which spearheaded modernization in mid-1980s. Notes, however, that CEPB's support does not guarantee success of the reform process, because traditional political sectors and the State bureaucracy oppose it.

3518 Mansilla, H.C.F. Repercusiones ecológicas y éticas del complejo coca/cocaína: la percepción de la problemática por los involucrados. La Paz: Sistema Educativo Antidrogas y de Movilización Social (SEAMOS), 1994. 107 p.: bibl. (Drogas, investigación para el debate; 7)

One of Bolivia's leading social scientists provides a short, succinct, and clear analysis of Bolivia's cocaine/coca situation. Analyzes attitudes of labor leaders, *campesinos* (coca growers), and members of political parties. Among numerous significant conclusions, most noteworthy states that both workers and coca growers suffer from a premodern mentality that translates into a basically undemocratic conservative political culture. Argues that these social groups are unlikely to accept the logic of representative democracy or environmental arguments against the production of coca and cocaine. Concludes that only education will overcome this mentality.

3519 Mayorga, Fernando. Discurso y política en Bolivia. La Paz: CERES; ILDIS, 1993. 239 p.: bibl.

Important analysis examines Bolivian political discourse since 1952. First part analyzes discourse of the national revolution and studies its long-term impact on Bolivian politics. Second part critically examines the variety of discourses that emerged during Bolivia's democratization process.

3520 Mendoza, William R. Los mercaderes de la muerte. Buenos Aires: Marymar, 1993. 167 p.: bibl., ill. (Temas de actualidad)

Assesses structure of and linkages between Bolivian drug organizations and challenges common assumption that they exist only as appendages of larger Colombian cartels. Description of each organization is based on police archives, published literature, and press accounts from Bolivia and Argentina.

3521 Mesa Gisbert, Carlos D. *De Cerca:* una década de conversaciones en democracia. La Paz: ILDIS; PAT; BBA, 1993. 666 p.: ill., index.

Transcribed interviews from television program *De Cerca* conducted by author from 1983–93. Interviewees are prominent political actors who played key roles in the democratization process, including Gen. Hugo Banzer Suárez, Gonzalo Sánchez de Lozada, Jaime Paz Zamora, Walter Guevara, Lydia Gueiler, and Gen. Guido Vildoso.

3522 Molina, Fernando. La historia de la participación popular. La Paz?: Ministerio de Desarrollo Humano, 1997. 1 v.

Entertaining history of Bolivia's "Participación Popular," an innovative decentralization scheme initiated in 1994 during the administration of Gonzalo Sánchez de Lozada (1993–97). "Participación Popular" has received much international attention and has been in some measure adopted by the World Bank as a worthy reproducible decentralization experiment. Relates idea's development by Sánchez de Lozada. See also items **3489, 3499,** and **3494.**

3523 Radio Fides (Bolivia). El año del cambio. La Paz: Editorial Mundy Color, 1994. 299 p.

Daily account of life in Bolivia during 1993, drawn mainly from radio and television accounts. Includes everything from Bolivia's soccer team world cup qualifying matches to reports on Sánchez de Lozada's first few months in office. Eduardo Pérez Iribarne, a Jesuit priest, is the director of Radio Fides and the anchor of one of Bolivia's most-watched evening newscasts.

3524 Rojas, Marta and **Mirta Rodríguez Calderón.** Tania, guerrillera heroica. Buenos Aires: R. Cedeño Editor, 1993. 159 p.

᛭ Short book appears to have actually been written by Guido "Inti" Peredo, chief of Bolivia's Ejército de Liberación Nacional who fought and died alongside Che Guevara in 1967. Provides interesting insights into the life of Tamara Haydee Bunke, alias "Tania." Tania became famous for her role in organizing the failed Ñancahuazú guerrilla experiment. Authors are Cuban journalists who apparently completed the book based on Inti's writings, snippets from Tania's diary, and interviews with Tania's parents and others. Fascinating reading provides insights into early phases of Che Guevara's Bolivian experience.

3525 Rojas Ortuste, Gonzalo. Democracia en Bolivia hoy y mañana: enraizando la democracia con las experiencias de los pueblos indígenas. La Paz: CIPCA, 1994. 152 p.: bibl., index. (Cuadernos de investigación; 41)

Proposes a model of consociational democracy that would consider needs of Bolivian indigenous groups. Argues that the model would create a more democratic political system by guaranteeing Bolivia's vast indigenous population direct representation while maintaining their core ethnic and cultural identity. Consociational arrangements have had short histories elsewhere in the world however, and nothing author argues suggests that his model would be more successful.

3526 Romero Ballivián, Salvador. Geografía electoral de Bolivia: así votan los bolivianos. La Paz: Centro Boliviano de Estudios Multidisciplinarios (CEBEM); ILDIS, 1993. 288 p.: bibl., ill.

Excellent contribution to the study of elections in Bolivia. Good electoral history from 1977–89; thorough analysis of the performance of major political parties in each election; and excellent statistical data examining electoral results in districts throughout Bolivia. Identifies party strongholds by district and demonstrates source of strength for political parties.

3527 San Martín Arzabe, Hugo. Sistemas electorales: adaptación del doble voto alemán al caso boliviano. La Paz?: Fundación Milenio, 1993. 78 p.: bibl.

The result of a report prepared for the Fundación Milenio, a private think tank linked to current President Gonzalo Sánchez de Lozada, study is representative of a large body of works related to Bolivian constitutional reform, specifically in regard to the electoral system. Provides an incomplete comparative introduction to electoral systems and a good discussion of the German electoral law which combines proportional representation and single member district systems. In 1994 Bolivia adopted a similar law, and beginning in 1997, 50 percent of the members of the Cámara de Diputados are elected using a single member district strategy. Author does not fully justify the application of this system to Bolivia.

3528 Sanabria G., Floren. Banzer: democracia y nacionalismo. La Paz: Empresa Editora Proinsa, 1990. 269 p.: ill.

Author defends Hugo Banzer Suárez's 1970s dictatorship and places the retired general among Bolivia's most important heroes. Banzer, in addition to his 1971–78 presidency, did assist in Bolivia's democratization by accepting the 1985 congressional election of Víctor Paz Estenssoro, and by providing criti-

cal political support in order to help stabilize the economy. Banzer's party, Acción Democrática Nacionalista, also co-governed with Jaime Paz Zamora from 1989–93. However, author does not attempt to balance these positive aspects of Banzer's career with his leadership of one of the most brutal and corrupt governments of the 20th century.

3529 Sandoval Rodríguez, Isaac. Los partidos políticos en Bolivia. La Paz: U.M.S.A., 1993 204 p.: bibl.

Good, albeit tedious, history of political parties in Bolivia. Unfortunately, work is difficult to read and use. Those interested are better off reading Herbert Klein's classic *Parties and political change in Bolivia, 1880–1952* (see HLAS 33:7699 and HLAS 34:2830) and Mario Rolón Anaya's *Política y partidos en Bolivia* (see HLAS 29:6383 and HLAS 55:3341).

3530 SEAMOS (Bolivia). Información sobre drogas: instituciones y recursos humanos en Bolivia. Dirección de Silvia Calderón Lora. La Paz: SEAMOS, 1993. 273 p. (Drogas, investigación para el debate; 4)

Basic directory lists institutions, psychologists, and other resources in Bolivia that provide drug addiction prevention and rehabilitation programs.

3531 SEAMOS (Bolivia). Narcotráfico en Bolivia: resúmenes analíticos, 1980–1993. Dirección de Silvia Calderón Lora. La Paz: SEAMOS, 1993. 276 p. (Drogas, investigación para el debate; 5)

Excellent annotated bibliography of several dozen articles and books published between 1980–93 on narcotics trafficking and related topics. Most of the publications are Bolivian and difficult to locate; SEAMOS apparently has original copies which can be used at their library. SEAMOS is a drug education and drug abuse prevention organization which has carried out several programs in Bolivia with some US and foreign funding.

3532 SEAMOS (Bolivia). Penalización o legalización de drogas en Bolivia. La Paz: SEAMOS, 1994. 145 p.: appendix, bibl., index. (Drogas: el debate boliviano; 9)

Transcribes debate sponsored by SEAMOS, Bolivia's drug abuse prevention organization, on drug legalization. In first section, journalist Jorge Canelas and sociologist H.C.F. Mansilla debate legalization and selective decriminalization of narcotics. In the second, Canelas and Mansilla defend their views before a panel of commentators. Reproduces a few documents on the issue including an interview with well-known legalization advocate and Nobel Prize winner Milton Friedman.

3533 Serrate Reich, Carlos. Vistazo al país: *Hoy.* v. 1–3. La Paz: Empresa Editora Siglo, 1994 3 v.: ill.

Three-volume collection of author's editorials previously published between 1976–94 in the La Paz newspaper *Hoy.* Author is a well-known and sometimes controversial journalist and diplomat whose work reveals his changing political views during this time period.

3534 Sivak, Martín. El asesinato de Juan José Torres: Banzer y el Mercosur de la Muerte. Buenos Aires: Ediciones del Pensamiento Nacional, 1998. 251 p.: bibl., ill.

First work of investigative journalism about the murder of Gen. Juan José Torres González, former *de facto* president of Bolivia. Torres was kidnapped and murdered in Buenos Aires in June 1976, presumably by members of an Argentine hit squad with links to the then military governments of Argentina and Bolivia. Concludes that conspiracy involved then Bolivian president Hugo Banzer Suárez; his cousin Eduardo Banzer, who was serving as Bolivian consul in Buenos Aires; Albano Harguindeguy, then Argentina's Interior Minister; members of Gen. Pinochet's Chilean intelligence service; and a host of other characters. Author interviewed over 60 people in Argentina, Bolivia, and Uruguay. If account is correct, investigation presents a very serious indictment of intelligence sharing by Argentine, Bolivian, and Chilean dictators in order to eliminate opposition.

3535 Soto S., César. Historia del Pacto Militar Campesino. Cochabamba, Bolivia: Ediciones CERES, 1994 70 p.: bibl.

Brief, interesting history of the pact between Bolivian armed forces and *campesinos* from early 1960s–74. Describes its formation thanks to Gen. René Barrientos Ortuño who mobilized and armed important peasantry sectors of Cochabamba's central valleys in order to catapult himself to power. Following his death, the pact grew fragile as successive military governments failed to reinforce es-

tablished patrimonial links. The pact essentially ended in Jan. 1974 when then President Gen. Hugo Banzer Suárez ordered the air force to strafe a peasant protest in the town of Tolata. Subsequent military governments had little capacity to mobilize the peasantry. See also item **3509.**

3536 Torrico V., Erick Rolando. Bolivia: izquierdas en transición. (*Nueva Soc.,* 141, enero/feb. 1996, p. 156–165, bibl., ill.)

Argues that the left in Bolivia, as elsewhere in the Americas, is undergoing a significant transformation. States that unless the left accommodates the current neoliberal regime and representative democracy, it will become at best marginal and at worst it will completely disappear.

3537 Torrico V., Erick Rolando. La privatización de los medios no aportó a la democracia. (*Rev. UNITAS,* 15, julio 1996, p. 35–41, ill.)

Respected Bolivian journalist argues that, although the media have played an important role in Bolivian politics since the transition to democracy, especially during elections, they have failed to contribute to the development of "genuine democratic culture." Author criticizes utilitarian relationship between the media and politics in Bolivia. Moreover, he points out an interesting trait of contemporary Bolivian journalism: that it is characterized by a troubling authoritarian legacy which is evident in journalists' view that they are always correct and always must have the final word. Author notes that this trait in particular does not contribute to Bolivia's democratization.

3538 Universidad Católica Boliviana. Instituto de Encuestas. Encuesta de percepción política. La Paz: Fundación Hanns-Seidel, 1993. 113 p.: ill.

Results of a good survey of Bolivia's prevailing political attitudes on Aug. 14, 1993, only days after President Gonzalo Sánchez de Lozada took office. Date is particularly useful, as Sánchez de Lozada achieved power with one of Bolivia's highest rates of popular support since the transition to democracy in 1982. Provides good data on opinions, attitudes, and behaviors of Bolivians. Shows, for example, that despite lack of confidence in political institutions such as parties, legislatures, and judiciaries, Bolivians preferred democracy to authoritarian government.

3539 Universidad Católica Boliviana. Instituto de Encuestas. Encuesta de percepción política V, Ciudad de La Paz. La Paz: Fundación Hanns-Seidel, 1994. 68 p.: ill., tables.

Results of a public opinion poll taken in La Paz in June 1994 provide interesting glimpse of urban political culture. Lists questions and includes short description of the methodology. No analysis of poll results.

3540 Violencias encubiertas en Bolivia. Coordinación de Xavier Albó y Raúl Barrios Morón. Coca, vida cotidiana y comunicación de Centro de Documentación e Investigación Bolivia (CEDIB), Patricia Cottle, Carmen Beatriz Ruiz y Juan Cristóbal Soruco. Violencia en la Región Andina: sintesis final de Equipo de la Asociación Peruana de Estudios e Investigación para la Paz. v. 2, La Paz: CIPCA; Aruwiyiri, 1993. 1 v. (CIPCA; 39)

Superb collection of articles on violence in Bolivia examines topics ranging from the war on drugs to everyday violence to media methods of reporting on recent terrorist attacks. Final chapter places Bolivian experience in a broader Andean context. For annotation of Vol. 1 see *HLAS* 55:3355 and 55:4979.

PERU

DAVID SCOTT PALMER, *Professor of International Relations and Political Science, Chairman of the Department of Political Science, and Founding Director, Latin American Studies Program, Boston University*

OVER THE MID TO LATE 1990s, Peruvian politics became more predictable and routinized. These were welcome developments after a turbulent decade of hyperinflation, economic stagnation and decline, intolerable levels of political violence, *autogolpe,* and international opprobrium (items **3556, 3593, 3582, 3583, 3603,** and **3570**).

From a field of 14 candidates, President Alberto Fujimori easily won the 1995 presidential race (with 64 percent in the first round). The elections followed the adjusted rules of the 1993 Constitution permitting immediate reelection and a return to counting percentages based on the valid vote rather than the total vote (i.e., including spoiled and blank votes as in 1985 and 1990) (items **3559** and **3590**). Quite unexpectedly, his supporters also won an absolute majority, (67 of 120 seats), in the one-chamber Congress, even though they received just 25 percent of the total vote. This outcome was largely due to much voter confusion when confronted with a cluttered field of 22 parties, a single list for each national electoral district, the option to specify two preferences from a single list, and abbreviated voting hours (item **3581**). International observer missions declared the results "free and fair" and the United States supported this position. Thus, despite persisting reservations in the minds of many, Peru returned to full standing as a functioning democracy (items **3576, 3566, 3581,** and **3551**).

Peru's economy continued to improve. Growth in 1994 was a record 13 percent, with the 1995 to 1997 average a more modest, but still healthy, 5 percent. Poverty levels declined slightly (from 47 to 45 percent), foreign investment levels remained high (with US investment increasing from $300 million in 1996 to just over $1 billion in 1996), and a significant debt reduction under a 1997 Brady Plan agreement (of $9.4 billion, or about 50 percent of upcoming obligations) gave Peru some breathing room in its international financial obligations. Nevertheless, even as economic and political stability were restored in Peru, many analysts became concerned over the country's continuing lack of political institutionalization, the influence of the armed forces, and President Fujimori's personalistic and authoritarian style of governance (items **3547** and **3555**).

On the day of his April 7, 1995 electoral victory, President Fujimori declared his commitment to "direct democracy, without parties or intermediaries between the President and the people." Because none of the established parties had received at least five percent of the vote in the presidential elections, under new procedures each party had to gather at least 600,000 signatures before being reregistered for participation in future elections. None had been approved as of late 1997. Other disquieting government initiatives included: 1) a June 1995 general amnesty for any abuses committed during the counterinsurgency campaign, 2) the concentration of more than 25 percent of the government budget in the Ministry of the Presidency, 3) the removal of three Supreme Electoral Tribunal judges who ruled against the constitutionality of a third election of the president, 4) the revocation of the citizenship of the majority owner of a television station that revealed telephone wiretapping of some 200 leading politicians, journalists, and business executives, and 5) the continuation of "faceless judges"in military trials of accused terrorists until October 1997.

Although incidents and deaths related to political violence continued to decline (to about 400 and 200 respectively in 1997), deep pockets of unrest remained. On December 18, 1996, the world was riveted when 14 Tupac Amaru Revolutionary Movement (MRTA) guerrillas seized control of the Japanese Ambassador's residence, taking over 500 hostages. Amidst on and off negotiations, the siege and stand-off continued for over four months. Then a spectacular assault on April 22, 1997 by approximately 180 specially-trained Peruvian military personnel successfully evacuated all but one of the remaining 42 hostages and killed all the guerrillas.

Although President Fujimori benefitted from this successful outcome by a temporary jump in popular support, his poll numbers soon fell to lows unprecedented in his seven-year presidency, declining to a mere 20 to 25 percent approval rating. For almost the first time, it appears that Fujimori might be vulnerable to defeat should he decide, as appears likely, to run for reelection yet again in April 2000. As of the end of 1997, the leading opposition candidate is the Mayor of Lima, Alberto Andrade.

3541 Adrianzén, Alberto. Partidos y orden social en el Perú. (*in* Democracia, etnicidad y violencia política en los países andinos. Lima: Instituto Francés de Estudios Andinos; Instituto de Estudios Peruanos, 1993, p. 29–41, bibl.)

Maintains that the crisis of politics and political parties since the 1980s is due to the voter belief that the country's political parties do not represent the will of the people and to questions about the legitimacy of old and new parties, resulting in a preference for independent candidates. Claims that the political system and parties in Peru have broken down because they have not been able to create a democratic order appropriate for Peru's new socioeconomic conditions. [S. Lastarria]

3542 Altamirano, Teófilo et al. El Perú frente al siglo XXI. Edición de Gonzalo Portocarrero Maisch y Marcel Valcárcel C. Lima: Pontificia Univ. Católica del Perú, Fondo Editorial, 1995. 670 p.: bibl., ill.

In commemoration of the 30th anniversary of the founding of the Social Sciences Faculty of the Catholic Univ. of Peru, faculty members offer wide-ranging analyses and projections on Peru's economy, demography, environment, society, culture, and politics, as well as comments on the role of social sciences and the university in development.

3543 Amat y León Ch., Carlos *et al.* Pensando el Perú: educación en derechos humanos y propuesta nacional para la democracia, la paz, y el desarrollo. Edición de Polo Coordinador de la Red Peruana de Educación en Derechos Humanos. Lima: Comisión Andina de Juristas, 1993. 205 p.

At the height of Peru's multiple crises, 15 leading Peruvian scholars and politicians provide a remarkable and diverse set of reflections on the basic requirements for restoring peace, progress, and tolerance in their beleaguered country.

3544 Arias Quincot, César. La modernización autoritaria: la nueva institucionalidad surgida a partir de 1990. Lima: Fundación Friedrich Ebert, 1994. 178 p.: bibl.

Valuable study of the challenges of forging a new constitution in the context of large-scale political violence and the assumption of sweeping presidential powers via *autogolpe*. Includes texts of President Fujimori's April 5, 1992 speech, the OAS resolution of April 13, and key decree laws of May 1992.

3545 Barrig, Maruja. The difficult equilibrium between bread and roses: women's organizations and democracy in Peru. (*in* The women's movement in Latin America: participation and democracy. Edited by Jane S. Jaquette. Boulder, Colo.: Westview Press, 1994, p. 151–175)

Significant overview and analysis of the emerging women's movement in Peru and its weakening due to strategic decisions, as well as due to Shining Path's policy of threatening and assassinating women's movement leaders.

3546 Becker, David G. Citizenship, equality, and urban property rights in Latin America: the Peruvian case. (*Stud. Comp. Int. Dev.*, 31 : 1, Spring 1996, p. 65–95, bibl.)

Pathbreaking analysis reconceptualizing democratization in Latin America to consider civil society more broadly as a society of law. Thus migrants' pursuit of property rights can be included, as they have a stake in democratic participation and capitalist development. The Institute of Liberty and Democracy's work with Lima squatters examined as a case study.

3547 Bernales Ballesteros, Enrique. Partidos políticos y democracia en el Perú. (*Social. Particip.*, 73, marzo 1996, p. 45–53)

Updates previous studies on Peru's political party crisis. Views the pre-1992 system as irreparable, but sees the absolute necessity of parties for democracy. Includes valuable historical overview of parties under Peruvian law, including the very negative effects on parties of post-*autogolpe* legislation. Concludes with specific recommendations for establishing a modern party system. Essential reading.

3548 Bernales Ballesteros, Enrique. Los poderes ejecutivo y legislativo en la constitución peruana de 1993. (*in* Divisiones de poderes. Buenos Aires: Centro Interdisciplinario de Estudios sobre el Desarrollo Latinoamericano de la Fundación Konrad Adenauer (CIEDLA); St. Augustin, Germany: Konrad-Adenauer-Stiftung, 1994, p. 121–182, bibl.)

Significant study, by a leading scholar and former senator, of both the legal and political contexts for replacing a "progressive" document (1979 Constitution) with a "reactionary" one (1993 Constitution), in which populist presidentialism is dramatically and systematically reinforced. Argues that the new constitution compounds the limitations of the old instead of rectifying them and is fundamentally flawed on both legal and political grounds.

3549 Cabieses, Hugo and **Ricardo Soberón Garrido.** Narcotráfico. (*Quehacer/Lima*, 102, julio/agosto 1996, p. 41–59, photos, tables)

Two articles offer extremely valuable analysis, with extensive data, of overproduction and dramatic decline in prices for Peruvian coca and cocaine derivatives. Concludes that sustained price increases are unlikely in the future and supports alternative development approaches. In the second article, Soberón Garrido discusses the dilemmas of military involvement in counternarcotics efforts and the extensive corruption that has resulted.

Cáceres Valdivia, Eduardo. The incorporation of economic, social, cultural, and indigenous people's rights into the agendas of human rights organizations in Peru. See item **1183.**

3550 Calvo Ospina, Hernando and **Katlijn Declercq.** Perú, los senderos posibles. Tafalla, Spain: Txalaparta, 1994. 222 p.: bibl. (Saila Gebara; 25)

A European Marxist perspective on Peru revealed through interviews in 1992 with church, Red Cross, and NGO officials; lawyers; generals; and Shining Path sympathizers.

Comunidades campesinas y nativas, en el nuevo contexto nacional. See item **1189.**

3551 Conaghan, Catherine M. Public life in the time of Alberto Fujimori. Washington: Woodrow Wilson International Center for Scholars, Latin American Program, 1996. 30 p. (Working paper series; 219)

Incisive analysis of the capacity of the Fujimori government to resist scrutiny and criticism regarding public controversies and actually to defy public opinion. A free press does not lead to government accountability in Peru, due largely to the fragmented state of society and the collapse of the party system. Significant contribution.

3552 Congreso Peruano de Ciencia Política, *1st, Lima, 1994.* Sociedad, partidos y estado en el Perú: estudios sobre la crise y el cambio; ponencias presentadas en el Primer Congreso Peruana de Ciencia Política celebrado en Lima del 8 al 10 de noviembre de 1994 organizado por el Centro de Investigación de la Facultad de Derecho y Ciencias Políticas de la Universidad de Lima y con el auspicio de la Sociedad Peruana de Ciencia Política. Coordinación de Carlos Fernández Fontenoy. Textos de Juan Abugattás A. *et al.* Lima: Univ. de Lima, 1995. 639 p.: bibl., ill.

Comprehensive overview of Peruvian politics by leading social scientists, including some comparative regional analyses. Focuses on the crisis of political paradigms, the political party crisis, democracy and its "reinvention," the armed forces, the new profile of Peruvian civil society, and State reform.

3553 Coral Cordero, Isabel. Desplazamiento por violencia política en el Perú, 1980–1992. (*in* Consulta sobre Desplazamiento y Refugio en la Región Andina, Lima?, 1993. Desplazados. Lima: Instituto de Defensa Legal, 1995, p. 73–121, tables)

Important contribution by a key participant in the effort to help those displaced by political violence to return to their homes. Analysis based on a survey of migrants pro-

vides much detail on economic status, causes of departure, educational levels, and occupations. Notes significance of Church assistance and a concomitant lack of government support.

3554 Cotler, Julio. Political parties and the problems of democratic consolidation in Peru. (*in* Building democratic institutions: party systems in Latin America. Edited by Scott Mainwaring and Timothy R. Scully. Stanford: Stanford University Press, 1995, p. 323–353, tables)

Peru's most established political sociologist analyzes the failure of Peru's historically fragmented, exclusionary, and personalist political parties to build an inclusive political system of institutionalized parties with the return to democracy in 1980. Documents the trajectory of political party decline through 1992.

3555 Crabtree, John. La crisis del sistema partidario peruano, 1985–1995. (*Apuntes/Lima*, 35, 1994, p. 19–36, table)

Valuable analysis, with ample detail and data, of the breakdown of the party system over the late 1980s and early 1990s and its replacement by a political "outsider" of a *democradura.* Sees some prospects for party rejuvenation based on analyses of municipal elections outside of metropolitan Lima.

3556 Degregori, Carlos Iván. Perú: redefinición del papel militar en un contexto de violencia subversiva y colapso del régimen democrático. (*in* Reconversión militar en América Latina. Coordinación de Gabriel Aguilera Peralta. Guatemala: FLACSO, 1994, p. 107–124, bibl., graph)

Tight, detailed analysis of the progressive "militarization of society" under President Fujimori. Includes an exhaustive overview of the military's often counterproductive counterinsurgency role in the 1980s and the political dynamics of the early 1990s that produced a civilian-controlled counterterrorism agreement in Congress, helping to provoke the *autogolpe.* Important contribution.

3557 Degregori, Carlos Iván *et al.* Las rondas campesinas y la derrota de Sendero Luminoso. Lima: IEP Ediciones, 1996. 269 p.: bibl., ill. (Estudios de la sociedad rural; 15)

Detailed, fieldwork-based analysis of Shining Path and its defeat in the Ayacucho region. Highlights the importance of guerrilla insensitivity to local realities and resulting peasant alienation, as well as the crucial role of local organized responses by peasant self-defense groups and evangelical Protestant churches. Major contribution.

3558 Durand, Francisco. From fragile crystal to solid rock: the formation and consolidation of a business peak association in Peru. (*in* Business and democracy in Latin America. Pittsburgh, Pa.: Univ. of Pittsburgh Press, 1995, p. 141–177)

Major case study, rich in detail, of the struggles, challenges, and eventual success of the Confederación Nacional de Instituciones Empresariales Privadas (CONFIEP) in the turbulent context of Peruvian politics in the 1980s and early 1990s. Documents CONFIEP's ability to become a dynamic, integrated, and inclusive spokesperson for the private sector.

3559 García Belaúnde, Domingo and **Pedro Planas Silva.** La constitución traicionada: páginas de historia reciente. Lima: Seglusa Editores, 1993. 321 p.: bibl.

Detailed critique of the 1993 Constitution and the Constitutional Congress that formulated it, emphasizing its tendencies toward autocracy and a reconcentration of presidential power. Largely a compilation of the authors' previously published newspaper, news magazine, and academic journal accounts.

3560 García Belaúnde, Domingo. The new Peruvian constitution, 1993. (*Jahrb. Öffentl. Rechts Gegenwart,* 43, 1995, p. 651–659)

Useful brief summary of Peru's 12th Constitution, focusing on historical background, the immediate political context of its formulation, and key provisions.

3561 García Belaúnde, José Antonio. El Perú en el Grupo Andino, 1992–1997: los años difíciles. (*Social. Particip.,* 78, junio 1997, p. 47–62, photos, tables)

Useful discussion of the failure of the Andean Pact due to its emphasis on import substitution industrialization approaches and Peru's withdrawal as the Fujimori government moved to an economic liberalization strategy.

3562 García-Sayán, Diego; Jorge Morelli Pando; and **Sinesio Jarama.** Perú-Ecuador: las cartas sobre la mesa. (*Quehacer/ Lima,* 94, marzo/abril 1995, p. 57–65, photos)

Three distinguished Peruvians and opinion leaders—an international lawyer and ex-UN Mission chief, a retired career diplomat and former two-time ambassador to Ecuador, and a retired army general and regional commander—offer their cautiously pessimistic views on the 1995 border conflict as peace talks began. Valuable benchmark.

3563 Gatti Murriel, Aldo and **Piedad Pareja Pflucker.** Democracia y participación. Lima: Fundación Friedrich Ebert, 1995. 129 p.: bibl.

Careful analysis of core characteristics of voting laws in Peru—such as secret, obligatory, and invalid—and their effects on voting patterns from 1980–94 in relation to political leadership, campaigning, electoral system efficiency, and the eligible voting population. Includes data for each election by department. Among other conclusions, expresses concern about declining rates of participation.

3564 Grompone, Romeo and **Carlos Mejía.** Nuevos tiempos, nueva política: el fin de un ciclo partidario. Lima: IEP, 1995. 110 p.: bibl., ill. (Col. mínima, 1019–4479; 32)

Provocative analysis of "the politics of antipolitics" of President Fujimori and the failures of parties and their leadership. In the context of party failure and presidential initiatives to keep parties marginalized, envisions the emergence of new grassroots institutional initiatives from an emerging civil society.

3565 Guzmán, León. Construcción del liderazgo y mito político: Abimael Guzmán, un revolucionario burócrata. (*in* Psicología de la acción política. Recopilación de Orlando D'Adamo, Virginia García Beaudoux e Maritza Montero. Buenos Aires: Paidós, 1995, p. 143–162, bibl., graph, table)

Cogent political-psychological analysis of Shining Path's leadership characteristics. Concludes that Guzmán combines a "charismatic authoritarian" personality and emphasis on organization, ideology, contemplation, and the elaboration of a revolutionary myth, which distinguishes him from most guerrilla leaders. Conclusions based on content analysis of four speeches and an interview.

3566 Hammergren, Linn A. The politics of justice and justice reform in Latin America: the Peruvian case in comparative perspective. Boulder, Colo.: Westview Press, 1998. 342 p.: bibl., index.

Comprehensive, detailed discussion of the judicial system of Peru by an academic specialist on the country and AID manager of administration of justice projects (includes cases on Colombia, El Salvador, and Costa Rica). Emphasizes the crisis of the late 1980s and 1990s and the Fujimori government reforms of 1992–95. Definitive treatment of a crucial component of democratic consolidation.

3567 Herzog, Kristin. Finding their voice: Peruvian women's testimonies of war. Valley Forge, Pa.: Trinity Press International, 1993. 272 p.: bibl., ill., index.

Windows on the "witness of women" of Peru and their perspectives on war and peace at the height of political violence, 1989–92, by a committed Catholic German-American. Includes careful and comprehensive analysis of women's issues and the women's movement in Peru. Important contribution.

3568 Implementación de políticas públicas en el Perú. Edición de Augusto Alvarez Rodrich y Gabriel Ortiz de Zevallos. Lima: Editorial Apoyo, 1995. 183 p.: ill.

A pioneering public policy approach towards understanding how politics functions in Peru, with eight case studies of initiatives in the 1990–92 period. These include telecommunications, social security, the 1992 budget, transportation, tax reform, and agriculture. Highlights the interactions between legislative and executive branches, and includes interviews with several government officials.

3569 Inca, Gerónimo. El ABC de Sendero Luminoso y del MRTA. Lima: Grupo Editorial G. Inca, 1994. 226 p.: ill.

Summary presentation of basic information on the organization, ideology, membership, and trajectory of Shining Path and MRTA through 1992. Appears to be based on government intelligence sources.

3570 Informe sobre la situación de los derechos humanos en el Perú en 1993. Lima: Coordinadora Nacional de Derechos Humanos, 1993. 111 p.: ill., tables.

Compact discussion of political violence and human rights violations in Peru in 1993 by the country's most respected human rights NGO. Includes detailed tables and charts showing incidence of violence, deaths, and disappearances.

3571 Informe sobre la situación de los derechos humanos en Perú. Washington: General Secretariat, Organization of American States, 1993. 105 p.: appendix.

Important benchmark study by the OAS on Peru and the 1992 *autogolpe* in the context of OAS responsibilities under the Santiago Accord of 1991 to review internal threats to democracy in member countries. Appendix includes reports of visits by the Interamerican Commission on Human Rights.

3572 Jochamowitz, Luis. Ciudadano Fujimori: la construcción de un político. Lima: PEISA, 1993. 346 p.: bibl., ill., photos. (Serie crónicas contemporáneas)

The well-written product of a *Caretas* reporter's research and interviews to produce a biography of Fujimori, a difficult undertaking due to now-closed public archives and unwillingness of family members to talk about their distinguished relative. Incomplete, unofficial, and extremely interesting. Includes fascinating photographs.

3573 Latin American Studies Association. The 1995 electoral process in Peru: a delegation report of the Latin American Studies Association. Miami, Fla.: North-South Center, Univ. of Miami, 1995. 35 p.

Using nine criteria of a democratic election, the pre-election evaluation used in this report assesses extent to which elections were free, fair, and representative in view of the 1992 *autogolpe* and other irregularities. According to key findings of report, "Peruvian democracy is a fragile enterprise, and overall the central government is not acting to fully strengthen the freedoms and civilian institutions that are the essential conditions of democracy" (p. 21). [D. Dent]

3574 Lauer, Mirko. Días divididos: columnas periodísticas de los años noventa. Lima: ADEC-ATC, 1994. 236 p.: index.

Compilation of selected newspaper and magazine commentaries (1990–93) by one of Peru's most able and acerbic columnists. Vehement critic of the Fujimori government after the 1992 *autogolpe*.

3575 Maraví Sumar, Milagros. Las instituciones de democracia directa en el Perú. (*in* Democracia directa. Buenos Aires: Abeledo-Perrot, 1997, p. 127–147)

After noting the importance of alternative mechanisms for popular expression in the informal sector, neighborhoods, peasant communities, and self-defense committees, lays out the 1993 Constitution provisions for a referendum, popular legislation initiatives, and popular recall of some local officials. Valuable contribution.

3576 Marquezado C., Hugo. Descentralización en el Perú: evaluación del gobierno de la región Chavín. Chimbote, Peru: ATUSPARIA; Lima: CEPES, 1993. 156 p.: bibl., ill.

A most valuable, if disheartening, case study of the failure of Peru's most recent experiment in political decentralization carefully documented by one of its elected practitioners. Demonstrates how the Fujimori Administration undermined this effort between 1990–93.

3577 Mauceri, Philip. State reform, coalitions, and the neoliberal *autogolpe* in Peru. (*LARR*, 30:1, 1995, p. 7–37, bibl.)

Thoughtful analysis of Fujimori's *autogolpe* of April 1992. Argues the *Fujimorazo* was the culminating response of an elite attempt to restructure the Peruvian State and its relations with society via a combination of neoliberal economic reforms and authoritarian political methods. While only analyzing Peru, this article has broader implications for other Latin American countries. [D. Dent]

3578 McCormick, Gordon H. Sharp dressed men: Peru's Túpac Amaru Revolutionary Movement. Santa Monica, Calif.: RAND, 1993. 73 p.: bibl., ill.

Valuable overview of the background, history, and trajectory of MRTA prior to Japanese Ambassador's residence takeover. Characterized as a "low profile revolutionary organization." Includes complete table of MRTA incidents (1984–1992) and comparisons with Shining Path.

3579 Moyano, María Elena. María Elena Moyano: en busca de una esperanza. Recopilación de Diana Miloslavich Túpac. Lima: Centro de la Mujer Peruana Flora Tristán, 1993. 109 p.: bibl., ill.

Tribute to a martyr in the cause of democracy over terrorism, the elected deputy mayor of Lima's largest "New Town," Villa El Salvador, who was assassinated by Shining Path guerrillas on Feb. 15, 1992. Provides, mostly in her own words, a powerful statement of courage, conviction, and capacity.

3580 Ossio A., Juan M. Las paradojas del Perú oficial: indigenismo, democracia y crisis estructural. Prólogo de Mario Vargas Llosa. Lima: Pontificia Univ. Católica del Perú, Fondo Editorial, 1994. 300 p.: bibl.

Insightful essays on the continued cultural duality of Peru, the lack of understanding by the dominant Hispanic component of the dominated Indian sector as reflected in the tragedies of Uchuraccay (and the resulting extension of the struggle against Shining Path), and suggested methods to preserve the indigenous culture within a modernizing society.

3581 Panfichi, Aldo *et al.* Los enigmas del poder: Fujimori, 1990–1996. Recopilación de Fernando Tuesta Soldevilla. Lima: Fundación Friedrich Ebert, 1996. 378 p.: bibl.

The most comprehensive treatment available in Spanish of Peruvian politics during the first six years of the Fujimori governments. Includes detailed, data-rich chapters by leading Peruvian and US political scientists who specialize in contemporary Peru in three main areas: process and political institutions, elections and parties, and public opinion.

3582 Pease García, Henry. Los años de la langosta: la escena política del fujimorismo. Lima: La Voz Ediciones, 1994. 439 p.: bibl.

Meticulous presentation and critique by a leading scholar and opposition politician of President Fujimori's first two and one-half years in power, with a postscript on the Constitution of 1993. Includes selected 1990–92 chronology of major developments from the DESCO database.

3583 Peru: human rights since the suspension of constitutional government. New York: Amnesty International, 1993. 46 p.

Report on the continuing human rights problems in Peru over the 13 months following the *autogolpe* of April 5, 1992, includes due process issues as well as information on multiple violations of individual rights. Very critical detailed study devoted primarily to government abuses.

3584 Perú, desafío democrático: bases del Proyecto Nacional hacia el siglo XXI. Recopilación de Manuel Dammert Egoaguirre. Recopilación de Mónica Vecco, Francisco Reyes y Francisco Mattos. Lima: Editora La República, 1993. 269 p.: ill. (some col.), maps.

Published product of a set of seminars on Peru's development prospects over the next 30 years in 18 key sectors—from environment to energy to democracy. Much detail, data, and analyses by leading Peruvians. Sponsored by *La República,* an opposition newspaper, but not partisan in approach.

3585 El poder en el Perú. Recopilación de Augusto Alvarez Rodrich. Lima: Editorial APOYO, 1993. 238 p.: bibl.

Brief essays by leading Peruvian academics and essayists on the changing power dynamics in Peru's public and private institutions, organizations, and groups over the 1980s and early 1990s. Suggest that, in Peru at least, constellations and dynamics of power are fluid.

3586 Podobnik, Bruce M. Revolutionary terrorism in the periphery: a comparative analysis of the Shining Path and the Khmer Rouge. (*in* Latin America in the world-economy. Westport, Conn.: Greenwood Press, 1996, p. 169–186, bibl.)

Valuable comparative analysis of two extreme movements. Although reflects fuller understanding of Cambodia than Peru, offers compelling insights on the significance of universities as incubators for revolutionary action in the context of increased government expenditures for education and contracting opportunities for graduates, as well as expansion by the revolutionary organizations into central government vacuums and inept government responses to the challenges posed.

3587 Quijano, Aníbal. El fujimorismo y el Perú. Lima: Seminario de Estudios y Debates Socialistas, 1995. 48 p.: bibl. (Cuadernos; 1)

Compilation of previously published analyses of contemporary Peruvian reality by a leading leftist scholar. Includes incisive critiques of the Fujimori government, his 1995 reelection, his intervention in the country's

public universities, and a concluding comment on the continued viability of socialism.

Remy, María Isabel. The indigenous population and the construction of democracy in Peru. See item **5064.**

Rocha V., Alberto. El redescubrimiento de la democracia en el Perú: aproximación general al debate en la década de los 80. See item **5066.**

3588 Rospigliosi, Fernando. La amenaza de la *Fujimorización:* gobernabilidad y democracia en condiciones adversas; Perú y los países andinos. (*in* Partidos y clase política en América Latina en los 90. San José: Instituto Interamericano de Derechos Humanos (IIDH); Centro de Asesoría y Promoción Electoral (CAPEL), 1995, p. 311–334)

Analysis of Peru's failure to sustain electoral democracy and the emergence of "directed democracy," not democratic consolidation, after Fujimori's *autogolpe.* Explains the situation as due to the failure of political parties, Fujimori's popularity, and the military's perceived need for a presidential advocate. Pessimistic about Peru's political future, and fears other fragile Andean democracies could follow a similar path.

3589 Rúa, Efraín. El crímen de La Cantuta: la desaparición y muerte de un profesor y nueve estudiantes que estremeció al país. Lima: Edición del autor, 1996. 140 p.

Detailed narration of the July 1992 military operation by the "Grupo Colina," uncovered by careful investigative journalism with help from offended military professionals. Includes trial, conviction, and subsequent pardon of the "Grupo" under with President Fujimori's June 1995 general amnesty. Also details university politics in the 1980s and then Rector Fujimori's interventionist role.

3590 Schmidt, Gregory D. Fujimori's 1990 upset victory in Peru: electoral rules, contingencies, and adaptive strategies. (*Comp. Polit.,* 28:3, April 1996, p. 321–354, graph, tables)

Groundbreaking analysis examines how the rules governing elections help determine outcomes. Among the most important rules in Peru's 1990 elections were: 1) allowing simultaneous candidacies for congress and the presidency, making independents viable; 2) a majority runoff format counting spoiled and blank ballots in the total, lowering the second place threshold; and 3) open list proportional representation, fostering splits within party coalitions.

Starn, Orin. Maoism in the Andes: The Communist Party of Peru-Shining Path and the refusal of history. See item **1225.**

3591 Starn, Orin. To revolt against the Revolution: war and resistance in Peru's Andes. (*Cult. Anthropol.*, 10:4, Nov. 1995, p. 547–580, bibl.)

Carefully documented and culturally grounded analysis of the rise of peasant patrols (*rondas campesinas*) in central and south-central highland Peru in the late 1980s "against the revolution waged in their name" (p. 548). Well before the Sept. 1992 capture of Guzmán, this popular movement sapped the strength and influence of Shining Path. Essential reading. For the sociologist's comment see item **5068.**

3592 Stern, Peter A. Sendero Luminoso: an annotated bibliography of the Shining Path guerrilla movement, 1980–1993. Foreword by Carlos Iván Degregori. New Mexico: SALALM Secretariat, General Library, Univ. of New Mexico, 1995. 388 p.: indexes.

Careful, noneditorialized annotations of selected articles on Shining Path (1,185 in all), plus a pithy summary essay. Essential reference.

3593 Stokes, Susan Carol. Democratic accountability and policy change: economic policy in Fujimori's Peru. (*Comp. Polit.*, 29:2, Jan. 1997, p. 209–227, graph)

Compelling analysis, based in part on interviews with key participants, of the dramatic shift in policy between Fujimori's electoral campaign and his presidency. In assessing the divergence, concludes that "bait and switch" tactics gained popular support because Fujimori responded to security concerns. Overlooks impact of successful inflation reduction policies.

3594 Stokes, Susan Carol. Economic reform and public opinion in Peru, 1990–1995. (*Comp. Polit. Stud.*, 29:5, Oct. 1996, p. 544–565, bibl., graphs, tables)

Sophisticated effort to explain public support for a president who implemented economic shock policies against the short term interests of most citizens. Concludes that overall ratings masked differences be-

tween levels of support by rich and poor and the pre- and post-*autogolpe* periods.

3595 Strong, Simon. Shining Path: a case study in ideological terrorism. (*in* Latin America and the Caribbean: prospects for democracy. Edited by William Gutteridge. Aldershot, England; Brookfield, Vt.: Ashgate, 1997, p. 207–235, map)

Useful overview of Shining Path's trajectory through 1993 by a close foreign observer. Sees Shining Path retaining its capacity and foreign links, and the government, due to its undemocratic nature and overreliance on military support, unlikely to be able to eliminate the organization.

3596 Los sucesos del Alto Huallaga: marzo, abril-mayo, 1994; Challhuayacu, Chavín de Pariarca, Cayumba Chico, Moyuna y Moena. Lima: Coordinadora Nacional de Derechos Humanos, 1994. 240 p.: map.

Details and testimonials of human rights abuses committed by the army on the local population in the Upper Huallaga Valley between March-May 1994. Documents the failure of government authorities at different levels to resolve abuses justly.

3597 Tamariz Lúcar, Domingo. Historia del poder: elecciones y golpes de estado en el Perú. Lima: J. Campodónico, 1995. 440 p.: bibl., ill., photos.

Ambitious and successful, one-volume treatment of Peru's poltical history, 1820–1992. Concentrates on the heads of State and their successes and failures. Tightly written and amply detailed, with many photographs.

3598 Tello, María del Pilar et al. El pacto: Perú, de la crisis al Acuerdo Nacional. Lima: Ediciones SAGSA, 1994. 266 p.

Interviews with 16 leading Peruvian politicians, academics, and military officials in 1992–93 (between the April 5, 1992 *autogolpe* and the Nov. 31, 1993 Constitutional Referendum). Includes an analysis of the referendum, noting the closeness of the vote created a basis for building a new political consensus.

3599 Toche, Eduardo. La pacificación en el Perú: buscando nuevos rumbos. (*Allpanchis/Cusco*, 29:49, primer semestre 1997, p. 243–258)

Valuable analysis of limits of pacification in Peru. Although Shining Path incidents declined by 75 percent through 1996, organization still operates over a wide geographical area. With civil defense committees controlled by the army, and police and armed forces increasingly corrupt, non-terrorist crime proliferates. Anticipates dire consequences for Peru's citizens.

3600 Torres y Torres Lara, Carlos. Los nudos del poder: una experiencia peruana de gobierno. Lima: Desarrollo y Paz, 1992. 197 p.

A compact, personal, but reasoned perspective on the challenges of being a cabinet minister in Peru in the early 1990s (Labor, Foreign Relations, and Prime Minister). Grist for bureaucratic politics analysts.

3601 Tuesta Soldevilla, Fernando. Sistema de partidos políticos en el Perú, 1978–1995. Lima: Fundación Friedrich Ebert, 1995. 149 p.: bibl.

Valuable overview and analysis of Peru's political parties by a leading Peruvian political scientist. Includes 20th-century historical background, legal framework, electoral system, relationship to legislative and executive powers, and party/party system characteristics over time, with electoral tables and party indicators.

3602 Vargas, Virginia and Victoria Villanueva. Between confusion and the law: women and politics in Peru. (*in* Women and politics worldwide. Edited by Barbara J. Nelson and Najma Chowdhury. New Haven, Conn.: Yale Univ. Press, 1994, p. 575–589)

Comprehensive overview of the three major strands of the women's movement in Peru—"a feminist stream, a community-based popular stream, and a traditional political stream" (p. 578)—in the context of an ethnically cleaved society and significant economic and political challenges. Optimistic in its projections of gaining strength over time.

3603 Vargas Llosa, Alvaro. The madness of things Peruvian: democracy under siege. New Brunswick, N.J.: Transaction Publishers, 1994. 173 p.: bibl., index.

Personal reflections and insights on Peruvian politics in the 1990s, articulately presented by a participant-observer. Identifies Fujimori with the death of democracy and the forging of a sinister alliance with the military, but ranges well beyond to reflect on the distant historical origins of Peru's political challenges.

Vargas Llosa, Mario. Desafíos a la libertad. See *HLAS 56:3742.*

3604 Vega-Centeno B., Imelda. Género y política: a propósito de la mujer en Sendero Luminoso. (*Bol. Am.*, 34:44, 1994, p. 207–213, bibl.)

After an incisive summary review of the male-dominant trajectory of Spanish and post-independent Peru, argues on the basis of only partially available evidence that Shining Path exploits the same feminine characteristics of the "machista-capitalist society of the *ancien regime* they are trying to overthrow." (p. 210) Preliminary, but important study.

CHILE

MICHAEL FLEET, *Associate Professor of Political Science, Marquette University*

THIS BIENNIUM'S MATERIALS on Chile reflect a declining interest in politics among Chileans. Compared to previous years, this volume includes more studies published outside Chile (in the US, Europe, and elsewhere in Latin America), and a larger number of journal articles, rather than commercially marketed books, among those produced in the country. It seems that publishers can not guarantee the sale of enough copies of books about politics to justify producing greater quantities. Evidence of declining political interest is also found in the December 1993 general elections, in which the percentage of eligible voters who actually voted was relatively high, but interest and enthusiasm were clearly much lower than in 1989. Materials during this period are dominated by personal portraits and testimonies (many of which have been produced by political parties and/or presses favorable to them), by proposals and discussions dealing with institutional reform, by studies of social forces and movements, and by analyses of national politics and parties.

One interesting example of portrait and testimonial literature is Santibáñez's account of Aylwin's early career and presidency, underscoring the skill with which the Christian Democratic president managed party and broader coalition problems (item **3662**). Sapag offers affectionate reminiscences and anecdotes of Cardinal Raul Silva Henríquez (item **3663**). Serrano and Scantlebury interview a number of the economists who played central policy-making roles during the 1940s, 1950s and 1960s (item **2107**). And Pinochet's Interior Minister Sergio Fernández offers a detailed, insider's account of policy and political decision-making during the early 1980s and in the year prior to the 1988 plebiscite (item **3619**). The latest volume of Pinochet's own memoirs makes for less than riveting reading (item **3645**), but Osorio and Cabezas offer enlightening portraits of a number of his cabinet ministers' closest collaborators (item **3641**). Pohorecky sheds light on reasons for which young activists including her son found the Manuel Rodríguez Patriotic Front to be an attractive option during the years of military rule (item **3648**).

Among works dealing with institutional reform, Tomassini's stand out. His edited volume offers reflections by Chileans, other Latin Americans, and Europeans on various aspects of administrative reform and modernization, State-civil societal relations, and specific policy questions (item **3652**). In his own work, he fashions an argument (with right-wing reform opponents in mind) linking enduring economic growth and efficiency to the greater equity and political stability that reforms might produce (item **2989**). In related essays, Lahera presses for more efficient, if more limited, regulation of certain markets (item **3632**), and Martner argues for the democratization of municipal governments which began in 1993 (item **3637**). On the issue of the controversial binomial electoral system imposed by Pinochet as he was leaving power, Rabkin argues persuasively that it has not had unduly disproportional effects, and has pushed the country's parties toward greater moderation and collaboration (*HLAS 55:3480*); Siavelis and Valenzuela take a different view, suggesting that its tendency to exclude smaller parties unwilling to join broader alliances could have destabilizing effects, and that electoral systems are generally less important in producing party-systems than historical and contextual factors which they should try to accommodate rather than neutralize (item **3666**). Two additional works worthy of note are the proceedings of a 1994 conference on political corruption (item **3621**), and retired Army Gen. Julio Canessa's reflections on the military interventions of 1924 and 1973 (item **3612**).

This period's material also includes a number of studies of social forces and movements. Schneider's study of neighborhood organizations offers detailed portraits of activists, and links higher levels of involvement in the mid-1980s protests to the presence of a Communist party nucleus and a tradition of political militancy (item **3664**). Oxhorn covers much of the same ground, but focuses on relations with national party organizations and developments beyond 1986 (item **3643**). Lowden analyzes the important role of the Catholic Church's *Vicaria de Solidaridad*, particularly during the 1970s and early 1980s (item **3635**). Hipsher stresses the willingness of local-level activists in Spain and Chile to lower their profiles when this was likely to make the transition smoother (item **3625**). Frohmann and Valdés attempt to explain why Chilean women have not parlayed their growing cultural influence into the political sphere (item **3620**). Finally, Rehren traces the evolution of entrepreneurial attitudes and loyalties prior to, during, and following the 1988 plebiscite (item **3653**).

Some interesting studies of parties and politics published during this biennium are Angell and Pollack's assessment of the December 1993 election (item **3608**), Spanish journalist Rafael Otano's masterful *Crónica de la transición* (item **3642**), Hite's insightful analysis of the evolution of leaders of the Chilean left (item **3626**), Scully's reflections on the remarkable persistence of the country's three ideological-political blocs (item **3665**), and a highly critical assessment of Chile's restored democracy by Galleguillos and Nef (item **3622**). Although there are fewer than in previous periods, this biennium includes several dramatic accounts of the activities of security forces during the years of military rule. Merino's *Mi verdad* is the confession of a *mirista* who spent 15 years working for the DINA and CNI (item **3638**). Caucoto and Salazar offer a thorough assessment of *Carabinero* involvement in the 1985 murders of three Communist party militants and the subsequent cover-up (item **3613**). *La Epoca* editor Manuel Salazar has written a forceful exposé of Manuel Contreras, the DINA, and their involvement in the murders of Ronnie Moffit and Orlando Letelier (item **3661**).

A final set of materials offer valuable insight into Chilean culture and society over the last 30 years. These include Lechner's thoughtful reflections on the political disaffection that has enveloped so many Chileans in recent years (item **3633**), Jadresic's assessment of post-military Chile's mental and spiritual health (item **3630**), Piñuel's analysis of the effects of television advertising in the 1988 plebiscite (item **3647**), and Duran's study of the impact of Chile's *El Mercurio* during the last year of the Allende government (item **3617**).

3605 Agosin, Marjorie. Tapestries of hope, threads of love: the arpillera movement in Chile, 1974–1994. Translated by Celeste Kostopulos-Cooperman. Photographs by Emma Sepulveda and Ted Polumbaum. Albuquerque: Univ. of New Mexico Press, 1996. 154 p.: bibl., ill. (some col.).

Arpilleras are burlap-backed tapestries depicting the experiences and emotions of women whose sons and husbands were arrested and never heard from again during the years of military rule. Agosin's narrative traces the *arpillera* movement from its early days under the promotion and protection of the Catholic Church's Vicaría de Solidaridad through the early 1990s, when newly reestablished civilian authorities decided not to more forcefully seek justice for victims of human rights abuses. The book includes 45 reproductions (on glossy plates), and the moving testimonies of a number of the *arpilleristas* themselves.

3606 Allamand Zavala, Andrés. La centroderecha del futuro. Santiago: Editorial Los Andes, 1993. 180 p. (Serie Política y sociedad)

An interesting collection of speeches and writings from 1990–93 by the influential, but frequently embattled, 39-year-old leader of the moderate right-wing Renovación Nacional party. Of particular interest are his thoughts on the transition to democracy, human rights abuses and national reconciliation, economic and political development, and developments within the rival Christian Democratic party.

3607 Angell, Alan and **Carol Graham.** Can social sector reform make adjustment sustainable and equitable?: lessons from Chile and Venezuela. (*J. Lat. Am. Stud.*, 27:1, Feb. 1995, p. 189–219)

Angell and Graham link the outcomes of market-oriented reform programs to improvements in social services systems (those delivering health care, education, social security, housing, and employment) that alleviate poverty, distribute the burden of reforms more equitably, and help to legitimize democratic institutions and processes. They point to the additional outlays required, resistant public sector agencies and unions, widespread corruption, political party influence in certain ministries, and low levels of organization among social service clients as factors obstructing social sector reform, and they argue that overcoming such obstacles will depend largely on political will and capability, not resources or autocratic methods.

3608 Angell, Alan and **Benny Pollack.** The Chilean elections of 1993: from polarisation to consensus. (*Bull. Lat. Am. Res.*, 14: 2, May 1995, p. 105–125, tables)

Another sterling piece of analysis from Oxford's Angell and the Chilean Benny Pollack, who teaches at the Univ. of Liverpool. The authors find that Chilean parties are weaker (they have less of a hold on a smaller number of militants) than in the past, that citizens are less interested in election campaigns generally, and that the electoral mechanisms imposed by Pinochet are pushing parties into broader coalitions (and improving their prospects for success) at the expense of political clarity.

3609 Aylwin Azócar, Andrés. Testimonio y compromiso por la paz: citas escogidas. Santiago: LOM Ediciones, 1993. 90 p.: ill.

Excerpts and citations from the speeches and writings of Andrés Aylwin, Chilean congressman, human rights activist, and the brother of Chilean president (1990–94) Patricio Aylwin. Something is lost, unfortunately, when his remarks are taken from their original texts and contexts, and strung together under broad thematic categories.

3610 Aylwin Azócar, Patricio. Crecimiento con equidad: discursos escogidos, 1992–1994. Edición de Secretaría de Comunicación y Cultura, Ministerio Secretaría General de Gobierno. Santiago: Editorial Andrés Bello, 1994. 494 p. (Col. Temas)

A collection of Aylwin's speeches made during the last two years of his presidency. Some deal with famous Chilean personalities (Bernardo O'Higgins, St. Teresa of the Andes, and Pablo Neruda); others cover subjects like political ethics and his government's economic and international policies.

Baraona Urzúa, Pablo; Martín Costabal Llona; and **Alvaro Vial.** Mil días, mil por ciento: la economía chilena durante el gobierno de Allende. See item **2073.**

Bartell, Ernest. Perceptions by business leaders and the transition to democracy in Chile. See item **2075.**

3611 Briones, Alvaro. El reflejo diferido: consideraciones acerca de la transición y la democracia en España y Chile. (*Rev. Occident.*, 179, abril 1996, p. 59–78)

An interesting essay by a moderate socialist who stresses parallels in the politi-

cal histories of these countries. He sees Chile's 1980 constitution playing the same decisively positive role that the monarchy played in Spain's transition, but argues that the Chilean military must accept responsibility for human rights violations under its rule if Chile's restored democracy is to emerge fully and endure.

Cáceres, Carlos F. et al. Las tareas de hoy: políticas sociales y económicas para una sociedad libre. See item **2078.**

3612 Canessa Robert, Julio. Quiebre y recuperación del orden institucional en Chile: el factor militar, 1924–1973. Santiago: Emérida Ediciones, 1995. 298 p.: bibl.

An articulate defense of the military interventions of 1924 and 1973 by a retired Army general and loyal backer of Pinochet. Some will challenge his assessment of the crises that gave rise to the coups. Others will ask if the military's cure was not worse than the disease at which it was aimed. But virtually all are likely to question his insistence on full autonomy and political competence for the armed forces, in defense of which he invokes Spanish falangist José Antonio Primo de Rivera.

3613 Caucoto Pereira, Nelson and **Héctor Salazar Ardiles.** Un verde manto de impunidad. Santiago: Ediciones Academia, Univ. Academia de Humanismo Cristiano; Fundación de Ayuda Social de las Iglesias Cristianas, 1994. 194 p.: ill.

An account of the brutal 1985 murders of three Communist party militants by agents of Chile's National Police, and of the efforts, over the next nine years, of independent prosecutors to bring those responsible to justice. Written by lawyers with access to prosecutorial files, it shows the extent to which personal and institutional moral decay permeated even the once widely admired Carabineros.

Cavendish, James C. Christian base communities and the building of democracy: Brazil and Chile. See item **3863.**

Caviedes, César N. Estudios sobre la variabilidad espacial del voto en América Latina. See item **2392.**

3614 Chuchryk, Patricia M. From dictatorship to democracy: the women's movement in Chile. (*in* The women's movement in Latin America: participation and democracy.

Edited by Jane S. Jaquette. Boulder, Colo.: Westview Press, 1994, p. 65–107)

A lengthy narrative of the women's movement stressing its roots in anti-military protests, its relationship to the broader opposition movement, and the prospects for feminist politics in a democratic Chile. Covers too much material to offer in-depth analysis of the many interesting issues it raises, but useful as context or background against which to look at them.

3615 Cuevas Farren, Gustavo. Proyección del gobierno militar en la modernización del país. Santiago: Univ. de Chile, Instituto de Ciencia Política, 1993. 79 p.: bibl.

An essay by a former advisor to Junta Member Admiral José Toribio Merino in which he attributes much of the political and economic success of the Aylwin government to foundations laid down under Pinochet. While making this argument in clear and coherent fashion, however, he fails to address the extent literature and thus leaves important issues and questions unresolved.

3616 Las deudas de la transición: balance de derechos humanos. Edición de Carlos López Dawson. Santiago: Comisión Chilena de Derechos Humanos; Ediciones Nacionales, 1994. 214 p.: bibl., ill.

The Commission finds that under the Aylwin government State institutions were operating normally, the powers and prerogatives of civilian authorities were honored by the military, and some of the human rights abuses committed under the military were brought to the attention of the general public. But it also notes problems with the "abusive methods" used by police to interrogate suspects and detainees, and with the government's general approach to juvenile delinquency.

3617 Durán, Claudio. *El Mercurio:* ideología y propaganda, 1954–1994; ensayos de interpretación bi-lógica y psico-histórica. v. 1, Propaganda de agitación en el período agosto 1972-marzo 1973. Santiago: Ediciones Chile y América-CESOC, 1995. 1 v.

A content analysis of the impact of the conservative Chilean newspaper during the latter stages of the Allende government. In a more evenly handed and socially scientific manner than most studies of Allende's overthrow, Durán examines the newspaper's se-

lection of news stories, editorials, headlines, and front-page photographs to demonstrates the paper's use of explicit and subconscious logic to build support for a military coup.

3618 Estudio nacional de opinión pública no. 1, tercera serie, noviembre-diciembre 1994. Santiago: Centro de Estudios Públicos, 1995. 182 p.: tables. (Documento de trabajo; 227)

The latest in a series of national opinion polls conducted by a respected center-right research center that began doing polls in 1986. Provides useful and reliable data regarding Chilean opinion of economic and political developments, ranking of contemporary problems, and assessment of the performance of the government (the newly installed Frei government) and of the country's major parties and political personalities.

3619 Fernández Fernández, Sergio. Mi lucha por la democracia. Santiago: Editorial los Andes, 1994. 332 p.: ill.

The Interior Minister between 1978–82, and again, in 1987–88. Fernández provides a detailed, insider's account of policy-making and political decision-making under the military government. Of particular interest are his analysis of the genesis of the 1980 Constitution, and his spirited, if not entirely persuasive, refutation of charges that Pinochet sought to have the 1988 plebiscite set aside once it was clear that he had lost.

Foxley, Alejandro. La economía política de la transición: el camino del diálogo. See item **2092.**

3620 Frohmann, Alicia and Teresa Valdés. Democracy in the country and in the home: the women's movement in Chile. (*in* The challenge of local feminisms: women's movements in global perspective. Boulder, Colo.: Westview Press, 1995, p. 276–301, photos, tables)

Frohmann and Valdés ask why women's groups have failed to project the enormous presence and influence they have achieved in the cultural sphere into the political arena. Authors speculate that groups' insistence on internal democracy makes it more difficult to articulate and project a single, coherent vision, and has prevented the emergence of forceful leaders capable of commanding the attention and respect of other political forces. For sociologist's comment see item **5166.**

3621 Fundación Eduardo Frei. La democracia combate la corrupción. Santiago: Ediciones ChileAmérica, 1994. 240 p.

A collection of papers and reflections on various aspects of corruption in post-military Chile. The presentations by former and current government officials, leading entrepreneurs, and others tell the reader little about the extent of problem, but make clear how a person's vantage point colors his (or her) perceptions of and preferred solutions for these problems.

3622 Galleguillos, Nibaldo and Jorge Nef. Chile: redemocratization or the entrenchment of counterrevolution? (in Latin America to the year 2000: reactivating growth, improving equity, sustaining democracy. New York: Praeger, 1992, p. 177–193, bibl.)

An analysis of Chile's post-military politics as the normalization of the counter revolution begun and sustained repressively under the military. The authors, for whom the character of a sociopolitical order is to be found in its class relations and in its distribution of wealth, power, and privilege, question the significance of "mere" political rights and liberties, and think that things were different in both respects prior to the 1973 coup.

Godoy Arcaya, Oscar and Salvador Valdés Prieto. Democracia y previsión en Chile: experiencia con dos sistemas. See item **2094.**

3623 González Errázuriz, Francisco Javier. Partido Demócrata Cristiano: la lucha por definirse. Chile: Instituto de Estudios Generales, 1989. 239 p.: bibl., ill., ports. (Serie Estudios históricos)

An account of the formative years of Chile's Christian Democratic Party from its origins as the rebellious youth wing of the traditionally Catholic Conservative Party to the military's 1973 overthrow of the Allende government. The author confines himself to party materials and accounts by party members, leaving untouched the extensive academic literature (Chilean, US, and European) that has developed in the last 15 years.

3624 Heine, Jorge. ¿Reforma o status-quo?: dilemas y desafíos del Estado en Chile. (Rev. Cienc. Polít./Santiago, 15:1/2, 1993, p. 7–20)

An essay by the president of the Chilean Political Science Association introducing a collection of papers given at the Associa-

tion's 1992 meeting on the subject of the reform of administrative or State structures. Useful in delineating issues of national debate. See items **2989** and **3652.**

3625 Hipsher, Patricia L. Democratization and the decline of urban social movements in Chile and Spain. (Comp. Polit., 28:3, April 1996, p. 273–297)

A useful review of the transition literature as it applies to the Spanish and Chilean cases. Explains the decline of urban social movements at crucial junctures in the transition process as the result of prudential calculi of elites and mass-movement activists alike. (Both groups agree that popular forces need to "settle for less," and otherwise alleviate the anxieties of pro-authoritarian economic and political elites, if they want to avoid a return to power by authoritarian elements.)

3626 Hite, Katherine. The formation and transformation of political identity: leaders of the Chilean left, 1968–1990. (J. Lat. Am. Stud., 28:2, May 1996, p. 299–328)

Analyzes the evolution of the more than 70 leftist leaders, blending recent work in "identity formation" with structural and rational choice approaches. Insisting that different people define themselves and their interests differently, she delineates a cognitive framework consisting of four "personality types" (the party loyalist, the personal loyalist, the thinker, and the pragmatist), and argues that each evolves somewhat differently in interaction with the political structural context in which they are embedded, and the formative (traumatic) experiences by which they have been conditioned.

3627 Hofmeister, Wilhelm. La opción por la democracia: democracia cristiana y desarrollo político en Chile, 1964–1994. Santiago: Konrad Adenauer Stifftung, 1995. 345 p.: bibl.

An account by a German political scientist of the PDC in the pre-1973 period, under the military, during the transition to democracy, and under the Aylwin government (1990–94). Unfortunately, it relies on already widely diffused electoral data and secondary material, shedding relatively little light on such issues as policymaking under the first Frei government (1964–70), the party's willingness to work with Allende, and the attitudes of party activists at the time of and following the coup. Also, it is hard to accept the author's contention that the party that has become increasingly pragmatic and consensus-oriented is still more progressive than its European counterparts.

3628 Hojman, D.E. Chile under Frei (again): the first Latin American tiger—or just another cat? (*Bull. Lat. Am. Res.*, 14:2, May 1995, p. 127–142, bibl.)

An analysis of the government of Eduardo Frei Ruiz-Tagle by a British economist who teaches at the Univ. of Liverpool. Hojman thinks that Chile is a young, inexperienced, and somewhat timid, tiger whose "neo-liberalism with a human face" will continue to provide it with steady growth, domestic and external stability, reduced poverty, and more equal income distribution for the remainder of Frei's term.

3629 Hoyl Cruz, Ana María. Canto a lo humano. Santiago?: Comunidad Monseñor Enrique Alvear, 199-? 421 p.

Interviews by a social worker whose clients were people who lived through the 1973 coup and the early years of military rule. Among those recounting their experiences are Vicaría lawyer Hernán Montealegre, Radio Chilena manager Alfredo Pesce, popular-sector priest Roberto Bolton, a number of women whose sons were killed by the military, and several local neighborhood leaders.

3630 Jadresic, Víctor. Los horizontes del chileno: ensayo. Santiago: Editorial Platero, 1993. 91 p.: bibl. (Serie Cobre menor)

A respected Chilean psychiatrist examines his country's state of health after three years of civilian rule. He is disturbed by the rising incidence of delinquency, drug addiction, terrorism, psychological depression, and other symptoms of social disintegration, warning that economic growth is a necessary but not sufficient condition of social progress. He fears that the unevenly distributed prosperity and the bureaucratization of both public- and private-sector life, will end up robbing many Chileans of their once indomitable spirits.

3631 Jorquera, Carlos. El Chicho Allende. Santiago: Ediciones Bat, 1990. 347 p.

An intimate and occasionally humorous portrait of Allende written by close friend and confidant Carlos "El Negro" Jorquera.

3632 Lahera, Eugenio. Gestión pública para el desarrollo nacional. (*Rev. Cienc. Polít.*/Santiago, 15:1/2, 1993, p. 187–209)

Lahera, who belongs to the PPD, offers a laundry list of institutions and processes that need to be reformed or coordinated. He calls for increased regulatory capability in those (relatively few) areas where regulations are needed or existing regulations need to be modified, and he urges candidates for public office to make specific proposals a part of their campaigns so that, once elected, they can claim a mandate for proceeding.

Lasagna Barrena, Marcelo. La política iberoamericana de España de cara a los noventa: la relación con Chile, 1982–1992. See item **4386.**

3633 Lechner, Norbert. Chile 2000: las sombras del mañana. (*Estud. Int.*/Santiago, 27:105, enero/marzo 1994, p. 3–11)

A masterfully written essay reflecting on the political disaffection and disillusionment that have emerged in Chile, despite the Aylwin's government's record of economic and political successes and continuing prosperity under Frei. In Lechner's view, a vague sense of satisfaction with the country's dynamic economy, and the expectation of most people that their situations will soon improve if they have not already, has produced a species of "blind triumphalism" that fails to see the costs of modernization and hence offers nothing (but more of the same) for the future. At the same time, demands for State (and political) protection and leadership, that have been displaced by seemingly irresistible market forces, nonetheless persist, casting misleading and ultimately disheartening "shadows" on the social landscape.

3634 Loveman, Brian. Chilean NGOs: forging a role in the transition to democracy. (*in* New paths to democratic development in Latin America. Edited by Charles A. Reilly. Boulder, Colo.: Lynne Rienner Publishers, 1995, p. 119–144, table)

A useful overview of the role of nongovernmental organizations during and following military rule. As private (i.e., independent of the state) organizations that have "public" (i.e., humanitarian or cooperative) purposes, NGOs are notoriously hard to describe concisely and generalize about. Loveman warns of possible loss of autonomy, credibility, and creativity under a resourceful and socially responsive democratic government, but does not have the space in which to examine fully experiences to date, the risks involved, and likely outcomes.

3635 Lowden, Pamela. Moral opposition to authoritarian rule in Chile, 1973–90. Houndmills, England: Macmillan Press; New York: St. Martin's Press, 1996. 228 p.: bibl., index. (St. Antony's series)

This study of the Vicaría de Solidaridad provides detailed coverage of its efforts on behalf of human rights during the early years (1973–82) of military rule. While the organization did much to strengthen the Church's credibility with popular sector Chileans, it may not offer a sufficient basis for generalizing about either the Church's moral authority generally or its role, particularly post-1983, in the transition to civilian rule.

3636 Macchiavello, Guido; Eduardo Miranda Salas; and Germán Urzúa Valenzuela. Humanismo y democracia. Santiago?: Corporación Educacional Pedro Aguirre Cerda, 1993. 123 p.

Philosophical essays on economic, political, and other themes written by self-described secular humanists (humanistas laicos) who are loosely connected to Chile's Radical Party.

3637 Martner, Gonzalo. Descentralización y modernización del Estado en la transición. Santiago: LOM, 1993. 185 p.

A selection of speeches, papers, and interviews given by the economist who was President Aylwin's Under Secretary for Regional Development and Administration from 1990–94. Offers the rationale that led the Aylwin government, in 1992, to institute the popular election of local mayors and council members, and the creation of new forms and channels of participation for local neighborhood and functional organizations.

3638 Merino Vega, Marcia Alejandra. Mi verdad: "más allá del horror, yo acuso—." Santiago: A.T.G.S.A., 1993. 150 p.: ill.

The confessions of a mirista who spent 15 years helping the DINA and the CNI in their dirty wars on regime critics and opponents. Merino concentrates on providing the names, affiliations, and involvements of those with whom she worked or had contact. What

she and the reader gain in terms of such detail, unfortunately, is at the expense of thoughtful reflection or assessment.

3639 Molina Silva, Sergio. Abriendo caminos. Santiago: Corporación de Investigaciones para el Desarrollo, 1993. 286 p.: ill.

A collection of speeches, seminar papers, and articles on social policy and development, stressing the importance of growth and equity, by the Christian Democratic economist who served as Budget Director in the Ibáñez and Alessandri governments, as Treasury Minister and head of CORFO under Eduardo Frei Montalva (1964–68), and, most recently, as Director of ODEPLAN and Minister of Planning and Cooperation under Patricio Aylwin (1990–93).

Muñoz G., Oscar and **Carmen Celedon.** Chile en transición: estrategia económica y política. See item **2114.**

3640 Novoa Monreal, Eduardo. Los resquicios legales: un ejercicio de lógica jurídica. Santiago: Ediciones Bat, 1992. 162 p.

A vigorous legal and political defense, some 20 years later, of the use of obscure provisions of the Chilean constitution to justify the Allende government's expropriation and/or operation of privately owned firms, by the man who discovered them, while serving as Chairman of President Allende's Council on State Security.

3641 Osorio, Víctor and **Iván Cabezas.** Los hijos de Pinochet. Santiago: Planeta, 1995. 342 p.: bibl., index. (Col. Chile—su historia inmediata)

Intimate biographies of 12 of Pinochet's "political" sons (i.e., ministers, advisors, counsellors, and administrative appointees like Sergio de Castro, José Piñera, Hernán Büchi, Carlos Cáceres, Francisco Javier Cuadra, Pablo Rodríguez, Miguel Kast, Jaime Guzmán, etc.), many of whom, although no longer "in power," head up parties, financial institutions, businesses that exert considerable influence over the daily lives and destinies of many Chileans.

3642 Otano, Rafael. Crónica de la transición. Santiago: Planeta, 1995. 387 p.: bibl., index. (Col. Chile—su historia inmediata)

This account of the demise of the Pinochet regime and of the Aylwin government that succeeded it is by far the best of the several published in recent years. The author, a Spanish journalist trained in theology and classical languages, is neither Chilean nor a politician himself, but has friends and confidants in all the right (and center-left) places, and has a remarkable feel for the flow and subtleties of Chilean politics. Otano argues that despite Chile's economic success and astute civilian leadership since 1990, General Pinochet remains a powerful and disruptive influence. Author also provides insightful analyses of the divisions afflicting opposition and Concertation parties alike, the power and cohesion of the president and his principal ministers and advisors (which Otano terms the "transversal" party), and the political management skills of key ministers like Krauss, Boeninger, and Correa.

3643 Oxhorn, Philip. Where did all the protesters go?: popular mobilization and the transition to democracy in Chile. (*Lat. Am. Perspect.*, 21:3, Summer 1994, p. 49–68, bibl., table)

Oxhorn revisits his earlier study of popular organizations under authoritarian and post-authoritarian regimes (see *HLAS 53: 4005*), noting the double paradox that their political significance is greater prior to the restoration of democratic institutions and processes and that their subsequently diminished impact makes them less threatening and therefore more likely to survive.

3644 Padilla Ballesteros, Elías. La memoria y el olvido: detenidos desaparecidos en Chile. Santiago: Ediciones Orígenes, 1995. 151 p.: bibl., ill.

A gripping study of fates of almost 1,200 Chileans who were arrested in the early years of military rule, were never heard from, and then were executed and buried in unmarked graves throughout the country. The author, a forensic anthropologist, argues for a public accounting of the circumstances of their deaths, the location and proper reburial of the remains of the dead, and the punishment of those responsible for crimes against humanity.

3645 Pinochet Ugarte, Augusto. Camino recorrido. v. 3, pt. 2. Santiago: Tall. Gráf. del Instituto Geográfico Militar de Chile, 1994. 3 v. in 4: ill.

In this final(?) installment of his memoirs, Pinochet attributes his defeat in the Oct. 1988 plebiscite to the opposition's demagoguery, the machinations of US Ambassador "Dirty Harry" Barnes, and the power of foreign money. He claims to have "expected" defeat well before Oct. 5th, denies attempting to persuade Junta members to nullify the plebiscite's results, and attributes the notion that he was unwilling to relinquish power to unavoidable delays in reporting the vote count and to the perverse imaginations of ideologically blinded journalists.

3646 Pinto Lagarrigue, Fernando. Alessandrismo versus Ibañismo. Santiago?: Editorial La Noria, 1995. 345 p.: bibl.

An account of the 26-year period between 1926–52 that attributes its volatility (there were 13 different chief executives) to the running antagonism between Arturo Alessandri Palma and General Carlos Ibáñez. Unfortunately, Pinto does little more than describe events, letting the sequenced facts speak for themselves, while failing to ask or answer questions that might tell us more.

3647 Piñuel Raigada, José Luis. La cultura política del ciudadano y la comunicación política en TV, en la transición política del plebiscito chileno. Madrid: Centro Español de Estudios de America Latina, CEDEAL, 1992. 218 p.: bibl., ill.

An in-depth study by Spanish and Chilean social scientists of television advertising in the 1988 plebiscite. Directed by Piñuel, a prominent Spanish communications theory expert, the study pieces together data from content analysis of televised advertising in the month preceding the plebiscite, and an attitudinal survey taken three weeks after it. Its findings challenge the view that the NO campaign's ads were responsible for the outcome. It argues, instead, that Pinochet was defeated by the country's political culture whose "social representations" predated the plebiscite, and were more compatible with NO campaign programming.

3648 Pohorecky, Adriana. Ignacio Valenzuela, fundador del Frente Patriótico Manuel Rodríguez: testimonios. Santiago: A. Pohorecky, 1995. 284 p.: ill.

An interesting, if somewhat melodramatic biography, compiled by the mother of Ignacio Valenzuela. A founder, active militant, and leading strategist of the Manuel

Rodríguez Patriotic Front, Valenzuela was shot to death by Chilean security forces in 1987. Pohorecky interweaves her own, deeply personal reflections with those of friends, relatives, and fellow-militants from whom she has collected letters, extensive interviews, and reflections.

3649 Ponce Durán, Pedro. Oscar Schnake Vergara: comienzos del socialismo chileno, 1933–1942. Santiago: Ediciones Documentas, 1994. 217 p.: bibl., ill. (Documentas/estudio)

A portrait of one of the founding members and early influential leaders of the Chilean Socialist Party. In the early 1940s, following an abortive attempt at his party's presidential nomination, Schnake abandoned party politics, serving as Chilean Ambassador to Mexico and France under President Juan Antonio Ríos, and later as Minister of Mining under Gabriel González Videla, before going on to the United Nations and later the Inter-American Development Bank.

3650 Pressaco, Carlos Fabián. Partidos políticos y rol del Estado en la economía: acuerdos e intereses. (*Rev. Cienc. Polít. /Santiago*, 15 : 1/2, 1993, p. 123–141)

A Chilean political scientist describes and assesses the role that the country's major political parties (the Christian Democrats, the Socialists, the Party for Democracy, National Renovation, and the Independent Democratic Union) assign the State with respect to the economy: the first three value the market, but are ready to restrict it in the interests of democracy; the latter two will sacrifice democracy for free market allocations and "the proper social order."

3651 Proceso legislativo chileno: un enfoque cuantitativo; la transición democrática, 1990–1994. Santiago: Proyecto de Modernización, Congreso Nacional de Chile, 1994. 80 p.: ill.

An analysis of legislative activity that differentiates bills (*proyectos de ley*) in terms of their origins (presidential message or congressional motion), the chamber that first takes them up, their subject matter, and their outcome (passage, withdrawal, rejection, and still pending status). Not surprisingly, bills submitted by the president have a much greater likelihood (63 percent) of passing than

do those emanating from either the Senate or the Chamber (7 percent).

3652 ¿Qué espera la sociedad del gobierno? Recopilación de Luciano Tomassini. Santiago: Univ. de Chile, Centro de Análisis de Políticas Públicas; Asociación Chilena de Ciencia Política, 1994. 336 p.: bibl.

A collection of essays dealing with various aspects of democracy, public policy(ies), and State-civil societal relations. Of particular note are former General Secretary of the Presidency Eduardo Boeninger's discussion of governability, the theoretical reflections of sociologists Raúl Urzua and Manuel Antonio Garretón, and Tomassini's own insistence on the need to adapt State functions and procedures to changes taking place in the economy and civil society.

3653 Rehren, Alfredo. Empresarios, transición y consolidación democrática en Chile. (*Rev. Cienc. Polít. /Santiago*, 17 : 1/2, 1995, p. 5–61)

An analysis of the political attitudes and sympathies of Chilean entrepreneurs prior to, during, and following the 1988 plebiscite. The image that emerges is one of loyalty to Pinochet and skepticism of his critics up through the plebiscite. But this may be because in the largely public materials on which Rehren relies entrepreneurs were seeking not to speak their minds freely but to reassure Pinochet (whose defeat was by no means certain).

3654 La renovación ideológica en Chile: los partidos y su nueva visión estratégica. Edición de Gustavo Cuevas Farren. Santiago: Univ. de Chile, Instituto de Ciencia Política, 1993. 163 p.: bibl.

A interesting collection of articles on ideological changes in Chile's major political parties. Of note are Garretón's introductory essay, in which he warns of a potential crisis occasioned by the dearth (due to social pacts) of debateable issues, and the comments of often critical academics following presentations by official representatives (e.g., Allamand, Molina, Walker, Dittborn, and Puccio) of the parties themselves.

3655 Richards, Ben. Proprietors not proletarians: the politics of housing subsidies under military rule in Chile. (*in* Authoritarianism in Latin America since independence.

Westport, Conn.: Greenwood Press, 1996,
p. 133–148, table)

A useful analysis of housing policies
and programs under the military government,
which, according to the author, were moderately successful: while not eliminating the
overall housing deficit, they kept it from rising further, they were relatively free of favoritism and corruption, and they were reasonably responsive to changing levels of need and
demand.

3656 Rivano, Luis. La CIA mató a Letelier:
otra hipótesis. Santiago: Ediciones de la
Librería de Luis Rivano, 1995. 142 p.: bibl., ill.

An account of the Letelier-Moffit assassinations by an eccentric, self-taught ex-
carabinero who operates a small bookstore in
Santiago, and has turned to investigative reporting after writing plays for both amateur
and professional theaters. Rivano concludes
that Michael Townley worked for both the
DINA and CIA, and that the latter organization probably ordered Orlando Letelier's death
and then had Contreras and Espinoza charged
and convicted.

3657 Rodríguez, Aniceto. Entre el miedo y la
esperanza: historia social de Chile. Caracas: Univ. Central de Venezuela, Ediciones
de la Biblioteca; Santiago: Editorial Andrés
Bello, 1995. 625 p.: bibl., ill. (Col. Historia;
24)

A rambling narrative of modern Chilean politics written by a moderate Socialist
who was a senator (1953–73), his party's secretary general (1965–71), and ambassador to
Venezuela, where he had lived 13 years in
exile, from 1990 until his death in 1995.
Among the subjects Rodríguez addresses are
his party's radicalization in the 1960s-70s,
its reunification and renovation in the 1980s,
and, during the same period, its gradual reconciliation with the Christian Democrats.

3658 Rodríguez, Laura. A quien quiera escu-
char. Santiago: Fundación Laura Rodríguez; Ediciones ChileAmérica CESOC, 1994.
220 p.

A collection of lectures, speeches, and
legislative initiatives (dealing with such topics as human rights, indigenous rights, wom-
en's rights, health care, and divorce) of the
former Humanist party president, feminist,
and deputy who died of cancer in 1992 at the
age of 35.

3659 Rojo Orrego, Emilio. La otra cara de la
Moneda: los cuatro años de Aylwin.
Santiago: Ediciones ChileAmérica CESOC,
1995? 149 p.: ill.

An account of the operations of the
Aylwin presidency by one of the newspaper
La Epoca's top political reporters. The author's coverage (of the roughly 30 face-to-face
meetings that Aylwin had with Pinochet, for
example) is less detailed and less colorful, but
probably more reliable, than those of other
observers, because of its more limited scope
(more the presidency's operations than its
policies), and because of his access to presidential palace secretaries Carlos Bascuñan
and Valentina Larraín Bunster.

3660 Ruiz de Giorgio, José. Los trabajadores
hacia el siglo XXI. Santiago: Comisión
Sudamericana de Paz, 1988. 202 p.

A collection of essays by a Christian
Democratic labor leader dealing with inter-
American affairs, pre-1973 Chilean politics,
human rights, external indebtedness, Chilean
labor history, and future prospects for organized labor. The author writes well, but offers
little analysis of the challenges that labor
faces in a post-military Chile in which the
potential costs of antagonizing entrepreneurial or military elites are very high.

3661 Salazar Salvo, Manuel. Contreras: historia de un intocable. Santiago: Grijalbo, 1995. 196 p.: bibl., ill. (Hojas nuevas)

A detailed account of Contreras's role
in the creation of the infamous DINA (Dirección de Inteligencia Nacional), its links to
security organizations in other countries (Argentina, Paraguay, Italy, and anti-Castro Cubans in the US and Venezuela), its pursuit of
critics and opponents of the Pinochet regime,
and of the ultimately successful 20-year effort
to identify and punish those who ordered Letelier assassinated.

3662 Santibáñez, Abraham. Patricio Aylwin
Azócar: su hora más gloriosa. Chile:
Editorial La Noria, 1994. 144 p.

A brief account of Aylwin's early career and presidency (1990–94) by a long-time
friend and collaborator. Although less detailed
and insightful than Otano's (item **3642**), it offers a balanced assessment of Aylwin's skillful
handling of challenges to Chile's transition to
democracy, and his maintenance of solid support for his government's economic and social
policies.

3663 Sapag Chain, Reinaldo. Mi amigo, el Cardenal. Santiago: Ediciones Copygraph, 1996. 236 p.

Reminiscences and anecdotes involving Chilean Cardinal Raúl Silva Henríquez by a layman who has been his informal liaison and confidant for more than 25 years. Sapag is more interested in Silva's sense of humor, and tastes in wine and people, than in his leadership style or political strategy. His narrative is too affectionate to be either critical or probing, but it still offers an abiding sense of Silva's humanity and astuteness.

3664 Schneider, Cathy Lisa. Shantytown protest in Pinochet's Chile. Philadelphia: Temple Univ. Press, 1995. 293 p.: bibl., ill., index, map.

A study of local-level social and political organizations during the early years of military rule and of the protest between 1983–86. The author points to the presence (or absence) of a strong Communist party nucleus and a historical tradition (pre-1973) of political involvement, not levels of poverty or unemployment, as factors determining the extent of politicization and involvement. She offers more detailed portraits of activists and organizations than Oxhorn, but less coverage of their relations with political parties, and of developments beyond 1986.

3665 Scully, Timothy R. Reconstituting party politics in Chile. (*in* Building democratic institutions: party systems in Latin America. Edited by Scott Mainwaring and Timothy R. Scully. Stanford: Stanford Univ. Press, 1995, p. 100–137, tables)

A survey of contemporary party politics that stresses the persistence of Chile's traditional ideological-political blocs (with parties at the left and right poles and in the middle ground between them), and newly rediscovered inclinations toward moderation and the formation of coalitions and alliances. Unlike Rabkin (*HLAS 55:3480*), he attributes the renewed appreciation for accommodation and compromise to the trauma of military rule, and not the electoral engineering of the outgoing Pinochet government.

3666 Siavelis, Peter and **Arturo Valenzuela.** Electoral engineering and democratic stability: the legacy of authoritarian rule in Chile. (*in* Institutional design in new democ-

racies: Eastern Europe and Latin America. Boulder, Colo.: Westview Press, 1996, p. 77–99, tables)

An analysis of the 1989 general elections with an eye to assessing the impact of the modified majority (binominal) electoral system imposed by Pinochet as he relinquished power to his democratically elected successor. The authors use the 1989 general election results to show that the system did help the right (one of its goals), but did not weaken the country's three traditional politico-ideological blocs or promote a two-party system (the other goal). They then use simulation tests to demonstrate the system's potential for volatility and destabilization. Unfortunately, they do not look at either the 1992 municipal or the 1993 general election results, nor do they directly addresses Rabkin's arguments (*HLAS 55:3480*), but they do make a strong case for looking beyond purely electoral-mechanical calculations to underlying, and possibly enduring, contextual factors.

3667 Silva, Eduardo. From dictatorship to democracy: the business-State nexus in Chile's economic transformation, 1975–1994. (*Comp. Polit.*, 28:3, April 1996, p. 299–320)

Silva extends his earlier studies of economic policy-making under Pinochet (*HLAS 53:4024 and 55:3485–3486*) to cover the post-military government of Christian Democrat Patricio Aylwin. Here, too, he stresses the importance of contacts and collaboration between business and government elites (the Chilean State's tight, hierarchical structure and the encompassing character of peak business associations greatly facilitate their collaboration), and argues that too much State autonomy would probably discourage positive business responses to liberalizing initiatives.

Silva, Eduardo. The State and capital in Chile: business elites, technocrats, and market economics. See item **2131.**

3668 Socialismo, 10 años de renovación, 1979–1989. v. 1, De la convergencia a la unidad socialista. v 2, El adios al marxismo-leninismo. Recopilación de Ricardo Nuñez. Santiago: Las Ediciones del Ornitorrinco, 1991. 2 v.

A two-volume compilation of essays, articles, and other materials that mark the transformation of Chile's once radical, Marxist-Leninist Socialists into a moderate, social democratic party. While providing an ample forum for representatives of the party's ultimately triumphant "renovated" elements, the collection offers virtually no coverage of traditional Socialists (Almeyda and others) who resisted the abandonment of marxism and confrontational politics well into the late 1980s.

3669 Thayer Arteaga, William. El senado en el presidencialismo y el parlamentarismo: evolución institucional y desafíos. 2. ed. Valparaíso, Chile: Ediciones Universitarias de Valparaíso, 1995. 79 p.: bibl.

An essay written by a former Christian Democrat who supported the military government and is one of the eight senators "designated" by Pinochet to keep his civilian successors from doing anything rash. Not surprisingly, Thayer stresses the dangers of direct representative democracy and the need for a legislative body comprising wiser, more experienced minds that can "moderate the transformative impulses of momentary majorities."

3670 Valdés, Gabriel. Para construir el futuro. Santiago: Editorial Los Andes, 1994. 174 p.: ill., ports. (Serie Política y sociedad)

A collection of speeches given by the President of the Chilean Senate during the presidency of his fellow Christian Democrat, and long standing intraparty rival, Patricio Aylwin. Of particular interest are his moving remarks at Jaime Guzmán's funeral, and the several occasions at which he argues for a mixed, presidential parliamentary system and against the 1980 Constitution's strengthening of president prerogatives.

3671 Verdugo, Patricia. Caso Arellano: los zarpazos del Puma. Santiago: CESOC; Ediciones ChileAmérica, 1989. 289 p.

A gripping account of the infamous flying death squad whose Oct. 1973 tour of Chilean provinces left a toll of 72 tortured and mangled bodies. Verdugo's analysis rests on interviews of the victims' families and the local military officials to whom most of the victims had surrendered voluntarily. The squad was led by Pinochet's "personal delegate," army Gen. Sergio Arellano Stark. He and others allegedly involved were spared ex-

posure and trial by the 1978 Law of Amnesty, and were later rewarded with promotions. The local officials who complained discreetly about violations of human rights and judicial procedures were punished and/or forced into early retirement. Arellano later sued Verdugo for libel, but when he objected to the court's hearing testimony from others in his squad the case was dismissed.

3672 Violencia y derechos humanos. Recopilación de Carlos López Dawson. Santiago: Comisión Chilena de Derechos Humanos; Editora Nacional de Derechos Humanos, 1993. 225 p.: bibl.

The proceedings of a 1991 Conference organized by the Chilean Human Rights Commission on different aspects of political violence. Includes presentations by leading Chilean political figures (Jorge Arrate, Maria Maluenda, and Genaro Arriagada) and noted academics and professionals (Sergio Garcia, Hugo Früling, Leon Rositcher, Luz Casanave, and Ana Cáceres).

3673 Zaldívar, Andrés. La transición inconclusa. Santiago: Editorial los Andes, 1995. 326 p.

A Christian Democratic senator and potential presidential candidate (in 2000) takes aim at the authoritarian tones of the 1980 Constitution, which continues to stifle the emergence of fully democratic rule in Chile. It lays bare the politics that helped hardline elements to dominate the drafting process and then rig the plebiscite. It is doubtful, however, that its reconstruction of events will win over anyone not already committed to full democratization.

3674 Zapata, Francisco. Transición democrática y sindicalismo en Chile. (*Foro Int.*, 32:5, oct./dic. 1992, p. 703–721, tables)

The well-known Mexican labor sociologist assesses the upsurge in strikes and tensions between workers and the government during the second year (1991) of the Aylwin government. He views the Concertation's commitment to growth with equity as a real limitation on its neoliberal policies, and not just a tactic for selling them. Believes that a more effective incorporation of workers and their representatives in the policymaking process will strengthen both the economy and the government's political base.

ARGENTINA, PARAGUAY, AND URUGUAY

PAUL H. LEWIS, *Professor of Political Science, Tulane University*

STUDENTS OF ARGENTINE politics have recently tended to write on two broad themes: civil-military relations and the effects of President Menem's neoliberal reforms. Study of the former has resulted in some horrifying accounts regarding the *proceso* and its consequences. Uriarte's *Almirante Cero*, a vivid biography of Admiral Massera (item **3776**), and Juvenal's *Buenos muchachos*, which documents the use of common criminals for "Dirty War" operations (item **3735**), are the best of this genre. Sain's two-volume *Los levantamientos carapintadas* is a useful description of the military's attempts to justify its actions and end the human rights trials (item **3767**). People associated with the *proceso* are by no means universally unpopular in Argentina, however. *Militares y politica* describes three cases of former provincial interventors who have since been democratically elected as governors (item **3737**).

The controversy over neoliberalism is inseparable from the personalities of Carlos Menem and his economics minister, Domingo Cavallo. There is an excellent biography of the latter in Santoro's *El hacedor* (item **3768**). Apart from the intelligentsia's usual disdain for capitalism, the uncontrolled corruption surrounding Menem's government provokes furious attacks. An accomplished example is Capalbo and Pandolfo's *Todo tiene precio*, a biography of one of Menem's shadiest cabinet ministers (item **3694**). More lighthearted is Walger's *Pizza con champán* (item **3780**), which tweaks the *nouveau riche.* On the other hand, "Civil-Military Relations and Argentine Democracy" by Zagorski (item **3781**), and Cavarozzi's "Los partidos politicos argentinos"(item **3697**), give Menem high marks for reconciling two previously alienated groups, the military and the entrepreneurs, and drawing them into the democratic mainstream.

Paraguayan writers, too, tend to divide their attention between two issues: the Stroessner period and the contemporary struggle to institutionalize democracy. Miranda's *Lucha armada en Paraguay* (item **3803**) and Esteche Notario's *Movimiento "14 de mayo"* (item **3793**) describe attempts by young guerrillas to invade Paraguay from exile during the early 1960s. Trinidad Alderete, on the other hand, offers a fairly objective portrait of Gen. Stroessner at the height of his power (item **3812**). *Pactos politicos,* by Frutos and Vera (item **3795**), examine the caudillo politics that formed a background to the *stronato.* Studies of the transition to democracy tend to be journalistic and quickly dated. One exception is Borda's "Empresariado y transición a la democracia en el Paraguay," which sheds light on the role of business in politics (item **3789**).

In Uruguay, Latin America's most developed welfare state, the challenge of neoliberalism has produced a societal split in which the traditional two-party system has given way to a four-party system. Two new parties of the left now control the Montevideo municipal government, while the traditional Colorados and Blancos alternate as heads the national government. There is, unfortunately, no book-length study of this interesting situation, but Mieres', "Venturas y desventuras de las izquierda uruguaya" (item **3830**), Perelli and Rial's, "Las elecciones uruguayas de noviembre de 1989" (item **3835**), Puchet Anyul's, "Elecciones, cambios politicos, y nuevos gobiernos en el Uruguay" (item **3840**) Rodriguez Larreta, "El 'plebiscito' municipal" (item **3842**) and Varela's, "Rasgos de la permanencia" (item **3847**) all treat various aspects of this multi-party system.

ARGENTINA

3675 Acuña, Carlos H. and **Catalina Smulovitz.** Militares en el Argentina: del gobierno a la subordinación constitucional. (*Rev. Parag. Sociol.*, 31:89, enero/abril 1994, p. 95–155)

Lengthy and useful survey of civil-military relations in Argentina, from the start of the *proceso* through Menem's pardon. Concludes that the zealous desire of the judiciary under Alfonsín to punish all human rights violators actually retarded the removal of the military's most anti-democratic elements.

3676 Ajuste y consenso en la era menemista: un nuevo mapa electoral. Argentina: Asociación Trabajadores del Estado, 1994. 60 p.: bibl., ill., map.

Maintains that a rise in absenteeism, blank ballots, and third parties, such as the Frente Grande, during the Oct. 1993 elections reflected discontent with Menem's policies. This conclusion, however, does not account for Menem's decisive reelection to a second presidential term.

3677 Alfonsín, Raúl. La reforma constitucional de 1994. Buenos Aires: Tiempo de Ideas, 1994. 111 p.: bibl. (Tiempo de ideas)

Argentina's ex-president, and head of the Radical Party suggests changes to the Constitution. He also explains to fellow party members why he agreed with President Menem's decision to call a constitutional convention.

Allub, Leopoldo. Impactos de las políticas de promoción agrícola en el desarrollo rural de la Provincia del San Juan. See item **5113.**

3678 Ancarola, Gerardo. Las tres etapas de la ciencia política argentina. (*Foro Polít.*, 9, dic. 1993, p. 85–100)

Describes the history of Argentine political science by examining the careers of three men: José Manuel Estrada (1842–92), Rodolfo Rivarola (1857–1942), and Mario Justo López (1915–89).

3679 Ansaldi, Waldo. Mediaciones políticas y construcción de la democracia argentina. (*Estudios/Univ. Córdoba*, 3, otoño 1994, p. 115–135, bibl.)

Uses a mainly historical approach to conclude that Argentine democracy has consistently been weakened by poorly organized political parties unable to withstand well-organized pressure groups.

3680 Argentina, the attack on the Third Infantry Regiment barracks at La Tablada: investigations into allegations of torture, "disappearances," and extrajudicial executions. New York: Amnesty International, 1990. 21 p.: appendix.

Investigates alleged leftist guerilla criminal acts during their Jan. 1989 attack on the La Tablada army barracks.

3681 Aznárez, Carlos and **Julio César Calistro.** Lorenzo: el padrino del poder sindical. Buenos Aires: Tiempo de Ideas, 1993. 221 p. (Col. Tiempo de ideas)

Ostensibly a biography of the metallurgical workers' boss, Lorenzo Miguel, work is actually a study of his powerful, corrupt union and its place in Argentina's labor movement. Examines Lorenzo Miguel's predecessors, Augusto Vandor and Jose Rucci focusing on their involvement in the CGT and Peronist politics, their gangs of thugs, and their coercive methods.

3682 Back in the saddle: a survey of Argentina. (*Economist/London*, 333:7891, Nov. 26/Dec 2, 1994, supplement, p. 3–18, graphs, photos)

Balanced account of the economic sucesses of Argentina's neoliberal reforms and their negative social consequences for the working and middle classes. Notes the widespread corruption under Menem and Argentina's ambivalent attitudes toward its South American neighbors.

3683 Beliz, Gustavo. Vale la pena: adiós a la vieja política. Buenos Aires: Editorial Sudamericana, 1992. 255 p.

President Menem's press secretary reconciles demands for economic efficiency imposed by global competition with the need to preserve the State's role as protector of the rights and well-being of its citizens. Author believes that the best means of balancing these demands lies in eliminating corruption and improving the quality of administration.

3684 Bermúdez, Norberto. La pista siria. Caracas: Ediciones de la Urraca, 1993. 227 p.: ill.

An Argentine journalist living in Spain details the international drug smuggling and money laundering activities of Menem's Syrian in-laws

3685 Bisciotti, Victorio O. Testigo y parte: historias de una pasión parlamentaria. Buenos Aires: Fundación Arturo Illia para la Democracia y la Paz, 1991? 1 v.

A Unión Cívica Radical national deputy writes his memoirs of the Alfonsín presidency. Polemic, and somewhat superficial.

3686 Blutman, Gustavo. Orden y desorden en la reforma del Estado argentino, 1989–1992. (*Rev. Ciclos*, 4:4, 1994, p. 53–93, bibl., table)

A good, though sometimes technical, survey of Menem's neoliberal reforms: privatization, deregulation, decentralization, and open markets. Discusses budget balancing through tax increases and spending cuts, and explains how government spending is curtailed by limiting the State's ability to borrow or print money.

3687 Bonilla Saus, Javier. Partidos y sistemas de partidos: historias y políticas en Argentina, Brasil y Uruguay. (*Secuencia/México*, 32, mayo/agosto 1995, p. 9–30, bibl., ill.)

Review and critique of three articles: Marcelo Cavarozzi on Argentine political parties, Waldo Ausaldi on Brazilian parties, and Gerardo Caetano on Uruguayan parties.

3688 Brizuela, Ricardo Eulogio. Pasajeros de la historia. v. 1, Isabel y los barquitos de Massera. Argentina: Servicios Periodísticos Especiales, 1993. v. 1.

Projected as the first of three volumes that will examine the history of the Peronist Movement from the fall of Isabel Perón to the election of Carlos Menem. The author is a Peronist journalist. Much of v. 1 deals with the travails of leading Peronists immediately after the 1976 coup.

3689 Brysk, Alison. From above and below: social movements, the international system, and human rights in Argentina. (*Comp. Polit. Stud.*, 26:3, Oct. 1993, p. 259–281)

Interesting description of how human rights groups inside Argentina worked with international groups to pressure the military leaders of the Proceso. For international relations specialist's comment, see item **4342.**

3690 Buchrucker, Cristián. Pensamiento político militar argentino: el debate sobre las hipótesis de guerra y la geopolítica. (*Estu-*

dios/Univ. Córdoba, 3, otoño 1994, p. 137–153, bibl.)

Geopolitical fears of invasions by Brazil and Chile have haunted Argentina's military since independence. The Cold War added fear of communist penetration. Because Argentine civilians seem relatively unconcerned with these "threats," the military views itself as the only group with a truly patriotic vision.

3691 Cabrera, Ernesto. La cuestión de la proporcionalidad y las elecciones legislativas en la República Argentina. (*Rev. Mex. Sociol.*, 54:4, oct./dic. 1992, p. 153–182, bibl., tables)

Uses simulated elections, based on data from the 1980s, to compare different systems of proportional representation to determine how closely they actually reflect voters' preferences.

3692 Caimari, Lila M. Perón y la Iglesia Católica: religión, Estado y sociedad en la Argentina, 1943–1955. Buenos Aires: Ariel Historia, 1995. 390 p.: bibl.

Scholarly work of the highest quality. Examines the evolution of Perón's relationship with the Catholic Church, from cautious alliance in 1946 to open hostility in 1954.

3693 Cao, Guillermo M. La huelga de los obreros de la carne de 1932: un aporte para una mejor comprensión del movimiento obrero anterior al peronismo. (*in* Historia de los argentinos. Argentina: Asociación de Fabricantes Argentinos de Coca-Cola, 1990, p. 69–97, bibl.)

Poor labor conditions in the meatpacking industry during the 1930s provided the initial source of support for the Peronist movement. The alliance of reactionary politicians and foreign companies, as well as the cultural gulf separating the older union leadership, with its European outlook, from the unskilled migrants from the interior, gave Perón his opportunity to win the loyalty of the masses.

3694 Capalbo, Daniel and **Gabriel Pandolfo.** Todo tiene precio: biografía no autorizada de José Luis Manzano. Buenos Aires: Planeta, 1992. 286 p.: bibl., ill. (Espejo de la Argentina)

First-rate biography of a young, up-and-coming Peronist politician: Jose Luis Manzano. From student radical to national deputy to minister of interior by the age of 40, this *aficionado* of fancy restaurants, Italian silk suits, and luxury apartments epitomizes the opportunism and corruption that comprise the seamy side of the Menem "miracle."

3695 Catterberg, Edgardo R. Los argentinos frente a la política: cultura política y opinión pública en la transición argentina a la democracia. Buenos Aires: Grupo Editorial Planeta, 1989. 159 p.: bibl., ill. (Col. Política y sociedad)

Opinion surveys conducted during the final year of the Proceso, Alfonsín's first year as president, and the later years of that administration allowed the author to chart changes in public attitude about democracy. Initial enthusiasm faded as socioeconomic problems mounted. The original pro-democratic consensus was as much a belief in democracy as a magical panacea as a reaction to the Proceso's horrors. By 1989 support for democracy mainly rested on a lack of consensus about an alternative.

3696 Cavarozzi, Marcelo and María Grossi. Argentina: from democratic reinvention to political decline and hyperinflation. (*in* Democratization and the State in the Southern Cone: essays on South American politics. Edited by Benno Galjart and Patricio Silva. Amsterdam: CEDLA, 1989, p. 129–157, bibl.)

Ambitious article tries to explain why the Radicals failed to consolidate their 1983 election victory and why the Peronists were able to make their comeback in 1989. Tantalizing asides about Alfonsín's attempt to establish personal domination over the UCR, and the long struggle of the Renovationist Peronists to overcome the unions' stranglehold over the party, but neither is sufficiently developed. Also avoids discussion of the Austral Plan, whose superficiality was the real cause of Alfonsin's failure.

3697 Cavarozzi, Marcelo. Los partidos políticos argentinos durante el siglo XX. (*Secuencia/México*, 32, mayo/agosto 1995, p. 31–48, bibl., ill.)

The modern Argentine party system has known two developmental phases. The first (1916–1983) failed to establish democracy because both the Radical and Peronist parties were led by populist demagogues who frightened entrepreneurs into the arms of the military. The second phase, beginning in 1983, enjoys a much broader consensus about the desirability of democracy. Also, Menem's inclusion of the economic elites in his ruling coalition is a political masterstroke.

3698 Cavarozzi, Marcelo and Vicente Palermo. State, civil society, and popular neighborhood organizations in Buenos Aires: key players in Argentina's transition to democracy. (*in* New paths to democratic development in Latin America. Edited by Charles A. Reilly. Boulder, Colo.: Lynne Rienner Publishers, 1995, p. 29–44)

Popular neighborhood organizations flourished during the Alfonsín Administration's early years, raising hopes of grassroots democracy. But Radical and Peronist party hacks have since taken control and the author believes the prospects for real popular participation are over.

3699 Cerruti, Gabriela. El jefe, vida y obra de Carlos Saúl Menem. Buenos Aires: Planeta, 1993. 397 p.: bibl., index. (Espejo de la Argentina)

Well-written and informed biography of Carlos Menem. Journalistic rather than scholarly. Recommended.

3700 Chanaguir, Elsa. El Partido Socialista y la convención reformadora de la provincia de Córdoba de 1923. (*Estudios/Univ. Córdoba*, 3, otoño 1994, p. 157–180, bibl.)

Describes the role of the Socialist party at the 1923 constitutional convention of Córdoba province.

3701 Chumbita, Hugo. El enigma peronista. Buenos Aires: Puntosur Editores, 1989. 189 p.: bibl.

A veteran Peronist offers an interpretative history of the movement. It is a national/populist phenomenon, like Getulio Vargas' following in Brazil, or Mexico under Lázaro Cárdenas. But little positive commentary can be offered about the pseudo-Peronist government of Carlos Menem.

3702 Córica, Juan Carlos. El desencuentro de los argentinos: efecto cultural y político, el antagonismo del pensamiento antagónico, un enfoque alternativo para revertirlo. Buenos Aires: Corregidor, 1993. 237 p.: bibl.

Argues for defending populist nationalism as a "third way" between the extremes of exploitative capitalism and Communist totalitarianism.

3703 Craviotti, Clara. Azúcar y conflictos en el norte argentino. Buenos Aires: Centro Editor de América Latina, 1992. 93 p.: bibl. (Biblioteca Política argentina; 360)

Sugar, an important crop in northwestern Argentina supports a peculiar society composed of many small planters, a few powerful mill owners, strongly organized factory labor, and provincial political machines. Until recently, sugar was protected and subsidized by the federal government, but attempts to open the economy have disrupted this way of life, often with violent results. An important study for understanding provincial politics.

3704 Dargoltz, Raúl Eduardo. El santiagueñazo: gestación y crónica de una pueblada argentina. Buenos Aires: El Despertador Ediciones, Sielp, 1994. 240 p.: bibl.

Riots erupted in the poor, remote province of Santiago del Estero on Dec. 16, 1993, resulting in the burning of the state house, legislature, courts, and the homes of leading citizens. The author traces the cause to President Menem's neoliberal policies, which pushed an already suffering population to the point of desperation.

3705 De Ipola, Emilio. Investigaciones políticas. Buenos Aires: Ediciones Nueva Visión, 1989. 156 p.: bibl. (Col. Cultura y sociedad)

Collection of previously published articles about Peronism, socialism, and contemporary Argentine culture by a Marxist social scientist.

3706 Del Brutto, Bibiana. Representación directa en la ciudad de Buenos Aires. Buenos Aires: Centro Editor de América Latina, 1994. 124 p.: bibl. (Biblioteca Política argentina; 457)

The city of Buenos Aires lacks the finances to provide its inhabitants with necessary services, including police protection. Moreover, its chief executive officer, the intendant, is an officer of the federal government and therefore not responsible to the local population. This book explores various possibilities for greater municipal autonomy, including constitutional changes, to improve the quality of life in the nation's capital. See also item **3726.**

3707 Di Tella, Torcuato S. Torcuato Di Tella: industria y política. Buenos Aires: Tesis, Grupo Editorial Norma, 1993. 165 p.: bibl., ill.

Biography of a leading Argentine industrialist of the 1930s-40s by one of his sons.

3708 Domingorena, Horacio Osvaldo. La agonía del Estado democrático. Buenos Aires: H.O. Domingorema, 1992. 105 p.: bibl.

Longtime Radical legislator and former president of Aerolíneas Argentinas decries the corruption that results from the proliferation of pressure groups, all of whom are trying to influence a powerful interventionist State.

3709 Fernández, Arturo. Las nuevas relaciones entre sindicatos y partidos políticos. Buenos Aires: Centro Editor de América Latina, 1993. 160 p.: bibl. (Biblioteca Política argentina ; 429)

Focusing on labor unions in Rosario, Argentina's second city, the author describes the strategies adopted by various unions to confront industrial and governmental downsizing. Because these neoliberal policies are being implemented by a Peronist government, labor is compelled to rethink its traditional allegiance to the Justicialist Party.

3710 Fernández Alberté, María Felisa. Descentralización política, o, dimensiones de la libertad. Buenos Aires: RundiNuskín Editor, 1992. 183 p.: bibl., index. (Col. Derecho)

Despite technological advances, nations and local communities are not obsolete. On the contrary, participatory democracy requires their revitalization.

3711 Ferreira Rubio, Delia and **Matteo Goretti.** La reforma constitucional argentina: ¿un presidente menos poderoso? (Contribuciones/Buenos Aires, 12 : 1, enero/marzo 1995, p. 69–89)

Brief, clear summary of the constitutional reforms instituted in 1994. Concludes that the new position of prime minister (jefe de gabinete) does not substantially change the presidentialist character of Argentina's government.

3712 Floria, Carlos. Votos y liderazgos en la transición argentina. (in Una tarea inconclusa: elecciones y democracia en América Latina, 1988–1991. San José: Instituto Interamericano de Derechos Humanos, Centro de Asesoría y Promoción Electoral, 1992, p. 467–484, tables)

Interpretive essay about Argentina's

transition to democracy, which the author believes to be permanent.

3713 Foradori, Carlos Mario. Pobreza política y el nuevo paradigma en la Argentina. Buenos Aires: Grupo Editor Latinoamericano, 1994. 152 p.: bibl. (Col. Estudios políticos y sociales. Col. Escritura de hoy)

Think-piece that offers a "new paradigm" to replace both the centralized bureaucratic State and the anarchic competition of a decentralized political system as avenues for more citizen participation.

3714 Fraga, Rosendo and **Marisa Szmukler.** Claves de la campaña electoral 1989. Buenos Aires: Editorial Centro de Estudios Unión para la Nueva Mayoria, 1989. 155 p. (Col. Análisis politico; 1)

Argentine electoral compaigning seldom uses television debates, telephone banks, or mass mailings. But radio and television ads are heavily used, as are opinion surveys. Carlos Menem was very effective with his automobile caravan, the "Menemovil," which brought him into direct contact with the voters. Interesting look at Argentine campaign styles and techniques of "image-building."

3715 Fraga, Rosendo. El ejército y Frondizi: 1958–1962. Buenos Aires: Emecé Editores, 1992. 310 p.: bibl.

Author's father was a general who participated in military blackmail against President Arturo Frodizi, then later became his War Secretary and defended him. The book is based on Gen. Fraga's notes and papers, as well as on interviews with other protagonists of the period. It is a useful supplement to works by Robert Potash and Alain Rouquié on civil-military relations during Frondizi's turbulent four years in office.

3716 Fraga, Rosendo. Las fuerzas armadas y los diez años de democracia. (*Todo es Hist.*, 317, dic. 1993, p. 21–25)

Compelling description of the low morale that pervades today's armed forces in Argentina.

3717 Franzé, Javier. El concepto de política en el socialismo argentino. (*Cuad. Hispanoam.*, 538, abril 1995, p. 57–67)

An essay on the political thought of Juan B. Justo placing him on the political spectrum between a Marxist and a Comtean.

3718 Frías, Pedro J. Federalismo y reforma del Estado en Argentina. (*Contribuciones/Buenos Aires*, 10:4, oct./dic. 1993, p. 39–48)

Supports the principle of subsidiarity, which would give Argentine provinces more control over education and other public services. However, the problem of revenue complicates all decentalization plans.

3719 Frondizi, Arturo. Los estados nacionales y las fuerzas armadas. (*Rev. Arg. Estud. Estrateg.*, 15, oct./dic. 1994, p. 11–19)

Argentina's ex-president wonders how to preserve the nation's identity in the face of seemingly inexorable pressures toward universalism. How far can national security be surrendered to transnational institutions? Frondizi argues that the armed forces, as part of the State, cannot be put at the service of others without compromising national sovereignty.

3720 Galasso, Norberto. De Perón a Menem: el peronismo en la encrucijada. Buenos Aires: Ediciones del Pensamiento Nacional, 1990. 158 p.

An intellectual of the nationalist left predicts that Menem's betrayal of Peronist principles will result in a mass exodus from the party.

3721 García, Héctor Ricardo. Cien veces me quisieron matar. Buenos Aires: Planeta, c1993. 318 p.

Autobiography of the owner of an Argentine multimedia empire. Describes his clashes with practically every government that came to power during the 1960s and 1970s, resulting in the loss of a television station, the closure of his newspaper and magazines, lawsuits, arrests, and attempts on his life.

3722 Garro, Alejandro M. Nine years of transition to democracy in Argentina: partial failure or qualified success? (*Columbia J. Transnatl. Law*, 31:1, 1993, p. 1–102)

Lengthy and wide-ranging essay on attempts (and some failures) since 1983 to establish the rule of law in Argentina. The author tends to editorialize about the advantages of US common law and constitutionalism, but there is much useful information about the Argentine legal system.

3723 Garzón Valdés, Ernesto. The Argentine military and democracy. (*Estud. Latinoam./Poland*, 14:pt. 2, 1992, p. 93–107, bibl.)

Defines State terrorism, provides a fascinating review of the arguments used to justify it, and offers suggestions on how to avoid it by infusing the military with democratic values.

Gibson, Edward L. The populist road to market reform: policy and electoral coalitions in Mexico and Argentina. See item **3053.**

3724 Gil, Germán Roberto. La izquierda peronista: para una interpretación ideológica, 1955–1974. Buenos Aires: Centro Editor de América Latina, 1989. 125 p.: bibl. (Biblioteca Política argentina; 253)

The Peronist left arose in reaction to attempts to supress the movement. Ironically, its great victory, in forcing the military to accept Perón's return to power, also led to its demise. Legitimated by elections, Perón isolated and attacked his young supporters. A familiar story, but well told and documented.

3725 Gillespie, Richard. John William Cooke: el peronismo alternativo. Buenos Aires: Cántaro Editores, 1989. 144 p.: bibl. (Col. de estudios socio-políticos; 4)

Biography of the man who headed the Peronist underground in Argentina before fleeing to Cuba. Converted to Communism, he became a hero to the Peronist left.

3726 Gobierno de la ciudad y crisis en la Argentina. Recopilación de Hilda Herzer y Pedro Pírez. Buenos Aires: Grupo Editor Latinoamericano, 1988. 233 p.: bibl. (Col. Estudios políticos y sociales)

Series of essays focus on the problems of Argentina's middle-sized cities. Though closer to the citizenry than the federal government, these cities lack funds to provide adequate services. Essays explore ways of decentralizing the State in order to make local government stronger. Should be read in conjunction with item **3706.**

3727 Gutiérrez, Alfredo. El derrumbe de la UCeDé: de Videla a Menem; la mutación liberal. Buenos Aires: Ediciones Letra Buena, 1992. 127 p. (Col. Transiciones; 7)

Traces the rise and fall of Alvaro Alsogaray's UCeDé, from its status as Argentina's principal neoliberal party in 1983 to its absorption by Carlos Menem's government and subsequent disappearance.

3728 Gutiérrez, María Alicia. Iglesia Catolica, Estado y democracia. Buenos Aires: Centro de Investigaciones Europeo-Latinoamericanas, 1993. 25 p.: bibl. (Serie Documentos de Trabajo EURAL; 52)

Thoughtful, carefully researched, well-written manuscript traces historical evolution of the relationship between the Catholic Church and democracy in Argentina. Highlights the distinctive institutional conduct, attitudes, and political role of the Argentine Church during the late military government (1976–83). This exceptionality in Argentina reveals a "theology of death" and Church complicity in State terrorism on a scale unknown in Latin America. [D. Dent]

3729 Hardoy, Emilio. No he vivido en vano: memorias. Buenos Aires: Marymar Ediciones, 1993. 478 p.

Posthumously published autobiography of a prominent conservative politician from Buenos Aires. Especially valuable for his recollections of the 1930s-40s.

3730 Hedges, Jill. Centre-provincial relations in Argentina, 1976–1991. Buenos Aires: Centro de Investigaciones Europeo-Latinoamericanas, 1993. 50 p.: tables. (Serie Documentos de Trabajo EURAL; 60)

Provides useful, hard-to-get information about local government in Argentina. Focuses on four provinces and their relations with the central government since 1976.

3731 Hedges, Jill. *Hasta sufrir en carne propia:* the Catholic Church and Peronismo in Argentina, 1943–1974. Buenos Aires: Centro de Investigaciones Europeo-Latinoamericanas, 1993. 48 p. (Serie Documentos de Trabajo EURAL; 56)

Analyzes Catholic Church's relationship to Perón. Demonstrates that each side manipulated the other.

3732 Hernández, Antonio Tomás. Los cien días que precedieron a Menem. Buenos Aires: Corregidor, 1989. 314 p.

Chronology of events during the 100 days before Carlos Menem's inauguration. Snapshots of local- and national-level political figures.

3733 Hora, Roy and **Javier Trímboli.** Entrevista a David Rock: el nacionalismo argentino coleccionó ideas europeas. (*Todo es Hist.*, 319, feb. 1994, p. 34–47, ill., photos)

Interview with a well-known British historian and author of several works on Argentina.

3734 La izquierda y La Tablada. Recopilación de Alberto Kohen y Rodolfo Mattarollo. Buenos Aires?: Ediciones Cuadernos de Ideas, 1989. 80 p.

The attack by leftist guerrillas on the La Tablada barracks in Jan. 1989 reminded Argentines of ERP and Montoneros terrorism. That put the left on the defensive. This collection of essays tries to restore the left's credibility by distancing it from La Tablada. See item **3680.**

3735 Juvenal, Carlos. Buenos muchachos: la industria del secuestro en la Argentina. Buenos Aires: Planeta, 1994. 340 p.: bibl., index. (Espejo de la Argentina)

The armed forces and security agencies often employed common criminals to carry out the ugliest tasks of the "Dirty War." Eventually the line between anti-subversive and just plain criminal activities became blurred, as kidnapping, confiscation, extortion, and murder were used against enemies of the State. Kidnapping rings are still active in the post-Proceso period, and are still protected, to some extent, by the police and intelligence agencies.

3736 Kaplan, Marcos. Estudios sobre política y derecho del petróleo argentino, 1907–1955. México: Univ. Nacional Autónoma de México, Instituto de Investigaciones Jurídicas, 1992. 263 p.: bibl. (Serie I—Estudios de derecho económico; 20)

Interpretive history of Argentina's oil industry up to Perón's 1955 overthrow. Emphasizes the rivalry between YPF and the foreign companies. Argues that YPF might have funtioned well if it had not been corrupted by Peronist bureaucracy and mismanagement, the Concordancia's deliberate sabotage, and Yrigoyen's indifference.

3737 Kozel, Andrés *et al.* Militares y política, 1983–1991: Rico, Bussi, Ruiz Palacios, Ulloa, Mittelbach y el CEMIDA. Recopilación de Pablo Lacoste. Buenos Aires: Centro Editor de América Latina, 1993. 144 p.: bibl. (Biblioteca Política argentina; 406)

Collection of essays attempts to explain the puzzling popularity of certain military men who held positions of responsibility under the Junta: Gen. Antonio Domingo Bussi (governor of Tucumán), Captain Jose David Ruiz Palacios (governor of Chaco) and Captain Roberto Ulloa (governor of Salta). All three have returned to power through elections. In addition, the notorious *carapintada,* Colonel Aldo Rico, heads Argentina's fourth-largest party at the national level.

3738 Krantzer, Guillermo and **Jorge Sánchez.** Regulaciones en el transporte urbano: el caso de Buenos Aires. (*EURE/Santiago,* 19:56, marzo 1993, p. 41–53, bibl.)

Urban transport poses a challenge to neoliberalism's faith in free enterprise because buses, subways, trains, and taxis require some degree of public regulation. They use public streets and public utilities, affect public safety as well as other forms of private property, and are crucial to the general economic life of the community. Thus, this sector's privatization in a metropolitan area like Greater Buenos Aires offers a rich area of study.

3739 Larriqueta, Daniel E. La maquinaria del poder. Buenos Aires: Ediciones de la Urraca, 1993. 164 p.

Author does not like Menem or his neoliberal reforms. Believes the latter, if not reversed, will harm more people than not. Separate chapters describe the decay of morals, education, government, the economy, and national defense.

3740 Lázara, Simón Alberto. Poder militar: origen, apogeo y transición. Buenos Aires: Editorial Legasa, 1988. 347 p. (Ensayo crítico)

The author, who is president of the Unified Socialist Party, a member of the World Council for Peace, and a member of the Permanent Assembly for Human Rights, locates the origins of the National Security Doctrine in the bourgeois doctrines of liberalism and Peronism.

3741 López, Ernesto. Ni la ceniza ni la gloria: actores, sistema político y cuestión militar en los años de Alfonsín. Buenos Aires: Univ. Nacional de Quilmes, 1994. 141 p.: bibl.

Study blames Argentina's civilian

elites for the country's frequent military interventions. The second half focuses on the Alfonsín Administration and its failure to establish civilian supremacy.

3742 Luciani, Tomás. El rey. Buenos Aires: Beas Ediciones, 1993. 220 p.: ill. (Col. Fax)

Laudatory biography of Ramon "Palito" Ortega, an Argentine singer who became involved with politics at President Menem's request. Ortega ran for governor of Tucumán on the Peronist ticket, as a desperate move to stop the popular Gen. Domingo Bussi.

3743 Maestre Wilkinsons, Eusebio. Argentina, 1983–1989. (*Secuencia/México*, 18, sept./dic. 1990, p. 153–178, ill.)

Argentine democracy remains fragile because more powerful interests continue to operate extra-legally, and economic sacrifices demanded by neoliberalism undermine popular support for constitutional government.

3744 Majul, Luis. Los dueños de la Argentina. v. 2, Los secretos del verdadero poder. Buenos Aires: Editorial Sudamericana, 1994. 2 v.: bibl.

Muckraking essays about how some of Argentina's richest men made their fortunes: Pérez Companc, Soldati, Roggio, and Pescamona. Good reading and good insight into Argentine culture. Could be read in conjunction with item **3755.** For annotation of vol. 1 see *HLAS 55:3551.*

3745 Martínez, Carlos et al. El Menemato: radiografía de dos años de gobierno de Carlos Menem. Buenos Aires: Ediciones Letra Buena, 1991. 264 p.: bibl. (Col. Actualidad política)

Seven hostile essays examine the negative aspects of Menem's first two years in office. Describe Menem's populist electoral campaign from his caravan, the *menemovil* and the economic crisis that forced Alfonsín to turn over power early. Then essays contrast Menem's "man of the people" political style with the corruption that pervades his government and the harsh economic consequences of neoliberalism. Also evaluate his pardons of convicted military chiefs and his pro-US foreign policy. Authors are puzzled by Menem's continued popularity and are alarmed by what they perceive to be a decline into barbarism.

3746 Martínez, Fabiana and **Susana Bonetto de Scandogliero.** Las palabaras de Menem: representaciones neoliberales en el discurso nacional populista. (*Anuario/Córdoba*, 1993, p. 85–126, bibl., graphs)

Content analysis of President Menem's speeches, as published in *Clarín* six months before and six months after the 1989 elections. Not surprisingly, they show that despite campaign promises, politicians may act very differently once elected to office.

3747 Marx, Jutta. Mujeres y partidos políticos: de una masiva participación a una escasa representación; un estudio de caso. Prólogo de Eva Giberti. Buenos Aires: Editorial Legasa, 1992. 199 p.: bibl.

Based in part on opinion surveys, but bolstered by other methods. Attemps to describe how, and to what extent, Argentine women participate in politics.

3748 McGuire, James W. Political parties and democracy in Argentina. (*in* Building democratic institutions: party systems in Latin America. Edited by Scott Mainwaring and Timothy R. Scully. Stanford, Calif.: Stanford Univ. Press, 1995, p. 200–246, tables)

Argentina's political parties traditionally have acted more like intransigent political movements' aims at hegemony rather than accepting democracy's inherent dependency on compromise. Moreover, their tenuous ties to important pressure groups like landowners, labor, or business, has caused the latter to reach their objectives, often by undemocratic means. Hopeful signs of change under Alfonsín have disappeared under Menem. A thought-provoking article and good summary of recent political trends.

3749 Méndez, Juan E. Truth and partial justice in Argentina: an update. New York: Human Rights Watch, 1991. 97 p. (An Americas Watch report)

Update of a 1987 report calling for the prosecution of former military leaders during the Proceso.

3750 Menem, Carlos Saúl. Tierra arrasada por la corrupción: discurso presidencial. (*in* Síntesis de Respondacon II, 2nd, Lima?, 1992. Combatiendo el fraude y la corrupción en los gobiernos. Lima: Colegio de Contadores Públicos de Lima, 1992, p. 139–146)

President Menem announces that he will not tolerate corruption in government.

Meza, Rubén Ariel. El triángulo de la opresión. See item **2970.**

3751 Moreno, Omar. La última oportunidad del sindicalismo argentino. (*in* Modelo neoliberal y sindicatos en América Latina. México: Fundación Friedrich Ebert, 1993, p. 45–77)

Can Argentina's labor unions meet the new global economy's demands for efficiency, productivity, and profitabilty? Author believes they should continue to play a major role in economic, political, and social policy-making, but President Menem is forcing unions to choose between following his neoliberal strategy or deserting the Justicialist party.

3752 Muchnik, Daniel. Identidad perdida: la menemización de la sociedad argentina. Buenos Aires: Editorial Galerna, 1994. 254 p.

Attacks Menem and Cavallo's neoliberal economic policies. Argentine industry, culture, and living standards are being sacrificed to an ideology that rewards corruption and speculation.

3753 Neuman, Elías. El abuso de poder en la Argentina y otros países latinoamericanos. Buenos Aires: Espasa Calpe, 1994. 190 p.: bibl. (Espasa hoy)

Inspired by the Proceso, study examines abuse of State power, especially the treatment of criminals and suspects. Also concerned with an alleged conspiracy between multinational corporations and the Catholic Church to eliminate human rights.

3754 Olgo Ochoa, Pedro. Años de furia y esperanza. Buenos Aires: Ediciones Corregidor, 1988. 157 p.

Short journalistic essays describing historic moments of peronismo from Oct. 17, 1945 to Perón's final days.

3755 Olivero, Roberto H. El financiamiento de partidos políticos en Argentina: un problema de cultura política y valores sociales. Prólogo del Dr. Alberto Antonio Spota. Buenos Aires: Instituto Internacional de Investigaciones Interdisciplinarias, 1994. 267 p.: bibl., index. (Col. Tesis y ensayos)

Analyzes corruption related to campaign financing in Argentina. Argues that there will be no change as long as Argentine society condones this behavior.

3756 Orlansky, Dora. Crisis y transformación del Estado en la Argentina, 1960–1993. (*Rev. Ciclos,* 4:4, 1994, p. 3–28, bibl., tables)

Public employment in Argentina has grown steadily in recent times. This growth was partially hidden under Alfonsín because it was counter-balanced by a decrease in national government positions. Under Menem, however, there have been significant cutbacks in public sector jobs. But if the civil service has suffered, there still are many political appointees, especially in the presidential staff and the Ministry of Interior.

3757 Pellet Lastra, Arturo. El Congreso por dentro: desde 1930 hasta nuestros días. Buenos Aires: Sainte Claire Editora, 1992? 306 p.: bibl., ill.

Very serious study examines why Congress does not play a stronger role in the national government. Details the various closures Congress has suffered in this century, and events leading up to them. Also analyzes how the two houses function, or fail to function, today. Author believes that legislative power is the best guarantee of democracy, and therefore views with concern Menem's constant accumulation of power.

3758 Pinedo, Enrique. Sesenta años a los tumbos: 1930–1990. Buenos Aires: Editorial Atlantida, 1992. 153 p.

A member of the Buenos Aires Conservative Party and the Jockey Club presents his opinions about Argentina's governments from Yrigoyen to Alfonsín.

3759 Pírez, Pedro. Las relaciones políticas en la configuración metropolitana: el caso de Buenos Aires. (*Estud. Sociol./México,* 11:33, sept./dic. 1993, p. 799–816, bibl., table)

Views Buenos Aires as a conglomerate of various political units: the intendency belongs to the national government and the municipal government; the Buenos Aires Provincial Government administers the suburbs. Each has its own jurisdiction and political style.

3760 Podetti, Mariana; María Elena Qués; and Cecilia Sagol. Política, medios y discurso en la Argentina. Buenos Aires: Centro Editor de América Latina, 1992. 113 p.: bibl. (Biblioteca Política argentina; 379)

Eight essays about "political discourse," which refers to political speeches, citizen response; and media reports within a continuous flow of information and reaction.

3761 Prévot Schapira, Marie-France. Du *welfare* à l'assistance: la décentralisation de l'intervention sociale en Argentine. (*Cah. Am. lat.*, 15, 1993, p. 29–50, table)

Effects on the poor when the State downsizes. Uncompetitive Argentine enterprises are failing, causing employment and poverty to increase. Welfare assistance, however, is being dismantled and provinces have too few resources to provide necessary aid.

3762 Ramos, Julio A. Los cerrojos a la prensa Buenos Aires: Editorial Amfin, 1993. 366 p.: bibl.

Publisher of *Ambito Financiero* accuses owner of *Clarín* of trying to create a news monopoly. In return for supporting military governments, he claims, *Clarín* was given control of the principal newsprint factory and has been allowed to buy newspaper companies as well as radio and television stations.

3763 Ratliff, William E. and Roger Fontaine. Argentina's capitalist revolution revisited: confronting the social costs of statist mistakes. Stanford, CA: Hoover Institution on War, Revolution, and Peace, Stanford Univ., 1993. 56 p.: bibl. (Essays in public policy; 41)

Useful survey of the first three years of President Menem's government emphasizes Cavallo's neoliberal reform program. Argues that reforms were long overdue.

3764 Rey, Alejandra and Luis Pazos. No llores por mí, Catamarca: la intriga política de un crimen. Buenos Aires: Editorial Sudamericana, 1991. 343 p.

A young woman, María Soledad, was raped and murdered in the Andean province of Catamarca, long the fiefdom of the Saadi family. As evidence began to point toward one of that family's young men, the investigation was halted. However, thanks to a courageous nun who organized street marches, the national government intervened. Gripping story of local intrigue and personal bravery.

3765 Riz, Liliana de and Catalina Smulovitz. Instauración democrática y reforma política en Argentina y Uruguay: un análisis comparado. (*Ibero-Am. Arch.*, 18:1/2, 1992, p. 181–224, bibl., tables)

A rather thin comparison of Argentina and Uruguay's failure to substantially reform either their government or political party structures.

3766 Sahni, Varun. Not quite British: a study of external influences on the Argentine Navy. (*J. Lat. Am. Stud.*, 25:3, Oct. 1993, p. 489–513, appendix, graphs, tables)

Effectively debunks, with a wealth of data, the commonly held notion that the Argentine navy is patterned after the British.

3767 Sain, Marcelo Fabián. Los levantamientos carapintada, 1987–1991. v. 1–2. Buenos Aires: Centro Editor de América Latina, 1994. 2 v. (241 p.): bibl. (Biblioteca Política argentina; 462–463)

Useful description and analysis of the three army revolts led by Cols. Rico and Seineldin between 1987–91. Provides history of recent civil-military relations in Argentina and discusses motives of various factions in the contemporary army.

3768 Santoro, Daniel. El Hacedor: una biografía política de Domingo Cavallo. Buenos Aires: Planeta, 1994. 421 p.: bibl., index. (Espejo de la Argentina)

Biography of Domingo Cavallo, Menem's powerful economic "wizard." Describes his rise to the top, despite having no party or family connections. Hated by old-time Peronists, he nevertheless continues to shape public policy with his firm neoliberal guidelines. Believable portrait of this controversial figure, based on careful and considerable research.

3769 Santoro, Daniel. Operación Condor II: la historia secreta del misil que desmanteló Menem. Buenos Aires: Ediciones Letra Buena, 1992. 127 p.: bibl., ill. (Col. Transiciones; 5)

History of Argentina's failed attempt to develop its own missile defense system. Accuses Menem of giving in to US pressure to dismantle the project and stunt the nation's technological growth.

3770 Scheetz, Thomas. El marco teórico, político y económico para una reforma militar en la Argentina. Buenos Aires: Centro de Investigaciones Europeo Latinoamericanos,

1993. 22 p.: bibl. (Serie de documentos de trabajo, EURAL; 50)

Suggests how the Argentine armed forces can redefine their role, reduce costs, and strengthen democratic values.

3771 Seoane, María and **Héctor Ruiz Núñez.** La noche de los lápices. Ed. definitiva. Buenos Aires: Planeta, 1992. 284 p.: bibl., ill. (Espejo de la Argentina)

Profiles of seven high school student activists who were arrested, tortured, and (except for one survivor) killed in La Plata by the Proceso. Sympathetic towards students, although it is clear they were involved in mass agitation work for the guerrillas. Worthwhile book, if read in conjunction with other works on the Dirty War.

3772 Serrafero, Mario Daniel. Cuestiones sobre la reforma constitucional. (*Desmemoria/Buenos Aires*, 1:3, abril/junio 1994, p. 9–16, photos)

As background to the constitutional convention of 1994, reviews the formal procedures and important questions, such as the immediate reelection of the president, that delegates will confront.

3773 Serrafero, Mario Daniel. Liderazgo y reelección presidencial en la Argentina. (*Desarro. Econ.*, 33:132, enero/marzo 1994, p. 565–586, tables)

Argues that Argentina's previous constitutional prohibition of immediate presidential reelection provided a safeguard against caesarism, a protection which was especially necessary when presidents were also head of their party.

3774 Spilimbergo, Jorge Enea. El fraude alfonsinista: historia crítica del radicalismo 1880–1988. 4. ed. Buenos Aires: Ediciones J. Hernández, 1989. 168 p.: bibl.

Polemical history of the Unión Civica Radical by a Marxist who thinks that the Radicals lost touch with the masses after Yrigoyen.

3775 Tcach, César. Partidos y pactos políticos en la Córdoba libertadora, 1955–1958. (*Estudios/Univ. Córdoba*, 3, otoño 1994, p. 17–30)

Focusing on Córdoba province, describes factional differences within the coalition that overthrew Perón in 1955.

3776 Uriarte, Claudio. Almirante Cero: biografía no autorizada de Emilio Eduardo Massera. Buenos Aires: Planeta, 1992. 352 p.: ill. (Espejo de la Argentina)

A superb biography of Admiral Emilio Massera, the navy's representative on the original Proceso junta. Essential reading for understanding the personalities and factional politics of the period.

3777 Uzal, Francisco Hipólito. Frondizi y Balbín: historia de un enfrentamiento. Prólogo de Emilia E. Menotti. Buenos Aires: Distribuidora y Editora Theoría, 1989. 176 p.: bibl. (Biblioteca de ensayistas contemporáneos)

The Radical Party has always been divided into national/populist and conservative wings. In the 1950s Frondizi led the former wing while Balbin headed the latter, and their struggle divided the party. Also divided the middle class and helped the Peronists' comeback. History of that fateful split.

3778 Viaggio, Julio José. La Tablada y el caso Puigjané : un proceso a la teología de la liberación. Buenos Aires: Editorial Cartago, 1990. 124 p.

Father Puigjane, a Franciscan monk, became involved with the Movimiento Todos para la Patria. The group started out doing charitable works in the slums, but was eventually was taken over by ex-guerrillas. In Jan. 1989 some of its members attacked the La Tabla army base. Although Puigjane was not among them, he was arrested, tried, and convicted. His lawyer claims he was railroaded because of his attachment to liberation theology.

3779 Viguera, Aníbal. Partidos y política en Argentina: reflexiones sobre una relación compleja. (*Secuencia/México*, 32, mayo/agosto 1995, p. 49–55, bibl., ill.)

Argentine parties in the past never really accepted the legitimacy of opposition. The fate of democracy depends on their overcoming such sectarianism.

3780 Walger, Sylvina. Pizza con champán: crónica de la fiesta menemista. 2. ed. Buenos Aires: Espasa Hoy, 1995. 328 p.: ill.

A selection of cynical but funny newspaper articles that look at the antics of the newly rich, famous, and powerful in Carlos Menem's *fin de siècle* Argentina.

3781 Zagorski, Paul W. Civil-military relations and Argentine democracy: the armed forces under the Menem government. (*Armed Forces Soc.*, 20:3, Spring 1994, p. 423–437)

Argues that Menem has been much more effective than Alfonsín in reforming and downsizing the military. Believes that Menem's pardons were an important step in calming the army's fears of civilian revenge and therefore decreased the likelihood of military intervention.

PARAGUAY

3782 Abente, Diego. A party system in transition: the case of Paraguay. (*in* Building democratic institutions: party systems in Latin America. Edited by Scott Mainwaring and Timothy R. Scully. Stanford: Stanford Univ. Press, 1995, p. 298–320, tables)

Excellent short history of Paraguay's political party system, especially its description of Colorado Party machine politics under Stroessner. Unfortunately, analysis does not extend beyond the 1989 elections, and so omits interesting recent developments.

3783 Ahumada Pacheco, Jaime. El gobierno y la administración pública local en los escenarios de la descentralización. (*Rev. Parag. Sociol.*, 31:90, mayo/agosto 1994, p. 169–200, bibl.)

Essay surveys problems and possibilities of establishing effective and responsible local government administration in Paraguay.

3784 Almada, Martín. Paraguay, la cárcel olvidada: el país exiliado—. 8. ed., con Anexo documental. Asunción: Ñandutí Vive; Intercontinental Editora, 1993. 289 p.: ill.

Personal account of a dissident Colorado who was arrested, tortured, and imprisoned for four years, until finally given the option of exile.

3785 Arditi, Benjamín. Adiós a Stroessner: la reconstrucción de la política en el Paraguay. Asunción: Centro de Documentación y Estudios : RP Ediciones, 1992. 224 p.: bibl., ill.

Examines Paraguay's gradual democratization since Stroessner fell. A Liberal Party activist, the author tends to underestimate the Colorados' resilience as well as the appeal

of other opposition parties, such as the Encuentro Nacional.

3786 Arriola Socol, Merardo. Una reconstrucción necesaria: nuestras experiencias de personas torturadas en el Paraguay de Stroessner. (*in* Salud psicosocial, cultura y democracia en América Latina: análisis de la violencia política. Asunción: Editora ATHYHA-IPD, 1993, v. 2, p. 27–51, bibl.)

Excerpts of testimony by former prisoners about their torture in Stroessner's jails. Most say that they never broke down and revealed information, claims that throw some doubt on the accuracy of their recollections.

3787 Balmelli, Carlos Mateo. Desarrollo institucional del Paraguay. (*Prop. Democrát.*, 1:1, enero/marzo 1994, p. 37–64, bibl.)

Reviews Paraguay's constitutional history, then discusses checks and balances and the separation of powers by the 1992 constitution.

3788 Boccia Paz, Alfredo; Myrian Angélica González; and **Rosa Palau Aguilar.** Es me informe: los archivos secretos de la policía de Stroessner. Asunción: CDE, 1994. 452 p.: bibl., ill.

Compilation of reports from the archive of Stroessner's police, with commentary by the author. Documents instances of torture and reveals the vast spy network that operated during the *stronato*.

3789 Borda, Dionisio. Empresariado y transición a la democracia en el Paraguay. (*Rev. Parag. Sociol.*, 30:86, enero/abril 1993, p. 31–66, appendix, tables)

In-depth article about Paraguay's increasingly important and complex business class. Full of hard-to-find facts and incisive analysis. Describes the sometimes complementary, sometimes conflictual, interests of the different sectors within the business community, both under the *stronato* and the Rodríguez Administration. Essential reading.

3790 Cardozo Rodas, Victorino. Lucha sindical y transición política en Paraguay, 1990. Heredia, Costa Rica: Editorial de la Univ. Nacional, 1992. 232 p.: bibl. (Col. Guayabo)

Useful description of Paraguay's labor union movement. Contains history of its evolution, an explanation of how competing labor federations differ, and the results of a survey of workers in the Asunción area. Somewhat polemical.

3791 Céspedes, Roberto Luis. Demanda social y política: autoritarismo en Paraguay, 1986–1988; senderos paralelos frente a una dictadura prologada. (*in* Movimientos sociales y política: el desafío de la democracia en América Latina. Santiago: CES Ediciones; Consejo Latinoamericano de Ciencias Sociales, 1990, p. 209–225, bibl.)

Written before Stroessner fell, article is a bit dated. Serves nevertheless as a good summary of the mounting problems the regime faced near its end.

3792 Estado, partidos políticos y sociedad: análisis de la transición política paraguaya. Asunción: Centro Paraguayo de Estudios Sociológicos, 1990. 52 p.: bibl.

Excellent collection of essays by a group of sociologists and economists describes how various aspects of post-Stroessner Paraguay are undermining modernization.

3793 Esteche Notario, Mario. Movimiento "14 de Mayo." Paraguay: s.n., 1989. 218 p.: ill.

Fascinating account of a guerrilla movement that grew out of the exiled Liberal Party and invaded Paraguay in 1960. Almost all were killed or captured. Author was a prisoner until mid-1961, when he escaped through the jungle and reached Brazil.

3794 Estigarribia V., Ricardo. ¿Privatización o estatismo?: defensa de las empresas monopólicas estratégicas del Estado paraguayo ante la política de privatización. Asunción: Editorial Latindata, 1994? 58 p.: bibl.

A member of the social-democratic Febrerista Party argues that strategic industries should be kept under State control.

3795 Frutos, Julio César and **Helio Vera.** Pactos políticos. Asunción: Editorial Medusa, 1993. 299 p.: bibl., ill., index.

Essential study on the period between the Triple Alliance War and the Chaco War. Important but much understudied period, especially since it gave rise to Paraguay's two main political parties. Treatment is refreshingly nonpartisan.

3796 Gagliardone, César R. Memorias gráficas y autobiográficas: un relato de la vida real. Asunción: Editora Litocolor, 1993. 193 p.: ill.

Memoirs of an army physician whose career, beginning in the Chaco War, included several appointments to the cabinet and a stint as Asunción's intendant. Format is based on interviews and previously published articles.

3797 Gatti Cardozo, Gustavo. El papel político de los militares en el Paraguay, 1870–1990. Asunción: Univ. Católica Nuestra Señora de la Asunción, 1990. 120 p.: bibl. (Biblioteca de estudios paraguayos; 35)

Civil-military relations in Paraguay have gone through various phases since 1870. *Caudillo* politics, which emerged from the anarchy that followed the Triple Alliance War, lasted until 1908. The country then enjoyed more or less civilian rule under the Liberal Party until 1936. The Chaco War introduced nationalist and revolutionary demands that the military attempted to channel and which ultimately culminated in the traumatic Civil War of 1947. From then until the fall of Stroessner in 1989, the military emphasized order over change. Now another phase has begun that will determine whether Paraguay will allow for democratic development, or remain under military control.

3798 Lara Castro, Jorge. Paraguay: crisis de la dictadura y dimensión política de la *democracia*. (*in* La democracia en América Latina: actualidad y perspectivas. Coordinación de Pablo González Casanova y Marcos Roitman Rosenmann. Madrid: Univ. Complutense de Madrid; México: Centro de Investigaciones Interdisciplinarias en Humanidades, UNAM, 1992, p. 105–115, bibl.)

Excellent analysis of the policies that made Stroessner's regime so successful during the 1970s and the contradictions that emerged to undermine it in the next decade.

3799 Lezcano G., Carlos María. Elecciones en el Paraguay. (*in* Una tarea inconclusa: elecciones y democracia en América Latina, 1988–1991. San José: Instituto Interamericano de Derechos Humanos, Centro de Asesoría y Promoción Electoral, 1992, p. 577–599, tables)

Useful summaries of political developments up to 1991.

3800 Lezcano G., Carlos María and **Carlos Martini.** Fuerzas armadas y democracia: a la búsqueda del equilibrio perdido; Paraguay, 1989–1993. Asunción: Centro de Documentación y Estudios (CED); Grupo de Ciencias Sociales (GCS), 1994. 315 p.: bibl., ill.

Collection of short essays, some of them newspaper articles, arguing that the coup that ousted Stroessner did not bring fundamental change to the ruling alliance of army, Colorado Party, and State.

3801 Mazacotte, Alejandro. El Estado paraguayo y la corrupción. Asunción: s.n., 1994. 319 p.: bibl.

An attack on the growth of government bureaucracy and corruption. Proposes several methods to reduce the State's role in the economy. Polemical, but well-informed.

3802 Meo, Carlos. El Cóndor traicionado—! Asunción: Editorial Idea, 1994. 154 p.

Geopolitical treatise argues that Paraguay should ally itself with Argentina, Uruguay, and Brazil to press for South American control over the Falkland Islands, Antarctica, and the eastern South Atlantic, which, according to author, belong to South America's natural "vital space."

Meza, Rubén Ariel. El triángulo de la opresión. See item **2970**.

3803 Miranda, Aníbal. Lucha armada en Paraguay. v. 1. Asunción: Miranda & Asociados, 1989- . 1 v: bibl., ill.

Polemic, but valuable study of the attempts by exile groups to invade Paraguay during the early 1960s. Describes Stroessner's repressive apparatus, and shows how the exiles' factionalism undermined their own efforts. Most interesting are the complex international maneuverings of Cuba, Argentina, Brazil, Venezuela, and the US in support of one side or the other.

3804 Palau Viladesau, Tomás. Tránsito a la democracia y hegemonía militar en el Paraguay. (in Propuestas políticas, comportamientos electorales y perspectivas de gobierno en el Cono Sur. Montevideo: OBSUR, 1991, p. 211–226)

Argues that while Paraguay's inexperienced peasantry look on with apathy, the "democratic transition" is being manipulated by an alliance consisting of international finance, the landed oligarchy, the armed forces, and the US Embassy. Somewhat dated. Does not discuss "Asunción Para Todos" nor the "Encuentro Nacional."

3805 Plate, Carlos F. Las fuerzas armadas y la democracia. Asunción: Editorial el Constitucionalista, 1994. 65 p.

Lengthy essay argues that the military should not interfere with politics. Interestingly, the author studied at West Point and the prologue was written by a general who served many years in Stroessner's cabinets.

3806 Rehren, Alfredo. Wasmosy frente al estado prebendario-clientelista: desafíos del liderazgo presidencial democrático. (Rev. Parag. Sociol., 31:90, mayo/agosto 1994, p. 147–168)

Evaluates the ability of democratically elected President Wasmosy to continue the democratic transition. Although the author of this work claims that Wasmosy has control over the armed forces, his hold on political authority seems tenuous. He is politically dependent on an alliance of military officers, Colorado politicians, and State contractors— a coalition that is nourished by the traditional one-party regime.

3807 La represión de las Ligas Agrarias Campesinas de Misiones: memorias, testimonies y comentarios. Asunción: Centro de Documentación y Estudios, 1993. 48 p.: photos, tables

Agrarian Leagues were cooperative communities sponsored by the Catholic Church during the 1970s. In April 1976 Stroessner, believing the Leagues were breeding grounds of peasant revolution, ordered soldiers to shut them down. This lengthy article uses interviews with survivors to show the military abused human rights.

3808 Riquelme, Marcial Antonio. Toward a Weberian characterization of the Stroessner regime in Paraguay: 1954–1989. (Rev. Eur., 57, Dec. 1994, p. 29–51, bibl., tables)

Reviews the taxonomic literature on comparative politics to find a suitable classification for the stronato, and concludes that it was a variation of "sultanism."

3809 Rivarola, Domingo M. Conservadurismo y cultura política en la transición. (Rev. Parag. Sociol., 31:90, mayo/agosto 1994, p. 231–249)

Paraguay has embarked on a gradual transition to democracy. Pace is slow because the economy is poor, middle class is weak, and culture is conservative. So far, intellectuals have failed to play any important role in this transition, mainly because they lack a secure foundation in society.

3810 Roa Bastos, Augusto. Política, poder y democracia en el Paraguay. (*Real. Econ./Buenos Aires*, 130, feb./marzo 1995, p. 100–108)

Paraguay's most celebrated author believes that only cultural and ethical changes can safegard against a return to tyranny.

3811 Schvartzman, Mauricio. Mito y duelo: el discurso de la "pre-transición" a la democracia en el Paraguay. Asunción: Base-IS, 1989. 157 p.: bibl.

"Myth" refers to the long-held belief among Stroessner's opposition that he would die in office and leave behind a power vacuum they could fill. However, his overthrow by another general left no vacuum. "Duel" refers to the struggle among parties and factions to influence Gen. Rodríguez. This study reveals that Paraguay still lacks a middle class strong enough to impose a liberal democracy. Based on public speeches by leading political figures, this book offers keen insights into Paraguay's political culture, which remain relevant even though Gen. Rodríguez has relinquished power to an elected civilian president.

3812 Trinidad Alderete, Paulo Rafael. El Stroessner desconocido: intimidades de su inmenso poder; testimonios anecdóticos. Asunción: Tall. Gráf. de la Rural Ediciones, 1993. 230 p.: ill.

Personal observation about Stroessner's personality, opinions, and governing style by a Colorado journalist who worked for a year in the presidential office. Not a laudatory biography, the book seeks to be objective. It reads like brief notes, perhaps from a diary, grouped under various subject headings. Fascinating reading, and certain not to please anyone in Paraguay.

3813 Valle Castillo, Miguelángel del. Así fue el golpe del 2 y 3 de febrero: caída de régimen; hechos y protagonistas reales. Asunción: Tall. Graf. San Nicolás, 1994? 243 p.: bibl., ill.

An analysis of the reasons Stroessner fell from power, and the initial steps taken afterwards to restore democracy. Highlight is description of the actual coup.

3814 Yaguareté. Nueva meditación sobre la identidad nacional: mediterraneidad, monarquía y república en el Paraguay. (*Cuad. Repub.*, 27, mayo 1995, p. 175–196)

Polemical essay "proving" that the Colorado Party is the only party in Paraguay that reflects the national culture.

3815 Zamorano, Carlos Mariano. Paraguay insurreccional del siglo XX. Buenos Aires: Editorial Sapucai, 1992. 129 p.: bibl., ill.

Short, superficial account of Paraguay's turbulent history since the Chaco War.

URUGUAY

3816 Achard, Diego. La transición en Uruguay. Montevideo: Ingenio en Servicios de Comunicación y Marketing, 1992. 440 p.: bibl.

Brief chronology of events related to the democratic transition, beginning with the 1980 constitutional plebescite. Includes interviews with eight leading figures involved in the process and a selection of previously unpublished documents.

3817 Barreiro, Fernando and **Anabel Cruz.** La dificultad de ser: organizaciones no gubernamentales en el Uruguay de hoy; el desafío de la democracia. Montevideo: Fundación de Cultura Universitaria; Instituto Latinoamericano de Estudios Transnacionales, Instituto de Comunicación y Desarrollo, 1988. 101 p.: bibl.

Authors perceive growth of nongovernmental organizations, such as those dealing with women, children, human rights, or the environment as special interests that pose a challenge to democratically elected authorities.

3818 Bottinelli, Oscar A. El sistema electoral uruguayo: descripción y análisis. Montevideo: PEITHO Sociedad de Análisis Político, 1991. 24 p.: tables. (Documento de Trabajo; 83)

Short and simple description of Uruguay's complicated electoral system. Proposes reform measures.

3819 Caetano, Gerardo. La partidocracia uruguaya: tradición y agenda reciente. (*Secuencia/México*, 32, mayo/agosto 1995, p. 103–134, bibl., ill.)

Uruguay's political system was long

characterized as a centralized, bureaucratic welfare state with a stable two-party system. This system began to break down in the mid-1950s as the economy slid into crisis. The military government further weakened the institutional order. Now the State is burdened by external pressure, and there are four parties competing for power.

3820 Caetano, Gerardo *et al.* Partidos y electores: centralidad y cambios. Montevideo: Centro Latinoamericano de Economía Humana; Ediciones de la Banda Oriental, 1992. 210 p.: bibl. (Col. Argumentos; 17)

Collection of short, easy-to-follow essays about Uruguay's party system, emphasizing the rise of nontraditional parties. Good introduction to the subject.

3821 Del PIT al PIT-CNT: ¿réquiem para el movimiento sindical? Montevideo: Instituto de Formación e Invetigación Sindical; Centro de Apoyo y Asesoramiento Sindical, 1991. 249 p.: bibl., ill.

Three authors associated with the trade unions describe their current deterioration in the face of privatization and free market reforms prompted in large part, by Mercosur.

3822 García Rey, José Manuel. Entrevista inédita a Wilson Ferreira Aldunate: la libertad electoral y el Partido Nacional. (*Cuad. Marcha*, 9:92, feb./marzo 1994, p. 25–30, ill.)

May 1985 interview with the now-deceased leader of the Blancos, while he was exiled in Madrid. Although this is the first time this interview has been published, it offers no surprises. Wilson took a straight nationalist line on foreign debt, relations with the US, and future of socialism in Uruguay.

3823 Gillespie, Charles Guy. State versus regime in the democratization of Uruguay. (*in* Democratization and the State in the Southern Cone: essays on South American politics. Edited by Benno Galjart and Patricio Silva. Amsterdam: CEDLA, 1989, p. 195–218, bibl., tables)

Includes a useful discussion of the recent military regime's failure to reform the policies that caused civilian rule to fail. Article demonstrates the military's inability to manage economic problems, in contrast to its ruthless application of political repression.

3824 González, Luis E. Continuity and change in the Uruguayan party system. (*in* Building democratic institutions: party systems in Latin America. Edited by Scott Mainwaring and Timothy R. Scully. Stanford, Calif.: Stanford Univ. Press, 1995, p. 138–163, tables)

The combination of proportional representation for both houses of Congress and the double simultaneous vote, in which voters first mark their preference for a party and then for one of its many lists, has caused great fractionalization. The two-party system before 1966 kept the problem within bounds, but the currrent four-party system makes it difficult for any party to govern.

3825 González, Luis Eduardo and **Charles Guy Gillespie.** Presidentialism and democratic stability in Uruguay. (*in* The failure of presidential democracy. Edited by Juan J. Linz and Arturo Valenzuela. Baltimore, Md.: Johns Hopkins Univ. Press, 1994, p. 225–252, bibl., tables)

Reviews Uruguay's many constitutions, with respect to legislative-execitive relations. Argues that the present constitution allows for an unusually powerful president in order to avoid stalemates that have arisen in past dictatorships.

3826 González Sierra, Yamandú. Continuidad y cambio en el movimiento sindical uruguayo: una perspectiva histórica de su problemática actual. Montevideo: Depto. de Asesoramiento Técnico Económico y Social, Centro Interdisciplinario de Estudios Sobre el Desarrollo-Uruguay, 1993. 98 p.: bibl., ill. (Cuadernos de información popular; 12)

Brief history of the Uruguayan trade union movement by a labor activist. Follows with an examination of the current crisis posed by the government's neoliberalism. Excellent chapter summarizes general trends undermining organized labor: more women in the workplace, the migration of industry out of Montevideo to the interior, and company downsizing and outsourcing. Offers few solutions, but urges a revitalization of the proletarian consciousness.

3827 Lanzaro, Jorge Luis. La *doble transición* en el Uruguay: gobierno de partidos y neo-presidencialismo. (*Nueva Soc.*, 128, nov./dic. 1993, p. 132–157, facsims.)

To deal with the double challenge of

restoring stable democracy and meeting challenges of the global economy, Uruguayans seem to be proceeding cautiously by streamlining the State, without relegating it to a secondary role.

3828 López-Alves, Fernando. Why not corporatism?: redemocratization and regime formation in Uruguay. (*in* Latin America in the 1940s: war and postwar transitions. Edited by David Rock. Berkeley: Univ. of California Press, 1994, p. 187–208)

Unlike its larger neighbors, Uruguay during the 1940s did not combine import substituting industrialization with corporativism or authoritarian government. The dominant Colorado Party did not attempt to destroy the labor movement or put it under State control. Yet, the decade's policies led to economic crisis and the collapse of democracy.

3829 Márquez Zacchino, Sergio. La revolución estafada: P.C.U y aparato armado; raportage a Elizardo Iglesias, ex integrante de la Cuarta Dirección del Partido Comunista del Uruguay. Montevideo: Ediciones de J. Darién; Vinten Editor, 1991. 100 p. (Col. Testimonios)

Lengthy interview with a young communist militant who was tortured and jailed by the military regime. He criticizes the old Communist party leadership for its ineptitude, and failing to prepare for the military's takeover.

3830 Mieres, Pablo. Venturas y desventuras de la izquierda uruguaya. (*Cuad. Marcha,* 9:90, dic. 1993, p. 27–30)

Good short discussion of Uruguay's contemporary left, the Frente Amplio and Nuevo Espacio. Despite various splits, the left is growing in popularity as a whole and may soon elect a national administration.

3831 El movimiento sindical en el Uruguay postdictatorial: los demonios, las máscaras y el espacio socialista. Montevideo: Instituto de Formación e Investigación Sindical; Centro de Apoyo y Asesoramiento Sindical, 1990. 153 p.: bibl.

Three essays by socialist supporters of the trade unions discuss how to revive the labor movement and "progressive thinking" in the face of a growing number of non-unionized workers, the rise of neoliberalism, the

challenge of technology, and the collapse of the Soviet bloc.

3832 Pallares, Laura and **Luis Stolovich.** Medios de comunicación masiva en el Uruguay: tecnología, poder y crisis. Montevideo: Centro Uruguay Independiente, 1991. 328 p.: bibl., ill., map. (Serie Los Poderosos; 5)

Authors are concerned about the power of Uruguay's capitalist media. They fear that a few large companies will control information sources and wield considerable influence over public opinion. Capitalists have also used technology to undermine the importance of labor unions.

3833 Pareja, Carlos; Martín Peixoto; and **Romeo Pérez Antón.** La alternativa parlamentarista. Montevideo: Centro Latinoamericano de Economía Humana; Ediciones de Ciencias Sociales, 1992. 172 p.: bibl.

Three Uruguayan political scientists explore pros and cons of a parliamentary system, as a way of making government more democratic and responsive.

3834 Pedoja Riet, Eduardo. Algunas causas que determinaron la derrota del Partido Nacional en 1966. (*Hoy Hist.,* 10:60, nov./dic. 1993, p. 34–38, photo)

Polemic against the Blanco Party government that ruled Uruguay from 1962–66. Argues that government leaders were unfaithful to traditional Blanco principles.

3835 Perelli, Carina and **Juan Rial.** Las elecciones uruguayas de noviembre de 1989. (*in* Una tarea inconclusa: elecciones y democracia en América Latina, 1988–1991. San José: Instituto Interamericano de Derechos Humanos, Centro de Asesoría y Promoción Electoral, 1992, p. 601–645, tables)

Very thorough examination of parties, personalities, factions, and issues influencing contemporary Uruguayan politics. The 1989 election is used as a starting point for examining voting trends and neoliberalism's impact on various issues. Essential essay for understanding this country's complicated political process.

3836 Perelli, Carina. The use of conservatism: women's democratic politics in Uruguay. (*in* The women's movement in Latin America: participation and democracy. Edited by Jane S. Jaquette. Boulder, Colo.: Westview Press, 1994, p. 131–149)

Uruguayan women, in their traditional roles as wives and mothers, used non-political tactics that helped create a favorable atmosphere for a return to democracy. Powerfully written and very insightful.

3837 Pereyra, Carlos Julio. La encrucijada nacional: poder civil, poder militar. Montevideo: Ediciones 504, 1988. 75 p.

Two speeches, from parliamentary records, of an Uruguayan senator. He opposed any amnesty for the leaders of the former military regime.

3838 Posadas, Juan Martín. Memorias del regreso: la vuelta de Wilson Ferreira al Uruguay. Montevideo: Editorial Fin de Siglo, 1993. 183 p. (Col. Uruguay XXI)

Personal recollections of resistance to military rule by a journalist and former senator for the National Party.

3839 Pucci, Francisco. Sindicatos y negociación colectiva, 1985–1989. Montevideo: CIESU, 1992. 135 p.: bibl.

Tied to the Frente Amplio, and especially to the Communist Party, Uruguay's leading labor federation has resisted recent government attempts to dismantle the old corporatist procedures that guided labor-management relations in favor of free collective bargaining.

3840 Puchet Anyul, Martín. Elecciones, cambios políticos y nuevos gobiernos en Uruguay. (Secuencia/México, 18, sept./dic. 1990, p. 203–228, graph, ill., tables)

Focusing on the 1989 elections, provides a good description of Uruguay's political factions and electoral laws.

3841 Rankin, Aidan. Reflections on the non-revolution in Uruguay. (New Left Rev., 211, May/June 1995, p. 131–143, table)

Lively description of the three-way struggle between Uruguay's two traditional parties and the leftist Frente Amplio, which has resulted in a deadlock between the national government and Montevideo's municipal government. So far, all of the principals have acted moderately by trying to preserve needed elements of the old welfare state, while also trying to adapt to the economic realities posed by neoliberalism.

Repression, exile, and democracy: Uruguayan culture. See item **5199**.

Riz, Liliana de and **Catalina Smulovitz.** Instauración democrática y reforma política en

Argentina y Uruguay: un análisis comparado. See item **3765**.

Roballo, Alba. Alba Roballo: pregón por el tiempo nuevo. See *HLAS 56:4150*.

3842 Rodríguez Larreta, Aureliano. El *plebiscito* municipal: una batalla romántica. (*Cuad. Marcha*, 9:87, sept. 1993, p. 42–45, bibl.)

The fact that the leftist Frente Amplio controls the city government of Montevideo, while the traditional parties control the other levels of government, leads to all sorts of constitutional confrontations. This article focuses on the issue of taxation, which is the real test of municipal autonomy.

3843 Roelofse-Campbell, Zélia. Redemocratization and amnesty in Uruguay: an interview with Alfonse Lessa. (*UNISA Lat. Am. Rep.*, 9:2, 1993, p. 39–41, photo)

Interview with an Uruguayan newspaper editor offers interesting insights into the plebescites on privatization and amnesty for the military chiefs.

3844 Sierra, Gerónimo de. Dictadura y restauración democrática en el Uruguay contemporáneo: límites y desafíos. (*in* La democracia en América Latina: actualidad y perspectivas. Coordinación de Pablo González Casanova y Marcos Roitman Rosenmann. Madrid: Univ. Complutense de Madrid; México: Centro de Investigaciones Interdisciplinarias en Humanidades, UNAM, 1992, p. 141–166, bibl.)

Interpretive essay by a Marxist about the decomposition of "bourgeois capitalist hegemony" in Uruguay. The author thinks that dependent capitalism is finished and that Uruguayans must choose between imperialistic neo-liberalism or socialism.

3845 Sierra, Gerónimo de. Elecciones uruguayas: cambios en el sistema de partidos y bloqueos emergentes. Montevideo: Centro Interdisciplinario de Estudios Sobre el Desarrollo (CIEDUR), 1994. 10 p.: tables.

A Marxist celebrates the forward progress of the Frente Amplio and looks forward to the day when the left will take control of the national government in addition to the city of Montevideo.

3846 Sierra, Gerónimo de. Reforma do Estado, modelos neoliberais e suas implicações para a democracia: o caso Uruguaio.

(*Cont. Int.*, 14:2, julho/dez. 1992, p. 241–267)

Offers a Marxist analysis of neoliberalism's impact on Latin America generally, and on Uruguayan democracy in particular. Suggests that international finance, in league with local business and agrarian elites, is working its evil will on "the People."

3847 Varela, Gonzalo. Rasgos de la permanencia de los partidos políticos uruguayos. (*Secuencia/México*, 32, mayo/agosto 1995, p. 135–141, bibl.)

Political parties traditionally have played an important role in Uruguayan politics, even more than pressure groups have. But now, given the exended economic crisis, the two traditional parties are losing their followers because they no longer have enough patronage to pass out.

3848 Villarreal, Nelson. La izquierda en Uruguay: impactos y reformulaciones, 1989–1992. Montevideo: Observatorio del Sur, 1992. 49 p.

A bibliography of books, documents, newspaper stories, and magazine articles published in Uruguay about the collapse of the USSR and its impact on the local left.

3849 Villarreal, Nelson. Neoconservadurismo y neoliberalismo, un intento de reformulación del capitalismo: consolidación y freno en Uruguay. 2a. ed. Montevideo: Observatorio del Sur, 1993. 74 p. (Transformaciones de fin de siglo; 2)

Written from a social Catholic viewpoint, this is a balanced but critical discussion of neoliberism's proponents, assumptions, and shortcomings as well as the reason for its current ascendancy.

BRAZIL

TIMOTHY J. POWER, *Assistant Professor of Political Science, Florida International University*

ON MARCH 15, 1995, Brazilian democracy celebrated its tenth birthday, and the consensus of observers was that the mid-1990s were crucial years for the country. The end of military rule in 1985 had led to widespread hopes for a stable democracy combined with economic growth and development, but the first eight years of the New Republic proved to be a roller-coaster ride of dashed expectations. An understanding of the convulsive nature of political and economic change during this first decade of civilian rule, the issues at stake, and the important events of the mid-1990s will clarify the choice of topics evident in recent scholarly literature on Brazilian government and politics.

The government of President José Sarney (1985–90) presided over an extended period of hyper-inflationary stagnation punctuated by major political battles—the most notable occurring during the National Constituent Assembly of 1987–88, which produced the country's current constitution. Although praised for its political inclusiveness, the constitution was widely criticized for its statist orientation at a time when most other countries were moving toward economic liberalization. President Fernando Collor de Mello came to power in 1990 promising to reorient Brazilian development away from State interventionism and toward market reliance. However, Collor's neoliberal reform policies failed to survive when the charismatic young populist fell from grace in a corruption scheme and subsequent impeachment in 1992. Neither Collor nor Sarney made much headway against Brazil's traditional nemesis, inflation, and their principal legacy was a parade of failed stabilization plans. Both presidents were handicapped by the weakness of the country's political institutions, particularly the party system and the national legislature, which made coalition building difficult.

Collor's vice president, Itamar Franco, took office in late 1992, and appeared initially to preside only over Brazil's economic and institutional paralysis. Early 1993 brought the darkest moments of Brazilian democracy to date, as analysts began to speak of a crisis of governability, and the media aired rumors of an impending military intervention. However, as the economy slowly revived from the Collor-induced recession, Franco made a fateful decision. In April 1993, he chose Fernando Henrique Cardoso as his Finance Minister. Cardoso, one of the region's most influential social scientists in the 1960s-70s, had become a widely respected senator in the 1980s. While in the Finance portfolio, Cardoso used his considerable negotiating skills to implement a new economic plan based on fiscal adjustment and the gradual introduction of a new currency (Brazil's sixth since 1985), the Real. Introducing the Plano Real in July 1994 was a turning point for a nation exhausted by a decade of economic failures. With the strong currency, inflation fell to near zero while a spending boom reignited the economy. Cardoso rode the Plan to a spectacular victory in the presidential elections of October 1994.

The success of the Real permitted Cardoso to construct a broad coalition, and in 1995–96, his government became the first in the new democracy to have widespread backing in both Congress and among the general public. By now far from his Marxist origins, Cardoso used his mandate to revive and accelerate the neoliberal adjustment initiated by Collor. By 1997, the similarity of the macroeconomic policies of these two presidents had been widely noted, and academic debate focused on the historical implications of this fact. There was no longer any doubt about the significance of the 1990s: Brazil was now abandoning the State-led development model that had prevailed since the 1930s in favor of the market orientation now dominant in Latin America. The buzzwords of Brazilian politics in the mid-1990s were liberalization, privatization, fiscal adjustment, neoliberalism, and globalization. As in neighboring countries, the shift in the development model was contested vigorously by the political left, public employees, and various rent-seeking social forces weaned on the developmentalist State. To achieve his economic reform goals, Cardoso began in 1995 to propose major amendments to the seven-year old constitution; his efforts provided Brazilian politicians with a daily source of debate and political action. As with previous presidents, Cardoso faced the difficulty of keeping his governing coalition intact in an environment of weak political institutions. Although the economy became somewhat more predictable and manageable in mid-decade, the polity did not follow suit.

If the foregoing is a reasonably accurate description of Brazil's recent travails, then the scholarly literature on Brazilian politics should logically parallel some of the concerns and issues raised in the turbulent 1990s. At first glance, the literature reviewed for *HLAS 57* appears exceedingly diverse. The largest group of contributions are studies of parties and elections. In second place are the general appraisals of the regime—either of democracy or the development model, but usually both together. In third place an ironic tie is found between the military and the organized left (the socialist Partido dos Trabalhadores, the two Communist or post-Communist parties, and the labor federations in their orbit). Other topics represented here include: social movements, human rights, and environmental activism; corruption and the Collorgate scandal of 1992; political economy studies of structural adjustment and/or State reform; and organized religion. The remaining contributions reviewed for this edition concern the 1993 plebiscite on parliamentary rule and the restoration of the monarchy, political elites, the National Congress, biographical studies, subnational and regional politics, and gender.

Much of the scholarly literature is devoted to three large clusters of topics. The first is political institutions, here broadly understood to include the party system, the electoral system, and the national legislature. The poor performance of Brazilian democracy in the late 1980s and early 1990s has frequently been traced to various deficiencies of these institutional arenas. The party system has been criticized as weak, fragmented, and incoherent; the national legislature has been portrayed as disorganized and inefficient; and the electoral system has been blamed for contributing to the foregoing weaknesses of parties and Congress. Moreover, the presidential system of government itself has been subject to withering academic attacks (the plebiscite held on April 21, 1993, in which Brazilian voters chose overwhelmingly to maintain presidentialism and reject parliamentary government, does not seem to have closed this debate). On the party system, the essay by Mainwaring is a lucid and penetrating discussion of the problem of weak parties (item **3915**); the book-length studies by Kinzo (item **3901**) and Nicolau (item **3932**) are less theoretical but are also valuable. The behavioral study by Limongi and Figueiredo challenges the conventional wisdom that Brazilian parties lack discipline (item **3913**), setting the stage for a vigorous debate over the proper characterization of the post-1985 party environment. On the topic of the National Congress, Ames' sophisticated study is a huge step forward in understanding legislative voting (item **3853**). On elections, there are numerous case studies of individual contests, especially the 1989 and 1994 presidential races. Dimenstein and Souza provide an excellent journalistic account of Cardoso's victory in 1994 (item **3870**). This and several other contributions reveal the recent "Americanization" of electoral campaigns in Brazil, as candidates rely increasingly on fund-raising, television access, marketing and focus groups, and the advice of professional political consultants.

The second group of contributions concerns progressive political and social movements. Over the past fifteen years, this category—including works on the Partido dos Trabalhadores (PT), organized labor, social movements, human rights organizations, environmental movements, the progressive wing of the Catholic Church, and other groups seeking social and political change—has consistently been one of the largest sources of scholarly output, as Brazilian and Brazilianist social scientists typically sympathize with the left. But there is also a practical reason for studying these groups. Progressive actors constitute a large part of Brazilian civil society, which has acquired unprecedented complexity, density and dynamism over the past decade. As argued by Viola and Nickel, progressive groups share a common interest in securing citizenship rights and the rule of law in Brazil because in the absence of these fundamental guarantees, progressive legislation has little meaning (item **3968**). A sobering report by the Univ. de São Paulo's pioneering center for the study of social violence shows how much farther Brazil must go in securing basic human rights (item **3872**). Human rights groups remain one of the few sources of knowledge about the urban settlements known as favelas, but Gay's comparative study breaks new ground in this area (item **3890**). Among recent contributions on the progressive Catholic Church, Hewitt's panel study of urban base communities is the most sophisticated (item **3894**). Turning to another largely urban actor, organized labor, the recent publications of Armando Boito Jr. provocatively revise earlier, more optimistic analyses of the *novo sindicalismo* of the late 1970s and early 1980s. The political party that emerged simultaneously with the *novo sindicalismo*, the PT, continues to expand its influence in the 1990s and is the subject of several contributions. Brazil's environmental movements are attracting increasing attention; the story of the rubber tappers of Acre is reviewed in Revkin's vivid biography of the late Chico Mendes (item **3947**) and in Keck's interpretive essay (item **3900**). Finally, after a long drought in which Brazilian agrarian movements were ignored by North American social science, the complementary books by Maybury-Lewis (item **3920**) and Pereira (item **3942**) break new ground in the study of rural workers.

The third broad group of contributions encompasses general appraisals of the political regime and the model of development. Although these are analytically distinguishable, many appraisals treat both economy and polity simultaneously as they review Brazil's trajectory since 1985. Within this group, two contributions are noteworthy. One is the felicitously conceived volume by Sola and Paulani, who, rather than chase the moving target of the 1990s, edited a retrospective review of the lessons of the turbulent 1980s (item **3909**). The other is Mainwaring's comparative essay on the political economy of democracy in the Southern Cone (item **2965**), which places the Brazilian experience in comparative perspective with Argentina, Uruguay, and Chile. As Cardoso pursues his reform agenda, his efforts will inspire even more spirited debate about neoliberalism and its social, political, and economic impacts. In coming years we can expect sustained academic attention to the public-private mix (State ownership versus privatization) and to the foreign-national mix (economic nationalism versus liberalization) in the politics of Brazilian economic development, especially in the form of sectoral and actor-oriented case studies. We can also expect more attention to the issue of State capacity, as in the recent work of Weyland (item **3970**). Clearly the advent of the neoliberal "revolution" is injecting new energy into comparative political economy approaches to Brazilian politics.

These three broad categories of research—political institutions, progressive movements and civil society, and the political economy of democracy and development—account for more than two thirds of all the citations to follow. A few observations are in order about the remaining literature. The Brazilian military continues to attract significant scholarly attention more than a decade after it withdrew from power. Most work on the military in the late 1980s and early 1990s stressed the continuation of military power and prerogatives, but recent research by Wendy Hunter disputes these earlier claims. In two provocative contributions (items **3897** and **3896**), Hunter argues instead that the logic of competitive democracy eroded military influence in important ways, and her unexpected findings are sure to spark further debate about civil-military relations in post-authoritarian regimes. As for remaining contributions reviewed this year, among the most noteworthy are Moises' impressive study of mass political culture in Brazil (item **3925**) and Leoni's fawning but still informative biography of Cardoso (item **3908**). The most outstanding recent contribution on Brazilian politics is Hagopian's beautifully written analysis of sub-national politics in Minas Gerais and its relationship to regime change (item **3893**).

No essay on the scholarly literature would be complete without suggestions for further research. First, the preoccupation with progressive actors is understandable, yet it must be balanced with sufficient attention to the political and social forces that tend to retard, not advance, social change in Brazil. Very little is known about rural elites, conservative parties and politicians, or right-wing pressure groups and social movements. Literature on the organization of the working class as traditionally defined abounds, but a useful study of white-collar unionism is lacking. There is a privileged stratum of middle-class public employees in Brazil whose interests are threatened by the changing role of the State and who are increasingly politically active, but about whom little is known. Third, the post-1988 administrative and fiscal decentralization has generated new patterns of political interaction, both in the relationship between the states and the federal government and within the internal politics of the states. The revolution in the federal structure of Brazil has important implications for political and economic development, but this revolution has not yet been the subject of systematic analysis. Any one of these topics would make an excellent doctoral dissertation. In a political system as rich and fascinating as Brazil's there is always room for further analysis, as both domestic and foreign observers will attest.

3850 Adriance, Madeleine. Base communities and rural mobilization in northern Brazil. (*in* Religion and democracy in Latin America. New Brunswick, N.J.: Transaction Publishers, 1994, p. 59–74, bibl.)

Stimulating study of grassroots Catholic groups (*Comunidades Eclesiais de Base*—CEBs), the Comissão Pastoral da Terra, and agrarian activism in the eastern Amazon region. Contradicts recent scholarship on religion and politics by claiming that CEBs are not in decline and that their success rests on commitment from local clergy rather than on support from bishops.

3851 Allen, Elizabeth. Calha Norte: military development in Brazilian Amazonia. (*in* Science, development and environment in Brazil: experiences and options for the future. Stockholm: Institute of Latin American Studies, Stockholm Univ., 1995, p. 197–226, bibl.)

Informative and well-researched overview of the military's pet project for the "development" of the northernmost reaches of Amazonia. Places military involvement in Amazon region in historical perspective. This excellent introduction to the social and political geography of the northern frontier is accessible to nonspecialists. See also item **3889.**

3852 Alvarez, Sonia E. The (trans)formation of feminism(s) and gender politics in democratizing Brazil. (*in* The women's movement in Latin America: participation and democracy. Edited by Jane S. Jaquette. Boulder, Colo.: Westview Press, 1994, p. 13–63)

Excellent overview examines relationship of feminist groups to the State. Popular oppositionist feminism in the 1970s was undercut by selective State incentives in the 1980s. The "professionalization" of feminism into pressure-group or NGO structures in the 1990s presents both opportunities and dangers. Author is thoroughly conversant with the movement, its main protagonists, and appropriate theories.

Amazônia: desenvolvimento ou retrocesso. See item **4466.**

3853 Ames, Barry. Electoral rules, constituency pressures, and pork barrel: bases of voting in the Brazilian Congress. (*J. Polit.*, 57:2, May 1995, p. 324–343, bibl., maps, tables)

Most sophisticated analysis to date of legislative voting in Brazil. Federal deputies are motivated by ideology, the necessity of reelection, the nature of their personal electorate, and their hunger for "pork." Presidential pork-barrel inducements are highly effective, and open-list proportional representation works against legislative accountability. These factors produce a congress largely unconcerned with policy matters. Recommended.

3854 Avelar, Lúcia. Mudanças estruturais, crise política e eleições. (*São Paulo Perspect.*, 8:2, abril/junho 1994, p. 53–60, tables)

Brief and practical introduction to political change in 1990s. Concludes that social and economic change are weakening domination by traditional elites.

3855 Benevides, Maria Victoria de Mesquita. A cidadania ativa: referendo, plebiscito e inciativa popular. São Paulo: Editora Ática, 1991. 208 p.: bibl. (Ensaios; 136)

Critique of representative democracy proposes the deepening of "semidirect" democracy in Brazil, with greater emphasis on referenda, plebiscites, and the people's right to initiate legislation. Good comparative references on these topics.

3856 Boito Júnior, Armando. De volta para o novo corporativismo: a trajetória política do sindicalismo brasileiro. (*São Paulo Perspect.*, 8:3, julho/set. 1994, p. 23–28, bibl.)

Provocative critique of the "neocorporatism" associated with the Central Única dos Trabalhadores (CUT). The "new unionism" of late 1970s was confrontational and offensive, but became defensive by late 1980s–early 1990s. This newly defensive stance led to internal fragmentation, and caused segments of organized labor to fall back on archaic institutions and methods dating from the populist era.

3857 Boito Júnior, Armando. O sindicalismo de Estado no Brasil: uma análise crítica da estrutura sindical. São Paulo: Editora Hucitec; Campinas, Brazil: Editora da Unicamp, 1991. 312 p.: (Estudos brasileiros; 28)

Critique of State-sponsored unionism in Brazil is grounded in solid historical research and inspired by revisionist Marxist approaches to ideology and State autonomy. Author concludes that six decades of tutelary unionism limited and fragmented the workers' movement.

3858 Boito Júnior, Armando. The State and trade unionism in Brazil. (*Lat. Am. Perspect.*, 21:1, Winter 1994, p. 7–23, bibl.)

Labor populism has largely faded as a political phenomenon, but its antidemocratic union structures persist. The Partido dos Trabalhadores (PT) and the Central Única dos Trabalhadores (CUT) energetically attack populist trade unionism but have failed to push for removal of its antidemocratic structures and to liberate themselves from the legacy of *peleguismo* (domination by co-opted union bosses). Provocative and well argued.

3859 Brazil. Congresso Nacional. Comissão Parlamentar Mista de Inquérito. Relatório final. Brasília: Centro Gráfico do Senado Federal, 1992. 369 p.

The final report of the 1992 congressional investigation into the Collorgate scandal that resulted in the indictment of Paulo César Farias and the impeachment of Fernando Collor de Mello.

3860 Broué, Pierre. Quand le peuple révoque le président: le Brésil de l'affaire Collor. Préface de Luis Favre. Annexe de Luis Inacio "Lula" da Silva. Paris: L'Harmattan, 1993. 171 p.: index. (Conjonctures politiques; 1)

Day-by-day chronology of "Collorgate" by a French Marxist historian who was visiting Brazil at the time. Useful for reconstructing the events.

3861 Campos, Roberto de Oliveira. Reflexões do crepúsculo. Rio de Janeiro: Topbooks, 1991. 262 p.: bibl., index.

Essays and speeches from the economist, congressman, and hard-line apostle of the free market system offer a critical right-wing view of the early Collor period. Author defends minority view that Collor was a timid and cautious neoliberal who did not move fast enough to reform Brazil's economy.

3862 Carone, Edgard. Da esquerda à direita. Belo Horizonte, Brazil: Oficina de Livros, 1991. 230 p.: bibl. (Col. Nossa terra)

Wide-ranging collection of essays covers history of ideology in Brazil—left, right, and center. Gives special attention to the Partido Comunista do Brasil in early 20th century.

3863 Cavendish, James C. Christian base communities and the building of democracy: Brazil and Chile. (*in* Religion and democracy in Latin America. New Brunswick, N.J.: Transaction Publishers, 1994, p. 75–91, bibl.)

Speculative treatment of the role of Christian base communities in democratic consolidation in the two countries suggests that while political activism may have declined following the transition to democracy, the communities remain valuable in transmitting democratic values to the wider population. Acknowledges that conclusions are tentative due to scarcity of empirical studies.

3864 Chaia, Vera Lúcia Michalany. A liderança política de Jânio Quadros, 1947–1990. Ibitinga, Brazil: Humanidades, 1992. 320 p.: bibl.

Well-researched overview of Jânio's career, from city councilman in 1947, to President in 1960, to mayor of São Paulo from 1985–88. Mostly descriptive, but nevertheless a valuable study of one of the most interesting public figures and most potent political machines of postwar Brazil.

Conference on Improving Prison Conditions in the Caribbean, *Port-of-Spain, 1991.* Improving prison conditions in the Caribbean. See item **3242.**

3865 Corporativismo e desigualdade: a construção do espaço público no Brasil. Organização de Renato Raul Boschi. Rio de Janeiro: IUPERJ; Rio Fundo Editora, 1991. 146 p.: bibl.

Distinguished social scientists present a collection of short essays on public and private power and on the notion of republican ethics in Brazil.

3866 Costa, Caio Túlio. O relógio de Pascal: a experiência do primeiro ombudsman da imprensa brasileira. São Paulo: Edições Siciliano, 1991. 263 p.

Diary of the first ombudsman (1989–91) at *Folha de São Paulo*, whose tenure coincided with a period in which the *Folha* was emerging as arguably the most politically influential newspaper in Brazil. Presents a fruitful study of journalistic ethics and the relationship between media and politics.

3867 A CUT e o movimento sindical internacional. v. 1–2. São Paulo: CEDI, 1991. 2 v.

Presents essays, interviews, and documents of the debate within the Central Única dos Trabalhadores over its proper relationship with the international labor federations. Helpful for understanding internal conflicts about independence versus solidarity.

3868 Dados biográficos dos presidentes do Senado Federal, 1826–1993. 3a. ed. Brasília: Senado Federal, Subsecretaria de Edições Técnicas, 1991. 90 p.: ill.

Includes short biographies and portraits or photographs of all Senate presidents through 1993. Excellent reference for historical research on Congress and politicians.

3869 A democracia como proposta. Rio de Janeiro: IBASE, 1991. 126 p.: bibl. (Col. Democracia; 1)

Collection of essays by progressive intellectuals who propose new concepts of democracy emphasizes social participation and policy alternatives to current wave of neoliberalism.

3870 Dimenstein, Gilberto and Josias de Souza. A história real: trama de uma sucessão. 2a. ed. São Paulo: Editora Ática; Folha de São Paulo, 1994. 242 p.: ill.

Tremendously engrossing account of the 1994 presidential campaign is written by two of Brazil's best political journalists in *The*

making of the president tradition. Authors had excellent inside access to Cardoso and Lula campaigns. Documents importance of the Plano Real to Cardoso's eventual victory. See also item **3964.**

3871 Diniz, Eugénio. Estratégia, informação e defesa nacional: entrevista do Almirante Mário César Flores a Eugénio Diniz. (*Novos Estud. CEBRAP*, 39, julho 1994, p. 115–132)

Flores is a former Navy Minister, and headed the Secretaria de Assuntos Estratégicos (SAE, formerly the Serviço Nacional de Informações—SNI). In this wide-ranging 1994 interview, he faces direct and provocative questions about the intelligence community, strategic planning, and the role of the armed forces in politics. Provides valuable insight into military thought.

3872 Os direitos humanos no Brasil. São Paulo: NEV; CTV, 1993. 107 p.: bibl., ill.

Wide-ranging report by the Univ. de São Paulo's pathbreaking, dynamic, and non-partisan Núcleo de Estudos da Violência covers crime, police violence, child abuse, neo-Nazism, and the death penalty. Documents Brazil's legal obligations in all of these areas. Sobering account but necessary to digest. Recommended.

3873 Draibe, Sônia Miriam. Etat de bien-être, inégalite et pauvreté au Brésil: les dilemmes actuels. (*Cah. Am. lat.*, 15, 1993, p. 73–87, bibl., tables)

Review of social policies effected since the 1930s emphasizes persistent regional inequalities. Social indicators reveal that, although much progress has been made, much remains to be achieved offers basic introduction to inequality and the welfare state.

3874 Economia e política da crise brasileira: a perspectiva social-democrata. Organização de Maurício Dias David. Apresentação de Hélio Jaguaribe. Rio de Janeiro: Rio Fundo Editora, 1991. 228 p.: bibl

Presents collection of essays by politicians and academics connected to the Partido da Social Democracia Brasileira (PSDB). Most of the PSDB luminaries are represented, as are politicians from Spanish and German socialist parties. Helpful for understanding PSDB's thought in its early years, before it came to power under Franco and Cardoso.

3875 As elites brasileiras e a modernização do setor público: um debate. Organização de Amaury de Sousa e Bolivar Lamounier. São Paulo: IDESP, Editora Sumaré, 1992? 61 p. (Série Seminários e debates; 0103-9539)

Interesting two-part report on State reform in Brazil provides results of survey of elite attitudes toward public sector performance, and presents a roundtable debate concerning the issues raised.

3876 Erundina, uma razão. São Paulo?: MPM/LINTAS; Assessoria de Impr. do Gabinete da Prefeita, 1991. 159 p.: ill.

Produced by the press office of the city government of São Paulo during the administration of Luiza Erundina de Souza of the Partido dos Trabalhadores, book documents the tenure of a Marxist woman at the helm of Latin America's industrial powerhouse. Although clearly a public relations effort, fruitful for the study of this crucial experiment in governance.

3877 A esquerda e o movimento operário, 1964-1984. v. 3, A reconstrução, 1964-1984. Organização de Celso Frederico. Belo Horizonte, Brazil: Oficina de Livros, 1991. 1 v.: index. (Nossa Terra)

Invaluable source for study of labor politics under military rule and during transition to democracy in early 1980s. Contains press clippings, manifestos, debates, and essays that reconstruct the transformations and internal debates of the union movement.

3878 Fernandes, Florestan. A transição prolongada: o período pós-constitucional. São Paulo: Cortez Editora, 1990. 239 p. (Biblioteca da educação. Série 2, Economía política; 2)

Collection of newspaper columns by the late Marxist sociologist cover period from the Assembléia Nacional Constituinte of 1987-88 to the inauguration of Collor in 1990. Valuable for a radical-left perspective of a crucial period of economic decline and impending presidential elections.

3879 Fernandes, Luis. Muito barulho por nada?: o realinhamento político-ideológico nas eleições de 1994. (*Dados/Rio de Janeiro*, 38:1, 1995, p. 107-144, appendices, bibl., graphs, tables)

Exhaustive analysis of 1994 elections includes presidential, congressional, gubernatorial, and state legislative results. Concludes

that 1994 saw a reconstitution of the political center (now with a center-right axis based on alliance of the Partido da Social Democracia Brasileira and the Partido da Frente Liberal), and that the left must also seek alliances if it is to have a chance at governing. Includes a wealth of electoral data.

3880 Figueiredo, Marcus. Volatilidade eleitoral em eleições parlamentares, 1950-1978. (*Opin. Públ.*, 3:3, dez. 1995, p. 97-127, bibl., tables)

A short introduction to the concept of electoral volatility includes a brief application to state-level election results in the 1950-62 and 1966-78 periods. The earlier period showed vote swings away from conservative parties, but trend was slowed by authoritarian manipulation of elections in the 1970s.

3881 Figueiredo, Rubens. Opinião pública, intencionalidade e voto. (*Opin. Públ.*, 2:2, dez. 1994, p. 73-82, graphs, tables)

Discussion of public opinion during 1994 presidential race is written by a political consultant. Survey data and focus groups identified some key characteristics sought by voters in their candidate. Sheds light on growing sophistication of political marketing in Brazil.

3882 Font, Mauricio A.; J. Timmons Roberts; and Katherine Ellison. Crisis and election: Brazil. (*Hemisphere/Miami*, 6:1, Winter/Spring 1994, p. 20-32, graph, photos)

Three brief articles on challenges facing Brazil during the transition to the Cardoso government include examinations of macroeconomic and environmental policy and a biography of Cardoso. Useful for nonspecialists.

3883 Formiga, Marcone. A república dos deslumbrados. São Paulo: Editora Brasiliense, 1992. 144 p.

A journalist's satirical yet insightful essays on the members of the Collor administration (1990-92) serve as a description of life in Brasília during the "República de Alagoas."

3884 Fórum Nacional Como Evitar uma Nova Década Perdida, *Rio de Janeiro*, 1991. O Brasil e as reformas políticas. Coordenação de João Paulo dos Reis Velloso. Rio de Janeiro: J. Olympio Editora, 1992. 135 p.: bibl.

Includes transcripts of symposium held by the Fórum Nacional in 1991. Several prominent political scientists and legislators discuss need for reform of democratic institutions. See also item **3885.**

3885 Fórum Nacional Idéias para a Modernização do Brasil, *Rio de Janeiro, 1988.* O leviatã ferido: a reforma do Estado brasileiro. Coordenação de João Paulo dos Reis Velloso. Rio de Janeiro: J. Olympio Editora, 1991. 139 p.: bibl., ill.

Symposium addresses need for modernizing public sector. Contains ideas of several prominent economists and political scientists. See also item **3884.**

3886 Franco, Tasso. O círculo do poder na Bahia. Salvador, Brazil: FPE, 1990? 375 p.: ill.

Using 1962 and 1986 gubernatorial races as case studies, describes various political machines and clans that have dominated Bahia in recent decades. Excellent road map for the labyrinth that is Bahia state politics.

3887 Freitas, Tiziana Severi; Paulo José Barbosa; and Tania Nobre Gonçalves Ferreira Amorim. Retórica, poder de decisão e grupos de pesquisa no Nordeste do Brasil. Recife, Brazil: Editora Universitária UFPE, 1993? 130 p.: bibl., ill. (Série Teses universitárias)

Serious and well-researched collaborative effort to reconstruct recent public policy decision-making in the Northeast focuses on three case studies: sugar-cane alcohol, petrochemicals, and aid to small rural producers.

3888 O futuro do Congresso brasileiro. Organização de Alzira Alves de Abreu e José Luciano de Mattos Dias. Rio de Janeiro: Fundação Getulio Vargas Editora, 1995. 185 p.

Collection of papers from a 1994 symposium on Congress includes addresses by legislators, political scientists, staff members, and lobbyists. Offers wide-ranging overview of deficiencies in the Congresso Nacional.

3889 Garrido, Luiz Fernando Azevedo. A presença militar brasileira na Amazônia como fator de dissuasão. (*Def. Nac.,* 770, out./dez. 1995, p. 93–117, bibl.)

An army major reviews most issues that have attracted foreign attention to the Amazon Basin. Criticizes international environmentalists, defenders of indigenous rights, and proponents of a "New World Order," who

are seen as interfering in the Amazon. As lead article in the most influential army publication, provides valuable insight into military thinking about the region. See also item **3851.**

3890 Gay, Robert. Popular organization and democracy in Rio de Janeiro: a tale of two favelas. Philadelphia, Pa.: Temple Univ. Press, 1994. 191 p.: bibl., ill., index, maps.

Compares two *favelas* in greater Rio de Janeiro, one based on clientelistic politics and the other on community activism. Using solid fieldwork, this profitable study of traditional politics and emerging political challenges is an excellent example of an interdisciplinary approach to the study of popular sectors.

3891 Genoino Neto, José. Repensando o socialismo: entrevista a Mauro Lopes. São Paulo: Editora Brasiliense, 1991. 63 p.

Transcript of lengthy interview with a fascinating figure in the Partido dos Trabalhadores (PT), a former guerrilla fighter who later became a master parliamentarian and leader of the PT's pragmatic wing. Genoino's case is essential for understanding the evolution of the left and new debates within socialism.

3892 Grau, Eros Roberto and **Luiz Gonzaga de Melo Belluzzo.** A corrupção no Brasil. (*Rev. Bras. Estud. Polít.,* 80, jan. 1995, p. 7–20)

Explores lack of republican tradition in Brazil. Impunity of elites and the toleration of corruption, leading inexorably to episodes like the Collor affair, are the effects of this political/cultural pattern. Provides little original information or analysis.

3893 Hagopian, Frances. Traditional politics and regime change in Brazil. Cambridge; New York: Cambridge Univ. Press, 1996. 317 p.: bibl., ill., index. (Cambridge studies in comparative politics)

Landmark study draws connections between subnational politics and macropolitical change in Brazil. Uses case study of Minas Gerais state to show persistence of traditional patronage politics under military rule and its repercussions in the subsequent democratic transition. Theoretically rich and cogently presented; a major contribution on Brazilian politics. Recommended.

3894 Hewitt, W.E. Religion and the consolidation of democracy in Brazil: the role of the *Comunidades Eclesiais de Base.* (*in* Religion and democracy in Latin America. New Brunswick, N.J.: Transaction Publishers, 1994, p. 45–58, bibl., tables)

Careful panel study of São Paulo *Comunidades Eclesiais de Base (CEB)* in 1984 and 1988 reveals a decline in community action function of CEBs, partially explained by weakening institutional support from the Church. With CEBs focusing more on winning legitimacy as mini-parishes, their external political salience is diminished. Strong methodology; excellent literature review.

3895 Hoge, James F. Fulfilling Brazil's promise: a conversation with President Cardoso. (*Foreign Aff.*, 74:4, July/Aug. 1995, p. 62–75, photo)

Interview granted by President Cardoso to editor of *Foreign Affairs* in April 1995 focuses mainly on economic policy, antipoverty measures, and US/Brazil relations. Essential for understanding transformation of Cardoso's political thought.

3896 Hunter, Wendy. Eroding military influence in Brazil: politicians against soldiers. Chapel Hill: Univ. of North Carolina Press, 1997. 243 p.: bibl., ill., index.

Major reconsideration of civil-military relations in post-authoritarian Brazil uses case studies of labor rights, federal budgeting, and control over Amazonia to argue that logic of competitive politics allowed civilian politicians to gradually erode military influence. Well researched and documented.

3897 Hunter, Wendy. Politicians against soldiers: contesting the military in post-authoritarian Brazil. (*Comp. Polit.*, 27:4, July 1995, p. 425–443, graph)

Disputes claim that transition to democracy left military power and prerogatives intact. Shows that logic of competition unleashed by political democracy positioned politicians against the military in a struggle for State resources, which has led to a significant erosion in the position of the armed forces. Theoretically elegant. Recommended.

3898 A Igreja e o exercício do poder. Organização de Maria Helena Arrochellas. 2. ed. Rio de Janeiro: Instituto de Estudos da Religião; Petrópolis, Brazil: Centro Alceu Amoroso Lima para a Liberdade, 1992. 187 p.: bibl., ill. (Cadernos do ISER; 26)

Contains collection of essays on recent changes within the Catholic Church written by intellectuals close to its progressive wing. Illustrates growing rift between the Vatican and the Catholic left in Brazil.

3899 Kasa, Sjur. Environmental reforms in Brazilian Amazonia under Sarney and Collor: explaining some contrasts. (*Ibero-Am./Stockholm*, 24:2, 1994, p. 42–63, bibl.)

Important article details contrasts in environmental policy under Sarney and Collor as a result of fundamentally different domestic political strategies. Valuable corrective to development theories that ignore national executives as independent actors.

3900 Keck, Margaret. Social equity and environmental politics in Brazil: lessons from the rubber tappers of Acre. (*Comp. Polit.*, 27:4, July 1995, p. 409–424)

The "Acre Story" represented an alliance between forest peoples and international environmentalists, in which the former were successfully able to shift their struggle from the local context to the more favorable international context. Interpretive essay provides insight into this unusual confluence of factors and cautions against making this case a paradigmatic one.

3901 Kinzo, Maria D'Alva Gil. Radiografia do quadro partidário brasileiro. São Paulo: Konrad-Adenauer-Stiftung, Centro de Estudos, 1993. 122 p.: bibl., ill. (Pesquisas; 1)

Excellent introduction to post-1985 party system contains a wealth of information about all of the relevant parties. One of the most practical sources on this topic. Recommended.

3902 Krieger, Gustavo; Fernando Rodrigues; and Elvis César Bonassa. Os donos do Congresso: a farsa na CPI do Orçamento. 2a. ed. São Paulo: Editora Atica, 1994. 237 p.: ill.

Three journalists from the *Folha de São Paulo* chronicle the 1993–94 congressional budget scandal that resulted in 18 expulsions. Discusses homicidal staffer at the center of the story, but also includes much data of macropolitical value. Documents lack of transparency in congressional budgeting process.

3903 Krieger, Gustavo; Luiz Antônio Novaes; and Tales Faria. Todos os sócios do presidente. Prefácio de Gilberto Dimenstein. São Paulo: Scritta Editorial, 1992. 195 p. (Atualidade)

Account written by three investigative journalists during Collorgate scandal of 1992 and published immediately before the impeachment vote in Congress. Helpful as a review of the day-by-day unfolding of the crisis.

3904 Lamounier, Bolivar. Brazil: toward parliamentarism? (*in* The failure of presidential democracy. Edited by Juan J. Linz and Arturo Valenzuela. Baltimore: Johns Hopkins Univ. Press, 1994, p. 253–293, tables)

Provides thorough historical overview of debate between parliamentarists and presidentialists in Brazil. Also covers period prior to 1993 plebiscite, analyzing survey results of both elite and mass opinion. The plebiscite itself is covered only in an afterword. One of the best sources in English on this topic. Recommended.

3905 Lamounier, Bolivar and **Amaury de Sousa.** Changing attitudes toward democracy and institutional reform in Brazil. (*in* Political culture and democracy in developing countries. Boulder, Colo.: Lynne Rienner Publishers, 1993, p. 295–326, tables)

Informative overview of elite and mass attitudes toward democracy in the late 1980s and 1990s focuses on three issue areas: expansion of political participation, electoral and partisan representation, and presidentialism versus parliamentarism concludes that despite lack of consensus on some institutional issues, Brazilian political culture is less hierarchical and elitist than traditional stereotypes suggest.

3906 Lamounier, Bolivar. O modelo institucional brasileiro, a presente crise e propostas de reforma. (*Ibero-Am. Arch.*, 18:1/2, 1992, p. 225–244, tables)

Links current institutional crisis to constitutional model introduced in the 1930s: plebiscitarian presidentialism, federalized proportional representation, and corporatist arrangements. Argues for adoption of parliamentarism. Effectively places current debates in historical perspective.

3907 Lampreia, Luiz Felipe. Relatório brasileiro sobre desenvolvimento social. (*Estud. Av.*, 9:24, maio/agôsto 1995, p. 9–74, bibl., graphs, photos, tables)

Report delivered by Brazilian foreign minister to the 1995 World Summit on Social Development in Copenhagen represents diagnosis and policy priorities of the Cardoso gov-

ernment. Provides balanced and self-critical, broad coverage of Brazilian development issues. Replete with useful data.

3908 Leoni, Brigitte Hersant. Fernando Henrique Cardoso: o Brasil do possível. Tradução de Dora Rocha. Rio de Janeiro: Editora Nova Fronteira, 1997. 360 p.: bibl., ill.

Admiring biography is based mostly on lengthy interviews with Cardoso's intellectual comrades, political associates, and family members. Author, a French journalist, finds a consistent ethos of pragmatism bridging Cardoso's two careers as sociologist and politician. Worthwhile reading as the first major biographical (as opposed to intellectual) study of this major figure. Only shortcoming is lack of critical perspective.

3909 Lições da década de 80. Organização de Lourdes Sola e Leda M. Paulani. São Paulo: Edusp, 1995. 287 p.: bibl., ill. (Seminários; 1)

Excellent collection of essays on the turbulent 1980s covers economic reform and stabilization, popular participation, political institutions, interest groups, and social policy, among other topics. Contributors include many distinguished Brazilian social scientists.

3910 Lima Júnior, Olavo Brasil de. Democracia e instituições políticas no Brasil dos anos 80. São Paulo: Edições Loyola, 1993. 162 p.: bibl., ill. (Col. Temas brasileiros; 9)

Broad overview of political institutions focuses on party fragmentation, electoral disproportionality, and importance of subnational politics to the party system. Useful for retracing party system change in 1980s; contains a wealth of data. For a synopsis of the book in article form, see item **3912.**

3911 Lima Júnior, Olavo Brasil de. As eleições gerais de 1994: resultados e implicações político-institucionais. (*Dados/Rio de Janeiro*, 38:1, 1995, p. 93–106, bibl., tables)

Brief overview of 1994 general elections contains complete results of legislative and executive contests. Argues that the elections did little to change the situation of party fragmentation.

3912 Lima Júnior, Olavo Brasil de. A reforma das instituições políticas: a experiência brasileira e o aperfeiçoamento democrático. (*Dados/Rio de Janeiro*, 36:1, 1993, p. 89–117, tables)

Abridged version of author's 1993 book (see item **3910**).

3913 Limongi, Fernando and **Argelina Chei-bub Figueiredo.** Partidos políticos na Câmara dos Deputados, 1989–1994. (*Dados/Rio de Janeiro*, 38:3, 1995, p. 497–525, bibl., tables)

Important article challenges conventional wisdom that Brazilian parties are undisciplined. Sophisticated study of 221 roll-call votes in the lower house of the Congresso Nacional shows that the seven largest parties are impressively cohesive and that members obey caucus leaders. Moreover, parties behave predictably along a clear ideological continuum. Unexpected findings certain to provoke vigorous debate. Recommended.

Linz, Juan José; Arend Lijphart; and **Arturo Valenzuela.** A opção parlamentarista. See item **2962.**

3914 Lopes, Roberto. Rede de intrigas. Rio de Janeiro: Editora Record, 1994. 360 p.: bibl., ill.

Provides encyclopedic, journalistic account of recent developments in Brazilian arms industry. Traces a network of military officers, weapons designers, arms exporters, and lobbyists that grew rapidly in 1980s. Specifically discusses Brazil's weapons markets in the Middle East.

3915 Mainwaring, Scott. Brazil: weak parties, feckless democracy. (*in* Building democratic institutions: party systems in Latin America. Edited by Scott Mainwaring and Timothy R. Scully. Stanford, Calif.: Stanford Univ. Press, 1995, p. 354–398, tables)

Focuses on Brazilian political parties in 1979–93 period. Includes historical background. Contrasts the ideological and programmatic parties of the left with the "catch-all" parties of the center and right. Examines economic crisis, presidentialism, electoral rules, television, and the interventionist State as obstacles to party development. Recommended as best English source on the topic.

3916 Mainwaring, Scott. Political parties and democratization in Brazil. (*LARR*, 30:3, 1995, p. 177–187, bibl., table)

Review essay covers important books by Antônio Lavareda, Maria D'Alva Gil Kinzo, and Margaret Keck; also cites numerous other recent works. Documents growing sophistication of political science research on Brazilian political parties.

3917 Mariz, Cecília. Religion and poverty in Brazil: a comparison of Catholic and Pentecostal communities. (*in* Religion and democracy in Latin America. New Brunswick, N.J.: Transaction Publishers, 1994, p. 93–100, bibl.)

Supports conventional wisdom that Catholic grassroots communities encourage political participation whereas Pentecostal groups do not. Focuses on similarities rather than differences: the communitarian and participatory organizational structures shared by both religions have similar outcomes in terms of social mobility and political effectiveness.

3918 Martins Filho, João Roberto. O palácio e a caserna: a dinâmica militar das crises políticas na ditadura, 1964–1969. São Carlos, Brazil: Editora da Univ. Federal de São Carlos, 1995. 204 p.: bibl., tables.

Well-researched account of the internal politics of the Castelo Branco and Costa e Silva administrations. Good documentation of the internecine struggles resulting in the radicalization of the military regime beginning in 1968; sensitive to hierarchy and interpersonal rivalries.

3919 Mathias, Suzeley Kalil and **Iara Beleli.** Os militares e as eleições de 1994: notas de pesquisa. (*Premissas/São Paulo*, 8, dez. 1994, p. 60–85)

A comparison of the discourse of senior military officers in the government with that of reservists conducted in their informal clubs and lobbies shows that reservists are far less democratic. However, the threat of renewed intervention is minimal when civilian groups maintain their positions. A helpful guide to intra-military cleavages in the mid-1990s, despite being theoretically weak.

3920 Maybury-Lewis, Biorn. The politics of the possible: the Brazilian rural workers' trade union movement, 1964–1985. Philadelphia, Pa.: Temple Univ. Press, 1994. 297 p.: bibl., index.

Wide-ranging study of the rural workers' movement under military rule describes a struggle of incipient popular organizations versus a repressive State apparatus and its propertied allies. Rare book-length study in English of contemporary agrarian politics in Brazil includes a fascinating concluding interview with Chico Mendes.

3921 Medeiros, Antônio Carlos de. The politics of decentralization in Brazil. (*Rev. Eur.*, 57, Dec. 1994, p. 8–27, bibl.)

Dense introduction to the relationship between democratization and decentralization in Brazil. Federalism and intergovernmental relations have changed substantially since early 1980s, creating new matrices of power at the subnational level. Addresses under-researches topic and corrects the tendency to study democratic consolidation only at the national level.

3922 Mendes, Antonio Manuel Teixeira and **Gustavo Venturi.** Eleição presidencial: o Plano Real na sucessão de Itamar Franco. (*Opin. Públ.*, 2:2, dez. 1994, p. 39–48, graphs, tables)

Analysis survey data from 1994 presidential race where Cardoso used his television time to advertise his paternity of the Plano Real. Explains direction, magnitude, and timing of reaction to the trumpeted connection between Cardoso and the Plano Real by examining voters' education, income, and employment status.

3923 Meneguello, Rachel. Electoral behaviour in Brazil: the 1994 presidential elections. (*Int. Soc. Sci. J.*, 146, Dec. 1995, p. 627–641, bibl., graphs, photos, tables)

Instructive overview of 1994 presidential campaign stresses role of the Plano Real and pocketbook voting. Draws heavily on several excellent large-N public opinion surveys. Concludes that the election turned on personalities and temporary policies, and that the problem of weak representative institutions has not changed.

3924 Mettenheim, Kurt von. The Brazilian voter: mass politics in democratic transition, 1974–1986. Pittsburgh, Pa.: Univ. of Pittsburgh Press, 1995. 295 p.: bibl., ill., index. (Pitt Latin American series. Pitt series in policy and institutional studies.)

Uses survey data from 1974, 1978, and 1982 elections. Analyzes voting and public opinion during the transition. Argues that voting studies need to be more open to national differences: Brazilian voters are less

driven by ideology than by plebiscitarian appeals and patronage-based machines.

3925 Moisés, José Alvaro. Os brasileiros e a democracia: bases sócio-políticas da legitimidade democrática. São Paulo: Editora Atica, 1995. 301 p.: bibl., ill. (Ensaios; 142)

Presents the most complete study to date of mass political culture in Brazil. Using exhaustive review of large-N surveys conducted between 1989–93, explores democratic legitimation compared with other post-authoritarian regimes. Concludes that transition generated mass support for democracy, but the basis for long-term legitimation is precarious due to crises of elites and institution building. Offers a wealth of data and insight. Recommended.

3926 Moisés, José Alvaro. Dilemmas of democratic consolidation in Brazil. (*in* Democratization and the State in the Southern Cone: essays on South American politics. Edited by Benno Galjart and Patricio Silva. Amsterdam: CEDLA, 1989, p. 158–175, bibl.)

Translation of essay written in 1988 reviews problems of the first three years of the democratic regime. Author cites heterogeneity of governing coalition, weakness of representative institutions, and legacy of authoritarian political culture as principal obstacles to democratic consolidation. Abstract and tentative in tone, given the brief experience with the new regime at the time.

3927 Monclaire, Stéphane. Le quasi-impeachment du président Collor. (*Rev. fr. sci. polit.*, 44:1, fév. 1994, p. 23–48)

Coverage of "Collorgate" and the presidential impeachment of 1992 includes retrospective analysis of the Collor administration and speculation about the subsequent Itamar Franco government. Places corruption scandal within the framework of the crisis of presidentialism. A good source on this crucial episode.

3928 Moraes, João Quartim de. A esquerda militar no Brasil. v.2, Da coluna à comuna. São Paulo: Edições Siciliano, 1991 1 v.

Vol. 2 of a carefully researched study of left-wing politics in the military focuses on 1920s and early 1930s. For annotation of vol. 1 see *HLAS* 55:3739.

3929 Morais, Fernando. Chatô, o rei do Brasil. São Paulo: Companhia das Letras, 1994. 732 p.: bibl., ill., index, map.

Widely admired biography of Assis Chateaubriand (1891–1968), Brazil's Hearst-like publishing magnate and political king-maker is valuable for retracing journalism and political intrigue from 1920s to military governments of 1960s. Recommended.

3930 Mota, Aroldo. História política do Ceará. v. 4, 1987–1991. Fortaleza, Brazil: s.n., 1985 1 v.

Chronicles crucial period in recent Northeast history when Tasso Ribeiro Jereissati was in his first term as governor of Ceará and Ciro Ferreira Gomes was elected mayor of Fortaleza. Purely descriptive, yet valuable as a record of the popular administration that turned Ceará away from traditional clientelistic politics.

3931 Nascimento, Elimar Pinheiro do. Adios señor presidente!! . . . análisis del proceso político de la renuncia de Collor de Mello. (*Ecuad. Deb.*, 33, dic. 1994, p. 64–85, bibl.)

Entertaining overview of "Collorgate" and the impeachment process compromises objectivity. Suggests precedent of presidential dismissal via impeachment may be used against a future government of the left.

3932 Nicolau, Jairo Marconi. Multipartidarismo e democracia: um estudo sobre o sistema partidário brasileiro, 1985–94. Rio de Janeiro: Fundação Getulio Vargas Editora, 1996. 118 p.: bibl., ill.

Theoretically well-informed and carefully presented work examines ways in which the electoral system affects the number of parties, and the consequences of party fragmentation for democratic consolidation. One of the best monographs yet to appear on the Brazilian party system.

3933 Nicolau, Jairo Marconi. Sistema eleitoral e reforma política. Rio de Janeiro: Foglio Editora, 1993. 117 p.: bibl., ill.

Written for a general audience yet academically sound, work offers clear and concise introduction to electoral system reform in Brazil. Also useful as a guide to electoral formulae around the world, showing various options that Brazil may consider.

3934 Nunes, Márcia Cavallaria; Örjan Olsén; and Joseph D. Straubhaar. O uso de pesquisas eleitorais em decisões de voto: as eleições brasileiras de 1989. (*Opin. Públ.*, 1:1, dez. 1993, p. 63–75, bibl., tables)

Uses survey research and multivariate statistical techniques to isolate the effect of published public opinion polls on voters' choice of presidential candidates in 1989. Concludes that impact of polling (i.e., on bandwaggoning, underdogging, or strategic voting) is mediated by educational level. Cautions that voters have other influences in addition to poll numbers.

3935 Ouvindo o Brasil: uma análise da opinião pública brasileira hoje. Organização de Bolivar Lamounier. São Paulo: IDESP, Editora Sumaré; IRS, 1992. 158 p.: bibl., ill.

Presents stimulating collection of brief reports on recent public opinion research projects. Addresses nationalism, business elites, labor issues, and support for democracy. Shows growing sophistication of opinion polling and political culture research.

3936 Partido Comunista do Brasil. Congresso, 7th, São Paulo, 1988. A política revolucionária do PCdoB. 2a. ed. São Paulo: Editora A. Garibaldi, 1989. 231 p.: ill.

Results of 7th Congress of the only unreconstructed Marxist-Leninist party still proposing State socialism and dictatorship of the proletariat document Party's response to 1987–88 constitutional convention. Valuable source for study of radical left. See also item **3937.**

3937 Partido Comunista do Brasil. Congresso, 8th, Brasília, 1992. O socialismo vive. 2a. ed. São Paulo: Editora A. Garibaldi, 1992. 108 p.

Results of the 8th Congress of the Partido Comunista do Brasil confirm Party's commitment to socialism. See also item **3936.**

3938 Partido dos Trabalhadores (Brazil). Secretaria Nacional de Assuntos Institucionais. O modo petista de governar. Organização de Jorge Bittar. São Paulo: Teoria & Debate, 1992. 324 p.: bibl. (Cadernos de teoria & debate; 2)

Presents outcome of series of self-evaluative seminars conducted in 26 municipalities governed by the Partido dos Trabalhadores. Facilitates understanding of Party's attempts to advance participation and equality while simultaneously addressing the nuts-and-bolts issues of local government.

3939 Pattnayak, Satya R. Determinants of military-civilian ties: a study of intra-elite bargaining in Brazil, 1964–1984. (*Int. Stud./New Delhi*, 31:2, April/June 1994, p. 171–187)

Review of military regime emphasizes factional conflicts within the armed forces. Relies heavily on secondary sources including the classic literature (Skidmore, Stepan, etc.).

3940 Payne, Leigh A. Brazilian business and the democratic transition: new attitudes and influence. (*in* Business and democracy in Latin America. Pittsburgh, Pa.: Univ. of Pittsburgh Press, 1995, p. 217–256, tables)

Nuanced discussion of business, public policy, and democracy from 1985–92 finds that business retains impressive resources, but is handicapped by internal diversity and poor leadership. Discredits authoritarian rule. Suggests that politicians can pursue social democratic policies by undermining the unity of organized business and appealing to its progressive elements.

3941 Payne, Leigh A. Brazilian industrialists and democratic change. Baltimore, Md.: Johns Hopkins Univ. Press, 1994. 216 p.: bibl., index.

Important study of business elites and their attitudes toward democratization in 1980s is based heavily on personal interviews with leading industrialists. Finds that many of the incentives that led these actors to support the coup of 1964 have changed or disappeared. Offers a worthwhile glimpse into the thinking of these elites.

3942 Pereira, Anthony W. The end of the peasantry: the rural labor movement in northeast Brazil, 1961–1988. Pittsburgh, Pa.: Univ. of Pittsburgh Press, 1997. 232 p.: bibl., index, maps. (Pitt Latin American series)

Study of emerging rural labor politics in the sugar zone of Pernambuco under military rule shows how popular movements contribute to both democratization and social change. Work is well-researched, sensitive to theory and history, and emphasizes ongoing changes in economic structure.

3943 Pinto, Céli Regina J. Donas-de-casa, mães, feministas batalhadoras: mulheres nas eleições de 1994 no Brasil. (*Estud. Fem.*, 2:2, 1994, p. 297–312, table)

Examination of women seeking office

in 1994 builds an interesting typology of candidacies, including spouse or relative of a well-known man (often proxy candidates in majoritarian elections), feminist activist, and female professional who downplays gender. Uses TV spots and endorsements to analyze the packaging of women candidates. For sociologist's comment see item **5282.**

3944 Um projeto para o Brasil: a proposta da Força Sindical. São Paulo: Geração Editorial, 1993. 654 p.: bibl., ill.

Presents massive compendium of national policies and reforms advocated by the moderate labor federation. This worthwhile introduction to public policy challenges facing Brazil in the 1990s includes broad coverage and high-quality analysis.

3945 Reale, Miguel. De Tancredo a Collor. São Paulo: Editora Siciliano, 1992. 350 p.

Presents distinguished jurist's comments on the early experience of the New Republic. Consists of reprints of column in the *Folha de São Paulo*, concerning mostly constitutional and legal aspects of democracy.

3946 Reforma eleitoral e representação política: Brasil anos 90. Organização de Hélgio Trindade. Porto Alegre, Brazil: Editora da Univ. Federal do Rio Grande do Sul, 1992? 290 p.:

Wide-ranging collection of essays and conference remarks on the topic of electoral system reform includes contributions by politicians, jurists, and political scientists.

3947 Revkin, Andrew. The burning season: the murder of Chico Mendes and the fight for the Amazon rain forest. Boston: Houghton Mifflin, 1990. 317 p., 16 p. of plates: bibl., ill., map.

A well-written and sympathetic biography of the late Chico Mendes, leader of the Acre rubber tappers who was assassinated in Dec. 1988. Uses biographical format successfully to probe the wider economic, social, and political questions of Amazonian development. Excellent for classroom use.

3948 Rocha, Geisa Maria. Redefining the role of the bourgeoisie in dependent capitalist development: privatization and liberalization in Brazil. (*Lat. Am. Perspect.*, 21:1, Winter 1994, p. 72–98)

Examines 1990s neoliberalism from an

orthodox dependency perspective. States that reforms under Collor are "compulsory ideological policy changes." Explains that neoliberalism shifts the responsibility for development from the State to the bourgeoisie, but the result is the perpetuation of dependency.

3949 Rodrigues, Leôncio Martins. Eleições, fragmentação partidaria e governabilidade. (*Novos Estud. CEBRAP,* 41, março 1995, p. 78–90, tables)

Straightforward overview reports that the tendency toward party system fragmentation was again confirmed in the 1994 elections. Hypothesizes that a fragmented Congress causes presidents to choose ministers purely for reasons of legislative support, thus compromising competent governance. Reviews the coalition potential of each of the major parties. Tables provide election results.

3950 Rone, Jemera. The struggle for land in Brazil: rural violence continues. Edited by Cynthia Arnson and Robert Kimzey. New York: Human Rights Watch, 1992. 108 p.: bibl. (An Americas Watch report.)

Sober and gripping chronicle of the repression of demands for agrarian reform includes several well-detailed case studies. Presents excellent background on the justice system and its uneven enforcement of the law.

3951 Rosa, Luiz Pinguelli; Fernando de Souza Barros; and Suzana Ribeiro Barreiros. A política nuclear no Brasil. São Paulo: Greenpeace, 1991. 148 p.: bibl., ill., maps.

Highly critical overview of nuclear policy from 1970s to early 1990s covers both domestic and international impact.

3952 Sadek, Maria Tereza Aina and **Bolivar Lamounier.** La elección presidencial de 1989: prospectos de la consolidación democrática en Brasil. (*in* Una tarea inconclusa: elecciones y democracia en América Latina, 1988–1991. San José: Instituto Interamericano de Derechos Humanos, Centro de Asesoría y Promoción Electoral, 1992, p. 493–521, graphs, tables)

Descriptive overview of 1989 presidential election contains a wealth of background information on the candidates, opinion polling, and characteristics of the electorate. A fine short introduction to this pivotal election.

3953 Sadek, Maria Tereza Aina. Opciones institucionales y consolidación democrática: un análisis del plebiscito de 1993 en Brasil. (*in* Partidos y clase política en América Latina en los 90. San José: Instituto Interamericano de Derechos Humanos (IIDH); Centro de Asesoría y Promoción Electoral (CAPEL), 1995, p. 365–385, tables)

Competent review of 1993 plebiscite on presidential versus parliamentary rule focuses on elite and mass opinion. Although sympathetic to parliamentarism, author gives a balanced assessment of reasons for victory of presidentialism. Good introductory study of the plebiscite.

3954 Sader, Emir and **Ken Silverstein.** Without fear of being happy: Lula, the Workers Party and Brazil. London; New York: Verso, 1991. 177 p.: bibl., index.

An intellectual of the Partido dos Trabalhadores (PT) and a US-based journalist produce a sympathetic portrait of the Party. Without being critical offers history and context of PT's phenomenal growth in 1980s. Title is an awkward translation of Lula's 1989 campaign slogan.

3955 Santos, Armando Alexandre dos. Ser ou não ser monarquista, eis a questão!. Prefácio de Bertrand de Orleans e Bragança. São Paulo: Artpress, 1990. 158 p.: bibl., ill.

Written in anticipation of the 1993 plebiscite on the restoration of the monarchy, book defends claim to the throne of H.R.I.H. Dom Luiz de Orleans e Bragança. Useful for historical research on the royal family.

3956 Santos, Murillo. O caminho da profissionalização das forças armadas. Rio de Janeiro: Gráfica Editora do Livro, 1991. 154 p.: bibl. (Col. Aeronáutica. Série Arte militar e poder aeroespacial; 4)

Air Force officer provides historical overview of military professionalization in Brazil, covering mostly late 19th and early 20th centuries. Worthwhile for military historians.

3957 Schneider, Ronald M. Brazil: culture and politics in a new industrial powerhouse. Boulder, Colo.: Westview Press, 1996. 255 p.: bibl., ill., index, maps. (Nations of the modern world. Latin America)

Country study intended for use in undergraduate courses on Latin American politics. Also includes chapters on economy, social problems, and culture and the arts. Lacks a unifying framework and is heavily descriptive. Relies heavily on a parade of statistics.

3958 Serra, José. Reforma política no Brasil: parlamentarismo x presidencialismo. São Paulo: Editora Siciliano, 1993. 219 p.

Newspaper columns written in 1987–92 by the influential economist who, as a member of the Partido da Social Democracia Brasileira (PSDB), served as federal deputy (and later senator) from São Paulo state. Covers extensively the institutional crisis and need for State reform; argues standard PSDB line in favor of parliamentary rule. Lucid, well-argued criticisms.

3959 O sindicalismo brasileiro nos anos 80. São Paulo: Paz e Terra, 1991. 196 p.: bibl., ill.

Five essays covering union politics in 1980s are written by leading scholars of labor in Brazil. These high quality essays represent one of the best volumes on this often-researched topic.

3960 Social democracia hoje: a alternativa social-democrata. Organização de Maurício Dias David. Rio de Janeiro: Fundação Teotônio Vilela, 1990. 284 p.: bibl. (Cadernos da social-democracia)

Collection of essays by leading luminaries of the Partido da Social Democracia Brasileira, published soon after its founding in 1988 offers insight into party ideology.

3961 Sodré, Nelson Werneck. A ofensiva reacionária. Rio de Janeiro: Bertrand Brasil, 1992. 315 p.: index.

Covering 1958–64 period, this is third volume in the memoirs of a leading intellectual with roots in the nationalist-developmentalist left wing of the army. Excellent source on the Instituto Superior de Estudos Brasileiros (ISEB), a prominent nationalist think tank. For annotation of first volume see *HLAS 30:2444,* and of the second volume, see *HLAS 53:4349.*

3962 Sola, Lourdes. Gobernabilidad, reforma fiscal y democratización: Brasil en una perspectiva comparada. (*Desarro. Econ.,* 33: 132, enero/marzo 1994, p. 483–514, bibl., tables)

Explores fiscal crisis of late 1980s–early 1990s, drawing connections to international pressures, ideological changes, and

domestic political incentives toward fiscal indiscipline. Solid introduction to State crisis and structural adjustment in Brazil; well-grounded in comparative political economy.

3963 Straubhaar, Joseph D. The electronic media in Brazil. (*in* Communication in Latin America: journalism, mass media, and society. Wilmington, Del.: Scholarly Resources, Inc., 1996, p. 217–243, tables)

Provides short but informative introduction to development of commercial radio and television in Brazil. Although analysis of State media policy and related political themes is meager, article warrants attention. Familiarity with sociology of television is indispensable for understanding Brazilian politics.

3964 Suassuna, Luciano and Luiz Antônio Novaes. Como Fernando Henrique foi eleito presidente. 2a. ed. São Paulo: Editora Contexto, 1994. 78 p.: ill. (Col. Vivendo a história)

Journalistic account of 1994 presidential campaign is similar in purpose to Dimenstein and Souza's work (see item **3870**). Worthwhile source provides detailed chronicle of the campaign.

3965 Trindade, Hélgio. Estado nacional, lógica liberal y representación política en Brasil. (*in* ¿Qué queda de la representación política? Caracas: Consejo Latinoamericano de Ciencias Sociales; Editorial Nueva Sociedad, 1992, p. 41–50)

Penetrating overview of the relationships between liberalism, State-building, and representation in Brazil. Historical priority of the elite has been building a national State rather than implementing liberalism in the political arena. Provides solid literature review.

3966 Trindade, Hélgio and Maria Izabel Noll. Rio Grande da América do Sul: partidos e eleições, 1823–1990. Porto Alegre, Brazil: Editora da Univ. Federal do Rio Grande do Sul; Editora Sulina, 1991? 96 p.: bibl., ill., maps.

Historical treatment of political competition in Rio Grande do Sul focuses on patterns of electoral geography.

3967 Viagem ao coração do Brasil. São Paulo: Scritta, 1994. 88 p.

Essays by intellectuals close to the Partido dos Trabalhadores (PT) reflect on Lula's tour through Brazil's interior—the (Caravana de Cidadania)- in early 1994. Documents social conditions in the interior and provides an interesting record of the early phase of the presidential campaign.

3968 Viola, Eduardo J. and James W. Nickel.
Integrando a defesa dos direitos humanos e do meio ambiente: lições do Brasil. (*Novos Estud. CEBRAP*, 40, nov. 1994, p. 171–184, bibl.)

Urges integration of Brazilian environmentalist and human rights movements which hold many common goals. Argues for a "greening" of the human rights agenda to emphasize the development model, poverty, and environmental degradation. Includes effective discussion of importance of securing the rule of law in Brazil, a matter of interest to both movements.

3969 Voto é marketing . . . o resto é política: estratégias eleitorais competitivas.
Organização de Rodolfo Grandi, Alexandre Marins e Eduardo Falcão. São Paulo: Associação Brasileira de Consultores Políticos; Edições Loyola, 1992. 249 p.: bibl., ill. (Col. Comunicação & marketing; 1)

Edited collection on political consulting in Brazil demonstrates phenomenal growth of this industry in the New Republic. Several leading consultants describe their recent candidates and campaigns.

3970 Weyland, Kurt Gerhard. Democracy without equity: failures of reform in Brazil. Pittsburgh, Pa.: Univ. of Pittsburgh Press, 1996. 293 p.: bibl., ill., index. (Pitt Latin American series)

Argues that Brazil's inability to implement major equity-enhancing reforms in post-1985 regime is result of personalist politics, a highly segmented society, and a lack of cohesion within the State apparatus. Case studies of health care, taxation, and social insurance provide an excellent window into policy-making in the new democracy.

3971 Zaverucha, Jorge. Forças armadas brasileiras: nova ordem mundial, velho papel social. (*in* Reconversión militar en América Latina. Coordinación de Gabriel Aguilera Peralta. Guatemala: FLACSO, 1994, p. 91–105, table)

Exploratory study of civilian control over the military compares Brazil with sev-

eral other countries experiencing recent transitions to democracy. Highlights 18 factors which may determine the degree of civilian supremacy in postauthoritarian regimes, and provides a brief discussion of each. Includes good catalog of variables and hypotheses.

JOURNAL ABBREVIATIONS

Allpanchis/Cusco. Allpanchis. Instituto de Pastoral Andina. Cusco, Peru.

Anu. Cienc. Soc. Anuario de Ciencias Sociales. Univ. Autónoma de Aguascalientes, Centro de Artes y Humanidades, Depto. de Sociología y Antropología. Aguascalientes, Mexico.

Anu. Inst. Chiapaneco Cult. Anuario Instituto Chiapaneco de Cultura. Instituto Chiapaneco de Cultura. Tuxtla Gutiérrez, Mexico.

Anuario/Córdoba. Anuario. Univ. Nacional de Córdoba, Facultad de Derecho y Ciencias Sociales, Centro de Investigaciones Jurídicas y Sociales. Córdoba, Argentina.

Apuntes/Lima. Apuntes. Univ. del Pacífico, Centro de Investigación. Lima.

Armed Forces Soc. Armed Forces & Society. Inter-Univ. Seminar on Armed Forces & Society. Univ. of Chicago. Chicago, Ill.

Bol. Am. Boletín Americanista. Univ. de Barcelona, Facultad de Geografía e Historia, Depto. de Historia de América. Barcelona.

Bol. Socioecon. Boletín Socioeconómico. Centro de Investigaciones y Documentación Socioeconómico (CIDSE), Univ. del Valle. Cali, Colombia.

Bull. Lat. Am. Res. Bulletin of Latin American Research. Society for Latin American Studies. Oxford, England.

Cah. Am. lat. Cahiers des Amériques latines. Paris.

Caribb. Q. Caribbean Quarterly. Univ. of the West Indies. Mona, Jamaica.

Caribb. Stud. Caribbean Studies. Univ. of Puerto Rico, Institute of Caribbean Studies. Río Piedras.

CEPAL Rev. CEPAL Review/Revista de la CEPAL. Naciones Unidas, Comisión Económica para América Latina. Santiago.

Cienc. Polít. Ciencia Política. Instituto de Ciencia Política de Bogotá; Tierra Firme Editores. Bogotá.

Cienc. Soc./Santo Domingo. Ciencia y Sociedad. Instituto Tecnológico de Santo Domingo.

Columbia J. Transnatl. Law. Columbia Journal of Transnational Law. Columbia Univ. School of Law. New York.

Comp. Polit. Comparative Politics. The City Univ. of New York, Political Science Program. New York.

Comp. Polit. Stud. Comparative Political Studies. Sage Publications, Thousand Oaks, Calif.

Cont. Int. Contexto Internacional. Instituto de Relações Internacionais, Pontifícia Univ. Católica. Rio de Janeiro.

Contribuciones/Buenos Aires. Contribuciones. Estudios Interdisciplinarios sobre Desarrollo y Cooperación Internacional. Konrad-Adenauer-Stiftung; Centro Interdisciplinario de Estudios Sobre el Desarrollo Latinoamericano (CIEDLA). Buenos Aires.

Controversia/Bogotá. Controversia. Centro de Investigación y Educación Popular (CINEP). Bogotá.

Cuad. Am. Cuadernos Americanos. Editorial Cultura. México.

Cuad. Hispanoam. Cuadernos Hispanoamericanos. Instituto de Cultura Hispánica. Madrid.

Cuad. Marcha. Cuadernos de Marcha. Eon Editores. Montevideo.

Cuad. Nuestra Am. Cuadernos de Nuestra América. Centro de Estudios sobre América. La Habana.

Cuad. Repub. Cuadernos Republicanos. Editorial Cuadernos Republicanos. Asunción.

Cuba. Stud. Cuban Studies. Univ. of Pittsburgh, Center for Latin American Studies. Pittsburgh, Penn.

Cuest. Polít. Cuestiones Políticas. Instituto de Estudios Políticos y Derecho Público, Facultad de Ciencias Jurídicas y Políticas, Univ. de Zulia. Maracaibo, Venezuela.

Cult. Anthropol. Cultural Anthropology: Journal of the Society for Cultural Anthropology. American Anthropological Assn.; Society for Cultural Anthropology. Washington.

Curr. Hist. Current History. Philadelphia, Penn.

Dados/Rio de Janeiro. Dados. Instituto Univ. de Pesquisas. Rio de Janeiro.

Def. Nac. A Defesa Nacional: Revista de Assuntos Militares e Estudo de Problemas Brasileiros. Rio de Janeiro.

Desarro. Econ. Desarrollo Económico. Instituto de Desarrollo Económico y Social. Buenos Aires.

Desmemoria/Buenos Aires. Desmemoria. Buenos Aires.

Dialect. Anthropol. Dialectical Anthropology. M. Nijhoff. Dordrecht, The Netherlands.

Diálogo Debate. Diálogo y Debate. Centro de Estudios para la Reforma del Estado. México.

ECA/San Salvador. Estudios Centro-Americanos: ECA. Univ. Centroamericana José Simeón Cañas. San Salvador.

Economist/London. The Economist. London.

Ecuad. Deb. Ecuador Debate. Centro Andino de Acción Popular (CAAP). Quito.

Estud. Av. Estudos Avançados. Univ. de São Paulo, Instituto de Estudos Avançados. São Paulo.

Estud. Fem. Estudos Feministas. CIEC, Escola de Comunicação, Univ. Federal do Rio de Janeiro.

Estud. Filos. Hist. Let. Estudios: Filosofía, Historia, Letras. Instituto Tecnológico Autónomo de México, Depto. Académico de Estudios Generales.

Estud. Int./Santiago. Estudios Internacionales. Instituto de Estudios Internacionales, Univ. de Chile. Santiago.

Estud. Latinoam./México. Estudios Latinoamericanos. Centro de Estudios Latinoamericanos (CELA), UNAM. México.

Estud. Latinoam./Poland. Estudios Latinoamericanos. Academia de Ciencias de Polonia, Instituto de Historia. Wrocław.

Estud. Polít./México. Estudios Políticos. Facultad de Ciencias Políticas y Sociales, UNAM. México.

Estud. Soc./Santo Domingo. Estudios Sociales. Centro de Estudios Sociales Juan Montalvo, SJ. Santo Domingo.

Estud. Sociol./México. Estudios Sociológicos. Centro de Estudios Sociológicos de El Colegio de México. México.

Estudios/Guatemala. Estudios. Instituto de Investigaciones Históricas, Antropológicas, y Arqueológicas, Univ. de San Carlos de Guatemala. Guatemala.

Estudios/Univ. Córdoba. Estudios. Centro de Estudios Avanzados, Univ. Nacional de Córdoba, Argentina.

EURE/Santiago. EURE: Revista Latinoamericana de Estudios Urbanos Regionales. Centro de Desarrollo Urbano y Regional, Univ. Católica de Chile. Santiago.

Foreign Aff. Foreign Affairs. Council on Foreign Relations, Inc. New York.

Foro Int. Foro Internacional. El Colegio de México. México.

Foro Polít. Foro Político. Instituto de Ciencias Políticas, Univ. del Museo Social Argentino. Buenos Aires.

Forum Libre. Forum Libre. Fondation Friedrich Ebert et Centre Pétion Bolivar. Port-au-Prince.

Hemisphere/Miami. Hemisphere. Latin American and Caribbean Center, Florida International Univ., Miami, Fla.

Hoy Hist. Hoy es Historia: Revista Bimestral de Historia Nacional e Iberoamericana. Editorial Raíces. Montevideo.

Ibero-Am. Arch. Ibero-Amerikanisches Archiv. Ibero-Amerikanisches Institut. Berlin.

Ibero-Am./Stockholm. Ibero-Americana: Nordic Journal of Latin American Studies. Institute of Latin American Studies, Univ. of Stockholm.

Index Censorsh. Index on Censorship. Writers & Scholars International. London.

Int. Labour Rev. International Labour Review. International Labour Office. Geneva.

Int. Soc. Sci. J. International Social Science Journal. Blackwell Publishers. Oxford, England.

Int. Stud./New Delhi. International Studies. Indian School of International Studies. New Delhi, India.

Iztapalapa/México. Iztapalapa. Univ. Autónoma Metropolitana, División de Ciencias Sociales y Humanidades. México.

J. Caribb. Hist. The Journal of Caribbean History. Caribbean Univ. Press. St. Lawrence, Barbados.

J. Caribb. Stud. Journal of Caribbean Studies. Assn. of Caribbean Studies. Coral Gables, Fla.

J. Commonw. Comp. Polit. The Journal of Commonwealth & Comparative Politics. Univ. of London, Institute of Commonwealth Studies. London.

J. Dev. Stud. The Journal of Development Studies. Frank Cass. London.

J. Interam. Stud. World Aff. Journal of Interamerican Studies and World Affairs. Institute of Interamerican Studies, Univ. of Miami. Coral Gables, Fla.

J. Lat. Am. Stud. Journal of Latin American Studies. Centers or Institutes of Latin American Studies at the Universities of Cambridge, Glasgow, Liverpool, London, and Oxford. Cambridge Univ. Press. London.

J. Peace Res. Journal of Peace Research. International Peace Research Institute, Universitetforlaget. Oslo.

J. Polit. The Journal of Politics. Univ. of Texas Press. Austin.

J. Polit. Mil. Sociol. Journal of Political and Military Sociology. Northern Illinois Univ., Dept. of Sociology. DeKalb, Ill.

J. Soc. Sci./Paramaribo. Journal of Social Sciences. Univ. van Suriname. Paramaribo.

Jahrb. öffentl. Rechts Gegenwart. Jahrbuch des öffentlichen Rechts der Gegenwart. Tübingen, Germany.

LARR. Latin American Research Review. Latin American Research Review Board. Univ. of New Mexico, Albuquerque, N.M.

Lat. Am. Perspect. Latin American Perspectives. Univ. of California. Newbury Park, Calif.

Lat. Am. Stud./Beijing. Latin American Studies. Institute of Latin American Studies. Beijing.

Lat. Am. Stud./Japan. Latin American Studies. Univ. of Tsukuba, Special Research Project on Latin America. Sakura-Mura, Japan.

Low Countries/Rekkem. The Low Countries: Arts and Society in Flanders and the Netherlands; a Yearbook. Flemish-Netherlands Foundation Stichting Ons Erfdeel. Rekkem, Belgium.

Memoria/CEMOS. Memoria: Boletín de CEMOS. Centro de Estudios del Movimiento Obrero y Socialista. México.

Mesoamérica/Antigua. Mesoamérica. Centro de Investigaciones Regionales de Mesoamérica. Antigua, Guatemala.

Mundo Nuevo/Caracas. Mundo Nuevo. Univ. Simón Bolívar, Instituto de Altos Estudios de América Latina. Caracas.

NACLA. NACLA: Report on the Americas. North American Congress on Latin America. New York.

New Left Rev. New Left Review. New Left Review, Ltd., London.

Novos Estud. CEBRAP. Novos Estudos CEBRAP. Centro Brasileiro de Análise e Planejamento. São Paulo.

Nueva Soc. Nueva Sociedad. Caracas.

Opin. Públ. Opinião Pública. Centro de Estudos de Opinião Pública (CESOP), Univ. Estadual de Campinas. Brazil.

Panorama Centroam. Pensam. Panorama Centroamericano: Pensamiento y Acción. Instituto Centroamericano de Estudios Políticos (INCEP). Guatemala.

Perf. Latinoam. Perfiles Latinoamericanos. Facultad Latinoamericana de Ciencias Sociales. México.

Planeac. Desarro. Planeación & Desarrollo. Depto. Nacional de Planeación. Bogotá.

Polít. Gob. Política y Gobierno. Centro de Investigación y Docencia Económicas. México.

Politeia/Caracas. Politeia. Instituto de Estudios Políticos, Univ. Central de Venezuela. Caracas.

Premissas/São Paulo. Premissas. Univ. Estadual de Campinas, Núcleo de Estudos Estratégicos. São Paulo.

Probl. Desarro. Problemas del Desarrollo: Revista Latinoamericana de Economía. Instituto de Investigaciones Económicas, UNAM. México.

Prop. Democrát. Propuestas Democráticas. Univ. Nacional de Asunción; Fundación Hanns Seidel. Asunción.

Quehacer/Lima. Quehacer. Centro de Estudios y Promoción del Desarrollo (DESCO). Lima.

Race Cl. Race & Class. Institute of Race Relations; The Transnational Institute. London.

Razón Fe. Razón y Fe. La Compañía de Jesús. Madrid.

Real. Econ./Buenos Aires. Realidad Económica. Instituto Argentino para el Desarrollo Económico (IADE). Buenos Aires.

Relaciones/Zamora. Relaciones. El Colegio de Michoacán. Zamora, Mexico.

Rev. Arg. Estud. Estrateg. Revista Argentina de Estudios Estratégicos. Olcese Editores. Buenos Aires.

Rev. Bras. Estud. Polít. Revista Brasileira de Estudos Políticos. Univ. de Minas Gerais. Belo Horizonte, Brazil.

Rev. Centroam. Econ. Revista Centroamericana de Economía. Univ. Nacional Autónoma de Honduras, Programa de Postgrado Centroamericano en Economía y Planificación. Tegucigalpa.

Rev. Ciclos. Revista Ciclos en la Historia, Economía y la Sociedad. Fundación de Investigaciones Históricas, Económicas y Sociales, Facultad de Ciencias Económicas, Univ. de Buenos Aires. Buenos Aires.

Rev. Cienc. Polít./Santiago. Revista de Ciencia Política. Instituto de Ciencia Política, Pontificia Univ. Católica de Chile. Santiago.

Rev. Cienc. Soc./Río Piedras. Revista de Ciencias Sociales. Univ. de Puerto Rico, Colegio de Ciencias Sociales. Río Piedras.

Rev. Colomb. Sociol. Revista Colombiana de Sociología. Depto. de Sociología, Univ. Nacional. Bogotá.

Rev. Eur. Revista Europea de Estudios Latinoamericanos y del Caribe = European Review of Latin American and Caribbean Studies. Center for Latin American Research and Documentation; Royal Institute of Linguistics and Anthropology. Amsterdam.

Rev. fr. sci. polit. Revue française de science politique. L'Association française de science politique. Paris.

Rev. Int. Sociol. Revista Internacional de Sociología. Consejo Superior de Investigaciones Científicas. Instituto de Economía y Geografía Aplicadas. Madrid.

Rev. Javer. Revista Javeriana. Provincia Colombiana de la Compañía de Jesús. Bogotá.

Rev. Mex. Sociol. Revista Mexicana de Sociología. Instituto de Investigaciones Sociales, Univ. Nacional Autónoma de México. México.

Rev. Occident. Revista de Occidente. Madrid.

Rev. Parag. Sociol. Revista Paraguaya de Sociología. Centro Paraguayo de Estudios Sociológicos. Asunción.

Rev. Rev. Interam. Revista/Review Interamericana. Inter-American Univ. Press. Hato Rey, Puerto Rico.

Rev. UNITAS. Revista UNITAS. Unión Nacional de Instituciones para el Trabajo de Acción Social. La Paz.

Rev. Univ. EAFIT. Revista Universidad EAFIT. Depto. de Comunicaciones, Univ. EAFIT. Medellín.

São Paulo Perspect. São Paulo em Perspectiva. Fundação SEADE. São Paulo.

SECOLAS Ann. SECOLAS Annals. Southeastern Conference on Latin American Studies; Thomasson Printing Co. Carrollton, Ga.

Secuencia/México. Secuencia. Instituto Mora. México.

Signs/Chicago. Signs. The Univ. of Chicago Press. Chicago, Ill.

Síntesis/Madrid. Síntesis. Asociación de Investigación y Especialización sobre Temas Latinoamericanos. Madrid.

Soc. Econ. Stud. Social and Economic Studies. Univ. of the West Indies, Institute of Social and Economic Research. Mona, Jamaica.

Social. Particip. Socialismo y Participación. Ediciones Socialismo y Participación. Lima.

Stud. Comp. Int. Dev. Studies in Comparative International Development. Transaction Periodicals Consortium, Rutgers Univ., New Brunswick, N.J.

Temas/Habana. Temas: Cultura, Ideología, Sociedad. Centro de Estudios Martianos. La Habana.

Todo es Hist. Todo es Historia. Buenos Aires.

Trace/México. Trace. Centre d'études mexicaines et centraméricaines. México.

UNISA Lat. Am. Rep. UNISA Latin American Report. Univ. of South Africa. Pretoria.

Vuelta/México. Vuelta. México.

World Policy J. World Policy Journal. World Policy Institute. New York.

World Polit. World Politics. Princeton Univ., Center of International Studies. Princeton, N.J.

INTERNATIONAL RELATIONS

GENERAL

G. POPE ATKINS, *Research Fellow, Institute of Latin American Studies, University of Texas at Austin, and Professor Emeritus of Political Science, United States Naval Academy*

RESEARCH AND WRITING on Latin American and Caribbean international relations during the biennium reflect the continuing, accelerated, and cumulative changes in both the global and Latin American regional systems, as well as the State and non-state actors' responses to them. As the contours of the "post-Cold War era" have become clearer, and related research trends fairly well established, it seems an appropriate time to evaluate current analysis of the region's international relations. The comments that follow update judgments made in previous *HLAS* volumes about events in Latin America and related scholarship.

In general, the works reviewed demonstrate vigorous and extensive analysis, but are nonetheless fragmented in conceptual and disciplinary terms. The volume of work remains high and the scope broad in terms of issues addressed and multidisciplinary contributions. While international relations scholarship in Latin American studies has been, and seems to remain, more willing to engage in conceptualizations and methods than other international studies within various social science disciplines, the abiding problem of linking works within some organizing framework is increasingly difficult. This difficulty is a reflection of changing real world circumstances and the associated phenomena and issues, and is analogous to the problem facing policymakers themselves.

Identifying the current era as "post-Cold War" reflects an understanding that previously utilized analytic and policy constructs are no longer valid; however, it detracts from a recognition that in Latin America certain important trends already were underway. As established patterns of global confrontation ended, Latin America was entering a new era characterized by the region's shift from authoritarian governments and State-dominated economies, the relative success of the Central American peace process, and the rise of drug trafficking as an international security issue, among other events. These issues in turn gave rise to other events and problems that attracted scholarly attention.

The new international phenomenon had a particularly significant impact on inter-American relations. Persistent problems whose resolution no longer depended on US Cold War security standards quickly became top priorities for Latin American States, US, and Canada. They turned their attention toward democratic development, human rights, State governance, civil-military relations, demilitarization, corruption, crime, and insurgency; economic integration, trade, investment, and debt; immigration and refugees; illicit drug traffic and its social, economic, and political complexities; the degradation of the physical environment and the achievement of "sustainable development;" and arms control and the clandestine arms trade. The Latin American States recognized these international issues as essentially extensions of their domestic concerns.

Dominant themes in the foreign policy analysis of Latin American States have been influenced by the difficult processes and mixed results of democratic and economic recovery and reform. In terms of foreign policy orientations, elected governments reconstituted regional collaboration in an effort called *concertación* (a concept going beyond mere policy "cooperation" to aspire to "harmonization"). In the wake of the isolation and isolationism of their military regimes, these governments wanted to be active participants in the evolving international system. They sought to maintain and expand relations with other States, international organizations, and nonstate actors. Attention is called to a multi-authored treatment of changing Latin American policy frameworks, which describes this new attitude (item **3988**).

Analysts of the US have paid particular attention to the impact of the Cold War's conclusion on policy-making. US decision makers abandoned their preoccupation with minimizing hostile foreign intrusions into the Americas and sought to define new policy goals. The Bush Administration adopted multilateralism and an economic focus, and acknowledged the essentiality of Latin American democracy; the Clinton Administration followed suit, making democracy and economics coequal components. Drug traffic presented special difficulties, seeming to replace the Central American conflict as the intractable problem compromising multilateralism and allowing "ends justifying means" calculations and activities. Military interventions in Panama (1989) and Haiti (1994) demonstrated the continued willingness of the US, in certain circumstances, to police the Caribbean, whether unilaterally or with multilateral cover.

Several senior US scholars have made major contributions to US policies. John Martz orchestrates a group of leading analysts who provide significant critiques of US policy in the context of a dramatically changing Latin America and the evolving post-Cold War period (item **4055**). In longer historical terms, Peter Smith provides an interdisciplinary "interpretive history" which seeks "to offer a conceptual framework for the comprehension of changing patterns of inter-American relations over a span of nearly two centuries," based on substantial evidence (item **4052**). Adding another major book to his long list of distinguished contributions, Frederick Pike offers a detailed examination of the Good Neighbor Policy (1933–45) and its continuing impact (item **4040**). David Dent edited a research handbook that admirably satisfies an important need to explore the literature of US policy-making toward Latin America (item **4054**).

Canada's increased activity in Latin America is notable. During the latter 1980s, Canada played a significant role in the Central American peace process, and in 1990 it became a full member of the OAS. A number of good academic treatments of Canada's new inter-American policies appeared and have been noted in previous volumes of the *HLAS*. Added to the list this biennium is James Rochlin's book, a chronicle and analysis of the evolution of Canada's foreign policy toward Latin America emphasizing the period of expanded involvement (item **4043**).

Other outside actors rekindled their interests and activities in Latin America and represented significant regional competition for the US. The European Union (and within the EU, Spain in particular) is of special importance. In 1991, the EU began to hold formal annual foreign ministry meetings with the Rio Group to discuss a wide range of subjects in addition to the central trade and investment issues; in December 1995 the EU signed an agreement with Mercosur opening free trade possibilities followed by accords with the Andean Community, Mexico, and Chile. Additionally, the EU continued its practice, begun during the peace process of high-level meetings with Central Americans. Within the significant body of work on Europe and Latin America, the publications of the Institute for European-Latin American Relations in Madrid are especially noteworthy for their analysis of European policies and points-of-view on the spectrum of Latin American and Caribbean issues. One of the Institute's recent contributions concerns the political economy of current foreign investment in the region (item **4006**).

Another characteristic of the current international era is the revival of international governmental organizations on all levels, with concomitant academic interest. Latin American and Caribbean governments revitalized their regional and subregional associations and their participation in the Inter-American System and United Nations. Latin American and Caribbean economic integration arrangements were animated, first as a function of *concertación* and further by the prospect of free trade with the US, which Latin American nations hedged by broadening their arrangements beyond the Western Hemisphere. *Concertación* also energized the region-wide political associations; the Latin American Economic System (SELA) restored its role as policy analyst and advocate, and the Rio Group emerged as a dynamic voice on a broad agenda of issues.

The formal Inter-American System had a significant, if ambiguous, renewal. The important participation of the OAS in the Central American peace process reversed much of its two-decade decline, with subsequent action and reform facilitated by a more positive Latin American nationalism, the United States' return to multilateralism, and Canada's new commitment to hemispheric affairs. Analysts cautioned that the new opportunities were tempered by the well-known political, financial, and administrative obstacles attendant to intergovernmental organizations, as well as the continuing reality of asymmetrical inter-American power relations. In any event, a general inter-American consensus emerged that the nature of the issues required a multilateral resolution and depended on favorable political and economic contexts within Latin America and the Caribbean. Thus democratic development and economic reform constituted the guiding norms in hemispheric relations; in fact, they were declared national and international security matters. Pope Atkins published an extensive reference guide to the evolution, institutions, purposes, policies, events, and personalities of the system (item **3978**).

The United Nations for the first time became overtly and actively involved in inter-American conflict resolution, breaking the established precedent of deferring to the Inter-American System on matters of peace and security. At the invitation of the Central American presidents, it became deeply involved in Central American peace operations, and developed a with the OAS a division of labor and resources between the two organizations. The UN was also involved with the Haiti crisis and continues as the sponsor of the international peacekeeping mission in that country. If this direct UN presence in matters of inter-American peace and security is sustained, it represents a historic new role for the organization.

Students of international relations have reemphasized concepts of globalization and transnationalization—and debated their precise meanings. In the Latin American context, globalization may be seen as a process of an outward expansion of relations with different characteristics at various system levels—that is, as a series of regional responses to global economic, political, and social change. These responses occur in the context of Latin American democratization. Even as the international system has become more interdependent globally, it has simultaneously been increasingly defined by regions. Latin American regional and intraregional units have, in recent years, actually increased their cohesion. Transnationalization accompanies globalization, while elevating the prominence of nonstate actors and intensifying their activities. Thus, elements of transnational phenomena merge with interstate relations and also evolve in a largely autonomous manner. Multinational corporations, political party organizations, labor associations, nongovernmental organizations, churches, communications and entertainment media, educational institutions, immigrants and refugees, tourists, artists, athletes, and others, as well as drug traffickers and other criminal elements, engage in a myriad of activities flowing across state boundaries creating their own economic, political, social, and cultural patterns. These linkages are not new, but in the early 1980s they increased rapidly and today seem unabated. The burgeoning phenomena require, and surely will receive, considerably more scholarly attention from several academic disciplines.

The enduring question of State sovereignty in Latin American international relations resurfaced in the new-era setting. If States cannot alone surmount the interstate and transnational problems, and if resolving them requires multilateral action, then the new meaning of international security requires a redefinition of sovereignty. Latin American and Caribbean states have acquiesced to a limited degree, but the majority remain particularly sensitive to anything that might legitimate US military force. Tom Farer edited an important, timely collection of essays in which distinguished experts tackle the conceptual and policy issues surrounding the key debate in inter-American action: sovereignty versus collective action for democracy (item **3985**).

3972 Advancing the Miami process: civil society and the Summit of the Americas. Edited by Robin L. Rosenberg and Steve J. Stein. Miami: North-South Center Press; Boulder, Colo.: Lynne Rienner Publishers, 1995. 453 p.: bibl., ill., index.

A thorough and useful documentary collection of official summit documents, publications of intergovernmental organizations, proposals from nongovernmental organizations and individuals, and some correspondence relating to the summit.

3973 Alvarez Gómez, Ana Josefina. Políticas antidrogas y proyecto neoliberal. (*Estud. Latinoam./México*, 2:4, julio/dic. 1995, p. 71–87)

Uses a typical economic analysis, treating drugs as any economic commodity. Concludes that a neoconservative policy has been counterproductive. [D. Story]

3974 América Latina y el Caribe ante el nuevo escenario europeo. Caracas: Sistema Económico Latinoamericano-SELA; Editorial Nueva Sociedad, 1993. 246 p.: bibl.

An analysis by SELA for its member States regarding the relations of Latin American and Caribbean countries and the subre-

gional integration organizations with the increasingly integrated European Community.

3975 América Latina y el Sudeste Asiático: perfiles de cooperación regional. Edición de Manfred Mols, Manfred Wilhelmy y Hernán Gutiérrez. Santiago: Univ. de Chile, Instituto de Estudios Internacionales, 1995. 386 p.

Seven German and Chilean analysts take on a little-researched topic in cross-regional interactions. Insightful appraisals of both significant relations and regional separation.

3976 Arenal, Celestino del. Política exterior de España hacia Iberoamérica. Madrid: Editorial Complutense, 1994. 299 p.: bibl.

Solid historical and policy analysis of Spanish purposes in Latin America. Emphasizes the orientation of democratic Spain from 1976–92 and the formation of an Ibero-American community.

3977 Astori, Danilo et al. La integración latinoamericana y sus problemas contemporáneos: foro, 22–23 de marzo de 1993, Montevideo, Uruguay. Montevideo: Fundación Rodney Arismendi, 1993? 169 p.: bibl.

Papers and commentaries that utilize Arismendi's Marxist perspective as point of departure to analyze Latin American integration problems and possibilities.

3978 Atkins, G. Pope. Encyclopedia of the Inter-American System. Westport, Conn.: Greenwood Press, 1997. 583 p.: appendices, bibl., ill., index, maps.

Multidisciplinary, scholarly work by well-known political scientist and specialist of inter-American relations. Foremost reference in the field. More comprehensive and up-to-date than Sheinin's (item **4050**) or Stoetzer's (*HLAS 55:3866*). Lengthy entries describe in historical perspective the major events and facets of the inter-American system (IAS) at all levels: national, regional, subregional, institutional (OAS, IDB, NAFTA, etc.), and personal/personnel. Each entry followed by section with leading, relevant sources in English and Spanish. Also includes useful bibliographic essay (p. 533–536) and extensive index (p. 536–561). Chronology and appendices include IAS membership, nine structural charts, and texts of OAS Charter and Rio Treaty. [L.C. Wilson]

3979 Atkins, G. Pope. Latin America in the international political system. 3rd ed. Boulder: Westview Press, 1995. 412 p.: bibl., index, maps.

New edition pays special attention to how the Cold War's conclusion along with regional political, economic, military, and social transformations changed the international system and the Latin American and Caribbean subsystems. See *HLAS 51:4134*.

3980 Baklanoff, Eric N. Spain's economic strategy toward the "nations of its historical community:" the "reconquest" of Latin America? (*J. Interam. Stud. World Aff.*, 38:1, Spring 1996, p. 105–127, bibl., table)

Spain's transformation from economic backwardness to prosperity and from Franco's authoritarianism to "parliamentary-monarchy" facilitated its economic presence in Latin America as counterpoise to the US; but constraints are presented by convergence of US and Latin American economic reform and free-trade agendas.

Bandeira, Moniz. O milagre alemão e o desenvolvimento do Brasil: as relações da Alemanha com o Brasil e a América Latina, 1949–1994. See item **4472.**

3981 Baranyi, Stephen. Peace missions and subsidiarity in the Americas: conflict management in the western hemisphere. (*Int. J./Toronto*, 50:2, Spring 1995, p. 343–369)

Thoughtful assessment of concerns that UN is overburdened with worldwide peace duties and suggestions that OAS play greater role in regional peacekeeping; recent experiences in Central America and Caribbean suggest limited possibilities for such peacekeeping operations and institutional divisions of labor.

Bejarano Avila, Jesús Antonio. Una agenda para la paz: aproximaciones desde la teoría de la resolución de conflictos. See item **2928.**

3982 Benchimol, Samuel. Eco-92: borealismo ecológico e tropicalismo ambiental. (*Ciênc. Tróp.*, 20:1, jan./junho 1992, p. 7–26)

Contrasts views from the Northern Hemisphere (*borealismo ecológico*) with those of the Southern Hemisphere (*tropicalismo ambiental*) on environmental and ecological issues prior to the 1992 UN Conference on Environment and Development in Rio de Janeiro. [S.D. Tollefson]

Benedetti, Mario. Perplejidades de fin de siglo. See *HLAS 56:3863.*

Benítez Manaut, Raúl. Centroamérica y el nuevo sistema internacional: negociaciones, paz, integración y geopolítica. See item **4143.**

3983 Berger, Mark T. Under northern eyes: Latin American studies and U.S. hegemony in the Americas, 1898–1990. Foreword by Jack W. Hopkins. Bloomington: Indiana Univ. Press, 1995. 583 p.: bibl., index. (Caribbean and Latin American studies)

Applying Gramscian world-system and related theories to evolution of Latin American studies in the US, Berger sees academic activity profoundly complementing continuous US imperial policies. Although the approach precludes much complexity, review of literature is exceptionally thorough and limited thesis itself well-argued. Almost 60 percent of book devoted to notes and bibliography.

3984 Bernal-Meza, Raúl et al. El nuevo orden mundial y nosotros: América Latina en el umbral del siglo XXI. Recopilación de Cristian Buchrucker y Oscar Armanda Mendoza. Argentina: FACSO; CEILA, 1993. 247 p.: bibl., ill.

Six Argentine scholars theorize about new post-Cold War global structures and analyze position of Latin American States and institutions within the *orden mundial.*

Bernecker, Walther L. Las relaciones entre Europa y Latinoamérica durante el siglo XIX: ofensivas comerciales e intereses económicos. See *HLAS 56 : 1003.*

3985 Beyond sovereignty: collectively defending democracy in the Americas. Edited by Tom J. Farer. Baltimore, Md.: Johns Hopkins Univ. Press, 1996. 428 p.: bibl., index. (An Inter-American dialogue book)

Seventeen distinguished experts tackle profound issues related to titled subject. Farer's lively introduction furnishes clear, insightful framework; subsequent chapters provide strong theoretical and empirical bases with high-quality scholarship. States receiving case study attention, however, are limited; key ones such as Brazil and Argentina are not included.

3986 Buchanan, Paul G. US defense policy for the western hemisphere: new wine in old bottles, old wine in new bottles, or something completely different? (*J. Interam. Stud. World Aff.*, 38 : 1, Spring 1996, p. 1–31, bibl.)

Complex argument that Cold War-era fear of internal Latin American enemies endures within US "defense hierarchy" and Latin American military circles that seek new missions in modified global circumstances; US perspectives dramatically changed on other issues due to lack of external threat and regional democratic resurgence.

3987 Calvert, Peter. The international politics of Latin America. Manchester, England; New York: Manchester Univ. Press; New York: St. Martin's Press, 1994. 271 p.: bibl., index. (Regional international politics series)

Relatively brief book on a large topic. Applies a comprehensive and combined international-domestic political systems organizing framework, guided by neo-realist conceptual assumptions.

3988 Cambio de paradigmas en América Latina: nuevos impulsos, nuevos temores. Edición de Manfred Mols *et al.* Caracas: Asociación Alemana de Investigación sobre América Latina (ADLAF); Fundación

Friedrich Ebert; Editorial Nueva Sociedad, 1994. 220 p.: ill., maps.

Multinational group of 18 contributors explore array of general and specific themes in Latin American foreign policy and international relations "en un mundo cambiente." Volume the result of 1993 conference of the sponsoring association and foundation.

Castañeda, Jorge G. La casa por la ventana. See item **3016.**

3989 Chabat, Jorge. Seguridad nacional y narcotráfico: vínculos reales e imaginarios. (*Polít. Gob.*, 1 : 1, enero/junio 1994, p. 97–123)

Argues that US policy toward drug trafficking has taken on strong national security implications and hence has become increasingly militarized. For political scientist's comment, see item **3018.** [D. Story]

3990 Cockcroft, James D. Latin America: history, politics, and U.S. policy. 2nd ed. Chicago: Nelson-Hall Publishers, 1996. 783 p.: bibl., ill., maps.

Substantially revised and retitled second edition of a thorough multidisciplinary textbook focusing on the elements of the subtitle. Authored by a pioneer of dependency theory. The first edition appeared in 1989. See *HLAS 53 : 4377.*

3991 Collective responses to regional problems: the case of Latin America and the Caribbean; a collection of essays from a project of the American Academy of Arts and Sciences. Edited by Carl Kaysen, Robert A. Pastor, and Laura W. Reed. Cambridge, Mass.: Committee on International Security Studies, American Academy of Arts and Sciences, 1994. 177 p.: bibl.

Brief, insightful essays and valuable commentary by conference participants at the Carter Center in Sept. 1993 (including former President Jimmy Carter and Haitian President Jean-Bertrand Aristide). Emphasis on legitimacy of collective international actions for peace, democracy, and human rights and accompanying ambivalence of many Latin Americans in terms of State sovereignty.

3992 Coloquio de Invierno, *Ciudad Universitaria, Mexico, 1992.* Los grandes cambios de nuestro tiempo: la situación internacional, América Latina y México. v. 1, La

situación mundial y la democracia. v. 2, Las
Américas en el horizonte del cambio. México:
Univ. Nacional Autónoma de México; Consejo Nacional para la Cultura y las Artes;
Fondo de Cultura Económica, 1992. 2 v.: bibl.
(Col. Tierra firme)
    Based on important two-week confer-
ence (Feb. 1992) at UNAM with authorative
experts from Latin America, the US, Europe,
Asia, and Africa. Twenty-five presentations
in vol. 1 address from various perspectives
the titled subject and related phenomena (security, ideology, ecology, development, communications, and problems of governance);
13 contributions in vol. 2 focus on elements
of development and modernity, social movements, future of democracy, and interstate
integration.

**3993 Comunidad latinoamericana o inicia-
tiva para las Américas, ¿alternativa o
destino?** Caracas: Fondo Latinoamericano de
Ediciones Sociales, 1992. 422 p.: bibl. (Col.
CLAT)
    Report of debates at conference initi-
ated by Central Latinoamericana de Trabajadores (Nov. 1991). Focuses on challenge of
President Bush's Enterprise for the Americas
Initiative and prospect of hemispheric free
trade. Participants representing Latin American labor movements and politicial and academic arenas agreed on necessity for Latin
American unity and community.

**3994 Cooperation or rivalry?: regional inte-
gration in the Americas and the Pacific
Rim.** Edited by Shōji Nishijima and Peter H.
Smith. Boulder, Colo.: Westview Press, 1996.
320 p.: bibl., index. (Latin America in global
perspective)
    Multinational group of 13 contributors
examine issues and themes of cooperation
and rivalry in integration theory and practice.
Case studies discuss the meaning of NAFTA,
and its possible expansion into a Western
Hemisphere Free Trade Agreement, for Latin
America and Pacific Rim. For economist's
comment see item **1287.**

**3995 Cumbre Iberoamericana, 2nd, Madrid,
1992.** Segunda Cumbre Iberoamericana, Madrid, España, 1992: discursos y documentos. 2. ed. México: Fondo de Cultura
Económica, 1993. 375 p. (Col. popular; 486)
    Serviceable documentary collection
of proceedings of second summit meeting of

leaders from Spanish America, Brazil, Spain,
and Portugal held in July 1992 in Madrid.

3996 Cuzán, Alfred G. The Latin American
Studies Association vs. the United
States: the verdict of history. (*Acad. Quest.*,
7:3, Summer 1994, p. 40–55)
    Based on review of LASA's "resolu-
tions, reports, and other official declaration
or statements," denounces organization's
radicalization during 1970s and its "profound
misunderstanding" regarding the nature of
the Sandinista and Castro regimes. Others
might find more complexity among LASA
members and their views than can reliably be
measured by official statements of business
meetings. For opposite view, see item **3983.**

**3997 El diálogo Unión Europea-América
Latina.** Bogotá?: FESCOL, 1995. 146 p.
    Useful primarily for perspectives of-
fered by 18 seminar participants, mostly ambassadors and other officials, who address
positions and policies of France, Spain, Italy,
Germany, Chile, Mexico, Rio Group, Andean
Group, MERCOSUR, and European Union.

**3998 Difficult liaison: trade and the environ-
ment in the Americas.** Edited by Heraldo Muñoz and Robin L. Rosenberg. Miami:
North-South Center, Univ. of Miami; New
Brunswick, N.J.: Transaction Publishers,
1993. 296 p.: bibl.
    Product of an OAS Seminar on Interna-
tional Trade and the Environment; 17 participants analyze, in papers and commentaries,
questions of international trade and environmental protection in contexts of interdependent global economy, problems of natural resources, certain Latin American structures
and processes, and other institutional and
juridical aspects.

3999 Drug trafficking in the Americas. Edited by Bruce M. Bagley and William O.
Walker III. Coral Gables, Fla.: Univ. of Miami,
North-South Center; New Brunswick, N.J.:
Transaction Publishers, 1994. 562 p.: bibl.
    Informative, encyclopedic compen-
dium of 28 chapters by established academic
experts, talented newcomers, and experienced
practiners; six chapters on US drug policy,
three on international dimensions, four on
Central America and the Caribbean, and
17 on Mexico and five South American
countries.

4000 Drugs in the Western Hemisphere: an odyssey of cultures in conflict. Edited by William O. Walker, III. Wilmington, Del.: Scholarly Resources, 1996. xxvii, 262 p.: bibl. (Jaguar books on Latin America; 12)

Walker adds to his authoritative works on drug trafficking with his original collection of 43 essays on the history of Latin American drug cultures, their place in individual societies, and Latin American and US efforts to control them.

4001 Encuentro de Integración para el Desarrollo Cultural de América Latina y el Caribe, *Manta, Ecuador, 1992.* Memorias: informe final. Manta, Ecuador: Univ. Laica Eloy Alfaro de Manabí, 1993. 238 p.: bibl., ill.

Volume contains presentations and final report issued at a 1992 conference on cultural integration organized in Ecuador with participants from Argentina, Brazil, Chile, Colombia, Costa Rica, Cuba, Dominican Republic, and Venezuela. Interesting analyses of some of these countries' cultural policies and prospects for cultural exchanges and cooperation at the regional level. [A. Vacs]

4002 Enfoques teóricos y metodológicos para el estudio de la política exterior. Edición de Roberto Russell. Buenos Aires: RIAL; Grupo Editor Latinoamericano, 1992. 159 p.: bibl. (Col. Estudios internacionales)

Useful collection of articles examining, from theoretical and methodological perspectives, the literature on foreign relations produced in some Latin American countries. General introduction by Russell is followed by well-documented essays on the evolution and current state of foreign relations studies in Argentina, Brazil, Chile, Colombia, and Mexico. [A. Vacs]

4003 España/América Latina: un siglo de políticas culturales. Coordinación de Pedro Pérez Herrero y Nuria Tabanera. Madrid: AIETI/Síntesis; OEI, 1993. 256 p.: bibl. (Monografías AIETI/Síntesis; 2)

Six insightful essays by eight Spanish and two Latin American historians analyze in chronological order official Spanish cultural policy toward Latin America from 1898–1992.

4004 Europe and Latin America in the world economy. Edited by Susan Kaufman Purcell and Françoise Simon. Foreword by Gonzalo de Las Heras. Boulder, Colo.: Lynne Rienner Publishers, 1994. 228 p.: bibl. ill., index.

Eight experts thoroughly discuss interregional economic relationships; roles of Germany, Spain, and Eastern Europe; and trilateral connections including the US, in context of accelerated economic integration in both regions combined with the end of Cold War. Statistical data included. For economist's comment see item **1311.**

4005 Falco, Mathea. U.S. drug policy: addicted to failure. (*Foreign Policy*, 102, Spring 1996, p. 120–133, graph)

In a brief, provocative essay, former US State Dept. official argues that strong US public support for antidrug programs in Latin America reflects mistaken but convenient view that outsiders are largely responsible for US domestic problems; US should concentrate on its own social predicament.

4006 Foreign direct investment in Latin America in the 1990s. Madrid: Institute for European-Latin American Relations; Washington: Inter-American Development Bank, 1996. 149 p.: bibl., ill.

Careful political-economic description and analysis of subject, addressed primarily to European audience but of general analytic interest. For economist's comment see item **1323.**

4007 Foreign policy and regionalism in the Americas. Edited by Gordon Mace and Jean-Philippe Thérien. Boulder, Colo.: Lynne Rienner Publishers, 1996. 259 p.: bibl., index.

Impatient with globalist assumptions concerning the nature of the current international system, authors convincingly argue that recent developments have created "a particularly favorable environment for the establishment of a new regional system of the Americas;" less persuasively predict an eventual "true community of American nations."

4008 Garay, Luis J. América Latina ante el reordenamiento económico internacional. Bogotá: Editorial Univ. Nacional, 1994. 288 p.: bibl. (Col. latinoamericana)

Informative analysis prescribes role of Latin American integration in current world process of "reconfiguring international economic space."

4009 Gaviria Trujillo, César *et al.* Doce ensayos sobre integración continental. Recopilación de Poly Hincapié Buchelli. Pre-

parada por el Instituto de Altos Estudios Jurídicos y Relaciones Internacionales de la Univ.
del Valle. Cali, Colombia: Univ. del Valle,
Centro Editorial, 1994. 208 p.: bibl., ill. (Ensayos; Textos universitarios)

A dozen thoughtful essays on Latin
American and hemispheric economic integration by 14 prestigious figures in Colombian
and inter-American public and academic life.

4010 Gilderhus, Mark T. Got a gringo on
their shoulders: U.S. relations with
Latin America. (*LARR*, 31:1, 1996, p. 189–
200)

Good comparative review of eclectic
set of ten diplomatic histories. Eight deal
with circum-Caribbean and two with Brazil.

4011 Griffith, Ivelaw L. From Cold War geopolitics to post-Cold War geonarcotics.
(*Int. J./Toronto*, 49:1, Winter 1993/94, p. 1–
36, table)

Substantial article argues that with end
of East-West conflict a prominent replacement for anachronistic geopolitics in inter-
American associations will be geonarcotics,
defined as "conflict and co-operation among
national and international actors that are
driven by the narcotics phenomenon."

4012 Hakim, Peter. NAFTA . . . and after: a
new era for the US and Latin America.
(*Curr. Hist.*, 93:581, March 1994, p. 97–102)

Projects other regional trade arrangements to follow NAFTA, as well as the possibility of more cooperation on political issues in the hemisphere.

4013 Harrison, Lawrence E. The Pan-American dream: do Latin America's cultural
values discourage true partnership with the
United States and Canada? New York: Basic-
Books, 1997. 319 p.: bibl., index.

Harrison continues his provocative
but hardly novel thesis established in prior
works, that the most important factor explaining US and Canadian "progress" and
Latin American "underdevelopment" is "the
contrast between Anglo-Protestant and Ibero-
Catholic culture." Thus his answer to subtitle question is "not necessarily" but a successful process will be very difficult.

Huang, Wendeng. Zhongguo Gongchandang
yu Lamei Zhendang Guanxide Xianzhuang yu
Qianjing [Present situation of, and prospects
for, relations between the Chinese Commu-

nist Party and Latin American political par-
ties]. See item **2950.**

4014 Hufbauer, Gary Clyde and **Jeffrey J.
Schott.** Western Hemisphere economic
integration. Washington: Institute of International Economics, 1994. 294 p.: bibl., index,
map.

Thorough analysis of processes and
consequences of proposals for extending
NAFTA throughout the Western Hemisphere;
seeks to assess both economic and political
consequences of several avenues that might
be followed, including impact on the global
trading system.

4015 Ianni, Octávio. O labirinto latinoamericano. Petrópolis, Brazil: Vozes,
1993. 142 p.:

An unrepentant neo-Marxist bemoans
the lack of integration in Latin America to
counter the "dominant" countries—the US,
England, and Germany. [S.D. Tollefson.]

**4016 Integración latinoamericana y territo-
rio: transformaciones socio-económi-
cas, políticas y ambientales en el marco de las
políticas de ajuste.** Recopilación de Pablo Ciccolella *et al.* Edición de Mariana Caspani y
Mariana Schweitzer. Buenos Aires: Instituto
de Geografía, Facultad de Filosofía y Letras,
Univ. de Buenos Aires; Ediciones CEUR,
1994. 541 p.: bibl., ill. (Serie Jornadas y
congresos)

Emphasizes structure of regional and
subregional integration organizations in
newly evolving global context.

**4017 Integrating the Americas: shaping
future trade policy.** Edited by Sidney
Weintraub. New Brunswick, N.J.: Transaction
Publishers, 1994. xxi, 197 p.: bibl., ill.

A leading (and realistic) advocate of
hemispheric free trade assembles nine other
experts to focus on new ideas concerning regional integration and implications for inter-
American relations; they offer suggestions
"for strengthening the separate integration
arrangements and analyze proposals for consolidating them into" a Western Hemisphere
free trade area.

**4018 The international dimensions of de-
mocratization: Europe and the Americas.** Edited by Laurence Whitehead. Oxford;
New York: Oxford Univ. Press, 1996. 443 p.:
bibl., index. (Oxford studies in democratization)

Seven of 14 chapters deal with the Americas, three others provide analytic context (four treat democratization in Europe). In Americas-specific chapters, leading scholars address themes related to Caribbean democracy, US human rights policy and "political development assistance," international political party associations, and international dimensions of development in Brazil and Chile.

4019 *Journal of Interamerican Studies and World Affairs.* Vol. 36, No. 3, Fall 1994. The Summit of the Americas: issues to consider. Coral Gables, Fla.: Univ. of Miami, Institute of Interamerican Studies.

Written on eve of Miami summit in Dec. 1994, expert articles offer good analyses of the inter-American issues considered at the meeting: democracy, environment, corruption, drugs, migration, security, trade, and sustainable development.

4020 *Journal of Interamerican Studies and World Affairs.* Vol. 39, No. 1, Spring 1997. Coral Gables, Fla.: Univ. of Miami, Institute of Interamerican Studies.

Good collection of articles, with provocative interpretations and informative analyses concerning overall condition of US policy, general relations with the hemisphere, and particular elements.

4021 Kaplan, Marcos. Integración internacional de América Latina: aspectos sociopolíticos. (*Perf. Latinoam.*, 3 : 4, junio 1994, p. 87–108)

Critical examination of attempts made since the 1950s to promote regional integration in Latin America. After pointing out main obstacles to successful integration, such as the lack of willingness to introduce structural changes, economic backwardness and dependency, and opposition to integration from some influential groups, the author emphasizes problems associated with current weakness of Latin American States as actors in process of economic development and integration. [A. Vacs]

Katada, Saori N. Two aid hegemons: Japanese-U.S. interaction and aid allocation to Latin America and the Caribbean. See item **1360.**

4022 Kenworthy, Eldon. America/Américas: myth in the making of U.S. policy toward Latin America. University Park: Pennsylvania State Univ. Press, 1995. 205 p.: bibl., ill., index.

Complex, sweeping, provocative interpretation of negative US cultural perceptions of Latin America and their influence on regional actions; argues that opinions rooted in myth of US exceptionalism and fear of extrahemispheric rivals, coupled with view of Latin Americans as culturally and politically inferior, results in both forceful and benign US paternalism.

4023 Krämer, Raimund. De una diplomacia desaparecida: la política exterior de la República Democrática Alemana y sus relaciones con Améria Latina. (*Estud. Int. /Santiago*, 28 : 110, abril/junio 1995, p. 174–197, tables)

Interesting exploratory overview of Latin America as case study in foreign policy of the German Democratic Republic's closed (for forty years) political system. Uses archival material available after 1990 reunification.

Latin America and the Caribbean: policies to improve linkages with the global economy. See item **4262.**

4024 Latin American environmental policy in international perspective. Edited by Gordon James MacDonald, Daniel Nielson, and Marc A. Stern. Boulder, Colo.: Westview Press, 1996. 304 p.: bibl., ill. (Latin America in global perspective)

Fourteen experts from US, Latin America, Europe, and Africa provide considerable information and realistic evaluations of inter-American environmental policy in terms of sustainable development. Assess impact of Latin American democratization, free trade, multilateral development banks, and nongovernmental organizations. Also compare problems in southern Africa and former USSR.

4025 Latin American nations in world politics. Edited by Heraldo Muñoz and Joseph S. Tulchin. 2nd ed. Boulder, Colo.: Westview Press, 1996. 285 p.: bibl., index.

Second edition of excellent multiauthored textbook (first ed. 1984) emphasizes themes and foreign policy theory, and addresses most individual Latin American and Caribbean States. Inclusion of otherwise good chapter on the USSR's relations seems incongruous. See *HLAS 47 : 7062.*

4026 Lerman Alperstein, Aída. Relaciones América Latina-Comunidad Europea. México: Univ. Autónoma Metropolitana,

Unidad Xochimilco, 1993. 121 p.: bibl., ill.
(Col. Ensayos)

Brief, straightforward analysis of economic and political dimensions of Latin American-European Community relations, including non-official interactions of international political party organizations.

4027 Li, Zhixiang. Zhongguo He Lamei Guojia Jingmao Guanxide Xianzhuang He Qianjing [Present situation of, and prospects for, economic and trade relations between China and Latin America]. (*Lat. Am. Stud./Beijing*, 1, 1995, p. 25–27)

Asserts that economic and trade relations, and scientific and technical cooperation, between China and Latin America have rapidly expanded during 1990s. However, China is faced with increasing challenges in exporting to Latin America. While prospects are good for further development of their relations, a number of problems such as reciprocal credit, export credit insurance, transportation, and trade legislation remain to be solved. Author is a researcher for the Chinese Ministry of Foreign Economic Relations and Trade. [M. Xianglin]

4028 Marini, Ruy Mauro. Latin America at the crossroads. (*Lat. Am. Perspect.*, 21:1, Winter 1994, p. 99–114)

In period of crisis for Marxist analysis, director of Centro de Estudios Latinoamericanos (CELA) of the Facultad de Ciencias Políticas y Sociales at the Univ. Nacional Autónoma de México, sees current world transformations and Latin America's position in it as part of two-decade process explainable in terms of Marxist theory of long cycles.

4029 Martin, Edwin M. Kennedy and Latin America. Lanham, Md.: Univ. Press of America, 1994. 485 p.: bibl., index.

The author, Assistant Secretary of State for Inter-American Affairs under President Kennedy, provides extensive, authoritative, and readable insider's view of policies and events.

Medeiros, Marcelo de Almeida. Relações externas do Mercosul: uma abordagem brasileira. See item **4498.**

4030 Missionaries of science: the Rockefeller Foundation and Latin America. Edited by Marcos Cueto. Bloomington: Indiana Univ. Press, 1994. 191 p.: bibl. (Philanthropic studies)

Concerns impact of American philanthropy on public health, agriculture, and science in Latin America and relations with State authority from 1920s-60s, with particular attention to Brazil and Mexico.

4031 Missoni, Eduardo and **María Inés Bussi.** Nunca aceptes carabelas de desconocidos. Bogotá: Ecoe Ediciones, 1993. 308 p.: bibl., ill.

Legal, organizational, and statistical data concerning Italy's development programs in Latin America within general policy context.

4032 Mita Barrientos, Fernando. El fenómeno del narcotráfico: enfoque nacional e internacional. La Paz: AVF Producciones, 1994. 630 p.: bibl.

Former judge and professor of criminology presents detailed treatment of drug traffic, its social and economic causes and consequences, drug cartels, and juridical considerations; chapters devoted to Latin American region and individual countries, the US, Europe, Asia, and Africa.

4033 Molineu, Harold. The inter-American system: searching for a new framework. (*LARR*, 29:1, 1994, p. 215–226)

Thorough comparative review of five books published between 1990–92, emphasizing early impact of the Cold War's conclusion (title refers to "inter-American relations" not formal hemispheric intergovernmental organizations).

4034 Money doctors, foreign debts, and economic reforms in Latin America from the 1890s to the present. Edited by Paul W. Drake. Wilmington, Del.: SR Books, 1994. 303 p.: bibl. (Jaguar books on Latin America; 3)

Superb collection of readings and documents, with enlightening introduction, about foreign economic advisers' influence on Latin American governments and private sectors. Four parts address "proconsul" period of US domination of the Caribbean (1898–1930), privatization and Kemmerer missions to Latin America (1917–31), IMF stabilization programs, and "Import Substitution and the New Academics." For economist's comment see *HLAS 55:1227.*

4035 The multilateral development banks. v. 4, Inter-American Development Bank by Diana Tussie. Boulder, Colo.: Lynne Rienner Publishers, 1996. 1 v.: bibl., index.

Informative description, analysis, and critique of bank's functions and operations. Includes eight chapters divided between two parts, "Historical Setting and Record of Performance" and "Development Agenda," with a final chapter on "looming development challenges."

4036 Nef, Jorge and **Ximena Núñez.** El monólogo interamericano: una visión histórica. (*Política/Santiago*, 32, primavera 1994, p. 81–112, bibl.)

Interesting, provocative, highly debatable. Conclusions are too sweeping for evidence presented (e.g., section on Cold War does not do justice to complexities of Latin American thrust for foreign policy autonomy); article's real value lies in questions posed about characteristics of post-Cold War era.

4037 Nieto-Navia, Rafael. Introducción al sistema interamericano de protección a los derechos humanos. Bogotá: Temis; San José: Instituto Interamericano de Derechos Humanos, 1993. 290 p.: bibl.

Good textbook presentation from historical, institutional, juridical, and philosophical perspective by former president of Inter-American Court of Human Rights and professor of international law in Colombia.

4038 O'Brien, Thomas F. The revolutionary mission: American enterprise in Latin America, 1900–1945. New York: Cambridge Univ. Press, 1996. 370 p.: bibl., ill., index. (Cambridge Latin American studies; 81)

Excellent exploration of US corporate culture's "revolutionary mission" to spread American materialist values and its consequent impact on Latin American societies; latter's reaction is a love-hate mix of acceptance and rejection. For historian's comment see *HLAS 56:1071.*

4039 Peceny, Mark. The Inter-American System as a liberal "pacific union?" (*LARR*, 29:3, 1994, p. 188–201)

Thoughtful, comparative review of nine books drawn together in terms of Immanuel Kant's maxim that liberal democracy and commerce lead to international cooperation and peace, a notion that has resurfaced in scholarly literature.

Pereira Castañares, Juan Carlos. España e Iberoamérica: un siglo de relaciones, 1836–1936. See *HLAS 56:1033.*

Perkins, M. Katherine and **Herbert R. Gilbert.** An economic analysis of U.S. narcotics control policy in the Caribbean and Latin America. See item **4279.**

4040 Pike, Fredrick B. FDR's Good Neighbor Policy: sixty years of generally gentle chaos. Austin: Univ. of Texas Press, 1995. 394 p.: bibl., ill., index.

In this thoughtful, thoroughly researched, balanced, and unorthodox analysis, Pike decides US noninterventionist orientation was based on Rooseveltian realism eschewing pressures on Latin Americans to accept US values (he assumed they would eventually converge) as counterproductive to achieving US goal of hemispheric stability and support for its strategic interests. For historian's comment see *HLAS 56:1074.*

4041 Pons Muzzo, Gustavo. Estudio histórico sobre el protocolo de Río de Janeiro: el Ecuador, país amazónico. Lima: s.n., 1994. 432 p.: bibl., ill., maps (some col.).

Detailed description and documentation of history of the Rio Protocol—attempting to settle the territorial dispute between Peru and Ecuador. Work traces period from treaty's 1992 signing through continuing conflict up to 1994.

4042 Los procesos de integración en América Latina: enfoques y perspectivas. Recopilación de Georges Couffignal y Germán A. de la Reza. Estocolmo: Instituto de Estudios Latinoamericanos, con el apoyo del Institut des hautes études de l'Amerique latine, París, 1996. 188 p.: bibl., ill.

Broad ranging set of papers analyze political and social as well as economic international elements of subregional integration in Latin America and the Caribbean.

La République dominicaine, la Guadeloupe et la Caraïbe. See item **4286.**

4043 Rochlin, James Francis. Discovering the Americas: the evolution of Canadian foreign policy towards Latin America. Vancouver, Canada: UBC Press, 1994. 300 p.: bibl., index, maps. (Canada and international relations, 0847–0510; 8)

Canadian professor chronicles and analyzes evolution of Canada's foreign policy toward Latin America, emphasizing period of increasing involvement since 1959.

4044 Rock, David. War and postwar intersections: Latin America and the United States. (*in* Latin America in the 1940s: war and postwar transitions. Edited by David Rock. Berkeley: Univ. of California Press, 1994, p. 15–40)

Possibility that US in 1940s might align with Latin American progressive forces, subdued first by fight against nazism and then by the containment of communism. Conclusion: "when powerful foreign nations dominated the strategic regions of Europe and Asia the United States turned toward Latin America; if the United States itself controlled these regions, it turned away. . . ." For historian's comment see *HLAS 56:1076.*

4045 Rodríguez Iturbe, José. Incertidumbre y búsqueda: la transición hacia un nuevo orden internacional desde la perspectiva de América Latina. (*Panorama Centroam. Pensam.,* 41, enero/marzo 1996, p. 45–59)

End of Cold War has generated uncertainty and search for a new order and reformulation of security doctrines and instruments; they will be based above all on indisputable reality of State interdependence.

4046 Roitman, Marcos. América Latina en el proceso de globalización: los límites de sus proyectos. México: Univ. Nacional Autónoma de México, Centro de Investigaciones Interdisciplinarias en Humanidades, Coordinación de Humanidades, 1994. 61 p.: bibl. (El mundo actual)

Helpful definitional-conceptual effort regarding rapidly evolving, but not well understood characteristic of post-Cold War international system and regional American subsystems.

4047 Rossiĭa-Latinskaĭa Amerika: tikhookeanskiĭ most. [Russia and Latin America: a Pacific Ocean bridge. Edited by Aleksandr Ivanovich Sizonenko.] Moscow: Russian Academy of Sciences, Institute of Latin American Studies, 1993. 80 p.: bibl.

Examines potential for increased trade of raw materials and manufactured and agricultural products between Siberia and Russia's Far East, and Mexico, Colombia, Peru, Chile, etc. Also notes possibilities for exchange of technical expertise and for cooperation on exploitation of Pacific Ocean resources, nuclear energy policies, and security issues. [B. Dash]

4048 Roubik, Caroline and **Marcela Schmidt.** Los orígenes de la integración latinoamericana. México: Instituto Panamericano de Geografía e Historia, 1994. 170 p.: appendix, bibl. (Pub./Instituto Panamericano de Geografía e Historia; 469)

Issued by one of the Specialized Organizations of the OAS; authors briefly (in 77 p. of text) assert and trace origins of Latin American political-economic union from 1810–90. Thirteen related official documents plus a useful bibliography are appended.

4049 Security, democracy, and development in U.S.-Latin American relations. Edited by Lars Schoultz, William C. Smith, and Augusto Varas. Miami: North-South Center, Univ. of Miami; New Brunswick, N.J.: Distributed by Transaction Publishers, 1994. 298 p.: bibl., ill., index.

Twelve Latin American and US scholars, in a set of solid contributions, examine various critical post-Cold War issues in terms of titled concepts. Emphasis on broad aspects of inter-American military relations and arms control.

4050 Sheinin, David. The Organization of American States. New Brunswick, N.J.: Transaction Publishers, 1996. 232 p.: indexes. (International organizations series; 11)

Carefully prepared scholarly work that fully annotates official and unofficial sources with 661 entries covering broad range of categories (various citations fall under more than one). A useful starting point for anyone interested in the organization of American states and Pan Americanism. Excellent index.

4051 Smith, Gaddis. The last years of the Monroe doctrine, 1945–1993. New York: Hill and Wang, 1994. 280 p.: bibl., index.

This epilogue to well-known history of Monroe Doctrine is a provocative interpretation of how US presidents resolved policy contradiction of accepting Soviet presence in the Caribbean while reaffirming tenets of Monroe Doctrine.

4052 Smith, Peter H. Talons of the eagle: dynamics of U.S.-Latin American relations. New York: Oxford Univ. Press, 1996. 389 p.: bibl., ill., index, maps.

In this "personal statement" Smith interprets and synthesizes years of research and reflection on two centuries of inter-American relations. Emphasis on structure, continuity, and change; divides system into three broad periods (Imperial Era, Cold War, and current Age of Uncertainty), defining characteristics and dynamics of each.

Toro Hardy, Alfredo. Bajo el signo de la incertidumbre. See item **4458.**

4053 Trías, Vivián. La rebelión de las orillas. Selección y prólogo de Carlos Machado. Montevideo: Ediciones de la Banda Oriental, 1989. 384 p.: bibl. (Selección de obras de Vivián Trías; 12. Serie Patria grande)

New edition of a series of articles on Third World and Latin American issues originally published between the 1950s–70s by the Uruguayan socialist thinker and politician. Includes Trías' essays on Latin America's popular and oligarchic nationalism, possibilities of regional integration, and several populist leaders. [A. Vacs]

4054 U.S.-Latin American policymaking: a reference handbook. Edited by David W. Dent. Westport, Conn.: Greenwood Press, 1995. 586 p.: bibl., ill., index.

Complete, well-conceived, highly useful reference work, with 24 experts contributing focused essays on inter-American and US domestic environments, policymaking structures, actors in US political system, and certain major policy issues.

4055 United States policy in Latin America: a decade of crisis and challenge. Edited by John D. Martz. Lincoln: Univ. of Nebraska Press, 1995. 424 p.: bibl., index.

Companion volume to superb *United States policy in Latin America: a quarter century of crisis and challenge, 1961–1986* edited by Martz in 1988 (see *HLAS 51:4207*) which follows its excellent example. Thirteen prominent scholars offer important critique of US policy, exploring processes, key bilateral relations, and critical problems in context of dramatically changing Latin American and evolving post-Cold War period.

4056 Vanney-Hryćko, Maria Aleksandra. Wpływ przemian w Unii Europejskiej na stosunki z Ameryką Łacińską [The effect of changes within the European Union on relations with Latin America]. Warszawa, Poland: Centrum Studiów Latynoamerykańskich (CESLA), Uniwersytet Warszawski,

1996. 26 p.: tables. (Dokumenty Robocze; 22)

Analyzes current events affecting the European Union and their influence on EU relations with Latin America. Includes the expansion of economic integration within the EU, the end of the Cold War, and the political transformation in Central and Eastern Europe. Also includes statistical tables on EU and Latin American trade during the 1980s and 1990s. [Z. Kantorosinski]

4057 Varas, Augusto. La seguridad del hemisferio occidental en el período posterior a la Guerra Fría. (*Estud. Int./IRIPAZ*, 2:4, julio/dic. 1994, p. 45–70, tables)

Thorough, subtle comparative analysis of diverse post-Cold War security-strategic thinking by US and Latin American policymakers on new agenda of top-priority issues: drugs, migration, environment, democracy and human rights, terrorism and subversion, territorial disputes, and weapons proliferation.

4058 Wiarda, Howard J. After Miami: the summit, the peso crisis, and the future of US-Latin American relations. (*J. Interam. Stud. World Aff.*, 37:1, Spring 1995, p. 43–68, bibl.)

A sober, balanced view of Latin America's politico-economic accomplishments—without idealizing these—over the past decade, as well as a solid assessment of the region's ongoing problems—without despairing of these. Wiarda's realistic analysis and caution concerning the malleability of deep-rooted sociocultural values are the major reasons that he believes political and economic development in Latin America is likely to be tentative. [D. Dent]

4059 Wiarda, Howard J. Democracy and its discontents: development, interdependence, and U.S. policy in Latin America. Lanham, Md.: Rowman & Littlefield Publishers, 1995. 376 p.: bibl., index.

Republication of Wiarda's prior writings on US post-Cold War policy reconsiderations, addressing Bush and Clinton processes, critical policy issues, five case studies, and aspects of Latin American politics; contributions are interesting but only loosely linked as a collection.

4060 Wiarda, Howard J. Iberia and Latin America: new democracies, new policies, new models. Lanham, Md.: Rowman &

Littlefield Publishers, 1996. 128 p.: bibl., ill., index.

Good concise introduction to complex connection of Spain and Portugal's histories, cultures, and policies with Latin America over past two decades; raises important questions regarding democratization and influence of external models and policy actions.

MEXICO AND CENTRAL AMERICA

DALE STORY, *Professor and Chair, Department of Political Science, University of Texas at Arlington*

WITH THE DEMISE OF THE COLD WAR and the concomitant security concerns in Central America, the literature on this region's international relations has become both less strident and less prolific. Not surprisingly, issues concerning US military operations and national security continue to be of critical importance to scholars and publishers. Hence, many studies issued this biennium have focused on the US invasion of Panama—the first use of military force after the Cold War—and fears about the Canal's vulnerability.

In an important article, Max Manwaring argues that the domestic dynamics of Panamanian development take precedence over concerns about international threats to the Canal. He believes that emphasizing political and economic stability in Panama would more effectively safeguard the Canal than would strict military protection (item **4180**). In another study, Eytan Gilboa, like Manwaring, contends that international geo-political objectives are less salient than regional, bilateral, and national priorities (item **4165**). Mark Falcoff's study, however, questions Panama's ability as a sovereign nation to maintain and administer the Canal (item **4160**). Falcoff argues that the final transfer of authority to Panama in 1999 will leave a potentially dangerous vacuum of experience and administrative acumen.

Studies of other Central American nations have focused on the aftermath of negotiated peace pacts emphasizing themes of consolidation, integration, and democratization. Olivier Dabene has stipulated that the short-term resolution to the Central American "crisis" of the 1980s has strengthened efforts for regional integration in the 1990s (item **4153**). While this current emphasis on cooperation and regionalism may ultimately be no more successful than earlier efforts, at least these initiatives are occurring in a much more optimistic environment. Karen Ponciano Castellanos' well-documented and thorough examination of the peace processes in El Salvador and Guatemala avoids such sweeping predictions (item **4187**). This empirical and historical work arrives at more broadly applicable conclusions regarding the consolidation of peace and stability. Terry Karl (item **4173**) and Ian Johnstone (item **4170**) focus on the most significant issue in regard to El Salvador—the peace pact of 1992 that ended approximately 12 years of internal conflict. Karl discusses several factors that insured the success of negotiations to end the civil strife: the apparent military stalemate between government and rebels, the willingness, by both sides, to compromise, and the effect of international pressure by multilateral actors such as the UN. On the latter point, Johnstone discusses the United Nations' success in promoting the 1992 accord and in maintaining peace in the area. Johnstone, a former UN official, argues that external organizations are necessary because they help opposing parties initiate and reach successful negotiations.

Richard Millett, a preeminent scholar of Central America, cautions against over-optimistic predictions regarding the future of peace and democracy in the region (item **4181**). Millett maintains that conditions of marginalization and poverty—the foundations of the conflicts—still exist today. The current period of relative peace and stability, he argues, may be short-lived unless measures are implemented that will permanently resolve the region-wide problem of socioeconomic disparity.

Much of the literature on Mexico continues to focus on postwar bilateral issues between the US and Mexico. The foremost concerns involve trade in general, and the North American Free Trade Agreement (NAFTA) in particular. Because of NAFTA's recent implementation, debate and discussion tend to revolve around the trade agreement's more immediate repercussions. Sidney Weintraub, a leading scholar of US-Mexico economic relations, advances a moderate prognosis regarding NAFTA's consequences (item **4133**). He argues that although the agreement is a positive step, it will not bring immediate prosperity to Mexico. Weintraub reaches similar conclusions in his essential monograph, *NAFTA at Three* (item **4134**). Though he foresees a number of positive outcomes from NAFTA (some job creation, a trade increase, and others), he cautions against judging NAFTA prematurely or expecting from it too much. Unlike the European Community, NAFTA is not an economic and monetary union, and its long-term consequences remain unknown.

Other authors explore graver concerns stemming from implementation of the agreement and examine its potential long-term consequences. Edward Williams argues that the economic infrastructure, particularly along the Mexico-US border region, cannot support the increased economic activity generated by the agreement. He asserts that this economic surge will exert a negative impact on both nations (item **4135**). Williams also discusses potential environmental and public health concerns. Carol Zabin and Sallie Hughes argue that increased Mexican migration to the US will be an unintended and costly result of NAFTA (item **4136**). According to these authors, an expanded Mexican agricultural export market will produce increased levels of internal migration toward northern Mexico; migration that will ultimately spill-over into the US.

The illegal drug trade, a topic once shunned by scholars, now appears prominently as a subject of serious study. More studies than ever are appearing that analyze drug policy of both Mexico and the US. Timothy Dunn's important work critiques US policy on both immigration and narcotics issues (item **4078**). Dunn argues that US efforts to stem the flow of illegal immigration and narcotics have led to a counter-productive militarization of the US-Mexico border region. Using the image of a US military helicopter hovering above undocumented Mexican workers, Dunn applies the theory of low-intensity conflict to the manner in which the United States fulfills its policy objectives. Two Mexican authors provide a more dispassionate analysis of anti-narcotics efforts. José Maria Ramos describes US efforts to halt the import of drugs from Mexico, and examines both social and political contexts of drug trafficking and policies designed to combat it (item **4109**). Maria Celia Toro has written an excellent overview of Mexico's drug market and its anti-drug policies (item **4126**). She reminds us that Mexico, a country with a relatively low level of domestic narcotics consumption, expends disproportionately high levels of economic resources and police and military efforts to enforce anti-drug policies.

Luis G. Zorrilla presents a rare, far-encompassing analysis of Mexico's international relations, detailing the evolution of Mexican foreign policy since the 1840s (item **4138**). The chronological organization of Zorrilla's exceptional multi-volume work facilitates a reader's understanding of the bilateral and multilateral relationships and predominant issues of each era.

MEXICO

4061 Abella Armengol, Gloria. La política exterior en el primer año de gobierno de Ernesto Zedillo. (*Relac. Int./México*, 69, enero/marzo 1996, p. 121–139, table)
Micro-study of initial year of the most recent Mexican presidential *sexenio*. Analyzes year in context of the country's "economic crisis," and argues that this crisis helps explain foreign policy decisions.

4062 Abella Armengol, Gloria. La política exterior en la administración de Carlos Salinas de Gortari: la propuesta del cambio estructural. (*Relac. Int./México*, 62, abril/junio 1994, p. 53–70)
Good overview of Salinas Administration's foreign policy objectives. Stresses the active yet pragmatic nature of Salinas' initiatives.

Alvarez, Robert R. Changing ideology in a transnational market: *chile* and *chileros* in Mexico and the US. See item **693.**

4063 Amador Zamora, Edgar Abraham. Entrando en órbita: las relaciones económicas México-Estados Unidos, 1821–1910, y la función de los poderes regionales. (*Clio/Sinaloa*, 11, mayo/agosto 1994, p. 45–79, bibl., graphs, tables)
Commendable study of growing economic relations between Mexico and US before the Mexican Revolution. Useful tables on trade.

4064 Arellanes Jiménez, Paulino Ernesto. El Tratado de Libre Comercio de América del Norte y la seguridad política nacional. (*Relac. Int./México*, 59, julio/sept. 1993, p. 27–38)
Views NAFTA debate from perspective of Mexico's national security and, ultimately, its sovereignty.

4065 Arrieta Munguía, Judith. La política exterior de México hacia la Unión Europea, 1990–1995. (*Rev. Mex. Polít. Exter.*, 49, invierno 1995/96, p. 123–148)
Traces Mexico's economic relations with Europe since 1960. Focuses on period following 1990 agreements.

4066 Ballesteros, Carlos. El concepto de seguridad ambiental y la integración del mercado norteamericano. (*Relac. Int./México*, 58, abril/junio 1993, p. 63–68)
Mexican perspective on the ecological debate surrounding NAFTA. Argues that the environment is a bilateral and transnational issue.

4067 Barragán F., Armando. La apertura comercial y sistema *antidumping* mexicano, 1987–1995. (*Relac. Int./México*, 70, abril/junio 1996, p. 85–91, graphs, table)
Argues that as Mexico has adopted one of the world's most open trade policies, it must also adopt policies to counteract unfair trade practices.

4068 Barry, Tom; Harry Browne; and Beth Sims. Crossing the line: immigrants, economic integration, and drug enforcement on the U.S.-Mexico border. Albuquerque, N.M.: Resource Center Press, 1994. 146 p.: bibl., map. (U.S.-Mexico series; 3)
Somewhat anecdotal study focusing on a variety of Mexico/US border issues, ranging from immigration to drugs. Useful introduction, but not essential for original research.

4069 Beltrán, Jesús Moisés. Los derechos laborales y la protección ambiental en las negociaciones del Tratado de Libre Comercio de América del Norte. (*Front. Norte*, 7:14, julio/dic. 1995, p. 81–94)
Examines connection between domestic political forces and international negotiations. Uses labor and environmental protection clauses in NAFTA as case studies.

4070 Bouzas, Roberto. El regionalismo en el Hemisferio Occidental: NAFTA, Mercosur y después. (*Desarro. Econ.*, 36, no. especial, verano 1996, p. 87–114, bibl.)
Traces popularity of "regionalism" from Mercosur to NAFTA through several other bilateral arrangements. Suggests that this phenomenon poses several dilemmas.

4071 Brunelle, Dorval and Christian Deblock. New issues on the NAFTA front. (*Int. J./Toronto*, 50:3, Summer 1995, p. 619–629)

Review article surveys five monographs on NAFTA published between 1993–94. Demonstrates how quickly publications on this issue become dated.

4072 Cárdenas Rodriguez, Héctor. México y la Cuenca del Pacífico. (*Rev. Mex. Polít. Exter.*, 44, otoño 1994, p. 104–116, tables)

Describes Mexico's recent attempts to establish a closer relationship with Pacific Rim countries. Ultimately recognizes limitations on such attempts due to dominance of bilateral relationship with US. See also item **4114**.

Castañeda, Jorge G. La casa por la ventana. See item **3016**.

4073 Center for Strategic & International Studies (Washington). NAFTA and sovereignty: trade-offs for Canada, Mexico, and the United States. Edited by Joyce Hoebing, Sidney Weintraub, and M. Delal Baer. Washington: Center for Strategic & International Studies, 1996. 153 p.: bibl. (Significant issues series, 0736–7136; v. 18, no. 4)

Argues that concerns regarding national sovereignty are unfounded and impede progress. Two authors from each of the three NAFTA countries discuss economic and political sovereignty.

4074 Chen Charpentier, Jorge. La política hacia Africa, Asia y Medio Oriente, 1988–1994. (*Rev. Mex. Polít. Exter.*, 44, otoño 1994, p. 117–130)

Brief article by a Mexican diplomat provides cursory look at his country's recent actions toward Africa, Asia, and the Middle East.

4075 Covián González, Miguel A. México en el surgimiento y la creación de la organización de las Naciones Unidas. (*Rev. Mex. Polít. Exter.*, 45, invierno 1994, p. 47–67)

Traces Mexico's international policy of "participation in order to influence" back to the post-World War II creation of the United Nations. See also items **4077** and **4130**.

4076 Dávila Aldás, Francisco R. El Tratado de Libre Comercio México-Estado Unidos y el desarrollo de México. (*Estud. Polit. / México*, 4:4, julio/sept. 1994, p. 63–95)

Examines impact of NAFTA on Mexican development, particularly in light of the

country's restructuring following the early-1980s crisis.

4077 Dávila Pérez, Consuelo. La participación de México en la Organización de las Naciones Unidas. (*Relac. Int. /México*, 68, oct./dic. 1995, p. 123–130)

Overview of Mexico's involvement with the UN in postwar era greatly exaggerates the role played by the UN and Mexico's influence within this international body. See also items **4075** and **4130**.

4078 Dunn, Timothy J. The militarization of the U.S-Mexico border, 1978–1992: low intensity conflict doctrine comes home. Austin: CMAS Books, Univ. of Texas at Austin, 1995. 307 p.: bibl., index, map.

Focuses on the growing militarization of US immigration and drug policy along Mexico/US border. Well-researched monograph examines potential for human rights violations by Border Patrol operations and other law enforcement efforts.

4079 Eisenhower, John S.D. Intervention!: the United States and the Mexican Revolution, 1913–1917. New York: W.W. Norton, 1993. 393 p.: bibl., ill., index, map.

Very readable and engaging summary of US involvement in early stages of the Mexican Revolution. Enlightening for new students, but adds little new information for scholars.

4080 Eisenstadt, Todd. Nuevo estilo diplomático: cabildeo y relaciones públicas, 1986–1991. (*Foro Int.*, 32:5, oct./dic. 1992 p. 667–702, graph, tables)

Discusses several factors that have influenced changes in Mexico/US relations: growing importance of US Congress, "intervening" events, dominance of the Mexican presidency, and Mexico's economic dependence.

4081 Endsley, Harry B. Dispute settlement under the CFTA and NAFTA: from eleventh-hour innovation to accepted institution. (*Hastings Int. Comp. Law Rev.*, 18:4, Summer 1995, p. 659–711, graphs, ill.)

Explores the dispute resolution mechanisms of NAFTA and its predecessor, the Free Trade Agreement between Canada and the US (CFTA). Includes several instructive graphs and charts.

Entre la guerra y la estabilidad política: el México de los 40. See item **3038.**

4082 Fernández Jilberto, Alex E. and **Barbara Hogenboom.** Mexico's integration in NAFTA: neoliberal restructuring and changing political alliances. (*in* Liberalization in the developing world: institutional and economic changes in Latin America, Africa, and Asia. London; New York: Routledge, 1996, p. 138–160, bibl.)

Argues that Mexico's "neoliberal restructuring" policies are counterproductive. Descriptions of the varying political alliances, particularly with regard to NAFTA, are insightful.

4083 Fuentes-Berain, Sandra. México y Canadá: la nueva frontera del norte. (*Rev. Mex. Polít. Exter.*, 44, otoño 1994, p. 14–30)

The Mexican Ambassador to Canada maintains that few nations in the world present more favorable conditions for significant and mutually beneficial relations than Canada and Mexico.

4084 Gaytán Guzmán, Rosa Isabel. La política exterior mexicana en el marco de los procesos mundiales de integración comercial. (*Relac. Int./México*, 58, abril/junio 1993, p. 25–37, tables)

Attempts to develop a theory linking international negotiations with stages of foreign commercial development. Focuses on Mexican industrial plans and decisions regarding GATT.

4085 González Souza, Luis. Soberanía herida: México-Estados Unidos en la hora de la globalización. v. 2, Integración política y desnacionalización cultural. México: Editorial Nuestro Tiempo, 1994. 1 v. (Col. Los grandes problemas nacionales)

Neo-dependency argument regarding Mexico/US relations provides unique perspective through emphasis on cultural penetration, e.g., by the mass media.

4086 Gordon Rapoport, Sara. México frente a Centroamérica. México: Univ. Nacional Autónoma de México, Instituto de Investigaciones Sociales, 1993. 116 p.: bibl. (Col. Sociedad y política)

Rigorous analysis of Mexico's role in Central American affairs during 1980s. Provides a perspective on Central America rarely emphasized.

4087 Grinspun, Ricardo and **Maxwell A. Cameron.** NAFTA and the political economy of Mexico's external relations. (*LARR*, 31:3, 1996, p. 161–188, bibl.)

Review article of 11 monographs on NAFTA suggests that most literature is overly optimistic regarding Mexico's ability to achieve a more equal relationship with its northern neighbor.

4088 Gutiérrez Vidal, Manuel and **Sárah Martínez Pellégrini.** El Tratado de la Unión Europea y el TLC: un análisis comparativo. (*Front. Norte*, 7:13, enero/junio 1995, p. 109–127, bibl., tables)

Compares international integration achieved by the European community to that achieved by NAFTA. The former established a common market; the latter, a free trade area.

Hakim, Peter. NAFTA . . . and after: a new era for the US and Latin America. See item **4012.**

4089 Hernández Martínez, Alfredo. El Acuerdo de Cooperación Laboral de América del Norte (ACLAN): negociación, contenido y perspectivas. (*Rev. Mex. Polít. Exter.*, 46, primavera 1995, p. 28–49, appendices, tables)

Examines non-immigration labor issues concerning bilateral economic links between Mexico and US. Includes useful summary table of events.

4090 Krugman, Paul. The uncomfortable truth about NAFTA: it's foreign policy, stupid. (*Foreign Aff.*, 72:5, Nov./Dec. 1993, p. 13–19)

Argues in favor of NAFTA, but recognizes that the debate in the US over the agreement has become polarized and bitter. See also item **4100.**

4091 Lechuga, Eduardo and **Jean-Louis Dupont.** La Comunidad Europea y sus relaciones con México. (*Foro Int.*, 33:2, abril/junio 1993, p. 419–439)

Recognizing the European Community as a model for economic integration, authors focus on key issues of the Community involving commercial interactions.

Lewis, David E. The Latin Caribbean and regional cooperation: a survey of challenges and opportunities. See item **4264.**

4092 Lotz, Hellmut. Myth and NAFTA: the use of core values in U.S. politics. (*in* Culture and foreign policy. Boulder, Colo.: Lynne Rienner Publishers, 1997, p. 73–96, bibl., graphs, tables)

Unusual piece begins with a philosophical and historical discussion of the "theory of myth," and eventually applies this conceptualization to the Gore-Perot debate on NAFTA.

4093 Lozoya, Jorge Alberto. México y la cooperación internacional. (*Rev. Mex. Polít. Exter.*, 44, otoño 1994, p. 131–140)

Fairly theoretical discussion of foreign policy issues unrelated to defense and national security, written by a high-ranking official of Mexico's Secretaría de Relaciones Exteriores.

4094 Martin, Philip. Mexican-U.S. migration: policies and economic impacts. (*in* Changing structure of Mexico: political, social, and economic prospects. Armonk, N.Y.: M.E. Sharpe, 1996, p. 145–156, graphs)

Short summary essay documents Mexican migration to US over time. Also examines impact of NAFTA and currency devaluations.

4095 Méndez Escobar, Francisca. La política de la Unión Europea hacia América Latina: el caso de México. (*Rev. Mex. Polít. Exter.*, 49, invierno 1995/96, p. 91–122, tables)

Summarizes development of the European Union; then analyzes its initiatives toward Mexico.

4096 Mexico. Secretaría de Relaciones Exteriores. La diplomacia ambiental: México y la Conferencia de las Naciones Unidas sobre Medio Ambiente y Desarrollo. Recopilación de Alberto Glender y Víctor Lichtinger. México: Secretaría de Relaciones Exteriores; Fondo de Cultura Económica, 1994. 431 p.: bibl., ill. (Sección de obras de política y derecho)

Lengthy compilation of scholarly essays related to a 1992 United Nations conference on the environment. Useful look at Mexican perspectives on these policy issues.

4097 Mexico. Secretaría de Salud. Programa nacional de acción: México y la Cumbre Mundial en Favor de la Infancia. 2. ed. México: Secretaría de Salud, 1992. 159 p.: ill.

Useful overview of "children's issues,"

examined in the context of Mexico's development and role in the international arena.

4098 Mexico-United States Border Governors' Conference, *11th, Monterrey, Mexico, 1993.* Eleventh Mexico-United States Border Governors' Conference. Monterrey, Mexico: Impresora y Editorial Plata, 1993? 155 p.: ill.

Very objective and straightforward summary of the 1993 Border Governors' Conference involving state governors from both countries. The focus, not surprisingly, was on impact of NAFTA.

4099 Mitos en las relaciones México-Estados Unidos. Recopilación de María Esther Schumacher. México: Secretaría de Relaciones Exteriores; Fondo de Cultura Económica, 1994. 528 p.: appendices, bibl. (Sección de obras de historia)

Bilateral compilation of scholarly essays from a 1992 conference on Mexico/US relations. Volume is quite broad in scope and lacks a clear focus; does include useful appendices of chronological events.

4100 Orme, William A. Myths versus facts: the whole truth about the half-truths. (*Foreign Aff.*, 72:5, Nov./Dec. 1993, p. 2–12)

Argues that NAFTA debate in US really centered on domestic political agendas and irreconcilable world views. More prescriptive than objective. See also item **4090.**

4101 Orme, William A. Understanding NAFTA: Mexico, free trade, and the new North America. Austin: Univ. of Texas Press, 1996. 335 p.: ill., index, map.

Very readable book written during height of NAFTA debate. Remains a valuable resource for discussing impact of the trade agreement in Mexico and US.

4102 Papademetriou, Demetrios G. Illegal Mexican migration in the United States and US responses. (*Int. Migr.*, 31:2/3, 1993, p. 314–348, tables)

Brief but useful overview of Mexican migration and US policy responses to this issue over time.

4103 Pérez, Al I. Free trade with Mexico and U.S. national security. (*in* Mexico faces the 21st century. Westport, Conn.: Greenwood Press, 1995, p. 119–136, table)

Economic analysis of NAFTA reaches a number of fairly common conclusions. Most laudable is the discussion of domestic political implications for Mexico.

4104 Pereznieto Castro, Leonel. Algunos aspectos del sistema de solución de controversias en el Tratado Norteamericano de Libre Comercio. (*Relac. Int./México*, 58, abril/junio 1993, p. 69–77)

Praises NAFTA's conflict resolution system. Gives overviews from both US and Mexican viewpoints.

4105 Piñón Antillón, Rosa María. El reto de México: desarrollo y mercados externos. (*Relac. Int./México*, 70, abril/junio 1996, p. 11–22, bibl., graphs, maps, tables)

Discusses shift in Mexico's economic development strategy from an inward-oriented approach before 1980 to a more outward-oriented policy since mid-1980s. Concludes that economic growth has not "trickled down" to alleviate marginality and poverty.

4106 La política internacional de México en el decenio de los ochenta. Compilación y presentación de César Sepúlveda. México: Fondo de Cultura Económica, 1994. 656 p.: bibl., indexes. (Sección de obras de política y derecho)

Highly commendable volume of essays by noted Mexican scholars emphasizes diversification of Mexican foreign policy, i.e., a discernible effort to move away from focus on bilateral relations with US.

Polska-Meksyk, 1918–1988: zbiór dokumentów i materiałów [Poland-Mexico, 1918–1988: a collection of documents and materials]. See *HLAS 56:1567*.

4107 Ponce Nava, Diana L. El derecho internacional sobre medio ambiente y desarrollo: la contribución mexicana. (*Rev. Mex. Polít. Exter.*, 47, verano 1995, p. 81–99)

Essentially a legal summary touching on international issues related to environmental protection and Mexico's contribution to negotiations.

4108 Prado, Irene Zea. La otra frontera: raíces históricas de la relación México-Centroamérica o el origen de un resentimiento. (*Relac. Int./México*, 59, julio/sept. 1993, p. 61–65)

Contrasts Mexico's struggle for political independence with that of Central American nations. Suggests that a differential hierarchy of political dependency existed between the dominant power of Spain (and later of the US) and the colony of Mexico, on the one hand, and Central American colonies on the other.

4109 Ramos, José María. Las políticas antidrogas y comercial de Estados Unidos en la frontera con México. Tijuana, Mexico: El Colegio de la Frontera Norte, 1995. 133 p.: bibl., ill.

Important book documents US efforts to stem narcotic flows from Mexico; places these policies in social and political contexts; and examines impact on specific border areas.

4110 Relaciones México-California: más allá de la frontera. Recopilación de Guillermo Ibarra Escobar. Culiacán Rosales, Mexico: Univ. Autónoma de Sinaloa; Sistema de Investigación del Mar de Cortés, 1997. 265 p.: appendix, bibl., graphs, maps, tables.

Uses examination of California to review the panorama of Mexico/US relations. Extensive appendix of statistical information.

4111 Retana Tello, Ismael Reyes. México frente al arbitraje internacional: el caso de El Chamizal. (*Rev. Mex. Polít. Exter.*, 43, abril/junio 1994, p. 98–111)

A Mexican diplomat reviews the classic case of El Chamizal as a case study of international arbitration.

4112 Rich, Paul. Mexican neoliberal nightmares: Tampico is not Taiwan. (*J. Interam. Stud. World Aff.*, 37:4, Winter 1995, p. 173–190, bibl.)

Review essay of eight fairly disparate monographs focused generally on issues of Mexico/US trade relations and NAFTA.

4113 Rodríguez Muñoz, María del Consuelo and **Gabriela Ugalde García.** Guía del Archivo de Límites y Ríos México-Guatemala, 1855–1986. Coordinación de Guadalupe Rodríguez de Ita. México: Secretaría de Relaciones Exteriores; Instituto Mora, 1993. 127 p. (Archivo histórico diplomático mexicano)

Detailed bibliographical and historical guide to Guatemala/Mexico relations. Notable primary research resource for scholars of this bilateral relationship.

4114 Roldán, Eduardo. Estrategia de la política exterior de México hacia el Pacífico. (*Rev. Mex. Polít. Exter.*, 43, abril/junio 1994, p. 66–80, graph, table)

Presents official Mexican viewpoint on the importance of the Pacific area to Mexico. See also item **4072.**

4115 Rosas, María Cristina. El Tratado de Libre Comercio de América del Norte: factores estratégicos. (*Rev. Ciclos*, 4:4, 1994, p. 95–118)

Discusses asymmetries among the three NAFTA partners. Recognizes potential for a Canadian-Mexican alliance.

4116 Rosas, María Cristina and **Pekka Valtonen.** El Tratado de Libre Comercio de América del Norte: desarrollo social y los dilemas de la agricultura mexicana. (*Rev. Mex. Cienc. Polít. Soc.*, 39:158, oct./dic. 1994, p. 23–41)

Examines regional impacts of NAFTA, especially regarding agriculture. Concludes that cultivation of Mexico's export-oriented agricultural commodities will likely increase (particularly in the northern region) at the expense of agricultural products for domestic consumption.

4117 Rosenzweig, Gabriel. La política de México hacia Europa, 1989–1994. (*Rev. Mex. Polít. Exter.*, 44, otoño 1994, p. 94–103, tables)

Summarizes important Mexican policy decisions toward Europe since 1989, and analyzes factors that helped shape such policy. Includes extensive data on economic interactions.

4118 Rossiĩa i Meksika: 100 let diplomaticheskikh otnosheniĩ. [Russia and Mexico: 100 years of diplomatic relations.] Edited by Anatoliĩ Danilovich Bekarevich and Aleksandr Ivanovich Sizonenko. Moscow: Academy of Sciences of the USSR, Institute of Latin American Studies, 1990. 173 p.: appendix, bibl.

Collection honors 100th anniversary (Dec. 1990) of the establishment of formal relations between Mexico and Russia/USSR. Includes contributions by historians at the Institute of Latin American Studies, who trace Russian sympathies toward, and interaction with, Mexico from early-19th century through Soviet period. Early Russian visitors to Mexico included scientists, journalists, military officers, and representatives of the mercantile Russian America Co. Also addressed are issues such as Russian/Soviet views of Mexican historical events, Soviet/

Mexican economic relations, and the work of Friendship Societies. Appendix includes historical documents. [B. Dash]

4119 Rozental, Andrés. La nueva etapa en las relaciones México-Estados Unidos. (*Rev. Mex. Polít. Exter.*, 44, otoño 1994, p. 7–13)

An approximation of the official Mexican government perspective, claims that NAFTA signals new era of Mexico/US interdependence.

4120 Ruelas, Ana Luz. México y Estados Unidos en la revolución mundial de las telecomunicaciones. México: Univ. Nacional Autónoma de México, Centro de Investigaciones sobre América del Norte (CISAN); Culiacán Rosales, Mexico: Univ. Autónoma de Sinaloa, Escuela de Historia, 1996. 307 p.: bibl., ill., map.

Interesting examination of telecommunications industry. Discussion ranges from economic and technological descriptions to case studies of the industry's standing within the US and Mexico.

4121 Sandéz Pérez, Agustín. Perspectivas de integración energética México-norteamericana: intercambios de electricidad y gas natural en el noroeste Mexicano. (*Estud. Front.*, 29, sept./dic. 1992, p. 9–55, bibl.)

Focuses on commercial exchange of energy products (particularly petroleum) as a nexus in the panorama of US/Mexico relations.

4122 Saunders, J. Owen. The NAFTA and the North American Agreement on Environmental Cooperation. (*in* Environmental policy: transnational issues and national trends. Westport, Conn.: Quorum Books, 1997, p. 61–85, bibl.)

Objective and legalistic treatise examines the compromises (or cooperation) on environmental issues that developed, outside of NAFTA, into the North American Agreement on Environmental Cooperation.

4123 Sherro, Stéphan. La Unión Europea como opción diversificadora: un recorrido crítico. (*Rev. Mex. Polít. Exter.*, 49, invierno 1995/96, p. 220–243, appendix, table)

Argues that positive and improving relations between Mexico and the European Union could become even better. Focus is on nexus among economic and political spheres.

4124 Solana, Fernando. Cinco años de política exterior. Prólogo de Modesto Seara Vázquez. México: Editorial Porrúa, 1994. 840 p.: index.

Compilation of essays from the Secretaría de Relaciones Exteriores of Mexico covering the period 1988–93.

Solveira de Báez, Beatriz. La Argentina, el ABC y el conflicto entre México y Estados Unidos, 1913–1916. See item **4368.**

4125 Suárez Farías, Francisco. Los gabinetes presidenciales de México y Estados Unidos durante los gobiernos de Miguel de la Madrid y Ronald Reagan. México: Univ. Autónoma Metropolitana, Unidad Xochimilco, 1994. 148 p.: bibl. (Col. Ensayos)

Fairly empirical comparison of Mexican and US executive branch cabinets during 1980s. Somewhat esoteric, but useful analysis of both administrations.

4126 Toro, María Celia. Mexico's "war" on drugs: causes and consequences. Boulder, Colo.: Lynne Rienner Publishers, 1995. 105 p.: bibl., ill., index, maps. (Studies on the impact of the illegal drug trade; 3)

Reminds readers that Mexico, a country with a relatively low level of domestic drug abuse, spends "substantial" portions of its police and military budgets combating drug traffic. All-too-brief overview of Mexico's drug market and anti-drug policies.

4127 Universidad Autónoma Chapingo (Mexico). Departamento de Sociología Rural. Emigración, derechos humanos y el TLC. México: Univ. Autónoma Chapingo, Depto. de Sociología Rural, 1995. 67 p.: bibl. (Col. de cuadernos sobre migración; 2)

Brief compilation of essays by Mexican scholars on Mexican immigration to US. Includes a few interesting case studies (focusing on specific Mexican regions), but lacks central thesis.

4128 Velázquez Flores, Rafael. Algunas reflexiones en torno al análisis de la política exterior de México. (Relac. Int./México, 62, abril/junio 1994, p. 7–19)

Attempts to methodically analyze Mexican foreign policy and connect it to national objectives.

4129 Velázquez Flores, Rafael. Introducción al estudio de la política exterior de México. México: Editorial Nuestro Tiempo, 1995. 302 p.: bibl.

Textbook study of Mexican foreign policy combines a chronological organization with case studies of regional issues and roles of domestic actors.

4130 Voz de México en la Asamblea General de la ONU, 1946–1993. Presentación de Manuel Tello. Recopilación de Olga Pellicer de Brody. México: Secretaría de Relaciones Exteriores; Fondo de Cultura Económica, 1994. 479 p. (Vida y pensamiento de México)

Reference work on Mexican presentations at the United Nations during postwar era. See also items **4075** and **4077.**

4131 Washington Office on Latin America. Mexican insights: Mexican civil society speaks to the United States. Washington: Washington Office on Latin America, 1995. 51 p.

Brief attempt, after the Chiapas uprising and implementation of NAFTA, to publicize within the US the opinions of important Mexican nongovernmental decision-makers.

4132 Weintraub, Sidney. The depth of economic integration between Mexico and the United States. (Wash. Q., 18:4, Autumn 1995, p. 173–184)

Contrasts perspectives of "inevitablists" (those who argue that US/Mexican economic integration will inevitably reach higher levels) with those of NAFTA proponents (who argue that NAFTA is necessary to increase such integration). For economist's comment, see item **1719.**

4133 Weintraub, Sidney. Mexico's foreign economic policy: from admiration to disappointment. (in Changing structure of Mexico: political, social, and economic prospects. Armonk, N.Y.: M.E. Sharpe, 1996, p. 43–54, graphs)

Noted economist examines watershed of change that has occurred in Mexican foreign economic policy in recent decades. Includes a number of enlightening graphs on changes in economic outcomes during the Salinas Administration.

4134 Weintraub, Sidney. NAFTA at three: a progress report. Washington: Center for Strategic & International Studies, 1997. 105 p.: bibl., ill., index. (Significant issues series ; v. 19, no. 1)

Very dispassionate and objective analysis of NAFTA three years after implementation. Predominantly positive conclusions about agreement's impact, but recognizes that its short-term significance should not be exaggerated.

4135 Williams, Edward J. NAFTA and beyond: the United States-Mexican borderlands in transition. (*in* Mexico faces the 21st century. Westport, Conn.: Greenwood Press, 1995, p. 137–151)

Argues that NAFTA will have both positive and negative implications for the Mexico/US border region. A positive effect is aggregate economic growth, but argues that existing infrastructure is insufficient to absorb this growth.

4136 Zabin, Carol and **Sallie Hughes.** Economic integration and labor flows: stage migration in farm labor markets in Mexico and the United States. (*Int. Migr. Rev.*, 29:2, Summer 1995, p. 395–422, bibl., graphs, maps, tables)

Argues that NAFTA likely will result in increased Mexican agricultural exports, leading to increased Mexican migration to US. Well-researched. Instructive tables and graphs.

Zea, Leopoldo. Chiapas, yunque de México para Latinoamérica. See item **3133.**

4137 Zhao, Suisheng. China's perceptions of NAFTA and changing roles in the Asia-Pacific. (*in* Cooperation or rivalry: regional integration in the Americas and the Pacific Rim. Boulder, Colo.: Westview Press, 1996, p. 225–242)

Begins with surprising claim (citing the Chinese news agency) that approval of NAFTA was one of the ten major international news events for China in 1993. Article then discusses Chinese interests in NAFTA.

4138 Zorrilla, Luis G. Relaciones políticas, económicas y sociales de México con el extranjero. v. 1–4. México: Offset Universal, 1993–. 4 v.: bibl., indexes.

Indispensable history of Mexico's foreign policy (1750–1940) focuses on the pertinent bilateral relationships of that era. Critical reference source.

CENTRAL AMERICA

4139 Araúz, Celestino Andrés. Panamá y sus relaciones internacionales. v. 1–2. Panamá: Editorial Universitaria, 1994. 2 v.: bibl. (Biblioteca de la cultura panameña; 15)

Exhaustive, ambitious, and lengthy historical study spans three centuries and culminates with the signing of the Panama Canal Treaties during the 1970s. Useful, detailed information on Panamanian international relations.

4140 Arias Calderón, Ricardo. Un rumbo racional y nacional con respecto a las bases y el Canal de Panamá. (*Panorama Centroam. Pensam.*, 44, oct./dic. 1996, p. 51–59)

Important and enlightening essay on Panamanian views toward mid-1990s negotiations with US concerning implementation of the Panama Canal Treaties.

4141 Baranyi, Stephen. Beyond traditional peace-keeping?: caveats from international theory and from UN experiences in Central America. (*Estud. Int./IRIPAZ*, 5:9, enero/junio 1994, p. 153–166)

Argues that the end of the Cold War has given the UN an enhanced role in international relations. Examines this thesis in context of Central America.

4142 Bayo, Francesc. El papel de España en la pacificación y democratización de América Central. (*in* International Congress of Americanists, *48th, Stockholm, 1994.* Problems of democracy in Latin America. Stockholm: Institute of Latin American Studies, Stockholm Univ., 1996, p. 106–123, bibl.)

Discusses Spanish relations with Central America over last 15 years. Focuses on three main themes: internal Spanish politics, Central American instability, and the region's geopolitical environment.

4143 Benítez Manaut, Raúl. Centroamérica y el nuevo sistema internacional: negociaciones, paz, integración y geopolítica. (*Estud. Int./IRIPAZ*, 2:4, julio/dic. 1994, p. 96–117)

First examines Latin America's role in the context of the "new political order" (i.e., post-Cold War era); then discusses the new geopolitical environment of Central America.

4144 Bermúdez Torres, Lilia. Percepciones centroamericanas sobre la política de promoción de la democracia de Estados Unidos. (*in* Estados Unidos desde América Latina: sociedad, política y cultura. México: Instituto de Investigaciones Dr. José María Luis Mora; Centro de Investigación y Docencia Económicas, El Colegio de México, 1995, p. 377–406, appendix)

Discussion of Central American perceptions of US policy on regional democratization. Based on 24 interviews with political actors in El Salvador, Nicaragua, and Panama. Admirable effort, but depends on a small number of highly selective interviews.

4145 Booth, John A. Central America and the United States: cycles of containment and response. (*Relac. Int./Heredia*, 48/49, tercer y cuarto trimestres 1994, p. 25–38, tables)

Not original research, but a good introduction to US policy toward Central America. Commendably offers several theoretical interpretations of this relationship, each of which stresses its inherent inequity and the primacy of security in US actions.

4146 Brown, Jeremy M. Explaining the Reagan years in Central America: a world system perspective. Lanham, Md.: Univ. Press of America, 1995. 300 p.: bibl., index.

Although the author, a former Special Forces soldier stationed in Latin America, admits to a "subjective" and even "personal" interest in Central America, he attempts to apply a series of fairly esoteric sociological theories to Central American crisis. Ultimately not a major contribution.

4147 Brown, Timothy C. The United States and Nicaragua: inside the Carter and Sandinista Administrations. (*J. Interam. Stud. World Aff.*, 36:2, Summer 1994, p. 207–219, bibl.)

Former US Foreign Service officer reviews two books on the fall of Somoza and subsequent Sandinista regime.

4148 Cardenal, Rodolfo. La segunda visita de Juan Pablo II: el desafío de la justicia y la reconciliación. (*ECA/San Salvador*, 51: 567–568, enero/feb. 1996, p. 29–46, photos)

Discusses the Pope's Feb. 1996 visit to El Salvador as it relates to issues of national reconciliation, social justice, and permanent peace. See also item **4159.**

4149 Centroamérica: balance de la década de los 80; una perspectiva regional. Coordinación de Marta Casaús Arzú y Rolando Castillo Quintana. Madrid: Fundación CEDEAL, 1993. 527 p.: bibl., ill., map.

Compilation of essays from noted Central American scholars. Various themes include democratization, case studies of US policy, and historical analysis of local oligarchies.

4150 Cole, Ronald H. Operation Just Cause: the planning and execution of joint operations in Panama, February 1988–January 1990. Washington: Joint History Office, Office of the Chairman of the Joint Chiefs of Staff, 1995. 88 p.: bibl., index, map.

US Joint Chiefs of Staff publication on the "planning and execution" of the Panama invasion (Operation Just Cause). Short but useful summary of events from US military perspective.

4151 Crónica de una infamia: la invasión a Panamá y el deber incumplido en salud. San José: LIL, 1993. 143 p.: bibl., ill.

Provides interesting twist on critiques of US invasion of Panama by focusing on public health issues. Useful for its analysis of public policy issues as well as for its understanding of foreign policy.

4152 Cruz, Arturo J. Estados Unidos y Centroamérica: la era del comercio. (*Rev. INCAE*, 8:2, 1995, p. 9–22)

Argues that US relations with Central America have undergone a transition from a geopolitical era to a trade era. More realistically, without a crisis to stoke the geopolitical fires, US policy is guided mostly by benign neglect.

4153 Dabène, Olivier. La invención y remanencia de una crisis: Centroamérica en los años 80. (*Anu. Estud. Centroam.*, 19:2, 1993, p. 25–50, tables)

Argues that Central American heads of State recast the "crisis" of the 1980s in regional terms, rather than addressing the separate and distinct national issues. This regionalization has led to a focus on integration during the 1990s.

4154 Delgado Diamante, Daniel. La neutralidad como mecanismo de seguridad del canal de Panamá. (*Tareas/Panamá*, 86, enero/abril 1994, p. 43–54)

Argues that neutrality of the Canal is the best (if not the only) means of guaranteeing its security.

4155 Díaz Córdova, Arturo. ¿Adónde va el diálogo político entre la comunidad CEE y Centroamérica? (*Estud. Int./IRIPAZ*, 3:5, enero/junio 1992, p. 59–74)

Focuses on evolution of the Central American Common Market, contrasting Central American experience with that of the European Union.

4156 Díaz Córdova, Arturo. El proceso de paz en El Salvador: la Comisión de la Verdad, análisis e implicaciones de su trabajo. (*Estud. Int./IRIPAZ*, 5:9, enero/junio 1994, p. 85–104)

Claims that the role of international organizations was central to the success of Salvadoran peace process. Useful analysis provides sound details regarding peace accords and international involvement in their development.

4157 Dierckxsens, Wim. De la globalización a la perestroika occidental. San José: DEI, 1994. 176 p.: bibl., ill. (Col. universitaria)

Interesting analysis of Central American development during post-Cold War era places region in a broader than usual international context.

4158 Escalante Herrera, Ana Cecilia. Cooperación para la democracia y el desarrollo en América Central: un reto para la política exterior de Estados Unidos en los años noventa. (*Relac. Int./Heredia*, 48/49, tercer y cuarto trimestres 1994, p. 13–23, bibl., tables)

Examines prospects for democracy in Central America and effects of this process on regional development. Useful data on US aid and investment.

4159 Escobar, Francisco Andrés. Totus tuus: Juan Pablo II en El Salvador. (*ECA/San Salvador*, 51:567–568, enero/feb. 1996, p. 47–57, photos)

Brief quotes from dozens of interviews with average citizens. Attempts to give a popular Salvadoran perspective regarding impact of Pope's Feb. 1996 visit. See also item **4148.**

4160 Falcoff, Mark. Panama's Canal: what happens when the United States gives a small country what it wants. Washington: AEI Press, 1998. 168 p.: bibl., index.

Author discusses the problems faced by former colonial territories (or smaller, "dependent" countries) when they assume responsibilities formerly undertaken by the US. Examines transfer of authority over Canal from US to Panama as a case study.

4161 Foro Centroamericano sobre la Integración de Panamá, *Panamá, 1991*. Actas. San José: FEDEPRICAP, 1992. 155 p.: bibl.

Transcript of a 1991 public- and private-sector-sponsored conference held in Panama City. All articles explore possibilities for Panama's incorporation into a Central American regional economic cartel.

4162 Fundación Istmeña de Estudios Económicos y Sociales (Panama). Seminario. El futuro del Canal de Panamá en el año 2000: informe del Seminario FIEES. Panamá: Fundación Istmeña de Estudios Económicos y Sociales, 1993. 111 p. (Serie FIEES; 1, agosto 1993)

Compilation of essays, mostly by Panamanian authors, on issues that may affect the Panama Canal after year 2000. Lacks central focus and integration of ideas.

4163 Gandásegui, Marco A. Las bases militares y las areas revertidas. (*Tareas/Panamá*, 95, enero/abril 1997, p. 13–29, table)

Dispassionate discussion of costs and benefits involved in allowing US military bases to continue operating in Panama into the next century.

4164 García-Sayán, Diego. El rol de las Naciones Unidas en los conflictos internos: el caso de El Salvador. (*Anal. Int.*, 2, abril/junio 1993, p. 51–69)

Examines roles that UN and its Secretary-General have played in the resolution of recent conflicts in El Salvador. Offers little concrete analysis.

4165 Gilboa, Eytan. The Panama invasion revisited: lessons for the use of force in the post Cold War era. (*Polit. Sci. Q.*, 110:4, Winter 1995/96, p. 539–562)

Analyzes significance of 1989 invasion of Panama—the first time US used military force after the Cold War. Discusses several critical mistakes and inconsistencies in US policy toward Panama.

4166 Gill, Lesley. Examining power, serving the State: anthropology, Congress and the invasion of Panama. (*Hum. Organ.*, 54:3, Fall 1995, p. 318–324, bibl.)

Somewhat unusual article is essentially an autobiography of an anthropologist serving as a US Congressional Fellow. Relates her efforts to write an op-ed piece on the US invasion of Panama.

4167 Gutiérrez Pita, José Ignacio. La neutralidad del Canal de Panamá. (*Tareas/Panamá*, 90, mayo/agosto 1995, p. 9–31)

Very brief treatise is essentially an historical overview of efforts to maintain the Panama Canal's "neutrality."

4168 Herrera Herrera, Carlos Eduardo. Cronología de la política exterior de Costa Rica: julio-septiembre de 1993. (*Relac. Int./ Heredia*, 47, segundo semestre 1994, p. 41–57)

Detailed daily journal of Costa Rican foreign policy kept over a three-month period in 1993.

4169 Informe sobre el cumplimiento de los acuerdos de paz al 31 de octubre de 1995. San Salvador: Gobierno de El Salvador, 1995? 50 leaves: ill.

Very brief analysis of Salvadoran peace treaty. Discusses effect on domestic politics and its economic impact.

4170 Johnstone, Ian. Rights and reconciliation: UN strategies in El Salvador. Boulder, Colo.: Lynne Rienner Publishers, 1995. 104 p.: bibl. (International Peace Academy occasional paper series)

Brief monograph written by UN official argues, using El Salvador as example, that UN peacekeeping missions can balance goals of peace and justice. Well-researched; includes dozens of original interviews.

4171 Jonas, Susanne. Dangerous liaisons: the U.S. in Guatemala. (*Foreign Policy*, 103, Summer 1996, p. 145–160, photo)

Prescriptive article argues that mid-1990s were critical years for the evolution of peace and democracy in Guatemala. Calls upon US to enhance reform by exercising positive influence.

4172 Jované, Juan. Cinco tesis sobre las bases nortamericanas en Panamá. (*Tareas/Panamá*, 95, enero/abril 1997, p. 31–38, table)

Among the better Panamanian discussions of concerns regarding the continued existence of US military bases in that country.

4173 Karl, Terry Lynn. El Salvador's negotiated revolution. (*Foreign Aff.*, 71:2, Spring 1992, p. 147–164)

Argues that 1992 Salvadoran domestic peace represents an important path-breaking compromise made possible by military stalemate, increasing flexibility during negotiations, and UN presence.

4174 Krenn, Michael L. The chains of interdependence: U.S. policy toward Central America, 1945–1954. Armonk, N.Y.: M.E. Sharpe, 1996. 228 p.: bibl., index. (Perspectives on Latin America and the Caribbean)

Historical analysis of theories of interdependence in US policy since World War II. Examines their application toward Central America from 1950s-80s.

4175 LeMoyne, James. El PNUD y la promoción de la gobernabilidad democrática en América Central. (*in* Gobernabilidad y desarrollo democrático en América Latina. New York: Programa de las Naciones Unidas y el Caribe para el Desarrollo. 1997, p. 220–241)

Author believes the UN will play a central role in Central America's transition to democracy.

4176 Leonard, Thomas M. Central America and the United States: overlooked foreign policy objectives. (*Americas/Francisc.*, 50:1, July 1993, p. 1–30)

Indirectly criticizes plethora of literature on US foreign policy toward Central America. Argues that Central American foreign policy objectives should also be considered.

4177 Leonard, Thomas M. Central America, U.S. policy, and the crisis of the 1980s: recent interpretations. (*LARR*, 31:2, 1996, p. 194–211)

Reviews eight English-language monographs concerning Central America's international involvement. Examines some important individual works, but strains to find connections among them.

4178 Leonard, Thomas M. An outpost of Cold War strategy?: the United States and Central America, 1944–1947. (*Rev. Rev. Interam.*, 25:1/4, enero/dic. 1995, p. 21–44)

Thorough examination of US relations with Central America. Argues that US policy was guided by regional concerns, rather than by emerging international dynamics.

4179 Manfredo, Fernando. The future of the Panama Canal. (*J. Interam. Stud. World Aff.*, 35:3, Fall 1993, p. 103–128)

Former administrator with the Panama Canal Commission and a negotiator of the treaties warns of potential pitfalls in their final implementation.

4180 Manwaring, Max G. The security of Panama and the Canal: now and for the future. (*J. Interam. Stud. World Aff.*, 35:3, Fall 1993, p. 151–170)

Argues that security of the Panama Canal is less an issue of conventional military strategy than one of political and economic stability.

Martin, Lisa L. and **Kathryn Sikkink.** U.S. policy and human rights in Argentina and Guatemala, 1973–1980. See item **4355.**

4181 Millet, Richard L. Central America's enduring conflicts. (*Curr. Hist.*, 93 : 581, March 1994, p. 124–128)

Contends that international (i.e., US) attention has shifted away from Central America, and argues that many conditions that gave rise to 1980s conflicts are still present.

4182 Murillo, Luis E. The Noriega mess: the drugs, the Canal, and why America invaded. Berkeley, Calif.: Video-Books, 1995. 1096 p.: bibl., ill., index, maps.

Lengthy account of Noriega years in Panama, written by an anti-Noriega activist. Extensive discussion may prove useful.

4183 Nuzzi O'Shaughessy, Laura. La verificación/observación internacional como medio demcrático de legitimación: los acuerdos centroamericanos de paz en Nicaragua y El Salvador. (*Relac. Int./Heredia*, 46, primer trimestre 1994, 31–40)

Argues that implementation components of verification are critical elements in legitimizing and preserving negotiated Central America peace accords.

4184 Orozco, Manuel Salvador. Aiding Central America: the three contexts of aid. (*Relac. Int./Heredia*, 51/53, 1995, p. 47–61, graphs, tables)

Well-argued article posits classic theory that aid is used essentially as leverage for political and/or economic objectives. Well substantiated by commendable presentation of data.

4185 Ortega Pinto, Herbert David. Naciones Unidas, acuerdos de paz y verificación internacional: el caso de El Salvador. (*Estud. Int./IRIPAZ*, 4:8, julio/dic. 1993, p. 83–91)

Useful case study of El Salvador, but real focus of article is UN's peacekeeping role as legally determined in the organization's charter and elsewhere.

4186 Padilla, Luis Alberto. La teoría de la resolución de conflictos y su aplicación al contexto socio político de Guatemala. (*Estud. Int./IRIPAZ*, 1:2, julio/dic. 1990, p. 60–73, bibl.)

Admirable attempt to apply conflict resolution theory to the Guatemala case; however, fails to sufficiently distinguish between international and domestic conflict.

4187 *Panorama Centroamericano: Temas y Documentos de Debate.* No. 60, nov./dic. 1995. Centro America 1995 de Edelberto Torres Rivas. Guatemala: Instituto Centroamericano de Estudios Políticos (INCEP).

General Spanish-language introduction to sociopolitical environment in Central America during mid-1990s. Nothing new for regional experts, but a good introduction for students and interested readers. Includes some useful tables.

4188 *Panorama Centroamericano: Temas y Documentos de Debate.* No. 64, julio/agosto 1996. El rol de la sociedad civil en los procesos de paz de Guatemala y El Salvador de Karen Ponciano Castellanos. Guatemala: Instituto Centroamericano de Estudios Políticos (INCEP).

Lengthy volume on domestic peace negotiations in these two Central American countries. Excellent, well-researched guide.

4189 Pastor, Robert A. The United States and Central America: interlocking debates. (*in* Double-edged diplomacy: international bargaining and domestic politics. Berkeley: Univ. of California Press, 1993, p. 265–299)

Former official of the Carter Administration and respected scholar posits need to analyze foreign policy on two levels—international negotiations and domestic bargaining—and applies this perspective to the most significant Central American issues.

4190 Paz Barnica, Edgardo. La Cumbre de las Américas y la prosperidad compartida. Madrid: Tecnos, 1996. 181 p. (Col. Ventana abierta)

Honduran perspective on potential Central American integration and cooperation.

Prado, Irene Zea. La otra frontera: raíces históricas de la relación México-Centroamérica o el origen de un resentimiento. See item **4108.**

4191 Queiser Morales, Waltraud. Intervention in the Cold War and post-Cold War era: lessons from Grenada and Panama.

(*SECOLAS Ann.*, 25, March 1994, p. 5–24)
Well-researched article compares a US
military campaign during Cold War (Grenada)
with another after Cold War (Panama).

4192   Quintero Russo, Carmen. Opiniones
y expectativas acerca del Canal de Panamá, bienes y áreas revertidas. Panamá:
Univ. de Panamá, Instituto del Canal de Panamá y Estudios Internacionales, 1994. 46 p.:
ill. (Serie Avance de investigación; 2)
Discusses results of Panamanian public opinion polls regarding the Canal and general issues concerning relations with US.
Relies strongly on surveys conducted in
Panama.

4193   Rhenán Segura, Jorge. Costa Rica y la
protección internacional de los derechos humanos, 1945–1995. (*Relac. Int./Here-
dia*, 50, 1995, p. 17–27, bibl.)
Briefly summarizes human rights record of Costa Rica, one of Central America's
most democratic nations. Cites specific post-
World War II accomplishments.

Rodríguez Muñoz, María del Consuelo and
Gabriela Ugalde García. Guía del Archivo de
Límites y Ríos México-Guatemala, 1855–
1986. See item **4113.**

4194   Rojas Aravena, Francisco. Centroamérica: dos años de trabajo por la paz.
(*Estud. Int./IRIPAZ*, 1:2, julio/dic. 1990,
p. 20–29)
Summarizes process leading up to, and
results of, the Esquipulas II agreement. Some
useful insights.

4195   Rojas Aravena, Francisco and **Luis G.
Solís Rivera.** De la guerra a la integración: la transición y la seguridad en Centroamérica. (*Polit. Estrateg.*, 60, mayo/agosto
1993, p. 27–40)
Examines how transition towards democracy and the process of rebuilding economic infrastructure have been affected by
internal military conflict and external influence (particularly from the US).

4196   Rojas Aravena, Francisco. Esquipulas:
un proceso de construcción de confianza. (*Estud. Int./IRIPAZ*, 4:8, julio/dic.
1993, p. 64–82, bibl.)
Central American peace process must
create a sense of confidence and legitimacy.
Discusses ways to achieve these goals.

4197   Sanahuja, José Antonio. Las relaciones
entre la Comunidad Europea y Centroamérica en los años noventa: continuidad,
reactivación, o cambio? Managua: Coordinadora Regional de Investigaciones Económicas
y Sociales (CRIES), 1994. 63 p.: bibl., ill. (Documento de trabajo / CRIES; 94/1)
Brief overview of Europe's motives and
objectives in its relations with Central America since 1984. Useful examination of trans-
atlantic relations.

4198   Simmons, Donald C. National sovereignty as an element of international
jurisprudence: a case study; the quest of Belizean separation from Guatemalan dominion.
(*in* Belize: selected proceedings from the second interdisciplinary conference. Lanham,
Md.: Univ. Press of America, 1996, p. 87–100,
bibl.)
Some interesting insights and details
regarding Belizean quest for independence.
However, the article is inadequately researched and provides little or no theoretical
framework.

4199   Smith, Christian Stephen. Resisting
Reagan: the U.S. Central America
peace movement. Chicago: Univ. of Chicago
Press, 1996. 464 p.: bibl., index.
Though more a study of US interest
groups and social movements, provides useful
information on US policy toward Central
America. Somewhat sympathetic toward the
peace movements' goals and to their definition of "harassment."

4200   Sobel, Richard. Contra aid fundamentals: exploring the intricacies and the
issues. (*Polit. Sci. Q.*, 110:2, Summer 1995,
p. 287–306, tables)
Little analysis, but useful source of basic "factual" information on US aid to Nicaraguan contras. Informative charts and tables.

4201   Sojo, Carlos. Centroamérica: la nueva
e inevitable integración. (*Relac. Int./
Heredia*, 42, primer trimestre 1993, p. 19–37,
ill., map, photos, tables)
Discusses Central America's unreal-
ized integration. Suggests that democratization of the region may make integration more
attainable during the 1990s than in previous
years.

4202   Soler, Ricaurte. La invasión de Estados
Unidos a Panamá: neocolonialismo en
la posguerra fría. 2. ed. Panamá: Tareas; Mé-

xico: Siglo Veintiuno Editores, 1992. 186 p.: bibl. (Historia inmediata)

Excellent critique of the US invasion places this event in its historical context. Less ideologically based than most studies on the subject.

4203 Soto, Alvaro de and **Graciana del Castillo.** Obstacles to peacebuilding. (*Foreign Policy*, 94, Spring 1994, p. 69–83)

Explores "proliferating challenges" that El Salvador peace process poses for the UN and other international bodies. Draws comparisons to other international "hot spots."

4204 St. Malo Arias, Guillermo de and **Godfrey Harris.** The Panamanian problem: how the Reagan Administration dealt with the Noriega regime. Los Angeles: Americas Group, 1993. 352 p.: bibl., ill., index, maps.

Journalistic summary of events leading up to 1989 US invasion. Also discusses impact of the invasion.

4205 Tack, Juan Antonio. Ilusiones y realidades en las negociaciones con los Estados Unidos de América. v. 1. Panamá: Manfer, 1995. 1 v: bibl., ill.

Objective historical description of Panamanian negotiations with US from 1896–1950s.

4206 Toussaint Ribot, Mónica. El papel de Estados Unidos en la disputa mexicano-guatemalteca por Belice. (*Relac. Int./México*, 61, enero/marzo 1994, p. 59–66)

Examines dispute over Belize from historical origins of Spanish and British involvement through more recent involvement of Mexico and Guatemala. Relatively little attention to US role.

4207 United Nations. Commission on the Truth. De la locura a la esperanza: la guerra de doce años en El Salvador; informe de la Comisión de la Verdad para El Salvador. (*ECA/San Salvador*, 48:533, marzo 1993, p. 159–323)

Detailed, lengthy series of case studies of human rights violations during 1980s Salvadoran "civil war."

4208 Van Tassell, Darin H. Operational code evolution: how Central America came to be "our backyard" in U.S. culture. (*in* Culture and foreign policy. Boulder, Colo.: Lynne Rienner Publishers, 1997, p. 231–261, ill., table)

Applies content analysis of US policymakers' declarations to substantiate conclusion that popular US attitudes toward Central America ("our backyard") stem from a cultural "operational code." Very admirable piece of research on ideology and cultural predilections in US foreign policy.

4209 Vargas Foronda, Jacobo. Guatemala-México: el fenomeno migatorio (acercamiento interpretativo). (*Estud. Int./IRIPAZ*, 1:2, julio/dic. 1990, p. 41–59)

Explores important immigration component of Mexico/Guatemala bilateral relations. Weakened by overdependence on quotes from other studies.

4210 Velásquez Pereira, José Luis. La política exterior soviética en Nicaragua, 1979–1989. (*Rev. Nicar.*, 1:2, agosto 1992, p. 12–48, bibl., graphs, photos, tables)

Discusses implications of Soviet role in Nicaragua during Sandinista regime. Outlines different phases of Soviet involvement.

4211 Villagrán Kramer, Francisco. El dilema de Belice: ¿pais caribeño o centroamericano? (*Estud. Int./IRIPAZ*, 2:4, julio/dic. 1994, p. 5–29)

Exhaustive examination of Belize's regional role. Focuses on country's identity crisis.

4212 Washington Office on Latin America. Demilitarizing public order: the international community, police reform and human rights in Central America and Haiti. Washington: Washington Office on Latin America, 1995. 69 p.: appendices.

Summarizes events of 1994 conference on demilitarization in Central America and the Caribbean. Focuses on strategies and policies for professionalizing both police and military forces.

4213 Weisskoff, Richard. Forty-one years of structural continuity and social change in Nicaragua, 1950–1991. (*J. Dev. Areas*, 28:3, April 1995, p. 379–392, tables)

Economic analysis of Nicaraguan development during postwar period. Relates economic development to international interference and domestic political changes.

4214 Zamora R., Augusto. El conflicto Estados Unidos-Nicaragua, 1979–1990. Managua: Fondo Editorial CIRA, 1996. 551 p.: bibl.

Lengthy and detailed analysis of US policy toward Nicaragua during 1980s, particularly aid to the Contras. Examines specific events in Nicaragua and US reactions to them, while also considering broader international context and influence of international organizations.

THE CARIBBEAN AND THE GUIANAS

DAMIAN J. FERNANDEZ, *Associate Professor of International Relations, Florida International University*
JACQUELINE ANNE BRAVEBOY-WAGNER, *Professor of Political Science, The City College and The Graduate School, University Center, CUNY*

GENERAL AND HISPANIC CARIBBEAN

WITH NOTABLE EXCEPTIONS, the literature considered for this volume can be summarized by the phrase, "old wine in new bottles." Neither the topics nor the approaches to them have altered significantly in the past years. This is surprising given that the end of the Cold War ushered in new expectations and concerns for the region, while calling into question the traditional scholarly paradigms (specifically, realism and Marxism). But the end of the Cold War also rendered the area less important to the US foreign policymakers and other international players. For the first time in decades there is no crisis and no international competition. Perhaps this will translate into reduced academic attention to the region.

Security continues to be a topic that draws attention, but with a new twist. Issues once deemed low politics, such as the drug trade, immigration, and the environment, are now of high import. The other recurrent topics are fairly typical ones: Cuban foreign policy, despite its decline since the late 1980s; US-Cuban relations; Dominican-Haitian affairs (see items **4303, 4275,** and **4258**); and regional integration in the Caribbean. Other timely issues produced several valuable articles, including the Haitian crisis of 1990 (items **4272** and **4297**) and the region's relations with Europe (items **4267** and **4256**). Few scholars addressed topics of international political economy.

One of the positive trends in the literature is the publication of valuable primary and secondary documents, as well as works of diplomatic history that rely on recently declassified sources. Two studies, one on the Bay of Pigs (item **4242**) and one on the Missile crisis (item **4229**) are excellent pieces of scholarship. Also noteworthy for its extensive and insightful use of the historical record is a work on the architect of Puerto Rico's industrialization policy (item **4269**).

In the future, one can only hope that highly studied topics, particularly US-Cuban relations, will one day benefit from historical hindsight, newly released documents, and fresh analysis. In the meantime, the literature produced inside Cuba, with a few important exceptions, still suffers from limits imposed by an ideological imperative. Whether the future literature on the general and specific aspects of the region's international relations is marked by topical and analytical continuity or by change will reflect whether the end of the Cold War represented a watershed or merely more of the same. [DJF]

NON-HISPANIC CARIBBEAN

Major changes have taken place in global relations in the 1990s and this has been reflected in the foci of the literature on Caribbean international relations: The new works deal less with "high politics"than with dilemmas of globalization, trade, and social policy, including environmental policy, drugs, human rights and democracy. The exception to this new thrust is the outpouring of work on Haiti. Not unexpectedly, the 1990s saw a spate of analyses and reports dealing with the overthrow of President Aristide, the subsequent years of negotiation, and the final US/UN intervention in Haiti.

The studies reviewed here are of variable quality and utility. The most serious analytical works employ political economic frameworks (items **4306, 4280,** and **4233**). The best issue-focused works provide rich detail on, for example, trade (item **4221**) and Haitian political history (item **4292**). Informative analyses of new issues are also offered by volumes on human rights and democracy (item **3243**) and on cultural relations between Latin America and the Caribbean (item **4230**). Finally, for pure informational value, there is a large volume of documentation from US Congressional and other intergovernmental sources.

Global change has been matched in academia by a certain invigoration of international relations theory. The theoretical debate has taken the form of discussions of various postmodern approaches, questions as to the very epistemological and paradigmatic foundations of the field, and certainly, attempts to modify existing models to include new actors and new assumptions. Regrettably, the Caribbean literature contributes little to this theoretical debate, preferring to continue the descriptive tradition. If anything, the rise of post-Cold War issues has led to a perceived need by scholars for more policy analysis and an attendant, unfortunate abandonment of incipient attempts at theoretical rigor. However, in this respect, two theoretically-oriented works deserve special mention, a class-structuralist interpretation of Caribbean international relations (item **4306**), and a rigorous methodological framework for analyzing conflict in the Caribbean (item **4271**).

The remarkable increase in the volume of works on Haiti is clearly the natural outgrowth of the political crisis. Many of these works have a very narrow focus and are publications of nongovernmental or US agencies (for example, item **4249** on the refugee issue; item **4283** on the demographic "time bomb;" or item **4250,** an interesting report on military-civilian relations during the intervention). A number of works are of rather limited descriptive value (for example, items **4284** and **4273**). The most useful work dealing with recent Haitian events is also the most comprehensive and analytical one (item **4233**).

Overall, while studies of Caribbean international relations in the 1990s are proving to be relatively rich in scope and detail, there continues to be a lack of good theoretical and rigorous methodological work, a lacuna that makes these contributions more useful for narrow policy and informational purposes than for broader comparative research in international relations. [JAB-W]

4215 Abrams, Elliot Marc. The shiprider solution: policing the Caribbean. (*Natl. Int.*, 43, Spring 1996, p. 86–92)
   Conservative reinterpretation of US security concerns in the post-Cold War era.
Argues that the US is the only power capable of guaranteeing security in the Caribbean. (Does not consider that the US has and might contribute to insecurity.)

4216 Artaud, Denise. Les Etats-Unis et leur arrière-cour: la défense de la troisième frontière. Paris: Hachette, 1995. 602 p.: bibl., index, map. (Col. Pluriel. Série Intervention)

Detailed history of the US-Central American relationship from the Monroe Doctrine to the Summit of the Americas. One of the few such works available in French. [J. Braveboy-Wagner]

4217 Azcuy, Hugo. Los derechos humanos en la política norteamericana y el caso cubano. (*Cuad. Nuestra Am.*, 10:20, julio/dic. 1993, p. 4-19)

Critical analysis of US human rights policy (1980s-90s) vis-à-vis Cuba. Since article was written, international opinion regarding the Castro government has changed.

4218 Azócar, Héctor C. La política de cooperación de Venezuela con el Caribe, perspectivas ante los nuevos procesos de integración subregional: la asociación de estados del Caribe. (*Econ. Cienc. Soc.*, 4, oct./dic. 1995, p. 153-167, bibl.)

Incomplete but useful chronological and descriptive account of Venezuela's policy toward the Caribbean.

4219 Basdeo, Sahedeo. CARIBCAN: a continuum in Canada-CARICOM economic relations. (*Caribb. Stud.*, 25:3/4, 1992, p. 189-219, table)

Highly informative review of Canada-Caribbean Community (CARICOM) relations. [J. Braveboy-Wagner]

4220 Bernell, David. The curious case of Cuba in American foreign policy. (*J. Interam. Stud. World Aff.*, 36:2, Summer 1994, p. 65-103, bibl.)

Original study on how scholarship on US-Cuban relations has helped shape Washington's policy toward Havana identifies three groups of scholars and how they have answered the question "why is Cuba a threat to the US?".

4221 The Caribbean: new dynamics in trade and political economy. Edited by Anthony T. Bryan. Coral Gables, Fla.: North-South Center, Univ. of Miami; New Brunswick, N.J.: Transaction Publishers, 1995. 1 v.: bibl.

Serious discussion of free trade and political economic issues affecting the Caribbean in the 1990s suggests some practical strategies for Caribbean survival in a difficult and challenging era. [J. Braveboy-Wagner]

4222 The Caribbean Basin: economic and security issues: study papers. Submitted to the Joint Economic Committee, Congress of the United States. Washington: U.S. G.P.O., Supt. of Docs., Congressional Sales Office, 1993. 425 p.: bibl., ill. (S. prt.; 102-110)

Economic analysis of the impact of the Caribbean Basin Initiative, the North American Free Trade Agreement, and other trading arrangements prepared for US Congress. Contains some useful details and data. [J. Braveboy-Wagner]

4223 El Caribe y Cuba en la posguerra fría. Recopilación de Andrés Serbín y Joseph S. Tulchin. Caracas: Instituto Venezolano de Estudios Sociales y Políticos (INVESP); Editorial Nueva Sociedad, 1994. 272 p.: bibl.

Most complete study available includes extensive coverage of Cuban-Caribbean relations from different perspectives. Ranges from issues of regime transition in the area to migration. Top experts in the field contributed chapters.

4224 Castro, Fidel. Diálogo del gobierno cubano y personas representativas de la comunidad cubana en el exterior, 1978. La Habana: Editora Política, 1994. 158 p.

Document on the dialogue between the Cuban government and groups of Cuban exiles in 1978.

4225 Castro, Fidel. Fidel en Brasil: selección de intervenciones; 14 al 19 de marzo de 1990. La Habana: Editora Política, 1990. 252 p.: ill. (Col. Olivo)

Speeches by and interviews of Fidel Castro during his visit to Brazil in 1990.

4226 Cedeño, Carmen *et al.* La cuestión haitiana en Santo Domingo: migración internacional, desarrollo y relaciones interestatales entre Haití y República Dominicana. Recopilación de Wilfredo Lozano. Santo Domingo: Facultad Latinoamericana de Ciencias Sociales, Programa República Dominicana; Coral Gables, Fla.?: Centro Norte-Sur, Univ. de Miami, 1993. 293 p.: bibl.

Interdisciplinary study on Haitian-Dominican relations includes chapters on migration, nationality, agricultural labor, and democratic consolidation.

4227 Comisión Económica para América Latina y el Caribe (CEPAL). Sede subregional de la CEPAL para el Caribe. Las relaciones entre América Latina y el Caribe. (*Relac. Int. / Heredia*, 43, segundo trimestre 1993, p. 37–54, bibl., tables)

Account by CEPAL of cooperative arrangements between the Caribbean and Latin America in the 1990s includes brief discussion on areas of conflict and cooperation.

4228 Cuba contra el narcotráfico internacional, 1987. Habana: Editorial José Martí, 1988? 55 p.: ill., maps, ports.

Engaging and illuminating testimonies of drug traffickers caught in Cuba.

Democracy and human rights in the Caribbean. See item **3243**.

4229 Dialogue in Havana: the Caribbean crisis. (*Int. Aff. /Moscow*, 10, Oct. 1992, p. 108–128)

Extracts from the record of a conversation between A. Mikoyan and F. Castro (Nov. 3, 1962). Valuable document for studying missile crisis.

4230 Distant cousins: the Caribbean-Latin American relationship. Edited by Anthony T. Bryan and Andrés Serbin. Coral Gables, Fla.: North-South Center Press, 1996. 135 p.: bibl., index.

Examines Latin America-Caribbean relationship from economic, cultural, ethnic, and literary perspectives. [J. Braveboy-Wagner]

4231 Dumas, John Reginald P. In the service of the public: articles and speeches 1963–1993, with commentaries. Kingston: Canoe Press, Univ. of the West Indies, 1995. 484 p.: bibl., ill.

Public policy practitioner and former diplomat's views of Trinidad and Tobago's international affairs, human resource management, ethnicity, and other topics. Although tone is non-academic, opinionated and prescriptive, work provides useful personal insights on trade issues, Trinidad and Tobago's diplomacy in Nigeria and India, and reactions to US positions regarding the UN.

4232 Dumornay, Jacques. Les Etats-Unis: de la doctrine de Monroë à la domination mondiale. Haïti: Bibliothèque nationale d'Haïti, 1995. 232 p.: bibl.

Proffers Haitian view of events in Haiti up to period before 1995 intervention. Author takes strong anti-US perspective while assessing history and growth of US domination of the region and the world. [J. Braveboy-Wagner]

4233 Dupuy, Alex. Haiti in the new world order: the limits of the democratic revolution. Boulder, Colo.: Westview Press, 1997. 234 p.: bibl., index.

Thorough treatment of Haiti's recent political history details policies and strategies of President Aristide and the US within an analytic framework, taking into account both foreign and domestic factors. [J. Braveboy-Wagner]

4234 Encuentro Latinoamericano y del Caribe, 4th, La Habana, 1994. Principales documentos. Recopilación de Ana R. Gort y María Cristina Zamora. La Habana: Editora Política, 1994. 101 p.;

Principal document of the 1994 meeting in Cuba of representatives of Latin American and Caribbean left reflects their position on a host of issues including women, the economy, and Native Americans.

4235 Feinsilver, Julie M. La actual integración de Cuba en los sistemas internacional y hemisférico. (*Estud. Int. /Santiago*, 17 : 107/108, julio-sept./oct.-dic. 1994, p. 513–525)

Reviews Cuba's integration in the international and regional systems in the early 1990s. Analysis of possibilities and constraints of full membership in the OAS and the IMF is noteworthy.

4236 Feinsilver, Julie M. Cuban biotechnology: the strategic success and commercial limits of a first world approach to development. (*in* Biotechnology in Latin America: politics, impacts, and risks. Wilmington, Del.: Scholarly Resources, 1995, p. 97–125)

Excellent description and analysis of success and limits of Cuba's biotechnology industry discusses difficulties facing a Third World country attempting to compete in a first world industry.

4237 Gerlus, Jean-Claude. The effects of the Cold War on U.S.-Haiti relations. (*J. Caribb. Stud.*, 9 : 3, Winter 1993/Spring 1994, p. 146–163)

An overview of US-Haiti relations from the 1950s–80s. [J. Braveboy-Wagner]

4238 Giacalone, Rita. La Asociación de Estados del Caribe: una institución para un proyecto político de región. (*Mundo Nuevo/ Caracas*, 18:1, enero/marzo 1995, p. 51–72, bibl.)

Argues that the Association of Caribbean States constitutes a political project, creating common institutions and identity. Rich in theoretical discussions on integration.

4239 Giacalone, Rita; Freddy A. Martínez; and Peter Verton. Curazao y Aruba: entre la autonomía y la independencia. Mérida, Venezuela: Univ. de Los Andes, Consejo de Desarrollo Científico, Humanístico y Tecnológico, 1990. 246 p.: bibl., maps.

Overview of the economic, political, and social situation of Aruba and Curaçao since 1969.

Giacalone, Rita. La política exterior de Venezuela en el Caribe oriental: ¿compatibilidad o competencia con Estados Unidos? See item **4448.**

Gilderhus, Mark T. Got a gringo on their shoulders: U.S. relations with Latin America. See item **4010.**

4240 Gill, Henry S.; Anthony P. Gonzales; and Roberto B. Saladín Selin. Haiti y República Dominicana: condiciones y perspectivas para su ingreso a la Comunidad del Caribe (CARICOM). Buenos Aires: Banco Interamericano de Desarrollo, Instituto para la Integración de América Latina/BID-INTAL, 1993. 288 p.: bibl. (Publicación; 412)

Exhaustive study of economic prospects and constraints of CARICOM membership for Haiti and Dominican Republic.

4241 Gleijeses, Piero. Cuba's first venture in Africa: Algeria, 1961–1965. (*J. Lat. Am. Stud.*, 28:1, Feb. 1996, p. 159–195, bibl.)

History of Cuba's involvement in Algeria, the rest of Africa, and the Middle East underscores non-rational bases of Cuba's foreign policy. Important contribution.

4242 Gleijeses, Piero. Ships in the night: the CIA, the White House and the Bay of Pigs. (*J. Lat. Am. Stud.*, 27:1, Feb. 1995, p. 1–42)

Comprehensive study of available US documents on the Bay of Pigs. Concludes that "the CIA and White House assumed they

were speaking the same language when, in fact, they were speaking in entirely different tongues."

4243 Gleijeses, Piero. Truth or credibility: Castro, Carter and the invasions of Shaba. (*Int. Hist. Rev.*, 18:1, Feb. 1996, p. 70–103)

Useful contribution to the history of Cuba's policy in Africa reveals aspects of Cuban and US decision-making.

4244 Graham, Pamela and Jonathan Hartlyn. The United States and the Dominican Republic toward the year 2000: marginality, unilateralism or cooperation? (*in* The Dominican Republic today: realities and perspectives. New York: Bildner Center for Western Hemisphere Studies, 1996, p. 123–150)

Excellent overview of issues in US-Dominican post-Cold War relations including finance investment, trade, democracy, drugs, migration and the environment. Examines marginality, unilateralism, and cooperation.

4245 Griffin, Clifford E. The illogic of the logic of US sanctions against Cuba. (*Caribb. Stud.*, 26:1/2, 1993, p. 161–174)

Articulate argument favoring US bargaining approach toward Cuba which "entails trading economic goods for political concessions" to convert economic power into political influence.

Griffith, Ivelaw L. Caribbean security: retrospect and prospect. See item **3246.**

4246 Grugel, Jean. Politics and development in the Caribbean Basin: Central America and the Caribbean in the New World Order. Bloomington: Indiana Univ. Press, 1995. 292 p.: bibl., index, map.

Introductory text to political and economic development of the Caribbean and Central America. Useful for undergraduate courses.

4247 Gunn, Gillian. Cuba in transition: options for U.S. policy. New York: Twentieth Century Fund Press, 1993. 117 p.: bibl., index.

Identifies US interests in Cuba, likely scenarios of political change on the island, and a policy course that might help secure Washington's priorities.

4248 Haiti: dangerous crossroads. Edited by Deidre McFadyen *et al.* from the North American Congress on Latin America

(NACLA). Boston, MA: South End Press, 1995. 256 p.: bibl., index.

Covers important issues, but the analysis is simplistic and more ideological than scholarly. Includes sections on US policy, the 1990 coup, and human rights.

4249 *Haïti Information Libre.* Vol. 9, No. 97, 1995? Paris: Haïti solidarité internationale.

Booklet of proposals published at the height of the Haiti crisis for integration of Haitian refugees in France. Includes an extract of an Amnesty International report on the status of refugees in the US and a debate on aspects of the 1995 elections.

4250 Hayes, Margaret Daly and **Gary F. Wheatley.** Interagency and political-military dimensions of peace operations: Haiti, a case study. Washington: Directorate of Advanced Concepts, Technologies, and Information Strategies, Institute for National Strategic Studies, National Defense Univ.: U.S. G.P.O. Supt. of Docs., 1996. xiv, 65 p.

Report of a defense workshop reviewing military operations in Haiti in 1995 contains useful information on coordination between military and civilian agencies. [J. Braveboy-Wagner]

4251 Hernández, Rafael. Aprendiendo de la guerra fría: la política de los Estados Unidos hacia Cuba y Viet Nam. (*Cuad. Nuestra Am.,* 10:20, julio/dic. 1993, p. 99–113)

Argues that Cuba and Vietnam remain unsolved issues of the Cold War and that US policies toward these countries have been intertwined with US domestic politics and reflect changes in US policy after the end of the Cold War. Shows the role of information and ideology in US foreign policy.

4252 Hernández, Rafael. La cuestión de la *solución del conflicto* entre los Estados Unidos y Cuba: precisiones, premisas, precauciones. (*Estud. Int./Santiago,* 27:107/108, julio–sept./oct.–dic. 1994, p. 424–446)

Offers thorough, but not new, discussion of obstacles and possibilities for a US-Cuban rapprochement.

4253 Hernández, Rafael. 1999: la lógica democrática y el futuro de las relaciones entre los Estados Unidos y Cuba. (*Casa Am.,* 36:201, oct./dic. 1995, p. 125–132)

Leading Cuban social scientist predicts and endorses a process of political and economic "openness" in Cuba, while continuing to straddle the fence by defending the one-party State. Assesses positive and negative impact of these developments on US-Cuban relations.

4254 Hernández, Rafael. El ruido y las nueces: el ciclo en la política de EE.UU. hacia Cuba. (*Rev. Rev. Interam.,* 22:3/4, otoño/invierno 1992, p. 82–98)

One of the best articles available on US-Cuban relations argues that Washington should change its policy toward the island. Lacks discussion from Cuban perspective.

4255 Hernández, Rafael. La seguridad nacional de Cuba y la cuestión de la base naval de Guantánamo. La Habana: Centro de Estudios sobre América, 1988. 16 leaves: bibl., ill. (Cuadernos CEA; 2)

Analysis of Guantánamo Base issue in US-Cuban relations argues that negotiation is a possibility.

4256 Hernández Arvelo, Miguel Angel. El Caribe, Estados Unidos y la Europa del 92: una relación cambiante. (*Mundo Nuevo/Caracas,* 16:2/3, abril/sept. 1993, p. 323–340)

Outlines history of US-Caribbean-EC relations. Specifically discusses Lomé and the development of nontraditional exports and free export zones.

4257 Imperial power and regional trade: the Caribbean Basin Initiative. Edited by Abigail Bess Bakan, David Cox, and Colin Leys. Waterloo, Ont.: Wilfrid Laurier Univ. Press, 1993. 276 p.: bibl., index.

Detailed analysis of impact of Caribbean Basin Initiative and CaribCan preferences on the Caribbean through 1989. [J. Braveboy-Wagner]

4258 Inoa, Orlando. Bibliografía haitiana en la República Dominicana. Río Piedras, P.R.: Facultad de Humanidades, Depto. de Historia, Univ. de Puerto Rico, Recinto de Río Piedras, 1994. 183 p.: index. (Serie bibliográfica; 2)

A useful tool for researchers interested in Domincan/Haitian relations. [J.M. Hernández]

4259 Jácome, Francine. La cooperación ambiental: retos para la asociación de estados del Caribe. (*Econ. Cienc. Soc.,* 4, oct./dic. 1995, p. 168–189, bibl.)

In-depth account of environmental issues confronting the Association of Caribbean States sets discussion within the theoretical framework of social movements.

4260 Kirk, John M. Descifrando la paradoja: la posición del Canada respecto de Cuba. (*Estud. Int./Santiago*, 27:107/108, julio–sept./oct.–dic. 1994, p. 570–585)

Examines Canadian-Cuban relations, specifically miscommunication, pragmatism, differences with Washington, and coexistence and mutual benefits.

4261 Koike, Yasuhiro. Imagen de Cuba entre los estudiantes japoneses: un análisis de las encuestas a los estudiantes universitarios de Japón. (*Iberoam./Tokyo*, 17:2, 1995, p. 71–85, tables)

Presents results of 13 questionnaires about the image of Cuba among university students in Japan. Includes basic topics such as the name of the Cuban leader, the US embargo against Cuba, and Cuban socialism. Helpful for both countries in developing mutual understanding in the future. [K. Horisaka]

4262 Latin America and the Caribbean: policies to improve linkages with the global economy. Santiago: United Nations, Economic Commission for Latin America and the Caribbean, 1994. 301 p.: bibl., ill.

Public policy document provides a comprehensive analysis of trade, investment and development linkages in Latin America and *some* Caribbean countries. [J. Braveboy-Wagner]

4263 León Rojas, Gloria María. La crisis de octubre y los *memorialistas* norteamericanos. (*Santiago/Cuba*, 76, julio/dic. 1993, p. 5–41)

Offers first-hand accounts of US policymakers (Kennedy, Sorensen, Schlesinger, Jr.) regarding the missile crisis from the perspective of a Cuban Marxist historian.

4264 Lewis, David E. The Latin Caribbean and regional cooperation: a survey of challenges and opportunities. (*J. Interam. Stud. World Aff.*, 37:4, Winter 1995, p. 25–55, bibl.)

Suggests strategic alliances the Caribbean might develop for the 1990s, including possibilities of deeper CARICOM-Hispanic Caribbean/Central American linkages. [J. Braveboy-Wagner]

4265 Lockward, Angel. Haiti: cronología de una crisis. Santo Domingo: s.n., 1993. 157 p.: bibl., ill. (some col.).

Journalistic account of the Haitian crisis of 1990.

4266 Lowenthal, Abraham F. The Dominican intervention. Baltimore: The Johns Hopkins Univ. Press, 1995. 262 p.: bibl., index, map.

Reprint of 1972 classic on US intervention in the Dominican Republic (1965). Excellent analysis of apparent non-rational bases of US actions contains a wealth of information.

4267 Loynaz Fernández, Verónica. Europa comunitaria y América Latina: el caso Cuba y sus desafíos. (*Rev. Rev. Interam.*, 22:3/4, otoño/invierno 1992, p. 56–81)

Descriptive survey of the issues (especially commercial) in Cuban-European relations.

4268 Maingot, Anthony P. Offshore secrecy centers and the necessary role of States: bucking the trend. (*J. Interam. Stud. World Aff.*, 37:4, Winter 1995, p. 1–24, bibl.)

Intelligent and groundbreaking article on the politics of corruption and the growing problem in the international relations of the Caribbean (including Florida). Covers impact on the State and role of non-State actors.

4269 Maldonado, A.W. Teodoro Moscoso and Puerto Rico's Operation Bootstrap. Gainesville: Univ. Press of Florida, 1997. 276 p.: bibl., ill., index.

Long overdue and of superb quality, this book examines the contribution of Moscoso (the architect of Operation Bootstrap) to the politics and economics of Puerto Rico. Describes the man, the times, and the place with illuminating stories. Valuable discussion of US-Puerto Rican relations, US-Latin American affairs, and the impact of industrialization on the society. Rich in detail.

4270 Maríñez, Pablo A. L'anti-haïtianisme de J. Balaguer. (*Rencontre/Haiti*, 5, 1993, p. 25–27)

Argues that President Joaquín Balaguer strengthened the role of racism and anti-haitianism.

4271 Mars, Perry. Foreign influence, political conflicts and conflict resolution in the Caribbean. (*J. Peace Res.*, 32:4, Nov. 1995, p. 437–451, bibl., tables)

Theoretical work analyzes patterns and characteristics of conflict in the Caribbean using an empirical approach. Draws on various theories of international relations conflict. Concludes that Caribbean conflict tends to be externally-induced and that the solutions employed tend to be authoritarian. [J. Braveboy-Wagner]

4272 Martin, Ian. Haiti: mangled multilateralism. (*Foreign Policy*, 95, Summer 1995, p. 72–89)
Examines role of human rights concerns on multilateral policy vis-à-vis Haiti in the early 1990s. Considers military intervention a failure partly because it neglected to focus on human rights.

4273 Mintz, Sidney W. Can Haiti change? (*Foreign Aff.*, 74:1, Jan./Feb. 1995, p. 73–86, photo)
An evaluation of Haiti's social structure in the context of the 1995 occupation. [J. Braveboy-Wagner]

4274 Moore, Fauzya A. The report of the West Indian commission: new directions for CARICOM? (*Soc. Econ. Stud.*, 43:2, June 1994, p. 149–172)
A good analytical review essay on the report of the West Indian Commission. [J. Braveboy-Wagner]

Morales Paúl, Isidro. La delimitación de áreas marinas y submarinas entre Venezuela y Trinidad & Tobago. See item **4453**.

4275 Muñoz, María Elena. Las relaciones domínico-haitianas: geopolítica y migración. Santo Domingo: Editora Alfa y Omega, 1995. 297 p.: bibl.
Historical overview of Dominican-Haitian relations to the 1990s, focusing on migration. Analysis is from the perspective of dependency theory.

4276 OECS seminar/workshop for aid proposal, preparation and presentation for OECS member governments funded by CIDA: OECS Conference Room, St. John's, Antigua, January 22–26th, 1990. St. John's: OECS, 1990. 173 p.: ill.
Summarizes comments from an aid proposal seminar. Useful for those interested in aid procedures and requirements of different donors. [J. Braveboy-Wagner]

4277 Paterson, Thomas G. Contesting Castro: the United States and the triumph of the Cuban Revolution. New York: Oxford Univ. Press, 1994. 364 p.: bibl., ill., index.
Engaging diplomatic history of US-Cuban relations focuses on the 1950s and early 1960s. Aims to explain reasons for the conflict between neighbors.

4278 Perera Gómez, Eduardo. La Unión Europea y Cuba: hacia un mayor realismo en las relaciones. (*Rev. Estud. Euro.*, 8:31, julio/sept. 1994, p. 25–59)
Insightful and balanced analysis of Cuban-European relations since the 1960s.

4279 Perkins, M. Katherine and **Herbert R. Gilbert.** An economic analysis of U.S. narcotics control policy in the Caribbean and Latin America. (*in* Association des études de la Caraïbe. Congrès, *13th*, *Pointe-à-Pitre*, *Guadeloupe*, *1988*. Etudes caraïbéennes: société et politique; actes. Toulouse, France; Presses de l'Institut d'études politiques de Toulouse; Pointe-à-Pitre: Centre d'études et de recherches caraïbéennes; Fort-de-France, Martinique: Univ. des Antilles et de la Guyane, 1991, p. 317–338, graphs, tables)
Brief and useful analysis of incentives to drug cultivation and trafficking as well as alternatives for US policy. [J. Braveboy-Wagner]

4280 Phillips, Peter. The crisis of hegemony in the Caribbean: U.S.-Caribbean relations in historical perspective. (*in* Association des études de la Caraïbe. Congrès, *13th*, *Pointe-à-Pitre*, *Guadeloupe*, *1988*. Etudes caraïbéennes: société et politique; actes. Toulouse, France; Presses de l'Institut d'études politiques de Toulouse; Pointe-à-Pitre: Centre d'études et de recherches caraïbéennes; Fort-de-France, Martinique: Univ. des Antilles et de la Guyane, 1991, p. 231–274, tables)
Thoughtful structural analysis of US-Caribbean relations through the 1980s. [J. Braveboy-Wagner]

4281 Pierre-Louis, Vincent Serge. Haití: protocolo estatal y servicio exterior. Santo Domingo: Editora El Nuevo Diario, 1994. 86 p.: bibl., ill.
General guide of functions related to the Haitian foreign ministry.

4282 Políticas de descolonización de las potencias en la región caribeña. Recopilación de Carmen Gautier Mayoral y Idsa E. Alegría Ortega. Recinto de Río Piedras: Centro de Investigaciones Sociales, Facultad de Ciencias Sociales, Univ. de Puerto Rico, 1994. 141 p.: bibl.

Collection of articles examines process and issues of decolonization in Puerto Rico, Virgin Islands, Guyana, and Guadeloupe. Includes chapters on the roles of the US and the UN.

4283 Preeg, Ernest H. The Haitian dilemma: a case study in demographics, development, and U.S. foreign policy. Washington: Center for Strategic and International Studies, 1996. 141 p.: 1 map. (Significant issues series, 0736-7136; v. 18, no. 1)

A report-style overview, with prescriptions, of Haitian development prospects and US foreign policy toward Haiti as of 1995. Focuses on demographic "time bomb" but arguments for the centrality of demography remain unconvincing.

4284 Queiser Morales, Waltraud. Caribbean intervention—then and now: the case of Haiti. (*South East. Lat. Am.*, 38:3, Winter 1995, p. 25–40)

Reviews US foreign policy toward Haiti from the Cold War era to the early 1990s. [J. Braveboy-Wagner]

4285 Reding, Andrew. Exorcising Haiti's ghosts. (*World Policy J.*, 13:1, Spring 1996, p. 15–26)

Plea for abolishing Haitian army and for constitutional reform. [J. Braveboy-Wagner]

4286 La République dominicaine, la Guadeloupe et la Caraïbe. Direction de Michel L. Martin, François Vellas et Alain Yacou. Paris: Economica, 1992. 213 p.: bibl., ill., maps.

Report of a conference held in 1992 to celebrate the quincentennial of the arrival of Columbus in the New World. Focuses on history of the Dominican Republic. Third part is of interest to international relations specialists, dealing with immigration and trade between the French Antilles and the Dominican Republic. Concludes that, unfortunately, these relations are very limited. [J. Braveboy-Wagner]

4287 Roberts, Matthew. Small islands, big media: challenges of foreign media in covering the Caribbean. (*Caribb. Q.*, 40:2, June 1994, p. 8–22)

Comments on lack of media coverage of the Caribbean region in Great Britain and attributes the lack to difficulties in finding correspondents and to US sphere of influence in the region. [B. Aguirre-Lopez]

4288 Rodríguez Chávez, Ernesto. Tendencias actuales del flujo migratorio cubano. (*Cuad. Nuestra Am.*, 10:20, julio/dic. 1993, p. 114–140, graphs)

Broad statistical overview on Cuban migration from 1980s to the early 1990s.

4289 Rotberg, Robert I. Clinton was right. (*Foreign Policy*, 102, Spring 1996, p. 135–141)

Argues that President Clinton's policy toward Haiti improved the situation in that country.

4290 Safie de Bendek, Evelyn and **Francisco Zacarías Bendek.** Política exterior dominicana en el área diplomática, comercial y financiera. Santo Domingo: Impr. Avelina Larancuent, 1996. 369 p.: bibl., ill.

Practical field guide for foreign affairs officials and businessmen in the Dominican Republic includes documents on trade and political matters. Lacks scholarly assessment of the country's foreign policy.

Schiller, Nina Glick; Linda Basch; and Cristina Szanton Blanc. From immigrant to transmigrant: theorizing migration. See item **897.**

4291 Schiller, Nina Glick. The implications of Haitian transnationalism for U.S.-Haiti relations: contradictions of the deterritorialized nation-state. (*J. Haitian Stud.*, 1:1, Spring 1995, p. 111–123, bibl.)

Discusses role of Haitian transmigrants in US/Haitian relations. Argues that a Haitian transnational identity, legitimized and nationalized under the concept of the "deterritorialized nation-state," has impacted US policy toward Haiti and Haitian refugees. Specifically, transmigrant agitation and political action in the US against the 1992 military dictatorship prevented US from recognizing the regime. Whether this transnational identity will serve the national interests of the US or of Haiti will depend on whether it is "defused" or "colonized" in the American process of nation-building. [L. Comitas]

4292 Schmidt, Hans. The United States occupation of Haiti, 1915–1934. New foreword by Stephen Solarz. New Brunswick, N.J.: Rutgers Univ. Press, 1995. 321 p.: bibl., ill., index, map.

Detailed and useful history of US intervention in Haiti (1915–34); originally published in 1971, and re-released in 1995 at the time of the US invasion of Haiti. Contains many interesting insights. [J. Braveboy-Wagner]

4293 Scott, Len and **Steve Smith.** Lesson of October: historians, political scientists, policy-makers and the Cuban missile crisis. (*Int. Aff./Moscow*, 70:4, Oct. 1994, p. 659–684)

The authors "call the received wisdom" about the October crisis into question due to evidence made available only recently. They conclude that no one "definite" version of the events is possible.

4294 Serbín, Andrés. Las desafíos del proceso de regionalización de la Cuenca del Caribe: integración, soberanía, democracia e identidad. (*Econ. Cienc. Soc.*, 4, oct./dic. 1995, p. 75–113, bibl.)

Thorough analysis of the process of integration discusses the impact of integration on sovereignty, democracy and identity.

4295 Serbín, Andrés. La paz en el Caribe: ¿una utopía posible? (*in* Association des études de la Caraïbe. Congrès, *13th*, Pointe-à-Pitre, Guadeloupe, *1988*. Etudes caraïbéennes: société et politique; actes. Toulouse, France; Presses de l'Institut d'études politiques de Toulouse; Pointe-à-Pitre: Centre d'études et de recherches caraïbéennes; Fort-de-France, Martinique: Univ. des Antilles et de la Guyane, 1991, p. 339–370)

A strong plea for greater cooperation between the Caribbean and Latin America and for the creation of a "zone of peace" in the Caribbean.

4296 Serbín, Andrés. Towards an Association of Caribbean States: raising some awkward questions. (*J. Interam. Stud. World Aff.*, 36:4, Winter 1994, p. 61–90, bibl.)

Raises key issues of viability, commonalities and differences, and variations in perception and priorities among the members of the Association of Caribbean States. [J. Braveboy-Wagner]

4297 Smith, Jennie. Politics of protection: the interdiction, repatriation and treatment of Haitian refugees since the coup d'etat of September 1991. (*J. Haitian Stud.*, 1:1, Spring 1995, p. 57–74, bibl.)

Summary of conduct of US policy of detaining and repatriating Haitian refugees since 1991 coup focuses on whether this policy was executed in order to deny entry or to protect refugees from the hazards of the high seas. Based on observations of the mistreatment of detainees at Guantanamo, the lack of due process in handling asylum claims, statements of officials, and attitudes culled from a limited number of US informants, author concludes that US policy was motivated by race and by a desire to exclude from entry a poor, uneducated, and culturally different people. [L. Comitas]

4298 Smith, Wayne S. Cuba después de la Guerra Fría: ¿cuál debería ser la política de los Estados Unidos? (*Estud. Int./Santiago*, 27:107/108, julio-sept./oct.-dic. 1994, p. 402–423)

Argues for a change in Washington's policy toward Havana to protect US political and economic interests. This article, like many others on US-Cuban relations, covers familiar territory.

4299 Suárez Salazar, Luis. Cuba: la política exterior en el período especial. (*Estud. Int./Santiago*, 27:107/108, julio–sept./oct.–dic. 1994, p. 307–334)

Overview of the island's foreign policy in the 1990s from the perspective of a Cuban "official" academic recommends economic competition and reforms that will help to reinsert Cuba in the global economy.

4300 Sutton, Paul. The "New Europe" and the Caribbean. (*Rev. Eur.*, 59, Dec. 1995, p. 37–57)

An informative discussion of the implications of the Single European Market for the Caribbean countries. [J. Braveboy-Wagner]

4301 Thorndike, Tony. The British Caribbean dependencies: prospects and possibilities. (*in* Association des études de la Caraïbe. Congrès, *13th*, Pointe-à-Pitre, Guadeloupe, *1988*. Etudes caraïbéennes: société et politique; actes. Toulouse, France; Presses de l'Institut d'études politiques de Toulouse; Pointe-à-Pitre: Centre d'études et de recherches caraïbéennes; Fort-de-France, Martinique: Univ. des Antilles et de la Guyane, 1991, p. 275–299, tables)

A general discussion of alternatives to independence for the British dependencies of Bermuda, Turks and Caicos, Virgin Islands, and Anguilla. [J. Braveboy-Wagner]

Torres-Rivas, Edelberto. Para entender El Caribe. See item **4931.**

4302 Vargas, Tahira. Levantamiento documental: la situación dominico-haitiana. (*Estud. Soc./Santo Domingo*, 27:98, oct./dic. 1994, p. 59–82, table)

Extensive bibliography on Dominican-Haitian relations.

4303 Vega, Bernardo. Etnicidad y el futuro de las relaciones dominico-haitianas. (*Estud. Soc./Santo Domingo*, 26:94, oct./dic. 1993, p. 29–44, ill.)

Focusing on 1980s–90s, author reviews "ethnic issue" in Dominican-Haitian relations. Although the discussion is shallow, the analysis of specific aspects (i.e., the role of the Dominican intellectuals) is a welcome addition to the literature.

4304 Venegas Delgado, Hernán. La confederación antillana: realidad y esperanza. (*Caribb. Stud.*, 27:1/2, Jan./June 1994, p. 118–127)

Stresses commonalities among Caribbean states and the promise of integration. [J. Braveboy-Wagner]

4305 Los vínculos ruso-cubanos, soviético-cubanos, siglos XVIII–XX. Academia de Ciencias de la URSS, Academia de Ciencias de Cuba. La Habana: Editorial de Ciencias Sociales, 1989. 276 p.: bibl. (Ediciones políticas)

A propaganda tract on Soviet-Cuban relations typical of the Cold War era.

Washington Office on Latin America. Demilitarizing public order: the international community, police reform and human rights in Central America and Haiti. See item **4212.**

4306 Watson, Hilbourne A. Globalization, liberalism and the Caribbean: deciphering the limits of nation, nation-state, and sovereignty under global capitalism. (*Caribb. Stud.*, 26:3/4, July/Dec. 1993, p. 213–264, bibl.)

Offers concise, class-structuralist interpretation of the significance of globalization for Caribbean international relations as an alternative to liberalist and realist perspectives. [J. Braveboy-Wagner]

4307 Wider Caribbean Environment and Development Conference, San Juan, P.R., 1992. Matching environmental solutions to development problems; San Juan, Puerto Rico, March 4–6, 1992. Sponsored by Commonwealth of Puerto Rico *et al.* San Juan: s.n., 1992. iii, 60 leaves.

Speeches and reports summarizing US and Caribbean views on environmental developments; conference proceedings.

4308 Written comments on H.R. 1403, Caribbean Basin Free Trade Agreements Act. Subcommittee on Trade of the Committee on Ways and Means, U.S. House of Representatives. Washington: U.S. G.P.O., Supt. of Docs., Congressional Sales Office, 1993. 178 p.: ill.

Caribbean Basin Initiative proposed revisions and comments by interest groups. [J. Braveboy-Wagner]

4309 Wrobel, Paulo S. Aspectos da política extrena independente: a questão do desarmamento e o caso de Cuba. (*Estud. Hist./Rio de Janeiro*, 12, julho/dez. 1993, p. 191–209)

Brief but useful study of Brazilian-Cuban relations in the late 1950s and early 1960s includes multilateral and bilateral dynamics.

Wucker, Michele. Democracy comes to Hispaniola. See item **3270.**

SOUTH AMERICA (Except Brazil)

ALDO C. VACS, *Professor of Government, Skidmore College*

LITERATURE ON SOUTH AMERICAN INTERNATIONAL RELATIONS published during this biennium includes an interesting mix of works examining both traditional and relatively new subjects. The more innovative research is primarily focused on the region's new security challenges; the drug problem; the processes of economic integration; the development of regional mechanisms for political-diplomatic cooperation; and connections between democratic consolidation, economic neoliberalism, and foreign policies. Traditional literature is dominated by analyses of border disputes, territorial issues, and relations between particular South American and extra-regional countries. There is an overall trend toward higher academic quality, even for border dispute analyses which have been typically affected by nationalistic biases. Studies are still largely concerned with or produced in the region's larger countries—Argentina, Chile, Colombia, Peru, and Venezuela—but there has been a noteworthy increase in the quality and quantity of the literature dealing with the foreign policies of smaller countries such as Ecuador and Uruguay.

The end of the Cold War, the Soviet Union's demise, the global process of economic and political liberalization, and the hesitant rise of a "new world order" have generated new security concerns for South American countries. Most authors agree that these new global circumstances have created a better opportunity for regional security cooperation, but many warn that this political environment will not lead, in the short term, to the emergence of unified South American defense mechanisms and procedures. Interesting studies of the emerging security challenges and opportunities include the book edited by Obando Arbulú on new security threats (item **4310**), Caro's analysis of confidence-building measures (item **4315**), and Donadio's work on regional defense integration (item **4317**). Among the most interesting studies devoted to security policies of specific countries are those by Diamint (item **4346**) and Montenegro on Argentina (item **4357**); Buitrago *et al.* on Colombia (item **4402**); and Mercado Jarrín on Peru (item **4427**).

The impact of drug traffic and production on foreign relations, particularly between Andean countries and the United States, has been the subject of notable critical studies by Riley (item **4331**) and Tokatlian (item **4407**). The most significant analyses concerning particular countries include those by Verdesoto on Bolivia-US relations (item **4381**), Reina on Colombian-US relations (item **4403**), and Obando Arbulú on Peru (item **4428**). Many authors criticize the repressive supply-side-focused policies of the US and insist on more cooperative, demand-focused sets of policies.

Renewed attempts to promote regional economic integration have fostered a substantial number of writings that analyze the evolution and prospects of these agreements and their corresponding institutional arrangements. Although most authors recognize current limitations of these attempts, they seem to have a relatively optimistic view of the prospects for Mercosur and a less sanguine one for the Andean Pact and admission to NAFTA. Some of the most important contributions on Mercosur include Hirst (item **4324**), Manzetti (item **4327**), Peña (item **4330**), and Yore and Palau (item **4318**). Interesting analyses of the Andean Pact include the volume published by CED-IRELA on its relations with the European Community (item **4316**) and the study by Basombrío Zender on Peru (item **4419**).

Existing agreements and institutional mechanisms for regional diplomatic-political cooperation—such as the Rio Group and the Group of Three—have also been the focus of some studies. In particular, the Group of Three (Colombia, Mexico and Venezuela) is the subject of some insightful examinations. Serbín and Romero edited a study concerning the Group's general features (item **4322**) and Tokatlian and Cardona wrote another on Colombia's relation to the Group (item **4408**).

Authors have assessed the links between democratic consolidation, economic neoliberalism, and national foreign policies in various ways. As in the cases of Argentina (items **4341** and **4360**) and Venezuela (item **4456**), some authors argue that the democratic administration's economic liberalism has had a substantial impact on foreign policies. Luján, by contrast, concludes that democratization and neoliberalism have had minimal effects on Uruguayan foreign policy (item **4440**).

Traditional issues, such as those related to territorial demarcation and border disputes, particularly between Bolivia-Chile, Ecuador-Peru, and Colombia-Venezuela, continue to generate considerable interest. Less stridently nationalistic analyses have given way to more objective studies; a noticeable trend that began with contributions reviewed in *HLAS 55*, and which appears to have continued during this last biennium. Among the valuable studies concerning territorial issues are those by Figueroa Pla (item **4376**) and Gumucio Granier (item **4377**) regarding Bolivia's exit-to-the-sea initiatives at different international organizations, Zapata's study of the Atacama desert dispute (item **4393**), Cardona *et al.*'s volume on the Colombian-Venezuelan dispute (item **4397**), Ferrero Costa's edited book on Peruvian-Ecuadorian relations (item **4430**), González Lapeyre's study of the evolution of Uruguay's borders (item **4435**), the Venezuelan Presidential Commission's report on the frontier policy toward Colombia (item **4449**) and Mendible's book on Venezuela's borders with Brazil (item **4452**).

There have also appeared a significant number of interesting publications concerning the evolution and prospects of relations between several individual South American countries with the US, Western Europe, Japan, and other extra-regional States. The abundance of these studies makes it difficult to enumerate all the valuable contributions that are reviewed in the following pages. In general terms, these works have extended the traditional focus on South American relations with the United States and Europe to include a growing interest in exploring and analyzing current and possible ties with nontraditional actors, such as those located in the Pacific basin (Japan, Taiwan, China, etc.), Africa, and Asia.

GENERAL

4310 Aliaga Rodríguez, José et al. Nuevas amenazas a la seguridad y relaciones civiles militares en un mundo en desorden. Edición de Enrique Obando Arbulú. Lima: CEPEI, 1994. 286 p.: bibl. (Serie Seminarios, mesas redondas y conferencias, 1017–5121; no. 16)

Collection of articles analyzing the impact of post-Cold War international circumstances on the emergence of new security threats and new relationships between civilians and military at the global and regional level. Particularly interesting are discussions of drug trafficking, political violence, and human rights, especially as it relates to Peru.

4311 Almeida, Paulo Roberto de. MERCO-SUR y la Unión Europea: de la cooperación a la asociación. (*in* International Congress of Americanists, *48th, Stockholm, 1994.* Los procesos de integración en América La-tina: enfoques y perspectivas. Stockholm: Institute of Latin American Studies, Stockholm Univ., 1996, p. 113–130)

Insightful and sober analysis of the prospects for association between the EU and Mercosur. Author is optimistic that further cooperation can be achieved, but is less sanguine about the prospects for formal association. [S.D. Tollefson]

4312 Barbosa, Rubens A. Intentos de integración en el Cono Sur hasta el Tratado de Asunción. (*Contribuciones/Buenos Aires,* 10:2, abril/junio 1993, p. 7–18)

Survey of Southern Cone integration efforts since 1941 leading to the formation of Mercosur. [S.D. Tollefson]

4313 Bizzozero, Lincoln. La agenda de las relaciones Comunidad Europea-países del MERCOSUR: perspectivas de la amplicación comunitaria. (*Rev. Estud. Euro.,* 8:31, julio/sept. 1994, p. 76–90)

Brief review of the sensitive issues—trade, financial flows, and development cooperation—affecting the relationship between Mercosur and the European Community as well as of the institutional ties established between both blocs during the 1990s.

4314 Bustos Ramírez, Juan. Coca-cocaína: entre el derecho y la guerra; política criminal de la droga en los países andinos. Barcelona: PPU, 1990. 146 p.: bibl. (Col. Derecho y estado)

Brief comparative analysis of anti-drug policies implemented by Andean countries emphasizing legal aspects. Concludes that the repressive approach is ineffective and calls for policies focused on the prevention and treatment of addiction, improvement of economic conditions, and measured use of penal sanctions.

4315 Caro, Isaac. Medidas de confianza mutua en Sudamérica. (*Estud. Int. /Santiago*, 28:109, enero/marzo 1995, p. 37–57, tables)

Brief review of the most important bilateral and multilateral confidence-building initiatives implemented in South America since 1990, including the agreements on: 1) nuclear proliferation and chemical weapons; 2) Argentine-British negotiations; 3) encounters between military representatives of Argentina, Brazil, Chile, Peru, and Uruguay; 4) Argentine-Brazilian nuclear cooperation; and 5) joint naval operations in the South Atlantic.

Cavagnari Filho, Geraldo Lesbat. América do Sul: alguns subsídios para definição da segurança nacional. See item **4476.**

Chuquihuara, Luis. Perú y Brasil entre el Pacífico y el Atlántico: espacio surandino e integración sudamericana. See item **4425.**

4316 Comunidad Europea, Pacto Andino: hacia la profundización de las relaciones birregionales. Quito: Corporación de Estudios para el Desarrollo; Madrid: Instituto de Relaciones Europeo-Latinoamericanas, 1993. 352 p.: bibl.

Excellent articles examine the economic and political relations between the European Community and the Andean Pact after the 1992 cooperation agreement was signed. Includes analyses of the evolution and prospects for political and inter-parliamentary dialogue, bilateral trade relations, commercial policies, and the role of private investment.

4317 Donadio, Marcela. Integración y defensa nacional en el Cono Sur. (*SER / Buenos Aires*, 8, oct. 1995, p. 60–70)

Interesting assessment of the possibilities of regional security integration in the Southern Cone. After examining the security positions stated by the governments of Argentina, Brazil, Chile, Paraguay, and Uruguay, author concludes that with the exception of Argentina and, to a lesser extent, Paraguay, the regional actors do not support defense integration and prefer to preserve autonomy.

4318 La estructura institucional y las negociaciones del Mercosur: los 30 primeros meses. Recopilación de Fátima Myriam Yore y Tomás Palau. Asunción: Ministerio de Relaciones Exteriores, Subsecretaría de Relaciones Exteriores para Asuntos Económicos; BASE-IS, 1994. 472 p.

Useful compilation of official documents related to the institutional conformation of Mercosur. Detailed chronological presentation of agreements reached at the ministerial summits, working groups, special meetings, and the joint parliamentary commission between Nov. 1991 and Dec. 1994.

4319 Estructura orgánica, toma de decisiones y atribuciones de representación externa. Buenos Aires: Editorial Fraterna; Consejo Argentino para las Relaciones Internacionales; ADEBA, 1993. 122 p.: bibl. (Temas del Mercosur)

Study of the organization and decision-making mechanisms and capacity for common external representation assigned to Mercosur in comparison to the European Community, ALALC, and the Andean Group. Recommends strengthening the joint decision-making mechanisms and authority of Mercosur to represent its member States within the international arena.

4320 Fraga, Jorge Alberto. La Antártida: reserva ecológica; al cumplir 30 años su tratado. Buenos Aires: Instituto de Publicaciones Navales, Centro Naval, 1992. 299 p.: bibl., 21 ill., maps. (Nonagésimo octavo libro de las Ediciones del Instituto de Publicaciones Navales. Vigésimo noveno libro de la Colección Estrategia.)

Informed study of the evolution, up to

1991, of the Antarctic system and the claims and controversies surrounding it, written by an Argentine rear admiral and former director of the National Antarctic Dept. Although defending Argentine territorial claims, its analysis of the different claims, approaches, and prospects is open-minded. Concludes that Argentina should avoid nationalistic posturing and adopt a flexible and pragmatic strategy aimed to preserve the Antarctic Treaty and System. Includes a useful documentary appendix reproducing several Argentine and international laws, declarations, treaties, conventions, and resolutions related to the Antarctic issue.

García Sayán, Diego; Jorge Morelli Pando; and **Sinesio Jarama.** Perú-Ecuador: las cartas sobre la mesa. See item **3562.**

4321 Garré Copello, Belter. El Tratado de Asunción y el Mercado Común del Sur (Mercosur): los megabloques económicos y América austral. Montevideo: Editoral Universidad, 1991. 320 p.

Examines the agreements that led to the creation of Mercosur [between Argentina, Brazil, Paraguay, and Uruguay]. After a detailed legal analysis of the contents of the 1991 "Treaty of Asuncion," author points out that it requires modifications to protect the interests of the smaller partners (particularly Uruguay) and recommends a more equitable and balanced structure.

4322 El Grupo de los Tres: asimetrías y convergencias. Edición de Andrés Serbín y Carlos A. Romero. Bogotá: Fundación Friedrich Ebert de Colombia; Caracas: Instituto Venezolano de Estudios Sociales y Políticos; Nueva Sociedad, 1993. 229 p.: bibl.

Excellent set of studies by different authors on the origins, evolution, and prospects for the Group of Three, conformed by Colombia, Mexico, and Venezuela in 1989. Enlightening analysis of the factors that facilitate or obstruct cooperation among these countries and of the gradual transformation of this group from a political agreement into a more economically oriented organization.

4323 Grupo de Río: documentos oficiales del principal foro político de América Latina y el Caribe. Santiago: BAT Ediciones, 1994. 321 p.

Useful compilation of the documents issued by the Rio Group—the Permanent

Mechanism for Political Consultation and Concertation created in Rio de Janeiro in 1986 whose members are Argentina, Bolivia, Brazil, Colombia, Ecuador, El Salvador, Mexico, Paraguay, Peru, Uruguay, and Venezuela—between 1986–93. Includes the final declarations issued by the presidential and foreign relations ministers' meetings as well as a number of communiques and declarations issued during specific occasions such as the meetings with the European Community, the peace process in Central America, the GATT Uruguay Round, democratic transitions, and the Haitian situation.

4324 Hirst, Mónica. La dimensión política del Mercosur: especificidades nacionales, aspectos institucionales y actores sociales. (*Perf. Latinoam.*, 3:4, junio 1994, p. 37–62, bibl.)

Excellent analysis of the political variables influencing the evolution of Mercosur. Discusses positive and negative external factors that affect the integration process: common democratization, cooperative nuclear policies, similarity of past neoliberal economic policies, differing political ideologies and foreign policies, divergent economic policies, and distinctive roles played by Congress, the military, entrepreneurs, organized labor, etc. Also analyzes the internal political dynamics of Mercosur, both in terms of institutional arrangements and actors, before reaching a cautiously optimistic conclusion about the prospects for further regional integration.

4325 Integración y formación: lecciones de la experiencia comunitaria europea y las perspectivas para el Mercosur. Recopilación de Pedro Daniel Weinberg. Montevideo: CINTERFOR/OIT, 1992. 267 p.: bibl. (Informes; 150)

Although mostly focused on the EC, contains some interesting articles on economic and trade relations between Latin America and the EC, and on the labor dimension of the process of integration in Mercosur.

4326 Lara Brozzesi, Claude. La doctrina latinoamericana y el sistema marítimo del Pacífico sudeste. Quito: El Duende, 1993. 540 p.: bibl.

Well-documented doctoral thesis written by Ecuadorian expert examines the Latin American contributions to the emergence and development of international maritime law. Discusses the law's application to the Southeastern Pacific region as it was translated in 1952 in the "Declaration of Santiago" and the creation of the Maritime System of the Southeastern Pacific (SMPSE) by Chile, Ecuador, and Peru. Shows how these important agreements and joint initiatives led to global acceptance of the 200-mile economic zone and the development of other principles included in the Law of the Sea. Earlier versions of some chapters were published as *El concepto territorialista latinoamericano en el derecho internacional del mar* (Quito: Banco Central del Ecuador, 1991).

4327 Manzetti, Luigi. The political economy of Mercosur. (*J. Interam. Stud. World Aff.*, 35:4, Winter 1993/94, p. 101–141, bibl., tables)

Critical examination of Mercosur's political economic features including the expectations of the four governments concerning security, commercial production and capital gains, and its institutional arrangements. Against this setting, the author analyzes the possible impact of disparities in the relative distribution of gains among the four partners that might result from differences in market size, external tariffs, macroeconomic policies, and domestic regulations.

4328 La mujer frente a la política internacional contemporánea. Asunción: Investigación, Comunicación y Desarrollo, 1993. 93 p.

Brief papers delivered at a 1992 seminar by the Brazilian and Uruguayan ambassadors to Paraguay and the Paraguayan vice-minister of foreign relations concerning Mercosur and their respective countries' foreign policies.

4329 Nuevos regionalismos: ¿cooperación o conflicto? Edición de Lincoln Bizzozero, Klaus Bodemer y Marcel Vaillant. Caracas: Univ. de la República Oriental del Uruguay; Fundación Friedrich Ebert en el Uruguay; Editorial Nueva Sociedad, 1994. 138 p.

The first section of this excellent collection of articles places Mercosur in the larger context of new regional agreements and the transformations in multilateral trade arrangements associated with the Uruguay Round of GATT. Other sections address the specific nature and prospects of the relations between Mercosur, the EC and the US. Authors explore from the Southern Cone perspective, the tensions between multilateralism vs. regionalism in an attempt to present the different commercial strategic options open to these countries in the 1990s.

4330 Peña, Félix. New approaches to economic integration in the Southern Cone. (*Wash. Q.*, 18:3, Summer 1995, p. 113–122)

Insightful article, written by former deputy manager for integration of the Inter-American Development Bank (1985–90) and Argentina's undersecretary for Mercosur and inter-American economic relations (1991–92), analyzes the evolution and prospects of regional integration. Author believes that Mercosur has been relatively successful and that further development depends on the strengthening of its institutional structure and the establishment of collective economic discipline.

Pérez Otermin, Jorge. Política exterior y profesionalismo diplomático. See item **4442.**

4331 Riley, Kevin Jack. Snow job?: the war against international cocaine trafficking. New Brunswick, NJ: Transaction Publishers, 1995. 315 p.: bibl., ill., index, maps.

Comprehensive analysis of the contents and impact of the source country control policies implemented by the US, particularly in reference to Bolivia, Colombia, and Peru. After detailed analysis of drug traffickers' ability to defeat "supply-side" policies, author recommends that the US pursue "strategic goals based on institutional building and regime stability," that is, to focus on strengthening the police and judicial capacities of Latin American governments to confront, control, and punish drug traffickers while also assisting governments with adequate interdiction, domestic enforcement, and treatment policies.

Santos, Luís Cláudio Vilafañe Gomes. A missão Especial nas Repúblicas do Pacífico e Venezuela. See item **4512.**

4332 Scuro Neto, Pedro. A rotinização do Mercosul. (*Rev. Bras. Polít. Int.*, 36:1, 1993, p. 124–133)

Gives a brief and sobering evaluation of Mercosur. [S.D. Tollefson]

4333 Seminário O Sul das Américas frente a Novos Desafios, *Brasília, 1995.* Anais. Brasília: FUNAG, 1995. 52 p.: ill.

Succinct, first-rate conference papers analyze Southern Cone integration. [S.D. Tollefson]

4334 Stahringer, Ofelia et al. La integración latinoamericana en el actual escenario mundial: de la ALALC.ALADI al Mercosur. Coordinación de Iris Mabel Laredo. Rosario, Argentina: Univ. Nacional de Rosario, Facultad de Ciencia Política y Relaciones Internacionales, 1992. 162 p.: ill.

Analyzes the Latin American integration process from the historical, economic, educational, and communicational perspectives. Three essays deal with the US role. Informative discussion of the integration initiatives' evolution since 1960 and of the role of education and communication in regard to this process.

4335 Stevens, Willy. Mercosur: a Latin American regional integration of the second generation. (*Stud. Dipl.*, 48:4, 1995, p. 49–63, tables)

Belgian diplomat examines the origins, evolution, and prospects of Mercosur from a European perspective. Considers Mercosur a successful initiative and proposes that cooperation with the EC will lead to the establishment of a free trade area with concessions on a reciprocal basis.

Trías, Vivián. La rebelión de las orillas. See item **4053.**

Trías, Vivián. Uruguay y sus claves geopolíticas. See item **4444.**

Vieira, Gleuber. Perspectivas para um futuro sistema de segurança hemisférica. See item **4527.**

ARGENTINA

4336 Angelone, Juan Pablo et al. Las relaciones Argentina-Estados Unidos, 1983–1993: variables para un análisis interpretativo. Edición de Alfredo H. Rizzo Romano y Artemio Luis Melo. Rosario, Argentina: Homo Sapiens Ediciones, 1993. 203 p.: bibl.

Group of international relations specialists from National Univ. of Rosario examines different aspects of bilateral relations during the first decade of democracy in Argentina. Articles of dissimilar quality among which the most informative and insightful are those that compare the foreign policies of the Alfonsín and Menem administrations and examine the current theoretical debate on Argentina's foreign policy.

4337 Anglaril, Nilda Beatriz. Argentina's relations with Africa: the myths and realities of co-operation between the countries of the Southern Hemisphere. Translated by Marcia Lockett. (*UNISA Lat. Am. Rep.*, 11:1, 1995, p. 4–15, ill.)

Well-documented historical and critical analysis of a seldom-studied aspect of Argentina's foreign polices. Argues that Argentina's approach to Africa since the late 1950s has been affected by a number of ideological positions such as those advocating either Third World solidarity and nonalignment or Western ascription and alignment. This approach has resulted in fluctuating and contradictory policies toward the region often characterized by a dissociation between the economic and political aspects of the relationship.

4338 Arena de Tejedor, Francesca et al. Argentina y Japón: se conocieron en el violento amanecer del mundo moderno. Buenos Aires: Centro Naval, Instituto de Publicaciones Navales, 1992. 320 p.: bibl., ill. (Nonagésimo noveno libro de las Ediciones del Instituto de Publicaciones Navales. Decimoséptimo libro de la Col. Historia)

Collection of articles published by the Argentine Naval Center on the early relations between Argentina and Japan. Although mostly focused on the experiences of Navy Captain Manuel Domecq García as naval attaché in Japan and his observations concerning the Russo-Japanese War (1905), some articles include interesting information on bilateral diplomatic and economic relations up to 1944.

4339 Azcoitia, Carlos Eduardo. La guerra olvidada: Argentina en la guerra del Congo. Prólogo de Arturo Frondizi. Buenos Aires: Marymar Ediciones, 1992. 299 p.: ill., map.

Collection of anecdotes and observations on the former Belgian Congo and the role of international peacekeepers written by one of the Argentine Air Force pilots who participated in the UN peace force sent to the Congo in 1960–63.

Bandeira, Moniz. Estado nacional e política internacional na América Latina: o conti-

nente nas relações Argentina-Brasil, 1930–
1992. See item **4471.**

4340 Bocco, Héctor Eduardo. La cooperación
nuclear Argentina-Brasil: notas para
una evaluación política. Buenos Aires: Facultad Latinoamericana de Ciencias Sociales,
Programa Argentina, 1989. 64 p.: bibl. (Serie
Documentos e informes de investigación; 82.
Area Relaciones internacionales)

Brief and informative monograph analyzes the evolution of the Argentine and Brazilian nuclear programs and policies and the
initial steps toward collaboration taken during the 1980s. Sheds light on the transition
from bilateral nuclear competition to cooperation and the recent move toward acceptance of the nonproliferation regime by both
countries.

4341 Boron, Atilio. Las transformaciones
del sistema internacional y las alternativas de la política exterior argentina. Buenos
Aires: Centro de Investigaciones Europeo-
Latinoamericanas, 1993. 33 p. (Serie Documentos de Trabajo EURAL; 53)

Critically analyzes the restructuring
of the international system during the 1990s,
and the Argentine government's attempt to introduce the country into the new world order
by implementing neoliberal economic policies and aligning with US political-diplomatic
and security issues. Concludes that, in the
current state of international transition
toward "neo-trilateralism," it will be more
effective and realistic for Argentina to adopt
a moderately independent foreign policy.

4342 Brysk, Alison. From above and below:
social movements, the international
system, and human rights in Argentina.
(*Comp. Polit. Stud.*, 26:3, Oct. 1993, p. 259–
281)

Interesting examination of the ways
in which Argentine human rights groups appealed to the international human rights regime and nongovernmental organizations and
combined the favorable responses of each
with their own domestic activities in order to
compel changes in the military government's
behavior (1976–83). For political scientist's
comment, see item **3689.**

4343 Ceresole, Norberto. Argentina y el
ocaso de los poderes hegemónicos de
la política mundial. Buenos Aires?: ILCTRI,
1992. 133 p.

Three geopolitical essays criticize Argentina's recent foreign policy from a nationalistic perspective. Believes that Menem's
abandonment of traditional Peronist policies
and his option for Western alignment were
the result of a "brilliant plot planned and executed by the Jewish-North American lobby
and the British and Israeli secret services" and
calls for a new role to be played by nationalistic army groups in formulating and implementing independent policies. Representative
sample of the unbalanced views held by these
military groups and their civilian allies who
opposed Alfonsín's and Menem's foreign
policies.

4344 Cortines, José Estanislao. Intereses
argentinos: conflictos en el Atlántico
Sur. Buenos Aires: Centro Naval, Instituto
de Publicaciones Navales, 1988. 204 p.: bibl.,
maps. (Col. Estrategia; 24° libro)

Study by retired Navy captain of the
geopolitical situation in the South Atlantic
and Argentine interests in the area. Emphasizes the political-strategic and economic importance of the South Western Atlantic and
Antarctica. Calls for an increased Argentine
naval presence in the territorial sea, infrastructural improvement, and development
of new occupation activities in the Estados
Island, Tierra del Fuego, and South Shetland
Islands.

**Curso Especial de Derecho Internacional
Público, 1st, Montevideo, 1989.** Primer Curso
Especial de Derecho Internacional Público:
nuestras fronteras; situación general y problemas. v. 1. See item **4433.**

4345 Delamer, Guillermo Ramón. Perspectivas de cooperación naval multinacio-
nal en el Atlántico Sur. Buenos Aires: Centro
de Estudios Unión Para la Nueva Mayoría,
1994. 20 leaves. (Cuaderno; 104)

Brief analysis of the prospects for multinational cooperation between the Argentine navy and those of other countries in the
South Atlantic. Reviews the existing joint naval operations and recommends their multi-
plication while moving toward an integrated
system of maritime traffic control.

4346 Diamint, Rut. La seguridad estratégica
regional y las medidas de confianza
mutua pensadas desde Argentina. (*Estud.
Int./IRIPAZ*, 4:7, enero/junio 1993, p. 29–46)

Informative discussion of Argentine

recent initiatives to promote mutual confidence measures at the regional level. Reviews measures such as those aimed to reduce tensions with Great Britain, control maritime traffic in the South Atlantic, develop collective security, coordinate military activities, and ban nuclear and chemical weapons.

4347 Docampo, César. El plan nuclear argentino y la problemática de la no proliferación. Buenos Aires: Centro de Investigaciones Europeo Latinoamericanos, 1993. 59 p.: bibl. (Serie documentos de trabajo, EURAL; 49)

Part one of this work describes the nonproliferation regime in terms of its treaties and organizations. Part two describes the evolution and components of Argentina's nuclear program and discusses how it has been impacted by the country's reluctance to accept the full scope nuclear safeguards until its acceptance by the Menem Administration.

4348 Elisalde, Roberto and **Gabriela Farran.** Peronismo, nacionalismo y relaciones con Estados Unidos: de Perón a Menem. (in Estado Unidos desde América Latina: sociedad, política y cultura. México: Instituto de Investigaciones Dr. José María Luis Mora; Centro de Investigación y Docencia Económicas, El Colegio de México, 1995, p. 322–345)

Critically analyzes the evolution of Peronist ideology concerning foreign relations—from Perón's "third position" to Menem's "realism"—focusing on the changes in Argentina's approach to the US.

4349 Figallo, Beatriz J. El protocolo Perón-Franco: relaciones hispano-argentinas, 1942–1952. Buenos Aires: Corregidor, 1992. 240 p.: bibl., index.

Well-researched historical study of the evolution of Argentine-Spanish relations from 1942–52. Focuses on the origins and application of commercial agreements signed in 1946 and 1948. Documentary sources, particularly those found in Spain's Ministry of Foreign Affairs, private archives, and interviews are used to examine the economic and political factors that led to the rise and decline of bilateral cooperation between the Perón and Franco governments.

4350 Figari, Guillermo Miguel. Pasado, presente y futuro de la política exterior argentina. Buenos Aires: Editorial Biblos, 1993. 251 p.: bibl.

Theoretical analysis and historical survey of the evolution of Argentina's foreign policy since the early-19th century until the mid-1990s. Uses a sociological-historical approach to examine the origins of Argentina's foreign policies after independence and its evolution through the phases of inwardly oriented growth, the inter-war period, the Cold War, and the transition from "Third Position" to Western alignment. Highlights interaction between domestic and international variables and the importance of cultural factors in shaping the dependent features of the country's foreign policies.

4351 Fraga, Jorge Alberto. Malvinas: evolución de la cuestión desde la guerra, 1982–1994. (*Rev. Mil.*, 732, abril/junio 1995, p. 69–79, maps, tables)

Transcript of a lecture given at the Navy Center by Argentine rear admiral which recounts the different stages of British-Argentine negotiations on the Falklands-Malvinas issue after the 1982 war.

4352 Gilbert, Isidoro. El oro de Moscú: la historia secreta de las relaciones argentino-soviéticas. Buenos Aires: Planeta, 1994. 446 p.: bibl., ill., index, maps. (Espejo de la Argentina)

Highly informative history of Argentine-Soviet relations that relies on personal interviews with Soviet and Argentine witnesses, primary and secondary sources, the author's 30 years experience as Tass correspondent in Argentina, and his close connections with local and Soviet Communists. Presents a fascinating picture of bilateral relations. Particularly interesting are examinations of relations between Argentine and Soviet Communist parties, activities of the KGB in Argentina, contacts between Peronist politicians and the USSR, and the evolution of bilateral relations during Argentina's last military regime (1976–83).

González Lapeyre, Edison. Los límites de la República Oriental del Uruguay. See item **4435.**

4353 La inserción de la Argentina en el mundo. v. 1–2. Dirección del trabajo de Ricardo H. Arriazu. Participaron en el equipo Marcos A. Buscaglia *et al.* Buenos Aires: Consejo Empresario Argentino, 1995. 2 v. (789 p.): ill.

Detailed study, commissioned by the

Argentine Entrepreneurial Council, of the nature and prospects of Argentina's integration into the world economy. Presents a model to assess the effectiveness of commercial policies, analyzes the evolution of Argentine policies and global economic trends, discusses different trade options with special emphasis on regional accords such as NAFTA and Mercosur, and finally assesses three trade policy alternatives: unilateral commercial opening, multilateral commercial liberalization, and regional trade agreements. Recommends further development of Mercosur to include services and a lower common external tariff while negotiating a free trade agreement with NAFTA.

Jensen, Brigitte. Ecueils et réussites de l'intégration Argentine-Brésil. See item **4493.**

4354 Lanata, Jorge and **Joe Goldman.** Cortinas de humo: una investigación independiente sobre los atentados contra la Embajada de Israel y la AMIA. Buenos Aires: Planeta, 1994. 217 p.: ill. (some col.). (Espejo de la Argentina)

Journalistic probe of the terrorist attacks against the Israeli embassy and the Jewish central association (AMIA). Criticizes governmental investigations and raises a number of questions concerning the authors of the motivations and circumstances surrounding the bombings. Does not offer convincing answers, but documents the inadequacy of governmental performance, raises doubts about Iranian participation, and suggests Syrian involvement.

4355 Martin, Lisa L. and **Kathryn Sikkink.** U.S. policy and human rights in Argentina and Guatemala, 1973–1980. (*in* Double-edged diplomacy: international bargaining and domestic politics. Berkeley: Univ. of California Press, 1993, p. 330–362)

Comparative study of US human rights policies toward both countries concludes that policy was more effective in Argentina's case because of "the temporary convergence of four necessary conditions: a small win-set in the United States, a sympathetic chief negotiator, a faction in the Argentine government willing to use outside pressures to pursue its own political goals internally, and the existence and active involvement of nongovernmental human rights organizations."

4356 Martorell, Francisco and **Jorge Ramírez Gaete.** Impunidad diplomática. 3a ed. Buenos Aires: Planeta, 1993. 238 p.

Journalistic account of the life and activities of Oscar Spinosa Melo, an associate of President Menem whose tenure as Argentine ambassador to Chile ended amid accusations of extortion, drug consumption, and debauchery. Even if some of the accusations remain unproven, the narrative highlights the problems arising from the personalistic practices in Argentina's foreign service.

4357 Montenegro, María Cristina. La política exterior de Menem: el rol de las FF.AA. y las misiones de paz en el Golfo Pérsico y Yugoeslavia. (*Anu. Cent. Estud. Av.,* 1994, p. 59–78, bibl.)

Critical examination of Menem's foreign policy, particularly focused on the Argentine military participation in the Persian Gulf and Yugoslavian UN initiatives. Concludes that these Argentine decisions were motivated by the desire to establish closer relations with the US, but that they did not serve any specific Argentine national interest.

4358 Mosquera, Carlos Julio. La conciencia territorial Argentina y el tratado con Chile de 1881/1893: una censurable custodia del patrimonio territorial. Buenos Aires: Círculo Militar, 1994. 605 p.: bibl., ill., maps. (Biblioteca del oficial; 757)

Retired general blames the pacifism, isolationism, legalism, moralism, and Eurocentricity of some members of Argentina's political and economic elite for engendering the lack of "territorial consciousness" that encouraged the acceptance of detrimental border agreements such as those signed with Chile in 1881/1893. Questionable facts and arguments but reflects the uncompromising nationalistic views of some significant military and political groups.

4359 Neves, Juan Carlos. The Argentine navy and United Nations peace-keeping operations in the Gulf of Fonseca. (*Nav. War. Coll. Rev.,* 47:1, Winter 1994, p. 40–67, map, table)

Informative examination of the role played in 1990–92 by four Argentine fast patrol boats in enforcing the Central American peace treaty regulations in the Gulf of Fonseca as part of the UN peace-keeping force. Interesting contribution to understanding the role of the Argentine navy in the new world order.

4360 La política exterior del gobierno de Menem: seguimiento y reflexiones al promediar su mandato. Rosario, Argentina: Ediciones CERIR (Centro de Estudios en Relaciones Internacionales de Rosario), 1994. 388 p.: bibl.

Comprehensive collection of high quality articles analyzing different aspects of Argentina's foreign policy during the first years of the Menem Administration (1989–93). Excellent introductory chapter discusses theoretical assumptions and perceptual factors shaping Argentina's new international strategy and their practical consequences. A series of case studies discussing the relations with Mercosur countries, the US, the post-Soviet republics, Western Europe, Japan, Africa and the Middle East. Also discusses the issues surrounding Antarctica and the Falkland-Malvinas in the context of Argentine foreign policy.

4361 Procile, Gabriel. The challenge of cooperation: Argentina and Brazil, 1939–1955. (*J. Lat. Am. Stud.*, 27:1, Feb. 1995, p. 129–159)

Article argues that the rivalry and suspicion characteristic of the bilateral relationship was moderated in this period by the interests of both countries in expanding trade and enhancing their international position. However, in a lesson applicable to current efforts at integration, bilateral cooperation was hampered by an inadequate institutional framework, triangular relations with the US, and domestic political shifts.

4362 Quijada, Mónica. *Zollverein* e integración sudamericana en la política exterior peronista, 1946–1955: análisis de un caso de nacionalismo hispanoamericanista. (*Jahrb. Gesch.*, 30, 1993, p. 371–408)

Analysis of the frustrated attempt made during the first Peronist government (1946–55) to create a South American customs union and establish the basis for regional economic integration. Among the obstacles faced in this attempt the author mentions US opposition, fear of Argentine expansionism and rejection of its hegemonic aspirations in neighboring countries, and Argentina's lack of economic capacity amid the crisis of the early 1950s to offer appropri-ate incentives for other countries to join the union.

4363 Rapoport, Mario and **Claudio Spiguel.** Estados Unidos y el peronismo: la política norteamericana en la Argentina, 1949–1955. Buenos Aires: Grupo Editor Latinoamericano, 1994. 314 p.: bibl., ill. (Col. Estudios internacionales)

Excellent study of US-Argentine economic and political negotiations during the last six years of Perón's first government. Well-documented work that relies mainly on US diplomatic communications and State Dept. documents to demonstrate the complex dynamics of the bilateral relations and to argue that contradictory domestic and international pressures led to a relationship characterized by both conflictive and cooperative elements.

4364 Redick, John R.; Julio C. Carasales; and **Paulo S. Wrobel.** Nuclear rapprochement: Argentina, Brazil, and the nonpoliferation regime. (*Wash. Q.*, 18:1, Winter 1995, p. 107–122)

Interesting examination of the evolution of Argentine-Brazilian nuclear relations from hostility and competition to cooperation and confidence-building. Among the factors leading to the change in relations, the authors emphasize economic and mutual security considerations, the transition to democracy, the move toward more liberal economic policies, and the existence of a supportive international climate.

4365 Rivadulla Barrientos, Daniel. La *amistad irreconciliable:* España y Argentina, 1900–1914. Madrid: Editorial MAPFRE, 1992. 269 p.: bibl., index. (Col. Relaciones entre España y América; 20. Col. MAPFRE 1492)

Well-documented historical study of the evolution of the political and diplomatic relations between Spain and Argentina from the late-19th century to the beginning of World War I. Particularly interesting are chapters devoted to the impact of Spanish immigration to Argentina on the bilateral relation and the evolution of the two countries' divergent commercial policies.

4366 Saavedra, Marisol. Argentina dentro del sistema interamericano entre 1945 y 1955. Buenos Aires: IDICSO, 1992. 119 p.: bibl. (Serie de investigaciones del IDICSO; 2)

Informative analysis, based mostly on secondary sources, of the role played by Argentina in the creation and initial period of the OAS, particularly in the Interamerican Economic and Social Council, the Interamerican Conferences of 1947, 1948, and 1954, and the Consultative Meeting of 1951. Useful addition to the literature on Peronist foreign policy highlighting the controversies between Argentina and the US on economic and strategic issues.

4367 Siepe, Raimundo; María Monserrat Llairo; and Nidia Gale. Perón y las relaciones económicas con el Este. Buenos Aires: Centro Editor de América Latina, 1994. 126 p.: bibl. (Biblioteca Política argentina; 467)

Informative study of the development of Argentine economic relations with the Eastern European countries during Perón's brief second administration (1952–55).

Solveira, Beatriz Rosario. El nudo ferroviario de Santa Cruz de la Sierra y la rivalidad argentino-brasileña. See item **4380.**

4368 Solveira de Báez, Beatriz. La Argentina, el ABC y el conflicto entre México y Estados Unidos, 1913–1916. Córdoba, Argentina: Centro de Estudios Históricos, 1994. 214 p.: bibl.

Detailed analysis of the diplomatic initiatives taken by Argentina—together with Brazil and Chile (the ABC)—to mediate US-Mexican relations and prevent further armed confrontations. Use of original documents from Argentine archives helps clarify Argentine objectives and role in the mediation and explain the relative success of the ABC initiative in 1914 and its ineffectiveness in following years.

4369 Spinosa Melo, Oscar. Sobre el volcán: memorias de un diplomático. Buenos Aires: Ediciones de la Urraca, 1993. 193 p., 8 p. of plates: ill. (some col.).

In his memoirs former Argentine ambassador to Chile rejects accusations of corruption that led to his dismissal and accuses foreign minister Di Tella and several other officials of conspiring against him. Unconvincing defense but some interesting information about internal workings of foreign relations ministry.

4370 Weinmann, Ricardo. Argentina en la Primera Guerra Mundial: neutralidad, transición política y continuismo económico.

Buenos Aires: Editorial Biblos; Fundación Simón Rodríguez, 1994. 168 p.: bibl. (Col. Cuadernos Simón Rodríguez; 27)

Well-researched study of the evolution of Argentina's policy of neutrality during World War I under Presidents Victorino de la Plaza and Hipólito Yrigoyen. Interesting comparative analysis of de la Plaza's economically motivated neutral policy and Yrigoyen's more nationalistic motivations.

BOLIVIA

4371 Arze Quiroga, Eduardo. Las relaciones internacionales de Bolivia, 1825–1990. La Paz: Editorial Los Amigos del Libro, 1991. lx, 522 p.: bibl., maps. (Col. Historia. Obras completas; 1)

Collection of essays by the late Bolivian politician, diplomat, and minister of foreign relations divided in five sections dealing with international relations from the historical and philosophical perspectives, geopolitical approaches, issues of national and collective security, Bolivia's land-locked situation, and the Chaco War. Excellent anthology of texts originally published in many different periodicals that offer interesting insights on Bolivia's foreign policies from the perspective of one of its main protagonists.

4372 Barrios Morón, Raúl. Bolivia & Estados Unidos: democracia, derechos humanos y narcotráfico, 1980–1982. La Paz: HISBOL; FLACSO, 1989. 203 p.: bibl.

Excellent study of the evolution of relations between Bolivia and the US in 1980–82. Analyzes the US reactions to the García Meza coup of 1980; the importance of the impact of drug traffic, human rights, and democratization in the context of the bilateral relations; and the role US pressures and sanctions have played in promoting Bolivia's democratic transition.

4373 Bedregal, Guillermo. La posición internacional de Bolivia: discursos del Ministro de Relaciones Exteriores y Culto en organismos internacionales. La Paz: Empresa Editora Urquizo, 1989. 67 p.

Brief volume containing several speeches made in 1988 by then minister of foreign relations on issues such as Bolivia's international economic relations, role in the nonaligned movement and the UN, and drug traffic.

4374 Encuentro de dos democracias. Cochabamba, Bolivia: Editorial los Amigos
del Libro; Ministerio de Informaciones de
Bolivia; Embajada de la República Federal de
Alemania, 1988. 91 p.: ill., ports. (Col. Bolivia
y el mundo; 265)

Pamphlet documenting visit of Richard
von Weizacker, President of the Federal Republic of Germany, to Bolivia in 1988 is an
official joint publication of the Bolivian foreign ministry and the German Embassy in
La Paz. Contains photographs and transcripts
of speeches delivered during the visit.
[E. Gamarra]

4375 Espada, Joaquín. Bolivia en la inter-
americanidad. Cochabamba, Bolivia:
Editorial Canelas, 1993. 281 p.

Collection of articles by Bolivian politician and former finance minister on international relations issues from the 1950s–80s.
Addresses topics such as the prospects for
regional economic integration, national and
collective security, and Bolivia's territorial
demands.

4376 Figueroa Pla, Uldaricio. La demanda
marítima boliviana en los foros internacionales. Santiago: Editorial Andrés Bello,
1992. 513 p.: bibl.

Detailed and comprehensive account
of Bolivia's diplomatic initiatives, in regional
and international organizations, to gain support for an exit to the Pacific Ocean. Original
because book is written by a Chilean diplomat who believes that Chile's democratization has created new possibilities for an ami-
cable solution to this conflict, although he
rejects any possibility of granting Bolivia a
sovereign corridor.

4377 Gumucio Granier, Jorge. El enclaustra-
miento marítimo de Bolivia en los foros del mundo. La Paz: Academia Boliviana
de la Historia, 1993. 590 p.: appendix, bibl.

Comprehensive historical analysis
of Bolivia's initiatives, in different international forums, to gain support in its quest for
access to the sea. Reviews Bolivia's diplomatic efforts in the League of Nations, the
UN, the Non-Aligned Movement and the
inter-American organizations. Informative
appendix reproduces many official Bolivian
documents (diplomatic notes and instruc-
tions, congressional resolutions and debates,
ministerial reports, laws and resolutions).

4378 Lizón, Ramiro Prudencio. En busca de
una solución al problema de la "Salida
al Mar" de Bolivia. (*Am. Merid.*, 7, julio 1987,
p. 7–15)

After rejecting unrealistic proposals for
a Bolivian enclave in Chilean territory south
of Arica and the internationalization of Arica's harbor, argues that the only practical
means of offering Bolivia an exit to the sea is
the creation of a territorial corridor north of
Arica.

4379 Piedra Fernández, Juan M. de la. Bolivia mar: Zofri Ilo. Lima: Haruki Abe
Producciónes, 1992. 166 p.: bibl., maps.

Informative, descriptive legal examination of the free international trade, industrial,
and touristic zone created in the area of Ilo
(Peru) to facilitate Bolivia's access to the sea
and promote economic growth in that region.

4380 Solveira, Beatriz Rosario. El nudo ferroviario de Santa Cruz de la Sierra y la rivalidad argentino-brasileña. (*Anu. Cent. Estud. Av.*, 1994, p. 93–118, bibl.)

Interesting historical analysis of the
Argentine-Brazilian attempts between 1920–
38 to impose their hegemony on Bolivia,
demonstrated by the race to control the rail-
road junction at Santa Cruz de la Sierra.

4381 Verdesoto, Luis and **Gloria Ardaya Salinas.** Entre la presión y el consenso: escenarios y previsiones para la relación Bolivia—Estados Unidos. La Paz: UDAPEX,
Min.RR.EE.; ILDIS, 1993. 282 p.: appendix,
bibl.

Well-documented 1993 study on the recent evolution and future prospects of Boliv-
ian-US relations. Comprehensive discussion
of the issues involved in the bilateral agenda,
particularly the problems of drugs, extradition, the role of the military, economic ties,
and the impact of US aid programs. Appendix
includes interesting interviews with Bolivian
policymakers, diplomats, and businessmen,
as well as a detailed chronology of the bilateral relations between Jan. 1986–June 1993.

CHILE

Benavides Correa, Alfonso. Perú y Chile: del
tratado y protocolo complementario de 1929
sobre Tacna y Arica a la convención de 1993
sobre pretendido cumplimiento de obligaciones. See item **4420.**

4382 Carvajal Prado, Patricio. Charaña: un acuerdo entre Chile y Bolivia y el tercero en discordia. Valparaíso, Chile: Empresa Editora Arquén, 1994. 220 p.: bibl., ill., maps.

Memoir by former foreign relations minister of Pinochet regime concerning negotiations that led to the Charaña agreement between Chile and Bolivia granting Bolivia access to the sea. Attributes failure of negotiations to Peruvian demands that would have adversely impacted Chilean sovereignty.

4383 De la reinserción a los acuerdos: la política exterior chilena en 1991. Santiago: FLACSO, 1992. 413 p.: index. (Serie Política exterior y relaciones internacionales)

Detailed chronological presentation of the evolution of Chile's foreign policy during 1991. Highlights the capacity of Aylwin's democratic administration to reach important border, economic and political-diplomatic agreements with countries in the Americas, Europe, and the Pacific basin. Useful and comprehensive reference work.

4384 Garay Vera, Cristián. Bibliografía y fuentes para la relación chileno-española entre 1936–1939. (*Rev. Chil. Humanid.*, 13, 1992, p. 117–131, appendix)

Informative annotated bibliography reviews published documents from the Chilean foreign relations ministry concerning Chile's relations with the Madrid and Burgos governments during the Spanish Civil War (1936–39).

4385 Gutiérrez B., Hernán. Presente y futuro de las relaciones entre Taiwan y Chile. (*Estud. Int. /Santiago*, 28:111, julio/sept. 1995, p. 308–322, tables)

Examines the evolution and prospects for Chilean and Taiwanese relations, focusing on economic aspects. Emphasizes importance for Chile of Taiwanese markets and possible investments.

4386 Lasagna Barrena, Marcelo. La política iberoamericana de España de cara a los noventa: la relación con Chile, 1982–1992. (*Rev. Cienc. Polít. /Santiago*, 26:1/2, 1994, p. 67–94, bibl., tables)

Examines the evolution and future of Spanish foreign policy toward Latin America. Focused on the development of Spain's bilateral ties with Chile between 1982–92. Interesting analysis documents improvement of

political-diplomatic ties as the process of Chilean democratization progressed, while showing that economic relations were not affected by these political situations. Concludes that the leading role taken by Spain in the European Community's relations with Latin America and the consolidation of Chile's democratic regime indicate excellent prospects for bilateral relations.

4387 Martínez Busch, Jorge. La Cuenca del Pacífico, su importancia económica y estratégica en el próximo siglo: una perspectiva chilena. (*Rev. Chil. Geopolít.*, 9:3, agosto 1993, p. 9–18, table)

Text of a speech by the commander-in-chief of the Chilean navy underscores the economic and strategic importance of the Pacific basin for Chile.

4388 Matus Baeza, Mario. Hacia una nueva política exterior de Chile. (*Estud. Int. / Santiago*, 26:104, oct./dic. 1993, p. 571–594, bibl.)

After reviewing some of the main global trends in the post-Cold War era, the author recommends that Chile's foreign policy should promote the country's development by using a flexible, adaptable, and coherent approach, implemented by a foreign relations ministry reorganized according to geographical areas. Also recommends the creation of task forces, a planning office and an economic negotiations section, and a special concentration on foreign investment promotion.

4389 Mezzano Lopetegui, Silvia. Chile e Italia: un siglo de relaciones bilaterales, 1861–1961. Santiago?: Ediciones Mar del Plata, 1994. 269 p.: bibl., ill.

Detailed chronology of Italian-Chilean relations from 1861–1961. Interesting details concerning influence of Italian immigrants on culture and politics as well as on the character of 20th-century diplomatic and economic relations.

4390 Morandé Lavín, José A. and **Roberto Durán Sepúlveda.** Percepciones en la política exterior chilena: un estudio sobre líderes de opinion pública. (*Estud. Int. /Santiago*, 26:104, oct./dic. 1993, p. 595–609, tables)

Presents and analyzes the opinions of 400 influential members of Chilean society concerning foreign policy. Results indicate that: 1) a slight majority sympathized with US policy concerning human rights; 2) a large majority believed the military intervention in foreign policy detrimental to the country's international image and projection; and 3) a majority favored economic objectives although they preferred Chile to deal with economic concerns independently from other countries of the region.

4391 Morandé Lavín, José A. Relaciones internacionales entre Chile y Estados Unidos durante el periodo de la restauración democrática, 1990–1993. (*Estud. Int./Santiago*, 28:111, julio/sept. 1995, p. 323–337, table)

Brief but informative examination of the evolution of bilateral diplomatic and economic ties during the first three years of the Aylwin Administration. Underscores the shift toward normalization of diplomatic relations while pointing out the continuity within the economic sphere.

Mosquera, Carlos Julio. La conciencia territorial Argentina y el tratado con Chile de 1881/1893: una censurable custodia del patrimonio territorial. See item **4358.**

Quintanilla Pérez, Victor. Problemas y consecuencias ambientales sobre el Bosque de Alerce, (*Fitzroya Cupressoides* (Mol) Johnst), debido a la explotación de la cordillera costera de Chile austral. See item **2828.**

Teniente Merino, el héroe de Laguna del Desierto. See item **2838.**

4392 Valenzuela Montenegro, Carlos. Cuando América descubra el mundo. Santiago: Tall. Gráf. de Editorial Universitaria, 1992. 175 p.: bibl., index.

Memoirs by former Chilean diplomat concerning his activities between 1947–84. Mostly personal recollections but contains some interesting information on Chile's foreign policies toward the US, the USSR, Mexico, Europe, and North Africa and concerning the country's initiatives in the UN and UNCTAD.

4393 Zapata, Francisco. Atacama, desierto de la discordia: minería y política internacional en Bolivia, Chile y Perú. México: Colegio de México, Centro de Estudios Internacionales y Centro de Estudios Sociológicos, 1992. 178 p.: bibl., maps.

Informative study of the development of conflictive relations between Bolivia, Chile, and Peru focused on the territorial dispute over the Atacama desert and its mineral resources. Analyzes impact of the evolving relations between the State and mining sector within the three countries in regard to the dispute. Conclusion reviews the possible effect of transnational capital, State enterprises, and integration efforts on the establishment of cooperative initiatives for the region's economic development.

4394 Zeballos, Estanislao Severo. La política exterior de Chile: dos conferencias, tres artículos y un discurso. Presentación y notas por Roberto Ortigueira. Introducción por el Dr. Raúl Rey Balmaceda. Buenos Aires: Librería Clásica, 1993. lix, 178 p.: bibl., ill., maps.

New edition of highly critical lectures, articles, and one speech on Chile's foreign policies delivered between 1898–1901 by Argentina's three-time minister of foreign relations. Biased nationalistic interpretations but helpful in tracing origins of the Argentine-Chilean territorial dispute that lasted until the 1990s.

COLOMBIA

4395 Angel Maya, Augusto et al. Medio ambiente y relaciones internacionales. Bogotá: Ediciones Uniandes; Tercer Mundo, 1992. 354 p.: bibl.

Articles from a seminar organized in Colombia in preparation for the 1992 Rio Earth Summit discuss global and national environmental issues and policies. Interesting analyses of the growing importance of environmental issues within global international relations. Followed by studies of environmental policies of the US, Venezuela, the Andean Group, and in Amazonia. Particularly valuable is the final section that contains Colombia's official proposal for environmental policies, critical analysis of official positions, and the agenda for the Rio summit.

4396 Bendeck Olivella, Jorge. La corbeta solitaria. Bogotá: Editorial Grijalbo, 1994. 149 p.: bibl., maps.

Concise and informative account of Colombian-Venezuelan border dispute. Written by Colombia's former minister of public works and transportation, describes evolution of Gulf of Venezuela boundary issue from independence through 1994. Relatively objective examination includes historical background, negotiations, agreements, and military incidents, the latter well illustrated with detailed maps. Rejects chauvinistic positions and concludes that remaining delimitation problems could be resolved peacefully in the context of a binational integration process.

4397 Cardona, Diego *et al.* Colombia-Venezuela: ¿crisis o negociación? Bogotá: CEI, UNIANDES; FESCOL, 1992. 120 p.: bibl.

Excellent study by a team of Colombian social scientists of the recent evolution of Colombian-Venezuelan relations and their process of integration. Analyzes Colombian and Venezuelan roles in the other country's foreign policy, evolution of bilateral relations (1989–92), commercial relations, and negotiations and agreements on border, commercial, transportation, energy, environmental, and other issues. Concludes that integration process has lost momentum and recommends the reduction of the number and complexity of issues under discussion, while focusing attention on implementation of agreements already reached.

4398 Fleischer, Lowell Ronald and Eduardo Lora. Colombian policy in the mid-1990s: a report of the CSIS Americas Program. Washington: Center for Strategic & International Studies, 1994. xi, 60 p.: bibl., ill., 1 map. (CSIS report)

Brief report on Colombia's situation in the aftermath of Ernesto Samper's Aug. 1994 presidential inauguration. Particularly interesting analysis of the liberal structural economic reforms and their impact on Colombia's trade policy. Authors believe that the economic liberalization process is likely to continue, and that it will help establish closer relations with the US if more effective measures are implemented against drug trafficking.

4399 García Olano, Enrique. La Comunidad Europea y Colombia: el nuevo orden mundial como entorno de las relaciones comerciales entre Colombia y la CE. Bogotá: Forum Pacis, 1994. 190 p.: bibl.

Particularly interesting is analysis of Colombia's direct relations with the European Community, and the impact of the special cooperation program on trade and economic relations between Bolivia, Colombia, Ecuador, Peru, and the EC.

4400 Gaviria Liévano, Enrique. Colombia en el diferendo con Venezuela. Colombia: Ediciones Jurídicas Gustavo Ibañez, 1994. 548 p.: bibl., maps.

Comprehensive diplomatic-legal review of Colombia's rights in regard to its border disputes with Venezuela. Due to the failure of direct negotiations, the author supports the application of an arbitration procedure specified in the Colombian-Venezuelan treaty of 1939.

Hacia una política para la frontera con Colombia. See item **4449.**

Hernández Carstens, Eduardo. Venezuela, ¿mutilada e invadida?: límites y población. See item **4450.**

4401 Jaramillo Correa, Luis Fernando. La política exterior colombiana. Bogotá: Ministerio de Relaciones Exteriores, Subdirección de Asuntos Culturales y Divulgación, 1991. 157 p.

Collection of speeches, interviews, and articles issued or published in 1990–91 by Colombia's foreign relations minister.

Los límites entre Venezuela y Colombia: documentos oficiales que los han establecido. See item **4451.**

4402 Pardo Rueda, Rafael *et al.* Orden mundial y seguridad: nuevos desafíos para Colombia y América Latina. Recopilación de Francisco Leal Buitrago y Juan Gabriel Tokatlian. Bogotá: Tercer Mundo Editores, 1994. 205 p.: bibl.

Interesting collection of essays on the national security challenges faced by Colombia and Latin America in the 1990s. The authors agree given the conditions created by the end of the Cold War—the rise of globalization and interdependence and the consolidation of democracy in Latin America—the old notions of national security focused on anticommunism, US leadership, the central role of the military and the regional hypotheses of conflict should be replaced by a new doctrine aimed at strengthening democracy, promoting South American cooperation, restructuring military-civilian relations, and facing new challenges. Particularly interesting are the articles studying Colombian issues, such as national defense and security between 1958–93, narcotraffic, control of light weapons, and relations between citizenry and police.

4403 Reina, Mauricio. Las relaciones entre Colombia y Estados Unidos, 1978–1986. Bogotá: Centro de Estudios Internacionales de la Univ. de los Andes, 1990. 61 p.: tables. (Serie Documentos Ocasionales; 15)

Excellent study of the evolution of Colombian-US relations during the Turbay (1978–82) and Betancur (1982–86) administrations. Well-documented article examines in detail the diplomatic, economic, and drug policy-related dimensions of the bilateral relationship. Concludes that Turbay's policy of close alignment with the US failed to gain any concessions, particularly in the economic area. On the other hand, Betancur's non-aligned approach in the first half of his administration seems to have created the conditions for some US economic concessions, paving the way for closer ties from 1984–86.

4404 Rodríguez Becerra, Manuel. Crisis ambiental y relaciones internacionales: hacia una estrategia colombiana. Bogotá: FESCOL; Fundación Alejandro Angel Escobar: CEREC, 1994. 203 p.: bibl., ill. (Serie ecológica; 6)

Written by Colombia's first minister of the environment, analyzes the antecedents and negotiations leading up to the 1992 Rio Earth Summit, as well as the issues, proposals, and agreements that were discussed at this UN-sponsored conference. Particularly interesting are the sections that analyze the new institutional arrangements and recent application of environmental rules by Colombian authorities.

4405 Rodríguez Gómez, Juan Camilo. Liderazgo y autonomía: Colombia en el Consejo de Seguridad de las Naciones Unidas, 1989–1990. Prólogo de Virgilio Barco. Bogotá: Facultad de Finanzas y Relaciones Internacionales, Univ. Externado de Colombia, Centro de Investigaciones y Proyectos Especiales, 1993. 276 p.: bibl., indexes. (Pre-textos; 3)

Study of the role played by Colombia during the two years (1989–90) that it was a member of the UN Security Council. Interesting analysis of Colombia's positions on issues such as the US downing of Libyan airplanes, the invasion of Panama, Namibia's independence, the Central American peace process, the Iraqi invasion of Kuwait, and

Haitian elections. Highlights importance of Colombia's commitment to nonintervention and peaceful resolution of disputes to explain some controversial decisions, such as the condemnation of US and Iraqi actions and the reluctance to interfere in Haiti's domestic political process.

4406 Rojas, Fernando *et al.* Colombia en la presidencia de los no alineados. Bogotá: Fundación Friedrich Ebert de Colombia, 1995. 109 p.

Collection of articles by Colombian international relations experts discusses the country's presidential role in the Non-Aligned Movement and advances policy recommendations. Authors agree that it is convenient for Colombia to promote a cooperative approach open to negotiation between the NAM and the global community and to develop a socioeconomic agenda. They do not, however, reach an agreement on the kind of leadership (pragmatic or idealistic, maximalist or minimalist) that would suit Colombia best.

Sureda Delgado, Rafael Angel. El Golfo de Venezuela: análisis histórico crítico de tres tesis para que Colombia no posea áreas marinas ni submarinas en la costa Guajira entre Castilletes y Punta Espada. See item **4457.**

4407 Tokatlian, Juan Gabriel. Drogas, dilemas y dogmas: Estados Unidos y la narcocriminalidad organizada en Colombia. Bogotá: CEI; TM Editores, 1995. 192 p.: bibl. (Estudios internacionales)

Insightful study of Colombia's drug problem. First chapters challenge some accepted ideas concerning the narcotics issue and its criminal, security, diplomatic, and military implications. Later chapters address its international aspects, focusing particularly on the role played by the US. Concludes that Colombian-US relations will become even more "complex, difficult and tense" as a result of tough US policies and the negative impact of Colombia's political weakness and disarray on the anti-drug effort.

4408 Tokatlian, Juan Gabriel and **Diego Cardona.** El Grupo de los Tres y la política exterior de Colombia: ¿alternativa o ilusión? (*Estud. Int./Santiago,* 26 : 104, oct./dic. 1993, p. 610–636, tables)

Analyzes the role played by the Group of Three (Colombia, Mexico, and Venezuela)

in the formulation and implementation of
Colombia's foreign policy. Authors point out
discrepancies between Colombian declarations of the Group's importance and the country's reluctance to take practical steps toward
integration. This discrepancy is attributed to
1) the lack of information, private participation, and a more coordinated governmental
approach; 2) the excessive emphasis on commercial aspects; and 3) the fluctuating domestic political and economic situations of the
three countries.

4409 Uribe Vargas, Diego. Los últimos derechos de Colombia en el Canal de Panamá: el Tratado Uribe Vargas-Ozores. Prólogo de Ricardo Sanchez A. Bogotá?: Facultad
de Derecho, Ciencias Políticas y Sociales y
Empresa Editorial, Univ. Nacional de Colombia, 1993. 428 p.: bibl., index.

Polemical historical study of the origins of Panamanian secession and the role
played by Colombian domestic actors and the
US government. The evolution of Colombian-
Panamanian relations since 1903, with particular reference to the issue of the Panama
Canal is also analyzed. Denounces support of
Panamanian separatism and its appropriation
of the Canal Zone but also criticizes the behavior of Colombian parties and administrations for generating Panamanian resentment,
opening doors to foreign intervention and failing to pay adequate attention to the inter-
oceanic canal issue. Interesting analysis of
Colombia's preferential rights of navigation
and transportation through the Canal and
Panamanian territory.

Vila Masot, Oscar. El Golfo de Venezuela: estudio de un caso de aguas históricas. See item
4459.

ECUADOR

4410 Acosta Yépez, Francisco. Ecuador y
Perú: ¿futuro de paz? Quito: Fundación
El Comercio, 1993. 186 p.: bibl., maps.

Comprehensive assortment of brief articles on the origins, evolution, and prospects
for solving the territorial dispute with Peru
written by well-known Ecuadorian politicians, diplomats, and international relations
specialists. Includes an excellent bibliography, maps, and a selection of official proposals
for resolving the dispute.

4411 Bonilla, Adrián. Las sorprendentes vir-
tudes de lo perverso: Ecuador y narcotráfico en los 90. Quito: FLACSO-Sede Ecuador, 1993. 103 p.: bibl. (Serie Ciencias
políticas)

Brief critical analysis of the international dimensions of the Ecuadoran drug trafficking problem. Reviews the repressive unilateral US approach to drug trafficking and
money laundering and Ecuador's compliant
response during the 1990s before concluding
this strategy has failed and should be replaced
by a cooperative multilateral approach. For
political scientist's comment see *HLAS
55:3214.*

Burgos, Hernando; Alberto Adrianzén; and
Martín Beaumont. Conflicto Perú-Ecuador:
cómo llegamos hasta aquí. See item **4422.**

**4412 El Ecuador y los problemas internacio-
nales.** Quito: Univ. Central del Ecuador, Facultad de Jurisprudencia, Ciencias
Políticas y Sociales, Escuela de Ciencias Internacionales, 1989. 351 p.: bibl., ill. (Col.
Ciencias internacionales)

Particularly interesting among the articles assembled in this collection are those
discussing institutions that participate in
Ecuador's foreign policy-making process, the
foreign debt problem, and the role played by
Ecuador in the UN, OAS, and OPEC. Includes
an interesting legal/technical article on Ecuador's position concerning satellite use of the
synchronic geostationary orbit crossing over
its territory.

García Sayán, Diego; Jorge Morelli Pando; and
Sinesio Jarama. Perú-Ecuador: las cartas sobre
la mesa. See item **3562.**

4413 Guzmán Polanco, Manuel de. Ecuador
en lo internacional: un cuarto de siglo,
1945–1970. (*in* El Ecuador de la Postguerra.
Quito: Banco Central de Ecuador, 1992, v. 2,
p. 411–457)

Historical account of the evolution
of Ecuador's foreign policies in the postwar
period until 1970. Informative study encompasses the most important aspects of Ecuador's international relations though the interpretation of some of them—such as the
conflict with Peru—are heavily influenced by
a nationalistic perspective.

4414 Hey, Jeanne A.K. Ecuadorean foreign
policy since 1979: ideological cycles or
a trend towards neoliberalism? (*J. Interam.*

Stud. World Aff., 37:4, Winter 1995, p. 57–88, bibl.)

Well-argued analysis of the evolution of Ecuador's foreign policies during the Roldós/Hurtado (1979–84), Febres Cordero (1984–88), and Borja (1988–92) administrations. Concludes that although ideological fluctuations resulted in different diplomatic cycles, the neoliberal economic policies showed a high degree of consistency.

4415 Hey, Jeanne A.K. Foreign policy options under dependence: a theoretical evaluation with evidence from Ecuador. (*J. Lat. Am. Stud.*, 25:3, Oct. 1993, p. 543–574)

Interesting analysis, from a dependency theory perspective, of Ecuador's foreign policies during the Hurtado (1981–84) and Febres Cordero (1984–88) administrations. First discusses Ecuador's economic dependence and the evolution of its domestic and international policies, then concludes that "Ecuador may only be able to design and implement foreign policy autonomously in those areas the USA considers unimportant."

Rada Jordán, Eduardo. Perú y Ecuador: frontera sangrienta. See item **4429.**

Relaciones del Perú con el Ecuador. See item **4430.**

PARAGUAY

4416 Herrera, Luis Alberto de. La diplomacia oriental en el Paraguay. v. 1. Prólogo de María Julia Ardao. Montevideo: República Oriental del Uruguay, Cámara de Representantes, 1989. 1 v.: bibl. (Serie Revisión historiográfica; 11)

Official reedition of the polemical historical study written by an Uruguayan politician on the origins of the War of the Triple Alliance against Paraguay. In this early manifestation of "historical revisionism" the author used materials left by his father—Uruguay's minister of foreign relations before the war—to document the aggressive policies of Argentina and Brazil against Paraguay.

Salum-Flecha, Antonio. Historia diplomática del Paraguay de 1869 a 1990. See *HLAS 56: 3166.*

4417 Salum-Flecha, Antonio. Itaipú: la soberanía sobre el antiguo Salto del Guaíra. (*Prop. Democrát.*, 1:1, enero/marzo 1994, p. 65–74)

Brief study of the evolution of Paraguayan-Brazilian relations focused primarily on negotiations concerning border disputes and Itaipú's hydroelectric dam. Points out that Paraguay would like to renegotiate Itaipú's treaty in order to sell its surplus electrical energy to any country, and not only to Brazil.

PERU

4418 Amayo, Enrique. La transoceánica Perú-Brasil: los contradictorios intereses de Estados Unidos y Japón. (*Allpanchis/ Cusco*, 27:45, primer semestre 1995, p. 37–88, appendices, bibl., graphs, maps)

Peruvian historian examines various alternatives for the construction of a transnational highway connecting the Brazilian Amazonia to the Peruvian coast. Examines the possible contradictory interests between Japan and the US before concluding that the highway should be controlled by a binational commission that would inscribe this project into the framework of South America's economic integration.

4419 Basombrío Zender, Ignacio and **Fernando González Vigil.** El Perú y el Grupo Andino: elementos para un debate nacional. Lima: Centro Peruano de Estudios Internacionales, 1993. 96 p.: bibl. (Documentos de trabajo; 16)

Two essays address Peru's partial withdrawal from the Andean Group and discuss the country's current positions and prospects. Both review Peru's options and recommend that the country remain in the regional organization and strengthen it.

4420 Benavides Correa, Alfonso. Perú y Chile: del tratado y protocolo complementario de 1929 sobre Tacna y Arica a la convención de 1993 sobre pretendido cumplimiento de obligaciones. Lima: Metrocolor, 1993. 173 p.: ill.

Critical analysis of the agreement signed in 1993 by Peru and Chile on the implementation of the 1929 protocol on Tacna and Arica. Denounces the agreement as an unnecessary surrender of Peruvian rights to the Arica harbor.

4421 Blacker Miller, Augusto. La propuesta inconclusa. Magdalena, Peru: Consorcio La Moneda, 1993? 353 p.: ill.

Memoirs written by former foreign relations minister (Nov. 1991-April 1992) of the Fujimori administration. Interesting details concerning the ministry's internal workings, Peru's international agenda, and the evolution of relations with Ecuador, Bolivia, Chile, and the US. Particularly intriguing is the discussion of Fujimori's palace coup of April 1992, the cabinet divisions, and the effects of the events on Peru's international relations.

4422 Burgos, Hernando; Alberto Adrianzén; and Martín Beaumont. Conflicto Perú-Ecuador: cómo llegamos hasta aquí. (*Quehacer/Lima,* 93, enero/feb. 1995, p. 5–38, maps, photos)

Articles summarize the origins and evolution of the Peruvian-Ecuadorian border dispute and analyze the last armed confrontation in early 1995, ending with the signing of the Itamaraty Peace Declaration in Feb. 1995. According to the authors, this Declaration represents the first occasion since 1942 on which Peru accepted the possibility of negotiating the territorial delimitation of the area.

4423 Carlos García Bedoya: una visión desde los 90. Lima: Mosca Azul Editores, 1993. 315 p.: bibl., ill.

Collection of articles in homage to the late Peruvian diplomat and foreign minister discusses his foreign relations ideas and strategies, as well as some of his initiatives on issues such as the law of the sea, territorial problems, Antarctica, and collective security.

4424 Castro Contreras, Jaime. Geopolítica: una visión del Perú y sus posibilidades. 2. ed. Lima: Editorial Distribuidora Buenaventura, 1994. 93 p.: ill. (some col.), maps.

Brief study of Peru's geopolitical situation and prospects. Calls for the formulation and implementation of a national development program focused primarily on Peruvian integration into the Pacific basin, and secondarily into the Orinoco, Amazon, and La Plata basins.

4425 Chuquihuara, Luis. Perú y Brasil entre el Pacífico y el Atlántico: espacio surandino e integración sudamericana. (*Allpanchis/Cusco,* 27:45, primer semestre 1995, p. 89–112, bibl., tables)

Briefly examines Peruvian-Brazilian relations including economic aspects and the prospects for cooperation and integration in the areas of transportation, energy, the Amazon Basin and frontier development. Closer relations could contribute to a merging of the Andean Pact and Mercosur, and the ultimate creation of a South American free trade area.

García Sayán, Diego; Jorge Morelli Pando; and Sinesio Jarama. Perú-Ecuador: las cartas sobre la mesa. See item **3562.**

4426 Mariátegui, Juan. El 5 de abril— y la política exterior peruana. Lima: s.n., 1993. 195 p.

Interviews and articles concerning the consequences of Fujimori's April 5, 1992 palace coup on Peru's international relations. Highly critical of Fujimori's actions, pointing out Peru's international isolation resulting from the democratic breakdown.

4427 Mercado Jarrín, Edgardo. Perú: perspectivas geopolíticas. Lima: Consejo Nacional de Ciencia y Tecnología; Instituto Peruano de Estudios Geopolíticos y Estratégicos, 1993. 381 p.: bibl., col. maps.

Comprehensive geopolitical study of Peru written by former prime minister and minister of war and foreign relations during the military regime. After a detailed analysis of Peru's domestic geopolitical resources and problems, its insertion in the Pacific Basin, and its relations with Bolivia, Ecuador, and Chile, the author calls for a 20-year National Agreement on social policies, elimination of subversion, consolidation of a consensual democracy, and an economic plan focused on agricultural, energy and educational modernizations.

4428 Obando Arbulú, Enrique. El narcotráfico en el Perú: una aproximación histórica. (*Anal. Int.,* 2, abril/junio 1993, p. 80–100)

Study of drug traffic from a Peruvian perspective underscores the economic factors that have led to an increase in coca production and the role played by the peasants, drug traffickers, military, and guerrilla groups in the evolution of the narcotics problem. Discusses the US anti-drug policy, the initiatives taken by the Fujimori Administration, and the 1991 and 1992 bilateral agreements. Concludes that a lack of funds for "alternative development" in production and the use of a repressive approach led to failure.

4429 Rada Jordán, Eduardo. Perú y Ecuador: frontera sangrienta. Lima: Editorial Minerva, 1995. 99 p.: ill.

Polemical presentation of the Peruvian-Ecuadorian border dispute from a Peruvian nationalistic perspective. Extremely biased but useful exposition of Peru's claims and views that help one understand how this border dispute has periodically erupted into armed conflict.

4430 Relaciones del Perú con el Ecuador. Edición de Eduardo Ferrero Costa. Lima: Centro Peruano de Estudios Internacionales, 1994. 290 p.: bibl., ill. (Serie Seminarios, mesas redondas y conferencias, 1017–5121; 17)

Excellent collection of papers by noted Peruvian specialists delivered at a seminar on relations with Ecuador. Includes chapters on the convergence of both countries' foreign policies in the international forums (Jorge Morelli Pando), security issues (Enrique Obando), bilateral commercial relations (Ignacio Basombrío), frontier integration (José A. García Belaúnde), and entrepreneurial relations (Luis Abugattas).

4431 Rivero, Oswaldo de. La protección internacional de los derechos humanos: la situación del Perú. (*Anal. Int.*, 2, abril/junio 1993, p. 70–79)

Former Peruvian ambassador discusses the country's human rights policies and its reponse to international pressures. Points out that Peru succeeded in making the UN Commission on Human Rights accept the notion that human rights violations practiced by anti-democratic guerrilla groups, such as Shining Path, should be reported and denounced. However, the Fujimori government has damaged its international image and hindered access to economic aid and loans by refusing to respond to the international organization's questions on disappearances, torture, and massacres and failing to stop these practices.

URUGUAY

4432 Bizzozero, Lincoln and **Carlos Luján.** La política exterior del gobierno de transición en Uruguay, 1985–1989. Montevideo: Facultad de Ciencias Sociales, Depto. de Posgrados, 1992. 90 p.: bibl.

Study of the foreign policy pursued by the democratic administration of Julio M. Sanguinetti. After analyzing the formulation,

agenda and implementation of Uruguay's foreign policy between 1985–89 the authors conclude there were some adjustments—particularly concerning the adoption of a more pragmatic and open diplomatic style—but that there was no significant break with the policies implemented by the authoritarian regime.

4433 Curso Especial de Derecho Internacional Público, 1st, Montevideo, 1989. Primer Curso Especial de Derecho Internacional Público: nuestras fronteras; situación general y problemas. v. 1. Publicación dirigida por Heber Arbuet Vignali. Montevideo: Fundación de Cultura Universitaria, 1989? 1 v.

Compilation of lectures delivered by a number of Uruguayan specialists on the evolution of the country's borders, with special reference to some of the problems faced with regard to Argentina and Brazil. Informative legal-historical review from a Uruguayan perspective.

4434 Flangini, Yamandú. El tratado del Río de la Plata y su frente marítimo: 20 años de vigencia. Montevideo: Arca, 1993. 256 p. (Nuevas fronteras)

Informative study of the Argentine-Uruguayan border dispute along the Río de la Plata and the negotiations leading to a mutually acceptable solution in 1973. The author, an Uruguayan navy officer who served in the foreign relations ministry, participated in the negotiations and mixes documental information with anecdotal recollections.

4435 González Lapeyre, Edison. Los límites de la República Oriental del Uruguay. Prólogo de Enrique Iglesias. 2. ed. actualizada. Montevideo: A.M. Fernández, 1992. 376 p.: bibl. (Ediciones jurídicas)

Updated version of a 1986 publication offers a complete historical, legal, and diplomatic analysis of the evolution of Uruguay's borders. As a former negotiator of the treaties with Argentina on the de la Plata and Uruguay rivers, the author offers particularly interesting insights.

4436 Gros Espiell, Héctor. Política exterior del Uruguay: marzo de 1990–julio de 1991. Montevideo: República Oriental del Uruguay, Ministerio de Relaciones Exteriores, Instituto Artigas del Servicio Exterior, 1991. 86 p.

Compilation of speeches delivered by

Uruguay's foreign relations minister at various domestic and international forums.

4437 Herrera, Luis Alberto de. La doctrina Drago y el interés del Uruguay. Montevideo: República Oriental del Uruguay, Cámara de Representantes, 1991. xlii, 234 p.: bibl., 1 ill. (Serie Actividad política, periodística y parlamentaria; 1)

Official reedition of the Uruguayan politician's essay on the Drago doctrine (originally published in 1908). It also includes a number of Herrera's congressional speeches and articles mostly on the issue of nonintervention.

4438 Herrera, Luis Alberto de. El Uruguay internacional: seguido de Labor diplomática en Norteamérica; selección de documentos. Montevideo: Cámara de Representantes de la República Oriental del Uruguay, 1988. 444 p.: ill., maps. (Serie Teorización política; 1)

Official reedition of the classic nationalistic defense of Uruguay's independence and sovereignty first published in 1912. Includes a selection of diplomatic communications sent by Herrera while he represented Uruguay before the US and Mexico.

4439 Kechichián, José. Aspectos sociales y políticos de la integración regional: Uruguay en la perspectiva del Mercosur. (*Perf. Latinoam.*, 3:4, junio 1994, p. 63–85)

Studies the impact of integration into Mercosur on Uruguay's political and economic situations. Points out potential danger of deindustrialization and negative social consequences of embracing a neoliberal strategy for regional integration. Calls for a more active role of the State in economic and social spheres.

4440 Luján, Carlos. Cambio de régimen y política internacional: el caso uruguayo. Montevideo: División Cultura, Intendencia Municipal de Montevideo, 1993. 147 p.: bibl. (Col. Los Premios. Primera serie)

Excellent study of the evolution of Uruguay's foreign policies in the context of its transition to democracy. Analyzes links between political regime and foreign policy, the continuities and changes in Uruguay's foreign policy agenda between 1985–90, and transformations in the decision-making process. Concludes that although there were important changes in style and decision-making mecha-

nisms, the regime change had a limited impact on foreign policy objectives.

4441 Luján, Carlos. Europa y Estados Unidos en la democratización uruguaya: cooperación internacional y relaciones bilaterales. (*Estud. Int./Santiago*, 27:106, abril/junio 1994, p. 129–161, tables)

Analyzes of the role played by Western European countries and the US in the process of Uruguayan democratization from the decline of its authoritarian regime to the mid-1990s. After discussing external diplomatic initiatives and economic influences, the author concludes that their impact on Uruguayan democratization was modest and that the main factors were endogenous, such as the existence of pro-democratic forces and culture.

4442 Pérez Otermin, Jorge. Política exterior y profesionalismo diplomático. Montevideo: Organización de los Estados Americanos, 1992. 50 p.: bibl.

Paper delivered by the director of the Artigas Institute of Foreign Service of Uruguay's ministry of foreign relations. Describes the institution's features and suggests ways to promote diplomatic professionalism and avoid political interferences in foreign service.

4443 Policy on the environment and development: Uruguay and the Rio de Janeiro World Conference. Coordinación de Mateo J. Magariños de Mello. Montevideo: Ministry of Foreign Affairs;: Ministry of Housing, Land Use Planning and Environment, 1992. 504 p.: bibl., ill.

Collection of papers on environmental problems and international policies produced by Uruguayan government officials and specialists in preparation for the 1992 UN Conference on the Environment and Development in Rio de Janeiro. Of particular interest are the articles concerning Uruguay's environmental policies and proposals, including those on its environmental agenda, and relations between environmental protection and human rights, transfrontier pollution, and trade and maritime policies.

Trías, Vivián. La rebelión de las orillas. See item **4053.**

4444 Trías, Vivián. Uruguay y sus claves geopolíticas. Prólogo de Rubén Cotelo. Montevideo: Ediciones de la Banda Oriental,

1991. 309 p.: bibl., map. (Selección de obras de Vivián Trías; 8. Serie Patria chica)

Reedition of Trías' 1972 analysis of Uruguay's geopolitical circumstances in the global and South American context. Outdated in many respects, but still useful for understanding the leftist nationalistic approach so influential during the 1960s–70s. Also includes a selection of journalistic articles on geopolitical issues, mostly focused on the South Atlantic.

VENEZUELA

4445 Cardozo de Da Silva, Elsa *et al.* Reforma y política exterior en Venezuela. Coordinación de Carlos A. Romero. Caracas: Instituto Venezolano de Estudios Sociales y Políticos; Editorial Nueva Sociedad, 1992. 273 p.: bibl., ill.

Collection of insightful articles analyze the features of Venezuela's foreign policy, its foundations, and decision-making processes. Discusses future prospects and recommends changes in the context of a more general process of State reform. Includes concise but well-documented studies of the evolution of Venezuela's foreign policy, its institutional complexity and economic aspects, the role of the military, and characteristics of the foreign service and diplomatic corps. Important contribution.

4446 Carnevali, Atilano. Atilano Carnevali, embajador de Venezuela, 1937–1959. Recopilación de Dinorah Carnevali de Toro. Caracas: Ministerio de Relaciones Exteriores, 1994. 920 p.: ill., index. (Biblioteca de política exterior; 9)

Selection of official documents related to or written by Ambassador Carnevali throughout his long diplomatic career as Venezuela's representative in Argentina, Brazil, Chile, Colombia, Great Britain, Italy, the OAS, and Peru.

4447 Consuegra C., José. Carlos Andrés Pérez: diplomacia directa. Caracas: Ediciones del Ministerio de la Secretaría de la Presidencia de la República, 1991. 275 p.: ill.

Friend and advisor of Carlos Andrés Pérez, presents a flattering account of presidential diplomatic activities during the first two years (1989–90) of Pérez's ill-fated second administration. Propagandistic work, however, allows for examination of Venezuela's foreign policy during this period, particularly the crucial role played by an activist president.

Ellner, Steve. Venezuela. See *HLAS 56:2655.*

Frota, Luciara Silveira de Aragão e. Documentos para una historia de las relaciones diplomáticas, Brasil-Venezuela, 1859–1900. See item **4486.**

4448 Giacalone, Rita. La política exterior de Venezuela en el Caribe oriental: ¿compatibilidad o competencia con Estados Unidos? (*in* Association des études de la Caraïbe. Congrès, *13th, Pointe-à-Pitre, Guadeloupe, 1988.* Etudes caraïbéennes: société et politique; actes. Toulouse, France; Presses de l'Institut d'études politiques de Toulouse; Pointe-à-Pitre: Centre d'études et de recherches caraïbéennes; Fort-de-France, Martinique: Univ. des Antilles et de la Guyane, 1991, p. 301–316)

Comparative analysis of US and Venezuelan foreign policies toward the island nations of the Eastern Caribbean. Shows that although both countries share certain objectives (promotion of political stability, economic development, and social progress in the region), differing methods and policies have led to confrontations (i.e., during US interventions and periods of occupation or when Venezuela offered economic aid to Grenada before the US invasion).

4449 Hacia una política para la frontera con Colombia. Caracas: Comisión Presidencial para Asuntos Fronterizos Colombo-Venezolanos, 1991. 216 p., 4 folded leaves of plates: ill., maps. (Serie Consultas)

Excellent collection of studies on border issues with Colombia delivered at a 1990 seminar organized by the Venezuelan presidential commission. Forgoing the usual chauvinistic approach, the authors, both civilian and military experts, present a comprehensive picture of the border problems, including different interpretations of Venezuela's foreign policies toward Colombia; studies of the economic, social, and ethnic characteristics of the border region; and analyses of the prospects for bilateral resolutions.

4450 Hernández Carstens, Eduardo. Venezuela, ¿mutilada e invadida?: límites y población. Caracas: M.A. García e Hijo, 1989. 172 p.: appendix, maps.

Polemical work by Venezuelan nationalistic politician denouncing Colombia's expansionism and Venezuela's lack of adequate frontier policies that have led, in his view, to the loss of important land and maritime territories. Also argues that the large number of Colombian migrants endangers Venezuela's sovereignty. A documentary appendix reproduces border agreements, arbitral decisions and proposals issued between 1881–1980.

Hugueney, Clodoaldo. La dimensión suramericana de la diplomacia brasileña. See item **4490.**

4451 Los límites entre Venezuela y Colombia: documentos oficiales que los han establecido. Recopilación de Tomás Polanco Alcántara y Eduardo Hernández Carstens. Caracas: Ediciones de la Academia Nacional de la Historia, 1993. 526 p.: bibl. (Biblioteca de la Academia Nacional de la Historia)

Compilation of official documents published by the Venezuela's National Academy of History concerning delimitation of borders with Colombia. Useful source that reproduces bilateral treaties, arbitral decisions, Venezuelan ministerial memoirs, diplomatic notes and communications, and transcripts of congressional debates and resolutions issued through 1941.

Mendible Z., Alejandro. Venezuela-Brasil: su acelerado acercamiento histórico. See item **4499.**

4452 Mendible Z., Alejandro. Venezuela y sus verdaderas fronteras con el Brasil: desde el Tratado de Tordesillas hasta la incursión de los garimpeiros. Caracas: Centro Abreu e Lima de Estudios Brasileños, Instituto de Altos Estudios de América Latina, Univ. Simón Bolívar, 1993. 349 p.: bibl.

Comprehensive well-researched study of the evolution of the Venezuelan-Brazilian border demarcation, from the colonial period to the 1990s. Examines diplomatic, political, economic, and demographic aspects of the bilateral interactions. Concludes with a discussion of problems generated during the late 1980s when the entry into Venezuelan territory of large numbers of Brazilian *garimpeiros* (illegal gold miners) led to diplomatic negotiations resulting in the creation of a binational aboriginal and ecological reserve.

4453 Morales Paúl, Isidro. La delimitación de áreas marinas y submarinas entre Venezuela y Trinidad & Tobago. Caracas:

Academia de Ciencias Políticas y Sociales, 1993. 193 p.: bibl., ill., maps. (Biblioteca de la Academia de Ciencias Políticas y Sociales. Serie Estudios; 9)

Comprehensive study written by chief of the Venezuelan delegation concerning the bilateral negotiations and contents of the agreement between Venezuela and Trinidad & Tobago delimitating the maritime and underwater jurisdictions of both countries. Interesting example of successfully negotiated resolution of a territorial dispute.

4454 Picón-Salas, Mariano. Mariano Picón-Salas, embajador de Venezuela. Recopilación de Delia Picón. Prólogo de Simón Alberto Consalvi. Presentación de Efraín Schacht Aristeguieta. Caracas: Instituto de Asuntos Internacionales, Ministerio de Relaciones Exteriores, 1987. 546 p.: ill., indexes. (Biblioteca de política exterior; 3)

Collection of official documents published by Venezuela's foreign relations ministry concerning Ambassador Picón-Salas activities within the ministry and as a Venezuelan representative to Czechoslovakia, the US, Colombia, Brazil, Mexico, and UNESCO.

Ramos, Danielly Silva. Brasil-Venezuela: a nova integração. See item **4507.**

4455 Schwartz, Rafael. Los Monjes: conflicto entre Venezuela y Colombia; la verdad histórica. 2. ed. Caracas: Bonalde Editores, 1993. 227 p.: bibl., ill., maps.

Defense of Venezuelan claims to archipelago in the Gulf of Venezuela currently disputed with Colombia. Interesting, albeit biased interpretation of conflict.

4456 Serbín, Andrés. A new approach to the world? the *gran viraje* and Venezuelan policy. (*in* Lessons of the Venezuelan experience. Edited by Louis W. Goodman *et al.* Washington: Woodrow Wilson Center Press, 1995, p. 365–386)

Insightful study of the impact on foreign policy of the *gran viraje* (great turnaround) since the Pérez Administration. Study states that as a result of this change Venezuelan new strategy calls for the "nation's insertion into the world economic system by reinforcing . . . both the comparative advantages offered by the oil industry . . . and the promotion of the growth of nontraditional exports." Thus, Venezuela's traditional non-aligned approaches are "being superseded increasingly by economic priorities such as the liberalization of trade, subregional integration, and the diversification of exports, free markets, and sources of investment and technology."

4457 Sureda Delgado, Rafael Angel. El Golfo de Venezuela: análisis histórico crítico de tres tesis para que Colombia no posea áreas marinas ni submarinas en la costa Guajira entre Castilletes y Punta Espada. Caracas: Academia de Ciencias Políticas y Sociales, 1994. 465 p.: appendix, bibl., index, maps. (Biblioteca de la Academia de Ciencias Políticas y Sociales. Serie Estudios; 42)

Venezuelan account of historical, diplomatic, and security reasons why Colombia should not possess maritime areas along the Guajira coast between Castilletes and Punta Espada. Biased, but includes a useful documental appendix and some interesting legal considerations.

4458 Toro Hardy, Alfredo. Bajo el signo de la incertidumbre. Caracas: Editorial Panapo; Tomotex, 1992. 143 p.

Collection of short essays by foreign relations specialist dealing with recent international and Venezuelan political developments. Particularly interesting are analyses Venezuela's crisis during the Carlos A. Pérez presidency and its impact on the country's foreign policy.

4459 Vila Masot, Oscar. El Golfo de Venezuela: estudio de un caso de aguas históricas. Caracas: Editorial Arte, 1992. 61 p.

Brief legal-historical study of the Venezuelan-Colombian territorial dispute concerning the Gulf of Venezuela. Claims that important elements of the 1891 arbitral decision by the Spanish crown were ignored, thereby making later agreements on border demarcation null and void. Concludes that, according to the original decision, Colombia does not have any territorial rights in the Guajira or Gulf waters.

4460 Vivas Gallardo, Freddy. Venezuela-Estados Unidos, 1939–1945: la coyuntura decisiva; las relaciones politicas y militares entre Venezuela y los Estados Unidos durante la Segunda Guerra Mundial. Caracas: Univ. Central de Venezuela, Facultad de Ciencias Jurídicas y Políticas, 1993. 343 p.: bibl., map.

Excellent analysis of the evolution of Venezuelan-US relations (bilateral, political, economic, and military contacts) during World War II. Argues that the 1939–45 marked a foreign policy turning point as Venezuela moved away from Europe and established a close, but subordinate association, with the US.

BRAZIL

SCOTT D. TOLLEFSON, *Assistant Professor, Department of Political Science, Kansas State University*

BRAZIL'S INTERNATIONAL RELATIONS LITERATURE is dominated this biennium by the theme of integration. This is a reflection of Brazil's membership, along with Argentina, Uruguay, and Paraguay, in Mercosul (Bolivia and Chile are associate members) (item **4333**). The literature on integration, however, is at times euphoric, lacking healthy skepticism, with the prominent exception of item **4517**.

Discussions of integration are not limited to Mercosul. Some focus on the relationship between Mercosul and the North American Free Trade Agreement (NAFTA) (item **4492**); others examine integration efforts in the Amazon region, and Brazil's relations with other areas of the world (item **4496**).

A second major theme concerns Brazil's position within the changing international system. Diplomats from Brazil's Ministry of Foreign Relations are among the most astute writers on this topic. Perhaps the most important volumes in this field are those edited by Gelson Fonseca and Sergio Henrique Nabuco de Castro (item **4522**). Other important works are those published by the Ministry of Foreign Relations (item **4491**) and Ricardo Antônio Seitenfus (item **4514**).

A third, more traditional area of study is Brazil's bilateral relations, especially those with the United States. Maria Helena Tachinardi avoids the dominant diplomatic history approach to provide the most fascinating book on the topic. She focuses on the "war of the patents" waged between the United States and Brazil (item **4521**). Brazil's relations with Germany are also the topic of several studies (item **4495**), as are Brazil's relations with the People's Republic of China, Japan, and various African countries.

Other prominent themes include the relationship between Brazil's environmental policies and the international system; geopolitics (item **4500**); and external security (items **4476, 4525,** and **4527**). René Armand Dreifuss has authored a particularly good study of Brazil's maritime policies (item **4483**).

In conclusion, the literature on Brazil's international relations is improving, demonstrating greater theoretical and methodological rigor. The gradual shift from descriptive diplomatic histories to more scholarly analyses augurs well for future studies.

4461 Abdenur, Roberto. Política externa e desenvolvimento. (*Polít. Extern./São Paulo*, 3:3, dez./fcv., 1994/95, p. 52–71, bibl.)

Author, Secretário-Geral of Brazil's Ministério das Relações Exteriores, examines relationship between the international system, Brazil's economic development, and Brazil's foreign policy. He is optimistic about Brazil's prospects, both internally and externally.

4462 Al-Safi, Mansour Saleh. Arábia Saudita: política externa e aspectos de suas relações com o Brasil. Brasília: Thesaurus, 1993. 242 p.: bibl., ill., map.

Saudi diplomat with ten years experience in Brazil provides overview of Saudi Arabia and its foreign policy, with an emphasis on relations with Brazil.

4463 Albuquerque, José Augusto Guilhon. Relações Brasil-Estados Unidos e a integração continental. (*Polít. Extern./São Paulo*, 5:1, junho/agôsto 1996, p. 3–19, bibl.)

Argues that the major obstacle to hemispheric integration is the contentious bilateral relationship between Brazil and the US. Brazil's strategy is one of "postponement"—denying the US greater access to markets in Latin America.

4464 Almeida, Paulo Roberto de. O Brasil e o Mercosur em face do NAFTA. (*Polít. Extern./São Paulo*, 3:1, junho/agôsto 1994, p. 84–96)

Highlights political dimensions of Mercosur and NAFTA and analyzes Brazil's relationship to each.

4465 Almeida, Paulo Roberto de. Estudos de relações internacionais do Brasil: etapas de produção historiográfica brasileira, 1927–1992. (*Rev. Bras. Polít. Int.*, 36:1, 1993, p. 11–36, bibl.)

Broad and interesting historiography of works published on Brazil's international relations.

Amayo, Enrique. La transoceánica Perú-Brasil: los contradictorios intereses de Estados Unidos y Japón. See item **4418.**

4466 Amazônia: desenvolvimento ou retrocesso. Coordenação de José Marcelino Monteiro da Costa. Belém, Brazil: Edições CEJUP, 1992. 351 p.: bibl., ill. (Col. Amazoniana; 2)

Eight scientists working in the Amazon collaborated on this volume with hopes of influencing the ECO-92 (Rio de Janeiro) discussions. Adherbal Meira Mattos is extremely nationalistic in his chapter entitled "O Interesse Nacional e os Interesses Internacionais na Amazônia Brasileira."

4467 Andrade, Antonio de. Brasil: ¿del Acuerdo Amazónico al Mercosur? (*Geosur/Montevideo*, 17:189/190, feb. 1996, p. 41–53, maps, tables)

Geopolitical analysis of the Acuerdo

Amazónico considers its relationship to Mercosur, to a potential Merconorte, and to other efforts at hemispheric integration.

4468 Andrade, Virgílio Moretzsohn de.
África, com ênfase nos países de língua portuguesa e Nigéria, Namíbia e África do Sul. (*Rev. Esc. Super. Guerr.*, 10:29, 1994, p. 9–31)
Speech by Brazilian diplomat given at the Escola Superior de Guerra in Rio de Janeiro provides excellent overview of Brazil's relations with sub-Saharan Africa.

4469 Arroi, Ana Carolina Machado. A política externa e o sistema brasileiro de telecomunicações por satélite. (*Cont. Int.*, 17:1, jan./junho 1995, p. 61–88)
Ambitious effort to examine the nexus between domestic public policy and foreign policy on issues relating to Brazil's satellite communications system. While scope of study is too broad for an article, addresses an important gap in the literature.

4470 Arruda, Antônio de. Aspectos da política externa brasileira. (*Rev. Esc. Super. Guerr.*, 10:29, 1994, p. 73–78, bibl.)
Traces, in succinct and theoretical fashion, the guiding principles of Brazil's foreign policy. Argues that Brazil should follow a more ambitious foreign policy.

4471 Bandeira, Moniz. Estado nacional e política internacional na América Latina: o continente nas relações Argentina-Brasil, 1930–1992. Brasília: Edunb; São Paulo: Editora Ensaio, 1993. 304 p.: bibl., index.
Impressive and fascinating historical account of the competition between Brazil and Argentina since 1930, culminating with their integration in Mercosur in 1991.

4472 Bandeira, Moniz. O milagre alemão e o desenvolvimento do Brasil: as relações da Alemanha com o Brasil e a América Latina, 1949–1994. São Paulo: Editora Ensaio, 1994. 246 p.: bibl., index.
Based on extensive primary sources, prolific historian analyzes Germany's role in shaping Brazil's foreign economic relations from 1949–94. Concludes that extensive economic ties between the two countries (including those in the nuclear sector) provided Brazil with greater leverage in its relations with the US.

Bocco, Héctor Eduardo. La cooperación nuclear Argentina-Brasil: notas para una evaluación política. See item **4340.**

4473 Brazil. Congreso Nacional. Senado Federal. Comissão de Relações Exteriores e Defesa Nacional. Relatório dos trabalhos e atividades da Comissão de Relações Exteriores e Defesa Nacional, biênio 1991–1992. Relato do Senador Irapuan Costa Júnior. Brasília: Senado Federal, 1993. 189 p.
Succinct yet important record of the Comission's activities between 1991–92. Includes many articles and speeches by Senator Irapuan Costa Júnior, President of the Commission.

4474 Brigagão, Clóvis. Margens do Brasil: ensaios de política global. Rio de Janeiro: Topbooks, 1995. 119 p.: bibl., ill.
Thirteen short essays discuss a range of topics from ecological security to nuclear energy.

4475 Carrilho, Arnaldo. O Brasil e a área econômica chinesa. São Paulo: Univ. de São Paulo, Instituto de Estudos Avançados, 1995. 31 p.: bibl., graphs, tables. (Col. documentos. Série assuntos internacionais; 37)
Anecdotal and rather insubstantial overview of Brazil's relations with China.

4476 Cavagnari Filho, Geraldo Lesbat. América do Sul: alguns subsídios para definição da segurança nacional. (*Premissas*/São Paulo, 6, abril 1994, p. 25–46)
Leading Brazilian expert on security issues traces major changes in the international system, considering their implications for security in South America generally and for Brazil specifically.

4477 Cervo, Amado Luiz. Dos tendencias de la política exterior del Brasil desde los años treintas. (*in* Colección nuestra patria es América: integración y política exterior. Quito: Editora Nacional, 1992, v. 6, p. 171–184, bibl.)
Overview of various Brazilian foreign policy models since beginning of Getúlio Vargas' presidency. Author favors integrationist model of 1990s.

4478 Cervo, Amado Luiz. Multiculturalismo e política exterior: o caso do Brasil. (*Rev. Bras. Polít. Int.*, 38:2, 1995, p. 133–146)

Provocative and compelling examination of the relationship between Brazil's "multiculturalism" and its foreign policy. Concludes that Brazil's ethnic groups have had only a marginal impact on the formulation of foreign policy.

Chuquihuara, Luis. Perú y Brasil entre el Pacífico y el Atlántico: espacio surandino e integración sudamericana. See item **4425.**

4479 Ciclo Nacional de Temas Estratégicos, 1st, Rio de Janeiro, 1994. Monopólio estatal do petróleo: anais. Rio de Janeiro: Escola Superior de Guerra, 1994? 75 p.

Experts, most of whom are sympathetic to State monopoly of Brazil's petroleum industry, debate privatization of that industry.

4480 Corrêa, Manoel Pio. O governo brasileiro frente a um caso de pirataria. (*Bol. Soc. Bras. Direito Int.*, 47:93/94, julho/dez. 1994, p. 37–42)

Laments the fact that in 1961 President Jânio Quadros granted political asylum to over 70 anti-Salazar Portuguese "pirates" who took over a Brazilian ship, the *Santa Maria*, on its way from Portugal to Rio de Janeiro.

4481 Corrêa, Manoel Pio. O mundo em que vivi. Rio de Janeiro: Expressão e Cultura, 1995. 1068 p.: ill., indexes.

In a lengthy anecdotal account, a Brazilian diplomat looks back on his years in the Ministério das Relações Exteriores.

Curso Especial de Derecho Internacional Público, 1st, Montevideo, 1989. Primer Curso Especial de Derecho Internacional Público: nuestras fronteras; situación general y problemas. v. 1. See item **4433.**

4482 O desafio internacional: a política exterior do Brasil de 1930 a nossos dias. Organização de Amado Luiz Cervo. Brasília: Editora UnB, 1994. 354 p.: (Col. Relações internacionais)

Important contribution to an understanding of Brazil's foreign policy since 1930. Includes chapters by leading experts: Clodoaldo Bueno (multilateral policy); Moniz Bandeira (the Americas); León E. Bieber (Europe); José Flávio Sombra Saraiva (Africa); and Antônio José Barbosa (China, Japan, Middle East, and North Africa). Cervo's insightful introductory chapter is required reading for

anyone interested in the historiography of Brazil's international relations.

4483 Dreifuss, René Armand. O mar e a Marinha no contexto das tendências de estruturação do novo cenário mundial. (*Premissas/São Paulo*, 4, agôsto 1993, p. 50–66)

One of Brazil's most astute observers of international relations links changes in the international system to Brazil's navy and its role and mission. Based on a lecture delivered at the Escola de Guerra Naval in Rio de Janeiro.

4484 Fórum Nacional Como Evitar uma Nova Década Perdida, Rio de Janeiro, 1991. A nova ordem internacional e a terceira revolução industrial. Coordenação de João Paulo dos Reis Velloso. Rio de Janeiro: J. Olympio Editora, 1992. 191 p.: bibl., ill.

Collection of ten papers by leading diplomats, scholars, and others considers various issues related to Brazil's insertion in the international system. Despite some valuable individual chapters, book lacks unifying theme. See also items **4492** and **4488.**

4485 Franco, Itamar. Discursos de política externa: de novembro de 1992 a maio de 1993. Brasília: Presidência da República Federativa do Brasil, 1993. 100 p.: ill.

Contains 12 uninspiring foreign policy speeches by Brazil's President Itamar Franco, from Nov. 1992-May 1993.

4486 Frota, Luciara Silveira de Aragão e. Documentos para una historia de las relaciones diplomáticas, Brasil-Venezuela, 1859–1900. (*Mundo Nuevo/Caracas*, 18:4, oct./dic. 1995, p. 553–575)

Describes Brazil's diplomatic relations with Venezuela after border between the two countries was established in 1859. Focuses on issue of border demarcation up to turn of the century.

Gilderhus, Mark T. Got a gringo on their shoulders: U.S. relations with Latin America. See item **4010.**

4487 Gonçalves, William da Silva and **Shiguenoli Miyamoto.** Os militares na política externa brasileria: 1964–1984. (*Estud. Hist./Rio de Janeiro*, 12, julho/dez. 1993, p. 211–246)

First-rate article analyzes military's role in Brazil's foreign policy from 1964–85. While noting differences between the military presidents, concludes that objective of the military government remained the same: to make Brazil a great world power.

4488 A grande crise: a nova (des)ordem internacional dos anos 80 aos 90. Organização de Paulo Gilberto Fagundes Vizentini. Petrópolis, Brazil: Vozes, 1992. 236 p.: bibl.

Various scholars consider the changing international system and its implications for Brazil. Similar to volume coordinated by Reis Velloso (item **4484**), but more focused along the lines of item **4492**.

4489 Grieco, Francisco de Assis. O Brasil e a nova geopolítica européia. São Paulo: Edições Aduaneiras, 1992. 221 p.: bibl.

Brazilian diplomat with extensive experience in European economic affairs assesses integration of Europe and its implications for Brazil. Solid and prescient.

Hoge, James F. Fulfilling Brazil's promise: a conversation with President Cardoso. See item **3895**.

4490 Hugueney, Clodoaldo. La dimensión suramericana de la diplomacia brasileña. (*Mundo Nuevo/Caracas*, 18:4, oct./dic. 1995, p. 517–531)

Traces Brazil's increasingly complex relations with Venezuela within the context of globalization and regionalization in the 1990s.

4491 Instituto de Pesquisa de Relações Internacionais (Brazil). Reflexões sobre a política externa brasileira. Brasília: Ministério das Relações Exteriores, Subsecretaria-Geral de Planejamento Político e Econômico, Fundação Alexandre de Gusmão, Instituto de Pesquisa de Relações Internacionais, 1993? 352 p.

Leading Brazilian diplomats, professors, journalists, and businessmen reflect on relationship between changes in the international system and the "national situation." Pt. 1 is thematic; Pt. 2 is a summary of four conferences. Most interesting are the exchanges between conference participants.

4492 Instituto Sul-Norte de Política Econômica e Relações Internacionais (Brazil). O Brasil frente a um mundo dividido em blocos. São Paulo: Nobel; Instituto Sul-Norte de Política Econômica e Relações Internacionais, 1994. 277 p.: bibl.

Important analysis of Brazil's foreign economic relations. Authors applaud Brazil's economic opening, but put forward the controversial argument that Brazil should, in addition to Mercosur, also link itself with US-led North American bloc, instead of becoming a small global trader. Rich with data. See also items **4484** and **4488**.

4493 Jensen, Brigitte. Ecueils et réussites de l'intégration Argentine-Brésil. (*Cah. Am. lat.*, 12, 1991, p. 74–88, bibl., tables)

Sectoral economic analysis of Brazil's integration with Argentina.

4494 José Guilherme Merquior, diplomata. Brasília: Fundação Alexandre de Gusmão, Instituto de Pesquisa de Relações Internacionais, 1993. 80 p.: bibl. (Col. Relações internacionais; 15)

José Guilherme Alves Merquior (1941–91) was one of Brazil's leading diplomats and experts on international relations. Book is a collection of five tributes by fellow diplomats. Includes text of Merquior's "O Problema da Legitimidade em Política Internacional."

4495 Lafer, Celso. Brasil-Alemanha no novo cenário internacional. (*Polít. Extern./São Paulo*, 4:3, dez./fev. 1995/96, p. 82–85)

Leading Brazilian scholar and diplomat traces history of Brazil's relations with Germany, focusing on economic ties. Lafer is optimistic that in the post-Cold War era, convergence of interests between the two countries will lead to a closer relationship.

4496 Lafer, Celso. O Brasil no mundo pós-Guerra Fria. (*in* A economia mundial em transformação. Rio de Janeiro: Fundação Getulio Vargas, Comitê de Cooperação Empresarial, Centro de Economia Mundial, 1994, p. 99–108)

Superb analysis examines Brazil's involvement in Mercosur and relations with the US, Europe, and Japan since the collapse of a bipolar system. Author refers frequently to his experience as foreign minister of Brazil.

4497 Lege, Klaus-Wilhelm. A abertura da economia brasileira e sua influência nas relações exteriores do Brasil. (*Rev. Bras. Polít. Int.*, 38:2, 1995, p. 59–98)

Analyzes relationship between Brazil's economic and foreign policies. Study is flawed methodologically because it is based almost exclusively on German sources and on a survey of German and Brazilian entrepreneurs. It nonetheless raises important questions.

4498 Medeiros, Marcelo de Almeida. Relações externas do Mercosul: uma abordagem brasileira. (*Rev. Bras. Polít. Int.*, 38:2, 1995, p. 31–58, graphs)

Insightful, theoretical assessment of Mercosur's current and potential relationship with 1) the rest of Latin America, 2) NAFTA, 3) the European Union, and 4) Asia. Focuses on Brazilian interests.

4499 Mendible Z., Alejandro. Venezuela-Brasil: su acelerado acercamiento histórico. (*Mundo Nuevo/Caracas*, 18:4, oct./dic. 1995, p. 533–551)

Historical but naive overview of relations between Venezuela and Brazil, from a Venezuelan perspective. Emphasizes importance of the 1859 treaty that established the border between the two countries.

Mendible Z., Alejandro. Venezuela y sus verdaderas fronteras con el Brasil: desde el Tratado de Tordesillas hasta la incursión de los garimpeiros. See item **4452.**

Mitre, Antonio and **Tania Quintaneiro.** Viagem conturbada por um rio tranqüilo: conflitos diplomáticos em torno da navegação do Amazonas no século XIX. See *HLAS 56:3334.*

4500 Miyamoto, Shiguenoli. Geopolítica e poder no Brasil. Campinas, Brazil: Papirus Editora, 1995. 257 p.: bibl., maps. (Estado e política)

Superb overview of influence of geopolitical thought on Brazil's development. Book astutely divided into three parts: theoretical considerations, chronological development of geopolitical thought in Brazil, and "grand themes" in Brazilian geopolitics.

4501 Moura, Gerson. Neutralidade dependente: o caso do Brasil, 1939–42. (*Estud. Hist./Rio de Janeiro*, 12, julho/dez. 1993, p. 177–180)

Argues that Brazil maintained a neutral position from 1939–42 in relation to World War II, but its "dependent" position (on the US) limited its foreign policy, forcing Brazil to join the Allies in the final years of the war.

4502 Ninomiya, Masato. O centenário do Tratado de Amizade, Comércio e Navegação entre Brasil e Japão. (*Rev. USP*, 28, dez./fev. 1995/96, p. 245–250, photo)

Brief account of the 1895 treaty signed between Brazil and Japan.

4503 Odell, John S. International threats and internal politics: Brazil, the European Community, and the United States, 1985–1987. (*in* Double-edged diplomacy: international bargaining and domestic politics. Berkeley: Univ. of California Press, 1993, p. 233–264)

Insightful and highly theoretical study of Brazil's trade with Europe and the US reveals major implications for US foreign policy.

4504 Oliveira, Henrique Altemani de. As relações Brasil-Africa. Brasília: Faculdade de Estudos Sociais Aplicados, Univ. de Brasília, 1992. 19 p.: tables. (Cadernos de Relações Internacionais; 4)

Examines Brazilian foreign policy toward Africa since 1960s, focusing on commercial ties. Includes trade data.

4505 Pinheiro, Letícia. Restabelecimento de relações diplomáticas com a República Popular da China: uma análise do processo de decisão. (*Estud. Hist./Rio de Janeiro*, 12, julho/dez. 1993, p. 247–270)

Focused study examines President Geisel's rapprochement with China. Methodologically rich, offers a model that could be applied to similar decisions.

4506 Pinto, Lenine. Natal, USA. Natal, Brazil: Econômico Empresa Jornalística, 1995. 254 p.: bibl., ill., index, maps.

Anecdotal and critical account of US military involvement in Natal during World War II. Despite some eyewitness observations by the author, book lacks focus and methodological rigor.

Procile, Gabriel. The challenge of cooperation: Argentina and Brazil, 1939–1955. See item **4361.**

4507 Ramos, Danielly Silva. Brasil-Venezuela: a nova integração. (*Rev. Bras. Polít. Int.*, 38:2, 1995, p. 99–111)

Balanced historical account of Brazilian-Venezuelan relations. Argues that increasingly close economic relations between Brazil and Venezuela in the 1990s are driven primarily by energy and mineral resources.

4508 Ribeiro, Osmar José de Barros. O tráfico de drogas no mundo e no Brasil. (*Def. Nac.*, 770, out./dez. 1995, p. 51–64)

Predictable overview of drug trafficking in Brazil written by a lieutenant colonel in Brazilian Army.

4509 Rodrigues, José Honório and Ricardo Antônio Silva Seitenfus. Uma história diplomática do Brasil, 1531–1945. Organização de Lêda Boechat Rodrigues. Rio de Janeiro: Civilização Brasileira, 1995. 512 p.: bibl., index.

Insightful, chronological analysis of Brazil's diplomatic relations from the colonial period through World War II. First two chapters and conclusion, in which underpinnings of Brazil's foreign relations are examined, are especially good.

4510 Roelofse-Campbell, Zélia. Brazil's new role in South and southern Africa: an interview with Luiz Felipe Lampreia. (*UNISA Lat. Am. Rep.*, 11:2, July/Dec. 1995, p. 51–53, map, photo)

Brief interview with Brazil's foreign minister focuses on Brazil's relations with South Africa (incipient and promising); Angola (close relations since Angola's independence in 1975); and Mozambique (modest but developing economic and military relations).

4511 Roelofse-Campbell, Zélia. A special relationship: Angola and Brazil; an interview with Albina de Assis Africano. (*UNISA Lat. Am. Rep.*, 11:2, July/Dec. 1995, p. 54–56, maps, photo)

Brief, unrevealing 1995 interview with Angola's Minister of Petroleum.

Salum-Flecha, Antonio. Itaipú: la soberanía sobre el antiguo Salto del Guaíra. See item **4417.**

4512 Santos, Luís Cláudio Vilafañe Gomes. A missão especial nas repúblicas do Pacífico e Venezuela. (*Textos Hist./Brasília,* 2:3, 1994, p. 123–147)

Breaks with conventional wisdom and argues that Brazil's foreign policy from independence to 1850 was inconsistent, reflecting domestic political weaknesses and domestic economic uncertainty. Brazil's foreign policy gained an enduring coherence only after 1851, when a "special mission" was sent to negotiate borders with Chile, Bolivia, Peru, Ecuador, Colombia, and Venezuela. Fascinating study.

4513 Saraiva, José Flávio Sombra. O Brasil e a ordem internacional. (*Humanidades/ Brasília*, 9:2, 1993, p. 137–141, bibl.)

Brief, incomplete assessment of Brazil's role in the New World (dis)Order.

4514 Seitenfus, Ricardo Antônio Silva. Para uma nova política externa brasileira. Porto Alegre, Brazil: Livraria do Advogado Editora, 1994. 247 p.: bibl.

Broad critique of Brazil's foreign policy. The author's "new agenda" stresses importance of regional cooperation and views Mercosur as a model for such cooperation. This perspective reflects author's involvement in 1987 creation of the Secretaria de Assuntos Internacionais do Estado do Rio Grande do Sul, the first body of its kind in Brazil.

4515 Silva, Alexandra de Mello e. O Brasil no continente e no mundo: atores e imagens na política externa brasileira contemporânea. (*Estud. Hist./Rio de Janeiro,* 15, jan./junho 1995, p. 95–118, bibl.)

Outstanding analysis of belief systems and perceptions of Brazil's foreign policymakers, from the Barão do Rio Branco (1850s) to San Thiago Dantas and Araújo Castro (1960s). Theoretically rich, article promises more than it delivers. Nonetheless, raises questions that deserve further attention.

4516 Silva, Alexandra de Mello e. A política externa de JK: Operação Pan-Americana. Rio de Janeiro: Fundação Getúlio Vargas, Centro de Pesquisa e Documentação de História Contemporânea do Brasil, 1992. 60 p.: bibl. (Texto CPDOC)

Argues succinctly that Operação Pan-Americana (1956–61) launched by Kubitschek affected Brazil's foreign policy for decades with its themes of multilateralism, development, and autonomy. Written initially as a master's thesis under the supervision of Gerson Moura.

4517 Silva, Celso de Souza e. A posição relativa do Brasil no quadro estratégico mundial. (*Rev. Bras. Polít. Int.*, 34:133/134, 1991, p. 5–14)

Brazilian diplomat considers Brazil's changing position within the international system, arguing that to improve its position, Brazil "must put its house in order."

4518 Silveira, Helder Gordim da. Brasil e Argentina: a guerra sul-americana nas projeções da razão estratégica, 1933–35. (*Biblos/Rio de Janeiro*, 8, 1996, p. 179–192)

An historian argues that during mid-1930s Argentina was most concerned with potential threats from Chile and Brazil. For Brazil, the greatest fear was that of an anti-Brazilian alliance among Argentina, Paraguay, and Uruguay (the colonial Viceroyalty of La Plata).

Solveira, Beatriz Rosario. El nudo ferroviario de Santa Cruz de la Sierra y la rivalidad argentino-brasileña. See item **4380.**

4519 Sousa, Jorge Luiz Prata de. Una dialéctica de exclusión mutua: Brazil y América Latina. (*in* Colección nuestra patria es América: integración y política exterior. Quito: Editora Nacional, 1992, v. 6, p. 251–258)

Argues that "masses" should be included in plans for Latin American integration. Naive and poorly argued.

4520 Streeter, Stephen M. Campaigning against Latin American nationalism: U.S. Ambassador John Moors Cabot in Brazil, 1959–1961. (*Americas/Francisc.*, 51:2, Oct. 1994, p. 193–218)

Examines recall of US Ambassador to Brazil John Moors Cabot. Concludes that individuals have limited ability to determine US foreign policy.

4521 Tachinardi, Maria Helena. A guerra das patentes: o conflito Brasil x EUA sobre propriedade intelectual. Prefácio de Fernando Henrique Cardoso. São Paulo: Paz e Terra, 1993. 266 p.: bibl., ill.

The author, a foreign affairs correspondent for *Gazeta Mercantil*, is one of Brazil's leading experts on foreign policy issues. Based on her master's thesis at Univ. of Brasília, work is a penetrating account of the tensions in Brazil/US relations regarding intellectual property issues in the pharmaceutical industry.

4522 Temas de política externa brasileira. v. 2, pts. 1–2. Organização de Gelson Fonseca Júnior e Sergio Henrique Nabuco de Castro. Brasília: Paz e Terra; IPRI, 1994. 1 v. in 2 pts. (Col. Relações internacionais)

Important work by leading Brazilian diplomats and professors. Pt. 1 analyzes Brazil's global standing from a multilateral perspective. Pt. 2 focuses on Brazil's bilateral relationships. Especially provocative is second chapter of the prologue which discusses Brazil's *sentimento de exclusão*. Essential reading for anyone interested in Brazil's for-

eign relations in the 1990s. For annotation of vol. 1, see *HLAS 55:4387.*

4523 Thorstensen, Vera; Yoshiaki Nakano; and Ernesto Lozardo. São Paulo e Brasil frente a um mundo dividido em blocos: o estado em busca de uma política de comércio externo. (*Polít. Extern./São Paulo*, 3:1, junho/agôsto 1994, p. 48–83, bibl., tables)

Examines role played by São Paulo state in Brazil's commercial relations. Contains abundant trade data.

4524 United Nations Conference on Environment and Development, *Rio de Janeiro, 1992*. Relatório da delegação brasileira. Apresentação de Celso Lafer. Brasília: Fundação Alexandre de Gusmão, Instituto de Pesquisa de Relações Internacionais, 1993. 144 p.: appendices. (Col. Relações internacionais; 16)

Report prepared by the Divisão do Meio Ambiente of Brazil's Ministério das Relações Exteriores analyzes the ECO 92 (Rio) conference in an historical context. Includes preface by Celso Lafer and various appendices related to Brazil's involvement in the conference.

4525 Vaz, Alcides Costa. Condicionantes das posições brasileiras frente ao desarmamento, regimes de controle de exportações e segurança regional. (*Premissas/São Paulo*, 4, agôsto 1993, p. 3–18)

Excellent overview and explanation of Brazil's changing positions, in 1993, on issues relating to disarmament, export controls, and regional security.

4526 Vidigal, Armando Amorim Ferreira. Uma estratégia marítima para o Brasil. (*Rev. Marít. Bras.*, 116:1/3, jan/março 1996, p. 55–90, appendix, graph, photos, tables)

Informative and critical examination of Brazil's maritime strategy gives special consideration to merchant marine.

4527 Vieira, Gleuber. Perspectivas para um futuro sistema de segurança hemisférica. (*Def. Nac.*, 765, julho/set. 1994, p. 4–13)

Calls for greater sub-regional security associations in South America, with Brazilian participation. South America's "geostrategic marginality" gives the region "space and opportunities to elaborate this thinking of sub-regional integration."

4528 **Vinhosa, Francisco Luiz Teixeira.** O Brasil e a Primeira Guerra Mundial: a diplomacia brasileira e as grandes potências. Rio de Janeiro: Instituto Histórico e Geográfico Brasileiro, 1990. 257 p.: bibl.

Well-researched historical account of Brazil's initial neutrality (1914–17) and subsequent participation (Oct. 1917–Nov. 1918) in World War I is followed by examination of Brazil's role in the peace conference.

4529 **Vizentini, Paulo Gilberto Fagundes.** Relações internacionais e desenvolvimento: o nacionalismo e a política externa independente, 1951–1964. Petrópolis, Brazil: Vozes, 1995. 325 p.: bibl., ill., maps.

Good chronological overview of Brazil's independent foreign policy from 1951–64.

4530 **Welch, Cliff.** Labor internationalism: U.S. involvement in Brazilian unions, 1945–1965. (*LARR*, 30:2, 1995, p. 61–89, bibl.)

Excellent review of relationship among Brazilian unions, the Brazilian State, and the US over two decades. Concludes that "Brazilian institutions demonstrated considerable autonomy vis-à-vis US efforts."

Wrobel, Paulo S. Aspectos da política externa independente: a questão do desarmamento e o caso de Cuba. See item **4309.**

4531 **Wrobel, Paulo S.** A diplomacia nuclear brasileira: a não-proliferação nuclear e o Tratado de Tlatelolco. (*Cont. Int.*, 15:1, jan./junho 1993, p. 27–55)

Excellent account of Brazil's position regarding the Treaty of Tlatelolco (1967) is written by a leading expert on Brazil's nuclear programs. Work is a revised chapter of author's Ph.D. dissertation.

4532 **Xavier, Renato.** O gerenciamento costeiro no Brasil e a cooperação internacional. Brasília: IPRI, 1994? 157 p.: bibl. (Col. Relações internacionais; 25)

Perceptive examination of Brazil's coastal zones monitoring system concludes that the country lacks effective control of these areas.

4533 **Zirker, Daniel.** Brazilian foreign policy and subimperialism during the political transition of the 1980s: a review and reapplication of Marini's theory. (*Lat. Am. Perspect.*, 21:1, Winter 1994, p. 115–131)

Thoughtful and sympathetic application of Brazilian sociologist Ruy Mauro Marini's Marxist subimperialist theory to Brazil.

JOURNAL ABBREVIATIONS

Acad. Quest.   Academic Questions. Transaction Periodicals Consortium, Rutgers Univ., New Brunswick, N.J.

Allpanchis/Cusco.   Allpanchis. Instituto de Pastoral Andina. Cusco, Peru.

Am. Merid.   América Meridional. Sociedad Regional de Ciencias Humanas. Montevideo.

Americas/Francisc.   The Americas. Academy of American Franciscan History. Washington.

Anál. Int.   Análisis Internacional. Centro Peruano de Estudios Internacionales. Lima.

Anu. Cent. Estud. Av.   Anuario Centro de Estudios Avanzados. Centro de Estudios Avanzados. Córdoba, Argentina.

Anu. Estud. Centroam.   Anuario de Estudios Centroamericanos. Univ. de Costa Rica. San José.

Biblos/Rio de Janeiro.   Biblos: Revista do Departamento de Biblioteconomia e História. Editora da Fundação Univ. do Rio Grande. Rio Grande, Brazil.

Bol. Soc. Bras. Direito Int.   Boletim da Sociedade Brasileira de Direito Internacional. Univ. de Brasília, Depto. de Ciência Política e Relações Internacionais. Brasília.

Cah. Am. lat.   Cahiers des Amériques latines. Paris.

Caribb. Q.   Caribbean Quarterly. Univ. of the West Indies. Mona, Jamaica.

Caribb. Stud.   Caribbean Studies. Univ. of Puerto Rico, Institute of Caribbean Studies. Río Piedras.

Casa Am.   Casa de las Américas. La Habana.

Ciênc. Tróp.   Ciência & Trópico. Fundação Joaquim Nabuco; Editora Massangana. Recife, Brazil.

Clío/Sinaloa.   Clío. Univ. Autónoma de Sinaloa, Escuela de Historia. Culiacán, Mexico.

Comp. Polit. Stud.   Comparative Political Studies. Sage Publications, Thousand Oaks, Calif.

Cont. Int. Contexto Internacional. Instituto de Relações Internacionais, Pontifícia Univ. Católica. Rio de Janeiro.

Contribuciones/Buenos Aires. Contribuciones. Estudios Interdisciplinarios sobre Desarrollo y Cooperación Internacional. Konrad-Adenauer-Stiftung; Centro Interdisciplinario de Estudios Sobre el Desarrollo Latinoamericano (CIEDLA). Buenos Aires.

Cuad. Nuestra Am. Cuadernos de Nuestra América. Centro de Estudios sobre América. La Habana.

Curr. Hist. Current History. Philadelphia, Penn.

Def. Nac. A Defesa Nacional: Revista de Assuntos Militares e Estudo de Problemas Brasileiros. Rio de Janeiro.

Desarro. Econ. Desarrollo Económico. Instituto de Desarrollo Económico y Social. Buenos Aires.

ECA/San Salvador. Estudios Centro-Americanos: ECA. Univ. Centroamericana José Simeón Cañas. San Salvador.

Econ. Cienc. Soc. Economía y Ciencias Sociales. Facultad de Ciencias Económicas y Sociales, Univ. Central de Venezuela. Caracas.

Estud. Front. Estudios Fronterizos. Instituto de Investigaciones Sociales, Univ. Autónoma de Baja California. Mexicali, Mexico.

Estud. Hist./Rio de Janeiro. Estudos Históricos. Centro de Pesquisa e Documentação de História Contemporânea do Brasil da Fundacão Gertulio Vargas. Rio de Janeiro.

Estud. Int./IRIPAZ. Estudios Internacionales: Revista del IRIPAZ. Instituto de Relaciones Internacionales y de Investigaciones para la Paz. Guatemala.

Estud. Int./Santiago. Estudios Internacionales. Instituto de Estudios Internacionales, Univ. de Chile. Santiago.

Estud. Latinoam./México. Estudios Latinoamericanos. Centro de Estudios Latinoamericanos (CELA), UNAM. México.

Estud. Polít./México. Estudios Políticos. Facultad de Ciencias Políticas y Sociales, UNAM. México.

Estud. Soc./Santo Domingo. Estudios Sociales. Centro de Estudios Sociales Juan Montalvo, SJ. Santo Domingo.

Foreign Aff. Foreign Affairs. Council on Foreign Relations, Inc. New York.

Foreign Policy. Foreign Policy. National Affairs Inc.; Carnegie Endowment for International Peace. New York.

Foro Int. Foro Internacional. El Colegio de México. México.

Front. Norte. Frontera Norte. Colegio de la Frontera Norte. Tijuana, Mexico.

Geosur/Montevideo. Geosur. Asociación Latinoamericana de Estudios Geopolíticos e Internacionales. Montevideo.

Haïti Inf. Libre. Haïti Information Libre. Haïti solidarité internationale. Paris.

Hastings Int. Comp. Law Rev. Hastings International and Comparative Law Review. Univ. of California, Hastings College of the Law. San Francisco, Calif.

Hum. Organ. Human Organization. Society for Applied Anthropology. New York.

Humanidades/Brasília. Humanidades. Editora Univ. de Brasília.

Iberoam./Tokyo. Iberoamericana. Univ. of Sofia. Tokyo.

Int. Aff./Moscow. International Affairs. Moscow.

Int. Hist. Rev. The International History Review. Univ. of Toronto Press. Downsview, Ontario, Canada.

Int. J./Toronto. International Journal. Canadian Institute of International Affairs. Toronto, Canada.

Int. Migr. International Migration = Migrations Internationales = Migraciones Internacionales. Intergovernmental Committee for European Migration; Research Group for European Migration Problems; International Organization for Migration. The Hague, Netherlands; Geneva, Switzerland.

Int. Migr. Rev. International Migration Review. Center for Migration Studies. New York.

J. Caribb. Stud. Journal of Caribbean Studies. Assn. of Caribbean Studies. Coral Gables, Fla.

J. Dev. Areas. The Journal of Developing Areas. Western Illinois Univ. Press. Macomb, Ill.

J. Haitian Stud. Journal of Haitian Studies. Haitian Studies Assn. Boston, Mass.

J. Interam. Stud. World Aff. Journal of Interamerican Studies and World Affairs. Institute of Interamerican Studies, Univ. of Miami. Coral Gables, Fla.

J. Lat. Am. Stud. Journal of Latin American Studies. Centers or Institutes of Latin American Studies at the Universities of Cambridge, Glasgow, Liverpool, London, and Oxford. Cambridge Univ. Press. London.

J. Peace Res. Journal of Peace Research. International Peace Research Institute, Universitetforlaget. Oslo.

Jahrb. Gesch. Jahrbuch für Geschichte von Staat, Wirtschaft und Gesellschaft Lateinamerikas. Köln, Germany.

LARR. Latin American Research Review. Latin American Research Review Board. Univ. of New Mexico, Albuquerque, N.M.

Lat. Am. Perspect. Latin American Perspectives. Univ. of California. Newbury Park, Calif.

Lat. Am. Stud./Beijing. Latin American Studies. Institute of Latin American Studies. Beijing.

Mundo Nuevo/Caracas. Mundo Nuevo. Univ. Simón Bolívar, Instituto de Altos Estudios de América Latina. Caracas.

Natl. Int. The National Interest. National Affairs. Washington.

Nav. War Coll. Rev. Naval War College Review. Newport, R.I.

Panorama Centroam. Pensam. Panorama Centroamericano: Pensamiento y Acción. Instituto Centroamericano de Estudios Políticos (INCEP). Guatemala.

Panorama Centroam. Temas. Panorama Centroamericano: Temas y Documentos de Debate. Instituto Centroamericano de Estudios Políticos (INCEP). Guatemala.

Perf. Latinoam. Perfiles Latinoamericanos. Facultad Latinoamericana de Ciencias Sociales. México.

Polít. Estrateg. Política y Estrategia. Academia Nacional de Estudios Políticos y Estratégicos. Santiago.

Polít. Extern./São Paulo. Política Externa. Paz e Terra. São Paulo.

Polít. Gob. Política y Gobierno. Centro de Investigación y Docencia Económicas. México.

Polit. Sci. Q. Political Science Quarterly. Columbia Univ., The Academy of Political Science. New York.

Política/Santiago. Política. Instituto de Ciencia Política, Univ. de Chile. Santiago.

Premissas/São Paulo. Premissas. Univ. Estadual de Campinas, Núcleo de Estudos Estratégicos. São Paulo.

Prop. Democrát. Propuestas Democráticas. Univ. Nacional de Asunción; Fundación Hanns Seidel. Asunción.

Quehacer/Lima. Quehacer. Centro de Estudios y Promoción del Desarrollo (DESCO). Lima.

Relac. Int./Heredia. Relaciones Internacionales. Escuela de Relaciones Internacionales, Univ. Nacional. Heredia, Costa Rica.

Relac. Int./México. Relaciones Internacionales. Centro de Relaciones Internacionales. Facultad de Ciencias Políticas y Sociales, Univ. Nacional Autónoma de México. México.

Rencontre/Haiti. Rencontre. CRESFED. Canapé Vert, Haiti.

Rev. Bras. Polít. Int. Revista Brasileira de Política Internacional. Instituto Brasileiro de Relações Internacionais. Rio de Janeiro.

Rev. Chil. Geopolít. Revista Chilena de Geopolítica. Instituto Geopolítico de Chile. Santiago.

Rev. Chil. Humanid. Revista Chilena de Humanidades. Facultad de Filosofía, Humanidades y Educación, Univ. de Chile. Santiago.

Rev. Ciclos. Revista Ciclos en la Historia, Economía y la Sociedad. Fundación de Investigaciones Históricas, Económicas y Sociales, Facultad de Ciencias Económicas, Univ. de Buenos Aires. Buenos Aires.

Rev. Cienc. Polít./Santiago. Revista de Ciencia Política. Instituto de Ciencia Política, Pontificia Univ. Católica de Chile. Santiago.

Rev. Esc. Super. Guerr. Revista da Escola Superior de Guerra. Escola Superior de Guerra, Divisão de Documentação. Rio de Janeiro.

Rev. Estud. Euro. Revista de Estudios Europeos. Centro de Estudios sobre Europa Occidental. La Habana.

Rev. Eur. Revista Europea de Estudios Latinoamericanos y del Caribe = European Review of Latin American and Caribbean Studies. Center for Latin American Research and Documentation; Royal Institute of Linguistics and Anthropology. Amsterdam.

Rev. INCAE. Revista INCAE. Instituto Centroamericano de Administración de Empresas. Alajuela, Costa Rica.

Rev. Marít. Bras. Revista Marítima Brasileira. Serviço de Documentação da Marinha, Ministério da Marinha. Rio de Janeiro.

Rev. Mex. Cienc. Polít. Soc. Revista Mexicana de Ciencias Políticas y Sociales. Facultad de Ciencias Políticas y Sociales, Univ. Nacional Autónoma de México. México.

Rev. Mex. Polít. Exter. Revista Mexicana de Política Exterior. Secretaría de Relaciones Exteriores; Instituto Matías Romero de Estudios Diplomáticos (IMPED). México.

Rev. Mil. Revista Militar. Círculo Militar, Buenos Aires.

Rev. Nicar. Revista Nicaragüense. Managua.

Rev. Rev. Interam. Revista/Review Interamericana. Inter-American Univ. Press. Hato Rey, Puerto Rico.

Rev. USP. Revista USP. Coordenadoria de Comunicação Social (CCS), Univ. de São Paulo.

Santiago/Cuba. Santiago. Univ. de Oriente. Santiago, Cuba.

SECOLAS Ann. SECOLAS Annals. Southeastern Conference on Latin American Studies; Thomasson Printing Co. Carrollton, Ga.

SER/Buenos Aires. Seguridad, Estrategia Regional en el 2000. Impresión Zona Gráfica. Buenos Aires.

Soc. Econ. Stud. Social and Economic Studies. Univ. of the West Indies, Institute of Social and Economic Research. Mona, Jamaica.

South East. Lat. Am. South Eastern Latin Americanist. South Eastern Council of Latin American Studies. Boone, N.C.

Stud. Dipl. Studia Diplomatica. Institut Royal des Relations Internationales. Bruxelles.

Tareas/Panamá. Tareas. Centro de Estudios Latinoamericanos (CELA). Panamá.

Textos Hist./Brasília. Textos de História. Pós-Graduação em História, Univ. de Brasília.

UNISA Lat. Am. Rep. UNISA Latin American Report. Univ. of South Africa. Pretoria.

Wash. Q. The Washington Quarterly. Georgetown Univ., The Center for Strategic and International Studies. Washington.

World Policy J. World Policy Journal. World Policy Institute. New York.

SOCIOLOGY

GENERAL

4534 América Latina: planteos, problemas, preguntas. Recopilación de Patricia Funes. Buenos Aires: M. Suárez, 1992. 161 p.: bibl.

Series of articles, based on a collective research project, offers some interesting insights giving greater precision to the notion of oligarchic States (referring to the regimes that prevailed in Latin America primarily between 1880s–1930s). Includes conceptual and comparative chapters and case studies of Chile, Ecuador, Peru, and Argentina. [R. Korzeniewicz]

4535 Berg, Hans van den. Bibliografía Aymara v. 1–3. Cochabamba: Univ. Católica Boliviana, 1994. 3 v.: ill., indexes.

Comprehensive social science bibliography of the Aymara peoples in Bolivia, Chile, and Peru. Updates author's earlier works as well as works by other authors such as Xavier Albó. [K. Healy]

Bronstein, Arturo S. Societal change and industrial relations in Latin America: trends and prospects. See item **2931.**

4536 Brunner, José Joaquín. América Latina, cultura y modernidad. México: Conscjo Nacional para la Cultura y las Artes; Grijalbo, 1992. 403 p.: bibl. (Claves de América Latina)

Stimulating, somewhat dated series of essays by a preeminent sociologist "thinking" about postmodernism in Latin America. [R. Korzeniewicz]

4537 Calvo Buezas, Tomás. Valores en los jóvenes españoles, portugueses y latino-americanos: problemas y esperanzas de los protagonistas del siglo XXI. Madrid: Libertarias/Prodhufi, 1997. 648 p.: bibl. (Ensayo; 110)

Massive and thorough inquiry conducted by Spanish social anthropologist into values, attitudes, beliefs, and ideals of youth in Iberia and Latin America (21 countries, including Puerto Rico and excepting Cuba). A total of 43,816 youngsters were polled (36,516 Latin Americans, 4,168 Spaniards, and 2,132 Portuguese). Reaches optimistic conclusion that most youth today are overall egalitarian, responsible, democratic, tolerant, and non-violent. [D. Martin]

4538 Carovano, Kathryn. A summary of substance-abuse patterns among women in Latin America and the Caribbean. (*in* Drug lessons & education programs in developing countries. New Brunswick, N.J.: Transaction Publishers, 1995, p. 141–151, bibl., table)

Contains data about different drugs and substances used by women in these regions. [B. Aguirre-López]

4539 Castro de la Mata, Ramiro and **Nils D. Noya T.** Coca: erythroxylum coca; erythroxylum novogranatense; bibliografía comentada. La Paz: Seamos, 1995. 306 p. (Drogas: investigación para el debate; 11)

Annotated bibliography on the coca plant covers historical literature from colonial period through the present. [K. Healy]

4540 Constructing collective identities and shaping public spheres: Latin American paths. Edited by Luis Roniger and Mario Sznajder. Brighton, England: Sussex Academic Press, 1998. 280 p.: bibl.

Collection of interdisciplinary essays on how collective identities have transformed the public sphere in Latin America since colonial times. Historians, anthropologists, sociologists, political scientists, and others shed light on colonial Cuzco, the regimes of Vargas and Perón, and issues in Argentina, Chile, Paraguay, Uruguay, and Latin America as a whole. [D. Martin]

4541 Encuentro Latinoamericano sobre la Biblioteca, la Lectura y el Niño Callejero, *1st, México, 1996.* Memoria. Recopilación de María Trinidad Román Haza. México: Univ. Nacional Autónoma de México, 1998. 234 p.: bibl. (Serie Memorias; 13)

Compilation of papers delivered at 1996 meeting on the impact of reading and access to public libraries on Latin American street children. Authors are sociologists, social workers, and educators. Countries are covered separately, as follows: Mexico (16 studies), Venezuela (3 studies), Bolivia (2 studies), and one study each for Honduras, Nicaragua, Guatemala, Dominican Republic, Colombia, Ecuador, Chile, Argentina, and Brazil. [D. Martin]

4542 Estrategias de desarrollo: intentando cambiar la vida. Recopilación y edición de Patricia Portocarrero Suárez. Lima: Flora Tristán Ediciones, 1993. 346 p.: bibl.

Excellent collection written by anthropologists, psychologists, sociologists, economists, historians, and lawyers includes studies on changing gender relations and identity; social, political, economic, and personal development; urban and rural work and production; and impacts of violence and civil war on women, gender relations, and development. Vargas' article provides historical context for the collection by looking at women's movements and the different forms of feminism in Latin America. Rivera, using oral tales and urban myths, reveals norms of feminine behavior and the consequences of ignoring those norms. Chávez looks at the growing proportion of women in the informal sector of the labor market. Concludes that despite growing recognition of gender equality, current conditions of poverty, economic crisis and restructuring, and political and street violence have a greater impact on women in their struggles to support themselves and their families. [S. Lastarria-Cornhiel]

4543 Fauquié Bescós, Rafael. La voz en el espejo. Caracas: Instituto de Altos Estudios de América Latina; Alfadil Ediciones, 1993. 110 p. (Col. Trópicos; 47)

Uses Carlos Fuentes' and Octavio Paz's essays as inspiration for reflecting on Latin American identity. Cites as a central idea Fuentes' proposal that Latin America was born from heresy, as well as Paz's concept of identity as mask. Shows interest in determining why authors write, and returns to this subject with regularity. For the author, literature is of interest primarily for its ideas. [R.L. Williams]

4544 Forment, Carlos A. Socio-historical models of Spanish-America democratization: a review and reformation. (*Estud. Latinoam./Poland*, 14:pt. 1, 1992, p. 113–239, bibl.)

Begins with analysis of more traditional/corporatist model of Spanish-America democratization offered by O'Donnell and Schmitter (see *HLAS 49:6025*). Then advances post-structuralist perspective on democracy. [B. Aguirre-López]

4545 Forum Internacional por la Revalorización de la Hoja de Coca, 2nd, Cusco, Peru, 1993. Compromiso nacional. Lima: ENACO; Univ. Nacional de San Antonio Abad, 1994. 140 p.: bibl.

Interesting collection by a diverse group of authors including medical doctors, anthropologists, chemists, lawyers, and nutritionists attempts to restore the positive social, medicinal, and nutritional characteristics of the coca leaf, the raw material for production of cocaine. Also suggests alternative industrial uses of coca. [S. Lastarria-Cornhiel]

4546 Fundación José Félix Ribas (Venezuela). Investigaciones en drogas: Perú, México, Ecuador, Colombia y Chile. Caracas: Fundación José Félix Ribas, CEDIF, 1996. 89 p.: bibl., graphs, tables. (Serie Investigaciones en drogas; 2)

Consists of five documented studies of drug use in Peru, Mexico, Ecuador, Colombia, and Chile. Compiled by recognized research specialists for Venezuelan think tank. Includes numerous tables, graphs, statistics, and bibliographies. [D. Martin]

4547 Instituto Latinoamericano de Servicios Legales Alternativos (Bogotá). Nuevos espacios para la lucha por los derechos humanos en América Latina. Bogotá: Instituto Latinoamericano de Servicios Legales Alternativos, 1995. 289 p. (Documentos; 12)

Compilation of papers from four conferences sponsored by Instituto Latinoamericano de Servicios Legales Alternativos represents viewpoints from across Latin America. Topics include economic and social rights in Mexico in light of NAFTA, rights in Southern Cone in relation to neoliberalism and democratic transition, indigenous rights, and evaluation of national protection of human rights in Colombia. [A. Ugalde]

4548 Instituto Latinoamericano de Servicios Legales Alternativos (Bogotá). El trabajo femenino en América Latina: los debates en la década de los noventa. Recopilación de Beatriz Bustos y Germán Palacio. Guadalajara, Mexico: Univ. de Guadalajara; Bogotá: Instituto Latinoamericano de Servicios Legales Alternativos, 1994. 311 p.: bibl., ill.

Collection of 12 papers from a seminar cosponsored by Univ. de Guadalajara and Instituto Latinoaméricano de Servicios Legales Alternativos in Bogotá. Works focus on general debates about women's work in Latin America, impacts of economic restructuring and industrialization, and issues surrounding the relationship of family to women's work. [A. Ugalde]

4549 Iwanowski, Zbigniew W. Latin American intelligentsia: changes in the structure, status and character. (*Estud. Latinoam./ Poland*, 14:pt. 1, 1992, p. 343–349)

Examines changing structure, status, and character of the Latin American intelligentsia. Mentions growing number of well-educated specialists, the decrease in their social status, and the effects of unemployment, increased inflation, wage freezes, and cuts in social expenditures. [B. Aguirre-López]

4550 Lancaster, Roger N. Sexual positions: caveats and second thoughts on "categories." (*Americas/Francisc.*, 54:1, July 1997, p. 1–16)

Discusses complexities of attempting sociological analyses of homosexuality. Offers accessible theoretical approaches to the topic, as well as examples from research on (homo)sexualities in the region (and beyond). Warns audience away from three different and misleading Scylla/Charybdis forms of error, and provides some positive guidelines for future work. More likely to be rewarding to those acquainted with the literature on sexuality. [T. Wickham-Crowley]

Lavrin, Asunción. Unfolding feminism: Spanish-American women's writing, 1970–1990. See *HLAS 56:1068*.

Moncayo Gallegos, Paco. Fuerzas armadas y sociedad. See item **5031**.

O'Brien, Thomas F. The revolutionary mission: American enterprise in Latin America, 1900–1945. See item **4038**.

4551 Pérez Herrero, Pedro and **María Jesús García-Arevalo.** La imagen de América Latina entre la población estudiantil española, 13–18 años. Madrid: Organización de Estados Iberoamericanos para la Educación, la Ciencia y la Cultura, 1994. 106 p.

Results of opinion poll conducted among 1,488 high school students in Spain (ages 13–18) concerning their views of Latin America and Latin Americans. Reveals interesting contrasts as to perceptions among females vis-à-vis males; urban vis-à-vis rural students; and private vis-à-vis public schools. [D. Martin]

Robben, Antonius C.G.M. Ethnographic seduction, transference, and resistance in dialogues about terror and violence in Argentina. See item **5143**.

4552 Situación de las mujeres y el VIH/ SIDA en América Latina: una agenda de investigación-acción. Recopilación de Blanca Rico G. *et al.* 1. ed. Cuernavaca, Mexico: Instituto Nacional de Salud Pública, 1997. 188 p. bibl.

Compilation of informative and documented articles on rate and nature of AIDS-HIV infection among women in Latin America. Authors are physicians, health, and socio-medical professionals. In addition to covering Latin American women as a whole, book devotes individual chapters to: Mexico, Guatemala, Costa Rica, Honduras, Nicaragua, Peru, Argentina, Chile, Uruguay, Brazil, and Hispanic females in the US. [D. Martin]

4553 Small, Stephen. Racial group boundaries and identities: people of 'mixed-race' in slavery across the Americas. (*Slavery Abolit.*, 15:3, Dec. 1994, p. 17–37)

Reviews creation of racial group boundaries and identities for people of mixed race. Compares British Caribbean and North American slavery systems. [B. Aguirre-López]

4554 Stolcke, Verena. The labors of coffee in Latin America: the hidden charm of family labor and self-provisioning. (*in* Coffee, society, and power in Latin America. Edited by William Roseberry, Lowell Gudmundson, and Mario Samper K. Baltimore: Johns Hopkins Univ. Press, 1995, p. 65–93)

Analyzes an often neglected dimension of labor systems in coffee cultivation: the role of the family as an ideal and as an actual set of relationships of social reproduction. Challenges "family-blind" and "gender-blind" studies which take the individual worker as their unit of analysis. Study's purpose is to draw attention to the relevance of family and gender relations (for their cultural-moral as well as socioeconomic dimensions) in analyses of socioeconomic process and change. [P. Lovell]

4555 El Sur también existe. Compilación y selección de Carlos Etchegoyhen. Montevideo: Edición Kairós; SCEA, 1991. 119 p.: bibl.

Selected essays and synthesis of monographs presented at a seminar on mental health and political repression in Argentina, Chile, and Uruguay. [R. Korzeniewicz]

Villamán P., Marcos. Religión y pobreza: una aproximación a los nuevos movimientos religiosos. See item **4941.**

MEXICO

ANTONIO UGALDE, *Professor of Sociology, University of Texas, Austin*
PATRICIA L. RICHARDS, *Department of Sociology, University of Texas, Austin*

DUE TO SPACE LIMITATIONS, the materials included in this section represent only a small fraction of the works examined this biennium. Almost all of the several hundred articles received for potential inclusion in *HLAS* 57 have been omitted, as have approximately half of the books. The selection of books over articles has some implications because the number of monographs and edited volumes published about Mexico by non-Mexican authors is negligible. The result is that our summary of the literature represents primarily the work of Mexican sociologists and it has been shown that the findings of Mexicans and foreign scholars do not always coincide (see items reviewed in *HLAS* 55, for example). On the other hand, the high quantity of volumes published in Mexico, particularly during times of extreme economic crisis, is indicative of the solid foundation of sociology in the country.

The lag between research and writing, publication, distribution, and library cataloging is long, as much as ten years in some cases. The delay varies according to the personal circumstances of researchers and the types of publications. For this reason, our biennial review covers many years. In the present volume we are abstracting publications from about 1990 to 1996 that include research carried out between the mid 1980s to about 1993. During these years Mexico experienced the most severe economic crisis in contemporary history and only timid programs to alleviate its devastating consequences for the poor and indigent; transcendental constitutional changes affecting land tenure and Church-State relations; reversals of longstanding economic policies, for example, the adherence of Mexico to GATT, the signing of North American Free Trade Agreement and its dramatic impact on Mexican business, and the privatization of hundreds of decentralized industries; and the significant erosion of the PRI's political power. The literature reviewed analyzes many of the sociopolitical consequences of these changes. Research on more recent events such as the emergence of guerrilla groups, including the much publicized movement in Chiapas, the growth of high-level corruption related to drug traffic, and increasing street violence has not yet reached library shelves.

Most authors decry the negative impact of neoliberal economic policies enacted to resolve the economic crisis, and the evidence presented to confirm their argumentation is overwhelming. By and large, scholars give a low grade to the National Solidarity Plan (Planasol), the program created to assist the poor during the economic crisis. The few whose findings support the government's contention that the program benefitted the poor found that among the poor, those better off were, in fact, its primary beneficiaries. Students who examine the agrarian question and rural conditions condemned the termination of land distribution and the end of the ejido system. In studies of the PRI, political sociologists continue to document corruption, bossism, political patronage, heavy-handed tactics and use of violence, together with a more recent loss of support among the urban poor, and even among labor, a traditional PRI stalwart.

Very few researchers provide a view of Mexico's future. Those who suggest that changes are inevitable do not indulge in political forecasting and suggest only that political modernization implies clean electoral processes and a genuine multi-party system. Social scientists who have examined electoral outcomes and other political events do not provide clear signs of the direction that the Mexican political system may take in the future. This ambivalence seems to suggest that anything is possible: genuine democratization through the modernization of the political system; severe political instability and chaos; political violence; or even revolution.

Sociologists interpret NAFTA as part of the trend towards a global economy under US hegemony. Theoretical studies and fieldwork assessments agree that the new export-oriented Mexican economy has caused additional poverty and suffering among the lower income groups. The work of rural sociologists confirms that rural "modernization" has produced impoverishment and ecological degradation.

Gender studies is a rapidly expanding field among Mexican sociologists. A sizeable number of volumes reviewed for this section concern women, dealing with topics as varied as health, work, poverty, identity, sexuality, and politics. Massolo's investigation of women and urban movements in Mexico during the 1970s is outstanding (item **4617**), and the Colegio de México's Interdisciplinary Program on Women Studies has contributed a wide range of noteworthy collections. We also noted an increased number of contributions in the field of sociology of health and illness. Some studies lack methodological sophistication, but there are solid contributions, for example, Mercado's study on diabetic patients (item **4620**).

Almost one third of the items reviewed dealt with social movements, an area that continues to be of great interest. As Mexico's urban population increases, we witness a growing interest in popular urban movements. Ramírez Sáiz's research on Guadalajara's urban movements is a monumental work (item **4656**). Housing and political behavior also attract the interest of urban sociologists. Researchers from both ends of the political spectrum consistently point out that social movements are currently the only available political alternative for the majority of Mexicans. Among studies of migration, there has been a shift from demographic issues to social problems and human rights of migrants. The lengthy volume edited by Sandoval Palacios is an excellent example of this new research direction (item **4663**).

In October of 1995, the historic center of Mexico City hosted the 20th Congress of the Latin American Association of Sociology. In spite of a change of venue with relatively short notice, it was well-organized and memorable. Mexican attendance was high in each of the seventeen different areas or specialties into which the program had been divided. The Congress thus allowed many Latin American sociologists to interact with prominent Mexican scholars and meet the very promising new generation of Mexican sociologists.

4556 Academia Mexicana de Derechos Humanos. La experiencia de refugio en Chiapas: nuevas relaciones en la frontera sur mexicana. México: Academia Mexicana de Derechos Humanos, 1993. 168 p.: bibl., ill.

Examines socioeconomic conditions of Guatemalan refugees in Chiapas and the impact of their arrival on local communities. Contends that common cultural background lessens conflict. Explores local/refugee relationships and border issues in terms of historical context of national formation of Mexico and Guatemala. Includes oral testimonies from individuals in six communities.

4557 La agricultura en tierras mexicanas desde sus orígenes hasta nuestros días. Coordinación de Teresa Rojas Rabiela. México: Consejo Nacional para la Cultura y las Artes; Grijalbo, 1991. 420 p.: bibl., ill., maps. (Los Noventa; 71)

Includes five articles on agricultural organization, land tenure, and cultivation methods since precolumbian period. Each contribution deals with a specific historical period: precolumbian, colonial, 19th century, the Porfiriato, and postrevolution. Descriptive, comprehensive, and useful overview.

4558 Aguilar, Adrián Guillermo; Boris Graizbord; and Alvaro Sánchez Crispín. Las ciudades intermedias y el desarrollo regional en México. México: Consejo Nacional para la Cultura y las Artes, Dirección General de Publicaciones; Univ. Nacional Autónoma de México, Instituto de Geografía; Colegio de México, Centro de Estudios Demográficos y de Desarrollo Urbano, 1996. 403 p.: appendices, bibl., maps, tables. (Regiones)

Evaluative study of policies adopted as a result of the 1984 Programa Nacional de Desarrollo y Vivienda, which established 59 medium-sized cities as investment priorities, focuses on regional and sectoral distribution of federal investment. Analysis is divided into four parts: urban structure and dynamics (1970–90); changes in urban-regional policy and public investment; strengthening of medium-sized cities (centering on agriculture, industry and tourism); and extension of social and physical infrastructure. Numerous tables cover general poverty indexes for medium-sized cities.

4559 Aguirre Benítez, Adán. Guerrero, economía campesina y capitalismo, 1960–1987. Chilpancingo, Mexico: Univ. Autónoma de Guerrero, Dirección de Investigación Científica, 1995. 262 p.: bibl., ill.

Insightful analysis of rural social classes and economic activities in the state of Guerrero discusses inter-class relations, the transformation suffered by peasantry, and peasants' increasing dependence on part-time wage labor. Final chapter presents rural and agricultural policies from Díaz Ordaz to Miguel de la Madrid, and consequences for Guerrero's rural dwellers.

4560 Alonso, Jorge. Por una alternativa a la inequidad: el Movimiento de Acción y Unidad Socialista. Guadalajara, Mexico: Centro Universitario de Ciencias Sociales y Humanidades, Univ. de Guadalajara, 1995. 402 p. (Col. Estado, cultura y sociedad)

Comprehensive volume examines history of Movimiento de Acción y Unidad Socialista (MAUS), its evolution as a social movement, role in political reform, and coalition with three other leftist groups during the 1970s. Applies MAUS experience to present-day leftist movement's search for future paths considering failure of communist and socialist regimes in Eastern Europe.

4561 Arance, Lidia Candi. México: factores psicosociales de la enfermedad de Chagas en Jalisco. (*Fermentum/Mérida*, 3/4:8/9, sept. 1993/abril 1994, p. 46–74, bibl.)

Chagas disease affects thousands of Mexicans, although public health authorities do not consider it a health problem. Examines population's awareness of the disease, causes, preventive measures, and therapy used. Discusses health education materials developed by the project. Methodology includes interviews with 62 mothers, attending physicians, and discussion groups.

4562 Arrieta Fernández, Pedro. La integración social de la Chontalpa: un análisis regional en el trópico mexicano. México: Univ. Iberoamericana; Gernika, 1994. 230 p.: bibl., ill. (Col. Estudios regionales; 2)

The region of Chontalpa in Tabasco was a pilot project in the comprehensive development of the Grijalva river basin. The project was completed in 1967 and this monograph is a 1976 impact evaluation. In spite of time elapsed, work is a useful case study of problems with planning from above, and a reminder of how little has been learned from past failures.

4563 Arroyo Alejandre, Jesús; Adrián De León Arias; and M. Basilia Valenzuela Varela. Migración rural hacia Estados Unidos: un estudio regional en Jalisco. México: Consejo Nacional para la Cultura y las Artes, 1991. 289 p.: bibl., ill.

Investigates relationship between regional development and migratory patterns, examining flow of population in regions with distinct forms and levels of socioeconomic development. Explores possibility of development policies that could increase retention of local population. Based mainly on interviews with 576 families in rural and semiurban areas with high levels of migration.

4564 Arroyo Mosqueda, Artemio. El mundo multiple: tradición y modernidad en la Huasteca Hidalguense. Pachuca, Mexico: Gobierno del Estado de Hidalgo, Instituto Hidalguense de Cultura, 1993. 69 p., 15 p. of plates: bibl., ill., maps (one folded). (Col. Lo nuestro)

Ethnological study of four rural communities examines geographical, historical, and contemporary factors influencing social structure and culture of the Nahua people. Questions possibility of maintaining ethnic identification in light of State development efforts. Emphasizes importance of festivals and language in culture retention.

4565 Astorga Almanza, Luis Alejandro. Mitología del "narcotraficante" en México. México: Univ. Nacional Autónoma de México; Plaza y Valdés Editores, 1995. 150 p.: bibl.

Provocative study uses interviews and historical materials to support contention that both legal codification and folk songs serve to mythologize drug trafficking. Suggests that legal/political sector contributes to the myth by addressing drug trafficking in terms of good and evil, while *corridos* of drug dealers propagate the myth among the people, serving as a collective catharsis.

4566 Azaola Garrido, Elena. Los niños de la correccional: fragmentos de vida. México: CIESAS, 1993. 61 p.: bibl.

Studies 100 8- to 14-year old boys at Mexico City's Escuela de Tratamiento para Menores Infractores. Examines institutional-

ization from perspective of inmates. Looks at material conditions and the role of sexuality. Based mainly on life histories acquired through group conversations, and on some individual and family interviews.

4567 Beraud Lozano, José Luis. Los movimientos sociales en la conformación territorial. Culiacán Rosales, Mexico: Univ. Autónoma de Sinaloa, 1995. 116 p.: bibl.

Reviews theses of social movement theorists and provides historical account of political mobilizations in Sinaloa. Access to land, decent prices for agricultural products, and better wages are common rural demands. Urban conflicts arise during land invasions, and demands include legalization of lots and access to affordable housing and basic services.

4568 Birn, Anne-Emanuelle. ¿El pasado como presagio? México, la salud pública y la Fundación Rockefeller. (*in* La medicina al final del milenio: realidades y proyectos en la sociedad occidental. Guadalajara, Mexico: Univ. de Guadalajara; Caracas: Asociación Latinoamericana de Medicina Social, 1995, p. 135–155)

Analyzes Foundation's role in fight against onchocerciasis, development of health services, and training of physicians. Suggests that in Mexico the Rockefeller Foundation favored biological over public health solutions, and encouraged importing technologies and models. Also maintains that these policies continue to influence health care service.

4569 Blancarte, Roberto. Recent changes in Church-State relations in Mexico: an historical approach. (*J. Church State,* 35:4, Autumn 1993, p. 781–805)

As part of his "modernization" attempt, President Salinas modified articles of the 1917 Constitution, limiting functions and status of churches. Explains forces behind changes and describes reaction of Catholic Church and suggests that reforms have eased relations between Church and the State without eliminating confrontations. For historian's comment see *HLAS 56:1418.*

4570 Boltvinik, Julio. Pobreza y estratificación social en México. Aguascalientes, Mexico: Instituto Nacional de Estadística, Geografía e Informática; México: Colegio de México; Instituto de Investigaciones Sociales de la Univ. Nacional Autónoma de México, 1994. 111 p.: bibl.

Quantitative study based on 1990 population census includes in-depth critique of advantages and limitations of methods and indicators used by researchers to measure poverty. Provides detailed explanation of procedures to construct social stratification scale. Finds that about two-thirds of Mexican population live in poverty.

4571 Brachet-Márquez, Viviane de. The dynamics of domination: State, class, and social reform in Mexico, 1910–1990. Pittsburgh, Pa.: Univ. of Pittsburgh Press, 1994. 251 p.: bibl., index. (Pitt Latin American series)

Masterfully discusses concept of "pact of domination" and provides basis for an analysis of contemporary history, organized by periods: 1910–40, 1940–70, and 1970–92. Argues that Mexico has avoided violent forms of social conflict resolution, not because of the strength of the State, but because the State's weaknesses have forced it to respond to pressures from below.

4572 Carmona, Fernando. Una alternativa al neoliberalismo: México y Latinoamérica 94. México: Editorial Nuestro Tiempo, 1993. 230 p.: bibl. (Col. Desarrollo)

Critically reviews shortcomings of neoliberal policies. Advances a number of common solutions including democratization and popular participation, reduction of North-South technological gap, fight against corruption, and Latin American integration to strengthen autochthonous capitalism in the region.

4573 Carrillo Viveros, Jorge. Dos décadas de sindicalismo en la industria maquiladora de exportación: examen en las ciudades de Tijuana, Juárez y Matamoros. México: Univ. Autónoma Metropolitana-Iztapalapa; M.A. Porrúa, 1994. 269 p.: bibl. (Las Ciencias sociales)

Comprehensive work utilizes official documents and other sources to analyze 142 labor conflicts in maquiladoras from 1968–87. Contends that unionism is functional to this industry. Sets forth model indicating that while unions in internally-oriented firms may function as mediator between management and workers, management in export-oriented firms have direct control over unions

and workers. This control results in unions' loss of negotiating power and the imposition of regressive contracts by management.

4574 Castaños, Carlos Manuel. Alternativas a la crisis rural en México. Chapingo, México: Agroecomunicación Saenz Colin, 1990. 391 p.: bibl., ill.

Agronomist's volume contains useful technical information for sociologists studying rural policies and conditions. *Inter alia,* explains why hybrid seeds (expected to be highly productive) do not perform as expected; gives reasons for lack of success of modernization efforts; and examines unused/ misused agricultural potential and inter-bureaucratic lack of coordination.

4575 Castillo Ochoa, Emilia. Los mineros de Cananea: proceso de trabajo y salud. Hermosillo, Mexico: Univ. de Sonora, División Ciencias Sociales, 1993. 127 p.: bibl.

Scholarly study of work environment and health conditions in mining town of north central Sonora, from 1980s-present.

4576 Chávez Galindo, Ana María; David Moctezuma Navarro; and Francisco Rodríguez Hernández. El combate a la pobreza en Morelos: aciertos y desaciertos de Solidaridad. Cuernavaca, Mexico: Univ. Nacional Autónoma de México, Centro Regional de Investigaciones Multidisciplinarias, 1994. 120 p.: bibl., ill.

Programa Nacional de Solaridad was created by the Mexican government to help the poor during the recent economic crisis by providing public services (water, electricity, health, and education), and aiding community construction of infrastructure. Assesses program and concludes that results were positive. However, the lowest decile of wealth distribution clearly received less than those above them. Also considers indirect consequences of the program such as increased community participation.

4577 Coloquio de Antropología e Historia Regionales, *11th, Zamora, Mexico, 1989.* Las realidades regionales de la crisis nacional. Recopilación de Jesús Tapia Santamaría. Zamora, Mexico: El Colegio de Michoacán, 1993. 799 p.: bibl., ill. (Col. Memorias)

Contains 25 papers, with comments by distinguished social scientists, from 1989 symposium. Presents impressive amount of information on a variety of topics. Most contributions examine consequences of modernization on quality of life and criticize Mexico's development approach.

4578 Coloquio Nacional de Investigadores, 2nd, México, 1988. Políticas urbanas y urbanización de la política. Coordinación de René Coulomb y Emilio Duhau. México: Univ. Autónoma Metropolitana, División de Ciencias Sociales y Humanidades, 1989. 259 p.: bibl. (Serie Sociología)

Nine presenters at 1988 colloquium comment on urban politics and local power; management of economic crisis in the Federal District; urban management, popular organizations and the State; and new political urban actors. Includes presentations and transcriptions of discussions. Provides comprehensive scholarly view of Mexican urban policies.

4579 La condición de la mujer en Jalisco. Recopilación de Rosa Rojas y María Rodríguez Batista. Guadalajara, Mexico: Univ. de Guadalajara, 1994. 203 p.: bibl.

Contains 23 short articles from conference held at Univ. de Guadalajara. Selections are divided among five distinct themes relating to women: politics and social organizations, education, health, work, and culture and art. Includes specific essays on women's participation in politics and female child employment.

4580 Cuéllar Vázquez, Angélica. La noche es de ustedes, el amanecer es nuestro: Asamblea de Barrios y Superbarrio Gómez en la Ciudad de México. México: Univ. Nacional Autónoma de México, Facultad de Ciencias Políticas y Sociales, 1993. 200 p.: bibl.

The 1985 earthquake in Mexico City presented conditions that prompted residents of stricken low-income neighborhoods to organize a grassroots movement to fight eviction. Examines history of the movement, its leader, its transformation into a political force, and its participation in 1988 presidential election supporting Cárdenas.

4581 Della Pergola, Sergio and Susana Lerner. La población judía en México: perfil demográfico, social y cultural. Jerusalem: Avraham Harman Institute of Contemporary Jewry, Hebrew Univ.; México: Centro de Estudios Demográficos y de Desarrollo Urbano, Colegio de México; Asociación Mexicana de Amigos de la Univ. Hebrea de Jerusalén,

1995. 188 p.: bibl., ill. (Jewish population studies; 26)

Based on 1991 Encuesta Sociodemográfica de la Población Judía de México, represents part of an international effort to document and analyze Jewish communities worldwide. Sample of 866 families includes self-identified cultural and/or religious Jews from various ethnic backgrounds. Focuses on population's origin, size, cultural-ethnic composition, family structure, schooling, economic activity, identity, religious participation and attitudes, continuities with Jewish communities in other countries, and unique attributes of Mexican Jews.

4582 Demographic dynamics of the U.S.-Mexico Border. Edited by John Robert Weeks and Roberto Ham-Chande. El Paso: Texas Western Press, Univ. of Texas at El Paso, 1992. 318 p.: bibl., ill., index, map.

Compilation of 15 articles of uneven quality and length from 1987 Binational Symposium on Population Issues along the US-Mexico Border held in Tijuana. Includes topics such as: border marriages, fertility on both sides of the border, emigration, infant mortality and family planning in northern Mexico, and economic impact of undocumented migrants in the US Southwest.

4583 Denman, Catalina A. Las repercusiones de la industria maquiladora de exportación en la salud: el peso al nacer de hijos de obreras en Nogales. Hermosillo, Mexico: Colegio de Sonora, 1991. 135 p.: bibl., ill., map. (Serie Cuadernos de trabajo; 2)

Divides random sample of 300 women who delivered at the Nogales hospital of the Instituto Mexicano de Seguro Social into two groups: women who worked in maquilas (n = 169) and those employed in the service sector (n = 131). Low birth weight risk factors coefficient correlates were calculated for groups. Results showed that maquila workers had a higher rate of low birth weights; however, sociodemographic characteristics differed so results should not be deemed conclusive.

4584 Desarrollo sustentable y participación comunitaria. Coordinación de Lucero Jiménez Guzmán. Cuernavaca, Mexico: Univ. Nacional Autónoma de México, Centro Regional de Investigaciones Multidisciplinarias, 1994. 127 p.: bibl.

Papers presented at a UNAM seminar partially sponsored by International Development Society approach development from a humanitarian and ecological perspective. Ranges from Gustavo Esteva's call for a radical reconception of development to Yolanda de los Reyes' evaluation of community participation in the Programa Nacional de Solidaridad.

4585 Durand, Jorge. Más allá de la línea: patrones migratorios entre México y Estados Unidos. México: Consejo Nacional para la Cultura y las Artes, 1994. 353 p.: bibl., ill., map. (Regiones)

Comprehensive study combines historical analysis, case study of a community in Guanajuato, and results of over 2,000 questionnaires from 11 communities in western Mexico, to explore patterns and cultural and economic impact of migration. Finds that migration has become a geographically and socioeconomically generalized phenomenon and that young people from poor neighborhoods and women have emerged as new migratory populations. Examines cultural impact of migration on children. Also discusses intended and unintended effects of Simpson-Rodino law.

4586 Economía contra sociedad: el Istmo de Tehuantepec, 1907–1986. Coordinación de Leticia Reina Aoyama. México: Nueva Imagen, 1994. 350 p.: bibl., ill.

First essay examines failed Ferrocarril Nacional de Tehuantepec from 1907–40. Following sections discuss unsuccessful efforts to modernize agriculture and introduce an industrial base to the region. Presents valuable information on Tablon irrigation dam, an excellent case study that exemplifies what can go wrong in large projects financed by multilateral banks. Important contribution to literature on development.

4587 Los empresarios ante la globalización. Coordinación de Ricardo Tirado. México: H. Cámara de Diputados, Instituto de Investigaciones Legislativas, LV Legislatura; Univ. Nacional Autónoma de México, Instituto de Investigaciones Sociales, 1994. 246 p.: bibl.

First six articles about Latin America provide information on State-private sector relations, political roles of business sector, and current transformations of business and industrial firms in light of economic globalization. Four contributions in pt. 2 provide a useful overview of the Mexican private sector's position regarding the country's participation in GATT and NAFTA. Discusses organization and modernization of sector, conflicts between large and small businesses, and lobbying strategies.

4588 Encuentro Nacional de Investigadores sobre la Familia, 1st, Tlaxcala, Mexico, 1993. Actas. v. 1–2. Coordinación de Dora Juárez Ortiz. Tlaxcala, Mexico: Univ. Autónoma de Tlaxcala, Depto. de Educación Especializada, Centro Universitario de Estudios para la Familia, 1994. 2 v.: bibl., ill.

Consists of 37 contributions of diverse quality from anthropology, sociology, psychology, education, and health. Some papers pertain to effects of socioeconomic change on the family, gender relations, and single mothers.

4589 Esteinou Madrid, Javier. La comunicación y la cultura nacionales: en los tiempos del libre comercio. México: Fundación Manuel Buendia, 1993. 287 p.: bibl. (Pistas)

Engaging volume contends that current Mexican conceptions of culture are narcissistic and regressive. Claims that State policies, mass media, neoliberalism, and free trade have created a consumer society and debilitated national identity. Advocates alternative conception of culture as general frame within which social, economic, and political activity take place, linking intellectual productivity and collective consciousness with resolution of structural conflicts. Suggests formulation of social liberalism policy which would support popular participation in creation of culture.

4590 Familia, salud y sociedad: experiencias de investigación en México. Guadalajara, Mexico: Univ. de Guadalajara; Cuernavaca, Mexico: Instituto de Investigación en Salud Pública; México: Centro de Investigaciones y Estudios Superiores en Antropología Social; Hermosillo, Mexico: Colegio de Sonora, 1993. 423 p.: bibl. (Col. Fin de milenio. Serie Medicina social)

Several of the 22 papers presented at a 1990 conference are written by well-known social and public health scientists. Some contributions discuss health topics including impact of female employment on family health, role of family in health care, and consequences of family migration on nutrition. Other contributions examine family organization and female employment.

4591 Foro sobre la Reforma Rural, 1st, México, 1988. Actas. México: Univ. Autónoma Chapingo, 1989? 239 p.

The 25 position papers presented at 1988 national symposium criticize rural and agricultural policies and lack of bureaucratic support to satisfy basic needs and demands of peasants and agricultural workers. Works also denounce increasing influence of agribusinesses and foreign interests. Provides useful overview of rural problems and advances solutions current conservative Mexican leaders most likely will reject.

4592 El futuro del campo: hacia una vía de desarrollo campesino. Coordinación de Ana de Ita Rubio. México: CECCAM; UNORCA; Fundación Friedrich Ebert, 1994. 176 p.: ill.

Critically reviews impact of neoliberal policies and NAFTA on traditional agriculture. Discusses policy recommendations for modernization of rural sector and protection of natural resources including sustainable agriculture, improved access to markets and loans, national food sufficiency, forest conservation, and price stability. Also examines recent conflicts between government and peasantry.

4593 García, Brígida and Orlandina de Oliveira. Trabajo femenino y vida familiar en México. México: El Colegio de México, Centro de Estudios Demográficos y de Desarrollo Urbano; Centro de Estudios Sociológicos, 1994. 301 p.: bibl.

Uses national fecundity surveys to examine changes in women's labor market participation from 1976–87. Employs questionnaires and in-depth interviews conducted in Mexico City, Tijuana, and Merida to analyze women's work outside the home. Focuses on structural factors that impact women's labor force participation, links between work and maternity and child care, changing gender roles, domestic violence, and differences between middle- and working-class women.

4594 García Barrios, Raúl; Luis García Barrios; and Elena Alvarez-Buylla. Lagunas: deterioro ambiental y tecnológico

en el campo semiproletarizado. México: Colegio de México, Programa sobre Ciencia, Tecnología y Desarrollo, 1991. 226 p.: bibl., ill.

Results of fieldwork conducted from 1984–86 demonstrate relationships between social institutions, natural resource management, and macroeconomic policies in San Andrés Lagunas. Analyzes historical, environmental, and technological issues relevant to *maíz* production, peasants' economic strategies, economic and social sources of environmental crisis, and potential role of peasants as social agents of conservation.

4595 Garrocho, Carlos. Análisis socioespacial de los servicios de salud: accesibilidad, utilización y calidad. Zinacantepec, Mexico: El Colegio Mexiquense, Sistema para el Desarrollo Integral de la Familia del Estado de México, 1995. 460 p.: bibl., ill.

Solid monograph by medical geographer examines accessibility and utilization of rural public services, and users' perceived quality. Study is based on a survey of 421 child users of a health clinic and a pediatric hospital in Toluca. Applies space location theory to reduce costs and improve services utilization.

4596 Garza Toledo, Enrique de la. Reestructuración productiva y respuesta sindical en México. México: Univ. Nacional Autónoma de México, Instituto de Investigaciones Económicas, 1993. 218 p.: bibl.

In 1980s Mexico entered a period of industrial reconversion. This excellent monograph examines technological and organizational changes and labor flexibility introduced in the private sector, including maquilas, and in public enterprises. Gives examples of reconversion in several industries such as textiles, automotive, Telmex, and Pemex.

4597 Gastélum Gaxiola, María de los Angeles. La migración de los trabajadores mexicanos indocumentados a los Estados Unidos. México: Coordinación General de Estudios de Posgrado, Facultad de Derecho, Univ. Nacional Autónoma de México, 1991. 381 p.: bibl., ill., maps. (Col. Posgrado; 6)

Thorough doctoral dissertation examines bilateral causes of international migration and its impact on Mexico's economy and society. Explores US immigration law and protection for undocumented workers under Mexican and international law. Contends that undocumented workers often are not aware of their rights. Issues general policy recommendations to reduce flow of illegal migrants, focusing on improving socioeconomic conditions in Mexico.

4598 Gestión urbana y cambio institucional. Coordinación de Antonio Azuela y Emilio Duhau. México: Univ. Autónoma Metropolitana, División de Ciencias Sociales y Humanidades, 1993. 259 p.: (Serie Sociología)

Collaborative effort consists of papers and debates presented at a colloquium held in Tlazcala between French and Mexican social scientists. Works are divided into three general themes: supply and demand of urban affairs management; local power, political culture, and social actors; and institutional change and social actors.

4599 Gledhill, John. Neoliberalism, transnationalization, and rural poverty: a case study of Michoacán, Mexico. Boulder, Colo.: Westview Press, 1995. 243 p.: bibl., ill., index, maps.

Based on 1990–91 fieldwork in rural Michoacán, subsequent short trips and secondary data, contends that migration at that time was a response to President Salinas' policies and US politics. Also analyzes conditions of migrants in US. Examines effects of migration on migrants' family, acculturation, and women's emancipation, among other topics.

4600 González de la Rocha, Mercedes. The resources of poverty: women and survival in a Mexican city. Oxford, England; Cambridge, Mass.: Blackwell, 1994. 311 p.: bibl., index, map. (Studies in urban and social change)

Updated, English-language version of *Los recursos de la pobreza: familia de bajos ingresos en Guadalajara* (see *HLAS 51:4586*). Original work is based on a small 1982 survey of households. English version includes more recent bibliographical references.

4601 González Salas, Carlos. Los trabajadores de Tampico y Ciudad Madero: un ensayo de sub-cultura laboral, 1886–1991. Ciudad Victoria, Mexico: Univ. Autónoma de Tamaulipas, Instituto de Investigaciones Históricas, 1993. 66 p.: bibl., ill.

Applies concept of subculture to groups of workers and analyzes impact of changes in working conditions on labor's val-

ues and attitudes, beginning with establishment of Waters Pierce oil refinery in 1886. Based on questionnaires administered to ex- and current workers in various occupations as well as to anarchist labor unions and groups.

4602 Gutiérrez Mejía, Irma Eugenia. Caminantes de la tierra ocupada: emigración campesina de la Huasteca hidalguense a las minas de Pachuca. México: Consejo Nacional para la Cultura y las Artes, 1992. 142 p.: bibl., ill. (Regiones)

Ethnography of Tetla, the sending community (pop. 505), precedes study of Pachuca, the receiving community. Survey of 125 Pachuca households in neighborhoods which supply laborers to local mines provides information on household composition, health status, and quality of life. Finds a high percentage of migrants from Tetla in these neighborhoods, and compares living conditions before and after migration.

4603 Guzmán Gómez, Carlota. Entre el deseo y la oportunidad: los estudiantes de la UNAM frente al mercado de trabajo. Cuernavaca, Mexico: Univ. Nacional Autónoma de México, Centro Regional de Investigaciones Multidisciplinarias, 1994. 261 p.: bibl.

Unique qualitative study consists of in-depth interviews of 205 students during their final year of studies in 10 different fields. Establishes a theoretical base in Bourdieu's concepts of habitus and social capital, and explores disparity between students' desires and job market realities. Concludes that, depending on their field of study, students approach the issue from four distinct perspectives.

4604 Hernández Díaz, Jorge; León Javier Parra Mora; and Manuel Matus Manzo. Etnicidad, nacionalismo y poder: tres ensayos. Oaxaca, Mexico: Univ. Autónoma Benito Juárez de Oaxaca, Secretaría Académica, 1993. 175 p.: bibl.

First essay critically reviews the position of many influential intellectuals (Vasconcelos, Aguirre Beltrán, Saénz, Caso, Gamio, and others) regarding indigenous assimilation. The second studies acculturation process of indigenous communities from 1900–present and identifies key events such as arrival of a school. Final essay provides general description of cultural components of present-day Zapotec communities in the Isthmus.

4605 Hernández Vicencio, Tania. Los gremios de taxistas en Tijuana: alternancia política y corporativismo cetemista. Tijuana, Mexico: El Colegio de la Frontera Norte, Depto. de Estudios Sociales, 1995. 107 p.: bibl. (Cuadernos; 7)

Case study emphasizes importance of local factors in modifying corporate structure. Focusing on period 1983–91, examines political influence of eight large taxi driver guilds associated with the Confederación de Trabajadores de México. Contends that, while guilds exercised forceful influence until 1989, PAN's reforms thereafter ended clientalistic relationship between government and corporations.

4606 Identidades, nacionalismos, y regiones. Recopilación de Ricardo Avila Palafox y Tomás Calvo Buezas. Guadalajara, Mexico: Univ. de Guadalajara; Madrid: Univ. Complutense de Madrid, 1993. 341 p.: bibl., ill. (Col. Fundamentos. Serie Laboratorio de Antropología)

Compilation of 17 papers from conference on internal demands for autonomy and self identity in context of globalization and advent of economic unions. Contributions pertain especially to Mexico and Spain; also includes selections on Germany, Canada, and France. Some papers deal with Chiapas and Veracruz, and elites in western Mexico.

4607 Imagen y realidad de la mujer. Recopilación de Inés Martínez de Castro, Edith Araoz Robles y Fernanda Aguilar Almada. Hermosillo, Mexico: El Colegio de Sonora; Unidad de Promoción Voluntaria de la Secretaría de Salud Pública del Estado de Sonora, 1995. 131 p.: bibl.

Collection of essays from two forums held in Hermosillo in 1994–95 looks at inconsistency between women's experience and cultural stereotypes by examining use of images as instruments of social control. Three sections focus on images of women in the arts; current problems, such as women's voice in electoral processes, population issues, and the informal economy; and reflections on menopause.

4608 Isaac, Claudia B. Class stratification and cooperative production among rural women in central Mexico. (*LARR*, 30:2, 1995, p. 123–150)

Lengthy research "note" uses Marxist

approach to explain failure of a rural women's cooperative in Querétaro. Contends that failure was due to class tensions resulting from patriarchy and dependent capitalism. Does not examine reasons for success of other cooperatives functioning under similar circumstances. Based on two months of participant observation, attempts to develop class faction categories.

4609 Kraemer Bayer, Gabriela and **Luis Alberto Solórzano Toscano.** Los productores de café en Zihuateutla, Pue.: origen, entorno y perspectivas. Texcoco, Mexico: Univ. Autónoma Chapingo, Dirección de Difusión Cultural, Depto. de Sociología Rural, 1990. 262 p.: bibl., ill. (Col. Cuadernos universitarios. Serie ciencias sociales; 8)

Demonstrates that deterioration of social and ecological conditions has led to changes in forms of production in subtropical area of Northern Sierra in Puebla, including a shift during 1970s from *cacique*-related traditional cultivation techniques to a two-tiered production system consisting of subsistence farming and contract work for large ranches and coffee plantations. Argues that both techniques are related to process of integrating peasant forms of production into capital accumulation. Methodology includes interviews, quantitative analysis of peasant economies, and geographical evaluation of land use.

4610 Lau, Rubén and **Víctor M. Quintana Silveyra.** Movimientos populares en Chihuahua. Ciudad Juárez, Mexico: Univ. Autónoma de Juárez, 1991. 119 p.: bibl. (Estudios regionales; 3)

Two essays examine popular movements from 1970–90. First describes political history of the Comité de Defensa Popular and its mobilizations centered around electoral processes. Second profiles actions and demands of major social movements during 1980s, focusing on sectors seeking better living and working conditions.

4611 LeVine, Sarah E. Dolor y alegría: women and social change in urban Mexico. Madison: Univ. of Wisconsin Press, 1993. 239 p.: bibl., ill., index. (Life course studies)

Fascinating ethnography focuses on ways in which urbanization and rapid social change have affected family life and women at various life stages, including childhood, adolescence, marriage, childbearing years, and old age. Based on interviews with 15 working-class women of distinct generational groups from a tenement neighborhood in Cuernavaca. Interviews were conducted semiweekly over a one-year span (1984–85). Additional chapter discusses women's roles and family relations during the 1990s.

4612 Linck, Thierry. El campesino despo-seido. Traducción de Luz María Santa María. Zamora, Mexico: Colegio de Michoa-cán; México: Centre d'Etudes Mexicaines et Centramericaines, 1988. 176 p.: bibl., ill., maps.

Analyzes methods of integrating peas-ant agriculture into the global system, includ-ing new technology, distinct market rela-tions, and State policies. Asserts that these factors weaken peasant economic and social structures, leading to dispossession of land and loss of culture and autonomy. Calls for alternative forms of development focusing on decentralization, peasant autonomy, and reconception of technology.

4613 Loaeza, Soledad. La experiencia mexi-cana de liberalización. (*Rev. Int. So-ciol.*, 7, 1994, p. 75–106, bibl.)

Mexico experienced gradual steps to-ward political liberalization until 1982, when President De la Madrid and later President Sa-linas introduced significant changes. Argues that liberalization in Mexico may lead to a fragmentation of political institutions, rather than a genuine democracy. Explains reasons for the outcome, and factors influencing the liberalization of Mexico's political system.

4614 Lomnitz-Adler, Claudio. Exits from the labyrinth: culture and ideology in the Mexican national space. Berkeley: Univ. of California Press, 1992. 386 p.: bibl., ill., index, maps.

Scholarly contribution to the under-standing of national culture. First part studies cultural production and ideology in Morelos and in the Huasteca Potosina. Second part fo-cuses on history of legitimacy and charisma in Mexican politics, and relationship between the national community and racial ideology. Based on extensive field work and participant observation.

Mallon, Florencia E. Peasant and nation: the making of postcolonial Mexico and Peru. See *HLAS 56:1350.*

4615 Martínez Velasco, Germán. Planta-ciones, trabajo guatemalteco y política migratoria en la frontera sur de México. Tux-tla Gutiérrez, Mexico: Gobierno del Estado de Chiapas, Consejo Estatal de Fomento a la In-vestigación y Difusión de la Cultura, Insti-tuto Chiapaneco de Cultura, 1994. 197 p.: bibl., ill. (Serie Nuestros pueblos)

Master's thesis examines relationship between border politics, migratory flows, and coffee plantations in Soconusco region of Chiapas. Views migration as consequence of oppression of indigenous communities in Guatemala as well as of structural need for labor force in coffee production. Concludes that ethnic identification and labor market transcend border, although migrants' status as foreigners increases potential for labor exploitation.

4616 Massey, Douglas S.; Luin Goldrin; and Jorge Durand. Continuities in transi-tional migration: an analysis of nineteen Mexican communities. (*Am. J. Sociol.*, 99:6, May 1994, p. 1492–1533, bibl., tables)

Data from 19 communities are used to explain similarities and differences of Mexi-can migration to US. During early phases, generally affluent males migrate to a few US locations. In time, the socioeconomic and gender base of migration is broadened and the number of locations increases.

4617 Massolo, Alejandra. Por amor y coraje: mujeres en movimientos urbanos de la ciudad de México. México: Colegio de Mé-xico, Programa Interdisciplinario de Estudios de la Mujer, 1992. 418 p.: bibl., maps.

Compelling exploratory investigation of women settlers in poor neighborhoods and their participation in social struggles during 1970s. Contends that although women were often the heart of social movements, their role has seldom been studied. Provides basic historical and theoretical/feminist frame-works. Mostly discusses life histories of four women and their recollections of popular struggles in three central and peripheral neighborhoods.

4618 Los medios y los modos: participación política y acción colectiva de las mu-jeres. Recopilación de Alejandra Massolo. México: Colegio de México, 1994. 212 p.: bibl.

Collection of five articles aims to debunk myth that political issues are not relevant to women by demonstrating women's leading roles in various social and political efforts. Two papers focus on women in the Partido Acción Nacional who are organizing against election fraud in Ciudad Juárez. Other articles examine Movimiento Urbano Popular in Veracruz, action networks in Mexico City, and a women's resistance organization in the mining community of Cananea, Sonora.

4619 Méndez García, Gloria. El industrialismo y los sindicatos en San Juan del Río, Querétaro. Querétaro, Mexico: Univ. Autónoma de Querétaro, Dirección Centros de Investigación, 1988. 226 p.: bibl., ill., map. (Temas de investigación; 15)

Queretaro's second city industrialized a few years before the economic crisis of the 1980s. After surveying Mexico's industrialization policies between 1970–84, work describes industrial growth in San Juan del Río and different types of labor unions, including independent, government, and "white" (organized by the firm). Case studies present labor tactics and outcomes of management-labor conflict.

4620 Mercado Martínez, Francisco Javier. La experiencia de la enfermedad crónica en un barrio urbano. Guadalajara, Mexico: Univ. de Guadalajara, 1996. 1 v.

Valuable contribution for understanding impact of diabetes on quality of patients' life. Based on clinical records, in-depth interviews, and three years of participant-observation of 50 adult patients (39 women, 11 men) in a poor neighborhood of Guadalajara, this is the most comprehensive study of its kind. Of interest to sociologists, medical anthropologists, and public health experts.

4621 Metz, Allan. Protestantism in Mexico: contemporary contextual developments. (*J. Church State,* 36:1, Winter 1994, p. 57–78)

Growth of Protestantism, specifically of Pentecostal and evangelical groups, in Mexico, in recent years has been phenomenal. Focuses on Catholic Church's reaction to the incipient loss of its monopolistic power and its attempts to maintain control. Examines 1988–92 period, during which articles of the Constitution governing religious institutions were revised.

4622 Meza, Armando. Movimiento urbano popular en Durango. México: CIESAS, 1994. 119 p.: bibl.

Presents organizational characteristics, demands, and outcomes of movement's efforts in three historical sequences—1972–79, 1980–86, and 1987–90. Details cases of land invasions, demands for water tariff reductions, confrontations between PRI-controlled unions and democratic leaders, and street vendors' fights with municipality. Considers role of political parties and evaluates Programa Nacional de Solidaridad.

4623 Mier y Terán, Marta. Fertility transition and women's life course in Mexico. New York: United Nations, 1993. 62 p.: bibl., ill.

Investigation uses data on women born between 1927–66 from Encuesta Mexicana de Fecundidad (1976) and Encuesta Nacional de Fecundidad y Salud (1987) to examine longitudinal impact of demographic, social, and economic changes on women's lives and fertility. Analyzes how members of different groups make life choices based on increasing opportunities, but also on restrictions resulting from historical events.

4624 La migración nacional e internacional de los oaxaqueños. Tijuana, Mexico: El Colegio de la Frontera Norte; Oaxaca, Mexico: Consejo Estatal de Población de Oaxaca, 1995. 286 p.: bibl., ill., maps.

Attempts to describe and quantify Oaxacan emigration using data from Censos de Población of 1950–90. Uses data from Proyecto Cañon Zapata and other Colegio de la Frontera Norte surveys to examine characteristics of undocumented migrants in US and those who have been deported.

4625 Moguel, Julio. Local power and development alternatives: an urban popular movement in northern Mexico. (*in* New paths to democratic development in Latin America. Edited by Charles A. Reilly. Boulder, Colo.: Lynne Rienner Publishers, 1995, p. 211–228)

Examines popular movements of northern Mexico, including the Comité de Defensa Popular de Durango "General Francisco Villa" (CDP). Finds that CDP's framework of growth rests on two fundamental principles: 1) sustained evolution of organizational methods and community development; and 2) sustained expansion of areas of influence and endeavor. [R.E. Looney]

4626 Morett Sánchez, Jesús Carlos. Alternativas de modernización del ejido. 2. ed. México: Instituto de Proposiciones Estratégicas; Editorial Diana, 1992. 223 p.: bibl., ill., maps.

Critiques legal and organizational structures of the *ejidos* written just before the 1992 constitutional reform of Article 27. Considers Article 27 obsolete and an impediment to modernization of the 28,000 *ejidos*. Many solutions coincide with President Salinas' proposed agricultural reform, but there are some important differences. Informative and well argued.

4627 Los movimientos sociales urbanos: un reto para la modernización. Coordinación de Hugo Esteve. México: Instituto de Proposiciones Estratégicas, 1992. 239 p.

Examines historical experience of Movimiento Urbano Popular and various social movement theories to determine both the characteristics of social movements, and their role in a modernizing world. Contends that social transformation depends on these movements, but that success depends on breaking with regional and sectoral politics in favor of long-term national-level goals.

4628 Mujer: trabajo, salud y conflictos sociales en Sonora. Recopilación de Inés Martínez de Castro, Fernanda Aguilar Almada y Edith Araoz Robles. Hermosillo, Mexico: El Colegio de Sonora, 1993. 154 p.: bibl., ill.

Includes 14 short articles from a conference held at Colegio de Sonora, separated into three categories: 1) women's participation in productive activities in and out of the home; 2) health issues pertaining to women and the family; and 3) women and social conflicts. Includes two contributions about violence against women.

4629 La mujer del México de la transición: memoria de un simposio. Recopilación de Patricia Galeana de Valadés. México: Federación Mexicana de Universitarias; Univ. Nacional Autónoma de México, Coordinación de Humanidades, Dirección General de Publicaciones, 1994. 191 p.: bibl., ill.

Collection of 17 papers presented at symposium of the Federación Mexicana de Universitarias analyzes role of women in economic transition. Ranges from academic papers to personal testimonies; themes include development in the university context, participation in public and private sectors, and information technology.

4630 Mujer rural y medio ambiente en la Selva Lacandona. Cuernavaca, Mexico: Univ. Nacional Autónoma de México, Centro Regional de Investigaciones Multidisciplinarias, 1994. 163 p.: bibl.

Focuses on indigenous and mestiza women's perceptions of environmental degradation in jungle in Chiapas. Based on 40 in-depth interviews and 121 questionnaires. Finds that women link deforestation to lack of natural resources and attribute this to health problems and nutritional needs. Contends that women's knowledge of jungle is a resource for redefining development.

4631 Las mujeres campesinas se organizan. Coordinación de Alejandra Safa Barraza y Erna Mergruen Rentería. México: UNORCA, 1993. 125 p.: graphs.

Examines 16 regional organizations encompassing 124 women's groups associated with the Red Nacional de Organizaciones de Mujeres Campesinas, a network organized by the Unión Nacional de Organizaciones Regionales Campesinas Autónomas (UNORCA). Diagnostic study focuses on nature of peasant women's work and possibility of participation in renumerated work. Includes 14 case studies of individual organizations.

4632 Las mujeres en la pobreza. México: El Colegio de México; Grupo Interdisciplinario sobre Mujer, Trabajo y Pobreza, 1994. 393 p.: bibl.

Collection of nine works explores relationships between social construction of gender, causes of poverty, and its intergenerational transmission. One section examines poor households, focusing on theoretical, conceptual, and methodological developments pertaining to inequality, poverty, and gender. Other sections discuss women's poverty in relation to urban and rural work, and mental and reproductive health. The final section addresses efforts of private and public sectors to counteract poverty.

4633 Mujeres, migración y maquila en la frontera norte. Recopilación de Soledad González Montes *et al.* México: Colegio de

México, Programa Interdisciplinario de Estudios de la Mujer; Tijuana, Mexico: Colegio de la Frontera Norte, 1995. 270 p.: bibl., ill.

Nine works utilize various methodologies to examine migration and maquiladoras in Tijuana and Ciudad Juárez focusing on gender relations, living conditions, and labor activities of women and families. Topics include international migration among undocumented women, family structure and women's work, and learning strategies in the electronic industry.

4634 Las mujeres y la salud. Recopilación de Soledad González Montes. México: Colegio de México, Programa Interdisciplinario de Estudios de la Mujer, 1995. 258 p.: bibl.

Six solid works analyze women's health and relevant sociocultural conditions. Contributions include a comparative analysis of attitudes and practices related to health, pregnancy, and contraception in two rural communities; an examination of the role of domestic medicine in rural areas; and a general revision of perspectives on the relationship between gender and health.

4635 Mummert, Gail. Tierra que pica: transformación social de un valle agrícola michoacano en la época post-reforma agraria. Zamora, Mexico: El Colegio de Michoacán, 1994. 214 p.: bibl., ill. (Col. Investigaciones)

Thorough case study utilizes both quantitative and qualitative methodology to analyze how post-land reform changes affected residents of Valle de Zacapu. Focusing on social implications of regional development, examines family strategies for social reproduction and life course decisions of different generations. Explores movements and interactions between *ejidal* community of Naranja de Tapia and city of Zacapu where an industrial plant was built in the late 1940s.

4636 Munguía, Miguel Angel. Estrategias de desarrollo rural: el actuar de organismos civiles. México: Univ. Autónoma Metropolitana, Unidad Xochimilco; EDUCE, 1993. 129 p.: bibl., ill. (Col. Ensayos)

Critically examines methodology of Fomento Cultural y Educativo, a nongovernmental organization in Jalapa, Veracruz, emphasizing consciousness-raising and popular participation. Concludes that network of civil organizations focusing on education, women, health, radio broadcasting, and small-scale coffee production was most effective in engendering rural development.

4637 Muro González, Víctor Gabriel. Iglesia y movimientos sociales en México: los casos de Ciudad Juárez y el Istmo de Tehuantepec. Puebla, Mexico: Red Nacional de Investigación Urbana; Zamora, Mexico: El Colegio de Michoacán, 1994. 263 p.

Analyzes role of Catholic Church in two regional social movements during 1970s and 1980s, providing historical and theoretical context and detailed descriptions. Contends that Church's involvement performed dual function of preserving Church's influence in a changing social arena, while strengthening the movements by giving their demands greater coherence and plausibility.

4638 El nuevo estado mexicano. v. 4, Estado y sociedad. Coordinación de Jorge Alonso, Alberto Aziz Nassif y Jaime Tamayo. Guadalajara, Mexico: Univ. de Guadalajara; México: Nueva Imagen, CIESAS, 1992. 1 v.

Nine critical essays by well-known authors (González Casanovas, De la Peña, Eduardo Menéndez, and others) examine role of government and public policies during 1980s. Some issues include health, education and technology policies, Church-State relations, political transformation toward modernization, and new political culture.

4639 Nuevos textos y renovados pretextos. Coordinación de Vania Salles y Elsie Mc Phail. México: Colegio de México, Programa Interdisciplinario de Estudios de la Mujer, 1994. 726 p.: bibl.

Broad-based collection of 19 papers focuses on presence and participation of women in Mexican society, including rural women's issues, urban women's work, health, sociodemographic aspects of women's work, family organization, power and political participation, and religion and kinship. Of special interest are Roberto Campos Navarro's paper on *curanderismo* and Rosa Aurora Espinosa Gómez's case study of expressions of power in Apaseo el Alto, Guanajuato, during late 1970s.

4640 Núñez Noriega, Guillermo. Sexo entre varones: poder y resistencia en el campo sexual. Hermosillo, Mexico: El Colegio de Sonora, Univ. de Sonora, 1994. 342 p.: bibl.

Incorporates theoretical perspectives of

Bourdieu and Foucault to interpret society's representation of erotic expressions between young men in Hermosillo. Examines impact of these representations on sexual and cultural practices of individuals. Deconstructs concept of homosexuality as historical creation non-representative of multifarious practices and self-conceptions. Based on 20 in-depth interviews, informal conversations, and participant and indirect observations.

4641 Ojeda de la Peña, Norma and **Silvia López.** Familias transfronterizas en Tijuana: dos estudios complementarios. Tijuana, Mexico: El Colegio de la Frontera Norte, Depto. de Estudios de Población, 1994. 74 p.: bibl., ill. (Serie Cuadernos; 6)

Notable contribution to literature on unique attributes of transborder families in Tijuana/San Diego region uses 38 life histories to analyze relationship between international migration, daily transborder migration, and formation of transborder families. Utilizes in-depth interviews to examine women's role in creating and maintaining cross-border social webs and their function in the social reproduction of transborder households.

4642 Ordóñez Morales, César Eduardo. Eslabones de frontera: un análisis sobre aspectos del desarrollo agrícola y migración de fuerza de trabajo en regiones fronterizas de Chiapas y Guatemala. Tuxtla Gutiérrez, Mexico: Univ. Autónoma de Chiapas. 1993. 139 p.: bibl., ill.

Explains causes of temporary labor migration from western highlands and southern coast of Guatemala to Soconusco in Chiapas. Finds that in Mexico, coffee and sugar plantations prefer Guatemalan *braceros* over native workers because they can be paid lower salaries, are more submissive, and can be exploited more easily.

4643 Ortega Aguirre, Maximino and **Ana Alicia Solís de Alba.** México, estado y sindicatos, 1983–1988. Coyoacán, Mexico: Centro de Reflexión Teológica. 1992. 125 p.: bibl.

Studies tactics used by President De la Madrid to control the official labor unions' demands, and to insure repression of independent unions during severe economic crisis of 1980s. Assesses consequences of federal labor law reforms, and concludes that organized labor's ability to negotiate wages and labor benefits was considerably weakened.

4644 Ortega Olivares, Mario. La utopía en el barrio. México: Univ. Autónoma Metropolitana, Unidad Xochimilco, División de Ciencias Sociales y Humanidades, Depto. de Relaciones Sociales, 1995. 333 p.: bibl., ill.

Criticizes government's incompetence during the reconstruction of Mexico City following 1985 earthquake, and its derailing of citizen efforts. Presents exhaustive information on reconstruction work by dwellers of Colonia Guerrero, a poor downtown neighborhood, and discusses limitations of grassroots mobilization. Explains reasons for failure of a health program based on community participation.

4645 Osorio Salgado, Isabel. Erradicación o radicación de la pobreza?: PRONASOL y territorio en el estado de Guerrero. Chilpancingo, Mexico: Univ. Autónoma de Guerrero, Dirección de Investigación Científica, 1995. 234 p.: bibl., ill., maps.

Reviews poverty reduction initiatives launched by Mexican governments of recent decades. In-depth study of Programa Nacional de Solidaridad (PRONASOL) in Guerrero shows that relatively high allocation of PRONASOL funds were spent primarily in urban areas and on infrastructure. Program's impact among rural poor was negligible.

4646 Oswald Spring, Ursula. Estrategias de supervivencia en la ciudad de México. Cuernavaca, Mexico: Univ. Nacional Autónoma de México, Centro Regional de Investigaciones Multidisciplinarias, 1991. 219 p.: bibl.

Responses to 1980s economic crisis in five Mexico City slums indicate that inhabitants reduced protein-caloric intake, increased labor participation in the informal sector, sold non-essential goods, borrowed money and food, and reduced all non-essential purchases. Describes nutritional consequences of food changes. Offers useful evaluation of government programs providing assistance to the poor such as the Centros Populares de Abasto, run by Compañía Nacional de Subsistencias Populares (Conasupo) and its distributors Dicconsa and Liconsa.

4647 Parra Mora, León Javier and **Jorge Hernández Díaz.** Violencia y cambio social en la región Triqui. Oaxaca, Mexico: Univ. Autónoma Benito Juárez de Oaxaca; Consejo Estatal de Población de Oaxaca, 1994. 293 p.: bibl., ill., index, maps.

Explains cultural and institutional factors supporting use of violence to settle political differences among Trique-speaking inhabitants of northwest Oaxaca. For many years, leadership patterns, family and social organization, and traditions reinforced political violence. However, since 1970s, acculturation and bilingualism, outmigration due to violence, and increasing mestizo influence have promoted political mediation for conflict resolution and introduced new social and political institutions.

4648 Partida Bush, Virgilio. Migración interna. Aguascalientes, Mexico: Instituto Nacional de Estadística, Geografía e Informática; México: El Colegio de México; Instituto de Investigaciones Sociales, Univ. Nacional Autónoma de México, 1994. 130 p.: bibl., ill.

Technical and quantitative study of 1960–90 migration, based on census data. Status and variables such as age, occupation, civil status, education, fertility, income, and infant mortality are cross-tabulated. Census data allow only for inter-state migration analysis.

4649 Peña, Guillermo de la. La cultura política mexicana: reflexiones desde la antropología. (*Estud. Cult. Contemp.*, 6:16/17, 1994, p. 153–166, bibl.)

Considers the nature of Mexican political culture and attempts to determine meaning of historical and religious symbols. Founding fathers' political behavior and corporate nature of PRI have left imprints on political culture. Discusses political socialization using life histories which show that first alliances are to the family, religious groups, and labor unions.

4650 Población y desigualdad social en México. Coordinación de Raúl Béjar Navarro y Héctor H. Hernández Bringas. Cuernavaca, Mexico: Univ. Nacional Autónoma de México, Centro Regional de Investigaciones Multidisciplinarias, 1993. 415 p.: bibl., ill., maps.

Solid contribution of 15 articles by leading researchers examines impact of 1980s economic crisis on wealth concentration and inequality, fertility, internal migration, mortality, health status, education, and indigenous populations. Also considers way-of-life adjustments during the crisis.

4651 Poder local en el Golfo de México. México: El Colegio de México, Centro de Estudios Sociológicos, 1995. 224 p.: bibl., ill. (Cuadernos del CES; 38)

First two papers examine political economy of agricultural municipalities in Veracruz and Tamaulipas. Third work deals with urbanization and local elites of Altamira, near Ciudad Madero. These ethnographic accounts emphasize interplay between politics and economics. Final item is a short comparative demographic analysis of population dynamics in two municipalities in Veracruz.

4652 Pries, Ludger. Movilidad en el empleo: una comparación de trabajo asalariado y por cuenta propia en Puebla. (*Estud. Sociol./México*, 11:32, mayo/agosto 1993, p. 475–496, bibl., graphs)

Follows employment shifts by age groups and occupations of 500 histories of workers in the automotive and textile industries, and in self-employed activities (small metal and mechanical shops, food and street vendors, public market vendors, and small shops). Contrary to previous assumptions, wage laborers are attracted to the informal sector, which is demonstrated by frequent voluntary shifts from salaried positions to self-employment.

Problemas socioreligiosos en Centroamérica y México: algunos estudios de caso. See item 4739.

4653 Ramírez Carrillo, Luis Alfonso. Secretos de familia: libaneses y élites empresariales en Yucatán. México: Consejo Nacional para la Cultura y las Artes, Dirección General de Publicaciones, 1994. 487 p.: bibl., ill. (Regiones)

Fascinating volume examines family history of Lebanese immigrants from time of arrival to consolidation as elites. Contends that extended families replaced certain functions of society and created conditions for competitive and profitable enterprise. Also looks at how elites that emerged from the middle class use coalitions. Analyzes relationship between political and economic aspects of social life. Based on case studies and historical analysis.

4654 Ramírez Carrillo, Luis Alfonso. Sociedad y población urbana en Yucatán, 1950–1989. México: Colegio de México, Centro de Estudios Sociológicos, 1993. 110 p.: bibl. (Cuadernos del CES; 36)

Describes changes in service and industrial sectors. Examines level of production, products manufactured, reasons for slow growth of maquila industries, and decreasing dominance of sisal. Discusses transformation of the labor force based on national population and economic censuses and data from the Cámaras Nacionales de Comercio e Industria and the Instituto Nacional de Estadística, Geografía e Informática.

4655 Ramírez Sáiz, Juan Manuel. Los caminos de la acción colectiva: "movimientos" urbanos, organizaciones ciudadanas y grupos vecinales de Guadalajara en los noventa. Zapopan, Mexico: El Colegio de Jalisco; México: Instituto Nacional de Antropología e Historia, 1994. 63 p.: bibl. (Ensayos jaliscienses)

Outlines theoretical approaches to analyze collective action. Describes sociopolitical context in which independent traditional organizations, new urban actors, and autonomous neighborhood groups emerged to pressure authorities addressing citizen rights and needs. Calls upon government to build channels facilitating collective action and communication between government and civil society.

4656 Ramírez Sáiz, Juan Manuel. Los movimientos sociales y la política: el Comité Popular del Sur en Guadalajara. Guadalajara, Mexico: Univ. de Guadalajara, Dirección de Publicaciones, 1995. 308 p.: bibl., ill. (Col. Fin de milenio. Biblioteca Movimientos Sociales)

Scholarly work examines an urban social movement in Guadalajara's shantytowns. Analyzes organizational characteristics of the movement, political behavior of leaders and membership, interactions with political parties and civil authorities at the municipal level, and accomplishments and failures. Provides insightful understanding of political parties' position regarding urban problems and the municipal electoral context.

4657 Ramírez Sáiz, Juan Manuel. La vivienda popular y sus actores: fondos públicos de vivienda, fundaciones privadas, organizaciones no gubernamantales (ONG) y movimiento urbano popular. Puebla, Mexico: Programa Editorial Red Nacional de Investi-

gación Urbana; Guadalajara, Mexico: CISMoS de la Univ. de Guadalajara, 1993. 309 p.: bibl., ill., maps.

Compares and discusses in detail internal dynamics of two social movements. One is a group of families soliciting housing funds from the Fondo Nacional de la Habitación Popular in Guadalajara, and the other is a Catholic Church-based organization whose members' dwellings were destroyed by the 1985 earthquake in Ciudad Guzmán.

4658 Regalado Santillán, Jorge. Lucha por la vivienda en Guadalajara: historia, política y organización social, 1980–1992. Guadalajara, Mexico: Centro Universitario de Ciencias Sociales y Humanidades, Univ. de Guadalajara, 1995. 258 p.: bibl., ill. (Col. Estado, cultura y sociedad)

Examines struggle for adequate housing by reviewing history of housing problems, government action, and political roots of popular urban movement focused on housing issues. Presents case study of the Foro de Lucha por la Vivienda organization. Analyzes reasons for lack of success of 1980s popular urban movement and acknowledges limitations including sectarianism and a focus on electoral issues rather than on poverty.

4659 Relaciones de género y transformaciones agrarias: estudios sobre el campo mexicano. Coordinación de Soledad González Montes y Vania Salles. México: El Colegio de México, Programa Interdisciplinario de Estudios de la Mujer, 1995. 337 p.: bibl., ill.

Eight works investigate impact of economic and political change and cultural transformations on evolution of rural women's work over the past century and, in particular, during the past decade. Focuses on various regions. Topics include migration, maternity, devaluation of women's work, and women's participation in regional economies.

4660 Rello, Fernando. Burguesía, campesinos y Estado en México: el conflicto agrario de 1976. Prólogo de Rodolfo Stavenhagen. Geneva: United Nations Research Institute for Social Development, 1987. 119 p.: bibl., maps. (Informe / United Nations Research Institute for Social Development; 86.4)

In 1976 Sinaloa and Sonora witnessed serious confrontations between the landless peasantry and farmers. Examines alliances between factions of the rural and industrial bourgeoisie, the bourgeoisie and the State, and the loss of power by Mexican political leaders who supported agrarian policies. Excellent study for understanding social class transformation in rural Mexico. For annotation of English-language version see *HLAS 51:1860*.

4661 Reunión Nacional de Diagnóstico sobre el Estado Actual y Perspectivas de las Ciencias Sociales en México, 1st, Cocoyoc, Mexico, 1993. Las ciencias sociales en México: análisis y perspectivas. Coordinación de Manuel Perló Cohen. México: Univ. Nacional Autónoma de México, Instituto de Investigaciones Sociales; Consejo Mexicano de Ciencias Sociales; Unidad Azcapotzalco, 1994. 287 p.: bibl., ill.

Assesses recent development of social sciences in Mexico, training of social scientists, and university admissions by discipline and region. Articles on current debates regarding the appropriateness of methods used to measure quality of research and publications are of particular interest. Also includes valuable discussions of the social impact and significance of social science research, and of public policy affecting this field.

4662 Reygadas, Luis; Gabriel Borunda; and Víctor Quintana. Familia y trabajo en Chihuahua: estrategias de inserción laboral de las familias rurales y urbanas del estado de Chihuahua. Ciudad Juárez, Mexico: Univ. Autónoma de Ciudad Juárez, 1994. 139 p.: bibl. (Estudios regionales; 9)

Analyzes labor force incorporation strategies which families used in response to State restructuring efforts based on interviews of 33 rural and 18 urban families. Strategies include increasing number of working members and heterogeneity of occupations and redistributing family roles. Presents policy recommendations that the State, private sector, and nongovernmental organizations could adopt to support families with scarce resources.

4663 Seminario Permanente de Estudios Chicanos y de Fronteras. Las fronteras nacionales en el umbral de dos siglos. Recopilación de Juan Manuel Sandoval Palacios. México: Instituto Nacional de Antropología e Historia, 1993. 420 p.: bibl. (Serie Antropología social. Col. científica; 267)

Presents papers from 1991 interna-

tional forum in Mexico City. Pt. 1 includes ten articles on border readjustments implemented by new international order, emphasizing NAFTA. Also examines recent border realignments in Europe and meaning of borders in Latin America. Pt. 2 concerns various aspects of Mexican migration (11 articles). Pt. 3 covers a variety of topics under the general title of migrants and refugee human rights in US and Mexico (22 articles). Last section includes studies of acculturation and transculturation along Mexico's northern and southern borders.

4664 Simbiosis de culturas: los inmigrantes y su cultura en México. Recopilación de Guillermo Bonfil Batalla. México: Consejo Nacional para la Cultura y las Artes; Fondo de Cultura Económica, 1993. 572 p.: bibl. (Sección de obras de historia)

Examines influential cultural contributions of immigrant groups in Mexico. Emphasizes medieval traditions, Islamic and African influences, contemporary Japanese values imported through trade, intellectual interest in cultural components and religions from India, cultural elements from the Middle East and Europe, and the ever-present US culture.

4665 Simposio Población y Sociedad, 2nd, México?, 1992. Población y sociedad. Coordinación de Emma Liliana Navarrete y Marta G. Vera Bolaños. México: El Colegio Mexiquense; COESPO, 1994. 442 p.: bibl., ill., maps.

Collection of 14 articles from second Simposio Población y Sociedad (1992) includes topics ranging from demographic studies on mortality, fertility, migration, urbanization, and labor force to broad issues such as midwives' training, women's participation in agricultural labor, access to education, and vocational training. All contributions refer to Mexico, with the exception of one chapter on mortality trends in Cuba.

4666 Sociedad, economía y cultura alimentaria. Recopilación de Shoko Doode Matsumoto y Emma Paulina Pérez López. Hermosillo, Mexico: Centro de Investigación en Alimentación y Desarrollo; México: Centro de Investigaciones y Estudios Superiores en Antropología Social, 1994. 452 p.: bibl., ill.

Multidisciplinary collection consists of 20 articles divided into seven sections. Themes include impact of internacionalization of agriculture on subsistence; national food policies; case studies in Sonora; relationship between food, nutrition, and health; historical analyses of food; culture and food; and an evaluation of Plan Sierra, an attempt at eco-development in the Dominican Republic.

4667 Las sociedades rurales hoy. Recopilación de Jorge Zepeda Patterson. Zamora, Mexico: Colegio de Michoacán; México: CONACYT, 1988. 552 p.: bibl., ill., maps.

Contains 34 contributions by many distinguished social scientists including Barkin, A. Bartra, Paré, Warman, Oswald, Esteva, Gordillo, and De la Peña. Papers were presented at a 1987 interdisciplinary conference in Zamora (Guanajuato), and are grouped in six categories: rural society towards the end of the century, rural policies, survival alternatives, organization of producers, old and new rural actors, and the future of rural Mexico.

4668 La sociología contemporánea en México: perspectivas disciplinarias y nuevos desafíos. Coordinación de Juan Felipe Leal *et al.* México: Facultad de Ciencias Políticas y Sociales, Dirección General de Asuntos del Personal Académico, Univ. Nacional Autónoma de México, 1994. 339 p.: bibl.

Indispensable for understanding theoretical influences, paradigm shifts, and contributions of Mexican sociologists to the discipline. Explains orientation and content of Mexican journals of sociology. Last six articles discuss crisis of the discipline in Latin America and tendencies and theoretical approaches of Latin American sociology. Of interest to students of sociology of knowledge.

4669 Sotelo Valencia, Adrián. México, dependencia y modernización. México: Ediciones El Caballito, 1993. 148 p.: bibl.

Engaging essay focuses on hypothesis that capitalist industrial conversion and technological modernization have driven Latin American crisis and promoted a new pattern of capitalist reproduction specializing in export production. Explains that development of this pattern depends on restructuring work force to maximize flexibility. Includes analysis of government, union, and business conversion projects, and of efforts to restructure work force. Emphasizes need for alternatives to neoliberalism.

4670 Stern, Claudio. La desigualdad socioeconómica en México: una revisión de las tendencias, 1895–1992. (*Estud. Sociol. / México,* 12:35, mayo/agosto 1994, p. 421–434, bibl., graphs, table)

Presents changes in social class, employment, and income distribution throughout the century using various sources (censuses, national household income and expenditures surveys, and secondary sources). Conclusions suggest that while from 1963–84 the middle class experienced notable income growth and improved income distribution, income distribution in the early 1990s eroded middle class gains.

4671 Szasz Pianta, Ivonne. Migración temporal en Malinalco: la agricultura de subsistencia en tiempos de crisis. México: El Colegio de México; Toluca, Mexico: El Colegio Mexiquense, 1993. 199 p.: bibl.

Comparative study of two villages in the state of Mexico evaluates relationship between temporary migration, conditions of labor market incorporation, and family demographic structure to determine conditions under which temporary migration emerges as strategy for subsistence. Analyzes role of temporary migration in reinforcing or altering reproduction of subsistence-oriented families. Based on a random sample of 140 households and additional in-depth interviews.

4672 Tabasco: realidad y perspectivas. v. 1–3. México: Gobierno del Estado de Tabasco; M.A. Porrúa, 1993. 3 v.: bibl., ill., maps.

Presents multidisciplinary collection of 126 articles divided into three broad sections: population and culture, economy and development, and politics and law. Specific topics include health and social welfare, development and the environment, the international context of economic relations, State reforms, and political organizations.

4673 La tarea de gobernar: gobiernos locales y demandas ciudadanas. Coordinación de Alicia Ziccardi. México: Instituto de Investigaciones Sociales, UNAM; M.A. Porrúa, 1995. 402 p.: bibl., ill. (Las Ciencias sociales)

Valuable study of municipal governments of Saltillo, León, Ciudad Juárez, Pátzcuaro, Durango, Mazatlán, Torreón, Toluca, and municipal delegation of Miguel Hidalgo in the Distrito Federal reports that four cities were governed by Partido Revolucionario Institucional (PRI), three by Partido Acción Nacional (PAN), and two by Partido de la Revolución Democrática (PRD) and Partido del Trabajo (PT). Essential for understanding current political transformation in Mexico and potential viability of decentralization.

4674 Trabajo, poder y sexualidad. Coordinación de Orlandina de Oliveira. México: El Colegio de México, 1989. 403 p.: bibl.

Collection of 13 works is product of a three-year workshop on condition of women. Focuses on themes related to work, family and reproduction, women's political participation, and identity and sexuality. Cortina's essay about women's role in a regional teachers' union is of particular interest.

4675 Vázquez, Lourdes Celina. Identidad, cultura y religión en el sur de Jalisco. Zapopan, Mexico: Colegio de Jalisco, 1993. 172 p.: bibl., ill.

Exploratory analysis of family organization, collective identity, and religious culture in diocese of Ciudad Guzmán contends that a resurgence of cultural manifestations and popular religion, influenced by the Catholic Church, has taken place in the region despite economic and political disarticulation. Based on 207 questionnaires administered in 23 towns.

4676 Vázquez Palacios, Felipe. Protestantismo en Xalapa. Jalapa, Mexico: Comisión Estatal Conmemorativa del V Centenario del Encuentro de Dos Mundos, Gobierno del Estado de Veracruz, 1991. 176 p.: bibl. (Col. V centenario; 2)

Pt. 1 traces historical roots and development of Protestantism in Jalapa. Survey of religious groups provides number of churches and temples and membership size. Followers are classified as convert, sinner, repentant, or fallen. In-depth interviews illustrate differences by type in performance of daily routines at home and at work.

4677 Velázquez Gutiérrez, Margarita. Políticas sociales, transformación agraria y participación de las mujeres en el campo: 1920–1988. Cuernavaca, Mexico: Univ. Nacional Autónoma de México, Centro Regional de Investigaciones Multidisciplinarias, 1992. 272 p.: bibl.

Historical overview describes rural and indigenous women's socioeconomic roles in agrarian sector during four distinct periods: consolidation of agrarian structure (1920–40), growth of agricultural production (1940–65), beginning of crisis (1965–82), and deepening of crisis (1982–88). Explains how agrarian and social policies have affected women's participation and marginalization. Attributes failure of development policies in part to lack of reflection on women's economic and social roles in agriculture.

4678 Villarreal, René. Liberalismo social y reforma del Estado: México en la era del capitalismo posmoderno. México: Nacional Financiera; Fondo de Cultura Económica, 1993. 395 p.: bibl., ill. (Nueva cultura económica)

Builds ideal model of social liberalism by removing excesses of socialism and laissez-faire capitalism, and merging their market and social aspects. Theory combines Locke's idea of limitations of power with principles from Keynesian economics. Attempts to demonstrate that social liberalism is the basis of Presidents De la Madrid and Salinas de Gortari's modernization policies.

4679 La voluntad de ser: mujeres en los noventa. Recopilación de María Luisa Tarrés. México: Programa Interdisciplinario de Estudios de la Mujer, El Colegio de México, 1992. 312 p.: bibl.

Worthwhile collection addresses women's integration into Mexican society and role in national modernization process. The 12 works are divided into three sections examining identity, work, and politics. Of particular interest are Brígida García and Orlandina de Oliveira's profile of women's labor market participation and Alejandra Massolo's essay on women and urban policy.

4680 Welti Chanes, Carlos. La fecundidad en México. Aguascalientes, Mexico: Instituto Nacional de Estadística, Geografía e Informática; México: Instituto de Investigaciones Sociales de la Univ. Nacional Autónoma de México, 1994. 251 p.: bibl., ill., index.

Quantitative technical study based on 1990 population census details fertility rates by age group, level of education, and state. Cross-tabulates fertility by rural-urban residency and ethnicity. Findings show significant fertility decline since 1986 national study.

Wiegand, Bruce. Petty smuggling as "social justice": research findings from the Belize-Mexico border. See item **4942.**

4681 Y ante todo la población rural persiste: efectos de la modernización económica en el campo mexicano. Recopilación de Jesús Arroyo Alejandre. Guadalajara, Mexico: Univ. de Guadalajara, Centro Universitario de Ciencias Económico Administrativas, 1995. 255 p.: bibl., ill.

Nine essays explore agricultural modernization strategies and their impact in Nayarit, Sonora, Jalisco, Michoacán, Baja California, and state of Mexico. Examines population movements, labor force transformation, environmental effects, economic outcomes, crop and technology changes, effects on poverty, and health consequences. Several contributions discuss NAFTA's role.

4682 Zabludovsky, Gina. Sociología y política, el debate clásico y contemporáneo. México: Facultad de Ciencias Políticas y Sociales de la UNAM; Grupo Editorial M.A. Porrúa, 1995. 302 p.: bibl. (Las Ciencias sociales)

Noteworthy contribution reflects on central problems of contemporary and classical theory and attempts to bridge European/US and Mexican thought. Addresses democracy and implications of globalization on social theory. Includes an imaginary dialogue between De Tocqueville and Lorenzo de Za-

vala, an analysis of challenges to the discipline using Gidden's "radicalized modernity" concept, and a diagnostic of sociology in Mexico.

4683 Zapata Martelo, Emma. Modernization, adjustment, and peasant production: a gender analysis. (*Lat. Am. Perspect.*, 23:1, Winter 1996, p. 118–130, bibl.)

Examines effects of Mexican agrarian policy on members of peasant family units. Also investigates how gender inequality causes effects to vary in relation to the role each member plays in the division of labor, control over productive resources, income, and access to State services. Explores cultural and intrafamilial impacts on these processes. For anthropologist's comment, see item **784.** [B. Aguirre-López]

4684 Zúñiga, Víctor. Monterrey: tres estudios urbanos. Monterrey, Mexico: Fondo Editorial Nuevo León, 1993. 208 p.: bibl., ill.

First study is a favorable evaluation of Fomento Metropolitano de Monterrey (FOMERREY), a municipal housing agency. Examines shifts in housing demand that took place since agency's creation in 1976, and quality of life in neighborhoods developed by agency. Second essay analyzes usage of open spaces in Ciudad Guadalupe, a dormitory town near Monterrey. Final chapter assesses preferences for urban dwelling among residents of eight middle-class neighborhoods.

CENTRAL AMERICA

TIMOTHY P. WICKHAM-CROWLEY, *Associate Professor of Sociology, Georgetown University*

THE RECENT LITERATURE in Central American sociology continues to blossom and diversify, even as some areas remain largely ignored. The decline of organized, civil war/revolutionary violence by the mid-1990s has unsurprisingly turned some scholars away from analyses of violence and toward examinations of "returns to normalcy." Each of these avenues toward more peaceful societies reveals its own complex costs and trade-offs, despite the welcomes given to peace processes. Sociological research that continues to concentrate on eras of violence is informed more by fine-grained, local research and is rooted less in a dependency perspective and more in political economy and/or political sociology in general. Class and ethnic inequalities, social movements, and State-oriented demands in particular have emerged as significant topics of study. These works help us to understand revolutionary processes and conflicts (before and after the transfer of power), as well as the dynamics of other social movements. Detailed work on upper-class family networks continues, following in the footsteps of Samuel Stone's *Heritage of the conquistadors*. Barrington Moore's classic study of Eurasian politics, *Social origins of dictatorship and democracy*, is still being employed critically, yet fruitfully, in several works; key here is the long-awaited study by Jeffery Paige on coffee and power during the 20th century (item **4733**).

All such macrosociological perspectives, dependency theory included, now find intellectual competition in a growing literature that is clearly sociological or historical-sociological in viewpoint, yet grows out of a text-oriented, cultural studies perspective. Various national political cultures are regarded as negotiated social creations, "contested terrains," where various subordinate or marginal groups create or are urged to create alternatives to the mainstream national culture; exemplars include David Whisnant's groundbreaking book on Nicaragua (item **4758**) and several works on Costa Rican national culture.

With regard to migration studies in this "postwar" period, increasing attention is being paid to the difficulties of returned migrants and also to migrants who may not return home even after the forces that prompted their departure have gone away. In these cases, their experiences in and impact upon their host-society-turned-new-home become central, with, of course, a focus on inter-ethnic tensions. Those studies are complemented by good research on internal migration and on migrants' lives in cities, which in turn is complemented by Portes and Lungo's new collection on urban dynamics (item **4752**).

Continuing previous patterns in research (and in activist writings), the dynamics and dangers of war, neoliberal policies at home, and changing experiences of a shifting global economy are routinely analyzed from the perspective of the society as a whole and across class and ethnic structures, in urban or agrarian settings. Many other studies examine how those processes differentially (and often for the worse) affect women's lives in particular. More and better studies thus focus on women's access to (*maquila*) jobs, to equal wages, to land, to incomes via the informal economy, and so forth. More generally, the literature on women's experiences continues to expand apace, to intersect with virtually all other topics of scholarly interest, and to move into new terrain, like a careful study of midwifery in El Salvador (item **4754**). Bibliographical guides and country-specific collections appear intermittently to help scholars sort through the growing mass of studies on women, even as newer and/or deeper studies focus on issues like male violence against women, especially in households (item **4741**). In the twin contexts of home and school, children are emerging as a new topic of research in works on their socialization, their varied experiences (including those of paid work or of war), and their own perceptions of society itself, all the topics of recent books. Yet the classic, focal triad of mother/father/child and their social interrelations are mostly ignored in recent writing. Perhaps this lacuna reflects some mix of the historical weakness of family sociology in Latin American studies, also the specifically feminist turn in much household research, and finally the sheer empirics of widespread father-absent households. Despite one good recent study of juvenile delinquency in Honduras (item **4711**) and Wiegand's work on the Belizean black market (item **4759**), the study of deviance, crime and criminology, so widely and deeply developed in North American sociology, still has very little counterpart literature within Central America. While one might include in this category the ample literature on terror and corruption, those studies tend to have a governmental rather than "street-crime" focus.

Core values and beliefs of the ordinary people of Central America still loom large. The literature on the increasingly competitive "religious economy" (to use North American sociologist Rodney Stark's term) of Central America continues to move away from simplistic views of the spread of evangelical Protestants and Protestantism as both conservative and imperialistic, for the good reason that careful evaluation suggests that their growing popularity owes quite little to such impulses. Research-based data and information, both qualitative and quantitative, enrich studies of evangelical belief and the evangelicals themselves. Importantly, much new work on the Catholic Church also seems to have been generated by the new religious dynamic of the region, and many studies, especially the statistical ones, systematically juxtapose profiles and responses of Catholics and evangelicals, including subgroups of each. Rarely do we find very large differences on core issues. The recent focus on giving voice to the evangelicals themselves, rather than imputing to them certain motives and attitudes, had its earlier yet still growing counterpart in many studies which recount the lives, words, and autobiographies of non-famous people. The selections that follow thus include, for example, letters from migrants in the United States to loved ones back home, the life-story of a Guatemalan Indian, and the voices of many and varied women.

4685 Abaunza, Humberto; Irela Solórzano; and Raquel Fernández. Una causa para rebeldes: identidad y condición juvenil en Nicaragua. Managua: Puntos de Encuentro, 1995. 219 p.: bibl., ill. (Puntos en agenda; 2)

In the early 1990s authors interviewed 295 girls and boys, ranging from infancy to near-adulthood, and from a wide range of backgrounds and regions, to try to get a "kid-centric" view of life. Their voices are blended into the largely descriptive, but still analytical text, with chapters devoted to self-identity, generations, concepts of sex and gender, family, sexuality and sex education, friends, couples, school, youth groups, work, politics, and their dreams for the future.

4686 El acceso de la mujer a la tierra en Costa Rica. 1. ed. San José, Costa Rica: Fundación Arias para la Paz y el Progreso Humano, 1992. 147 p.: bibl.

One of a series of publications devoted to analyzing land availability for women in Central America focuses on sexual discrimination, economic handicaps, participation in agrarian reform programs, and the impact of new legislation.

4687 El acceso de la mujer a la tierra en Guatemala. Coordinación de Jorge Escoto et al. Colaboración de Edgar Gutiérrez y Marta Gutiérrez. Coordinación institucional de Carmen Lucía Pellecer. San José: Fundación Arias para la Paz y el Progreso Humano: Agrupación de Mujeres Tierra Viva, 1993. 215 p.: bibl., ill.

One of a series of "investigation-action" studies drawing on existing work and community-based interviews with women. Parallel, but not identically-structured, volumes have appeared for Costa Rica, El Salvador, Honduras, and Nicaragua. The excellent Guatemala volume sets out the rural context for women's lives and focuses on women's access to land (crucial to the study of rural class relations). Also discusses women in rural politics and agrarian movements, and recommends policy changes.

4688 Aguilar Revelo, Lorena et al. ¿Feminismo en Costa Rica?: testimonios, reflexiones, ensayos. San José: Editorial Mujeres, 1995. 231 p.: bibl., ill. (Col. Ensayo)

Twelve feminist contributors, many who head organizations (governmental or not), address a wide range of issues with different expository aims. Sociologically most interesting are a survey-based analysis of Afro-Costa Rican women and an anthropologist's report on indigenous women. The personal testimonials also can be used as a selective data source on women's experiences in Costa Rica.

**4689 Alternativas campesinas: moderniza-
ción en el agro y movimiento campesino en Centroamérica.** Coordinación de
Klaus-Dieter Tangermann y Ivana Ríos
Valdés. Managua: Latino Editores; CRIES,
1994. 320 p.: bibl., ill.

Rich collection of well-researched essays on economies and peasant movements.
The topical chapters are filled with comparative data, usually from five or six of the Central American nations, and cover issues like
democracy, small producers, access to land,
marketing, credit, etc. The book also contains
careful country studies of national peasant
movements in Costa Rica, Panama, Honduras, and El Salvador, and is largely policy-
oriented, while still scholarly in style and
presentation.

4690 Bailey, Adrian J. and **Joshua G. Hane.**
Population in motion: Salvadorean refugees and circulation migration. (*Bull. Lat.
Am. Res.,* 14:2, May 1995, p. 171–200, appendices, bibl., tables)

Unusual study in its argument that
neither permanent nor departure-and-return
migration is likely to be the "final" destination for Salvadoran (refugee-?) migrants of the
1980s and beyond. Authors argue that the impulses for migration cannot be narrowly categorized as political or economic, but are typically a mixture of both; make the case that
international remittances are a clear sign of a
transnational community of Salvador-identi-
fied people; provide valuable data on the
traits of emigrants and on the sheer numbers
of returning migrants; and finally argue that
local ostracism back home (i.e., they are sus-
pected of being unpatriotic) and self-selection
for migration itself (especially personality attributes) will create a population of imperma-
nently rooted Salvadorans who will shuttle
back and forth for the foreseeable future.

4691 Bastos, Santiago and **Manuela Camus.**
Sombras de una batalla: los desplaza-
dos por la violencia en Ciudad de Guatemala.
Guatemala: FLACSO, 1994. 170 p.: bibl., ill.

This study of indigenous peoples of
Guatemala, all displaced by violence to Guatemala City, puts its subjects' voices front
and center. Several dozen respondents, originally from Izabal and El Quiché departments,
discuss a wide variety of topics, from the conditions behind their flights to their deep religiosity. Statistical data allow us to see their

social profiles and to contrast them with another indigenous group living in the capital
city by choice.

**4692 Between the lines: letters between
undocumented Mexican and Central
American immigrants and their families and
friends.** Translated, edited, and with an introduction by Larry Siems. Preface by Jimmy
Santiago Baca. Hopewell, NJ: Ecco Press,
1992. 335 p.

These 1990–92 letters are a rich trea-
sure worthy of use by anthropologists, sociologists, political scientists, and historians;
the usual methodological objections about a
small, selective, and literate sample should be
bracketed here. Separate sections focus on the
US arrival, life back home, love letters, and
sections devoted to a few specific groups. All
letters appear in Spanish with facing-page English translations.

4693 Binford, Leigh. The El Mozote massacre: anthropology and human rights.
Tucson: Univ. of Arizona Press, 1996. 282 p.:
bibl., ill., index, maps. (Hegemony and
experience)

Through fieldwork among the surprisingly numerous survivors, the author reconstructs the recent social structure, culture,
and history of the northeastern Salvadoran
village of Segundo Montes before, during,
and after the infamous massacre. She tries to
place anthropology squarely into political issues, but also focuses on the people's oral testimonies more than on her own ethnography,
especially resisting the easy/total categorization of the survivors as victims. For the ethnologist's comment see item **702.**

4694 Blumburg, Rae Lesser *et al.* Women's
work, wealth, and family survival
strategy: the impact of Guatemala's ALCOSA
agribusiness project. (*in* Women, the family,
and policy: a global perspective. Edited by Esther Ngan-ling Chow and Catherine White
Berheide. Albany: State Univ. of New York
Press, 1994, p. 117–141, bibl., tables)

Study uses a 1985 data set on female
workers from a foreign subsidiary, ALCOSA,
in addition to earlier studies. Relates them to
a "women-in-development" theoretical approach, which criticizes the assumption that
households simply respond in mechanical
ways to macroeconomic and other structural
forces. The central finding: women who con-

trolled independent sources of income—not simply any economic labors—exerted greater leverage than women without such resources, both in domestic decision-making and in decisions about births and family size.

4695 Brett, Edward T. The impact of religion in Central America: a bibliographical essay. (*Americas/Francisc.*, 49:3, Jan. 1993, p. 297–341, bibl.)

Provides listings and commentary on both the Catholic Church and Protestant upswings, and comprises both historical and contemporary (to the early 90s) studies. Coverage and extensive listings for Guatemala, El Salvador, and Nicaragua (where the pre-1970 period is not slighted), with fewer materials for Costa Rica and fewer yet for Honduras. Covers Spanish- and English-language publications, the latter including a number of dissertations and theses. Authors from many different disciplines.

4696 Cabrera Arias, Magela. Crisis urbana y movimientos sociales: Panamá 1970–1992. Panamá: Impr. Universitaria, 1993. 125 p.: bibl., ill., maps.

The span of this empirically focused work is actually wider than the title suggests, extending its analyses back to the 1920s. Throughout, the changing role of the State in economic life, specifically with respect to the housing sector, is related to popular needs, demands, and movements. Both empirical and analytical, the study's data range from the content of national laws to the popular collective actions taken in various districts of Panama City.

4697 Casaús, Marta Elena. La pervivencia de las redes familiares en la configuración de la elite de poder centroamericana: el caso de la familia Díaz Durán. (*Anu. Estud. Centroam.*, 20:2, 1994, p. 41–69, tables)

Study contributes a more elaborated theory and well-researched data on yet one more of the powerful family lineages and networks that scholars have been studying in Central America, the Díaz Durán family (part of a larger project the author is pursuing). Family networks emerge and are maintained via marriage, business, social closeness, formal associations, and, most originally, the formation of their own "organic intellectuals". The latter are especially relevant in this case because of the key intellectual/dip-lomatic roles the family has played in Guatemalan history, most notably in the democratic opening of the 1980s.

4698 Chávez Borjas, Manuel. Cómo subsisten los campesinos: estrategia reproductiva de las familias campesinas, bajo la persistencia de la economía de subsistencia en el occidente de Honduras. Tegucigalpa: Editorial Guaymuras, 1992. 141 p.: bibl., ill. (Col. Códices)

Focuses on subsistence farmers in western Honduras. Examines familial, religious, and economic lives of users of *ejidal* (communal) land, created in the economic interstices left by capitalistic agriculture. Carefully studies the *cofradías*, including some transcribed rites, arguing that the religious brotherhoods play a critical community-preserving role.

4699 Las clases sociales en Panamá: grupos humanos, clases medias, elites y oligarquía. Recopilación de Marco A. Gandásegui *et al.* Panamá: CELA, 1993. 182 p.: bibl.

Somewhat misleadingly titled volume really collects four essays published between 1949–75 on the middle classes, human groups, and on nation-and-oligarchy. The essays range in flavor from straightforwardly Marxist to idiosyncratic sociology. Informative, particularly the lead editor's own contribution on the concentration of economic power during the 1960s.

4700 The Costa Rican women's movement: a reader. Edited by Ilse Abshagen Leitinger. Pittsburgh, Pa.: Univ. of Pittsburgh Press, 1997. 385 p.: bibl., ill., map. (Pitt Latin American series)

Thirty-four short contributions make this akin to a reference work, albeit one varying greatly in flavor, topic, and scholarliness, i.e., from group self-promotion to politico-legal endorsements to scholarly pieces. Among the scholarly topics: colonial women, 19th-century women, feminist organizational theorizing, popular music, caesarean births, and women at the Univ. de Costa Rica (where they are one-third of faculty). Almost all social-feminist topics are touched on, save perhaps language; sexuality, violence, disability, class/race/gender, art and artists, and more.

4701 Cuevas Molina, Rafael. Traspatio florecido: tendencias de la dinámica de la cultura en Centroamérica, 1979–1990. Heredia, Costa Rica: EUNA, 1993. 176 p.: bibl. (Col. Cubujuquí)

Five nations are viewed through a theoretical lens combining Gramscian and cultural-studies views with more traditional Marxism, with only Sandinista culture being praised. While a broad, anthropological definition of culture is advanced, elite-produced and -distributed arts and letters and the mass media are the foci here. A search for changes in "revolutionary" cultures (e.g., the Christian Base Communities) coexists uneasily with dismissals of the also-new cultures of evangelical Christians. Many and varied observations pepper the analysis, e.g., the feminization of Costa Rican literary culture.

4702 Dary, Claudia. Entre el hogar y la vega: estudio sobre la participación femenina en la agricultura de El Progreso. Guatemala: FLACSO, 1994. 174 p.: bibl., maps.

Close examination of several hamlets of Guatemala, where a long dry spell and consequent, disproportionate male departures led to fundamental shifts in gender roles in agriculture, with women involved in a wide array of activities. Uses field notes, survey and official data, and interviews with women; these also detail artisanal activities and credit (-seeking) histories, and show new opportunities alongside constraints on women's actions, both old and new.

4703 De Vries, Peter. Unruly clients in the Atlantic zone of Costa Rica: a study of how bureaucrats try and fail to transform gatekeepers, communists and preachers into ideal beneficiaries. Amsterdam: CEDLA, 1997. 250 p.: bibl., ill., maps. (Latin America Studies; 78)

Examines relations between Costa Rican peasants and the bureaucracy. Highly critical of the discourse of development, mainly because of the power it confers on bureaucratic actors determined to change to lives of people through administrative means. Examines what "development" means to ordinary people, and how "development" is both discursively and organizationally constructed as an idea suffusing the hopes of people searching for a better life. [R. Hoefte]

4704 Diskin, Martin. Distilled conclusions: the disappearance of the agrarian question in El Salvador. (*LARR*, 31:2, 1996, p. 111–126, bibl., tables)

See item **4747.**

4705 Edelman, Marc and **Mitchell A. Seligson.** La desigualdad en la tenencia de la tierra: una comparación de los datos de los censos y de los registros de propiedad en el sur de Costa Rica en el siglo XX. (*Anu. Estud. Centroam.*, 20:1, 1994, p. 65–113, bibl., graph, maps, tables)

Very careful juxtaposition of land tenure data for the canton of Coto Brus, Costa Rica drawn from two different sources, agrarian censuses and land-registry data, finds neither data-set wholly satisfactory. Like many historians, authors suggest that biased data will be generated when the State tries, for purposes probably not shared with its citizenry, to collect such information from them. Since many studies of land concentration (e.g., gini indexes) and peasant grievances (perhaps revolutionary?) in Central America routinely draw on agrarian census data, this study undermines the empirical footings on which such arguments are constructed. For related information see item **4747.**

4706 El Salvador a fin de siglo. Recopilación de Rafael Guido Béjar y Stefan Roggenbuck. San Salvador: Fundación Konrad Adenauer, 1995. 325 p.: bibl.

Eight essays focusing primarily on political economy and demography. Most interesting are Molina on the "exhaustion" of yet another externally "imposed" economic model (i.e., neoliberalism), with a call for a truly integrated, national model of development; Montoya's solid description of agriculture; and the longest piece, Huezo's manifesto on cultural decadence and renovation.

El Salvador hacia el año 2000: una plataforma de política económica y social de consenso. See item **1783.**

4707 Engle, Patrice L. Father's money, mother's money, and parental commitment: Guatemala and Nicaragua. (*in* EnGENDERing wealth and well-being: empowerment for global change. Boulder, Colo.: Westview Press, 1995, p. 155–179, tables)

Late 1980s survey of just under 100 poor households, each in or near the two capital cities, to determine whether men and women allocate their earnings differently within the household, especially with respect to indirect anthropometric measures of children's nutrition. Controlling for the family's overall wealth, mothers' outside-work status had a clearly positive effect on Nicaraguan children, and the percent of family income she earned had a positive effect in Guatemala. Fathers' incomes also correlated positively with well-being, more so with older, legally married, at-home, employed fathers. The theoretical setting and cross-national comparisons round out the analysis.

4708 Enríquez, Laura J. Agrarian reform and class consciousness in Nicaragua. Gainesville: Univ. Press of Florida, 1997. 214 p.: bibl., index, maps.

Close study of the changing political responses of two peasant populations whose neighboring regions near the Pacific coast experienced different impacts from the Sandinista agrarian reforms. Shows the irony of some reform-beneficiaries turning against their benefactor-regime, a more likely event when productive relations become privatized. Argues, contra Huntington, that demobilization of various social groups will work against the achievement of development goals.

4709 Everingham, Mark. Revolution and the multiclass coalition in Nicaragua. Pittsburgh, Pa.: Univ. of Pittsburgh Press, 1996. 234 p.: bibl., index. (Pitt Latin American series)

Deepens and qualifies recent theories stressing the special vulnerabilities of neopatrimonial dictatorships to revolutionary overthrows. An intensive analysis of Nicaraguan social actors and movements, crucial events, and economic processes is supplemented by contrasts with other Latin American cases, especially El Salvador. Far more depth, nuance, and sense of missed historical possibilities than in the usual writings on the topic.

4710 Figueroa, Faizury. El sida en Honduras. Tegucigalpa: CEDOH, 1993. 86 p.: bibl., ill., map.

Solid study on the growth of risk groups and on the sexual behaviors associated with AIDS; the stigmatizing quality of the sickness; and the institutional responses by public health and other officials in Honduras, which harbors three-fifths of all Central American AIDS cases. Unlike the US pattern, cases are fully one-third female. Skilled male laborers are also hard hit, as are ages 20–40, and heterosexuals of both sexes (c. 70 percent of all cases), the last generally not drug-related in origin.

4711 Flores Varela, Hiram and **María del Carmen Sauceda Guerra.** Familia y delincuencia juvenil en Honduras. San Pedro Sula, Honduras: Central Editorial, 1994. 100 p.: bibl., ill.

Two psychiatrists closely studied 196 lower-class juvenile delinquents (and their families) whose court cases were from 1979–80. The study's lack of randomness is a partial flaw. The typical delinquents, three-fourths males, are products of urban life, not of the process or rural uprooting; come from disintegrated families (neither two-parent nor extended), where parents' mental afflictions and low IQ were common, the discipline of children chaotic, and affection largely absent. Offenses ranged widely, including some striking ones, e.g., males who committed sexual violations victimized younger boys more often than girls.

4712 Freyermuth Enciso, Graciela and **Nancy Godfrey.** Refugiados guatemaltecos en México: la vida en un continuo estado de emergencia. México: Centro de Investigaciones y Estudios Superiores en Antropología Social; Tuxtla Gutiérrez, Mexico: Instituto Chiapaneco de Cultura, 1993. 112 p.: bibl., ill., maps.

Close, careful study of the health conditions Guatemalan refugees first faced in Chiapas and in the Yucatán, after fleeing "the first emergency": poverty and repression. Later emergencies arose from refugees seeking asylum and then from being transferred to Campeche and Quintana Roo. Those events at times complicate their core problems, including very high (if later falling) rates of illness and death.

4713 Gindling, T.H. ¿Por que las mujeres ganan menos que los hombres en Costa Rica? (*Cienc. Econ./San José,* 13:1/2, enero/dic. 1993, p. 3–31, bibl., tables)

Econometric analysis of a question examined in many world nations. The 1989 survey data show a scant three and a half percent salary-edge for Costa Rican men, far less than commonly found elsewhere. Women actually have more education on average than men, work in better-paid sectors of the economy, and thus, should have higher pay. Concludes, less surprisingly, that the deficit occurs because, other factors being equal, women suffer "discrimination . . . in the labor market."

4714 Goldenberg, Olga and **Víctor H. Acuña Ortega.** Género en la informalidad: historias laborales centroamericanas. San José: FLACSO, 1994. 235 p.: bibl.

Offers series of "testimonials" from five of the six countries of Spanish Central America (not El Salvador). Additionally, provides the theoretical, historical, and methodological background for the testimonials that follow, and attempts to analyze narratives in a theoretically nuanced way, focusing on the subtle and not-so-subtle links between gender identity, household relations, and work experiences in the informal sector.

4715 González, Simeón. Panamá, 1968– 1990: ensayos de sociología política. Panamá: Univ. de Panamá, 1994. 319 p. bibl.

Readers can embrace, contend with, or read around the author's brief for socialism and the various Marxist perspectives he brings to bear on the Panamanian economy, class structure, and State patterns. Analysis covers more than the promised two decades and is rich with data and theory on this understudied nation. Focus on the rise, structural patterns, and fall of "torrijismo," i.e., the period of rule by Omar Torrijos.

4716 González O., Alfonso. Costa Rica, el discurso de la patria: estructuras simbólicas del poder. San José: Editorial de la Univ. de Costa Rica, 1994. 215 p.: bibl.

Theoretically varied content analysis of national newspaper stoics (1950–86) sees Costa Rican national political culture as centered on discourses of patria, independence, liberty, democracy, and peace, perspectives deemed "exhausted" compared to Marxian viewpoints. Analysis includes a questionable attempt to relate the grammatical gender of Spanish terms to social gender. Also offers a conceptualization of the "psychogenesis" of the "collective imagination." No consideration is given to the measurement/theory problems in conflating elite-created news or views with popular viewpoints.

4717 Hammond, John L. Popular education in the Salvadoran guerrilla army. (*Hum. Organ.*, 55:4, Winter 1996, p. 436–445)

Based on multiple visits, author looks at the FMLN's educational project, focusing on the aims, needs, organization, and agendas of the revolutionaries-turned-educators. Does not ignore the tensions and ambivalences, especially among some recruits who rejected

formal political work and indoctrination. Argues that educational efforts were a crucial FMLN morale builder. For the ethnologist's comment see item **734.**

4718 Hawley, Susan. Protestantism and indigenous mobilisation: the Moravian church among the Miskitu Indians of Nicaragua. (*J. Lat. Am. Stud.*, 29:1, Feb. 1997, p. 111–129)

During the mid-1980s, the Atlantic-coast Miskitus became a key anti-governmental force against newly installed Sandinistas. This study examines ever more influential role of Moravian Church in mobilizing the Miskitus and defining the ideological character of their struggle against the government.

4719 Herrera, Michele. Bibliografía sobre mujer en El Salvador, 1902–1994. San Salvador: Instituto de Estudios de la Mujer Norma Virginia Guirola de Herrera, 1995. 190 p.: appendix, bibl. (Col. CEMUJER)

A valuable, if flawed asset on the topic. Listed, not annotated, sources comprise only those written in El Salvador itself (not "published," since many are theses). Four chapters are devoted to different loci of publication, especially several NGOs and universities. The remaining chapter devotes ten pages to works written by men. With an average of just five titles per page the overall volume-length is misleading. Some entries are missing key bibliographic information. Appendix grids are used to map out thematic changes over the decades.

4720 Hooks, Margaret. Guatemalan women speak. Introduction by Rigoberta Menchú. Washington: Ecumenical Program on Central America and the Caribbean, 1993. 133p.: bibl., port., map.

Interviews with more than 40 Guatemalan women in the late 1980s, all but two in Spanish (even though they were mostly ethnically indigenous). Notes that most successful interviews came when the subject herself "directed" the process. Their voices tell a series of clear "short stories" on wide array of themes, roughly grouped together under the headings of work, being Indian, family, and resistance.

4721 Houtart, François and **Geneviève Lemercinier.** La mujer urbana: visión del mundo, religión y dimensión ético-política.

Managua: Ediciones Nicarao, 1993. 114 p.: bibl.

Based on a multi-question scale, the authors posit five types of religiosity (traditional, transitional, modern-social, modern-cum-economic liberalism, and "unknown"). Interviews with 200 women of Managua (half Catholic and half Protestants [the latter of two types]) serve to place them among the five types, with comparisons made on range of attitudes and traits: class distribution, family planning and abortion, schooling, etc. Religious confessions are analyzed separately.

4722 Instituto Universitario de Opinión Pública. La religión para los salvadoreños en 1995. (ECA/San Salvador, 50:563, sept. 1995, p. 849–862, graphs, tables)

A survey of religious beliefs and traditions of 1,211 adults across the nation provides descriptive data, at times compared to 1988 results. Just under one-fourth claim no religion (an increase from 15 percent), 57 percent are Catholic (33 percent practicing), and 18 percent "evangelicals." Religious comparisons across carefully defined classes turn up results both surprising and not. Catholics cite as reasons for their faith both tradition and family upbringing; evangelicals cite other reasons. Few differences split Catholics and Evangelicals on the perceived justice of the Salvadoran social system.

4723 Jonas, Susanne. Transnational realities and anti-immigrant state policies: issues raised by the experiences of Central American immigrants and refugees in a trinational region. (in Latin America in the world-economy. Westport, Conn.: Greenwood Press, 1996, p. 117–132, bibl.)

Examines emergence of a trinational region, El Salvador/Guatemala, Mexico, and the southwestern US, conditioned partly by the world economy, and by contradictory circumstances within the US where intense economic demands for cheap labor, especially in agriculture belie anti-immigrant policies. Mexico and the US southwest are experiencing tensions over (de-)democratization in a two-tiered society of citizens living with an increasing number of noncitizens.

4724 Kutsche, Paul. Two truths about Costa Rica. (in Latin American male homosexualities. Albuquerque: Univ. of New Mexico Press, 1995, p. 111–137)

The author contrasts his own "contract" model, applied to men with (any) homosexual experience, to Jacobo Schifter's "oppression" model (see HLAS 53:5112) centered on the smaller group of self-identified, exclusively gay men. The contract model perceives a fairly sex-tolerant society, albeit one where homosexual expressions are limited by family obligations, apartment/housing shortages, and the small-town, non-anonymous ambience. The oppression model, built on analogies to class and gender oppression, finds lack of space for gays within an anti-gay society. Interesting contrasts with other Latin American nations and the US.

4725 Kutsche, Paul. Voices of migrants: rural-urban migration in Costa Rica. Gainsville: Univ. Press of Florida, 1994. 248 p.: bibl., ill., index, maps.

Verbatim or near-verbatim 1981–84 interviews with 14 Costa Ricans (ten men, four women) provide information about life histories of migrants to San José. Strong opening chapters provide the context for migration and the interview-years. Conclusion relates their narratives to Costa Rican "exceptionalism" and other value-patterns.

4726 Lara Martínez, Carlos Benjamin. Salvadoreños en Calgary: el proceso de configuración de un nuevo grupo étnico. San Salvador: Concultura, 1994. 135 p.: bibl.

Author marshals a variety of sociological and anthropological theories, four months of participant-observation notes, and other types of data to understand a "new ethnic group" being born among the roughly 300 Salvadorans who moved to Calgary since the mid-1980s. Their "pilgrimage" pushes them toward the Canadian values of success, individualism, materialism, and freedom (and away from their opposites), despite contrarian trends: suspicion of Canadian ways (e.g., footloose young people) and the preservation of distinctive group identities via compadrazgo, friendships, and soccer teams.

4727 Low, Setha M. Spatializing culture: the social production and social construction of public space in Costa Rica. (Am. Ethnol., 23:4, Nov. 1996, p. 861–879, bibl., photos)

Based on field-trips and primary research, author brings an anthropological approach to the study of the built environment.

Contrasts public use of older Parque Central, historically an elite strolling ground transformed into a place for pensioners and informal economic activities, and the newer Plaza Central. The latter reveals a greater variety of users, but also generates among some a sense of fear. For ethnologist's comment see item 748.

4728 Macdonald, Mandy and **Mike Gatehouse.** In the mountains of Morazán: portrait of a returned refugee community in El Salvador. London: Latin American Bureau; New York: Monthly Review Press, 1995. 219 p.: ill., index, maps.

During the 1989 uprising, 8,000 refugees began their return to an FMLN zone of influence at Ciudad Segunda Montes, a process soon followed by the authors' two years of research visits. Topical chapters provide short vignettes on the issues a rebuilding community faces in the context of a concluding civil war. Rich in voices and descriptions (alongside some boosterism), thin in social theorizing (understandable, given the authors' aims).

4729 Medina, Laurie Kroshus. Development policies and identity politics: class and collectivity in Belize. (*Am. Ethnol.*, 24:1, Feb. 1997, p. 148–169, bibl.)

Uses a Marxian-cum-cultural-studies view of the various citrus-industry social classes to bring the idea of identity-politics and its viewpoint/discourses to the analysis of class relations. The success of small growers in increasing their powers and coherence (unlike large growers) is contrasted with the spatial/economic divisions that, along with ethnic cleavages, have segmented the citrus industry's wage-workers. Rich economic detail plus additional political background. For the ethnologist's comment see item 750.

4730 Menjívar, Cecilia. Salvadorian migration to the United States in the 1980s: what can we learn about it and from it? (*Int. Migr.*, 32:3, 1994, p. 371–401, bibl.)

Uses survey data, interviews, and ethnographic fieldwork in combination with migration theory to examine economic versus political motivations for migration; to discuss the migrants' political and economic reception in the US; and to study the role and importance of social networks in the resettlement process. In the process of examining these issues, the author questions the common assumption that migrant networks always provide safe and welcoming havens.

4731 Moberg, Mark. Transnational labor and refugee enclaves in a Central American banana industry. (*Hum. Organ.*, 55:4, Winter 1996, p. 425–435, bibl., tables)

Many Central American refugees fled to Belize in the 1980s, accentuating Belizean tensions with Hispanophone Central America. The immigrants themselves were divided by national origin and religion, weakening their collective actions as workers. Author asserts that many such immigrants will not return home, but neither will they (easily) become Belizean—becoming perhaps "transnationals"—thus transforming that nation permanently, but not through egalitarian assimilation. For ethnologist's comment see item 877.

4732 Moreno Martín, Florentino. Infancia y guerra en Centroamérica. San José: FLACSO, 1991. 243 p.: ill.

Studies how the experience of war affects children's development. Children aged eight to 14, numbering 891 in all, were interviewed in 1989 in Nicaraguan war zones, Honduran contra refugee camps, and (as a control of sorts) in Extremadura, Spain. The use and review of the socialization literature is not impressive, but this topic is infrequently studied. Children in war show a widespread acceptance of a polarized view of social relations, and girls and boys often diverge sharply and develop sex-differentiated orientations toward warfare.

4733 Paige, Jeffery M. Coffee and power: revolution and the rise of democracy in Central America. Cambridge, Mass.: Harvard Univ. Press, 1997. 447 p.: bibl., index.

Extraordinary wealth and variety of historiographical, interview, and statistical data undergird a critical application of Barrington Moore's theses on revolution and democracy to the cases of Costa Rica, El Salvador, and Nicaragua. Three different class-and-state structures, largely generated by their coffee economies, are analyzed by dividing the upper classes into (purely) agrarian elites and their agroindustrial (processor/exporter) counterparts. A deepening split between them paved the recent path toward democratization in both El Salvador and Nica-

ragua. Costa Rica's earlier, smoother democratization is accounted for by the processor-
grower social pact of the 1930s. Yet all three
arrived at more democratic, though flawed,
neoliberal systems by the 1990s.

**4734 PARLACEN; PREALC/OIT; and
UNICEF.** Los niños trabajadores en
Centroamérica. San José: Facultad Latinoam-
ericana de Ciencias Sociales (FLACSO), 1994.
108 p.: bibl., graphs, tables. (Cuadernos de
Ciencias Sociales; 66)

Survey-based data and analysis on the
levels, profiles, and socioeconomic impacts of
child labor in five countries of Spanish Central America (Nicaragua is excluded). By 1990
there were about one million child laborers
regionwide. They were most common in, and
contributed the greatest share of income to,
indigent families, and were more commonly
illiterate than their nonworking age peers.
Each nation is also analyzed separately.

**4735 El paso del cometa: Estado, política so-
cial y culturas populares en Costa Rica,
1800/1950.** Recopilación de Iván Molina Jiménez y Steven Palmer. San José: Editorial Porvenir; Plumsock Mesoamerican Studies,
1994. 232 p.: bibl., ill., map. (Col. Ensayos)

A close look by social historians at the
"underside" of Costa Rican history, using
many legal records as sources. Authors encounter variations of Costa Rican national
culture, which seems less unified than previously characterized. Class/race/gender recur
as thematics and cleavages in the essays,
which cover rape and incest, prostitution,
witchcraft charges, labor culture, the reaction
to Halley's Comet (1910), and heroin use.

4736 Pérez Sáinz, Juan Pablo. Imaginarios
sociales sobre el trabajo: percepciones
empresariales y sindicales en la industria de
exportación de Costa Rica y República Dominicana. (*Rev. Eur.*, 61, Dec. 1996, p. 65–94,
bibl.)

Careful, interview-based comparison
of new export-oriented industries in the two
nations and, within those sectors, different
groups' perceptions of salaries, working conditions, etc. Focal groups are unionists, employers, and Costa Rica's "solidarists" (workers in company-store, company-benefits
firms). Similar work forces in both nations—
typically more young, female, and unmarried—produce differing national responses.

4737 Picado, Miguel. La Iglesia costarricense
entre el pueblo y el Estado: de 1949 a
nuestros días. San José: Guayacán, 1989.
323 p.: bibl.

A political sociology of Catholicism in
Costa Rica since the late 1940s, with a rich
gathering of Catholic perspectives ranging
from the Costa Rican grassroots all the way
up to the papacy. From a left-Catholic perspective the author traces changes from the
1950s-60s symbiosis of welfare-state and a
proreformist church, through a later preferential option for the middle classes (N.B., not
the poor), and to the more recent alleged ex-
haustion/crisis of the national welfare state,
itself paralleled by the growth of both neoconservative Catholics and Protestant evangelical groups.

**4738 Los pobres explican la pobreza: el caso
de Guatemala.** Guatemala: Univ. Rafael Landívar, Instituto de Investigaciones
Económicas y Sociales, 1995. 226 p.: bibl.
(Serie económica)

Conversational interviews with 627
people, focus groups, and direct observation
of the Guatemalan poor are used to determine
their concept of poverty, its causes and consequences. The poor are far less likely to view
poverty as a result of God's will, destiny, or
personal laziness, and more as due to low
wages (100 percent of respondents name this),
lack of access to land (ca. 60 percent), or high
prices (ca. 85 percent).

**4739 Problemas socio-religiosos en Centro-
américa y México: algunos estudios de
caso.** Recopilación de Rodolfo Casillas R.
México: Sede Académica de México, Facultad
Latinoamericana de Ciencias Sociales, 1993.
151 p.: bibl. (Cuadernos de FLACSO; 3)

Theoretical and sometimes empirical
essays treat a variety of topics, including the
increasing plurality of religious beliefs and
practices; increasing secularization via modernization; and the occasional recognition of
the "religious field" as a "marketplace" of
competing groups. Empirically interesting are
Samandú on Nicaraguan Pentecostals; González on Mexican popular Catholicism and
syncretism; Gama, who adds much theoretical care to his study of Jehovah's Witnesses
in Mexico; and the editor on migration and
religious uniformity/diversity in Mexican
history.

4740 Purcell, Trevor W. Banana fallout: class, color, and culture among West Indians in Costa Rica. Foreword by R.S. Bryce-Laporte. Los Angeles: Center for Afro-American Studies, Univ. of California, 1993. 197 p.: bibl., ill., index. (Afro-American culture and society, 0882–5297; 12)

Extended exploration of blacks in Costa Rica shows the deep cultural division between San José and the Caribbean coast. Highlights dependence of the region on banana exports. Includes detailed and unique analysis of the ethnic ecology and social stratification of the city of Limon and the import of skin color and language. For ethnologist's comment, see *HLAS 55 : 826.* [B. Aguirre-López]

4741 Quirós Rodríguez, Edda and **Olga Barrantes Romero.** ¿—y vivieron felices para siempre?: manifestaciones y efectos en las mujeres de algunas formas de violencia en la vida cotidiana. San José: Centro Nacional para el Desarrollo de la Mujer y la Familia, 1994. 182 p.: appendices, bibl., ill.

Survey of 1,312 women from metropolitan San Jose touches on many themes, but focuses on male aggression against female partners, married or not. An unmined wealth of data lies in the appendices. Authors' wide-ranging feminist theorizing seeks a broad understanding of the data patterns. Some such findings and conceptual usages parallel studies done elsewhere. Violence and aggression are defined in extremely broad terms (including "stony silence"), an example of questionable conceptual looseness here and there.

4742 Randall, Margaret. Sandino's daughters revisited: feminism in Nicaragua. New Brunswick, N.J.: Rutgers Univ. Press, 1994. 327 p.: bibl., ill.

A completely new and different book from her earlier *Sandino's Daughters.* The core is a dozen lengthy interviews with feminist women (all but one), hence not randomly drawn from Nicaraguan society. Randall opens the volume with a useful, wide-ranging interpretative survey of history, politics, and the social situation of women. One observation that sticks: women who most resembled men in their conduct rose highest under Sandinista rule.

4743 Las reglas del juego: límites y libertades . . . para la juventud en Nicaragua. Recopilación de Irela Solórzano y Humberto

Abaunza. Managua: Puntos de Encuentro, 1994. 278 p.: bibl., ill. (Puntos en agenda; 1)

Contributors provide rich and varied groundings for their key claims that young and teenage Nicaraguans are exposed to sexist and "adultist" portrayal or treatment in textbooks, news stories, television ads and programs, the legal code, and religious life. A prologue sharply contrasts Sandinista rule with its successor in such matters, yet materials are actually drawn from both periods. Few theoretical surprises, but noteworthy data collection.

4744 Rosero Bixby, Luis and **John B. Casterline.** Difusión por interacción social y transición de la fecundidad: evidencia cuantitativa y cualitativa de Costa Rica. (*Notas Pobl.,* 23 : 61, junio 1995, p. 29–78, bibl., graphs, map, tables)

A new wrinkle in the study of Costa Rica's decline in birth rates, the rapidity of which had few global counterparts. Argues that a "contagion" process diffused the idea and practice of fertility limitation across social groups and geographic regions (paralleling the European historical findings of van de Walle and Knodel). Authors use both long-term vital statistics and focus-group interviews with women.

4745 Saakes, Sylvia and **Flor de María Zúñiga.** Mujeres en tiempo de guerra: Nueva Guinea, Nicaragua. Managua: Instituto de Investigaciones Mujer y Cambio, 1993. 133 p.: bibl.

Qualitative interviews held around the time of the 1990 national elections, along with a statistical base, provide rich data for this self-identified feminist research project. Among the striking results: the threats of war per se are less central than, for example, often successful economic adaptations to male absences by multi-woman households; women are more willing to carry out male roles than vice-versa; men used domestic violence against a majority of women interviewed.

4746 Sánchez Lang, Rosamaría and **Mariana Aburto Chavarría.** Concepciones prevalecientes en la sociedad nicaragüense acerca de las niñas y los niños. Metodología de René Urroz Alvarez. Managua: Rädda Barnen de Suecia, 1994. 75 p.: bibl., ill.

An unusual study contrasts how a national sample of adults and children—the latter analyzed as a whole and separated by sex and rural-urban residence—differ in their perceptions of children and childhood. Topics include the traits of children; their social and political rights; education; household obligations; views of sexuality and of parenting; violence; work; mass media perceptions; etc.

4747 Seligson, Mitchell A. Thirty years of transformation in the agrarian structure of El Salvador, 1961–1991. (*LARR*, 30:3, 1995, p. 43–74, bibl., graphs, tables)

A key, empirical, air-clearing debate on rural El Salvador. Draws on a 1991–92 large sample survey to challenge the common assertion that the nation had a growing (relatively and absolutely) landless and land poor population who also were the foundation of insurrectionary support for revolution during the civil war. Instead argues for a decline in such numbers during 1961–91. Diskin's critique (see item **4704**) focuses on assumptions that lead to sharp underestimates of landless and land poor; Paige (see item **5083**) additionally criticizes Seligson's use of Prosterman's rural instability index as a good guide to sources of rural insurrectionary potential; and Seligson defends his numbers and argues for new directions in the study of "who rebels" in the countryside. For the ethnologist's comment see item **767** and for the economist's comment see item **1792**.

4748 Shepherd, Frederick M. Church and State in Honduras and Nicaragua prior to 1979. (*in* Religion and democracy in Latin America. New Brunswick, N.J.: Transaction Publishers, 1994, p. 117–133, bibl.)

Views the Church in both nations as an "external actor" in national political life, parallel to the political or economic roles played by the US government (mainly Nicaragua) or investors (mainly Honduras). In Nicaragua, the Church played a key role in bringing Somoza legitimacy in his rise to power, and stood close by the family dynasty until about 1970, when subgroups began the move leftward. Its Honduran counterpart had a more "arms-length" relationship with the State by the 1950s and was clearly in the reformist vanguard by the late 1960s–early 1970s, when even governments were reformist. The Vatican II reforms and the 1968 Medellín conference more sharply influenced Nicaraguan events than Honduran ones because of those differing contexts.

4749 El significado de la maquila en Guatemala: elementos para su comprensión. Ciudad de Guatemala: Asociación para el Avance de las Ciencias Sociales en Guatemala, 1994. 224 p.: bibl., ill, map. (Cuadernos de investigación; 10)

Thorough 1992 study adds much to our understanding of cross-border textile industries: variation, because it focuses on Guatemala and includes the candy industry; depth, because it ranges from the global economic context, to national developmental challenges, to industrial sectors and firms, to structured interviews, especially with female workers; and balance. Of special interest: the *maquilas'* global linkages, women's interview comments, and union-organizing efforts.

4750 Sociedad participativa en El Salvador. Recopilación de Rafael Guido Béjar y Stefan Roggenbuck. San Salvador: Fundación Konrad Adenauer; Depto. de Sociología y Ciencias Políticas, UCA, 1995. 209 p.: bibl.

Studies the role nongovernmental organizations and (a revitalized?) civil society have played and can play in El Salvador. Varied topics include the changing Catholic Church; social-movement and labor-union activity; the cultural-poetical analysis of Salvadorans as "people on the cross;" and a broad overview of the (necessarily conflictual) role that NGOs will play as society reorganizes itself in an era of reduced State efforts.

4751 Spalding, Rose J. Capitalists and revolution in Nicaragua: opposition and accommodation, 1979–1993. Chapel Hill: Univ. of North Carolina Press, 1994. 332 p.: bibl., index, map.

Interview-based and theoretically rich study traces the changing fortunes and positions of various subgroups of Nicaragua's economic elite up to and through the Sandinista revolutionary era. Shifts led in the end to a "reshuffling" of that bourgeoisie, by the 1990s changed greatly from the Somoza era. Political economy and political sociology are used with care and clarity. Crisply argued comparisons/contrasts with Chile, Mexico, and Peru. Meticulous research.

4752 Urbanización en Centroamérica. Coordinación de Alejandro Portes y Mario Lungo. San José: FLACSO, 1992. 289 p.: bibl., maps.

Exceptionally well researched and

data-rich study. A brief summary chapter on recent Caribbean Basin urban trends is followed by two longer in-depth studies of Costa Rican changes (esp. in metropolitican San José) and of Guatemala City. Close attention is paid to 30–40 years of economic changes, including topics such as migration, *maquiladoras*, the informal sectors, economic differences across the capital-city areas, and urban policies.

4753 Vega R., Isabel. Trabajo productivo de la mujer y cambio en los roles familiares: el caso de Costa Rica. (*Anu. Estud. Centroam.*, 20:1, 1994, p. 133–151, bibl.)

Author proposes a family-interaction-centered view of women's roles in both family and labor market as an antidote to feminism which, she argues, makes both theoretically and politically central the world of paid, material work and the pursuit of economic equality. Using both Costa Rican survey data and studies from the US, argues that the family universe has its own internal dynamics rooted in the interaction of its members (interactions affected by, but not reducible to either external economic involvements or national gender ideologies); questions simple visions of male "domination" and female "subordination;" sees spaces where women are increasingly protagonists in their own family lives; and suggests further exploration of these ideas.

4754 Velásquez, José Humberto. La partera salvadoreña. San Salvador: Univ. de El Salvador, Editorial Universitaria, 1996. 139 p.: bibl., ill. (Col. Antropología e historia; 1)

The unusual topic of midwives and midwifery is carefully analyzed with quantitative data and theoretical force. Rejects the understanding of midwives as an expression of an older and popular culture, instead placing them structurally in a political economy where limited state resources and efforts can indirectly benefit from the activities of underpaid (yet still trained) midwives, as self-employed providers of health care. Includes a wealth of statistics.

4755 Vigor, Catherine. Atanasio: parole d'Indien du Guatemala. Paris: L'Harmattan, 1993. 203 p.: bibl. (Recherches & documents. Amériques latines)

A rich autobiographical "life" of a Guatemalan man of Quiché-Maya background.

Good exemplar of a 1990s contribution to the genre of "giving voice" to one of the heretofore voiceless, including his reflections on his youth, education, and work; war, elders, and medicine among his people; and commentaries on violence in the "savage nation" of Guatemala. The thorny sampling issue remains: are such highly literate, well-read persons typical of their own peoples?

4756 Vilas, Carlos María. Estado, clase y etnicidad: la Costa Atlántica de Nicaragua. México: Fondo de Cultura Económica, 1992. 453 p.: bibl., index. (Col. popular; 472)

A welcome book on this understudied region and its peoples. Long sections are each given over to the earlier history, post-WWII development, and to an extended and deep narrative-cum-analysis of the region's ethnic-based tensions with the FSLN. A flexible Marxian political-economic view can be embraced or ignored; it is rich when read either way, including a wry coda on the "unequal development of socialist revolutions" (i.e., not capitalism).

4757 Vilas, Carlos María. Transición desde el subdesarrollo. Caracas: Editorial Nueva Sociedad, 1989. 218 p.: bibl.

Work focuses on Central American events before and after the Sandinistas' 1979 ascent to power in Nicaragua, but prior to their 1990 electoral defeat, and weaves together analyses of socioeconomic transformations, regime-types and transitions, and international pressures to understand (especially but not only) the transformations of Nicaraguan State and society. The most distinctive contributions include a focus on the working class, both as participants in insurrections and as foci of postrevolutionary policy.

4758 Whisnant, David E. Rascally signs in sacred places: the politics of culture in Nicaragua. Chapel Hill: Univ. of North Carolina Press, 1995. 582 p.: bibl., ill., index, maps.

Anthropology meets cultural studies (popular and otherwise) and historiography with a remarkable theoretical and investigative depth. A wide range of topics includes the title essay on 19th-century culture; culture under Somoza (the elder) and resistance to that culture; Sandinista culture and resistance thereto; 19th-century looting of antiquities; gender; the political cultures surrounding Rubén Darío and Augusto Sandino; and effective introductory and concluding remarks.

4759 Wiegand, Bruce. Black money in Belize: the ethnicity and social structure of black-market crime. (*Soc. Forces,* 73:1, Sept. 1994, p. 135–154, bibl.)

Sociologists now commonly perceive economic markets as social structures and the author applies that idea in analyzing one of the East Indians' economic niches (their involvement in the black-marketing of US dollars) in Belize, seen as part of that community's social exchange network. The Indians' ethnic solidarities cement their intra- and transnational trading networks, largely conducted in US dollars, and generate unregistered dollars by underinvoicing, customs evasion, smuggling, etc. A useful contrast with Belizean mestizos' contraband activities also enriches the discussion of black markets and ethnicity, the latter finally seen as not being the explanation of the former.

4760 Woods, Louis A.; Joseph M. Perry; and Jeffrey W. Steagall. The composition and distribution of ethnic groups in Belize: immigration and emigration patterns, 1980–1991. (*LARR,* 32:3, 1997, p. 63–88, map, tables)

Authors use 1980 and 1991 Belizean censuses and the 1990 US census to document the rapidly changing patterns of ethnicity in Belize, mostly generated recently by immigration from Hispanic Central America and emigration to the United States. Despite that recent focus, the long-run view of Belizean ethnic complexity is also noted. Descriptive, statistical detail abounds—data often absent, assumed, or glossed over in other recent studies of Belize. Includes breakdowns of the population by district and by urban/rural residence, by ethnic groups, and by immigrants' countries of origin.

4761 Zub Kurylowicz, Roberto. Protestantismo y elecciones en Nicaragua: estudio sobre la estratificación socio-religiosa y las actitudes político-electorales de los protestantes en Nicaragua. Managua: Ediciones Nicarao; CIEETS, 1993. 119 p.: bibl.

Analysis of the results of a late-1991 survey (i.e., after the Sandinista election loss) of 248 Protestants drawn from church-member lists in or near Managua. While the numbers from each denomination are thus small, ca. 30–60, the sheer variety of groups—Baptists, Assembly of God, Church of God etc.—allows the author to make reasonable (if still tentative) assertions about the social and economic positions, political sympathies, and voting patterns of Protestants, which appear, not as monolithically conservative (although that tilt is clearly present), but as substantially varied in both their politics and social profiles.

THE CARIBBEAN AND THE GUIANAS

BENIGNO E. AGUIRRE-LOPEZ, *Professor, Department of Sociology, Texas A&M University*

AN IMPORTANT THEME in recent literature on the Caribbean region is pan-national cultural, social and political integration, illustrated by reports showing the continuing problems in the West Indies (item **4811**) and in the Caribbean (items **4781** and **4817**). One complexity of integration is the anomalous status of Cuba, the largest island country in the region, which, despite its many efforts, has been largely excluded from regional integration. Studies of the region's relations with the US continue to thrive. Particularly noteworthy among reports of these international exchanges are the issue of economic remittances of transnational Caribbean communities in the US (item **4850**), the expansion and impact of Cuban and Caribbean religions into the US (item **4790**), the growing importance in the Caribbean of Pentecostalism (item **4941**), and the influence of US immigration and drug policies (item

4931). Unintended effects of economic adjustment policies from these international exchanges are the aggravation of ethnic antagonisms and political instability (item **4918**). Despite optimism in the region for the promise of democracy and free enterprise, research shows the devastating effects of chronic and pervasive poverty aggravated by austerity programs of international monetary agencies. Other topics of interest to regional specialists are urbanization processes and their links to macroeconomic forces (item **4934**) and life chances and survival strategies of women (items **4920** and **4870**).

Cuba continues to attract a significant portion of the attention of specialists, although there is a greater emphasis on other countries of the region. African religious expressions in Cuba attract considerable research attention (item **4788**). Recent research often carried out in Cuba expresses a welcome and much needed willingness to analyze the social costs of continuing with the present government. Information about effects of the economic crisis which began in 1989 and of the government programs created to alleviate its effects are available. Studies documenting demographic impacts are particularly worthwhile (item **4823**), including a drop in national fertility indices from already comparatively low levels (item **4825**), a decline in health and educational benefits (item **4828**), two often-mentioned achievements of the revolutionary government (items **4929** and **4935**), labor market dislocations (item **4814**), the resurgence and changing nature of organized religion (items **4779** and **4772**) and efforts of artists and intellectuals to chart a new course (items **4868** and **4818**). The growing recognition that racism persists in Cuba is also important (items **4776** and **4827**). For too long, the revolutionary dogma declared all social inequality as the result of social class exploitation rather than racist discriminatory practices. Fortunately, this assumption has been largely abandoned. Likewise, the significant topic of political centralization and the failures of the present government's policies designed to strengthen local governments have also received careful treatment (item **4816**). Among the top scholarship are studies enhancing an understanding of Cuban culture centered on the meaning and practice of citizenship (item **4777**); the influence of black people on Cuban culture and society (item **4792**); and the experience of exile, an ever-present reality in imagining the Cuban nation (item **4915**).

The nature of Puerto Rican national culture and identity continues to attract research attention. The celebrated interpretation of José Luis González is included here (item **4837**). One work explores the relationship between national culture and politics (item **4813**). Migration to and from the US may become a politically controversial topic as many well-trained Puerto Rican workers moved to the US after the US Congress annulled special tax advantages for US corporations doing business on the island. This augured to have devastating consequences for the Puerto Rican economy (items **4845, 4882,** and **4874**). A welcome research theme is the ecology of San Juan (item **4923**). Hopefully, more work on human ecology will be forthcoming. Studies of places such as the beautiful Bay of Mayagüez decimated by industry are still needed. Other topics in need of greater research attention are illegal land occupation by the poor (item **4786**) and crimes of passion. One recent innovative research effort conceptualizes crime in Puerto Rico from the perspective of social power, both at the macro or structural and micro or interpersonal levels of analyses (item **4916**). It explores the roots of crime in colonial and sexist relationships. Another research effort looks at the Cuban community in Puerto Rico as a middleman minority (item **4798**).

The nature and change of the national political system and the economic crisis dominates scholarship on the Dominican Republic. Studies of the impact of the economic crisis on family life and on marriage and other forms of intimate relations are included (item **4930**). Research on women and street children documents chronic poverty and the government's indifference to their plight (items **4834, 4793,** and **4763**). Also there is an extended analysis of the lasting remnants of "caudillismo," a long standing political tradition antedating R. Trujillo's government which militates against the establishment of democracy (items **4862** and **4804**). Balaguer's waning influence and the recent presidential elections may augur the beginning of yet another epoch in Dominican politics. Another promising line of research is on social movement organizations, documenting how the mass of the people organize and attempt to change political and economic power to better reflect their needs (item **4938**). Research has demonstrated the lack of effective public health programs (item **4767**). The "Haitian question," or the meaning and effects of Haitian immigration for the culture and society of the Dominican Republic, continues to attract attention (item **4805;** see also *HLAS 56:1984*). Results of national surveys of internal (item **4903**) and international (item **4902**) migrants, first-hand accounts of illegal emigration to Puerto Rico and subsequently to the US (item **4869**), and a demographic profile of Dominicans in Puerto Rico (item **4888**) are now available.

There is comparatively slightly greater research interest in Haiti which provides hope for the improvement of social science research and adds to our understanding of Haitian society. Major themes are the analysis of the continuing impact of the legacies of the Duvalier period on present-day political processes (items **4928** and **4794**), class formations (item **4894**), and the difficulty of establishing a demo cratic polity (items **4940** and **4895**). The current legal system has come under scrutiny, particularly in its inability to protect the rights of women and children (items **4824, 4859** and **4851**). Also worthwhile in the recent scholarship are the studies of Haitian legends and myths (item **4810**) and the impact of internal migration on urban culture (item **4866**).

In Jamaica, scholarship on the Rastafari Movement continues to thrive (item **4846**). Lewis' recent book-length monograph is an important addition to this burgeoning literature, showing the Rastafari experience in the US, its symbols, and its material culture (item **4858**). Other studies examine the internationalization of the movement (items **4922** and **4836**). The report of a national task force charged with examining crime and the fear of crime was also published (item **4907**), as was a monograph on the subject (item **4842**). Both argue for a structural understanding of crime behavior as caused by poverty. Other significant research includes an extended argument on how best to preserve Jamaican culture (item **4883**), an exploration of Jamaican women's identity (item **4787**), and an investigation of the determinants of the use of health care services (item **4854**). The use of theater as a tool for stopping violence against women is one of the most interesting documented efforts to solve this important problem (item **4830**).

Other island nations in the Caribbean are also represented in recent scholarship, including a social history of the people of Guadeloupe (item **4905**) and Guyana (item **4925**). A biography of Walter Rodney offers in-depth coverage of his relationship with the government of Guyana (item **4835**). Another important research effort is a collection of articles on social history of the Bahamas (item **4877**). Work on Barbados examines crime (item **4890**), television viewing habits (item **4891**), gender stereotypes (item **4889**), the continuation of racism during the post independence period (item **4769**), and typical experiences of immigrants in England (item **4796**). A similar study examines the experiences of immigrants from Guyana in France (item **4921**). Grenada's political system and its recent revolutionary transformation are the topics of recent scholarship (items **4843** and **4803**), as is the grassroots movements in Dominica (item **4912**). Family land tenure in St. Lucia is the topic of two monographs (items **4766** and **4806**). In Trinidad and Tobago, the results of the 1990 census have been published (item **4932**). Other important contributions examine the carnival as a vehicle for social change (item **4946**), the history of Chinese immigration (item **4876**), the assimilation of Indian immigrants, and the function of religion in structuring the Indian community (items **4864** and **4927**).

4762 Acosta-Belén, Edna and **Christine E. Bose.** Colonialism, structural subordination, and empowerment: women and the development process in Latin America and the Caribbean. (*in* Women in the Latin American development process. Philadelphia: Temple Univ. Press, 1995, p. 15–36, bibl.)

Examines the many facets of the status of women in the development of the Caribbean region and the continued impact of colonialism on women's subordination.

4763 Aguilar, Gracia. Una opción obligada: el palomo y su realidad. (*Estud. Soc. / Santo Domingo*, 28:102, oct./dic. 1995, p. 69–97, bibl.)

A heart-rending, ethnographic, participant-observation study of street children (*palomos*) in the Dominican Republic. Identifies important cultural patterns characterizing status such as typical family background, street experiences, the use of inhalants (*cemento*), and the failure of institutions.

Angrosino, Michael V. The Indo-Caribbeans: evolution of a group identity. See item **789.**

4764 Argüelles Mederos, Aníbal. Les systèmes divinatoires de la Règle Ocha à Cuba. (*Soc. Compass*, 41:2, June 1994, p. 293–301, bibl.)

Detailed examination of the cult of Ocha in Cuba discusses its African origins, beliefs, the importance of myths, religious agents, divinities, and divinatory systems.

4765 Austin-Broos, Diane J. Politics and the Redeemer: State and religion as ways of being in Jamaica. (*NWIG*, 70:1/2, 1996, p. 59–90, bibl.)

Examines transformation of the relation between experience of religion and experience of race and class as exemplified by Pentecostals in Jamaica. Argues that Pentecostalism in Jamaica displaces and reconstructs many aspects of the discourse of race and class. For ethnologist's comment see item **790.**

Austin-Broos, Diane J. Race/class: Jamaica's discourse of heritable identity. See item **791.**

Aymer, Paula L. Uprooted women: migrant domestics in the Caribbean. See item **793.**

4766 Barrow, Christine. Family land and development in St. Lucia. Cave Hill, Barbados: Institute of Social and Economic Research, Eastern Caribbean, Univ. of the West Indies, 1992. 83 p.: bibl., maps. (Monograph series; 1)

Examination of family land tenure in Saint Lucia reviews its legal foundation and impact of banana production and population growth.

4767 Batista del Villar, Guarocuya. Cinco ensayos sobre la salud de los dominicanos. Santo Domingo: Asociación Medica Dominicana, 1994. 132 p.: bibl., ill., maps. (Col. AMD-Centenaria; 7)

Reviews state of public health in the Dominican Republic, including effects of economic underdevelopment. Includes chapters on education, the structural difficulties of the public health system, and the continued poor state of the peoples' health.

Baud, Michiel. Una frontera para cruzar: la sociedad rural a través de la frontera dominico-haitiana, 1870–1930. See *HLAS 56:1984.*

4768 Baver, Sherrie L. Including migration in the development calculus: the Dominican Republic and other Caribbean countries. (*LARR*, 30:1, 1995, p. 191–202)

Reviews seven books on the socio-economic impact of migration flows into Caribbean countries.

Using the Dominican Republic as a case study, discusses cycles of penetration, incorporation, and out-migration and offers policy recommendations for both the sending and receiving countries.

4769 Beckles, Hilary. Independence and the social crisis of nationalism in Barbados. (*in* Caribbean freedom: society and economy from emancipation to the present. Kingston, Jamaica: Ian Randle Publishers, 1993, p. 528–539, tables)

Examines post-independence social crisis of nationalism in Barbados. Focuses on the continued subordination of blacks and their inability to access power and resources.

4770 Benítez Nazario, Jorge. Puerto Rican political parties and poor communities: the erosion of the political parties' social base. (*Rev. Adm. Pública/México*, 26, 1993/94, p. 185–199, bibl.)

Discusses relationship between political parties and poor communities in Puerto Rico. Suggests that a huge gap exists between poor communities' demands on existing political parties and what those political parties offer them, and that the gap erodes the political parties' social base in the country.

4771 Bennett, Wycliffe. Questions of identity, democracy and broadcasting: the case of Jamaica. (*Caribb. Q.*, 40:2, June 1994, p. 23–32)

Reviews the complex nature of broadcasting in Jamaica and the problems resulting from the affiliation of the national broadcast system with the ruling party. Governmental influence is seen as threatening the credibility of the news.

4772 Berges Curbelo, Juana; René Cárdenas Medina; and Elizabeth Carrillo García. Le pastorat du protestantisme historique à Cuba: ses approches sociol-religieuses et la nouvelle théologie cubaine. (*Soc. Compass*, 41:2, June 1994, p. 273–291, bibl.)

Reviews history of Protestantism in Cuba and the changes it has experienced since 1959. Emphasizes changes in the theology of Protestant denominations as a means of adapting to the ideology of the Castro regime.

Berleant-Schiller, Riva and **Bill Maurer.** Women's place is every place: merging domains & women's roles in Barbuda & Dominica. See item **799.**

4773 Bernard, Jean Maxius and **Barbara Orvis De Zalduondo.** Les conditions sanitaires dans les bidonvilles haïtiens: le cas de Cité-Soleil. (*Bull. Bur. natl. ethnol.*, 1993–1994, p. 69–88, bibl., map, table)

Examines public health situation in the infamous Cité-Soleil slum. Includes information on the history of the area, the rural origin of many of its inhabitants, population density, family and marriage characteristics, and the problems faced by sanitation programs.

Bernard, Jean Maxius. Le fêtes champêtres et la religion populaire en Haïti. See item **800.**

Besson, Jean and **Barry Chevannes.** The continuity-creativity debate: the case of Revival. See item **803.**

Birth, Kevin K. Most of us are family some of the time: interracial unions and transracial kinship in eastern Trinidad. See item **810.**

4774 Birth, Kevin K. Trinidadian times: temporal dependency and temporal flexibility on the margins of industrial capitalism. (*Anthropol. Q.*, 69:2, April 1996, p. 79–89, bibl.)

Discusses reasons why young men in rural Trinidad who attend secondary school have a more difficult time making a living than those who do not attend. Draws attention to the importance of multiple occupations for people who live on the margins of industrial capitalism. For ethnologist's comment see item **811.**

4775 Black, M.L. My mother never fathered me: rethinking kinship and the governing of families. (*Soc. Econ. Stud.*, 44:1, March 1995, p. 49–71, bibl.)

Reviews parliamentary debates surrounding child support law in Antigua. Investigates connections between kinship and gender ideology and practice and State governance of families in the country. Demonstrates how commonsense understanding of kinship influences lawmaking. For ethnologist's comment see item **859.**

4776 Bobes, Velia Cecilia. Cuba y la cuestión racial. (*Perf. Latinoam.*, 5:8, enero/junio 1996, p. 115–139, bibl.)

Wide-ranging study of race relations in Cuba includes sections on the confluence of race and class in the republican period, the emphasis on class rather than race differences during the revolutionary period, and the continuation of racism in society and culture.

4777 Bobes, Velia Cecilia. La utilidad de la virtud: un estudio de la ciudadanía en Cuba, 1898–1994. (*Perf. Latinoam.*, 4:7, dic. 1995, p. 199–224, bibl.)

Wide-ranging study examines citizenship in Cuba, from late-19th century to present. Discusses meaning and practice of citizenship as status and activity. Also discusses historical evolution of citizenship and impact of the post-1959 revolution.

4778 Bolland, O. Nigel. The politics of freedom in the British Caribbean. (*in* The meaning of freedom: economics, politics, and culture after slavery. Pittsburgh, Pa.: Univ. of Pittsburgh Press, 1992, p. 113–146, bibl.)

Examines the meaning of "freedom" to former slaves in the British Caribbean and the forms of domination that replaced slavery. Reviews the post-emancipation domination techniques used by ruling elites, the role of the State and its support of planter hegemony, and the struggles and accommodations of labor in a free market.

4779 Bonome Moreno, Pedro; Gustavo Véliz Olivarez; and Zeida Sánchez Alvisa. Social functions and evolution of Catholicism in Cuban society. (*Soc. Compass,* 41:2, June 1994, p. 255–271)

Reviews changing roles of Catholicism and the Catholic Church in the lives of the Cuban people. Identifies three historical stages in the Church-nation relationship: colonial, neocolonial, and revolutionary. Also identifies different evangelical activities carried out by the Church during each of the three stages.

4780 Boulbés, D.C. Vers une maitrise du phenomene nataliste? (*Etud. Guad.,* 5, fév. 1992, p. 134–146, bibl., graphs)

Reviews post-1969 demographic patterns in Guadeloupe. Discusses demographic effects of present-day age structure of the population, high rate of emigration of young people to France, and labor force inelasticities.

4781 Boxill, Ian. Ideology and Caribbean integration. Kingston: Consortium Graduate School of Social Sciences, Univ. of the West Indies, Mona Campus, 1993. 128 p.: bibl., ill. (New generation series, 0799–0057)

Thoroughly reviews regional integration efforts by Caribbean nations. Analyzes Caribbean Free Trade Association (CARIFTA) and Caribbean Community (CARICOM), and points out their weaknesses. Argues for the need for a regional ideology, including a pan-national identity, agreed-upon explanations for causes of shared past problems and ways

to solve them, and consensus on building successful regional integration. See also item **4817.**

4782 Boxill, Ian. The two faces of Caribbean music. (*Soc. Econ. Stud.,* 43:2, June 1994, p. 33–56, bibl.)

Examines contradictory nature of reggae and calypso music in Caribbean society. Emphasizes contributions of this music to the creation of mass culture and to the history, political dynamics, and racial and cultural identity of the Caribbean people. For music specialist's comment see *HLAS 56:4722.*

4783 Bravo, Ernesto Mario. La biomedicina en Cuba: desarrollo en el subdesarrollo. Puebla, Mexico: Benemérita Univ. Autónoma de Puebla, 1993. 163 p.: bibl., ill.

Review of biomedicine in Cuba includes short descriptions of research and personal narratives and biographies of some important scientists working in Cuba in the area of biomedicine.

4784 Brea, Rafael and **José Millet.** The African presence in the carnivals of Santiago de Cuba. Translated by Katheryn A. Thompson. (*J. Caribb. Stud.,* 10:1/2, Winter 1994/Spring 1995, p. 30–49, bibl.)

Explores influence of African presence on Cuban culture. Examination of Carnival of Santiago de Cuba shows that African music, art, song, and dance have become integral parts of Cuban culture and identity. For ethnologist's comment see item **814.**

4785 Brennan, Lance; John McDonald; and **Ralph Shlomowitz.** Long-term change and sex differences in the heights of Afro-Caribbeans and Indo-Caribbeans. (*Soc. Econ. Stud.,* 44:1, March 1995, p. 73–93, bibl., graph, tables)

Quantitative analysis examines long-term changes in the statures of the descendants of African and Indian migrants in the Caribbean area. Long-term change is adduced by comparing the stature of African-born slaves in 1813 and Indian-born indentured workers in 1905–1913 with that of their descendants in the 1960s.

4786 Brentlinger, John. Villa Sin Miedo, presente! Fotografías de Mel Rosenthal. México: Claves Latinoamericanas, 1989. 161 p.: bibl., photos.

Describes the attempt by approximately 300 families of poor, homeless Puerto Ricans to occupy Dolores Farm in Nov. 1980. Gives a sympathetic account of their community development, their hopes and struggles for a place to live, and their treatment by police and other government agencies.

4787 Brice-Baker, Janet R. West Indian women of color: the Jamaican women. (*in* Women of color: integrating ethnic and gender identities in psychotherapy. New York: Guilford Press, 1994, p. 139–160, bibl.)

Exploration of Jamaican women's identity reviews issues of immigration, gender, sexuality, family dynamics, and race. Also reviews the historical and contemporary background for these practices as they affect women.

Browne, Katherine E. The informal economy in Martinique: insights from the field, implications for development policy. See item **815.**

4788 Cabrera, Lydia. Religious syncretism in Cuba. (*J. Caribb. Stud.*, 10:1/2, Winter 1994/Spring 1995, p. 84–94)

Discusses interplay between Santería with its African roots and the Christian-based religions of the Europeans. Explains how Afro-Cuban religions survived through Cuban slave system. Compares religious experiences of slaves in Cuba with those of slaves in the US where white domination and resistance to African religious beliefs were much stronger.

4789 Cáceres Ureña, Francisco. Algunas manifestaciones de los desequilibrios regionales en la República Dominicana. (*Polít. Gob.*, 3:1, 1996, p. 35–54, tables)

Summarizes results of the 1993 national census, stratified by region.

4790 Canizares, Raul José. Santeria: from Afro-Caribbean cult to world religion. (*Caribb. Q.*, 40:1, March 1994, p. 59–63)

Examines transformation of Santería from a geographically-specific to a world religion. Stresses growth among non-Hispanic believers and evolution of "traditional" Santería religion to accomodate the new believers. Discusses penetration into US and implications of this phenomenon.

4791 Casimir, Jean. The Caribbean: one and divisible. Santiago: Comisión Económica para América Latina y el Caribe

(CEPAL), 1992. 207 p.: bibl. (Cuadernos de la CEPAL, 0252–2195; 66)

Sociological analysis of Caribbean societies includes chapters on the creoles, freedmen, Caribbean regions, emergence of Caribbean nations, chronic problems of the economy, development, and culture and power.

4792 Castellanos, Jorge and Isabel Castellanos. Cultura afrocubana. v. 4, Letras, música, arte. Miami, Fla.: Ediciones Universal, 1994. 1 v. bibl., indexes. (Col. Ebano y canela)

Fourth and final volume of a monumental work on the influence of blacks on Cuba's culture. Centers on Cuban literature, arts, and music, and includes chapters on the presence of black culture and social organization in Cuban novels (1900–59), short stories, poetry, music, and painting.

4793 Castillo Ariza, Marina. Familias y pobreza: menores deambulantes en República Dominicana. (*Nueva Soc.*, 129, enero/feb. 1994, p. 90–103, bibl., tables)

A study of street children in Santo Domingo uses information collected from children who work in the streets and other public spaces, those who live in the streets, and others who are institutionalized. Examines type of work, theft, prostitution, poverty, and family developmental stages including relations with parents.

4794 Castor, Suzy. Démocratie et société en Haïti. (*Rencontre/Haiti*, 5, 1993, p. 16–20)

Essay on the political conditions in Haiti reviews class dynamics, weaknesses in the economy and its dependence on foreign capital, and the conservative functions of the Duvalier State.

Castro Pereda, Rafael. Idioma, historia y nación: ensayos de Rafael Castro Pereda y documentos históricos sobre la *Ley del Idioma.* See *HLAS 56:2118.*

4795 Catasús Cervera, Sonia I. The sociodemographic and reproductive characteristics of Cuban women. Translated by Barbara N. Gantt. (*Lat. Am. Perspect.*, 23:1, Winter 1996, p. 87–98, bibl.)

Examines dynamics of certain characteristics of Cuban women. Analyzes reproductive behavior, variables associated with this behavior, and demographic characteristics of Cuban families.

4796 Chamberlain, Mary. Family narratives and migration dynamics: Barbadians to Britain. (*NWIG,* 69:3/4, 1995, p. 253–275, bibl.)

Study of Barbados immigrant families and communities in Britain uses oral history. Examines migrants' international movements, the impact of migration on their culture, and their adjustments.

4797 Chevannes, Barry. Sexual behavior of Jamaicans: a literature review. (*Soc. Econ. Stud.,* 42:1, March 1993, p. 1–45, bibl., tables)

Documents sexual behavior among the Jamaican people. Discusses sexual and mating patterns and the integration of sexual mores into Jamaican cultural practices. Identifies topics on which further research is needed.

4798 Cobas, José A. and **Jorge Duany.** Los cubanos en Puerto Rico: economía étnica e identidad cultural. San Juan: Editorial de la Univ. de Puerto Rico, 1995. 252 p.: bibl., index. (Col. caribeña)

In-depth qualitative study of post-1959 Cuban immigration to Puerto Rico interprets Cubans as forming a middleman minority on the island. Includes chapters on the middleman minority thesis, a history of migration, the emergence of a Cuban ethnic economy, and the social organization of the community. Also available in English (Gainesville: Univ. Press of Florida, 1997).

Colón, Jesús. The way it was, and other writings. See *HLAS 56:3554.*

4799 Combe, Georges. L'explosion conflictuelle: de la signification des conflits sociaux. (*Etud. Guad.,* 5, fév. 1992, p. 36–57, tables)

Analysis of old and new forms of collective action in Guadeloupe discusses causes of social conflict in the island nation. Reviews socio-structural, socio-psychological, and legal factors, and the failure of labor regulations. Includes the frequency of various forms of labor unrest.

4800 Comité de Estudios para la Reforma Educacional en Cuba (US). La educación en Cuba: pasado, presente y futuro. United States: Endowment for Cuban American Studies, 1993. 193 p.: bibl., ill.

Reviews Cuba's formal educational system. Includes chapters on changes in the system from 1959–91, and considers future of Cuban education during a post-Castro government.

4801 Congreso Nacional de Administradores de Recursos Humanos, 1st, Santo Domingo, 1992. Antecedentes y perspectivas de la administración de los recursos humanos. Santo Domingo: ADOARH, 1992. 189 p.: ill.

Includes proceedings of conference on human resources held in the Dominican Republic.

4802 Constant, Fred. Religion, ethnicité et politique en Caraïbe. (*Rev. fr. sci. polit.,* 44:1, fév. 1994, p. 49–74, appendix, bibl.)

Synthesizes scholarly works on religion, ethnicity, and politics in the Caribbean. Questions the validity of three extant approaches to ethnicity and religion: primordialist, instrumentalist, and ideological.

4803 Cooper, Carolyn. Grenadian popular culture and the rhetoric of revolution: Merle Collins' *Angel.* (*Caribb. Q.,* 41:2, June 1995, p. 57–70, appendix)

An extended commentary on the novel *Angel* (Seattle, Wash.: Seal Press, 1988). Characters reflect evolution of radical nationalist politics in Grenada, from idealistic promises of the revolution to often grim political reality.

4804 Cordero, Margarita. Autoritario y democracia en la política dominicana. (*Estud. Soc./Santo Domingo,* 28:101, julio/ sept. 1995, p. 109–116)

Essay on political practices in the Dominican Republic examines lasting effect of Trujillo's dictatorship on political culture of the country.

4805 Corten, André and **Isis Duarte.** Quinientos mil Haitianos en Republica Dominicana. (*Estud. Soc./Santo Domingo,* 27:98, oct./dic. 1994, p. 7–36, bibl., tables)

Review of "Haitian Question" in the Dominican Republic offers estimates of Haitian immigrants and of Dominicans of Haitian origin. Includes sections on Haitians' participation in the labor force, the impact of Haitian immigration on Dominican presidential politics, and the dynamics of political interdependence of the two countries.

4806 Crichlow, Michaeline A. An alternative approach to family land tenure in the Anglophone Caribbean: the case of St. Lucia. (*NWIG*, 68:1/2, 1994, p. 77–99, bibl., tables)

Discusses development and structure of family land tenure in the Caribbean island of Saint Lucia. Argues that development was the result of previous links to world markets. Documents history of family land tenure, economic pressures to sell lands, and the relationship between accessibility to land and family relations. For ethnologist's comment see *HLAS 55:786.*

4807 Cros Sandoval, Mercedes. Mariel and Cuban national identity. Miami, Fla.: Editorial SIBI, 1985. 78 p.

Study of Cubans who immigrated to US in 1980 includes results of a survey of 439 respondents. Presents a cultural-attitudinal typology of the immigrants, their typical mode of survival in Cuba, and their symbolic import to the Cuban exile community in Florida or as representation of Cuba's national identity under socialism.

4808 Cuba: National Report, World Summit for Social Development, Copenhagen, 1995. La Habana: International Conference Center, 1995. 105 p.: graphs, tables.

Calls for implementation of economic and social policies to ameliorate poverty in underdeveloped countries in Latin America. Pays particular attention to income distribution/redistribution, social security/welfare, and access to social services.

4809 Cuban festivals: an illustrated anthology. Edited by Judith Bettelheim. New York: Garland Pub., 1993. 261 p.: bibl., ill., index. (Studies in ethnic art; 3. Garland reference library of the humanities; 1444)

Presents an ethnography of the carnival in Santiago de Cuba and translation of the work of Fernando Ortiz on the Day of Kings national festival. Includes a glossary of carnival terms by Cuban researchers Rafael Brea and José Millet, and a personal recollection of carnival by Pedro Pérez Sarduy.

4810 Déita. La légende des loa du vodou haïtien. Haïti: Déita, 1993. 398 p.: bibl., ill., index.

Provides three-part detailed description of legends of Haitian people. Stresses themes of legend, associated mythical beings and powers, and relationships to Voodooism.

4811 Demas, William G. Towards West Indian survival: an essay. Black Rock, St. James, Barbados: West Indian Commission Secretariat, 1990? 74 p.: bibl. (Occasional paper; 1)

Official international commission's report on the present difficulties and prospects of the West Indies includes sections on the changing world environment, West Indies achievements and shortcomings, problems of development, and emergence and facilitation of a pan-national West Indian community and culture.

4812 Dembicz, Andrzej. Entre la Granja del Pueblo y la Cooperativa de Producción Agropecuaria: un ensayo de interpretación de condicionantes de las actitudes campesinas cubanas contemporáneas. (*in* Society of Caribbean Research. International Conference, *1st, Berlin, 1988.* Alternative cultures in the Caribbean. Frankfurt: Vervuert Verlag, 1993, p. 265–277, tables)

Review of Cuban agriculture up to 1986 emphasizes emergence of governmental cooperatives and their implications for the *campesinado.* Also reviews some important problems the new system created, such as sectoral inefficiencies, cost overruns, and poor investment decisions.

4813 Díaz, José O. Status, *caudillismo* e identidad: recent work on Puerto Rico. (*LARR*, 29:2, 1994, p. 212–222)

Reviews six books on Puerto Rican politics and culture. Discusses political status of Puerto Rico, *caudillismo*, and ethnic identity.

4814 Díaz-Briquets, Sergio. Collision course: labor force and educational trends in Cuba. (*Cuba. Stud.*, 23, 1993, p. 91–112)

Examines labor market dislocations in Cuba after the collapse of the Soviet Bloc. Notes shortages in material goods and energy supply. Pays attention to policy changes implemented by the Cuban government to ease the crisis and to implications of this new plan for the people of Cuba.

Díaz Quiñones, Arcadio. La memoria rota. See *HLAS 56:3600.*

4815 Díaz-Stevens, Ana María. La Misa Jíbara como campo de batalla sociopolítica en Puerto Rico. (*Rev. Cienc. Soc./Río Piedras,* 30:1/2, enero/junio 1993, p. 139–161, bibl., ill.)

Case study focuses on the expulsion of a community of Dominican brothers at Comerío. Finds that the group had developed theological symbols favorable to the nationalist movement in Puerto Rico and to the Latin American liberation theology movement. Includes sections on Catholic theology and liturgy, and information on the conflicts leading to the expulsion.

4816 Dilla Alfonso, Haroldo; Gerardo González Núñez; and Ana Teresa Vincentelli. Participación popular y desarrollo en los municipios cubanos. Caracas: Fondo Editorial Tropykos, 1994. 173 p.: bibl.

Reviews history of local governments, or *municipios.* After briefly reviewing legal and political characteristics of local governments in the pre-1959 period, work focuses on the years following the 1959 revolution. Presents information from a systematic survey of *municipios* in four central cities conducted during 1989–91. Offers a detailed analysis of *poder popular* and its local organs. Discusses community and political participation, relative freedom of elections, continued discrimination against women in local elections, and failures of local governments.

4817 Diversidad cultural y tensión regional: América Latina y el Caribe. Coordinación de Francine Jácome. Caracas: Instituto Venezolano de Estudios Sociales y Políticos; Editorial Nueva Sociedad, 1993. 143 p.: bibl., ill.

Extended review studies cultural similarities and differences between English- and Spanish-speaking Caribbean nations, and the difficulties the latter create for regional integration. Examines the mass media, the anomaly of Cuba, oral literature and stereotypes, and ethnic identity, among other topics. See also item **4781.**

4818 Dóriga, Enrique L. Cuba 1995: vivencias personales. Lima: Univ. del Pacífico, Centro de Investigación (CIUP), 1996. 88 p. (Documentos de trabajo; 23)

Book-length monograph on present situation in Cuba includes chapters on the

revolutionary government, its public policy successes, the Special Period, difficulties of daily living (lack of food, education, and health care), emergence of the Catholic Church, the phenomenon of tourism and its impact on society, and widespread grievances and forms of protest.

Double passage: the lives of Caribbean migrants abroad and back home. See item **822.**

Drayton, Kathleen B. White man's knowledge: sex, race and class in Caribbean English language textbooks. See item **823.**

Duany, Jorge. The creation of a transnational Caribbean identity: Dominican immigrants in San Juan and New York City. See item **824.**

4819 Duany, Jorge. Imagining the Puerto Rican nation: recent works on cultural identity. (*LARR,* 31:3, 1996, p. 248–267, bibl.)

Reviews five books devoted to cultural and national identity of the Puerto Rican people. Lanny Thompson argues that US political and economic domination of Puerto Rico is predicated on unequal cultural relations between the two countries. The book edited by J.M. Carrion *et al.* contains 16 essays devoted to Pedro Albizu Campos, a prominent figure in Puerto Rico's history. The book edited by S. Alvarez-Curbelo and M. Castro gathers six papers analyzing foundational myths about Puerto Rico's history. A.D. Quinones has assembled nine of his literary essays dealing with the last 40 years of Puerto Rican cultural history. C.A. Torre edited a multidisciplinary volume containing 14 essays devoted to various aspects of Puerto Rican social and political life.

Duany, Jorge. Transnational migration from the Dominican Republic: the cultural redefinition of racial identity. See item **825.**

4820 Duharte Jiménez, Rafael. Cuba: identidad cultural, mestizaje y racismo; encuentros y desencuentros de la cultura cubana. (*Am. Indíg.,* 52:3, julio/sept. 1992, p. 159–167)

Summarizes experience of blacks in Cuba. Includes sections on slavery, the reality of mestizaje, and the continuation of racism.

4821 Dunn, Hopeton. Caribbean telecommunications policy: fashioned by debt, dependency and under-development. (*Caribb. Q.,* 40:2, June 1994, p. 33–56, bibl., tables)

Examines Caribbean telecommunications policies and their dependence on external capital, notably British. Local population's limited knowledge of technical matters has also helped to keep control of the telecommunications industry in the hands of the multinational firm Cable and Wireless (West Indies) Limited.

4822 Espín Guillois, Vilma. La mujer en Cuba; familia y sociedad: discursos, entrevistas, documentos. La Habana: Impr. Central de las FAR, 1990. 266 p.: bibl., ill.

Cuban Government's official perspective on Cuban women is presented by the long-time president of the Federación de Mujeres Cubanas, a quasi-governmental organization. Includes speeches and interviews on the subject of Cuban women.

Ethnicity, race and nationality in the Caribbean. See item **828.**

4823 La familia cubana: principales rasgos sociodemográficos que han caracterizado su desarrollo y dinámica. (*in* Cambios en el perfil de la familia: la experiencia regional. Santiago: Naciones Unidas, Comisión Económica para América Latina y el Caribe, 1993, p. 251–274, bibl., tables)

Demographic study of Cuba in late 1980s includes sections on birth, death, migration, age structure, and housing shortage. One section explains how social change has impacted the developmental stages of families in the island. Also addresses marriage formation (particularly age at marriage), fertility behavior, household characteristics, family composition, women's labor force participation, and the aging of the population.

4824 Fanfant, F.E. La recherche de la paternité. (*Haïti Inf. Libre*, 9:98, 1996, p. 25–32, photos)

Reviews the legal history and the present lack of satisfactory legislation in Haiti regulating the establishment of the rights and duties of fatherhood.

4825 Farnós Morejón, Alfonso. Cuba: perspectivas demográficas en el siglo XXI. (*in* El poblamiento de las Américas, *Veracruz*, 1992. Actas. Liège, Belgium: International Union for the Scientific Study of Population, 1992, v. 4, p. 195–212, bibl., tables)

Reviews recent demographic patterns in Cuba and the effects of the Special Period on these patterns. Discusses demographic effects of present-day issues including extremely low national fertility, international and internal migration flows, and the decline in the size of Havana. Offers population projections by age up to the year 2025.

4826 Faxas, Laura. El empresariado dominicano: ¿de clase dominante autoritaria a clase dirigente democrática? (*Estud. Soc.* / Santo Domingo, 28:100, abril/junio 1995, p. 63–102, bibl., facsim., tables)

Shows a pre-1980 absence of shared political consciousness among business people and its emergence in more recent years. Discusses Trujillo and Balaguer periods and State actions during their administrations which propitiated business people's political quiescence. Concluding section reviews the economic crisis of the 1980s and the reinsertion of business actors in politics.

4827 Fernandez, Nadine T. The color of love: young interracial couples in Cuba. (*Lat. Am. Perspect.*, 23:1, Winter 1996, p. 99–117, bibl.)

Ethnographic study of interracial couples in Cuba documents prevalence of black male-white female couples and continued racism of many Cuban families.

4828 Ferriol, Angela and **Alfredo González.** Cuba: política social en el ajuste económico. (*Caribb. Stud.*, 26:1/2, 1993, p. 81–111)

Offers detailed evaluation of needed economic adjustments in Cuba during the Special Period. Highlights problems of unemployment and underemployment, informal economy, salary imbalances, consumer behavior, deterioration of selected health indices, disconnection between educational training and labor force needs of the economy, housing deficits, and food allocations.

Flores, Juan. Divided borders: essays on Puerto Rican identity. See *HLAS 56:3601.*

4829 Ford-Smith, Honor. An experiment in popular theatre and women's history: *Ida Revolt inna Jonkonnu Stylee.* (*in* Subversive women: women's movements in Africa, Asia, Latin America and the Caribbean. Atlantic Highlands, N.J.: Zed Books Ltd., 1995, p. 147–164)

Examines role of popular theater for tradition of feminism in Jamaica. Discusses attempt of the Caribbean Popular Theater Exchange to make history available to broader society through theatrical performances.

4830 Ford-Smith, Honor. No! to sexual violence in Jamaica. (*in* Women and violence. Edited by Miranda Davis. London; Atlantic Highlands, N.J.: Zed Books Ltd., 1994, p. 225–229)

Relates the history and methods of Sistren, a working-class theater in Jamaica dedicated to stopping violence against women. Discusses tactics to curb the voilence including use of the theater and the media, and working with the young. Also discusses network of self-help groups formed as a result of Sistren's activities. See also item **4944.**

4831 Fuente García, Alejandro de la. Raça e desigualdade em Cuba, 1899–1981. (*Estud. Afro-Asiát.*, 27, abril 1995, p. 7–43, bibl., graphs, tables)

Wide-ranging empirical study, based on colonial and republican Cuban censuses, examines social situation of blacks in Cuba. Documents improvements in life expectancy and education during the post-1959 revolutionary period.

4832 Gabriel, Jean Michel. Comportements des haïtiens face aux dictons populaires. (*Bull. Bur. natl. ethnol.*, 1993–1994, p. 57–68, bibl., tables)

Reviews content of Haitian popular sayings and their ties to popular beliefs. Categorizes them as popular, instructive, telepathic, or mystic and tranquilizing sayings.

4833 Gautier Mayoral, Carmen. Puerto Rico: el efecto de los ajustes sobre la "democracia" y la descolonización a fines del siglo XX. (*Rev. Cienc. Soc./Río Piedras*, 30:1/2, enero/junio 1993, p. 3–26, ill.)

Reviews social problems caused by the colonial status of Puerto Rico and anticipated minimal effects of recent changes in the political status of Puerto Rico.

4834 *Género y Sociedad.* Vol. 1, no. 2, sept./dic. 1993. Posición socio-cultural y económica de la mujer en la República Dominicana de Clara Báez y Ginny Taulé. Santo Domingo: INTEC, Centro de Estudio del Género.

In-depth study examines social conditions of women in the Dominican Republic during post-1980 economic crisis. Includes sections on demographic patterns, work, education, health and nutrition, legal rights and protections, government programs, matrimony, and changes needed to bring about gender equality in the country.

4835 Gibbons, Arnold. Walter Rodney and his times. v. 1, Identity and ideology. Introduction by Wole Soyinka. Georgetown: Guyana National Printers Limited, 1994. 1 v.

First volume of biography of Walter Rodney consists of six chapters, roughly covering the historical context to his work, early intellectual ideas, relations with the Rastafari movement, contributions to the ideology and practice of black power, the problems of national development, and socialism in Africa. His work is understood in the context of England's colonial influence on Guyana, relations with the People's National Congress, and the struggle of Third World people to gain independence and self-determination.

4836 Gjerest, Heidi. First generation Rastafari in St. Eustatius: a case study in the Netherlands Antilles. (*Caribb. Q.*, 40:1, March 1994, p. 64–77, bibl.)

Shows transformations that Rastafari undergoes when separated from its point of origin. Examines Rasta settlement and subsistence patterns, social structure, diet and hygiene, ideology, and social gatherings.

Glazier, Stephen D. New religious movements in the Caribbean: identity and resistance. See item **835.**

Gmelch, George and **Sharon Bohn Gmelch.** The parish behind God's back: the changing culture of rural Barbados. See item **836.**

4837 González, José Luis. Puerto Rico: the four-storeyed country and other essays. Translated by Gerald Guinness. Princeton, N.J.: M. Wiener Pub., 1993. 135 p.: bibl.

Controversial, much commented on interpretation of Puerto Rican culture is written by a well-known writer and social critic who insists on importance of the African roots of the Puerto Rican nation and of the mestizos. Includes chapters on Puerto Rican literature and art. For historian's comment see *HLAS 56:2155.*

4838 Gopaul-McNicol, Sharon-Ann. An examination of racial attitudes of pre-school children in the English-speaking Caribbean. (*Caribb. Stud.*, 25:3/4, 1992, p. 389–400, bibl., tables)

Studies the environmental origin of white bias in pre-school children. Examines the influence of colonial rule; actions and racial biases of pre-school teachers; continuing discrimination against blacks in the mass media; and the political, economic, and social institutions of the region.

4839 Greene, John Edward. Race, class and gender in the future of the Caribbean: an overview. (*in* Association des études de la Caraïbe. Congrès, *13th, Pointe-à-Pitre, Guadeloupe, 1988*. Etudes caraïbéennes: société et politique; actes. Toulouse, France: Presses de l'Institut d'études politiques de Toulouse, 1991, p. 71–89, graphs)

Examines changes in the racial and class composition of the Caribbean population and their effects on kinship, status, social mobility, and stratification in this area. Discusses impact of changing gender relations on the dominant patterns of race and class.

4840 Gullick, C.J.M.R. Afro-American religious mindsets. (*Bull. Lat. Am. Res.*, 13:3, Sept. 1994, p. 319–326, bibl.)

Review of three books on Caribbean Afro-American religious mindsets focuses on intercultural communication among religions. Particular mindsets of differing religions influence the communication. Suggests differences result from various social structures, cultural beliefs, and cultural activities, all of which require proper cultural translation in order to understand fully the role of mindsets in religion.

4841 Gurak, Douglas T. and Mary M. Kritz. Social context, household composition and employment among migrant and nonmigrant Dominican women. (*Int. Migr. Rev.*, 30:2, Summer 1996, p. 399–422, bibl., graph, tables)

Examines effects of social composition on the employment status of females in the Dominican Republic and female immigrants from the Dominican Republic residing in New York City. Explores structural factors in the context of the Dominican Republic and

New York City that might account for the differing rates of employment.

Handwerker, W. Penn. Why violence?: a test of hypotheses representing three discourses on the roots of domestic violence. See item **841**.

Hay, Fred J. Microethnography of a Haitian boutique. See item **842**.

4842 Headley, Bernard D. The Jamaican crime scene: a perspective. Mandeville, Jamaica: Eureka Press, 1994. 182 p.: bibl., index.

Extended social commentary examines mostly male criminal behavior in Jamaica. Concludes that criminal behavior is the result of unequal opportunities. Identifies structural crises of 1960s as key determinants of subsequent crime. Offers detailed analysis of the causes of different types of crimes and specific recommendations to ameliorate the problem of crime. See also item **4907**.

4843 Henry, Paget. Grenada and the theory of peripheral transformation. (*Soc. Econ. Stud.*, 39:2, June 1990, p. 151–192, bibl.)

Examines theory of "peripheral transformation" and its applicability to understanding the impact of socialism in Grenada. Examines rise and fall of socialism and problems of political legitimization. Points to discrepancy between theories of socialist transformation and reality for developing nations.

4844 Hernández Angueira, Luisa. El *Estado Benefactor* y la pobreza en la mujer puertorriqueña. (*Rev. Adm. Pública/México*, 26, 1993/94, p. 319–328, bibl.)

Analyzes structural constraints impacting low-income women. Explores problem of poverty, the AFDC program and its impact on women, and the contradiction between greater demand for skilled labor and lower level of support for those in need.

4845 Hernández Cruz, Juan E. and Clara G. Muschkin. Corrientes migratorias en Puerto Rico = Migratory trends in Puerto Rico. Recopilación de Juan E. Hernández Cruz. San Germán, P.R.: Univ. Interamericana de Puerto Rico, 1994. 195 p.: bibl., ill. (Estudios sobre la sociedad y cultura puertorriqueña; Centro de Investigaciones del Caribe y América Latina; 4)

Collection of articles, most written by Hernández Cruz, focuses on societal impact and social organization of Puerto Rican migration to and from the mainland. Examines effects of migration on local government, demographic structure, labor force, and family.

4846 Herrera B., María del Socorro. Los Rastafari de Jamaica: movimiento social de resistencia. (*Am. Negra*, 9, junio 1995, p. 109–133, bibl., photo)

Interprets Rastafari as a nativistic social movement. Offers detailed analysis of social and cultural changes in the movement since its inception in late 1950s, and of the evolution of Rastafari communities and their ideology. Includes material on the meaning of hair styles, food habits, language, use of marijuana, reggae music, as well as on relations with the Jamaican State.

4847 Ho, Christine G.T. The twin processes of racialization and ethnification among Afro-Trinidadian immigrants in Los Angeles. (*Caribb. Q.*, 41:3/4, Sept./Dec. 1995, p. 99–122, bibl.)

Analyzes development of racial consciousness and racial-ethnic identity among Afro-Trinidadian immigrants in Los Angeles. Relates how Afro-Trinidadians grasp racial dynamics in the US in their quest for upward mobility. For ethnologist's comment see item **845.**

4848 Hoetink, Harmannus. Ideology, intellectuals, identity: the Dominican Republic 1880–1980; some preliminary notes. (*in* Intellectuals in the twentieth-century Caribbean. London: Macmillan Caribbean, 1992, v. 2, p. 132–144)

Examines several changes in Dominican society over the last 100 years. Key areas showing shifts are ideology, intellectual trends, dependence on external academic models of thought, and national and racial identity.

4849 Institut national de formation professionnelle (Haiti). Políticas de empleo y capacitación de jóvenes en Haití. (*in* Capacitación y empleo de jóvenes en América Latina: informe completo, Belo Horizonte, noviembre 1989. Montevideo: CINTERFOR/OIT, 1991, p. 195–200)

Summarizes labor force statistics, causes of unemployment and underemployment, and efforts to improve the structure of employment in Haiti.

4850 Itzigsohn, José. Migrant remittances, labor markets, and household strategies: a comparative analysis of low-income household strategies in the Caribbean Basin. (*Soc. Forces*, 74:2, Dec. 1995, p. 633–655, bibl., tables)

Statistical analysis shows importance of economic remittances for subsistence and social mobility of low-income families and households in the cities of Santo Domingo, Guatemala, Kingston, and Port-au-Prince.

4851 Joanis, Mirlène. Le droit des enfants dans la famille haïtienne. (*Haïti Inf. Libre*, 9:98, 1996, p. 9–15, photos)

Describes the predicament of young people in Haiti. Notes their physical and sexual abuse, their sexist education, and their victimization by laws.

4852 Jorge, Antonio. An objectless revolution: Cuba's nominal socialism as a personal project. (*Rev. Interam. Bibliogr.*, 43:2, 1993, p. 287–298)

Critical review of the book *The Cuban Revolution into the 1990s: Cuban perspectives* (see *HLAS* 55:3119). Analyzes logical fallacies and ideological biases of the book. Asserts that the book reflects fundamental traits of the totalitarian society in which it was produced.

4853 Jutkowitz, Joel M. and **Orlando Hernández.** Linking research to message construction: the use of focus groups in the Dominican Republic. (*in* Drug lessons & education programs in developing countries. New Brunswick, N.J.: Transaction Publishers, 1995, p. 105–116, ill., tables)

Examines use of focus groups in developing necessary information to organize a mass campaign against drug abuse by adolescents. Dramatic content and realism, rather than ridicule, seem more effective for prevention.

Koningsbruggen, Petrus Hendrikus van. The spirit of Canboulay: the socio-cultural autonomy of the Trinidad Carnival. See item **853.**

4854 Lavy, Victor; Michael Palumbo; and **Steven N. Stern.** Health care in Jamaica: quality, outcomes, and labor supply.

Washington: World Bank, 1995. 30 p.: bibl. (LSMS working paper; 116)

Investigates relationships among labor force participation, health outcomes, and quality of health care in Jamaica. Develops an econometric model linking demand for health care, health status outcomes, and labor force participation.

4855 Lefever, Harry G. Unraveling the web of "Anansi the Spider": the trickster in the West African diaspora. (*J. Caribb. Stud.,* 9:3, Winter 1993/Spring 1994, p. 247–265, table)

Describes folklore of the peoples of Tortuguero, an African diaspora town on the Atlantic Coast of Costa Rica. Offers folk story of "Anansi the Spider" as an example. Work examines model of reality the folklore advances and the functions it serves.

LeFranc, Elsie. The meaning of sexual partnerships: re-examining the Jamaican family system. See item **860**.

4856 LeFranc, Elsie. Status group formation in small communities: a case study of a Dominican small-farming village. Mona, Jamaica: Institute of Social and Economic Research, Univ. of the West Indies, 1993. 106 p.: bibl., ill. (Working paper; 39)

Study of peasant community life in the West Indies is based on fieldwork in a village in Dominica. First chapter presents the peasantry in Caribbean societies as an integral component of capitalism. Social network analysis is used to document the existence of clusters of social relationships and of mutual aid among peasants. Identifies a typology of such mutual aid social relationships. For ethnologist's comment, see *HLAS 55: 815.*

4857 Leo-Rhynie, Elsa. The Jamaican family: continuity and change. Kingston: The Grace, Kennedy Foundation, 1993. 69 p.: bibl. (Grace, Kennedy Foundation lecture; 1993.)

Essay on Jamaican family patterns and socialization identifies social problems threatening the family such as increasing poverty, substandard educational institutions, and teenage pregnancy.

4858 Lewis, William F. Soul rebels: the Rastafari. Foreword by Serena Nanda. Edited by Joan Young Gregg. Prospect Heights, Ill.: Waveland Press, 1993. 139 p.: bibl., ill., map.

Book-length monograph on the Rastafari uses both historical and participant observation ethnographic methods. Contains chapters on history of the movement, its adaptation to the urban area of Kingston, relationships with the Jamaican State, growth of Rastafari in the US, symbolism, problems with the law, and status of the social movement—or its evolution from charisma to institution.

4859 Lhérisson, Dilia Lemaire. La réalité légale des enfants en Haïti. (*Haïti Inf. Libre,* 9:98, 1996, p. 17–23, photos)

Reviews the *de facto* and *de jure* rights of young children in Haiti and the difficulties created by polygamous practices in the country. Documents the lack of State-funded institutions protecting young children.

4860 Lowe, Agatha. Themes of war, politics and health education in calypso music. (*Caribb. Q.,* 39:2, June 1993, p. 56–72, bibl.)

Discusses social and historical context of protest and struggle in calypso music. Explores political expression of these ideas in the music. In addition, author finds that health care issues such as AIDS prevention, family planning, and drug abuse are also effectively expressed through the music.

4861 Lozano, Wilfredo. Migración e informalidad en República Dominicana. (*Cienc. Soc./Santo Domingo,* 18:3, julio/sept. 1993, p. 254–270)

Examines post-1950 labor force migration patterns. Traces links between immigration of Haitians into agriculture and urban labor markets and the emigration of Dominicans to New York.

4862 Lozano, Wilfredo. Tradición caudillista y cambio político en República Dominicana, 1966–1994. (*Perf. Latinoam.,* 5:8, enero/junio 1996, p. 29–50, bibl.)

Analyzes *caudillista* political tradition in the Dominican Republic and its forms of expression during both authoritarian and populist regimes. Includes sections on the origin of the Balaguer Government and the contemporary crisis of caudillo politics.

4863 Lutjens, Sheryl L. Remaking the public sphere: women and revolution in Cuba. (*in* Women and revolution in Africa, Asia, and the New World. Edited by Mary Ann Té-treault. Columbia, S.C.: Univ. of South Carolina Press, 1994, p. 366–393)

Examines changing women's roles in Cuba resulting from changes of late 1980s and Cuba's continued commitment to socialist ideals. Discusses reorganization of the public sphere during the rectification period and the role of gender. Concludes by discussing the dangers of privatization. For political scientist's comment see item **3352.**

Mahabir, Kumar. Whose nation is this?: the struggle over national and ethnic identity in Guyana. See item **863.**

4864 Maharaj, Ashram B. The pandits in Trinidad: a study of a Hindu institution. Foreword by P.K. Misra. Trinidad: Indian Review Press, 1991. 96 p.

Study of the orthodox Sanatanist sect in Trinidad is based in part on interviews conducted during 1987–91 with pandits and other key East Indian informants. Examines the caste system from which the sect originates, its links to immigration, and the importance of the pandits for the Hindu community in the island.

4865 Malo de Molina, Gustavo F. El bohío cubano. (*Anu. Etnol./Habana*, 1988, p. 50–66, bibl.)

Detailed examination of the Cuban *bohío* includes its historical evolution as well as origins of the term, comparisons to buildings in Venezuela, building materials and technology, and existing typologies.

4866 Manigat, Sabine. Migración y movimientos sociales en Haití. (*Cienc. Soc./Santo Domingo*, 18:3, julio/sept. 1993, p. 271–280)

Comments on the relationship between social movements and migration in Haiti, the transformation of the culture of Port-au-Prince by rural immigrants, and the growth of other urban centers in Haiti.

4867 Martínez, Juan A. Cuban art and national identity: the Vanguardia painters, 1927–1950. Gainesville: Univ. Press of Florida, 1994. 189 p.: bibl., ill. (some col.), index.

Presents in detail the work of Cuban painters in the Vanguardia art movement of 1927–50. Includes chapters on the artistic context of the movement, contemporary so-

cial movements, the search for national identity, and biographies of Lam, Pelaez, Enriquez, Ponce, Abela, Gattorno and Victor Manuel.

Martínez, Samuel. Indifference with indignation: anthropology, human rights, and the Haitian bracero. See item **864.**

Martínez, Samuel. The masking of history: popular images of the nation on a Dominican sugar plantation. See item **865.**

4868 Martínez Pérez, Liliana. Los riesgos de la identidad en Cuba. (*Perf. Latinoam.*, 3:4, junio 1994, p. 169–192)

Detailed study examines attempts at cultural change in Cuba during post-1959 revolutionary period and reactions of the government and political elite. Includes information on recent attempts by artists and social scientists to bring about alternative cultural change.

4869 Martínez Rosario, Raúl. Puerto Rico, una ruta incierta al norte: la travesía en yola. Santo Domingo: Centro Editorial, 1993. 177 p.

First-person, ethnographic account of illegal immigration from the Dominican Republic to Puerto Rico, and eventually to Chicago. Describes dangers, fears experienced during the trip by sea, and difficulties illegal immigrants face in finding work and evading detection by government and immigration officials in both Puerto Rico and the mainland.

4870 Martínez Vergne, Teresita. The liberation of women in the Caribbean: research perspectives for the study of gender relations in the post-emancipation period. (*Caribb. Stud.*, 27:1/2, Jan./June 1994, p. 5–36)

Reviews contemporary scholarship on women in the Caribbean. Includes sections on slavery, post-slavery class relationships, and family and household dynamics. See also item **4878.**

4871 Marvel, Thomas S. Antonin Nechodoma, architect 1877–1928: the Prairie School in the Caribbean. Gainesville: Univ. Press of Florida, 1994. 223 p.: bibl., ill., index, maps.

In-depth study examines buildings designed by Antonin Nechodoma in Puerto Rico and the influence of the Prairie School on his work. Includes chapters on Nechodoma's training in Chicago and residence in the Dominican Republic, as well as extended assessments of his building designs in Puerto Rico.

4872 Matibag, Eugenio D. Voodoo origins of Afro-Cuban culture. (*J. Caribb. Stud.*, 10:1/2, Winter 1994/Spring 1995, p. 50–65)

Reviews history of the West African slave trade and Yoruba origins of Afro-Cuban culture. Includes discussion of the myth of Ile Ife and the rise and fall of Oyo. Concludes by analyzing Yoruba practices in contemporary Cuba.

4873 Matos Moquete, Manuel. Contexto sociocultural del prejuicio antihaitiano de los dominicanos: una investigación de ONÈ-RESPE. (*Estud. Soc./Santo Domingo*, 29:104, abril/junio 1996, p. 75–86, bibl.)

Presents extended discourse on race relations in Haiti and the Dominican Republic from the perspective of a Dominican writer and based on research by the group Equipo Onè-Respe.

4874 Meléndez, Edwin. Puerto Rican migration and occupational selectivity, 1982–1988. (*Int. Migr. Rev.*, 28:105, Spring 1994, p. 49–67, bibl., graphs, tables)

Offers a statistical examination of the migration of Puerto Ricans to and from the mainland. Research finds no evidence of occupational selectivity among Puerto Rican emigrants, with the exception of farm workers, laborers, and craft and kindred workers who are overrepresented in emigration to the US.

4875 Millet, José and **Alexis Alarcón.** El culto de los gemelos en el vodú cubano. (*Del Caribe*, 23, 1994, p. 99–103, photos)

Ethnographic study examines voodoo religious cult practice in Cuba and the relative importance of twins in its pantheon of supernatural forces and divinities.

4876 Millett, Trevor M. The Chinese in Trinidad. Port of Spain: Inprint Caribbean, 1993. 321 p.: bibl., ill., index, maps.

History of Chinese immigrants in Trinidad since 19th century includes descriptions of commercial activities, voluntary associations, cultural traits, ethnic identity, and evolving generational differences.

4877 Modern Bahamian society. Edited by Dean Walter Collinwood and Steve Dodge. Parkersburg, Iowa: Caribbean Books, 1989. 278 p.: bibl., map.

Lengthy collection of articles on the social history of contemporary Bahamian society contains works by distinguished specialists. Includes sections on politics, economics, and culture. Includes essays by R. Ramsaran on the economy, D.L. Johnson on Black Tuesday, C.P. Hughes on symbolic race relationships, and J. Levey on ethnography of small village life.

4878 Mohammed, Patricia. Nuancing the feminist discourse in the Caribbean. (*Soc. Econ. Stud.*, 43:3, Sept. 1994, p. 135–167, bibl.)

Considers continued relevance of feminist scholarship for understanding Caribbean society. Argues for creative adaptation of feminist scholarship to the lives of the people of the region, and for the value of scholarship in achieving an appreciation of the origin and continuation of patriarchy. See also item **4870.**

4879 Morel, Edmundo and **Manuel Mejía.** Los impactos de los desalojos: la constitución o reconstitución de las identidades. (*Estud. Soc./Santo Domingo*, 26:94, oct./dic. 1993, p. 45–74, bibl.)

Critically assesses the impact of urban renewal in Santo Domingo on approximately 30,000 displaced families. Stresses importance of individual and collective identity of displaced people, continued importance of their neighborhood identification, and solidarity created by religious beliefs.

4880 Mujer y estadísticas: memorias del primer seminario. Producción ejectutiva y técnica, y edición de Evelyn Otero Figueroa. Puerto Rico: Pro Mujer, Colegio Universitario de Cayey, UPR, 1992. 1 v.: bibl., ill.

Proceedings of a conference on statistics about women in Puerto Rico includes chapters on statistics in education, health, labor force participation, and the informal economy. Also discusses potential availability and use of existing data sources such as the Commonwealth Government and US Bureau of the Census.

4881 Muñoz Tábora, Jesús. La cultura garífuna en el contexto musical Afro Caribe. (*Acervo/Tegucigalpa*, 1, mayo/junio/julio 1994, p. 30–37, bibl.)

Studies impact of African culture on Caribbean music and dance expressions. Discusses the music of Cuba, Haiti, Dominican Republic, Trinidad, Guyana, and coastal Honduras.

Murray, David A.B. The cultural citizen: negations of race and language in the making of Martiniquais. See item **878.**

4882 Muschkin, Clara G. and **George C. Myers.** Return migrant status and income attainment in Puerto Rico. (*Soc. Econ. Stud.*, 42:1, March 1993, p. 149–170, bibl., tables)

Discussion of Puerto Rican return migration questions human capital assumption that return migrants have greater potential for economic success than non-migrants. Reviews prior research on return migrants in Puerto Rico. Uses US Bureau of the Census information to show that migratory behavior does not correlate positively with economic attainment.

4883 Nettleford, Rex M. Inward stretch, outward reach: a voice from the Caribbean. London: Macmillan Caribbean, 1993. 209 p.: bibl., index.

In this collection of articles by a noted Jamaican intellectual, one of the recurrent themes is the preservation of Jamaican and Caribbean culture and the use of education, the arts, dance, festivals, and the mass media.

4884 Nicholls, David. Lebanese of the Antilles: Haiti, Dominican Republic, Jamaica, and Trinidad. (*in* The Lebanese in the world: a century of emigration. London: Centre for Lebanese Studies, 1992, p. 339–360)

Examines migration flows from Lebanon into the Caribbean islands, focusing specifically on their presence in Haiti, Dominican Republic, Jamaica, and Trinidad. Emphasizes marriage patterns, types of employment, religious customs, and links with Lebanon.

4885 O'Callaghan, Evelyn. (Ex)tending the boundaries: early travel writing by women and the construction of the "West In-dies." (*Caribb. Stud.*, 27:3/4, July/Dec. 1994, p. 255–277, bibl.)

Analyzes "travel writing" narrative style characteristic of women's literature in the Caribbean. Argues that this style contributed to the representation of the West Indies region in literary and art work.

Olwig, Karen Fog. The migration experience: Nevisian women at home & abroad. See item **882.**

Oostindie, Gert. Ethnicity, nationalism and the exodus: the Dutch Caribbean predicament. See item **883.**

4886 Oropesa, R.S. Normative beliefs about marriage and cohabitation: a comparison of non-Latino whites, Mexican Americans, and Puerto Ricans. (*J. Marriage Fam.*, 58:1, Feb. 1996, p. 49–62, bibl., tables)

Discusses impact of ethnic, socioeconomic, and cultural variables on attitudes towards marriage and singlehood among non-Latino whites, Mexican Americans, and mainland Puerto Ricans.

4887 Ortiz, Vilma. Migration and marriage among Puerto Rican women. (*Int. Migr. Rev.*, 30:2, Summer 1996, p. 460–484, appendix, bibl., graphs, tables)

Examines the effects of family indicators on migration by women from Puerto Rico to US, and return, in the 1980s. Suggests that unmarried women are more likely to migrate from and return to Puerto Rico, and that women married for longer periods of time are the least likely to migrate.

Parry, Odette. Equality, gender and the Caribbean classroom. See item **885.**

4888 Pascual Morán, Vanessa. La migración dominicana indocumentada a Puerto Rico: ¿marginación o movilidad social? (*Rev. Adm. Pública/México*, 26, 1993/94, p. 275–304, bibl., tables)

Reviews history of migration between Puerto Rico and the Dominican Republic and the economic crisis creating massive Dominican emigration. Includes demographic analysis of emigrants from the Dominican Republic, what is known about these undocumented immigrants in Puerto Rico, their dependence on agricultural work, and the increasing difficulty of the agricultural sector in Puerto Rico.

4889 Payne, Monica A. The nature and extent of Barbadian adolescents' sex-stereotyping of occupations. (*Soc. Econ. Stud.*, 42:2/3, June/Sept. 1993, p. 135–151, bibl., tables)

Reviews gender stereotyping of occupations by Barbadian adolescents. Stereotyping was stronger for perceived "competence" than for "eligibility." Notes that stereotyped views on eligibility for occupations have lessened, but a perception of lower competence for women in traditionally male occupations still remains. This is especially true among male adolescents.

4890 Payne, Monica A. and **Adrian Furnham.** Perceptions of crime and delinquency in Barbados. (*Soc. Econ. Stud.*, 39:2, June 1990, p. 135–150, bibl., tables)

Investigates how people of Barbados evaluate 50 delinquent and criminal offenses. Finds that offenses' relative degree of seriousness varies according to respondents' age group, religious affiliation, and gender. Discusses implications of findings for law enforcement, mass media's shaping of public opinion toward criminal offenses, and public awareness campaigns.

4891 Payne, Monica A. Television viewing habits of Barbadian adolescents: a preliminary study. (*Soc. Econ. Stud.*, 40:3, Sept. 1991, p. 91–114, bibl., tables)

Reviews impact of program content on television viewing habits of Barbados adolescents. Notes programs watched by adolescents, and records viewing patterns according to time of day, day of the week (weekdays and weekends), late night, and video watching. Differences in viewing patterns were associated with respondents' gender, age, and type of school attended.

4892 Peláez Martínez, Roberto et al. El médico de la familia y la medicina general integral en la República de Cuba. (*Interciencia/Caracas*, 20:4, July/Aug. 1995, p. 212–214, bibl., tables)

Reviews success of the family doctor program and its link to preventive medicine.

Pereira, Joe. Gun talk and girls' talk: the DJ clash. See item **886.**

Pérez Sáinz, Juan Pablo. Imaginarios sociales sobre el trabajo: percepciones empresariales y sindicales en la industria de exportación de Costa Rica y República Dominicana. See item **4736.**

Phillips, Daphne. The family in crisis: explaining the new phenomenon of street children in Trinidad. See item **887.**

4893 Picó, Fernando. Coffee and the rise of commercial agriculture in Puerto Rico's highlands: the occupation and loss of land in Guaonico and Roncador (Utuado), 1833–1900. (*in* Coffee, society, and power in Latin America. Edited by William Roseberry, Lowell Gudmundson, and Mario Samper K. Baltimore: Johns Hopkins Univ. Press, 1995, p. 94–111, tables)

Examines struggles associated with rise of commercial agriculture in Puerto Rico. Studies the occupation and subsequent loss of land by first settlers in Guaonico and Roncador during 1833–1900. Identifies five stages of land occupation by these landholders and offers five explanations for their loss of land in these regions.

4894 Pierre-Charles, Gérard. Los actores sociales en el proceso político. (*Cienc. Soc./Santo Domingo*, 18:3, julio/sept. 1993, p. 299–318)

Comments on the political dynamics of the 1986–92 transitional period in Haiti. Argues that important segments of the middle classes were weakened prior to and during this time period, and shows implications of this weakening for the prospects of democracy.

4895 Pierre-Charles, Gérard. El difícil camino del cambio democrático en Haití. (*Perf. Latinoam.*, 5:8, enero/junio 1996, p. 51–78)

Reviews evolution towards democracy in Haiti and present-day efforts to invigorate local governments and citizen participation in politics.

4896 Portes, Alejandro; José Itzigsohn; and Carlos Dore-Cabral. Urbanization in the Caribbean Basin: social change during the years of the crisis. (*LARR*, 29:2, 1994, p. 3–37, bibl., maps, tables)

Reviews recent Latin American urbanization theories which focus on changes in urban primacy, spatial polarization within the cities, the urban informal economy, increased participation of the region in the global economy, and the economic crisis of the last two decades.

4897 Pouchet Paquet, Sandra. Surfacing: the counterhegemonic project of representation, identification, and resistance in nineteenth-century African Caribbean women's texts. (*Caribb. Stud.*, 27:3/4, July/Dec. 1994, p. 278–297, bibl.)

Discusses 19th-century African Caribbean women's texts reflecting their quest for cultural legitimacy and autonomy. Reconstructs Caribbean women's aesthetic, literary culture, and narrative styles.

4898 Praeger, Michèle. Of masters and maroons. (*J. Caribb. Stud.*, 9:3, Winter 1993/Spring 1994, p. 178–193)

Presents a historiographical perspective of *marronage*, the flight from slavery. Reviews different theoretical perspectives and also delineates creation and origins of a slave identity.

Price, Richard. Duas variantes das relações raciais no Caribe. See item **889**.

4899 Puerto Rican women and children: issues in health, growth, and development. Edited by Gontran Lamberty and Cynthia T. García Coll. New York: Plenum Press, 1994. 285 p.: bibl., ill., index. (Topics in social psychiatry. The language of science)

Wide-ranging, lengthy collection of papers on Puerto Ricans on the mainland and the island includes Clara E. Rodriguez's historical review of Puerto Rican immigration to the US. Other chapters present information on Puerto Rican fertility, the problem of AIDS, bilingual education, pediatric care, and children's health and physical growth.

4900 Quintero Rivera, Angel G. El tambor oculto en el cuatro: la melodización de ritmos y la etnicidad cimarroneada en la caribeña cultura de la contraplantación. (*Bol. Am.*, 33:42/43, 1992/93, p. 87–106, music)

Traces importance of salsa music as a symbol of Puerto Rican national identity, and places it in the context of counter- or oppositional culture. Shows African roots of the music and its similarity to the Puerto Rican *bomba*.

Quintero Rivero, Angel G. The somatology of manners: class, race and gender in the history of dance etiquette in the Hispanic Caribbean. See item **893**.

4901 Race, class & gender in the future of the Caribbean. Edited by John Edward Greene. Mona, Jamaica: Institute of Social & Economic Research, Univ. of the West Indies, 1993. 138 p.: bibl., ill.

Collection of articles on the theme of class, race, and gender in Caribbean societies includes G.W. Roberts' chapter on the history of vital statistics registrations, R. Reddock's chapter on the autonomy and primacy of gender, H. McKenzie's chapter on family forms, and J.E. Greene's introductory chapter on models of race and ethnic relations, as well as other commentaries. For ethnologist's comment see *HLAS 55: 827*.

4902 Ramírez, Nelson. La emigración dominicana hacia el exterior: análisis de los resultados del cuestionario de hogar ampliado, encuesta demográfica y de salud 1991, Endesa 91. Santo Domingo: Instituto de Estudios de Población y Desarrollo, 1993. 40 leaves: bibl., ill. (Serie monográfica; 01)

Study of Dominican external migration presents results of the 1991 national survey of families on health and demography. Estimates numbers for international migration of Dominicans, and relates characteristics of the emigrants and of return migrants.

4903 Ramírez, Nelson. Las migraciones internas en República Dominicana: análisis de los resultados del cuestionario de hogar ampliado, encuesta demográfica y de salud de 1991. Santo Domingo: Instituto de Estudios de Población y Desarrollo, 1993. 48 leaves: bibl., ill. (Serie monográfica; 02)

Study of internal migration in the Dominican Republic presents results of 1991 national survey of families on health and demography. Documents regional net migration gains and sociodemographic differences between migrants and non-migrants.

4904 Ramoutar, Karen M. The impact of punishment threats on crime in a Caribbean community. (*Soc. Econ. Stud.*, 44:1, March 1995, p. 31–47, appendix, bibl., tables)

Examines the problem of deterrence and the effect of punishment on the occurrence of crime. Presents an empirical test of four types of punishment threats on self reports of crime in Barbados. Discusses effects of stigma from peers, threat of guilt, legal punishment, and the perceived rewards from involvement in crime.

4905 Rauzduel, Rosan. Introduction à la sociologie du développement de la Guadeloupe. Paris: Publisud, 1995. 118 p.: bibl. (Manuels 2000)

Summarizes important aspects of the history of the people of Guadeloupe, including their social stratification system; the geopolitical relationship vis-à-vis other West Indian nations, the US, and France; a synthesis of theories of national development; and the accomplishments and failures of development policy in Guadeloupe.

Razak, Victoria M. Carnival in Aruba: history and meaning in Aruba's bacchanal. See item **894.**

4906 Reddock, Rhoda. The early women's movement in Trinidad and Tobago, 1900–1937. (in Subversive women: women's movements in Africa, Asia, Latin America and the Caribbean. Atlantic Highlands, N.J.: Zed Books Ltd., 1995, p. 101–120)

Examines impact of the nationalist framework on the women's movement in Trinidad and Tobago from 1900–37 and the differing attitudes of black, white, middle-class, and working-class women.

4907 Report of the National Task Force on Crime. Kingston: Jamaica Printing Services, 1993. 113 p.: ill.

A national task force evaluation of the crime problem in Jamaica reviews statistics on various categories of crime. Includes a straightforward statement about the causes of crime and ameliorating the crime problem to creating a just society. See also item **4842.**

4908 Richardson, Mary F. Fear of success and gender-role stereotyping. (Soc. Econ. Stud., 42:2/3, June/Sept. 1993, p. 153–174, bibl., tables)

Qualitative examination of stories written by Jamaican teenagers in response to cues concerning male and female success. Boys and girls characterized both male and female cues according to commonly held gender stereotypes.

4909 Richardson, Mary F. "Fear of success" and Jamaican adolescents. (Soc. Econ. Stud., 40:2, June 1991, p. 63–82, bibl., graph, tables)

Examines "fear of success" responses of Jamaican adolescents and male and female

attitudes toward success. Documents effects of age, gender cues, and type of educational environment.

4910 Ríos, Palmira N. Gender, industrialization, and development in Puerto Rico. (in Women in the Latin American development process. Philadelphia: Temple Univ. Press, 1995, p. 125–148, bibl., tables)

Reviews gender divisions in the labor market, industrialization, and economic development in Puerto Rico. Also examines effects of Operation Bootstrap (a modernization program to improve economic conditions) on three distinct stages of the industrialization process. Delineates characteristics of gender-typed manufacturing activities (especially in the petrochemical sector) as well as the influence of gender on economic development policies.

4911 Rivera Ramos, Alba Nydia. Personalidad puertorriqueña: mito o realidad. Río Piedras, P.R.: Editorial Edil, 1993. 139 p.

Sociopsychological study of the national character of the Puerto Rican people includes chapters on males, females, and children. Emphasizes impact of US relations and presence on Puerto Rican culture and personal identity.

4912 Riviere, Bill. Reminiscences concerning mass work among farmers in Dominica, 1976–1980. (Soc. Econ. Stud., 42:2/3, June/Sept. 1993, p. 261–282, appendix)

Discusses grassroots movements formed in Dominica during 1976–80. These years were a time of political uncertainty and constitutional transformation. Paper explains peasant-based political movements, and includes information about the members of these movements, their mobilization against the political regime, creation of the organizations, the importance of farmers in the mass revolt, and the electoral campaigns.

Rodney, Walter. The birth of the Guyanese working class and the first sugar strikes, 1840/41 and 1847. See item **3276.**

4913 Rodríguez, Juan M. and **Arthur J. Mann.** The Puerto Rican entrepreneur: personal and company characteristics. (Caribb. Stud., 27:1/2, Jan./June 1994, p. 85–102, bibl., tables)

Statistical description of 904 Puerto

Rican entrepeneurs and their businesses. Describes their two principal difficulties: capital and high operational costs, and personnel relationships.

4914 Rodríguez Chávez, Ernesto. Tendencias actuales del flujo migratorio cubano. (*Caribb. Stud.*, 26:1/2, 1993, p. 127–159)

Provides thorough description of the major issues surrounding Cuban emigration since mid-1980s, and gives Cuban government's statistics on legal and illegal emigrants. Examines the recently-created Program Exodus sponsored by the Cuban American National Foundation, and the special situation of Cuban deportees in prison in the US.

4915 Rojas, Rafael. Insularidad y exilio de los intelectuales cubanos. (*Estud. Filos. Hist. Let.*, 11:43, invierno 1995/96, p. 69–83)

Encyclopedic essay reviews the presence of the reality of exile both as a spiritual and a spatial experience in Cuban culture and national identity. Also examines its manifestation in the life and works of arguably the most noted intellectuals in the history of Cuba from colonial times to the present. For political scientist's comment, see item **3363.**

4916 Román, Madeline. Estado y criminalidad en Puerto Rico: un abordaje criminológico alternativo. San Juan: Publicaciones Puertorriqueños, 1993. 145 p.: bibl.

Reviews criminal and penal practices in Puerto Rico. Includes chapters on the history of crime and punishment, social control mechanisms, prison system, drug-related crimes, and crimes of passion (mostly against women).

4917 Rosario, Pedro Juan del. Azúcar, agroempresas y campesinos en la República Dominicana. (*Rev. Eme-Eme*, 19:90/91, sept. 1991/abril 1992, p. 11–32, bibl.)

Extended commentary examines crisis of sugarcane production in the Dominican Republic. Argues for the need for a new national agricultural policy to facilitate agricultural production by small farmers.

Ryan, Selwyn D. Gobernabilidad democrática y condiciones sociales en el Caribe anglófono. See item **3253.**

4918 Ryan, Selwyn D. Structural adjustment and the ethnic factor in Caribbean societies. (*in* Democracy in the Caribbean: political, economic, and social perspectives. Baltimore: The Johns Hopkins Univ. Press, 1993, p. 122–142, tables)

Examines role of economic structural adjustment policies in ethnic relationships in Trinidad, Tobago, and Guyana, and the possibility that these new policies may increase ethnic rivalry and competition for resources. Power-sharing techniques are offered to avoid the political and social crisis that may occur as a result of the increased competition.

4919 Safa, Helen Icken. Gender implications of export-led industrialization in the Caribbean Basin. (*in* EnGENDERing wealth and well-being: empowerment for global change. Boulder, Colo.: Westview Press, 1995, p. 89–112, tables)

Critical examination of export-led industrialization in the Caribbean region focuses on the garment and textile industry and its impact on gender relationships in the Dominican Republic and Puerto Rico. Reviews the promises, achievements, and failure of Operation Bootstrap, and its impact on female employment.

4920 Safa, Helen Icken. The myth of the male breadwinner: women and industrialization in the Caribbean. Boulder, Colo.: Westview Press, 1995. 208 p.: bibl., ill., index. (Conflict and social change series)

Comparative sociohistorical study examines interplay of the economy and gender relationships in Cuba, Puerto Rico, and the Dominican Republic. Offers extended treatment of the impact of Operation Bootstrap on Puerto Rican women and gender relationships, the impact on women of the Dominican Republic's economic crisis and export manufacturing option of the 1980s, and the development of mass organizations for women in Cuba.

4921 Sainte-Rose, Pierre-Leval. Le retour des migrants aux Antilles et en Guyane Françaises. (*in* Association des études de la Caraïbe. Congrès, *13th, Pointe-à-Pitre, Guadeloupe, 1988*. Etudes caraïbéennes: société et politique; actes. Toulouse, France; Presses de l'Institut d'études politiques de Toulouse; Pointe-à-Pitre: Centre d'études et de recherches caraïbéennes; Fort-de-France: Univ. des Antilles et de la Guyane, 1991, p. 117–143, tables)

A study of migration to France from the French Antilles. Includes information on the demographic and work situation of the migrants in the metropolis, as well as detailed information on the return migrants to French Guiana occasioned by the economic crisis and increasing xenophobia against immigrants current in France.

4922 Savishinsky, Neil J. Transitional popular culture and the global spread of the Jamaican Rastafarian movement. (*NWIG*, 68:3/4, 1994, p. 259–281, bibl.)

Examines spread of the Rastafarian movement and its impact on world culture. Author notes growing use of low-cost technologies (cassettes, VCRs, etc.) enabling "Rasta" culture to expand throughout the world, and political, ideological, and musical influences of reggae on popular culture.

4923 Seguinot Barbosa, José. La ecología urbana de San Juan: una interpretación geográfico-social. San Germán: Univ. Interamericana de Puerto Rico, Recinto de San Germán; Centro de Investigaciones del Caribe y América Latina, 1995. 25 p. (Documentos de Trabajo; 66)

Reviews growth of population and attendant ecological changes in the San Juan area, emphasizing social geography of the metropolis. Focuses on ecological adaptation, including changes in vegetation, topography, coasts, climate, and quality of life in the metropolitan area, and shows that such changes reflect the social, cultural, and economic forces that have shaped Puerto Rico since European colonization, including the resulting changes to vegetation, topography, coasts, climate, and quality of life in the metropolitan area.

4924 Serra Deliz, Wenceslao. La construcción social de la imagen de la mujer en el refranero puertorriqueño. (*in* Asssociation des Études de la Caraïbe. Congrès, *13th, Pointe-à-Pitre, Guadeloupe, 1988.* Etudes caraïbéennes: société et politique; actes. Toulouse, France; Presses de l'Institut d'études politiques de Toulouse; Pointe-à-Pitre: Centre d'études et de recherches caraïbéennes; Fort-de-France: Univ. des Antilles et de la Guyane,

1991, p. 31–69, bibl.)

Synthesis of Puerto Rican popular sayings or *refranes* looks at their verbal aggresivity against women, their conception of gender relations, and their portrayal of women as evil, dumb, mentally incompetent, and morally defective.

4925 Smith, Raymond T. "Living in the gun mouth:" race, class, and political violence in Guyana. (*NWIG*, 69:3/4, 1995, p. 223–252, bibl., table)

Analyzes collective memory creating the political identity of the people of Guyana. Examines independence from Britain, the conflict among various ethnic groups, and the presence of social stratification and inequality juxtaposed to a national ideology of equality. For ethnologist's comment see item **901.**

Stevens, Alta Mae. The symbolic significance of *manje* in Haitian culture. See item **905.**

4926 Stubbs, Jean. Revolutionizing women, family, and power. (*in* Women and politics worldwide. Edited by Barbara J. Nelson and Najma Chowdhury. New Haven, Conn.: Yale Univ. Press, 1994, p. 189–207)

Reviews active contribution of women in the shaping of Cuba as a nation. Discusses history of the women's movement, the revolutionary changes since late 1950s, and participation of women in different spheres of life such as family, employment, politics, and media.

4927 Sudama, Trevor. The political uses of myth, or, Discrimination rationalized: a collection of articles. Trinidad: T. Sudama, 1993? 296 p.

Journalist's wide-ranging collection of commentaries and extended analyses focus on problems of intergroup relations in Trinidad and the continued difficulties of indigenous peoples.

4928 Tardieu-Dehoux, Charles. Education et culture en Haïti après quarante ans de pouvoir noir et de régime duvaliérien. (*in* Association des études de la Caraïbe. Congrès, *13th, Pointe-à-Pitre, Guadeloupe, 1988.* Études caraïbéennes: société et politique; actes. Toulouse, France; Presses de l'Institut d'études politiques de Toulouse; Pointe-à-Pitre: Centre d'études et de recherches caraïbéennes; Fort-de-France: Univ. des Antilles et de la Guyane, 1991, p. 91–116, table)

An analysis of education and culture during the 30 years of the Duvalier dictatorship and its continued effects during the period of transition to democracy. Analyzes the Duvalierist ideology of *classe moyenne* and the use (and misuse) of State power for the personal enrichment of the powerful. Also identifies the elitist emphasis of Haiti's educational system.

4929 Tejada, Alonso Aurelio. Cuba: efectos sociales de la introducción de la lógica del mercado. (*Estud. Latinoam. /México,* 1:2, 1994, p. 131–141)

Analysis of the social impact of the introduction of market forces in Cuba as a means to adapt to the economic crisis known as the Special Period. Points out the problems of lack of food and inability to consume, deterioration of health and education sectors, price inflation, the coexistence of both dollar and peso internal economies. Author worries about the resulting social "deformations" and proposes strengthening local governments as a way to deal with them.

4930 Tejada Holguín, Ramón. La juventud dominicana: ¿divino tesoro o infernal problema? (*Poblac. Desarro.,* 5, 1995, p. 9–29, tables)

Summary of recent national surveys of the effect of the economic crisis on the family and the institution of marriage. Includes sections on survival strategies, emerging forms of intimacy among young people, relationship between sexual relations and pregnancy, economic activities of youth and their participation in internal and international migratory flows.

4931 Torres-Rivas, Edelberto. Para entender El Caribe. (*Perf. Latinoam.,* 5:8, enero/junio 1996, p. 9–28, bibl.)

Examines the future of regional integration; the impact of US immigration and drug traffic policies on the region; and the value of a democratic polity in Cuba, Puerto Rico, and the Dominican Republic.

4932 Trinidad and Tobago. Central Statistical Office. 1990 population and housing census. v. 1, pt. 1. Port of Spain: Central Statistical Office, 1993. 1 v.

Part of a series, volume presents partial results of the 1990 national census of population of Trinidad and Tobago. Focuses on age, religion, ethnicity, and education.

4933 Tujibikile, Muamba. Las Cachúas: revelación de una historia encubierta. Santo Domingo: Ediciones CEPAE, 1993. 75 p.: bibl., ill.

Documentary of the survival of African culture in the Dominican Republic examines use of masks (*Mascaras Cachuas*) in public celebrations and the meanings of such celebrations for the people of the the town of Cabral. Considers the changes that tourist-oriented carnivals bring to this collective practice.

4934 Urbanización en el Caribe. Coordinación de Alejandro Portes y Mario Lungo. San José: FLACSO, 1992. 349 p.: bibl., ill.

Comparative, historical study of Caribbean urbanization includes chapters by S. Manigat on Haiti, D. Gordon and S. Dixon on Jamaica, and W. Lozano and I. Duarte on the Dominican Republic. Each chapter reviews governmental economic policy and its effects on urban areas, class divisions, urban ecological differentiation, and internal and international migration.

4935 Valdés Fernández, María Teresa and Edith Felipe Duyos. La crisis y el ajuste cubano en los noventa: apuntes en torno a lo social. (*Perf. Latinoam.,* 5:8, enero/junio 1996, p. 97–114)

A dynamic view of the myriad difficulties faced by the Cuban people during the Special Period and the widespread poverty of the nation.

4936 Vargas, Julio César. La caficultura dominicana: estudio de la región central. Santo Domingo: Ediciones CEPAE, 1993. 92 p.: bibl., ill.

Monograph on coffee production in the Dominican Republic includes chapters on the history of coffee production, effects of State intervention, characteristics of coffee-growing central region, coffee growers' voluntary associations, and the future of the coffee industry.

4937 Vargas, Manuel. Culture, ideology, and dwelling in two Dominican villages. (*NWIG,* 70:1/2, 1996, p. 5–38, bibl., maps)

Discusses differing responses of two

Dominican communities to natural disasters and attempts at modernization. Argues that ethnic ideologies of the two distant geographic regions conditioned the way they engaged both phenomena. For ethnologist's comment, see item **908.**

4938 Vargas, Tahira. Las organizaciones de base de Santo Domingo. (*Estud. Soc. / Santo Domingo*, 27:97, julio/sept. 1994, p. 91–112, tables)

Analysis of social movement organizations in the Dominican Republic includes a typology of these organizations, their relative frequency by region of the country, and discussion of their structures. Also includes discussion of internal organizational processes such as elections, leadership circulation, decision making, division of labor, conflict resolution, and their needs and problems.

4939 Vásquez, Sonia. Liderazgo de las mujeres en las luchas populares urbanas. (*Estud. Soc. /Santo Domingo*, 28:102, oct./ dic. 1995, p. 7–19, bibl., ill.)

Study of the relationship between the declining living conditions of women in the Dominican Republic and their participation in social movements protesting the suffering of the people. Includes a section on the issue of individual and collective identities.

4940 Verger, Jean-Claude de. Haïti: vive la démocratie! Val-d'Or, Canada: D'ici et d'ailleurs, 1994. 254 p.: bibl. (Col. Propos d'ici; 3)

Analyzes possibilities for democratic politics in Haiti. Includes evaluation of Haitian institutions, and points out need for the mental liberation of its people. Compares Haiti to the Canadian system of politics. Includes text of the 1987 Haitian Constitution and Bill of Rights.

4941 Villamán P., Marcos. Religión y pobreza: una aproximación a los nuevos movimientos religiosos. (*Estud. Soc. /Santo Domingo*, 26:94, oct./dic. 1993, p. 75–96, tables)

Study of Pentecostalism in Latin America is based on first-hand observations in Santo Domingo. Documents the extraordinary growth of Pentecostalism, calculated at 25 percent annually, and relates it to the crisis of civilization and modernity, particularly chronic and pervasive poverty and the inward turn to spirituality. Explains the growth of Pentecostalism by showing the fit between

Pentecostalism's messianic-apocalyptic explanation of mankind's fate and the present-day economic hopelessness of the people of the region.

4942 Wiegand, Bruce. Petty smuggling as "social justice": research findings from the Belize-Mexico border. (*Soc. Econ. Stud.*, 42:1, March 1993, p. 171–193, bibl.)

Examines conditions of petty smuggling along the Belize-Mexico border, placing particular emphasis on social determinants of smuggling. Examines conflict among social classes, in which peasantry views smuggling as social justice.

4943 Wilk, Richard R. Beauty and the feast: official and visceral nationalism in Belize. (*Ethnos/Stockholm*, 58:3/4, 1993, p. 295–316, bibl.)

Examines attempts by Belizean government to encourage nationalist feelings in the country. Such attempts include government-sponsored beauty pageants. Also notes non-government-sanctioned trends such as the emergence of a national cuisine.

4944 Wilson, Gladstone. The Sistren Theatre Collective: Jamaica. (*in* Alternative media: linking global and local. Paris: UNESCO, 1993, p. 41–49, bibl.)

Examines class relationships and accommodation among women members of Sistren, as well as origins of the theater in the first Manley Government. See also item **4830.**

4945 Wiltshire, Rosina. Problems of environmental degradation and poverty with particular emphasis on women and children of island nations. (*in* Women and children first: environment, poverty, and sustainable development. Rochester, Vt.: Schenkman Books, 1993, p. 69–92, bibl., tables)

Outlines the philosophical and theoretical underpinnings of present development strategies, and the link between environmental degradation, marginalization of women and children, and increasing poverty in the Caribbean. Discusses major regional environmental problems and related human activities.

Women & change in the Caribbean: a Pan-Caribbean perspective. See item **913.**

4946 Wüst, Ruth. The Trinidad Carnival: a medium of social change. (*in* Society of Caribbean Research. International Conference *1st, Berlin, 1988*. Proceedings. Frankfurt: Vervuert Verlag, 1993, p. 149–159)

Examines transformative nature of Trinidad's carnival as a means of bringing about social change. Reviews historical factors which led to the modern-day festival, the relationship between the people of Trinidad and the colonial government which maintained law and order, and the people's use of carnival customs and practices as a means of social criticism.

Yelvington, Kevin A. Flirting in the factory. See item **915**.

Yelvington, Kevin A. Producing power: ethnicity, gender, and class in a Caribbean workplace. See item **917**.

4947 Zequeira Sánchez, Mario and **Isabel Valdivia Fernández.** El papel del cultivo del café para le sociedad y la economía cubana. (*Caravelle/Toulouse*, 61, 1993, p. 129–136, bibl.)

Presents historical account of production of coffee in Cuba, from its introduction and development by French families fleeing the Haitian Revolution. Notes the political activism of coffee producers and the typical familial unit of production of coffee growers.

4948 Zimbalist, Andrew. Baseball and society in the Caribbean. (*NWIG*, 68:1/2, 1994, p. 101–104, bibl.)

Reviews two books which look at impact of baseball on Caribbean society. The first book discusses integration of baseball into Dominican life, offering a historical account of the growing popularity of the sport. The second looks at the contradictory nature of Cuban society and at baseball in Cuba, particularly its relationship to the US Major Leagues up to the 1960 series.

4949 Zorrilla, Carmen *et al.* Acquired Immune Deficiency Snydrome (AIDS) in women and children in Puerto Rico. (*in* Puerto Rican women and children: issues in health, growth, and development. New York: Plenum Press, 1994, p. 55–70, bibl.)

Analyzes patterns of development of AIDS epidemic in Puerto Rico and the ways it has affected women and children. Contains recommendations for development of culture-sensitive HIV prevention programs in Puerto Rico.

COLOMBIA AND VENEZUELA

WILLIAM L. CANAK, *Professor of Sociology, Middle Tennessee State University*

Colombian and Venezuelan sociologists face difficult times in the late 1990s. Their world is defined by a weak economy and labor market, low real wages, job loss due to public sector austerity, and inadequate external funding for research and institutional support.

Since the inception of professional sociology in Colombia, a legacy of commitment to progressive and active research has marked the discipline as a target for conservatives. Today, some sociologists who work with popular reformist organizations in rural or urban contexts face death threats from leftist guerillas, from right wing paramilitaries, and from narcotics Mafia. Many are taking low profiles and others have emigrated since the May 1999 assassination of Hernan Henao Delgado, Director of the Instituto de Estudios Regionales. The Univ. Nacional (Bogotá) remains at the epicenter of conflict, while private institutes such as the Caja de la Mujer and CINEP continue with funding from public and private sources in Europe (principally the Netherlands and Germany).

Colombia's sociological community has gone through a crisis marked by threats, violence, repression, organizational changes, and shifts in dominant research trends. Academic sociology proliferated in 1960s with the Alliance for Progress, Peace Corps, development of extension systems supporting rural development, and an increased role for sociology in designing policy and advising program implementation. International luminaries such as Albert Hirschman (economics) and Gene Havens (sociology) worked actively in Colombia. Analysis of peasant movements and the "agrarian question" dominated Colombian sociology. In the 1980s and 1990s Colombian sociology began shifting its focus toward such topics as urbanization, the informal economy and drug economy, and violence. In the 1990s, Colombian sociology's stress on political economy continues, but the context of social and political violence has driven many sociologists to adopt lower profiles while they struggle to continue a tradition of "action research" and commitment to social justice.

Venezuelan sociologists have seen the deterioration of public and private organizational infrastructures. Professional associations lack resources, but active memberships sustain their activities supporting a wide range of sociological specialites. Nevertheless, while sociologists may struggle with bureaucratic restrictions, the community of researchers is growing and they continue to work without facing repression. Venezuelans commonly regard sociologists as open-minded social critics, and thus as a threat to policymakers and political leaders. While sociological research in Venezuela mirrors core themes in North American sociology, emphasizing family, social psychology, crime and deviance, demography, and race and gender, recent years have shown evidence of a deepening caution. Given the turbulent economic and political environment, the sociological community has polarized into very leftist and very conservative factions. In 1990 the Venezuelan government began the *Programa de Proción al Investigador* establishing a nationally sponsored research capacity. Unfortunately, this effort has suffered from modest funding and serious delays in payments to researchers.

COLOMBIA

Antropología en la modernidad. See item 1122.

4950 Archila Neira, Mauricio and **Alvaro Delgado Guzmán.** ¿Dónde está la clase obrera?: huelgas en Colombia 1946–1990. Bogotá: Centro de Investigación y Educación Popular, 1995. 173 p.: graphs, tables. (Documentos ocasionales; 72)

Important contribution to research on strikes in Colombia provides extensive statistics and a useful historical review. Core reference for Latin American labor and labor relations research.

Arias Londoño, Melba. Mujer, sexualidad y ley. See item **3369.**

4951 Betancourt E., Darío and **Martha Luz García Bustos.** Contrabandistas, marimberos y mafiosos: historia social de la mafia colombiana, 1965–1992. Bogotá: T.M. Editores, 1994. 318 p.: bibl., map. (Académica. Sociología y política)

Benchmark contribution to historical political economy of organized crime in Colombia focuses on three variables: sociopolitical and cultural contexts; illicit and legal markets; and organizations linked to organized crime groups and their structure and behavior. Vital reading for understanding modern Colombia.

4952 Colombia. Departamento Administrativo Nacional de Estadística. Las estadísticas sociales en Colombia. Bogotá: Depto. Administrativo Nacional de Estadística, 1993. 870 p.: bibl., ill.

Massive and important "social indicators" statistical reference tool includes data on demography, poverty, family, education, and other basic descriptors of Colombian society.

4953 Conde Jorrín, Javier and **Antonia Santos Pérez.** Tejido social y red asociativa en Bogotá: ¿hacia prácticas emancipatorias? (*in* Las ciudades hablan: identidades y movimientos sociales en seis metrópolis latinoamericanas. Caracas: Editorial Nueva Sociedad, 1994, p. 109–128)

Analysis of urban social movements in four Bogotá zones focuses on origins and internal dynamics of change. Incorporating recent social movement research in Colombia, considers elements of Colombian urban life such as violence, patriarchy, group identity, and celebrations (*fiestas*). Also contrasts networks of clientelism embracing traditional, deep-rooted popular movements with new movements marked by a less extensive popular base but more administrative structure. Authors note a developing situation wherein a newly legitimate State incorporates these groups.

4954 Corsetti, Giancarlo; Massimo Tommasoli; and Maura Viezzoli. Migrantes y colonos de la sierra en la selva tropical colombiana: la cooperación técnica italiana dentro del sistema amazónico para la planificación de la energía. Rome: Bulzoni, 1987. 321 p.: bibl., ill.

Comparative investigation of two Colombian Amazon region areas uses family interviews, interviews with local public officials, and direct observation of the community. Concludes that migration is part of a continuous and unstable process as high fertility rates induce second-generation migration to urban areas.

4955 Dombois, Rainer. Trabajadores en el cambio industrial: estudio de una empresa del sector automotriz. Bogotá: Univ. Nacional de Colombia, Depto. de Sociología, 1992. 221 p.: bibl. (Condiciones de trabajo en la industria colombiana)

Case study of Surcarr automobile factory describes management policy changes implemented following 1980s economic crisis, and their impact on organizational structure and labor relations. Presents sound comparative perspective in its portrayal of the transformation from traditional authoritarian to contemporary human resources practices. See also items **4970, 4987,** and **4988.**

4956 Drogas, poder y región en Colombia. v. 1. Economía y política, v. 2. Impactos locales y conflictos. Recopilación de Ricardo Vargas M. Bogotá: Cinep, 1994. 2 v.: bibl., ill.

Broad-ranging essays cover Colombia's drug economy from numerous perspectives including macroeconomic, political, human rights, consumption, prevention policies, and crime. Well-established researchers provide solid introduction to Colombian view of this controversial issue.

4957 Dureau, Françoise; Carmen Elisa Flórez; and María Cristina Hoyos. Las formas de movilidad de la población de Bogotá y su impacto sobre la dinámica del area metropolitana: metodología de un sistema de encuestas. (*Desarro. Soc.*, 34, sept. 1994, p. 73–94, bibl., tables)

Research survey focuses on migration to Bogotá and within metropolitan area. Targets types of spacial mobility and impact on local areas, combining demographic and anthropological methodologies. Concludes that advanced methods can be successfully applied in Colombia to study national migration patterns and produce more accurate national statistics.

4958 Dureau, Françoise; María Cristina Hoyos; and Carmen Elisa Flórez. Soacha: un barrio de Bogotá; movilidad y acceso a la vivienda de la población de los sectores orientales del municipio. (*Desarro. Soc.*, 34, sept. 1994, p. 95–147, bibl., graphs, maps, photos, tables)

Using data from a 1993 household survey conducted by Centro de Estudios sobre Desarrollo Económico (CEDE) and ORSTOM, work examines social and demographic dynamics of one middle-class illegal urban housing settlement.

4959 Echeverri, Rafael and Carmen Elisa Flórez. El cambio social en Colombia y sus repercusiones en la familia. (*in* Cambios en el perfil de la familia: la experiencia regional. Santiago: Naciones Unidas, Comisión Económica para América Latina y el Caribe, 1993, p. 231–250, bibl., tables)

Examines profoundly transformative impact of economic and social change on the structure of Colombian families. Analyzes demographic changes and the changed role of women in society and the family.

4960 Echeverri Angel, Ligia. Familia y vejez: realidad y perspectiva en Colombia. 2. ed. Bogotá: Tercer Mundo Editores, 1994. 174 p.: bibl.

Quantitative study focuses on implications of Colombian demography for social policies affecting the aged.

4961 En busca de la estabilidad perdida: actores políticos y sociales en los años noventa. Recopilación de Francisco Leal Buitrago. Bogotá: TM Editores; IEPRI; Colciencias, 1995. 331 p.: bibl. (Sociología y política)

Essays by leading Colombian political economists review various aspects of contemporary Colombia including political parties, the congress, justice system, military, Catholic Church, social movements, and reform policies. Excellent review of the current scene.

4962 Encuentro Niñez y Juventud: una Mirada desde la Universidad, *Bogotá, 1994.* Niños y jóvenes en la Colombia de hoy: memorias. Recopilación de Ernesto Durán S. Bogotá: Univ. Nacional de Colombia, Grupo Niñez y Juventud, PRIAC-UN, 1995. 127 p.: bibl.

Sixteen interdisciplinary essays from 1994 meeting on children and youth are written by faculty of the Univ. Nacional. Focuses on political and economic conditions affecting children and youth, but also offers proactive policies to meet their needs, in the tradition of Colombian "action research."

4963 Fajardo Montaña, Darío. Espacio y sociedad: formación de las regiones agrarias en Colombia. Bogotá: Corporación Colombiana para la Amazonia-Araracuara, 1993. 261 p.: bibl., maps. (9589537936)

Historical analysis of product markets, spacial differentiation, distribution of activities, migration and colonization, violence, and State structure and policies is an important contribution to agrarian research and will be cited extensively.

4964 Friedemann, Nina S. de. Vida y muerte en el Caribe afrocolombiano. (*Ecos/Santo Domingo,* 3:4, 1995, p. 193–206, bibl.)

Anthropological analysis of African belief systems and their reflections in the practices of the people of Palenque and El Manzanillo. Includes descriptions of the meaning of death and its cultural expressions in food and music. [B.E. Aguirre-López]

4965 Gladden, Kathleen. La reestructuración industrial: el subcontrato y la incorporación de la fuerza de trabajo femenina en Colombia. (*Bol. Am.,* 35:45, 1995, p. 101–120, bibl., tables)

Analysis of subcontracting in clothing industry evaluates role of formal and informal sectors, access to markets, and control of resources. Focuses on women's labor.

4966 Gómez Alzate, Camilo. La cara social del sector informal. Bogotá: FIEL, Instituto de Estudios Sociales Juan Pablo II, 1992.

255 p.: appendix, bibl. (Col. Horizontes de solidaridad; 6)

Based on a four-city survey, focused interviews with expert informants, a survey of Bogotá street workers, and participant observation research, work profiles economic and social structure of Colombia's informal economy. The quantitative appendix is valuable.

4967 Gómez Jiménez, Alcides. Economía campesina y condiciones agroalimentarias: el salto social y el reto de los problemas estructurales. (*Chungará/Arica,* 23, dic. 1989, p. 65–83, bibl., tables)

Compares rural development policies under Gaviria and Samper administrations, each emphasizing neoliberal strategies. Focuses on differences in expenditures and concludes that policies have strong similarities despite contrasting perceptions and rhetoric.

Jimeno, Myriam and **Ismael Roldán.** Las sombras arbitrarias: violencia y autoridad en Colombia. See item **1134.**

4968 Legrand, Catherine *et al.* El agro y la cuestión social. Bogotá: Banco Ganadero; Caja Agraria; VECOL; T.M. Editores, 1994. 417 p.: bibl., ill., map. (Académica. Economía agraria. Minagricultura 80 años)

Important contribution to Colombian rural studies includes sections on colonization and conflict, rural poverty, rural social movements, rural development, and government policies promoting rural peace. Provides good overview as well as a solid bibliographic foundation for research on these topics.

4969 Londoño Vélez, Argelia and **Gloria María Jaramillo Villegas.** Las mujeres remiendan la pobreza: diagnóstico del estado de las organizaciones de mujeres del Departamento de Antioquia. Medellín, Colombia: Centro de Investigaciones Sociales, CIS, Facultad de Ciencias Sociales y Humanas, Universidad de Antioquia, 1994. 167 p.: appendix, bibl. (Centro de Investigaciones Sociales, Universidad de Antioquia; 1)

Useful analysis of women's organizations in Antioquia details range of government and grassroots groups working to improve women's situation in the home, workplace, and elsewhere. Appendix lists groups by purpose or service provided and location.

López Alvarez, Luis. Literatura e identidad en Venezuela. See *HLAS 56:3648.*

4970 López Pino, Carmen Marina and **Gina Loreno Castellanos S.** Arbitrariedad y benevolencia en el trabajo industrial: estudio en la empresa Indugras. 2. ed. Bogotá: Univ. Nacional de Colombia, Depto. de Sociología, 1992. 219 p.: bibl., ill. (Condiciones de trabajo en la industria colombiana)

Historical case study based on interviews with managers and employees evaluates industrial organization and labor relations. Reviews processes or organizational expansion, restructuring, and human resource policies. See also items **4955, 4987,** and **4988.**

Muñoz Vila, Cecilia and **Ximena Pachón C.** La aventura infantil a mediados de siglo: los niños colombianos enfrentan cambios sociales, educativos y culturales que marcarán su futuro. See item **1138.**

4971 Osorio Pérez, Flor Edilma. La jefatura femenina de hogar en zonas de violencia. (*Cuad. Desarro. Rural*, 32, primer semestre 1994, p. 39–52, bibl.)

Theoretical discussion of women's household leadership is based on a review of three regions marked by high levels of violence.

4972 Palacio Valencia, María Cristina and **Laura Cecilia Castaño de Romero.** La realidad familiar en Manizales: violencia intrafamiliar. Bogotá: Ministerio de Salud, Instituto Nacional de Salud, División de Investigaciones Especiales; Univ. de Caldas, Facultad de Desarrollo Familiar, Centro de Investigaciones, 1994. 170 p.: bibl., ill.

Part of a long-term project analyzing family violence in Manizales, study targets risk factors and combinations of these factors associated with family violence. Data based on household survey; solid sampling methodology. Concludes that violence exists in all socioeconomic strata. Important contribution to Colombian family studies. See also item **4973.**

4973 Palacio Valencia, María Cristina. La violencia familiar en Manizales: investigaciones I. Manizales, Colombia: Univ. de Caldas, Facultad de Desarrollo Familiar, 1993. 48 p.: bibl., ill. (Serie Documentos de familia; 6)

Useful analysis of family violence is based on police reports (1,938 cases) from 1987–89. See also item **4972.**

4974 La política social en los 90. Recopilación de Yolanda Puyana y Camilo González Posso. Bogotá: Indepaz, 1994. 267 p.: bibl.

Eclectic collection of 25 chapters covering the range of Colombian social and political institutions is organized into seven themes: neoliberal policies; social development; ethnic and territorial laws; political participation; women, family, and marginalized sectors; education and health; and science and culture. Excellent introduction to contemporary Colombia.

4975 Rico-Velasco, Jesús. Demografía social y salud pública. 2. ed. Cali, Colombia: Univ. del Valle, 1993. 274 p.: ill., map. (Col. Edición previa. Serie Investigación)

Mainstream demographic profile of Colombia surveys population composition, distribution, fecundity, mortality, and others. Includes chapters on the health care system. Solid reference work.

4976 Rojas Guerra, José María. La bipolaridad del poder local: Caldono en el Cauca indígena. Cali, Colombia: Univ. del Valle, 1993. 130 p.: bibl., maps. (Col. Edición previa. Serie Investigación)

Insightful analysis examines local community power and emergence of an indigenous group's political awareness in the context of a mayoral election.

4977 Rojas Guerra, José María. Comunidad y liderazgo campesino en Colombia. Cali, Colombia: Univ. del Valle, 1994. 93 p.: bibl., ill.

Presents final report of extensive project investigating peasant organizations and grassroots leadership.

4978 Salazar J., Alonso and **Ana María Jaramillo A.** Medellín: las subculturas del narcotráfico. Bogotá: CINEP, 1992. 168 p., 1 folded leaf: bibl., map. (Col. Sociedad y conflicto)

Important contribution describes the social, economic, and political history of Medellín that gave rise to an organized criminal economy. Portrays synthesis of this economy with existing formal institutions.

4979 El salto social en discusión. Coordinación de Eduardo Lora y Cristina Lanzetta. Bogotá: FEDESARROLLO; Tercer Mundo Editores, 1995. 297 p.: bibl. (Economía colombiana)

Comprehensive critical work evaluates Colombian social policy implemented under the national development plan. Solid work, and a good starting point for those interested in the political economy of development.

4980 Sánchez, Fabio and Jairo Núñez. ¿Por qué los niños pobres no van a la escuela?: determinantes de la asistencia escolar en Colombia. (*Planeac. Desarro.*, 26:4, oct./dic. 1995, p. 73–118, appendices, bibl., tables)

Wide-ranging, quantitative, policy-oriented analysis of Colombian education concludes that educational policy has greatest impact on poor families. Simulates impact of student assistance rates on the poorest children in primary grades. Examines funding, inequality, and quality in Colombian education. Asserts that second poorest quintile responds to education policies more strongly than the poorest segment of the population.

4981 Seminario Nacional Familia, Infancia y Calidad de Vida, *Barranquilla, Colombia, 1992.* Síntesis y conclusiones. Barranquilla, Colombia: Ediciones Uninorte, 1993. 106 p.: bibl.

Report summarizing 1992 conference offers a wide-ranging introduction to research on the Colombian family, child welfare, and quality of life.

4982 Tenjo, Jaime. Labor markets, the wage gap and gender discrimination: the case of Colombia. (*in* Case studies on women's employment and pay in Latin America. Washington: World Bank, 1992, p. 149–168, bibl., tables)

Using sample from 1979 household survey by the Depto. Administrativo Nacional de Estadística, examines causes of gender "wage gap" in Colombia. Reviews impact of differences in productivity, working conditions, and discrimination. Concludes that wage gap is smaller than in developed countries. Presents some evidence of "female ghetto" occupations such as domestic service and clerical jobs. For economist's comment see item **2012.**

4983 Tobasura, Isaías. El campesino colombiano: modernización sin modernidad. (*Cuad. Desarro. Rural*, 32, primer semestre 1994, p. 19–30)

Theoretical analysis examines social change processes integrating peasants with

national culture through secularization, modernization, and rationalization of daily life.

4984 Villarreal Méndez, Norma. El camino de la utopía feminista en Colombia, 1975–1991. (*in* Mujeres y participación política: avances y desafíos en América Latina. Bogotá: TM Editores, 1994, p. 181–204, bibl.)

Evaluates Colombian women's movement over two periods. During the first period, 1975–82, new groups were formed, society became radicalized, and civil society faced an increasingly repressive State. During the second, 1983–91, despite efforts to reach a negotiated settlement to the social conflict, violence intensified, producing a general consensus about the need for institutional change to create channels for participation and to foster political resolution of the conflicts.

4985 Violencia en la región andina: el caso Colombia. Bogotá: CINEP; APEP, 1993. 357 p.: bibl., ill.

The Centro de Investigación y Educación Popular, a well-known Colombian research center, coordinated analysis for this work as part of a multi-cultural project organized by the Asociación Peruana de Estudios y Investigaciones para la Paz. Investigates the culture of violence including its impact on daily life, the media, and the economy, as well as its relationship with narcotics and organized crime. Contributors are well-established scholars.

4986 Wade, Peter. The cultural politics of blackness in Colombia. (*Am. Ethnol.*, 22:2, May 1995, p. 341–357, bibl.)

Traces history of Colombia's black social movement, evaluating its interaction with indigenous peoples' movements. Analyzes emergence of competing concepts of black "racial" identity, linking this analysis to cultural politics and pointing out implications for social scientists studying such groups.

4987 Weiss de Belalcázar, Anita. La empresa colombiana entre la tecnocracia y la participación: del taylorismo a la calidad total. Bogotá: Univ. Nacional de Colombia, Depto. de Sociología, 1994. 208 p.: (Serie Condiciones de trabajo en la industria colombiana)

Analyzes historical changes in organizational structure, management practices, and labor relations. Key document for students of Colombian and Latin American industrial and labor relations. See also items **4988, 4970,** and **4955.**

4988 Weiss de Belalcázar, Anita and **Wigberto Castañeda H.** Estrategias empresariales y diferenciación obrera: estudio en la empresa Colpartes. 2. ed. Bogotá: Univ. Nacional de Colombia, Depto. de Sociología, 1992. 233 p.: bibl. (Condiciones de trabajo en la industria colombiana)

Significant contribution to political economy of industry and labor. Identifies determinants of organizational forms and links this research to important historical investigations by Alfred Chandler, Neil Fligstein, and William Roy evaluating business structure in the US. Labor market and business/union analysis adds depth and new insights to this field. See also items **4987, 4970,** and **4955.**

VENEZUELA

4989 Abreu Sojo, Iván. Los rumores en Venezuela: elementos para su estudio. Recopilación de José Agustín Catalá. Caracas: Centauro, 1993. 471 p.: bibl., ill.

Based on 1990–91 interviews and survey data from Caracas, explores public opinion dynamics of rumor in Venezuelan society, with particular reference to political stress.

4990 Andrade, Raiza; Yubirí Aragort; and **Juan Díaz G.** Las formas que asume la producción informal de vivienda en Mérida. (*Fermentum/Mérida,* 1:1, mayo/agosto 1991, p. 40–58, bibl.)

Analyzes four Mérida neighborhoods, focusing on grassroots land invasions and housing solutions addressed by government policies. Evaluates social dynamics of an informal economy linked to producing housing for low-income urban populations.

4991 Balliache, Dilcia and **Carlos Eduardo Febres.** Participación de la mujer en los sindicatos de Venezuela: estudio de caso—Sindicatos del Area Metropolitana Interna de Caracas. Mérida, Venezuela: Univ. de Los Andes, Consejo de Publicaciones; Instituto Latinoamericano de Investigaciones Sociales, 1993. 194 p.: bibl., ill. (Col. Ciencias sociales. Serie Sociología)

Excellent historical and quantitative

analysis of women's labor force participation and their role in labor organizations reviews patterns of discrimination, gender relations, and legislation.

4992 Bolívar Chollett, Miguel and **Francisco Javier Velasco.** La familia en una época de crisis y transformaciones de la sociedad venezolana. (*in* Cambios en el perfil de la familia: la experiencia regional. Santiago: Naciones Unidas, Comisión Económica para América Latina y el Caribe, 1993, p. 413–429, bibl.)

Historical profile of the Venezuelan family examines effects of sociocultural change on family structure, poverty and family survival strategies, social policy and the family, and sources of statistical data on the family. Useful reference document.

4993 Bolívar Chollett, Miguel. Población y sociedad en la Venezuela del siglo XX. Caracas: Fondo Editorial Tropykos; Ediciones FACES/UCV, 1994. 267 p.: bibl.

Useful, integrated review of 20th-century Venezuelan demographic trends.

4994 Bravo Dávila, Luis Alfonso. Cambio social, criminalidad y control del crimen en Margarita, 1960–1986. Caracas: Univ. Central de Venezuela, Consejo de Desarrollo Científico y Humanístico, 1993. 361 p.: bibl. (Col. Estudios)

Historical case study of Venezuelan Caribbean island of Margarita focuses on period 1960–86, 11 years previous to and 5 years following the year when island became a free trade zone. Charts demographic, economic, political, urban, and legal changes. Presents critical examination of official crime statistics, the criminal justice system, and the underground economy.

4995 Caminos, Guiomar. Reflexiones acerca del descenso de la fecundidad en Venezuela. (*Rev. Geogr. Venez.,* 33, 1992, p. 261–275, bibl., table)

Examines causes for declining overall fertility rate in Venezuela. Concludes that family survival strategies, not increased education or women's increased labor force participation, explain this decline.

4996 Delahaye, Olivier. El Estado entre los pactos locales y los organismos multilaterales: una reflexión sobre la política venezolana de tierras. (*Tierra Firme,* 13:52, oct./dic. 1995, p. 527–549, bibl., tables)

Review of Venezuelan rural development policy focuses on government's role in the various regions, the impact of policy on land ownership patterns, and agricultural property markets in each region.

4997 El desarrollo humano en Venezuela: pobreza, deuda social y equidad. Recopilación de Bernardo Kliksberg. Caracas: Programa de las Naciones Unidas para el Desarrollo; Monte Avila Editores Latinoamericana, 1994. 337 p.: appendices, bibl., ill. (Perspectiva actual)

Based on research funded by United Nations Development Programme, provides comprehensive review of Venezuelan human resources. Sections cover employment and income, education, health, social security, public safety, justice, women's status, infants, culture, urban life, and management. Statistical appendices give important historical data.

4998 Evans, Ronald. Salud y enfermedad en las areas urbanas, con referencia especial a Caracas. (in La urbe latinoamericana: balance y perspectivas a las puertas del tercer milenio. Recopilación de Giuletta Fadda. Caracas: Univ. Central de Venezuela, 1993, p. 209–235, bibl., graphs, tables)

Provides epidemiological profile for Caracas of infant and general population mortality within the context of the social ecology of urban health.

4999 Froehle, Bryan T. Religious competition in contemporary Venezuela. (in Organized religion in the political transformation of Latin America. Lanham, Md.; New York: Univ. Press of America, 1995, p. 125–152, tables)

Reviews recent evangelical initiatives of Roman Catholics and Protestants in Venezuela. Evaluates organizational and institutional characteristics; analyzes geographical focus of activities and populations affected. Includes case study of a new Catholic urban project in Caracas, 1960–70. Concludes that Catholicism's structure and resources limit its ability to absorb new congregants, while evangelicals are continuing to expand.

5000 García-Guadilla, María Pilar. Gender, environment, and empowerment in Venezuela. (in EnGENDERing wealth and well-being: empowerment for global change. Boulder, Colo.: Westview Press, 1995, p. 213–237)

Analyzes Venezuela'a environmental movement, focusing on women's groups. Concludes that main factors affecting women's environmental political activity are definition of demands, choice of strategy, and degree of media attention.

5001 Hurtado Salazar, Samuel and Alberto Gruson. Gerencias campesinas en Venezuela. Caracas: Univ. Central de Venezuela, Consejo de Desarrollo Científico y Humanístico, 1993. 325 p.: bibl., ill. (Col. Estudios)

Quantitative study of rural household strategies and management is based on a survey of 546 (out of a total of 1,953) households in 22 communities. This theoretically and methodologically sophisticated agrarian research has significant policy implications. High-quality work is sure to be influential.

5002 Iranzo, Consuelo. La sociología del trabajo en Venezuela. (Rev. Econ. Sociol. Trab., 23/24, marzo/junio 1994, p. 167–179, bibl.)

Useful summary of Venezuelan research on unions, labor relations, labor markets, informal economy, work structures, and labor conditions. Excellent starting point for research on labor issues in Venezuela.

5003 Jiménez, Oswaldo et al. La pobreza: una discusión necesaria. (Fermentum/ Mérida, 2:3, enero/abril 1992, p. 99–114, bibl., photos, tables)

Brief descriptive review of growing poverty in Venezuela and in the city of Mérida focuses on causes linked to the global economy, national policies, and the current economic and political crises.

5004 Marcano, Esther Elena. La crisis del agua en Caracas: elementos para el análisis de la política urbana. Caracas: Univ. Central de Venezuela, Consejo de Desarrollo Científico y Humanístico, 1993. 252 p.: bibl., ill.

Analysis of water services for metropolitan Caracas provides unique perspective on interaction of urban space, politics, and economic interests. Good urban political economy study with a policy focus.

5005 Márquez, Gustavo and Clementina Acedo. Origen y desarrollo del seguro social en Venezuela. (Espac. Temas Cienc. Soc., 2, 1995, p. 7–65, graphs, tables)

Important contribution to Latin American social security research provides analytic and quantitative history of Venezuelan social security policies. Concludes with recommendations for regional decentralization and revised funding.

5006 Mujeres, una fuerza social en movimiento. Coordinación de Carol Delgado Arria. Caracas: Ediciones Los Heraldos Negros, 1995. 143 p.: ill.

Summarizes conference on the status of women in Venezuela. Reviews themes of women and power, political participation, violence, and women's socioeconomic status.

5007 Pérez Schael, María Sol. Petróleo, cultura y poder en Venezuela. Caracas: Monte Avila Editores Latinoamericana, 1993. 235 p.: bibl. (Perspectiva actual)

Useful historical review of policies of 20th-century regimes emphasizes that cognitive assumptions dominating leaders' decisions were a result of the petroleum economy.

5008 Pilato Díaz, Elsa and **Mirka Torres Acosta.** Mercado y expectativas profesionales en el área de la comunicación del sector público en Venezuela. (*Cuad. Comun.*, 2, 1995, p. 33–51, appendix, bibl., tables)

Based on a survey of 38 organizations, analyzes professional communication in public administration.

Pollak-Eltz, Angelina. Anima worship in Venezuela. See item **888.**

5009 Pollak-Eltz, Angelina. La religiosidad popular en Venezuela. Caracas: San Pablo, 1994. 192 p.: bibl. (Ensayos San Pablo; 1)

Phenomenological analysis of Venezuelan popular religious practice provides insightful, rich review of grassroots religious identity.

5010 Rakowski, Cathy A. Planned development and women's relative power: steel and forestry in Venezuela. (*Lat. Am. Perspect.*, 22:2, Spring 1995, p. 51–75, bibl.)

Diverse economic and normative factors influence women's independent decision-making at home and at work. Study compares longitudinal data from two communities, one a steel mill town and the other a producer of forest products. Concludes that potential for change in gender relations is highly selective; however, non-economic factors such as legal

rights and access to housing and social services set a base for women's empowerment.

5011 Silva Villanueva, Narsa. Perfil ocupacional del comunicador social en la empresa privada venezolana. (*Cuad. Comun.*, 2, 1995, p. 53–79, appendix, bibl., tables)

Based on a survey of 48 companies in various industries, examines communication and information processes.

5012 Tricás, Jorge. El gran juego del tiempo democrático: visión sociológica de la actualidad venezolana. Caracas: Ediciones Centauro, 1993. 257 p.: bibl.

A "critical sociology" work evaluates a Venezuelan power structure dominated by groups controlling the coffee and petroleum sectors. Examines groups' impact on State structure and policy and on social and economic inequality, assessing the consequences for 1990s crisis.

5013 Universidad de los Andes (Mérida, Venezuela). Los indicadores sociales en Venezuela. Mérida, Venezuela: Univ. de los Andes, Consejo de Publicaciones; ILDIS, 1993. 129 p.: appendices, bibl. (Col. Ciencias sociales. Serie Sociología)

Offers useful brief review of data sources and social indicator definitions. Offers good reference material for researchers planning quantitative studies in Venezuela. Appendices inventory social indicators, their operational definitions, sources, dates, and population coverage.

5014 La violencia en Venezuela. Caracas: Monte Avila Editores; Univ. Católica Andrés Bello, 1993. 299 p.: bibl., ill. (Perspectiva actual)

Part of a comparative project studying violence in Andean countries organized by the Asociación Peruana de Estudios para la Paz, this empirical study explores violence in various social contexts and institutions. Examines the culture of violence, violence and the State and political system, role of the communications media, and drugs. Includes a case study of a Caracas *barrio*. Concludes that various forms of violence have significantly increased as Venezuelan institutions have lost both legitimacy and a capacity to provide resources supportive of civil society.

5015 Vivancos Cabello, Francisco and **Luis Pedro España.** La crisis que nos falta por recorrer: prospectiva social de Venezuela,

1992–2005. Caracas: Instituto Latinoamericano de Investigaciones Sociales; Editorial Nueva Sociedad, 1993. 145 p.: bibl., ill.

Using social and economic indicators, explores potential evolution of conditions in Venezuela. Aimed at developing policies to prevent social problems.

ECUADOR

AMALIA M. ALBERTI, *Independent Consultant, c/o United States Agency for International Development, San Salvador*

THE SUBSTANTIAL NUMBER of thought-provoking contributions reviewed here this biennium offers evidence of the increasing interest in Ecuadorian indigenous cultures, ethnicity, and societal evolution. Several works focus on the role of education in a multicultural society; Cliche's work is noteworthy for its comparison of indigenous and non-indigenous children (item **5018**). Kanagy's study on the successful Protestant conversion movement provides insight into an aspect of sociocultural change seldom considered (item **5028**). Espinosa's analysis of indigenous elements in mestizo ethnic identity offers a new perspective on a familiar theme, thus generating unanticipated findings (item **5023**).

Inspired by the Fourth World Conference of Women (Beijing 1995), works relating to women and gender issues abounded. In a number of cases, data was gathered from similar sources and in-depth analysis is lacking. Despite a tendency toward superficiality and a failure to address the ethnic dimension of gender, the volume is generally well done and does provide helpful explanations of the data as presented. (item **5032**).

In recent years there has been a notable decline in the number of works focusing on changes in the Ecuadorian agricultural sectors. Considering the changes occurring throughout the country, there must be serious adjustments within the agricultural sector as well. However, the available research belies this interpretation; recent works on rural areas focus on the cultural aspect of social organization, thereby neglecting the economic element.

Campesinos del Mira y del Chanchán. v. 1. See item **1150**.

5016 Centro de Estudios de Población y Paternidad Responsable (Ecuador). Ecuador: encuesta demográfica y de salud materna e infantil; informe general; ENDEMAIN-94. Quito: Centro de Estudios de Población y Paternidad Responsable, 1994. 320 p.: ill.

This is the fifth in a series of maternal and infant health surveys, and the first designed to be representative at the level of each of ten highland and five coastal provinces, as well as at the national level. Subjects covered include general demographic characteristics of women between 15 and 49 years of age, general housing conditions, fertility and family planning, infant and maternal health and mortality, and characteristics of the school-age population (not gender-disaggregated).

5017 Centro de Planificación y Estudios Sociales—CEPLAES (Ecuador). La dimensión de género en las políticas y acciones ambientales ecuatorianas. Recopilación de Silvia Vega Ugalde. Quito: CEPLAES; UNFPA, 1995. 136 p.: bibl.

Collection of seven predominantly theoretical essays (first presented at a seminar in 1995) explores issues of gender within the context of national environmental policy in Ecuador. Several authors consider a correlation between feminism and environmental theory. Other essays examine gender and the environment within a specific geographical context, such as the municipal district of Quito.

5018 Cliche, Paúl and Fernando García. Escuela e indianidad en las urbes ecuatorianas. Quito: EB/PRODEC, 1995. 398 p.: bibl., ill.

Comparative study focuses on indigenous and non-indigenous children between ages six and twelve, in 12 non-randomly selected elementary schools in four cities: Quito, Guayaquil, Machala, and Riobamba. Offers select results and discussion of academic achievement, self-esteem, attitudes, and aspirations. Data are disaggregated by sex and ethnic identification. Questionnaires and interview guides included.

5019 Comisión Económica para América Latina y el Caribe (CEPAL). La perdurabilidad de los lazos de parentesco en la reproducción social en Ecuador. (in Cambios en el perfil de la familia: la experiencia regional. Santiago: Naciones Unidas, Comisión Económica para América Latina y el Caribe, 1993, p. 275–304, bibl., tables)

Focusing on eight marginal barrios of four cities (Quito, Guayaquil, Riobamba, and Esmeraldas), this carefully documented study analyzes survival strategies associated with different family types. Considers productive and reproductive roles within the household and the pressures of formal or informal employment options as they relate to family type.

5020 Comité Ecuatoriano de Cooperación con la Comisión Interamericana de Mujeres. Diagnóstico de la situación de la mujer en el Ecuador, 1980–1994: informe nacional para la Cuarta Conferencia Mundial sobre la Mujer, Beijing, 1995. Quito: CECIM, 1994. 281 p.: bibl., ill.

Report prepared for the Fourth World Conference on Women (Beijing, 1995) includes gender-disaggregated data on poverty, employment, access to land, access to education, health practices, and violence. In some cases data are disaggregated by geographic area (urban/rural), and some tables compare data over time; however, none of the material is disaggregated by ethnicity. Good explanatory text for each subject area.

5021 Costales, Piedad Peñaherrera de and Alfredo Costales Samaniego. Lo indígena y lo negro. Quito: Instituto Andino de Artes Populares del Convenio Andrés Bello, 1995. 162 p.: bibl., ill., music.

Cultural account of the *Jahuay*, a ritual of music and song for farming, especially the harvest. Includes variations of verses, descriptions and illustrations of instruments, and musical scores. Based on research begun in the 1940s by Piedad and Alfredo Costales.

5022 Encuentro-Taller de Teoria Feminista, 1st, Ballenita, Ecuador, 1986–1987. Tomando fuerzas para volar con fibra: memoria. Quito: Centro Acción de la Mujer; Centro de Información y Apoyo a la Mujer, 1988? 117 p.: ill.

Personal accounts of two encounter groups, one addressing feminist theory held in 1985, and the other focusing on politics and power held in 1987. Topics covered include the intersection of sex and class, feminism and feminist theory, political organization and participation, and issues of power and autonomy. Concludes with a discussion of strategies.

5023 Espinosa Apolo, Manuel. Los mestizos ecuatorianos y las señas de identidad cultural. Quito: Ediciones Centro de Estudios Felipe Guamán Poma de Ayala, 1995. 245 p.: bibl.

Carefully documented study investigates significance of mestizo identity. Author defines it as a process of Hispanic acculturation enriched with a Quichua cultural core that determines its unique final form, rather than as a rejection of indigenous identification (p. 53). Racial and cultural elements are considered separately.

5024 Goffin, Alvin Matthew. The rise of Protestant evangelism in Ecuador, 1895–1990. Gainesville: Univ. Press of Florida, 1994. 189 p.: bibl., ill., index, maps.

Review of Protestantism in Ecuador. Provides historical account of religious activities. Documents struggle of Protestant denominations to gain recognition from the Catholic Church and acceptance by indigenous communities. [B. Aguirre-López]

5025 Hombre y Ambiente. No. 30, enero/marzo 1994. Quito: Ediciones Abya-Yala.

Issue reports on conflict between petroleum-extracting interests and human rights in Amazon region of Ecuador. Report hinges on government's legal responsibility to protect human rights, but also considers moral obligation and responsibility of private companies and international credit sources. Provides data documenting levels of contamination. Includes recommendations from social, legal, and financial perspectives.

5026 Informe Social Ecuador. No. 1, 1993. Ajuste y situación social. Quito: Instituto Latinoamericano de Investigaciones Sociales.

Analyzes social impact of economic adjustment policies. Compares data over intervals ranging from eight to 25 years. Synthesizes various social and economic policy alternatives to address an increasingly inequitable distribution of economic resources. Concludes with specific recommendations for implementing those alternatives. Includes indicators developed for the study as indices of basic needs.

5027 Instituto Ecuatoriano de Investigaciones y Capacitación de la Mujer. Investigación de datos estadísticos sobre la mujer ecuatoriana: demografía, salud, educación y empleo. Quito: IECAIM, 1992. 173 p.: bibl., ill.

Includes data on demographics, health, education, and employment of women from 1990 national census. Cites and compares findings with preceding years. Some tables disaggregated by location (urban/rural). Ethnicity is discussed in a separate chapter without statistics.

5028 Kanagy, Conrad L. The formation and development of a Protestant conversion movement among the highland Quichua of Ecuador. (in Religion and democracy in Latin America. New Brunswick, N.J.: Transaction Publishers, 1994, p. 135–147, bibl.)

Provocative article explores factors leading to successful entry of Protestantism into an indigenous area of Chimborazo prov., beginning in the 1960s. Documents role of Protestantism in the community, including its involvement in social and economic development. Hypothesizes about possible changes

to that role as political, social, and economic conditions in the region evolve.

5029 León, Guadalupe. Del encubrimiento a la impunidad: diagnóstico sobre violencia de género; Ecuador, 1989–1995. Quito: CEIME Ediciones, 1995. 294 p.: bibl., ill.

Author traces changing attitudes towards acts of sexual violence from acceptance or denial to impunity. Includes quotes from victims, perpetrators, service officials, and doctors, almost all of whom rationalize such violence. Concludes with strategies and options for individuals, institutions, and social movements to create conditions of greater social equity.

5030 Luna Tamayo, Milton. Las trampas históricas de la industria ecuatoriana: su frustrada constitución como clase. (in Colección nuestra patria es América: historia económica de América Latina. Edited by Jorge Nuñez Sánchez. Quito: Editora Nacional, 1992, v. 7, p. 205–238, tables)

Tracks formation of an industrial sector in Ecuador, contrasting coastal patterns with those of the northern and southern sierra. Cites evidence of growing interest in capitalism and industrialization from the early 1900s in all regions, but counters with examples of regional resistance against efforts to facilitate importation of machinery and raw materials and exportation of finished products.

Maiguashca, Juan. Los sectores subalternos en los años 30 y el aparecimiento del velasquismo. See *HLAS 56:2745.*

5031 Moncayo Gallegos, Paco. Fuerzas armadas y sociedad. Quito: Corporación Editora Nacional, 1995. 194 p.: bibl. (Biblioteca de ciencias sociales; 44)

Begins with a historical account of international conflict and the need for national defense. Then discusses the armed forces in Latin America. Concludes with a specific description of the role of the armed forces in Latin America, and in Ecuador in particular. Projects potential roles armed forces could play in the future, such as supporting human rights or protecting the environment.

5032 Ramón Valarezo, Galo. El regreso de los runas: la potencialidad del proyecto indio en el Ecuador contemporáneo. Quito: COMUNIDEC; Fundación Interamericana, 1993. 349 p.: bibl., maps.

Ten independent but complementary essays address issues of ethnicity, class, and nationality. Topics, considered from an ethnic perspective, include access to land, natural health beliefs and practices, natural resource management and environmental sustainability, conflict and conflict resolution, political participation, and aspects of acculturation including access to and effects of formal education. Ethnic revitalization is the underlying theme.

5033 Tenorio Ambrossi, Rodrigo; María Soledad Jarrín S.; and **Paul Bonilla S.** La cultura sexual de los adolescentes. Quito: Ediciones Abya-Yala; UNFPA, 1995. 542 p.: appendices, bibl., ill.

Interviews with one thousand 10–19 year old Ecuadorian youths, almost evenly divided between males and females, and highland and coastal residents. Questionnaires and interview guides not included. Descriptive discussion of adolescents' responses to

open-ended interview questions. Minimal reference made to differentiating characteristics of respondents. Limited quantitative data presented as annexes but not discussed or analyzed in the text.

5034 Yáñez Cossío, Consuelo. La educación indígena en el Ecuador: estudio introductorio. Quito: Instituto de Capacitación Municipal; Ediciones de la Univ. Politécnica Salesiana, 1995? 258 p.: bibl., ill. (Historia de la educación y el pensamiento pedagógico ecuatorianos; 5)

Well-documented report traces attitudes toward and efforts to encourage indigenous education from conquest to contemporary bilingual education programs. Considers cultural implications of exclusively Spanish language programs that are based on the traditional primary school curriculum. Includes personal accounts of abuse, humiliation, and rejection experienced by indigenous students.

PERU

SUSANA LASTARRIA-CORNHIEL, *Professor, Land Tenure Center, University of Wisconsin*

PERU HAS SUFFERED a series of political and economic crises since the mid-1970s. Thus, it is not surprising that the prevailing theme among sociological publications is poverty, reflecting the unrelenting economic crisis that Peru and its people have suffered for several decades. The other dominant cross-cutting theme is violence: violence resulting from poverty, political struggle, and crime. Sociological publications of this period can be categorized into the following areas: gender and sexuality, youth and family, urban studies, agrarian issues, violence and the State, and ethnicity. These are obviously highly interrelated categories and many publications fall into several at the same time.

A great number of publications examine gender relations (at both personal and societal levels, and as affected by State policy). The specific topics studied include violence against women (including prostitution, abortion, and sexual abuse), employment conditions and opportunities, gender identity (old and new norms of femininity and masculinity, mariana/marimacha models of women), women's movements and organizations, peasant women, and sexual identity (homosexuality). The most frequently used research methods are case studies and oral testimonies. Two outstanding publications in this category are edited volumes by foremost experts on gender issues: P. Portocarrero's *Estrategias de desarrollo* (from the NGO, Centro Flora Tristan) (item **4542**) and P. Ruiz-Bravo's *Detras de la puerta* (from La Catolica University's Gender Studies Program) (item **5052**).

Agrarian issues, another important theme this biennium, also cover a broad spectrum of social and political phenomena: peasant production, indigenous identity, peasant militia, and the impact of State economic policies on the rural sector, particularly the peasantry. Changing State policy toward agriculture (the agrarian reform of the 1970s, land parcelation in the 1980s, and rural land market liberalization in the 1990s) and macroeconomic policies (particularly structural adjustment policies) has had, and continues to have, deep impacts on the peasant sectors. Some of these publications reveal that while impacts are generally overwhelmingly negative for smallholder farmers and their families, there are some positive effects which should be and can be nurtured by both State policy and NGO programs.

During the period under review, SEPIA (Seminario Permanente de Investigación Agraria), an organization of different professionals working in the rural sector, held its sixth congress in Cajamarca in August 1995. The themes were articulation and tendencies of rural markets, cultural changes and political behavior of rural society, and sustainable rural development. SEPIA is one of the most important professional organizations and forums for debate and discussion of rural issues. Papers presented at the congress are published in book form and provide a reference source for the problems and issues being debated in rural Peru.

Adrianzén, Alberto. Partidos y orden social en el Perú. See item **3541.**

Aibar Ray, Elena. Identidad y resistencia cultural en las obras de José María Arguedas. See *HLAS 56:3623.*

5035 Alarcón G., Walter. Ser niño: una nueva mirada de la infancia en el Perú. Lima: IEP; Unicef, 1994. 203 p.: bibl. (Serie Infancia y sociedad; 1)

An excellent compilation of information on the conditions of underprivileged children in Peru who make up over 60 percent of the population under the age of 18. These children at risk are found working in the street, often homeless, and are sometimes caught in the civil war. Alarcon used several different sources of secondary data including national surveys, as well as original data gathered from in-depth interviews and a survey applied in metropolitan Lima.

5036 Alfaro M., Julio. Los gremios rurales: rol de las organizaciones rurales en la década de los noventa. Lima: Fundación Friedrich Ebert, 1994. 174 p.: bibl.

This study of contemporary farm workers' unions and federations is based on an analysis of structured interviews with members and leaders of these unions. Other chapters present an analysis of the unions' social pacts with other unions, the State and local government, agroindustry, and NGOs and their positions on State policy regarding land markets, free markets, the environment, and technology transfers.

5037 Balbi Scarneo, Carmen Rosa. Sindicalismo y flexibilización del mercado de trabajo en el Perú. (*Debates Sociol.,* 19, 1994, p. 91–117, bibl., graphs)

The labor unions and federations, which strongly represented, defended, and protected the urban wage labor force for many decades, currently finds itself powerless and unable to protect workers from deteriorating working conditions and falling wages. Balbi examines the economic and political conditions, as well as the problems within the labor movement, which during the 1990s debilitated the labor unions, resulting in the loss of stable employment and work benefits for the majority of workers.

5038 Barrig, Maruja. Seis familias en la crisis. Lima: ADEC-ATC, 1993. 118 p.: bibl.

Six families, interviewed during 1992, are used as case studies to demonstrate the different survival strategies used by poor households in a society where unemployment and underemployment are high, inflation is out of control, and social services are practically nonexistent. One significant factor in these survival strategies was the important role of women, not only in contributing to family income and care, but also in organizing and maintaining community activities to gather and extend their meager resources.

5039 Blondet, Cecilia. Out of the kitchens and onto the streets: women's activism in Peru. (*in* The challenge of local feminisms: women's movements in global perspective.

Boulder, Colo.: Westview Press, 1995, p. 251–275, photos, table)

Blondet traces the emergence of women's movements in Peru during the last few decades—movements based on social, economic, and ethnic/racial factors spawned by economic and political crises. Deep social polarization together with radically declining living standards for the majority of the population have resulted in women uniting around different issues. Many of these organizations disappear once a particular problem is resolved. Blondet attempts to explain why this occurs in spite of attempts to create a coherent and unified alliance of women activists around an agenda. For historian's comment see *HLAS 56:2760.*

5040 Concurso de Testimonio Campesino "Historia de mi Organización," Lima, 1988. Sólo organizados podemos vencer: Concurso de Testimonio Campesino Historia de mi Organización. Introducción de Carlos Iván Degregori. Lima: Servicios Educativos Rurales, 1989. 234 p.

This collection of oral testimonies from a diverse group of peasants presents a view of their organizations and society and in their own beautifully articulated words. These testimonies reveal continued oppression despite the demise of the oligarchic system of abuse and domination, and great difficulties in the development of peasant organizations and the establishment of viable, non-patronizing relations with State agencies and other social groups. Particularly interesting are the women peasants who demand their own rights and their own voice in private and public affairs independent of their relationships with men.

5041 Cotler, Julio. Política y sociedad en el Perú: cambios y continuidades. Lima: IEP, 1994. 235 p.: bibl., ill. (Serie Perú problema, 0079–1075; 23)

Collection of articles by one of the most original political scientists in Peru covers 30 years of sociopolitical thought. Describes a time of great social change which saw the invalidation of traditional social stratification based on a colonial criteria of ethnicity, the creation of new social and political institutions, and the development of new public expectations of the State. Concludes, in part, that the great inequalities based on ethnicity and class have not disappeared and

that the country still faces the challenge of building a democratic and cohesive society.

Damonte V., Gerardo. Componentes de la cultura urbana en el Perú. See item **1192.**

5042 Debate Agrario. No. 14, junio/sept. 1992 [and] No. 15, oct./dic. 1992. Lima: Centro Peruano de Estudios Sociales (CEPES).

Six articles in these two issues examine both the survival of and changes in peasant communities and peasant families as they attempt to protect their resources against capitalist agriculture: 1) the historical tendencies in the legal process of recognizing peasant communities from 1920 to the present (Trivelli, v. 14); 2) legislative changes needed to modernize peasant communities (Castillo, v. 14); 3) the historical development and modernization of a peasant community in a cotton-growing area of the coast (Revesz, v. 14); 4) use of communal farms and land tenure by smallholder peasants to protect themselves against some capitalist tendencies and to take advantage of others (Pérez, v. 15); and 5) modernizing tendencies, including urbanization, of peasant communities (Caballero, v. 14, and Soto, v. 15).

5043 Degregori, Carlos Iván. Identidad étnica: movimientos sociales y participación política en el Perú. (*in* Democracia, etnicidad y violencia política en los países andinos. Lima: Instituto Francés de Estudios Andinos; Instituto de Estudios Peruanos, 1993, p. 113–133, bibl.)

Degregori maintains that ethnicity remains an important factor in the identity of Peruvians and that it continues to contribute to social stratification, politics, cultural activities, and social movements. Also argues that its expression and dynamic is different in Peru from other Andean countries.

5044 Dietz, Henry. Peru's Sendero Luminoso as a revolutionary movement. (*J. Polit. Mil. Sociol.*, 18:1, Summer 1990, p. 123–149, bibl.)

A study of Sendero Luminoso examines its history, including conditions that engendered its emergence, ideology, goals, leadership, internal organization, international connections, and government responses (through three administrations) to its activities. The author locates Sendero Luminoso within revolutionary movements in general, and attempts to determine whether Sendero Luminoso will attain its goals.

5045 Eguren, Fernando. Sociedad rural: el nuevo escenario. (*Debate Agrar.*, 13, enero/mayo 1992, p. 85–99)

Argues that the Peruvian peasant (or smallholder producer) is dynamic, progressive, and more than willing to produce for the market. Unfortunately, recent State policies, based on structural adjustment rationale, favor the large and medium agriculturist producing for the export market, effectively excluding the peasant producer. This tendency is likely to aggravate violence in the rural sector.

Encuentro Binacional Perú-Bolivia, *La Paz, 1991.* El Lago Titicaca: análisis peruano-boliviano de las relaciones entre el ambiente y el desarrollo social; memorias. See item **5085.**

5046 Fuller Osores, Norma J. Dilemas de la femineidad: mujeres de clase media en el Perú. Lima: Fondo Editorial, Pontificia Univ. Católica del Perú, 1993. 232 p.: bibl.

Using sources such as oral interviews and the media, an anthropologist and psychologist examines the changing attitudes and images of middle-class women, the different roles and contexts of women (such as working women, mothers, wives), and the changing socialization of different generations. This publication contributes greatly towards an understanding of the changing relations between women, on the one hand, and men, family, and society, on the other, that has been occurring in Peru. Similar studies about other women in Peruvian society would help reveal the different realities in which women work and live.

5047 García Núñez, Gonzalo. Perú: la visión de los peruanos excluidos; balance y perspectivas, 1950–1995. Lima: Mosca Azul Editores, 1995. 138 p.: bibl., ill.

The explicit focus of this study is the impact of recent neoliberal (structural adjustment) economic and social policies on a significant sector of the Peruvian population, deepening their poverty and marginalizing their participation in the economy. Author asserts that in urban areas, unemployment and underemployment has increased; and in rural areas, poverty has increased due to the elimination of agricultural production credit and the creation of an agricultural land market.

5048 Gonzales de Olarte, Efraín. El ajuste estructural y los campesinos. Lima: IEP; Ayuda en Acción-Perú, Action Aid-UK, 1996. 138 p.: bibl., ill. (Col. Mínima; 33)

This little volume looks at the result of market-oriented macroeconomic policies on the peasantry. The impact of the stabilization policies of the 1980s-early 1990s are examined through a case study in the highlands of Cajamarca. The structural adjustment programs of the 1990s are studied in four regions of the highlands and the coast. A balanced examination reveals that both negative and positive effects are experienced by the peasantry, and that State policy should be an investment in human capital through education, health services, and infrastructural services.

5049 Grompone, Romeo. Perú: la vertiginosa irrupción de Fujimori; buscando las razones de un sorprendente resultado electoral. (*Rev. Mex. Sociol.*, 54:2, oct./dic. 1990, p. 177–203, bibl., graphs)

In an attempt to explain why Fujimori defeated Vargas Llosa, the favored presidential candidate in the 1990 Peruvian elections, that author gives an excellent account of the state of politics and political parties in Peru for the last few decades, particularly the reasons politicians and political parties have been discredited. For political scientist's comment, see *HLAS 55:3377.*

5050 Guzmán Barcos, Virginia and **Alicia Pinzás Stoll.** Biografías compartidas: redes sociales en Lima. Lima: Centro de la Mujer Peruana Flora Tristán, 1995. 199 p.

Interesting oral history of a working-class, migrant woman in Lima discusses her personal background and the process of becoming a community organizer and leader. This fascinating and revealing account also examines the dialogue process between the working class woman and the middle-class professionals that interact with her, as well as the methodological problems of studies in which persons of different cultural backgrounds and ideologies interact.

5051 Huber, Ludwig. *Depués de Dios y La Virgen está la ronda:* las rondas campesinas de Piura. Lima: Instituto de Estudios Peruanos; Instituto Francés de Estudios Andinos, 1995. 132 p.: bibl. (Col. Mínima; 31)

One of many social phenomena that emerged from the civil war between Sendero

Luminoso and the Peruvian military is the peasant militia, called *rondas campesinas*. This ethnographic work on several *rondas campesinas* in the highlands of Piura examines the nature of these *rondas:* whether they are creations of the military and therefore pawns to be used against the people, or an expression of popular movement and part of the construction of a civil society.

5052 Kogan, Liuba *et al.* Detrás de la puerta: hombres y mujeres en el Perú de hoy. Recopilación de Patricia Ruiz-Bravo. Lima?: Pontificia Univ. Católica del Perú, Facultad de Ciencias Sociales, Programa de Estudios de Género, 1996. 310 p.: bibl.

A collection of articles by a broad range of social scientists that examines the many different aspects of changing gender relations in contemporary Peru. These aspects include gender identity of different groups of women, from working class to elite, rural to urban; sexuality; gender identity of men, including concepts of masculinity; representation of women in Peruvian literature; legislation that affects gender relations such, as domestic violence and labor laws. Valuable bibliography on gender readings in Peru.

5053 López Jiménez, María Angeles. La or- ganización popular en Lima: de la tradición comunitaria a la participación ciudadana. (*in* Las ciudades hablan: identidades y movimientos sociales en seis metrópolis latinoamericanas. Caracas: Editorial Nueva Sociedad, 1994, p. 233–250)

A study of the small organizations in low-income urban neighborhoods in Lima, known as *asentamientos humanos* or *asentamientos populares,* created around particular interests or groups, such as mothers, juveniles, or young adults. These minor organizations emerge out of the poverty and desperate living and working conditions that persons in the *asentamientos* face. For related information from a different perspective, see item **5060.**

Malengreau, Jacques. Trashumancia, migraciones y restructuraciones étnicas entre sierra y selva al norte de Chachapoyas, Perú. See item **1204.**

Mallon, Florencia E. Peasant and nation: the making of postcolonial Mexico and Peru. See *HLAS 56:2791.*

5054 Marañón, Boris. Obreros en la industria esparraguera: Valles de Chao-Virú e Ica. (*Debate Agrar.,* 17, dic. 1993, p. 27–52, graphs, photo, tables)

The export of nontraditional agricultural products has been advanced as an alternative to the low farm prices and incomes in South America. Marañón examines one such crop, asparagus, grown on the Peruvian coast; in particular, the working conditions (including income levels) of those who labor in the fields are presented. Concludes that while this industry represents modern agriculture and offers high earnings for investors, it does not mean progress for its workers. The latter are mostly temporary workers who are employed for less than half a year, earning low wages, and receiving no social services nor benefits.

5055 Montoya, Rodrigo. Al borde del naufragio: democracia, violencia y problema étnico en el Perú. Lima: SUR Casa de Estudios del Socialismo, 1992. 118 p.: bibl. (Cuadernos de SUR)

Beautifully written collection of essays delineates the debate in Peru on different aspects of ethnicity: ethnic identity (what does it mean to be Peruvian? indigenous?), democracy (how can a society be democratic when a significant number of ethnic groups are denied democratic participation?), and political violence (structural violence from both the right and the left suffered by ethnic minorities).

5056 Montoya, Rodrigo. Lucha por la tierra, reformas agrarias y capitalismo en el Perú del siglo XX. Lima: Mosca Azul Editores, 1989. 279 p.: bibl., ill.

This well-know scholar of the Peruvian peasantry has collected in this volume a series of chapters on 20th-century peasant struggles, looking at ethnic and class conflicts and identity issues. Also offers a study of the 1969 agrarian reform and its impacts on class structure and conflict, with a view to the current situation and future tendencies in the rural sector, particularly in the highlands.

5057 Mujeres peruanas: la mitad de la po- blación del Perú a comienzos de los **noventa.** Edición de Amelia Fort. Investigación de Amelia Fort *et al.* Lima: CENTRO-Instituto de Estudios Socioeconómicos y Fomento del Desarrollo, por encargo de ACDI, 1993. 257 p.: bibl.

Useful volume on women and the conditions under which they live and work in Peru. Census data and national surveys, as well as historical and legal information were used to draw a diagnostic picture of different aspects (demographic, legal, cultural, educational, employment, etc.) of women's lives in contemporary Peru. While some of the chapters are excellent reference sources (for example, educational levels of women), other chapters (such as the cultural history of women in Peru) offer interesting narratives.

5058 Los nuevos limeños: sueños, fervores y caminos en el mundo popular. Taller de Estudios de las Mentalidades Populares, TEMPO. Edición de Gonzalo Portocarrero Maisch. Lima: SUR Casa de Estudios del Socialismo; TAFOS, 1993. 399 p.: bibl., ill.

Collection presents a social psychological picture of the residents of contemporary Lima, a city of diverse cultural traditions. Oral testimonies are deconstructed to demonstrate different aspects of these urban residents: work cultures; political values, attitudes, and organization; religious beliefs; art and culture; as well as the challenges that today's urban youth face.

5059 Nugent, David. Building the State, making the nation: the bases and limits of State centralization in "modern" Peru. (*Am. Anthropol.*, 96:2, June 1994, p. 333–369, bibl., map)

This analysis of political, social, and economic development of an isolated region on the eastern side of the Andes, Chachapoyas, rejects the thesis that State and society are necessarily opposing forces. Attempts to show that the relations between State and society are both conflictive and cooperative and that the dynamic between them leads to fragmentation and consolidation of the State and national culture.

5060 Olivera Cárdenas, Luis. Lima y su organización urbano-popular. (*in* Las ciudades hablan: identidades y movimientos sociales en seis metrópolis latinoamericanas. Caracas: Editorial Nueva Sociedad, 1994, p. 221–231)

Olivera looks at the nature and capacity of neighborhood organizations in low-income urban neighborhoods in Lima, known as *asentamientos humanos* or *asentamientos populares*, as they confront and negotiate

with State agencies and struggle to meet the needs of the neighborhoods. Four historical periods are described as these organizations deal with changing economic conditions, different government administrations, and different urban policies.

5061 Ordóñez Bustamante, Dwight and **María del Pilar Mejía Fritsch.** El trabajo infantil callejero en Lima: aproximación descriptiva. Lima: CEDRO, 1994. 126 p.: bibl. (Línea verde; 1)

In addition to presenting the working and living conditions of children who work in the street, this publication explores the methodological difficulties of collecting information on these children. While acknowledging the great contribution of studies based on oral testimonies from street children, this study attempts to arrive at objective and generalized conclusions about working children.

5062 Picht, Hans-Joachim. Conflictos intercomunales en los Andes centrales. (*Debate Agrar.*, 23, dic. 1995, p. 37–50)

Decades of conflict between two villages in the central Andes are traced to show that the decline of customary communal authority and the imposition of local structures, governing institutions, and authorities by the State gave rise to economic and spatial destructuring of the Andean communities. Communities were drawn into fighting over scarce resources (such as arable land, wood) when boundaries were redrawn and traditional authority institutions no longer functioned adequately.

5063 Portocarrero Maisch, Gonzalo. Racismo y mestizaje. Lima: Sur Casa de Estudios del Socialismo, 1993. 297 p.: bibl.

Valuable collection of essays studies violence in Peru as an answer or reaction to the racial oppression and cruelty inherited from the colonial period. The three sets of essays look at social interaction between those who dominate (based on fear and guilt) and those who are dominated (based on resentment and hate), at physical traits and reactions to them, and the different strategies, particularly improved economic status, utilized by the oppressed to overcome racial prejudice.

5064 Remy, María Isabel. The indigenous population and the construction of democracy in Peru. (*in* Indigenous peoples and democracy in Latin America. New York: St. Martin's Press, 1994, p. 107–130)

Traces the efforts of indigenous populations during the last 100 years to be recognized both as indigenous and as citizens of the country; as different from other Peruvians because of their cultural and ethnic heritage, but still citizens of the same democracy. As ethnic and cultural minorities, these indigenous groups mobilize themselves to demand their legal rights as citizens, and to demand an end to abuses and discrimination.

5065 Riofrío, Gustavo and **Romeo Grompone.** Lima: ¿para vivir mañana? Lima: CIDIAG/FOVIDA, 1991. 391 p.: bibl., ill.

An introductory section presents the principal characteristics (demographic, economic, political, and institutional) and problems (urban sprawl, economic inequality, poor and inexistent infrastructure) of Lima. The next two sections are case studies of Villa El Salvador, perhaps the best known (because of its conflictive and political origins, as well as its community organizations) of the squatter settlements that surround Lima, and the work undertaken by women in the poorer sectors of the city to improve health and food services.

5066 Rocha V., Alberto. El redescubrimiento de la democracia en el Perú: aproximación general al debate en la década de los 80. (in Democracia, etnicidad y violencia política en los países andinos. Lima: Instituto Francés de Estudios Andinos; Instituto de Estudios Peruanos, 1993, p. 167–192, table)

An interesting typology of political intellectuals looks at how they perceive democracy and the development of democracy in Peru. Examines six "think tanks" from different political tendencies, describing the evolution of their thinking during the 1980s. Most remarkable are the different interpretations of each group for the same period of events.

5067 Scott, Alison MacEwen. Divisions and solidarities: gender, class and employment in Latin America. London; New York: Routledge, 1994. 281 p.: bibl., ill., index, map.

Using both survey and case study data on working class persons in Lima, Scott argues that class fragmentation among the urban poor has been exaggerated and distorted. In addition to divisions between formal and informal sectors, aspects such as gender and skill, family affiliation, and the changing labor market are just as important, if not more so, when studying employment structure and divisions.

5068 Starn, Orin. To revolt against the Revolution: war and resistance in Peru's Andes. (Cult. Anthropol., 10:4, Nov. 1995, p. 547–580, bibl.)

The rondas campesinas or peasant patrols were widely formed in the late 1980s and early 1990s in the Peruvian highlands to protect villages against attacks by Sendero Luminoso. Starn recounts the history of these rondas campesinas as a counterrevolutionary social movement within the context of contemporary nationalism and popular culture. For political scientist's comment, see item **3591.**

Stokes, Susan Carol. Cultures in conflict: social movements and the State in Peru. See item **1226.**

5069 Sulmont, Denis. La sociología del trabajo en el Perú. (Rev. Econ. Sociol. Trab., 23/24, marzo/junio 1994, p. 156–166, bibl.)

Useful review of sociological analysis undertaken since the 1950s of the Peruvian work force and business owners and management. Offers a good overview of the development of this analysis as historical events occurred in Peru and the focus of sociologists shifted.

5070 Taipe Campos, Néstor Godofredo. Movimientos campesinos en Colcabamba, 1970–1990. Lima: CEAR; Editorial Horizonte, 1993. 228 p.: bibl., map. (Realidad peruana; 20)

This sociohistorical account of Colcabamba, located in the southern end of the central Andes, follows the social changes that occurred in an area typical of Peru's rural history. Focuses on 1970–90 and the impact of internal and external social changes on the peasantry and on haciendas and peasant communities. Several background chapters provide context by examining control of the land and peasant labor prior to 1970.

5071 Ugarteche, Oscar. Historia, sexo y cultura en el Perú. Lima: Movimiento Homosexual de Lima, 1993. 49 p.: bibl., ill.

This essay examines the contradictory behaviors and attitudes toward sexuality and homosexuality in Peru by looking at preco-lumbian sexuality, which was tolerant of different sexual expressions, and the imposition of the repressive Spanish sexuality based on human reproduction, female virginity, and monogamous sexual activity. The influence of religion, economic development, and devastating plagues on attitudes toward sexuality is also examined.

5072 Urrutia, Jaime. Relaciones laborales, empleo agrícola y sociedad rural en Cajamarca. (*Debate Agrar.*, 24, junio 1996, p. 93–114, map, tables)

This interesting article examines an important phenomenon, which initially appears contradictory, among smallholders in the highlands: off-farm employment as a strategy to maintain peasant agriculture. A study of several provinces in Cajamarca finds that traditional agriculture, using family labor, peasant technology, and planting mainly subsistence crops, is able to survive because part of the family finds off-farm work, often in other regions, bringing in wages to complement peasant production.

5073 Vattuone, María Elena et al. De la costa a la sierra: mujer campesina. Recopilación de Emma Zevallos Aguilar. Lima: Editor Stilo Novo, 1994. 164 p.: bibl., ill.

This book actually contains two studies on rural women, one done on the coast (Ica) and the other in the highlands (Ancash). Both studies attempt to understand the intrahousehold dynamics of peasant production and household reproduction. Focuses on the changing roles of women due to deteriorating rural conditions and prolonged economic crisis. Underlying both analyses is the complementary sexual division of labor in rural areas based on gender subordination.

5074 Vélez Ubilluz, Luis Felipe. Ser niño y pobre en la Región Grau. Piura, Peru: Instituto de Pedagogía Popular, 1990. 53 p.: bibl., ill. (Serie Ñari-walác; 1)

Presents diagnosis of children under 14 years of age in the northern region (Region Grau) of Peru motivated by a debate regarding a proposed education program. The diagnosis involves not only preschool and elementary education, but also children's nutritional status and health. Focuses on children living in marginal urban areas and working children. Using census and survey data, the author confirms that children from poor families who work are more likely to abandon school, eat poorly, and become ill. This publication, together with many other studies undertaken in the last decade, demonstrate the dire effects of the economic crisis and structural adjustment on families and especially on children.

5075 Villalobos Dador, Raúl et al. Rol de la mujer en sistemas de riego. Puno, Peru: Instituto de Investigaciones para el Desarrollo Social del Altiplano-UNA; Servicio Holandés de Cooperación Técnica y Social: Consejo Andino de Manejo Ecológico, 1993. 95 p.: bibl.

Looks at the role of women in the development and maintenance of irrigation systems in a community in the high Andes of Puno using various research methods including observation, unstructured interviews, and surveys. One conclusion is that while women work as hard if not harder than men in agricultural work, including irrigating the fields, they have minimal input in the administration and organization of irrigation systems at the community level and in household decision-making.

5076 Wilson, Fiona. Género y clase en un pueblo de los Andes. (*in* Mujeres latino americanas: diez ensayos y una historia colectiva. Lima: Flora Tristán Centro de la Mujer Peruana, 1988, p. 95–142, bibl., table)

This article looks at the interaction of various social dimensions—class, gender, and ethnicity—during a period of rapid social change when the relations of domination shifted. The time and place is a small, provincial town in the central Peruvian Andes at the end of the 19th century and the social phenomenon when a mercantile class of both white and indigenous merchants was developing. Outlines struggle of this emerging class with the old elite (large landowners) and the differentiated impact of this process on women from the two different ethnic groups.

Zamudio, Delia. Piel de mujer. See item **1231.**

BOLIVIA AND PARAGUAY

KEVIN J. HEALY, *Foundation Representative, Inter-American Foundation, Rosslyn, Virginia*

BOLIVIA

ONCE AGAIN, THE DOMINANT THEME of the biennium in Bolivia is the role of ethnicity in national politics and society. There are new and insightful interpretations of the contemporary historical evolution of ethnicity in politics (items **5078** and **5080**), as well as an analysis of the contradictions of the Confederación Sindical Unica de Trabajadores Campesinos de Bolivia (CSTUCB) led by the Tupak Katari indigenous movement (items **5097** and **5086**). These works offer a critical perspective of the commitment to Andean cultural values and institutions by this widely esteemed social movement in social science literature.

Indigenous cultural issues also rise in publications about the medical and spiritual practices of traditional healers in the Bolivian Andes (item **5077**), the Bolivian Catholic Church's inculturation approach to evangelization among the Aymara in recent decades (item **5091**), and the diversity of agricultural ritual among communities in the Andean region of Charazani (item **5095**). An important contribution to the political economy of cultural change is the work on Guarani Indian communities analyzing how households straddle between market and non-market strategies in meeting subsistence needs and maintaining a strong ethnic identity (item **5108**).

Bolivia's coca-cocaine literature continues to grow, although not at the same rate as in the past. An important contribution is the edited volume on the multifaceted coca-cocaine issue that uses multidisciplinary analytical tools (item **5082**). The volume contains various angles of this controversial issue's effect on the economy, society and international relations. The material is fresh and the focuses often are innovative given the framework being used. There are new publications produced by the Bolivian NGO SEAMOS in this collection which are less analytical.

Gender research continues to loom large in this collection of publications. The focus is on discrimination toward migrant women (item **5084**); grassroots development experiences (item **5094**), including a small-scale sweater-knitting enterprise (item **5096**); and women's participation as leaders in political parties (item **5098**).

PARAGUAY

In Paraguay, as in Bolivia, ethnic representation in the political sphere is a major theme. Some publications examine the level of political development attained by the country's largest and most representative indigenous organization, especially its progress in securing new land rights for its members (items **5104** and **5107**).

New perspectives on gender issues abound in Paraguay as well. One work addresses the impact of educational reform for university women (item **5100**), and another analyzes reproductive behavior (item **5103**).

The production of new data and interpretations on the Paraguayan peasant sector has slowed in recent years, especially relating to understanding the rapidly expanding impact of globalization on Paraguayan society and economy. Instead, interest has focused on providing a profile of institutions working toward developmental and sociopolitical changes in the countryside as a statement about the growth in civil society, useful sociological contributions for grassroots activism (items **5102** and **5106**).

BOLIVIA

5077 Alba Fernández, Juan José. Jampiris y médicos en Raqaypampa. Cochabamba, Bolivia: IIHCE; CENDA, 1995. 88 p.: ill. (Cuadernos de investigación. Serie Estudios de la cultura; 2)

Insightful work examines medical and related spiritual practices of the traditional healers (pampa jampiri) in the Cochabamba mountain zone of Rayqaypampa, and healers' responses to presence of modern medicine in Western health clinics, including the program in which author was involved.

5078 Albó, Xavier. And from Kataristas to MNRistas?: the surprising and bold alliance between Aymaras and neoliberals in Bolivia. (in Indigenous peoples and democracy in Latin America. New York: St. Martin's Press, 1994, p. 55–79)

Traces politics of a Bolivian movement oriented toward formation of a pluricultural, multi-ethnic nation. Examines the rise of the Katarismo phenomenon in 1970s, its trajectory during first years of 1980s, and its demise during middle of the decade. Even though the Kataristas failed to maintain their broad-based social movement, this nation-building process, also influenced by important currents emanating from eastern lowland ethnopolitics, resulted in the election of Víctor Hugo Cárdenas, an Aymara leader, to the vice presidency. Article presents excellent overview of the political parties, individual political actors, and important changes and events involved in this process of shaping a "new ethnic consciousness" and related programs in Bolivia during 1990s. For political scientist's comment see item **3485.**

Balboa Valencia, Alfredo and **Julio César Córdova.** La juventud alteña: entre la integración e identificación socio-cultural aymara y occidental y sus formas de relación social. See item **1072.**

5079 Bolivia en la hora de su modernización. Recopilación de Mario Miranda Pacheco. México: Univ. Nacional Autónoma de México, 1993. 444 p.: bibl., ill. (Serie Nuestra América; 40)

Leading Bolivian intellectuals provide their interpretations of the many complex and contradictory facets of Bolivia's economic, political, and societal experience with modernization and neoliberalism.

5080 Calla Ortega, Ricardo. Hally hayllisa huti: identificación étnica y procesos políticos en Bolivia, 1973–1991. (in Democracia, etnicidad y violencia política en los países andinos. Lima: Instituto Francés de Estudios Andinos; Instituto de Estudios Peruanos, 1993, p. 57–81)

Analyzes evolution of "ethnopolitics" and "ethno-elites" within Bolivia's political systems over the past three decades. Provocative analysis divides this process into two periods: 1973–85 and 1986–91. Argues that main opposition to neoliberal economic policies in Bolivia evolved from class-based politics to ethnopolitics.

5081 Centro de Estudios Regionales para el Desarrollo de Tarija (Bolivia). Primera aproximación al impacto social y económico de la coca-cocaína en el Departamento de Tarija. La Paz: SEAMOS, 1993. 95 p.: bibl. (Drogas, investigación para el debate; 6)

Commissioned report on the increased illegal narcotrafficking activity in the city of Yacuiba on Bolivia/Argentina border provides a general analysis, neglecting much of the related social sciences literature. Does provide interesting figures for a geographic area about which little has been written.

5082 Coca, cocaine, and the Bolivian reality. Edited by Madeline Barbara Léons and Harry Sanabria. Albany: State Univ. of New York Press, 1997. 310 p.: bibl., ill, index, maps.

Edited volume of contributions from Bolivian, American, and British political scientists, development sociologists, anthropologists, and historians examines impacts of the coca/cocaine economy on Bolivian society and politics, and on the US, in recent years. Together these works constitute the most complete, updated collection of analyses about this controversial public policy issue affecting US/Bolivian relations.

5083 Corzón, Carmelo. Danzas y vestimentas folklóricas de Bolivia. La Paz: Producciones CIMA, 1994. 80 p.: bibl., col. ill. See item **4747.**

5084 Criales, Lucila. Mujer y conflictos socio-culturales: el caso de las migrantes de Caquiaviri en la ciudad de La Paz. La Paz: Aruwiyiri; Taller de Historia Oral Andina, 1994. 76 p.: bibl. (Serie Mujer)

Contemporary examination of women

from the Caquiaviri zone of the Altiplano who migrated to La Paz. Thin volume discusses the ethnic and gender discrimination they experienced, as well as the entrepreneurial success some achieved. Demonstrates the complexities and ambiguities of assimilating the dominant Western culture, while also asserting one's own culture within an urban milieu.

5085 Encuentro Binacional Perú-Bolivia, La Paz, 1991. El Lago Titicaca: análisis peruano-boliviano de las relaciones entre el ambiente y el desarrollo social; memorias. Edición de César A. Quiroz Peralta. Bogotá: SECAB, 1992. 209 p. (Ciencia y tecnología; 25)

Papers and government reports on current environmental conditions and changes in Lake Titicaca are presented by professional representatives from public and private Peruvian and Bolivian entities. Volume demonstrates the bilateral interest in Lake Titicaca that underpins the institutional efforts and collaborative agreements of these neighboring countries.

5086 Hahn, Dwight R. The use and abuse of ethnicity: the case of the Bolivian CSUTCB. (*Lat. Am. Perspect.*, 23:2, Spring 1996, p. 91–106, bibl.)

Argues that the national peasant confederation, Confederación Sindical Unica de Trabajadores Campesinos de Bolivia (CSUTCB), failed to represent the genuine interests of its constituents. Despite its explicitly pro-ethnicity platform, the Confederación promoted improvements (subsidized credit, farm equipment) within a capitalist marketing system instead of working to maintain cultural and material self-sufficiency, which would have been more consistent with the indigenous rural economy.

5087 Instituto Nacional de Estadística (Bolivia). Bolivia: encuesta nacional de demografía y salud, 1994; informe resumido. La Paz: Instituto Nacional de Estadística, 1994. 23 p.: ill. (some col.)

National survey conducted in Bolivia in late 1993 covers statistical information on maternal/child health practices and health service coverage, family planning, and demography. Data is useful for making comparisons both among Bolivian regions and internationally, and could be compared with data from a

similar survey conducted in 1989 (*Maternal and child health in Bolivia: report on the in-depth DHS survey in Bolivia, 1989*. Columbia, Md.: Institute for Resource Development/Macro Systems, 1991).

5088 Justiniano, José Guillermo. Opción cero. La Paz: SEAMOS, 1994. 219 p.: bibl. (Drogas, el debate boliviano; 11)

Collection focuses on Bolivian government's plan (Opción Cero), to resettle coca leaf growers en masse from the Chapare region to another part of the country. Includes views of social scientists, US and Bolivian government policymakers, journalists, political activists, and other opinion makers.

5089 Knowlton, David. Desengaño y desesperación: narrativas populares y elecciones del 85. (*Rev. Mus. Nac. Etnogr. Folk.*, 4:4, 1991, p. 1–21, bibl.)

Analyzes narratives of Bolivian working class citizens during 1985 presidential campaign. Argues that they represent a view of Bolivian politics framed in the idioms of popular culture by including folk tales and vivid social class analysis.

5090 Lanza, Gregorio. La coca prohibida: producción, transformación y persecución a fines del siglo XX. La Paz: SNV-Bolivia; CEDIB, 1995. 150 p.: bibl., ill. (Trabajos del Servicio Holandés; 9)

Excellent introduction to conditions of coca leaf and cocaine production in Bolivia and to the impact of US and Bolivian drug policy. Written by a critic of the prohibitionist approach.

Mita Barrientos, Fernando. El fenómeno del narcotráfico: enfoque nacional e internacional. See item **4032.**

Morales Durán, Agustín. Fiestas de Tarija: cuentos testimoniales de medio siglo. See *HLAS 56:3654.*

5091 Orta, Andrew. From theologies of liberation to theologies of inculturation: Aymara catechists and the *second evangelization* in highlands Bolivia. (*in* Organized religion in the political transformation of Latin America. Lanham, Md; New York: Univ. Press of America, 1995, p. 97–124)

Penetrating analysis of the role of Catholic catechists in the post-Vatican II, post-liberation theology ideology and practice of inculturation in the Bolivian Altiplano. A fine contribution about an important topic that has received little attention.

5092 Pacheco Balanza, Diego. El indianismo y el discurso de la "utopía" en Bolivia. (*Rev. Mus. Nac. Etnogr. Folk.*, 4:4, 1991, p. 23–110, tables)

Schematic presentation of highland indigenous organizations and political parties.

5093 Patrinos, Harry Anthony and **George Psacharopoulos.** The cost of being indigenous in Bolivia: an empirical analysis of educational attainments and outcomes. (*Bull. Lat. Am. Res.*, 12:3, Sept. 1993, p. 293–309, graph, tables)

Uses a simple human capital model to study effects of ethnicity on income in urban Bolivia. Regression results (for men only) suggest that traditional experience, education, and social variables account for 72 percent of the observed differences, while 28 percent was unexplained and thus related to unobserved factors such as discrimination, labor market segmentation, and uncaptured social effects. A useful paper on a little-studied topic. [J. Franks]

5094 Peredo, Elizabeth; Ruth Volgger; and **Ineke Dibbits.** Trenzando ilusiones: reflexiones y propuestas para una metodología de trabajo con mujeres. La Paz: TAHIPAMU, 1994. 124 p.: bibl.

Three professional women share their reflections on educational and income-generating projects and activities conducted with low-income women by their NGO over a ten-year period in the city of El Alto, adjacent to La Paz. Assumes a critical, soul-searching tone for finding the most effective ways to empower women.

5095 Rösing, Ina. Paraman Purina—llamar la lluvia. (*Yachay/Cochabamba*, 10:18, segundo semestre 1993, p. 143–202, bibl., tables)

Describes and analyzes the diversity of agricultural rituals for invoking rainfall among communities in the zone of Charazani. Provides insightful observations of common elements and details such as the elaborate prayers offered to sacred mountains and lakes and relates role of Andean ritual specialists. Argues that Catholic elements of these rituals may not be what a superficial analysis would determine. For annotation of the English-language version see item **1095.**

5096 Salinas Mulder, Silvia. Mujeres: historias de una experiencia. La Paz: Centro de Desarrollo y Fomento a la Auto-Ayuda (CEDEFOA), 1993. 170 p., 5 p. of plates: ill.

Relates story of a women's sweater-knitter organization in the La Paz barrio of Munaypata. Organization is schematic, but work includes interesting testimonies about the women's family life and organizational participation.

5097 Ströbele-Gregor, Juliana. Culture and political practice of the Aymara and Quechua in Bolivia: autonomous forms of modernity in the Andes. (*Lat. Am. Perspect.*, 23:2, Spring 1996, p. 72–90, bibl.)

Rendition of the political crisis suffered by the Katarista *sindicatos* in Bolivia in the 1980s, when the contradictions between Western-style unionism and communal ethno-cultural values and norms became exacerbated. Discusses persistence and strength of Andean cultural forms within Bolivia's peculiar process of modernity.

Wood, Bill and **Harry Anthony Patrinos.** Urban Bolivia. See item **2210.**

5098 Zabala, María Lourdes. Nos/otras en democracia: mineras, cholas y feministas, 1976–1994. La Paz: ILDIS, 1995. 316 p.: bibl., ill. (Serie Mujer; 3)

Provides historical perspective of women's contributions to social and political change in Bolivia, beginning with late-1970s miners' wives' hunger strike, marking the opening to democracy, to the present. Pays special attention to the support of gender issues by the political party Consciencia de Patria (CONDEPA), nongovernmental organizations associated with the Movimiento de Izquierda Revolucionario (MIR), and others.

PARAGUAY

5099 Centro Paraguayo de Estudios de Población. Paraguay: las políticas de población en un nuevo tiempo político. Asunción: Centro Paraguayo de Estudios de Población (CEPEP), 1993. 78 p.: bibl., ill. (Centro Paraguayo de Estudios de Población; 3)

Series of concise articles by notable Paraguayan intellectuals links population trends to health, environment, education, and employment.

5100 Corvalán, Graziella. Los estudios de la mujer y la reforma educativa en el Paraguay. (*Enfoques Mujer*, 31, junio 1994, p. 13–22, photos)

Analyzes advances achieved by women via university curriculum reform over the past decade, and obstacles and challenges for making further changes. Contends that gender themes must acquire a respected role within public discussions and that politicians and intellectuals must participate in validating and accepting these themes.

5101 Dávalos, Myriam Cristina and José Carlos Rodríguez. Censo de organizaciones campesinas, 1992–1993. Asunción: Centro de Documentación y Estudios, 1994. 240 p.: bibl., tables.

Contains descriptive features and organizational characteristics of Paraguayan peasant organizations. See also item **5102.**

5102 Dávalos, Myriam Cristina and José Carlos Rodríguez. Guía de organizaciones campesinas, 1992–1993. Asunción Centro de Documentación y Estudios, 1994. 300 p.: index, maps.

Source book lists many local peasant organizations in the countryside. Includes brief organizational profile for each group. See also item **5101.**

5103 Heikel, María Victoria. Sexualidad y comportamiento reproductivo de la mujer campesina. (*Enfoques Mujer*, 31, junio 1994, p. 8–12, photos)

Insightful and provocative analysis of recent data taken from 42 life histories examines patterns of sexual and reproductive behavior of peasant women in rural Paraguay. Within this framework, research focuses on relations within the family, between the couple, and among the wider community.

5104 Kidd, Stephen W. Los indígenas del Paraguay durante la transición. (*Rev. Parag. Sociol.*, 31:90, mayo/agosto 1994, p. 209–229, bibl.)

Critical analysis of State policy and actions toward indigenous land rights under the Rodríguez government, following its ratification of the progressive ILO Convention 169. Includes commentary on level of political organization of indigenous peoples in Paraguay and on their allies within civil society.

5105 Palau, Tomás. Modificación de patrones migratorios y movilidad transfronteriza en el Paraguay. (*Rev. Parag. Sociol.*, 31:90, mayo/agosto 1994, p. 113–129, bibl., table)

Examines new Paraguayan migration patterns shaped by economic transformations due to increasing globalization of the national economy. The "commuter informal" system of transnational organization is creating binational consumers and students, as well as new social and occupational configurations, in the frontier zones where these migrations are occurring.

5106 Palau, Tomás. La promoción de organizaciones campesinas, ONGs y la cooperación para el desarrollo. Asunción: Programa de Estudios Agrarios y Campesinos BASE, Investigaciones Sociales, 1995. 126 p.: bibl., tables. (Documento de trabajo; 70)

Profiles civil society in terms of development of nongovernmental organizations and grassroots federations in rural Paraguay. Provides sophisticated and useful analysis of the role, performance, aspirations, and limitations of nongovernmental actors in rural development who work within the difficult conditions of prevailing agrarian structures and dominant national economic trends favoring economic elites rather than the peasantry.

5107 Prieto, Esther. Indigenous peoples in Paraguay. (*in* Indigenous peoples and democracy in Latin America. New York: St. Martin's Press, 1994, p. 235–258, appendices)

Although author's notion of a Paraguayan indigenous movement is slightly exaggerated, work offers a critical discussion of the indigenous situation in the country. Of particular interest is her discussion of the 1990s constitutional changes supporting customary indigenous rights, bilingual education, recognition of cultural heritage, and efforts to preserve and develop ethnic identity.

5108 Reed, Richard K. Household ethnicity, household consumption: commodities and the Guarani. (*Econ. Dev. Cult. Change*, 44:1, Oct. 1995, p. 129–145, tables)

Using household survey data from Guarani indigenous communities, author argues that the purchase of commodities does not inevitably destroy indigenous cultural systems, as some analysts have argued. Data show that the key to preventing complete commercial integration and the resulting cultural assimilation is maintenance of a solid base within the subsistence economy and of corresponding locally-based networks of mutual support.

5109 Rodríguez Marín, Rafael. Actitudes frente a la norma del castellano paraguayo en la ciudad de Asunción. (*Rev. Parag. Sociol.*, 31:90, mayo/agosto 1994, p. 75–84)

Analyzes linguistic preferences and practices in the capital city of Asunción.

5110 Smith, Russel E. Trabajadores y transición paraguaya en perspectiva comparada: un estudio introductorio. (*Rev. Parag. Sociol.*, 31:90, mayo/agosto 1994, p. 131–145, bibl.)

Historical analysis of evolution of the *sindicato* as an institution representing and advocating workers' rights within Paraguay throughout the 20th century is placed within a wider, comparative Latin American focus. Includes analysis of Céspedes' work *Autoritarismo, sindicalismo y transición en Paraguay*, focusing mainly on *sindicato* activity during the transition period to democracy in Paraguay.

5111 Villagra, María Susana; Gladys Casaccia; and María Teresa Ayala. Organizaciones campesinas en el Paraguay. v. 2, La búsqueda de la autoexpresión. Dirección de Susana López de Quevedo. Asunción: Centro Interdisciplinario de Derecho Social y Economía Política, Univ. Católica, 1989. 1 v.: bibl. (Serie Investigaciones/CIDSEP; 8)

Critique of contemporary agrarian policies and land tenure systems in Paraguay. Advocate of small farm agriculture and farmers' organizations. For annotation of vol. 1 see *HLAS 51:4862.*

ARGENTINA, CHILE AND URUGUAY

ROBERTO PATRICIO KORZENIEWICZ, *Assistant Professor, Department of Sociology, University of Maryland, College Park*

ARGENTINA

CONTINUING TRENDS OF RECENT YEARS, the social science literature in Argentina has shifted its scope and focus. As mentioned in the previous edition of the *Handbook*, this has been in part a consequence of the fact that financial constraints have restricted both academic research and the opportunities to publish works intended for scholarly consumption. Simultaneously, there have been two significant developments shaping the organization of social science research. First, the consolidation of democratic rule together with deepening economic reforms have changed the immediate agenda of social scientists, promoting a growing concern with assessing the social impact of recent economic and institutional transformations. Second, a broader shift within the social sciences has promoted greater attention to processes of social differentiation other than class stratification (such as gender or ethnic differentiation).

The principal area of sociological research and publication has been the social impact of structural adjustment policies. Several studies have sought to assess overall changes in the distribution of income, to provide a more detailed understanding of trends in the evolution of poverty, and to identify which social groups have been more vulnerable to poverty and/or unemployment in recent years (items **5139** and **5134**). A related area of inquiry has been the impact of the budget cutbacks and new priorities that have come to shape State social spending. Here, the main effort of both quantitative and qualitative studies has been to identify which sectors of the population have been affected by recent changes in social spending, which individual and collective strategies are deployed by these vulnerable sectors, and what types of social programs are most likely to effectively reach their intended beneficiaries.

This general interest about the social impact of structural adjustment is related to two additional sets of literature. First, several studies have sought to provide a more detailed understanding of social policy options by focusing on the recent organizational transformations undergone by State agencies, enterprises, and professionals within more specific areas of social spending. A particularly good example of such research is the study of the public health sector conducted by Jorge M. Katz (item **5128**). Also within this general interest on the social impact of structural adjustment, many qualitative studies have focused on more specific groups within the population. For example, several authors have focused on the survival strategies deployed by young men and women to deal with limited job opportunities, and others have sought to identify the types of characteristics that may make specific groups within the elderly population more vulnerable to poverty.

Another significant area of sociological publication is gender relations, although many of these publications are destined for general consumption and/or political advocacy, and academic studies are considerably fewer in number. However, there have been several noteworthy publications in this area, seeking to evaluate changes in the status of women by focusing on issues such as patterns of female labor force participation and the characteristics of labor market segregation and discrimination.

In economic sociology, an important literature focuses on patterns of competition and innovation in key areas of production. One of the concerns within this literature is to identify the organizational characteristics that have been most likely to lead to innovation and/or the establishment of successful market niches. In particular, several of these studies have focused on agricultural enterprises (often, fresh fruit producers) in the western and southern areas of the country, and have sought to evaluate, for example, whether innovation has been most likely among small or large enterprises. This literature on economic sociology is guided partly by a concern with assessing the impact of regional trade agreements and/or new patterns of competition on established local producers (particularly small enterprises or family farmers) and the labor force in general, as well as with identifying the type of technologies that might maximize production and employment opportunities for these groups.

In political sociology, several studies continue to focus on the institutional transformations accompanying the consolidation of democracy. Some of these studies analyze social patterns in voting behavior. Others seek to evaluate and debate whether the consolidation of formal democratic procedures (such as elections) has been accompanied by an advance or retreat in broader dimensions of democracy that are of substantive importance to its very existence. Of course, depending on the author, such alternative dimensions are defined as being of greater or lesser importance than the formal democratic procedures involved in elections, and might include such issues as prevailing levels of transparency/corruption in public administration, or the expansion/limitation of citizenship rights. Here too, an evident concern is to assess the degree to which the changes associated with structural adjustment and economic restructuring are compatible with the consolidation of democratic values and institutions.

Beyond these issues, more traditional areas of inquiry continue to attract academic interest. There have been several good publications on changing demographic patterns, focusing for example on gender differences in the recent evolution of mortality rates, or on patterns of sexual behavior and fertility among the youth (item **5137**). Several studies in urban sociology have sought to identify the organizational and political causes of the deterioration of basic services and the environment in Buenos Aires. There is also a continuing interest in migration, from the perspective of both current trends and historical patterns. Finally, as indicated in the entries below, there is also continuing interest in the long-term consequences of the terror and violence experienced under military rule.

Some of the areas attracting social science research would benefit from more detailed, microsociological studies of the issues in question (as carried out in other areas of research, such as the studies of poverty and unemployment among the youth). For example, more detailed reconstructions of the strategic choices that allowed some enterprises to gain significant competitive advantages relative to other producers might produce important insights for the study of the relationship between organizational patterns and innovation among agricultural producers. In other areas, such as the study of gender differentiation, it might be useful to develop a broader, comparative approach to the study of labor market segmentation and discrimination. Situating patterns of gender differentiation in Argentina within the broader context of similar patterns in other areas (such as the Southern Cone as a whole, or countries characterized by similar levels of urbanization) might help to identify the most salient trends and characteristics of the particular country in question.

Finally, sociological studies in Argentina might fruitfully explore the topic of social inequalities. In particular, greater research is needed on the relationship of social inequality to economic growth (for example, as mediated by patterns of educational achievement), the relationship of different forms of social differentiation (such as gender or ethnicity) to overall patterns of inequality, and the historical evolution of social inequality under the different political arrangements of the 20th century.

CHILE

Several trends reported in the last review of sociology in Chile continue in the 1990s. The professionalization of the discipline, the enduring impact of years of dictatorship on the university system, and the decline of independent research institutions, have continued to narrow the scope of issues considered within the field. On the other hand, accompanying high rates of economic growth over the late 1980s and early 1990s, there have been fewer contributions focusing on the overall social impact of structural adjustment. Instead, most works have turned their attention toward examining changing social conditions among more specific sectors of the population.

A major area of concern has been in assessing the rise and decline of organizational efforts among what came to be known as "new social movements" (centered, for example, around women, the youth, and poor urban dwellers). These studies have focused on the internal development of these organizations, on the networks established between these organizations and their constituencies, and on the relationship between these organizations and more traditional political forces (such as existing political parties and State agencies). Additionally, several of these studies have sought to evaluate the effectiveness of State agencies in providing services for different constituencies.

A second major area of concern has been in identifying the changing relationship between social forces (such as entrepreneurs, trade unions, or the peasantry) and existing political arrangements. Most of these studies note that the last decade has brought a profound transformation in this relationship, and seek to assess the impact of these changes for the immediate and long-term future of democracy. For the most part, these studies adopt an optimistic perspective on these changes, emphasizing that corporatism has ceased to be a central mechanism for exercising political influence, that consensus on the basic rules of the game has been reached among key political players, and that these trends bode well for the future of democracy. Less systematic attention has been paid to enduring authoritarian traits (such as the persistent political influence of the military through informal and formal mechanisms).

But perhaps the most striking feature of publications in recent years has been the strong focus on women. There are several issues explored within this literature. Many studies have sought to highlight the importance of domestic violence and sexual harassment in shaping everyday life (primarily in contemporary times, but also from a historical perspective). Others focus on the hidden experience of specific groups of women (such as workers in different areas of production or single mothers). This strong emphasis on women's issues is part of a regional trends toward such concerns, but is particularly strong in the case of Chile.

Finally, there are several good-quality studies focusing on more traditional areas of concern within sociology (such as trends in the relative intensity of different social problems). Particularly noteworthy are studies on the social dynamics of criminal activity in Santiago (item **5162**), and on the problems confronting the organization of public health services (items **5159** and **5158**).

URUGUAY

The literature on Uruguay shows that there is an intense concern with evaluating the social impact of recent economic reforms. As in the case of Argentina, many of these studies seek to identify sectors of the population that might be particularly vulnerable to poverty and/or exclusion, to explain the causes of this vulnerability, and to identify individual, collective, and public strategies that might effectively reduce this vulnerability. A large number of publications (both detailed research studies and overviews prepared for general advocacy and consumption) deal with the impact of poverty and unemployment on children and the youth.

There is also a continuing concern with more established areas of inquiry. Many publications continue to analyze the characteristics of democratic institutions in the 1990s, with several studies focusing specifically on the relationship between democracy and processes shaping the country's identity and national formation. Also, a considerable number of publications deal with the changing status of women and processes of gender differentiation, with several studies showing a considerable increase in female labor force participation and educational achievement after the late 1970s (item **5194**).

ARGENTINA

5112 Achard, Diego; Manuel Flores Silva; and Luis E. González. Las élites argentinas y brasileñas frente al Mercosur. Buenos Aires: Banco Interamericano de Desarrollo, Instituto para la Integración de América Latina, 1994. 208 p.: bibl. (Publicación/BID/INTAL; 418)

Uses survey data and detailed interviews with entrepreneurs from Brazil and Argentina to assess attitudes towards Mercosur, especially areas of potential convergence or conflict.

5113 Allub, Leopoldo. Impactos de las políticas de promoción agrícola en el desarrollo rural de la Provincia del San Juan. (*Cuad.*

Desarro. Rural, 32, primer semestre 1994, p. 5–18, bibl., graphs, map, tables)

Combining field research with official production data, argues that State efforts to promote agricultural technological innovation through special incentives tend to favor large-scale enterprises, and that special promotion efforts are needed to aid small- and medium-sized producers.

5114 Auyero, Javier. Otra vez en la vía: notas e interrogantes sobre la juventud de sectores populares. Buenos Aires: Espacio Editorial, 1993. 149 p.: bibl. (Cuaderno/Fundación del Sur; GECUS, 2; Sociología de la cultura)

Study of social life among urban youth in poorer neighborhoods of Buenos Aires contains some useful anecdotal insights.

5115 Bandieri, Susana. Historia regional y relaciones fronterizas en los Andes meridionales: el caso del Neuquén, Argentina. (*Siglo XIX*, 4 : 12, mayo/agosto 1995, p. 49–73, map)

Argues that throughout 19th and much of the 20th century, territorial boundaries between Chile and Argentina did not impede an intense commercial and interethnic exchange that bridged official frontiers. Hence, greater attention should be paid to the specific characteristics of each border area.

5116 Belmartino, Susana and **Carlos Bloch.** El sector salud en Argentina: actores, conflictos de intereses y modelos organizativos, 1960–1985. Argentina: Representación OPS/OMS Argentina, Organización Panamericana de la Salud; Oficina Sanitaria Panamericana Regional de la Organización Mundial de la Salud, 1994. 379 p.: bibl. (Publicación; 40)

Very good, detailed study of evolution of Argentina's health system in recent decades emphasizes political shifts in corporate alliances as a crucial component of this evolution.

Brysk, Alison. From above and below: social movements, the international system, and human rights in Argentina. See item **4342.**

5117 Celton, Dora Estela. Informe demográfico de la provincia de Córdoba. Córdoba, Argentina: Centro de Estudios Avanzados, Univ. Nacional de Córdoba, 1994. 103 p.: bibl. (Col. Debates)

Useful, short monograph on demographic trends in the province.

5118 Deutsche Bank. La juventud argentina: una comparación de generaciones. Buenos Aires: Planeta, 1993. 316 p.: appendix, ill. (Espejo de la Argentina)

Describes results of a detailed, large-scale survey exploring social and political attitudes of youth (n=1,019 ages 14–24) and compares these attitudes to an additional sample (n=1,002) of older individuals. Rather superficial, but reports some interesting results and provides a detailed appendix with the survey data.

5119 Eisenberg, Ellen. Argentine and American Jewry: a case for contrasting immigrant origins. (*Am. Jew. Arch.*, 47 : 1, Spring/Summer 1995, p. 1–16, photos)

Focusing on Jewish immigrants to Entre Ríos prov., and drawing on arguments made elsewhere regarding the character of Italian migration, this brief article suggests that original background of Jewish immigrants, rather than the characteristics of the host countries, might explain the greater institutional strength of the Jewish community in the US as compared to Argentina.

5120 Estudios inconformistas sobre la clase obrera argentina: 1955–1989. Recopilación de Patricia M. Berrotarán y Pablo A. Pozzi. Argentina: Ediciones Letra Buena, 1994. 246 p.: bibl. (Col. Temas de historia)

Uneven collection of essays focuses on patterns of organization and action among sectors of the working class of Buenos Aires and Rosario. Several articles use oral histories to provide narratives on topics such as labor conflicts or changes in the organization of the workplace.

5121 Forni, Floreal H. and **Laura M. Roldán.** Pobreza, políticas sociales y de empleo. v. 1. Buenos Aires: Ministerio de Trabajo y Seguridad Social, Programa Nacional de Asistencia Técnica para la Administración de los Servicios Sociales en la República Argentina, 1993. 1 v.: bibl., ill. (Documento de trabajo; 16)

Short commissioned monograph is primarily a methodological assessment of the measurement of poverty and employment in Argentina, suggesting possible areas for future research and providing a short, annotated bibliography of relevant contributions. See also item **5122.**

5122 Forni, Floreal H. and **Laura M. Roldán.** Trayectorias laborales de residentes de áreas urbanas pobres: un estudio de casos en el conurbano bonaerense. (*Desarro. Econ.*, 35 : 140, enero/marzo 1996, p. 585–599)

Effectively combining case study histories and ethnographic observations, argues that sensitivity to the different dimensions shaping poverty (such as specific interactions between patterns of residence and labor market participation) provides a more accurate basis for identifying which social groups are most susceptible to poverty, and which measures might be most effective in targeting these problems. See also item **5121.**

5123 Fundacíon Alumbrar (Argentina). La adolescente embarazada. Buenos Aires: Grupo Editor Latinoamericano, 1994. 193 p.: bibl. (Col. Temas)

Based on organizational experience of an NGO serving adolescent mothers, and drawing on authors' therapeutic and medical experience, volume is intended as introductory resource. Also recounts organizational experience of a short-lived home for adolescent mothers.

5124 Geldstein, Rosa N. Los roles de género en la crisis: mujeres como principal sostén económico del hogar. Buenos Aires: Centro de Estudios de Población, 1994. 146 p.: bibl. (Cuaderno del CENEP, 0326–1095; 50)

Good, detailed analysis of patterns of women's labor force participation in the midst of late-1980s economic crisis.

5125 Golbert, Laura; Susana Lumi; and **Emilio Tenti Fanfani.** La mano izquierda del estado: la asistencia social según los beneficiarios. Buenos Aires: Miño y Dávila Editores, 1992. 160 p.: bibl. (Col. Políticas públicas)

Interviews with residents in poor neighborhoods of Buenos Aires are used to assess effectiveness of existing social programs and to delineate areas in need of further attention.

5126 Grushka, Carlos O. Mortalidad adulta en Argentina: tendencias recientes, causas y diferenciales. (*Notas Pobl.*, 23 : 61, junio 1995, p. 111–146, bibl., graphs, tables)

Good study examines changes in adult mortality rates from 1980–90. A reduction in the mortality rate for diseases of the circulatory system was key to a decline of 14 percent in overall adult mortality rates. Using data on the country's provinces, study also finds a strong relationship between mortality rates and socioeconomic status for women, but not for men, and provides a preliminary explanation of this pattern.

5127 Informe nacional: situación de la mujer en la última década en la República Argentina. Argentina: Centro Nacional de Coordinación Preparatorio de la IV Conferencia Mundial de la Mujer: Consejo Nacional de la Mujer, 1994. 159 p.: bibl.

Official report provides a general overview and useful statistics on the status of women.

5128 Katz, Jorge M. El sector salud en la República Argentina: su estructura y comportamiento. México: Fondo de Cultura Económica, 1993. 369 p.: bibl., ill. (Serie de economía/Fondo de Cultura Económica)

Excellent analysis of Argentine health system includes overview of historical trends, and specific case studies of several provinces (Buenos Aires, Córdoba, Corrientes, Neuquén, Salta, San Juan) and of the city of Rosario (Santa Fé prov.). Studies emphasize uneven quality of health services across the country. Evaluates policy options regarding administrative regulation and decentralization.

5129 Lo Vuolo, Rubén Mario and **Alberto C. Barbeito.** La nueva oscuridad de la política social: del estado populista al neoconservador. Buenos Aires: Miño y Dávila Editores, 1993. 246 p.: bibl. (Col. Políticas públicas)

Good analysis of the demise of a "welfare state" in Argentina.

5130 Macri, Mariela and **Solange Van Kemenade.** Estrategias laborales en jóvenes de barrios carenciados. Buenos Aires: Centro Editor de América Latina, 1993. 98 p.: bibl. (Biblioteca Política argentina; 413)

Authors use a detailed 1988 survey of 25 young men and women in a precarious neighborhood on the outskirts of Buenos Aires to provide some interesting insights into work strategies during a period of crisis.

5131 Mafud, Julio. Los dueños del país: sociología de la clase alta argentina. Buenos Aires: Editorial Distal, 1993. 224 p.: bibl.

Posthumous publication of rather traditional anecdotal essays on the ruling class in Argentina. Seeks to explain endurance of upper class by emphasizing its cultural/normative cohesion and continued control of key mechanisms of wealth (landholding, financial institutions).

5132 Manzanal, Mabel. Estrategias de sobrevivencia de los pobres rurales. Buenos Aires: Centro Editor de América Latina, 1993. 107 p.: bibl. (Biblioteca Política argentina; 437)

Brief but useful study uses census data to estimate prevalence of poverty in different rural areas of Argentina. Follows with a review of the secondary literature (case studies) to assess poor households' survival strategies. Concludes by outlining policy implications for alleviation of poverty.

5133 Míguez, Daniel. Spiritual bonfire in Argentina: confronting current theories with an ethnographic account of Pentecostal growth in a Buenos Aires suburb. Amsterdam: CEDLA, 1998. 204 p. (Latin America Studies; 81)

Examines political, cultural, social, and religious factors to explain the increasing popularity of Pentecostalism in Argentina. Based on a case study of Villa Eulalia, a suburb of Buenos Aires, argues that a series of structural transformations to society in 1980s led to the growth of Pentecostalism. Drawing on the theory, practice, and concept of social identity, author challenges some of the more widely accepted theories for explaining the success of Pentecostalism in Latin America. [R. Hoefte]

5134 Minujin Z., Alberto and **Gabriel Kessler.** La nueva pobreza en la Argentina. Buenos Aires: Editorial Planeta, 1995. 278 p.: bibl., ill. (Temas de hoy. Ensayo)

Effectively combines detailed case studies and quantitative survey data to provide an overview of impoverishment patterns in Argentina in early 1990s. Intended primarily for general rather than academic audiences.

5135 Miranda, Omar A. El cambio técnico en la fruticultura familiar del Alto Valle de Río Negro. (*Ruralia/Buenos Aires*, 6, sept. 1995, p. 28–46, bibl., tables)

A careful study of technological change, family labor, and productivity in different types of farms (small and large, modern and traditional). Small farms effectively in-

corporate new technologies with continued reliance on unremunerated family labor. See also items **5151** and **5152.**

5136 Mujeres latinoamericanas en cifras. v. 1, Argentina. Coordinación de Teresa Valdés y Enrique Gomáriz. Madrid: Instituto de la Mujer, Ministerio de Asuntos Sociales de España; Santiago: Facultad Latinoamericana de Ciencias Sociales (FLACSO), 1992. 1 v.

Thorough statistical overview of the economic, social, and political status of women in Argentina. Part of a broader survey of the status of women in Latin America.

Oro, Ari Pedro. A desterritorialização das religiões afro-brasileiras. See item **5279.**

5137 Pantelides, Edith A; Rosa N. Geldstein; and Graciela Infesta Domínguez. Imágenes de género y conducta reproductiva en la adolescencia. Buenos Aires: Centro de Estudios de Población, 1995. 143 p.: bibl. (Cuadernos del CENEP; 51)

Excellent study of patterns of sexual behavior among Argentine youth uses survey data to compare the impact of gender images among different social strata.

5138 Pírez, Pedro. Buenos Aires Metropolitana: política y gestión de la ciudad. Buenos Aires: Centro Editor de América Latina, 1994. 181 p.: bibl., maps. (Sociedad y cultura)

Good analysis of urban development emphasizes institutional constraints on planning and policy implementation that result from a deficit of city-wide public organizations and collective actors.

5139 Política social: la cuenta pendiente — claves para enfrentar la pobreza en la Argentina. Recopilación de Gustavo Béliz. Buenos Aires: Editorial Sudamericana: Fundación Konrad Adenauer, 1995 329 p.: bibl.

Good overview of recent changes in the characteristics of poverty and the social policies implemented by the State. Provides statistical overview of recent trends in poverty and income distribution, an assessment of patterns of State expenditure in some relevant areas, and a discussion of policy alternatives.

5140 Pozzi, Pablo A. and **Alejandro Schneider.** Combatiendo al [sic] capital: crisis y recomposición de la clase obrera argentina,

1983–1993. Buenos Aires: El Bloque Editorial, 1994. 221 p.: bibl.

Assesses extent of the crisis undergone by organized labor using secondary literature, survey data, and interviews with informants. Also identifies potential forms of innovative organization that may develop in the future.

Ratliff, William E. and **Roger Fontaine.** Argentina's capitalist revolution revisited: confronting the social costs of statist mistakes. See item **3763.**

5141 Redondo, Nélida. Reestructuración económica y envejecimiento poblacional. Buenos Aires: Ediciones Imago Mundi, 1994. 143 p.: bibl. (Col. Argentina debate)

Useful overview of trends regarding the elderly in Argentina situates their contemporary status within a historical perspective. Also identifies groups at risk within the relevant population, and outlines policy options.

5142 Rinesi, Eduardo. Seducidos y abandonados: carisma y traición en la "transición democrática" argentina. Buenos Aires: Manuel Suárez, 1993. 158 p. (La carabela perdida)

Compilation of thoughtful essays on contemporary social sciences and democracy in Argentina includes a creative interpretation of influential texts.

5143 Robben, Antonius C.G.M. Ethnographic seduction, transference, and resistance in dialogues about terror and violence in Argentina. (*Ethos/Society*, 24:1, March 1996, p. 71–106, bibl.)

Analysis of tape recordings of interviews conducted by the author provides thoughtful reflections on the dynamics involved in generating information through personal informants. Pays particular attention to methodological and ethical implications.

5144 Sartori, María Gabriela. La barbarie oligárquica: violencia y salud mental. Buenos Aires: El Bloque, 1993. 206 p.: bibl. (Col. Testimonios del sur)

Uses psychoanalytic perspective to study the forms of violence that accompanied military rule after 1976. Interviews provide anecdotal evidence of the impact of imprisonment on mental health. Argues that developing social links with other prisoners was crucial for maintaining mental health under repressive conditions.

5145 Suárez Lastra, Facundo. La reina en jaque. Buenos Aires: Distribuye Editorial Sudamericana, 1994. 189 p.: bibl.

Author, a long-time participant in municipal politics, argues that the city of Buenos Aires is on the verge of collapse (i.e., a deterioration of basic services, an inability to ensure sufficient fiscal resources, persistent official corruption, and growing environmental pollution). Calls for introduction of institutional mechanisms to ensure greater democratic participation in municipal affairs.

5146 Torrado, Susana. Procreación en la Argentina: hechos e ideas. Buenos Aires: Ediciones de la Flor; Centro de Estudios de la Mujer, 1993. 397 p.: bibl., ill.

Examines evolution of demographic patterns in Argentina from 1870s-1990s. Differentiating fertility patterns by social strata, argues that high birth rates among poor and marginal groups are a consequence of public policies that prevent easy access to modern birth control.

5147 Universidad de Buenos Aires. Facultad de Ciencias Sociales. Instituto de Investigaciones. Acciones colectivas y organización cooperativa: reflexiones y estudios de caso. Recopilación de Norma Giarracca. Buenos Aires: Centro Editor de América Latina; Univ. de Buenos Aires, Facultad de Ciencias Sociales, Instituto de Investigaciones, 1994. 173 p.: bibl. (Bibliotecas universitarias. Sociedad y cultura)

Good analysis of cooperatives links case studies to the general literature and evaluates both successful and failed experiences of organization.

5148 Universidad de Buenos Aires. Facultad de Ciencias Sociales. Instituto de Investigaciones. Conflicto obrero: transición política, conflictividad obrera y comportamiento sindical en la Argentina, 1984–1989. Coordinación de Ernesto Villanueva. Quilmes: Univ. Nacional de Quilmes, 1994. 154 p.: bibl.

Good, detailed analysis of labor conflicts in Argentina.

5149 Universidad Nacional de San Juan (Argentina). Instituto de Investigaciones Socioeconómicas. Violencia juvenil. Dirección de María Daniela Puebla. San Juan, Argentina: Editorial Fundación Univ. Nacional de San Juan, 1992. 154 p., 1 folded leaf: bibl., ill.

Short, uneven criminology study provides ethnographic observations on leisure activities among urban youth in San Juan. Explains why other social agents within communities studied perceive activities as either criminal or legitimate.

5150 Universidad Nacional del Comahue (Argentina). Campesinado y ganadería transhumante en Neuquén. Buenos Aires: Editorial La Colmena, 1993. 225 p.: bibl., ill., maps.

Competent analysis of migrant sheep herders in western Argentina provides detailed account of household survival strategies and income-generating activities.

5151 Universidad Nacional del Comahue (Argentina). El minifundio en el Alto Valle del Río Negro: estrategias de adaptación. Neuquén, Argentina: Univ. Nacional de Comahue, Facultad de Ciencias Agrarias, Facultad de Humanidades, 1994. 204 p.: bibl., ill., maps.

Good analysis of characteristics of agricultural production gives particular emphasis to recent changes affecting the fresh fruit industry, especially the impact of changes on the alternative economic strategies available to small producers. See also items **5152** and **5153.**

5152 Universidad Nacional del Comahue (Argentina). Trabajo y cambio técnico: el caso de la agroindustria frutícola en el Alto Valle. Coordinación de Mónica Bendini y Cristina Pescio. Buenos Aires: Editorial La Colmena, 1996. 287 p.: bibl., tables.

Good study of changes in organization of production and work in the fresh fruit industry includes detailed evaluation of technological changes affecting workplace and of shifts in patterns of labor demand throughout the production cycle. See also items **5151** and **5153.**

5153 Wainerman, Catalina. ¿Segregación o discriminación?: el mito de la igualdad de oportunidades. (*Bol. Inf. Techint*, 285, oct./dic. 1995, p. 59–75)

Although brief and written primarily for a non-specialized public, article provides a useful overview of gender differentiation and patterns of labor market segregation and discrimination. See also items **5151** and **5152.**

5154 Waisbord, Silvio. El gran desfile: campañas electorales y medios de comunicación en la Argentina. Buenos Aires: Editorial Sudaméricana, 1995. 204 p.: bibl.

Interesting political analysis of recent elections in Argentina emphasizes growing importance of electoral campaigns as old political alliances weaken.

5155 Zorrilla, Rubén H. El fenómeno Menem. Buenos Aires?: Grupo Editor Latinoamericano, 1994. 144 p.: bibl. (Col. Estudios políticos y sociales)

Sociological interpretation of recent political changes in Argentina contends that apparent centralization of power under the Menem Administration conceals a remarkable strengthening of civil society. For example, according to author, apparent growth of government corruption under Menem actually may reflect greater transparency of political transactions to inquiry by agents of civil society.

CHILE

5156 Arteaga, Ana María and Virginia Figueroa. La salud de las mujeres en Chile: repertorio de investigaciones, 1985–1992. Santiago: Centro de Estudios para el Desarrollo de la Mujer, 1993. 245 p.: ill., index.

Thorough annotated bibliography of research projects on women's health conducted between 1985–92.

5157 Baltra Montaner, Lidia. Rompiendo el aislamiento campesino: una experiencia de comunicación, multimedios. Santiago: Ediciones ICECOOP, 1987. 233 p. (Col. Análisis; Serie Documentos)

Detailed analysis describes efforts to develop new media (independent newspapers and radio programs) among the peasantry in Chile. Emphasizes problems that prevented greater and sustained direct participation of peasant communities in the projects.

Bandieri, Susana. Historia regional y relaciones fronterizas en los Andes meridionales: el caso del Neuquén, Argentina. See item **5115.**

5158 Centro de Estudios Públicos (Chile). La salud en Chile: evolución y perspectivas. Edición de Ernesto Miranda R. Santiago:

Centro de Estudios Públicos, 1994. 301 p.: bibl., ill.

Very good description of evolution of public health system in Chile includes chapters providing historical background as well as comparative perspective on problems and solutions in other countries.

5159 Centro de Estudios Públicos (Chile). La salud en el siglo XXI: cambios necesarios. Recopilación de Juan Giaconi G. Santiago: Centro de Estudios Públicos, 1995. 231 p.: bibl., ill.

Excellent analysis of the future direction of public health policy in Chile.

5160 Chile. Ministerio de Planificación y Cooperación. Programas sociales: su impacto en los hogares chilenos; Casen 1990. Santiago: MIDEPLAN, 1990. 283 p.: bibl., graphs, tables.

Official government publication uses the results of a large national survey (*Encuestra de Caracterización Socioeconómica Nacional*) to provide a detailed analysis of poverty, income distribution, and the extent to which social policies effectively target the neediest sectors of the population.

5161 Chile. Servicio Nacional de la Mujer. De mujer sola a jefa de hogar: género, pobreza y políticas públicas. Recopilación de María Elena Valenzuela, Sylvia Venegas, y Carmen Andrade. Santiago: Servicio Nacional de la Mujer, 1994. 471 p.: bibl., ill.

Several articles use results of large-scale surveys to analyze relative prevalence of female-headed households among different sectors of the population and to evaluate relative vulnerability of these households to poverty. Other articles evaluate effectiveness of a broad range of social policies in areas such as education, employment, and housing. Very good, detailed collection.

5162 Cooper Mayr, Doris. Delincuencia común en Chile. Santiago: LOM Ediciones, 1994. 232 p.: bibl.

Combining survey data with in-depth interviews with prisoners, book provides useful analysis of delinquency patterns in Chile. Distinguishes five patterns of criminal behavior that are shaped by ethnicity, gender, and urban/rural residence. Carefully delineates social norms characterizing criminal culture of Santiago.

5163 Délano Azócar, Bárbara and **Rosalba Todaro C.** Asedio sexual en el trabajo. Santiago: Ediciones CEM, 1993. 109 p.: bibl.

Reviews results of 1991 survey of 1,200 employees in Greater Santiago. Results suggest high levels of sexual harassment. Based on these findings, authors call for legal measures to attack harassment in the workplace.

5164 Desarrollo Campesino (Chile). El campesinado chileno: sus organizaciones productivas; factores de éxito y fracaso en su funcionamiento interno. Santiago: Instituto Chileno de Educación Cooperativa; Instituto de Sociología de la Univ. Católica de Chile; Desarrollo Campesino, 1988. 383 p.: bibl., ill.

Dated study of 50 organizations of small agricultural producers seeks to elucidate opportunities and constraints that characterize different forms of coordinating authority and leadership. Overall, study finds that producers have a very limited involvement with their organizations.

5165 Díaz B., Ximena and **Norah Schlaen.** La salud ignorada: trabajadoras de la confección. Santiago: Ediciones Centro de Estudios de la Mujer, 1994. 201 p.: bibl., ill.

Author uses a detailed representative survey of 325 female workers in the clothing industry to identify health concerns and to make relevant policy recommendations.

Errázuriz K., Ana María. Análisis espacial de la natalidad en Chile: 1952–1989. See item **2802.**

5166 Frohmann, Alicia and **Teresa Valdés.** Democracy in the country and in the home: the women's movement in Chile. (*in* The challenge of local feminisms: women's movements in global perspective. Boulder, Colo.: Westview Press, 1995, p. 276–301, photos, tables)

Brief but thoughtful history of the women's movement in Chile focuses on the role of women's organizations in promoting a transition to democracy and on the challenges faced by the movement under democracy. See also item **5169.** For political scientist's comment see item **3620.**

5167 Fundación para la Protección de la Infancia Dañada por los Estados de Emergencia (Chile). Infancia y represión: historias para no olvidar; experiencia clínica con niños y familias que han vivido la represión política. Santiago: Fundación PIDEE, 1992. 279 p.: bibl., ill.

Detailed case histories and an evaluation of the impact of different therapeutical approaches make this work a valuable resource on families and children victimized by political repression.

Gangas Geisse, Mónica and **Ana María Errázuriz K.** Diferenciación interna de la fuerza de trabajo en la provincia de San Antonio. See item **2806.**

5168 Garretón Merino, Manuel Antonio. La faz sumergida del iceberg: estudios sobre la transformación cultural. Santiago: LOM; CESOC Ediciones, 1993. 233 p.

Collection of essays by one of the most respected political scientists in Latin America provides a stimulating interpretation of current patterns of political change. Argues that rather than experiencing a demise of institutional politics, Chile is characterized by new patterns of interaction between traditional political structures and new types of social demands.

5169 Gaviola Artigas, Edda; Eliana Largo; and **Sandra Palestro.** Una historia necesaria: mujeres en Chile, 1973–1990. Santiago: Akí & Aora, Ltd., 1994. 256 p.: bibl., ill.

Oral histories and documents of the period are effectively combined in this narrative of the trajectory of women's organizations during the Pinochet regime and the transition to democracy. See also item **5166.**

Gill, Indermit S. Is there sex discrimination in Chile?: evidence from the CASEN survey. See item **2093.**

5170 Guevara Tapia, Soledad. Madresolterismo: estructuras y vivencias en sectores populares. Santiago: Univ. Academia de Humanismo Cristiano, Ediciones Academia, 1994. 146 p.: bibl.

Testimonies of 50 women from marginal neighborhoods in Santiago are used to evaluate the social and cultural background of single mothers and the impact of their status on educational attainment and living conditions. Interesting anecdotal insights.

5171 Guillaudat, Patrick and **Pierre Mouterde.** Les mouvements sociaux au Chili, 1973–1993. Paris: L'Harmattan, 1995. 303 p.: bibl., index. (Recherches & documents Amériques latines)

Serious interpretation of role of social movements in Chile during the Pinochet military dictatorship and its immediate aftermath is based primarily on secondary materials rather than on original research.

5172 Guzman, Virigina; Sandra Lerda; and **Rebeca Salazar.** La dimensión de género en el quehacer del Estado. Santiago: Centro de Estudios de la Mujer, Ediciones CEM, 1994. 101 p.: bibl.

Using the experience of Chile as a case study, work offers useful insights into the difficulties involved in creating State agencies to promote gender equality. Provides a good critical evaluation of the institutional trajectory of a key State agency (Servicio Nacional de la Mujer).

5173 Hurtado, Victoria; Guadalupe Santa Cruz; and **Alejandra Valdés.** Un indecente deseo: Escuela de Formación de Líderes Mujeres; 1995. 194 p.: bibl., ill.

Provides detailed account of content of workshops and readings used in this training school. Topics range from historical patterns of gender differentiation to strategies and styles of political leadership.

5174 Instituto Nacional de Estadísticas (Chile). Mujeres de Chile: radiografía en numeros; 8 de marzo 1994, Día Internacional de la Mujer. Santiago: Instituto Nacional de Estadísticas, 1994. 85 p.: bibl., ill.

Useful statistical survey and synthesis of the current status of women in Chile.

5175 Iturriaga, Maria Alicia. Niños de padre ausente: un estudio de la relación entre la madre soltera y sus niños. Santiago: Ediciones Academia; Univ. Adademia de Humanismo Cristiano, 1994. 141 p.: bibl.

Reviewing the pertinent secondary literature, and emphasizing an anecdotal account of selected life histories, author advances hypothesis that children raised in female-headed families are likely to reproduce the same family structure in their subsequent relationships.

5176 Larrain Heiremans, Soledad. Violencia puertas adentro: la mujer golpeada. Prólogo de Fernando Lolas Stepke. Santiago: Editorial Universitaria, 1994. 149 p.: bibl. (Col. Punta de lanza)

One of the best studies of patterns of domestic violence in Santiago, work shows good command of the relevant literature and uses careful survey of 1,000 women of different social strata to ascertain variables most likely to put women at risk for domestic violence.

5177 Montecino Aguirre, Sonia. Sangres cruzadas: mujeres chilenas y mestizaje. Santiago: Servicio Nacional de la Mujer, 1993. 61 p.: bibl., ill. (Col. Mujeres en la cultura chilena; 1)

Although brief and produced primarily for popular consumption, work provides interesting comments on contrasting status of white and indigenous women in mixed sexual unions, as well as on hidden role of mestizaje in shaping early social relations in Chile.

5178 Montero, Cecilia. El actor empresarial en transición. (*Colecc. Estud. CIEPLAN*, 37, junio 1993, p. 37–68, bibl.)

Very good analysis of changing relationship in Chile between entrepreneurs as a political force and the State.

5179 Osorio Alvarez, Emilio Antonio. Los escenarios de vida de los niños y mujeres en Chile: vulnerabilidad, extrema pobreza y disparidad espacial. Santiago: Fondo de las Naciones Unidas para la Infancia, Oficina de Area para Argentina, Chile y Uruguay, 1990. 127 p.: bibl., ill.

Competent, critical evaluation of trends in extreme poverty in Chile tracks changes between 1970–89, focusing on vulnerability of women, children, and particular regions.

Raczynski, Dagmar. Políticas sociales y programas de combate a la pobreza en Chile: balance y desafíos. See item **2122.**

5180 Richard, Nelly. La insubordinación de los signos: cambio político, transformaciones culturales y poéticas de la crisis. Santiago: Editorial Cuarto Propio, 1994. 126 p.: bibl. (Serie Debates)

Cultural critique of social science and political change in Chile.

Rodríguez, Aniceto. Entre el miedo y la esperanza: historia social de Chile. See item **3657.**

5181 Salman, Ton. The diffident movement: generation and gender in the vicissitudes of the Chilean shantytown organizations, 1973–1990. (*Lat. Am. Perspect.*, 21:3, Summer 1994, p. 8–31, bibl.)

Competent effort to explain initial importance of informal organizations in challenging dictatorial rule and their later withdrawal during the democratic transition. Drawing on interviews, author argues that this pattern was an outcome of high level of participation of previously unorganized women and youth (but not adult males). For annotation of author's dissertation on this subject (in Dutch language) see *HLAS* 55:5069.

5182 Santelices, Marisol. Mal amor: violencia entre cuatro paredes. Santiago: Ediciones CEM, 1991. 223 p.: bibl.

Uses in-depth interviews with abused women from different social strata to provide case studies of abusive relationships and an analysis of patterns of behavior and outcomes that characterize domestic violence.

5183 Schkolnik, Mariana and **Berta Teitelboim G.** Pobreza y desempleo en poblaciones: la otra cara del modelo neoliberal. Santiago: Programa de Economía del Trabajo, Academia de Humanismo Cristiano, 1988. 347 p.: bibl., ill. (Col. Temas sociales; 2)

Based on detailed 1986 surveys, provides a primarily qualitative assessment of the survival strategies used by the poor in several *poblaciones* around Santiago.

5184 Seminario Modelos Teóricos y Metodológicos de Intervención en Violencia Doméstica y Sexual, *Santiago, 1991*. Actas. Recopilación de Ana Cáceres O., Valentina Martínez M. y Diana Rivera O. Santiago: Casa de la Mujer La Morada; Instituto de la Mujer; Servicio Evangélico para el Desarrollo, 1993. 126 p.: bibl.

The results of a 1991 seminar, volume contains useful chapters reviewing various strategies for intervention in domestic and sexual violence. Includes appropriate policy recommendations.

5185 Valdés, Ximena; Loreto Rebolledo G.; and **Angélica Willson Aedo.** Masculino y femenino en la hacienda chilena del siglo XX. Santiago: FONDART; CEDEM, 1995. 122 p.: bibl., ill.

Very good work of 20th century social history draws on photographs, life histories, and documents to analyze patterns of gender differentiation and work on large rural farms.

5186 Venegas, Sylvia. Una gota al día—un chorro al año: el impacto social de la expansión frutícola. Santiago: Grupo de Estudios Agro-Regionales, Univ. Academia de Humanismo Cristiano, 1992. 289 p.: bibl.

Very good study of labor relations in the Chilean fresh fruit industry. Quantitative survey data and in-depth interviews are competently used to analyze heterogeneous labor market and prevailing working conditions in this important area of economic activity.

URUGUAY

5187 Bango, Julio and Juliana Martinez Franzoni. En tránsito-: realidades y actitudes de los jóvenes uruguayos. Coordinación de María Elena Laurnaga. Montevideo: Foro Juvenil, 1991? 164 p.: bibl., ill., map.

Competent overview of the characteristics of Uruguayan youth in early 1990s.

5188 Conferencia Episcopal del Uruguay. Comisión de Pastoral Popular. La fiesta hoy: estudio interdisciplinario sobre la fiesta. Montevideo: C.P.P.-C.E.U., 1992. 240 p.: bibl.

Results of a 1991 conference on festive celebrations, called by the Comisión de Pastoral Popular de la Conferencia Episcopal del Uruguay. Most articles focus on ritualized festivities, particularly (although not exclusively) those of a religious nature. Includes observations by a movie critic, a psychiatrist, a sociologist, and theologians.

5189 Errandonea, Alfredo. Actores cooperativos en un contexto de retracción del sector público: el caso uruguayo. (*Rev. Cienc. Soc./Montevideo,* 8:9, nov. 1993, p. 7–15, bibl., tables)

Using survey data and secondary sources, argues that economic restructuring in Uruguay has been accompanied by a significant increase in the number of cooperative organizations.

5190 Filgueira, Fernando. Un estado social centenario: el crecimiento hasta el límite del estado social batllista. Montevideo: PEITHO, Sociedad de Análisis Político, 1991. 70 p.: bibl., tables. (Documento de trabajo; 81)

Good analysis of the history of the welfare state in Uruguay includes evaluation of policy options for the current period of political and administrative reform.

5191 Filgueira, Nea. Crisis y cambio en la sociedad uruguaya: la situación de la mujeres. Montevideo: Grupo de Estudios sobre la Condición de la Mujer en el Uruguay (GRECMU), 1991. 64 p.: tables (Serie Lila; 21)

Good review of historical trends affecting the status of women in Uruguay pays close attention to recent changes in patterns of labor force participation.

5192 Identidad uruguaya: mito, crisis o afirmación? Recopilación de Hugo Achugar y Gerardo Caetano. Montevideo: Ediciones Trilce, 1992. 174 p.: bibl. (Col. Desafíos)

Includes a dozen articles presented at a 1992 seminar, representing a range of approaches to national identity. Most are intelligent and stimulating reflections of processes shaping identity and national formation.

5193 Instituto Goethe de Montevideo. La medicalización de la sociedad. Montevideo: Nordan Comunidad; Goethe-Institut, 1993. 251 p.: bibl., ill. (Ecoteca; 6)

Product of a 1993 workshop sponsored by Instituto Goethe de Montevideo, work examines origins and consequences of the rise of medicine as a specialized field of knowledge and professional practice. Some articles take a general approach, but most focus on the particular experience of Uruguay.

5194 Longhi, Augusto. Sobre la dinámica de la oferta de trabajo y sus determinantes: Montevideo, 1968–1988. (*Rev. Cienc. Soc./Montevideo,* 8:8, marzo 1993, p. 47–62, bibl., graph, tables)

Competent article uses official data to analyze labor market changes in Montevideo. Shows that a significant increase in overall labor supply occurred after late 1970s, driven primarily by incorporation of women (and also youth) into the labor force, and characterized by growing levels of educational achievement.

5195 Luján, Carlos. ¿Quienes son los jóvenes uruguayos más desfavorecidos?: un análisis de la Primera Encuesta Nacional de la Juventud. Montevideo: Comisión Económica para América Latina y el Caribe, Oficina de Montevideo; Instituto Nacional de Estadística, 1994. 71 p.: bibl.

Good, brief analysis of a large-scale survey of Uruguayan youth (n=6547, ages 15–29) identifies characteristics that promote social mobility, and those that lead to cycles of poverty and lack of access to educational resources.

5196 Míguez, Hugo Adolfo. Patrones socio-culturales del uso de drogas. Montevideo: Presidencia de la República Oriental del Uruguay, Junta Nacional de Prevención y Represión del Tráfico Ilícito y Uso Abusivo de Drogas, 1993. 169 leaves.

Interesting use of participant observation to evaluate drug consumption patterns among youth in Punta del Este and surrounding communities. Provides detailed observations, but makes few references to relevant literature.

5197 Morás, Luis Eduardo. Los hijos del Estado: fundación y crisis del modelo de protección-control de menores en Uruguay. Montevideo: Depto. de Sociología de la Facultad de Ciencias Sociales: Servicio Paz y Justicia Uruguay, 1992. 187 p.: bibl.

Brief overview of development of State policies vis-à-vis juvenile delinquency focuses on three historical turning points: the rise of such policies in the 1930s; the initial crisis of welfare policies in the 1950s; and the fiscal crisis of the 1980s (accompanied by a perceived wave of juvenile crime and calls for the greater use of punishment as a response).

5198 Núñez Panzardo, José Pedro. Infancia y pobreza en el Uruguay. Melo, Uruguay: Casa de la Mujer; Movimiento Paulina Luisi, 1990. 125 p.: bibl., graphs, ill., tables.

Creative use of graphs and tables illustrates patterns of poverty among children and youth in Uruguay.

Oro, Ari Pedro. A desterritorialização das religiões afro-brasileiras. See item **5279.**

5199 Repression, exile, and democracy: Uruguayan culture. Edited by Saúl Sosnowski and Louise B. Popkin. Translated from the Spanish by Louise B. Popkin. Durham, N.C.: Duke Univ. Press, 1993. 259 p.: bibl. (Latin America in translation/en traducción/em tradução)

Most of the essays in this book were originally presented at a 1986 conference on Uruguay (see *HLAS 50:3550*); however, several of the chapters were updated immediately prior to publication. Overall, work serves as excellent document on prevailing cultural perspectives in initial years of the return to democracy. Several articles provide a stimulating perspective on dictatorship and democracy.

5200 Riella, Alberto. Agricultores familiares: ¿agentes de transformación agraria? (*Rev. Cienc. Soc./Montevideo*, 8:9, nov. 1993, p. 86–93)

Brief article draws on field research in Salto to argue that, rather than gradually disappearing in the face of new patterns of regional competition, family farms play an important role in developing innovative areas of production and in effectively incorporating new technologies and forms of organization.

5201 Rodríguez Villamil, Silvia. El trabajo de las mujeres en Uruguay: pautas históricas en relación con los cambios en las ideologías de género. Montevideo: Grupo de Estudios sobre la Condición de la Mujer en el Uruguay (GRECMU), 1992. 48 p.: tables (Serie Lila; 27)

Somewhat sketchy, but overall good reconstruction of changes in female labor force participation. Emphasizes role played by social and political movements.

5202 La salud de los uruguayos: cambios y perspectivas. Montevideo: Organización Panamericana de la Salud, Oficina Sanitaria Panamericana, Oficina Regional de la Organización Mundial de la Salud; Editorial Nordan-Comunidad, 1994. 149 p.: bibl., ill. (Ecoteca; 9)

Good overview of health trends and health services in Uruguay identifies current problems, the strategies of political parties towards health issues, and possible future directions.

5203 Seminario Proyectos y Políticas Culturales en el Uruguay hacia el siglo XXI, *Montevideo, 1990.* Cultura(s) y nación en el Uruguay de fin de siglo. Recopilación de Hugo Achugar. Montevideo: LOGOS; FESUR, 1991. 230 p.: bibl.

The product of a 1990 seminar and debate involving intellectuals of various backgrounds (e.g., sociologists, artists, cultural entrepreneurs) provides stimulating reflections on the new characteristics of culture and democracy in Uruguay in the 1990s.

5204 Tornaría de Gadea, Carmen. La creación de una nueva dimensión de lo político a través de las mujeres. Montevideo: Fundación PLEMUU, 1990. 59 p.: ill.

Although fundamentally for general distribution, short booklet contains some interesting observations on the development of women's organizations in recent decades.

BRAZIL

PEGGY A. LOVELL, *Associate Professor of Sociology, University of Pittsburgh*

ONE OF THE MOST INTERESTING TRENDS in the sociological literature produced on Brazil in the mid-1990s was the increasing centrality of race. Previous studies of race focused primarily on social stratification, whereas much of the literature reviewed in this volume considers race in shaping all social relations. Leading studies examine the relationship between race and violence, gender, identity, social movements, political change, labor, the media and religion. The racial character of Brazil's national identity as inspired by Gilberto Freyre is the subject of a book which offers a new and rich interpretation of Freyre's major works (item **5212**). One provocative article analyzes the interrelations between racial, social and cultural dimensions of constructing black identity (item **5291**).

Feminist scholars continue to lead the discipline in their theoretical, methodological and empirical analyses of the sociology of gender. *Estudos Feministas* is an excellent journal of leading scholarship in this field. Studies on education, work, family, domestic violence, protest, health, sexuality and political participation have moved beyond a singular focus on women. Instead, gender is examined as a relational concept where the emphasis is on the differential experiences of women and men. Two historical studies are an analysis of coffee cultivation challenging both "family-blind" and "gender-blind" analyses of socioeconomic process and change (item **4554**) and a study of changing gender ideologies (item **5219**). Other works provide important summaries of Brazil's feminist movement and women's political history (items **5300** and **5297**).

Sociologists of Brazil continue to examine social violence and human rights abuses. Centers for the study of violence have been established at several universities including the Nucleo de Estudos da Violencia at the Univ. de São Paulo. Notable contributions in this area are an analysis of racial discrimination in the criminal justice system (item **5285**) and two vivid accounts of human rights violations (items **5237** and **5206**).

Two traditional areas of interest have been religion and the environment. Sociologists of religion continue to contribute a number of studies on the growth of Protestant fundamentalist groups, cleavages within the Catholic Church, and religious behavior and attitudes (items **5225, 5259,** and **5260**). However, fewer environmental studies were produced in this period, reflecting an overall decline in attention to the social implications of environmental change.

Achard, Diego; Manuel Flores Silva; and **Luis E. González.** Las elites argentinas y brasileñas frente al Mercosur. See item **5112.**

5205 Adorno, Sérgio. Discriminação racial e justiça criminal em São Paulo. (*Novos Estud. CEBRAP*, 43, nov. 1995, p. 45–63, graphs, tables)

Identifies differential access to criminal justice experienced by blacks and whites in São Paulo by analyzing the distribution of judicial sentences. Despite nearly identical crime rates for blacks and whites, blacks tend to be harassed more by police and face greater obstacles in their defense and access to justice, resulting in harsher sentences. Concludes that color remains a powerful instrument for discrimination in the criminal justice system.

5206 Adorno, Sérgio. A violência na sociedade brasileira: um painel inconcluso em uma democracia não consolidada. (*Soc. Estado*, 10:2, julho/dez. 1995, p. 299–342, bibl.)

Despite Brazil's recent democratic gains, human rights violations persist. Argues that social conflicts are caused by an endemic violence rooted in social structure and customs. The torture of prisoners, murder of rural workers, killing of street children, domestic violence, lynchings, and extermination of ethnic minorities are examined against the asymmetry between social and political rights, the absence of institutional political and public mediations, and the dominant political culture of authoritarianism.

5207 Agier, Michel. Racism, culture and black identity in Brazil. (*Bull. Lat. Am. Res.*, 14:3, Sept. 1995, p. 245–264, bibl.)

Provocative analysis examines interrelations among racial, social, and cultural dimensions of the construction of black identity in Bahia. The political and internal transformations of black culture (Afro-Bahian religion, carnival, leisure, and political groups) are examined in light of socioeconomic restructuring and the historical and contemporary reproduction of racism.

5208 Aguiar, Neuma. Rio de Janeiro plural: um guia para políticas sociais por gênero e raça. Rio de Janeiro: Editora Rosa dos Tempos; IUPERJ, 1994. 168 p.: bibl., ill.

Statistical analysis based on the Pesquisa Nacional por Amostra de Domicílios (PNAD) for 1988 examines relative social status of white and black women and men in metropolitan Rio de Janeiro. Focuses on work, education, women's health, domestic violence, and women's organizations and political participation.

5209 A AIDS no Brasil, 1982–1992, Organização de Richard Guy Parker *et al.* Rio de Janeiro: ABIA; IMS-UERJ; Relume Dumará, 1994. 360 p.: bibl., ill., map. (Col. História social da AIDS; 2)

Second volume in the series *Historia social da AIDS*, this multidisciplinary collection of essays draws upon seminar series held by the Instituto de Medicina Social of the Univ. do Estado do Rio de Janeiro. Papers examine epidemiology of AIDS, its social impact, and its impact on politics and civil society. Concludes with a proposal to develop an AIDS program.

5210 Alencar, José Almino de and **Edgar Coelho de Andrade.** O uso de contraceptivos no Brasil: uma análise da prevalência de esterilização feminina. (*Dados/Rio de Janeiro*, 36:3, 1993, p. 419–439, tables)

Uses empirical analysis to examine social and demographic characteristics of Brazil's sterilized female population. Compares results with characteristics of the institutions and agents that provide birth-control methods. Documents the spread of sterilization from more affluent to poorer classes.

5211 Andrews, George Reid. Brazilian racial democracy, 1900–90: an American counterpoint. (*J. Contemp. Hist.*, 31:3, 1996, p. 483–507)

Examines impact of external factors on Brazilian racial politics and racial thought. Studies dialogue between national scholars and intellectuals, and the transnational flow of ideas, images, practices, and institutions. Argues that the dialogue of the 1990s presages another shift in Brazilian conceptualizations of a multiracial society.

5212 Araújo, Ricardo Benzaquen de. Guerra e paz: Casa-Grande & Senzala e a obra de Gilberto Freyre nos anos 30. Rio de Janeiro: Editora 34, 1994. 215 p.: bibl.

Prize-winning book analyzes Gilberto Freyre's 1930s texts. Two-part analysis provides a commentary on the key substantive themes in *Casa-grande & senzala* and a critique of later texts. Traces themes Freyre developed in his analysis of the colonial era and later applied to the 19th century.

5213 Barbosa, Luiz C. The people of the forest against international capitalism: systemic and anti-systemic forces in the battle for the preservation of the Brazilian Amazon rainforest. (*Sociol. Perspect.*, 39:2, 1996, p. 327–331, bibl., table)

Links rapid deforestation in Amazon region to Brazilian government's alliance with global institutions. Argues that changes in global ecopolitics beginning in mid-1980s strengthened attempts by various social groups (e.g. rubber tappers) to gain political leverage, create extractive reserves, and bring about the demarcation of indigenous lands. Concludes that a world-systems approach is critical for understanding environmental problems in developing countries.

5214 Barros, Henrique de. Just one foot in the market: internal strategies of small horticultural farmers in Northeast Brazil. (*Bull. Lat. Am. Res.*, 12:3, Sept. 1993, p. 273–292, bibl., tables)

Focuses on survival strategies used by small farmers in Pernambuco. Demonstrates ways in which producers have adapted to agricultural modernization by resisting wage-work and investing instead in small-commodity production.

5215 Barsted, Leila de Andrade Linhares. Violência contra a mulher e cidadania: uma avaliação das políticas públicas. Rio de Janeiro: CEPIA, 1994. 61 p.: bibl. (Cadernos CEPIA; 1)

Initial publication of CEPIA (Cidadania, Estudo, Pesquisa, Informação, Ação), a nonprofit institute dedicated to research on issues of social rights, analyzes relationship between State and society in creating and applying policies to prevent violence against women. Examines role of the feminist movement, legislation, progress, and impasses of public services and the judicial system. Offers recommendations for change.

5216 Bava, Silvio Caccia and Laura Mullahy. Making cities livable: local initiatives in solid waste and public transportation management in Brazil. (*in* New paths to democratic development in Latin America. Edited by Charles A. Reilly. Boulder, Colo.: Lynne Rienner Publishers, 1995, p. 99–117)

Examines the experience of Pólis (Instituto de Estudos, Formação e Assessoria em Políticas Sociais), a pioneering nonpartisan organization in São Paulo, that provides assistance to urban community groups. This grassroots support agency addresses issues of poverty and inequitable public policies and services. Documents role of Pólis in developing a public transportation system and cost-sharing programs.

5217 Beaney, Peter. The irrigated El Dorado: State-managed rural development, redemocratisation and popular participation in the Brazilian Northeast. (*Bull. Lat. Am. Res.*, 12:3, Sept. 1993, p. 249–271, bibl.)

Uses a detailed case study of a rural development project to examine interaction between State and peasant action. Relates local struggles over rural development to a broader

political economy of State intervention and agrarian social relations.

5218 Berquó, Elza and Maria Coleta F.A. de Oliveira. Casamento em tempos de crise. (*Rev. Bras. Estud. Popul.*, 9:2, julho/dez. 1992, p. 155–167, bibl., graphs, tables)

Examines relationship between Brazil's 1980s economic crisis and nuptiality. Documents decline in marriages throughout the country. Women's roles and expectations are being redefined and alternatives to marriage are emerging.

5219 Besse, Susan Kent. Restructuring patriarchy: the modernization of gender inequality in Brazil, 1914–1940. Chapel Hill: Univ. of North Carolina Press, 1996. 285 p.: bibl., index.

Falling comfortably between women's history and political history, book examines changing gender ideologies. Focusing primarily on urban upper classes, author studies changing interactions between women and men in the family, schools, labor market, professions, polity, and culture.

5220 O Brasil social: realidades, desafios, opções. Coordenação de Roberto Cavalcanti de Albuquerque. Rio de Janeiro: Instituto de Pesquisa Econômica Aplicada, 1993. 544 p.: bibl., ill. (IPEA; 139)

Empirically-based study analyzes social consequences of uneven development in Brazil during last two decades. Draws on social, economic, and political indicators; documents social inequality in income, education, housing, and demographic outcomes. Examines trajectories for development, and offers ideas for combating poverty and redistributing wealth.

5221 Brazilian issues on education, gender and race. Organized by Elba Siqueira de Sá Barretto and Dagmar M.L. Zibas. Translated by Jonathan Hannay. São Paulo: Fundação Carlos Chagas, 1996. 342 p.: bibl., ill.

Includes articles by researchers from the Fundação Carlos Chagas, an interdisciplinary research institution dedicated to studying relations between education and Brazil's social problems, educational evaluation, and gender and race relations. Articles are representative of work developed in recent years by Fundação researchers and focus on the social and educational issues facing Brazil at the dawn of a new century.

5222 The Brazilian puzzle: culture on the borderlands of the Western world. Edited by David J. Hess and Roberto A. da Matta. New York: Columbia Univ. Press, 1995. 306 p.: bibl., index, map.

Collection of essays written by Brazilian and American scholars considers many aspects of Brazilian society and culture. Divided into four sections: "Brazilian Styles of Social Relations," "Race, Class, and Gender in a Changing Culture," "Ideologies and Cultures on an International Stage," and "Brazilian Society: Macrostructures in Comparative Perspective." Essays share a comparative and cultural perspective, bringing out the hierarchical and personalistic structures of Brazilian society.

5223 Brown, Diana DeGroat. Umbanda: religion and politics in urban Brazil. New York: Columbia Univ. Press, 1994. 256 p.: bibl., index.

Explores history and development of Umbanda from its beginnings in Rio de Janeiro during 1920s to late 1970s. Describes changes in ritual forms, geographic distribution, and increase in followers as Umbanda was transformed from marginal to a widely accepted religion.

5224 Bruschini, Cristina and **Sandra Ridenti.** Trabalho domiciliar masculino. (*Estud. Fem.*, 3:2, 1995, p. 363–392, table)

Based on quantitive and qualitative data from São Paulo, study contrasts character of female versus male home-based labor. Finds that men's work in this sector—in contrast to women's—is defined as more qualified, specialized, formalized, and structured. Unlike women, who are often motivated by domestic reponsibilities, men choose to engage in home-based work due to factors such as autonomy, time flexibility, and cost efficiency.

5225 Burdick, John. Gossip and secrecy: women's articulation of domestic conflict in three religions of urban Brazil. (*in* Gender and religion. Edited by William H. Swatos. New Brunswick, N.J.: Transaction Publishers, 1994, p. 173–190, bibl.)

Ethnographic study of a working-class community examines how women seeking help in coping with domestic conflict choose among the Catholic Church, Pentecostalism, and Afro-Brazilian Umbanda. Finds that women often prefer the secrecy offered by Pentecostalism and Umbanda in contrast to the Catholic Church where they can be vulnerable to gossip.

5226 Cardoso, Fernando Henrique. Livros que inventaram o Brasil. (*Novos Estud. CEBRAP*, 37, nov. 1993, p. 21–35)

In his 1993 Aula Magna lecture to students of the Instituto Rio Branco (a school for diplomats), Cardoso (then Ministro das Relações Exteriores) discusses significance of the contributions of Gilberto Freyre, Sérgio Buarque de Holanda, and Caio Prado Júnior to the interpretation of Brazilian social reality.

5227 Cardoso, Nara Maria Batista and **Patrícia Krieger Grossi.** Mulheres en relacionamentos violentos: factores de permanência. (*Veritas/Porto Alegre*, 39:154, junho 1994, p. 211–229, bibl.)

Based on data collected from battered women in Porto Alegre, authors examine factors affecting women's decisions to leave or stay in violent relationships. Findings suggest that a woman's socioeconomic level, number of children, family background, existence and strength of a social support network, fear of reprisal from the batterer, and hope of an improved relationship are key factors in her decision. Discusses cycles of marital violence and offers suggestions for intervention.

5228 Carvalho, José Jorge de. Images of the black man in Brazilian popular culture. Brasília: Depto. de Antropologia, Univ. de Brasília, 1996. 22 p.: bibl. (Série Antropologia; 201)

Explores complex universe of images, stereotypes, values, and ideals of black masculinity projected within Brazil using cultural texts such as popular songs, magazine and newspaper articles, films, etc.

5229 Carybé. Os deuses africanos no candomblé da Bahia = African gods in the candomblé of Bahia. Apresentação de Antônio Carlos Magalhães. Introdução de Jorge Amado e Carybé. Textos de Pierre Fatumbi Verger e Waldeloir Rego. Edição de Bruno Furrer. 2a. ed. Salvador, Brazil: Editora Bigraf, 1993. 263 p.: bibl., col. ill.

Revised edition of *Iconografia dos deuses africanos no candomblé da Bahia*. Stunning productions of watercolors by Carybé (representing 30 years of his art) document Bahian Candomblé. Text in English and

Portuguese includes chapters on African myths and rituals in Bahia (by Waldeloir Rego) and the orishas of Bahia (by Pierre Fatumbi Verger).

5230 Castro, Mary Garcia. Gênero e poder no espaço sindical. (*Estud. Fem.*, 3:1, 1995, p. 29–51, photo)

Investigates sexual division of power in labor unions by referencing a case study of the Sindicato dos Bancários da Bahia. Examines debates concerning quotas, the gendered structure of space, changes in the social politics of labor, and the ways in which gender intersects with race, ethnicity, class, and age. Finds that women's increasing participation has contributed to a revitalization of organized labor. Critical and thought-provoking essay.

5231 Castro, Mary Garcia. Mulher negra, resistência e cidadania: e o lugar da mulata. (*Presença Mulher*, 7:28, nov. 1995, p. 26–33)

Presents reflections on resistance, diversity, and social justice for women of color. Considers validity of the concept of citizenship in projects related to identity and collective action. Relates manner in which racism is exercised through exotica.

5232 Castro, Mary Garcia. Raça, gênero e sindicato em tempos de globalização. (*Cad. CEAS*, 166, nov./dez. 1996, p. 36–51)

Discusses convergence of race, gender, and unionization within a perspective of globalization. Examines current debate on developing a Brazilian equivalent of affirmative action and comments on the challenges and lessons to be learned from the US experience.

5233 Cohn, Amelia. NGOs, social movements, and the privatization of health care: experiences in São Paulo. (*in* New paths to democratic development in Latin America. Edited by Charles A. Reilly. Boulder, Colo.: Lynne Rienner Publishers, 1995, p. 85–98)

Describes Brazilian health care system and two peri-urban popular community movements. Discusses role of social movements and NGOs in promoting community participation in health care reform and policy.

5234 A criança menorizada: banco de referências bibliográficas. São Paulo: Núcleo de Estudos da Violência, Univ. de São

Paulo, 1991. 120 p.: indexes. (Série Dossiê NEV, 0103–7390; 3)

Bibliography of 265 publications produced from 1988–90 on violence against children and adolescents.

5235 Criminalidade urbana e violência: o Rio de Janeiro no contexto internacional. Coordenação de Luiz Eduardo Soares. 3a ed. Rio de Janeiro: Núcleo de Pesquisa/ISER, 1993. 1 v.: bibl., graphs, tables. (Série Textos de pesquisa)

Empirical analysis of urban crime in Rio de Janeiro (city and state) from 1985–92 compares crime rates with those of other countries. Chiefly graphs and tables.

5236 De Vos, Susan. Análisis preliminar acerca de las madres solteras, jefas de hogar, en Brasil durante 1970 y 1980. (*Notas Pobl.*, 22:59, junio 1994, p. 155–181, bibl., tables)

Analyzes census data from 1970 and 1980 to investigate a rise in female-headed households. Finds that unmarried mothers from 15–49 headed about 1/4 of all female-headed households in Brazil by 1980. Discusses data problems that make firm conclusions impossible.

5237 Dimenstein, Gilberto. Democracia em pedaços: direitos humanos no Brasil. São Paulo: Companhia das Letras, 1996. 262 p.: bibl.

Investigative journalist presents the major human rights problems confronting contemporary Brazil. Offers a vivid account of the human and social realities provoking documented violence over the past eight years by Human Rights Watch/Americas and the Núcleo de Estudos da Violência of the Univ. de São Paulo. Examines causes, consequences, and State response to violence against children, prisoners, the landless, blacks, the indigenous population, and women. Told through personal narratives of victims, survivors, and activists.

5238 Diniz, Eli. Governabilidade, democracia e reforma do Estado: os desafios da construção de uma nova ordem no Brasil dos anos 90. (*Dados/Rio de Janeiro*, 38:3, 1995, p. 385–415, bibl.)

Discusses governability in relation to public sector reform and the demands raised by consolidation of democracy. Critically reviews conventional concepts of governability and proposes an alternative focus which views the public sector as including society and politics. Presents a new paradigm for public sector reform, redefining the prevailing concept of State autonomy and the public management model.

5239 Draibe, Sônia Miriam and **Marta Teresa S. Arretche.** Involving civil society: Brazil. (*in* Strategies to combat poverty in Latin America. Washington: Inter-American Development Bank; Baltimore: John Hopkins Univ. Press, 1995, p. 85–148, appendices, bibl., graphs, tables)

Reviews Brazil's social policies and federal social security system. Identifies and evaluates programs and forms of expenditure geared specifically to the poor. Results confirm that the poorest benefit the least. Suggests ways to reach the poorest groups through cooperation between the State, NGOs, and philanthropic programs.

5240 Duarte, Lyz Elizabeth Amorim Melo. A participação da Igreja Católica na questão agrária no Brasil. (*Ciênc. Hum. Rev./ Goiânia*, 2:1/2, jan./dez. 1991, p. 83–106, bibl.)

Analyzes Catholic Church's position on agrarian reform from 1950s-70s. Documents controversy concerning viability of small landholders, as well as scholars' attempts to legitimize or reject the Church's support (as published in the document *Igreja e problemas da terra*) of small landholders' struggle for land.

5241 Fausto Neto, Ana Maria Quiroga. Violência e dominação: as favelas voltam à cena. (*Soc. Estado*, 10:2, julho/dez. 1995, p. 417–438, bibl.)

Examines new dynamics of poverty within shantytowns whereby laws are not equal for all and the poor's identity as "worker" is confused with that of "bandit." In this context, coinciding with a decline in neighborhood associations, organized crime's authority gains legitimacy. Argues that State policies controlling narcotraffic veil the important issues of social exclusion and the consequences of globalization.

5242 Fernandes, Rubem César. Kościół katolicki w Brazylii i w Polsce [The Catholic Church in Brazil and Poland]. Selection and preface by Marcin Kula. Warszawa: Centrum Studiów Latynoamerykańskich, Uniwersytet Warszawski, 1996. 58 p.: bibl. (Kokumenty Robocze; 20)

In this collection of five previously published articles, a Brazilian social anthropologist analyzes similarities and differences of the Catholic Church in Brazil and Poland. Three articles originally appeared in Polish-language journals, one in *Social Science Information* (Vol. 24, No. 4, 1985) and one in *Religião e Sociedade* (Vol. 15, No. 2–3, 1990). [Z. Kantorosinski]

5243 Fighting for the soul of Brazil. Edited by Kevin Danaher and Michael Shellenberger. New York: Monthly Review Press, 1995. 272 p.: bibl., index, map.

Diverse collection of articles includes eyewitness reports, interviews, and political and economic analyses dealing with the 1994 elections, the impeachment of President Collor, the subculture of abandoned street children, changes in Amazonia, and popular protest.

5244 Fonseca Sobrinho, Délcio da. Estado e população: uma história do planejamento familiar no Brasil. Rio de Janeiro: Editora Rosa dos Tempos, 1993. 203 p.: bibl., ill.

Provides a history of family planning by focusing on three distinct phases: pronatalism (19th century-1964), anti-natalism (1964–74), and family planning (1974–83). Analyzes effects of international and national debates and social movements on State policies of fertility control.

5245 Font, Mauricio A. Labor system and collective action in a coffee export sector: São Paulo. (*in* Coffee, society, and power in Latin America. Edited by William Roseberry, Lowell Gudmundson, and Mario Samper K. Baltimore: Johns Hopkins Univ. Press, 1995, p. 181–205, tables)

Explores labor systems and patterns of social relations and social conflict generated in the coffee economy of São Paulo state from 1889–1930. Reconsiders *colono* system in light of structural complexity, presenting evidence from strikes and other forms of participation and conflict in the coffee zone. Findings suggest that the extent to which landlords succeed in proletarianizing or enserfing direct cultivators depends on landlords' access to the labor supply and their ability to monopolize land and related economic opportunities, both of which ultimately hinge on access to State power.

5246 Furuya, Yoshiaki. Possessão e discurso: os "caboclos" nas religiões afro-amazônicas. (*Lat. Am. Stud./Japan*, 13, 1994, p. 73–88)

Based on fieldwork conducted in Belém, Pará, study examines historical and social formation of Afro-Brazilian religion in the Amazon. Compares and contrasts Afro-Amazonian religion with Afro-Brazilian religions found in other regions of the country.

5247 Gilliam, Angela and Onik'a Gilliam. Negociando a subjetividade de mulata no Brasil. (*Estud. Fem.*, 3:2, 1995, p. 525–543)

Vivid and personal account of racial consciousness in Brazil as experienced by a North American anthropologist and her daughter. Examines fluid nature of racial identity and the interplay between appearances and the juxtaposition of black Brazilian and North American women.

5248 Gomes-Neto, João Batista and Eric A. Hanushek. Causes and consequences of grade repetition: evidence from Brazil. (*Econ. Dev. Cult. Change*, 43:1, Oct. 1994, p. 117–148, graphs, tables)

Relying on a unique data set for students in northeast Brazil, study considers ways in which the schooling system and individual students interact in determining enrollment patterns in primary school. Tests various hypotheses about the determinants and effects of grade repetition. Concludes that low performance is a key element in repetition; however, repetition improves achievement. Discusses implication of mandatory promotion policies.

5249 Goza, Franklin. Brazilian immigration to North America. (*Int. Migr. Rev.*, 28:105, Spring 1994, p. 136–152, bibl., graph, tables)

Comparative study of Brazilian immigration to Canada and the US focuses on origins of recent immigrants, their labor force activities, social adaptation, and future aspirations.

5250 Green, James N. The emergence of the Brazilian gay liberation movement, 1977–1981. (*Lat. Am. Perspect.*, 21:1, Winter 1994, p. 38–55)

Follows development of the gay movement in São Paulo, which emerged from the interaction between the international gay movement and the changing political situation in Brazil. Discusses polarization within the movement.

5251 Grün, Roberto. Identidade e representação: os judeus na esfera política e a imagem na comunidade. (*Rev. Bras. Ciênc. Sociais*, 26:9, out. 1994, p. 123–148, bibl., tables)

Explores self-representation and identity of the Jewish community in São Paulo. Focuses on political attitudes and participation. Documents voting patterns for Jewish political candidates from 1950–90.

5252 Guimarães, Antônio Sérgio Alfredo. 'Raça,' racismo e grupos de cor no Brasil. (*Estud. Afro-Asiát.*, 27, abril 1995, p. 45–63, bibl.)

Discusses definitions of "race" that have been applied to Brazil. Argues that the distinctions between color groups in Brazil are founded on a form of racism defined by the denial of racial differences. Concludes that most studies of race relations in Brazil are based on a North American paradigm and as a result tend to deny the existence of multiple racial categories within Brazil.

5253 Guimarães, Antônio Sérgio Alfredo. Racismo e anti-racismo no Brasil. (*Novos Estud. CEBRAP*, 43, nov. 1995, p. 26–44)

Examines links between Brazil's outdated yet persistent myth of racial equality and European and North American theories of race. Demonstrates how the language of class and color in Brazil "naturalizes" inequalities that might otherwise tarnish the country's reputation as a racial democracy.

5254 Guimarães, Carmen Dora. Mulheres, sexualidade e AIDS: um projeto de prevenção. (*in* Alternativas escassas: saúde, sexualidade e reprodução na América Latina. São Paulo: Fundação Carlos Chagas; Rio de Janeiro: Editora 34, 1994, p. 249–281, bibl.)

Describes AIDSCOM, a program initiated by the Sociedade Civil Bem Estar Familiar no Brasil (BEMFAM) and USAID. The project was centered in two lower-middle-class neighborhood health clinics and involved 250 women between 21 and 30. Objective was to collect data about sexual attitudes and condom use, with the goal of developing interventions giving women the incentive to talk about their experiences with their sexual partners and increase use of condoms. Summarizes the three phases of the project and offers conclusions.

5255 Hasenbalg, Carlos. Entre o mito e os fatos: racismo e relações raciais no Brasil. (*Dados/Rio de Janeiro*, 38:2, 1995, p. 355–374, bibl.)

Identifies two central characteristics of a peculiarly Latin American type of race relations: the ideal of whitening (*branqueamento*) and the elite ideology of racial harmony, tolerance, and the absence of prejudice and discrimination. Reviews recent empirical and ethnographic studies of social mobility and inequality.

5256 Hasenbalg, Carlos. Perspectivas sobre raza y clase en Brasil. (*Estud. Soc./Hermosillo*, 12:34, enero/abril 1994, p. 75–99, tables)

Empirical study based on census and national survey data examines labor market inequalities between white and Afro-Brazilian women and men. Concludes that, despite gains in human capital (e.g., education), occupational and wage discrimination persist. Women and Afro-Brazilians continue to be excluded from the most prestigious and better-paid occupations.

5257 Hasenbalg, Carlos. Racial inequalities in Brazil and throughout Latin America: timid responses to disguised racism. (*in* Constructing democracy: human rights, citizenship, and society in Latin America. Boulder, Colo.: Westview Press, 1996, p. 161–175, bibl., tables)

Analyzes significance of race for extension of citizenship rights in contemporary Latin America, particularly Brazil. Reviews evolving perspectives of race relations and offers updated analysis of social position of Afro-Brazilians. Suggests a number of strategies that nascent democratic systems might pursue in an effort to overcome racial discrimination.

5258 Hermann, Jacqueline and **Leila de Andrade Linhares Barsted.** O judiciário e a violência: a ordem legal e a (des)ordem familiar. Rio de Janeiro: CEPIA, 1995. 135 p.: appendix, bibl. (Cadernos CEPIA; 2)

CEPIA's (Cidadania, Estudo, Pesquisa, Informação, Ação) second study explores the judicial system's response to violence against women. Emphasizes need for a gendered per-

spective within analyses of public policy. Appendix includes Interamerican and UN declarations against domestic violence.

5259 Hewitt, W.E. The changing of the guard: transformation in the politico-religious attitudes and behaviors of CEB members in São Paulo, 1984–1993. (*J. Church State*, 38:1, Winter 1996, p. 115–136, tables)

Examines evolving character of political and religious attitudes and behaviors of members of several Christian Base Communities. Focuses on members' changing demographic characteristics, religious and political beliefs and attitudes, and group participation. Finds that, unlike the older activists, new members tend to have conservative attitudes and prefer devotional religious activities over political participation. Discusses factors and future implications of these changes for the Communities.

5260 Hewitt, W.E. Popular movements, resource demobilization, and the legacy of Vatican restructuring in the Archdiocese of São Paulo. (*Can. J. Lat. Am. Caribb. Stud.*, 18:36, 1993, p. 1–24, tables)

Examines effect of recent conservative pressures on the Archdiocese of São Paulo, formerly one of Brazil's most socially active churches. Argues that Vatican-sponsored dismantling of the local Church in 1989 led to a fragmentation of São Paulo's resource base, decreasing popular mobilization. Assesses implications of these changes for the continued political involvement of the Brazilian Church.

5261 Ianni, Octávio. A sociologia de Florestan Fernandes. (*Rev. USP*, 29, março/maio 1996, p. 26–33, photos)

Identifies and discusses five central themes explored by Florestan Fernandes, the author of critical sociology in Brazil: classical and contemporary sociological theory, Marxist theory, contemporary Brazilian social theory, social change, and social class.

5262 Indicadores sociais: uma análise da década de 1980. Rio de Janeiro: Fundação Instituto Brasileiro de Geografia e Estatística, Diretoria de Pesquisas, 1995. 361 p.: bibl., col. ill.

Statistical indicators reflect the socioeconomic transformation of Brazilian society during 1980s. Based on 1980 Pesquisa Nacional por Amostra de Domicílios (PNAD) and 1991 Censo Demográfico, analysis examines recent demographic trends, health and nutrition, families, children and adolescents, work and wages, basic sanitation, education, and political participation. An important source for recent sociodemographic change.

5263 Iyda, Massako. Cem anos de saúde pública: a cidadania negada. São Paulo: Editora UNESP, Fundação para o Desenvolvimento da UNESP, 1994. 148 p.: bibl. (Col. Prismas)

Examines public health conditions in São Paulo in five distinct periods: before 1889, 1889–1930, 1930–45, 1945–64, and 1964–78. Analyzes roles of the State, technical bureaucrats, scientific knowledge, and individual/collective relationships for each period. Sophisticated theoretical and empirical framework places the relationship between State and society at the center of the analysis.

5264 Kassouf, Ana L. and Benjamin Senauer. Direct and indirect effects of parental education on malnutrition among children in Brazil: a full income approach. (*Econ. Dev. Cult. Change*, 44:4, July 1996, p. 817–837, appendices, tables)

Examines direct and indirect effects of parental education on malnutrition among preschool children, using anthropometric measures from the 1989 *Perfil estatístico de crianças e mães no Brasil*. Finds that the most serious malnutrition among preschoolers was stunting and that malnutrition was widespread among children of parents with little or no education.

5265 Lam, David and Robert F. Schoeni. Effects of family background on earnings and returns to schooling: evidence from Brazil. (*J. Polit. Econ.*, 101:4, Aug. 1993, p. 710–740, bibl., graphs, tables)

Attempts to determine, first, whether family background characteristics affect conventional return-to-schooling estimates and, second, whether family background has an impact on wage earnings. Finds that parental characteristics, especially the schooling of fathers-in-law, have considerable impact on wages. Findings are interpreted as evidence that parental characteristics represent unobservable worker attributes rather than nepotism in the labor market. For economist's comment see item **2358.**

5266 Lebon, Nathalie. Professionalization of women's health groups in São Paulo: the troublesome road towards organizational diversity. (*Organization/London*, 3:4, 1996, p. 588–609)

Studies origin, characteristics, and organizational diversity of the women's health movement in São Paulo as a specific example of a social movement. Examines ways in which organizational change occurs and effects of change on identity of these groups. Concludes with a discussion of advantages and problems of organizational diversity.

5267 Leslie, Michael. The representation of blacks on commercial television in Brazil: some cultivation effects. (*INTERCOM/São Paulo*, 18:1, jan./junho 1995, p. 94–107, bibl., tables)

Compares media portrayal of black Brazilians with TV viewers' opinions about Afro-Brazilians. Controlling for education and race of the viewer, findings show divergence between TV content and the objective conditions of blacks. Discusses the effects of media images on racial attitudes.

Malczewski, Zdzisław. Obecność Polaków i Polonii w Rio de Janeiro. See *HLAS 56:3329.*

5268 Martins, José de Souza. A reprodução do capital na frente pioneira e o renascimento da escravidão no Brasil. (*Tempo Soc./São Paulo*, 6:1/2, junho 1995, p. 1–25, bibl.)

Argues that the rapid territorial expansion of capital that took place in Amazonia in the mid-1960s reinforced slavery-like conditions through debt or peonage. Contemporary peonage is characterized by extreme physical violence against workers, often culminating in the murder of those who try to escape. Central thesis is that peonage through debt is an extreme variety of overexploited wage work under conditions of primitive capital accumulation.

5269 Moreira, Diva and Adalberto Batista Sobrinho. Casamentos inter-raciais: o homem negro e a rejeição da mulher negra. (*in* Alternativas escassas: saúde, sexualidade e reprodução na América Latina. São Paulo: Fundação Carlos Chagas; Rio de Janeiro: Editora 34, 1994, p. 81–107, bibl., tables)

Based on surveys conducted among interracial couples in Belo Horizonte, Salvador, and São Paulo, this unique article explores issues of racial identity and the persistence of the ideology of whitening (*branqueamento*).

5270 Moss, Philip and **Chris Tilly.** Competências "indefinidas" e raça: uma investigação sobre os problemas de emprêgo dos homens negros. (*Estud. Afro-Asiát.*, 29, março 1996, p. 55–84, bibl., tables)

Investigates changes in skill requirements and effects of these changes on black men's access to entry-level jobs. Using open-ended interviews of managers of four industries, findings show that managers report that "soft skills" (e.g., motivation and ability to interact well with customers and co-workers) are increasingly important. However, managers view black men as lacking such skills.

5271 Motta, Roberto da. Sacrifício, mesa, festa e transe na religião afro-brasileira. (*Horiz. Antropol.*, 1:3, 1995, p. 31–38, bibl.)

Discusses ritual acts of animal sacrifice, trance, and dance in the religions of Candomblé of Bahia and Xangô of Recife.

5272 Moura, Edila Arnaud Ferreira *et al.* Zona Franca de Manaus: os filhos da era eletroeletrônica. Belém, Brazil: Associação de Universidades Amazônicas; Univ. Federal do Pará, 1993. 141 p.: bibl., ill. (Série Pobreza e meio ambiente na Amazônia; 2)

Part of series published by the Associação de Universidades Amazônicas and the Univ. Federal do Pará which examines effects of colonization and changes in land use on children's health, education, and socioeconomic conditions in various regions and states of Amazonia.

5273 Os muitos Brasis: saúde e população na década de 80. Organização de Maria Cecília de Souza Minayo. São Paulo: Editora Hucitec; Rio de Janeiro: ABRASCO, 1995. 356 p.: bibl., computer disk, ill., maps. (Saúde em debate; 79)

Essays on public health examine health outcomes during 1980s. Findings reveal the prevalence of cardiovascular disease, the impact and causes of violent death among the young, an increase of AIDS cases, new forms of infectious and parasitic diseases, the permanence of hunger, and an increase in both life expectancy and the elderly population.

5274 Mulher brasileira é assim. Organização de Heleieth Iara Bongiovani Saffioti e Monica Muñoz Vargas. Brasília: Fundo das

Nações Unidas para a Infância; Rio de Janeiro: Editora Rosa dos Tempos; Núcleo Interdisciplinar de Pesquisa e Ação Social, 1994. 283 p.: bibl.

Anthology organized by the Núcleo Interdisciplinar de Pesquisa e Ação Social of Rio de Janeiro includes articles on women's participation in Brazilian society. Papers explore issues of education, work, health, violence, identity, political participation, and citizenship.

5275 Muller, Keith D. and **Maria do Carmo Oliveira.** Gender and the criminal justice system: Northeast Brazil. (*Pap. Proc. Appl. Geogr. Conf.*, 20, 1997, p. 293–296)

Examines phenomenon of increasing numbers of women entering law enforcement, judicial, and political-related occupations in the region. Forsees a continuance of this trend. [K.D. Muller]

5276 Nelson, Sara. Constructing and negotiating gender in women's police stations in Brazil. (*Lat. Am. Perspect.*, 23:1, Winter 1996, p. 131–148, bibl.)

Drawing on both quantitive and qualitative data, study examines São Paulo's first women's police stations and considers their current status. Discusses complex political issues involved as the dynamics of a liberalizing state and the women's movement are negotiated in an institutional, bureaucratic setting.

5277 Novaes, Regina Celia Reyes. Pentecostal identity in rural Brazil. (*Soc. Compass*, 41:4, Dec. 1994, p. 525–535)

Based on an ethnographic study of a Northeast community in Paraíba, article examines significance for rural workers of leaving the Catholic Church and converting to Pentecostalism. Focuses on the questions and arguments used to attract new followers.

5278 Nunes, Maria José Fontelas Rosado. De mulheres, sexo e Igreja: uma pesquisa e muitas interrogações. (*in* Alternativas escassas: saúde, sexualidade e reprodução na América Latina. São Paulo: Fundação Carlos Chagas; Rio de Janeiro: Editora 34, 1994, p. 175–203, bibl.)

Based on interviews with women who are active in Christian Base Communities in São Paulo, study examines ambiguities and contradictions between Church teachings and issues of contraceptives and sexuality. Analyzes how religious beliefs interact with the role of the State, the media, and feminist movements.

5279 Oro, Ari Pedro. A desterritorialização das religiões afro-brasileiras. (*Horiz. Antropol.*, 1:3, 1995, p. 69–79, bibl.)

Presents data on Afro-Brazilian religions in Brazil, Argentina, and Uruguay. Examines their expansion, distinctive characteristics, and adaptation to modern society.

5280 Ottmann, Götz. Movimentos sociais urbanos e democracia no Brasil: uma abordagem cognitiva. (*Novos Estud. CEBRAP*, 41, março 1995, p. 186–207, bibl.)

Based on an analysis of urban movements in Metropolitan São Paulo from 1940–late 1980s, author refutes perspective that political significance of the "new avant-garde" is declining. Argues that pessimism concerning social movements is rooted in the unrealistically short time frame of analysis, whereas adopting a wider time frame would offer a view of social movements as a cyclical phenomenon, revealing their fluid and contextual identities.

5281 Pace, Richard. The new amazons in Amazon town?: a case study of women's public roles in Gurupá, Pará, Brazil. (*J. Anthropol. Res.*, 51:3, Fall 1995, p. 263–278, bibl., tables)

Based on fieldwork between 1983–91, explores why most of the political, judicial, education, and health care positions in this community are occupied by women. Examines national patterns of gender roles and public occupations, cultural views on gender stereotypes, historical precedent of women in public roles in Gurupá, and influence of feminism and liberation theology. Offers three reasons to explain the domination of women in the public sphere: male outmigration; expansion of government bureaucracy; and the community's reputation as a safe place (in an otherwise dangerous region), which is appropriate for professional women.

5282 Pinto, Céli Regina J. Donas-de-casa, mães, feministas batalhadoras: mulheres nas eleições de 1994 no Brasil. (*Estud. Fem.*, 2:2, 1994, p. 297–312, table)

During the 1994 elections in Brazil, women candidates gained considerable ground. Examines presence of a feminist agenda and the defense of women's rights in the discourse of women candidates, with special attention to the state of Rio Grande do Sul. For political scientist's comment see item **3943**.

5283 Prandi, Reginaldo. Deuses africanos no Brasil contemporâneo: introdução sociológica ao Candomblé de hoje. (*Horiz. Antropol.*, 1:3, 1995, p. 10–30, appendix, bibl., tables)

Analyzes growth of Candomblé as a religion without racial boundaries. Argues that the ritual nature of Candomblé appeals to the demands of disenchanted metropolitan workers. Includes charts on the principal attributes of the *orixás*.

5284 Rago, Margareth. A sexualidade feminina entre o desejo e a norma: moral sexual e cultural literária feminina no Brasil, 1900–1932. (*Rev. Bras. Hist.*, 14:28, 1994, p. 28–44)

Analyzes novels written by women in Brazil in the first decades of 20th century, exploring how women questioned male culture and expressed gendered differences.

5285 Ribeiro, Carlos Antonio Costa. Cor e criminalidade: estudo e análise da justiça no Rio de Janeiro, 1900–1930. Rio de Janeiro: Editora UFRJ, 1995. 167 p.: bibl., ill.

Pathbreaking study examines whether judicial decisions are influenced by race. Findings suggest that skin color was a central factor in the unequal application of the law: blacks were more likely than whites—accused of the same crime—to be imprisoned and receive harsh sentences. Also, if the accused was black, poor, and male, and the victim was white, the probability of a guilty verdict and the degree of punishment was disproportionally high. Highly recommended.

Roberts, J. Timmons. Expansion of television in eastern Amazonia. See item **2910**.

5286 Roberts, J. Timmons and F. Nii-Amoo Dodoo. Population growth, sex ratios, and women's work on the contemporary Amazon frontier. (*Yearbook/CLAG*, 21, 1995, p. 91–105)

Analysis of 1991 census data and 1990 survey data shows relationship between population growth, sex ratios, and women's labor force participation. [K.D. Muller]

5287 Roberts, J. Timmons. Subcontracting and the omitted social dimensions of large development projects: household survival at the Carajás mines in the Brazilian Amazon. (*Econ. Dev. Cult. Change*, 43:4, July 1995, p. 735–758)

Examines local responses to the Brazilian State-owned firm Companhia Vale do Rio Doce's (CVRD) use of low-paid, subcontracted workers. Finds that migrants are forced to split their families in order to lower living expenses; to participate in urban squatter invasions; and to work in or buy from semilegal informal markets. Such practices allow CVRD to produce ore more cheaply and may ultimately contribute to the continued depression in world iron ore prices. Based on data from local, state, and federal governments; the mining company; and household surveys.

5288 Rosemberg, Fúlvia and Regina Pahim Pinto. Criança pequena e raça na PNAD 87. São Paulo: Fundação Carlos Chagas, 1997. 1 v.

Based on 1987 Pesquisa Nacional por Amostra de Domicílios (PNAD), examines differing social conditions among Afro-Brazilian and white children up to age six. Focuses on five themes: population, family, income, education, and basic sanitation. Discusses racial classification in Brazil and the relationship between racial differences in these indicators and residential segregation.

5289 Rosemberg, Fúlvia and Edith Piza. Illiteracy, gender and race in Brazil. (*in* Gender dimensions in education in Latin America. Washington: Organization of American States, 1995, p. 49–71)

Examines principal trends in illiteracy as observed through longitudinal demographic census analysis. Finds that gender and race differentially affect educational opportunities. Authors' focus is on interaction between gender and race in access to education.

5290 Sallum Júnior, Brasílio. Labirintos: dos generais à Nova República. São Paulo: Curso de Pós-Graduação em Sociologia, Depto. de Sociologia da Faculdade de Filosofia, Letras e Ciências Humanas da Univ. de São Paulo; Editora Hucitec, 1996. 199 p.: bibl., ill.

Return to democracy was never the desired outcome of Brazil's military government despite its initiation of the *abertura*. Sallum argues that this dynamic political transition is the result of the country's relations in the international sphere, internal economic processes, and the democratization of society. Recommended.

5291 Sansone, Lívio. O local e o global na Afro-Bahia contemporânea. (*Rev. Bras. Ciênc. Sociais*, 10:29, out. 1995, p. 65–84, bibl.)

Focusing on youth in metropolitan Salvador, work describes changes in racial categories, the development of a new black Bahian culture, and the combination of new black international symbols with traditional Afro-Bahian symbols. Based on fieldwork conducted in lower-class neighborhoods in Salvador.

5292 Santos, Helio. Uma teoria para a questão racial do negro brasileiro: a trilha do círculo vicioso. (*São Paulo Perspect.*, 8:3, julho/set. 1994, p. 56–65, bibl., graph)

Uses an interdisciplinary approach to develop a theoretical framework to analyze and challenge contemporary racial inequality.

5293 Schwarcz, Lilia Moritz. O espetáculo das raças: cientistas, instituições e questão racial no Brasil, 1870–1930. São Paulo: Companhia das Letras, 1993. 287 p.: bibl., ill. (some col.), index, map.

Based on analysis of historical documents from the turn of the century, examines discourse of nation building and scientific racism. Focuses on dialogue among medical professionals, scientists, university faculty, and scholars at state and federal institutions. Explores liberal and racist paradoxes of this debate and its impact on national identity.

5294 Segato, Rita Laura. Cidadania: por que não?; Estado e sociedade no Brasil à luz de um discurso religioso afro-brasileiro. (*Dados/Rio de Janeiro*, 38:3, 1995, p. 581–601, bibl.)

Analyzing role of Afro-Brazilian religion in social protest, study offers a critique of minority politics as the only avenue for resolving political disputes. Calls attention to the demand for more sophisticated and radical political voices.

5295 Simpósio sobre o Fenômeno Chamado Dekassegui, *São Paulo, 1991*. Dekassegui. Organização de Masato Ninomiya. São Paulo: Estação Liberdade; Sociedade Brasileira de Cultura Japonesa, 1992. 247 p.: bibl., ill.

Collection of conference papers on the

migration of Brazilian workers of Japanese descent to Japan focuses on political, judicial, social, psychological, cultural, and economic aspects of this labor migration.

5296 Soares, Luiz Eduardo et al. Violência e política no Rio de Janeiro. Rio de Janeiro: ISER; Relume Dumará, 1996. 309 p.: bibl., ill.

Edited volume of essays by researchers at the Nucleo de Pesquisas of the Instituto de Estudos da Religião (ISER) examines relationships between urban violence and race, gender, poverty, and age. Includes studies documenting rates of violence, political inefficiency, public responses, and campaigns against violence.

5297 Soares, Vera et al. Brazilian feminism and women's movements: a two-way street. (*in* The challenge of local feminisms: women's movements in global perspective. Boulder, Colo.: Westview Press, 1995, p. 302–323, photos, table)

Reviews Brazil's feminist movement during the past two decades. Provides brief history of the feminist movement; examines relationships between feminist and women's movements and the State; and discusses issues and challenges for the future.

5298 Stubbe, Hannes. Moleques: afrobrasilianische Strassenkinder. (*in* Brasilien: die Unordnung des Fortschritts. Frankfurt: Vervuert Verlag, 1994, p. 263–308, bibl., graphs, tables)

Study of Afro-Brazilian street children examines present status of research on topic and makes recommendations for further in-depth analyses. Includes extensive data and excellent bibliography. [C.K. Converse]

5299 Sutton, Alison. Slavery in Brazil: a link in the chain of modernisation; the case of Amazonia. London: Anti-Slavery International, 1994. 158 p.: bibl., ill., map. (Human rights series; 7)

Based on field research for Anti-Slavery International (interviews with workers, their families, the police, government officials, and social activists), author examines relationships between environmental destruction, migrant labor, and human rights abuses. Documents accounts of debt bondage in forest clearing, charcoal burning, rubber tapping, and mining in Amazonia. Foreword by José de Souza Martins.

5300 Tabak, Fanny. Women in the struggle for democracy and equal rights in Brazil. (*in* Women and politics worldwide. Edited by Barbara J. Nelson and Najma Chowdhury. New Haven, Conn.: Yale Univ. Press, 1994, p. 127–141)

Summarizes Brazilian women's political history. Briefly discusses suffragist movement, women's organizations, women's struggles for political representation following Brazil's return to democracy, women's participation in writing the 1988 Constitution, social movements, health care reform, and future prospects.

5301 Telles, Vera da Silva. Família e trabalho: precariedade e pauperismo na Grande São Paulo. (*Rev. Bras. Estud. Popul.*, 11:2, julho/dez. 1994, p. 187–223, bibl., tables)

Based on data from the 1980s, article analyzes employment conditions and verifies existence of sex and age discrimination. Focuses on ways in which women and youth experience labor market inequalities and the effects of these inequalities on the family.

5302 Thomas, Dorothy Q. In search of solution: women's police stations in Brazil. (*in* Women and violence. Edited by Miranda Davis. London; Atlantic Highlands, N.J.: Zed Books Ltd., 1994, p. 32–43, ill.)

Summarizes report written by staff members of Human Rights Watch who traveled to Brazil in 1991. Examines role of women's movement and impact of women's police stations, assessing response of Brazilian government to problems of domestic violence.

5303 O trabalho invisível: estudos sobre trabalhadores a domicílio no Brasil. Organização de Alice Rangel de Paiva Abreu e Bila Sorj. Rio de Janeiro: Rio Fundo Editora, 1993. 132 p.: bibl.

Papers presented at the 1992 Seminário Trabalho a Domicílio no Brasil focus on contracted domestic labor in Rio de Janeiro and São Paulo.

5304 Twine, Francine Winddance. O hiato de gênero nas percepções de racismo: o caso dos afro-brasileiros socialmente ascendentes. (*Estud. Afro-Asiát.*, 29, março 1996, p. 37–54, bibl.)

Examines gender gap in reported encounters of racism in a small urban community in Rio de Janeiro state. Provides an ethnographic case study of perceptions of "everyday racism." Focuses on occupational segregation and interracial relationships. Concludes that men experience more racism at work and in interracial relationships.

Vilas, Carlos María. De ambulancias, bomberos y policias: la política social del neoliberalismo. See item **1477.**

5305 **Waisbord, Silvio.** Contando histórias de corrupção: narrativa de telenovela e moralidad populista no caso *Collorgate*. (*Comun Polít.*, 3 : 2, maio/agôsto 1996, p. 95–110)
Analysis of language of the Brazilian press (*Veja* and *Istoé*) examines coverage of the Collorgate affair. Discusses role of journalism as a moral agent in the new democracy.

5306 **Wolfe, Joel.** Working women, working men: São Paulo and the rise of Brazil's industrial working class, 1900–1955. Durham, N.C.: Duke Univ. Press, 1993. 312 p.: bibl., ill., index, map.
Based on archival data on oral histories, work examines rise of Brazil's industrial working class by focusing on female and male textile and metallurgical workers in São Paulo. Analyzes interactions between workers, union leaders, industrialists, and State policymakers. Finds distinct and sometimes contradictory gender discourses of work, organization, protest, and politics. For historian's comment see *HLAS 54:3453.*

5307 **Yazbek, Maria Carmelita.** Classes subalternas e assistência social. São Paulo: Cortez Editora, 1993. 184 p.: bibl.
Originally a doctoral thesis, study examines role of social assistance. Uses personal narratives to explore issues of identity, daily life, and hopes and dreams of the poor.

JOURNAL ABBREVIATIONS

Acervo/Tegucigalpa. Acervo: Revista Hondureña de Cultura. Ministerio de Cultura, Instituto del Libro y el Documento. Tegucigalpa.

Am. Anthropol. American Anthropologist. American Anthropological Assn., Washington.

Am. Ethnol. American Ethnologist. American Ethnological Society. Washington.

Am. Indíg. América Indígena. Instituto Indigenista Interamericano. México.

Am. J. Sociol. American Journal of Sociology. Univ. of Chicago. Chicago, Ill.

Am. Jew. Arch. American Jewish Archives. Cincinnati, Ohio.

Am. Negra. América Negra. Pontificia Univ. Javeriana. Bogotá.

Americas/Francisc. The Americas. Academy of American Franciscan History. Washington.

Anthropol. Q. Anthropological Quarterly. Catholic Univ. of America, Catholic Anthropological Conference. Washington.

Anu. Estud. Centroam. Anuario de Estudios Centroamericanos. Univ. de Costa Rica. San José.

Anu. Etnol./Habana. Anuario de Etnología. Academia de Ciencias de Cuba; Editorial Academia. La Habana.

Bol. Am. Boletín Americanista. Univ. de Barcelona, Facultad de Geografía e Historia, Depto. de Historia de América. Barcelona.

Bol. Inf. Techint. Boletín Informativo Techint. Organización Techint. Buenos Aires.

Bull. Bur. natl. ethnol. Bulletin du Bureau national d'ethnologie. Bureau national d'ethnologie. Port-au-Prince, Haiti.

Bull. Lat. Am. Res. Bulletin of Latin American Research. Society for Latin American Studies. Oxford, England.

Cad. CEAS. Cadernos do Centro de Estudos e Ação Social (CEAS). Salvador, Brazil.

Can. J. Lat. Am. Caribb. Stud. Canadian Journal of Latin American and Caribbean Studies. Univ. of Ottawa. Ontario, Canada.

Caravelle/Toulouse. Caravelle. Cahiers du monde hispanique et luso-brésilien. Univ. de Toulouse, Institute d'études hispaniques, hispano-americaines et luso-brésiliennes. Toulouse, France.

Caribb. Q. Caribbean Quarterly. Univ. of the West Indies. Mona, Jamaica.

Caribb. Stud. Caribbean Studies. Univ. of Puerto Rico, Institute of Caribbean Studies. Río Piedras.

Chungará/Arica. Chungará. Univ. del Norte, Depto. de Antropología. Arica, Chile.

Cienc. Econ./San José. Ciencias Económicas. Instituto de Investigaciones en Ciencias Económicas, Univ. de Costa Rica. San José.

Ciênc. Hum. Rev./Goiânia. Ciências Humanas em Revista. Instituto de Ciências Humanas e Letras, Univ. Federal de Goiás. Goiânia, Brazil.

Cienc. Soc./Santo Domingo. Ciencia y Sociedad. Instituto Tecnológico de Santo Domingo.

Colecc. Estud. CIEPLAN. Colección Estudios CIEPLAN. Corporación de Investigaciones Económicas para Latinoamérica. Santiago.

Comun. Polít. Comunicação & Política. Centro Brasileiro de Estudos Latino-Americanos. Rio de Janeiro.

Cuad. Comun. Cuadernos de Comunicación. Escuela de Comunicación Social, Univ. Católica Andrés Bello. Caracas.

Cuad. Desarro. Rural. Cuadernos de Desarrollo Rural. Instituto de Estudios Rurales, Pontificia Univ. Javeriana. Bogotá.

Cuba. Stud. Cuban Studies. Univ. of Pittsburgh, Center for Latin American Studies. Pittsburgh, Penn.

Cult. Anthropol. Cultural Anthropology: Journal of the Society for Cultural Anthropology. American Anthropological Assn.; Society for Cultural Anthropology. Washington.

Dados/Rio de Janeiro. Dados. Instituto Univ. de Pesquisas. Rio de Janeiro.

Debate Agrar. Debate Agrario. Centro Peruano de Estudios Sociales (CEPES). Lima.

Debates Sociol. Debates en Sociología. Pontificia Univ. Católica del Perú, Depto. de Ciencias Sociales. Lima.

Del Caribe. Del Caribe. Casa del Caribe. Santiago, Cuba.

Desarro. Econ. Desarrollo Económico. Instituto de Desarrollo Económico y Social. Buenos Aires.

Desarro. Soc. Desarrollo y Sociedad. Univ. de los Andes, Facultad de Economía, Centro de Estudios sobre el Desarrollo Económico (CEDE). Bogotá.

ECA/San Salvador. Estudios Centro-Americanos: ECA. Univ. Centroamericana José Simeón Cañas. San Salvador.

Econ. Dev. Cult. Change. Economic Development and Cultural Change. Univ. of Chicago, Research Center in Economic Development and Cultural Change. Chicago, Ill.

Ecos/Santo Domingo. Ecos. Instituto de Historia, Univ. Autónoma de Santo Domingo.

Enfoques Mujer. Enfoques de Mujer. Grupo de Estudios de la Mujer Paraguaya, Centro Paraguayo de Estudios Sociológicos. Asunción.

Espac. Temas Cienc. Soc. Espacio: Temas de Ciencias Sociales. Escuela de Ciencias Sociales, Univ. Católica Andrés Bello. Caracas.

Estud. Afro-Asiát. Estudos Afro-Asiáticos. Centro de Estudos Afro-Asiáticos. Rio de Janeiro.

Estud. Cult. Contemp. Estudios sobre las Culturas Contemporáneas. Centro Universitario de Investigaciones Sociales, Univ. de Colima. México.

Estud. Fem. Estudos Feministas. CIEC, Escola de Comunicação, Univ. Federal do Rio de Janeiro.

Estud. Filos. Hist. Let. Estudios: Filosofía, Historia, Letras. Instituto Tecnológico Autónomo de México, Depto. Académico de Estudios Generales.

Estud. Latinoam./México. Estudios Latinoamericanos. Centro de Estudios Latinoamericanos (CELA), UNAM. México.

Estud. Latinoam./Poland. Estudios Latinoamericanos. Academia de Ciencias de Polonia, Instituto de Historia. Wrocław.

Estud. Soc./Hermosillo. Estudios Sociales. El Colegio de Sonora. Hermosillo, Mexico.

Estud. Soc./Santo Domingo. Estudios Sociales. Centro de Estudios Sociales Juan Montalvo, SJ. Santo Domingo.

Estud. Sociol./México. Estudios Sociológicos. Centro de Estudios Sociológicos de El Colegio de México. México.

Ethnos/Stockholm. Ethnos. Statens Etnografiska Museum. Stockholm.

Ethos/Society. Ethos. Society for Psychological Anthropology; Univ. of California, Los Angeles.

Etud. Guad. Etudes Guadeloupéennes. Association guadeloupéenne de recherches et d'études. Abymes, Guadeloupe.

Fermentum/Mérida. Fermentum: Revista Venezolana de Sociología y Antropología. Univ. de los Andes. Mérida, Venezuela.

Género Soc. Género y Sociedad. Centro de Estudio del Género. Santo Domingo.

Haïti Inf. Libre. Haïti Information Libre. Haïti solidarité internationale. Paris.

Hombre Ambient. Hombre y Ambiente. Ediciones Abya-Yala. Quito.

Horiz. Antropol. Horizontes Antropológicos. Programa de Pós-Graduação em Antropologia Social da Univ. Federal do Rio Grande do Sul. Porto Alegre, Brazil.

Hum. Organ. Human Organization. Society for Applied Anthropology. New York.

Inf. Soc. Ecuad. Informe Social Ecuador. Instituto Latinoamericano de Investigaciones Sociales (ILDIS). Quito.

Int. Migr. International Migration = Migrations Internationales = Migraciones Internacionales. Intergovernmental Committee for European Migration; Research Group for European Migration Problems; International Organization for Migration. The Hague, Netherlands; Geneva, Switzerland.

Int. Migr. Rev. International Migration Review. Center for Migration Studies. New York.

Interciencia/Caracas. Interciencia. Asociación Interciencia. Caracas.

INTERCOM/São Paulo. INTERCOM: Revista Brasileira de Comunicação. Sociedade Brasileira de Estudos Interdisciplinares da Comunicação (INTERCOM). São Paulo.

J. Anthropol. Res. Journal of Anthropological Research. Univ. of New Mexico. Albuquerque, N.M.

J. Caribb. Stud. Journal of Caribbean Studies. Assn. of Caribbean Studies. Coral Gables, Fla.

J. Church State. Journal of Church and State. J.M. Dawson Studies in Church and State, Baylor Univ., Waco, Tex.

J. Contemp. Hist. Journal of Contemporary History. Sage Publications. London.

J. Lat. Am. Stud. Journal of Latin American Studies. Centers or Institutes of Latin American Studies at the Universities of Cambridge, Glasgow, Liverpool, London, and Oxford. Cambridge Univ. Press. London.

J. Marriage Fam. Journal of Marriage and the Family. Univ. of Nebraska-Lincoln.

J. Polit. Econ. Journal of Political Economy. Univ. of Chicago. Chicago, Ill.

J. Polit. Mil. Sociol. Journal of Political and Military Sociology. Northern Illinois Univ., Dept. of Sociology. DeKalb, Ill.

LARR. Latin American Research Review. Latin American Research Review Board. Univ. of New Mexico, Albuquerque, N.M.

Lat. Am. Perspect. Latin American Perspectives. Univ. of California. Newbury Park, Calif.

Lat. Am. Stud./Japan. Latin American Studies. Univ. of Tsukuba, Special Research Project on Latin America. Sakura-Mura, Japan.

Notas Pobl. Notas de Población. Centro Latinoamericano de Demografía. Santiago.

Novos Estud. CEBRAP. Novos Estudos CEBRAP. Centro Brasileiro de Análise e Planejamento. São Paulo.

Nueva Soc. Nueva Sociedad. Caracas.

NWIG. New West Indian Guide/Nieuwe West Indische Gids. KITLV Press. Leiden, The Netherlands.

Organization/London. Organization. Sage Publications. London.

Pap. Proc. Appl. Geogr. Conf. Papers and Proceedings of the Applied Geography Conferences. Dept. of Geography, Kent State Univ.; State Univ. of New York (SUNY) at Binghamton.

Perf. Latinoam. Perfiles Latinoamericanos. Facultad Latinoamericana de Ciencias Sociales. México.

Planeac. Desarro. Planeación & Desarrollo. Depto. Nacional de Planeación. Bogotá.

Poblac. Desarro. Población y Desarrollo. Asociación Dominicana Pro Bienestar de la Familia (PROFAMILIA). Santo Domingo.

Polít. Gob. Política y Gobierno. Centro de Investigación y Docencia Económicas. México.

Presença Mulher. Presença da Mulher. Editora Liberdade Mulher. São Paulo.

Rencontre/Haiti. Rencontre. CRESFED. Canapé Vert, Haiti.

Rev. Adm. Pública/México. Revista de Administración Pública. Instituto de Administración Pública. México.

Rev. Bras. Ciênc. Sociais. Revista Brasileira de Ciências Sociais. Associação Nacional de Pós-Graduação e Pesquisa em Ciências Sociais. Rio de Janeiro.

Rev. Bras. Estud. Popul. Revista Brasileira de Estudos de População. Associação Brasileira de Estudos Populacionais. São Paulo.

Rev. Bras. Hist. Revista Brasileira de História. Associação Nacional dos Professores Universitários de História (ANPUH). São Paulo.

Rev. Cienc. Soc./Montevideo. Revista de Ciencias Sociales. Facultad de Ciencias, Depto. de Sociología, Fundación de Cultura Universitaria. Montevideo.

Rev. Cienc. Soc./Río Piedras. Revista de Ciencias Sociales. Univ. de Puerto Rico, Colegio de Ciencias Sociales. Río Piedras.

Rev. Econ. Sociol. Trab. Revista de Economía y Sociología del Trabajo. Ministerio de Trabajo y Seguridad Social. Madrid.

Rev. Eme-Eme. Revista Eme-Eme. Univ. Católica Madre y Maestra. Santiago de los Caballeros, Dominican Republic.

Rev. Eur. Revista Europea de Estudios Latinoamericanos y del Caribe = European Review of Latin American and Caribbean Studies. Center for Latin American Research and Documentation; Royal Institute of Linguistics and Anthropology. Amsterdam.

Rev. fr. sci. polit. Revue française de science politique. L'Association française de science politique. Paris.

Rev. Geogr. Venez. Revista Geográfica Venezolana. Univ. de los Andes. Mérida, Venezuela.

Rev. Int. Sociol. Revista Internacional de Sociología. Consejo Superior de Investigaciones Científicas. Instituto de Economía y Geografía Aplicadas. Madrid.

Rev. Interam. Bibliogr. Revista Interamericana de Bibliografía. Organization of American States. Washington.

Rev. Mex. Sociol. Revista Mexicana de Sociología. Instituto de Investigaciones Sociales, Univ. Nacional Autónoma de México. México.

Rev. Mus. Nac. Etnogr. Folk. Revista del Museo Nacional de Etnografía y Folklore. MUSEF Editores. La Paz.

Rev. Parag. Sociol. Revista Paraguaya de Sociología. Centro Paraguayo de Estudios Sociológicos. Asunción.

Rev. USP. Revista USP. Coordenadoria de Comunicação Social (CCS), Univ. de São Paulo.

Ruralia/Buenos Aires. Ruralia: Revista Argentina de Estudios Agrarios. FLACSO; Ediciones Imago Mundi. Buenos Aires.

São Paulo Perspect. São Paulo em Perspectiva. Fundação SEADE. São Paulo.

Siglo XIX. Siglo XIX. Facultad de Filosofía y Letras, Univ. Autónoma de Nuevo León. Monterrey, Mexico.

Slavery Abolit. Slavery & Abolition. Frank Cass & Co., Ltd., London.

Soc. Compass. Social Compass. The International Catholic Institute for Social-Ecclesiastical Research. The Hague.

Soc. Econ. Stud. Social and Economic Studies. Univ. of the West Indies, Institute of Social and Economic Research. Mona, Jamaica.

Soc. Estado. Sociedade e Estado. Univ. de Brasília, Depto. de Sociologia. Brasília.

Soc. Forces. Social Forces. Univ. of North Carolina Press. Chapel Hill, N.C.

Sociol. Perspect. Sociological Perspectives. Pacific Sociological Assn.; JAI Press, Inc. Greenwich, Conn.

Tempo Soc./São Paulo. Tempo Social. Faculdade de Filosofia, Letras e Ciências Humanas, Depto. de Sociologia, Univ. de São Paulo.

Tierra Firme. Tierra Firme. Caracas.

Veritas/Porto Alegre. Veritas. Pontificia Univ. Católica do Rio Grande do Sul. Porto Alegre, Brazil.

Yachay/Cochabamba. Yachay. Facultad de Filosofía y Ciencias Religiosas, Univ. Católica Boliviana. Cochabamba, Bolivia.

Yearbook/CLAG. Yearbook. Conference of Latin Americanist Geographers; Ball State Univ., Muncie, Ind.

ABBREVIATIONS AND ACRONYMS

Except for journal abbreviations which are listed: 1) at the end of each major disciplinary section (e.g., Anthropology, Economics, Geography, etc.); 2) after each journal title in the *Title List of Journals Indexed* (p. 753); and 3) in the *Abbreviation List of Journals Indexed* (p. 769).

a.	annual
ABC	Argentina, Brazil, Chile
A.C.	antes de Cristo
ACAR	Associação de Crédito e Assistência Rural, Brazil
AD	Anno Domini
A.D.	Acción Democrática, Venezuela
ADESG	Associação dos Diplomados de Escola Superior de Guerra, Brazil
AGI	Archivo General de Indias, Sevilla
AGN	Archivo General de la Nación
AID	Agency for International Development
a.k.a.	also known as
Ala.	Alabama
ALADI	Asociación Latinoamericana de Integración
ALALC	Asociación Latinoamericana de Libre Comercio
ALEC	*Atlas lingüístico etnográfico de Colombia*
ANAPO	Alianza Nacional Popular, Colombia
ANCARSE	Associação Nordestina de Crédito e Assistência Rural de Sergipe, Brazil
ANCOM	Andean Common Market
ANDI	Asociación Nacional de Industriales, Colombia
ANPOCS	Associação Nacional de Pós-Graduação e Pesquisa em Ciências Sociais, São Paulo
ANUC	Asociación Nacional de Usuarios Campesinos, Colombia
ANUIES	Asociación Nacional de Universidades e Institutos de Enseñanza Superior, Mexico
AP	Acción Popular
APRA	Alianza Popular Revolucionaria Americana, Peru
ARENA	Aliança Renovadora Nacional, Brazil
Ariz.	Arizona
Ark.	Arkansas
ASA	Association of Social Anthropologists of the Commonwealth, London
ASSEPLAN	Assessoria de Planejamento e Acompanhamento, Recife
Assn.	Association
Aufl.	Auflage (edition, edición)
AUFS	American Universities Field Staff Reports, Hanover, N.H.
Aug.	August, Augustan
aum.	aumentada
b.	born (nació)
B.A.R.	British Archaeological Reports
BBE	Bibliografia Brasileira de Educação
b.c.	indicates dates obtained by radiocarbon methods

BC	Before Christ
bibl(s).	bibliography(ies)
BID	Banco Interamericano de Desarrollo
BNDE	Banco Nacional de Desenvolvimento Econômico, Brazil
BNH	Banco Nacional de Habitação, Brazil
BP	before present
b/w	black and white
C14	Carbon 14
ca.	*circa* (about)
CACM	Central American Common Market
CADE	Conferencia Anual de Ejecutivos de Empresas, Peru
CAEM	Centro de Altos Estudios Militares, Peru
Calif.	California
Cap.	Capítulo
CARC	Centro de Arte y Comunicación, Buenos Aires
CARICOM	Caribbean Common Market
CARIFTA	Caribbean Free Trade Association
CBC	Christian base communities
CBD	central business district
CBI	Caribbean Basin Initiative
CD	Christian Democrats, Chile
CDHES	Comisión de Derechos Humanos de El Salvador
CDI	Conselho de Desenvolvimento Industrial, Brasília
CEB	comunidades eclesiásticas de base
CEBRAP	Centro Brasileiro de Análise e Planejamento, São Paulo
CECORA	Centro de Cooperativas de la Reforma Agraria, Colombia
CEDAL	Centro de Estudios Democráticos de América Latina, Costa Rica
CEDE	Centro de Estudios sobre Desarrollo Económico, Univ. de los Andes, Bogotá
CEDEPLAR	Centro de Desenvolvimento e Planejamento Regional, Belo Horizonte
CEDES	Centro de Estudios de Estado y Sociedad, Buenos Aires; Centro de Estudos de Educação e Sociedade, São Paulo
CEDI	Centro Ecumênico de Documentos e Informação, São Paulo
CEDLA	Centro de Estudios y Documentación Latinoamericanos, Amsterdam
CEESTEM	Centro de Estudios Económicos y Sociales del Tercer Mundo, México
CELADE	Centro Latinoamericano de Demografía
CELADEC	Comisión Evangélica Latinoamericana de Educación Cristiana
CELAM	Consejo Episcopal Latinoamericano
CEMLA	Centro de Estudios Monetarios Latinoamericanos, Mexico
CENDES	Centro de Estudios del Desarrollo, Venezuela
CENIDIM	Centro Nacional de Información, Documentación e Investigación Musicales, Mexico
CENIET	Centro Nacional de Información y Estadísticas del Trabajo, Mexico
CEOSL	Confederación Ecuatoriana de Organizaciones Sindicales LIbres
CEPADE	Centro Paraguayo de Estudios de Desarrollo Económico y Social
CEPA-SE	Comissão Estadual de Planejamento Agrícola, Sergipe
CEPAL	Comisión Económica para América Latina y el Caribe
CEPLAES	Centro de Planificación y Estudios Sociales, Quito
CERES	Centro de Estudios de la Realidad Económica y Social, Bolivia
CES	constant elasticity of substitution
cf.	compare
CFI	Consejo Federal de Inversiones, Buenos Aires
CGE	Confederación General Económica, Argentina
CGTP	Confederación General de Trabajadores del Perú
chap(s).	chapter(s)
CHEAR	Council on Higher Education in the American Republics

Cía.	Compañía
CIA	Central Intelligence Agency
CIDA	Comité Interamericano de Desarrollo Agrícola
CIDE	Centro de Investigación y Desarrollo de la Educación, Chile; Centro de Investigación y Docencias Económicas, Mexico
CIDIAG	Centro de Información y Desarrollo Internacional de Autogestión, Lima
CIE	Centro de Investigaciones Económicas, Buenos Aires
CIEDLA	Centro Interdisciplinario de Estudios sobre el Desarrollo Latinoamericano, Buenos Aires
CIEDUR	Centro Interdisciplinario de Estudios sobre el Desarrollo Uruguay, Montevideo
CIEPLAN	Corporación de Investigaciones Económicas para América Latina, Santiago
CIESE	Centro de Investigaciones y Estudios Socioeconómicos, Quito
CIMI	Conselho Indigenista Missionário, Brazil
CINTERFOR	Centro Interamericano de Investigación y Documentación sobre Formación Profesional
CINVE	Centro de Investigaciones Económicas, Montevideo
CIP	Conselho Interministerial de Preços, Brazil
CIPCA	Centro de Investigación y Promoción del Campesinado, Bolivia
CIPEC	Consejo Intergubernamental de Países Exportadores de Cobre, Santiago
CLACSO	Consejo Latinoamericano de Ciencias Sociales, Secretaría Ejecutiva, Buenos Aires
CLASC	Confederación Latinoamericana Sindical Cristiana
CLE	Comunidad Latinoamericana de Escritores, Mexico
cm	centimeter
CNI	Confederação Nacional da Indústria, Brazil
CNPq	Conselho Nacional de Pesquisas, Brazil
Co.	Company
COB	Central Obrera Boliviana
COBAL	Companhia Brasileira de Alimentos
CODEHUCA	Comisión para la Defensa de los Derechos Humanos en Centroamérica
Col.	Collection, Colección, Coleção
col.	colored, coloured
Colo.	Colorado
COMCORDE	Comisión Coordinadora para el Desarrollo Económico, Uruguay
comp(s).	compiler(s), compilador(es)
CONCLAT	Congresso Nacional das Classes Trabalhadoras, Brazil
CONCYTEC	Consejo Nacional de Ciencia y Tecnología (Peru)
CONDESE	Conselho de Desenvolvimento Econômico de Sergipe
Conn.	Connecticut
COPEI	Comité Organizador Pro-Elecciones Independientes, Venezuela
CORFO	Corporación de Fomento de la Producción, Chile
CORP	Corporación para el Fomento de Investigaciones Económicas, Colombia
Corp.	Corporation, Corporación
corr.	corrected, corregida
CP	Communist Party
CPDOC	Centro de Pesquisa e Documentação, Brazil
CRIC	Consejo Regional Indígena del Cauca, Colombia
CSUTCB	Confederación Sindical Unica de Trabajadores Campesinos de Bolivia
CTM	Confederación de Trabajadores de México
CUNY	City University of New York
CUT	Central Unica de Trabajadores (Mexico); Central Unica dos Trabalhadores (Brazil); Central Unitaria de Trabajadores (Chile; Colombia); Confederación Unitaria de Trabajadores (Costa Rica)
CVG	Corporación Venezolana de Guayana
d.	died (murió)

DANE	Departamento Nacional de Estadística, Colombia
DC	developed country; Demócratas Cristianos, Chile
d.C.	después de Cristo
Dec./déc.	December, décembre
Del.	Delaware
dept.	department
depto.	departamento
DESCO	Centro de Estudios y Promoción del Desarrollo, Lima
Dez./dez.	Dezember, dezembro
dic.	diciembre, dicembre
disc.	discography
DNOCS	Departamento Nacional de Obras Contra as Secas, Brazil
doc.	document, documento
Dr.	Doctor
Dra.	Doctora
DRAE	*Diccionario de la Real Academia Española*
ECLAC	UN Economic Commision for Latin America and the Caribbean, New York and Santiago
ECOSOC	UN Economic and Social Council
ed./éd.(s)	edition(s), édition(s), edición(es), editor(s), redactor(es), director(es)
EDEME	Editora Emprendimentos Educacionais, Florianópolis
Edo.	Estado
EEC	European Economic Community
EE.UU.	Estados Unidos de América
EFTA	European Free Trade Association
e.g.	*exempio gratia* (for example, por ejemplo)
ELN	Ejército de Liberación Nacional, Colombia
ENDEF	Estudo Nacional da Despesa Familiar, Brazil
ERP	Ejército Revolucionario del Pueblo, El Salvador
ESG	Escola Superior de Guerra, Brazil
estr.	estrenado
et al.	*et alia* (and others)
ETENE	Escritório Técnico de Estudos Econômicos do Nordeste, Brazil
ETEPE	Escritório Técnico de Planejamento, Brazil
EUDEBA	Editorial Universitaria de Buenos Aires
EWG	Europaische Wirtschaftsgemeinschaft. *See* EEC.
facsim(s).	facsimile(s)
FAO	Food and Agriculture Organization of the United Nations
FDR	Frente Democrático Revolucionario, El Salvador
FEB	Força Expedicionária Brasileira
Feb./feb.	February, Februar, febrero, febbraio
FEDECAFE	Federación Nacional de Cafeteros, Colombia
fev./fév.	fevereiro, février
ff.	following
FGTS	Fundo de Garantia do Tempo de Serviço, Brazil
FGV	Fundação Getúlio Vargas
FIEL	Fundación de Investigaciones Económicas Latinoamericanas, Argentina
film.	filmography
fl.	flourished
Fla.	Florida
FLACSO	Facultad Latinoamericana de Ciencias Sociales
FMI	Fondo Monetario Internacional
FMLN	Frente Farabundo Martí de Liberación Nacional, El Salvador
fold.	folded
fol(s).	folio(s)

FPL	Fuerzas Populares de Liberación Farabundo Marti, El Salvador
FRG	Federal Republic of Germany
FSLN	Frente Sandinista de Liberación Nacional, Nicaragua
ft.	foot, feet
FUAR	Frente Unido de Acción Revolucionaria, Colombia
FUCVAM	Federación Unificadora de Cooperativas de Vivienda por Ayuda Mutua, Uruguay
FUNAI	Fundação Nacional do Indio, Brazil
FUNARTE	Fundação Nacional de Arte, Brazil
FURN	Fundação Universidade Regional do Nordeste
Ga.	Georgia
GAO	General Accounting Office, Wahington
GATT	General Agreement on Tariffs and Trade
GDP	gross domestic product
GDR	German Democratic Republic
GEIDA	Grupo Executivo de Irrigação para o Desenvolvimento Agrícola, Brazil
gen.	gennaio
Gen.	General
GMT	Greenwich Mean Time
GPA	grade point average
GPO	Government Printing Office, Washington
h.	hijo
ha.	hectares, hectáreas
HLAS	*Handbook of Latin American Studies*
HMAI	*Handbook of Middle American Indians*
Hnos.	hermanos
HRAF	Human Relations Area Files, Inc., New Haven, Conn.
IBBD	Instituto Brasileiro de Bibliografia e Documentação
IBGE	Instituto Brasileiro de Geografia e Estatística, Rio de Janeiro
IBRD	International Bank for Reconstruction and Development (World Bank)
ICA	Instituto Colombiano Agropecuario
ICAIC	Instituto Cubano de Arte e Industria Cinematográfica
ICCE	Instituto Colombiano de Construcción Escolar
ICE	International Cultural Exchange
ICSS	Instituto Colombiano de Seguridad Social
ICT	Instituto de Crédito Territorial, Colombia
id.	*idem* (the same as previously mentioned or given)
IDB	Inter-American Development Bank
i.e.	*id est* (that is, o sea)
IEL	Instituto Euvaldo Lodi, Brazil
IEP	Instituto de Estudios Peruanos
IERAC	Instituto Ecuatoriano de Reforma Agraria y Colonización
IFAD	International Fund for Agricultural Development
IICA	Instituto Interamericano de Ciencias Agrícolas, San José
III	Instituto Indigenista Interamericano, Mexico
IIN	Instituto Indigenista Nacional, Guatemala
ILDIS	Instituto Latinoamericano de Investigaciones Sociales
ill.	illustration(s)
Ill.	Illinois
ILO	International Labour Organization, Geneva
IMES	Instituto Mexicano de Estudios Sociales
IMF	International Monetary Fund
Impr.	Imprenta, Imprimérie
in.	inches
INAH	Instituto Nacional de Antropología e Historia, Mexico

INBA	Instituto Nacional de Bellas Artes, Mexico
Inc.	Incorporated
INCORA	Instituto Colombiano de Reforma Agraria
Ind.	Indiana
INEP	Instituto Nacional de Estudios Pedagógicos, Brazil
INI	Instituto Nacional Indigenista, Mexico
INIT	Instituto Nacional de Industria Turística, Cuba
INPES/IPEA	Instituto de Planejamento Econômico e Social, Brazil
INTAL	Instituto para la Integración de América Latina
IPA	Instituto de Pastoral Andina, Univ. de San Antonio de Abad, Seminario de Antropología, Cusco, Peru
IPEA	Instituto de Pesquisa Econômica Aplicada, Brazil
IPES/GB	Instituto de Pesquisas e Estudos Sociais, Guanabara, Brazil
IPHAN	Instituto de Patrimônio Histórico e Artístico Nacional, Brazil
ir.	irregular
IS	Internacional Socialista
ITESM	Instituto Tecnológico y de Estudios Superiores de Monterrey
ITT	International Telephone and Telegraph
Jan./jan.	January, Januar, janeiro, janvier
JLP	Jamaican Labour Party
Jr.	Junior, Júnior
JUC	Juventude Universitária Católica, Brazil
JUCEPLAN	Junta Central de Planificación, Cuba
Kan.	Kansas
km	kilometers, kilómetros
Ky.	Kentucky
La.	Louisiana
LASA	Latin American Studies Association
LDC	less developed country(ies)
LP	long-playing record
Ltd(a).	Limited, Limitada
m	meters, metros
m.	murió (died)
M	mille, mil, thousand
M.A.	Master of Arts
MACLAS	Middle Atlantic Council of Latin American Studies
MAPU	Movimiento de Acción Popular Unitario, Chile
MARI	Middle American Research Institute, Tulane University, New Orleans
MAS	Movimiento al Socialismo, Venezuela
Mass.	Massachusetts
MCC	Mercado Común Centro-Americano
Md.	Maryland
MDB	Movimiento Democrático Brasileiro
MDC	more developed countries
Me.	Maine
MEC	Ministério de Educação e Cultura, Brazil
Mich.	Michigan
mimeo	mimeographed, mimeografiado
min.	minutes, minutos
Minn.	Minnesota
MIR	Movimiento de Izquierda Revolucionaria, Chile and Venezuela
Miss.	Mississippi
MIT	Massachusetts Institute of Technology
ml	milliliter
MLN	Movimiento de Liberación Nacional

mm.	millimeter
MNC	multinational corporation
MNI	minimum number of individuals
MNR	Movimiento Nacionalista Revolucionario, Bolivia
Mo.	Missouri
MOBRAL	Movimento Brasileiro de Alfabetização
MOIR	Movimiento Obrero Independiente y Revolucionario, Colombia
Mont.	Montana
MRL	Movimiento Revolucionario Liberal, Colombia
ms.	manuscript
M.S.	Master of Science
msl	mean sea level
n.	nació (born)
NBER	National Bureau of Economic Research, Cambridge, Massachusetts
N.C.	North Carolina
N.D.	North Dakota
NE	Northeast
Neb.	Nebraska
neubearb.	neubearbeitet (revised, corregida)
Nev.	Nevada
n.f.	neue Folge (new series)
NGO	nongovernmental organization
NGDO	nongovernmental development organization
N.H.	New Hampshire
NIEO	New International Economic Order
NIH	National Institutes of Health, Washington
N.J.	New Jersey
NJM	New Jewel Movement, Grenada
N.M.	New Mexico
no(s).	number(s), número(s)
NOEI	Nuevo Orden Económico Internacional
NOSALF	Scandinavian Committee for Research in Latin America
Nov./nov.	November, noviembre, novembre, novembro
NSF	National Science Foundation
NW	Northwest
N.Y.	New York
OAB	Ordem dos Advogados do Brasil
OAS	Organization of American States
Oct./oct.	October, octubre, octobre
ODEPLAN	Oficina de Planificación Nacional, Chile
OEA	Organización de los Estados Americanos
OIT	Organización Internacional del Trabajo
Okla.	Oklahoma
Okt.	Oktober
ONUSAL	United Nations Observer Mission in El Salvador
op.	opus
OPANAL	Organismo para la Proscripción de las Armas Nucleares en América Latina
OPEC	Organization of Petroleum Exporting Countries
OPEP	Organización de Países Exportadores de Petróleo
OPIC	Overseas Private Investment Corporation, Washington
Or.	Oregon
OREALC	Oficina Regional de Educación para América Latina y el Caribe
ORIT	Organización Regional Interamericana del Trabajo
ORSTOM	Office de la recherche scientifique et technique outre-mer (France)
ott.	ottobre

out.	outubro
p.	page(s)
Pa.	Pennsylvania
PAN	Partido Acción Nacional, Mexico
PC	Partido Comunista
PCCLAS	Pacific Coast Council on Latin American Studies
PCN	Partido de Conciliación Nacional, El Salvador
PCP	Partido Comunista del Perú
PCR	Partido Comunista Revolucionario, Chile y Argentina
PCV	Partido Comunista de Venezuela
PD	Partido Democrático
PDC	Partido Demócrata Cristiano, Chile
PDS	Partido Democrático Social, Brazil
PDT	Partido Democrático Trabalhista, Brazil
PDVSA	Petróleos de Venezuela S.A.
PEMEX	Petróleos Mexicanos
PETROBRAS	Petróleo Brasileiro
PIMES	Programa Integrado de Mestrado em Economia e Sociologia, Brazil
PIP	Partido Independiente de Puerto Rico
PLN	Partido Liberación Nacional, Costa Rica
PMDB	Partido do Movimento Democrático Brasileiro
PNAD	Pesquisa Nacional por Amostra Domiciliar, Brazil
PNC	People's National Congress, Guyana
PNM	People's National Movement, Trinidad and Tobago
PNP	People's National Party, Jamaica
pop.	population
port(s).	portrait(s)
PPP	purchasing power parities; People's Progressive Party of Guyana
PRD	Partido Revolucionario Dominicano
PREALC	Programa Regional del Empleo para América Latina y el Caribe, Organización Internacional del Trabajo, Santiago
PRI	Partido Revolucionario Institucional, Mexico
Prof.	Professor, Profesor(a)
PRONAPA	Programa Nacional de Pesquisas Arqueológicas, Brazil
prov.	province, provincia
PS	Partido Socialista, Chile
PSD	Partido Social Democrático, Brazil
pseud.	pseudonym, pseudónimo
PT	Partido dos Trabalhadores, Brazil
pt(s).	part(s), parte(s)
PTB	Partido Trabalhista Brasileiro
pub.	published, publisher
PUC	Pontifícia Universidade Católica
PURSC	Partido Unido de la Revolución Socialista de Cuba
q.	quarterly
rev.	revisada, revista, revised
R.I.	Rhode Island
s.a.	semiannual
SALALM	Seminar on the Acquisition of Latin American Library Materials
SATB	soprano, alto, tenor, bass
sd.	sound
s.d.	*sine datum* (no date, sin fecha)
S.D.	South Dakota
SDR	special drawing rights
SE	Southeast

SELA	Sistema Económico Latinoamericano
SEMARNAP	Secretaria de Medio Ambiente, Recursos Naturales y Pesca, Mexico
SENAC	Serviço Nacional de Aprendizagem Comercial, Rio de Janeiro
SENAI	Serviço Nacional de Aprendizagem Industrial, São Paulo
SEP	Secretaría de Educación Pública, Mexico
SEPLA	Seminario Permanente sobre Latinoamérica, Mexico
Sept./sept.	September, septiembre, septembre
SES	socioeconomic status
SESI	Serviço Social da Indústria, Brazil
set.	setembro, settembre
SI	Socialist International
SIECA	Secretaría Permanente del Tratado General de Integración Económica Centroamericana
SIL	Summer Institute of Linguistics (Instituto Lingüístico de Verano)
SINAMOS	Sistema Nacional de Apoyo a la Movilización Social, Peru
S.J.	Society of Jesus
s.l.	*sine loco* (place of publication unknown)
s.n.	*sine nomine* (publisher unknown)
SNA	Sociedad Nacional de Agricultura, Chile
SPP	Secretaría de Programación y Presupuesto, Mexico
SPVEA	Superintendência do Plano de Valorização Econômica da Amazônia, Brazil
sq.	square
SSRC	Social Sciences Research Council, New York
STENEE	Empresa Nacional de Energía Eléctrica. Sindicato de Trabajadores, Honduras
SUDAM	Superintendência de Desenvolvimento da Amazônia, Brazil
SUDENE	Superintendência de Desenvolvimento do Nordeste, Brazil
SUFRAMA	Superintendência da Zona Franca de Manaus, Brazil
SUNY	State University of New York
SW	Southwest
t.	tomo(s), tome(s)
TAT	Thematic Apperception Test
TB	tuberculosis
Tenn.	Tennessee
Tex.	Texas
TG	transformational generative
TL	Thermoluminescent
TNE	Transnational enterprise
TNP	Tratado de No Proliferación
trans.	translator
UABC	Universidad Autónoma de Baja California
UCA	Universidad Centroamericana José Simeón Cañas, San Salvador
UCLA	University of California, Los Angeles
UDN	União Democrática Nacional, Brazil
UFG	Universidade Federal de Goiás
UFPb	Universidade Federal de Paraíba
UFSC	Universidade Federal de Santa Catarina
UK	United Kingdom
UN	United Nations
UNAM	Universidad Nacional Autónoma de México
UNCTAD	United Nations Conference on Trade and Development
UNDP	United Nations Development Programme
UNEAC	Unión de Escritores y Artistas de Cuba
UNESCO	United Nations Educational, Scientific and Cultural Organization
UNI/UNIND	União das Nações Indígenas

UNICEF	United Nations International Children's Emergency Fund
Univ(s).	university(ies), universidad(es), universidade(s), université(s), universität(s), universitá(s)
uniw.	uniwersytet (university)
Unltd.	Unlimited
UP	Unidad Popular, Chile
URD	Unidad Revolucionaria Democrática
URSS	Unión de Repúblicas Soviéticas Socialistas
US	United States
USAID	*See* AID.
USIA	United States Information Agency
USSR	Union of Soviet Socialist Republics
UTM	Universal Transverse Mercator
UWI	Univ. of the West Indies
v.	volume(s), volumen (volúmenes)
Va.	Virginia
V.I.	Virgin Islands
viz.	*videlicet* (that is, namely)
vol(s).	volume(s), volumen (volúmenes)
vs.	versus
Vt.	Vermont
W.Va.	West Virginia
Wash.	Washington
Wis.	Wisconsin
WPA	Working People's Alliance, Guyana
WWI	World War I
WWII	World War II
Wyo.	Wyoming
yr(s).	year(s)

TITLE LIST OF JOURNALS INDEXED

For journal titles listed by abbreviation, see *Abbreviation List of Journals Indexed*, p. 769.

21st Century Policy Review. I.A.A.S. Publishers. Langley Park, Md. (21st Century Policy Rev.)

Academic Questions. Transaction Periodicals Consortium, Rutgers Univ., New Brunswick, N.J. (Acad. Quest.)

Acervo: Revista Hondureña de Cultura. Ministerio de Cultura, Instituto del Libro y el Documento. Tegucigalpa. (Acervo/ Tegucigalpa)

Acta geographica. Société de Géographie. Paris. (Acta geogr.)

Agricultural History. Agricultural History Society. Univ. of Calif. Press. Berkeley. (Agric. Hist.)

Agroforestry Systems. Kluwer Academic Publishers. Dordrecht, The Netherlands. (Agrofor. Syst.)

Allpanchis. Instituto de Pastoral Andina. Cusco, Peru. (Allpanchis/Cusco)

Amazonía Peruana. Centro Amazónico de Antropología y Aplicación Práctica, Depto. de Documentación y Publicaciones. Lima. (Amazonía Peru.)

América Indígena. Instituto Indigenista Interamericano. México. (Am. Indíg.)

América Meridional. Sociedad Regional de Ciencias Humanas. Montevideo. (Am. Merid.)

América Negra. Pontificia Univ. Javeriana. Bogotá. (Am. Negra)

American Anthropologist. American Anthropological Assn., Washington. (Am. Anthropol.)

American Antiquity. The Society for American Archaeology. Washington. (Am. Antiq.)

The American Economic Review. American Economic Assn., Evanston, Ill. (Am. Econ. Rev.)

American Ethnologist. American Ethnological Society. Washington. (Am. Ethnol.)

American Jewish Archives. Cincinnati, Ohio. (Am. Jew. Arch.)

American Journal of Sociology. Univ. of Chicago. Chicago, Ill. (Am. J. Sociol.)

The Americas. Academy of American Franciscan History. Washington. (Americas/ Francisc.)

Amérindia. Association d'Ethnologistique Amérindienne (AEA). Paris. (Amérindia/ Paris)

Analecta Praehistorica Leidensia. Leiden Univ. Press. Leiden, The Netherlands. (Analecta Praehist. Leiden.)

Anales de la Asociación Argentina de Economía Política. Facultad de Ciencias Económicas, Univ. Nacional de Cuyo. Mendoza, Argentina. (An. Asoc. Argent. Econ. Polít.)

Anales del Instituto de la Patagonia: Serie Ciencias Humanas. Univ. de Magallanes. Punta Arenas, Chile. (An. Inst. Patagon./ Hum.)

Análisis Económico. Ediciones UDAPE (Unidad de Análisis de Políticas Económicas). La Paz. (Anál. Econ./La Paz)

Análisis Internacional. Centro Peruano de Estudios Internacionales. Lima. (Anál. Int.)

Ancient Mesoamerica. Cambridge Univ. Press. Cambridge, England. (Anc. Mesoam.)

Andean Past. Latin American Studies Program, Cornell Univ., Ithaca, N.Y. (Andean Past)

Andes: Boletín de la Misión Arqueológica Andina. Univ. of Warsaw. Warsaw, Poland. (Andes/Warsaw)

Andes: Revista de la Facultad de Ciencias Sociales. Univ. Nacional de San Antonio Abad del Cusco, Facultad de Ciencias Sociales. Cusco, Peru. (Andes/Cusco)

Annals of the Association of American Geographers. Lawrence, Kan. (Ann. Assoc. Am. Geogr.)

Annals of the Carnegie Museum. Carnegie Museum of Natural History. Pittsburgh, Penn. (Ann. Carnegie Mus.)

Annual Review of Anthropology. Annual Reviews, Inc., Palo Alto, Calif. (Annu. Rev. Anthropol.)

Anthropologica. Depto. de Ciencias Sociales, Pontificia Univ. Católica del Perú. Lima. (Anthropologica/Lima)

Anthropological Quarterly. Catholic Univ. of America, Catholic Anthropological Conference. Washington. (Anthropol. Q.)

L'Anthropologie. Institut de paleontologie humaine. Paris. (Anthropologie/Paris)

Anthropology and Education Quarterly. Council on Anthropology and Education. Washington. (Anthropol. Educ. Q.)

Anthropos. International Review of Ethnology and Linguistics. Anthropos-Institut. Freiburg, Switzerland. (Anthropos/Switzerland)

Antiquity. A Quarterly Review of Archaeology. The Antiquity Trust. Cambridge, England. (Antiquity/Cambridge)

Antropológica. Fundación La Salle de Ciencias Naturales; Instituto Caribe de Antropología y Sociología. Caracas. (Antropológica/Caracas)

Anuario. Univ. Nacional de Córdoba, Facultad de Derecho y Ciencias Sociales, Centro de Investigaciones Jurídicas y Sociales. Córdoba, Argentina. (Anuario/Córdoba)

Anuario. Centro de Estudios Superiores de México y Centroamérica, Univ. de Ciencias y Artes del Estado de Chiapas. Tuxtla Gutiérrez, Mexico. (Anuario/Tuxtla Gutiérrez)

Anuário Antropológico. Tempo Brasileiro. Rio de Janeiro. (Anu. Antropol.)

Anuario Centro de Estudios Avanzados. Centro de Estudios Avanzados. Córdoba, Argentina. (Anu. Cent. Estud. Av.)

Anuario de Ciencias Sociales. Univ. Autónoma de Aguascalientes, Centro de Artes y Humanidades, Depto. de Sociología y Antropología. Aguascalientes, Mexico. (Anu. Cienc. Soc.)

Anuario de Estudios Americanos. Consejo Superior de Investigaciones Científicas; Univ. de Sevilla, Escuela de Estudios Hispano-Americanos. Sevilla, Spain. (Anu. Estud. Am.)

Anuario de Estudios Centroamericanos. Univ. de Costa Rica. San José. (Anu. Estud. Centroam.)

Anuario de Etnología. Academia de Ciencias de Cuba; Editorial Academia. La Habana. (Anu. Etnol./Habana)

Anuario Estudios Sociales. El Colegio de Puebla. México. (Anu. Estud. Soc.)

Anuario IEHS. Univ. Nacional del Centro de la Provincia de Buenos Aires, Instituto de Estudios Histórico-Sociales. Tandil, Argentina. (Anu. IEHS)

Anuario Instituto Chiapaneco de Cultura. Instituto Chiapaneco de Cultura. Tuxtla Gutiérrez, Mexico. (Anu. Inst. Chiapaneco Cult.)

Apuntes. Univ. del Pacífico, Centro de Investigación. Lima. (Apuntes/Lima)

Archaeoastronomy. Science History Publications. Giles, England. (Archaeoastronomy/England)

Archaeology. Archaeology Institute of America. New York. (Archaeology/New York)

Archaeology and Anthropology. Ministry of Education and Cultural Development. Georgetown, Guyana. (Archaeol. Anthropol.)

Archè. Faculdades Integradas Candido Mendes, Ipanema. Rio de Janeiro. (Archè/Rio de Janeiro)

Archiv für Völkerkunde. Museum für Völkerkunde in Wien und von Verein Freunde der Völkerkunde. Vienna. (Arch. Völkerkd.)

Arctic and Alpine Research. Institute of Arctic and Alpine Research, Univ. of Colorado. Boulder. (Arctic Alpine Res.)

Argentina: a country for investment and growth. Ministerio de Economía y Obras y Servicios Públicos. Buenos Aires. (Argent. Ctry. Investm. Growth)

Armed Forces & Society. Inter-Univ. Seminar on Armed Forces & Society. Univ. of Chicago. Chicago, Ill. (Armed Forces Soc.)

Arqueología. Instituto Nacional de Antropología e Historia. México. (Arqueología/México)

Arqueología Contemporánea. Programa de Estudios Prehistóricos. Buenos Aires. (Arqueol. Contemp.)

Arqueología Mexicana. Instituto Nacional de Antropología e Historia, Editorial Raíces. México. (Arqueol. Mex.)

Arquivos do Museu de História Natural. Univ. Federal de Minas Gerais. Belo Horizonte, Brazil. (Arq. Mus. Hist. Nat.)

The Banker. Financial Times Business Publishing Ltd., London. (Banker/London)

Beyond Law = Más Allá del Derecho. Instituto Latinoamericano de Servicios Legales Alternativos. Bogotá. (Beyond Law)

Biblos: Revista do Departamento de Biblioteconomia e História. Editora da Fundação

Univ. do Rio Grande. Rio Grande, Brazil. (Biblos/Rio de Janeiro)

Boletim da Sociedade Brasileira de Direito Internacional. Univ. de Brasília, Depto. de Ciência Política e Relações Internacionais. Brasília. (Bol. Soc. Bras. Direito Int.)

Boletim de Integração Latino-Americana. Ministério das Relações Exteriores, Subsecretaria-Geral de Asuntos de Integração, Econômicos e de Comercio Exterior, Grupo de Estudos Técnicos. Brasília. (Bol. Integr. Lat.-Am.)

Boletim do Museu Paraense Emílio Goeldi. Nova série: antropologia. Conselho Nacional de Desenvolvimento Científico e Tecnológico, Instituto Nacional de Pesquisas da Amazônia. Belém, Brazil. (Bol. Mus. Para. Goeldi)

Boletim Paulista de Geografia. Associação dos Geógrafos Brasileiros. Seção Regional de São Paulo. São Paulo. (Bol. Paul. Geogr.)

Boletín Americanista. Univ. de Barcelona, Facultad de Geografía e Historia, Depto. de Historia de América. Barcelona. (Bol. Am.)

Boletín de Antropología. Univ. de Antioquia. Medellín, Colombia. (Bol. Antropol./ Antioquia)

Boletín de Estudios Geográficos. Univ. Nacional de Cuyo. Mendoza, Argentina. (Bol. Estud. Geogr.)

Boletín de la Sociedad Chilena de Arqueología. Sociedad Chilena de Arqueología. Santiago. (Bol. Soc. Chil. Arqueol.)

Boletín de Lima. Revista Cultural Científica. Lima. (Bol. Lima)

Boletín del Museo Arqueológico de Quibor. Museo Arqueológico de Quibor. Quibor, Venezuela. (Bol. Mus. Arqueol. Quibor)

Boletín del Museo Chileno de Arte Precolombino. Santiago. (Bol. Mus. Chil. Arte Precolomb.)

Boletín del Museo del Oro. Banco de la República. Bogotá. (Boletín/Bogotá)

Boletín Informativo. Museo de Táchira. San Cristóbal, Venezuela. (Bol. Inf./San Cristóbal)

Boletín Informativo Techint. Organización Techint. Buenos Aires. (Bol. Inf. Techint)

Boletín Socioeconómico. Centro de Investigaciones y Documentación Socioeconómico (CIDSE), Univ. del Valle. Cali, Colombia. (Bol. Socioecon.)

Bulletin. Société suisse des américanistes; Musée et institut d'éthnographie. Geneva. (Bulletin/Geneva)

Bulletin de la Société d'histoire de la Guadeloupe. Archives départamentales avec le concours du Conseil général de la Guadeloupe. Basse-Terre, Guadeloupe. (Bull. Soc. hist. Guadeloupe)

Bulletin de l'Institut français d'études andines. Lima. (Bull. Inst. fr. étud. andin.)

Bulletin du Bureau national d'ethnologie. Bureau national d'ethnologie. Port-au-Prince, Haiti. (Bull. Bur. natl. ethnol.)

Bulletin of Eastern Caribbean Affairs. Univ. of West Indies. Cave Hill, Barbados. (Bull. East. Caribb. Aff.)

Bulletin of Latin American Research. Society for Latin American Studies. Oxford, England. (Bull. Lat. Am. Res.)

Bulletin of the International Committee on Urgent Anthropological and Ethnological Research. International Union of Anthropological and Ethnological Sciences. Vienna. (Bull. Int. Anthropol. Ethnol. Res.)

Cadernos de Sociologia. Univ. Federal do Rio Grande do Sul, Programa de Pós-Graduação em Sociologia. Porto Alegre, Brazil. (Cad. Sociol.)

Cadernos do Centro de Estudos e Ação Social (CEAS). Salvador, Brazil. (Cad. CEAS)

Cahiers des Amériques latines. Paris. (Cah. Am. lat.)

Les Cahiers d'Outre-Mer. Institut de géographie de la Faculté des lettres de Bordeaux; Institut de la France d'Outre-Mer; Société de géographie de Bordeaux. Bordeaux, France. (Cah. Outre-Mer)

Cambridge Archaeological Journal. Cambridge Univ. Press. Cambridge, England. (Camb. Archaeol. J.)

Canadian Journal of Latin American and Caribbean Studies. Univ. of Ottawa. Ontario, Canada. (Can. J. Lat. Am. Caribb. Stud.)

Caravelle. Cahiers du monde hispanique et luso-brésilien. Univ. de Toulouse, Institute d'études hispaniques, hispano-americaines et luso-brésiliennes. Toulouse, France. (Caravelle/Toulouse)

Caribbean Geography. Univ. of the West Indies, Dept. of Geography. Kingston, Jamaica. (Caribb. Geogr.)

Caribbean Journal of Science. Univ. of Puerto Rico. Mayagüez, Puerto Rico. (Caribb. J. Sci.)

Caribbean Quarterly. Univ. of the West Indies. Mona, Jamaica. (Caribb. Q.)

Caribbean Studies. Univ. of Puerto Rico, Institute of Caribbean Studies. Río Piedras. (Caribb. Stud.)

Caribena: cahiers d'études américanistes de la Caraïbe. Centre d'études et de recherches archéologiques (CERA). Martinique. (Caribena/Martinique)

Casa de las Américas. La Habana. (Casa Am.)

Centroamérica Internacional. Facultad Latinoamericana de Ciencias Sociales (FLACSO). San José. (Centroam. Int.)

CEPAL Review/Revista de la CEPAL. Naciones Unidas, Comisión Económica para América Latina. Santiago. (CEPAL Rev.)

Cerámica de Cultura Maya. Temple Univ., Dept. of Anthropology. Philadelphia, Penn. (Cerám. Cult. Maya)

Cespedesia. Depto. del Valle del Cauca. Cali, Colombia. (Cespedesia/Cali)

Chungará. Univ. del Norte, Depto. de Antropología. Arica, Chile. (Chungará/Arica)

Ciência & Ambiente. Univ. Federal de Santa Maria. Santa Maria, Brazil. (Ciênc. Amb.)

Ciência & Trópico. Fundação Joaquim Nabuco; Editora Massangana. Recife, Brazil. (Ciênc. Tróp.)

Ciência Hoje. Sociedade Brasileira para o Progresso da Ciência. Rio de Janeiro. (Ciênc. Hoje)

Ciencia Hoy. Asociación Ciencia Hoy; Morgan Antártica. Buenos Aires. (Cienc. Hoy)

Ciencia Política. Instituto de Ciencia Política de Bogotá; Tierra Firme Editores. Bogotá. (Cienc. Polít.)

Ciencia y Sociedad. Instituto Tecnológico de Santo Domingo. (Cienc. Soc./Santo Domingo)

Ciencias Económicas. Instituto de Investigaciones en Ciencias Ecónomicas, Univ. de Costa Rica. San José. (Cienc. Econ./San José)

Ciências Humanas em Revista. Instituto de Ciências Humanas e Letras, Univ. Federal de Goiás. Goiânia, Brazil. (Ciênc. Hum. Rev./Goiânia)

Clío. Univ. Autónoma de Sinaloa, Escuela de Historia. Culiacán, Mexico. (Clío/Sinaloa)

Clio: Série Arqueológica. Univ. Federal de Pernambuco. Recife, Brazil. (Clio Arqueol./Recife)

Colección Estudios CIEPLAN. Corporación de Investigaciones Económicas para Latinoamérica. Santiago. (Colecc. Estud. CIEPLAN)

Columbia Journal of Transnational Law. Columbia Univ. School of Law. New York. (Columbia J. Transnatl. Law)

Comparative Political Studies. Sage Publications, Thousand Oaks, Calif. (Comp. Polit. Stud.)

Comparative Politics. The City Univ. of New York, Political Science Program. New York. (Comp. Polit.)

Comparative Studies in Society and History. Society for the Comparative Study of Society and History; Cambridge Univ. Press. London. (Comp. Stud. Soc. Hist.)

Computer Applications and Quantitative Methods in Archaeology. BAR. Oxford. (CAA/Oxford)

Comunicação & Política. Centro Brasileiro de Estudos Latino-Americanos. Rio de Janeiro. (Comun. Polít.)

Conjonction. Bulletin de l'Institut français d'Haïti. Port-au-Prince. (Conjonction/Port-au-Prince)

Contemporary Issues in Social Science: a Caribbean Perspective. Univ. of the West Indies, Faculty of Social Sciences, ANSA McAL Psychological Research Centre. St. Augustine, Trinidad. (Contemp. Issues. Soc. Sci. Caribb. Perspect.)

Contexto Internacional. Instituto de Relações Internacionais, Pontifícia Univ. Católica. Rio de Janeiro. (Cont. Int.)

Contribuciones. Estudios Interdisciplinarios sobre Desarrollo y Cooperación Internacional. Konrad-Adenauer-Stiftung; Centro Interdisciplinario de Estudios Sobre el Desarrollo Latinoamericano (CIEDLA). Buenos Aires. (Contribuciones/Buenos Aires)

Controversia. Centro de Investigación y Educación Popular (CINEP). Bogotá. (Controversia/Bogotá)

Cuadernos Americanos. Editorial Cultura. México. (Cuad. Am.)

Cuadernos de Arquitectura Mesoamericana. Facultad de Arquitectura, Univ. Nacional Autónoma de México. México. (Cuad. Arquit. Mesoam.)

Cuadernos de Comunicación. Escuela de Comunicación Social, Univ. Católica Andrés Bello. Caracas. (Cuad. Comun.)

Cuadernos de Desarrollo Rural. Instituto de Estudios Rurales, Pontificia Univ. Javeriana. Bogotá. (Cuad. Desarro. Rural)

Cuadernos de Economía. Univ. Nacional de Colombia. Bogotá. (Cuad. Econ./Bogotá)

Cuadernos de Economía. Pontificia Univ.

Católica de Chile, Instituto de Economía. Santiago. (Cuad. Econ./Santiago)

Cuadernos de Geografía. Univ. de Cádiz. Cádiz, Spain. (Cuad. Geogr./Cádiz)

Cuadernos de Historia. Univ. de Chile, Facultad de Humanidades y Educación, Depto. de Ciencias Históricas. Santiago. (Cuad. Hist./Santiago)

Cuadernos de Historia y Arqueología. Casa de Cultura, Núcleo del Guayas. Guayaquil, Ecuador. (Cuad. Hist. Arqueol.)

Cuadernos de Marcha. Eon Editores. Montevideo. (Cuad. Marcha)

Cuadernos de Nuestra América. Centro de Estudios sobre América. La Habana. (Cuad. Nuestra Am.)

Cuadernos del CLAEH. Centro Latinoamericano de Economía Humana. Montevideo. (Cuad. CLAEH)

Cuadernos del Instituto Nacional de Antropología y Pensamiento Latinoamericano. Ministerio de Cultura y Educación. Buenos Aires. (Cuad. Antropol. Pensam. Latinoam.)

Cuadernos Hispanoamericanos. Instituto de Cultura Hispánica. Madrid. (Cuad. Hispanoam.)

Cuadernos Prehispánicos. Seminario de Historia de América, Univ. de Valladolid. Spain. (Cuad. Prehispánicos)

Cuadernos Republicanos. Editorial Cuadernos Republicanos. Asunción. (Cuad. Repub.)

Cuba: Handbook of Trade Statistics. Central Intelligence Agency, Directorate of Intelligence. Washington. (Cuba Handb. Trade Stat.)

Cuba in Transition: Papers and Proceedings of the . . . Annual Meeting of the Association for the Study of the Cuban Economy. Florida International Univ. Miami; Assn. for the Study of the Cuban Economy. Washington. (Cuba Transit.)

Cuban Studies. Univ. of Pittsburgh, Center for Latin American Studies. Pittsburgh, Penn. (Cuba. Stud.)

Cuestiones Políticas. Instituto de Estudios Políticos y Derecho Público, Facultad de Ciencias Jurídicas y Políticas, Univ. de Zulia. Maracaibo, Venezuela. (Cuest. Polít.)

Cultural Anthropology: Journal of the Society for Cultural Anthropology. American Anthropological Assn.; Society for Cultural Anthropology. Washington. (Cult. Anthropol.)

Current Anthropology. Univ. of Chicago. Chicago, Ill. (Curr. Anthropol.)

Current History. Philadelphia, Penn. (Curr. Hist.)

Current Sociology/La Sociologie Contemporaine. International Sociological Assn. Sage Publications. Thousand Oaks, Calif. (Curr. Sociol.)

Dados. Instituto Univ. de Pesquisas. Rio de Janeiro. (Dados/Rio de Janeiro)

Debate Agrario. Centro Peruano de Estudios Sociales (CEPES). Lima. (Debate Agrar.)

Debates en Sociología. Pontificia Univ. Católica del Perú, Depto. de Ciencias Sociales. Lima. (Debates Sociol.)

A Defesa Nacional: Revista de Assuntos Militares e Estudo de Problemas Brasileiros. Rio de Janeiro. (Def. Nac.)

Del Caribe. Casa del Caribe. Santiago, Cuba. (Del Caribe)

Desarrollo Económico. Instituto de Desarrollo Económico y Social. Buenos Aires. (Desarro. Econ.)

Desarrollo y Energía. Instituto de Economía Energética. Río Negro, Argentina. (Desarro. Energ.)

Desarrollo y Sociedad. Univ. de los Andes, Facultad de Economía, Centro de Estudios sobre el Desarrollo Económico (CEDE). Bogotá. (Desarro. Soc.)

Desmemoria. Buenos Aires. (Desmemoria/ Buenos Aires)

Dialectical Anthropology. M. Nijhoff. Dordrecht, The Netherlands. (Dialect. Anthropol.)

Diálogo Andino. Univ. de Tarapacá. Arica, Chile. (Diálogo Andin.)

Diálogo y Debate. Centro de Estudios para la Reforma del Estado. México. (Diálogo Debate)

Documents D'Anàlisi Geogràfica. Dept. de Geografia, Univ. Autònoma de Barcelona. Bellaterra, Spain. (Doc. Anàl. Geogr.)

The Eastern Anthropologist. Ethnographic & Folk Culture Society. Lucknow, India. (East. Anthropol.)

Ecologie Humaine. Laboratorie d'écologie humaine. Aix-en-Provence, France. (Ecol. Hum.)

Economía. Univ. de San Buenaventura. Cali, Colombia. (Economía/Cali)

Economía. Depto. de Economía, Pontificia Univ. Católica del Perú. Lima. (Economía/ Lima)

Economia Internazionale. Instituto de Economia Internazionale. Genova, Italy. (Econ.
Int./Genova)

Economía Mexicana. Centro de Investigación
y Docencia Económicas. México. (Econ.
Mex.)

Economía y Ciencias Sociales. Facultad de
Ciencias Económicas y Sociales, Univ.
Central de Venezuela. Caracas. (Econ.
Cienc. Soc.)

Economía y Desarrollo. Univ. de La Habana,
Instituto de Economía. La Habana. (Econ.
Desarro./Habana)

Economic and Social Progress in Latin America. Inter-American Development Bank.
Washington. (Econ. Soc. Prog. Lat. Am.)

Economic Development and Cultural Change.
Univ. of Chicago, Research Center in Eco-
nomic Development and Cultural Change.
Chicago, Ill. (Econ. Dev. Cult. Change)

Economic Geography. Clark Univ., Worcester, Mass. (Econ. Geogr.)

The Economist. London. (Economist/London)

Ecos. Instituto de Historia, Univ. Autónoma
de Santo Domingo. (Ecos/Santo Domingo)

Ecuador Debate. Centro Andino de Acción
Popular (CAAP). Quito. (Ecuad. Deb.)

Enfoques de Mujer. Grupo de Estudios de la
Mujer Paraguaya, Centro Paraguayo de Es-
tudios Sociológicos. Asunción. (Enfoques
Mujer)

Ensayos sobre Política Económica. Banco de
la República, Depto. de Investigaciones
Económicas. Bogotá. (Ens. Polít. Econ.)

Environmental Management. Springer-Verlag
New York, Inc. New York. (Environ.
Manag.)

Erdkunde. Archiv für Wissenschaftliche Geographie. Univ. Bonn, Geographisches Institut. Bonn, Germany. (Erdkunde/Bonn)

Espace Caraïbe. Maison des Pays Ibériques,
Univ. M. de Montaigne, Bordeaux, France;
Centre d'Études et de Recherches Caraï-
béennes, Univ. des Antilles et de la Guy-
ane, Pointe-à-Pitre, Guadeloupe. (Espace
Caraïbe)

Espacio: Temas de Ciencias Sociales. Escuela
de Ciencias Sociales, Univ. Católica Andrés
Bello. Caracas. (Espac. Temas Cienc. Soc.)

Estadística & Economía. Instituto Nacional
de Estadísticas. Santiago. (Estad. Econ.)

Estudios. Instituto de Estudios Económicos sobre la Realidad Argentina y Latinoamericana; Fundación Mediterránea. Cór-

doba, Argentina. (Estudios/Fundación
Mediterránea)

Estudios. Instituto de Investigaciones Históricas, Antropológicas, y Arqueológicas, Univ.
de San Carlos de Guatemala. Guatemala.
(Estudios/Guatemala)

Estudios. Centro de Estudios Avanzados,
Univ. Nacional de Córdoba, Argentina.
(Estudios/Univ. Córdoba)

Estudios Atacameños. Univ. del Norte, Museo de Arqueología. San Pedro de Atacama,
Chile. (Estud. Atacameños)

Estudios Centro-Americanos: ECA. Univ.
Centroamericana José Simeón Cañas. San
Salvador. (ECA/San Salvador)

Estudios de Economía. Depto. de Economía,
Univ. de Chile. Santiago. (Estud. Econ./
Santiago)

Estudios del Hombre. Depto. de Estudios del
Hombre, Univ. de Guadalajara. Guadalajara, Mexico. (Estud. Hombre)

Estudios Económicos. Univ. Nacional del Sur.
Bahía Blanca, Argentina. (Estud. Econ./Ba-
hía Blanca)

Estudios Económicos. El Colegio de México.
México. (Estud. Econ./México)

Estudios: Filosofía, Historia, Letras. Instituto
Tecnológico Autónomo de México, Depto.
Académico de Estudios Generales. (Estud.
Filos. Hist. Let.)

Estudios Fronterizos. Instituto de Investiga-
ciones Sociales, Univ. Autónoma de Baja
California. Mexicali, Mexico. (Estud.
Front.)

Estudios Geográficos. Instituto de Economía
y Geografía Aplicadas, Consejo Superior de
Investigaciones Científicas. Madrid. (Estud.
Geogr./Madrid)

Estudios Internacionales. Instituto de Estudios Internacionales, Univ. de Chile. Santiago. (Estud. Int./Santiago)

Estudios Internacionales: Revista del IRIPAZ.
Instituto de Relaciones Internacionales y
de Investigaciones para la Paz. Guatemala.
(Estud. Int./IRIPAZ)

Estudios Jaliscienses. Univ. de Guadalajara.
Guadalajara, Mexico. (Estud. Jalisc.)

Estudios Latinoamericanos. Centro de Estudios Latinoamericanos (CELA), UNAM.
México. (Estud. Latinoam./México)

Estudios Latinoamericanos. Academia de
Ciencias de Polonia, Instituto de Historia.
Wrocław. (Estud. Latinoam./Poland)

Estudios Políticos. Facultad de Ciencias Políticas y Sociales, UNAM. México. (Estud. Polít./México)

Estudios Públicos. Centro de Estudios Públicos. Santiago. (Estud. Públicos)

Estudios sobre las Culturas Contemporáneas. Centro Universitario de Investigaciones Sociales, Univ. de Colima. México. (Estud. Cult. Contemp.)

Estudios Sociales. Corporación de Promoción Universitaria. Santiago. (Estud. Soc./Santiago)

Estudios Sociales. Centro de Estudios Sociales Juan Montalvo, SJ. Santo Domingo. (Estud. Soc./Santo Domingo)

Estudios Sociales. El Colegio de Sonora. Hermosillo, Mexico. (Estud. Soc./Hermosillo)

Estudios Sociológicos. Centro de Estudios Sociológicos de El Colegio de México. México. (Estud. Sociol./México)

Estudios y Perspectivas en Turismo. Centro de Investigaciones, Estudios Turísticos. Buenos Aires. (Estud. Perspect. Turismo)

Estudos Afro-Asiáticos. Centro de Estudos Afro-Asiáticos. Rio de Janeiro. (Estud. Afro-Asiát.)

Estudos Avançados. Univ. de São Paulo, Instituto de Estudos Avançados. São Paulo. (Estud. Av.)

Estudos Econômicos. Univ. de São Paulo, Instituto de Pesquisas Econômicas. São Paulo. (Estud. Econ./São Paulo)

Estudos Feministas. CIEC, Escola de Comunicação, Univ. Federal do Rio de Janeiro. (Estud. Fem.)

Estudos Históricos. Centro de Pesquisa e Documentação de História Contemporânea do Brasil da Fundacão Gertulio Vargas. Rio de Janeiro. (Estud. Hist./Rio de Janeiro)

Estudos Ibero-Americanos. Pontifícia Univ. Católica do Rio Grande do Sul, Depto. de História. Porto Alegre, Brazil. (Estud. Ibero-Am./Porto Alegre)

Estudos Leopoldenses. Faculdade de Filosofia, Ciências e Letras. São Leopoldo, Brazil. (Estud. Leopold.)

Estudos Sociedade e Agricultura. Depto. de Letras e Ciências Sociais, Curso de Pós-graduação em Desenvolvimento, Agricultura e Sociedade, Instituto de Ciências Humanas e Sociais, Univ. Federal Ruaral do Rio de Janeiro. (Estud. Soc. Agric.)

Ethnohistory. American Society for Ethnohistory. Duke Univ., Durham, N.C. (Ethnohistory/Society)

Ethnology: An International Journal of Cultural and Social Anthropology. Univ. of Pittsburgh, Penn. (Ethnology/Pittsburgh)

Ethnos. Statens Etnografiska Museum. Stockholm. (Ethnos/Stockholm)

Ethos. Society for Psychological Anthropology; Univ. of California, Los Angeles. (Ethos/Society)

Etnología: Boletín del Museo Nacional de Etnografía y Folklore. La Paz. (Etnología/La Paz)

Etudes créoles. Comité international des études créoles. Montréal. (Etud. créoles)

Etudes Guadeloupéennes. Association guadeloupéenne de recherches et d'études. Abymes, Guadeloupe. (Etud. Guad.)

EURE: Revista Latinoamericana de Estudios Urbanos Regionales. Centro de Desarrollo Urbano y Regional, Univ. Católica de Chile. Santiago. (EURE/Santiago)

Expedition. Univ. Museum, Univ. of Pennsylvania. Philadelphia, Penn. (Expedition/Philadelphia)

The Explorers Journal. New York. (Explor. J.)

Fermentum: Revista Venezolana de Sociología y Antropología. Univ. de los Andes. Mérida, Venezuela. (Fermentum/Mérida)

Filhos da Terra. Núcleo de Pesquisa e Estudos Históricos, Instituto de Filosofia e Ciências Sociais, Univ. Federal do Rio de Janeiro. (Filhos Terr.)

Finance and Development. International Monetary Fund; The World Bank. Washington. (Financ. Dev.)

Focaal: Tijdschrift voor Antropolgie. Stichting Focaal. (Focaal/Nijmegen)

Foreign Affairs. Council on Foreign Relations, Inc. New York. (Foreign Aff.)

Foreign Policy. National Affairs Inc.; Carnegie Endowment for International Peace. New York. (Foreign Policy)

Forest & Conservation History. Forest History Society; Duke Univ. Press. Durham, N.C. (For. Conserv. Hist.)

Forest Ecology and Management. Elsevier Scientific Publishing Company. Amsterdam. (For. Ecol. Manage.)

Foro Internacional. El Colegio de México. México. (Foro Int.)

Foro Político. Instituto de Ciencias Políticas, Univ. del Museo Social Argentino. Buenos Aires. (Foro Polít.)

Forum Libre. Fondation Friedrich Ebert et

Centre Pétion Bolivar. Port-au-Prince. (Forum Libre)

Frontera Norte. Colegio de la Frontera Norte. Tijuana, Mexico. (Front. Norte)

Gaceta Arqueológica Andina. Instituto Andino de Estudios Arqueológicos. Lima. (Gac. Arqueol. Andin.)

Género y Sociedad. Centro de Estudio del Género. Santo Domingo. (Género Soc.)

Geoarchaeology. John Wiley. New York. (Geoarchaeology/New York)

Geofísica Internacional. Univ. Nacional Autónoma de México, Instituto de Geofísica. México. (Geofís. Int.)

Geografia. Associação de Geografia Teorética. Rio Claro, Brazil. (Geografia/Rio Claro)

The Geographical Journal. The Royal Geographical Society. London. (Geogr. J.)

The Geographical Review. American Geographical Society. New York. (Geogr. Rev.)

Geographische Rundschau. Zeitschrift für Schulgeographie. Georg Westermann Verlag. Braunschweig, Germany. (Geogr. Rundsch.)

Geoistmo. Asociación de Profesionales en Geografía de Costa Rica. San José. (Geoistmo/San José)

GeoJournal. D. Reidel Publishing Co., Boston, Mass. (GeoJournal/Boston)

The Geological Society of America Bulletin. Geological Society of America. Boulder, Colo. (Geol. Soc. Am. Bull.)

Geopolítica. Instituto de Estudios Geopolíticos. Buenos Aires. (Geopolítica/Buenos Aires)

Geosul. Depto. de Geociências, Univ. Federal de Santa Catarina. Florianópolis, Brazil. (Geosul/Florianópolis)

Geosur. Asociación Latinoamericana de Estudios Geopolíticos e Internacionales. Montevideo. (Geosur/Montevideo)

Global Environmental Change: Human and Policy Dimensions. Butterworth-Heinemann. Guildford, England. (Glob. Environ. Change)

Global Finance Journal. JAI Press, Greenwich, Conn. (Glob. Financ. J.)

Haïti Information Libre. Haïti solidarité internationale. Paris. (Haïti Inf. Libre)

Harvard Business Review. Graduate School of Business Administration, Harvard Univ., Boston. (Harv. Bus. Rev.)

Hastings International and Comparative Law Review. Univ. of California, Hastings College of the Law. San Francisco, Calif. (Hastings Int. Comp. Law Rev.)

Hemisphere. Latin American and Caribbean Center, Florida International Univ., Miami, Fla. (Hemisphere/Miami)

Herencia. Programa de Rescate y Revitalización del Patrimonio Cultural. San José. (Herencia/San José)

Higher Education. Kluwer Academic Publishers. Dordrecht, Netherlands. (High. Educ.)

Histórica. Pontificia Univ. Católica del Perú, Depto. de Humanidades. Lima. (Histórica/Lima)

Historical Archaeology. Society for Historical Archaeology. Bethlehem, Penn. (Hist. Archaeol.)

History of Religions. Univ. of Chicago. Chicago, Ill. (Hist. Relig.)

Hombre y Ambiente. Ediciones Abya-Yala. Quito. (Hombre Ambient.)

Hombre y Desierto: Una Perspectiva Cultural. Univ. de Antofagasta, Instituto de Investigaciones Antropológicas. Antofagasta, Chile. (Hombre Desierto)

L'Homme. Laboratoire d'anthropologie, Collège de France. Paris. (Homme/Paris)

Horizontes Antropológicos. Programa de Pós-Graduação em Antropologia Social da Univ. Federal do Rio Grande do Sul. Porto Alegre, Brazil. (Horiz. Antropol.)

Hoy es Historia: Revista Bimestral de Historia Nacional e Iberoamericana. Editorial Raíces. Montevideo. (Hoy Hist.)

Human Ecology. Plenum Publishing Corp., New York. (Hum. Ecol.)

Human Organization. Society for Applied Anthropology. New York. (Hum. Organ.)

Humanidades. Editora Univ. de Brasília. (Humanidades/Brasília)

Ibero-Americana: Nordic Journal of Latin American Studies. Institute of Latin American Studies, Univ. of Stockholm. (Ibero-Am./Stockholm)

Ibero-Amerikanisches Archiv. Ibero-Amerikanisches Institut. Berlin. (Ibero-Am. Arch.)

Iberoamericana. Vervuert Verlagsgesellschaft. Frankfurt. (Iberoam./Frankfurt)

Iberoamericana. Univ. of Sofia. Tokyo. (Iberoam./Tokyo)

Index on Censorship. Writers & Scholars International. London. (Index Censorsh.)

Información. Centro de Estudios Históricos y Sociales, Univ. Autónoma de Campeche.

Campeche, Mexico. (Información/Campeche)

L'information géographique. Paris. (Inf. géogr./Paris)

Informe Económico. Banco Nacional de Cuba. La Habana. (Inf. Econ./Habana)

Informe Social Ecuador. Instituto Latinoamericano de Investigaciones Sociales (ILDIS). Quito. (Inf. Soc. Ecuad.)

Integración Latinoamericana. Instituto para la Integración de América Latina. Buenos Aires. (Integr. Latinoam.)

Interciencia. Asociación Interciencia. Caracas. (Interciencia/Caracas)

INTERCOM: Revista Brasileira de Comunicação. Sociedade Brasileira de Estudos Interdisciplinares da Comunicação (INTERCOM). São Paulo. (INTERCOM/São Paulo)

International Affairs. Moscow. (Int. Aff./Moscow)

The International History Review. Univ. of Toronto Press. Downsview, Ontario, Canada. (Int. Hist. Rev.)

International Journal. Canadian Institute of International Affairs. Toronto, Canada. (Int. J./Toronto)

International Journal of Comparative Sociology. York Univ., Dept. of Sociology and Anthropology. Toronto, Canada. (Int. J. Comp. Sociol.)

International Labour Review. International Labour Office. Geneva. (Int. Labour Rev.)

International Migration = Migrations Internationales = Migraciones Internacionales. Intergovernmental Committee for European Migration; Research Group for European Migration Problems; International Organization for Migration. The Hague, Netherlands; Geneva, Switzerland. (Int. Migr.)

International Migration Review. Center for Migration Studies. New York. (Int. Migr. Rev.)

International Organization. World Peace Foundation; Univ. of Wisconsin Press. Madison. (Int. Organ.)

International Social Science Journal. Blackwell Publishers. Oxford, England. (Int. Soc. Sci. J.)

International Studies. Indian School of International Studies. New Delhi, India. (Int. Stud./New Delhi)

Investigación Agraria: Economía. Instituto

Nacional de Investigaciones Agrarias. Madrid. (Invest. Agrar.)

Investigaciones Geográficas. Instituto Universitario de Geografía, Univ. de Alicante. Murcia, Spain. (Invest. Geogr./Murcia)

Iztapalapa. Univ. Autónoma Metropolitana, División de Ciencias Sociales y Humanidades. México. (Iztapalapa/México)

Jahrbuch des öffentlichen Rechts der Gegenwart. Tübingen, Germany. (Jahrb. öffentl. Rechts Gegenwart)

Jahrbuch für Geschichte von Staat, Wirtschaft und Gesellschaft Lateinamerikas. Köln, Germany. (Jahrb. Gesch.)

Jamaica Journal. Institute of Jamaica. Kingston. (Jam. J.)

Journal of American Folklore. American Folklore Society. Washington. (J. Am. Folk.)

Journal of Anthropological Research. Univ. of New Mexico. Albuquerque, N.M. (J. Anthropol. Res.)

Journal of Archaeological Method and Theory. Plenum Pub. Corp. New York. (J. Archaeol. Method Theory)

Journal of Archaeological Research. Plenum Press. New York. (J. Archaeol. Res.)

Journal of Archaeological Science. Academic Press. New York. (J. Archaeol. Sci.)

The Journal of Caribbean History. Caribbean Univ. Press. St. Lawrence, Barbados. (J. Caribb. Hist.)

Journal of Caribbean Studies. Assn. of Caribbean Studies. Coral Gables, Fla. (J. Caribb. Stud.)

Journal of Church and State. J.M. Dawson Studies in Church and State, Baylor Univ., Waco, Tex. (J. Church State)

The Journal of Commonwealth & Comparative Politics. Univ. of London, Institute of Commonwealth Studies. London. (J. Commonw. Comp. Polit.)

Journal of Contemporary History. Sage Publications. London. (J. Contemp. Hist.)

The Journal of Developing Areas. Western Illinois Univ. Press. Macomb, Ill. (J. Dev. Areas)

Journal of Development Economics. North-Holland Publishing Co., Amsterdam, The Netherlands. (J. Dev. Econ.)

The Journal of Development Studies. Frank Cass. London. (J. Dev. Stud.)

Journal of Ethnobiology. Center for Western Studies. Flagstaff, Ariz. (J. Ethnobiol.)

Journal of Field Archaeology. Boston Univ.,

Boston, Mass. (J. Field Archaeol.)

Journal of Geography. National Council of Geographic Education. Menasha, Wis. (J. Geogr.)

Journal of Haitian Studies. Haitian Studies Assn. Boston, Mass. (J. Haitian Stud.)

Journal of Interamerican Studies and World Affairs. Institute of Interamerican Studies, Univ. of Miami. Coral Gables, Fla. (J. Interam. Stud. World Aff.)

Journal of International Economics. Amsterdam. (J. Int. Econ.)

Journal of Latin American Anthropology. American Anthropological Assn. Arlington, Va. (J. Lat. Am. Anthropol.)

Journal of Latin American Lore. Univ. of California, Latin American Center. Los Angeles, Calif. (J. Lat. Am. Lore)

Journal of Latin American Studies. Centers or Institutes of Latin American Studies at the Universities of Cambridge, Glasgow, Liverpool, London, and Oxford. Cambridge Univ. Press. London. (J. Lat. Am. Stud.)

Journal of Marriage and the Family. Univ. of Nebraska-Lincoln. (J. Marriage Fam.)

Journal of Peace Research. International Peace Research Institute, Universitetforlaget. Oslo. (J. Peace Res.)

The Journal of Peasant Studies. Frank Cass & Co., London. (J. Peasant Stud.)

Journal of Political and Military Sociology. Northern Illinois Univ., Dept. of Sociology. DeKalb, Ill. (J. Polit. Mil. Sociol.)

Journal of Political Economy. Univ. of Chicago. Chicago, Ill. (J. Polit. Econ.)

The Journal of Politics. Univ. of Texas Press. Austin. (J. Polit.)

Journal of Social Sciences. Univ. van Suriname. Paramaribo. (J. Soc. Sci./Paramaribo)

Journal of the Royal Anthropological Institute. The Royal Anthropological Institute. London. (J. Royal Anthropol. Inst.)

Journal of the Steward Anthropological Society. Urbana, Ill. (J. Steward Anthropol. Soc.)

Journal of World Prehistory. Plenum Press. New York. (J. World Prehist.)

Lateinamerika Studien. Univ. Erlangen-Nürnberg, Sektion Lateinamerika. Nürnberg, Germany. (Lat.am. Stud./Nürnberg)

The Latin American Anthropology Review. Society for Latin American Anthropology. Fairfax, Va. (Lat. Am. Anthropol. Rev.)

Latin American Antiquity. Society for American Archaeology. Washington. (Lat. Am. Antiq.)

Latin American Indian Literatures Journal. Geneva College. Beaver Falls, Penn. (Lat. Am. Indian Lit. J.)

Latin American Perspectives. Univ. of California. Newbury Park, Calif. (Lat. Am. Perspect.)

Latin American Research Review. Latin American Research Review Board. Univ. of New Mexico, Albuquerque, N.M. (LARR)

Latin American Studies. Univ. of Tsukuba, Special Research Project on Latin America. Sakura-Mura, Japan. (Lat. Am. Stud./Japan)

Latin American Studies. Institute of Latin American Studies. Beijing. (Lat. Am. Stud./Beijing)

Leguas: Revista Argentina de Geografía. Univ. Nacional de Cuyo, Facultad de Filosofía y Letras. Mendoza, Argentina. (Leguas/Mendoza)

Les Dossiers d'Archéologie. Editions Faton. Dijon, France. (Doss. d'Archéol.)

The Low Countries: Arts and Society in Flanders and the Netherlands; a Yearbook. Flemish-Netherlands Foundation Stichting Ons Erfdeel. Rekkem, Belgium. (Low Countries/Rekkem)

Luso-Brazilian Review. Univ. of Wisconsin Press. Madison, Wis. (Luso-Braz. Rev.)

Memoria: Boletín de CEMOS. Centro de Estudios del Movimiento Obrero y Socialista. México. (Memoria/CEMOS)

Meridiano: Revista de Geografía. Centro de Estudios Alexander von Humboldt. Buenos Aires. (Meridiano Rev. Geogr.)

Mesoamérica. Centro de Investigaciones Regionales de Mesoamérica. Antigua, Guatemala. (Mesoamérica/Antigua)

Mexicon. K.-F. von Flemming. Berlin, Germany. (Mexicon/Berlin)

Mitteilungen der österreichischen Geographischen Gesellschaft. Verleger, Herausgeber und Eigentümer. Vienna. (Mitt. österr. Geogr. Ges.)

Montalbán. Univ. Católica Andrés Bello, Facultad de Humanidades y Educación, Institutos Humanísticos de Investigación. Caracas. (Montalbán/Caracas)

Mountain Research and Development. International Mountain Society. Boulder, Colo. (Mt. Res. Dev.)

Mundo Nuevo. Univ. Simón Bolívar, Instituto de Altos Estudios de América Latina. Caracas. (Mundo Nuevo/Caracas)

NACLA: Report on the Americas. North

American Congress on Latin America. New York. (NACLA)

Nariz del Diablo. Centro de Investigaciones y Estudios Socio-Económicos. Quito. (Nariz Diablo)

National Geographic Magazine. National Geographic Society. Washington. (Natl. Geogr. Mag.)

The National Interest. National Affairs. Washington. (Natl. Int.)

Nature: International Weekly Journal of Science. Macmillan Magazines. London. (Nature/London)

Naval War College Review. Newport, R.I. (Nav. War Coll. Rev.)

New Left Review. New Left Review, Ltd., London. (New Left Rev.)

New West Indian Guide/Nieuwe West Indische Gids. KITLV Press. Leiden, The Netherlands. (NWIG)

NewsWARP. Wetland Archaeology Research Project, Fursdon Mill Cottage. Thorverton, England. (NewsWARP/Thorverton)

Notas de Población. Centro Latinoamericano de Demografía. Santiago. (Notas Pobl.)

Nova Economia. Depto. de Ciências Econômicas, Univ. Federal de Minas Gerais. Belo Horizonte, Brazil. (Nova Econ.)

Novedades Económicas. Fundación Mediterránea. Córdoba, Argentina. (Noved. Econ.)

Novos Estudos CEBRAP. Centro Brasileiro de Análise e Planejamento. São Paulo. (Novos Estud. CEBRAP)

Nueva Antropología. Nueva Antropología. México. (Nueva Antropol.)

Nueva Economía. Academia Nacional de Ciencias Económicas. Caracas. (Nueva Econ./Caracas)

Nueva Sociedad. Caracas. (Nueva Soc.)

Nütram. Centro Ecuménico Diego de Medellín. Santiago. (Nütram/Santiago)

Opinião Pública. Centro de Estudos de Opinião Pública (CESOP), Univ. Estadual de Campinas. Brazil. (Opin. Públ.)

Organization. Sage Publications. London. (Organization/London)

OSO. Stichting Instituut ter Bevordering van de Surinamistick (IBS) te Nijmegen. Nijmegen, The Netherlands. (OSO/Netherlands)

El Otro Derecho. Instituto Latinoamericano de Servicios Legales Alternativos (ILSA). Bogotá. (Otro Derecho)

Paisajes Geográficos. Centro Panamericano de Estudios e Investigaciones Geográficas. Quito. (Paisajes Geogr.)

Panorama Centroamericano: Pensamiento y Acción. Instituto Centroamericano de Estudios Políticos (INCEP). Guatemala. (Panorama Centroam. Pensam.)

Panorama Centroamericano: Temas y Documentos de Debate. Instituto Centroamericano de Estudios Políticos (INCEP). Guatemala. (Panorama Centroam. Temas)

Papers and Proceedings of the Applied Geography Conferences. Dept. of Geography, Kent State Univ.; State Univ. of New York (SUNY) at Binghamton. (Pap. Proc. Appl. Geogr. Conf.)

Perfiles Latinoamericanos. Facultad Latinoamericana de Ciencias Sociales. México. (Perf. Latinoam.)

Pesquisa e Planejamento Econômico. Instituto de Planejamento Econômico e Social. Rio de Janeiro. (Pesqui. Planej. Econ.)

Pesquisas. Instituto Anchietano de Pesquisas. São Leopoldo, Brazil. (Pesquisas/São Leopoldo)

Petermanns Geographische Mitteilungen. Justus Perthes. Gotha, Germany. (Petermanns Geogr. Mitt.)

Planeación & Desarrollo. Depto. Nacional de Planeación. Bogotá. (Planeac. Desarro.)

Planejamento e Políticas Públicas. Instituto de Pesquisa Econômica Aplicada (IPEA). Brasília. (Planej. Polít. Públicas)

Plantation Society in the Americas. Univ. of New Orleans. (Plant. Soc. Am.)

Población y Desarrollo. Asociación Dominicana Pro Bienestar de la Familia (PROFAMILIA). Santo Domingo. (Poblac. Desarro.)

Politeia. Instituto de Estudios Políticos, Univ. Central de Venezuela. Caracas. (Politeia/Caracas)

Política. Instituto de Ciencia Política, Univ. de Chile. Santiago. (Política/Santiago)

Política Externa. Paz e Terra. São Paulo. (Polít. Extern./São Paulo)

Política y Estrategia. Academia Nacional de Estudios Políticos y Estratégicos. Santiago. (Polít. Estrateg.)

Política y Gobierno. Centro de Investigación y Docencia Económicas. México. (Polít. Gob.)

Political and Legal Anthropology. American Anthropological Assn., Assn. for Political and Legal Anthropology (a division of AAA). Washington. (PoLAR/Washington)

Political Science Quarterly. Columbia Univ.,

The Academy of Political Science. New York. (Polit. Sci. Q.)

Prehistoria: Revista del Programa de Estudios Prehistóricos. Consejo Nacional de Investigaciones Científicas y Técnicas. Buenos Aires. (Prehistoria/Buenos Aires)

Premissas. Univ. Estadual de Campinas, Núcleo de Estudos Estratégicos. São Paulo. (Premissas/São Paulo)

Presença da Mulher. Editora Liberdade Mulher. São Paulo. (Presença Mulher)

Presencia. Centro de Investigaciones Tecnológicas y Científicas. San Salvador. (Presencia/San Salvador)

Principes. International Palm Society. Lawrence, Kan. (Principes/Lawrence)

Problemas del Desarrollo: Revista Latinoamericana de Economía. Instituto de Investigaciones Económicas, UNAM. México. (Probl. Desarro.)

The Professional Geographer. Assn. of American Geographers. Washington. (Prof. Geogr.)

Propuestas Democráticas. Univ. Nacional de Asunción; Fundación Hanns Seidel. Asunción. (Prop. Democrát.)

Publicaciones. Univ. Nacional de Córdoba, Facultad de Filosofía y Humanidades. Córdoba, Argentina. (Publicaciones/Córdoba)

Pueblos Indígenas y Educación. Ediciones Abya-Yala. Quito. (Pueblos Indíg. Educ.)

Pumapunku. Centro de Investigaciones Antropológicas Tiwanaku. La Paz. (Pumapunku/La Paz)

Quantum. Facultad de Ciencias Económicas y de Administración. Montevideo. (Quantum/Montevideo)

The Quarterly Journal of Economics. Cambridge, Mass. (Q. J. Econ.)

Quaternary Research. Academic Press. New York. (Quat. Res./New York)

Quehacer. Centro de Estudios y Promoción del Desarrollo (DESCO). Lima. (Quehacer/Lima)

Rábida. Patronato Provincial del V Centenario del Descubrimiento. Huelva, Spain. (Rábida/Huelva)

Race & Class. Institute of Race Relations; The Transnational Institute. London. (Race Cl.)

Razón y Fe. La Compañía de Jesús. Madrid. (Razón Fe)

Realidad Económica. Instituto Argentino para el Desarrollo Económico (IADE). Buenos Aires. (Real. Econ./Buenos Aires)

Reforma Agrária. Asociação Brasileira de Reforma Agraria (ABRA). Campinas, Brazil. (Reforma Agrár.)

Relaciones. El Colegio de Michoacán. Zamora, Mexico. (Relaciones/Zamora)

Relaciones Internacionales. Escuela de Relaciones Internacionales, Univ. Nacional. Heredia, Costa Rica. (Relac. Int./Heredia)

Relaciones Internacionales. Centro de Relaciones Internacionales. Facultad de Ciencias Políticas y Sociales, Univ. Nacional Autónoma de México. México. (Relac. Int./México)

Religion and the Social Order. JAI Press; Assn. for the Sociology of Religion. Greenwich, Conn. (Relig. Soc. Order)

Rencontre. CRESFED. Canapé Vert, Haiti. (Rencontre/Haiti)

Res. Peabody Museum of Archaeology and Ethnology, Harvard Univ., Cambridge, Mass. (Res/Harvard)

Research & Exploration. National Geographic Society. Washington. (Res. Explor.)

The Review of Black Political Economy. National Economic Assn.; Atlanta Univ. Center. Atlanta, Ga. (Rev. Black Polit. Econ.)

The Review of Economics and Statistics. Elsvier Science Publishers BV. Amsterdam. (Rev. Econ. Stat.)

Revista Andina. Centro Bartolomé de las Casas. Cusco, Peru. (Rev. Andin.)

Revista Argentina de Estudios Estratégicos. Olcese Editores. Buenos Aires. (Rev. Arg. Estud. Estrateg.)

Revista Bimestre Cubana. Sociedad Económica de Amigos del País. La Habana. (Rev. Bimest. Cuba.)

Revista Brasileira de Ciências Sociais. Associação Nacional de Pós-Graduação e Pesquisa em Ciências Sociais. Rio de Janeiro. (Rev. Bras. Ciênc. Sociais)

Revista Brasileira de Comércio Exterior. Fundação Centro de Estudos do Comércio Exterior. Rio de Janeiro. (Rev. Bras. Comér. Exter.)

Revista Brasileira de Economia. Fundação Getúlio Vargas, Instituto Brasileiro de Economia. Rio de Janeiro. (Rev. Bras. Econ.)

Revista Brasileira de Estudos de População. Associação Brasileira de Estudos Populacionais. São Paulo. (Rev. Bras. Estud. Popul.)

Revista Brasileira de Estudos Políticos. Univ. de Minas Gerais. Belo Horizonte, Brazil. (Rev. Bras. Estud. Polít.)

Revista Brasileira de Geografia. Conselho Nacional de Geografia, Instituto Brasileiro de Geografia e Estatística. Rio de Janeiro. (Rev. Bras. Geogr.)

Revista Brasileira de História. Associação Nacional dos Professores Universitários de História (ANPUH). São Paulo. (Rev. Bras. Hist.)

Revista Brasileira de Política Internacional. Instituto Brasileiro de Relações Internacionais. Rio de Janeiro. (Rev. Bras. Polít. Int.)

Revista Centroamericana de Economía. Univ. Nacional Autónoma de Honduras, Programa de Postgrado Centroamericano en Economía y Planificación. Tegucigalpa. (Rev. Centroam. Econ.)

Revista Chilena de Antropología. Depto. de Antropología, Univ. de Chile. Santiago. (Rev. Chil. Antropol.)

Revista Chilena de Geopolítica. Instituto Geopolítico de Chile. Santiago. (Rev. Chil. Geopolít.)

Revista Chilena de Historia Natural. Valparaíso, Chile: Sociedad de la Biología de Chile. (Rev. Chil. Hist. Nat.)

Revista Chilena de Historia y Geografía. Sociedad Chilena de Historia y Geografía. Santiago. (Rev. Chil. Hist. Geogr.)

Revista Chilena de Humanidades. Facultad de Filosofía, Humanidades y Educación, Univ. de Chile. Santiago. (Rev. Chil. Humanid.)

Revista Ciclos en la Historia, Economía y la Sociedad. Fundación de Investigaciones Históricas, Económicas y Sociales, Facultad de Ciencias Económicas, Univ. de Buenos Aires. Buenos Aires. (Rev. Ciclos)

Revista Colombiana de Antropología. Ministerio de Educación Nacional, Instituto Colombiano de Antropología. Bogotá. (Rev. Colomb. Antropol.)

Revista Colombiana de Sociología. Depto. de Sociología, Univ. Nacional. Bogotá. (Rev. Colomb. Sociol.)

Revista da Escola Superior de Guerra. Escola Superior de Guerra, Divisão de Documentação. Rio de Janeiro. (Rev. Esc. Super. Guerr.)

Revista de Administración Pública. Instituto de Administración Pública. México. (Rev. Adm. Pública/México)

Revista de Análisis Económico. Programa de Postgrado en Economía, ILADES/Georgetown Univ., Santiago. (Rev. Anál. Econ.)

Revista de Arqueología. Zugento Ediciones. Madrid. (Rev. Arqueol./Madrid)

Revista de Arqueologia. Sociedade de Arqueologia Brasileira. São Paulo. (Rev. Arqueol./São Paulo)

Revista de Arqueología Americana. Instituto Panamericano de Geografía e Historia. México. (Rev. Arqueol. Am.)

Revista de Ciencia Política. Instituto de Ciencia Política, Pontificia Univ. Católica de Chile. Santiago. (Rev. Cienc. Polít./Santiago)

Revista de Ciencias Sociales. Facultad de Ciencias, Depto. de Sociología, Fundación de Cultura Universitaria. Montevideo. (Rev. Cienc. Soc./Montevideo)

Revista de Ciencias Sociales. Univ. de Puerto Rico, Colegio de Ciencias Sociales. Río Piedras. (Rev. Cienc. Soc./Río Piedras)

Revista de Economía. Banco de la Provincia de Córdoba. Córdoba, Argentina. (Rev. Econ./Argentina)

Revista de Economía. Banco Central de Uruguay. Montevideo. (Rev. Econ./Uruguay)

Revista de Economia Política. Centro de Economia Política. São Paulo. (Rev. Econ. Polít.)

Revista de Economía y Sociología del Trabajo. Ministerio de Trabajo y Seguridad Social. Madrid. (Rev. Econ. Sociol. Trab.)

Revista de Economía y Trabajo. Programa de Economía del Trabajo. Santiago. (Rev. Econ. Trab.)

Revista de Estudios Europeos. Centro de Estudios sobre Europa Occidental. La Habana. (Rev. Estud. Euro.)

Revista de Geografía Norte Grande. Pontificia Univ. Católica de Chile. Santiago. (Rev. Geogr. Norte Gd.)

Revista de Indias. Consejo Superior de Investigaciones Científicas, Instituto Gonzalo Fernández de Oviedo. Madrid. (Rev. Indias)

Revista de la Integración y el Desarrollo de Centroamérica. Banco Centroamericano de Integración Económica. Tegucigalpa. (Rev. Integr. Desarro. Centroam.)

Revista de la Universidad del Valle de Guatemala. Univ. del Valle de Guatemala. Guatemala. (Rev. Univ. Val. Guatem.)

Revista de la Universidad Nacional de Río Cuarto. Río Cuarto, Argentina. (Rev. Univ. Nac. Río Cuarto)

Revista de Occidente. Madrid. (Rev. Occident.)

Revista de Sociología. Depto. de Sociología, Facultad de Ciencias Sociales, Univ. de Chile. Santiago. (Rev. Sociol./Santiago)

Revista del Banco de la República. Bogotá. (Rev. Banco Repúb./Bogotá)

La Revista del Centro de Estudios Avanzados de Puerto Rico y el Caribe. San Juan. (Rev. Cent. Estud. Av.)

Revista del Museo de Arqueología, Antropología e Historia. Univ. Nacional de Trujillo, Museo de Arqueología. Trujillo, Peru. (Rev. Mus. Arqueol. Antropol. Hist.)

Revista del Museo de Historia Natural de San Rafael. Mendoza, Argentina. (Rev. Mus. Hist. Nat. San Rafael)

Revista del Museo Nacional de Etnografía y Folklore. MUSEF Editores. La Paz. (Rev. Mus. Nac. Etnogr. Folk.)

Revista do BNDES. Banco Nacional de Desenvolvimento Econômico e Social. Rio de Janeiro. (Rev. BNDES)

Revista do CEPA. Centro de Ensino e Pesquisas Arqueológicas, Faculdades Integradas de Santa Cruz do Sul. Santa Cruz do Sul, Brazil. (Rev. CEPA)

Revista do Museu de Arqueologia e Etnologia. Univ. de São Paulo. (Rev. Mus. Arqueol. Etnol.)

Revista Econômica do Nordeste. Banco do Nordeste do Brasil, Depto. de Estudos Econômicos do Nordeste. Fortaleza, Brazil. (Rev. Econ. Nordeste)

Revista Eme-Eme. Univ. Católica Madre y Maestra. Santiago de los Caballeros, Dominican Republic. (Rev. Eme-Eme)

Revista Española de Antropología Americana. Facultad de Geografía e Historia. Univ. Complutense de Madrid. (Rev. Esp. Antropol. Am.)

Revista Europea de Estudios Latinoamericanos y del Caribe = European Review of Latin American and Caribbean Studies. Center for Latin American Research and Documentation; Royal Institute of Linguistics and Anthropology. Amsterdam. (Rev. Eur.)

Revista Geográfica. Univ. de Los Andes. Mérida, Venezuela. (Rev. Geogr./Mérida)

Revista Geográfica. Instituto Panamericano de Geografía e Historia, Comisión de Geografía. México. (Rev. Geogr./México)

Revista Geográfica de Chile. Instituto Geográfico Militar. Santiago. (Rev. Geogr. Chile)

Revista Geográfica Venezolana. Univ. de los Andes. Mérida, Venezuela. (Rev. Geogr. Venez.)

Revista INCAE. Instituto Centroamericano de Administración de Empresas. Alajuela, Costa Rica. (Rev. INCAE)

Revista Interamericana de Bibliografía. Organization of American States. Washington. (Rev. Interam. Bibliogr.)

Revista Internacional de Sociología. Consejo Superior de Investigaciones Científicas. Instituto de Economía y Geografía Aplicadas. Madrid. (Rev. Int. Sociol.)

Revista Javeriana. Provincia Colombiana de la Compañía de Jesús. Bogotá. (Rev. Javer.)

Revista Marítima Brasileira. Serviço de Documentação da Marinha, Ministério da Marinha. Rio de Janeiro. (Rev. Marít. Bras.)

Revista Mexicana de Ciencias Políticas y Sociales. Facultad de Ciencias Políticas y Sociales, Univ. Nacional Autónoma de México. México. (Rev. Mex. Cienc. Polít. Soc.)

Revista Mexicana de Política Exterior. Secretaría de Relaciones Exteriores; Instituto Matías Romero de Estudios Diplomáticos (IMPED). México. (Rev. Mex. Polít. Exter.)

Revista Mexicana de Sociología. Instituto de Investigaciones Sociales, Univ. Nacional Autónoma de México. México. (Rev. Mex. Sociol.)

Revista Militar. Círculo Militar, Buenos Aires. (Rev. Mil.)

Revista Nacional. Ministerio de Instrucción Pública. Montevideo. (Rev. Nac./Montevideo)

Revista Nicaragüense. Managua. (Rev. Nicar.)

Revista Paraguaya de Sociología. Centro Paraguayo de Estudios Sociológicos. Asunción. (Rev. Parag. Sociol.)

Revista/Review Interamericana. Inter-American Univ. Press. Hato Rey, Puerto Rico. (Rev. Rev. Interam.)

Revista UNIBE de Ciencia y Cultura. Univ. Iberoamericana. Santo Domingo. (Rev. UNIBE)

Revista UNITAS. Unión Nacional de Instituciones para el Trabajo de Acción Social. La Paz. (Rev. UNITAS)

Revista Universidad EAFIT. Depto. de Comunicaciones, Univ. EAFIT. Medellín. (Rev. Univ. EAFIT)

Revista Universitaria de Geografía. Univ. Nacional del Sur. Bahía Blanca, Argentina. (Rev. Univ. Geogr.)

Revista USP. Coordenadoria de Comunicação Social (CCS), Univ. de São Paulo. (Rev. USP)

Revue française de science politique. L'Association française de science politique. Paris. (Rev. fr. sci. polit.)

Runa. Archivo para las Ciencias del Hombre;
Univ. de Buenos Aires, Facultad de Filosofía
y Letras, Instituto de Antropología. (Runa/
Buenos Aires)

Ruralia: Revista Argentina de Estudios Agrarios. FLACSO; Ediciones Imago Mundi.
Buenos Aires. (Ruralia/Buenos Aires)

Saguntum: Papeles del Laboratorio de Ar-
queología de Valencia. Univ. de València,
Facultat de Geografia i Història, Depto. de
Prehistòria i Arqueologia. Valencia, Spain.
(Saguntum/Valencia)

Santiago. Univ. de Oriente. Santiago, Cuba.
(Santiago/Cuba)

São Paulo em Perspectiva. Fundação SEADE.
São Paulo. (São Paulo Perspect.)

Sarance. Instituto Otavaleño de Antropología.
Otavalo, Ecuador. (Sarance/Otavalo)

Schweizerische Amerikanisten Gesellschaft.
Société suisse des américanistes. Genève.
(Schweiz. Amer. Ges.)

Science. American Assn. for the Advancement of Science. Washington. (Science/
Washington)

SECOLAS Annals. Southeastern Conference
on Latin American Studies; Thomasson
Printing Co. Carrollton, Ga. (SECOLAS
Ann.)

Secuencia. Instituto Mora. México. (Secuen-
cia/México)

Seguridad, Estrategia Regional en el 2000. Impresión Zona Gráfica. Buenos Aires. (SER/
Buenos Aires)

Senderos. Biblioteca Nacional de Colombia.
Bogotá. (Senderos/Bogotá)

Siglo XIX. Facultad de Filosofía y Letras,
Univ. Autónoma de Nuevo León. Monterrey, Mexico. (Siglo XIX)

Signos Universitarios: Revista de la Universidad del Salvador. Univ. del Salvador. Buenos Aires. (Signos Univ.)

Signs. The Univ. of Chicago Press. Chicago,
Ill. (Signs/Chicago)

Síntesis. Asociación de Investigación y Especialización sobre Temas Latinoamericanos.
Madrid. (Síntesis/Madrid)

Slavery & Abolition. Frank Cass & Co., Ltd.,
London. (Slavery Abolit.)

Social and Economic Studies. Univ. of the
West Indies, Institute of Social and Eco-
nomic Research. Mona, Jamaica. (Soc.
Econ. Stud.)

Social Compass. The International Catholic
Institute for Social-Ecclesiastical Research.
The Hague. (Soc. Compass)

Social Forces. Univ. of North Carolina Press.
Chapel Hill, N.C. (Soc. Forces)

Socialismo y Participación. Ediciones Socialismo y Participación. Lima. (Social.
Particip.)

Sociedade e Estado. Univ. de Brasília, Depto.
de Sociologia. Brasília. (Soc. Estado)

Sociological Perspectives. Pacific Sociological
Assn.; JAI Press, Inc. Greenwich, Conn.
(Sociol. Perspect.)

South Eastern Latin Americanist. South Eastern Council of Latin American Studies.
Boone, N.C. (South East. Lat. Am.)

Southern Economic Journal. Chapel Hill,
N.C. (South. Econ. J.)

Studia Diplomatica. Institut Royal des Relations Internationales. Bruxelles. (Stud.
Dipl.)

Studies in Comparative International Development. Transaction Periodicals Consortium, Rutgers Univ., New Brunswick, N.J.
(Stud. Comp. Int. Dev.)

SWI Forum voor Kunst, Kultuur en Wetenschop. De Stichting. Paramaribo, Suriname.
(SWI Forum)

Tareas. Centro de Estudios Latinoamericanos
(CELA). Panamá. (Tareas/Panamá)

Temas: Cultura, Ideología, Sociedad. Centro
de Estudios Martianos. La Habana. (Temas/
Habana)

Temas de Coyuntura. Instituto de Investigaciones Económicas y Sociales, Univ. Católica Andrés Bello. Caracas. (Temas Coyunt./Caracas)

Tempo Social. Faculdade de Filosofia, Letras
e Ciências Humanas, Depto. de Sociologia,
Univ. de São Paulo. (Tempo Soc./São Paulo)

Textos de História. Pós-Graduação em História, Univ. de Brasília. (Textos Hist./Brasília)

Third World Planning Review. Liverpool
Univ. Press. Liverpool, England. (Third
World Plan. Rev.)

Third World Quarterly. Third World Foundation; New Zealand House. London. (Third
World Q.)

Tierra Firme. Caracas. (Tierra Firme)

Todo es Historia. Buenos Aires. (Todo es
Hist.)

Trace. Centre d'études mexicaines et centraméricaines. México. (Trace/México)

El Trimestre Económico. Fondo de Cultura
Económica. México. (Trimest. Econ.)

Umbrales. Univ. Mayor de San Andrés. La
Paz, Bolivia. (Umbrales/La Paz)

UNISA Latin American Report. Univ. of

South Africa. Pretoria. (UNISA Lat. Am. Rep.)

Universitas Económica. Pontificia Univ. Javeriana, Facultad de Ciencias Económicas y Administrativas. Bogotá. (Univ. Econ.)

Universum. Univ. de Talca. Talca, Chile. (Universum/Talca)

Veritas. Pontificia Univ. Católica do Rio Grande do Sul. Porto Alegre, Brazil. (Veritas/Porto Alegre)

Vínculos. Museo Nacional de Costa Rica. San José. (Vínculos/San José)

Vuelta. México. (Vuelta/México)

Wampum. Archeologisch Centrum. Leiden, The Netherlands. (Wampum/Leiden)

The Washington Quarterly. Georgetown Univ., The Center for Strategic and International Studies. Washington. (Wash. Q.)

Weltwirtschaftliches Archiv. Zeitschrift des Institut für Weltwirtschaft an der Christians-Albrechts-Univ. Kiel. Kiel, Germany. (Weltwirtsch. Arch.)

World Archaeology. Routledge & Kegan Paul. London. (World Archaeol.)

The World Bank Economic Review. World Bank. Washington. (World Bank Econ. Rev.)

World Development. Pergamon Press. Oxford, England. (World Dev.)

The World Economy. Basil Blackwell. London. (World Econ.)

World Policy Journal. World Policy Institute. New York. (World Policy J.)

World Politics. Princeton Univ., Center of International Studies. Princeton, N.J. (World Polit.)

Yachay. Facultad de Filosofía y Ciencias Religiosas, Univ. Católica Boliviana. Cochabamba, Bolivia. (Yachay/Cochabamba)

Yearbook. Conference of Latin Americanist Geographers; Ball State Univ., Muncie, Ind. (Yearbook/CLAG)

Zeitschrift für Ethnologie. Deutschen Gesellschaft für Völkerkunde. Verlag Albert Limbach. Braunschweig, Germany. (Z. Ethnol.)

ABBREVIATION LIST OF JOURNALS INDEXED

For journal titles listed by full title, see *Title List of Journals Indexed*, p. 753.

Acad. Quest. Academic Questions. Transaction Periodicals Consortium, Rutgers Univ., New Brunswick, N.J.

Acervo/Tegucigalpa. Acervo: Revista Hondureña de Cultura. Ministerio de Cultura, Instituto del Libro y el Documento. Tegucigalpa.

Acta geogr. Acta geographica. Société de Géographie. Paris.

Agric. Hist. Agricultural History. Agricultural History Society. Univ. of Calif. Press. Berkeley.

Agrofor. Syst. Agroforestry Systems. Kluwer Academic Publishers. Dordrecht, The Netherlands.

Allpanchis/Cusco. Allpanchis. Instituto de Pastoral Andina. Cusco, Peru.

Am. Anthropol. American Anthropologist. American Anthropological Assn., Washington.

Am. Antiq. American Antiquity. The Society for American Archaeology. Washington.

Am. Econ. Rev. The American Economic Review. American Economic Assn., Evanston, Ill.

Am. Ethnol. American Ethnologist. American Ethnological Society. Washington.

Am. Indíg. América Indígena. Instituto Indigenista Interamericano. México.

Am. J. Sociol. American Journal of Sociology. Univ. of Chicago. Chicago, Ill.

Am. Jew. Arch. American Jewish Archives. Cincinnati, Ohio.

Am. Merid. América Meridional. Sociedad Regional de Ciencias Humanas. Montevideo.

Am. Negra. América Negra. Pontificia Univ. Javeriana. Bogotá.

Amazonía Peru. Amazonía Peruana. Centro Amazónico de Antropología y Aplicación Práctica, Depto. de Documentación y Publicaciones. Lima.

Americas/Francisc. The Americas. Academy of American Franciscan History. Washington.

Amérindia/Paris. Amérindia. Association d'Ethnologistique Amérindienne (AEA). Paris.

An. Asoc. Argent. Econ. Polít. Anales de la Asociación Argentina de Economía Política. Facultad de Ciencias Económicas, Univ. Nacional de Cuyo. Mendoza, Argentina.

An. Inst. Patagon./Hum. Anales del Instituto de la Patagonia: Serie Ciencias Humanas. Univ. de Magallanes. Punta Arenas, Chile.

Anál. Econ./La Paz. Análisis Económico. Ediciones UDAPE (Unidad de Análisis de Políticas Económicas). La Paz.

Anál. Int. Análisis Internacional. Centro Peruano de Estudios Internacionales. Lima.

Analecta Praehist. Leiden. Analecta Praehistorica Leidensia. Leiden Univ. Press. Leiden, The Netherlands.

Anc. Mesoam. Ancient Mesoamerica. Cambridge Univ. Press. Cambridge, England.

Andean Past. Andean Past. Latin American Studies Program, Cornell Univ., Ithaca, N.Y.

Andes/Cusco. Andes: Revista de la Facultad de Ciencias Sociales. Univ. Nacional de San Antonio Abad del Cusco, Facultad de Ciencias Sociales. Cusco, Peru.

Andes/Warsaw. Andes: Boletín de la Misión Arqueológica Andina. Univ. of Warsaw. Warsaw, Poland.

Ann. Assoc. Am. Geogr. Annals of the Association of American Geographers. Lawrence, Kan.

Ann. Carnegie Mus. Annals of the Carnegie Museum. Carnegie Museum of Natural History. Pittsburgh, Penn.

Annu. Rev. Anthropol. Annual Review of Anthropology. Annual Reviews, Inc., Palo Alto, Calif.

Anthropol. Educ. Q. Anthropology and Education Quarterly. Council on Anthropology and Education. Washington.

Anthropol. Q. Anthropological Quarterly. Catholic Univ. of America, Catholic Anthropological Conference. Washington.

Anthropologica/Lima. Anthropologica. Depto. de Ciencias Sociales, Pontificia Univ. Católica del Perú. Lima.

Anthropologie/Paris. L'Anthropologie. Institut de paleontologie humaine. Paris.

Anthropos/Switzerland. Anthropos. International Review of Ethnology and Linguistics. Anthropos-Institut. Freiburg, Switzerland.

Antiquity/Cambridge. Antiquity. A Quarterly Review of Archaeology. The Antiquity Trust. Cambridge, England.

Antropológica/Caracas. Antropológica. Fundación La Salle de Ciencias Naturales; Instituto Caribe de Antropología y Sociología. Caracas.

Anu. Antropol. Anuário Antropológico. Tempo Brasileiro. Rio de Janeiro.

Anu. Cent. Estud. Av. Anuario Centro de Estudios Avanzados. Centro de Estudios Avanzados. Córdoba, Argentina.

Anu. Cienc. Soc. Anuario de Ciencias Sociales. Univ. Autónoma de Aguascalientes, Centro de Artes y Humanidades, Depto. de Sociología y Antropología. Aguascalientes, Mexico.

Anu. Estud. Am. Anuario de Estudios Americanos. Consejo Superior de Investigaciones Científicas; Univ. de Sevilla, Escuela de Estudios Hispano-Americanos. Sevilla, Spain.

Anu. Estud. Centroam. Anuario de Estudios Centroamericanos. Univ. de Costa Rica. San José.

Anu. Estud. Soc. Anuario Estudios Sociales. El Colegio de Puebla. México.

Anu. Etnol./Habana. Anuario de Etnología. Academia de Ciencias de Cuba; Editorial Academia. La Habana.

Anu. IEHS. Anuario IEHS. Univ. Nacional del Centro de la Provincia de Buenos Aires, Instituto de Estudios Histórico-Sociales. Tandil, Argentina.

Anu. Inst. Chiapaneco Cult. Anuario Instituto Chiapaneco de Cultura. Instituto Chiapaneco de Cultura. Tuxtla Gutiérrez, Mexico.

Anuario/Córdoba. Anuario. Univ. Nacional de Córdoba, Facultad de Derecho y Ciencias Sociales, Centro de Investigaciones Jurídicas y Sociales. Córdoba, Argentina.

Anuario/Tuxtla Gutiérrez. Anuario. Centro de Estudios Superiores de México y Centroamérica, Univ. de Ciencias y Artes del Estado de Chiapas. Tuxtla Gutiérrez, Mexico.

Apuntes/Lima. Apuntes. Univ. del Pacífico, Centro de Investigación. Lima.

Arch. Völkerkd. Archiv für Völkerkunde. Museum für Völkerkunde in Wien und von Verein Freunde der Völkerkunde. Vienna.

Archaeoastronomy/England. Archaeoastronomy. Science History Publications. Giles, England.

Archaeol. Anthropol. Archaeology and Anthropology. Ministry of Education and Cultural Development. Georgetown, Guyana.

Archaeology/New York. Archaeology. Archaeology Institute of America. New York.

Archè/Rio de Janeiro. Archè. Faculdades Integradas Candido Mendes, Ipanema. Rio de Janeiro.

Arctic Alpine Res. Arctic and Alpine Research. Institute of Arctic and Alpine Research, Univ. of Colorado. Boulder.

Argent. Ctry. Investm. Growth. Argentina: a country for investment and growth. Ministerio de Economía y Obras y Servicios Públicos. Buenos Aires.

Armed Forces Soc. Armed Forces & Society. Inter-Univ. Seminar on Armed Forces & Society. Univ. of Chicago. Chicago, Ill.

Arq. Mus. Hist. Nat. Arquivos do Museu de História Natural. Univ. Federal de Minas Gerais. Belo Horizonte, Brazil.

Arqueol. Contemp. Arqueología Contemporánea. Programa de Estudios Prehistóricos. Buenos Aires.

Arqueol. Mex. Arqueología Mexicana. Instituto Nacional de Antropología e Historia, Editorial Raíces. México.

Arqueología/México. Arqueología. Instituto Nacional de Antropología e Historia. México.

Banker/London. The Banker. Financial Times Business Publishing Ltd., London.

Beyond Law. Beyond Law = Más Allá del Derecho. Instituto Latinoamericano de Servicios Legales Alternativos. Bogotá.

Biblos/Rio de Janeiro. Biblos: Revista do Departamento de Biblioteconomia e História. Editora da Fundação Univ. do Rio Grande. Rio Grande, Brazil.

Bol. Am. Boletín Americanista. Univ. de Barcelona, Facultad de Geografía e Historia, Depto. de Historia de América. Barcelona.

Bol. Antropol./Antioquia. Boletín de Antropología. Univ. de Antioquia. Medellín, Colombia.

Bol. Estud. Geogr. Boletín de Estudios Geográficos. Univ. Nacional de Cuyo. Mendoza, Argentina.

Bol. Inf./San Cristóbal. Boletín Informativo. Museo de Táchira. San Cristóbal, Venezuela.

Bol. Inf. Techint. Boletín Informativo Techint. Organización Techint. Buenos Aires.

Bol. Integr. Lat.-Am. Boletim de Integração Latino-Americana. Ministério das Relações Exteriores, Subsecretaria-Geral de Asuntos de Integração, Econômicos e de Comercio Exterior, Grupo de Estudos Técnicos. Brasília.

Bol. Lima. Boletín de Lima. Revista Cultural Científica. Lima.

Bol. Mus. Arqueol. Quibor. Boletín del Museo Arqueológico de Quibor. Museo Arqueológico de Quibor. Quibor, Venezuela.

Bol. Mus. Chil. Arte Precolomb. Boletín del Museo Chileno de Arte Precolombino. Santiago.

Bol. Mus. Para. Goeldi. Boletim do Museu Paraense Emílio Goeldi. Nova série: antropologia. Conselho Nacional de Desenvolvimento Científico e Tecnológico, Instituto Nacional de Pesquisas da Amazônia. Belém, Brazil.

Bol. Paul. Geogr. Boletim Paulista de Geografia. Associação dos Geógrafos Brasileiros. Seção Regional de São Paulo. São Paulo.

Bol. Soc. Bras. Direito Int. Boletim da Sociedade Brasileira de Direito Internacional. Univ. de Brasília, Depto. de Ciência Política e Relações Internacionais. Brasília.

Bol. Soc. Chil. Arqueol. Boletín de la Sociedad Chilena de Arqueología. Sociedad Chilena de Arqueología. Santiago.

Bol. Socioecon. Boletín Socioeconómico. Centro de Investigaciones y Documentación Socioeconómico (CIDSE), Univ. del Valle. Cali, Colombia.

Boletín/Bogotá. Boletín del Museo del Oro. Banco de la República. Bogotá.

Bull. Bur. natl. ethnol. Bulletin du Bureau national d'ethnologie. Bureau national d'ethnologie. Port-au-Prince, Haiti.

Bull. East. Caribb. Aff. Bulletin of Eastern Caribbean Affairs. Univ. of West Indies. Cave Hill, Barbados.

Bull. Inst. fr. étud. andin. Bulletin de l'Institut français d'études andines. Lima.

Bull. Int. Anthropol. Ethnol. Res. Bulletin of the International Committee on Urgent Anthropological and Ethnological Research. International Union of Anthropological and Ethnological Sciences. Vienna.

Bull. Lat. Am. Res. Bulletin of Latin American Research. Society for Latin American Studies. Oxford, England.

Bull. Soc. hist. Guadeloupe. Bulletin de la Société d'histoire de la Guadeloupe. Archives départementales avec le concours du Conseil général de la Guadeloupe. Basse-Terre, Guadeloupe.

Bulletin/Geneva. Bulletin. Société suisse des américanistes; Musée et institut d'éthnographie. Geneva.

CAA/Oxford. Computer Applications and Quantitative Methods in Archaeology. BAR. Oxford.

Cad. CEAS. Cadernos do Centro de Estudos e Ação Social (CEAS). Salvador, Brazil.

Cad. Sociol. Cadernos de Sociologia. Univ. Federal do Rio Grande do Sul, Programa de Pós-Graduação em Sociologia. Porto Alegre, Brazil.

Cah. Am. lat. Cahiers des Amériques latines. Paris.

Cah. Outre-Mer. Les Cahiers d'Outre-Mer. Institut de géographie de la Faculté des lettres de Bordeaux; Institut de la France d'Outre-Mer; Société de géographie de Bordeaux. Bordeaux, France.

Camb. Archaeol. J. Cambridge Archaeological Journal. Cambridge Univ. Press. Cambridge, England.

Can. J. Lat. Am. Caribb. Stud. Canadian Journal of Latin American and Caribbean Studies. Univ. of Ottawa. Ontario, Canada.

Caravelle/Toulouse. Caravelle. Cahiers du monde hispanique et luso-brésilien. Univ. de Toulouse, Institute d'études hispaniques, hispano-americaines et luso-brésiliennes. Toulouse, France.

Caribb. Geogr. Caribbean Geography. Univ. of the West Indies, Dept. of Geography. Kingston, Jamaica.

Caribb. J. Sci. Caribbean Journal of Science. Univ. of Puerto Rico. Mayagüez, Puerto Rico.

Caribb. Q. Caribbean Quarterly. Univ. of the West Indies. Mona, Jamaica.

Caribb. Stud. Caribbean Studies. Univ. of Puerto Rico, Institute of Caribbean Studies. Río Piedras.

Caribena/Martinique. Caribena: cahiers d'études américanistes de la Caraïbe. Centre d'études et de recherches archéologiques (CERA). Martinique.

Casa Am. Casa de las Américas. La Habana.

Centroam. Int. Centroamérica Internacional. Facultad Latinoamericana de Ciencias Sociales (FLACSO). San José.

CEPAL Rev. CEPAL Review/Revista de la CEPAL. Naciones Unidas, Comisión Económica para América Latina. Santiago.

Cerám. Cult. Maya. Cerámica de Cultura Maya. Temple Univ., Dept. of Anthropology. Philadelphia, Penn.

Cespedesia/Cali. Cespedesia. Depto. del Valle del Cauca. Cali, Colombia.

Chungará/Arica. Chungará. Univ. del Norte, Depto. de Antropología. Arica, Chile.

Ciênc. Amb. Ciência & Ambiente. Univ. Federal de Santa Maria. Santa Maria, Brazil.

Cienc. Econ./San José. Ciencias Económicas. Instituto de Investigaciones en Ciencias Económicas, Univ. de Costa Rica. San José.

Ciênc. Hoje. Ciência Hoje. Sociedade Brasileira para o Progresso da Ciência. Rio de Janeiro.

Cienc. Hoy. Ciencia Hoy. Asociación Ciencia Hoy; Morgan Antártica. Buenos Aires.

Ciênc. Hum. Rev./Goiânia. Ciências Humanas em Revista. Instituto de Ciências Humanas e Letras, Univ. Federal de Goiás. Goiânia, Brazil.

Cienc. Polít. Ciencia Política. Instituto de Ciencia Política de Bogotá; Tierra Firme Editores. Bogotá.

Cienc. Soc./Santo Domingo. Ciencia y Sociedad. Instituto Tecnológico de Santo Domingo.

Ciênc. Tróp. Ciência & Trópico. Fundação Joaquim Nabuco; Editora Massangana. Recife, Brazil.

Clio Arqueol./Recife. Clio: Série Arqueológica. Univ. Federal de Pernambuco. Recife, Brazil.

Clío/Sinaloa. Clío. Univ. Autónoma de Sinaloa, Escuela de Historia. Culiacán, Mexico.

Colecc. Estud. CIEPLAN. Colección Estudios CIEPLAN. Corporación de Investigaciones Económicas para Latinoamérica. Santiago.

Columbia J. Transnatl. Law. Columbia Journal of Transnational Law. Columbia Univ. School of Law. New York.

Comp. Polit. Comparative Politics. The City Univ. of New York, Political Science Program. New York.

Comp. Polit. Stud. Comparative Political Studies. Sage Publications, Thousand Oaks, Calif.

Comp. Stud. Soc. Hist. Comparative Studies in Society and History. Society for the Comparative Study of Society and History; Cambridge Univ. Press. London.

Comun. Polít. Comunicação & Política. Centro Brasileiro de Estudos Latino-Americanos. Rio de Janeiro.

Conjonction/Port-au-Prince. Conjonction. Bulletin de l'Institut français d'Haïti. Port-au-Prince.

Cont. Int. Contexto Internacional. Instituto de Relações Internacionais, Pontificia Univ. Católica. Rio de Janeiro.

Contemp. Issues. Soc. Sci. Caribb. Perspect. Contemporary Issues in Social Science: a Caribbean Perspective. Univ. of the West Indies, Faculty of Social Sciences, ANSA McAL Psychological Research Centre. St. Augustine, Trinidad.

Contribuciones/Buenos Aires. Contribuciones. Estudios Interdisciplinarios sobre Desarrollo y Cooperación Internacional. Konrad-Adenauer-Stiftung; Centro Interdisciplinario de Estudios Sobre el Desarrollo Latinoamericano (CIEDLA). Buenos Aires.

Controversia/Bogotá. Controversia. Centro de Investigación y Educación Popular (CINEP). Bogotá.

Cuad. Am. Cuadernos Americanos. Editorial Cultura. México.

Cuad. Antropol. Pensam. Latinoam. Cuadernos del Instituto Nacional de Antropología y Pensamiento Latinoamericano. Ministerio de Cultura y Educación. Buenos Aires.

Cuad. Arquit. Mesoam. Cuadernos de Arquitectura Mesoamericana. Facultad de Arquitectura, Univ. Nacional Autónoma de México. México.

Cuad. CLAEH. Cuadernos del CLAEH. Centro Latinoamericano de Economía Humana. Montevideo.

Cuad. Comun. Cuadernos de Comunicación. Escuela de Comunicación Social, Univ. Católica Andrés Bello. Caracas.

Cuad. Desarro. Rural. Cuadernos de Desarrollo Rural. Instituto de Estudios Rurales, Pontificia Univ. Javeriana. Bogotá.

Cuad. Econ./Bogotá. Cuadernos de Economía. Univ. Nacional de Colombia. Bogotá.

Cuad. Econ./Santiago. Cuadernos de Economía. Pontificia Univ. Católica de Chile, Instituto de Economía. Santiago.

Cuad. Geogr./Cádiz. Cuadernos de Geografía. Univ. de Cádiz. Cádiz, Spain.

Cuad. Hispanoam. Cuadernos Hispanoamericanos. Instituto de Cultura Hispánica. Madrid.

Cuad. Hist. Arqueol. Cuadernos de Historia y Arqueología. Casa de Cultura, Núcleo del Guayas. Guayaquil, Ecuador.

Cuad. Hist./Santiago. Cuadernos de Historia. Univ. de Chile, Facultad de Humanidades y Educación, Depto. de Ciencias Históricas. Santiago.

Cuad. Marcha. Cuadernos de Marcha. Eon Editores. Montevideo.

Cuad. Nuestra Am. Cuadernos de Nuestra América. Centro de Estudios sobre América. La Habana.

Cuad. Prehispánicos. Cuadernos Prehispánicos. Seminario de Historia de América, Univ. de Valladolid. Spain.

Cuad. Repub. Cuadernos Republicanos. Editorial Cuadernos Republicanos. Asunción.

Cuba Handb. Trade Stat. Cuba: Handbook of Trade Statistics. Central Intelligence Agency, Directorate of Intelligence. Washington.

Cuba. Stud. Cuban Studies. Univ. of Pittsburgh, Center for Latin American Studies. Pittsburgh, Penn.

Cuba Transit. Cuba in Transition: Papers and Proceedings of the . . . Annual Meeting of the Association for the Study of the Cuban Economy. Florida International Univ. Miami; Assn. for the Study of the Cuban Economy. Washington.

Cuest. Polít. Cuestiones Políticas. Instituto de Estudios Políticos y Derecho Público, Facultad de Ciencias Jurídicas y Políticas, Univ. de Zulia. Maracaibo, Venezuela.

Cult. Anthropol. Cultural Anthropology: Journal of the Society for Cultural Anthropology. American Anthropological Assn.; Society for Cultural Anthropology. Washington.

Curr. Anthropol. Current Anthropology. Univ. of Chicago. Chicago, Ill.

Curr. Hist. Current History. Philadelphia, Penn.

Curr. Sociol. Current Sociology/La Sociologie Contemporaine. International Sociological Assn. Sage Publications. Thousand Oaks, Calif.

Dados/Rio de Janeiro. Dados. Instituto Univ. de Pesquisas. Rio de Janeiro.

Debate Agrar. Debate Agrario. Centro Peruano de Estudios Sociales (CEPES). Lima.

Debates Sociol. Debates en Sociología. Pontificia Univ. Católica del Perú, Depto. de Ciencias Sociales. Lima.

Def. Nac. A Defesa Nacional: Revista de Assuntos Militares e Estudo de Problemas Brasileiros. Rio de Janeiro.

Del Caribe. Del Caribe. Casa del Caribe. Santiago, Cuba.

Desarro. Econ. Desarrollo Económico. Instituto de Desarrollo Económico y Social. Buenos Aires.

Desarro. Energ. Desarrollo y Energía. Instituto de Economía Energética. Río Negro, Argentina.

Desarro. Soc. Desarrollo y Sociedad. Univ. de los Andes, Facultad de Economía, Centro de Estudios sobre el Desarrollo Económico (CEDE). Bogotá.

Desmemoria/Buenos Aires. Desmemoria. Buenos Aires.

Dialect. Anthropol. Dialectical Anthropology. M. Nijhoff. Dordrecht, The Netherlands.

Diálogo Andin. Diálogo Andino. Univ. de Tarapacá. Arica, Chile.

Diálogo Debate. Diálogo y Debate. Centro de Estudios para la Reforma del Estado. México.

Doc. Anàl. Geogr. Documents D'Anàlisi Geogràfica. Dept. de Geografia, Univ. Autònoma de Barcelona. Bellaterra, Spain.

Doss. d'Archéol. Les Dossiers d'Archéologie. Editions Faton. Dijon, France.

East. Anthropol. The Eastern Anthropologist. Ethnographic & Folk Culture Society. Lucknow, India.

ECA/San Salvador. Estudios Centro-Americanos: ECA. Univ. Centroamericana José Simeón Cañas. San Salvador.

Ecol. Hum. Ecologie Humaine. Laboratorie d'écologie humaine. Aix-en-Provence, France.

Econ. Cienc. Soc. Economía y Ciencias Sociales. Facultad de Ciencias Económicas y Sociales, Univ. Central de Venezuela. Caracas.

Econ. Desarro./Habana. Economía y Desarrollo. Univ. de La Habana, Instituto de Economía. La Habana.

Econ. Dev. Cult. Change. Economic Development and Cultural Change. Univ. of Chicago, Research Center in Economic Development and Cultural Change. Chicago, Ill.

Econ. Geogr. Economic Geography. Clark Univ., Worcester, Mass.

Econ. Int./Genova. Economia Internazionale. Instituto di Economia Internazionale. Genova, Italy.

Econ. Mex. Economía Mexicana. Centro de Investigación y Docencia Económicas. México.

Econ. Soc. Prog. Lat. Am. Economic and Social Progress in Latin America. Inter-American Development Bank. Washington.

Economía/Cali. Economía. Univ. de San Buenaventura. Cali, Colombia.

Economía/Lima. Economía. Depto. de Economía, Pontificia Univ. Católica del Perú. Lima.

Economist/London. The Economist. London.

Ecos/Santo Domingo. Ecos. Instituto de Historia, Univ. Autónoma de Santo Domingo.

Ecuad. Deb. Ecuador Debate. Centro Andino de Acción Popular (CAAP). Quito.

Enfoques Mujer. Enfoques de Mujer. Grupo de Estudios de la Mujer Paraguaya, Centro Paraguayo de Estudios Sociológicos. Asunción.

Ens. Polít. Econ. Ensayos sobre Política Económica. Banco de la República, Depto. de Investigaciones Económicas. Bogotá.

Environ. Manag. Environmental Management. Springer-Verlag New York, Inc. New York.

Erdkunde/Bonn. Erdkunde. Archiv für Wissenschaftliche Geographie. Univ. Bonn, Geographisches Institut. Bonn, Germany.

Espac. Temas Cienc. Soc. Espacio: Temas de Ciencias Sociales. Escuela de Ciencias Sociales, Univ. Católica Andrés Bello. Caracas.

Espace Caraïbe. Espace Caraïbe. Maison des Pays Ibériques, Univ. M. de Montaigne, Bordeaux, France; Centre d'Études et de Recherches Caraïbéennes, Univ. des Antilles et de la Guyane, Pointe-à-Pitre, Guadeloupe.

Estad. Econ. Estadística & Economía. Instituto Nacional de Estadísticas. Santiago.

Estud. Afro-Asiát. Estudos Afro-Asiáticos. Centro de Estudos Afro-Asiáticos. Rio de Janeiro.

Estud. Atacameños. Estudios Atacameños. Univ. del Norte, Museo de Arqueología. San Pedro de Atacama, Chile.

Estud. Av. Estudos Avançados. Univ. de São Paulo, Instituto de Estudos Avançados. São Paulo.

Estud. Cult. Contemp. Estudios sobre las Culturas Contemporáneas. Centro Universitario de Investigaciones Sociales, Univ. de Colima. México.

Estud. Econ./Bahía Blanca. Estudios Económicos. Univ. Nacional del Sur. Bahía Blanca, Argentina.

Estud. Econ./México. Estudios Económicos. El Colegio de México. México.

Estud. Econ./Santiago. Estudios de Economía. Depto. de Economía, Univ. de Chile. Santiago.

Estud. Econ./São Paulo. Estudos Econômicos. Univ. de São Paulo, Instituto de Pesquisas Econômicas. São Paulo.

Estud. Fem. Estudos Feministas. CIEC, Escola de Comunicação, Univ. Federal do Rio de Janeiro.

Estud. Filos. Hist. Let. Estudios: Filosofía, Historia, Letras. Instituto Tecnológico Autónomo de México, Depto. Académico de Estudios Generales.

Estud. Front. Estudios Fronterizos. Instituto de Investigaciones Sociales, Univ. Autónoma de Baja California. Mexicali, Mexico.

Estud. Geogr./Madrid. Estudios Geográficos. Instituto de Economía y Geografía Aplicadas, Consejo Superior de Investigaciones Científicas. Madrid.

Estud. Hist./Rio de Janeiro. Estudos Históricos. Centro de Pesquisa e Documentação de História Contemporânea do Brasil da Fundação Gertulio Vargas. Rio de Janeiro.

Estud. Hombre. Estudios del Hombre. Depto. de Estudios del Hombre, Univ. de Guadalajara. Guadalajara, Mexico.

Estud. Ibero-Am./Porto Alegre. Estudos Ibero-Americanos. Pontificia Univ. Católica do Rio Grande do Sul, Depto. de História. Porto Alegre, Brazil.

Estud. Int./IRIPAZ. Estudios Internacionales: Revista del IRIPAZ. Instituto de Relaciones Internacionales y de Investigaciones para la Paz. Guatemala.

Estud. Int./Santiago. Estudios Internacionales. Instituto de Estudios Internacionales, Univ. de Chile. Santiago.

Estud. Jalisc. Estudios Jaliscienses. Univ. de Guadalajara. Guadalajara, Mexico.

Estud. Latinoam./México. Estudios Latinoamericanos. Centro de Estudios Latinoamericanos (CELA), UNAM. México.

Estud. Latinoam./Poland. Estudios Latinoamericanos. Academia de Ciencias de Polonia, Instituto de Historia. Wrocław.

Estud. Leopold. Estudos Leopoldenses. Faculdade de Filosofia, Ciências e Letras. São Leopoldo, Brazil.

Estud. Perspect. Turismo. Estudios y Perspectivas en Turismo. Centro de Investigaciones, Estudios Turísticos. Buenos Aires.

Estud. Polít./México. Estudios Políticos. Facultad de Ciencias Políticas y Sociales, UNAM. México.

Estud. Públicos. Estudios Públicos. Centro de Estudios Públicos. Santiago.

Estud. Soc. Agric. Estudos Sociedade e Agricultura. Depto. de Letras e Ciências Sociais, Curso de Pós-graduação em Desenvolvimento, Agricultura e Sociedade, Instituto de Ciências Humanas e Sociais, Univ. Federal Ruaral do Rio de Janeiro.

Estud. Soc./Hermosillo. Estudios Sociales. El Colegio de Sonora. Hermosillo, Mexico.

Estud. Soc./Santiago. Estudios Sociales. Corporación de Promoción Universitaria. Santiago.

Estud. Soc./Santo Domingo. Estudios Sociales. Centro de Estudios Sociales Juan Montalvo, SJ. Santo Domingo.

Estud. Sociol./México. Estudios Sociológicos. Centro de Estudios Sociológicos de El Colegio de México. México.

Estudios/Fundación Mediterránea. Estudios. Instituto de Estudios Económicos sobre la Realidad Argentina y Latinoamericana; Fundación Mediterránea. Córdoba, Argentina.

Estudios/Guatemala. Estudios. Instituto de Investigaciones Históricas, Antropológicas, y Arqueológicas, Univ. de San Carlos de Guatemala. Guatemala.

Estudios/Univ. Córdoba. Estudios. Centro de Estudios Avanzados, Univ. Nacional de Córdoba, Argentina.

Ethnohistory/Society. Ethnohistory. American Society for Ethnohistory. Duke Univ., Durham, N.C.

Ethnology/Pittsburgh. Ethnology: An International Journal of Cultural and Social Anthropology. Univ. of Pittsburgh, Penn.

Ethnos/Stockholm. Ethnos. Statens Etnografiska Museum. Stockholm.

Ethos/Society. Ethos. Society for Psychological Anthropology; Univ. of California, Los Angeles.

Etnología/La Paz. Etnología: Boletín del Museo Nacional de Etnografía y Folklore. La Paz.

Etud. créoles. Etudes créoles. Comité international des études créoles. Montréal.

Etud. Guad. Etudes Guadeloupéennes. Association guadeloupéenne de recherches et d'études. Abymes, Guadeloupe.

EURE/Santiago. EURE: Revista Latinoamericana de Estudios Urbanos Regionales. Centro de Desarrollo Urbano y Regional, Univ. Católica de Chile. Santiago.

Expedition/Philadelphia. Expedition. Univ. Museum, Univ. of Pennsylvania. Philadelphia, Penn.

Explor. J. The Explorers Journal. New York.

Fermentum/Mérida. Fermentum: Revista Venezolana de Sociología y Antropología. Univ. de los Andes. Mérida, Venezuela.

Filhos Terr. Filhos da Terra. Núcleo de Pesquisa e Estudos Históricos, Instituto de Filosofia e Ciências Sociais, Univ. Federal do Rio de Janeiro.

Financ. Dev. Finance and Development. International Monetary Fund; The World Bank. Washington.

Focaal/Nijmegen. Focaal: Tijdschrift voor Antropolgie. Stichting Focaal.

For. Conserv. Hist. Forest & Conservation History. Forest History Society; Duke Univ. Press. Durham, N.C.

For. Ecol. Manage. Forest Ecology and Management. Elsevier Scientific Publishing Company. Amsterdam.

Foreign Aff. Foreign Affairs. Council on Foreign Relations, Inc. New York.

Foreign Policy. Foreign Policy. National Affairs Inc.; Carnegie Endowment for International Peace. New York.

Foro Int. Foro Internacional. El Colegio de México. México.

Foro Polít. Foro Político. Instituto de Ciencias Políticas, Univ. del Museo Social Argentino. Buenos Aires.

Forum Libre. Forum Libre. Fondation Friedrich Ebert et Centre Pétion Bolivar. Port-au-Prince.

Front. Norte. Frontera Norte. Colegio de la Frontera Norte. Tijuana, Mexico.

Gac. Arqueol. Andin. Gaceta Arqueológica Andina. Instituto Andino de Estudios Arqueológicos. Lima.

Género Soc. Género y Sociedad. Centro de Estudio del Género. Santo Domingo.

Geoarchaeology/New York. Geoarchaeology. John Wiley. New York.

Geofís. Int. Geofísica Internacional. Univ. Nacional Autónoma de México, Instituto de Geofísica. México.

Geogr. J. The Geographical Journal. The Royal Geographical Society. London.

Geogr. Rev.   The Geographical Review. American Geographical Society. New York.

Geogr. Rundsch.   Geographische Rundschau. Zeitschrift für Schulgeographie. Georg Westermann Verlag. Braunschweig, Germany.

Geografía/Rio Claro.   Geografia. Associação de Geografia Teorética. Rio Claro, Brazil.

Geoistmo/San José.   Geoistmo. Asociación de Profesionales en Geografía de Costa Rica. San José.

GeoJournal/Boston.   GeoJournal. D. Reidel Publishing Co., Boston, Mass.

Geol. Soc. Am. Bull.   The Geological Society of America Bulletin. Geological Society of America. Boulder, Colo.

Geopolítica/Buenos Aires.   Geopolítica. Instituto de Estudios Geopolíticos. Buenos Aires.

Geosul/Florianópolis.   Geosul. Depto. de Geociências, Univ. Federal de Santa Catarina. Florianópolis, Brazil.

Geosur/Montevideo.   Geosur. Asociación Latinoamericana de Estudios Geopolíticos e Internacionales. Montevideo.

Glob. Environ. Change.   Global Environmental Change: Human and Policy Dimensions. Butterworth-Heinemann. Guildford, England.

Glob. Financ. J.   Global Finance Journal. JAI Press, Greenwich, Conn.

Haïti Inf. Libre.   Haïti Information Libre. Haïti solidarité internationale. Paris.

Harv. Bus. Rev.   Harvard Business Review. Graduate School of Business Administration, Harvard Univ., Boston.

Hastings Int. Comp. Law Rev.   Hastings International and Comparative Law Review. Univ. of California, Hastings College of the Law. San Francisco, Calif.

Hemisphere/Miami.   Hemisphere. Latin American and Caribbean Center, Florida International Univ., Miami, Fla.

Herencia/San José.   Herencia. Programa de Rescate y Revitalización del Patrimonio Cultural. San José.

High. Educ.   Higher Education. Kluwer Academic Publishers. Dordrecht, Netherlands.

Hist. Archaeol.   Historical Archaeology. Society for Historical Archaeology. Bethlehem, Penn.

Hist. Relig.   History of Religions. Univ. of Chicago. Chicago, Ill.

Histórica/Lima.   Histórica. Pontificia Univ. Católica del Perú, Depto. de Humanidades. Lima.

Hombre Ambient.   Hombre y Ambiente. Ediciones Abya-Yala. Quito.

Hombre Desierto.   Hombre y Desierto: Una Perspectiva Cultural. Univ. de Antofagasta, Instituto de Investigaciones Antropológicas. Antofagasta, Chile.

Homme/Paris.   L'Homme. Laboratoire d'anthropologie, Collège de France. Paris.

Horiz. Antropol.   Horizontes Antropológicos. Programa de Pós-Graduação em Antropologia Social da Univ. Federal do Rio Grande do Sul. Porto Alegre, Brazil.

Hoy Hist.   Hoy es Historia: Revista Bimestral de Historia Nacional e Iberoamericana. Editorial Raíces. Montevideo.

Hum. Ecol.   Human Ecology. Plenum Publishing Corp., New York.

Hum. Organ.   Human Organization. Society for Applied Anthropology. New York.

Humanidades/Brasília.   Humanidades. Editora Univ. de Brasília.

Ibero-Am. Arch.   Ibero-Amerikanisches Archiv. Ibero-Amerikanisches Institut. Berlin.

Ibero-Am./Stockholm.   Ibero-Americana: Nordic Journal of Latin American Studies. Institute of Latin American Studies, Univ. of Stockholm.

Iberoam./Frankfurt.   Iberoamericana. Vervuert Verlagsgesellschaft. Frankfurt.

Iberoam./Tokyo.   Iberoamericana. Univ. of Sofia. Tokyo.

Index Censorsh.   Index on Censorship. Writers & Scholars International. London.

Inf. Econ./Habana.   Informe Económico. Banco Nacional de Cuba. La Habana.

Inf. géogr./Paris.   L'information géographique. Paris.

Inf. Soc. Ecuad. Informe Social Ecuador. Instituto Latinoamericano de Investigaciones Sociales (ILDIS). Quito.

Información/Campeche. Información. Centro de Estudios Históricos y Sociales, Univ. Autónoma de Campeche. Campeche, Mexico.

Int. Aff./Moscow. International Affairs. Moscow.

Int. Hist. Rev. The International History Review. Univ. of Toronto Press. Downsview, Ontario, Canada.

Int. J. Comp. Sociol. International Journal of Comparative Sociology. York Univ., Dept. of Sociology and Anthropology. Toronto, Canada.

Int. J./Toronto. International Journal. Canadian Institute of International Affairs. Toronto, Canada.

Int. Labour Rev. International Labour Review. International Labour Office. Geneva.

Int. Migr. International Migration = Migrations Internationales = Migraciones Internacionales. Intergovernmental Committee for European Migration; Research Group for European Migration Problems; International Organization for Migration. The Hague, Netherlands; Geneva, Switzerland.

Int. Migr. Rev. International Migration Review. Center for Migration Studies. New York.

Int. Organ. International Organization. World Peace Foundation; Univ. of Wisconsin Press. Madison.

Int. Soc. Sci. J. International Social Science Journal. Blackwell Publishers. Oxford, England.

Int. Stud./New Delhi. International Studies. Indian School of International Studies. New Delhi, India.

Integr. Latinoam. Integración Latinoamericana. Instituto para la Integración de América Latina. Buenos Aires.

Interciencia/Caracas. Interciencia. Asociación Interciencia. Caracas.

INTERCOM/São Paulo. INTERCOM: Revista Brasileira de Comunicação. Sociedade Brasileira de Estudos Interdisciplinares da Comunicação (INTERCOM). São Paulo.

Invest. Agrar. Investigación Agraria: Economía. Instituto Nacional de Investigaciones Agrarias. Madrid.

Invest. Geogr./Murcia. Investigaciones Geográficas. Instituto Universitario de Geografía, Univ. de Alicante. Murcia, Spain.

Iztapalapa/México. Iztapalapa. Univ. Autónoma Metropolitana, División de Ciencias Sociales y Humanidades. México.

J. Am. Folk. Journal of American Folklore. American Folklore Society. Washington.

J. Anthropol. Res. Journal of Anthropological Research. Univ. of New Mexico. Albuquerque, N.M.

J. Archaeol. Method Theory. Journal of Archaeological Method and Theory. Plenum Pub. Corp. New York.

J. Archaeol. Res. Journal of Archaeological Research. Plenum Press. New York.

J. Archaeol. Sci. Journal of Archaeological Science. Academic Press. New York.

J. Caribb. Hist. The Journal of Caribbean History. Caribbean Univ. Press. St. Lawrence, Barbados.

J. Caribb. Stud. Journal of Caribbean Studies. Assn. of Caribbean Studies. Coral Gables, Fla.

J. Church State. Journal of Church and State. J.M. Dawson Studies in Church and State, Baylor Univ., Waco, Tex.

J. Commonw. Comp. Polit. The Journal of Commonwealth & Comparative Politics. Univ. of London, Institute of Commonwealth Studies. London.

J. Contemp. Hist. Journal of Contemporary History. Sage Publications. London.

J. Dev. Areas. The Journal of Developing Areas. Western Illinois Univ. Press. Macomb, Ill.

J. Dev. Econ. Journal of Development Economics. North-Holland Publishing Co., Amsterdam, The Netherlands.

J. Dev. Stud. The Journal of Development Studies. Frank Cass. London.

J. Ethnobiol. Journal of Ethnobiology. Center for Western Studies. Flagstaff, Ariz.

J. Field Archaeol. Journal of Field Archaeology. Boston Univ., Boston, Mass.

J. Geogr. Journal of Geography. National Council of Geographic Education. Menasha, Wis.

J. Haitian Stud. Journal of Haitian Studies. Haitian Studies Assn. Boston, Mass.

J. Int. Econ. Journal of International Economics. Amsterdam.

J. Interam. Stud. World Aff. Journal of Interamerican Studies and World Affairs. Institute of Interamerican Studies, Univ. of Miami. Coral Gables, Fla.

J. Lat. Am. Anthropol. Journal of Latin American Anthropology. American Anthropological Assn. Arlington, Va.

J. Lat. Am. Lore. Journal of Latin American Lore. Univ. of California, Latin American Center. Los Angeles, Calif.

J. Lat. Am. Stud. Journal of Latin American Studies. Centers or Institutes of Latin American Studies at the Universities of Cambridge, Glasgow, Liverpool, London, and Oxford. Cambridge Univ. Press. London.

J. Marriage Fam. Journal of Marriage and the Family. Univ. of Nebraska-Lincoln.

J. Peace Res. Journal of Peace Research. International Peace Research Institute, Universitetforlaget. Oslo.

J. Peasant Stud. The Journal of Peasant Studies. Frank Cass & Co., London.

J. Polit. The Journal of Politics. Univ. of Texas Press. Austin.

J. Polit. Econ. Journal of Political Economy. Univ. of Chicago. Chicago, Ill.

J. Polit. Mil. Sociol. Journal of Political and Military Sociology. Northern Illinois Univ., Dept. of Sociology. DeKalb, Ill.

J. Royal Anthropol. Inst. Journal of the Royal Anthropological Institute. The Royal Anthropological Institute. London.

J. Soc. Sci./Paramaribo. Journal of Social Sciences. Univ. van Suriname. Paramaribo.

J. Steward Anthropol. Soc. Journal of the Steward Anthropological Society. Urbana, Ill.

J. World Prehist. Journal of World Prehistory. Plenum Press. New York.

Jahrb. Gesch. Jahrbuch für Geschichte von Staat, Wirtschaft und Gesellschaft Lateinamerikas. Köln, Germany.

Jahrb. öffentl. Rechts Gegenwart. Jahrbuch des öffentlichen Rechts der Gegenwart. Tübingen, Germany.

Jam. J. Jamaica Journal. Institute of Jamaica. Kingston.

LARR. Latin American Research Review. Latin American Research Review Board. Univ. of New Mexico, Albuquerque, N.M.

Lat. Am. Anthropol. Rev. The Latin American Anthropology Review. Society for Latin American Anthropology. Fairfax, Va.

Lat. Am. Antiq. Latin American Antiquity. Society for American Archaeology. Washington.

Lat. Am. Indian Lit. J. Latin American Indian Literatures Journal. Geneva College. Beaver Falls, Penn.

Lat. Am. Perspect. Latin American Perspectives. Univ. of California. Newbury Park, Calif.

Lat. Am. Stud./Beijing. Latin American Studies. Institute of Latin American Studies. Beijing.

Lat. Am. Stud./Japan. Latin American Studies. Univ. of Tsukuba, Special Research Project on Latin America. Sakura-Mura, Japan.

Lat.am. Stud./Nürnberg. Lateinamerika Studien. Univ. Erlangen-Nürnberg, Sektion Lateinamerika. Nürnberg, Germany.

Leguas/Mendoza. Leguas: Revista Argentina de Geografía. Univ. Nacional de Cuyo, Facultad de Filosofía y Letras. Mendoza, Argentina.

Low Countries/Rekkem. The Low Countries: Arts and Society in Flanders and the Netherlands; a Yearbook. Flemish-Netherlands Foundation Stichting Ons Erfdeel. Rekkem, Belgium.

Luso-Braz. Rev. Luso-Brazilian Review. Univ. of Wisconsin Press. Madison, Wis.

Memoria/CEMOS. Memoria: Boletín de CEMOS. Centro de Estudios del Movimiento Obrero y Socialista. México.

Meridiano Rev. Geogr. Meridiano: Revista de Geografía. Centro de Estudios Alexander von Humboldt. Buenos Aires.

Mesoamérica/Antigua. Mesoamérica. Centro de Investigaciones Regionales de Mesoamérica. Antigua, Guatemala.

Mexicon/Berlin. Mexicon. K.-F. von Flemming. Berlin, Germany.

Mitt. österr. Geogr. Ges. Mitteilungen der österreichischen Geographischen Gesellschaft. Verleger, Herausgeber und Eigentümer. Vienna.

Montalbán/Caracas. Montalbán. Univ. Católica Andrés Bello, Facultad de Humanidades y Educación, Institutos Humanísticos de Investigación. Caracas.

Mt. Res. Dev. Mountain Research and Development. International Mountain Society. Boulder, Colo.

Mundo Nuevo/Caracas. Mundo Nuevo. Univ. Simón Bolívar, Instituto de Altos Estudios de América Latina. Caracas.

NACLA. NACLA: Report on the Americas. North American Congress on Latin America. New York.

Nariz Diablo. Nariz del Diablo. Centro de Investigaciones y Estudios Socio-Económicos. Quito.

Natl. Geogr. Mag. National Geographic Magazine. National Geographic Society. Washington.

Natl. Int. The National Interest. National Affairs. Washington.

Nature/London. Nature: International Weekly Journal of Science. Macmillan Magazines. London.

Nav. War Coll. Rev. Naval War College Review. Newport, R.I.

New Left Rev. New Left Review. New Left Review, Ltd., London.

NewsWARP/Thorverton. NewsWARP. Wetland Archaeology Research Project, Fursdon Mill Cottage. Thorverton, England.

Notas Pobl. Notas de Población. Centro Latinoamericano de Demografía. Santiago.

Nova Econ. Nova Economia. Depto. de Ciências Econômicas, Univ. Federal de Minas Gerais. Belo Horizonte, Brazil.

Noved. Econ. Novedades Económicas. Fundación Mediterránea. Córdoba, Argentina.

Novos Estud. CEBRAP. Novos Estudos CEBRAP. Centro Brasileiro de Análise e Planejamento. São Paulo.

Nueva Antropol. Nueva Antropología. Nueva Antropología. México.

Nueva Econ./Caracas. Nueva Economía. Academia Nacional de Ciencias Económicas. Caracas.

Nueva Soc. Nueva Sociedad. Caracas.

Nütram/Santiago. Nütram. Centro Ecuménico Diego de Medellín. Santiago.

NWIG. New West Indian Guide/Nieuwe West Indische Gids. KITLV Press. Leiden, The Netherlands.

Opin. Públ. Opinião Pública. Centro de Estudos de Opinião Pública (CESOP), Univ. Estadual de Campinas. Brazil.

Organization/London. Organization. Sage Publications. London.

OSO/Netherlands. OSO. Stichting Instituut ter Bevordering van de Surinamistick (IBS) te Nijmegen. Nijmegen, The Netherlands.

Otro Derecho. El Otro Derecho. Instituto Latinoamericano de Servicios Legales Alternativos (ILSA). Bogotá.

Paisajes Geogr. Paisajes Geográficos. Centro Panamericano de Estudios e Investigaciones Geográficas. Quito.

Panorama Centroam. Pensam. Panorama Centroamericano: Pensamiento y Acción. Instituto Centroamericano de Estudios Políticos (INCEP). Guatemala.

Panorama Centroam. Temas. Panorama Centroamericano: Temas y Documentos de Debate. Instituto Centroamericano de Estudios Políticos (INCEP). Guatemala.

Pap. Proc. Appl. Geogr. Conf. Papers and Proceedings of the Applied Geography Conferences. Dept. of Geography, Kent State Univ.; State Univ. of New York (SUNY) at Binghamton.

Perf. Latinoam. Perfiles Latinoamericanos. Facultad Latinoamericana de Ciencias Sociales. México.

Pesqui. Planej. Econ. Pesquisa e Planejamento Econômico. Instituto de Planejamento Econômico e Social. Rio de Janeiro.

Pesquisas/São Leopoldo. Pesquisas. Instituto Anchietano de Pesquisas. São Leopoldo, Brazil.

Petermanns Geogr. Mitt. Petermanns Geographische Mitteilungen. Justus Perthes. Gotha, Germany.

Planeac. Desarro. Planeación & Desarrollo. Depto. Nacional de Planeación. Bogotá.

Planej. Polít. Públicas. Planejamento e Políticas Públicas. Instituto de Pesquisa Econômica Aplicada (IPEA). Brasília.

Plant. Soc. Am. Plantation Society in the Americas. Univ. of New Orleans.

Poblac. Desarro. Población y Desarrollo. Asociación Dominicana Pro Bienestar de la Familia (PROFAMILIA). Santo Domingo.

PoLAR/Washington. Political and Legal Anthropology. American Anthropological Assn., Assn. for Political and Legal Anthropology (a division of AAA). Washington.

Polít. Estrateg. Política y Estrategia. Academia Nacional de Estudios Políticos y Estratégicos. Santiago.

Polít. Extern./São Paulo. Política Externa. Paz e Terra. São Paulo.

Polít. Gob. Política y Gobierno. Centro de Investigación y Docencia Económicas. México.

Polit. Sci. Q. Political Science Quarterly. Columbia Univ., The Academy of Political Science. New York.

Politeia/Caracas. Politeia. Instituto de Estudios Políticos, Univ. Central de Venezuela. Caracas.

Política/Santiago. Política. Instituto de Ciencia Política, Univ. de Chile. Santiago.

Prehistoria/Buenos Aires. Prehistoria: Revista del Programa de Estudios Prehistóricos. Consejo Nacional de Investigaciones Científicas y Técnicas. Buenos Aires.

Premissas/São Paulo. Premissas. Univ. Estadual de Campinas, Núcleo de Estudos Estratégicos. São Paulo.

Presença Mulher. Presença da Mulher. Editora Liberdade Mulher. São Paulo.

Presencia/San Salvador. Presencia. Centro de Investigaciones Tecnológicas y Científicas. San Salvador.

Principes/Lawrence. Principes. International Palm Society. Lawrence, Kan.

Probl. Desarro. Problemas del Desarrollo: Revista Latinoamericana de Economía. Instituto de Investigaciones Económicas, UNAM. México.

Prof. Geogr. The Professional Geographer. Assn. of American Geographers. Washington.

Prop. Democrát. Propuestas Democráticas. Univ. Nacional de Asunción; Fundación Hanns Seidel. Asunción.

Publicaciones/Córdoba. Publicaciones. Univ. Nacional de Córdoba, Facultad de Filosofía y Humanidades. Córdoba, Argentina.

Pueblos Indíg. Educ. Pueblos Indígenas y Educación. Ediciones Abya-Yala. Quito.

Pumapunku/La Paz. Pumapunku. Centro de Investigaciones Antropológicas Tiwanaku. La Paz.

Q. J. Econ. The Quarterly Journal of Economics. Cambridge, Mass.

Quantum/Montevideo. Quantum. Facultad de Ciencias Económicas y de Administración. Montevideo.

Quat. Res./New York. Quaternary Research. Academic Press. New York.

Quehacer/Lima. Quehacer. Centro de Estudios y Promoción del Desarrollo (DESCO). Lima.

Rábida/Huelva. Rábida. Patronato Provincial del V Centenario del Descubrimiento. Huelva, Spain.

Race Cl. Race & Class. Institute of Race Relations; The Transnational Institute. London.

Razón Fe. Razón y Fe. La Compañía de Jesús. Madrid.

Real. Econ./Buenos Aires. Realidad Económica. Instituto Argentino para el Desarrollo Económico (IADE). Buenos Aires.

Reforma Agrár. Reforma Agrária. Asociação Brasileira de Reforma Agraria (ABRA). Campinas, Brazil.

Relac. Int./Heredia. Relaciones Internacionales. Escuela de Relaciones Internacionales, Univ. Nacional. Heredia, Costa Rica.

Relac. Int./México. Relaciones Internacionales. Centro de Relaciones Internacionales. Facultad de Ciencias Políticas y Sociales, Univ. Nacional Autónoma de México. México.

Relaciones/Zamora. Relaciones. El Colegio de Michoacán. Zamora, Mexico.

Relig. Soc. Order. Religion and the Social Order. JAI Press; Assn. for the Sociology of Religion. Greenwich, Conn.

Rencontre/Haiti. Rencontre. CRESFED. Canapé Vert, Haiti.

Res. Explor. Research & Exploration. National Geographic Society. Washington.

Res/Harvard. Res. Peabody Museum of Archaeology and Ethnology, Harvard Univ., Cambridge, Mass.

Rev. Adm. Pública/México. Revista de Administración Pública. Instituto de Administración Pública. México.

Rev. Anál. Econ. Revista de Análisis Económico. Programa de Postgrado en Economía, ILADES/Georgetown Univ., Santiago.

Rev. Andin. Revista Andina. Centro Bartolomé de las Casas. Cusco, Peru.

Rev. Arg. Estud. Estrateg. Revista Argentina de Estudios Estratégicos. Olcese Editores. Buenos Aires.

Rev. Arqueol. Am. Revista de Arqueología Americana. Instituto Panamericano de Geografía e Historia. México.

Rev. Arqueol./Madrid. Revista de Arqueología. Zugento Ediciones. Madrid.

Rev. Arqueol./São Paulo. Revista de Arqueologia. Sociedade de Arqueologia Brasileira. São Paulo.

Rev. Banco Repúb./Bogotá. Revista del Banco de la República. Bogotá.

Rev. Bimest. Cuba. Revista Bimestre Cubana. Sociedad Económica de Amigos del País. La Habana.

Rev. Black Polit. Econ. The Review of Black Political Economy. National Economic Assn.; Atlanta Univ. Center. Atlanta, Ga.

Rev. BNDES. Revista do BNDES. Banco Nacional de Desenvolvimento Econômico e Social. Rio de Janeiro.

Rev. Bras. Ciênc. Sociais. Revista Brasileira de Ciências Sociais. Associação Nacional de Pós-Graduação e Pesquisa em Ciências Sociais. Rio de Janeiro.

Rev. Bras. Comér. Exter. Revista Brasileira de Comércio Exterior. Fundação Centro de Estudos do Comércio Exterior. Rio de Janeiro.

Rev. Bras. Econ. Revista Brasileira de Economia. Fundação Getúlio Vargas, Instituto Brasileiro de Economia. Rio de Janeiro.

Rev. Bras. Estud. Polít. Revista Brasileira de Estudos Políticos. Univ. de Minas Gerais. Belo Horizonte, Brazil.

Rev. Bras. Estud. Popul. Revista Brasileira de Estudos de População. Associação Brasileira de Estudos Populacionais. São Paulo.

Rev. Bras. Geogr. Revista Brasileira de Geografia. Conselho Nacional de Geografia, Instituto Brasileiro de Geografia e Estatística. Rio de Janeiro.

Rev. Bras. Hist. Revista Brasileira de História. Associação Nacional dos Professores Universitários de História (ANPUH). São Paulo.

Rev. Bras. Polít. Int. Revista Brasileira de Política Internacional. Instituto Brasileiro de Relações Internacionais. Rio de Janeiro.

Rev. Cent. Estud. Av. La Revista del Centro de Estudios Avanzados de Puerto Rico y el Caribe. San Juan.

Rev. Centroam. Econ. Revista Centroamericana de Economía. Univ. Nacional Autónoma de Honduras, Programa de Postgrado Centroamericano en Economía y Planificación. Tegucigalpa.

Rev. CEPA. Revista do CEPA. Centro de Ensino e Pesquisas Arqueológicas, Faculdades Integradas de Santa Cruz do Sul. Santa Cruz do Sul, Brazil.

Rev. Chil. Antropol. Revista Chilena de Antropología. Depto. de Antropología, Univ. de Chile. Santiago.

Rev. Chil. Geopolít. Revista Chilena de Geopolítica. Instituto Geopolítico de Chile. Santiago.

Rev. Chil. Hist. Geogr. Revista Chilena de Historia y Geografía. Sociedad Chilena de Historia y Geografía. Santiago.

Rev. Chil. Hist. Nat. Revista Chilena de Historia Natural. Valparaíso, Chile: Sociedad de la Biología de Chile.

Rev. Chil. Humanid. Revista Chilena de Humanidades. Facultad de Filosofía, Humanidades y Educación, Univ. de Chile. Santiago.

Rev. Ciclos. Revista Ciclos en la Historia, Economía y la Sociedad. Fundación de Investigaciones Históricas, Económicas y Sociales, Facultad de Ciencias Económicas, Univ. de Buenos Aires. Buenos Aires.

Rev. Cienc. Polít./Santiago. Revista de Ciencia Política. Instituto de Ciencia Política, Pontificia Univ. Católica de Chile. Santiago.

Rev. Cienc. Soc./Montevideo. Revista de Ciencias Sociales. Facultad de Ciencias, Depto. de Sociología, Fundación de Cultura Universitaria. Montevideo.

Rev. Cienc. Soc./Río Piedras. Revista de Ciencias Sociales. Univ. de Puerto Rico, Colegio de Ciencias Sociales. Río Piedras.

Rev. Colomb. Antropol. Revista Colombiana de Antropología. Ministerio de Educación Nacional, Instituto Colombiano de Antropología. Bogotá.

Rev. Colomb. Sociol. Revista Colombiana de Sociología. Depto. de Sociología, Univ. Nacional. Bogotá.

Rev. Econ./Argentina. Revista de Economía. Banco de la Provincia de Córdoba. Córdoba, Argentina.

Rev. Econ. Nordeste. Revista Econômica do Nordeste. Banco do Nordeste do Brasil, Depto. de Estudos Econômicos do Nordeste. Fortaleza, Brazil.

Rev. Econ. Polít. Revista de Economia Política. Centro de Economia Política. São Paulo.

Rev. Econ. Sociol. Trab. Revista de Economía y Sociología del Trabajo. Ministerio de Trabajo y Seguridad Social. Madrid.

Rev. Econ. Stat. The Review of Economics and Statistics. Elsvier Science Publishers BV. Amsterdam.

Rev. Econ. Trab. Revista de Economía y Trabajo. Programa de Economía del Trabajo. Santiago.

Rev. Econ./Uruguay. Revista de Economía. Banco Central de Uruguay. Montevideo.

Rev. Eme-Eme. Revista Eme-Eme. Univ. Católica Madre y Maestra. Santiago de los Caballeros, Dominican Republic.

Rev. Esc. Super. Guerr. Revista da Escola Superior de Guerra. Escola Superior de Guerra, Divisão de Documentação. Rio de Janeiro.

Rev. Esp. Antropol. Am. Revista Española de Antropología Americana. Facultad de Geografía e Historia. Univ. Complutense de Madrid.

Rev. Estud. Euro. Revista de Estudios Europeos. Centro de Estudios sobre Europa Occidental. La Habana.

Rev. Eur. Revista Europea de Estudios Latinoamericanos y del Caribe = European Review of Latin American and Caribbean Studies. Center for Latin American Research and Documentation; Royal Institute of Linguistics and Anthropology. Amsterdam.

Rev. fr. sci. polit. Revue française de science politique. L'Association française de science politique. Paris.

Rev. Geogr. Chile. Revista Geográfica de Chile. Instituto Geográfico Militar. Santiago.

Rev. Geogr./Mérida. Revista Geográfica. Univ. de Los Andes. Mérida, Venezuela.

Rev. Geogr./México. Revista Geográfica. Instituto Panamericano de Geografía e Historia, Comisión de Geografía. México.

Rev. Geogr. Norte Gd. Revista de Geografía Norte Grande. Pontificia Univ. Católica de Chile. Santiago.

Rev. Geogr. Venez. Revista Geográfica Venezolana. Univ. de los Andes. Mérida, Venezuela.

Rev. INCAE. Revista INCAE. Instituto Centroamericano de Administración de Empresas. Alajuela, Costa Rica.

Rev. Indias. Revista de Indias. Consejo Superior de Investigaciones Científicas, Instituto Gonzalo Fernández de Oviedo. Madrid.

Rev. Int. Sociol. Revista Internacional de Sociología. Consejo Superior de Investigaciones Científicas. Instituto de Economía y Geografía Aplicadas. Madrid.

Rev. Integr. Desarro. Centroam. Revista de la Integración y el Desarrollo de Centroamérica. Banco Centroamericano de Integración Económica. Tegucigalpa.

Rev. Interam. Bibliogr. Revista Interamericana de Bibliografía. Organization of American States. Washington.

Rev. Javer. Revista Javeriana. Provincia Colombiana de la Compañía de Jesús. Bogotá.

Rev. Marít. Bras. Revista Marítima Brasileira. Serviço de Documentação da Marinha, Ministério da Marinha. Rio de Janeiro.

Rev. Mex. Cienc. Polít. Soc. Revista Mexicana de Ciencias Políticas y Sociales. Facultad de Ciencias Políticas y Sociales, Univ. Nacional Autónoma de México. México.

Rev. Mex. Polít. Exter. Revista Mexicana de Política Exterior. Secretaría de Relaciones Exteriores; Instituto Matías Romero de Estudios Diplomáticos (IMPED). México.

Rev. Mex. Sociol. Revista Mexicana de Sociología. Instituto de Investigaciones Sociales, Univ. Nacional Autónoma de México. México.

Rev. Mil. Revista Militar. Círculo Militar, Buenos Aires.

Rev. Mus. Arqueol. Antropol. Hist. Revista del Museo de Arqueología, Antropología e Historia. Univ. Nacional de Trujillo, Museo de Arqueología. Trujillo, Peru.

Rev. Mus. Arqueol. Etnol. Revista do Museu de Arqueologia e Etnologia. Univ. de São Paulo.

Rev. Mus. Hist. Nat. San Rafael. Revista del Museo de Historia Natural de San Rafael. Mendoza, Argentina.

Rev. Mus. Nac. Etnogr. Folk. Revista del Museo Nacional de Etnografía y Folklore. MUSEF Editores. La Paz.

Rev. Nac./Montevideo. Revista Nacional. Ministerio de Instrucción Pública. Montevideo.

Rev. Nicar. Revista Nicaragüense. Managua.

Rev. Occident. Revista de Occidente. Madrid.

Rev. Parag. Sociol. Revista Paraguaya de Sociología. Centro Paraguayo de Estudios Sociológicos. Asunción.

Rev. Rev. Interam. Revista/Review Interamericana. Inter-American Univ. Press. Hato Rey, Puerto Rico.

Rev. Sociol./Santiago. Revista de Sociología. Depto. de Sociología, Facultad de Ciencias Sociales, Univ. de Chile. Santiago.

Rev. UNIBE. Revista UNIBE de Ciencia y Cultura. Univ. Iberoamericana. Santo Domingo.

Rev. UNITAS. Revista UNITAS. Unión Nacional de Instituciones para el Trabajo de Acción Social. La Paz.

Rev. Univ. EAFIT. Revista Universidad EAFIT. Depto. de Comunicaciones, Univ. EAFIT. Medellín.

Rev. Univ. Geogr. Revista Universitaria de Geografía. Univ. Nacional del Sur. Bahía Blanca, Argentina.

Rev. Univ. Nac. Río Cuarto. Revista de la Universidad Nacional de Río Cuarto. Río Cuarto, Argentina.

Rev. Univ. Val. Guatem. Revista de la Universidad del Valle de Guatemala. Univ. del Valle de Guatemala. Guatemala.

Rev. USP. Revista USP. Coordenadoria de Comunicação Social (CCS), Univ. de São Paulo.

Runa/Buenos Aires. Runa. Archivo para las Ciencias del Hombre; Univ. de Buenos Aires, Facultad de Filosofía y Letras, Instituto de Antropología.

Ruralia/Buenos Aires. Ruralia: Revista Argentina de Estudios Agrarios. FLACSO; Ediciones Imago Mundi. Buenos Aires.

Saguntum/Valencia. Saguntum: Papeles del Laboratorio de Arqueología de Valencia. Univ. de València, Facultat de Geografia i Història, Depto. de Prehistòria i Arqueologia. Valencia, Spain.

Santiago/Cuba. Santiago. Univ. de Oriente. Santiago, Cuba.

São Paulo Perspect. São Paulo em Perspectiva. Fundação SEADE. São Paulo.

Sarance/Otavalo. Sarance. Instituto Otavaleño de Antropología. Otavalo, Ecuador.

Schweiz. Amer. Ges. Schweizerische Amerikanisten Gesellschaft. Société suisse des
américanistes. Genève.

Science/Washington. Science. American
Assn. for the Advancement of Science.
Washington.

SECOLAS Ann. SECOLAS Annals. Southeastern Conference on Latin American Studies; Thomasson Printing Co. Carrollton, Ga.

Secuencia/México. Secuencia. Instituto
Mora. México.

Senderos/Bogotá. Senderos. Biblioteca Nacional de Colombia. Bogotá.

SER/Buenos Aires. Seguridad, Estrategia
Regional en el 2000. Impresión Zona Gráfica.
Buenos Aires.

Siglo XIX. Siglo XIX. Facultad de Filosofía
y Letras, Univ. Autónoma de Nuevo León.
Monterrey, Mexico.

Signos Univ. Signos Universitarios: Revista
de la Universidad del Salvador. Univ. del Salvador. Buenos Aires.

Signs/Chicago. Signs. The Univ. of Chicago
Press. Chicago, Ill.

Síntesis/Madrid. Síntesis. Asociación de
Investigación y Especialización sobre Temas
Latinoamericanos. Madrid.

Slavery Abolit. Slavery & Abolition. Frank
Cass & Co., Ltd., London.

Soc. Compass. Social Compass. The International Catholic Institute for Social-Ecclesiastical Research. The Hague.

Soc. Econ. Stud. Social and Economic Studies. Univ. of the West Indies, Institute of Social and Economic Research. Mona, Jamaica.

Soc. Estado. Sociedade e Estado. Univ. de
Brasília, Depto. de Sociologia. Brasília.

Soc. Forces. Social Forces. Univ. of North
Carolina Press. Chapel Hill, N.C.

Social. Particip. Socialismo y Participación.
Ediciones Socialismo y Participación. Lima.

Sociol. Perspect. Sociological Perspectives.
Pacific Sociological Assn.; JAI Press, Inc.
Greenwich, Conn.

South East. Lat. Am. South Eastern Latin
Americanist. South Eastern Council of Latin
American Studies. Boone, N.C.

South. Econ. J. Southern Economic Journal.
Chapel Hill, N.C.

Stud. Comp. Int. Dev. Studies in Compara-
tive International Development. Transaction
Periodicals Consortium, Rutgers Univ., New
Brunswick, N.J.

Stud. Dipl. Studia Diplomatica. Institut
Royal des Relations Internationales.
Bruxelles.

SWI Forum. SWI Forum voor Kunst, Kultuur en Wetenschop. De Stichting. Paramaribo, Suriname.

Tareas/Panamá. Tareas. Centro de Estudios
Latinoamericanos (CELA). Panamá.

Temas Coyunt./Caracas. Temas de Coyuntura. Instituto de Investigaciones Económicas
y Sociales, Univ. Católica Andrés Bello.
Caracas.

Temas/Habana. Temas: Cultura, Ideología,
Sociedad. Centro de Estudios Martianos. La
Habana.

Tempo Soc./São Paulo. Tempo Social. Faculdade de Filosofia, Letras e Ciências Humanas, Depto. de Sociologia, Univ. de São Paulo.

Textos Hist./Brasília. Textos de História.
Pós-Graduação em História, Univ. de Brasília.

Third World Plan. Rev. Third World Planning Review. Liverpool Univ. Press. Liverpool, England.

Third World Q. Third World Quarterly.
Third World Foundation; New Zealand
House. London.

Tierra Firme. Tierra Firme. Caracas.

Todo es Hist. Todo es Historia. Buenos
Aires.

Trace/México. Trace. Centre d'études mexicaines et centraméricaines. México.

Trimest. Econ. El Trimestre Económico.
Fondo de Cultura Económica. México.

21st Century Policy Rev. 21st Century
Policy Review. I.A.A.S. Publishers. Langley
Park, Md.

Umbrales/La Paz. Umbrales. Univ. Mayor
de San Andrés. La Paz, Bolivia.

UNISA Lat. Am. Rep. UNISA Latin American Report. Univ. of South Africa. Pretoria.

Univ. Econ. Universitas Económica. Pontificia Univ. Javeriana, Facultad de Ciencias Económicas y Administrativas. Bogotá.

Universum/Talca. Universum. Univ. de Talca. Talca, Chile.

Veritas/Porto Alegre. Veritas. Pontificia Univ. Católica do Rio Grande do Sul. Porto Alegre, Brazil.

Vínculos/San José. Vínculos. Museo Nacional de Costa Rica. San José.

Vuelta/México. Vuelta. México.

Wampum/Leiden. Wampum. Archeologisch Centrum. Leiden, The Netherlands.

Wash. Q. The Washington Quarterly. Georgetown Univ., The Center for Strategic and International Studies. Washington.

Weltwirtsch. Arch. Weltwirtschaftliches Archiv. Zeitschrift des Institut für Weltwirtschaft an der Christians-Albrechts-Univ. Kiel. Kiel, Germany.

World Archaeol. World Archaeology. Routledge & Kegan Paul. London.

World Bank Econ. Rev. The World Bank Economic Review. World Bank. Washington.

World Dev. World Development. Pergamon Press. Oxford, England.

World Econ. The World Economy. Basil Blackwell. London.

World Policy J. World Policy Journal. World Policy Institute. New York.

World Polit. World Politics. Princeton Univ., Center of International Studies. Princeton, N.J.

Yachay/Cochabamba. Yachay. Facultad de Filosofía y Ciencias Religiosas, Univ. Católica Boliviana. Cochabamba, Bolivia.

Yearbook/CLAG. Yearbook. Conference of Latin Americanist Geographers; Ball State Univ., Muncie, Ind.

Z. Ethnol. Zeitschrift für Ethnologie. Deutschen Gesellschaft für Völkerkunde. Verlag Albert Limbach. Braunschweig, Germany.

SUBJECT INDEX

Abaj Takalik Site (Guatemala). Ball Games, 273.

Abandoned Children. Brazil, 5243. Colombia, 1138.

Abdenur, Roberto, 4461.

Abolition (slavery). Elites, 798. Montserrat, 798.

Abused Children. See Child Abuse.

Acawai (indigenous group). Human Ecology, 983. Religious Life and Customs, 983. Rites and Ceremonies, 983. Shamanism, 983.

Accompong, Jamaica (town). Maroons, 801.

Acculturation. Argentina, 1059. Belize, 4731. Bolivia, 1085. Chile, 1108. Chontal, 774. Family and Family Relations, 1072. French Caribbean, 892. Indigenous Peoples, 695. Mass Media, 1072. Mexican-American Border Region, 4663. Mexico, 695, 4663. Museums, 892. Salvadorans, 4726.

Achaninca (indigenous group). Development, 1015.

Achuar (indigenous group). Ethnography, 999. Human Ecology, 998. Social Life and Customs, 999. Symbolism, 998.

Acre, Brazil (state). Environmental Protection, 3900. Forests and Forest Industry, 2865. Rubber Industry and Trade, 3900.

Adolescents. See Teenagers; Youth.

Adult Education. Brazil, 2358. Family and Family Relations, 2358. Wages, 2358.

Advertising. Ecuador, 2033.

African Development Bank, 4035.

African Influences. Brazil, 974, 2924, 5223, 5229, 5271, 5279, 5283, 5291. British Caribbean, 869. Caribbean Area, 918, 4964. Colombia, 861, 1127, 4964. Costa Rica, 4855. Cuba, 814, 974, 4764, 4784, 4788, 4792, 4872. Dominican Republic, 4933. Jamaica, 803. Popular Music, 4881. Puerto Rico, 4837, 4900. Religious Life and Customs, 974. Trinidad and Tobago, 834, 847.

Africano, Albina de Assis, 4511.

Africans. Dominican Republic, 865. Return Migration, 858.

Afro-Americans. See Africans; Blacks.

Aged. Argentina, 5141. Colombia, 4960.

Agostini, Alberto María de, 2754.

Agrarian Reform. See Land Reform.

Agribusiness, 1423. Guatemala, 4694. Mexico, 4591. Puerto Rico, 4893.

Agricultural Colonization. Andean Region, 2647. Argentina, 2739. Colombia, 4963, 4968. Costa Rica, 2496, 4705. Ecuador, 1168. Mexico, 2550. Peru, 2647. Puerto Rico, 4893. Venezuela, 4996.

Agricultural Credit. Brazil, 2878. Colombia, 2003. Costa Rica, 1762. Guatemala, 1794. Honduras, 1817. Nicaragua, 1829. Peru, 2147.

Agricultural Development, 1461. Andean Region, 2647. Argentina, 5113. Bolivia, 2204, 2211, 3513. Brazil, 2375. Caribbean Area, 1890. Central America, 1743, 2478. Chile, 2788, 2830. Chontal, 2529. Colombia, 4963. Dominican Republic, 2471. Ecuador, 2029, 2055. Guatemala, 1794. Mesoamerica, 12. Mexico, 784, 1500, 1502, 1531, 1655, 1705, 2529, 4574, 4612, 4681. Montserrat, 797. Paraguay, 2217. Peru, 2156, 2172, 2647, 5054. Sex Roles, 784. Venezuela, 1944, 1964.

Agricultural Development Projects. See Development Projects.

Agricultural Ecology, 2447. Andean Region, 2581. Bolivia, 2673. Brazil, 2375. Quechua, 2673.

Agricultural Geography. Argentina, 2757. Bolivia, 2211. Brazil, 2881. Colombia, 4963. Costa Rica, 2489. Mexico, 4557.

Agricultural Industries, 1423. Argentina, 2257, 2310, 5152. Brazil, 2357. Caribbean Area, 2462. Dominican Republic, 4917. Economic Liberalization, 1470. Ecuador, 2017. Globalization, 1470. Jamaica, 1866. Mexico, 770, 1493, 1601, 1699. Modernization, 1470. Neoliberalism, 1470. Peru, 2017, 2155, 2159, 5036. Venezuela, 1950.

Agricultural Labor. Andean Region, 1036. Barbados, 794. Bolivia, 2191, 5086. Brazil, 2350, 2357, 3920, 3950. Chile, 2840, 5185. Civil Rights, 864. Coffee Industry and Trade, 5245. Ecuador, 2022. El Salvador, 1792. Family and Family Relations, 4554. Guatemala, 4702. Haiti, 864. Mexico, 1721, 4659. Paraguay, 5101–5102. Peru, 1206, 5036, 5040, 5054, 5056, 5070, 5072, 5075. Puerto Rico, 4888. Quality of Life, 2357. Trade Unions, 3920. US, 4127, 4723. Women, 1036, 2840, 4659, 4702.

Agricultural Policy, 1343, 1736, 2438. Andean Pact, 2042. Andean Region, 2042. Argentina, 5113. Bolivia, 2211, 3513. Brazil, 2338, 2375, 3920. Caribbean Area, 2462. Central America, 1736, 1743, 2476, 2478, 4689. Chile, 2136. Colombia, 1985, 1992, 2003, 4963, 4967. Costa Rica, 1736, 1760, 1770, 1775. Cuba, 1910, 1920, 1923, 4812. Dominican Republic, 2471, 4917. Ecuador, 2017, 2029, 2061. El Salvador, 1777. Exports, 2029. Family and Family Relations, 4683. Guatemala, 4687. Honduras, 1811, 1814–1815. Mexico, 1493, 1500, 1520, 1530–1531, 1552, 1578, 1601–1602, 1607, 1631, 1655, 3044, 4116, 4136, 4574, 4591–4592, 4612, 4660, 4666, 4677, 4683. Montserrat, 797. Nicaragua, 1821, 1823, 1829, 1832, 1835–1836. Paraguay, 2216–2218, 5106, 5111. Peru, 2017, 2145, 2147–2148, 2174, 5036, 5045, 5048, 5051. Venezuela, 1964, 1973.

Agricultural Productivity. Amazon Basin, 2060. Andean Region, 2658. Argentina, 2696. Cuba, 1910. Dominican Republic, 4917. Ecuador, 2055, 2060. El Salvador, 1727. Guatemala, 727. Mexico, 703, 1607, 1636, 4116, 4574. Nahuas, 703. Nicaragua, 1727, 1823, 1830. Peru, 2148. South America, 2390. Uruguay, 5200. Women, 2060.

Agricultural Subsidies. Chile, 2136. Trinidad and Tobago, 1878.

Agricultural Systems. Amazon Basin, 2887. Andean Region, 1038. Argentina, 2757. Brazil, 2357. Central America, 2483. Cuba, 4812. Haiti, 795. Indigenous Peoples, 1038. Kinship, 1200. Mayas, 116. Mesoamerica, 62. Mexico, 1601, 4557. Paleo-Indians, 116. Paraguay, 5111. Peru, 1229, 2172. Poor, 1470. Precolumbian Civilizations, 62, 137. Trinidad and Tobago, 1878.

Agricultural Technology, 1342, 1423. Andean Region, 1045. Argentina, 5113, 5135. Bo-

livia, 2192. Brazil, 2375. Chile, 2088. Guatemala, 1794. Honduras, 1812. Indigenous Peoples, 1045, 1191. Mexico, 1602, 1619, 4557, 4574, 4594, 4612. Oral Tradition, 1188. Peru, 1188, 1191. Uruguay, 5200.

Agriculture. European Influences, 1756. Haiti, 2468.

Agroindustry. See Agricultural Industries.

Aguaruna (indigenous group). Kinship, 996. Marriage, 996. Sex Roles, 996. Social Life and Customs, 996.

Aguascalientes, Mexico (city). Industry and Industrialization, 1483.

Aguascalientes, Mexico (state). Agricultural Technology, 1619. Economic Conditions, 1482. Engineering, 1619. Social Conditions, 1482. Social Sciences, 1619.

AIDS. Brazil, 5209, 5254. Honduras, 4710. Puerto Rico, 4899, 4949. Women, 4552, 5254.

Airlines. Colombia, 2606.

Aisén, Chile (prov.). Description and Travel, 2810. Discovery and Exploration, 2810. Geography, 2787. History, 2787. Human Geography, 2792. Physical Geography, 2792.

Akwē Shavante. See Xavante.

ALADI. See Asociación Latinoamericana de Integración.

Alakaluf. See Alacaluf.

Alarcón Rivera, Fabián, 2037.

Albizu Campos, Pedro, 4819.

Alcohol and Alcoholism. Indigenous Peoples, 1149. Mexico, 718. Tzotzil, 718. Women, 718.

Alcohol Fuel Industry. Brazil, 2364.

Alessandri, Arturo, 3646.

Alfaro Vive, Carajo! (Ecuadorian guerrilla group), 3441.

Alfonsín, Raúl, 3677, 3685, 3695, 3698, 3741, 3774, 4336.

Allende Gossens, Salvador, 2073, 2075, 3617, 3631, 3633, 3640.

Almada, Martín, 3784.

Alsogaray, Alvaro, 3727.

Altos Hornos de México. History, 1629.

Amazon Basin. Agricultural Development, 2884. Agricultural Systems, 2887. Agriculture, 2880, 2920. Archaeological Surveys, 458. Archaeology, 455, 651. Christian Base Communities, 3850. City Planning, 2868. Climatology, 2859. Coffee Industry and Trade, 2060. Conservation, 2608, 2643, 2858, 2920. Cultural Geography, 2880. Cultural Identity, 934, 2910. Deforestation,

2859, 2923. Demography, 5286. Development, 2397, 4466. Development Projects, 2886, 3851. Ecology, 2411, 2859, 2880, 2886, 2894, 2900, 2922. Economic Conditions, 934, 2621. Economic Development, 2871. Economic Geography, 2880. Economic Integration, 4418. Employment, 5286. Environmental Degradation, 2890, 2923, 5299. Environmental Policy, 934, 2397, 2411, 2886, 2922, 3899, 4466. Environmental Pollution, 2891, 2917. Environmental Protection, 2858, 2920, 5213. Ethnobotany, 2873. Ethnoecology, 931, 936. Ethnohistory, 928, 932, 946, 1013. Ethnology, 932, 946. Explorers, 2873. Fish and Fishing, 2880, 2909. Folk Religion, 5246. Folklore, 2921. Foreign Influences, 934. Forests and Forest Industry, 2902, 2920. Frontier and Pioneer Life, 2895. Geographical History, 2644. Geomorphology, 2644. Historiography, 1013. Households, 2643. Human Adaptation, 471. Human Ecology, 936, 998. Human Geography, 3851. Indigenous Peoples, 471, 926, 928, 946. Internal Migration, 2884. Land Invasions, 945. Land Settlement, 2880. Land Tenure, 926, 939, 2894. Land Use, 2060, 2608, 2887, 2894, 2920. Medical Anthropology, 935, 997. Medical Care, 935. Mestizos and Mestizaje, 970. Military Policy, 3851, 3889. Minerals and Mining Industry, 2856. Natural Resources, 2615. Paleo-Indians, 409, 455, 461, 471. Paleoecology, 409. Paleogeography, 409. Palms, 2870, 2902. Peasants, 2643. Physical Geography, 2880. Political Economy, 2856. Popular Religion, 1009. Population Growth, 5286. Precolumbian Civilizations, 403. Precolumbian Land Settlement Patterns, 461. Public Health, 2579. Rainforests, 2921, 3947, 5213. Reforestation, 2923. Regional Planning, 2868. Religious Life and Customs, 1009. Research, 2864. Research Institutes, 2864. Roads, 2893, 4418. Rural Development, 931. Social Change, 2920. Social Conditions, 2621. Social Marginality, 2895. Social Structure, 2895. Soils, 2900. Sustainable Development, 934, 2858, 2864–2865. Television, 2910. Traditional Farming, 931. Traditional Medicine, 935, 997. Urbanization, 2856, 2868. Violence, 945. Water Conservation, 2922. Water Supply, 2922. Women, 2060.
Amazonas, Brazil (state). Demography, 2883. Economic Development, 2907. Economic

Policy, 2907. Fish and Fishing, 2896. Migration, 2883. Urbanization, 2883.
Amazonas, Colombia (commisary. Conservation, 2608.
Amazonas, Colombia (commisary). Land Use, 2608.
Amazonas, Peru (dept.), 4410. Ethnic Groups and Ethnicity, 1204. Migration, 1204.
Ameller Gatica, Agustín, 3487.
Americans (US). Brazil, 2874, 4506. Mexico, 2555.
Anaya Sanabria, Herbert, 3171.
Ancash, Peru (dept.). Glaciers, 2639. Households, 5073. Peasants, 5073. Sex Roles, 5073. Women, 5073.
Andean Pact, 3561, 4316, 4419, 4425. Agricultural Policy, 2042. Ecuador, 2026. Trade Policy, 2042.
Andean Region. Agricultural Colonization, 2647. Agricultural Development, 2647. Agricultural Ecology, 2581. Agricultural Labor, 1036. Agricultural Policy, 2042. Agricultural Productivity, 2658. Agricultural Systems, 1038. Agricultural Technology, 1045. Archaeology, 406, 574. Boundaries, 4410. Censuses, 2657. Child Development, 1068. Cities and Towns, 1037. City Planning, 2578. Civilization, 1193. Climatology, 2585, 2658, 2670. Clothing and Dress, 1071. Coca, 2577. Cocaine, 2577. Community Development, 5062. Conservation, 2583. Costume and Adornment, 1071. Cults, 1060. Cultural Development, 643, 1193. Cultural History, 1037. Deforestation, 2637. Demography, 2657. Description and Travel, 2576. Deserts, 2837. Drug Traffic, 2577. Ecology, 2580, 2584, 2692. Economic Conditions, 1244. Economic Development, 1193, 1447. Economic History, 1040. Elites, 5076. Environmental Degradation, 2692. Ethnic Groups and Ethnicity, 5076. Family and Family Relations, 1039. Farms, 2657. Forests and Forest Industry, 2583. Geographers, 2580. Geographical History, 2575, 2842. Glaciers, 2585, 2670. Global Warming, 2670. Herders and Herding, 1098. Historical Geography, 2578, 2580. Human Ecology, 1198. Indigenous Art, 1071, 1106. Indigenous Music, 1071. Indigenous/Non-Indigenous Relations, 1037, 1040. Kinship, 1042. Land Use, 2627, 2637. Latin American Area Studies, 1207. Maps and Cartography, 2684. Mortuary Customs, 408. Paleo-Indians, 406, 449. Pa-

Brazil, 3908. Chile, 3638, 3641, 3645, 3663. Cuba, 3351. Guatemala, 4755. Indigenous Peoples, 1054. Jamaica, 840. Mexico, 65, 1599, 3126. Nicaragua, 3226. Paraguay, 3796. Peru, 3572. Political Prisoners, 3638. Presidents, 3645. Quiché, 4755. Venezuela, 3472.

Biological Diversity, 1316, 2408, 2447. Bolivia, 2668. Colombia, 2597. Costa Rica, 2490. Peru, 2145, 2664.

Biotechnology, 1332. Cuba, 1921, 4236. Mexico, 3050.

Birds. Argentina, 2747, 2756. Bolivia, 2747. Chile, 2747, 2786. Paraguay, 2747, 2843. Río de la Plata, 2843. Symbolism, 69.

Birth Control. Argentina, 5137, 5146. Bolivia, 5087. Brazil, 5210, 5244. Ecuador, 5016. Mexico, 2541. Social Classes, 5210. Venezuela, 4995.

Birth Rate. Chile, 2802. Costa Rica, 4744. Mexico, 2541.

Bishop, Maurice, 3273.

Black Carib (indigenous group). Migration, 866. Popular Music, 4881. US, 866. Women, 866.

Black Market. Belize, 4759. Cuba, 2467. Ethnic Groups and Ethnicity, 4759. Jamaica, 1880.

Blacks. Anthropometry, 4785. Barbados, 4769. Belize, 3148. Brazil, 5207, 5228, 5231, 5246, 5257, 5267, 5270, 5291, 5294. Caribbean Area, 4835, 4840. Colombia, 861, 1127, 1132–1133, 1144, 3383, 4986. Costa Rica, 4740, 4855. Cuba, 4792, 4820, 4831. Cultural Identity, 920, 5207, 5228. Ecuador, 1150, 5021. Employment, 5270. Folk Music, 5021. Folk Religion, 5246. Guyana, 4835. Peru, 1231. Political Development, 5294.

Boa Vista, Brazil (city). Population Growth, 2856.

Bogotá, Colombia (city). Children, 1138. Demography, 4957. Households, 4958. Informal Sector, 4966. Migration, 4957. Political Culture, 1122. Social Mobility, 4958. Social Movements, 4953. Urban Sociology, 1134, 4953, 4958. Violence, 1134.

Bolívar, Venezuela (state). Ecology, 2590. Mountaineering, 2590. Natural History, 2590.

Bolivia. Congreso Nacional, 3487.

Bolivia. Congreso Nacional. Cámara de Diputados. Comisión de Constitución, Justicia y Policía Judicial, 3508.

Bolivian Revolution (1952), 3519.

Bolsa de Mercadorias & Futuros (Brazil), 2346.

Bonampak Site (Mexico), 252.

Boni (Surinamese people). Cultural Identity, 807. French Guiana, 807.

Borderlands. Mexico, 4663.

Borja, Rodrigo, 3435, 4414.

Bororo (indigenous group). Cosmology, 952. Indigenous/Non-Indigenous Relations, 952. Social Life and Customs, 952.

Bosch, Juan, 3259.

Botany. Colombia, 2613. Costa Rica, 2489. History, 2433. Venezuela, 2589.

Boundaries. Andean Region, 4410. Argentina/Chile, 5115. Belize, 2574. Belize/Mexico, 4942. Brazil/Venezuela, 4486, 4499. Chiefdoms, 561. Ecuador/Peru, 2624. Guatemala, 2574. Guatemala/Mexico, 4113. Land Use, 2510. Mesoamerica, 164. Mexico, 2574. Nicaragua, 2510. Uruguay, 4433, 4435.

Boundary Disputes, 4057. Argentina/Chile, 2763, 2767, 2793, 2803, 2838. Argentina/Uruguay, 4433–4435. Bolivia/Chile, 2813, 4378, 4382. Brazil/Paraguay, 4417. Brazil/Uruguay, 4433. Brazil/Venezuela, 4452. Chile/Peru, 2813, 4420. Colombia/Venezuela, 2609, 4396, 4400, 4449–4451, 4455, 4457, 4459. Ecuador/Peru, 2633, 3562, 4041, 4410, 4429. Mexico/US, 4111. Trinidad and Tobago/Venezuela, 4453.

Bourterse, Desire Delano, 3316.

Boyacá, Colombia (dept.). Archaeology, 548.

Brasília, Brazil (city). Food Supply, 2892.

Brazil. Assembléia Nacional Constituente (1987–1988), 976.

Brazil. Congresso Nacional, 3853, 3888.

Brazil. Congresso Nacional. Câmara dos Deputados, 3913.

Brazil. Congresso Nacional. Senado Federal, 3868.

Brazil. Congresso Nacional. Senado Federal. Comissão de Relações Exteriores e Defesa Nacional, 4473.

Brazil. Congresso Nacional. Senado Federal. CPI do Orçamento, 3902.

Brazil. Marinha, 4483.

Brazil. Ministério das Relações Exteriores, 4481.

Brazilians. Canada, 5249. Japan, 5295. US, 5249.

Briano, Juan, 2709.

British Caribbean. African Influences, 869. Central-Local Government Relations, 3252. Civil Rights, 3251. Decentralization, 3252. Freedmen, 4778. Judicial Process, 3251.

Cerén Site (El Salvador), 241.

Cerro Ñañañique Site (Peru), 614.

Chachapoyas, Peru (town). Migration, 1204.

Chaco, Argentina (prov.). Deforestation, 2718. Land Settlement, 2707. Migration, 2724. Urban History, 2724.

Chaco War (1932–1935), 3815.

Chalcatzingo Site (Mexico), 75.

Chamococo (indigenous group). Acculturation, 1022. Kinship, 1022. Myths and Mythology, 1022. Social Life and Customs, 1022.

Chamorro, Violeta, 3226.

Chamorro Cardenal, Pedro Joaquín, 3216.

Chamula. *See* Tzotzil.

Chan Chan Site (Peru), 653–654.

Chaparé, Bolivia (region). Coca, 2678. Rain and Rainfall, 2678.

Chateaubriand Bandeira de Melo, Francisco de Assis, 3929.

Chavín (indigenous group). Animals, 645. Archaeology, 606–607, 642. Artifacts, 642. Iconography, 606–607. Material Culture, 645. Precolumbian Art, 606–607. Precolumbian Pottery, 642. Social Structure, 645.

Chayahuita (indigenous group). History, 1001. Myths and Mythology, 1001. Religious Life and Customs, 1001. Social Life and Customs, 1001. Traditional Medicine, 1001.

Chayantaka, Bolivia (town). Textiles and Textile Industry, 1082.

Chemical Industry. Mexico, 1717.

Chiapas, Mexico (state). Acculturation, 695. Agricultural Labor, 4615. Archaeological Surveys, 145. Archaeology, 66. Artifacts, 255. Catholic Church, 3021, 3042. Cattle Raising and Trade, 1650. Ceramics, 259. Chol, 691. Coffee Industry and Trade, 4615. Deforestation, 4630. Environmental Degradation, 4630. Excavations, 67, 255. Farms, 701. Guatemalans, 4556, 4615, 4642. Human Rights, 3063–3064. Indigenous/Non-Indigenous Relations, 737. Indigenous Peoples, 747, 3021, 3064, 3109. Indigenous Policy, 761, 3086. Indigenous Resistance, 758. Insurrections, 714, 761, 3063–3064, 3108, 3120. Mayas, 66–67, 758. Migrant Labor, 4642. Migration, 775. Mortuary Customs, 145. Neoliberalism, 2543. Political Culture, 3022. Poor, 714. Precolumbian Architecture, 67, 294–295. Precolumbian Art, 314. Precolumbian Civilizations, 255. Precolumbian Sculpture, 295. Refugees, 4556, 4712. Repression, 3063. Rescue Archaeology, 167. Revolutions and Revolutionary

Movements, 3007, 3024, 3034, 3062, 3096, 3108–3109, 3120, 3127, 3133. Rural Development, 4630. Rural Sociology, 706. Social Classes, 3022. Social Conditions, 3021. Social History, 3021. Social Life and Customs, 706. Social Marginalization, 3022. Social Movements, 3048. Structural Adjustment, 714. Sustainable Agriculture, 701, 2543. Murals, 252.

Chibcha (indigenous group). Archaeology, 530. Infant Mortality, 534. Nutrition, 534. Textiles and Textile Industry, 555.

Chicago, Illinois (city). Dominicans, 4869. Mexican Americans, 779.

Chicanná Site (Mexico), 179.

Chicanos. *See* Mexican Americans; Mexicans.

Chicha. Colombia, 1136. Indigenous Peoples, 1136.

Chichén Itzá Site (Mexico), 40, 87–88, 324, 710.

Chichimecs (indigenous group). Precolumbian Trade, 71.

Chiefdoms. Boundaries, 561. Colombia, 536, 549. Ecuador, 536, 561, 1150. Paleo-Indians, 536. Panama, 331.

Chihuahua, Mexico (state). Cities and Towns, 2517. Economic Forecasting, 1556. Economic Policy, 1556. Elections, 2996. Free Trade, 1556. Geomorphology, 2517. Government, Resistance to, 692. Households, 4662. Industry and Industrialization, 1556. Precolumbian Architecture, 73. Precolumbian Land Settlement Patterns, 73. Social Life and Customs, 692. Social Movements, 4610. Social Structure, 692. Urban Areas, 2517. Urbanization, 2517.

Child Abuse. Bibliography, 5234. Brazil, 3872, 5234. Colombia, 1138. Haiti, 4851.

Child Development. Andean Region, 1068. Argentina, 1068. Brazil, 5264. Colombia, 1138.

Childbirth. Mexico, 4583. Peru, 1187.

Children. Belize, 821. Bolivia, 5087. Brazil, 5234, 5272, 5288. Central America, 4732, 4734. Civil War, 4732. Colombia, 1989, 4962, 4981. Dominican Republic, 4793. Ecuador, 5018. Haiti, 4851, 4859. Labor Market, 1989, 4734. Labor Supply, 4734. Mexico, 4097. Nicaragua, 4685, 4746. Peru, 5035, 5074. Poor, 5074. Public Opinion, 4746. Puerto Rico, 4899. Race and Race Relations, 4838. Repression, 5167. Uruguay, 5198.

Chile. Congreso Nacional, 3651.

Chile. Congreso Nacional. Senado, 3669.
Chile. Dirección de Inteligencia Nacional, 3661.
Chile. Servicio Nacional de la Mujer, 5172.
Chileans. Argentina, 2767.
Chiloé, Chile (prov.). Description and Travel, 2790. Social Life and Customs, 2790.
Chimborazo, Ecuador (prov.). Agricultural Technology, 1171. Archaeology, 558. Horticulture, 1171. Indigenous Peoples, 5028. Modernization, 1171. Peasant Movements, 2618. Protestantism, 5028. Rural Development, 2618. Rural-Urban Migration, 1171. Sex Roles, 1171. Stone Implements, 558.
Chimu (indigenous group). Archaeology, 629, 654. Precolumbian Pottery, 622.
Chinese. Mexican-American Border Region, 2537. Mexico, 2537. Migration, 2424. Trinidad and Tobago, 4876.
Chinese Communist Party, 2950.
Chiriguano (indigenous group). Cultural Identity, 1021. Land Tenure, 1021. Religious Life and Customs, 1021. Traditional Medicine, 1021.
Chiripá (indigenous group). Conservation, 2847. Cultural Identity, 1028. Forests and Forest Industry, 1028, 2847. Human Ecology, 1028. Indigenous/Non-Indigenous Relations, 1028. Judicial Process, 1019. Myths and Mythology, 1017. Religious Life and Customs, 1017. Rites and Ceremonies, 1017. Shamanism, 1017. Social Life and Customs, 1019. Social Structure, 1019, 1028. Sustainable Development, 2847. Traditional Medicine, 1017.
Chiriquí, Panama (prov.). Archaeological Surveys, 333. Land Tenure, 1844.
Chocó, Colombia (dept.). African Influences, 861. Blacks, 3383. Description and Travel, 2605. Ethnic Groups and Ethnicity, 2605. Guerrillas, 3383. Indigenous Peoples, 988. Religious Life and Customs, 861.
Chol (indigenous group). Cultural Identity, 691. Migration, 775. Oral History, 691.
Cholula, Mexico (town). Excavations, 103. Precolumbian Architecture, 103.
Chontal (indigenous group). Acculturation, 774. Agricultural Development, 2529. Catholicism, 765. Indigenous/Non-Indigenous Relations, 774. Religious Life and Customs, 765. Rites and Ceremonies, 765.
Christian Base Communities. Brazil, 3850, 3863, 3894, 3917, 5259, 5278. Chile, 3863. Democratization, 3863, 3894. Political Participation, 3917. Social Mobility, 3917.

Christian Democracy. Central America, 3139. Nicaragua, 3214.
Christianity. Indigenous Peoples, 1075. Jamaica, 792. Trinidad and Tobago, 834.
Chronicles. See Crónicas.
Chubut, Argentina (prov.). Discovery and Exploration, 2716. Historical Geography, 2716.
Chubut River Basin (Argentina). Agricultural Colonization, 2739. Description and Travel, 2739. Germans, 2739.
Church Architecture. El Salvador, 204.
Church History. Argentina, 3692, 3731. Chile, 3663. Costa Rica, 4737. Cuba, 4779. Honduras, 4748. Mexico, 4569, 4637. Nicaragua, 4748.
Church-State Relations, 2986. Argentina, 3692, 3728, 3731. Brazil, 5260. Costa Rica, 4737. Cuba, 3332, 3366, 4779. El Salvador, 4148. Honduras, 4748. Mexico, 3019, 3069, 4569, 4621, 4638. Nicaragua, 4748. Paraguay, 3807.
CIA. See United States. Central Intelligence Agency.
Cities and Towns, 2396, 2434, 2442. Argentina, 2765. Bolivia, 2671, 2674. Brazil, 2869, 2905, 2912–2913. Caribbean Area, 4934. Central America, 2479. Chile, 2804, 2818, 2824. Costa Rica, 2491. Cuba, 2452. Cultural Development, 643. Land Use, 2800. Mayas, 20. Mesoamerica, 20. Mexico, 2517, 4558. Olmecs, 20. Peru, 2648. South America, 2429.
Citizenship. Brazil, 5231, 5257. Chile, 1108. Cuba, 4777. Race and Race Relations, 5257.
City Planning, 2396. Amazon Basin, 2868. Andean Region, 2578. Argentina, 2761, 2765, 2772, 5138. Bolivia, 3500, 3505. Brazil, 2908, 2912, 5216. Chile, 2789, 2804, 2818, 2824. Guatemala, 2507. Mexico, 1608, 1644, 1691, 2534, 2549, 2567, 4558, 4684.
Ciudad Guzmán, Mexico (city). Popular Religion, 4675. Religious Life and Customs, 4675. Social Movements, 4657.
Ciudad Juárez, Mexico (city). Political Participation, 2998. Women, 2998.
Civil-Military Relations, 4310, 5031. Argentina, 3675, 3715, 3723, 3741, 3767, 3770, 3781. Bolivia, 3490, 3501, 3506, 3535. Brazil, 3871, 3896–3897, 3919, 3928, 3939, 3971. Chile, 3615. Democratization, 3971. Ecuador, 3426, 3428, 5031. El Salvador, 3178. Haiti, 3278, 4250. Honduras, 3207. Mexico, 3003, 3019, 3051, 3128. Paraguay,

3797, 3800, 3805. Peru, 3556, 3596, 3603. Uruguay, 3837.

Civil Rights. Agricultural Labor, 864. Argentina, 3749. Brazil, 3872. Colombia, 1126, 3379, 3381. El Salvador, 3180. Guatemala, 713, 3188, 3190, 3194. Haiti, 864, 3291. Honduras, 3199. Mayas, 713. Mexico, 744, 2997, 3029. Mixtec, 744. Peru, 3571, 3583. Puerto Rico, 3314. Suriname, 3319.

Civil Service. Argentina, 2246, 3756. Haiti, 3280. Mexico, 3070.

Civil War. Central America, 2928, 4181, 4732. Children, 4732. Colombia, 2928, 3389. Economic Indicators, 3389. El Salvador, 3145, 3162, 3172, 3183, 4173, 4207. Guatemala, 2505, 3145, 3185. Nicaragua, 4745. Peru, 5035. Women, 4745.

Clarín (Buenos Aires, Argentina), 3746, 3762.

Class Conflict. *See* Social Classes; Social Conflict.

Clergy. Chile, 3663. Cuba, 3332. Honduras, 3198. Mexico, 3042.

Clientelism. Brazil, 3890, 3893. Colombia, 3382, 3393, 4953. Mexico, 3045, 3058.

Climatology. Amazon Basin, 2859. Andean Region, 2585, 2658, 2670. Argentina, 2693, 2777. Bolivia, 2666, 2670. Chile, 2693. Cultural Collapse, 122, 228. Mesoamerica, 122. Mexican-American Border Region, 2535. Mexico, 2553. Peru, 2658. South America, 2390, 2427. Southern Cone, 2693. Yucatán Peninsula, 53.

Clinton, Bill, 4289.

Clothing and Dress. Andean Region, 1071.

Clothing Industry. Caribbean Area, 4919. Chile, 5165. Colombia, 4965. Peru, 2164. Public Health, 5165. Sex Roles, 4919. Women, 4965, 5165.

Coahuila, Mexico (state). Agricultural Development, 1705. Archaeology, 143. Balance of Payments, 1549. Commerce, 1549. Development Projects, 1705. Economic Forecasting, 1549. Industry and Industrialization, 1549.

Coaiquer. *See* Cuaiquer.

Coal Mining. *See* Minerals and Mining Industry.

Coalitions. Nicaragua, 4709.

Coastal Areas. Brazil, 4532. Chile, 2834, 2839. Land Use, 2834.

Cobaría (indigenous group). Myths and Mythology, 990. Oral Tradition, 990. Rites and Ceremonies, 990. Social Structure, 990.

Coca, 4545. Andes Region, 4314. Bibliography, 4539. Bolivia, 2204, 2577, 2678, 3491,

3498, 3518, 5081–5082, 5088, 5090. Climatology, 2678. Colombia, 2577. Paleo-Indians, 511. Peru, 1176, 2577, 4428. Quechua, 1176.

Cocaine. Andean Region, 4314, 4331. Bibliography, 4539. Bolivia, 2577, 3491, 3518, 5081–5082, 5088, 5090. Colombia, 2577, 3374. Peru, 2577, 4428. US, 4331.

Cochabamba, Bolivia (dept.). Cities and Towns, 2671, 2674. Commerce, 2674. Cultural History, 2671. Deforestation, 2683. Excavations, 444. Indigenous/Non-Indigenous Relations, 2686. Peasants, 2687. Precolumbian Land Settlement Patterns, 2686. Precolumbian Pottery, 444. Soil Erosion, 2687. Spaniards, 2686. Trade Unions, 2687. Traditional Medicine, 5077.

Cochabamba,, Bolivia (dept.). Trees, 2683.

Cochabamba, Bolivia (dept.). Urbanization, 2671.

Coclé, Panama (prov.). Land Tenure, 1844.

Codices. Dresden, 299–300, 309. Madrid, 299. Mixtec, 302, 316. Zouche-Nuttall, 320.

Coffee Industry and Trade, 1671. Agricultural Labor, 5245. Amazon Basin, 2060. Brazil, 5245. Central America, 3140. Colombia, 1984, 1998, 2000. Costa Rica, 1766, 3140, 4733. Cuba, 4947. Dominican Republic, 4936. Ecuador, 2060. El Salvador, 3140, 4733. Family and Family Relations, 4554. Mexico, 1671–1672, 1707, 4609. Nicaragua, 3140, 3225, 4733. Sex Roles, 4554.

Colca River Basin (Peru). Agricultural Systems, 669. Colonial Architecture, 2654. Commerce, 1214. Farms, 2661. Indigenous Peoples, 2654, 2661. Irrigation, 2661. Terracing, 669, 2661. Traditional Farming, 669.

Cold War, 4033. Haiti, 4284.

Colha Site (Belize), 231–232, 236, 253. Precolumbian Sculpture, 23. Stone Implements, 224–225, 271.

Colima, Mexico (state). Agricultural Productivity, 1636.

Collective Bargaining. Uruguay, 3839.

Collective Memory. Dominican Republic, 865. Grenada, 3271. Maroons, 809, 906. Peru, 1181.

Collor de Mello, Fernando Affonso, 3859–3861, 3883, 3899, 3903, 3927, 3931, 5243, 5305.

Colombians. Venezuela, 4450.

Colón, Honduras (dept.). Land Tenure, 1813. Land Use, 1813.

Colonial Administration. Caribbean Area,

Construction Industry. Mexico, 738.

Consultores Asociados—CONAS (Cuba), 1914.

Consumption (economics). Colombia, 1122, 2005. Trinidad and Tobago, 872, 1873.

Contact. See Cultural Contact.

Contras. See Counterrevolutionaries.

Contreras Sepúlveda, Manuel, 3661.

Cooke, John William, 3725.

Cooperatives, 5147. Artisanry, 772. Cuba, 1910, 1920, 4812. Cuna, 772. Economic Liberalization, 5189. Haiti, 1907. Mexico, 4608. Nicaragua, 696, 721, 1822. Panama, 772, 1843. Peru, 2169. Social Classes, 4608. Sugar Industry and Trade, 2169. Uruguay, 5189. Women, 772, 4608.

Copán Site (Honduras), 156, 207, 212, 229. Environmental Degradation, 256. Historical Demography, 257. Lime and Lime Making, 152. Precolumbian Architecture, 195. Precolumbian Land Settlement Patterns, 23.

Copper Industry and Trade. Chile, 2079, 2096, 2135, 2785. Mexico, 2524. Peru, 2640.

Córdoba, Argentina (prov.). Constitutions, 3700. Demography, 5117. Excavations, 412. Political History, 3700, 3775. Political Parties, 3700, 3775. Socialism and Socialist Parties, 3700.

Coricancha Temple Site (Cuzco, Peru), 672.

Corn. Mexico, 1550.

Corporación Nacional del Cobre de Chile (CODELCO), 2079, 2096.

Corporación Venezolana de Guayana, 1946, 1972.

Corporatism, 2980. Brazil, 3856, 3865. Mexico, 3027, 3038. Uruguay, 3828.

Corrêa, Manoel Pio, 4481.

Corrientes, Argentina (city). Urban History, 2725.

Corruption. Bolivia, 3488. Brazil, 3914. Chile, 2101. Colombia, 3415. Peru, 3549, 3599.

Corruption in Politics. See Political Corruption.

Cortés, Hernán, 77.

Cosmology. Aztecs, 297. Indigenous Peoples, 735. Mayas, 29, 266, 298. Mesoamerica, 735. Peru, 1199, 1216, 1220–1221. Precolumbian Civilizations, 371. Puerto Rico, 371. Shamanism, 982. Taino, 367. Traditional Medicine, 1199, 1201, 1216.

Cost and Standard of Living. Barbados, 1887. Cuba, 4814. Intellectuals, 4549. Mexico, 1541, 1574, 1640, 1689. Peru, 5039. Southern Cone, 2979.

Costa, Caio Túlio, 3866.

Costa e Silva, Arthur da, 3918.

Costa Júnior, Irapuan, 4473.

Costa Rican Development Corporation. See Corporación Costarricense de Desarrollo.

Costume and Adornment. Andean Region, 18, 1071. Brazil, 958. British Caribbean, 378. Cakchikel, 736. Guatemala, 736. Indigenous Peoples, 18, 958. Mesoamerica, 18. Monserrat, 378. Peru, 1217. Precolumbian Civilizations, 378.

Cotacachi, Ecuador (town). Festivals, 1162. Popular Culture, 1162. Social Life and Customs, 1162.

Cotton Industry and Trade. Paraguay, 2214.

Counterinsurgency. El Salvador, 3162. Peru, 3556.

Counterrevolutionaries. Nicaragua, 3215, 4200.

Coups d'Etat, 2943. Chile, 3612, 3617, 3622, 3629. Ecuador, 3444. Guatemala, 3187. Haiti, 4248. Paraguay, 3800, 3811, 3813. Peru, 3597. Trinidad and Tobago, 3320–3321. Venezuela, 3447, 3462.

Courts. Jamaica, 856.

Cozumel Island (Mexico). Excavations, 276. Precolumbian Land Settlement Patterns, 276. Precolumbian Pottery, 258.

Crafts. See Artisanry.

Credit. Ecuador, 2021. Guatemala, 1796. Mexico, 1511, 1555. Nicaragua, 1820. Peru, 2152.

Crime and Criminals. Argentina, 5149. Barbados, 4890, 4904. Brazil, 3872, 5205, 5235, 5241, 5285, 5296. Chile, 5162. Colombia, 4951, 4978, 4985. Costa Rica, 4735. Jamaica, 4842, 4907. Peru, 3599. Puerto Rico, 4916. Uruguay, 5197. Venezuela, 4994.

Criollos. Trinidad and Tobago, 810.

Crónicas. Chile, 2819. Mexico, 30.

Cuaiquer (indigenous group). Collective Memory, 1159. Political Culture, 1159.

Cuban American National Foundation (US), 4914.

Cuban Americans. Cultural Identity, 4807.

Cuban Missile Crisis (1962), 4229, 4263, 4293.

Cuban Revolution (1959), 3355, 4277.

Cuban Revolution into the 1990s: Cuban perspectives, 4852.

Cubans. Puerto Rico, 4798. US, 4807, 4914.

Cuello Site (Belize), 182. Mortuary Customs, 219.

Cuenca, Ecuador (city). Archaeology, 581.

Cuexcomate Site (Mexico), 137.

Dependency, 2985, 3990. Bolivia, 2193. Brazil, 3948. Cultural Relations, 4085. French Caribbean, 3305. Guadeloupe, 3305. Martinique, 3305. Mexico, 4669.

Deregulation, 1432. Argentina, 2255, 2294, 2297, 2310. Central America, 1748. Mexico, 1492, 1589, 1616. Panama, 1841. Venezuela, 1969.

Desana (indigenous group). Cosmology, 971. Myths and Mythology, 971.

Desaparecidos. *See* Disappeared Persons; Missing Persons.

Description and Travel, 2444. Andean Region, 2576. Argentina, 2734, 2739. Brazil, 2387, 2436. Chile, 2790, 2810, 2833, 2835. Colombia, 2598–2599, 2605, 2607. Mexico, 1497. Patagonia, 2698, 2739, 2741, 2810. Peru, 2645, 2651, 2663, 3550. South America, 2406. Uruguay, 2849–2850. Venezuela, 2586.

Desertification. Bolivia, 2677.

Deserts. Andean Region, 2837. Chile, 2837.

Devaluation of Currency. *See* Exchange Rates.

Developing Countries. Income Distribution, 4808. Poverty, 4808. Social Policy, 4808.

Development. Amazon Basin, 2397. Brazil, 3907, 3948. Central America, 1744. Colombia, 1129. Costa Rica, 4703. Economic Policy, 1260, 1455. Environmental Protection, 1309. Mexico, 4572. Sex Roles, 1015. Technological Innovations, 1443. Universities, 3542. Women, 1129.

Development Projects, 2446. Bolivia, 2197, 2203–2204. Brazil, 2372, 2376, 5217. Colombia, 1129, 4954. Costa Rica, 1759. Ecuador, 1166. Environmental Degradation, 978, 2376. Mexico, 1502, 1532, 1602, 1705, 4562, 4576, 4586.

Devil and commodity fetishism in South America, 1132.

Di Peso, Charles Corradino, 52.

Di Tella, Torcuato S., 3707, 4369.

Dictators. Dominican Republic, 4862. Panama, 3239. Paraguay, 3798.

Dictatorships, 2943, 2951, 2970. Argentina, 2970. Chile, 3614. Cuba, 3328, 3331, 3362. Dominican Republic, 2970. Panama, 3239. Paraguay, 2970, 3791, 3798. Uruguay, 3816, 3825.

Diplomatic History, 4023. Argentina, 4337–4338, 4348–4350, 4356, 4358, 4365. Bolivia, 4371. Brazil, 4010, 4481, 4486, 4505, 4509, 4512, 4515, 4520, 4528. Canada,

4043. Caribbean Area, 4010, 4280. Central America, 4697. Chile, 4384, 4392. Colombia, 4403. Cuba, 4241, 4277. Cuba/US, 4242. Guatemala, 4697. Japan, 4338. Mexico, 4111, 4118. Spain, 4349, 4365, 4384. Uruguay, 4438. US, 4044, 4051, 4055, 4277, 4280, 4284, 4520. Venezuela, 4446, 4454, 4460, 4486.

Diplomats. Argentina, 4369. Bolivia, 4376. Brazil, 4481, 4494, 4515. Chile, 4376. Dominican Republic, 3267, 4290. Haiti, 4281. US, 3198, 4520.

Dirty War (Argentina, 1976–1983), 3735, 3771.

Disappeared Persons. Argentina, 3680, 3771. Central America, 3144. Chile, 3605, 3613, 3644. Peru, 3589.

Disarmament. *See* Arms Control.

Discourse Analysis. Cultural Identity, 948. Jamaica, 848. Markets, 1210. Mayas, 307. Peru, 1210. Quechua, 1173, 1178.

Discoverie of Guiana, 843, 912.

Discovery and Exploration, 2385, 2394. Argentina, 2689. Caribbean Area, 334, 354. Chile, 2689, 2810, 2819. Paleogeography, 393. Patagonia, 2810. Southern Cone, 2691. The Guianas, 843.

Discrimination. Argentina, 5153. Brazil, 5285, 5288, 5301. Jamaica, 1895. Trinidad and Tobago, 1877.

Diseases. Argentina, 5126. Bolivia, 1094. Brazil, 5273. Carib, 358. Caribbean Area, 358. Chile, 2823. Ecuador, 2036. Honduras, 4710. Mexico, 4561, 4568, 4620. Peru, 1202–1203. Social Structure, 1202.

Displaced Persons. Colombia, 3376, 3398.

Dispute Resolution, 4081, 4170, 4203. El Salvador, 4164. Guatemala, 4186. Mexico/US, 4104.

Dissenters. Cuba, 3346. Paraguay, 3784.

Distribution of Wealth. *See* Income Distribution.

Distrito Federal, Brazil. Urbanization, 2863.

Distrito Federal, Mexico. Political Geography, 2521. Urban Policy, 4578.

Documentation Centers. *See* Libraries.

Dollarization. Cuba, 1938, 1940, 3354.

Domecq García, Manuel, 4338.

Domestic Animals. Paleo-Indians, 16. Traditional Medicine, 1201.

Domestic Violence. *See* Family Violence.

Domestics. Brazil, 5303.

Dominican Republic. Secretaría de Relaciones Exteriores, 4290.

2082, 2119. Colombia, 1983. Costa Rica, 1767. Cuba, 4235. Dominican Republic, 4240. Exports, 1350. Haiti, 4240. Jamaica, 1880. Labor and Laboring Classes, 1462. Mexico, 1626, 1635, 1643, 1653, 1676, 1692, 1708, 1719, 4082. Mexico/US, 4132. North America, 1639, 1642, 1653, 1719. Panama, 4161. Private Enterprise, 1463. South America, 2238, 2278, 2665, 4318, 4362, 4418. Southern Cone, 2097, 2221, 2734, 2848, 4319, 4321, 4324, 4327, 4330. Statistics, 1249, 1348. Trade Unions, 1476. Uruguay, 2233, 4439. US, 1719.
Economic Liberalization, 1236, 1258, 1312, 1318, 1326, 1328–1329, 1333, 1340, 1380, 1389, 1407, 1426, 1432, 1454. Agriculture, 1474. Argentina, 2311, 2322, 2769. Banking and Financial Institutions, 1384. Bolivia, 2190. Brazil, 2351, 2365, 2382, 3948. Central America, 1748–1749. Chile, 2065, 2083, 2110, 2125–2126, 3667. Colombia, 1975, 4398. Cooperatives, 5189. Costa Rica, 1774. Democratization, 1373. Ecuador, 2036. El Salvador, 1782. Foreign Investment, 1472. Income Distribution, 1315. Industrial Productivity, 1256. Jamaica, 1884. Mexico, 1486, 1545, 1589, 1591, 1617, 1653, 1677, 1703, 1720, 3045, 3071, 3099, 4613. Nicaragua, 1824. Paraguay, 2216. Peru, 2148, 2161, 3561. Political Reform, 1373. Poverty, 1277, 1449. Rural Conditions, 2216. Social Marginality, 1278. Social Policy, 1278. Uruguay, 2224, 2234, 2237, 5189. Venezuela, 1945. Wages, 1315.
Economic Models, 1276, 1292, 1336, 1356, 1389, 1391, 1409, 1449, 1480. Argentina, 2265. Bolivia, 2196, 3497. Caribbean Area, 1859, 1890. Central America, 1730, 1734. Chile, 2079, 2082. Colombia, 1990, 1997, 2010. Costa Rica, 1768, 1770. Ecuador, 2026, 2060. El Salvador, 4706. Guatemala, 1795. Honduras, 1810. Industrial Productivity, 1675. Inflation, 1319. Jamaica, 1881, 1883, 1892. Mexico, 1501, 1503–1504, 1509, 1518–1519, 1528–1529, 1579, 1591, 1609, 1667, 1674–1675, 1723, 3077, 4678. Neoliberalism, 1591. Nicaragua, 1831. Peru, 2158. Uruguay, 2241–2242.
Economic Planning. See Economic Policy.
Economic Policy, 1270–1271, 1292, 1305, 1312, 1389, 1416, 1469, 1478, 1480, 1495, 1564, 1692, 2438, 2935, 2938, 2989. Argentina, 2247, 2252–2254, 2256, 2260–2261, 2272, 2274, 2282–2283, 2307, 2311, 2314, 2322, 2720–2721, 3682, 3704, 3739, 3751–

3752, 3763, 4341, 4367. Bahamas, 1891. Bolivia, 2185, 2187, 2193–2194, 2196, 2199–2200, 2205. Brazil, 2335, 2348, 2355, 2359, 2365, 2378, 2871, 3861, 3882, 3895, 3909, 3962, 4497. Caribbean Area, 1849, 1852, 1854–1855, 1858, 1900, 4221, 4246. Central America, 1728–1730, 1734, 2476, 4246. Chile, 1560, 2063–2067, 2070, 2072–2074, 2078, 2081, 2083, 2085, 2089, 2092, 2100, 2106–2107, 2109, 2114, 2125, 2131, 2137, 3610, 3639, 3650. Colombia, 1975, 1983, 1985, 1987–1988, 1990–1991, 1993, 1996, 2002, 2010–2011, 4398. Costa Rica, 1757, 1765, 1768, 1770–1771, 1774–1775, 1855, 3153. Cuba, 1912–1913, 1924, 1927–1930, 1932–1934, 1939, 3327, 3330, 3337, 3344, 3347, 4299, 4828, 4929. Curaçao, 1908. Democratization, 2952. Development, 1260, 1455. Dominican Republic, 1855, 1862, 3268. Ecuador, 2028, 2034, 2036, 2038–2039, 2043, 2046, 2054, 2056, 2062, 3425, 3435–3436, 3438, 4414, 5026. El Salvador, 1777, 1780, 1783, 1787, 1793. Environmental Protection, 1325. Exchange Rates, 1272. Grenada, 1896. Guatemala, 1795, 1800, 1802. Haiti, 1904, 4283. Honduras, 1806, 1808–1811, 1814, 1816, 1818. Income Distribution, 1261, 1341, 1408. Jamaica, 1855, 1871, 1882, 1884, 1893. Labor and Laboring Classes, 1366. Mexico, 725, 770, 1272, 1483, 1486–1487, 1492, 1495, 1499, 1518, 1525, 1539, 1542–1543, 1545, 1547–1548, 1551, 1559–1560, 1564, 1572, 1577, 1579, 1583, 1585, 1591, 1597, 1603, 1605, 1610–1611, 1613–1614, 1616–1617, 1620, 1622, 1624, 1626–1627, 1631, 1634, 1643, 1646, 1648, 1651, 1654, 1658–1659, 1666, 1669, 1677, 1683, 1689–1692, 1699, 1703, 1722, 1725, 2544, 3015, 3046, 3057, 3071, 3080, 3082, 3098, 3119, 4082, 4105, 4133, 4572, 4592, 4596, 4613, 4669, 4678. Nicaragua, 696, 1819–1823, 1831, 1834, 1836, 1838. Panama, 1840–1841, 3227. Peru, 1495, 2144, 2158, 2160, 2162, 2168, 2173, 2178, 3568, 3577, 3593–3594, 5047–5048. Poverty, 1260, 1273, 1349. Puerto Rico, 4269. Suriname, 1909. Technological Development, 1266. Trinidad and Tobago, 1894. Uruguay, 2226, 2234, 3821, 3823, 3827–3828. US, 770, 1699. Venezuela, 1945, 1948, 1957, 1969, 1972, 2028, 3481, 3483, 4456.
Economic Sanctions, European. Haiti, 1905.
Economic Sanctions, US. Cuba, 4245. Haiti, 1905.
Economic Stabilization, 1306, 1314, 1326,

Media, 3402. Mexico, 3070. Montserrat, 798. Nicaragua, 3140, 3224–3225, 4709, 4733, 4751. Peru, 3577, 5076. Precolumbian Civilizations, 343. Puerto Rico, 3311. South America, 2690. State Reform, 3875. Venezuela, 2592, 5012.

Emancipation. *See* Abolition.

Embera (indigenous group). Rites and Ceremonies, 988. Shamanism, 988.

Emigrant Remittances. Americans, 2555. Caribbean Area, 4850. Nicaraguans, 1738. Salvadorans, 1738, 1793, 4690.

Emigration and Immigration. *See* Migration.

Employee Management. Uruguay, 2240.

Employment. Argentina, 2272, 2312, 2713, 5121, 5124, 5130. Banana Trade, 877. Barbados, 1872. Blacks, 5270. Bolivia, 2202. Brazil, 2332, 2337, 2367–2368, 2377, 5256, 5270, 5301. Central America, 1735, 1739, 1741, 4714. Chile, 2080, 2105, 2124, 2129. Colombia, 2012, 4982. Demography, 1310. Dominican Republic, 4841. Ecuador, 2031, 2040. Globalization, 2177. Haiti, 4849. Informal Sector, 2180. Jamaica, 812, 1879, 1888, 1892. Mexican Americans, 779. Mexico, 1567, 1590, 1700, 1721, 4593, 4603, 4652, 4662. Minerals and Mining Industry, 1888. Nicaragua, 1827, 1833, 1838. Peru, 2150, 2177, 2179–2180, 5037, 5067. Race and Race Relations, 5256. Racism, 1877. Secondary Education, 811, 4774. Sexism, 2150, 2202. Students, 4603. Trinidad and Tobago, 811, 917, 1877, 4774. Urban Areas, 1827. Uruguay, 2220, 2236, 5194, 5201. Women, 1248, 1307, 1403, 1442, 1586, 1590, 1700, 1735, 1838, 1879, 2012, 2040, 2337, 2368, 4542, 4548, 4593, 5275. Youth, 2236.

Empresa de los Ferrocarriles del Estado de Chile, 2123.

Endangered Species. Chile, 2836.

Energy Consumption. Argentina, 2766.

Energy Policy, 2438. Brazil, 2364. Colombia, 2008. Dominican Republic, 1863. Ecuador, 3432. Mexico, 4121. Rural Development, 3432.

Energy Sources. Brazil, 2370.

Energy Supply. Ecuador, 3432. Finance, 1453.

Engineering. Mexico, 1619.

Engineers. Argentina, 2709.

Enterprise for the Americas Initiative, 3993.

Entidad Binacional Yacyretá (Argentina and Paraguay), 2212.

Entre Ríos, Argentina (prov.). Jews, 5119.

Entrepreneurs. Chile, 2125, 3653, 5178. Ecua-

dor, 2021. Mexican Americans, 779. Mexico, 693, 3130. Panama, 1843. Peru, 2165, 2648, 3558. Puerto Rico, 4913. Shrimp Industry, 2594. US, 693. Venezuela, 1954, 2594. Women, 3130.

Environmental Conservation. Ecuador, 2035, 2049.

Environmental Degradation, 2389. Amazon Basin, 2890. Andean Region, 2692. Argentina, 2717, 2720, 2778. Bolivia, 2679. Brazil, 978, 2327, 2890, 2904, 5213, 5299. Caribbean Area, 4945. Central America, 2484. Chile, 2839. Costa Rica, 1758, 2492, 2494. Deforestation, 1267. Development, 2958. Development Projects, 978. Economic Development, 2327. French Guiana, 2463. Guadeloupe, 2463. Honduras, 1807. Jamaica, 2460. Land Tenure, 1758. Martinique, 2463. Mesoamerica, 256. Mexico, 1625, 4594, 4630. Nicaragua, 1832, 1834. Panama, 731, 2513. Poverty, 4945. Venezuela, 685.

Environmental Policy, 1309, 1325, 1410, 2438, 2449, 2694, 3982, 3998, 4024. Amazon Basin, 2397, 2411, 2886, 2922, 3899, 4466. Argentina, 2262, 2270, 2276, 2775. Banana Trade, 1756. Belize, 2488. Bolivia, 3505, 5085. Brazil, 3882, 3899–3900, 4466, 4524. Caribbean Area, 2469, 4259, 4307. Central America, 2477. Chile, 2814, 2825–2826. Colombia, 2386, 2600, 2610, 2612, 4395, 4404. Costa Rica, 2497. Cuba, 2415. Dominican Republic, 2461. Economic Development, 2430. Ecuador, 2029, 2052, 2626, 5017. El Salvador, 1777, 2501. Guatemala, 2506. Guyana, 1897. Mexico, 4066, 4096. Panama, 777. Peru, 2154, 5085. Uruguay, 2853–2854, 4443.

Environmental Pollution. Amazon Basin, 2891, 2917. Argentina, 2697, 2701–2702, 2717, 2745. Belize, 2488. Brazil, 2327, 2891, 2917. Central America, 2477. Chile, 2826. Colombia, 2600. Costa Rica, 2494, 2498. Dominican Republic, 2466, 2474. Ecuador, 2052, 5025. Mexican-American Border Region, 2535, 2571. Mexico, 1566. Minerals and Mining Industry, 2638. Panama, 2512. Peru, 2638, 2640. Petroleum Industry and Trade, 5025. Puerto Rico, 2453. Uruguay, 2854. Water Supply, 2453.

Environmental Protection, 1331, 1411, 3982, 3998. Amazon Basin, 2858. Argentina, 2778. Bibliography, 2903. Bolivia, 2679. Brazil, 2879, 2903, 2915, 2925, 3882, 3900, 5213. Caribbean Area, 2464, 2469. Central

2206, 2363, 2367. Chile, 2071, 2110, 2133, 2135, 2811. Costa Rica, 4736. Cuba, 1915. Dominican Republic, 2456, 4736. Economic Integration, 1350. Ecuador, 2029, 2044, 2055, 2061. El Salvador, 1781, 1784, 1788. Electronic Industries, 1289. Exchange Rates, 1400. Guatemala, 1802. Income Distribution, 1279. Industry and Industrialization, 1413. Labor and Laboring Classes, 4736. Manufactures, 1350, 1378, 2363. Mexico, 770, 1496, 1506, 1557, 1645, 1695, 1699, 1706. Nicaragua, 1820, 1835. Panama, 1840. Peru, 2157, 2169, 5045. Rural Development, 1279. Uruguay, 2224.

External Debt, 1253, 1329, 1334, 1337, 1402, 1440. Argentina, 2703. Bibliography, 1283, 1363. Costa Rica, 1776. Cuba, 1940. Demography, 1468. Economic History, 1296. Ecuador, 2054, 2062. Mexico, 1535, 1577, 1599, 1610–1611, 1634, 1649, 1662–1663. Nicaragua, 1820. Uruguay, 2232. Venezuela, 1960.

Falkland/Malvinas War (1982), 2763, 4351.

Family and Family Relations, 1313, 1403, 4548. Acculturation, 1072. Adult Education, 2358. Agricultural Labor, 4554. Andean Region, 1039. Antigua and Barbuda, 859, 4775. Bolivia, 5096. Brazil, 2356, 2358, 5219, 5225, 5227, 5265, 5301. Caribbean Area, 4870. Central America, 4714. Chile, 5167, 5175. Coffee Industry and Trade, 4554. Colombia, 1138, 4959, 4971–4974, 4981. Costa Rica, 4753. Cuba, 4795, 4823, 4926. Dominican Republic, 4793, 4930. Ecuador, 5019. Guatemala, 1799, 4694. Haiti, 4824, 4859. Honduras, 4698, 4711. Indigenous Peoples, 1039, 1179. Jamaica, 812, 856, 860, 1881, 4857. Labor Supply, 2356. Law and Legislation, 856. Mexico, 783, 4588, 4590, 4593, 4611, 4628, 4662, 4674, 4683. Paraguay, 5103. Peru, 5038, 5052. Repression, 5167. Saint Kitts and Nevis, 882. Saint Lucia, 4806. Social Change, 4959. Trinidad and Tobago, 887. Venezuela, 4992.

Family Planning. See Birth Control.

Family Violence. Antigua, 841. Barbados, 841. Brazil, 5215, 5225, 5227, 5258, 5302. Chile, 5176, 5182, 5184. Colombia, 4972–4973. Costa Rica, 4741. Ecuador, 5029. Mexico, 4628. Nicaragua, 4745. Peru, 5052. Public Policy, 5215, 5258. Research, 841.

Far East. See East Asia.

Farias, Paulo César, 3859–3860, 3903.

Farms. Andean Region, 2657. Argentina,

2097, 2318, 2757. Caribbean Area, 1733. Central America, 1733. Chile, 2097. Costa Rica, 1760, 2499. Cuba, 1910. Guatemala, 727, 1801. Haiti, 2468. Honduras, 1812. Mexico, 701. Paraguay, 2216. Peru, 2657, 2661, 5036, 5042, 5072. Uruguay, 5200.

Favelas. See Slums; Squatter Settlements.

Feather-Work. Exhibitions, 929. Photography, 929.

Febres Cordero, León, 4414–4415.

Federación de Mujeres Cubanas, 4822.

Federal-State Relations. Brazil, 3921, 4514. Mexico, 3059, 3076. Venezuela, 1963.

Federalism. Brazil, 2340, 3921.

Feminism, 2954. Bolivia, 5098. Brazil, 3852, 5297. Caribbean Area, 4878. Chile, 3614, 3620, 3658, 5166, 5169. Colombia, 4984. Costa Rica, 4688, 4700. Cuba, 3352, 4926. Ecuador, 5022. Jamaica, 4829. Mexico, 3066–3067, 3103. Nicaragua, 4742. Peru, 3545, 3602, 5039. Popular Theater, 4829. Research, 4878. Southern Cone, 2956. Trinidad and Tobago, 4906. Uruguay, 5204. Writing, 1385.

Fernandes, Florestan, 5261.

Fernández Fernández, Sergio, 3619.

Ferreira Aldunate, Wilson, 3822, 3838.

Fertility. See Human Fertility.

Fertilizers and Fertilizer Industry. Mexico, 2557.

Festivals. Cuba, 4809. Dominican Republic, 4933. Ecuador, 1148. Haiti, 800. Indigenous Peoples, 1148. Peru, 1227. Uruguay, 5188.

Finance. Argentina, 2317. Brazil, 2362. Caribbean Area, 1846, 1851, 1867. Chile, 2077, 2081, 2086. Costa Rica, 1772. Dominican Republic, 1861. Economic Development, 1429. Ecuador, 2016. El Salvador, 1779. Guatemala, 1797. Mexico, 1492, 1511, 1513, 1623, 1656, 1658, 1718, 3057. Peru, 2144. Uruguay, 2230. Venezuela, 3477.

Financial Institutions. See Banking and Financial Institutions.

Financial Markets, 1372. Barbados, 1870. Economic Development, 1282.

Fiscal Policy, 1314. Brazil, 2336, 2366. Chile, 1999. Colombia, 1990, 1999, 2009. Mexico, 1528, 1546, 1582. Nicaragua, 1820, 1831. Peru, 2161. Venezuela, 1960, 1963.

Fish and Fishing. Amazon Basin, 2909. Argentina, 2267, 2276. Belize, 852. Brazil, 2896, 2909. Caribbean Area, 366. Chile, 2120. Montserrat, 366.

Fisheries. Argentina, 2267, 2701. Chile, 2120.

Ecuador, 2635. Livestock, 2635. Mexico, 1628, 2531. Peru, 2165. Sex Roles, 5185.

Haitians. Bibliography, 4258. Dominican Republic, 4226, 4258, 4270, 4275, 4805, 4861. Refugees, 4297. US, 4291.

Hallucinogenic Drugs. Colombia, 992. Mortuary Customs, 673. Paleo-Indians, 673. Peru, 1195. Traditional Medicine, 1203.

Harakmbet. *See* Mashco.

Hardoy, Emilio, 3729.

Haro, Cristóbal de, 2689.

Havana. *See* La Habana, Cuba (city).

Health Care. *See* Medical Care.

Henequen Industry and Trade. Mexico, 1716, 2536, 2545.

Herders and Herding. Andean Region, 1098. Argentina, 5150. Bolivia, 1098.

Hidalgo, Mexico (state). Archaeological Surveys, 79, 136, 184. Archaeology, 79. Human Remains, 211. Indigenous Peoples, 4564. Minerals and Mining Industry, 4602. Mortuary Customs, 211. Obsidian, 79, 184. Precolumbian Architecture, 88. Rural-Urban Migration, 4602.

Hieroglyphics. *See* Epigraphy; Inscriptions; Writing.

Higher Education. Anthropology, 1174. Ecuador, 2041. Mexico, 1573, 4661. Peru, 3587. Research Institutes, 2960.

Hinduism. Caribbean Area, 2464. Environmental Protection, 2464. Trinidad and Tobago, 4864.

Hispanic Caribbean. Dance, 893. Social Life and Customs, 893.

Historians. Argentina, 3733. Chile, 2808.

Historic Preservation. *See* Conservation and Restoration.

Historical Demography, 2451. Belize, 220. Bolivia, 444. British Caribbean, 379. Carib, 358. Caribbean Area, 358. Diseases, 1008. Ecuador, 2629. Honduras, 257. Indigenous Peoples, 2629. Mayas, 45, 257. Mesoamerica, 45. Mexico, 105, 2532. Monserrat, 379. Peru, 1008. Taino, 341. Venezuela, 680, 4993.

Historical Geography, 2394, 2402, 2405, 2407, 2418, 2420, 2444, 2448, 2450, 2611. Andean Region, 2578, 2580. Argentina, 2769, 2773, 2781, 2803. Belize, 232. Bolivia, 2675. Brazil, 2867. Central America, 2479. Chile, 2803, 2808, 2819. Colombia, 1125, 2611, 2616. Costa Rica, 2496. Guatemala, 226, 240, 2502–2504. Honduras, 2508. Law and Legislation, 2867. Mexico, 2526–2527, 2558–2559, 2561, 2573. Nicaragua, 2509. Peru, 2642, 2663, 2675. Precolumbian Civi-

lizations, 2509. Puerto Rico, 4923. Research, 2867. South America, 2441. Venezuela, 2591.

Historiography, 1225. Archaeology, 10. Aztecs, 47. Brazil, 4465. Indigenous Peoples, 912, 1013. International Relations, 4465. Maroons, 4898. Zoque, 747.

Hmong. French Guiana, 817.

Holanda, Sérgio Buarque de, 5226.

Home Industries. Brazil, 5224.

Homosexuality, 4550. Brazil, 5250. Costa Rica, 4724. Mexico, 4640. Peru, 5071. Precolumbian Civilizations, 5071.

Horticulture. Brazil, 5214. Guatemala, 1801.

Hospitals. Panama, 3228.

Hotel Industry. Barbados, 1869. Belize, 2485.

Houk, James Titus, 847.

Households, 1245. Amazon Basin, 2643. Argentina, 2286, 2300, 5124. Brazil, 5236, 5287. Caribbean Area, 4850. Central America, 1726, 1739, 4714. Chile, 2068, 2095, 5161. Colombia, 4971. Costa Rica, 1726. Cuba, 4823. Ecuador, 5019. Guatemala, 1726, 1799, 1803, 4707. Honduras, 1726. Indigenous Peoples, 1147. Jamaica, 812, 1881. Mexico, 697, 738, 1487, 1541, 1586, 1612, 1652, 2068, 4593, 4632, 4662. Migration, 4850. Nahuas, 697. Nicaragua, 696, 1825, 4707. Panama, 1839. Peru, 1202, 2643, 5038, 5073. Tarasco, 686. Venezuela, 5001. Women, 1881.

Housing. Argentina, 2746. Ecuador, 2024. Interest Rates, 1527. Mexico, 738, 1521, 1527, 2562, 4657–4658. Panama, 4696. Paraguay, 2213. Social Movements, 4657–4658.

Housing Policy. Chile, 3655. Grenada, 1857. Mexico, 1521. Panama, 4696. Paraguay, 2213. Saint Lucia, 1857. Saint Vincent and the Grenadines, 1857. Venezuela, 1947, 4990.

Hoy, 3533.

Huaca Rajada Site (Sipán, Peru), 603.

Huanca (indigenous group). Precolumbian Pottery, 620.

Huancavelica, Peru (dept.). Agricultural Labor, 5070. Haciendas, 5070. Land Tenure, 5070. Rural Sociology, 5070.

Huao (indigenous group). Evangelicalism, 1006. Indigenismo and Indianidad, 3429. Indigenous Resistance, 1006, 3429.

Huari (indigenous group). Pottery, 602. Precolumbian Land Settlement Patterns, 671.

Huarochirí, Peru (prov.). Archaeology, 635. Ethnohistory, 635.

Huastec (indigenous group). Cultural Identity, 4564. Social Structure, 4564.

Huasteca Region (Mexico). Indigenous Peoples, 4564. Minerals and Mining Industry, 4602. Political Culture, 4614. Rural-Urban Migration, 4602.

Huichol (indigenous group). Indigenous/Non-Indigenous Relations, 762. Religious Life and Customs, 762. Shamanism, 762. Social Life and Customs, 762.

Huitoto. See Witoto.

Human Adaptation. Amazon Basin, 471. South America, 400.

Human Ecology, 2410, 2412, 2611. Amazon Basin, 998. Andean Region, 1198. Argentina, 2740, 2775. Brazil, 978. Chile, 520, 2839. Colombia, 2611. Cuba, 2415. Development, 2958. Indigenous Peoples, 1191. Peru, 1191, 1198, 2664. The Guianas, 983.

Human Fertility. Argentina, 5146. Bolivia, 5087. Colombia, 4975. Cuba, 4795, 4825. Ecuador, 5016. Mexico, 4623, 4680. Paraguay, 5103. Puerto Rico, 4899. Social Change, 4623. Venezuela, 4995.

Human Genetics. Trinidad and Tobago, 844.

Human Geography, 2410, 2414, 2416. Argentina, 2727, 2732, 2770. Bolivia, 3510. Brazil, 2877, 2879. Chile, 2792, 2802, 2806, 2808, 2833. Dominican Republic, 4937. Mexico, 2538. Patagonia, 2792. Puerto Rico, 4923.

Human Physiology. Martinique, 833.

Human Remains. Archaeological Dating, 218. Belize, 186. Brazil, 470, 485. Central America, 35. Colombia, 534. Ecuador, 591. Mayas, 35. Mexico, 35. South America, 401.

Human Resources. Dominican Republic, 4801. Structural Adjustment, 1415, 1435.

Human Rights, 3753, 3991, 4547, 4555. Argentina, 3675, 3680, 3689, 3749, 3753, 4342, 4355. Bolivia, 3496, 3498. Brazil, 976, 3872, 3950, 3968, 5206, 5237, 5285, 5299. Caribbean Area, 3243. Central America, 3138, 3141, 3144, 4212. Chile, 2087, 3605–3606, 3609, 3611, 3616, 3629, 3635, 3644, 3658, 3672, 4390. Colombia, 3379–3381, 3388. Costa Rica, 4193. Cuba, 3336, 3357, 3366, 4217. Ecuador, 5025. El Salvador, 702, 3166, 3171, 3180, 3183, 4207, 4693. Guatemala, 3188–3191, 3194, 4355. Haiti, 864, 3285–3286, 3290–3291, 4212, 4248, 4272. Honduras, 3199, 3201. Indigenous Peoples, 1183. International Relations, 4193. Latin America, 4037. Mayas, 749. Mexico, 744, 2997, 3029, 3063–3064, 3089, 3100, 3125, 4663. Mixtec, 744. Nicaragua, 3222. Panama, 3238. Paraguay, 3807. Peru, 1183, 3543, 3570–3571, 3583, 3589, 3596, 4431.

Suriname, 3319. Uruguay, 4443. US, 4078, 4217.

Humanism. Chile, 3636, 3658.

Humboldt, Alexander von, 2651.

Hurricanes. Mexico, 2553.

Hurtado, Osvaldo, 4414–4415.

Hydration Rind Dating. See Archaeological Dating.

Hydroelectric Power. Argentina, 2212. Brazil, 4417. Paraguay, 2212, 4417.

Hydrology. South America, 2390.

Ibáñez del Campo, Carlos, 3646.

Ica, Peru (dept.). Households, 5073. Peasants, 5073. Sex Roles, 5073. Women, 5073.

Iconography. Aztecs, 297. Brazil, 488, 5229. Caves, 304. Mayas, 58, 130, 161. Mesoamerica, 253. Mochica, 674. Peru, 605.

Identidad Nacional: Memoria, Actualidad y Proyeccions. Seminario, 5192.

Illegal Aliens. US, 712, 4597.

Illegal Aliens, Dominican. Puerto Rico, 4869. US, 4869.

Illegal Aliens, Mexican. US, 2546. 2556, 4624.

Illiteracy. See Literacy and Illiteracy.

Illness. See Diseases.

Ilo, Peru (city). Free Trade, 4379. Tourism, 4379.

Imbabura, Ecuador (prov.). Ethnohistory, 1150.

Immigration. See Migration.

Import Substitution, 1340, 1362, 1375, 1378, 2980. Argentina, 2266. Bahamas, 1898. Caribbean Area, 1849. Industry and Industrialization, 1464. Mexico, 1611, 1635. Nicaragua, 1831. Peru, 3561. Uruguay, 3828.

Imports and Exports. See International Trade.

Inca Influences. Chile, 526.

Incas. Archaeological Dating, 383. Architecture, 504, 672. Argentina, 419, 2727. Artisanry, 419. Censuses, 2652. Chile, 509, 526. Commerce, 419. Cultural Development, 389, 572. Ecology, 2580. Ecuador, 572. Ethnology, 644. History, 621. Material Culture, 419. Monuments, 672. Mortuary Customs, 657. Political Culture, 621. Political Institutions, 389. Population Growth, 2652. Precolumbian Land Settlement Patterns, 671. Precolumbian Pottery, 620, 622. Roads, 391, 509, 526. Social Structure, 621. Warehouses, 636.

Income. Brazil, 2329. Chile, 2101. Guatemala, 4707. Nicaragua, 4707.

Income Distribution, 1241, 1245, 1288, 1330, 1375, 1379, 1402, 1424, 1430, 1434, 1439.

925, 978. Syncretism, 1075. Textiles and Textile Industry, 555, 1082. Time, 1212. Traditional Medicine, 751, 941. Trinidad and Tobago, 810, 4927. Urban Areas, 2210, 5093. Utopias, 1166. Views of, 87, 912, 977, 1046, 1166, 1211. Warfare, 402. Wars of Independence, 1145. Women, 704, 1160, 4720.

Indigenous Peoples, Views of. Franciscans, 30.

Indigenous Policy, 6, 1041. Argentina, 1030. Bolivia, 1091, 3525. Brazil, 947–948, 955, 962–963, 965, 976. Chile, 1120. Colombia, 1124, 1126, 1128, 1135, 1145. Ecuador, 1146, 1155, 1157, 5032. Guatemala, 687, 719, 781. Guyana, 831–832, 896. Mexico, 761, 3022, 3029, 3041, 3086, 3109. Nicaragua, 733. Paraguay, 1020, 1029, 1033, 5104, 5107. Peru, 1183, 1189. Venezuela, 989. Viceroyalty of New Spain, 760.

Indigenous Resistance, 933. Brazil, 955–956, 976. Chile, 1105, 1112. Ecuador, 1006, 1155, 1163, 1166, 3429. Mapuche, 1105. Mayas, 749, 758.

Industrial Development Projects. *See* Development Projects.

Industrial Policy, 1362, 1378. Argentina, 2255, 2262, 2270–2271, 2275, 2293, 2299, 2310, 2316. Bolivia, 2192, 2200. Brazil, 2345, 2378. Chile, 2053, 2128, 5178. Costa Rica, 3153. Ecuador, 2053. Export Promotion, 1469. Jamaica, 2053. Mexico, 1483, 1494, 1510, 1526, 1536–1537, 1594, 1616, 1622, 1686, 1693, 3056, 4587, 4596, 4669. Peru, 2175–2176. Technological Innovations, 1469. Venezuela, 1951–1955, 1957, 1970, 1972.

Industrial Productivity. Argentina, 2310. Brazil, 2351. Chile, 2135. Economic Liberalization, 1256. Economic Models, 1675. Mexico, 1510, 1540, 1587, 1675–1676. Peru, 2176.

Industrial Relations. Canada, 1615. Colombia, 4950, 4955, 4970, 4987–4988. Guyana, 3277. Mexico, 1588, 1615. Southern Cone, 2932. US, 1615. Venezuela, 5002.

Industrialists. Argentina, 3707. Brazil, 3941. Ecuador, 3433. Uruguay, 2221.

Industry and Industrialization, 1263, 1274, 1434, 2221, 2980. Argentina, 2254, 2257, 2293, 2299, 2319, 2717. Bolivia, 2209. Brazil, 2335, 2345, 2352, 2361, 2377, 2380. Central America, 1741. Chile, 2071, 2128, 2135, 2832. Colombia, 2600, 4970, 4988. Cuna, 772. Dominican Republic, 1860. Ecuador, 2052, 5030. Exports, 1413. Import Substitution, 1464. Labor and Laboring

Classes, 1510. Mexico, 1483, 1494, 1508–1510, 1537, 1549, 1556, 1558, 1594, 1617, 1622, 1646, 1667, 1670, 1675, 1683, 1686, 1693, 1701, 1711, 2552, 2562. Nicaragua, 1831. Panama, 772, 1840. Peru, 2175–2176, 3561. Puerto Rico, 4269, 4910. Sex Roles, 4910. Uruguay, 2221, 2224, 3826, 3828. Venezuela, 1942, 1951–1955, 1957, 1972. Women, 5010.

Infant Mortality. Chile, 1115. Venezuela, 4998.

Infants. Mexico, 4583.

Inflation. Argentina, 2273, 2313, 3696. Barbados, 1876. Bolivia, 2205. Brazil, 2329, 2371, 2383. Central America, 1737. Chile, 1560, 2129. Colombia, 1980. Costa Rica, 1774. Economic Models, 1319. Ecuador, 2016, 2038. Exchange Rates, 1276, 1361. Haiti, 1901. Mexico, 1501, 1560, 1604, 1656. Nicaragua, 1824. Peru, 3593, 5038. Public Finance, 1409. Trinidad and Tobago, 1873.

Informal Labor. *See* Informal Sector.

Informal Sector, 1428, 1466. Argentina, 2298. Bolivia, 2183, 2198. Central America, 1735, 1739, 4714. Chile, 2053. Colombia, 4966. Ecuador, 2053. El Salvador, 1790. Employment, 2180. Guatemala, 2507. Haiti, 1902. Jamaica, 2053. Labor Market, 1943. Martinique, 815. Mexico, 1524, 1590, 4652. Nicaragua, 1826, 1837. Peru, 2179–2180, 3575. Political Participation, 3575. Poverty, 1438. Research, 1290. Social Classes, 815. Uruguay, 2855. Venezuela, 1943, 5002. Wages, 1386, 1739. Women, 4542.

Information Science. Chile, 2830. Geography, 2830.

Information Services. Brazil, 2872. Nongovernmental Organizations, 1399.

Ingapirca Site (Ecuador), 568.

Inscriptions. Bibliography, 452. Brazil, 452. Easter Island, 503.

Instituto Agrario Nacional (Venezuela), 989.

Instituto Ecuatoriano de Seguridad Social, 2047.

Instituto Histórico e Geográfico Paraibano (Brazil), 460.

Instituto Nacional de Biodiversidad—INBio (Costa Rica), 1398.

Instituto Superior de Estudos Brasileiros, 3961.

Insurance. Chile, 2084. Unemployment, 2084.

Insurrections. Aymara, 1073. Bolivia, 1073. Ecuador, 1155. El Salvador, 3162–3163, 3169, 3177. Grenada, 3324. Indigenous

4372, 4381, 5082. Brazil, 4368, 4461, 4464–
4465, 4473–4474, 4477, 4482–4483, 4485,
4487–4488, 4491, 4494, 4496–4497, 4509,
4515–4517, 4522, 4525, 4528–4529. Brazil/
Africa, 4468, 4504, 4510. Brazil/Angola,
4510–4511. Brazil/China, 4475, 4505. Bra-
zil/Cuba, 4225, 4309. Brazil/Germany,
4495. Brazil/Guyana, 832. Brazil/Japan,
4418, 4502. Brazil/Mozambique, 4510. Bra-
zil/Paraguay, 4417. Brazil/Peru, 4418, 4425.
Brazil/Portugal, 4480. Brazil/Saudi Arabia,
4462. Brazil/South Africa, 4510. Brazil/
South America, 4512, 4527. Brazil/Uru-
guay, 4433. Brazil/US, 3895, 4361, 4463,
4501, 4506, 4520–4521, 4530. Brazil/Vene-
zuela, 4452, 4486, 4499. British Caribbean/
UK, 4301. British Guiana/Canada, 3274.
British West Indies/Latin America, 4230.
Caribbean Area, 4268, 4306. Caribbean
Area/Cuba, 4223. Caribbean Area/Domini-
can Republic, 4286. Caribbean Area/Euro-
pean Union, 4256. Caribbean Area/Latin
America, 4227, 4295. Caribbean Area/US,
4215–4216, 4256, 4280, 4448, 4931. Caribbean Area/Venezuela, 4218, 4448. Central
America, 4143, 4176–4177. Central Amer-
ica/European Union, 4197. Central Amer-
ica/Mexico, 4086. Central America/Spain,
4142. Central America/US, 4108, 4144–
4146, 4149, 4152, 4158, 4174, 4178, 4181,
4189, 4195, 4199, 4208. Chile, 4368, 4383,
4387, 4390, 4392–4393. Chile/Italy, 4389.
Chile/Peru, 4420. Chile/Spain, 4384, 4386.
Chile/Taiwan, 4385. Chile/US, 3656, 4391.
Colombia, 4401, 4405–4407. Colombia/
Mexico, 4408. Colombia/Panama, 4409.
Colombia/US, 3407–3408, 4403, 4409. Co-
lombia/Venezuela, 4397, 4400, 4408, 4449,
4451, 4455. Costa Rica, 4193. Cuba/Africa,
4243. Cuba/Algeria, 4241. Cuba/Asia, 1918.
Cuba/Brazil, 1918. Cuba/Canada, 4260.
Cuba/Caribbean Area, 1918. Cuba/Europe,
1918, 4267. Cuba/European Union, 4278.
Cuba/Japan, 4261. Cuba/Mexico, 1918.
Cuba/North America, 1918. Cuba/US,
1916, 1941, 3343, 4217, 4220, 4242–4243,
4245, 4247, 4251–4255, 4277, 4298. Cuba/
USSR, 4305. Dominican Republic, 4290.
Dominican Republic/Guadeloupe, 4286.
Dominican Republic/Haiti, 3270, 4226,
4258, 4265, 4275, 4302–4303, 4805. Do-
minican Republic/US, 3259, 4244, 4266.
Dutch Caribbean/The Netherlands, 3300–
3301, 3304. Ecology, 4066. Ecuador, 4412–

4413. Ecuador/Peru, 3562, 4422, 4430. Ecua-
dor/US, 4411. Guadeloupe, 4905. Guate-
mala/Mexico, 4113, 4209. Guatemala/US,
3193, 4171, 4355. Guyana, 901. Haiti, 3286.
Haiti/US, 4232–4233, 4237, 4248, 4250,
4283–4284, 4289, 4291, 4297. Historiography, 4465. Honduras/US, 3207. Human
Rights, 4193. Jamaica/US, 3292. Latin
America/Canada, 4043. Latin America/
China, 2950. Latin America/European
Union, 4026. Latin America/Germany,
4015, 4023. Latin America/Great Britain,
4015. Latin America/Japan, 1360. Latin
America/Portugal, 4060. Latin America/
Russia, 4047. Latin America/Southeast
Asia, 3975. Latin America/Spain, 3976,
3980, 4003, 4060. Latin America/US, 1360,
3133, 3983, 3986, 3989–3991, 4010, 4013,
4015, 4018, 4022, 4029–4030, 4040, 4044,
4049–4052, 4054–4055, 4058–4059, 4216,
4269, 4437. Mexico, 3038, 4074–4075,
4077, 4093, 4096–4097, 4106, 4124, 4128–
4130, 4138. Mexico/Canada, 4083, 4115.
Mexico/Europe, 4117. Mexico/European
Union, 4123. Mexico/Pacific Area, 4072,
4114. Mexico/Russia, 4118. Mexico/US,
725, 1640, 3003, 3016, 3018, 3080, 3083,
3095, 3133, 4068, 4072, 4079–4080, 4085,
4087, 4099, 4108, 4110–4111, 4119, 4131,
4368. Mexico/USSR, 4118. Mexico/Vene-
zuela, 4408. Nicaragua/US, 3215, 3225,
4147, 4200, 4214. Nicaragua/USSR, 4210.
Panama, 4139. Panama/US, 3229, 3234,
4140, 4151, 4160, 4163, 4165, 4172, 4179,
4182, 4192, 4202, 4204–4205, 4409, 4172.
Paraguay, 4416. Peru, 4393, 4421, 4423–
4424, 4426–4427, 4431. Peru/Brazil, 4418.
Peru/Japan, 4418. Peru/US, 4418, 4428.
Portugal/Spain, 2688. Puerto Rico/US,
3312–3313, 4269, 4813. Reference Books,
4002. Reference Works, 4054. South America, 4518. South America/Europe, 4311.
South America/European Union, 4313.
South America/US, 4444. Suriname/The
Netherlands, 3315. Trinidad and Tobago,
4231. Trinidad and Tobago/Venezuela,
4453. Uruguay, 4432, 4436, 4440, 4442. Ur-
uguay/Europe, 4441. Uruguay/Mexico,
4438. Uruguay/US, 4437–4438, 4441. US/
Japan, 4418. Venezuela, 4445–4447, 4454,
4458. Venezuela/US, 4448, 4460.
International Trade, 1240, 1257, 1406, 3994,
3998, 4353. Argentina, 2276, 2322. Central
America/Mexico, 1751. Chile, 2130. Costa

Kaingangue (indigenous group). Ethnography, 969. Rites and Ceremonies, 969.

Kalinya. *See* Carib.

Kamairuá (indigenous group). Oral Tradition, 972.

Kamaiurá (indigenous group). Ethnohistory, 949. Myths and Mythology, 972. Oral History, 949. Religious Life and Customs, 972. Social Life and Customs, 972.

Kaminaljuyu Site (Guatemala), 235.

Katarismo Movement (Bolivia), 1092, 3485–3486, 5078, 5097.

Kayapó. *See* Cayapo.

Kekchi (indigenous group). Cultural Identity, 781. Religious Life and Customs, 781. Social Life and Customs, 781.

Kelly, Isabel Truesdell, 142.

Kennedy, John Fitzgerald, 4029.

Keta-Kara Site (Argentina), 429.

Kidnapping. Argentina, 3735. Colombia, 3377.

Kings and Rulers. Mayas, 68, 306, 312.

Kingston, Jamaica (city). Households, 812. Rastafarian Movement, 4858. Women, 812.

Kinship. Agricultural Systems, 1200. Andean Region, 1042. Antigua and Barbuda, 859, 4775. Caribbean Area, 805, 868, 4839. Curaçao, 785. Dominica, 4856. Ecuador, 1172. Guyana, 871. Indigenous Peoples, 1026. Land Tenure, 868. Law and Legislation, 859, 4775. Maroons, 919. Mayas, 102. Mexico, 711, 783. Peru, 1200. Race and Race Relations, 810. Research, 1042. Trinidad and Tobago, 810.

Kinte, Kunta, 3383.

Klink, Amyr, 2691.

Kogi. *See* Kagaba.

Kogi: una tribu de la Sierra Nevada de Santa Marta, Colombia, 1139.

Krahó. *See* Craho.

Kubitschek, Juscelino, 4516.

Kuna. *See* Cuna.

Kwaiker. *See* Cuaiquer.

La Guajira, Colombia (dept.). Description and Travel, 1125. Historical Geography, 1125.

La Habana, Cuba (city). Black Market, 2467. Demography, 4825.

La Pampa, Argentina (prov.). City Planning, 2765. Demography, 2713. Employment, 2713. Regional Planning, 2765. Rural-Urban Migration, 2713. Urban Areas, 2765. Cities and Towns, 2765.

La Paz, Bolivia (city). Aymara, 1074. City Planning, 3500. Environmental Degrada-
tion, 3500. Indigenous Peoples, 1074. Political Culture, 3539. Public Opinion, 3539. Religious Life and Customs, 1096. Rural-Urban Migration, 5084. Social Movements, 5096. Urban Policy, 3500. Urban Sociology, 5084. Women, 5084.

La Paz, Bolivia (dept.). Excavations, 450. Geomorphology, 2681. Maps and Cartography, 2669, 2681.

La Rioja, Argentina (prov.). Manufactures, 2706.

La Tablada, Argentina (military base), 3680, 3734, 3778.

La Violencia. *See* Violencia, La (Colombia).

Labor and Laboring Classes, 1353, 1466. Argentina, 2755, 3709, 5120, 5122, 5140, 5148. Bolivia, 2182, 2184, 5089. Brazil, 3856, 5306. British Guiana, 3276. Caribbean Area, 1848, 1850. Central America, 1741. Chile, 2806, 3660, 3674, 5186. Colombia, 1989, 4950. Costa Rica, 4736. Cuba, 3364. Dominican Republic, 1864, 4736. Economic Integration, 1462. Economic Policy, 1366. Ecuador, 2023, 2040. Exports, 4736. Fruit Trade, 5186. Guadeloupe, 4799. Guyana, 3276. Industry and Industrialization, 1510. Jamaica, 1875, 1895, 4854. Mexico, 1488, 1510, 1522, 1586–1587, 1600, 1673, 1723, 2516, 3006, 3114, 4601, 4652. Neoliberalism, 2946. Paraguay, 3790. Peru, 5037, 5067, 5069. Statistics, 2023. Trinidad and Tobago, 916–917. Uruguay, 2220, 2226, 2236, 3826, 3831. Venezuela, 5002. Women, 2040.

Labor Market, 1466. Argentina, 2268, 2272, 2281, 2293, 2301, 2305, 2307–2308, 2320, 5121–5122, 5153. Barbados, 1872. Bolivia, 2182, 2184. Brazil, 2333, 2347, 2367. Caribbean Area, 1850. Central America, 4734. Children, 1989, 4734. Chile, 2093, 2102, 2117, 2122, 2124, 2129. Colombia, 1989, 1995, 1997, 2006, 2012, 2014, 4988. Costa Rica, 4713, 4753. Cuba, 4814. Ecuador, 2040. El Salvador, 1790. Export Trading Companies, 2240. Globalization, 1444. Guatemala, 1803. Honduras, 1806. Informal Sector, 1943. Jamaica, 1892, 1895. Mexico, 1700, 2546, 4603. Paraguay, 3790. Peru, 2146, 2150, 2179, 5067. Structural Adjustment, 1435. Technological Development, 2333. Uruguay, 2233, 2240. US, 2546. Venezuela, 1943, 1955, 5002. Women, 1248, 1997, 2014, 2040, 2102, 2150, 4753.

Labor Movement. Argentina, 3681, 5120, 5140, 5148. Bolivia, 2182, 5097. Brazil,

nals, 4978. Drug Traffic, 4978. Social History, 4978. Street-Railroads, 1974. Transportation, 1974.

Mediation, International. *See* International Arbitration.

Medical Anthropology, 927, 941, 973. Amazon Basin, 935, 997. Argentina, 1051. Bolivia, 1069, 1080, 1087–1088, 1094. Brazil, 973. Chile, 1103, 1110, 1116. Colombia, 1136. Ecuador, 1003, 1005. Mapuche, 1110. Peru, 1199, 1203, 1213.

Medical Care, 1335, 1450. Amazon Basin, 935. Argentina, 2275, 5116. Bolivia, 5087. Brazil, 5233, 5263. Chile, 5158. Colombia, 4975. Costa Rica, 1773. Cuba, 3339, 4892. Economic Liberalization, 1397. Ecuador, 5016. Educational Models, 1684. Infants, 5016. Jamaica, 4854. Mexico, 1514, 1684, 4561, 4568, 4590, 4620. Panama, 1839. Peru, 1213. Uruguay, 2227. Women, 5016.

Medical Education. Mexico, 4568.

Medicinal Plants, 941. Bolivia, 1069, 1088. Brazil, 2924. Colombia, 992. Ecuador, 1003. Mexico, 2433, 2519. Peru, 1182. Rainforests, 937. Rites and Ceremonies, 1182.

Medicine. Argentina, 1051. Chile, 1110. Cuba, 4783, 4892. Mexico, 4568. Uruguay, 5193.

Medrano, Juan Ramón, 3175.

Menchú, Rigoberta, 704.

Mendes, Chico, 3920, 3947.

Mendoza, Argentina (city). City Planning, 2772. Environmental Pollution, 2745. Poor, 2745.

Mendoza, Argentina (prov.). Agriculture, 2736. Colonization, 2749. Demography, 2700. Economic History, 2768–2769. Economic Liberalization, 2769. Elites, 2755, 2768–2769. Environmental Degradation, 2717. Environmental Pollution, 2717. Geology, 2719, 2780. Grazing, 2768. Historical Geography, 2769. Industry and Industrialization, 2717. Italians, 2755. Labor and Laboring Classes, 2755. Land Settlement, 2700. Land Use, 2728, 2736. Latifundios, 2749. Migration, 2726, 2755, 2769. Minerals and Mining Industry, 2719. Petroleum Industry and Trade, 2719. Physical Geography, 2780. Poor, 2717. Rural-Urban Migration, 2748. Spaniards, 2755. Squatter Settlements, 2726. Wine and Wine Making, 2728, 2748, 2768–2769.

Menem, Carlos Saúl, 2282, 2311, 3676, 3682, 3684, 3699, 3732, 3739, 3742, 3745–3746,

3749–3752, 3757, 3763, 3768, 3780–3781, 4336, 4347, 4360, 5155.

Mental Health. Political Prisoners, 5144. Repression, 4555.

Mercado Común Centroamericano, 4155.

Mercantile System. Paraguay, 2217.

Merchant Marine. Brazil, 4526.

Mercosul. *See* Mercosur.

Mercosur, 1237, 1328, 1352–1353, 1380, 1392–1393, 1410, 1421, 1445, 1458, 1462–1463, 1476, 2082, 2138, 2215, 2221, 2233, 2241, 2278, 2288, 2291, 2296, 2331, 2341, 2353, 2359, 2374, 2381–2382, 2848, 3821, 3984, 4070, 4311–4313, 4318–4319, 4321, 4324–4325, 4327–4328, 4330, 4332–4335, 4353, 4360, 4425, 4439, 4464, 4467, 4471, 4496, 4498, 4514, 5112.

Mercurio (Santiago, Chile), 3617.

Mérida, Venezuela (city). Informal Sector, 4990. Land Invasions, 4990. Poverty, 5003. Squatter Settlements, 4990. Housing, 4990.

Merino Correa, Hernán, 2838.

Merino Vega, Marcia Alejandra, 3638.

Merquior, José Guilherme, 4494.

Mestizos and Mestizaje, 743. Amazon Basin, 970. Argentina, 1059. Brazil, 970. Chile, 5177. Colombia, 1137, 1144. Cuba, 4820. Cultural Identity, 1184, 5023. Ecuador, 5023. Myths and Mythology, 1205. Nicaragua, 743. Peru, 1185, 1205, 1227, 5063.

Metal-Work. Argentina, 3681.

Metallurgy. Mesoamerica, 85. Paleo-Indians, 665.

Methodology. Geography, 2877. Sociology, 5143.

Mexica. *See* Aztecs.

Mexicali Valley (Mexico). Chinese, 2537. Migration, 2537.

Mexican-American Border Region. Acculturation, 4663. Chinese, 2537. Climatology, 2535. Commerce, 1714. Demography, 4582. Drug Enforcement, 4078. Drug Traffic, 4068, 4109. Economic Development, 4135. Energy Supply, 4121. Environmental Pollution, 2535, 2571. Family and Family Relations, 4633, 4641. Households, 4641. Human Rights, 4078. International Trade, 1621. Maquiladoras, 1706, 2515, 4573, 4633. Migrant Labor, 4633. Migration, 2515, 2537, 2546, 4068. Public Works, 4135. Quality of Life, 4633. Tourism, 1714. Urbanization, 1706, 2515.

Mexican Americans. Acculturation, 771. Employment, 779. Entrepreneurs, 779. Mar-

Movimiento Nacional Cimarrón (Colombia), 3383.
Movimiento Nacionalista Revolucionario (Bolivia), 3485–3487, 3517.
Movimiento Quintín Lame (Colombia), 1130, 3413.
Movimiento Revolucionario Túpac Amaru, 3569, 3578.
Movimiento Todos para la Patria (Argentina), 3778.
Movimiento Urbano Popular (Mexico), 4627.
Moyano, María Elena, 3579.
Muisca. See Chibcha.
Multinational Corporations, 1256, 1263, 1321, 1375. Brazil, 2860. Caribbean Area, 4821. Jamaica, 1879. Mexico, 1516. Regional Integration, 1299. Women, 1879.
Mummies. Chile, 494–496.
Municipal Government, 2971–2972, 3196, 3424. Argentina, 3706, 3726, 3730, 3759, 5138, 5145. Brazil, 3876, 3938. British Caribbean, 3252. Chile, 3637. Colombia, 3385. Costa Rica, 3158. Cuba, 3327, 3335, 4816. Democratization, 1436. Ecuador, 3424. El Salvador, 3174. Globalization, 1436. Haiti, 4895. Honduras, 3196. Mexico, 2551, 3061, 4578, 4598, 4656, 4673. Nongovernmental Organizations, 3061. Paraguay, 3783. Peru, 3579. Uruguay, 3841–3842. Venezuela, 3454.
Municipal Services, 2971.
Mural Painting. Conservation and Restoration, 176. Mayas, 98, 176, 244, 264, 293. Mexico, 27.
Murals. Mayas, 252.
Murder. Argentina, 3764.
Museo Frissell de Arte Zapoteca (Mexico), 237.
Museums. Acculturation, 892. Belize, 890. French Caribbean, 892. French Guiana, 890. Political Ideology, 890.
Musical Instruments. Bolivia, 1083, 1086. Ecuador, 5021. Indigenous Peoples, 1083, 1086.
Muslims. Trinidad and Tobago, 850.
Myths and Mythology, 938. Animals, 3, 115, 942. Aztecs, 96. Bolivia, 1094. Carib, 361. Chile, 1111. Colombia, 1143. Haiti, 4810. Jamaica, 370. Mapuche, 1111. Mesoamerica, 115. Mestizos and Mestizaje, 1205. Oral Tradition, 924. Peru, 1205, 1220–1223, 1230, 1232. Quiché, 95. Taino, 362, 367, 370.
Nahuas (indigenous group). Agricultural Productivity, 703. Cultural Identity, 697, 4564.

Households, 697. Law and Legislation, 703. Oral History, 703. Oral Tradition, 756. Plants, 2533. Popular Culture, 756. Rites and Ceremonies, 756. Salt and Salt Production, 70. Social Structure, 766, 4564.
Naj Tunich Site (Guatemala), 277, 281.
Napo, Ecuador (prov.). Deforestation, 2050. Economic Conditions, 2621. Land Tenure, 2050. Land Use, 2050. Social Conditions, 2621.
Narcotics Policy. Panama, 3234.
Nariño, Colombia (dept.). Archaeology, 546, 550. Rock Art, 550.
Nasca. See Nazca.
Natal, Brazil (city). Americans, 4506.
National Autonomy. See Autonomy.
National Characteristics. Argentina, 3719, 3733. Belize, 4211. Colombia, 1144. Cuba, 4807. Ecuador, 2631. Latin America, 4540. Mexico, 707. Paraguay, 3814. Uruguay, 5192.
National Defense. See National Security.
National Identity. See National Characteristics.
National Parks and Reserves. See Parks and Reserves.
National Patrimony. Chile, 521.
National Security, 3186, 3985, 4049, 4057, 4310, 4402. Argentina, 4345–4346, 4364. Brazil, 3871, 4364, 4473, 4476. Caribbean Area, 4215. Colombia, 3400, 4402. Cuba, 4255. El Salvador, 3161. Guatemala, 3186. Mexico, 3003, 3018, 3032, 4064. Panama, 4180. South America, 4476. Southern Cone, 4317. US, 3989, 4145.
Nationalism, 4053. Argentina, 3702, 3733, 4348. Barbados, 4769, Belize, 4943. Brazil, 4529. Chile, 2808. Cuba, 3354, 3360, 3365. Dominica, 826. Ecuador, 2624. Government Publicity, 4943. Guatemala, 719. Mexico, 3039. Peru, 3591, 5068. Popular Culture, 4943. Puerto Rico, 3310. Uruguay, 5192.
Nationalization. Mexico, 1614.
Nattino Allende. Santiago, 3613.
Natural Disasters. Chile, 2796. Guatemala, 2503.
Natural History. Argentina, 2705. Bolivia, 2673. Brazil, 2387. Chile, 2831. Colombia, 2599, 2602, 2613. Patagonia, 2705. Peru, 2651. Quechua, 2673. South America, 2406. Venezuela, 2590.
Natural Resources, 2402. Amazon Basin, 2615. Argentina, 2320, 2693, 2701, 2770.

Pampas, Argentina (region). Climatology, 2777. Colonization, 2777. Trees, 2759.

Pan-Americanism, 4323, 4437.

Panama Canal, 2511, 4160, 4162, 4180, 4182, 4205, 4409. Geopolitics, 2511. Land Use, 2511. Neutrality, 4154, 4167. Public Opinion, 4192.

Panama Canal Treaties (1977), 4139–4140, 4160, 4179.

Panama Invasion (1989), 4150–4151, 4165–4166, 4182, 4191, 4202, 4204.

Pané, Ramón, 362, 367.

Pantanal, Brazil (region). Rock Art, 465.

Papermaking. Argentina, 2262, 2270.

Pará, Brazil (state). Agricultural Development, 2884. Archaeological Surveys, 468. Fisheries, 2909. Forests and Forest Industry, 2902. Indigenous Peoples, 969. Internal Migration, 2884. Palms, 2902. Rock Art, 468.

Paracas Site (Peru), 649, 667.

Parada Maluenda, José Manuel, 3613.

Paraguayan War (1865–1870), 4416.

Paraíba do Sul River Valley, Brazil. Economic Development, 2911. Industry and Industrialization, 2911. Urbanization, 2911.

Paramaribo, Suriname (city). Ethnic Groups and Ethnicity, 909.

Paramilitary Forces. Colombia, 3376–3377, 3395, 3397.

Paramos (geographical feature). Andean Region, 2584. Colombia, 2604, 2614. Ecuador, 2634.

Paraná, Brazil (state). Agricultural Credit, 2878. Soybeans, 2878.

Paratii (ship), 2691.

Parenthood. Haiti, 4824.

Parks and Reserves. Argentina, 2733. Central America, 2477. Colombia, 2601. Ecuador, 2617, 2630. Nongovernmental Organizations, 2630. Venezuela, 2596.

Parliamentary Systems. *See* Political Systems.

Partido Acción Nacional (Mexico), 2995, 3013, 3026, 3060, 3065, 3129, 3132, 4605.

Partido Blanco. *See* Partido Nacional (Uruguay).

Partido Colorado (Paraguay), 3784, 3800, 3806, 3812, 3814.

Partido Colorado (Uruguay), 3828.

Partido Comunista de Colombia, 3403.

Partido Comunista de Cuba, 3327, 3358.

Partido Comunista de El Salvador, 3170.

Partido Comunista de la Argentina, 4352.

Partido Comunista del Peru, 1225.

Partido Comunista del Uruguay, 3829.

Partido Comunista do Brasil, 3862, 3936–3937.

Partido Conservador de Nicaragua, 3212.

Partido da Social Democracia Brasileira, 3874, 3958, 3960.

Partido de la Revolución Democrática (Mexico), 3026, 3043, 3084, 3100, 3105, 3117–3118, 3125.

Partido Demócrata-Cristiano (Chile), 3623, 3627, 3667, 3670, 3673.

Partido dos Trabalhadores (Brazil), 3858, 3891, 3938, 3954, 3967.

Partido Liberal de Honduras, 3202–3203.

Partido Mexicano Socialista, 3094.

Partido Nacional (Uruguay), 3822, 3834, 3838.

Partido Radical (Chile), 3636.

Partido Revolucionario de Trabajadores (Colombia), 3413.

Partido Revolucionario Dominicano, 3259.

Partido Revolucionario Institucional (Mexico), 3002, 3009, 3012, 3026–3028, 3052–3054, 3068, 3079, 3092–3093, 3107, 3132–3133, 4649.

Partido Revolucionario Obrero Clandestino Unión del Pueblo—PROCUP (Mexico), 3040.

Partido Social Cristiano (Ecuador), 3420.

Partido Social Cristiano Nicaragüense, 3214.

Partido Socialista (Chile), 3657, 3668.

Partido Unidad Social Cristiana (Costa Rica), 3157.

Partido Verde Ecologista de México, 3123.

Pasto, Colombia (city). Carnival, 1137. Mestizos and Mestizaje, 1137.

Pasto (indigenous group). Oral History, 1141. Oral Tradition, 1141.

Patagonia (region). Agricultural Colonization, 2739. Animal Remains, 422. Archaeology, 413, 422. Colonization, 2749. Description and Travel, 2698, 2739, 2741, 2754, 2810. Discovery and Exploration, 2810. Expeditions, 2698, 2754. Geography, 2787. Geopolitics, 2763. Germans, 2739. History, 2787. Human Geography, 2792. Latifundios, 2749. Minerals and Mining Industry, 2741. Mountaineering, 2698. Natural History, 2705. Obsidian, 436. Physical Geography, 2792. Pictorial Works, 2705. Rock Art, 422. Stone Implements, 422.

Paucartambo, Peru (town). Social Life and Customs, 1200.

Paz, Octavio, 3126.

Paz, La. *See* La Paz, Bolivia.

Paz Zamora, Jaime, 3495, 3508.

Peace. Caribbean Area, 3981, 4295. Central

America, 2477, 3981, 4141, 4183, 4194, 4196, 4359. Chile, 3609. El Salvador, 767, 1778–1779, 1788, 1793, 3145, 3176, 4156, 4164, 4169, 4173, 4185, 4203, 4747. Guatemala, 3145, 3185, 4171. Haiti, 4250. Peru, 3599.

Peasant Movements. Bolivia, 3509, 3535, 5086. Brazil, 2897, 3920, 3942. Central America, 4689. Chile, 5164. Colombia, 3386, 4968, 4977. Dominica, 4912. Ecuador, 2618. Mexico, 3022, 3044, 4567, 4631. Nonviolence, 3386. Paraguay, 5101–5102, 5106, 5111. Peru, 5051. Women, 4631.

Peasant Uprisings. Bolivia, 3509, 3535. Brazil, 2897. Peru, 5051.

Peasants. Amazon Basin, 2643. Andean Region, 2657. Argentina, 5132. Bolivia, 2204, 2687, 3518, 5086. Caribbean Area, 4856. Central America, 3134, 4689. Chile, 5157, 5164. Colombia, 3386, 4983. Communication, 5157. Costa Rica, 3134, 4703, 4705. Cuba, 4812. Dominica, 4856, 4912. Dominican Republic, 908, 4917. Ecuador, 2022. El Salvador, 1727. Evangelicalism, 746. Guatemala, 727, 3192, 4687, 4702. Haiti, 1903, 2468. Honduras, 3208. Mass Media, 5157. Mexico, 1490, 1628, 4612, 4667, 4677. Montserrat, 797. Nicaragua, 1727, 1832, 1836–1837, 3134, 4708. Paraguay, 2218, 3807. Pentecostalism, 5277. Peru, 1188, 1229, 2145, 2156, 2158, 2172, 2643, 2657, 3557, 3575, 3591, 5036, 5040, 5042, 5045, 5048, 5051, 5056, 5068, 5073. Political Participation, 3575. Sex Roles, 700, 784, 4683. Social Change, 4983. Venezuela, 5001. Women, 700, 784, 4677, 4702.

Peddlers. See Informal Sector.

Peñon del Rio Site (Ecuador), 593.

Pensions, 1275, 1382, 1394, 1450. Chile, 1275, 1382. Economic Liberalization, 1397. Privatization, 1396.

Pentecostalism, 2975, 4941. Argentina, 5133. Brazil, 3917, 5277. Cultural Identity, 1104. Dominican Republic, 4941. Jamaica, 790, 820, 4765. Peasants, 5277. Political Participation, 3917. Social Change, 5133. Social Mobility, 3917.

People's Revolutionary Government (Grenada), 3272.

Pequeño Hogar Alumbrar (Buenos Aires), 5123.

Pérez, Carlos Andrés, 1969, 3451, 3457, 3474, 4447, 4456, 4458.

Pérez Alfonzo, Juan Pablo, 1968.

Periodicals, US. Caribbean Area, 3248.

Pernambuco, Brazil (state). Agricultural Geography, 2881. Agricultural Productivity, 2881. Horticulture, 5214. Labor Movement, 3942. Peasant Movements, 3942. Rock Art, 464. Sugar Industry and Trade, 2881.

Perón, Juan Domingo, 1057, 2970, 3692–3693, 3731, 3754, 3775, 4348–4349, 4362–4363, 4366–4367.

Peronism, 3053, 3688, 3693, 3696, 3701, 3705, 3724–3725, 3740.

Personal Narrative. See Autobiography; Oral Tradition.

Pesquisa Nacional por Amostra de Domicílios (Brazil), 2337, 2356, 2360, 5208, 5262, 5288.

Pesticides. Costa Rica, 2494. Mexico, 2557.

Petén, Guatemala (dept.). Archaeological Geography, 93. Archaeological Surveys, 189, 240. Cave Paintings, 281. Linguistics, 740. Mayas, 93, 189. Precolumbian Architecture, 239.

Petrochemical Industry. Argentina, 2270, 2297. Venezuela, 1950.

Petroglyphs. See Rock Art.

Petróleo Brasileiro, S.A., 1479.

Petróleos del Perú, 2170.

Petroleum Industry and Trade. Argentina, 2294, 2297, 2719, 3736. Brazil, 4479. Colombia, 1981, 1987, 1991, 2004, 2011, 4970. Dominican Republic, 1863. Ecuador, 5025. Environmental Pollution, 5025. Geology, 2437. Mexico, 1507, 1681, 1688, 1712, 4121. Peru, 2170. South America, 2437. Trinidad and Tobago, 1894. US, 1712. Venezuela, 1966, 1968, 1970, 3479, 3481, 5007.

Petroleum Industry and Trade, US. Ecuador, 1006, 3429.

Pharmaceutical Industry. Argentina, 2323. Brazil, 4521.

Philanthropists. US, 4030.

Philosophy of Liberation. See Liberation Theology.

Photography. Satellites, 2421. South America, 2421.

Physical Anthropology. Mexico, 82, 768.

Physical Geography, 2385, 2395, 2444. Andean Region, 2576. Argentina, 2711. Brazil, 2877, 2879. Chile, 2792, 2833. French Guiana, 2473. Patagonia, 2787, 2792. Venezuela, 2591.

Physicians. Cuba, 4892. Uruguay, 5193.

Phytogeography. See Biogeography.

Piauí, Brazil (state). Archaeology, 466, 472, 477. Excavations, 477. Paleo-Indians, 466, 472. Rock Art, 477.

Political Geography, 2392. Bolivia, 3526. Chile, 2392. Colombia, 3406. Ecuador, 3427. Globalization, 2445.

Political History, 2937, 3990. Argentina, 2245, 2247, 3678–3679, 3688, 3690, 3692, 3695, 3697, 3700–3701, 3705, 3715, 3720, 3724, 3727, 3729, 3731, 3754, 3756, 3758, 3774–3775, 3777, 3779, 4348. Bahamas, 4877. Belize, 3149, 3151, 4206. Bolivia, 3506–3507, 3516, 3528–3529. Brazil, 3864, 3878, 3906, 3909, 3918, 3929, 3945, 5290. Central America, 3147, 4149. Chile, 2942, 3612, 3619, 3623, 3626–3627, 3631, 3640–3641, 3644–3646, 3648–3649, 3652, 3657, 3661. Colombia, 4403. Costa Rica, 3147. Cuba, 3351. Dominican Republic, 3257, 3259, 3264, 4266, 4286, 4862. Ecuador, 3431. El Salvador, 3170, 3175, 3181. Europe, 4446. Grenada, 3271, 4843. Guatemala, 2505, 3147, 3195. Haiti, 3278, 3282–3283, 4233, 4794. Honduras, 3197, 3205, 3211, 4748. Jamaica, 3292–3293. Mexico, 2942, 3005, 3038, 3116, 3122. Nicaragua, 3214, 3216, 3225, 4147, 4709, 4748. Panama, 3231, 3236, 3238–3239, 4699, 4715. Paraguay, 3782, 3793, 3795, 3798, 3803, 3808, 3812, 3815. Peru, 3547, 3597, 3601, 3603, 5041. Puerto Rico, 3309. South America, 4446. Southern Cone, 2956. Suriname, 3315, 3318. Uruguay, 3819, 3824–3825, 3828–3829, 3834, 3838. Venezuela, 3456, 3462–3463, 3472, 3478–3479, 3483–3484, 4458, 5007.

Political Ideology, 2931, 2966, 2991. Argentina, 3688, 3752, 4348. Brazil, 3862. Chile, 3626, 3654. Cuba, 3334, 3338, 3340, 3356, 3359. Ecuador, 4414. El Salvador, 3169. Haiti, 4928. Museums, 890. Nicaragua, 3219. US, 4208, 4251. Venezuela, 3452.

Political Institutions. Bolivia, 3503. Brazil, 3888, 3906, 3909–3910, 3912, 3923, 3925. British Caribbean, 3255. Chile, 3632, 3643, 5168. Colombia, 3387. Dominican Republic, 3257, 3261, 3265. Ecuador, 2020, 2034. Haiti, 3279, 4940. Mexico, 2994, 3011, 3019, 3097. Peru, 3585. Puerto Rico, 4813. Venezuela, 5014.

Political Integration, 4048. Uruguay, 4439.

Political Left, 2978, 2991, 4234. Argentina, 3725, 3734. Bolivia, 3516, 3536. Brazil, 3878, 3891, 3898. Catholic Church, 3898. Chile, 3626. Colombia, 3403. Cuba, 3338. Honduras, 3200. Mexico, 3040, 3049, 3084, 3094, 4560. Uruguay, 3830, 3845, 3848.

Political Opposition. *See* Opposition Groups.

Political Participation, 2992–2993, 3710. Argentina, 3695, 3698, 3713, 3747. Brazil, 3909, 3924–3925, 5300. Chile, 2072, 3620, 3647, 5181. Colombia, 3405, 4974. Cuba, 3327, 4816. Decentralization, 3196. Dominican Republic, 4826. Ecuador, 3425, 3440. El Salvador, 4750. Grenada, 3272. Guyana, 3276. Haiti, 3281, 4895. Honduras, 3196. Indigenous Peoples, 3440. Informal Sector, 3575. Literacy and Illiteracy, 3272. Mexico, 3035, 3079, 3103, 3130, 4580, 4618. Nicaragua, 3223. Panama, 3230. Peasants, 3575. Peru, 3545, 3563, 3575, 3602, 5043, 5049. Southern Cone, 2956. Trinidad and Tobago, 3325. Women, 2927, 2954, 2956, 2992–2993, 2998, 3072, 3103, 3130, 3281, 3545, 3602, 3620, 3747, 4618, 5282, 5300. Youth, 3223, 3230.

Political Parties, 2936, 2944, 2966. Argentina, 3679, 3685, 3687, 3696–3698, 3700–3701, 3705, 3709, 3720, 3727, 3747–3748, 3751, 3755, 3765, 3773, 3775, 3777, 3779. Bolivia, 3487, 3504, 3506, 3511–3512, 3516, 3526, 3529, 5092. Brazil, 3687, 3879, 3901, 3910–3913, 3915–3916, 3932, 3949, 3954, 3960. Central America, 3135–3136, 3139, 3142. Chile, 2073, 3606, 3608, 3618, 3623, 3627, 3649–3650, 3654, 3658, 3665, 3667–3668. Colombia, 3368, 3387, 4961. Costa Rica, 3135, 3157. Ecuador, 2020, 3416, 3418, 3423, 3430–3431, 3433. El Salvador, 3135. Guatemala, 3195. Honduras, 3202–3204, 3206, 3211. International Relations, 2950. Mexico, 2995, 3012, 3026, 3031, 3054–3055, 3068, 3073, 3079, 3088, 3094, 3132, 4673. Nicaragua, 3212, 3214, 3220. Panama, 3236. Paraguay, 3782, 3785, 3792, 3806. Peru, 3541, 3547, 3551–3552, 3554–3555, 3564, 3581, 3588, 3601, 5049. Puerto Rico, 3311, 4770. Research, 3916. Southern Cone, 2956. Trinidad and Tobago, 3322. Uruguay, 3687, 3765, 3820, 3824, 3829, 3834–3835, 3840–3842, 3845, 3847. Venezuela, 3445–3446, 3449–3450, 3456, 3470, 3478–3479, 3484.

Political Persecution. Argentina, 3721, 3735, 3771. Chile, 3629, 3638, 3661, 5167. El Salvador, 3183. Guatemala, 3191. Paraguay, 3788. Peru, 3571. Suriname, 891. Youth, 3771.

Political Philosophy. Argentina, 3702, 3717. Chile, 3610.

Political Platforms. Bolivia, 3504.

Political Prisoners. Argentina, 3771, 5144. Biography, 3638. Chile, 3638, 3671, 5167.

Cuba, 3355, 3362. Mental Health, 5144.
Paraguay, 3784, 3786, 3793. Women, 3355,
3362.
Political Psychology. Chile, 5180. Colombia,
3392. Peru, 3565. Voting, 3392.
Political Reform, 1368, 1407, 2957, 3710. Argentina, 3682, 3686. Bolivia, 3503, 3515,
3527. Brazil, 3869, 3884, 3905–3906, 3933,
3944, 3946. Chile, 3607, 3624, 3632, 3668,
5168. Colombia, 3384, 3387, 3399, 4961.
Cuba, 1932, 3334, 3336, 3347–3348. Dominican Republic, 3256, 3260–3261, 3266.
Economic Liberalization, 1373. Haiti, 3282.
Mexico, 3019, 3027, 3080, 3083, 3097,
3129, 4673. Nicaragua, 3217. Peru, 3566.
Uruguay, 3818, 3823. Venezuela, 3460.
Political Science, 2929, 2989. Colombia,
3410. Reference Books, 2987. Research,
2987. Textbooks, 3197.
Political Sociology. Argentina, 5155. Bahamas, 3298. Brazil, 3854, 3896, 3963, 3970,
5206. Caribbean Area, 4791. Chile, 5168,
5171. Colombia, 3393, 3415. Costa Rica,
4737. Ecuador, 3433. Guyana, 901, 4925.
Haiti, 3283, 4894, 4940. Jamaica, 3294–
3296. Mexico, 3022, 4613–4614, 4649,
4682. Montserrat, 3297. Nicaragua, 3221.
Puerto Rico, 3311, 3314, 4770, 4833. Suriname, 3317. Trinidad and Tobago, 3321.
Uruguay, 5199. Venezuela, 2592, 5012.
Political Stability. Central America, 3135,
3142. Ecuador, 3431, 3444. El Salvador,
1778. Panama, 4180. Peru, 3585. Venezuela,
3467.
Political Systems, 2962, 2984. Argentina,
3687, 3697, 3713, 3759, 3765. Bolivia, 3503,
3515. Brazil, 2962, 3687, 3855, 3904, 3906,
3910, 3912, 3931–3932, 3953, 3958. Central
America, 3136, 3147. Chile, 3666–3667,
3670. Colombia, 3387, 3401. Costa Rica,
3147, 3152. Cuba, 3335, 3361, 3365. Democracy, 2988. Ecuador, 2020. El Salvador,
3169, 3173. Guatemala, 3147. International
Relations, 3979, 3987. Mayas, 44, 55. Mesoamerica, 44, 81. Mexico, 3011, 3085. Paraguay, 3782, 3798, 3806. Peru, 3541, 3547,
3551, 3554–3555, 3564, 3581, 3585, 3590,
3601. Southern Cone, 2988. Uruguay, 3687,
3765, 3819–3820, 3824–3825, 3827–3828,
3833, 3835, 3842, 3845. Venezuela, 3446,
3448–3450, 3460, 3469, 3471.
Political Theory, 2937. Bolivia, 3507. Brazil,
4533. Caribbean Area, 4271, 4294. Colombia, 3403. Democratization, 4544. Ecuador,
4415. Foreign Policy, 4533. Mexico, 4682.

Political Thought, 2981, 4039, 4534, 4536. Argentina, 2929, 3717. Bolivia, 3519. Brazil,
3862, 3865, 3874, 4500. Chile, 2989, 3636.
Colombia, 3410. Cuba, 3356, 4915. Ecuador, 3443. Mexico, 3096, 4682. Peru, 3574.
Politicians. Argentina, 3678, 3694, 3725,
3729, 3732, 3740, 3760, 3768. Bolivia,
3485–3486, 3513, 3521. Brazil, 3868, 3883,
3896, 3952. Caricature, 3434. Chile, 3618,
3632, 3642, 3648–3649, 3659, 3670, 3673.
Cuba, 3349. Ecuador, 2020, 3423, 3430,
3434. Grenada, 3273. Mexico, 3017, 3023,
3070, 3093, 3110, 3115, 3117, 3121, 4125.
Nicaragua, 3216. Paraguay, 3796. Peru,
3541, 3582, 5049. Suriname, 3316, 3318.
Trinidad and Tobago, 3323, 3326. Uruguay,
3816, 3822. US, 4125. Venezuela, 3474.
Women, 3943.
Pollution. See Environmental Pollution.
Pontificia Universidad Católica del Perú,
1174.
Poor. Agricultural Systems, 1470. Argentina,
2279, 2286, 2300, 2302, 2305, 2717, 2745–
2746, 5125, 5130. Brazil, 5239, 5241, 5272,
5307. Central America, 2476. Children,
5074. Chile, 2122, 3664, 5183. Cultural
Identity, 5307. Ecuador, 2046. El Salvador,
767, 1792, 4747. Employment, 5130. Grenada, 1857. Guatemala, 2507, 4738. Honduras, 1810. Insurrections, 714. Mexico,
714, 716, 725, 1490, 1586, 4600. Nicaragua,
1828. Paraguay, 2213, 2218. Peru, 1226,
2141, 2153, 3546, 5035, 5038, 5053, 5065,
5067, 5074. Puerto Rico, 4770, 4786, 4844.
Saint Lucia, 1857. Saint Vincent and the
Grenadines, 1857. Urban Areas, 716. Uruguay, 2239. Venezuela, 1947.
Popenoe, Dorothy Hughes, 149.
Popol Vuh, 95, 229, 3193.
Popular Culture, 13. Andean Region, 1049.
Belize, 5089. Bolivia, 4943. Brazil, 5222,
5228. Caribbean Area, 886, 4883, 4964. Colombia, 1137. Costa Rica, 4855. Cuba, 814,
4784. Dance, 1066. Dominican Republic,
4933. Grenada, 4803. Haiti, 4832. Jamaica,
4883. Nationalism, 4943. Peru, 1209, 3591,
5058, 5068. Puerto Rico, 4924. Rastafarian
Movement, 4922. Reggae Music, 4922. Research, 1049. Social Change, 4946. Trinidad
and Tobago, 4946.
Popular Movements. See Social Movements.
Popular Music. African Influences, 4881. Caribbean Area, 4782, 4881. Peru, 1209.
Popular Religion. Amazon Basin, 1009. Brazil,
5260. Ecuador, 1165. Haiti, 800. Jamaica,

Programa de Desarrollo Rural Integrado (Colombia), 1129.

Programa de Difusión Campesina (Chile), 5157.

Programa Grande Carajás (Brazil), 2372, 2890.

Programa Nacional de Solidaridad (Mexico), 3027, 3045, 3102, 4576, 4584, 4622, 4645.

Property. Argentina, 2323. Costa Rica, 1770. Economic Development, 1280. Nicaragua, 1829. Peru, 3546. Private Enterprise, 1280.

Protectionism. Argentina, 2264, 2296. Barbados, 1887. Brazil, 2354. Chile, 2126. Costa Rica, 1768. Panama, 1840. Uruguay, 2225.

Protestant Churches, 2975. Cuba, 4772. Mexico, 4676. Peru, 3557.

Protestantism, 2930, 2945, 2975. Central America, 4695. Costa Rica, 4737. Cuba, 4772. Ecuador, 5024, 5028. Indigenous Peoples, 5028. Mexico, 4621, 4676. Mosquito, 4718. Nicaragua, 4718, 4761. Peru, 1224. Venezuela, 4999.

Protestants, 2945, 2975. Nicaragua, 4761.

Protests. Brazil, 5243. Chile, 3643, 3664. Cuba, 4818.

Proyecto Andino de Tecnologías Campesinas (Peru), 1191, 1193.

Public Administration, 1416. Argentina, 3683. Bolivia, 3499. Brazil, 3853, 3927, 3949, 5238. Chile, 2112, 3637. Colombia, 3390, 3400. Communication, 5008. Costa Rica, 3154. Dominican Republic, 3256. Haiti, 3280. Jamaica, 3293. Mexico, 2997, 3017, 3046, 3074, 3078, 3110. Paraguay, 3783. Private Enterprise, 1418, 1425. Trinidad and Tobago, 3322, 4231. Venezuela, 5008.

Public Administraton. Caribbean Area, 3249.

Public Debt. Brazil, 2326. Economic History, 1296.

Public Education. Mexico, 1574.

Public Enterprises. Argentina, 2285, 2311. Banking and Financial Institutions, 1409. Brazil, 4479. Caribbean Area, 3249. Chile, 2108, 2785. Mexico, 1526, 4596. Uruguay, 2228, 2237. Venezuela, 1946.

Public Finance, 1281, 1286, 1308, 1327, 1375, 1390, 1426, 1440, 1467. Argentina, 2277, 3686. Bolivia, 2199, 2205. Brazil, 2336, 2362, 2366. Costa Rica, 1774. Decentralization, 1295. Dominican Republic, 3268. Inflation, 1409. Mexico, 1577. Social Policy, 1345.

Public Health, 2416. Amazon Basin, 2579. Argentina, 5116, 5126, 5128. Bibliography, 5156. Bolivia, 3499. Brazil, 2919, 5209, 5233, 5254, 5263–5264, 5273. Chile, 5156, 5158–5159, 5165. Colombia, 4974–4975. Cuba, 3339. Dominican Republic, 4767, 4903. Haiti, 4773. Jamaica, 4854. Mexico, 4561, 4568, 4575, 4590, 4595, 4634, 4666. Panama, 4151. Puerto Rico, 4899, 4949. Refugees, 4712. Research, 5156. Uruguay, 5202. Venezuela, 4998. Women, 4634.

Public Investments, 1235. Argentina, 2294, 2321. Brazil, 2362. Caribbean Area, 1859. Electricity, 2321. Mexico, 1515, 1571, 1577, 1668, 1709, 2568, 4558. Uruguay, 2231.

Public Opinion, 4551. Argentina, 3695. Barbados, 4890. Bolivia, 3516, 3538–3539. Brazil, 3875, 3881, 3904–3905, 3922–3923, 3934–3935, 3952–3953. Central America, 4144. Children, 4746. Chile, 3618, 4390. El Salvador, 3166. Mexico, 3000–3001, 3069, 3101, 4131. Panama, 4140, 4172, 4192. Peru, 3551, 3581, 3594, 5049. Spain, 4551. Underdevelopment, 1417. Uruguay, 3832. US, 1417. Venezuela, 3445, 3452, 3464, 4989.

Public Policy. Brazil, 3869, 3887, 3907, 3940, 3944, 3970, 5215, 5238, 5258. Cuba, 4814, 4818, 4863. Ecuador, 3436, 3438. Family Violence, 5215, 5258. International Economic Relations, 1254. Mexico, 1540, 3018, 3113, 4128, 4638. Panama, 4151. Peru, 3573. Regional Development, 1473. Suriname, 3319. Venezuela, 5003, 5007.

Public Transportation. See Local Transit; Transportation.

Public Works, 1390. Colonial History, 2418. Haiti, 4773. Investments, 1456. Mexico, 1498, 2570, 4576.

Publishers and Publishing. Brazil, 3929.

Puebla, Mexico (city). Employment, 4652. Informal Sector, 4652. Labor and Laboring Classes, 4652. Land Use, 2528. Urban Planning, 2567. Urban Policy, 2567. Urbanization, 2567.

Puebla, Mexico (state). Agricultural Labor, 4609. Agricultural Systems, 4609. Archaeological Surveys, 177. Coffee Industry and Trade, 4609. Economic Development, 1508, 1711. Economic History, 1508. Housing, 2562. Industry and Industrialization, 1508, 1711, 2562. Oral Tradition, 756. Paleo-Indians, 177. Precolumbian Art, 106. Precolumbian Civilizations, 43. Precolumbian Land Settlement Patterns, 43. Precolumbian Pottery, 106. Regional Planning, 2528. Rites and Ceremonies, 756. Urban Policy, 2562. Urbanization, 2562.

Puerto Real Site (Haiti), 364.

Recessions. Ecuador, 2019.

Recife, Brazil (city). Food Industry and Trade, 2882.

Reclamation of Land. *See* Land Invasions; Land Reform; Land Tenure.

Red Nacional de Organizaciones de Mujeres Campesinas (Mexico), 4631.

Redemocratization. *See* Democratization.

Redistribution of Wealth. *See* Income Distribution.

Reference Books, 3978. Chile, 2798. Mexico, 3106. Peru, 1215. Political Science, 2987.

Referendums. Brazil, 3904, 3953. Chile, 3619, 3647, 3653, 3666, 3673. Peru, 3598. Puerto Rico, 3306, 3308, 3312–3313. Uruguay, 3816, 3843.

Reforestation. Amazon Basin, 2923. Brazil, 2898.

Refugees. Belize, 4731. El Salvador, 4728. Public Health, 4712.

Refugees, Guatemalan. Mexico, 4556, 4712.

Refugees, Haitian, 3290. France, 4249. US, 4249, 4297.

Refugees, Indigenous. Guatemala, 4691.

Refugees, Salvadoran. Belize, 2487.

Reggae Music, 886. Caribbean Area, 4782. Popular Culture, 4922.

Regional Development. Argentina, 2292, 2295, 2312. Brazil, 2340–2341, 2373, 2926. Caribbean Area, 1854. Central America, 2480. Chile, 5179. Decentralization, 1473. Dominican Republic, 4789. Mexico, 2558–2559, 3030, 4563. Migration, 4563. Private Sector, 1473. Public Policy, 1473. Statistics, 3030. Venezuela, 3480, 4996.

Regional Integration, 1324, 1339, 1352, 1381, 1411, 4016, 4021, 4042, 4312, 4333, 4408, 4463, 4527. Andean Region, 2042. Argentina, 2283. Bolivia, 3492. Brazil, 2331, 2341, 4467, 4477, 4490, 4514. Brazil/Latin America, 4519. Brazil/Venezuela, 4507. British Caribbean, 3255. Caribbean Area, 1849, 1853, 4218, 4238, 4264, 4271, 4294, 4296, 4304, 4781, 4817, 4931. Central America, 1729, 1734, 1745, 1747, 1749, 2480, 4153, 4264. Chile, 2130. Colombia, 3391. Cuba, 4235. Latin America, 4015. Multinational Corporations, 1299. South America, 4362, 4425. Southern Cone, 2130, 2734, 4317, 4319, 4324, 4330, 4335, 4346, 4361. Statistics, 1348. Uruguay, 2233, 4439.

Regional Planning. Amazon Basin, 2868. Argentina, 2765. Brazil, 2907–2908. Chile, 3637. Colombia, 3406. Honduras, 1806. Mexico, 1585, 1644, 1691, 1716, 1722, 2528, 2565, 4558, 4562. Uruguay, 2851.

Regionalism, 4007, 4329, 4334. Argentina, 2275. Chile, 2816. Ecuador, 3427. Historiography, 1014. Mexico, 4606. Peru, 1014. Venezuela, 3480.

Reichel-Dolmatoff, Gerardo, 1139.

Reina, Carlos Roberto, 3206.

Religion and Politics, 2986. Brazil, 3850, 3917. British Guiana, 3274. Cuba, 4772. Nicaragua, 4761. Peru, 1224. Puerto Rico, 4815.

Religious Life and Customs. African Influences, 974. Andean Region, 1047, 1060, 1065. Argentina, 5133. Barbados, 836. Bolivia, 1075, 1095–1096, 5095. Brazil, 975, 5225. Caribbean Area, 4840, 4964. Central America, 4695, 4739. Coca, 1176. Cuba, 3366, 4772. Cuna, 769. Democratization, 2930. Dominican Republic, 4879, 4941. Ecuador, 1165, 5024. El Salvador, 4722. Haiti, 795. Indigenous Peoples, 1047. Jamaica, 790, 792, 803, 820, 848, 4765. Mexico, 4621, 4739. Nicaragua, 4721. Panama, 769. Peru, 1181, 1196, 1224, 1227. Puerto Rico, 4815. Quechua, 1176. Research, 1095. Spiritualism, 975. Suriname, 902. Trinidad and Tobago, 834, 837, 847, 850. Uruguay, 5188. Venezuela, 888, 4999, 5009. Women, 1096, 5225. Zapotec, 19.

Remittances. *See* Emigrant Remittances.

Remote Sensing. Archaeology, 328. Costa Rica, 328.

Renovación Nacional (Chile), 3606.

Repression. Argentina, 5144. Brazil, 3920, 3950. Children, 5167. Chile, 5167. Family and Family Relations, 5167. Haiti, 3291. Mental Health, 4555. Mexico, 3063.

Rescue Archaeology. *See* Salvage Archaeology.

Research. Anthropology, 843. Cuba, 4783. Feminism, 4878. Guyana, 831. Mexico, 4661. Political Parties, 3916. Political Science, 2987. Poverty, 1265. Sociology, 5143.

Research Institutes. Higher Education, 2960. Privatization, 2960–2961.

Return Migration. Africans, 858. Barbados, 822. Dominican Republic, 4902. French Caribbean, 4921. Peru, 1180. Puerto Rico, 4882.

Return Migration, African. Ghana, 858.

Revolutionaries, 2947. Chile, 3648. Paraguay, 3807. Peru, 3565, 3586, 3591–3592, 3595, 3599, 3604, 4431. Universities, 3586.

Revolutions and Revolutionary Movements, 2947, 2976. Caribbean Area, 2969. Central America, 4757. Colombia, 3370. Cuba, 2969, 3329, 3350, 3352, 3360. Dominican

Social origins of dictatorship and democracy, 2951.

Social Policy, 1270, 1286, 1407, 1465, 1478, 2935. Argentina, 2256, 2259, 2285, 2314, 3751, 3761, 3763, 5116, 5121, 5128–5129, 5132, 5139, 5141. Belize, 750, 4729. Brazil, 3873, 3895, 3907, 3909, 3970, 5220, 5239, 5263, 5307. Chile, 2063–2064, 2072, 2078, 2100, 2122, 3639, 3652, 5159–5161, 5172. Colombia, 1983, 4960, 4962, 4968, 4979. Costa Rica, 1771. Cuba, 3337, 3347, 4828. Developing Countries, 4808. Dominican Republic, 1865. Economic Liberalization, 1278. El Salvador, 1783. Guatemala, 1795, 1800. Honduras, 1809–1810. Mexico, 1499, 1514, 1542, 2544, 3019, 3102, 4571, 4576, 4638, 4662, 4677. Peru, 2141, 2153, 3568. Poverty, 1273. Puerto Rico, 4833, 4844. Quality of Life, 1239. South America, 4325. Trinidad and Tobago, 4231. Uruguay, 2226, 5190, 5197. Venezuela, 1958, 3465, 3482–3483, 4992, 4997, 5015.

Social Prediction. Chile, 3630, 3633. Mexico, 1632.

Social Relations. *See* Social Life and Customs.

Social Sciences. Argentina, 5142. Mexico, 707, 1619, 4661, 4682. Peru, 3542. Research, 4661.

Social Security, 1322, 1382, 1394–1395, 1450, 1459. Argentina, 2275, 2290, 2311. Brazil, 2328. Caribbean Area, 1851. Chile, 2045, 2087, 2090, 2094, 2111. Costa Rica, 1773, 3159. Economic Liberalization, 1397. Ecuador, 2045, 2047. El Salvador, 1785. Foreign Investment, 2090. Privatization, 1396, 2045. Venezuela, 5005.

Social Services. Argentina, 5123, 5125, 5128. Brazil, 5210, 5216, 5239, 5276. Chile, 3607. Colombia, 4969, 4981. Mexico, 4576. Peru, 5060. Uruguay, 5202. Venezuela, 3459.

Social Structure, 1330. Andean Region, 1198. Argentina, 5131, 5133. Aztecs, 32, 36. Barbados, 4769. Brazil, 3970, 5206, 5222, 5253. British Caribbean, 4778. Caribbean Area, 4791, 4839. Central America, 4149. Chile, 2794. Colombia, 1144. Costa Rica, 4740. Diseases, 1202. Dominica, 4856. Ecuador, 1168. Guadeloupe, 4905. Guatemala, 708. Guyana, 4925. Haiti, 4273. Indigenous Peoples, 1168. Intellectuals, 4549. Mesoamerica, 81, 755. Mexico, 692, 717–718, 766, 773, 3041. Nahuas, 766. Otomí, 717. Peru, 1206, 5041, 5053. Trinidad and Tobago, 851, 915. Tzotzil, 718. Venezuela, 2592, 5012. Zapotec, 773.

Social Values. Cuba, 3329. Jamaica, 820. Youth, 4537.

Social Welfare, 1465. Argentina, 5125. Brazil, 3873, 5307. Children, 4097. Chile, 3630. Colombia, 4962, 4981. Haiti, 4859. Mexico, 4097, 4590. Puerto Rico, 4844. Structural Adjustment, 1427. Uruguay, 5190, 5197.

Socialism and Socialist Parties, 2967, 2978. Argentina, 3700, 3705, 3717. Brazil, 3874, 3891, 3960. Central America, 4757. Chile, 3632, 3649, 3657, 3668. Grenada, 1896, 4843. Mexico, 3049, 4560. Nicaragua, 4742. Peru, 3587. Uruguay, 3822, 3844, 4053. Venezuela, 3458, 3469.

Sociology. Mexico, 4668. Research, 4668.

Soconusco, Mexico (region). Agriculture, 1715. Coffee Industry and Trade, 1672. Ecology, 1715.

Sodré, Nelson Werneck, 3961.

Soil Erosion. Andean Region, 2575, 2627. Argentina, 2750. Bolivia, 2687. Brazil, 2857. Ecuador, 2623, 2627. Mesoamerica, 256. Mexico, 2530.

Soils. Amazon Basin, 2900. Argentina, 2696. Brazil, 2857, 2875. Mexico, 2522.

Somoza Debayle, Anastasio, 1835, 4147.

Sonora, Mexico (state). Archaeological Surveys, 172. Artifacts, 172. Cattle Raising and Trade, 1661. Ecology, 2525. Economic Forecasting, 1661. Economic Policy, 1534. Food Supply, 4666. Labor and Laboring Classes, 4575. Minerals and Mining Industry, 4575. Peasants, 1661, 4660. Plants, 2525. Public Health, 4575. Social Policy, 1534. Women, 4628.

Southern Peru Copper Corporation, 2640.

Souza, Luiza Erundina de, 3876.

Sovereignty, 1445, 3985, 4073. Aruba, 4239. Belize, 4198. Caribbean Area, 4294, 4306. Chile, 4382. Curaçao, 4239. Dutch Caribbean, 4239. Mexico, 3032, 3039, 4064.

Spaniards. Argentina, 2755. Bolivia, 2686. Relations with Carib, 358. Relations with Taino, 334.

Spanish Civil War (1936–1939). Bibliography, 4384. Chile, 4384.

Spanish Conquest. Argentina, 2744. Mayas, 208. Mexico, 77, 92.

Spanish Influences. Chile, 2808. Guatemala, 708.

Spanish Language. Paraguay, 5109. Peru, 1227.

Spinosa Melo, Oscar, 4356, 4369.

Spiritualism. Brazil, 975. Cultural Identity, 975.

Spores, Ronald, 38, 365.

Cuba, 3364. Economic Integration, 1476. Ecuador, 3422. Guyana, 3277. Honduras, 3205. Maquiladoras, 4573. Mexico, 1522, 1567, 3025, 3081, 3114, 3131, 4596, 4605, 4619, 4643. Neoliberalism, 3422. Nicaragua, 1838. Panama, 3237. Paraguay, 3790, 5101, 5110. Peru, 5036–5037, 5069. Uruguay, 2238, 3821, 3826, 3831–3832, 3839. Venezuela, 3455, 3484, 4991, 5002. Women, 4674, 5306.

Traditional Farming. Paraguay, 2845. Rural Development, 931.

Traditional Medicine, 937, 941, 973. Amazon Basin, 935, 997. Argentina, 1051. Aymara, 1080, 1201. Bolivia, 1069, 1080, 1087–1088, 5077. Brazil, 973. Chile, 1103, 1110. Colombia, 992, 1143. Cosmology, 1199, 1201, 1216. Domestic Animals, 1201. Ecuador, 1005. Hallucinogenic Drugs, 1203. Mapuche, 1103, 1110. Maroons, 910. Mexico, 751, 2519, 4639. Paleo-Indians, 8. Peru, 1195–1196, 1199, 1201, 1203, 1213, 1216. Precolumbian Civilizations, 8. Shamanism, 927. Shuar, 1005. Sources, 1088. Suriname, 910. Women, 4639.

Transnational Corporations. *See* Multinational Corporations.

Transportation. Argentina, 2250, 2751. Bolivia, 2665. Chile, 2123. Colombia, 1974, 2606. Ecuador, 2032. Mesoamerica, 57. Mexico, 1572, 1647, 2564. Peru, 2142. South America, 2417.

Travelers. Brazil, 2387. Chile, 2819.

Treaties. Argentina, 4358. Brazil, 4417. Caribbean Area, 4308. Central America, 4359. Chile, 4358. Colombia, 3379, 4400, 4409. Ecuador, 4041. El Salvador, 4169. Mexico, 1544. Panama, 3229, 4409. Paraguay, 4321, 4417. Peru, 4041. South America, 2450. Venezuela, 4400.

Trees. Argentina, 2771. Bolivia, 2683. Chile, 2827–2828.

Trinidad and Tobago. Social Life and Customs, 854.

Trinidadians. Cultural Identity, 845, 4847. Race and Race Relations, 845, 4847. US, 845, 4847.

Trio (indigenous group). Indigenous Languages, 816. Traditional Medicine, 937.

Trique (indigenous group). Political Culture, 4647. Social Change, 4647. Violence, 4647.

Troll, Carl, 2580.

Trujillo, Peru (city). History, 1227.

Trujillo Molina, Rafael Leónidas, 2970, 4804.

Tucanoan (indigenous group). Cultural Development, 986. Cultural Identity, 985. Educational Models, 986. Indigenismo and Indianidad, 985. Shamanism, 986.

Tucma. *See* Diaguita.

Tucumán, Argentina (city). Housing, 2746. Poor, 2746. Rural-Urban Migration, 2746. Sewage Disposal, 2714. Urban History, 2714. Urbanization, 2714. Water Supply, 2714.

Tucumán, Argentina (prov.). Economic Development, 2315. Elections, 3742. Governors, 3742. Structural Adjustment, 2315.

Túcume Site (Peru), 630.

Tucuna (indigenous group). Indigenous Art, 1123.

Tula Site (Mexico), 88, 136, 211. Obsidian, 136.

Tumaco-La Tolita Sites (Colombia and Ecuador). Precolumbian Art, 1123.

Tunja, Colombia (town). Archaeology, 548.

Tupi (indigenous group). Precolumbian Land Settlement Patterns, 475.

Tupi-Guarani (indigenous group). Cannibalism, 950. Cosmology, 950. Precolumbian Pottery, 462. Religious Life and Customs, 950. Rites and Ceremonies, 950.

Turbay Ayala, Julio César, 4403.

Tzeltal (indigenous group). Cultural History, 763. Cultural Identity, 763. Migration, 775.

Tzotzil (indigenous group). Alcohol and Alcoholism, 718. Social Structure, 718. Women, 718.

Uaxactún Site (Guatemala), 323.

Ubbelohde-Doering, Heinrich, 629.

Ubico, Jorge, 3195.

Uchuraccay, Peru (city). Terrorism, 3580.

Umbanda (cult), 5223.

UN. *See* United Nations.

UNAM. *See* Universidad Nacional Autónoma de México.

Underdevelopment. Public Opinion, 1417.

Underemployment. Bolivia, 2184. Chile, 2124. Nicaragua, 1827. Peru, 2167, 5038.

Underwater Archaeology. Mesoamerica, 155.

Unemployment. Argentina, 2269, 2275, 3761, 5130. Brazil, 2361. Chile, 2084, 2124, 2129, 5183. Insurance, 2084. Mexico, 1584, 1606, 1673. Nicaragua, 1824, 1833. Peru, 5038. Technological Innovations, 2361. Uruguay, 2222.

Unesco, 4454.

Unidad Democrática y Popular (Bolivia), 3487.

Unidad Popular (Chile), 2073–2074, 3640.

AUTHOR INDEX

Agreda Ugas, Víctor, 2139

La agricultura en tierras mexicanas desde sus orígenes hasta nuestros días, 4557

Agricultura orgánica: experiencias de cultivo ecológico en la Argentina, 2696

Agricultura y campesinado en Guatemala: una aproximación, 1794

Agroeconomía de la papa en México, 1481

Agua y medio ambiente en Buenos Aires, 2697

Aguascalientes en los noventas: estrategias para el cambio, 1482

Agudelo Cáceres, Lilian, 3445

Aguerre, Ana M., 418

Aguiar, Maria Suelí de, 921

Aguiar, Neuma, 1403, 5208

Aguilar, Adrián Guillermo, 1554, 1691, 4558

Aguilar, Alice, 452

Aguilar, Gracia, 4763

Aguilar, José Víctor, 1780

Aguilar, Víctor, 2140

Aguilar Almada, Fernanda, 4607, 4628

Aguilar Barajas, Ismael, 1483

Aguilar de León, Juan de Dios, 3184

Aguilar Monteverde, Alonso, 1484

Aguilar O., Carlos, 1821

Aguilar Revelo, Lorena, 4688

Aguilera A., Nelson, 493

Aguilera-Alfred, Nelson, 2021

Aguilera Ortega, Jesús, 2514

Aguilera Peralta, Gabriel Edgardo, 3185–3186

Aguinaga C., Consuelo, 2046

Aguinis, Ana María Meirovich de, 1237

Aguirre Benítez, Adán, 4559

Aguirre Tirado, Leonardo, 567

Aguirrechu, Iraida, 3327

Agurto Vílchez, Sonia, 1833

Ahumada Pacheco, Jaime, 3783

A AIDS no Brasil, 1982–1992, 5209

Aitken, Brian, 1238

Aiyer, Sri-Ram, 1478

Ajuste y consenso en la era menemista: un nuevo mapa electoral, 3676

Ajustes, políticas sociales y fondos de inversión en América Latina, 1239

Ajustes y desajustes regionales: el caso de Jalisco a fines del sexenio salinista, 1485

Akademiïa nauk SSSR., 4305

Al-Safi, Mansour Saleh, 4462

Alameda Ospina, Raúl, 1240

Alarcón, Alexis, 4875

Alarcón, Marleni M., 602

Alarcón Aliaga, Carlos, 2638

Alarcón G., Walter, 5035

Alarcón González, Diana, 1486–1490

Alba Fernández, Juan José, 1069, 5077

Alba Vega, Carlos, 3056

Albarracín-Jordán, Juan, 438

Albeck, María Ester, 406

Albert, Bruce, 943–944

Albó, Xavier, 689, 3485–3486, 3540, 5078

Albornoz D., Marcelo, 2080

Albornoz Guarderas, Vicente, 2016

Albuquerque, José Augusto Guilhon, 4463

Albuquerque, Paulo Tadeu de Souza, 453

Albuquerque, Roberto Cavalcanti de, 5220

Alcalá Delgado, Elio, 690

Alcántara Saez, Manuel, 3241

Alcina Franch, José, 1–2, 297

Alcocer V., Jorge, 3031

Alconini Mujica, Sonia, 439–440

Alegría, Ricardo E., 352

Alegría Olazábal, Tito, 1491, 2515

Alegría Ortega, Idsa E., 4282

Alejos García, José, 691

Alemán, Estela, 1822

Alencar, José Almino de, 5210

Alès, Catherine, 922

Alfaro M., Julio, 5036

Alfaro Montaro, Petra, 3446

Alfonsín, Raúl, 3677

Alford, Alan, 1492

Aliaga Rodríguez, José, 4310

Allaire, Louis, 334

Allamand Zavala, Andrés, 3606

Allegretti, Mary Helena, 2858

Allen, Catherine J., 1173

Allen, Elizabeth, 3851

Allen, Rose Mary, 787–788

Allender, Darrell, 2485

Allub, Leopoldo, 5113

Almada, Martín, 3784

Almeida, Alfredo Wagner Berno de, 945

Almeida, Paulo Roberto de, 4311, 4464–4465

Almeida Vinueza, José, 1146

Alonso, Ana María, 692

Alonso, Jorge, 3035, 4560, 4638

Alonso, Márcio, 481–482

Alonso Santos, José Luis, 2475

Alpinistas de Lecco en la Patagonia, 2698

Alsogaray, Alvaro, 2247

Altamirano, Teófilo, 689, 1174–1175, 3542

Alternativas campesinas: modernización en el agro y movimiento campesino en Centroamérica, 4689

Alternativas de Desarrollo (Association), 1769

Alternativas para el desarrollo agroindustrial, 1493

Altimir, Oscar, 1241–1242

Arnáiz Burne, Stella Maris, 2488
Arnauld, Charlotte, 157
Arnold, Denise Y., 1042, 1071
Arnold, Philip J., 24, 124
Arnove, Robert F., 1247
Arnson, Cynthia, 3950
Aroche Reyes, Fidel, 1503
Aronson, Meredith, 158
Arosemena, Guillermo, 2018–2019
Arqueología Contemporánea, 387
Arqueología de rescate, Oleoducto Vasconia-Coveñas: un viaje por el tiempo a lo largo del Oleoducto; cazadores-recolectores, agroaleareros y orfebres, 529
Arqueología del occidente y norte de México, 25
Arqueología Mexicana, 26–27, 159
La arqueología mexicana en el umbral del siglo XXI: proyectos especiales de arqueología, 28
Arqueología nos empreendimentos hidrelétricos da ELETRONORTE: resultados preliminares = Archeology in the hydroelectric projects of ELETRONORTE: preliminary results, 455
Arquez, Graciela S., 2702
Arquivos do Museu de História Natural, 456
Arrazcaeta, Roger, 337
Arraztoa Jaimerena, María Teresa, 2927
El arreglo de los pueblos Indios: la incansable tarea de reconstitución, 695
Arreola, Daniel David, 2517
Arreola Ayala, Alvaro, 2518
Arretche, Marta Teresa S., 5239
Arriagada, Irma, 1248
Arriaza, Bernardo T., 494–496
Arriazu, Ricardo H., 4353
Arrieta Abdalla, Mario, 2204
Arrieta Fernández, Pedro, 4562
Arrieta Munguía, Judith, 4065
Arriola, Carlos, 1708, 2995
Arriola Palomares, Joaquín, 1780
Arriola Socol, Merardo, 3786
Arrizabalo Montoro, Xabier, 2070
Arrochellas, Maria Helena, 3898
Arroi, Ana Carolina Machado, 4469
Arroyo, Barbara, 160
Arroyo, Mónica, 2703
Arroyo Alejandre, Jesús, 1485, 4563, 4681
Arroyo Ferreyros, Juan Carlos, 2142
Arroyo Mosqueda, Artemio, 4564
Arruda, Antônio de, 4470
Arrue, Wille, 1051
Arsenault, Daniel, 605
Artana, Daniel, 2253

Artaud, Denise, 4216
Arte indígena en Colombia: cultures del món, Castell de Bellver, 1123
El arte rupestre en la arqueología contemporánea, 388
Arteaga, Ana María, 5156
Arteta Villavicencio, Gustavo, 2020
Arvanitis, Reyes, 1717
Arvelo, Lilliam, 679
Arze Quiroga, Eduardo, 4371
Asamblea de la Sociedad Civil (Guatemala), 1795
Asambleas provinciales de balance del Partido Comunista de Cuba: 5 de enero al 24 de febrero de 1991, 3327
Asaro, Frank, 560
Aschero, Carlos A., 411
Ashby, Timothy, 3292
Ashdown, Peter David, 3148
Asociación Chilena de Ciencia Política, 3652
Asociación de Bancos Argentinos, 2272
Asociación de Ingenieros Consultores de Chile, 2826
Asociación de Instituciones de Promoción y Educación (Bolivia), 3489
Asociación de Promoción Agraria (Peru), 2148
Asociación Dominicana de Administradores de Recursos Humanos, 4801
Asociación Española de Empresas de Ingeniería y Consultoras, 2826
Asociación Geológica de Mendoza, 2719
Asociación Latinoamericana de Integración (Montevideo), 1249
Asociación Nicaragüense Pro-Derechos Humanos, 3222
Asociación para el Avance de las Ciencias Sociales en Guatemala, 4749
Asociación Peruana de Estudios e Investigaciones para la Paz (Lima), 3540, 5014
Asociación Trabajadores del Estado (Buenos Aires, Argentina), 2255
Assies, Willem, 2865
Associação de Universidades Amazônicas (Brazil), 5272
Associação Nacional das Instituições do Mercado Aberto (Brazil), 2325–2326
Association des dîplomés d'écoles supérieures de commerce, 1851
Association for European Research on the Caribbean and Central America. Conference, *9th, Maastricht, Netherlands*, 1727
Association of Caribbean Economists, 1852
Astorga Almanza, Luis Alejandro, 4565
Astori, Danilo, 3977
Athens, J. Stephen, 561

Atkins, G. Pope, 3978–3979
Atlas agropecuario de Costa Rica, 2489
Atlas de las plantas de la medicina tradicional
  mexicana, 2519
Auge exportador chileno: lecciones y desafíos
  futuros, 2071
Augustin, Gurulf, 1866
Augustine, C., 1846
Auroi, Claude, 5
Ausaldi, Waldo, 3687
Austin-Broos, Diane J., 790–792, 4765
Austral, Antonio G., 412
La autonomía del Banco de la República:
  economía política de la reforma, 1978
Auyero, Javier, 5114
Avalos Gutiérrez, Ignacio, 1942
Avalos Huertas, Antonio, 1504
Avanzando en equidad: un proceso de integra-
  ción al desarrollo, 1990–1992, 2072
Avelar, Lúcia, 3854
Avella Gómez, Mauricio, 1979
Avila, Patricia, 1664
Avila Palafox, Ricardo, 142, 4606
Avirama, Jesús, 1124
Avril, Prosper, 3278
Axline, W. Andrew, 1847
Ayala, María Teresa, 5111
Ayala Lafée, Cecilia, 678
Ayala Mora, Enrique, 3443
Ayala R., Patricia, 504
Aylwin Azócar, Andrés, 3609
Aylwin Azócar, Patricio, 3610
Aymer, Paula L., 793
Azaola Garrido, Elena, 4566
Azara, Félix de, 2843
Azcoitia, Carlos Eduardo, 4339
Azcuy, Hugo, 4217
Aziz Nassif, Alberto, 2996, 4638
Aznárez, Carlos, 3681
Azócar, Héctor C., 4218
Azpiazu, Daniel, 2254–2255
Azuela, Antonio, 4598
Babb, Florence E., 696
Bacigalupo, Ana Mariella, 1099
Back in the saddle: a survey of Argentina,
  3682
Back to the ballot box: evaluating Venezuela's
  1995 state and local elections, 3449
Baer, Gerhard, 994
Baer, M. Delal, 1639, 4073
Baer, Werner, 1250–1252, 1425, 2327
Báez, Clara, 4834
Báez, Luis, 3351
Báez Cubero, Lourdes, 697
Bagella, Michele, 1253

Bagley, Bruce Michael, 3999
Bähr, Jürgen, 2866
Bailey, Adrian J., 4690
Baines, Stephen Grant, 947–948
Baja California (Mexico). Secretaría de Desa-
  rrollo Económico. Dirección de Asesoría
  y Gestoría, 1645
Bakan, Abigail Bess, 4257
Baklanoff, Eric N., 3980
Balazote Oliver, Alejandro Omar, 1052, 1063–
  1064
Balbi Scarneo, Carmen Rosa, 5037
Balboa Valencia, Alfredo, 1072
Baldivia Urdininea, José, 2198
Baldó, Josefina, 1947
Ballesteros, Carlos, 4066
Balliache, Dilcia, 4991
Ballistrieri, Carlos A., 2704
Ballón Aguirre, Enrique, 995
Balmaceda, Felipe, 1790
Balmelli, Carlos Mateo, 3787
Balslev, Henrik, 2584
Baltra Montaner, Lidia, 5157
Balvín Díaz, Doris, 2640
Balze, Felipe A.M. de la, 2253
Banco Central de Chile, 2086
Banco Central de Honduras. Departamento de
  Estudios Económicos, 1804
Banco Central de Honduras. Sección Cuentas
  Nacionales, 1805
Banco Centroamericano de Integración Eco-
  nómica, 1745
Banco de México, 1505
Banco de Occidente (Colombia), 2602
Banco del Estado (Ecuador). Programa de De-
  sarrollo Municipal, 3424
Bandeira, Moniz, 4471–4472
Bandieri, Susana, 5115
Bang, Joon, 2257
Bango, Julio, 5187
Bannister, Geoffrey J., 1506
Bant, Astrid A., 996
Banzo, Mayté, 2520
Barabas, Alicia M., 698, 933
Barajas, Adolfo, 1980
Baranyi, Stephen, 3981, 4141
Baraona Urzúa, Pablo, 2073
Barba, Josep, 441
Barbeito, Alberto C., 2256, 5129
Barbery, Efraín, 441
Barbira-Freedman, Françoise, 935
Barbosa, Débora Rocha, 457
Barbosa, Fernando de Holanda, 2328
Barbosa, Luiz C., 5213
Barbosa, Márcia, 457

Elter, Doris, 2087
The emergence of pottery: technology and innovation in ancient societies, 7
Emigracja, Polonia, Ameryka Łacińska: procesy emigracji i osadnictwa Polaków w Ameryce Łacińskiej i ich odzwierciedlenie w świadomości społecznej. [Emigration, Poland, Latin America: the processes of emigration and Polish settlement in Latin America and their image in the social consciousness.], 2409
Emmanuel, Patrick A.M., 3245, 3254
Emmerich, Gustavo Ernesto, 2518
Empleo, cuello de botella del ajuste, 2031
Empresa, crisis y desarrollo, 1564
Empresa Metropolitana de Planejamento da Grande São Paulo, 2908
Los empresarios ante la globalización, 4587
En busca de la estabilidad perdida: actores políticos y sociales en los años noventa, 4961
En el nombre del señor: shamanes, demonios y curanderos del norte del Perú, 1196
Encalada Reyes, Marco A., 2052
Enciso, Braida Elena, 530, 535, 537
Enciso, Miguel Angel, 1020
Encontro Internacional Pobreza e Meio Ambiente: Alternativas Contra a Destruição, Belém, Brazil, 1994, 2446
Encontro Nacional de Economia, 22nd, Florianópolis, Brazil, 1994, 2343
Encuentro Binacional Perú-Bolivia, La Paz, 1991, 5085
Encuentro de dos democracias, 4374
Encuentro de Historiadores en Puerto Rico, Río Piedras, P.R., 1990, 3310
Encuentro de Integración para el Desarrollo Cultural de América Latina y el Caribe, Manta, Ecuador, 1992, 4001
Encuentro de Investigadores de la Costa Ecuatoriana en Europa, 1st, Barcelona, 1993, 575
Encuentro Internacional por la Rehabilitación de los Barrios del Tercer Mundo, 1st, Caracas, 1991, 1947
Encuentro Internacional sobre Situación Actual de la Familia Indígena en la Subregión Andina, Riobamba, Ecuador, 1993, 1039
Encuentro Latinoamericano sobre la Biblioteca, la Lectura y el Niño Callejero, 1st, México, 1996, 4541
Encuentro Latinoamericano y del Caribe, 4th, La Habana, 1994, 4234
Encuentro Nacional de Investigadores sobre la Familia, 1st, Tlaxcala, Mexico, 1993, 4588

Encuentro Niñez y Juventud: una Mirada desde la Universidad, Bogotá, 1994, 4962
Encuentro-Taller de Teoria Feminista, 1st, Ballenita, Ecuador, 1986–1987, 5022
Endsley, Harry B., 4081
Enfoque integral de la salud humana en la Amazonia, 2579
Enfoques teóricos y metodológicos para el estudio de la política exterior, 4002
Engle, Patrice L., 4707
Enright, Michael J., 1957
Enríquez, Laura J., 4708
Ensayos sobre la economía de la Ciudad de México, 1565
Entre la guerra y la estabilidad política: el México de los 40, 3038
The environmental dimension in development planning, 1309
La equidad en el panorama social de América Latina durante los años ochenta, 1310
Equipo Onè-Respe (Dominican Republic), 4873
Erbsen de Maldonado, Karin, 3139
Ereira, Alan, 1128
Erfani, Julie A., 3039
Erickson, Clark L., 624
Eróstegui T., Rodolfo, 2192
Errandonea, Alfredo, 5189
Errázuriz K., Ana María, 2797, 2802, 2806
Erundina, uma razão, 3876
Escaith, Hubert, 1737
Escalante, Ricardo, 3457
Escalante Gutiérrez, Carmen, 1228
Escalante Herrera, Ana Cecilia, 4158
Escalante Moscoso, Javier F., 443
Esch-Jakob, Juliane, 1075
Escobal D'Angelo, Javier, 2139
Escobar, Arturo, 1129
Escobar, Francisco Andrés, 4159
Escobar, Gabriela Martínez, 1190
Escobar H., Guillerno León, 3385
Escobedo, Héctor L., 133–135
Escola, Patricia, 420
Escola Superior de Guerra (Brazil), 4479
Escoto, Jorge, 4687
Los escuadrones de la muerte en El Salvador, 3167
Escuela Politécnica Nacional, 2625
Escuela Superior de Guerra Aérea (Peru), 4310
Eskeland, Gunnar S., 1566
Espada, Joaquín, 4375
España, Luis Pedro, 5015
España/América Latina: un siglo de políticas culturales, 4003
Espín Guillois, Vilma, 4822

Espinal, Carlos, 2579
Espino Z., Darinel, 3229
Espinosa, Myriam Amparo, 1130
Espinosa Apolo, Manuel, 5023
Espinosa Gómez, Rosa Aurora, 4639
Espinosa Ojeda, Bernarda, 1103
Espinoza, Isolda, 1822
Espinoza Valle, Víctor Alejandro, 1567
Los espíritus aliados: chamanismo y curación
  en los pueblos indios de Sudamérica, 927
Esponda Jimeno, Víctor Manuel, 22
A esquerda e o movimento operário, 1964–
  1984, 3877
Esquivel Trianot, Ricardo, 1131
Essman M., Alejandro, 2816
Estabilización y crecimiento: nuevas lecturas
  de macroeconomía colombiana, 1987
Estado de México: perspectivas para la década
  de los 90, 1568
Estado, partidos políticos y sociedad: análisis
  de la transición política paraguaya, 3792
Estado y nación: las demandas de los grupos
  étnicos en Guatemala, 719
Esteche Notario, Mario, 3793
Esteinou Madrid, Javier, 4589
Esteve, Hugo, 1539, 3040, 4627
Estigarribia V., Ricardo, 3794
Estrada Alvarez, Jairo, 2935
Estrada Belli, Francisco, 194
Estrategias de desarrollo: intentando cambiar
  la vida, 4542
Estrategias para superar la pobreza: seminario
  aniversario, Caracas, 29 al 31 de enero de
  1996, 1958
Estrella, Eduardo, 941
Estrella Valenzuela, Gabriel, 2541
La estructura institucional y las negocia-
  ciones del Mercosur: los 30 primeros
  meses, 4318
Estructura orgánica, toma de decisiones y
  atribuciones de representación externa,
  4319
La estructuración de las capitales centro-
  americanas, 2479
Estudio ambiental nacional, 2854
Estudio de la pobreza en Nicaragua: docu-
  mento de trabajo, 1825
Estudio integral de la frontera México-Belice,
  2542
Estudio nacional de opinión pública no. 1, ter-
  cera serie, noviembre-diciembre 1994,
  3618
Estudios argentinos para la integración del
  Mercosur, 2278
Estudios arqueológicos del período formativo

en el sur-este de Cochabamba, 1988–1989,
  444
Estudios inconformistas sobre la clase obrera
  argentina: 1955–1989, 5120
Etchegoyhen, Carlos, 4555
Eternod, Marcela, 1600
Etheart, Bernard, 3284
Ethnicity and employment practices in the
  public and private sectors in Trinidad and
  Tobago, 1877
Ethnicity in the Caribbean: essays in honor of
  Harry Hoetink, 827
Ethnicity, markets, and migration in the An-
  des: at the crossroads of history and anthro-
  pology, 1040
Ethnicity, race and nationality in the Carib-
  bean, 828
Etnohistoria del Amazonas, 928
Europe and Latin America in the world econ-
  omy, 1311, 4004
An evaluation of government's subsidy and
  incentive programmes in relation to the
  dairy and meat industries in Trinidad and
  Tobago: a report submitted to the cabinet
  appointed Commission of Enquiry into the
  Meat and Dairy Industry of Trinidad and
  Tobago. Dept. of Agricultural Economics
  and Farm Management, Faculty of Agricul-
  ture, the University of the West Indies,
  St. Augustine, Trinidad and Tobago, 1878
Evans, Ronald, 4998
Everingham, Mark, 4709
Evolución reciente de la pobreza en el Gran
  Buenos Aires, 1988–1992, 2279
Exposición sobre la política monetaria: para
  el lapso 1º. de enero de 1995–31 de diciem-
  bre de 1995, 1569
Eyre, L. Alan, 2460
Fábregas Puig, Andrés, 3041
Fähmel Beyer, Bernd Walter Federico, 59–60
Fahsen, Federico, 323
Fairlie Reinoso, Alan, 1312
Faissol, Speridão, 2877
Fajardo Montaña, Darío, 4963
Falabella, Fernanda, 502
Falaha Lumi, Boris, 2088
Falcão, Eduardo, 3969
Falchetti de Sáenz, Ana María, 538
Falco, Mathea, 4005
Falcoff, Mark, 4160
Falconer, Steven E., 23
Fallas, Helio, 1732, 1761
La familia cubana: principales rasgos socio-
  demográficos que han caracterizado su de-
  sarrollo y dinámica, 4823

Familia, salud y sociedad: experiencias de investigación en México, 4590
Familia y futuro: un programa regional en América Latina y el Caribe, 1313
Fanelli, José María, 1292, 1314, 2280
Fanfant, F.E., 4824
Fanta, Gloria, 2240
Fanzares, Anna, 2898
Faraco, Francisco José, 1959
Fárber, Guillermo, 1616
Farer, Tom J., 3985
Farfán Lovatón, Carlos, 625
Faria, Tales, 3903
Farné, Stefano, 1315
Farnós Morejón, Alfonso, 4825
Farran, Gabriela, 4348
Farrell, Terrence W., 1850
Faruqi, Shakil, 1320
Fash, Barbara, 195
Fash, William L., 195
Fassin, Dedier, 1044
Faugère-Kalfon, Briggitte, 61
Fauquié Bescós, Rafael, 4543
Fausto Neto, Ana Maria Quiroga, 5241
Fávero V., Gabriel del, 2814
Faxas, Laura, 4826
Fazio, Carlos, 3042
Febres, Carlos Eduardo, 4991
FEDEPRICAP (Organization), 1732, 1747
Federação das Indústrias do Estado de Rondônia (Brazil), 2344
Federación Internacional de Comites pro Derechos Humanos en Cuba, 3341
Federación Mexicana de Universitarias, 4629
Federación Unitaria de Trabajadores de Honduras, 3210
Federarbeiten der Indianer Südamerikas: aus der Studiensammlung Horst Antes; Rautenstrauch-Joest-Museum, 30 September 1994 bis 28; Januar 1995, Reiss-Museum der Stadt Mannheim, 16. März bis 18. Juni 1995, 929
Fedick, Scott L., 62, 196–197, 292
Fedorova, I.K., 503
Feinman, Gary M., 198
Feinsilver, Julie M., 1316, 1921, 3339, 4235–4236
Felipe, Jesus, 1317
Felipe Duyos, Edith, 4935
Feliú, Manuel, 2089
Felix, David, 1318
Feliz, Raúl Aníbal, 1319, 1570–1571
Feltenstein, Andrew, 1572
Femenías, Blenda, 2661
Ferbel, Peter J., 380

Ferguson, R. Brian, 930
Fernandes, Florestan, 3878
Fernandes, Luis, 3879
Fernandes, Rubem César, 5242
Fernández, Arturo, 1416, 3709
Fernández, Diego E., 1988
Fernández, Fiz Antonio, 8
Fernández, Luis Fernando, 1736
Fernandez, Nadine T., 4827
Fernández, Nuria, 3043
Fernández, Oscar, 1584
Fernández, Raquel, 4685
Fernández, Raúl, 2317
Fernández Alberté, María Felisa, 3710
Fernández Dávila, Enrique, 136
Fernández Fernández, Sergio, 3619
Fernández Font, Marcelo, 1922
Fernández Fontenoy, Carlos, 3552
Fernández Guerrero, Mariana, 3048
Fernández Jilberto, Alex E., 4082
Fernández Juárez, Gerardo, 1076–1081
Fernández Pérez, Joaquín, 2843
Fernández Pérez, Manuel, 1686
Fernández Poncela, Anna M., 720
Fernández Saavedra, Gustavo, 2190
Fernández Vásquez, Rodrigo, 2479
Ferpozzi, Luis Humberto, 2777
Ferraz, João Carlos, 2345
Ferreira, Alcides, 2346
Ferreira, Mariana Kawall Leal, 954
Ferreira, Reymi, 3502
Ferreira Falcón, Magno, 2212
Ferreira Rubio, Delia, 3711
Ferrer Fougá, Hernán, 2803, 2813
Ferrer Regales, Manuel, 2410
Ferrero Costa, Eduardo, 4430
Ferriol, Angela, 4828
Ferrufino, Alfonso, 3503
Festival international de l'indianité, 1st, Saint-François, Guadeloupe, 1990, 829
Ffrench-Davis, Ricardo, 1236, 1298
Fialko, Vilma, 238
Field, Les W., 721
Fields, Virginia M., 130
Figallo, Beatriz J., 4349
Figari, Guillermo Miguel, 4350
Fighting for the soul of Brazil, 5243
Figueiredo, Adma Hamam de, 2878
Figueiredo, Argelina Cheibub, 3913
Figueiredo, Luiz Carlos, 2385
Figueiredo, Marcus, 3880
Figueiredo, Rubens, 3881
Figueras, Alberto José, 2281
Figueras, Miguel Alejandro, 1923
Figueroa, Adolfo, 2151

Gatehouse, Mike, 4728
Gatti Cardozo, Gustavo, 3797
Gatti Murriel, Aldo, 3563
Gatto, Francisco, 2283
Gautier Mayoral, Carmen, 4282, 4833
Gautreaux Piñeyro, Bonaparte, 3259
Gavilán, Jorge, 2718
Gaviola Artigas, Edda, 5169
Gaviria Liévano, Enrique, 4400
Gaviria Trujillo, César, 1975, 4009
Gay, Robert, 3890
Gaytán Guzmán, Rosa Isabel, 4084
Geldstein, Rosa N., 5124, 5137
Gellert, Gisela, 2502
Gelles, Paul H., 1190, 1197
Género y Sociedad, 4834
Genin, Didier, 1038
Genoino Neto, José, 3891
GEODE Caraïbe, 2463
Geografía de San Luis: el hombre y la tierra, 2732
Geografía del medio ambiente: una alternativa del ordenamiento ecológico, 2415
Geografia e meio ambiente no Brasil, 2879
Geoistmo, 2416
Georgescu-Pipera, Constantino, 2417
Georgescu-Pipera, Paul, 2417
Gerlus, Jean-Claude, 4237
Gershenberg, Irving, 1879
La gestión ambiental en el Ecuador, 2626
Gestión urbana y cambio institucional, 4598
Ghysels, Joris, 1827
Giacalone, Rita, 4238–4239, 4448
Giaconi G., Juan, 5159
Giarracca, Norma, 5147
Gibbons, Arnold, 4835
Gibson, Edward L., 3053
Giddings, John Calvin, 2645
Gigliotti, Adriana, 2241
Gil, Beatriz, 5057
Gil, Germán Roberto, 3724
Gil-Díaz, Francisco, 1582
Gilbert, Herbert R., 4279
Gilbert, Isidoro, 4352
Gilboa, Eytan, 4165
Gilderhus, Mark T., 4010
Gilhodes, Pierre, 3387
Gill, Henry S., 4240
Gill, Indermit S., 2093
Gill, Lesley, 4166
Gillespie, Charles Guy, 3823, 3825
Gillespie, Richard, 3725
Gillespie, Susan D., 210
Gilliam, Angela, 5247
Gilliam, Onik'a, 5247

Gindling, T.H., 1763, 4713
Ginóbili de Tumminello, María Elena, 1056
Ginocchio, Luis, 2155
Giordani, Jorge, 3458
Giraldo, Javier, 3388
Giraud, Michel, 833
Girelli, Maribel, 465
Girón, Alicia, 1329, 1492
Girot, Pascal O., 2480
Gisbert, María Elena, 2191
Gitli, Eduardo, 1740
Giudice, Luis A., 2733
Gjerest, Heidi, 4836
Gladden, Kathleen, 4965
Glade, Alfonso A., 2836
Glade, William P., 1264, 1330
Glazier, Stephen D., 834–835
Gledhill, John, 725, 4599
Gleich, Albrecht von, 1374
Gleijeses, Piero, 4241–4243
Glender, Alberto, 4096
Gligo, Nicolo, 1331
Glikman, Pablo, 2027
Globalización, economía y proyecto neoliberal en México, 1583
Globalización y fuerza laboral en Centroamérica, 1741
Glynn, Carolyn, 2993
Gmelch, George, 822, 836
Gmelch, Sharon Bohn, 836
Gnecco, Cristóbal, 539–542, 547
Gnivecki, Perry L., 338
Gobierno de la ciudad y crisis en la Argentina, 3726
Godard, Henry, 2033
Godfrey, Brian J., 2868
Godfrey, Nancy, 4712
Godínez, José Alberto, 1621
Godio, Julio, 2946
Godoy, Ricardo, 726
Godoy Arcaya, Oscar, 2094
Goffin, Alvin Matthew, 5024
Golbert, Laura, 2269, 5125
Goldenberg, Olga, 4714
Goldin, Liliana R., 727
Goldman, Joe, 4354
Goldrin, Luin, 4616
Goldstein, Daniel J., 1332
Goldwasser, Michael, 837
Gollás, Manuel, 1584
Gomáriz, Enrique, 5136
Gomes-Neto, João Batista, 5248
Gómez, Emeterio, 1962
Gómez Alzate, Camilo, 4966
Gómez Flores, Ramiro, 1585

Grieco, Francisco de Assis, 4489
Griffin, Clifford E., 4245
Griffith, Ivelaw L., 3243, 3246–3247, 4011
Griffith, Winston H., 1853
Grimaldi, Víctor, 3260
Grindle, Merilee S., 2034
Grinspun, Ricardo, 4087
Griscom, Bronson W., 242
Grompone, Romeo, 3564, 5049, 5065
Groot, Jan P. de, 1727
Groot, Silvia W. de, 838
Gros Espiell, Héctor, 4436
Grosjean, Martin, 513
Gross, Liza, 2947
Gross, Patricio, 2809
Grosse, Robert E., 1334, 1338, 1880
Grosse Ickler, Juan Augusto, 2810
Grossi, María, 3696
Grossi, Patrícia Krieger, 5227
Grossman, Lawrence S., 2462
Group of Thirty, 1371
Grove, David C., 215
Grube, Nikolai, 72, 101, 303–304
Grugel, Jean, 4246
Grün, Roberto, 5251
Grupioni, Luís Donisete Benzi, 963, 977
El Grupo de los Tres: asimetrías y convergencias, 4322
Grupo de Río: documentos oficiales del principal foro político de América Latina y el Caribe, 4323
Grupo Interdisciplinario sobre Mujer, Trabajo y Pobreza (Mexico), 4632
Grupo Permanente de Estudio sobre Riego (Peru), 2646
Grushka, Carlos O., 5126
Gruson, Alberto, 5001
Guadeloupe, Martinique et Guyane dans le monde américain: réalités d'hier, mutations d'aujourd'hui, perspectives 2000, 2463
Gualdrón Sandoval, Jesús, 2935
Guallart Martínez, José María, 2419
Guaña, Pablo, 1161
Guandinango, Angel, 1162
Guardia, Alexis, 2095
Guardia Butrón, Fernando, 2671
Guardia Quirós, Jorge, 1764
Guastavino, Carlos Alberto, 2771
Guatemala: ONG's y desarrollo; el caso del altiplano central, 1798
Guatemala: impunity—a question of political will, 3189
Guatemala, 1800

Guatemala. Procurador de los Derechos Humanos, 3190
Guatemala, la búsqueda de la verdad, 3191
Guber, Rosana, 1057
Guderjan, Thomas H., 216, 247
Gudiño de Muñoz, Maria Elina, 2736
Gudynas, Eduardo, 2400
Gueron, Gabrielle, 1963
Guerra-Borges, Alfredo, 1742
Guerrini, Owen, 2096
Guevara Sánchez, Arturo, 73–74
Guevara Tapia, Soledad, 5170
Guffroy, J., 614
Guhl, Ernesto, 2386
Guia de fontes para a história indígena e do indigenismo em arquivos brasileiros: acervos das capitais, 960
Guido Béjar, Rafael, 4706, 4750
Guidon, Niède, 466
Guidugli, Odeibler Santo, 2883
Guillaudat, Patrick, 5171
Guillaume-Gentil, M. Nicolas, 576
Guillén, Ann Cyphers, 75
Guillermoprieto, Alma, 2948
Guimarães, Antônio Sérgio Alfredo, 5252–5253
Guimarães, Carmen Dora, 5254
Guionneau-Sinclair, Françoise, 731
Guliaev, Valerii Ivanovich, 393
Gullick, C.J.M.R., 4840
Gumucio Granier, Jorge, 4377
Gundermann Kroll, Hans, 1108
Gunn, Gillian, 4247
Gurak, Douglas T., 4841
Gutiérrez, Alejandro, 1964
Gutiérrez, Alfredo, 3727
Gutiérrez, María Alicia, 3728
Gutiérrez, María J., 2728
Gutiérrez, Mario A., 1339
Gutiérrez, Ramón, 2744
Gutiérrez, Ricardo, 3168
Gutiérrez, William, 2461
Gutiérrez Arriola, Angelina, 1587
Gutiérrez B., Hernán, 3975, 4385
Gutiérrez Condori, Ramiro, 1083
Gutiérrez Haces, Teresa, 2548
Gutiérrez Mejía, Irma Eugenia, 4602
Gutiérrez Pita, José Ignacio, 4167
Gutiérrez Rojas, Edith, 3509
Gutiérrez Urdaneta, Luis, 1912
Gutiérrez Vidal, Manuel, 4088
Gutmann, Matthew C., 732
Guzmán, León, 3565
Guzman, Viriginia, 5172
Guzmán, Yuyú, 2737

Payne, Leigh A., 1418, 3940–3941
Payne, Monica A., 4889–4891
Paysans, systèmes et crise: travaux sur l'agraire haïtien, 1903, 2468
Paz, Josef, 115
Paz, María Fernanda, 2403
Paz, Octavio, 3096–3097
Paz Barnica, Edgardo, 4190
Paz Sánchez, Fernando, 1655
Pazos, Luis, 1656–1657, 3764
Peart, Kenloy, 1893
Pease García, Henry, 3582
Pécaut, Daniel, 3396–3397
Peceny, Mark, 4039
Pechman, Clarice, 1338
Pedler, D.R., 492
Pedoja Riet, Eduardo, 3834
Peixoto, Martín, 3833
Peláez López, Antonio, 2410
Peláez Martínez, Roberto, 4892
Pelissero, Norberto A., 429
Pellecer, Carlos Manuel, 3193
Pellerin, Joel, 2906
Pellet Lastra, Arturo, 3757
Pellicer de Brody, Olga, 4130
Peña, Félix, 4330
Peña, Guillermo de la, 4649
Peña, Julio, 2120
Peña, Martín Rodolfo de la, 2756
Peña Gómez, José Francisco, 3263
Penal Reform International (London), 3242
Peñaloza Webb, Miguel, 1658–1659
Peñaloza Webb, Tomás, 1659
Peñaranda de Del Granado, Susana, 3495
Pendergast, David M., 359
Peniche Patrón, Noé Antonio, 1660
Peniche Rivero, Piedad, 2536
People of the peyote: Huichol Indian history, religion & survival, 762
Perales, Iosu, 3168
Peralta, Fabián, 2033
Peralta Toro, Fernando, 2825
Peraza Lope, Carlos, 258
Perdomo, Rodulio, 1814
Pereda, Isabel, 1061
Peredo, Elizabeth, 5094
Peredo, Guido Inti, 3524
Pereira, Anthony W., 3942
Pereira, Joe, 886
Pereira, Valia, 3470
Pereira Herrera, David M., 2686
Perelli, Carina, 3835–3836
Perera Gómez, Eduardo, 4278
Peres, Wilson, 1516

Pereyra, Carlos Julio, 3837
Pereyra, Daniel, 2973
Pérez, Al I., 4103
Pérez, Brittmarie Janson, 3233
Pérez, Carlos Andrés, 3474
Pérez, Jesús, 2591
Pérez, Niurka, 1920
Pérez, Rodolfo, 2291
Pérez Amat, M.E., 1054
Pérez Antón, Romeo, 3833
Pérez Arrarte, Carlos, 2852
Pérez Barrero, María Delia, 2312
Pérez Bugallo, Rubén, 1062
Pérez Gollán, José Antonio, 430
Pérez Guzmán, Diego, 3398
Pérez Herrero, Pedro, 4003, 4551
Pérez Iribarne, Eduardo, 3523
Pérez López, Emma Paulina, 1661, 4666
Pérez-López, Jorge F., 1935
Pérez Motta, Eduardo, 1686
Pérez Olivares, Enrique, 3157
Pérez Oropeza, M. Inés, 2196, 2198
Pérez Otermin, Jorge, 4442
Pérez Romagnoli, Eduardo E., 2513, 2768
Pérez Rosales, Laura, 761
Pérez Ruiz, Wilfredo, 2659
Pérez Sáinz, Juan Pablo, 1741, 2507, 4736
Pérez Schael, María Sol, 5007
Pérez-Stable, Marifeli, 3360
Pérez Villanueva, Omar Everleny, 1936
Pereznieto Castro, Leonel, 4104
Peri Fagerstrom, René, 2838
Periodismo, Derechos Humanos y Control del Poder Político en Centroamérica (Seminar), *San José, 1993,* 3141
Peritore, N. Patrick, 1576, 3050
Perkins, M. Katherine, 4279
Perló Cohen, Manuel, 4661
Perreault, Thomas, 2630
Perrotta, Elena, 1061
Perry, Guillermo E., 1273, 1426
Perry, Joseph M., 4760
Perry, William, 3476
Perspectivas de las relaciones civiles militares en El Salvador: San Salvador, 7 de octubre de 1993, 3178
Perspectivas regionales en la arqueología del suroccidente de Colombia y norte del Ecuador, 547
Persson, Annika, 1770
Perú: crisis y desafío, 2162
Peru: human rights since the suspension of constitutional government, 3583
Perú, desafío democrático: bases del Proyecto Nacional hacia el siglo XXI., 3584

Serbín, Andrés, 3481, 4223, 4230, 4294–4296, 4322, 4456
Seró, Liliana, 1030
Serra, Antônio de Castro Queiroz, 2381
Serra, José, 3958
Serra Deliz, Wenceslao, 4924
Serra Puche, Jaime, 1693
Serrafero, Mario Daniel, 3772–3773
Serrano Camarena, Antonio, 1632
Serrano Pérez, Margarita, 2107
Serrano Redonnet, Antonio E., 2741
Serrate Reich, Carlos, 3533
Servicio Holandés de Cooperación Técnica y Social. SNV-Bolivia, 5090
Servicios Educativos Rurales (Peru), 5040
Serviço Nacional de Aprendizagem Industrial (Brazil). Departamento Regional de São Paulo, 2377
Seventh Palenque round table, 1989, 130
Sguiglia, Eduardo, 2310
Shady Solís, Ruth, 663
Shafer, Harry J., 224
Shapiro, Dolores J., 975
Shapiro, Helen, 2378
Sharer, Robert J., 131–132
Sharon, Douglas, 1199
Sheahan, John, 1449
Sheets, Payson D., 328
Sheinin, David, 4050
Shellenberger, Michael, 5243
Shelton, Catherine N., 333
Shepherd, Frederick M., 4748
Sherraden, Margaret S., 1450, 1514, 3005
Sherro, Stéphan, 4123
Sherzer, Joel, 769
Shimada, Izumi, 407, 664–665
Shirley, Mary M., 1451
Shlomowitz, Ralph, 4785
Shome, Parthasarathi, 1452
Short, Margaret I., 3366
Siavelis, Peter, 3666
Siddique, Saud, 1453
Sieder, Rachel, 3209
Siegel, Peter E., 371–372
Siembieda, William J., 1694
Siems, Larry, 4692
Siepe, Raimundo, 4367
Sierra, Gerónimo de, 1454, 3844–3846
Sierra, Malú, 1119
Sierra, Pablo, 2299
Sierra Camacho, María Teresa, 976
Sierra Restrepo, Alberto, 2598
Sierra Sosa, Thelma Noemí, 276
Sievers, Merten, 2428

Siffre, Michel, 277
Sigmund, Paul E., 2983
El significado de la maquila en Guatemala: elementos para su comprensión, 4749
Sikkink, Kathryn, 4355
Silencing a people: the destruction of civil society in Haiti, 3291
Silgado Ferro, Enrique, 2441
Sills, Erin O., 2918
Silva, Alexandra de Mello e, 4515–4516
Silva, Aracy Lopes da, 977
Silva, Celso de Souza e, 4517
Silva, Ciléa Souza de, 2919
Silva, Eduardo, 2131, 3667
Silva, Fabíola Andréa, 489
Silva, Mauro José da, 2881
Silva, Paulo R. Palhano, 2901
Silva, Pedro Luiz Barros, 2340
Silva Herzog Flores, Jesús, 1626
Silva Léon, Gustavo A., 2595
Silva Rhoads, Carlos, 314
Silva-Santisteban, Fernando, 631
Silva Villanueva, Narsa, 5011
Silveira, Helder Gordim da, 4518
Silveira, Maria Laura, 2445
Silveira, Sara, 2240
Silverman, Gail P., 1222–1223
Silverman, Helaine, 666–667
Silvers, Arthur L., 1695
Silverstein, Ken, 3954
Simbiosis de culturas: los inmigrantes y su cultura en México, 4664
Simmons, Donald C., 4198
Simmons, Scott E., 278
Simon, Françoise, 1311, 4004
Simoneau, Karin, 1034
Simonsen, Mario Henrique, 2379
Simpósio Brasileiro de Geoprocessamento, 2nd, São Paulo, 1993, 2398
Simposio de Investigaciones Arqueológicas en Guatemala, 7th, Museo Nacional de Arqueología y Etnología, 1993, 133
Simposio de Investigaciones Arqueológicas en Guatemala, 8th, Guatemala, 1994, 134
Simposio de Investigacions Arqueológicas en Guatemala, 9th, Museo Nacional de Arqueología y Etnología, Guatemala, 1995, 135
Simposio Estado de Conservación de la Fauna de Vertebrados Terrestres de Chile, Santiago, 1987, 2836
Simpósio Indios e Não Indios—uma Interação Desigual no Limiar do Século XXI, Campinas, Brazil, 1991, 940

Solórzano, Irela, 4685, 4743
Solórzano Toscano, Luis Alberto, 4609
Solveira, Beatriz Rosario, 4380
Solveira de Báez, Beatriz, 4368
Solyman-Golpashini, Valentine, 1342
Sondrol, Paul C., 2984
Sorenson, John L., 17
Sorj, Bila, 5303
Soruco, Juan Cristóbal, 3540
Sosa Elízaga, Raquel, 2985
Sosnowski, Saúl, 5199
Sotelo Valencia, Adrián, 4669
Soto, Alvaro de, 4203
Soto Reyes, Ernesto, 1583
Soto S., César, 3535
Sotomayor, María Lucía, 2605
Sousa, Amaury de, 3875, 3905
Sousa, Jorge Luiz Prata de, 4519
Souza, Baltazar M. de, 2901
Souza, Josias de, 3870
Souza, Maria Adélia Aparecida de, 2445
Spalding, Rose J., 3224, 4751
Spence, Jack, 3179
Spence, Michael W., 280
Spencer, Charles S., 365, 683
Spencer, David E., 3177
Spier, Fred, 1224
Spiguel, Claudio, 4363
Spilimbergo, Jorge Enea, 3774
Spinosa Melo, Oscar, 4369
Spoor, Max, 1727, 1821, 1830, 1836
Spores, Ronald, 38
Springer, Gary L., 1698
Sprout, Ronald, 1460
Squeo, Francisco, 2837
St. Antony's College (University of Oxford), 3635
St. Malo Arias, Guillermo de, 4204
Stahl, Peter W., 327
Stahringer, Ofelia, 4334
Staller, John Edward, 590
Stambouli, Andrés, 3478
Standen, Vivien G., 525
Stanford, Lois, 770, 1699
Stanish, Charles, 447–448
Stark, Barbara, 139
Starn, Orin, 1215, 1225, 3591, 5068
The state of world rural poverty: a profile of Latin America and the Caribbean, 1461
Statistical synthesis of Chile, 1988–1992, 2132
Steadman, Sharon R., 140
Steagall, Jeffrey W., 4760
Stearman, Allyn MacLean, 1031
Steele, Diane, 1700, 1803

Stefañuk, Miguel Angel, 2776
Stehberg Landsberger, Rubén, 526
Stein, Ernesto, 1324
Stein, Steven J., 3972
Steiner, Roberto, 1412, 1978, 1987
Stemper, David Michael, 552, 554
Stephens, John D., 1883, 2951
Stern, Charles R., 436
Stern, Claudio, 4670
Stern, Marc A., 4024
Stern, Margaret J., 2634
Stern, Peter A., 3592
Stern, Steven N., 4854
Sternberg, Hilgard O'Reilly, 2443, 2922
Stevens, Alta Mae, 905
Stevens, Willy, 4335
Stewart-Gambino, Hannah W., 2975, 2986
Stokes, Anne V., 373
Stokes, Susan Carol, 1226, 3593–3594
Stolcke, Verena, 4554
Stolovich, Luis, 1462–1463, 3832
Stone, Andrea Joyce, 281
Stone, Carl, 3295–3296
Stone, Rosemarie, 3296
Stone-Miller, Rebecca, 668
Strategie rozwojowe i polityka przemysłowa wybranych krajów Azji i Ameryki Łacińskiej: praca zbiorowa, 1464
Strategies to combat poverty in Latin America, 1465
Straubhaar, Joseph D., 3934, 3963
Streeter, Stephen M., 4520
Streicker, Joel, 1142
Ströbele-Gregor, Juliana, 1096, 5097
Strong, Simon, 3595
Stuart, David, 306, 319
Stubbe, Hannes, 5298
Stubbs, Jean, 4926
Stumpo, Giovanni, 1263
Suárez, Carlos, 1954
Suárez, Jorge, 2780
Suárez, Luis Gaspar, 3236
Suárez Aguilar, Estela, 1701
Suárez Farías, Francisco, 4125
Suárez Lastra, Facundo, 5145
Suárez-Orozco, Carola, 771
Suárez-Orozco, Marcelo M., 771
Suárez Salazar, Luis, 4299
Suárez Soruco, Ramiro, 2437
Suassuna, Luciano, 3964
Sucesión pactada: la ingeniería política del salinismo, 3115
La sucesión presidencial en México, 1928–1988, 3116
Los sucesos del Alto Huallaga: marzo, abril–